In the Land of a Thousand Gods

In the
Land of a
Thousand
Gods

A History of
Asia Minor
in the Ancient
World

Christian Marek

IN COLLABORATION WITH PETER FREI
TRANSLATED BY STEVEN RENDALL

PRINCETON UNIVERSITY PRESS
PRINCETON AND OXFORD

Library of Congress Cataloging-in-Publication Data

Names: Marek, Christian, 1950– author. | Frei, Peter, 1925– | Rendall, Steven, translator.
Title: In the land of a thousand gods : a history of Asia Minor in the ancient world /
Christian Marek, in collaboration with Peter Frei ; translated by Steven Rendall.
Other titles: Geschichte Kleinasiens in der Antike. English
Description: Princeton : Princeton University Press, 2016. | "First published in German
under the title Geschichte Kleinasiens in der Antike, by Christian Marek, © Verlag C.H.
Beck oHG, München 2010." | Includes bibliographical references and index.
Identifiers: LCCN 2015039751 | ISBN 9780691159799 (hardcover : alk. paper)
Subjects: LCSH: Turkey—History—To 1500.
Classification: LCC DS155 .M3713 2016 | DDC 939/.2—dc23 LC record available at
http://lccn.loc.gov/2015039751

British Library Cataloging-in-Publication Data is available

This book has been composed in Garamond Premier Pro
with Frutiger lt cond. for display

Printed on acid-free paper. ∞

Printed in the United States of America

1 3 5 7 9 10 8 6 4 2

For Sebastian

Contents

Preface to the English Edition

The text has been revised, corrected, and at many points updated, as has the Bibliography and the lists of rulers in the Appendix. Reviewers of the German edition rightly pointed out that the thematic Bibliography did not make it easy to find the names of individual contributors to the field; for that reason, I have added an alphabetical list of authors with references to the numbers under which they are listed in the Bibliography. The notes have been supplemented with references to new source material and literature where this seemed indispensable. Chapter 2, on modern fieldwork in Asia Minor, has not been updated for good reasons: ongoing ramifications are difficult to follow, and current international fieldwork in Turkey is complex and short-lived. Some reviewers complained about the omission of Byzantine history in the book's conclusion; however, I cannot meet this demand and stand by the reasons I have given.

I thank my translator, Steven Rendall, who has done a great job on a particularly challenging project full of idiosyncrasies and thorny jargon in a field of scholarship that covers a whole range of disciplines from classics to oriental studies, linguistics, archaeology, prehistory, and anthropology. My Zurich team has once again contributed: Max Gander, a specialist in Hittite and Near Eastern Studies, has revised Chapters 4 and 5, while Janett Schröder, a postgraduate student in ancient history, carefully read the drafts of other chapters. Dr. Ursula Kunnert again helped in many ways.

I owe much gratitude to Princeton University Press, and especially to Al Bertrand, Hannah Paul, Quinn Fusting, and Sara Lerner for having the courage to publish in English a book of such size and on such a topic, and for their unfailing support and advice. I also wish to adress particular appreciation to Cyd Westmoreland and Maria E. denBoer for admirably tackling the enormous tasks of copyediting and indexing. Peter Thonemann, whom I also thank here, was the first to urge me to arrange to have this book appear in English translation. Clearly, all shortcomings and errors on the following pages are my own.

Zurich, January 2016

Preface to the Second German Edition

A gratifyingly great interest in this volume has made a second edition necessary only a few months after the appearance of the first. Apart from a few small corrections, it was possible to reprint the text unchanged. However, the recent discovery, in the town of Milas in southwestern Turkey, of a princely tomb containing a splendid marble sarcophagus from the fourth century BCE shows that in the archaeological "El Dorado" that is Turkey there have already been new developments that have attracted the attention of experts in the field. The owner of this tomb may have been a member of the family of Maussollos (377–353 BCE).

Shortly before the reprinting begin, I received the sad news of the death of my co-author, Peter Frei. Up to the last, he had worked tirelessly on the great corpus of sources from the city of Dorylaion in western Anatolia. With Peter Frei's death, research on Asia Minor has lost a scientist of worldwide renown. I dedicate this edition to my friend in grateful memory.

Taşköprü/North Turkey, Summer 2010
Christian Marek

Preface

The cultural area designated by the concept "Asia Minor" is now better known as Turkey—a country that many readers will have come to know as travelers. It impresses us by the plenitude and multiplicity of the various remains of prehistoric, Hittite, Phrygian, Iranian, Greek, and Roman sites from a distant past whose fascination attracts tourists interested in cultural history from all over the world, year after year. What the evidence of these cultures presented here shows very clearly is that they not only have a distant relationship to Europe, but they also proceed from a region in which the foundations of European cultural development were laid. The history of Turkey—including its most ancient history—is more relevant to our current concerns than ever, because an often-heated debate has arisen over the question as to whether this Islamic country is part of Europe or not.

The present book—as its sheer size already suggests—is certainly not a "brief introduction" to be read in haste, but it is conceived and written in such a way as to be accessible not only to the specialist but also to the general reader interested in history.* For that reason I have included genealogies, maps, and illustrations, as well as dates, translations, and explanations of words and technical terms in ancient languages that may sometimes be superfluous for scholars and perhaps occasionally problematic. On the same grounds, it seemed indispensable to provide additional guidance by appending chronological lists of rulers and a chronological table, and to make deeper study easier by providing a bibliography divided according to epochs and subject areas. The comprehensive lists of rulers in the Appendix are taken from various scholarly works and represent the present state of knowledge; I cannot claim to have undertaken an independent attempt to check in the sources the details of the chronology of the different rulers. The bibliography is generally limited to a selection of books (monographs) on Asia Minor; journal articles are mentioned only where books leave certain gaps. The titles are numbered successively. In the body of the text and the notes, primary and secondary sources listed in the bibliography are referred to by their numbers and short titles.

---

* On the spelling of names and words in foreign languages: to prevent "the magic of arbitrary signs [from] introducing useless pedantry into books that are relatively oriented toward the general reader" (Oleg Grabar, *Die Entstehung der islamischen Kunst*, Köln 1977, 10), I have reduced the use of diacritical signs and specialized transcriptions when reproducing ancient Egyptian, Hittite, Assyrian, Persian, Arabic, Greek, etc., names and thus have accepted a few inconsistencies. Thus I use the Anglicized form "Sasanid" when referring to the dynasty but give its founder's name as "Sāsān," and "Bīlād Rūm" in the context of a quotation from Ibn Baṭṭūta, but otherwise "Rum." Names of kings known from history books, such as Shapur and Ardashir, are not transcribed as "Šābuhr" and "Ardaxšīr," nor are the inevitably numerous transcriptions of words in ancient Greek given with accent and long-syllable signs. Popular forms of famous names (Mark Antony, Herodotus) have been treated as exceptions from the regular spelling (Marcus Antonius, Herodotos).

Seen from the point of view of cultural history, the unique mediating position of ancient Asia Minor between East and West might seem to require an explanatory approach that makes use of abstract concepts and models. But for an attempt like this one, which seeks to represent such a wide-ranging subject on the basis of the present state of scholarly knowledge, it may be more appropriate to eschew theorizing as much as possible. I see my task as being rather to remain as close as I can to the sources; and since the records are fragmentary, that means that I must often acknowledge that we do not know some things, or do not know them well enough to arrive at a clear conception of them. It goes without saying that no historian writes without making choices and shaping and coloring his material. In addition, I have not always refrained from making judgments on controversial questions, even if a full scholarly demonstration cannot be given in this book.

I am deeply indebted to many persons and institutions; they are so numerous that I cannot mention them all here. First of all, to my friend and predecessor in the chair at Zurich, Peter Frei. My desire to attempt a history of Asia Minor in antiquity would not have been realized had he not assured me that he would contribute the sections in which the historian has to base himself primarily on cuneiform and hieroglyphic sources. The description of the culture of the ancient Phrygians is also his.

Our contribution owes as much to our continuing passion for the country and its manifest, immense riches from the depths of history as it does to scholarly work conducted at our desks and in the field. Peter Frei first encountered Turkey in 1958, when he took part in the Zurich medievalist Marcel Beck's "Journeys to the Orient." He has been doing research on the territory of the Phrygian metropolis Dorylaion since 1976. From 1979 to the present I myself have repeatedly traveled in the area between Edirne and Cukurca, Knidos and Hopa, Anamur and Sinop; carried out epigraphic surveys; and participated in excavations in Kaunos and Pompeiopolis (Paphlagonia). Our scientific interests have been made fruitful at the university in lectures, seminars, and colloquia (sometimes presented jointly) on the ancient history of the country. To have awakened a similar passion in young researchers is surely a teacher's finest reward.

I give special thanks to Werner Eck and Georg Petzl. As profound connoisseurs of Asia Minor and models for my scholarly work, they have both done me the great favor of reading the thick typescript of this book and eliminating many errors and weaknesses in it. Valuable suggestions were also made by our friends and colleagues Manuel Baumbach, Anne Kolb, Wolfram Martini, Andreas Müller-Karpe, Alexander Michael Speidel and Lâtife Summerer, all of whom I thank most heartily. I owe thanks to my colleagues Andreas Schachner, the director of the excavations in the Hittite capital, Ḫattusa, and Klaus Schmidt, who excavated the Neolithic shrine of Göbekli Tepe, for generously providing up-to-date maps and illustrations.

On the long road from the first drafts to the print-ready typescript, I was accompanied by my colleagues and students in Zurich. A priceless contribution to the book was made by: Ursula Kunnert, herself *rerum orientalium perita* and a trusted associate in my research on Asia Minor; my two assistants, Max Gander—a budding expert on the Hittites and a researcher in the area of the geography of Asia Minor in the second millenium BCE, and Emanuel Zingg—a philologist and researcher on Isocrates; and my doctoral student, Marco Vitale, a specialist in ancient history who does research on the Roman provincialization of Asia Minor; their efforts were more valuable to me than my thanks here can express. And I want to thank another member of this team, our secretary Monika Pfau, who helped proofread the typescript.

Here I would also like to express my gratitude to the University of Zurich—my *alma mater Turicensis* since 1994. I am aware that not all German-speaking institutions provide an academic milieu in which the kind of research work that underlies this book can be pursued undisturbed.

I offer my heartiest thanks to the Gerda Henkel Foundation for having included this volume in its "Historische Bibliothek" and for its substantial contribution to the costs of printing it. Last but certainly not least, I express my special gratitude to the C.H. Beck publishing house. Most authors can probably only dream of receiving the kind of backing and encouragement provided me by Beck's readers and editors with the commitment, expert knowledge of ancient history, and tireless precision of Dr. Stefan von der Lahr and the meticulous technical support of his colleagues Heiko Hortsch, Peter Palm, and his assistant Andrea Morgan.

Over the long years of work on this book I have been sustained by the love and patience of my wife Ruxandra, and I hope that my son Sebastian will graciously accept this monster of a book, which is dedicated to him, and perhaps someday forgive me for occasionally neglecting him to undertake the necessary travels and research.

Zurich, January 2010

Acronyms and Abbreviations

AA   *Archäologischer Anzeiger*

ActaAntHung   *Acta archaeologica Academiae scientiarum hungaricae*

ADerg   *Arkeoloji Dergisi*

AE   *Année épigraphique*

AfO   *Archiv für Orientforschung*

AJA   *American Journal of Archaeology*

AJPh   *American Journal of Philology*

AM   *Athenische Mitteilungen*

AMI   *Archäologische Mitteilungen aus Iran*

AMS   *Asia Minor Studien*

AnatA   *Anatolia Antiqua*

AncCivScytSib   *Ancient Civilizations from Scythia to Siberia*

AnnPisa   *Annali della scuola normale superiore di Pisa*

ANRW   *Aufstieg und Niedergang der Römischen Welt*

AnSt   *Anatolian Studies*

AoF   *Altorientalische Forschungen*

AuA   *Antike und Abendland*

AvP   *Altertümer von Pergamon*

BCH   *Bulletin de correpondance hellénique*

Beih.   *Beiheft*

BICS   *Bulletin. Institute of Classical Studies, University of London*

BJb   *Bonner Jahrbücher*

BMC   British Museum Coins

Broughton, MRR   Broughton, The Magistrates of the Roman Republic

BSR   *Papers of the British School at Rome*

BullAcadBelgique   *Bulletins de l'Académie Royale des Sciences, des Lettres et des Beaux Arts de Belgique*

CAH   *Cambridge Ancient History*

CIL   *Corpus Inscriptionum Latinarum*

ClPhil   *Classical Philology*

CMG   *Corpus Medicorum Graecorum*

CRAI   *Comtes rendus de l'Académie des inscriptions et belles-lettres*

CSHB   *Corpus Scriptorum Historiae Byzantinae*

DBH   *Dresdner Beiträge zur Hethitologie*

DialHistAnc   *Dialogues d'histoire ancienne*

DNP   *Der Neue Pauly*

EHR   *English Historical Review*

EpigrAnat   *Epigraphica Anatolica*

FD   *Fouilles de Delphes*

FGrHist   *Fragmente der Griechischen Historiker*

Fr   Fragment

GrRomByzSt   *Greek, Roman and Byzantine Studies*

HA   *Historia Augusta*

HdO   *Handbuch der Orientalistik*

HZ   *Historische Zeitschrift*

I.   Inscriptions

IAG   *Iscrizioni agonistiche grece*

IG   *Inscriptiones Graecae*

IGR   *Inscriptiones Graecae ad Res Romanas Pertinentes*

IK   *Inschriften Griechischer Städte aus Kleinasien*

ILS   *Inscriptiones Latinae Selectae*

IstMitt   *Istanbuler Mitteilungen*

JbAC   *Jahrbuch für Antike und Christentum*

JHS   *Journal of Hellenic Studies*

JNES   *Journal of Near Eastern Studies*

JNG   *Jahrbuch für Numismatik und Geldgeschichte*

JRA   *Journal of Roman Archaeology*

JRS   *Journal of Roman Studies*

KBo   *Keilschrifttexte aus Boghazköi*

KUB   *Keilschrifturkunden aus Boghazköi*

LACL   *Lexikon der Antiken Christlichen Literatur*

LdH   *Lexikon des Hellenismus*

MAMA   *Monumenta Asiae Minoris Antiqua*

MDOG   *Mitteilungen der Deutschen Orientgesellschaft*

MedAnt   *Mediterraneo antico. Economie, società, culture*

MinEpigrP   *Minima epigraphica et papyrologica*

Moretti, IGUR   Moretti, *Inscriptiones Graecae Urbis Romae*

MünstBeitr   *Münstersche Beiträge zur antiken Handelsgeschichte*

MusHelv   *Museum Helveticum*

NAGW   *Nachrichten der Akademie der Wissenschaften in Göttingen*

NüBlA   *Nürnberger Blätter zur Archäologie*

NumChron   *Numismatic Chronicle*

OGIS   *Orientis Graecae Inscriptiones Selectae*

ÖJh   *Jahreshefte des Österreichischen archäologischen Institutes in Wien*

Oliver   Oliver, *Greek Constitutions of Early Roman Emperors*

PCG   *Poetae Comici Graeci*

PG   *Patrologia Graeca*

PL   *Patrologia Latina*

PSI   *Pubblicazioni della Società Italiana per la ricerca dei papiri greci e latini in Egitto*

PY   *Pylos-Tafeln (Linear B)*

RE Paulys Realencyclopädie der classischen Altertumswissenschaft

REA Revue des études anciennes

RECAM Regional Epigraphic Catalogues of Asia Minor

RMD Roman Military Diplomas

RNum Revue numismatique

Robert, OMS Robert, Opera Minora Selecta

RStorAnt Rivista storica dell'antichità

SBBerlin Sitzungsberichte der Deutschen Akademie der Wissenschaften zu Berlin, Klasse für Sprachen, Literatur und Kunst

SBMünchen Bayerische Akademie der Wissenschaften, Philosophisch-Historische Klasse, Sitzungsberichte

SBWien Sitzungsberichte der Österreichischen Akademie der Wissenschaften

SchwMBl Schweizer Münzblätter

SchwNumRu Schweizerische numismatische Rundschau

ScrClIsr Scripta Classica Israelica

SEG Supplementum Epigraphicum Graecum

Sherk, RDGE Sherk, Roman Documents from the Greek East

SMEA Studi micenei ed egeo-anatolici

SNG, SNG Aulock Sylloge Nummorum Graecorum, Sylloge Nummorum Graecorum, Aulock

StBoT Beih. Studien zu den Boghazköi-Texten, Beihefte

StBoT Studien zu den Boghazköi-Texten

StTroica Studia Troica

StV Staatsverträge des Altertums

SVF Stoicorum veterum Fragmenta

Syll.3 Sylloge Inscriptionum Graecarum

TAM Tituli Asiae Minoris

TAPhA Transactions of the American Philological Association

TH(eth) Texte der Hethiter

TIB Tabula Imperii Byzantini

VA Philostratos, Vita Apollonii

VDI Vestnik drevnej istorii

VS Philostratos, Vitae Sophistarum

Welles, RC Welles, Royal Correspondence in the Hellenistic Period

WUNT Wissenschaftliche Untersuchungen zum Neuen Testament

WürbJb Würzburger Jahrbücher für die Alterumswissenschaft

ZAntChr Zeitschrift für Antike und Christentum

ŽivaAnt Živa antika. Antiquité vivante

ZPE Zeitschrift für Papyrologie und Epigraphik

ZSav Zeitschrift der Savigny-Stiftung für Rechtsgeschichte

In the Land of a Thousand Gods

CHAPTER 1

Introduction: Anatolia between East and West

Asia Minor and Ancient World History

The part of the ancient world that projects from the continent of Asia to the Mediterranean and is called Asia Minor almost coincides with modern-day Turkey. A history of Turkey has to begin with the Turks.[1] However, for a history of Asia Minor, there is no unifying thread of this kind: it is shot through with a mixture of peoples and cultures, migrations, occupations and retreats, and shifting empires and states. Nonetheless, its location between seas and continents and its nature lend this peninsula a continuity over time in three respects: its "orientation,"[2] its "mixture,"[3] and its function as a "bridge."[4]

The secularism introduced by Mustafa Kemal—Atatürk—less than a century ago has ultimately resulted in Turkey's being strongly oriented toward the West. Despite Atatürk's deliberate choice to locate a new capital in Ankara, in the middle of Anatolia, intellectual life, money, and trends are still concentrated in Istanbul—a city whose old center is on the European continent. From this city the sultans ruled a multi-ethnic empire that once stretched from Yemen to Transylvania and from the Atlas mountains to the Caucasus. The Turks had been in Anatolia long before they conquered Constantinople (subsequently known as Istanbul) in 1453 and had established several other empires there in addition to the Ottoman empire. They first encountered an imperial structure that was already decadent in many places; they called it "Rum." The name is still found in many forms. The Anatolian Greeks who occupied part of the area up until Atatürk's time were called "Rum" (as opposed to the Greeks of Greece, who were called "Yunan" [Ionians]). Places in both eastern and western Anatolia bore names containing the element "rum," such as the city Erzurum or the fortress of Rumeli Hisarı on the Bosporus, which Sultan Mehmet II began to build in 1451, before the general attack on the capital (Figure 1). Jalāl ad-Dīn, the master (*mevlâna*) of Persian Islamic mysticism in the thirteenth century, came from Balkh, but used the name "Rūmī," alluding to his second homeland, the Sultanate of Rum that had emerged around the ancient city of Ikonion (Konya).

In Arabic, Persian, and Turkish, "rum" is the word for Rome and the Romans. Used in reference to the Greeks of the Christian Byzantine Empire, "rum" implies the continuity of the ancient Roman Empire in the Byzantine millennium, whose new capital Constantinople had been founded on the Bosporus by Constantine the Great around 330 CE.

1. The fortress of Rumeli Hisarı, at the narrowest point of the Bosporus.

Constantine's abandonment of "Eternal Rome," the city built on seven hills along the Tiber, as the capital of this empire had been preceded by a shift in the latter's center of gravity that had begun much earlier, and at the end of the third century had already led the Emperor Diocletian to take up residence in Nikomedeia (today İzmit) on the Sea of Marmara. From an Anatolian point of view, the seat of the imperial government was here in Nikomedeia, as it was later on the Bosporus on the western periphery. The orientation toward the West that had characterized the eastern provinces of the Roman Empire for more than 300 years continued. When Emperor Jovian made peace with the Persians in 363 CE and ceded to them the city of Nisibis on the Tigris (now Nusaybin on the Turkish-Syrian border), the latter's inhabitants were gripped by despair; they wanted to remain Romans (Ammianus 25, 8, 13).

An orientation toward political and cultural centers of gravity outside the country reaches far back into Anatolian history. Asia Minor itself became the center of an outwardly expanding empire only under the Hittites, in the second millennium BCE. Seen from the capital Ḫattusa, at the height of its development the Hittite state was oriented toward the southeast. So were the succeeding smaller states. Power, wealth, and splendor were located in Egypt, Babylon, and Nineveh. The rise of the Median and Persian empires, along with new kingdoms with their centers in Ekbatana, Susa, and Persepolis, altered this force field only slightly.

In the Persian epoch, for the first time a split between the Aegean and the Euphrates appeared in Anatolia's orientation. In the seventh and sixth centuries BCE, attractive power still radiated from the eastern palaces. In the world of high cultures, the Greeks lived on a remote coast and looked with admiration toward Asia. Their tyrants held court on the Lydian and Persian model. They also owed their literary and scientific achievements to the "simple fact" that they were "the most eastern of the westerners," that is, they were the first receivers among the latter.[5] But in the fifth and fourth centuries, the Anatolians—the most western of the easterners—began to change their orientation, no doubt under the influence of the development of the power of Athens after the repulse of the Persians: Lycian princes spoke Greek, read Greek literature, and were fond of Greek pictorial art. Lycians and Carians built communities (*poleis*) on the Greek model and settled on the Mediterranean. In the third and second centuries, after Alexander's campaigns, this reorientation became more and more extensive: the Greek language and the culture of the *polis* spread to middle and eastern Anatolia, Cappadocians contributed to art and rhetoric in Greek cities, and kings bore the title "Friend of the Greeks." Rome's expansion into the Hellenistic world increased this tendency. The new superpower in the West controlled the Anatolian princes through the medium of Hellenization in the wake of the allied Kingdom of Pergamon. Asia Minor resisted direct Roman rule for only a short time, throwing itself into the arms of a King of Pontos of Iranian descent. However, Pompey's and Octavian's victories over the eastern kingdoms clearly showed what the future would hold. In less than fifty years, the Anatolian land mass became a series of Roman provinces. But the West did not rule it completely. Urban civilization ebbed away as one approached the Euphrates. Armenia, which faced in both directions, provided a latent field of tension between East and West until the end of the ancient world.

Nonetheless, at no point in its history can Anatolian culture be neatly divided up into eastern and western. As far back as we can trace events, there was always a mixture. Imperial structures were preceded or accompanied by new settlements of peoples and ethnic groups who brought with them multiple proximities, overlaps, and fusions with earlier inhabitants: the (Latin) Romans, Celts, Jews, Macedonians, Iranians, Greeks, Arameans, and Assyrians settled the area in large numbers before the Rum and Turkish settlements. The old Anatolian kingdoms, those of the Lydians, the Phrygians, the Urartians, and the Hittites, can also be traced back to immigrants. Traditions brought into the country and those already existent there blended, and neither of them remained what it was. Hittite culture cannot be understood without the synthesis of Hattian, Luwian, Hurrian, and Semitic elements; nor are the Ionian Greeks of Miletus in the sixth century BCE identical in every respect with the Greeks in Athens and on Euboea. Their symbiosis with Asians is evident. Gods like Zeus or Men in the Phrygia of the second century CE are not Greek but Anatolian gods, and despite its origin and widespread dissemination, a religion like the cataphrygian heresy, so-called "Montanism"—an apocalyptic Christian movement—is characteristically Anatolian.

The third constant consists of Anatolia's role in transmitting culture (a "bridge"). The ancients made daring sea voyages and followed long caravan routes, on which a few people crossed continents and geographical spaces that were not rediscovered and made permanently accessible until the sixteenth century. Nonetheless, the ancient European civilization of the countries around the Mediterranean saw barriers in three directions: to the west, an ocean, not every part of which could be reached by conventional seafaring; to the north, an indeterminate multitude of barbarian peoples living in dark forests, endless steppes, and unbearably cold areas; to the south, deserts, heat, and wild animals. Although it had been circumnavigated by the Phoenicians, Africa remained a closed continent, even if its geographical outpost, Egypt, remained a source of fascination as the oldest cultural center. Only the east differed fundamentally from the other cardinal directions in this respect. Here there was no clear boundary at which the known world stopped. One country followed another like pearls on a string, the homelands of ancient high culture where there were permanent dwellings; writing was practiced; states were constructed and governed; laws were issued; and things produced, exchanged, and built. Only India, to which Alexander marched his armies and which Trajan's yearning reached, represented an approximate limit. The closure to the north and south, and the openness to the east, must have given commerce to and from the Mediterranean world its enduring longitudinal axis.

Anatolia lay between: "Asia minor as a bridge between East and West."[6] The metaphor of the bridge, which has become classical, is apt: ideas, craft skills, knowledge, and commodities passed through the peninsula from east to west and from west to east, and not only by land. Between the Levant and the Aegean, seafaring peoples groped their way along the south coast of Asia Minor in both directions. Long-distance relationships go far back into prehistory: we read and understand—on the basis of traces left by a past that antedates writing, when people were becoming sedentary—the migration of key elements of cultural practice from the East to Europe: the oldest writings come from the Orient to the West in the Bronze Age. The alphabet, myths, cosmology, mathematics, "money," music, and finally even Christianity followed. The polis, technology, architecture, baths, streets, and the theater moved in the opposite direction. The vigorous proliferation of cities is a special mission that finally became, in the Imperial period, the foundation of the "system" itself. In this respect Asia Minor differs from much of the Roman Empire—Gaul, Germany, the lands along the Danube, and Egypt.

This book seeks to provide a historical overview of Anatolia as a bridge and a melting pot, of the changing orientations, mixtures, and transmissions, from prehistory to the heyday of the Roman provinces. No other study has thus far done so. There is only the brief summary *Kleinasien in der Antike* written by Elmar Schwertheim, a specialist in ancient history at the University of Münster and published in 2005. The Roman period, which is the best documented in the sources, has been described in great detail by two works written in English. In 1993, Stephen Mitchell of the University of Exeter published a two-volume study, *Anatolia. Land, Men and Gods in Asia Minor*. He focuses on the central Anatolian context in the Roman period, giving special attention to the rise of Christianity. A work by David Magie, professor of classics at Princeton University, *Roman Rule in Asia Minor* (also in two volumes), offers a comprehensive bibliography of sources and literature, but was published more than four decades earlier. Beginning with the older periods, Magie describes the process of Roman expansion down to the age of the soldier-emperors.

It is true that the history of Asia Minor can hardly be abstracted from the general history of great ancient empires. Nevertheless, wherever possible I have avoided exceeding the geographical limits of our discussion. So far as the temporal boundaries are concerned, I do not continue all the way to the end of the ancient culture of Asia Minor, which survived the Arab expansion of the seventh century and gradually disappeared only in the middle of the Byzantine age. But although I conclude this account before Constantine, that endpoint is not an arbitrary one. With the tetrarchy, the reorganization of the provinces, Christian domination, and the Byzantine Empire, a period begins in Asia Minor whose richness and peculiar tradition cannot be squeezed into a closing chapter, but can be described only as a special historical epoch.

For more than a half century discoveries and research in the area of Asia Minor have increased exponentially. I have striven to take the current state of the field into account. It goes without saying that in view of the dimensions of the body of source material, the subject requires a compromise. Comprehensiveness—including everything, the essential trait of a genuine handbook—cannot be achieved here. Above all, the mass of archaeological and epigraphic sources excludes from the outset the possibility of presenting the material in a form similar to the one Magie attempted; the result would not only exceed the scope of the book but also make it questionable whether the latter could be completed at all. Since modern research on all aspects of life in ancient Asia Minor has long since exceeded the capacity of any single academic discipline, when one ventures to produce a synthesis, here as elsewhere in studies on the ancient world, the individual's competence encounters its limits.

In the past, scholars far more capable than I hesitated to undertake a "History of Asia Minor," and for good reasons. Louis Robert, the great Parisian scholar on ancient history, conducted excavations in Klaros and Amyzon; traveled through large parts of Turkey; and presented his phenomenal knowledge of the ancient geography, monuments, and documents of this land in countless articles and books—but never attempted an overall survey of it. He would certainly have disapproved of such a project.

The Name of the Land

In neither the cuneiform languages of Mesopotamia, Syria, and Anatolia itself, nor in ancient Egyptian, was there a name for the whole peninsula of Asia Minor. The Greeks originally called the land (according to a *scholion* on *Odyssey* 7, 8) simply "the mainland," and in the fifth century BCE, the Greek historian Herodotus still occasionally used this expression in contrast to the offshore islands (e.g., Herodotus 1, 169.174). Our geographical idea of Asia goes back to a Greek expression that apparently already occurs in the Mycenaean period on a Linear-B tablet from Pylos: *a-si-*

wi-ja, used here to designate the ancestry of a slave girl from the area on the eastern shore of the Aegean (PY Fr 1206). Concerning the older sources or origin of the word "Asia," there is presently no general agreement, not even regarding which language it actually comes from. It may be derived from the name of the area in western Asia Minor that in the second millennium BCE the Hittites called "Assuwa." Thus in a document of a certain King Tudḫaliya (probably Tudḫaliya I), we find: "When I had destroyed the land of Assuwa, I came back to Ḫattusa" (*Annals of Tudḫaliya*, v. II 33 f.).[7] Another interpretation connects Assuwa with the place-name Assos in the Troad, and the Indo-Germanist Jakob Wackernagel has already traced the name "Asia" (originally from *Assia chora*—"Assian land") back to this place-name.[8]

In Homer's *Iliad* there is a passage (2, 459 ff.) where the Achaean army's invasion of the land of the Trojans is compared with the arrival of a swarm of birds: "And as the many tribes of winged fowl, wild geese or cranes or long-necked swans on the Asian mead (*asio en leimoni*) by the streams of Caystrius, fly this way" (trans. Murray). However, this is problematic, insofar as readings other than the one adjective *asios* are conceivable. The word occurs unambiguously as the adjective *asis* ("Asian") around 700 BCE in a fragment of Hesiod: *en asidi aie*, "in Asian earth."[9] The noun *Asie, Asia* is also attested in the lyric poetry of the seventh and sixth centuries BCE: Archilochos, who speaks of the sheep-raising Asia (Fr. 226 West), Sappho (Fr. 55, 4 Diehl), and Mimnermos (Fr. 12, 2 Diehl). In each case the context indicates that "Asia" refers only to a very limited area in western Asia Minor.

As used by Herodotus, the term extended to the continent lying across from Europe and Libya (Africa), that is, to the land mass constituted by Asia Minor, Syria, Mesopotamia, and Persia. People knew that India and Arabia existed, but they had no precise idea of them—not to mention of the true dimensions of the continent. Likewise, the Romans used the term—following Greek tradition—to refer to the whole continent, but they also used it to refer to the province constructed out of the heritage of the Kingdom of Pergamon, which included large parts of western Anatolia. The first writer who clearly distinguished the continent from the peninsula (that is, Asia Minor as corresponding approximately to the borders of modern-day Turkey) was the geographer Strabo, an Anatolian from Amaseia (today Amasya) who had been given a Greek education and wrote in the time of the Emperors Augustus and Tiberius. In the Roman world, the term "Asia" continued to have three meanings: first, a continent opposed to Europe and Libya; second, a peninsula; and third, a province. Thus the province is also mentioned in the Bible (Acts 20:16): "For Paul had decided to sail past Ephesos, so that he might not have to spend time in Asia."

We first encounter the term "Asia Minor" in Claudius Ptolemaios (Ptolemy), a mathematician and geographer of the second century CE whose world-picture dominated the European and Arabic (cf. "Al-Magest") Middle Ages.[10] In contrast, the name "Anatolia" appears later. Greek *anatole* means "sunrise" or "east"; Latin has the corresponding word *oriens*. In the late Roman Empire (after Diocletian, end of the third century CE), the provinces were reorganized and the whole of the Orient put under a *praefectus praetorio per Orientem*, whose title was translated in Greek as *epar-*

chos Anatolikon praitorion. The term was also used in the narrower field of military administration. In the seventh century CE, when the Byzantine Empire was divided up into military districts or "themes" (*themata*), one of the latter was named *Anatolikon* and included a large part of Asia Minor from the coast of the Aegean to Isauria (a mountainous region south of present-day Konya); its capital was Amorion. This district, whose extent was steadily altered, existed at least into the eleventh century, and the terms used by Arab geographers and historians of the ninth and tenth centuries ultimately go back to it: *al-natulus, al-natulik*.

Geography

Asia Minor is a rectangular peninsula projecting into the eastern Mediteranean whose longer, east-west sides follow an S-curve (Map 1a,b). It extends about 1,500 kilometers from east to west, if we take the borders of modern Turkey as our point of reference. The rectangle's north-south sides are 500–600 kilometers long, narrowing to 480 kilometers at the place the Greeks called *Isthmos*. Taking the Asian part of Turkey as our basis, the total surface area is 756,855 square kilometers, the most extensive land mass in the Roman Empire, larger than Spain (about 580,000 square kilometers) or Gaul (about 550,000 square kilometers).

It is a mountainous land, situated in the Alpide belt of fold-mountains[11] that stretches from the Atlas, Pyrenees, and Alps in the west to the Balkans, Zagros, the Hindu Kush, Karakoram, and Himalayas, and continues as far as Indonesia. On the peninsula, this belt has northern and southern fold zones that surround the central high plateau. On the southeast border, the Arabian plate begins; the rift that runs from the lakes of East Africa north through the Red Sea, Lebanon, and Syria abuts the Taurus Mountains north of Antakya in an arc that swings off to the northeast.

Northern Asia Minor

The north is traversed by the broad band of parallel rifts and faults of the Pontic Mountains. Elevations around the Sea of Marmara are relatively low, rarely over 1,500 meters. Beyond the Bosporus, the Istranca (Strandzha) Mountains in eastern Thrace stretch from the rugged plateau of the Bithynia peninsula as far as the lower Sakarya (Sangarios) River. Between the southern shore of the Sea of Marmara and the Valley of Bakır Çay (Kaikos) is a volcanic rock plateau that rises as high as 1,300 meters and drains into the Aegean, through the Bakır Çay, Gediz, and Menderes rivers, as well as into the Sea of Marmara and the Black Sea, through the Simav and Sakarya rivers. Northeast of the Sakarya plain a small strip of land along the coast separates the zone of the western Pontic Mountains, which are 200 kilometers wide in places and very steep, from the central Anatolian massif. Three main mountain ranges can be distinguished: the coast range (north of Kastamonu, rising to more than 2,000 meters); behind it, and separated by the valleys of the Filyos and

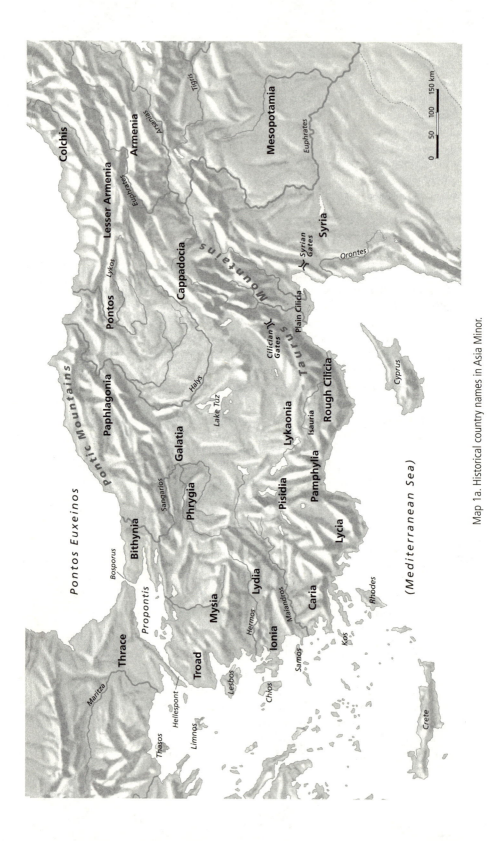

Map 1a. Historical country names in Asia Minor.

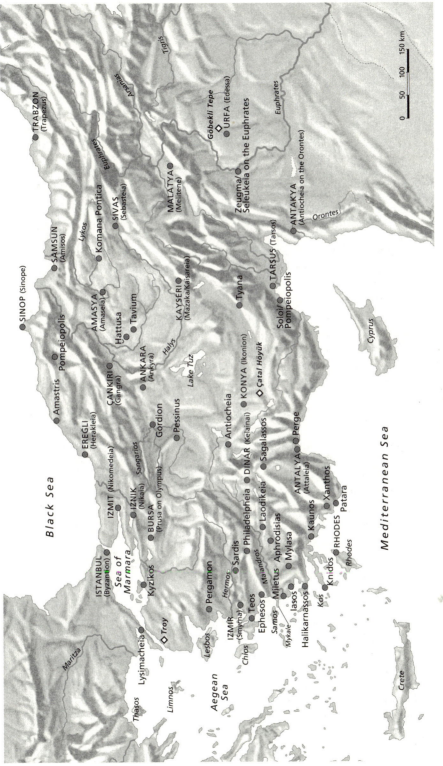

Map 1b. Important places. Maps drawn by Peter Palm, Berlin.

Gökırmak rivers, are the Bolu and Ilgaz Dağları ranges (as high as 2,588 meters); to the south, separated by the valleys of Gerede Çay and Devrez Çay, the Köroğlu Dağları range. From approximately the middle of the southern range, a ridge runs south almost as far as the basin of Lake Tuz, with a few higher points, such as Elma Dağ on the east, Ayaş Dağ on the west, and the Karaca and Paşa Dağları in the south; Ankara lies in a depression on this ridge.

Farther east, the Pontic range is more clearly articulated by narrow valleys and broader lowlands; especially notable are the valleys of the Kelkit and Çoruh, the Suluova (Merzifon), and the basins of Erbaa, Zile, Turhal, Tokat, and Niksar. The East Pontos coastal range rises almost 4,000 meters above Yusufeli. The prevailing cliff coast in the north is interrupted for long stretches only by the alluvial plains in the Sinop peninsula, Bafra and Çarşamba Ovaları, which project into the Black Sea. Travel along the Black Sea coast and between it and the high plateau is difficult: for a long time, ancient harbors were connected only by sea; no continuous coastal road has been proven before the period of the Roman Empire. The relief offers favorable routes from the interior to the coasts only on the western and eastern edges of the middle Pontos arc, from the Bolu Ovası through the valleys of the Mengen Çay and Devrek Çay into the alluvial plains of the Filyos delta and in the east through the basin system between the Kızılırmak and Yeşilırmak rivers down toward Samsun. In antiquity, the rivers played a limited role in transportation; they are navigable with boats and small ships upstream from their mouths for only a short distance, as far as the gorges, and beyond them, on the high plateau.[12] The Sakarya (Sangarios) River, the second-longest in Asia Minor, is already mentioned in Homer; it may be the river called Sahiriya in Hittite sources. It begins in the central massif, first curves around to the east, then west of Ankara it turns abruptly to the west, and finally, after a further curve to the north, breaks through the Pontos range and flows into the Black Sea. The Filyos (Billaios) River, the longest river in northern Anatolia after the Sakarya, follows a similar looping course. The climatic differences between the coastline and the plateau are very great. On the coast, a subtropical climate with luxuriant vegetation prevails. The heaviest annual precipitation in Turkey, 4,045.3 millimeters, was registered in 1931, east of Rize, in the legendary Colchis of antiquity. A continental climate prevails on the south side of the main mountain range, with cold, dry winters and humid, cool summers.

The Aegean Coast

The west coast is sharply divided, even cut up, as a result of folds and rifts running toward the west. The sea penetrates deeply into the rift zones and forms nine large bays that cut from 30 to 100 kilometers into the land. Between Edremit and Aydın (that is, in the largest part of the coastal region), rivers broaden into alluvial plains that are as wide as 12 kilometers and reach far into the interior; they are suitable for transportation and agriculture (Bakır Çay, Gediz, Küçük, and Büyük Menderes). In contrast, the southern section is characterized by craggy promontories extending into the sea, such as the Bodrum peninsula and especially the Reşadiye peninsula south of the bay of Gökova. Further north, in the interior the mountains run east and west. South of Aydın the relief becomes more uneven, with folds running northwest to southwest and north to south.

Central and Eastern Anatolia

The northwestern and western boundaries of the central Anatolian massif along the basin of the Sea of Marmara and the Aegean are hard to determine precisely; the plateau as a whole slopes slowly down to the west, although on both sides of the great river valleys there are ridges as high as 2,000 meters. The northeastern and eastern part of the central plateau, around Çankırı, Çorum, Amasya, and Tokat, is more clearly divided up and more humid than the southern half and offers fertile land for agriculture and livestock raising.

Central Anatolia is not a unified whole; it consists of high plains, mountain ranges, and peaks of various kinds of stone and origin; however, geological folds are rarer. The rises on the broad plains constitute no obstacles to transportation. A large part of this area lies inside the bend of the Kızılırmak ("Red River"), the longest river in Asia Minor. Fed by smaller tributaries east of Sivas, it first flows south in a broad curve through Cappadocia. Then, to the east of Lake Tuz ("Salt Lake"), it turns north and breaks through the Pontos Mountains and empties into the Black Sea. Its Greek name, *Halys* ("salt") was connected in antiquity with the salt deposits in the Cappadocian region of Ximene; the first mention of it by the Greeks is in Aeschylus's tragedy *The Persians* (866). The Hittites called it the Marassantiya.[13]

West and south of the Kızılırmak, in the parallelogram between Eskişehir, Konya, Niğde, and Ankara, hilly land and flat plains prevail. Everyone familiar with Anatolia understands the metaphor of "rolling hills" and loves the "apparent gentleness of the terrain, the rounding of the ridges and crests and the widespread areas that are still strikingly flat even in their relative high position above the valleys."[14] Low rises divide this plateau into three flat parts: the Sakarya valley, the Lake Tuz basin, and the Konya plains, which extend the farthest to the south, as far as the inner side of the arc of the Taurus Mountains.

East of a line running from Niğde through Nevşehir to Tokat, the central massif rises toward the east Anatolian high plateau. The latter is fissured by deep river valleys and divided by high mountain ranges and large volcanic peaks. The plains themselves are partly a product of the volcanoes in the middle of them, and the tuff landscape west of Kayseri is particularly bizarre (Figure 2).

These formations are the result of the erosion of lava and ash deposits proceeding from eruptions of Erciyas Dağ and Hasan Dağ. In the north, broader valleys divide up the parallel ranges along the east Pontos coast; for example, the Aşkale plain between Erzincan and Erzurum, and, farther east, the valleys of the upper Euphrates and upper Aras. North of the Aras valley rises the volcanic plateau of Kars, with a group of smaller volcanoes. At the eastern end and south of this mountain axis are

2. Tuff landscape in Cappadocia.

the volcanoes of Mt. Ararat, Little Ararat, Süphan Dağ, Nemrud Dağ, and the Bingöl Dağları range. At 5,156 meters, the majestic Mt. Ararat is the highest peak in Asia Minor (Figure 3). In Armenian, it is called *Masis*; in Greek, *Baris*; and in Turkish, *Ağrı Dağ*. The name "Ararat," which is used only in the European tradition, comes from the Old Testament (Gen. 8:4), where it designates the place where Noah's Ark landed. The reference is to the Armenian upland (Jerome translates it as *super montes Armeniae*—"on the mountains of Armenia"); the name comes from the Assyrian name for the region, *Urartu* (p. 99 f.). It is not entirely clear when this name came into use; the earliest attested uses appear to go back to the fourteenth century CE. Even today, attempts are repeatedly made, on foot and by air, to locate the Ark. In a book describing his travels in the Orient (partly copied from other authors, partly imagined), the fourteenth-century author who wrote under the name John Mandeville says that with God's help, a monk had managed to take with him a splinter of wood from the Ark.[15] The first known attempt to climb the mountain was made in 1707 by a professor of botany from Aix-en-Provence, Joseph Pitton de Tournefort (p. 20), but the summit was first reached by a German, Friedrich Parrot, in 1829.[16] The volcano last erupted in 1840.

Lake Van, which Strabo calls *Thospitis*, lies at an altitude of 1,720 meters above sea level and is the largest lake in Turkey. It is remarkable for its depth (more than 250 meters near its shores) and its high soda ash content. Strabo (11, 14, 8) described it as "containing soda." The fertile land along its shores already attracted settlers even in prehistoric times. South of the Van basin the Cilo and Sat Moun-

3. Mt. Ararat seen from the west.

tains rise as high as 4,000 meters and form a dividing wall between it and the steppe in northern Iraq.

The Euphrates and Tigris, which were, along with the Nile, the original life-giving rivers of the most ancient cultures, on the eastern plateau are not the broad, slow-moving waterways of Mesopotamia, but instead are torrents that cut deeply through the terrain, flowing rapidly through curves and canyons, and are dangerous for navigation. Particularly in the middle stretches of the Euphrates, gorges (sometimes with vertical rock walls) alternate with broader, intermontane basins, such as those around Erzincan, Elazığ, and Malatya, or, on the Murat, a large Euphrates tributary, around Bingöl.

Southern Asia Minor

As in the north, along the steep cliffs of the S-shaped coast south of the Taurus massif there are large alluvial plains in only a few places: on the Gulf of Antalya and between Mersin and the Bay of İskenderun.

The name "Taurus" (Turkish *Toros*) is first mentioned in Greek by Aristotle; the Greeks connected it with the homophonous word for "bull" (Dionysios Periegetes 641 Müller; Stephanos of Byzantion p. 608, 16–19 Meineke s. v.), associating its form with the humped back or its nature with the wildness of the bull. Libanios (*or.* 9, 92), a rhetorician and writer of the fourth century CE, gives another etymology:

the mountain range is supposed to have been the first to emerge from the flood-waters and dry out, and for that reason was given the name *Tersia*, from *tersaino* ("dry out"). The Taurus Mountains can be divided into two segments: the western segment (Lycian Taurus) forms a barrier between the Aegean and the Mediterranean coasts. Its topography is complex. Above Antalya, axes running southwest to north-east and axes running north to south intersect; extensive basins (the Elmalı plateau) are imbedded in the high ranges; in the high ridges that continue toward the north and intersect the Cilician Taurus Mountains that swing northwest, broad corridors form the basins of Lake Eğridir, Lake Beyşehir, and Lake Suğla. East of these lakes and before the Taurus range, the Ala-Dağ and Alaca-Dağ massifs rise out of the plateau to form the western boundary of the Konya plain.

The Cilician Taurus range[17] consists of rugged limestone and karst formations that tower over the coast. Behind them rise still higher massifs of granite that in the north decline into hills and finally into the plains of the southern part of the central massif. This folded zone is broken up by the Göksu (Kalykadnos) and, at the "Cilician Gates" (see Figure 69), by the Pozantı Çay, which cuts a thousand meters deep into the terrain. Above the Cilician alluvial plain the mountains divide into two main ranges, the Taurus and the Anti-Taurus, running southwest to northeast.

The Arabian Plate

The Arabian plate has a gentle topography. A series of broad, hilly plateaus level out to form the Euphrates basin in the southwest, the Harran plains in the middle, and the Tigris basin in the northeast. The plain is divided by the heights of the Karaca Dağ volcano (1,957 meters) that precede the plateau and the lower, lengthy ridge of the "Tur Abdin" north of Mardin.

✦ ✦ ✦

Taken as a whole, Anatolia has an extremely varied topography with sharp climatic contrasts. The broad "bridge" of the central massif is easily crossed but does not offer good conditions for settlement, at least in its dry southern part. Intense seismic activity is highly characteristic of Anatolia. Since the time of the Roman Empire, more than 800 earthquakes have been noted and reported. Antiquity has handed down to us harrowing testimonies to the regularly recurring suffering of the people—for instance, in Libanios's plaintive monody (*or.* 61) on Nikomedeia or on the tombstones of children who were killed (see Figure 92).

CHAPTER 2

Modern Fieldwork in Asia Minor

The analysis of ancient cultures in the area of Turkey is a central topic in the modern history of science. One has only to consider, to name three examples, what Troy is for the history of archaeology, the cuneiform archives of Ḫattusa for the linguistics and philology of ancient languages and literatures, and the Monumentum Ancyranum (the Temple of Augustus and Rome in Ankara) for ancient history. Whereas the Hittites, Hurrians, and Urartians first became known to us through archaeological finds, it was especially the Greek and Latin literature on Asia Minor that had been handed down from the archaic period through the Middle Ages and Renaissance that conveyed to its readers in every age the picture of a densely settled, civilized part of the ancient world. When at the same time that ancient culture was being reborn in early modern Europe, this region finally passed into the permanent possession of the Ottoman Empire, and this awareness faded away: readers and interpreters of the ancient texts lacked the visual impact of and physical encounter with the world from which these texts arose and to which they bore witness. Here I can offer only a brief sketch of the recovery of this knowledge. In doing so, the discussion is limited to travel, discovery, and excavation in the area, though they constitute only part of the relevant research. Even in this context selection and limitation are called for: today, Höyük and Tepe are of no less interest to researchers on antiquity than the acropolis and agora. Nonetheless, I largely forgo discussion of cultures without writing and emphasize Hittite and "classical" civilization. In Chapter 3, which is based exclusively on archaeology, major prehistoric sites and the research on them are presented.

It is difficult to pinpoint the beginning of the long process of regaining reliable knowledge about the ancient geography and topography of Asia Minor. One of the most important thematic strands in travel to and exploration of important sites of the past starts in Christian late antiquity; for example, it becomes visible in the first authentic pilgrimage account of the journey to the Orient undertaken in around 385 CE by Egeria, a noblewoman from Gaul or Spain (*Peregrinatio Sanctae Egeriae*). This lady's curiosity was entirely focused on Biblical sites and the tombs of saints and martyrs, and her travel guide was the Holy Scriptures she brought with her. Egeria's extant report mentions Anatolia only on her return trip and offers no details at all concerning the long, difficult route over the Taurus Mountains; she considers worth close examination only the site connected with St. Thecla near *Seleucia Hisauriae* (Seleukeia on the Kalykadnos River, in Isauria, now Silifke).

From the Fourteenth to the Nineteenth Centuries:
Pilgrims, Clergymen, Diplomats, Merchants, and Scientists

The French term *voyageurs* generally has come to be used to designate travelers who since the early modern period went to the Orient to learn about it (see Figure 4). Most of them did not travel alone but rather in groups, and before the middle of the fifteenth century their routes in Asia Minor crossed the borders of various territories ruled by Christians and by Turkish emirs. As a rule, they traveled through the Ottoman Empire with the sultan's permission and a letter of recommendation from him, accompanied by a *dragoman* (interpreter), an armed escort, a servant and cook, and riding and pack horses.

It was probably in 1333 that a Muslim pilgrim named Ibn Baṭṭūta, from Tangier in Morocco, boarded in Latakiya a Genoese ship headed for the land of the Turks. Eight years earlier he had traveled to Mecca, and finally returned thirty years later, after travels in the Near East, India, and China. This land of Bilād al-Rūm, he declared, "is one of the finest regions in the world; in it God has brought together the good things dispersed through other lands. Its inhabitants are the comeliest of men in form, the cleanest in dress, the most delicious in food, and the kindliest of God's creatures." He continues:

> Wherever we stopped in this land, whether at hospice or private house, our neighbours both men and women (who do not veil themselves) came to ask after our needs. When we left them to continue our journey, they bade us farewell as though they were our relatives and our own kin, and you would see the women weeping out of grief at our departure.[1]

Ibn Baṭṭūta spoke no Turkish and was dependent on interpreters in his entourage or in his host's home. He was chiefly interested in shrines, mosques, and tombs. But he also provides lively descriptions of the land and people, clothing, manners and customs, agricultural products, and foods, and he repeatedly reports on his encounters with the local notables. However, he very seldom mentions pre-Islamic relics or historical events and persons: for instance, he notes that people say Konya was founded by Alexander. In Selçuk he mentions, in addition to the Isa Bey mosque, the large church built with enormous stones, and says that the philosopher Aflāṭūn (Plato) lived in Pergamon—confusing him with the physician Galen. But in Amasya, which is praised by him for its beautiful gardens, trees, and fruit, he says nothing about the tombs of the kings cut into the rock cliffs.

In the Middle Ages, the route through Anatolia was not completely closed to Christian pilgrims from the West; however, most of them traveled by sea, and if they visited any cities, then only port cities, and even these usually only on the coasts of the Mediterranean.[2] In 1498 the Florentine priests Bonsignore di Francesco di Andrea Bonsignori and Bernardo Michelozzi, who were interested in archaeological

HALTE DES VOYAGEURS PRÈS DE DOURLACH, DANS LA CARIE.

4. Engraving from Marie-Gabriel-Florent-Auguste Comte de Choiseul-Gouffier, *Voyage pittoresque dans l'Orient Ottoman*, Paris 1782. Print in private possession of author.

sites, traveled there by land and by sea: from Constantinople they went to Bursa, visited the ruins of Kyzikos and Ilion (Troy), sailed on to Mytilene and back to the coast, traveled overland, via Foca (Phokaia), to İzmir, and then sailed via Chios to Palestine.[3] Pilgrims who crossed Anatolia—often on their way back from the Holy Land—chose different routes, through the Cilician Gates above Tarsos and via Ankara, or climbed (as did Arnold von Harff, a knight from Cologne, in 1499) up the valley of the Gök Su (Kalykadnos) River into the Taurus Mountains, passing through Anatolia via Karaman (Laranda), Konya, and Bursa.[4]

For Christians, Asia Minor was not simply a land to be passed through on the way to Palestine. Even today American and European groups travel to the sites where the Apostle Paul was active. In the past, clergymen and missionaries made many a discovery; knowledge of the Bible and learned curiosity went hand in hand. Thus in the seventeenth century (1668–1671) the English chaplain in Constantinople, Thomas Smith,[5] visited the seven cities mentioned in the Apocalypse of St. John and noted, in addition to those already known (Pergamon, Smyrna, Ephesos, Sardeis, and Philadelpheia), also the sites of Thyateira and Laodikeia. Edmund Chishull, the vicar of Walthamstow near London and a chaplain in Smyrna, was also interested in antiquities.[6] In 1739, his countryman Richard Pococke, the archdeacon of Dublin and bishop of Ossory and Meath, traveled from Smyrna through the

Maeander valley into the interior of Phrygia, where in 1740 he was the first European to obtain information about the existence of the ruins of Pessinus.[7] A Florentine abbot, Domenico Sestini, published his notes on a journey undertaken in 1781 all the way through Anatolia and down the Tigris to Basra.[8] In 1833 the British chaplain Francis Arundell discovered Antiocheia in Pisidia.[9] Competent in Arabic, Turkish, Armenian, Persian, Hebrew, Syrian, and Sanskrit, the Lazarist Eugène Boré, from Angers in western France, was long active in Ankara, where he founded a school for poor Armenians; his travels through Bithynia and Paphlagonia in 1838 produced a great deal of information on ancient ruins and discoveries of inscriptions.[10] The five-volume fundamental study on the cave churches of Cappadocia was completed in the first half of the twentieth century by the French Jesuit priest Guillaume de Jerphanion.[11] Among the researchers on Asia Minor who have made a name for themselves, Sir William Ramsay (p. 24 f.), for example, was particularly fascinated by the Christian areas and sites, and his countryman William Calder "had first arrived in 1908 with the Old Testament strapped to one ankle and the New to the other."[12]

From the late Middle Ages on, envoys and ambassadors constituted an important group of researchers on antiquity in Turkey. The Castilian nobleman Ruy Gonzales de Clavijo was sent to Tamerlane's court in Samarkand by Henry III of Castile between 1403 and 1406. He mentions walls, bridges, and church buildings in a few cities on the Turkish coast of the Black Sea, which were then controlled partly by the Turks, partly by the Genoese, and partly by the Empire of Trebizond.[13] In the sixteenth century, when European courts were more and more frequently sending legations to the new great power on the Bosporus, the Flemish diplomat Ogier Ghiselin de Busbeq resided in Asia Minor on several occasions. In 1554 Ferdinand I sent him to Sultan Suleiman II in Constantinople; he remained on diplomatic assignment in Turkey until 1562. When Busbeq arrived there, the sultan was away, waging war, and Busbeq followed him via Ankara and Çorum as far as Amasya. The journey to Amasya is described in the first of four letters to Busbeq's friend Nicolas Michault,[14] and we also have the notes taken by his companion, the Viennese humanist Hans Dernschwam, who came from Bohemia; they were first published in the nineteenth century.[15] We owe to Busbeq not only the introduction of lilacs, tulips, and hyacinths into Central Europe, but also the discovery of the temple in Ankara, where the inscriptions giving an account of the deeds of the Emperor Augustus were found.

Contributions to research on archaeology were made especially by diplomats who lived for long periods in the provinces of the Ottoman Empire:

the British consul in Smyrna, William Sherard, made expeditions between 1705 and 1716, for example to Aphrodisias, from which he brought back copies of inscriptions, including fragments of Diocletian's so-called "Prices Edict";[16]

Pascal Fourcade, Napoleon's consul in Sinop (1802–1812), who explored the site of Pompeiopolis in Paphlagonia and discovered the most important rock-cut tomb in northern Asia Minor;[17]

the French consul in Aleppo, Louis-Alexandre Corancez, who on returning home in 1812 brought along a description of the ruins of Side;[18]

the British Consul-General in Erzurum, James Brant, who traveled through eastern Anatolia in 1835 and 1838, between the Black Sea and Diyarbakır;[19]

the Russian Privy Councilor Nicolai Chanykoff, who in 1846 noted the rock-cut graves, inscriptions, and antique spolia in northern Asia Minor;[20] and

the British vice-consul in Trebizond (Trabzon), Alfred Biliotti, who was the first to describe the ruins of Satala on the Euphrates (which were recognized only later as the remains of a Roman legionary fortress) after visiting them in 1874.[21]

Alongside the diplomats there have been, ever since the fourteenth century, the commercial travelers, merchants, and officers from the port cities (Genoa, Venice, and Ancona), as well as the agents of western trading companies on the Bosporus and in Smyrna and other ports. Here the Italian businessman Ciriaco Pizecolli from Ancona stands out. Between 1430 and 1452 he made four journeys to western Asia Minor. Of his works, which were rich in observations on antiquities, only a few fragments were found and published centuries later.[22] The diamond dealer and traveler in India, Jean-Baptiste Tavernier, also reported on his overland journeys through Anatolia.[23] Around 1688 Daniel Cosson, from Leiden, the vice-consul of the Dutch trade association, was murdered in a village near Smyrna. This businessman and avid collector of inscriptions owed his classical training to the German philologist and professor in Leiden, Friedrich Gronovius.[24] Jacques Spon, an art dealer from Lyon, also wrote down the inscriptions on hundreds of ancient stones while traveling through western Asia Minor in 1676 with the English botanist George Wheler.[25] Plagiarism already took place at that time: copies of inscriptions from Anatolia made by Arthur Pullinger, an agent for the Levant Company in the silk and textile trade in Aleppo ca. 1725–1739, were appropriated by the Anglican bishop Richard Pococke without acknowledging their original source.[26] Andreas David Mordtmann, Sr., was a renowned researcher on antiquity who worked in Constantinople as a manager for the Hanseatic League. He explored northern Anatolia and composed his *Skizzen und Reisebriefe aus Kleinasien* (*Sketches and Travel Letters from Asia Minor*, 1850–1859).

In 1750, three wealthy and classically trained young Englishmen from Oxford and an Italian set out on a journey to the Orient, which—after one of them had died in Asia Minor—took the others to Palmyra and Baalbek. Their journey has been reconstructed from the papers of one of the participants, Robert Wood.[27] Wood and his companions left descriptions, maps, and sketches of many sites of ruins between the Dardanelles and Mylasa, the most valuable of them being those of the Temple of Artemis in Sardeis and the Temple of Artemis Leukophryene in Magnesia on the Maeander, which they did not, however, recognize as the Ionian Magnesia. Together with Wood's further notes on Kyzikos, Lampsakos, Pergamon, Teos, Ephesos, Miletus, Halikarnassos, Keramos, and Laodikeia on the Lykos, they constitute one of the most comprehensive dossiers on ancient architectural remains on the west coast of Asia Minor and are still important for archaeological research today.

Copies of ancient stone inscriptions were more and more in demand. The first large collection was produced by two extraordinary researchers: the French scholar and tutor of Charles-Louis-Napoleon Bonaparte (Emperor Napoleon III), Philippe le Bas, and an Englishman born and naturalized in France, William Henry Waddington, who read classics at Trinity College, Cambridge, and later became prime minister of France (1871).[28] Le Bas, who discovered Alinda and Labraunda in Caria, reflects the spirit of the long-since flared-up competition in searching out unknown antiquities: "I left Mylasa, having squeezed every last drop of juice from the lemon. In future, travelers can dispense with going there. I have not left them the slightest kernel to find."[29]

Since the eighteenth century, there has been an increasing number of organized expeditions to the Orient sponsored by European institutions and governments. Joseph Pitton de Tournefort, the botany professor from Aix-en-Provence who tried to climb Mt. Ararat, had been assigned by the king of France to conduct research on the flora of the East on the basis of ancient writings.[30] Paul Lucas was also sent to the Orient by Louis XIV; he so fantastically adorned his impressions on two journeys through the tuff landscape of Cappadocia that no one believed him.[31] Carsten Niebuhr, the father of the later equally well-known historian of antiquity, Barthold Georg Niebuhr, was the first in a series of great European researchers on Arabia. He studied mathematics in Göttingen and took part in the Danish expedition to the Orient that left Copenhagen in 1760. He was the only participant who returned alive.[32] His copies of inscriptions from Iran helped Georg Friedrich Grotefend decipher cuneiform script in 1802. The research done in Ionia between 1764 and 1765 by Richard Chandler, a fellow of Magdalen College, Oxford, was conducted on behalf of the Society of Dilettanti. It was published in 1769 under the title *Ionian Antiquities*.[33] Three years later appeared the *Voyage pittoresque*, a report written by Marie-Gabriel-Florent-Auguste Comte de Choiseul-Gouffier, d'Alembert's successor in the Académie française, on his crossing of the Lycian-Carian borderland on the Gulf of Fethiye.[34] Joseph Freiherr von Hammer-Purgstall, an Austrian orientalist and diplomat, traveled nearby in 1802 and was the first to record Carian alphabetic writing on a rock-cut tomb there.[35] A researcher on the Orient from London, William George Browne, the discoverer of the Siwah oasis, crossed Turkey several times between 1802 and 1813, and wrote down his impressions.[36] While traveling from eastern Anatolia toward Teheran, he was murdered by bandits. In 1829 the young Hessian cuneiform scholar Friedrich Eduard Schulz, from Gießen, met with the same fate in Kurdistan, which was nearly inaccessible to foreigners. He had been on his way to investigate, on behalf of the French Société Asiatique, inscriptions near Lake Van and Lake Urmia.[37] We owe to him the first close examination of the Urartian capital Tuspa, and he also discovered the Kelischin ("blue stone") stele, which is bilingual, Assyrian-Urartian, and is important for research on those languages.

Cartographers, Specialists in Natural History, and Archaeologists up to the First World War

The age of intensive exploration of ancient Asia Minor by European travelers began in the nineteenth century, after Napoleon's expedition to the Orient (he landed in Egypt in 1798). To the amateurs—diplomats, clergymen, merchants—we can add a group of men who wanted to study the geography, geology, and flora of the country and were especially concerned with cartographic depiction, though they also paid close attention to the antiquities: natural scientists, engineers, physicians, and officers. In 1800 the Old Phrygian rock-cut tombs and monuments were discovered by the English artillery officer William Martin Leake while on an expedition across Anatolia.[38] We owe to a captain working for the East India Company, John MacDonald Kinneir, the discoverer of Susa, observations from northern Asia Minor made between 1808 and 1814.[39] In his book *Karmania, or a Brief Description of the South Coast of Asia Minor and the Remains of Antiquity* (London, 1817), the English admiral and hydrographer Sir Francis Beaufort provided a description of the sites of Patara, Phaselis, and Soloi. Many discoveries of ancient sites, especially in west-central Anatolia, such as the ruins of Aizanoi and Synnada, were made by the French engineer and cartographer Camille Callier during his travels in that area in 1830–1831; he also determined the location of the Cilician and Syrian Gates through the Taurus and Amanos Mountains, as well as that of ancient Samosata on the Euphrates.[40]

Soon thereafter, in 1834, Charles Texier from Versailles found walls that later proved to be those of the Hittite capital Ḫattusa; for Texier, who had studied mathematics, chemistry, and Greek, that was not his only glorious chapter; he also was the first to make known the ruins of the Temple of Artemis in Magnesia on the Maeander (which had already been visited by Robert Wood), and following his investigations in Assos, the reliefs from the Temple of Athena were taken to Paris. Between 1839 and 1848 he wrote his comprehensive *Description de l'Asie Mineure*. William Francis Ainsworth, a physician and geologist, collected the materials for his *Travels and Researches in Asia Minor* (1842) during the Royal Geographical Society's Euphrates expedition carried out three years earlier. He measured Mons Casius—on the Turkish-Syrian border south of Antakya—and discovered the ruins of Apameia in northern Syria.

William John Hamilton must be considered an outstanding figure in the research of that time. Born in London, during his studies in Göttingen he turned first toward philology and history, but later became a natural historian with an emphasis on geology. Between 1835 and 1837 he traveled from Smyrna to large parts of western, northern, central, and eastern Anatolia. Among his works are descriptions, invariably accompanied by detailed geological studies—of the central Anatolian *katakekaumene* (literally, "scorched") landscape and the coast between Sinop and Trabzon, in which he draws on Xenophon and Strabo. He climbed Erciyas Dağ and crossed the tuff terrain of Cappadocia.[41]

Advances in knowledge of the southwest coast of Asia Minor were achieved mainly by Englishmen: Sir Charles Fellows, who explored the almost unknown interior of Lycia and discovered the ruins of Xanthos in 1838, while on an expedition from Smyrna, became the father of Lycian archaeology. On a second trip the following year he reached the Arykandos valley and Milyas and Kibyratis. The legendary English ship *Beacon* carried several researchers and also served to carry away objects discovered in the ancient ruins. The "Xanthian marbles," including the Nereid monument (p. 168) have been treasures of the British Museum ever since.[42] Aboard the *Beacon*, Captain Hoskyn discovered Kaunos in 1840.[43] The following year, under the command of Thomas Graves, the ship went on a research voyage led by Fellows, in which the physician and natural historian Edward Forbes and the naval officer Thomas Abel Brimige Spratt also participated.[44] Among the discoveries made was Termessos in Pisidia. At about the same time Ludwig Ross, from Holstein, and a teacher at a *Gymnasium* in Posen (today Poznan), Julius August Schönborn, explored the interior of Caria and Lycia; Schönborn found the Heroon of Trysa.[45] Rough Cilicia, which was still largely unexplored as late as the middle of the nineteenth century, was first crossed by the Prussian officer Fischer, followed soon afterward by the Austrian botanist Theodor Kotschy.[46] Among German travelers there arose the curious notion of colonizing the fertile stretches of land in the north and in the south of Asia Minor.[47]

The reports of researchers on Turkey up to the middle of the nineteenth century were taken into account in the monumental work *Die Erdkunde von Asien* written by Carl Ritter from Quedlinburg (1779–1859), which appeared in nineteen volumes between 1832 and 1859. The work combines ancient written sources and the accounts of modern *voyageurs* in a regional study that offered a wealth of materials unparalleled at that time. At about the same time Albert Forbiger, the rector of the Nicolai Gymnasium in Leipzig, produced the first and still only comprehensive, three-volume handbook of ancient geography (Asia is covered in volume II). In 1861, Ritter's student Heinrich Kiepert brought out the *Atlas Antiquus*, on the basis of which his son, Richard Kiepert, tried to produce an atlas of the whole of the ancient world, *Formae orbis antiqui*, but was unable to complete it. Among the most comprehensive reports of this period are those of two pioneers who were in the service of the Russian government. After resigning as an attaché at the Russian embassy in Constantinople, the geologist Piotr Alexandrovich Tschichatschew made six journeys through Asia Minor between 1848 and 1853. Heinrich Kiepert edited his notebooks and published them in abbreviated form in 1867.[48] Between 1855 and 1860, Xavier Hommaire de Hell, who was also a geologist and an engineer, roamed around Bithnyia, Paphlagonia, Pontos, Armenia, Azerbaijan, and Persia, accompanied by the painter Jules Laurens, whose enchanting watercolors of landscapes and ruins are now preserved in Paris. Hommaire de Hell died in Isfahan when he was only thirty-six years old.[49]

In the nineteenth century, officials at the Porte began to devote attention to the exact cartography of Asia Minor and to import expert know-how from Europe. The cartography of eastern, northern, and central Anatolia in particular owed its unprecedented level to a group of German officers. The instruments they used were clocks, compasses, and barometers. The most prominent of these officers was Helmuth Karl Bernhard Graf von Moltke, who was later to be the victorious general at the battles of Königgrätz and Sedan, and one of the founders of the German Empire proclaimed in 1871. By the time he died at the age of ninety-one, Moltke had become a legend as a soldier and a writer, like the later "Lawrence of Arabia." In 1835 he was assigned as a military advisor to the Porte when the latter was waging war against the renegade governor of Egypt, Mehmed Ali. During a four-year journey through eastern Anatolia, Moltke prepared the maps (published in 1852–1858) that were used by the Turkish general staff until well into the twentieth century. On a *kellek* (a raft made of animal hides), he floated down the upper Euphrates. Among his discoveries was an Urartian rock inscription found farther to the west than any other. His *Letters about Conditions and Events in Turkey, Written during the Years from 1835 to 1839* and especially his *Unter dem Halbmond. Erlebnisse in der alten Türkei* became widely known.

The writings of the Prussian cavalry captain Walther von Diest about his travels through Phrygia, Bithnyia, and Paphlagonia (1866) are not inferior in vividness and accuracy to Moltke's reports from the Euphrates region. Following in von Diest's footsteps in the north, Captains Maercker and Schäffer, along with First Lieutenants von Flottwell, Kannenberg, von Prittwitz, and Gaffron, in 1893 were the first to explore more fully the mouth of the river the ancients called the Halys (now known as the Kızılırmak) and its many gorges.[50] Around the turn of the twentieth century, their insights were broadened by the German geographer and geologist Richard Leonhard, who made three journeys through Paphlagonia and wrote a 400-page monograph on the area that appeared in 1915. Among other things, it contained new, precise information on the antiquities in the region, and especially the first comparative studies of Paphlagonian rock-cut tombs, with splendid photographs that were still taken on glass plates.

The descriptions of their horseback travels from village to village given by the Prussian officers and the geographer Leonhard offer an absorbing picture of the happiness and burdens—and the difficulties and dangers—they encountered on roads through the interior of late Ottoman Anatolia untraveled by other foreigners. The mountainous, densely forested terrain, and cold and rainy weather confronted researchers with harder tests than those they faced in the Mediterranean zones. Thus on November 1, 1886, Diest noted: "The horses were dreadfully soaked, the rain continued with only brief interruptions. On my way, I sketched the itinerary on the rubber cuffs of my coat." Then come further enchanting views, such as that of Amasra, the ancient Sesamos-Amastris:

A marvelous sight, one of the most beautiful of our journey, lay before us. Rocky islands stretched far out into the broad, sunlight-saturated sea, with its shimmering garland of pearls foaming at their feet, while on their cliffs glowed the white walls of the

Turkish houses, surrounded by medieval walls, lushly overgrown with dark green foliage, the whole blaze of colors standing out against the boundless surface of the blue Pontos Euxeinos.[51]

The local officials seemed especially suspicious of measurements and cartographic drawings, and people withheld information. Leonhard and Flottwell sensed distrust: "In the cities I was thought to be a spy, and in the villages an official working for the Turks who was supposed to conscript the men. The women often screamed when they saw me coming."[52] Certain localities had to be avoided because of cholera. Seeking refuge for the night in a *misafırodası* (guest room), they were plagued by myriad bedbugs and fleas, against which Persian insect powders were completely ineffective. Bands of robbers made roads and villages unsafe; a ringleader who had been wounded in a fight and taken prisoner was summarily shot by the local *Kaimakam* (administrator) before the visitors' eyes. Dogs were ubiquitous and posed the greatest danger:

> Every flock and every village is guarded by a number of these enormous animals. In packs of six to eight, they attack any stranger like charging cavalry, with a vehemence and fury that one hardly expects from dogs. Woe to him who cannot defend himself; he will inevitably be torn to pieces. The shepherds think a long time before calling off their dogs, and then it is still a question whether the dogs will obey them.[53]

Today, researchers traveling through these villages are still commonly confused by the kind of information that Flottwell encountered among the peasants: "Turks are so loath to tell a questioner something he will find displeasing that the information one receives regarding distances is very unreliable. As among Pomeranians a 'not very great' distance often turns out to be quite long, the Turk says: 'you'll be there in two hours,' but when after two hours one asks the same question, the reply is the same: 'in two hours.'"[54] However, these travelers also praise, as have countless others since Ibn Baṭṭūta, the exuberant hospitality found in most places. Thus an English researcher who was journeying through eastern Anatolia put it this way: "I received amazing hospitality, north of Malatya, leaving a trail of slaughtered sheep."[55]

The earliest true experts in the domain of studies on antiquity who undertook expeditions to these areas on the Black Sea and the neighboring regions in central Anatolia were archaeologists and epigraphists, first of all Georges Perrot, who was sent there in 1861 by Napoleon III to pursue scientific research—Perrot was accompanied by the architect and artist Edmond Guillaume—and Perrot's countrymen Doublet, Legrand, and Mendel, as well as Gustav Hirschfeld from Königsberg and Ernst Kalinka from Austria. The Scot William Mitchell Ramsay first went to Asia Minor in 1881 on a research grant; later knighted and appointed professor of archaeology at Oxford and professor of humanities at Aberdeen, Ramsay made several trips to the region before the First World War, especially in western and central Phrygia, Pisidia, and Lycaonia,[56] and published his *Historical Geography of Asia Minor* in 1890 and the two-volume study *Cities and Bishoprics of Phrygia* from 1895 to 1897.[57] Exploring central Phrygia, he was joined by Gertrude Bell, at that time already a distinguished traveler, archaeologist, and writer on the Near and Middle East, and together with her he excavated the site known as "A thousand and one churches" (Binbir Kilise). In 1914, during excavations in Psidian Antiocheia, Ramsay found fragments of a third copy (after those of Ankyra and Apollonia) of the *res gestae*, the account of the Emperor Augustus's deeds. John Robert Sitlington Sterrett of Boston traveled partly with Ramsay and partly on his own; he undertook the study of inscriptions at the American excavation of Assos and in Tralleis, and in 1884–1885 he searched for inscriptions throughout large parts of central Anatolia.[58] The Englishmen J.G.C. Anderson, J.A.R. Munro, F. B. Welch, and D. G. Hogarth, along with the Belgians Franz and Eugène Cumont and Henri Grégoire, journeyed through Pontos, Lesser Armenia, and Cappadocia. Their reports and copies of inscriptions are collected in the volumes of the *Studia Pontica*.[59] Grégoire, who put together a collection of Christian texts, also explored Cappadocia's cave churches in greater detail.[60]

The culture and language of the Urartians on Lake Van attracted more interest. British excavations at Toprakkale Castle in 1879 produced few results. A few years after the path-breaking research done by Eduard Schulz, all the members of a scientific expedition, including the German scholar R. Rosch, were killed in the same area.[61] New explorations were led by the orientalist Carl Friedrich Lehmann-Haupt in 1898–1899 in the area of the eastern Black Sea and the Caucasus, Armenia, Azerbaijan, and northern Mesopotamia. Members of his group also encountered perils. His adventurous travel writings, *Armenien einst und jetzt* (*Armenia Past and Present*), published in three volumes from 1910 to 1931, illustrate the wealth in historical relics, the ethnic-cultural and religious contradictions, and the enormous difficulties of traveling in this area (Figure 5). On almost every page, Lehmann-Haupt correlates his own observations of the country, people, languages, sites, and objects, as well as his descriptions of monuments and readings of inscriptions in Old Assyrian, Urartian, Greek, Syrian, and Arabic languages with the testimonies of ancient literature. His detailed reflections concern, for instance, the route described in the *Anabasis* and factual elements in Xenophon or the identification of Tigranocerta, the capital of the Armenian Empire founded by Tigranes II in the first century BCE.

Toward the end of the nineteenth and early in the twentieth century, several expeditions, especially epigraphic ones, were conducted in the west and southwest: Alfred Philippson traveled through Mysia and the adjoining parts of Bithynia and Phrygia.[62] A selection of Karl Buresch's unpublished papers appeared posthumously as *Aus Lydien. Epigraphisch-geographische Reisefrüchte* in 1898.[63] The Austrians Josef Keil and Anton von Premerstein made three journeys in the same area in 1906, 1908, and 1911.[64] Along with Ramsay, von Premerstein later evaluated the new text fragments of the *res gestae* from Apollonia. Gustav Hirschfeld visited Pamphylia in 1874,[65] Eugen Petersen, a professor of archaeology in Dorpat, and Felix von Luschan, an archaeologist, physician, and anthropologist, traveled through Lycia, Milyas, and Kibyratis from 1882 to 1885.[66] *Städte Pamphyliens und Pisidiens* (1890–1892) was based on the travel experiences of the Viennese art-lover and patron Karl Graf Lanckoroński, the scion of a Polish noble family. The large-format volumes

5. Kurdish mountain country west of Hakkari. Note the rough terrain.

offer photographs and multicolored drawings of exceptional quality of, for instance, the layouts of the cities of Selge, Termessos, and Sagalassos. Otto Benndorf and Georg Niemann reported on southwest Asia Minor, and Rudolf Heberdey, Ernst Kalinka, and Adolf Wilhelm reported on Cilicia, where Theodore Bent was able to observe the ruins of the temple of Zeus Olbios in 1890.[67]

The Beginning of the Excavations

In the second half of the nineteenth century, Europeans and Americans began to excavate archaeologically promising sites in Turkey. Their motives varied and were not limited to the spirit of research. The British Museum, which was founded in the eighteenth century and has been housed in its current building since 1848, competed with the Louvre in the purchase of antiquities. Museums in other cities, such as Berlin and Vienna, followed suit. At the time, the removal of antiquities, which has since been sharply criticized, took place with the consent of the Turkish government. In 1856 Sir Charles Newton, formerly an assistant in the British Museum's Antiquities Department and later vice-consul in Mytilene, discovered the remains of the Mausoleum at Halikarnassos—a funeral monument that in antiquity had been considered one of the wonders of the world because of its architecture and especially its sculptural decoration—from which he shipped sculptures and parts to London. In 1858 he had archaic sitting figures, a lion, and a sphinx from the Sacred Way at Didyma brought to the museum. In 1860 Newton returned to the British Museum, where he directed the Department of Greek and Roman Antiquities.[68] A few years later John Turtle Wood began, with the permission of the Turkish government, a search for one of the wonders of the world, the Temple of Artemis in Ephesos, at first at his own expense, and then with the support of the British Museum.[69]

The archaeological sensations, which had up to that point been made known to the European public mainly by Britons, were soon thereafter supplemented by Germans working in Miletus, Troy, and Pergamon. After a French expedition of 1868, Theodor Wiegand began excavations in 1899 in Miletus, from which the structural elements of the two-story ornamental façade of the market portal were shipped off to Berlin.[70] French excavations in Didyma in 1872–1873 and 1895–1896 preceded those of the Germans, and their discoveries ended up in the Louvre. Together with Hubert Knackfuß, Wiegand excavated in Didyma between 1905 and 1913 and again in 1924–1925, and he was the first to uncover the enormous temple (see Figure 41).[71]

The name of Heinrich Schliemann is inseparable from that of Troy. The son of a Protestant minister from Mecklenburg, he was a citizen of the world and a wealthy businessman who treated himself to the study of classical philology at the Sorbonne when he was in his middle forties. His fascination with Homer led him to search for the ruins of ancient Ilios, the scene of Homer's *Iliad*. From his new home in Greece he traveled to the Troad (northwestern Anatolia; see Map 1a) for the first time in 1868, and the following year published *Itaque, le Péloponnèse, Troie. Recherches archéologiques*, on the basis of which the University of Rostock awarded him a doctorate. Following an idea that had been put forward by others long before, he looked for Troy under the hill of Hisarlık (p. 60 f.) and there undertook the first of his excavations from 1870 to 1873 and the second in 1879. The first excavation already struck gold, the "Treasure of Priam," which can perhaps be considered, along with Howard Carter's discovery of Tutankhamen's tomb in the Egyptian Valley of the Kings in 1922, as the most spectacular in the history of archaeology. Schliemann established a Trojan collection in Athens, which he bequeathed to the German people. Transported from Berlin to Russia during the Second World War, this treasure still gives rise to diplomatic tugs of war between Berlin, Moscow, and Ankara.[72] During Schliemann's lifetime and afterward, his claim to have discovered "Homeric" Troy was highly controversial. Although it was firmly rejected by professionals in the field, his claim continues to be a subject of discussion even today. The excavation carried out by Schliemann's follower Wilhelm Dörpfeld (1893–1894) later acquired its true scientific significance as a cornerstone of modern stratigraphy, whose findings structure whole systems of chronologies of early ceramics.

The history of the excavation of Pergamon is no less sensational. In it are intertwined politics and diplomacy between Berlin and the Sublime Porte, road and railway construction in Turkey, Kaiser Wilhelm II's fascination with archaeology, the history of the German Archaeological Institute, and much more. It all began with the activities of German construction contractors in Turkey and the transport to Berlin of reliefs from the Great Altar. The massive sculptures made a powerful im-

6. Portrait gallery in the excavation house at Priene: Carl Humann, Osman Hamdi Bey, and Theodor Wiegand.

pression, and the attention given to the site in western Anatolia increased enormously. The "Pasha of Pergamon," Carl Humann (1839–1896), was an engineer and entrepreneur from Essen who was also an architectural researcher and a pioneering archaeologist. He began excavating Pergamon in 1878. In 1882 he produced in Ankara the first complete cast of the long inscription at the Monumentum Ancyranum and near the site of the Hittite capital in Boğazköy casts of the sculptures at the Yazılıkaya sanctuary. In 1883 he and Otto Puchstein were the first archaeologists to examine the shrine on the Nemrud Dağ, which the engineer Karl Sester had discovered in eastern Anatolia. Between 1891 and 1893 Humann excavated the Temple of Artemis in Magnesia on the Maeander. In 1895 he collaborated in the Austrian excavation of Ephesos, and from 1895 to 1899 he excavated, along with Theodor Wiegand and Hans Schrader, the ancient Ionian city of Priene. Highly distinguished by the end of his career, Humann died in Smyrna after a life spent in the Orient. In 1967, his remains were transferred to Pergamon. The list of Humann's successors who carried on (with interruptions) the excavations at Pergamon corresponds to the chapters of German archaeological history: Alexander Conze, Wilhelm Dörpfeld, Theodor Wiegand (Figure 6).[73]

Between 1881 and 1884 Otto Benndorf, an archaeology professor from Vienna, explored central Lycia on behalf of the Austrian Academy of Sciences, partly in collaboration with von Luschan and Graf Lanckoroński; reliefs from the Heroon of Trysa were transported to the Austrian capital.[74] Then, encroaching on the Englishmen's turf, Benndorf led the Austrian excavation in Ephesos, which had been begun in 1895. At that time Humann suspected that the Altar of Artemis "was located under the English rubble, and the devil knows whether the Englishmen will allow us to dig on their terrain."[75]

Osman Hamdi Bey, from a wealthy Istanbul family, studied law in Paris between 1860 and 1869. There he became a painter, an art lover, and an art connoisseur. After his return to Istanbul he embarked on a career that culminated in his appointment as Director of Museums at the Sublime Porte in 1881 (see Figure 6). He not only founded the Archaeological Museum of Istanbul but also led the first Turkish research at Nemrud Dağ, at the shrine of Hekate in Lagina, and at Sidon, where the so-called Sarcophagus of Alexander was excavated and sent to the Istanbul museum.[76] The discovery of Hittite culture in particular was to be of great importance for the growth of Turkish archaeology in the following period. Before the excavations began, the ruins at Boğazköy had been visited by many European scholars. After Heinrich Barth carried out a short excavation in Yazılıkaya in 1858, the Frenchman Ernest Chantre first began a dig in Boğazköy in 1893–1894. No one knew anything about a Hittite capital called Ḫattusa when in 1904 the Englishman John Garstang applied for permission to conduct excavations on the site. This project fell through when the German emperor personally intervened with Sultan Abdul Hamid II on behalf of the Assyriologist Hugo Winckler. Together with Theodor Makridi Bey, the curator of the museum in Istanbul under Osman Hamdi Bey, Winckler began excavations at the site in 1906. The inscriptions discovered there proved, even before Hittite was deciphered by Bedřich Hrozný in 1915, that they were in the capital of the great empire.

Even before the First World War, spectacular discoveries had shed light on the culture of the late Hittite principalities of southern Anatolia. Felix von Luschan conducted excavations in Zincirli between 1888 and 1902.[77] After Henderson's initial excavations made "Hittite" discoveries in the 1880s, David George Hogarth began his archaeological investigations in Karkamiš in 1910. The planned route of the Berlin-Baghdad railway to be built under German direction was supposed to cross the Euphrates at precisely this point, and the Germans threatened to deprive the excavators of the local labor force.

One assistant in the team was Thomas Edward Lawrence, whose book *The Seven Pillars of Wisdom* later made him famous as Colonel "Lawrence of Arabia," after he had helped organize the Arab uprising against the Turks (Figure 7). As a young graduate of Oxford and an expert on "medieval pottery," he investigated Syria's crusader castles, on foot and in the summer heat, and thus commended himself as the kind of English archaeologist who was not deterred by the most difficult conditions— "extremely indifferent to what he eats or how he lives"[78]—and not eager to leave the Orient for a seat at the high table and a chair in the Bodleian.

In the spring 1911 the renowned archaeologist Gertrude Bell (see p. 24 f.) visited Karkamiš. She sipped a cup of tea and offered advice about digging technique, while the hitherto hapless young assistants Thompson and Lawrence boasted about their erudition. Lawrence wrote in a letter: "She was taken (in five minutes) over Byzantine, Crusader, Roman, Hittite, and French architecture (my part) and over Greek folklore, Assyrian architecture, and Mesopotamian ethnology (by Thompson); prehistoric pottery and telephoto lenses, Bronze Age metal technique, Meredith, Anatole France, and the Octobrists (by me): the Young Turk movement, the construct state in Arabic, the price of riding camels, Assyrian burial customs, and German methods of excavation with the Baghdad railway (by Thompson)." By the end, apparently, "she was getting more respectful."[79]

7. Karkamiš excavation team, with T. E. Lawrence in the middle of the front row. © The Trustees of the British Museum, London.

Lawrence sent an anonymous letter to the *Times* (published on August 9, 1911, under the title "Vandalism in Upper Syria and Mesopotamia"), in which he lamented with bitter irony the destruction of historical relics in Aleppo, Urfa, Biredjik, and Rum Kale, and accused the Germans of wanting to use material from Karkamiš to build the Baghdad railway. But at the beginning of the 1912 season he made friends with the engineers, and they agreed that it was to the advantage of both sides to remove the stones that were blocking further digging and use them for constructing the railway. The Karkamiš excavation was initially unsuccessful under Hogarth, but under Leonard Woolley the site became known as the "metropolis of hieroglyphs" when unique reliefs and especially inscriptions were discovered there.[80]

From the Interwar Period to the Present

In the Turkish national state founded by Mustafa Kemal Atatürk after the First World War, Kurt Bittel resumed the excavation of Ḫattusa in 1931 and continued this work, with a long interruption during the Second World War, until 1978. Other members of the team were the architect Rudolf Naumann and the Hittite scholars Helmuth Theodor Bossert, Hans Gustav Güterbock, and Heinrich Otten. In 1978 the direction of the excavations was taken over by the architect Peter Neve, in 1994 by Jürgen Seeher, a specialist in prehistory, and in 2006 by Andreas Schachner, an archaeologist specializing in the Near East. Excavations of Hittite sites had long since begun in other places. Tahsin Özgüç excavated Maşathöyük in 1945 and from 1973 to 1984; Aygül and Mustafa Süel have been excavating Ortaköy, near Çorum, since 1990, and Andreas and Vuslat Müller-Karpe have been excavating Kuşaklı, south of Sivas, since 1992. In the 1990s, the Karlsruhe architectural researcher Wulf Schirmer carried out an architectural survey of a large, late Hittite complex on the volcanic cone of the Göllü-Dağ in southwest Cappadocia.

Bossert and Güterbock played a key role in training a group of Turkish scholars who were to become influential in the development of scientific research on antiquity and teaching in the new Kemalist republic. Bossert became a professor in Istanbul in 1934 and a Turkish citizen in 1947. With his German student Franz Xavier Steinherr and his Turkish students Bahadir Alkım, Selim Dirvana, Halet Çambel, and Muhibbe Darga, all of whom were polyglots, he devoted himself chiefly to research on Hittite hieroglyphics, and between 1947 and 1957 he excavated Karatepe in Cilicia, where sensational discoveries were made. From these C. W. Ceram took the inspiration for his popular book on Hittite research, *Enge Schlucht und Schwarzer Berg* (1955; the English translation was published as *The Secret of the Hittites: The Discovery of an Ancient Empire* in 1956). The exploration of Hittite and Luwian hieroglyphic monuments was carried further by David Hawkins and Halet Çambel, who published their monumental corpus in 1999–2000. In addition, between 1980 and 2004 Horst Ehringhaus produced a survey of Hittite rock reliefs in the time of the Great Empire.

The invitation extended by Atatürk to scientists proscribed in Nazi Germany was accepted not only by the Jewish specialist on the ancient Orient, Benno Landsberger, and by Clemens Emin Bosch, a specialist on ancient history, but also by Hans Gustav Güterbock, who taught for years in Ankara before moving to Uppsala and then to Chicago (1948–1949). Among his most important students were Nimet Dincer and her later husband, Tahsin Özgüç, who in 1947 began with the excavations in Kültepe near Kayseri. Even before the Nazis seized power in Germany, the Istanbul department of the German Archaeological Institute (whose first director was Martin Schede, until 1938), was established in 1929, and the Turkish Historical Society (*Türk Tarih Kurumu*) was founded in Ankara in 1931. Atatürk wanted talented young Turks to study abroad in Europe, and among the first of them were Sedat Alp and Ekrem Akurgal, who studied languages in the elite institution in Schulpforta (near Leipzig) that had been made famous in the nineteenth century by Nietzsche and Wilamowitz. Both went on to study in Berlin, Alp with Johannes Friedrich, Akurgal with Gerhard Rodenwaldt. Alp returned to Turkey in 1940, Akurgal in 1941.

Ekrem Akurgal[81] is considered the true Nestor of modern Turkish archaeology. The second and third generations of his students are now working at numerous excavation sites. Born in 1911 near Caesarea in what was then Ottoman Palestine, he spent his childhood and school days in Adapazarı and Istanbul before going to Germany. In 1941 he became a professor at the University of Ankara's Faculty of Language, History, and Geography, which had been opened five years earlier, and continued to teach there until 1981. His research projects extended to the whole of Anatolia, but the focus was on the archaeology of Greek culture in western Asia Minor. It is true that his first excavation, carried out with Nimet and Tahsin Özgüç in 1945, was in Zela, in Pontos, but from 1948 to 1952 he excavated the archaic Smyrna in Bayraklı with John Cook, and continued his work there from 1967 to shortly before his death in 2002. In the 1950s, 1960s, and 1970s, he led excavations on the Aeolian coast in Pitane, Kyme, and Phokaia, on the Ionian coast in Erythrai, and on the Carian coast on the Halikarnassos peninsula. With the Münster archaeologist Ludwig Budde, he conducted three campaigns in Sinop, the most important Greek colony on the Black Sea, and on the Propontis he worked in Kyzikos and Daskyleion, whose location, up to that time still a matter of debate, he was able to determine.

From 1932 to 1938 Carl Blegen directed the University of Cincinnati's excavations in Troy and once again attracted international attention to the archaeology of the Trojan War. Manfred Korfmann, a specialist in prehistory from Tübingen, Germany, finally resumed the excavations in 1988 and before his death in 2005 significantly enlarged the radius of research around the hill. Since then Ernst Pernicka, an archaeologist at the University of Tübingen, has assumed the direction of excavations. The directors of the German Archaeological Institute in Istanbul—Erich Boehringer, Wolfgang Radt, and Felix Pirson—continued the German tradition after the Second World War in Pergamon. Long-term and still continuing research was conducted in Miletus by the architectural historian Wolfgang Müller-Wiener, director of the German Archaeological Institute in his time, and Volkmar von Graeve, an archaeologist from Bochum; in the 1990s the team included the specialist in prehistory Wolf-Dietrich Niemeyer, whose work focused particularly on the Mycenaean period. Miletus's most outstanding temple, the Didymaion uncovered by Wiegand, was examined and restored after excavations there were resumed in 1962 by the archaeologist Klaus Tuchelt[82] (director from 1978 on), who extended the excavation area around the Sacred Way that ends in the temple district and the extant architecture nearby, followed in 2002 by Andreas Furtwängler. The architectural researcher Lothar Haselberger found ancient payrolls and building plans that were scratched into the marble of the inner courtyard's walls. Similar discoveries in Priene and Sardeis seem to confirm that such wall and floor surfaces in ancient structures were commonly used as drawing boards. In Priene the older German investigation was resumed by the Munich architectural historian and director of the German Archaeological Institute, Wolf Koenigs, and by the archaeologists Wulf Raeck (Frankfurt) and Frank Rumscheid (Kiel, Germany).[83] In the ruins of the city overlooking the Maeander valley, studies of ancient city planning and the evolution of Hellenistic-Roman domestic architecture have become the focus of interest. Aizanoi in Phrygia, fifty-four kilometers southwest of Kütahya, has a Temple of Zeus dating from Roman times that is among the best preserved in Anatolia and has developed into one of the larger German Archaeological Institute projects. Begun in 1926 to 1928 by Krencker and Schede, since 1970 the excavations have been extended to the baths and gymnasium, the stadium-theater complex, the colonnaded street, and other discoveries in the surrounding area made by the architectural researchers Rudolf Naumann (the third director, after Schede and Bittel, of the German Archaeo-

8. Ephesos, façade of the Celsus library and the south gate of the *agora*.

logical Institute in Istanbul) and Klaus Rheidt.[84] Rheidt was followed by the Freiburg archaeologist Ralf von den Hoff, who gave special attention to the Hellenistic phase of the city's development.

Hellenistic-Roman Ephesos has no doubt become the most imposing object of twentieth-century classical archaeology in Turkey concentrating on the architecture of ancient city centers. The excavations conducted by the Austrian Archaeological Institute from 1895 to 1913 and from 1926 to 1935 under Benndorf, Heberdey, Wilberg, and Keil were resumed after the Second World War by Franz Miltner from 1954 to 1959. Greek researchers had already undertaken restoration work in 1919 on the Basilica of St. John and the Church of Mary; Miltner carried out the first anastyloses (i.e., restoration using the original architectural elements to the greatest degree possible) in the area of the city, including that of the Temple of Hadrian. Under Fritz Eichler (1959–1969), Anton Bammer began excavating the Artemision. Finally, under the direction of the president of the Austrian Archaeological Institute, Hermann Vetters (until 1987), excavations at Ephesos underwent a phase in which large areas were uncovered and Roman buildings were re-erected, culminating in the terrace-house and library projects. While the former brought to light for the first time in the province a kind of interior architecture dating from the Roman Imperial period that is otherwise known only from Pompeii, the restored south gate of the agora and the restoration of the Celsus library by Friedmund Hueber and Volker Michael Strocka, completed in 1978, convey a vivid impression of the magnificence of the capital city of Asia during the Roman Empire (Figure 8).

However, a price was paid for the splendid achievements of archaeologists and engineers, since many investigations of the ruins could be made only by destroying existing late antique buildings.[85] Here as elsewhere, excavation sites developed into large construction sites, and the sites both profited and suffered from the increasing mass tourism. Under Vetter's successors Gerhard Langmann, Stefan Karwiese, Fritz Krinzinger, and (since 2008) Sabine Ladstätter and Johannes Koder, the construction of the largest archaeology park in Turkey advanced and currently attracts more than a million visitors per year.

Besides the one in Smyrna, a few smaller, notable sites are scattered over Ionia and Aiolis. In 1984 Orhan Bingöl began an excavation project in Magnesia, Ephesos's southern neighbor, on the lower Maeander, and in 2004 Vedat İdil of the University of Ankara began another in Nysa on the middle stretch of the river.[86] Theodor Makridi and Charles Picard had already carried out investigations in Klaros before the First World War, and between 1950 and 1960 Jeanne and Louis Robert excavated the site of the important oracle of Apollo. The Turks Mustafa Uz and Numan Tuna did research on the temple of Dionysos in Teos; Güven Bakır and Yaşar Ersoy worked in Klazomenai, where Greek excavations of the archaic necropolis had already taken place between 1919 and 1921; Ömer Özyiğit in Phokaia (Foca); and Ersin Doğer in Aigai.

Complex anastyloses of ancient stone architecture somewhat comparable to those in Ephesos and Pergamon accompanied the American excavations of Sardeis and Aphrodisias. In 1958 George M. A. Hanfmann resumed, under the sponsorship of the American School of Oriental Research at Harvard and Cornell Universities, the excavation work in the Lydian capital that was continued after 1977 by Crawford H. Greenwalt, Jr., of the University of California, Berkeley, and since 2008 has been directed by Nicholas D. Cahill, Professor of Art History at the University of Wisconsin, Madison. The enormous gymnasium-bath complex with the Jewish synagogue built into the south wing of the *palaistra* (a rectangular court in the architectural context of a gymnasium) was completely reconstructed, including the roof.[87] In Aphrodisias, which is located in the highlands of Caria, the initial French excavations (Paul Gaudin) between 1904 and 1913 were followed by Italian excavations (Giulio Jacopi) from 1937 to 1939. The excavations carried out there by Kenan Erim of New York University from 1961 to 1990, and from 1993 on by R.R.R. Smith (Oxford) and Christopher Ratté (currently at the University of Michigan) yielded, among other things, rich discoveries of large sculptures from the Roman Imperial period that can be attributed to the activity of a school of sculpture in the city.[88]

A series of important archaeological sites emerged in southwestern Asia Minor between the Maeander and the Pamphlyian plain. In the nineteenth century, Hierapolis, Pergamon's colony and, in the Imperial period, a big city on the upper reaches of the Maeander, had already attracted the attention of the Germans Humann, Cichorius, Judeich, and Winter before Paolo Verzone began the Italians' systematic excavations in 1957.[89] After 1960, Italian expeditions also worked in the coastal city of Iasos; begun under Doro Levi (the director of the Italian School of Archaeology in Athens) and continued by Clelia Laviosa and Fede Berti (the director of the National Archaeological Museum of Ferrara), these expeditions investigated the Hellenistic, Roman, and Byzantine structures in the large settlement area that covers a peninsula.[90]

In Knidos, the American archaeologist Iris Cornelia Love had since 1967 sought in vain the Aphrodite sculpted by the Greek master Praxiteles, which stood, according to the Roman writer Pliny the Elder (*nat.* 36, 22), in a shrine in the city.[91] In 1987 the direction of the excavations was taken over by Ramazan Özgan of the University of Konya.[92] In the 1980s and 1990s the Turkish archaeologists Yussuf Boysal and Çetin Şahin did research in Stratonikeia and Lagina, while Ümit Serdaroğlu examined the Imperial period temple of the Carian Zeus Lepsynos in Euromos. Since 1948, Swedish expeditions under Pontus Hellström and Lars Karlsson have studied the shrine of Carian Zeus Labrandeus in the mountains of inner Caria,[93] and Danish expeditions under Kristian Jeppesen and Poul Pedersen have made new discoveries at the site of the Mausoleum at Halikarnassos.

In the late 1940s Jeanne and Louis Robert excavated the Temple of Artemis of Amyzon in northwestern Caria, and the excavations in Kaunos that were begun in 1966 by Baki Öğün of the University of Ankara have been directed since 2001 by his student Cengiz Işık.[94] Lycia's most important dynastic seat, Xanthos, and the neighboring shrine of Leto, have been French excavation sites since 1950, first under Pierre Demargne, then under Henri Metzger and Christian Le Roy, and finally under Jacques de Courtils.[95] Here, in the center of the specifically Lycian-Greek mixed culture of the classical and Hellenistic periods, came to light an especially precious linguistic testimony—the Aramaic-Lycian-Greek *trilingue*, a document in three languages—that finds a parallel only in the later discovery of the *bilingue* of Kaunos, which is bilingual in Greek and Carian. The port city of Patara on the coast of western Lycia, with whose investigation and preservation Fahri Işık and his wife Havva Işkan, of the University of Antalya, Turkey, have been concerned since 1988,[96] contained the rubble of an equally exceptional monument from the time of the Emperor Claudius (41–54 CE), which the epigraphers Sencer Şahin and Mustafa Adak reconstructed. Inscribed on it is a road map of the province of Lycia with indications of the distances between cities. Havva Işkan also conducted excavations in Tlos, in the upper valley of the Xanthos. The German archaeologist Jürgen Borchhardt investigated the great Lycian rock necropolis of Myra and began excavations farther east in Limyra, where he discovered in 1969 the heroon of the dynast Perikles. Since 1975 he has been a professor at the University of Vienna. He pursued the work in Limyra and in 2002 handed over its leadership to the Viennese archaeologist Thomas Marksteiner. The name Cevdet Bayburtluoğlu, of the University of Ankara, is associated with long-term research on the nearby city of Arykanda.[97]

Still farther to the east, the great excavation sites on the south coast become rarer: after the Second World War, the Istanbul archaeologist Arif Müfid Mansel conducted excavations in the extensive fields of ruins in Perge and Side, the former in 1946, the latter in 1957. At both sites his student Jale İnan directed the work from

1975 on.[98] The excavation project in Perge also remained at the University of Istanbul after 1988, when Haluk Abbasoğlu took it over. Since that time, in addition to important discoveries of sculptures, splendidly decorated marble sarcophagi have been salvaged from the necropolis. Wolfram Martini, an archaeologist from Giessen, Germany, carried out surveys on the acropolis.[99] In Cilicia, genuinely systematic excavations have been conducted over a long period of time in Anemurion (1960s–1980s) by Elizabeth Alföldi-Rosenbaum and James Russell, as well as in Elaiussa Sebaste, headed up by Eugenia Equini Schneider, an archaeologist at the University of Rome (La Sapienza) since 1995.

If we go farther northwest and north from Pergamon, we also find few excavation sites other than Troy. The American excavations, begun in Assos by Henry Bacon and Joseph Clark from 1881 to 1883 in the Doric Temple of Athena (reliefs were sent to Boston at that time as well)—the agora, the theater, and the necropolis—were taken up again a century later by Ümit Serdaroğlu[100] and recently continued by Nurettin Arslan. Since 1997 the Münster historian of antiquity Elmar Schwertheim has been excavating the early Hellenistic foundation of Alexandria Troas, which was later a Roman colony. Turkish projects at the Temple of Apollo Smintheus, directed by Coşkun Özgünel; the Imperial period temple in Kyzikos, directed by Abdullah Yaylalı and (recently) Nurettin Koçhan; the marble quarries on the island of Prokonnesos, directed by Nuşin Asgari; since 1988 the Persian satrap's residence Daskyleion near Bandırma, under Tomris Bakır of the University of İzmir; and finally the theater excavations led by Bedri Yalman in Nikaia (İznik) since 1980 remain for the time being the only noteworthy ones in this region.

So far as the Greco-Roman civilization of the south coast of the Black Sea is concerned, this region has been neglected to an extent that is impossible to understand from a scientific point of view. After Akurgal's and Budde's excavations in Sinop, two larger projects were begun in Paphlagonia for the first time, that of the Munich archaeologist Lâtife Summerer in Pompeiopolis and that in Hadrianopolis directed by an archaeologist from İzmir, Ergün Laflı.

The European tunnel vision focused on the Greek classics and their ancient posterity in Hellenistic and Roman imperial art and architecture has—with the exception of the Hittite capital Ḫattusa—resulted in only scant attention being given to the large interior areas of Asia Minor. National traditions clung to the excavation sites with temples, halls, theaters, baths, and palaces, and to them flowed most of the money; the methodical approach to the ancient cultures of the land was in danger of being constricted. From the outset, John Garstang wanted to give a decidedly different emphasis to the British Institute of Archaeology at Ankara (BIAA), founded in 1948 at the urging of Seton Lloyd. Assessing the activities in one part of Turkey between 1971 and 1978, Stephen Mitchell and Anthony W. McNicoll lodged a complaint against an archaeology whose interest in the heritage of the past resembled that of a nineteenth-century museum.[101] In opposition to the latter they argued for an approach to research on the model of the English "New Archaeology." Perhaps the most consistent attempt to transfer this concept into reality was the Aşvan project. This hill, which rises out of the plain on the south bank of the Murad Su not far from Elaziğ, was settled from the Bronze Age down to the Middle Ages, and the BIAA director, David French, chose the village lying at its foot as the object of an ambitious human-environment study from prehistory to the present. Near the settlement site, which had very little to offer in the way of architecture or human artifacts, campaigns were conducted between 1970 and 1973 that, by using extremely refined sieving techniques, sought to make paleobotanical discoveries; locate animal bones, charcoal, and so forth; draw conclusions regarding the living conditions in the epochs concerned; and compare them—this was considered especially important—with the living conditions of the present inhabitants of the village. The project was not approved by the establishment in London, which gave priority to ceramics, artifacts, and buildings.[102] More than three decades later, however, much has changed in the "classical" sites as well: today, several excavation and survey projects in Turkey can claim to approach the ideals of the New Archaeology.

At a certain distance from the sites on the coast mentioned up to this point, are middle-sized and larger enterprises on the Anatolian plateau that can be mentioned. Among these are, for instance, the Belgian excavations in Sagalassos in Pisidia, where Marc Waelkens of the University of Leuven is working with a large team. With regard to the methodological plurality of the historical and scientific-technical research in use there and the funds invested, this excavation corresponds most closely to the aforementioned ideal. Pierre Lambrechts and subsequently John Devreker of the University of Ghent devoted themselves to the old Tolistobogii center, Pessinus in Galatia. Gordion, an Old Phrygian metropolis, is not far from Pessinus. After Gustav and Alfred Koerte conducted in 1900 excavations on the tumuli and the hill where the city was located, work under the leadership of Rodney S. Young of the University of Pennsylvania Museum (Machteld J. Mellink, a specialist in prehistory, was a member of his team) began there in 1949 and was continued by Keith deVries in 1974 and by Kenneth Sams in 1987. One of the most important Byzantine sites, Amorion, lies in this part of west-central Anatolia. The first excavations there were conducted by Martin Harrison in 1988 and are currently being continued by Chris Lightfoot.[103]

Among the outstanding Iron Age sites east of Ankara we may mention the Kerkenes Dağ project of Geoffrey and Françoise Summers of the Middle East Technical University in Ankara (since 1993), which succeeded in determining an Iron Age city layout by using modern technical survey tools, and the German-American-Turkish investigations of Eski Kahta and Nemrud Dağ. Following Humann, Puchstein, and Hamdi Bey in the nineteenth century, in 1938 Rudolf Naumann and Friedrich Karl Dörner made new discoveries. In 1951 Dörner found a cult relief, a stone processional way, rock inscriptions, and the acropolis of Arsameia on the Nymphaios, where he began excavations shortly afterward. At the same time, an American expedition directed by Theresa Goell began work on the Nemrud Dağ. The 2,150-meter-high mountain, with its artificially raised tumulus quickly became a tourist attraction in eastern Anatolia, not least as a result of a flood of illustrated publications, among which were many amateurish, enthusiastic, and misleading representations. In 1987 and 1988 Dörner's students Elmar Schwertheim, Sencer Şahin, and Jörg Wagner attempted to sound, by means of geophysical measurements, the inside of the tumulus, but they achieved no results that led further.[104] In 1968 Dörner, who had also conducted surveys in Bithnyia, had already founded the Forschungsstelle Asia Minor at the University of Münster, where under the leadership of Elmar Schwertheim a center for research on Asia Minor was established. There, Commagene remained an emphasis; the main shrine of the god Jupiter Dolichenus, a deity of worldwide significance during the Imperial period, has been explored and excavated since 2001 by Engelbert Winter, who had a few years earlier also discovered two large Mithras cult shrines at the foot of the hill-settlement of Doliche.[105] In Commagene, Samosata wholly disappeared, and Zeugma partly disappeared, beneath the waters of reservoirs; but before they did, emergency excavations were carried out there, in Zeugma by a Turkish-French-Swiss expedition beginning in 1996. Excavation and restoration in the Roman villa quarter with splendid mosaics are still being continued today under Kutalmiş Görkay of the University of Ankara.

In addition to the truly prehistoric sites where discoveries have been made, in Eastern Anatolia three further historical areas have moved into archaeology's field of view: the Roman border defenses on the Euphrates, the neo-Assyrian and neo-Hittite sites, and the Urartians' settlements and fortresses. In all these areas British researchers have made progress by digging. For instance, Richard Harper excavated the late Roman fort near Pağnik; in the 1980s David French excavated Tille-Höyük on the Euphrates; and in the 1950s Charles Burney carried out surveys of several fortresses in the Turkish part of the Urartian empire, and for one season in 1965, the excavation at Kayalıdere on the middle Arsanias (Murad-Su). In the 1960s, important Urartian fortresses were excavated: one in Altıntepe on the upper Euphrates by Tahsin Özgüç, two sites near Lake Van, in Adilcevaz by Emin Bilgiç and Baki Öğün, and in Çavuştepe by Arif Erzen (Figure 9). The Bronze Age site of Kültepe near Kayseri, which is the most important site in early Anatolian history before the Hittites, will be discussed later (pp. 64–67).

From Voyageur to Survey

Fieldwork beyond excavation began to change after the Second World War; there were no longer *voyageurs* of the old kind who crossed the territory on horseback. Greater distances were covered by means of off-road vehicles, even if nostalgic writers expressed their scorn for them: "the lone archaeologist incarcerated in a tin box misses much while driving."[106] The notion of the *voyage* was replaced by the English concept of the survey; the latter's "extensive" form, covering wider areas, concentrated mostly on certain kinds of material. In addition, other, more sophisticated forms have developed, such as the so-called intensive survey, in which individual researchers walk small areas or groups of several researchers walk a territory divided up

9. Urartian site at Cavuştepe, south of Lake Van.

into grid squares to document over large areas the remains of walls, the rubble of settlements, and scattered findings of all kinds.[107]

John M. Cook was a pioneer of historical regional studies in the Troad; he made multiple journeys from 1959 to 1969 that led, for instance, to the discovery of the ancient Greek town of Gergis.[108] In the 1990s, the philologist Josef Stauber completed a study devoted in particular to Homeric topography. Surveys in Mysia, Aiolis, and Lydia with primarily epigraphic interests were carried out by Elmar Schwertheim from Münster; Hasan Malay of the University of İzmir; Georg Petzl, a philologist from Cologne, Germany; and Peter Herrmann, an ancient historian from Hamburg. The project of producing a corpus series of the inscriptions in Asia Minor, *Tituli Asiae Minoris* (TAM), which was initiated by the Austrian Academy of Sciences and was intended to supplement the Berlin *Inscriptiones Graecae* (IG), began with Ernst Kalinka's edition of the Greek and Lycian inscriptions from Lycia (1901 and 1920). In 1981 and 1989 Herrmann published the results of his research in northeastern Lydia in two fascicles of volume V of the TAM series; Petzl extended the Lydian corpus by adding a third fascicle in 2007 covering the city of Philadelpheia and its territory. In Mysia the area around Pergamon has recently been examined more closely, with Felix Pierson's investigations of Pergamon's main port, the polis Elaia, on the one hand, and with the Atarneus survey conducted by Martin Zimmermann, an ancient historian from Munich, on the other hand.

Milesia—Miletus's territory—has been thoroughly investigated by surveys made in the 1980s and 1990s by Walter Voigtländer, a specialist in prehistory, and the archaeologist Hans Lohmann.[109] Lohmann also subjected to an intensive survey Mykale, a mountain ridge across from Samos, to which it had been difficult to gain access up to that point, because it was in a restricted military zone. He succeeded in finding previously unknown ruins there. After the Second World War, Caria has become one of the privileged areas for survey research: the territory was of special interest to Louis Robert, who planned a documentation of Mylasa in addition to his studies on Amyzon and Tabai.[110] The Englishman George Bean, still remembered by the natives as "Mr. Thousand" (*bin bey*) or "Giant Pagan" (*koca gavur*) because of his size, traveled a great deal in the southwest from 1946 to 1952 and published, in addition to his epigraphic findings, popular travel guides.[111] In the 1960s the Swede Paavo Roos produced a fundamental typology of Caria's rock-cut tombs.[112] At that time, Wolfgang Radt, who later led excavations at Pergamon, was examining not far away the remains of so-called Lelegian settlements on the Halikarnassos peninsula.[113] The ruins south of it, in Carian Chersonnesos, have been under excavation since 2005 by the archaeologist Winfried Held. Numerous inscriptions and discoveries regarding the historical topography of western and southern Caria were collected by Wolfgang Blümel of the University of Cologne and the Turkish-French team under the leadership of Pierre Debord (Bordeaux) and Ender Varinlioğlu (Ankara).[114] For several years, the territory of Herakleia on the slopes of Mt. Latmos has been the object of a multidisciplinary survey conducted by Anneliese Peschlow-Bindokat,[115] and a new inventory of topographical discoveries and archaeological relics resulted from the travels of Hans Lohmann and Werner Tietz in the area on the border between Caria and Lycia on the Gulf of Fethiye.[116]

In neighboring Lycia, still more intense international activity has prevailed over the past decades. In 2004 Hansgerd Hellenkemper and Friedrich Hild published the results of topographical studies on Lycia and Pamphylia in Byzantine times (*Tabula Imperii Byzantini* 8). Earlier, George Bean had also traveled in these areas[117] with his countryman Martin Harrison. The name of the small city Oinoanda in northern Lycia has become known to broader scientific circles because of the discovery, at the end of the nineteenth century, of fragments of a large inscription in which an Epicurean of the Roman Imperial period sought to set forth his master's teachings for the public. This text is of great importance for the history of philosophy. In 1968 a philosophy student, M. F. Smith, discovered 38 new fragments,[118] and the BIAA decided to undertake its own systematic survey of Oinoanda. The latter began in 1974 under the direction of Alan S. Hall and ended in 1983 with the completion of a map of the city and an epigraphic exploitation of eighty-six other pieces of the Epicurus inscription. This was immediately followed by a survey in the city of Balboura, not far to the north, which was carried out by James Coulton from 1985 to 1988. In

Oinoanda international and multidisciplinary research continues to the present day, and more and more fragments of the Epicurus-inscription come to light.[119] Kibyratis, which lies somewhat farther to the north, has recently been investigated by the epigrapher Thomas Corsten of the University of Heidelberg.[120]

In southern Lycia the surveys conducted by the architectural historian Wolfgang Wurster and the epigrapher Michael Wörrle have done pioneering work. Wurster investigated and compared a series of large and small seats of dynasts, while Wörrle shed light on the history and geography of Lycia as a whole as reflected in recently discovered inscriptions of exceptional richness.[121] These were followed in the 1990s by the University of Tübingen's Kyaneai project, directed by Frank Kolb, whose intensive surveys of the settlement structure of a city territory in central Lycia produced findings of unprecedented density and complexity. The significance of this project goes beyond Asia Minor itself, particularly with regard to the question of the relationship between city centers and rural settlement units. In its framework and in its wake, smaller individual projects led by Kolb's students followed: Andreas Thomsen's architectural documentation of the ruins on the Avşar-Tepesi; Christina Kokkinia's new interpretation of the Opramoas inscription from Rhodiapolis; and the research done in Teimiusa, Phellos, and Tyberissos by Martin Zimmermann and Christof Schuler.[122] The Austrian Thomas Marksteiner's field research—beyond the excavation of Limyra that he led—is situated farther east, and Mustafa Adak has added to our knowledge of the topography and epigraphy of the border area between eastern Lycia and Pamphylia.[123]

British and American activities extended from northern Lycia deep into central Anatolia: in the second half of the 1920s and in the 1930s the newly founded American Society for Archaeological Research in Asia Minor initiated and financed several research trips that ranged from the coasts of Rough Cilicia to the whole of Phrygia and the neighboring areas. A concept was developed that calls for all ancient relics found on the surface to be photographed and described, area by area, and then published in regional corpora under the title *Monumenta Asiae Minoris Antiqua* (MAMA). Among the most important researchers taking part in the fieldwork were the American William Hepburn Buckler from Baltimore, a co-founder of the Society, and the Scot William Moir Calder, a fellow at Oxford and professor in Manchester and Edinburgh who had earlier worked with Ramsay in Lycaonia; between 1908 and 1954 he undertook seventeen expeditions to Asia Minor. Other participants included Archibald Cameron and Christopher William Machell Cox (later knighted), whose copies of more than 1,200 inscriptions were published only much later by Barbara Levick, Stephen Mitchell, and others in *MAMA* IX–X.[124] From this research also proceeded Calder and Bean's *Classical Atlas of Asia Minor*, published by the BIAA in 1957. It was again Bean who in the 1950s made advances in Pisidia's highlands with regard to Graf Lanckoroński's research.[125] Between 1982 and 1996 Stephen Mitchell carried out, on behalf of the BIAA, a site survey of the cities of Antiocheia, Kremna, Sagalassos, and Ariassos, and traveled through various rural regions as well. If we also take into consideration the contributions of Bean, Hall,

Ballance, Mitford, and French, we could say that Pisidia "is BIAA territory,"[126] were it not for the research done by Hartwin Brandt, Bülent İplikçioğlu, and Marc Waelkens, the latter being a former member of Mitchell's survey team.[127]

In Phrygia, Emilie Haspels, continuing Sir William Ramsay's work, provided the first comprehensive documentation of the central highlands (the "city" of Midas) in her 1971 work *The Highlands of Phrygia. Sites and Monuments*, followed by Dietrich Berndt's 2005 study.[128] After earlier research by Louis Robert and Georges Radet, among others, Thomas Drew-Bear and Christian Naour undertook to investigate the epigraphy of this enormous area in the 1970s; since Naour's untimely death in a car accident, Drew-Bear has continued the museum and field work, year after year.[129] Marc Waelkens prepared a large study on so-called door-stones, parts of ancient tombs that are found primarily in Phrygia.[130] The results of Peter Frei's investigation of the territory of Dorylaion (now Eskişehir) in the 1980s and 1990s, also with an emphasis of epigraphy, will be published in his edition of a volume in the TAM series. Clemens Emin Bosch, who taught ancient history at the University of Istanbul, did outstanding work on the epigraphy of Galatia. In addition to important numismatic studies, his monograph *Quellen zur Geschichte der Stadt Ankara* (1967) is a milestone in research. Stephen Mitchell included in volume II of the series *Regional Epigraphic Catalogues of Asia Minor* (RECAM) the material I. W. Macpherson collected in the area around the city and published in his 1958 Cambridge doctoral dissertation. Together with David French, Mitchell published the first volume of a new Ankyra corpus in 2012. The fortresses of Galatia are dealt with in the surveys conducted by Levent Egemen Vardar from Ankara. In the 1990s Karl Strobel of Klagenfurt, Austria, and Christoph Gerber of Heidelberg investigated Tavium in eastern Galatia (Büyük Nefes Köy, near Yozgat). The Byzantine area was dealt with in a volume of *Tabula Imperii Byzantini* (TIB) published in 1984 by Klaus Belke and Marcel Restle.

Michael Gough, following in the footsteps of Ramsay, Swoboda,[131] and others, went farther, exploring the site of the Alahan monastery in Lycaonia and church buildings in Rough Cilicia between 1952 and 1972. Gough also studied the great ruins of the city of Anazarbos. In the 1990s, Gabriele Mietke of the State Museums in Berlin carried out a research project on early Byzantine churches in Cilicia; work on towers and settlements was done by Serra Durugönül, who established a center for research on Cilicia at Mersin University. For the TIB, Friedrich Hild and Hansgerd Hellenkemper invested many years in survey work on the whole area that is particularly rich in late antique and Byzantine ruins (TIB, vol. 5, 1990).

After surveys made between 1930 and the 1980s, the epigraphy of that region was represented in two MAMA volumes, several different reports, and a monograph.[132] Mustafa Sayar, an ancient historian from Istanbul, carried out new surveys that yielded a rich trove of inscriptions; he also discovered the previously unknown Seleucid fortress of Karasis, whose architectural plan is currently the subject of an international project.

Cappadocia has produced fewer finds. A survey made by the Hamburg archaeologist Dietrich Berges in the 1990s documented ancient remains in the area of Tyana; Berges presented his results together with Johannes Nollé's compilation of the inscriptions.[133] Since the first investigations carried out by Biliotti in 1874 and Hogarth in 1894, the boundary of the Roman Empire on the Euphrates between Commagene and Trapezus (now Trabzon) in Pontos and Cappadocia has become the domain of British survey researchers. Starting in 1963, Timothy Mitford explored, mostly on foot, the whole length of the borderline.[134] After Biliotti, the Cumont brothers, Timothy Mitford, and Chris Lightfoot,[135] the Roman legionary garrison at Satala was explored by the Swiss expedition led by Martin Hartmann (2004). In 1997, Mitford published the inscriptions that were discovered. Anthony Bryer and David Winfield investigated the primarily Byzantine relics found at the northernmost point of the Roman frontier, in Trapezus and in the whole Pontic part of the Turkish Black Sea coast, and published the results in a monumental study in 1985.[136] In the 1980s, the long-time BIAA director David French, who was originally a specialist in prehistory, turned to research on the Roman road system and the collection of milestones throughout Asia Minor; he also published numerous newly discovered inscriptions, as well as a corpus of the city of Sinop.[137] Among the fieldwork projects in the interior of Pontos are those of Bernard Rémy, the director of the École française Istanbul, in Sebastopolis, and those of Eckart Olshausen, an ancient historian from Stuttgart, in central Pontos. Of the ancient relics found in this area of the interior and in neighboring Paphlagonia, the rock-cut tombs are the most prominent. The Mainz archaeologist Robert Fleischer has recently investigated the larger ones in Pontos. After Hubertus von Gall's study, the numerous monuments in Paphlagonia required a new, more complete treatment, which F. Eray Dökü has now provided in his dissertation in Turkish.[138] This area had been earlier roamed by the Italian archaeologist Giulio Jacopi[139] in the 1930s, by Ahmet Gökoğlu, a museum director from Kastamonu, in the 1950s, and by the Englishman David Wilson in the 1960s. I have carried out nineteen epigraphic surveys in northern Asia Minor between 1983 and 2009, and since 2006 my team and I have been doing research on the inscriptions of Pompeiopolis. The walls of Amasra, on the Black Sea coast, have been subjected to a more precise investigation by Stephen Hill and James Crow.[140] In 1997 the director of the BIAA, Roger Matthews, began an interdisciplinary survey in southern Paphlagonia. Klaus Belke has authored a volume of the TIB (vol. 9, 1996) devoted to the region of Paphlagonia and Honorias.

Research and discoveries in the most western of the ancient lands of northern Asia Minor, Bithynia, also still lag behind those in the Aegean and Mediterranean regions. In addition to local projects, Friedrich Karl Dörner's and Sencer Şahin's comprehensive surveys have contributed to our knowledge of the topography and epigraphy of this region. Dörner collected and edited the epigraphic material from the Bithnyian peninsula (except for Chalkedon) for volume 4 of the TAM (1978).[141] Şahin's surveys covered the largest city territory in Bithynia, that of Nikaia. He him-

self brought out the corpus of the inscriptions from this city, initiated and shep-
herded the edition of other corpora of Prusias on the Hypios, Kios, Apameia, and
Bithynion-Klaudiupolis, and in several studies put the historical geography of western Bithynia on a new basis.[142]

Inscriptions and Coins

Field research projects have greatly increased in number over recent years and cannot
be further pursued here in all their current ramifications. In conclusion, we must cast
one more look on the enormous number of inscriptions and coins found and published individually or in collections. So far as corpora of inscriptions from all over
Asia Minor are concerned, the hieroglyphic corpus is unique, insofar as in it a coherent plan is consistently followed. Of all kinds, whether cuneiform, hieroglyphic, or
alphabetic, Greek inscriptions on stone offer by far the most productive epigraphic
documentation (cf. p. 181). There are hundreds of thousands of them. The obstacles
to producing a comprehensive corpus were and are of other dimensions. Time soon
swept aside the editions of Le Bas and Waddington, and of Boeckh and Franz in the
Corpus Inscriptionum Graecarum, not merely because of the increased number of
inscriptions found, but also because of methodological weaknesses in these early
works. After Ulrich von Wilamowitz-Moellendorff took over the "marshy corpus
matter" in 1902 and excluded Asia Minor from the new plan for the IG, no unified
concept could any longer develop in this area. Competing national attempts to establish supraregional corpora—TAM, MAMA, RECAM—remained fragmentary.
Today, the most comprehensive collection, with more than fifty volumes, *Inschriften
griechischer Städte aus Kleinasien* (*IK*), brings together collections and studies with
such different goals that one could better speak of a conglomerate than of an organized project to produce city corpora.[143] On the Greek epigraphy of Asia Minor, the
work of Louis Robert surpasses all others. Turkish researchers specializing in epigraphy emerged later and are still smaller in number than Turkish archaeologists; they
cannot all be mentioned here. At the outset stands Zafer Taşlıklıoğlu, who worked as
an assistant in classical philology under Ronald Syme, George E. Bean, and Walther
Kranz in Istanbul and later taught this subject himself as a professor and director of
the same institute. His research on inscriptions concentrated on Thrace and the area
around the Sea of Marmara. Among his students are Hasan Malay, İsmail Kaygusuz,
and Mustafa Sayar.[144] The development of the discipline in Turkey also owes much
to Sencer Şahin and Ender Varinlioğlu.

In Asia Minor, from the time of the Lydian Empire in the sixth century BCE to
the Byzantine era, coins were minted that are now found in museums and collections throughout the world. The purely aesthetic interest in the minor art of coins,
which was primarily focused on silver and gold, has long since been overtaken by the
basic historical discipline of numismatics, which seeks to find "princes of a lost
world," particularly among the mass-produced, rather "unattractive frogs" of bronze

coins minted by cities during the Roman Imperial period.[145] Given Johannes Nollé's estimate of the number of such coins—1 million—it is not surprising that attempts to produce overall corpora for Asia Minor have been up to this point even more fundamentally doomed to failure than editions of inscriptions on stone: the difficulties are of a different and greater kind than in epigraphy. A general publication on Asia Minor has nonetheless been envisaged. But William Henry Waddington, Ernest Babelon, and Théodore Reinach were no more able to advance their *Recueil générale des monnaies grecques d'Asie Mineure* beyond the beginnings than the Berlin Academy was able to realize the *Corpus nummorum*,[146] or Clemens Emin Bosch his general catalog of coins from Asia Minor. Apart from these attempts, scientific editions of larger holdings are scattered among museums; private collections; and regional, city-based, and thematic corpora. The Swiss textile manufacturer and collector Friedrich Imhoof-Blumer (*Kleinasiatische Münzen* 1–2, 1901–1902), who collaborated on the Berlin coin corpus, was one of the leading experts on the ancient coins of Asia Minor and became the pioneer of a modern methodology. We also owe advances to Hans von Aulock, an excellent amateur scholar and great collector, like Imhoof, as well as to Andrew Burnett, Michel Amandry, and Pere Pau Ripollès, the editors of the volumes of *Roman Provincial Coinage* that have appeared up to this point. This monumental work lists approximately 100,000 coins for the period up to the end of the Julio-Claudian era, most of them from Asia Minor, but it neither claims nor seeks to be absolutely complete, even within these limits. Thus at this point such a diversification of the sources has emerged that projected research under a thematic aspect already has to conquer terra incognita in the material. Major regional collections have been and still are partly in private hands and are published by the collectors themselves or, in fortunate cases, are made accessible to scientific study. For instance, Imhoof-Blumer's collection in the Winterthur Museum, Switzerland, is the core of the second volume of Hansjörg Bloesch's catalogue of the *Griechische Münzen in Winterthur*, which is dedicated to Asia Minor; in a series of volumes, von Aulock has dealt with the areas of Lycaonia, Pisidia, and Phrygia;[147] Henry Clay Lindgren has published important Asia Minor holdings; Edoardo Levante has published a comprehensive Cilicia collection; and Johannes Nollé and Ruprecht Ziegler have studied coins from Pamphylia and Cilicia held by various collectors in the Pfalz region, Germany, and in Düsseldorf.[148] Corpora for particular cities are becoming increasingly numerous; Dietrich Klose's corpus for Smyrna is very comprehensive.[149] There are whole volumes devoted to representations of gods on coins,[150] mintages representing the concept of *homonoia* ("order and unity"),[151] Hadrian's cistophoric (bearing the image of a casket) coinages,[152] and many other topics.

Modern numismatics does not stick to the object, but instead includes the whole spectrum of kinds of sources in the interpretation of coins. This self-evident but difficult-to-fulfill ambition was that of the same Louis Robert who dominated Greek epigraphy. In particular, municipal coinages under the Romans have up to this point been the subject of few monographic analyses. Peter Robert Franke's book *Kleinasien zur Römerzeit* (1968) is helpful for an exemplary overview.

Sabahat Atlan can be considered a genuine pioneer in classical numismatics in Turkey. She was a student of Clemens Emin Bosch in Istanbul and published a study on coins from Side. She has an outstanding successor in Koray Konuk, the editor of the first volume on Turkey in the series *Sylloge Nummorum Graecorum* (SNG).[153] Work on ancient coins is confronted by huge tasks in Turkey alone, where the coins accumulated in large and small museums, excavation depots, and private collections remain largely unexamined; approximately 800,000 coins, seals, and casts are currently stored in Istanbul.

✦ ✦ ✦

Research on the ancient cultures of Anatolia is not a matter of isolated specialization. The most experienced digger with the most intimate knowledge of ceramic styles, the expert on Persian-period wall painting or early Christian church architecture, the interpreter of the poetry of Apollonius of Rhodes or Quintus of Smyrna, or of the prose of Aelius Aristides, the decipherer of epichoric alphabetical writing on stone, or the interpreter of Anatolian linguistic remains in toponymy and anthroponymy—all their results emerge into the light of historical knowledge only when they are related to one another:

> It is contrary to the spirit of scientific inquiry when disciplinary groups, which were in any case formed accidentally, build their own hutches with a wolf trap in front of the door, and would like to reserve their own little showcase; and then they want to sing the praises of 'multidisciplinary' contacts. To do that is to take an enormous step backwards. Our science is not pursued by lining up cubes in a row, each in its little compartment, identified with nice labels, dabbed, sealed up, and sterilized. It is each individual's brain that makes the synthesis, and to achieve it one has to work—work hard—following the documents wherever they lead us.[154]

CHAPTER 3

From Prehistory to the Oldest Written Culture

Paleolithic, Mesolithic (ca. 2,000,000–10,000 BCE)

Relics of early humans in Anatolia go back to before 20,000 BCE and thus far into the Paleolithic or Old Stone Age. Hunters of large animals left traces of themselves in camps and caves that they occupied seasonally, and in some places also permanently, from which they went out in groups to hunt and to which they returned with their prey to butcher it. There they also made their tools and found shelter. In all of Asia Minor, more than fifty sites have been thoroughly investigated. In the Urfa region of the northern Fertile Crescent, more than 130 open camps have been found, and it is no accident that the first Paleolithic axe was already discovered there (near Birecik) in the nineteenth century. Discoveries in other regions are less numerous but nevertheless significant: bones of Neanderthals in the Karain cave, twenty-seven kilometers northwest of Antalya, and not far away, on the east coast of Lycia, relics of the Belbaşı and Beldibi cultures (see the Chronological Table in the Appendix). A key place in research is occupied by the Yarımburgaz cave, twenty kilometers northwest of Istanbul, which was inhabited or visited from the Paleolithic down into the Roman-Byzantine period (with interruptions). Prehistoric wall paintings have been discovered in the easternmost part of Anatolia, as well as in the south and west, in the Kızların cave near Van, in Beldibi near Antalya, and recently in the Latmos mountain range, not far from the Aegean coast. These paintings depict animals and humans—individuals, pairs, and groups. However, they do not date from the Old Stone Age, but certainly from one of the following epochs.[1]

Neolithic, Chalcolithic (ca. 10,000–3500 BCE)

Today, traditional terms such as pre-pottery Neolithic and Chalcolithic—the New Stone Age without ceramics and the transitional period between the Stone and Bronze ages—must no longer be understood literally as temporal horizons. It has turned out that ceramics were already being produced in the pre-pottery period, and copper and lead jewelry were produced in the late Neolithic.[2]

Anatolia's southeast flank projects directly into a zone where the transition to rain-fed agriculture and permanent settlements producing food on the basis of domesticated animals and cultivated plants took place in the early history of humanity.

This is the zone of the so-called Fertile Crescent, on the slopes of the mountains running from the Persian Gulf through Kurdistan and on to Palestine. In prehistoric times, this transition took place essentially during the pre-pottery phase of the New Stone Age, and this is what gives this period its exceptional significance in Anatolia as well: people repeatedly speak of the "Neolithic Revolution"—the sedentarization of humans—even though part of modern research has sought to emphasize that we are in fact dealing with transformations that proceeded at different rates, depending on the region and perhaps also independently of one another. Why, how, and in what stages and with what interruptions this transformation took place in Anatolia, whether it is connected with a specific conception of the early Anatolian (e.g., as the bearer of a common linguistic family)—these are the guiding questions of prehistory, and their importance far transcends Anatolia.

Since advances in the settlement areas of western, northern, central, eastern, and southeastern Anatolia, which differ greatly in natural environment and climate (see Chapter 1), cannot be connected with one another in any simple way, it continues to be difficult to define a typically Anatolian model of development between the Middle East and Europe. In addition, the maps based on survey and excavation results still have large blanks, and the field research done during the transition from the twentieth century to the twenty-first is going through a dynamic phase. In any case, the conception of Asia Minor as a "bridge between Asia and Europe," stretched to cover all historical periods, can be confirmed, if not (yet) traced precisely, insofar as there was a prehistoric transmission of agriculture, domestication, and processing techniques from the Orient to the Occident.[3] It is beyond doubt that the routes by which cultivated grains; domesticated animals like sheep, goats, and cattle; and crafts like ceramics, stone-cutting techniques, and metallurgy spread must have passed across Anatolia and over the straits to southeastern Europe. According to the latest investigations using DNA, all present-day cattle in Central Europe are descended from the ones domesticated in the Near East in the early Neolithic, although an independent domestication of European cattle was possible.[4]

Isolated sedentary cultures comparable to those in the Levant first appear in Asia Minor between 8300 BCE and 7600 BCE, after nomadic or semi-nomadic hunter-gatherer groups occupied ecologically attractive niches in the lowlands. Except for farther-reaching migrations made by individual groups, the hunting and gathering activity remained within a radius of about five kilometers from the camp. There are several models on which one can imagine a gradual, experimental change in strategies of self-sufficiency. Certainly, long-term and also periodic settlement must have been favored by the existence of abundant wild grains or vegetables and finally led to experimental attempts to grow them. This may also have been promoted by greater planned management of the game hunted: groups of hunters may have recognized the advantage of fencing in wild herds, whether to hunt the animals more easily, or to keep them away from crops in the fields or from stored food supplies. Sooner or later, more systematic control of game stocks meant feeding them. And to do that, it was necessary to store up more plant material.

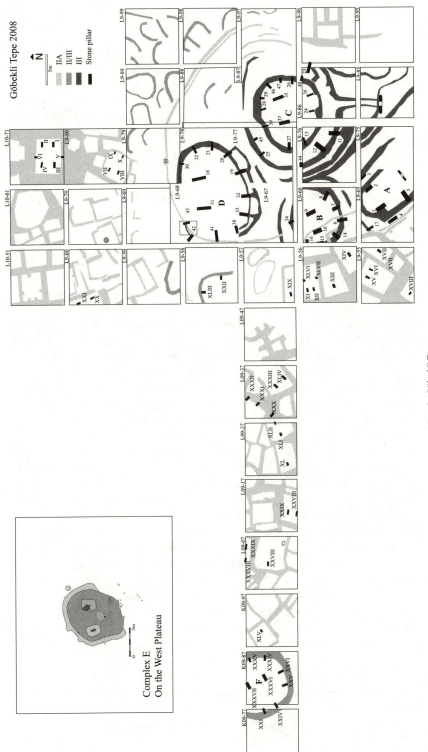

Map 2. Göbekli Tepe.

However, the conditions under which advances toward sedentariness took place are not discussed solely on the level of strategies of self-sufficiency. The investigation of a site the German prehistorian Klaus Schmidt has been excavating on Göbekli Tepe, fifteen kilometers northeast of Urfa on the northern edge of the plain of Harran, has made it possible to develop fascinating alternatives (Map 2).[5] There we find ourselves on the northern, hilly flank of the Fertile Crescent, in an area at the intersection of the trade routes and immediately adjacent to the north Syrian and north Mesopotamian cultural areas, where approximately one-third of all the extensively investigated or excavated Neolithic sites in Turkey are concentrated. It is a successively expanded and rebuilt complex that for monumentality has no peer in the pre-pottery Neolithic of the Middle East. The architecture (hearths or fireplaces are lacking) clearly had an exclusively or at least primarily religious function. On the south side of the hill, in the older, pre-pottery stratum III (PPNA, i.e., ca. 9600 to 8800 BCE), four round to oval *temene* (shrines) surrounded by circular perimeter walls were excavated. In their interior spaces stand, in their original places (in situ) on terrazzo floors, monolithic T-shaped pillars in a symmetrical arrangement. These pillars are three to five meters high and weigh as much as ten tons. There are as many as twelve smaller pillars on the periphery, with their capitals oriented toward the middle of the space and connected with each other by walls or stone benches, as well as a pair of especially large and carefully worked pillars in the center. Southwest and north of these enclosures and in the more recent stratum II (PPNB, i.e., ca. 8800 to 6800 BCE) are rectangular spaces with less numerous and smaller pillars about 1.5 meters high. Many of these pillars—twenty-two of thirty-seven in the older stratum III—are decorated with reliefs; here and there pairs of arms on the shaft still make clear the anthropomorphic shape. On the broad or frontal side of the capital and on the shaft, numerous images of animals and other motifs are carved, most of them with astonishing skill (Figure 10). In a secondary context—in the circular structures and around them—stone statuary of animal heads and bodies, and ithyphallic animal and idol-like human figures were excavated. Deeply cut into an elevated floor plate in enclosure A is a drawing of a woman—the only one found so far. She is squatting, with her legs spread, and something shapeless and long hangs from her vagina; it is impossible to decide whether this is meant to represent birth or sexuality. Perhaps people later than the builders carved this drawing; it is hard to fit it into the program of the original enclosures. Apart from this drawing, the iconography of Göbekli Tepe is exclusively male. Above all, individual animals and groups of animals are depicted, and are distributed in the enclosures, probably in accord with a deliberately chosen pictorial program. Snakes, foxes, and boars appear most often, along with aurochs, cranes, wild sheep, wild asses, gazelles, and leopards (or lions). A finely worked stone sculpture of a vulture's head was found in the rubble. The T-shaped pillar in enclosure D, excavated in 2006, has an unusually rich pictorial program with H-shaped symbols, a large scorpion, an ithyphallic man without a head, and a vulture. However, the interpretation of this program remains difficult, and since the investigation is ongoing, statements about it must be provisional. Many

10. T-shaped pillar in Göbekli Tepe. On the front side of the capital and on the side of the shaft appears a dense series of images of birds; four-footed animals; snakes; a scorpion; an ithyphallic, headless man; and several other objects whose nature cannot be clearly determined. Photo courtesy DAI, Orient Department (photo: Klaus Schmidt).

questions arise: Can one establish relationships between these representations and the animal species hunted (and proven by investigations on animal bones found there)? Up to now, the results tend to indicate that the pictorial series does not represent the wild animals chiefly hunted in the area, and thus we can hardly speak of a pure hunting cult. Does the correct interpretation lie in totemic or shamanic performances? Can these spaces be described as temples at all, and if so, how many people gathered there for what kind of rites? The difference in the height of some of the pillar placements seems to exclude the possibility that they functioned to hold up a roof, which makes one think of open-air religious structures made of enormous monoliths like those at Stonehenge. The construction, decoration, and operation of these shrines presupposes a powerful elite capable of planning and organization. In any case, large groups must have been regularly brought together over a long period of time. None of the enclosures was built before the ninth millennium BCE.

The immediate environment includes a series of other, though somewhat later sites, including a village on the Gürcütepe. The pre-pottery Neolithic settlement Nevali Çori, which lies farther north on the right bank of the Euphrates,[6] stands in a narrowly delimited temporal, architectonic, and iconographic context with Göbekli Tepe. The eastern part of the site, which had been under excavation by the prehistorian Harald Hauptmann since 1991 (it is now flooded by Atatürk Reservoir), went through five phases of construction and also has an enormous building (188 square meters) of the highest quality. In front of the inner walls plastered with clay and in the middle of the space (with a terrazzo floor) stand T-shaped pillars connected by a stone bench. Here, the base for a religious statue and the monumental stone statuary found in secondary structures also leave no doubt that the building, which may perhaps also be an open-air enclosure, functioned as a *temenos*, that is, a sacred precinct. Among the statues (some of them larger than life) and stone relief sculptures are animal and human heads and bodies, as well as composite human-animal figures; an enormous bird (a vulture?) repeatedly appears sitting on a human head. And there is no lack of representations of women. On one relief, big-bellied women (?) dance on either side of a huge Euphrates tortoise. About 700 clay figurines, most of them anthropomorphic and including naked female sitting figures (once again), a few pregnant women, and mothers with children, do not come from the context of the religious site. In addition, Nevali Çori has an extensive residential and storage area: twenty-nine buildings, most of them rectangular, between 13 and 18 meters long and 5.5 to 6 meters wide, with elaborate internal partitioning; stone bases for roof-supporting posts were found at a distance of 1.20 meters from foundations made of clay-mortared limestone masonry. Polished axes and other stone and metal artifacts (copper beads) point to relatively advanced techniques of workmanship. Here, the basis for subsistence was also hunting, and no less than fifty-six animal species are attested. Bodies were buried under the floors in the building. We will encounter this remarkable mode of human burial in other places as well. Numerous further discoveries in the Urfa region, including a Neolithic sculpture in Urfa itself, are so closely related to those in Nevali Çori that the assumption of a contemporary complex of settlements around a center (Urfa?) is inevitable. The importance of the discoveries in Nevali Çori and Göbekli Tepe is still hard to estimate. With regard to the dimensions and decoration of the shrines, one can only point out that the beginnings of religious architecture in Mesopotamia, the Ubaid- and Uruk V–IV-period temples built a thousand years later (fifth to the fourth millennia BCE), were significantly smaller and humbler.

At about the same time, not far to the east of Urfa, near Ergani in Diyarbakır province, humans settled for more than half a millennium an area on a hill of about 300 meters by 150 meters: Çayönü.[7] Taken as a whole, the excavations carried out between 1964 and 1988 and recently resumed have revealed a varied architecture, remains of skeletons, and artifacts whose richness is unsurpassed. Among the types of buildings—round, oval, cellular, and spacious structures belonging to different phases of construction—the "grill-plan house," so called because of its foundation, is represented by more than thirty examples. The stone foundations mortared with clay have several parallel, unconnected or meandering walls in front of a small, subdivided rectangle that is extended by a room or courtyard (with an oven). In the mud-brick buildings erected over them, these walls provided ventilation and drainage channels to ensure dry floors. In Çayönü as well, the presence of religious spaces has been proven: the "Bench Building," with its stone benches on the interior walls; the "Flagstone Building," with its large floor slabs; and above all the "Skull Building" and the "Terrazzo Building," in which a large number of human skulls and skeletons were ritually buried. Noteworthy are traces of human blood (hemoglobin crystals) on a stone slab or the stone rim of a pit in the floor. Did human sacrifices take place there? Thirty percent of the hundreds of human bones found belonged to children under sixteen years of age. Especially well-preserved skeletons of young women from a complex in the eastern sector throw light on a sad individual fate: a pregnant woman apparently died giving birth to a twin, with which she was buried, the other twin still in her body. As only seldom elsewhere in Anatolia, the discoveries made in Çayönü allow us to draw conclusions concerning body size, life expectancy, and mortality rates of genders and age groups, as well as the bases of the inhabitants' diet. Wheat is found in both wild and cultivated forms, along with barley, vetches, lentils, almonds, and pistachios; wild game is still at least as important as cultivated crops and includes aurochs, deer, and wild boars (with the highest rate of meat consumption among settlers in the older strata), bears, foxes, hares, and other wild animals. Goats were not yet domesticated, but sheep probably were, and interestingly, so were dogs (*Canis familiaris*). The earliest proof of copper-working with hammers and annealing (no smelting yet) was found in Çayönü and Aşıklı Höyük in Cappadocia.

Villages inhabited year-round were permanently established in great numbers during the two and a half millennia between 7600 and 5000 BCE, and not only in the southeast and south of Turkey. Special tools, such as those indispensable for field cultivation, textile production (at first from plant materials, such as flax), and finally pottery making, became widespread. Woven baskets and jars made of wood or stone probably appeared early, along with clay containers dried in the sun before fired ceramics were invented. Their forms and decorations are key discoveries for the definition of the temporal and spatial limits of cultures, that is, of the appearance of typical characteristics behind which stands a specific creative will. These cultures are not necessarily connected with particular peoples or groups of people; their spread cannot be interpreted simply as migrations, and their names generally stand only for the places in which the corresponding ceramics were first found.

Up to this point, the Aegean and Mediterranean coasts south of the Taurus Mountains have been little represented, mainly in the area around Mersin and Tarsos. In eastern Anatolia, Çafer Höyük occupies a key position: this pre-pottery Neolithic village on a hill forty kilometers northeast of Malatya has been only partly excavated;[8] a few building foundations divided into small spaces were found there (no grill-plan buildings). The Neolithic topography of Thrace and the Sea of Marmara region is difficult to determine because of major changes in the seacoast, lakes, and marshy areas. The Late Neolithic-Chalcolithic village of Ilıpınar, near İznik (ca. 5200–4800 BCE) offers important discoveries. The late Neolithic ceramics from

Fikirtepe were widely distributed, for instance as far as Thessaly. Northern Anatolia and the arc of the Pontos are still largely unknown territory; one lonely outpost of research in this region is Demirci Höyük near Eskişehir. This site was inhabited down to the middle Chalcolithic; then came an interruption until it was resettled in the late Chalcolithic and Bronze Age. Some pottery from the older settlement was found in the clay walls of the Bronze Age settlement.

The situation is entirely different on the northern edge of the western Taurus range: in the area containing lakes Acıgöl, Burdur, Eğridir, Beyşehir, and Suğla, on the hills around the lakeshores, there is clearly a settlement area dating from the Neolithic to the early Chalcolithic. Hunting was still predominant in the pre-pottery Neolithic village of Suberde, on the western shore of Lake Suğla: in one of the largest collections of animal bones from Anatolia (more than 300,000), sheep and goats that were obviously not yet domesticated are preponderant. And plants used for food do not belong to cultivated species (ca. 6500–5600 BCE). In contrast, in the sixth millennium BCE people in Erbaba, ten kilometers north-northwest of Beyşehir, ate only cultivated species. They lived in stone houses with small rooms that were entered through the roof. The village of Hacılar on the plain of Burdur was abandoned in the pre-pottery Neolithic and then resettled and strongly fortified in the Late Neolithic. It had large, two-story buildings with complexes of rooms grouped around courtyards. Again there was a "shrine" with a stone table (for sacrifices?), in which the dead were buried in the floor. Many clay figures represent women, girls, matrons, pregnant women, nursing mothers, who were standing, leaning, and enthroned, including a "Mistress of the Animals." The inhabitants knew how to spin and weave, and they had pottery workshops in which they made ceramics painted with reddish-brown motifs.

To the east of this lake region, we come to the high plains between Konya and Niğde, which are now semi-arid. At the edge of the Cilician arc of the Taurus Mountains and at the foot of the conical volcanoes, conditions must have been more favorable to rain-fed farming—farming that can succeed without artificial irrigation—in the Neolithic than they are today. Here, on the Cappadocian plateau, outstanding villages—Aşıklı Höyük, Köşk Höyük, and Can Hasan—have been excavated. Among the skulls buried in the buildings of Köşk Höyük, two covered with plaster like the earlier ones known from Jericho (compare p. 56 on Çatal Höyük) are particularly striking.

On the plain of Konya, fifty-six kilometers southeast of the city of Konya, lies the site of Çatal Höyük, which still shapes like no other our image of Anatolian prehistory in general.[9] Its size, its architecture, the wealth of tools and small discoveries, and above all its breathtaking world of images in wall paintings and in statuary give it a special status in all of Turkey; the excavator James Mellaart even spoke of a "town" instead of a "village" (Figure 11). Surveys in the surrounding area seem to exclude the possibility that this place had neighbors of the same size and quality at that time. On the hill, which is up to seventeen meters high and has a surface area of 13.5 hectares, excavations were conducted in a southwestern section between 1960

11. Çatal Höyük, Neolithic building with "horned altars."

and 1967, and in a northern section from the mid-1990s on. Twelve strata date from the late pre-pottery period down to the ceramic Neolithic (ca. 7000–5500 BCE); the architecture of stratum VI A was completely destroyed by a catastrophic fire. More than 150 rooms are known, but certainly many more remain to be found. According to current estimates, at times more than 5,000 people may have lived in this place in as many as 1,000 rooms. With regard to their use, we can distinguish living and storage rooms, but in many buildings, decorations, statuary, and small discoveries indicate religious activities. These were earlier defined as "shrines," but they are neither architectonically distinct from the dwellings, nor do they lack traces of habitation, such as stoves and ovens. To judge by their number and their integration into larger complexes of rooms, they may be the domestic shrines of clans and not real temples. Up to now, no public building type in a narrower sense has been found. The buildings do not stand on stone foundations; sun-dried clay bricks (some as long as ninety-five centimeters) were laid up in massive, self-supporting wooden frames made of oak and juniper (today, a similar construction method is still found in Anatolian farmhouses). These walls were plastered and topped with roofs that may have been flat and made of earth resting on wooden beams and covered with reeds or straw. The buildings were entered through the roofs; there were no entrances at ground level. In the northern section alone a street seems to have run along the side of a complex.

In addition to hunting, which plays a dominant role in the imagery, the basis for subsistence was chiefly the cultivation of emmer wheat, einkorn wheat, barley, and vegetables (peas). As a result of the catastrophic fire in stratum VI, charred fragments of textiles made of flax have been preserved over the millennia. In addition to stone tools (arrow- and spearheads, daggers and axes), the rooms in stratum IX contained jewelry made of copper and lead. Çatal Höyük seems to be the oldest known site where copper was smelted and lead melted. The discovery of clay shards that were monochrome and for the most part unpainted, along with intact clay jars and a few wooden ones, allows us to surmise that the ceramics from Çatal Höyük were of relatively subordinate importance. The case is completely different for the wall paintings, reliefs, and statuary. The walls are covered with hand prints and geometrical patterns whose meaning may be partly symbolic ("*kilim* patterns"); representations of humans and animals; and large pictorial compositions with ritual pre-hunt scenes, in which a group of armed hunters dances around an enormous prey, while a woman with protruding buttocks, perhaps a priestess, looks on.

In excavator James Mellaart's opinion, these wall paintings were not permanent decorations of the interior rooms but were instead produced on the occasion of an (unknown) event and later covered over with fresh plaster. This was repeated perhaps three times in the course of five generations, so that most of the time the wall had a monochrome appearance. Large, painted plaster reliefs of wild animals, such as a pair of leopards and several horizontal and vertical rows of images of horned ox heads (*bucrania*) on the wall or along the benches decorate these sanctuaries, along with anthropomorphic figures in childbirth posture, with raised arms and spread legs. The many clay and stone statues of men and women (roughly five to twenty centimeters high) come mainly from these rooms.

The object that serves as a "brand label" for Çatal Höyük was found in a grain container in one of the rooms in stratum II: a female sitting figure with pendulous breasts and a protuberant belly, from which a fetus is emerging through an opening, is enthroned atop a seat flanked by large predatory cats (Figure 12). Other sitting figures of women with large bellies and thighs hold their breasts in their hands. The religious significance of these figures is beyond question, but what they represent and exactly what function they fulfilled in the corresponding sites remains uncertain. Were they simple votive offerings of human images or genuine religious images of divinities, and as such objects of veneration and prayer? Can one already speak of "divinities" at all, or do these figures refer to impersonal supernatural powers?

In Çatal Höyük there were also ritual burials under the floors of certain rooms. The remains of more than 400 skeletons were discovered, a few of which were painted. A building excavated between 1995 and 1997 (Building 1) on the north side of the hill allows us to discern a clear separation of the living space in the southern part (access to which was also gained from the roof by means of a ladder) from the northern and eastern burial areas, divided between children and adults. The most recent burial inside this building is a headless skeleton of a man. Perhaps when the house was abandoned the skull may have been taken along for use as a "foundation deposit"—the ritual addition to the foundation of a new building, intended to safeguard it from collapsing—or as a precious object of ancestor worship. Excavations in 2004 unearthed a skull covered with plaster and painted red—the only one

12. Seated figure of a woman from Çatal Höyük, now in the Museum of Anatolian Civilizations, Ankara.

found here to date (see p. 54 on Köşk Höyük); it was held in the arms of the skeleton of a woman. In quite a few places the concentration of child burials is striking. Jewelry was buried with children and women, weapons and belt buckles (made of bone) with men. A noteworthy hypothesis was put forward by the excavator James Mellaart, who suggested that human skeletons were buried only after the bodies had been placed on elevated platforms, where they were protected from wild mammals but exposed to insects and vultures that stripped away their flesh. Is this procedure depicted in the wall paintings in which vultures attack dead, headless bodies? Insofar as they seem to symbolize death, perhaps they can be compared to the enormous birds sitting on the heads of people in the statuary of Nevali Çori and Göbekli Tepe.

These sensational images have given rise to wide-ranging reflections on the history and nature of religious representations. Female figures, some with protuberant lower bodies and buttocks, large breasts and thighs, giving birth or nursing, are well known in Africa, Asia, and Europe during the Neolithic. One of the earliest examples, from Mureybet on the middle Euphrates (Iraq), dates from the beginning of the tenth millennium BCE. However, we can hardly deny the peculiarly Anatolian continuity of this one particular type, which reaches from the sitting woman giving birth from Çatal Höyük to the representations of the great Anatolian Mother, and perhaps even to the early Aegean period and the Archaic age in Greece: the cult statue of Hera of Tiryns in Crete and the older cult statue of Athena Polias were images of sitting goddesses. As the protectress of hunters and givers of life, this ancient image of the woman belongs to the broader context of the fertility of humans, animals, and the earth. The sacrificial rite in Çatal Höyük obviously also seems to be established by the prominent representation of the noblest sacrificial animal, the ox. The pair of horns appears later as a sacred symbol connected with a sacrificial animal not only in Anatolia (e.g., in the early Bronze Age horned altar of Beycesultan), but also in the Minoan-Mycenaean culture of Crete.[10] "In the background stands the hunter's custom of partially giving back, the symbolic restitution of the killed wild animal."[11] The question of ritual sacrifices of humans, especially children, in the skull sites in Çayönü, Hacılar, and Çatal Höyük remains unanswered. Large cemeteries outside the settlements at this time are not known, but that does not mean that they did not exist. The number of individuals buried in the buildings in Çatal Höyük cannot approach that of the overall number of those who died during the long phase of settlement in these buildings, which raises the question of where the rest of them were buried. The burial or preservation of human skulls or skeletons in these rooms is a practice that is not peculiar to Anatolia but is widespread in the Middle East. It can be understood as a form of ancestor worship, and when accompanied by items buried with the dead, it certainly allows us to conclude that these people believed in a life after death.

It is more difficult to draw conclusions about subject areas other than the history of religion. The societies in Nevali Çori, Çayönü, Çatal Höyük, and elsewhere were based on the division of labor—but to what extent, if we go beyond the division of labor between men and women that is obvious in the discoveries made? The stone reliefs at Göbekli Tepe were certainly made by specialists. Wealth is unmistakable, and yet it seems to be equally distributed: up to this point no luxurious building, palace, or princely tomb from this period has been found anywhere. However, without powerful individuals, leaders, and priests, the relics can hardly be understood; a radical egalitarianism seems to be out of the question from the outset. But had social elites and claims to political leadership developed with access to resources, indeed, to territory? We cannot say to what extent societies like these defined themselves as a unit, or where the "foreign" began. We do not know their language or the names that they gave themselves and other natural and supernatural things. It is hard to determine what the rich nonfigural motifs on painted ceramics might express, especially whether they conveyed a message that went beyond the merely decorative, and if so, what it was. The Stone Age Anatolian also battled and killed his fellow humans. The inhabitants of Çatal Höyük were armed to the teeth, but war and fighting among humans were not among the motifs of their images. It is clear that weapons were not used solely for hunting, and that wounds cutting all the way to the bone were not simply caused by accidents. Conflicts are just as likely as clashes between neighboring groups. But were there long wars between large groups over land or hunting grounds?

In general, the question of exchange and trade already arises for the Neolithic as well. Obsidian from Cappadocia's volcanoes and from the region west of Lake Van (Nemrud Dağ), whose flakes made especially sharp blades, found its way into the southern Levant (Tell es-Sultān [Jericho]). Whether this took place through middlemen, and how many of them there were, remains unknown. The idea of traders, or even caravans, traveling over long distances raises the question of the density of village settlement along the routes and, of course, the risks involved in travel. Wandering groups of shepherds and hunters might also have played an important role in distributing many other desired commodities, such as metal, ceramics, textiles, and also certain foodstuffs. It is harder to prove the existence of market centers with barter economies. Can Çatal Höyük claim to have played such a role? Most questions regarding the highly important Neolithic remain unanswered.

Research on the Chalcolithic in Anatolia shows a clear rise in settlement activity. Between about 5000 and 3700 BCE, thousands of villages sprang up all over Anatolia, and it can be proven that there were contacts, indeed amalgamations, between settlement centers to form genuine cultural zones in various regions, for example, between the Konya plain and west Cilicia (Mersin). But the boundaries of these zones continue to be a subject of debate. In the southeast, the so-called Halaf and Ubaid cultures occupy a prominent place because of the wide distribution of their respective types of decorated ceramics, which were named after the sites where they were first discovered, Tall Halaf and Tall al Ubaid in Mesopotamia. In the far west, a settlement (Miletus I) emerged in the second half of the fourth millennium BCE on two small islands in the Latmian Gulf, where Miletus later grew up on the continent.[12]

Early and Middle Bronze Age (ca. 3000 to 1700 BCE)

Traditional periods divide the Bronze Age into three main parts, Early (3000–2000 BCE), Middle (2000–1700 BCE), and Late (1700–1200 BCE), abbreviated in English as EB, MB, and LB, respectively. The production of bronze, an alloy of copper and tin in a ratio of 8:1, gradually established itself in the course of the third millenium and gives the period its name. The increasing importance of metals—copper, tin (its presence in Anatolia is contested), gold, and silver provided the basis for the rise to wealth and power of some places in Anatolia. Settlements bore the stamp of social differentiation: in their fortresses, the heads of local societies built temples, expensive houses, and palaces, and buried their dead in special tombs with more valuable gifts than the rank and file received.

At the same time, the Sumerian-Akkadian high cultures of neighboring Mesopotamia produced political structure, systematic administration and cultivation of the flat land, organized trade, and above all writing. Just as for the West, Iraq is today an El Dorado of black gold, around 3000 BCE Anatolia emerged in the context of covetous glances on the part of the Mesopotamian local princes and merchants because of its deposits of metals that the land on the Euphrates and the Tigris wholly lacked. As part of a counterflow to the delivery of these metals, sooner or later the managers of long-distance trade introduced writing to Anatolia.

In the early Bronze Age, Anatolia was still far from being a cultural unit. Which regions were connected or corresponded to one another on the basis of types of architecture and ceramics, other artifacts, or forms of burial—where the boundaries of these cultures lay—is a complicated subject that cannot be elaborated on here.[13] I once again limit this discussion to highlighting a few key sites.

For millennia, nothing Anatolian is comparable to the enormous Neolithic cult-sites in the Urfa region. We know that in the fourth millennium BCE there were structures in Mesopotamia that have been called "temples." In connection with this phenomenon in late Chalcolithic and early Bronze Age Anatolia, Arslantepe and Beycesultan can be mentioned first and foremost.

The early culture on Arslantepe ("Lion Hill"), a place in eastern Anatolia six kilometers northeast of Malatya and not far from the right bank of the Euphrates, is approximately contemporary with the flourishing of Uruk in Mesopotamia (second half of the fourth millennium BCE). Between ca. 3300 and the beginning of the third millennium, powerful local lords established themselves on this hill, which had already been settled in the Chalcolithic. There they built the monumental double temples and decorated them with reliefs and wall paintings.[14] Other remains of buildings contained thousands of clay seals with about 150 different styles of figural motifs (including a few cylinder seals), indicating a highly developed administration of large quantities of centrally stockpiled food supplies and objects. Relationships with Mesopotamia are obvious. This high culture, in which social stratification and a rudimentary form of political organization are in any case discernible, came to an abrupt end. It was followed by a much poorer development of the hill.

Beycesultan is located in the west, on the upper Büyük Menderes (Meander), about fifty-six kilometers northwest of Dinar.[15] On a double hill separated by a saddle, forty different strata were excavated during the 1950s. Twenty of them date from the fifth and fourth millennia BCE, and twenty more from the fourth to the second millennia. In the early Bronze Age a rather large walled city arose there that almost covered the entire hill, a built-up area of about 800 by 300 meters. In the center, pairs of temples belonging to different construction phases were discovered, consisting of two adjacent rectangular cult rooms with a vestibule and a smaller room for priests at the rear. The construction type, which is similar to that of a *megaron* (p. 61), contains in its interior elaborate furnishings for its cultic function: in the eastern part of the main room, two flat steles with a clay horned altar in front of them represent the core of the sanctuary; behind the steles, beyond a small opening between them, a basin for libations (drink offerings) is embedded in the floor, accompanied by a sacrificial niche in the wall containing a "blood altar."

An irony of the history of research in the nineteenth century—or more precisely, an error made by Heinrich Schliemann—identified the ruins on the hill of Hisarlık on the Dardanelles as Priam's castle and thus put them at the absolute center of the archaeology of early history, indeed of archaeology itself. The site lies on the periphery of early Bronze Age Anatolia, in the network of a material culture that includes, in addition to the northwest coast of Asia Minor, part of Bulgaria, the European part of Turkey, and a few islands in the Aegean. Of its eight main strata, the oldest, I–III, belong to the early Bronze Age, while IV and V belong to the middle Bronze Age (ca. 3000 to 1700 BCE). Troy I and II are to be dated roughly to the period between 3000 and 2400. Atop the hill is a circular fortress; the walls of air-dried clay bricks rise from the steeply sloping stone base. Access to the interior is provided by ramps and gates. Older and more recent, symmetrically aligned forms of a rectangular building type that is generally known by the name *megaron* were constructed on the platform, which is about 110 meters across. In Homer, the Greek word *megaron* designates the main hall of the royal palace (as in *Odyssey* 17, 604). The long walls of the rectangle are extended on both sides and form a porch at the entrance. The oldest example of this kind of building in Troy Ia deviates from the type insofar as it has a kind of apse. The largest of these buildings, with a surface area 35 by 12.5 meters, has been interpreted as the local ruler's dwelling or assembly hall. In Troy I, pottery was still made by hand; it was first turned on a wheel in Troy II. Schliemann gave the two-handled cups the appropriate Homeric name: *depas amphikypellon* (*Iliad* 1, 584). The most spectacular discovery in these strata was Schliemann's "Treasure of Priam": according to the discoverer's report, this treasure must have been stashed in the wall by someone who left the castle in a hurry. The collection runs to more than 8,800 individual items, including a few precious ones of pure gold, whose immortal fame is connected with the photo of the beautiful Sophie Schliemann wearing shining jewelry (Figure 13). The later fate of the treasure in the nineteenth and twentieth centuries (p. 27) is perhaps even more breathtaking than its historical importance for early third millennium BCE.

A settlement probably accompanied the castle. There is still no consensus as to where its periphery is to be located. About 200 meters from the castle walls, a ditch with postholes in front of and behind it was found and excavated over a length of about forty meters: were these the remains of a palisade around Troy II? It cannot be proven that this Troy of the oldest phase dominated the whole of northwest Asia Minor and controlled maritime commerce by means of the straits that lie at its doorstep, even though this claim is found in the literature. It was already clear during Schliemann's lifetime that this much older settlement has nothing to do with Homer's Trojan War or Priam's palace.

In contrast to the Neolithic-Chalcolithic burials under the floors of buildings that we have encountered in southern and southeastern Anatolia, archaeology has also discovered large, extramural cemeteries from the Bronze Age in western and central Anatolia, in which most of the dead were buried in clay *pithoi* (large urns), while people of higher ranks were also buried in stone-lined shaft or stone cist graves, with precious furnishings. There is a large Bronze Age necropolis near Demirci Höyük, not far from Eskişehir on the Sakarya, and discoveries from the shaft graves

13. Sophie Schliemann wearing jewelry from the "Treasure of Priam." Photo courtesy AKG-Images, Berlin.

of the local elite of Alaca Höyük, about forty kilometers northeast of the later Hittite capital Ḫattusa, in the bend of the Halys River, go back to the period between ca. 2500 and 2100 BCE. Artfully cast standard holders, bronze solar disks, metal vessels, and gold jewelry underline the wealth of the pre-Hittite population in this region. Beyond the Taurus Mountains, in the Cilician plain, Bronze Age Tarsos developed into a walled city with (probably) two-story dwellings that were entered directly from the street.

There exists a fancifully embroidered narrative about the founder of the Mesopotamian dynasty of Akkad, Šarrukin (the Biblical "Sargon"), titled "The Epic of the King of the Battle."[16] To come to the aid of Akkadian merchants, he is supposed to have undertaken a campaign against a city in Asia Minor called Purušḫanda. The event may be fictitious, and the reference to the Central Anatolian trading city of Purušḫanda/Purušḫattum known later (cf. p. 65) may be an anachronism, but Akkadian trade relationships with a city in Anatolia as early as 2300 are not impossible. We must move only a few centuries later to find in Anatolia the prelude to written culture. Archaeology casts a bright light on a place in which a flourishing settlement with monumental architecture existed before trade actually brought to it the art of writing and even a school for scribes. Kültepe (Turkish "Ash heap") is located at a historic intersection on the Cappadocian plateau, twenty-one kilometers northeast of the present city of Kayseri. I return to the script phase of its history in greater detail in Chapter 4. Strata XVIII–XI belong to phases of settlement in the early Bronze Age and provide proof that this was also the center of a regional power with wide-ranging connections with the Orient, with Syria, and perhaps with Mesopotamia. The religious building from the late phase of this epoch, dated ca. 2100, provides what is essentially the easternmost example of a *megaron* yet found in Anatolia, more than half a millennium before the appearance of this type of structure in the Aegean world. Among the exceptional discoveries made in round stone tombs with a separate chamber for the furnishings are alabaster figurines, small sitting figures, and remarkable idols with round bodies from which two "bottle necks" with mushroom-shaped heads protrude. Kültepe is the center of a kind of pottery, the much-discussed Cappadocian polychrome pottery, that was widely distributed.

The lordly economic and administrative center already found in Arslantepe and a thousand years later in Kültepe is a phenomenon of the greatest importance. From Mesopotamian written sources we are familiar with the structures known as palaces, which must be understood not merely as buildings that served as a ruler's residence, but in an abstract sense as an economic and administrative system. One of the most imposing of these centers was found in stratum V of Beycesultan. However, here we are already in a period (early second millennium) in which writing was being practiced in Kültepe, whereas not a single written document from this time was found in Beycesultan. The "Burnt Palace" on the easternmost hill can in fact claim to be a palace in the architectural sense; it is a complex with a surface area of seventy meters by forty-five meters, with forty-seven rooms built on stone bases with clay-brick walls and timbering (Figure 14).

We do not know what kind of population these early princedoms (if we can call them that) produced in the various regions on the soil of Asia Minor, in Troy, Beycesultan, Alaca Höyük, Demirci Höyük, Tarsos, Arslantepe, Kültepe, and elsewhere. It has been suggested that there was a Luwian immigration even before the beginning of the early Bronze Age. It was thought that the widespread use of the Luwian language in the Asia Minor of the second millennium (as proven by the epigraphic testimonies) would allow inferences to be made about the people and its early history. But exactly what *Luwiya* designates is far from clear. We can say little more than that it referred to the bearer of a common language—not necessarily a people and certainly not a political structure. In any case, Luwian is Indo-European. The Indo-European family of languages in Anatolia, represented there by various idioms since the second millenium (p. 69 f.), presupposes an older Anatolian ancestor. This hypothetical linguistic stage is known as "Proto-Anatolian." When and by what routes speakers of this language first migrated to Anatolia, where they settled, who they influenced, and what influenced them in turn, remains unknown. Attempts to connect them with archaeological discoveries from periods before writing are built on sand. Their first representatives of whom we can form a concrete idea are the Hittites.

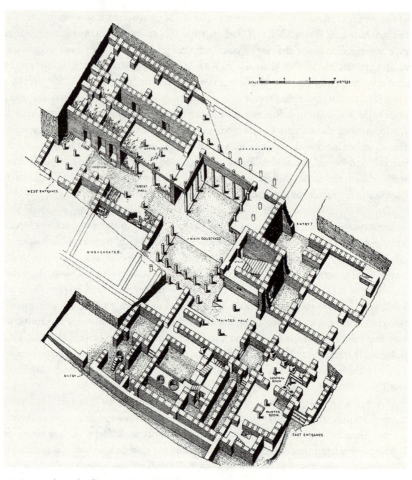

14. Beycesultan, the "Burnt Palace." Reconstruction drawing. Image from Seton Lloyd and James Mellaart (1965), *Beycesultan 2. Middle Bronze Age Architecture and Pottery* (Occasional publications of the British Institute at Ankara 8). © London, British Institute at Ankara: fig. A13.

Before the Assyrians (ca. 2000 to 1700 BCE)

During the third millennium, Mesopotamian texts still have nothing to say about Asia Minor—except for the previously mentioned stories from twenty-fourth century BCE, according to which King Sargon of Akkad undertook a campaign into the interior of Anatolia. It was probably at the end of this millennium that Assyrian merchants began to settle in Anatolia. It is to them that we owe the earliest written documents from Asia Minor, all of them in the Akkadian language and written in cuneiform script (p. 68 f.). The site where most of the discoveries were made is the previously mentioned Kültepe, near Kayseri. The first written tablets were found there in 1871. A few smaller excavations were followed by Bedřich Hrozný's 1925 excavations, which produced about 1,000 texts.[17] In the early second-millennium phase, the city named Kaneš (in the later, Hittite form, Nesa),[18] on the hill, must be distinguished from the quarter known as "Kārum" (Assyrian "quay," "harbor," "emporium"), on the plain. As the texts tell us, such transfer points also emerged in many other places in Anatolia. By definition, these were originally stopping places, which then gradually grew to become colonies of foreign merchants. In Kārum-Kaneš, five levels are distinguished: two of them from an old period without writing dated to the end of the third and the beginning of the second millennium BCE (IV–III), two with writing, the earlier one in the twentieth and nineteenth centuries BCE (II), the later one between ca. 1833 and 1719 BCE (Ib), as well as a more recent one without writing (Ia).

Representatives of large trading companies that had their headquarters in the capital, Assur, provided commercial connections between Mesopotamia and Anatolia. Donkey caravans ensured a well-organized transportation system. Although we can speak of a private business community, the Assyrian state exercised a certain supervision over the whole. This required precise reporting in addition to extensive correspondence (some of it private), and thus in the heyday of this trade in the nineteenth and eighteen centuries BCE, a great deal was written and archived. A comparable wealth of economic texts is not found in any other period of antiquity. To date, more than 20,000 clay tablets have been found, most of which have not been published. "Letters" consist of tablets written on both sides and inserted into clay envelopes that also bear writing and seals stamped by the sender. The documents provide manifold insights into Anatolia's complex economic life as well as its political, legal, social, cultural, and ethnic relationships.

The main features of trade can be described as follows. Anatolia had numerous copper, silver, and gold mines. Near the mines were storage and transfer sites; a series of these are known by name—Turḫumit and Tišmurna are often mentioned—but cannot be located with certainty. Copper was apparently mined primarily in the area north and northeast of Ankara, and it reached large trading centers via transfer points. One of these centers was a place called Purušḫattum, which has been identified with Acem Höyük, on the southern edge of Lake Tuz, which competed with Kaneš. Using donkey caravans, the Assyrians transported out of their homeland chiefly tin, wool, and textiles. Anatolia lacked tin, and the Assyrians held a regular monopoly on supplying it to markets in Asia Minor and sometimes outside it (though of course they too had to import it from elsewhere), and this gave them a privileged position with respect to the natives.[19] However, why they were able to sell so much wool in Anatolia remains a puzzle. They used the imported commodities to pay for silver, gold, and especially copper in the form of bars. As a rule, they obtained the metal directly from the palace, which delivered it to them via an office set up in the trade quarter. But it would be a mistake to assume that the merchants transported the copper to Assur. Instead, they sold it in Anatolia, primarily in exchange for silver and gold, which were what they really wanted. An Assyrian who sold gold to a foreigner was in danger of being put to death by the state; only "brothers," that is, fellow Assyrians, were allowed to trade in precious metals with one another. Thus copper bars constituted the most important means of payment, accepted in Assyrians' business dealings everywhere, and for their customers, first and foremost the palaces, the metal provided the raw material for bronze utensils and weapons. Two units of wool were worth one unit of copper, while silver was valued in relation to copper at a ratio of about 1:60–90 (depending on the place and the quality). Long-distance traders from Assur were not entirely without competitors in Anatolian markets. There were also merchants from Ebla in northern Syria, who bought copper and paid in silver.

Considerable light is shed on the Anatolian context. There were already well-organized states, most of which formed a geographical unit. About twenty of these are known. They were ruled by native princes (Assyrian *rubāum*), a few of whom had supra-regional influence and bore the title of Great King (Assyrian *rubāum rabium*). Among themselves the small states constituted an international system. The prince and his personal entourage were responsible for administration and the economy; collectively, they were known as *ekallum*, "the palace," a constitutive element in politics and economy that was widespread in the cultural world of the whole second millennium. Assyrian merchants had to cultivate good relationships with palace dignitaries, many of whose titles have come down to us. After Kārum became a regular colony of resident wholesalers, Assyrian officials also established themselves there. These officials maintained diplomatic relations with Anatolian princes and served as intermediaries for the emissaries of the city of Assur. The palace levied import and transit duties and punished smugglers. The records provide abundant testimony regarding legal matters, such as debt with interest rate agreements (default interest), rights of preemption at the palace, and partnership contracts. For the most part, the Assyrians seem to be in the better position. This is also shown statistically, because where debts are concerned, they are almost always the creditors and are seldom found in the role of debtors.

Kārum's commercial quarter was not inhabited solely by foreigners; Anatolians also lived there. However, they seem not to have been true business partners, but rather people who lent "money" (reckoned in silver or copper), sold slaves and everyday items (e.g., food), and also provided services. Many texts show that there were mixed marriages, chiefly between Assyrian men and Anatolian women, who were often second wives (*amtum*-wives) in addition to the main wife (*aššutum*). An exceptional case is the Assyrian woman Ištarbasti, who took an Anatolian as her second husband. We learn this from a letter from her father, in which he complains that he had to pay another five minas of silver as a dowry.[20] Since at all times many Assyrians were on the road with caravans, their wives—as housekeepers, managers, and mistresses—had an independent authority over the servants (a typical verb for their function was *naṣarum*, which means something like "guarding"). They appear under their own names and with their own seals in documents regarding transactions. In any case, mixed marriages were genuine marriages and not concubinages. But we know of no case in which an Assyrian returned to his homeland and took his Anatolian wife back with him.

We know little about the ethnic and linguistic affiliations of the Assyrians' native partners, the inhabitants of Asia Minor. Conclusions can be drawn only from the personal names here; extremely few loan words appear. The Assyrians apparently acquired no knowledge of the Anatolian languages of their host country; instead the Anatolians learned the language and the writing of the Semites. In doing so, they naturally made mistakes, such as the confusion of masculine and feminine genders. No matter how hazy our image of the "speechless" people on Kültepe is, it is certain that in their environment not only proto-Hattic and Hurrian groups (cf. p. 70 f.) but also the Indo-European Luwians and Hittites had already long since settled in and inhabited the city of Kaneš, which they called "Nesa." In the Hittite's self-image, this was their city, after which their own language was named: *nasili* or *nesumnili*. They seem to have become so prominent in this place that Tahsin Özgüç, an expert on the Hittites, called it the oldest Hittite capital;[21] they might even be responsible for the decline of Assyrian trade relationships with Kārum-Kaneš. The texts also record unrest. Thus one trader writes in a letter: "The country is in an uproar! As soon as peace returns, I shall leave."[22] At that time as nowadays, prolonged blockades of the trade routes were fatal for business. Writings found outside Kültepe also testify to the presence of the Assyrians. The only recently begun excavation of Kayalıpanar near Sivas (west of the Hittite city of Sarissa, p. 88 f.), with its residential buildings from the eighteenth century BCE, uncovered cylinder seals and a trade document in Old Assyrian.

CHAPTER 4

The Late Bronze and Iron Age

The Rise and Heyday of the Hittite Empire
(Eighteenth to Twelfth Centuries BCE)

The Hittites

A few general preliminary remarks will be helpful in understanding the context. For the purpose of defining periods, three different chronological systems are used for the first half of the second millennium (the so-called short, middle, and long chronologies). The difference between them consists in each case of about sixty-four years. The temporal limits are usually based on the short chronology (which fixes the reign of Ḥammurāpi of Babylon to 1728–1686 BCE), but often also on the middle chronology (which fixes Ḥammurāpi's reign to 1792–1750 BCE). For the second half of the millennium, Egypt offers the most comprehensive and reliable chronological system, though many questions have recently been raised in this connection as well. Here I use the dates most often found in the scholarly literature, without making any claims regarding their accuracy. In addition, thanks to the Assyrian tradition, from the twelfth century on events can be precisely dated when we have enough details. Unfortunately, the Hittites themselves did not date their documents. For genuine dating we are mostly dependent on arguments based on content. "Synchronisms," that is, the alignment of the same events in different chronological systems, are important. Difficulties sometimes arise when attempting to attribute a frequently appearing royal name to a particular individual; for example, the name Ḥattusili/Labarna (p. 71 f.) or the precise identification of the rulers of the so-called Middle Kingdom. This leads to the same king sometimes bearing different ordinal numbers in order to determine his position in the dynasty (e.g., Tudḫaliya I/II). These complicated questions cannot be further explored here.[1] (For a comparative table of differing lists of kings, see the Appendix).

So far as sources are concerned, we are dealing with a time in which the art of writing had become widespread, at least in the upper and middle levels of the society, to meet economic and social requirements. In general, two writing systems were used. In Egypt there was hieroglyphic writing, in which the form of the signs still clearly bore the trace of their original pictorial character. In the Middle East, cuneiform writing was used, in which the signs no longer have much to do with the original pictures. The writing is called "cuneiform" because the marks constituting the

15. Luwian hieroglyphic inscription (the so-called "Südburginschrift") in Ḫattusa.

signs have the shape of a wedge (Latin *cuneus*). This cuneiform script was also the Hittites' most important form of writing. They adopted it in a Babylonian version proceeding from northern Syria—exactly when, we do not know, but probably before the sixteenth century BCE. However, they also wrote with hieroglyphs, using a pictographic script that they apparently invented themselves, modeled on the Egyptian script. In the second millennium this script was used primarily for monumental texts (especially inscriptions on buildings) and for seals (Figure 15).

Writing occurred in many domains of public, religious, and also private life, though as a rule the texts were produced by professional scribes. Everywhere in the East, the medium for cuneiform script was clay tablets, which were normally stored unfired, though sometimes they were accidentally hardened—for example, as a result of war or a disastrous fire. This gave them the solidity that has allowed them to endure down to the present day. They were originally collected unfired in archives that were preserved in their original form in some places in Mesopotamia. The most important archives for Hittite history are found in the capital, Ḫattusa, near the modern-day village of Boğazkale (earlier Boğazköy), about 120 kilometers east of Ankara.[2] The tablets found there are the foundation of our knowledge. Smaller archives have been found in a few other places in the empire. Naturally, sources on Hittite history have also been discovered outside Asia Minor. In particular, we have important texts from Egypt, the land of writing. But documents from northern Syria and Mesopotamia also provide information about the Hittites.

Peoples and Languages

The age of the Hittites is a time in which we encounter many peoples and languages in Asia Minor. The writings found in Ḫattusa prove that seven different languages were in use: Hattian, Hittite, Palaic, Luwian, Hurrian, Akkadian, and Sumerian.[3] Here they are briefly presented and their names explained, so far as necessary and possible.

The part of Anatolia in which we find the Hittites—the later areas of eastern Phrygia and Cappadocia—was at that time populated by the Hattian people (they are now also called "proto-Hattians"), who spoke Hattian, a language that we know from Hittite religious texts. It was in that land, the land of the Hattians, that the Hittites established their empire. The name was transferred to them, and from then on they were known as the "people of Hatti." This is an eminently political term. It is what they were called all over the ancient East, as the founders of a large empire, and it is also the term that was applied later to their successors as chieftains of small principalities. The term "Hittite," which we conventionally use to refer to them, goes back to the word used in the Old Testament. They called their own language "Nesite," after the name of their early capital, Nesa (p. 67). Only when this language was deciphered by the Czech scholar Bedřich Hrozný in 1915 was access finally gained to the Hittite past.

The Hittites' ethnic background and language are part of a larger unit that includes related linguistic groups that are not unambiguously identified as peoples, and still less as political entities or states. They are referred to as the Anatolian family of the Indo-Europeans. The Luwians, who inhabited southern Asia Minor from the west coast to Cilicia and there established various states, belonged to the same family. Their language may have been spoken in everyday life in the Hittite area as well. We know it from Hittite religious texts. It survived the fall of the empire. The peoples whom we meet in southern Anatolia in the first millennium, the so-called Late or Hieroglyphic Hittites—and later the Carians, Lycians, Cilicians, and others whose last traces disappear only at the end of the Roman Empire—were the descendants of relatives of the older Luwian-speaking population. Palaic is a special variety of Anatolian language, which was spoken in northwestern Asia Minor.

Two groups of people and languages in particular stand outside this family. The Kaska, a people we know virtually nothing about, lived on the north coast of Asia Minor. The Hittites were hostile to them: in their view, the Kaska were barbarians who behaved like brigands and with whom they were in constant conflict. More important are the Hurrians. So far as we know, their original home was in eastern Anatolia, in the Armenian highlands. From there they pushed south and southwest, and in the sixteenth and fifteenth centuries BCE they founded various kingdoms in northern Mesopotamia and northern Syria that will be discussed later in this chapter. Their language, Hurrian, we know from a series of texts, especially from the Hittite area, but also from outside it. A little-known Indo-Aryan group (simply called "Aryans") was connected with the Hurrians and gained importance by introducing and developing horse breeding. Its members left behind them a few names of gods and persons also found later in India, as well as terms from the domain of horse breeding and training.

History of the Hittite Empire

As their language shows, the Hittites were an Indo-European people. That means that they presumably migrated from southern Russia to their later homeland in central Anatolia. Unfortunately, we know little about this movement. Whether it was made together by the whole Anatolian group, what route it took, and when it occurred, remain unknown to us. It has been suggested that the route ran primarily over the western slope of the Caucasus, but that remains unproven. So far as the date is concerned, we have to assume that it all took place in the late third millennium BCE. In any case, Hittites were certainly living in central Anatolia in the eighteenth century (p. 67). Hittite history is divided on the model of Egyptian history into the three periods of the Old, Middle, and New kingdoms, preceded by the Kussara Dynasty as a kind of prelude.

THE KUSSARA DYNASTY

Our first information, even though it is rather suggestive, is derived from the previously mentioned Assyrian sources, in which Hittite names appear. We first encounter Hittites as political actors in the eighteenth century, under the Kussara Dynasty, after which the period can be named (the record consists of a single text; see the list of Hittie rulers in the Appendix). It has not been proven that the leading family, which came from Kussara (a place that has not been located with certainty), belonged to the Hittite people, but there are good grounds for thinking that it did.[4] Under the kings Pithana and Anitta, it succeeded in dominating large parts of central Anatolia. At that time the city of Nesa (the Assyrian trading colony Kaneš) became its center. Anitta is credited with having produced the first extant text in Hittite, the oldest known text in an Indo-European language. He also conquered, among other places, the later capital of Hattusa, which he caused to be destroyed: "And I took it [Hattusa] at night by storm. Whoever after me becomes king and resettles Hattusa, [let] the Stormgod of the Sky strike him."[5] However, this episode appears to us as a sort of snapshot. Afterward, there is no further information for a long time. We do not know what happened.

THE OLD KINGDOM

A new beginning followed in the seventeenth century. The dynasty under which it occurred—this one certainly Hittite—also came from Kussara; but it cannot be determined whether there was a relationship to the Kussara dynasty of the earlier period. At its origin there seems to have been a ruler named Labarna, who was responsible for the rise of the new dynasty. We cannot say how he created his power center in central Anatolia. In any event, he was able to extend the kingdom in all directions, allegedly as far as the coast of the Black Sea and northern Syria. It was he who once again conquered the city of Hattusa and made it the capital—despite Anitta's curse. That was probably why he changed his original name, Labarna, to Hattusili, "the man from Ḫattusa." However, certain passages in the sources suggest that Labarna and Ḫattusili were two different kings, but this is a very controversial question that we cannot go into here. The real breakthrough into the greater world was achieved by Ḫattusili's successor Mursili I, who may have been the former's grandson. In northern Syria he conquered the important center Ḫalab (Aleppo), and in 1595 or 1531 BCE (depending on the chronological system used) he succeeded in taking Babylon after a campaign straight across Mesopotamia. This was an enormous undertaking, whose background remains hidden to us. He was not able to hold Babylon, but this conquest was also a turning point in Babylonian history; the famed Ḫammurāpi dynasty was replaced by the Kassites, who had emigrated from Iran and seized power.

Soon thereafter the Hittite empire collapsed. The causes were internal and external processes that mutually strengthened each other. So far as internal politics is concerned, we see a phenomenon that runs throughout Hittite history like a thread: constant competition within the royal extended family destabilized the situation, and the leaders of noble families probably also pursued their own interests. There had already been problems of succession during the last days of Ḫattusili. Mursili was murdered after his return from Babylon. The resulting confusion led to a breakdown of the empire. Several rulers subsequently died violent deaths. In addition, there were external threats: the Hurrians established themselves in the south. They succeeded in building political structures in northern Syria. In this connection we should mention first the construction of the Mittani Empire, which extended over all of Syria and far to the west. In the north, it was the Kaska who invaded Hittite territories from their ancestral area and robbed and sacked them. Nonetheless, one of the Hittite rulers, Telipinu (ca. 1500 BCE), attempted to achieve an internal political consolidation by creating a set of rules that was supposed to govern succession to the throne; he tried to use these rules to straighten out the relationship between rulers: "So I, Telipinu, summoned an assembly in Ḫattusa. From now on in Ḫattusa, let nobody do evil to a son of the family and draw a dagger on him."[6] Several of these norms even endured, but the difficult situation at that time could not be resolved by them alone.

THE MIDDLE KINGDOM

The time of the Middle Kingdom, essentially the fifteenth and early fourteenth centuries BCE, is a dark period.[7] We do not know whether we can put all the kings in the right order, and in particular cases the chronology is not at all clear.

The political threat from outside the kingdom remained. As before, it was the Kaska in the north and the Hurrian Mitanni in the south who were pressuring the Hittites. However, the Hittites also had rivals in Anatolia. On all sides, vassals were breaking away and posing an additional threat to the empire. In the southwest, the Arzawa Empire arose as a competing great power that maintained diplomatic relations with Egypt. This is shown by the so-called Arzawa letters from the Egyptian archive of Amarna, in which the ruler communicated with the Egyptian pharaoh in Hittite, the language of their common enemy (p. 89). Farther in the west as well, there were conflicts with hostile local powers. There, the Aḫḫiyawa, who were probably Mycenaean Greeks (see below), were active. Thus the Hittite Empire was at times limited to its heartland in central Anatolia. Individual rulers such as Tudḫaliya I tried to halt this development, but succeeded in doing so only temporarily.

In this period that was so difficult for the Hittites, an international system of relations among states grew up for the first time in history, a system that included the whole of the then known world, and that may be characterized as a genuine "concert of great powers," indeed, a genuine globalization. Its first phase began in the late seventeenth century, when the Egyptians invaded the Middle East and entered into a decades-long military competition with the Mitanni for control of northern Syria. In the east lay another great power, Babylon. This situation led to manifold belligerent and peaceful relations among these powers, in which Egypt was, for economic reasons, the strongest power.

The New Kingdom (Empire Period)

The Hittite Empire achieved an enduring consolidation around the middle of the fourteenth century BCE. Numerous sources now shed light on the course of events. A ruler named Suppiluliuma, a great-grandson (?) of Tudḫaliya I, was able, in the beginning as crown prince, to gain firm control over large parts of Anatolia in the north and the west, and he even pushed as far as northern Syria. There the battles led to the weakening and finally the destruction of the Hurrian Mitanni empire, which suffered from internal dissensions. Mitanni states continued to exist as Hittite vassal states. To secure the arrangement, a secundogeniture system was established in northern Syria, at Karkamiš on the Euphrates; that is, one of the Hittite king's sons was made king there and founded a dynasty, though of course he remained his father's subject. He and his successors exercised a kind of supervision over all of northern Syria.

The consequences of this expansion of power were significant. The Hittite Empire was thereby connected with the rest of the known world; it appeared as a powerful partner in the group of great powers. In Syria, the Hittites and the Egyptians henceforth confronted each other, the former ruling the north, the latter the south, more or less as the Ptolemaic and Seleucid kings did more than a thousand years later (pp. 211–213). There were battles but also attempts at cooperation. Thus the widow of an Egyptian king—probably the wife of Amenhotep IV (Akhenaten) or of Tutankhamen, who had died in 1336 (or 1323)—asked that a Hittite prince be sent to become her husband.[8] But the Hittite bridegroom was murdered on his way to Egypt. During the same period another great power emerged: the destruction of the Mitanni Empire enabled the Assyrians, who had up to that point been Mitanni subjects, to make their own wide-ranging claims only a short time later, under Adadnārāri (1295–1264). Their relationship to the Hittites was generally tense.

Then began the second phase of the international system outlined above. It was characterized by an alternation of armed conflict to resolve competing claims and attempts at a policy relying on the balance of powers. In a later treaty Egypt, Babylonia, Ḫanigalbat (an empire in upper Mesopotamia), and Assyria are explicitly named as great powers and potential adversaries of the Hittite king.[9] Strictly regulated diplomatic relations existed between the leading states. Kings addressed one another as "Brother"; granting permission to use this form of address signified recognition of great-power status. There was even an international diplomatic language; interestingly, this function was performed by the Babylonian language of the time. Economic exchange reached a significant level; trade caravans were constantly under way. Egypt considered itself the supreme power in this area and exploited its economic strength in political ways as well. The end of Suppiluliuma's reign was marred by an epidemic of plague that had been brought in from the south and that raged for decades. His son and successor Arnuwanda II died—whether of this plague, we do not know—after ruling for only a few years. Arnuwanda's brother Mursili II was confronted by a general secession of his vassals that had been provoked by the usual difficulties accompanying a transition in power. However, by forceful action he was able to restore the former situation. We are well informed about this, even in its details, because his campaign reports, the *Annals*, are for the most part extant: "Since I sat down on my father's throne, I have ruled ten years as king. These enemy lands I overcame with my own hands. The enemy lands which the royal princes and lords overcame are not included here. Whatever more the Sungoddess of Arinna, my lady, repeatedly gives to me (to do), I will carry it out and put it down (on clay)."[10]

In the north, he repelled the always active Kaska. He was also able to subjugate the Arzawa Empire, thereby gaining access to western Asia Minor and making the position of the Hittites considerably stronger. He managed to do the same thing in Syria. However, the eastern border with Assyria remained endangered. Mursili's son Muwatalli saw the Hittite position in Syria as being threatened by the energetic policy pursued by the Nineteenth-Dynasty pharaohs, and especially by Ramses II (1279–1213). A conflict between the two great powers was brewing, and the Hittites made careful preparations for it. These went so far that the seat of government was moved from Ḫattusa toward the south, to Tarḫuntassa "in the Lower Land," apparently so that the capital might be closer to the endangered region. War finally broke out, and a battle was fought near the city Qadeš (in the area of modern-day Homs) in the fifth year of Rameses II's reign—in May 1274 BCE. Only a few Hittite reports on this event have been preserved, but thanks to Egyptian reports, we are quite well informed regarding it. It is the first battle in world history whose course we are more or less able to reconstruct. It seems to have ended with a victory by the Hittites. But since their goal was generally defensive, the actual outcome was the preservation of the status quo; northern Syria remained in the hands of the Hittites, while the south remained Egyptian. Further fighting took place with the Kaska, whereas the situation in the West was apparently on the whole stable.

Muwatalli's successor was Urhi-Teššub, one of his sons by a secondary wife, who took the throne name of Mursili (III). He came into conflict with his uncle Hattusili, and after a certain number of years (we do not know exactly how many) he was over-thrown by the latter and taken to northern Syria, whence he eventually made his way to Egypt.

This Hattusili (III) had previously distinguished himself as a military leader and administrator. He justified what he had done in a kind of autobiography: "Ištar's divine providence I will proclaim. Let man hear it!"[11] However, it seems that his act of violence resulted in at least latent tensions within the nobility. Hattusili turned out to be a reformer. Hattusa, which had already under Mursili III become the capital again, was now expanded. But above all, the king sought to achieve a peaceful settlement with Egypt. In the twenty-first year of the reign of Ramses II, in November 1259, a treaty regulating relations between the two most important great powers was concluded. Its text has been preserved on temple walls in Egypt and in the Babylonian language in the archive of Boğazköy. It is the first extant peace treaty in history; a copy of it can be seen in the United Nations assembly hall in New York. The treaty's content is noteworthy. It included a nonaggression pact and provided for mutual aid in the event of war. The prevailing rules regarding succession to power were recognized by both sides. Political refugees were to be handed over, but had to be treated leniently:

> [And if] a single man flees from [Hatti, or] two men, [or three men, and they come to] Ramses, Beloved [of Amon, Great King, King] of Egypt, his brother, [then Ramses], Beloved of Amon, Great King, [King of Egypt, must seize them and send them] to Hattusili, his brother—for they are brothers. But [they shall not punish them for] their offenses. They shall [not] tear out [their tongues or their eyes]. And [they shall not mutilate (?)] their ears or [their] feet. [And they shall not destroy (?) their households, together with their wives] and their sons.[12]

In fact, the treaty produced a long-lasting peace settlement that was the foundation for a period of genuine collaboration. The partners to the treaty strengthened it by the marriage of one of Hattusili's daughters to Ramses II, which was preceded by years of negotiations. At the same time the Hittites succeeded in maintaining control of the situation in western Asia Minor.

However, a new foreign policy front appeared in the east: the Assyrians grew more aggressive, and violent conflicts became more numerous. Secundogenitures—that is, the rule of the king's sons, who could not rise to the imperial throne—became more important in the government of the whole empire. In northern Syria (Karkamiš) and also in southern Anatolia (Tarhuntassa) these secundogenitures gained more independence, so that in modern research they are often considered to be semi-autonomous. Hattusili's son and successor Tudhaliya IV continued his father's efforts at reform. Among his vigorous actions within the empire were an apparently methodical expansion and further massive development of the capital and its shrines. But he was concerned above all with a reorganization of the administration and of religion. We are relatively well informed about this by the clay tablet archive in Boğazköy.

The conflict in the east grew more intense. The Assyrians attempted to invade northern Syria, and though the battles remained limited, they obviously put the Hittites in difficulty. The Hittites repeatedly attempted to arrive at a settlement with the Assyrians. An interesting testimony to this is provided by a letter that Tudḫaliya sent to the Assyrian king, Tukulti-Ninurta, in 1244: "[You] acceded to the position [of your father], now protect your father's borders! . . . As [he] protected the borders, do not debase his name! [As] the gods [have] granted [him] their grace, so [may they now] grant it to you!"[13]

Tudḫaliya's son Arnuwanda III died after a short reign. He was succeeded by his brother Suppiluliuma II, under whom the empire suffered its catastrophe, which we discuss later in this chapter.

The Culture

STATE, SOCIETY, AND ECONOMY

The supreme arbiter of the Hittite state was the king, who was closely connected with the gods. The king's title meant "My Sun," and that was also what he called himself. Thus he represented (on the Egyptian model?) an embodiment of the sun god, and was that god's protégé. Accordingly, the winged sun served as a symbol of the king (Figure 16; cf. Figure 18). However, while he was alive the king was never referred to as a god, but rather as the "beloved of" a named god. He was deified only after his death (when used in reference to the king, the phrase "to become a god" meant "to die"). His functions concerned all areas of the state. He was the high priest, the supreme judge, the supreme commander of the army; he made all decisions regarding internal matters, had all goods at his disposal, and personally directed foreign policy. Alongside him stood the queen, whose title was "tawananna," and who had a very independent position. She remained queen for life, even after the death of her spouse, and his successor's wife's position was subordinate to hers. Occasionally there were political differences between the king and queen.

Correspondence, for example with Egypt, was conducted in the names of both King Ḫattusili III and his wife Puduḫepa. Puduḫepa exercised a significant influence in the cultural domain as well. Signs of women's extensive independent position in Hittite society are also encountered elsewhere. In general, Hittite society, like all Indo-European societies, was organized in a thoroughly patriarchal way. However, provisions attesting to an equal status for women can be found to a significant extent in Hittite law: the punishment for killing a woman is the same as that for killing a man; a woman can own property, and in the event of divorce may receive half the common property, and on the death of her husband she may also receive his share of the property; after a divorce, the mother may be granted custody of the children. But regarding pay for physical and nonphysical labor, men and women were treated unequally—as they still are today—to the disadvantage of the latter, in a ratio of 10:6.[14]

16. Yazılıkaya: god with king and winged sun.

The king resided in a palace that had numerous rooms as well as a storehouse and an archive (p. 85). But he did not reside solely in the capital; on extended journeys, especially for religious and military purposes, he often set up headquarters in the provinces for lengthy periods. In addition to the king, members of the royal family and selected officials, who represented a kind of nobility, also shared in governing. In the Old Kingdom (seventeenth to sixteenth centuries BCE) the nobility had a very independent position: a council of nobles (*pankus*) advised the king. A tendency to feudalization manifested itself early on. The king compensated noble officials by according them landed property. He thus achieved the enhancement of loyalty on the part of the nobles. This increased considerably in the New Kingdom (middle of the fourteenth century to 1200 BCE) and made the monarch's position seem stronger than ever before—the council of nobles is no longer mentioned. With respect to the military, a war-chariot corps acquired great importance; its members and also civil officials were granted fiefdoms by the king. The nobles conferred them in turn on farmers and craftsmen. Thus the broader strata of society were included in the system of fiefs. However, later on efforts were made to turn the holders of sovereignty into genuine government officials. The kings of the New Kingdom issued detailed written instructions that had to be confirmed by oath.

They were called *ishiul* (bond or obligation): "Tablet One of the obligations for all the temple personnel finished."[15]

In the international domain, a sharper distinction between "equal" and "dependent" states was made. The the feudal system's concepts were transferred to the relations between dependent states. In a conquered area the ruling king or his family were usually allowed to continue to rule, and the relationships were regulated by a treaty that was also called—significantly—a *ishiul* or "bond": "In the future this shall be [your] regulation (*ishiul*). [Observe it.] It shall be placed under oath for you."[16] The vassal remained sovereign within his land, but did not pursue an independent foreign policy and agreed to provide the Hittite king with military support. Each partner to the treaty guaranteed the legitimacy of the other's dynasty. Sometimes, especially in the city-states of northern Syria, Hittite secundogenitures were set up.

Thus the Hittite Empire had a relatively loose structure. Around the heart of the empire, the Hatti Land, there was a system of vassal states that were connected with the center by treaties. However, this system of dominion and alliance reacted sensitively to outside pressure that might weaken allegiance. Therefore the Hittite king's personal abilities were always of the greatest importance, both within the empire and in the relationships with his vassals. Thus succession to the throne almost always entailed problems of sovereignty, since a new king first had to prove his ability and bind the vassals to him.

Positive law had great influence among the Hittites. Relations among individuals and among institutions had to be clearly regulated, and these regulations were made permanent by putting them in writing. The above-mentioned set of rules (p. 72) had been created and put into writing by Telipinu in the period of the Old Kingdom. Several versions of a Hittite collection of laws are extant, and succeed one another chronologically. The oldest probably comes from the Old Kingdom. It refers to still older law. Criminal law does not follow the principle of the *lex talionis*, which aims at equivalent retribution. Instead, the idea of compensation is primary: "If anyone blinds a free person or knocks out his tooth, they used to pay 40 shekels of silver. But now he shall pay 20 shekels of silver."[17]

Agriculture represented—as it did throughout antiquity—the most important economic sector. Levies on subjects and especially on vassals contributed to the royal revenues; moreover, a large part of the latter came from war booty. Consequently the king set great store by the profitable exploitation of the land to maintain his household. Levies were closely connected with land ownership. The peasants were personally free, and many of them owned a small piece of land, but many also worked lands owned by nobles or by temples. In contrast, the "deported"—that is, foreign population groups deported after a successful war—were directly dependent and were assigned to temples or nobles as workers. The numerous staff for the great temples was recruited from these groups and used in maintaining the household, livestock raising, management, crafts, and agriculture. In Asia Minor, this system became traditional and continued into the Roman Imperial period. It was known under the Greek name of *hierodulia*—temple servitude. A text from Ḫattusa mentions an economic complex consisting of 208 individuals, including eighteen priests, twenty-nine musicians, fifty-two scribes, thirty-five augurs, and ten singers for songs in the Hurrian language. In addition to these temple officials, the complex also had its own slaves, though they seem not to have been very numerous.

Among the arts and crafts, pottery was of particular importance (p. 83). So were the production of textiles, mining, and metalworking, especially in bronze. Iron was already known and became an item of trade after the middle of the second millennium, but it was very expensive. Craftsmen usually worked for a lord. We know little about the organization of construction work. Trade was of some importance, since the Hittites were dependent on imports. To what extent there was private trade is not made clear by the sources, and opinions differ on this point. In any case, we know that there were merchants to whom the king guaranteed privileges. But we know little about them, especially since no genuinely commercial texts are extant. Trade played a major role in the international framework. This becomes clear, for instance, by the efforts made under Tudḫaliya IV to establish a trade embargo against the Assyrians:

> Since the King of Assyria is My Majesty's enemy, he shall be your enemy. Your merchant shall not go to Assyria, and you shall not allow his merchant into your land. He shall not pass through your land. But if he comes into your land, seize him and send him off to My Majesty. This matter [shall be placed] under [oath] for you.[18]

RELIGION

Religion and religious thought were of great importance in the lives of the Hittites, as is proven by the large number of religious texts. We know many of their divinities. The Hittites themselves spoke of the "thousand gods of Hatti":

> I have now placed these words under oath for you, and we have now summoned the Thousand Gods to assembly in this matter. The Sun-god of Heaven, the Sun-goddess of Arinna, the Storm-god of Heaven, the Storm-god of Hatti, . . . (sixteen lines of divine names) heaven, the earth, the great sea—they [shall be witness].[19]

Some of these gods are only local forms of more comprehensive figures; that is, the particular divinity connected with a place is similar to many others in specific qualities, whether it is as a sun, mother, tutelary, weather, or mountain divinity. Once adopted, even in the wake of conquests, all cults were continued. We find clear tendencies toward syncretism only in the thirteenth century, when the higher Hittite gods were equated with Hurrian gods, perhaps for political reasons—for example, to promote some unification of the empire's ideology—but they probably reflect chiefly the Hurrians' cultural influence.

The most important gods of the era of the empire were obviously Hattian in ancestry; that is, they were adopted from the earlier native population of the center of the empire. Imperial gods were the storm god and the sun goddess of Arinna, though we do not know where the city of Arinna was. In comparison to the Hurrian influences visible in the Imperial period, old Indo-European religious ideas probably played only a small part. The sole clearly Indo-European divinity is Sius, the god of the early Kussara Dynasty (p. 71). The name is related etymologically to the Greek word "Zeus" and the Latin "Jupiter."

Just as in the Greek tradition, the gods were conceived as persons but with capabilities and qualities exceeding those of humans; they are spared human weaknesses by their immortality and special powers. Humans are the gods' slaves. Their conduct must be in accord with ethical demands. If people sin, they will be punished, and their sins will also affect the lot of their posterity. The gods ensure that contracts and treaties, including those between states, are fulfilled. Humans must subject themselves to the gods' desire for justice, but they can also hope to receive divine mercy.

Naturally, it is important for humans to know the will of the gods. Thus the institution of the oracle, which was quite systematized, had an exalted status.[20] Strong Mesopotamian influences are discernible in this area. By means of sacrifices and festivals, people constantly strove to incline their divine lords to mercy. Festivals were held throughout the year and in various places; the king's presence was frequently necessary for them to be carried out. If he neglected this duty, the result could even be defeats in war. However, the will of the superior power could be influenced by magic. That is why we find numerous rituals that include magical practices. In this field as well, influences from northern Syria and Mesopotamia played a significant role. The Hittites had a deep-seated fear of hostile magic, of black magic: anyone who resorted to it was susceptible to severe punishment.

The Hittites worshiped their gods in temples, very large complexes of buildings with storerooms, regular economic units that corresponded to the palace. In the middle of temple lay the holy of holies, in which the image of the god was placed.

17. Twelve-gods-relief from Yazılıkaya.

18. Hittite spring shrine in Eflatun Pınar.

But there were also sacred sites in nature. Near the capital lay the rock shrine of Yazılıkaya. The latter is the modern Turkish name; it means "inscribed rock"; the Hittite name is unknown to us. On the walls of the main chamber of this shrine has been chiseled a representation of the two festive processions of the gods and goddesses; the two processions, which are led by the storm god and the sun goddess, meet in the middle. It is thought that the New Year's festival, in which all the respective gods come together, was celebrated in this place. In a second chamber, we find other divinities; the group of the so-called twelve gods (Figure 17), who also participate in the processions in the main chamber, is particularly noteworthy. A few figures are designated by Hurrian names given in hieroglyphic inscriptions—one of the clearest proofs of the tendency to syncretism. Tudḫaliya IV obviously played a major role in the development of this sacred site, since his figure appears as an observer in two different places (see Figure 16).

Finally, we may mention the spring shrine at Eflatun Pınar in south-central Anatolia as another of the Hittites' main religious sites. In the stone frame surrounding the spring basin are two facing structures made of huge ashlars. One of these structures—partly under water—has been preserved in excellent condition. The wall facing the center of the spring is artfully decorated with horizontal and vertical reliefs depicting a group of mountain gods, hybrid creatures, and winged suns arranged around a pair of divinities enthroned in the middle (Figure 18). This representation of the gods, which probably dates from the period of the empire (fourteenth to thirteenth centuries BCE), is considered one of the Hittites' highest quality works in stone known to us.[21]

Certainly, much in the Hittites' religion seems weird and odd, but even today a perceptible deep spirituality still emanates from it. Thus remarkable statements regarding human sinfulness are combined with the expression of great trust in the protection a divinity can provide:

> So it happens that people always sin. My father sinned as well and he transgressed the word of the Storm-god of Hatti, my lord. But I did not sin in any way. Nevertheless, it so happens that the father's sin comes upon his son, and so the sin of my father came upon me too. I have just confessed it to the Storm-god of Hatti, my lord, and to the gods, my lords. It is so. We have done it. But because I have confessed the sin of my father, may the soul of the Storm-god of Hatti, my lord, and of the gods, my lords, be appeased again.[22]

> Istar, My Lady, took me to her in every respect. Whenever illness befell me, sick as I was, I looked on (it) as the goddess' providence. The goddess, My Lady, held me by the hand in every respect. But, since I was a man divinely provided for, since I walked before the gods in divine providence, I never did an evil thing against man.[23]

We will find, in later propiatory inscriptions dating from a millennium and a half later, in the Anatolia of the first to the third centuries CE, other texts that are spiritually related to these ancient testimonies (pp. 523–525).

LITERATURE

The literature of the Hittites covers a wide range of different genres.[24] For example, part of it consists of literary genres that grew out of a certain subject field, especially religious texts (prayers, rituals, rules for sacrifices, festival texts, omen and oracle texts, etc.) and even library catalogs. Many texts concern legal and constitutional matters: governmental regulations, laws, treaties with great powers and with vassals, official instructions, court records, letters (correspondence among members of the royal family and especially between the king and his officials),[25] reports from government officials, and the kings' reports on their deeds (annals).

From this final group emerged a kind of narrative literature that represents a significant cultural achievement on the part of the Hittites. In it, they created the first genuine historical writing.[26] They clearly made an effort to represent events and processes as they actually happened—for example, by not omitting failures. These works offer vivid descriptions of events as well as reflections on their circumstances; above all, their own actions are reflected and explained to provide a lesson for future conduct. Thus treaties have a historical introduction that recounts the essential facts regarding previous common relationships. This holds also for Telipinu's "constitution" in the Old Kingdom and Ḫattusili III's "autobiography." Subsequently, the Hittite achievement in the field of historiography probably also functioned to some extent as a model. The Assyrian royal annals presumably continue the Hittite narrative tradition, but they do not attain the level of the Hittite accounts, because the Assyrian rulers' self-awareness made them less concerned with knowledge than with glorifying their deeds.

There is little narrative literature in the stricter sense. Narratives concern mainly myths and legends and thus have a religious background. They came in part from Mesopotamia (the epic of Gilgamesh, while others were taken from the Hurrians, especially after the influence of Hurrian culture increased in the thirteenth century BCE. Nonetheless, they represent our sole access to the world of Hurrian legend: their themes are chiefly the change and overthrow of divine dynasties, as we encounter them later in the early Greek tradition—first of all around 700 BCE in Hesiod's *Theogony* (p. 131).

What is entirely lacking in the Hittite tradition is independent poetry, even if poetic forms sometimes appear in religious liturgical texts.

Sculpture and Architecture

Our knowledge of this aspect of Hittite culture comes chiefly from the period of the empire. Strong influences from Mesopotamia, and also partly from Egypt, are evident in all domains; some of them are probably Hurrian. Although the Hittites elaborated on foreign material, taken as a whole their artistic creation makes a unified and independent impression.

With few exceptions, ceramics as art objects play a subordinate role; they are utensils. Vessels in the form of animals (*rhyton*) were used in religious ceremonies; terra cotta articles are also known. We have only a few remains of mural painting, whereas glyptics—the art of stone carving—has an important place, as is shown above all by the stamp seals.

However, sculpture is of great significance. Large statuary certainly existed, but almost all extant sculpture is small, and some of it is in bronze. The monumental gate sculptures with apotropaic (warding off evil) significance (e.g., Ḫattusa's lions, the sphinxes in Alaca Höyuk, and the god of Ḫattusa's so-called King's Gate) are distinguished by a high degree of vividness and a delicate modeling of facial features and body forms. Relief sculptures are also preserved. In this connection the orthostats of Alaca Höyuk's city walls should be mentioned; their flat and not fully shaped reliefs indicate that their creators had not yet mastered the art of composition. In contrast, the reliefs of the shrines at Eflatun Pınar (p. 81 f.) and at Yazılıkaya (near Boğazkale) are of higher quality. They show an effort to create an overall composition. Rock reliefs are found in various parts of Asia Minor (e.g., Muwatalli in the hinterland of Adana, the royal relief of Karabel in the west, and the deity at Sipylos near Manisa).[27] The Hittites' artistic expressions suggest that they cultivated a special religious relationship to mountains, crags, and stone.

The Hittites achieved a great deal in the domain of architecture. They had a marked sense for monumentality, which is seen in the adaptation of buildings to the area around them. This is also shown by their city planning. In addition to settlements on the plains that were sealed with the characteristic mounds (*Höyük*) after they were abandoned, mountain towns were also built. Large settlements had perimeter walls. Among the innovations are the casemate wall technology used in Hittite fortifications and the posterns, whose function has not yet been explained, as well as the huge double gates and towers that punctuate the walls at regular intervals and have crenellated battlements. A rigorous alignment of the buildings inside is found only rarely, as for example in Sarissa (p. 88). The palaces in more elevated situations are fortified and clearly demarcated from the rest of the residential quarters. Temples were not oriented in accord with the cardinal directions but rather placed to their best advantage as architecture.

However, our ability to make statements about Hittite architecture is limited, because for the most part only the foundations remain. In any case, the constituent elements of their buildings are bases made of large blocks of stone—limestone or greenish-black gabbro, of especially high quality in Ḫattusa—on which clay-brick walls with timber framework were built. The walls were subdivided by low-reaching windows; the roofs of the buildings were flat. Large inner courtyards and rooms provided space and lent an impression of monumentality. In the sanctuary of temples stood the image of the god, in metal or in wood, but we do not have a single example of these images. To gain a more precise notion of Hittite architecture, Chapter 5 examines more closely a few archaeological sites, and in particular the capital city.

Asia Minor in the Age of the Hittites

The attempt to gain reliable knowledge regarding the geography of Asia Minor in the age of the Hittites encounters a whole series of problems that are difficult to resolve. There is in fact a great deal of geographical information in the texts, but we have only a few fixed reference points that allow us to arrange it into a map.

Users of schematic maps with names and borders between countries or states in the age of the Hittites should be aware that in many cases these are based only on hypotheses. No reliable picture of the arrangement of states can be constructed on the basis of written testimonies regarding political relationships. Even more or less clearly indicated vicinities in the texts still give us no information concerning the exact location and extent of an area, and series or successions of names of countries in such sources cannot be simply translated into physical geography, especially since a series is not necessarily based on a geographical principle of organization. It is methodologically suspect to assign a country name to a particular region simply because there is "no longer any place" for such a territory elsewhere. Thus so far as large parts of Asia Minor are concerned, scientific discussion is still preliminary. The historical geography of the far west is particularly controversial, since it is connected to heatedly debated questions regarding the presence of Mycenaean Greeks and the existence of a Bronze Age city of Ilios/Troy ("Wilusa") shrouded in legend.[28]

Northern Anatolia and the Center of the Empire (Land of Hatti)

In north-central Anatolia, in the bend of the Halys, lies Ḫattusa (Turkish Boğazköy, "gorge village," today called Boğazkale, "gorge castle"). The earliest reference to this Hittite city is found in an eighteenth-century BCE text from Mari on the Euphrates.

In the empire period, when the Hittites were players in the concert of international powers, the city lay more on the margin than at the center of the region over which it claimed sovereignty. Its extensive urban area stretched over a raised area of rocky knolls; at its eastern end it was bounded by the deep gorge that gave the modern village its name (Map 3). Various periods of construction can be discerned, the oldest of which points to the time of the Hittites' Hattian predecessors. With an area of 181 hectares, Ḫattusa was one of the largest cities of that period, even if the whole enclosed space was not, of course, settled. The great fortifications extend to the open west side, opposite the gorge; they consist of a wall, originally eight meters high and strengthened by regularly placed towers, that has been traced over a distance of six kilometers. The older, northern perimeter wall is pierced by several tunnels (posterns). The more recent, southern wall, with the Lion Gate and the Royal Gate, surrounds the upper city (Figure 19).

The palace, built on a rocky ridge now known as the Büyükkale, dominates the city from above (Figure 20). It is difficult to determine the exact function of its individual spaces, though an official instruction for the bodyguard indicates that the royal family's residence, the storage and housekeeping areas, cult rooms, and lodgings for officials and the guard must have been located there. The palace's pillared, walled inner courtyards are typical. On the sides of the largest, so-called middle courtyard" are the building—possibly the palace library—in whose interior about 5,000 fragments of clay tablets were found and a two-story building with a wooden portico on the upper floor that apparently served as an audience hall for the ruler.

To date, more than thirty structures in the area of the capital have been identified as temples; the largest of them include whole groups of courtyards, halls, and rooms, which identify the temple, just as it does the palace, as a storage and housekeeping center. None of the structures can at present be attributed to a specific divinity with certainty. The main temple on the plain was probably erected where the city's oldest religious site was located and may have been dedicated to the two supreme gods of the empire, the storm god and the sun goddess of Arinna. In its storerooms, some of which had more than one floor, thousands of cuneiform tablets were found even during the initial excavation campaigns. All other temple structures are located in the upper city, quite close to one another, so that it is possible to speak of a more or less sacred precinct devoted exclusively to religious goals.[29]

Up to the present, purely residential quarters for an urban population have been excavated only in the lower city; therefore the number of inhabitants, probably mainly people serving the palaces and temples, can only be estimated. A clue is offered by the gigantic underground grain depots in the northwestern part of the city, in which several thousand tons of barley and wheat were stored. Seven springs and several ponds lie in the city. Its infrastructure also included a freshwater supply provided by rain and spring water and a system of drains under the streets. Ḫattusa's necropolises have yet to be discovered. Only a few dozen graves from the early days of the city have been found. In contrast to Pharaonic Egypt, not a single royal tomb has been proven to exist in Hittite Anatolia.

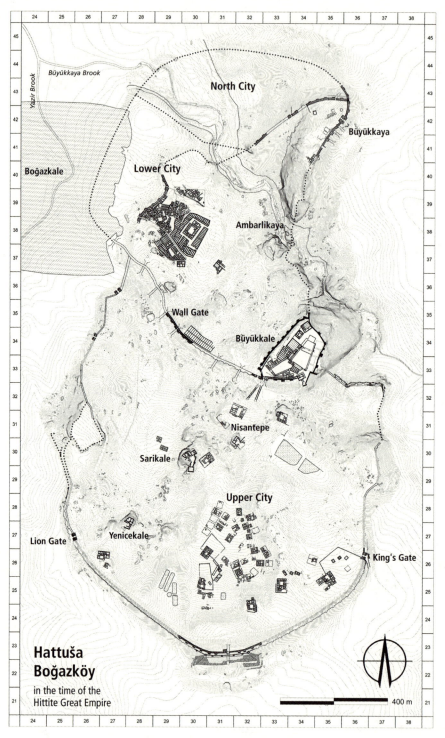

Map 3. Topography of the Hittite capital, Ḫattusa.

19. The "Royal Gate" in Ḫattusa.

20. Ḫattusa, view of the lower city from the Büyükkale.

Outside the capital only a few sites with complex architecture from the time of the Hittite Empire have been systematically investigated, and up to now discoveries of Hittite cuneiform texts—indices of an administrative or cultural center of at least regional significance—are scattered over a handful of places in the area around Ḫattusa. Tarsos in Cilicia and a few sites in northern Syria, including Karkemiš, Emar, and Ugarit, are the only other centers at this time that are far outside this area. I have already mentioned the town of Alaca Höyük northwest of Ḫattusa, with its rich Bronze Age tombs (p. 61 f.). There we find another Hittite city that has been quite well investigated. It has a city wall with orthostats—large, rectangular cut stones—a sphinx gate, and a temple complex in which archaeologists found statu-ettes in gold, ivory, and bronze. We are still not certain what the name of this city was.

More recent excavations and discoveries of texts throw more light on three places in particular: Sapinuwa in Ortaköy near Çorum, Tapikka (Maşathöyük), and Sarissa (Kuşaklı), south of Sivas. Sarissa is the easternmost city in the Anatolian highland ("upper country") where Hittite cuneiform texts were found; it is one of the Hittite provincial sites of the Imperial period that has been most intensively investigated. In more than one respect, Sarissa seems to have been a "small Ḫattusa." Its center was also surrounded by a wall and was entered through four gates that were closed and sealed at night; a clay seal was found there that corresponds to a text from the capital that describes this procedure in great detail. Inside Sarissa several sacred sites have been partly excavated; the largest had at least 110 rooms, as well as an extensive ser-vice wing in which beer, among other things, was kept. A huge storehouse at the southern tip of the perimeter wall held about 820 tons of grain that could have fed the inhabitants for more than a year if necessary—another facility that is also found in the capital. Ponds, some of which were within the city walls, and water supply systems corresponded to the water tanks in Ḫattusa. The clay tablets found in several areas were religious in content. In combination with texts from Ḫattusa, they refer to an important festival in the shrine of the "Ḫuwasi-stones" outside the city, which had been visited by the Great King, and the discovery of a clay seal even provides the name of a local king, "Mazitima."

Cuneiform tablets have also recently came to light in Kayalıpınar, west of the modern town of Sivas, and Oymaağaç near Vezirköprü, southwest of Samsum.

SOUTHERN AND WESTERN ANATOLIA

For the purposes of strategy and transportation, the alluvial plain in classical Cilicia, which lay on the border with Syria, was always a key position. In the age of the Hit-tites, this area was known as Kizzuwadna and was incorporated into the empire by Suppiluliuma I. Ḫattusili III married a princess who came from this region, probably thus strengthening the ties between the center and the periphery of the empire. The most important centers in the area are now occupied by the modern cities of Tarsus (Tarsos in classical sources, certainly to be equated with Hittite Tar-ša) and Mersin; the latter's ancient name we still do not know for sure.

So far as the countries of Tarḫuntassa and Lukka are concerned, the prevailing view is that they too lay on the Mediterranean coast. On the west, Tarḫuntassa bordered on Kizzuwadna. The previously mentioned thirteenth-century bronze tablet, on which the treaty between the Great King Tudḫaliya IV and the king of Tarḫuntassa was inscribed, offers a valuable reference point, because it connects the place name Parḫa with the name of the river Kastariya, which probably refers to the later city of Perge on the Kestros (near modern-day Antalya).[30] This river forms the border; west of it lay hostile area. Especially in later times, Tarḫuntassa was of considerable importance. When the Hittite Empire finally collapsed, this country was one of the three parts of the empire.

Records from the middle of the second millennium refer to a land of Luwiya that lay somewhere to the south or southwest, whereas later texts also speak of Lukka lands, whose inhabitants carried out predatory raids on Cyprus and were for the most part hostile to Hatti as well. Both names remind us of the name of the Greek country Lycia, which has led researchers to connect the Lycian peninsula with them. This conjecture seems plausible for Lukka, although the Lukka lands are supposed to have extended beyond Lycia. The grounds for this conjecture cannot, however, be presented here.[31]

The determination of the exact location and extent of Arzawa in western, southern, or southwestern Asia Minor is based on hypotheses. It was inhabited by Luwians, and in the fifteenth century BCE it was a powerful state. The names of three of its rulers are known. Pharaoh Amenophis III (1390–1352) corresponded with a king Tarḫundaradu, who had promised him his daughter as a wife; the pharaoh sent gifts but was unmoved by the gifts he received in return. The king of Arzawa wrote to the pharaoh in Hittite—a rare exception in the Amarna correspondence, which was conducted mainly in Akkadian—and even asked that the answer might be given him in Hittite. About two generations later, Arzawa was conquered and destroyed by Mursili II. The defeated usurper Uḫḫaziti had resided in a place named Apasa, which has been hypothetically equated with the later Ephesos. But where was the residence of Great Arzawa? One candidate—though not generally accepted—is Beycesultan in the upper valley of the Maeander, which we have already encountered. This hill town was impoverished after it was destroyed around 1750 BCE (p. 60), but in the period of Tarḫundaradu, around 1450, it experienced a boom with new settlement until it was finally abandoned in 1180. Unfortunately, because of the lack of written documents, Beycesultan cannot be connected with any of the regional states of that period.

The destruction of this empire is linked to the names of small states that are involved in the debate regarding the location of Arzawa. One of them bears the name "Mira" and was probably in the valley of the Maeander. Most researchers think that the land of the Seḫa River lay to the north of it (perhaps in the valley of the Hermos River). The boundary between the two seems to have run near the rock-cut relief of Karabel mentioned by Herodotus, twenty kilometers east of the great city of İzmir, as a review of the hieroglyphics made by the English researcher John David Hawkins has suggested. A further hieroglyphic inscription found far to the south has been interpreted as a boundary marker between Mira and the Hittite central empire. The German archaeologist Anneliese Peschlow-Bindokat discovered it at Suratkaya, on the Anadolu Pass east of Lake Bafa, in the summer of 2000. In this text, a man from Mira seems to be mentioned, among others; another name is found in a cartouche (a framed group of signs containing the ruler's name). However, the interpretation of the name as Kupanta-Kurunta, a nephew of Mursili II, like the interpretation of the whole inscription as a boundary marker, is rather unlikely.

If we now turn to the Aegean coast of Asia Minor, the notion that there had long been contacts with the islands lying offshore, sometimes within sight, does not seem very surprising. We find evidence suggesting that people from Minoan Crete traded with Asia and also probably settled there, in Miletus and other places farther south, including Iasos and Knidos.[32] But research has long given special attention to the question as to whether and where there were Greeks on the western edge of the Hittite-Luwian world of states in the time of the Hittite Empire. This question is connected with the search for the earliest appearance of Greeks in Asia in general. It is well known that the deciphering of the Linear B script by Michael Ventris and John Chadwick in 1954 proved that the language of the texts written on clay tablets in the seats of power in Crete and in Greece was Greek. But most of what has been preserved in this script consists only of inventories. The names of countries or places of origin of persons—especially of women, who were probably slaves, on tablets from Pylos in the Peloponnese—may perhaps point to places in Asia, including Miletus and Knidos: *mi-ra-ti-ja* (PY Aa 798 + Ab 573), *ki-ni-di-ja* (PY Aa 792; Ab 189; An 292). These are the oldest references to Asian matters in Mycenaean Greek. But that tells us little about the presence of Greeks in Asia. It is more exciting to look in the opposite direction, from the Hittites toward the west: an ongoing controversy is entwined around the so-called Aḫḫiyawa problem. Aḫḫiyawa was the name of a kingdom in the southwest or west that is known to have existed as early as the Middle Kingdom. However, whether it was on the mainland of Asia Minor or—and this seems more likely, at least for its capital—outside Anatolia, is not completely clear. In any event, Aḫḫiyawa was always independent and for a time even had great-power status. For the most part, its relationship to the Hittites was tense. In 1924 the Swiss orientalist Emil O. Forrer identified the inhabitants of this area with the Mycenaean Greeks, whom Homer calls *Achaioi* (Achaeans, older form *Akhaiwoi*). His main argument is the phonic similarity of the two names. This interpretation was the subject of a vigorous scholarly controversy during the interwar period; the identification of the Aḫḫiyawa with the Achaeans was subsequently taken up again by the Hittitologist Hans G. Güterbock. Even today there is no real proof for such an equation, but it is nevertheless generally accepted on the basis of general considerations regarding the historical context. Here it is not possible to examine in detail the fragmentary reports concerning conflicts and relationships. But if the identification is correct, then another question arises: where was the center of Aḫḫiyawa? Was it in the Peloponnese (Mycenae), central Greece (Thebes), Rhodes, or even Crete? The corresponding name has not yet been found in extant Linear-B tablets. An inscription discovered in 1997 at Cineköy, not far from Adana in Cilicia, deserves special attention in this connection. It is written in two languages, hieroglyphic Luwian and Phoenician, and dates from the eighth century BCE. The Luwian version mentions a place name in Cilicia: Ḫiyawa (the Phoenician translation gives a different name in this passage). If we assume that it is the same word as "Aḫḫiyawa" and not—as has also been argued[33]—an accidental echo of it, then we have to ask how the name happens to appear so far from the location of Aḫḫiyawa in the time of the Hittites, which has been sought—as we have already seen—in the area of Crete, the Aegean, or Greece. Archaeological evidence makes the presence of Greeks in Cilicia as early as the eighth century BCE at least probable. The word would then apply to a place in Cilicia or a part of the Cilician plains that was inhabited by Greeks. On that assumption, "Aḫḫiyawa" would mean "Land [or place] of the Greeks." If we grant the correctness of the equation, this would strengthen Forrer's hypothesis.

Independently of the problem of the Achaean/Aḫḫiyawa names, certain claims can now be based on archaeology. In the case of Miletus—whose equation with Millawata/Millawanda in Hittite texts is widely accepted, but has not been proven—and its broader environment, settlement by Greeks during the age of the Hittite Empire can be proven.[34] This is based chiefly on Mycenaean pottery for everyday use found in Miletus and on a Mycenaean tomb type (the chamber tomb), which also exists in Samos, Kos, and the Bodrum peninsula (Müsgebi and Pilavtepe). Apparently the area around Miletus became a kind of Greek Peraia (bridgehead) that may have belonged to the Aḫḫiyawa kingdom for a time. A burned layer in Miletus may go back to the violent destruction of the settlement and is connected with the campaigns in the west waged under Mursili II.

However, the relationships between Bronze Age Greeks and the Hittites were not intensive. There are no references to the Hittites even in Mycenaean Greece, and conversely, only a few discoveries of Mycenaean objects from the second millennium BCE have been found in the Hittite area. Whether Hittite construction methods provided a direct model for the cyclopean walls in Mycenae and Tiryns and for the Lion Gate in Mycenae, or whether Ḫattusa was known at all in Greece, remain open questions.[35] There is not the slightest evidence to support the view that Mycenaean Greeks could read cuneiform script and understand the contemporary "world language," Akkadian; not even King Tarḫundaradu's scribe in Arzawa in southern or western Anatolia could do that (p. 89). In any case, there is no mention of Achaeans in the Amarna correspondence.

TROY AND THE NORTHWEST

We have no certain knowledge about northwestern Asia Minor, either. Names of countries in the Hittite period—Masa, Karkisa—have been proposed for the wider area of the later Mysia and Bithynia, and Wilusa for the coastal area of the Troad.

Troy flourished again in the second millennium, after a period—between about 2490 and 1700 BCE—during which it consisted chiefly of village settlements.

Scholars speak of the Troy VI level, which is divided into eight (or more recently, nine) sublevels. It is distinguished by the construction of a new, circular fortification. A part of the wall about 350 meters long has been preserved; its stone base is 4 to 4.5 meters wide and 4 meters high. Several rather large, free-standing buildings can be proven to have existed. At that time the place obviously had a certain importance as a regional center of power. It was destroyed in the thirteenth century. Troy VII a (recently, the level is called VI i) continues the culture of level VI. This settlement subsided in rubble and ashes ca. 1190/80 BCE (?)—at least according to the chronology established by the excavator Manfred Korfmann. Troy VII b1-2, the following period, still belongs to the old tradition, and then comes the real break. However, after the catastrophic fire ca. 1020 BCE, settlement did not cease completely. A new era is distinguished by new architecture and new ceramics that show relationships with the Balkans. We call this phase Troy VIII.

Naturally, in this context the question of the historicity of the Trojan War arises. The state of the historical sources is complicated, but I will outline it briefly. However, before doing so, let us consider the history of the question itself. The ancient Greek writers were firmly convinced that the war for Troy actually occurred. They made various calculations and observations regarding when and where it took place. Their dates for the destruction of Troy fluctuate between 1300 and 1150 BCE (in our chronology). However, this is not a scientific chronology, but rather consists of convoluted extrapolations and learned speculations: so far as historical writing is concerned, for the Greeks the time before 700 was *terra incognita*, as Walter Burkert put it.[36] That the "Ilios" of the Homeric epic (the name "Troïē" also occurs) is to be sought in this part of Asia Minor at all is suggested by a whole series of topographic details given in the *Iliad* itself, especially the reference to the Greeks' ship harbor "at the Hellespont" (the Greek name for the Dardanelles; see especially *Iliad* 12, 30; 15, 233, and other passages), and also to Mt. Ida, the River Skamandros, and so forth. In any case, the poet was thinking of this landscape when he represented the scene of the war. Greeks had really settled there by the seventh century BCE at the latest, and they lived in a city named "Ilion"; their descendants claimed that Homer's *Ilios* had been there. But this claim had already been contradicted in antiquity by scholars who located Troy farther inland. The European Middle Ages and the early modern period knew the legendary material chiefly through Virgil's epic—the *Aeneid*. In the debate regarding the site, the ruins of Alexandria Troas were prominent for a while, and then a hill called Ballı Dağ. In the eighteenth century the Greco-Roman Ilion was rediscovered where the hill with the Turkish name of Hisarlık (i.e., "castle ruins") is located. The idea that the legendary Ilios/Troy must have been on this site was published in 1822 by the Scot Charles McLaren, and the Englishman Frank Calvert was active there before Heinrich Schliemann made the sensational "discovery" of Troy his own.

The development of the excavations and the ongoing debates concerning their results need not occupy us here. It is well known that at the beginning of the twenty-first century a new controversy over the interpretation of the discoveries flared up with such shocking violence that it was even discussed in the mass media. The controversy turns on the settlement traditionally labeled Troy VII a (VI i), because it was destroyed in precisely the same time span to which the Greeks had assigned the fall of Troy. Here we must consider, as the ancient historian Justus Cobet reminds us, that "What was found by excavation was simply the place to which the legend alluded . . . what these walls once saw and what led to their destruction is a different question."[37] Here the complex difficulties begin: the existing discoveries made by excavation do not provide an unambiguous answer to the question of the cause of the settlement's destruction. A decision for this or that version, war or no war, is based on interpretation. If we decide that the interpretation "war" is correct, we will not have gained much—and certainly not enough to connect the fate of the ruins with the narrative of Agamemnon's and Menelaus's campaign against Troy. The problems increase still more when trying to connect the imaginary overall picture of the city and Priam's castle with the results of archaeological research. In Homer, the whole city is surrounded by walls; but the poet says nothing about a perimeter wall around the castle. However, what archaeology has been able to establish up to this point reverses this relationship: Troy VI–VII had a massive wall around the castle, but there was no wall around the city. Interpretations of the function of a ditch or moat running some 400 meters south of the castle on the plains as intended to hinder invaders, interpretations of the remains of buildings and discoveries with a view to establishing that Troy was a city with a high population density, an economic power with vital trade relationships, do not stand up to criticism. Their supporters fail not only to confirm Homer's Troy, but also to assign this castle a political and economic significance comparable to that of important palace centers.[38]

Archaeology normally achieves the desirable certainty as to the ancient name of an excavated site by discovering written documents. That is how we know that Kārum Kaneš was discovered at the "ash hill" (Kültepe) and that Ḫattusa was discovered near Boğazköy. Except for the discovery of a seal irrelevant to our question, up to this point excavations at Hisarlık—the modern name for the supposed site of Troy—have not yielded any written documents at all. Individuals searching for circumstantial evidence of Homeric material are hoping to find in written sources outside Troy a second strand in addition to the discoveries made by excavation. Since from the Greece of the second millennium BCE only unproductive inventories in Linear-B script on clay tablets have been found,[39] they scrutinize the Egyptian and especially the Hittite literature from the empire period for references to the existence of an *Ilios* or *Troia*. This has now been going on for a long time, but with new discoveries and the progress made by philology and linguistics in dealing with textual material, in the twentieth and at the beginning of the twenty-first centuries the debate has come to a head. The focal point of the debates is the place-name "Wilusa," which occurs several times in the fragments of Hittite records, and which is equated with (W)Ilios. Wilusa appears as an area ruled by regents. Of importance is the emergence in the thirteenth century of a King Alaksandu of Wilusa, one of Muwatalli's vassals who is identified with Alexandros of Ilios, that is, with the Paris of the Troy legend. The place name Taruisa also appears, and has been equated with Troy. These similarities in place-names have much to be said for them from a linguistic standpoint, but taken by themselves they are again not conclusive. A weighty objection arises from the fact that in contrast to Homer's usage, which relates Ilios and Troy to parts or aspects of one and the same place, a Hittite text uses "Wilusa" and "Taruisa" to designate different areas. Unfortunately, all references in the few extant cuneiform fragments are too vague to allow a precise geographical localization.

Thus the outcome of the debate remains in doubt. Perhaps we will get lucky, and future discoveries will allow us to learn more details regarding the Hittite history of the northwestern corner of Asia Minor and also make progress toward answering the question as to the historical core of the Troy legend. Much that could also be brought to bear on the argument cannot be discussed here for reasons of length. But in conclusion we may ask how a historical event that we are supposed to assume to be the nucleus of the Troy legend could be handed down for five hundred and more years without the slightest trace of it ever put into writing. And even if we grant that much, we may still have the greatest doubt that the historical substance, no matter how reliable, could be preserved without being repeatedly poetically elaborated and reshaped to the point that it became unrecognizable.

End of the Empire, the Invasion of the Sea Peoples, and the Dark Age (ca. 1200–800 BCE)

The abrupt end of the Hittite Empire was accompanied by corresponding events in many places in Hittite Anatolia at about the same time (end of the thirteenth century and beginning of the twelfth century). The destruction of Ḫattusa is dated to between 1220 and shortly after 1200. Primarily the public buildings (the palace on Büyükkale and the temple) were affected.

The course of the great catastrophe is not known in detail. Political and economic phenomena of degeneration had enormous effects in all the empires of the region. In the late phase, economic difficulties, especially in agriculture, loomed. A genuine food shortage seems to have occurred in the heartland, but its causes may have been complex. We even read of aid provided by the Egyptians. In the fifth year of his reign, the Pharaoh Merenptah (1224–1204 BCE) reports: "I caused grain to be taken in ships to sustain this land of Hatti."[40] It is thought that at that time the Kaska attacked the center and that the capital fell victim to them. Finally, internal uprisings, perhaps induced by the conflict in loyalties that had continued since Ḫattusili III usurped the throne, are blamed for the destruction of the empire in the heartland. In Syria, secessionist movements were in the offing, and the federated states of Karkamiš and Tarḫuntassa acted quite independently.

In contrast, the cause of the final collapse is seen more narrowly as the result of the extensive migration from the Balkans toward the east—the invasion of the so-called sea peoples. Archaeologically, burned levels from this time can be proven at various sites, though it is not clear how closely they relate to the same series of events.[41] The discoveries made on Büyükkale, Ḫattusa's palace district, are striking in that only a few objects from the time of its destruction—objects of the kind that would normally belong to the inventory of a palace operation—were found under the heavy rubble of the walls and roofs that had collapsed. The palace seems to have been abandoned, indeed cleaned out, even before it was destroyed. Written sources that guide us on the events come from Egypt and Ugarit on the Syrian coast. The royal annals of the Middle Assyrian period (primarily those of Tiglatpilesar I, 1115–1093) shed light on the situation in the highlands. The Egyptian sources speak of "peoples from the islands of the sea" who attacked Egypt, but the notion of "islands of the sea" is often used mythically and cannot be located precisely in actual geography.[42] An initial invasion from the west occurred in 1219, or possibly 1208, during the reign of Pharaoh Merenptah; inhabitants of Asia Minor certainly took part in it. A second invasion (it is uncertain how it was connected with the first one) occurred in 1177, during the reign of Ramses III. Evidently it was a kind of migration, which approached Egypt from the north by land and by sea. The names of the peoples mentioned refer in part to the Balkans. It is expressly emphasized that no land stood up to the invaders. The land of the Hatti and other countries were annihilated. Then the pharaoh was able to stop the movement in Palestine. One of the sea peoples, the Philistines, settled in Palestine. They gave the country the name "Palestine." Reports from Ugarit (tablets that were found in a kiln but had not yet been fired at the time of the destruction) mention attacks from the sea and Hittite battles at sea off the south coast of Asia Minor and around Cyprus. A Hittite text written under the last Hittite king, Suppiluliuma II, also reports on naval battles around Cyprus.

Efforts to put the fall of the empire in Anatolia into temporal alignment with the general history of events have been based primarily on an Assyrian report from the year of King Tiglatpilesar I's accession to the throne (1115 BCE). According to this document, battles between the Assyrians and the Muški occurred, and the next year there were battles against the Kaska in northern Mesopotamia. Thus while the Hittite king was fighting the sea peoples in the south and was probably defeated by them, the Kaska and other invaders in the highlands were overrunning the Hittite center and then advancing farther to the southeast. The result was an unmistakable cultural rupture in central Anatolia. Whereas in the south and southeast many place-names have continued to exist down to the present day—Niğde, Adana, Malatya, and others—there was no comparable continuity in the middle of the region.[43] The external marks of civilization, such as the active use of writing and monumental architecture, largely disappear. Much the same happens in Greece. Since in the world of that time the written sources were completely drying up or greatly diminishing, historians speak of the Dark Age. However, the "dark" periods were regionally variable in duration. In the east and southeast, the tradition remained partially intact. This holds without qualification for Egypt and Assyria. In the west, the tradition resumes between the eighth and the sixth centuries BCE, through the Greek literature that was then emerging.

✦ ✦ ✦

The Hittite Empire has a special status in the history of Asia Minor. For the first, and for ages the only, time—and this holds true long after antiquity— almost the whole of the Asia Minor peninsula was politically dominated and culturally shaped by a people residing in Anatolia. The Hittites were a land power that came out of the interior of Anatolia, expanded overland, and entered into conflict and exchange with the great neighboring cultures of the Middle East. It is no accident that the Hittite heritage long remained alive in this zone of contact—so that the name of this people even appears in the Bible—whereas in the west it disappeared and in the whole of the Greek and Latin literature of classical antiquity the Hittites are not mentioned at all. This people and its history were recovered only in the twentieth century. In 1834 Charles Texier thought he had discovered in the ruins of Ḫattusa the Medes' city of Pteria, and at the end of the nineteenth century there was still speculation about the identity of the site, because the language of its written documents was not understood. A learned French Dominican, Father Jean-Vincent Scheil, was the first to realize that cuneiform texts were the written form of the "Hittite" language. Only with the beginning of excavations in 1906 under the direction of Theodor Makridi Bey and Hugo Winckler were scholars sure of where the Hittites were located, and with Bedřich Hrozný's successful decipherment in 1915, the door to a new world was opened for numerous new discoveries that have since been intensively investigated by excavations that are still ongoing. Work on texts, monuments, and objects is now advancing vigorously and has recently stimulated a discussion about specifically Anatolian historical and cultural contexts, including the Anatolian "continuity thesis" (p. 131).

Small States, Peoples, and New Kingdoms (ca. 1000–550 BCE and Later)

The collapse of the international system of states around and after 1200 BCE created a power vacuum from the Aegean realm to Syria and Palestine that allowed a series of migrations and enabled small states and new kingdoms to develop. This situation in the Orient did not change until the rise of the new Assyrian Empire in the tenth century. Basically, the motives were the same as those that had driven the Assyrians westward about a thousand years earlier: to secure a reliable supply of metals, wood for construction, and other valuable goods (e.g., horses). Initially the Assyrians' advances occurred sporadically, but from the eighth century on they established a permanent dominion over part of Asia Minor. Until ca. 700 their power extended as far as the coast of the Levant, Cyprus, and Cilicia. In the first half of the following century, Egypt fell under their control (671–655 BCE) until Psammetichus I freed himself from them and founded a new dynasty. A large portion of the resident population was deported from many areas, for example Cilicia, and Assyrians and Babylonians settled in them instead. The Assyrian Empire succumbed to the Babylonians and Medes only toward the end of the seventh century BCE.

The Hittite-Luwian linguistic and cultural tradition remained alive in the area of the Assyrian Empire as far as Cappadocia and Cilicia. The domain of these chieftains was traditionally conceived by its people as *Ḫatti*. Alongside it, the power of the Phoenician monarchies grew. But above all, the rise of a Semitic people called the Aramaeans belongs to this era. They advanced out of deserts and into the civilized areas, and they gradually prevailed everywhere. In the east, the kingdom of a people linguistically related to the Hurrians, the Urartians, was established on the Anatolian high plateau and lasted for about two centuries before collapsing.

Traces of the old Anatolian tradition found farther west come from a later period: the Lydians are considered to be the descendants of relatives of the Hittite-Luwian population, and idioms related to Luwian are also found on the southwest and southern coasts of Asia Minor—though very late (fifth to third century BCE)—among the Carians, the Lycians, and perhaps the Sidetans. However, the ancestry and earlier history of these peoples remain unknown to us. Central and western Anatolia was overrun by migrations, apparently from the Balkans. The Phrygian Empire emerged on the high plains of Anatolia. After destruction caused by renewed barbarian invasions, the expanding Lydian Empire rose up from the valley of the Hermos to that of the Halys. Settlements of Aeolian, Ionian, and Dorian Greeks on the Aegean and Mediterranean coasts had close contacts with the Phrygians, Lydians, Carians, and Lycians. After 700, new waves of Greek emigrants spread along the Propontis (Sea of Marmara) and the south coast of the Black Sea.

According to archaeological criteria, the Iron Age begins in the last centuries of the second millennium. The use and production of iron quickly spread. However, the precise contexts in which this major development in cultural history took place are as yet undetermined and remain an object of scholarly debate.

The written sources concerning this time come only in part from Asia Minor itself; much is described from the external perspective of the dominant Assyrian power, which at times annexed Cilicia (Qu'e) and part of Cappadocia (Tabal) as western provinces. For the region of southeastern Anatolia and northern Syria, the corpus of hieroglyphic Luwian inscriptions from the Iron Age published by John David Hawkins and Halet Çambel is of outstanding importance. From their area of distribution also come inscriptions on stone in Semitic alphabets (Phoenician, Aramaic), whereas in the highlands the Urartians composed their inscriptions in Assyrian cuneiform script. Carians, Lycians, Sidetans, and Lydians used—like the Phrygians and the Greeks—their own alphabets. However, by far the majority of the texts were written after the middle of the sixth century. The Greek literary tradition in western Anatolia begins in the seventh century BCE. The cultural and historical developments are so different that it would be inadvisable to present the events in Asia Minor in a strictly chronological manner; therefore let us examine the individual locations where they took place.

The Neo-Hittite Period (ca. Eleventh to Eighth Centuries BCE)

In southeastern Anatolia—in the area of the Taurus Mountains, Cilicia, and northern Syria—the "neo Hittite" small states survived and deliberately continued the traditions of the age of the Hittite Empire. Their rulers had names like Suppiluliuma, Muwatalli, and Labarna, and they bore the same titles as the kings of the Imperial period (for a list of states and rulers, see the Appendix). They used hieroglyphic script in everyday life: most of the extant documents in that script come from this period. The language is clearly Luwian (distinguished by some scholars as "Hieroglyphic Luwian"). The script was apparently felt to be typically Hittite and was an element of the tradition. Later on, Phoenician and Aramaic were also used in these areas. Among the most important states and localities, the one that already existed under the empire as a secundogeniture should be presented first: Karkamiš on the Euphrates. Today we can trace the local dynasty of the son of Suppiluliuma I over five generations down to a certain Kuzi-Teššub. In northern Syria, Karkamiš also played a leading political role for a time, but in any case it remained a cultural center where sculptures and inscriptions were found (p. 30), and that exercised a supraregional influence.[44]

In northern Syria we find Tell Ahmar; Aleppo, with a recently excavated shrine to the storm god on the citadel; also Samal (now Zincirli), where relief inscriptions in alphabetical script and proper names indicate a mixed Luwian-Semitic culture; and Hamath (Hama). Near and in the Taurus Mountains to the north, we know the principalities of Kummuḫ, the later kingdom of Commagene, Milid (Malatya), and Gurgum (Maras), west of the Euphrates.

On this side of the Amanos Mountains, principalities have been located near Antakya (Unqi) and on the Cilician plains (Que), the center of Que apparently lying underneath the modern city of Adana. Tell Tayinat in the Amuq plain (near Antakya) is probably the capital of the kingdom W/Palastin, which was apparently powerful between the 11th and 9th centuries BCE. Recent epigraphic discoveries contribute to our knowledge of its relevance and of its rulers. The relationship of W/Palastin to the "Philistines," located farther to the south, remains unclear.[45] The Karatepe excavation site in the Ceyhan valley, where a bilingual Phoenician-Luwian hieroglyphic inscription was found, also belongs in this context. According to Assyrian sources, the Land of Tabal lay north of the Cilician Taurus Mountains. Thanks primarily to the well-preserved eighth-century stone reliefs in İvriz (Figure 21), we know the names of princes of Tuwana (the later Tyana). A few years ago the remains of complex architecture (houses and a representative central building) and a few sculptures from the late Hittite period were found not far from Niğde, on the rim of the crater of the 2,000-meter-high Göllu Dağ. These discoveries raise the question of whether a large, late Hittite mountain shrine was located there, accompanied by a seasonal residential complex used by participants in festivals.

A coherent history of these small states cannot be narrated. Certainly they shared no sense of belonging together. The course of events in this region was determined by the previously mentioned general factors—first of all the constant infiltrations of

21. Stone relief from Ivriz. God with bundle of wheat and bunches of grapes; opposite facing, King Warpalawas.

the Aramaeans spreading from northern Syria that had been taking place since the tenth century BCE, and second the Assyrian conquests that began in the ninth century: Salmanassar III's campaigns (858–824) already forced Tabal and Qu'e to pay tribute; Kummuh was constantly threatened, and in 708 BCE it was incorporated into the Assyrian empire as the last late Hittite small state.

Numerous sculptures from the time of these principalities have been preserved: statues and reliefs on orthostats and stone walls. As already mentioned, the traditions of the Hittite Empire were continued in these principalities, but at the same time influences proceeding from the Semitic tribes in the environment were also absorbed. However, from an artistic point of view the extant monuments are not very developed.

Urartians (ca. Ninth to Sixth Centuries BCE)

It has been proven that Hurrian tribes settled in eastern Anatolia and in the bordering areas of Iran and Armenia from the eighteenth century BCE on. In the fourteenth century, the Nairi Lands are mentioned in this region, and from the thirteenth century on the name Uruaṭru/i is attested. The center of this culture lay in the area of Lake Van, the heart of the kingdom that was later called Urartu. In using this name, modern scholarship follows Assyrian terminology; earlier, in German scholarship the name Chalder—after their main god, Ḫaldi—was used to designate the inhabitants.[46] The corresponding state called itself Biainili. The name Urartu appears in the Old Testament in connection with the story of the Flood in the form *'arārāt*, which is used to refer to the country. (Not until the Middle Ages was the name "Ararat" used to designate the highest mountain in the region; see p. 12). The most important sources for the history of Urartu are Assyrian campaign reports. From the ninth century on, these are supplemented by a few royal inscriptions made under Urartian kings, initially in Assyrian, and then, after ca. 820 BCE, in the native language written in Assyrian cuneiform script. This language has still not been fully understood.

At first, smaller states divided up the area among themselves, but in the ninth century they appear to have been unified. We find the first mention of a king of Urartu in 856. The kingdom was involved in constant battles with the Assyrians and at times competed with them for power. During the period of Assyrian weakness from the end of the ninth century to the middle of the eighth, Urartu expanded greatly, reaching as far as Cilicia and northern Mesopotamia. However, in 714 BCE an Assyrian attack put an end to Urartu's great-power status, and toward the end of the century it was threatened and weakened by the Cimmerians, who invaded it from northern Asia Minor. In the seventh or the sixth century, Urartu disappears from history without a trace, and the reasons for this—why and how it happened—remain hidden from us. Its end may be connected with the Armenian immigration, which also remains, however, completely incomprehensible for us.

The political and cultural achievements of the Kingdom of Urartu are impressive: in a short time, its rulers constructed a state on the Assyrian model with a well-structured bureaucratic apparatus. The kings bore names such as Sardur, Argišti, and Rusa (for a list, see the Appendix). They presented their successes in military bulletins, introducing them with the formula "Saith the King," which we meet again later in the inscriptions of the Iranian Achaemenids. No literature in the strict sense has come down to us from the Urartians. But they made great achievements in architecture and metalworking. The Urartians worshipped their gods in temples whose appearance is known to us through representations on Assyrian reliefs. The earlier assumption that they were related architectonically to the type of the Greek temple is probably not correct. Significant remains of many fortifications have been found on rock formations that are difficult to access. In the cities there were blocks of multi-storied apartment buildings. Among the outstanding products of the art of metalworking in Urartu are large bronze kettles resembling tripods. They were widely distributed in the Mediterranean world of that time. Whether these were examples of the Urartians' export commodities or imitations of their products remains an open and controversial question. In the area inhabited by the Urartians, the natural conditions were not favorable for agriculture; it was pursued all the more intensively.

Lake Van was alkaline and could not be used as a reservoir of fresh water, so canals, irrigation systems, and terraces on hillsides were constructed.

As has been said, we still remain in the dark regarding the ancestry and origins of the Armenians who settled in the area of the Urartians after the latter disappeared from history. We do not know the provenance of the name Herodotus uses for them, the *Armenioi* (the name for the country, Armenia, first appears in Xenophon). The Persians called the land or the people *Armina*. As is usual in such cases, among the Greeks there were stories about a mythical ancestor, Armenos, who came from Thessaly and accompanied the Argonauts to Armenia. His followers—according to the myth—then divided up the enormous area among themselves, and their Thessalian origin could still be discerned in the Armenians' clothing, their long mantles, and their way of riding their horses. In modern times as well, there has been much speculation concerning their origin, but the sources do not provide an adequate basis for proof. There are also too few archaeological discoveries from the phase between the sixth and fourth centuries BCE. Despite the clear influence of their neighbors, who spoke Luwian and Hurrian-Urartian as well as Caucasian and Semitic tongues, Armenian has been identified as an Indo-European language. The Armenians produced texts in their own language only after they adopted the Greek alphabet shortly after 400 CE; from the preceding millennium only a few inscriptions and coins minted in Aramaic and Greek have come down to us.

Lycians, Carians, and Sidetans (ca. Seventh to Fourth Centuries BCE)

Far from the region of the late Hittite small states, other members of this large family of languages can be recognized in the formerly Luwian domain of southwest Asia Minor. There are two peoples, the Lycians and the Carians, from whom we have documents (exclusively inscriptions) in their languages, which are related to Luwian and are also called late Luwian.[47] This term simply refers to the fact that both form a dialect group with Luwian, and not that they are descendants of it.

Homer is the oldest textual source that mentions both peoples, and the Greeks connected the origins of both of them with Crete. Caria and Lycia are among the most heavily researched ancient areas of Asia Minor in general; but we know next to nothing about them from the Dark Age to the middle of the first millennium.

The epigraphic tradition of the over 200 known inscriptions in the Lycian language—there are two different versions of Lycian, called the A and B dialects—begins only in the sixth century BCE. Longer texts, such as the one on the pillar at Xanthos and the trilingual inscription from the Letoon (Lycian, Greek, and Aramaic), allow specialists to penetrate deeper into this language than into Carian. The Lycians, as they were called by the Greeks, did not use the name Lukka, but instead called themselves Termiles. In addition to the inscriptions, most of which are short—for example, owners' inscriptions at tomb façades—we find characteristically Lycian sculptural elements. In this connection, the "architecture" of tomb façades cut into the rock and minted coins may be mentioned, although in both domains Greek in-

22. The Carian-Greek bilingual inscription from Kaunos, fourth century BCE.

fluences are already apparent. Already in the eighth and seventh centuries BCE we find Greek pottery in Lycia. Nevertheless, an independent religious and also political tradition can be seen, and the sepulchers allow us to draw conclusions about many aspects of the society and culture. Basing himself on the testimony of ancient authors—Herodotus and Herakleides Pontikos.—Johann Jakob Bachofen attributed a form of matriarchy to the Lycians, but modern research does not support this thesis.[48] Lycian society did not cease to exist when the language disappeared from history after 300 BCE, and a number of phenomena from the time of the Roman Empire can still be considered as peculiarly Lycian.

Like the Lycians, the Carians also composed their texts in an alphabetic script, which both groups probably learned from the Greeks, even if there is no prevailing agreement among experts on this point.[49] The forms and sounds of the Carian, Lycian, and Greek alphabets differ considerably from one another. For linguists, Carian is a harder nut to crack than Lycian; a consensus regarding its decipherment was first achieved after the discovery of a relatively long Carian-Greek bilingual text in Kaunos (Figure 22). About 200 inscriptions in this idiom are extant, and paradoxically, only a minority of them comes from the Carian homeland. Most of these very short texts come from Egypt and were made after 700 BCE, since the Carians served the Empire on the Nile as soldiers, and many of them made it their new homeland. Slightly fewer than fifty inscriptions on stone from Caria itself belong to a significantly later period than those from Egypt; none of them can be proved to be older than the fourth century BCE. Dialectal differences can be discerned—for example, between the interior of Caria and Kaunos on the south coast—and in addition there are also differences in the way particular signs in the alphabet are used. The ancient history of this people is full of riddles, and the relation to Karkisa, a name in Hittite for a country, is completely unclear.

Only ten inscriptions on stone and legends on coins prove that there was an epichoric (regional) language and alphabetic script peculiar to Pamphylia, which is called Sidetic, because most of the discoveries come from Side. What may be the oldest of these inscriptions, though it is Sidetic, comes from Perge; it is scratched on the bottom of a jar from the sixth century BCE. We still lack sufficient grounds for classifying this as a Late Luwian language along with Lycian and Carian.

Phrygians (ca. Eleventh to Sixth Centuries BCE)

The written sources for the history and culture of the Phrygians are few: isolated reports are found in Assyrian documents, campaign bulletins, letters, and royal proclamations. We can learn more from the Greek tradition, though it does not provide us with a coherent picture, either. The inscriptions in the Phrygian language that come from central Anatolia are divided into two groups. First, the Old Phrygian texts written in Phrygian script, which date from the eighth to the third centuries BCE. There are only a few of these (somewhat more than fifty on stones and about 190 on pottery and utensils), and above all they are difficult to understand. Second, the New Phrygian inscriptions (somewhat fewer than a hundred) written in Greek script; they date from the second and especially the third centuries CE, and almost all of them have to do with tombs. Their content is not entirely intelligible to us either. Naturally, these more recent documents contribute nothing to our knowledge of the history of the Phrygian people.[50]

This makes the extensive archaeological research even more significant. It has yielded much relevant material and enabled us to gain knowledge regarding developments in particular places and the connections among them. But up to this point it has not been possible to integrate all these individual bits of knowledge and results into a generally accepted larger picture.

As their language shows, the Phrygians were an Indo-European people. They probably entertained close relations with the Greeks of the second millennium BCE. This is shown, for example, by the loan-words from Mycenaean Greek. Most scholars accept that the Phrygians must have migrated from the Balkans to Anatolia in the twelfth century at the earliest, but probably later. This European ancestry of the Phrygians is universally asserted by ancient sources, and it has been claimed that the name of a people, the "Bryges" (or "Briges"), attested in Thrace and Macedonia in the first millennium was the Phrygians' original name.

The process of Phrygian migration is comprehensible only hypothetically. In this context archaeological evidence is particularly significant. After the breakdown of the Hittite Empire, both old, native groups and immigrant groups settled in

Anatolia and apparently lived in small states. In the discoveries made, we can discern connections with the Balkan–North Aegean realm that can be traced back to a migration. Thus there seems to have been a context into which the Phrygian immigration could be integrated. Perhaps we should envisage the possibility of several migrations, or a continuous stream of immigrants out of the northwest. However, skeptical researchers question whether the Phrygians were a group that had immigrated at all.

Their connection with the people known as the Muški raises a special problem. This connection arises because an Assyrian text of the late eighth century BCE (p. 105) refers to the Phrygian Midas as the king of this people. However, the Muški are definitely a people of eastern Asia Minor, who are mentioned by Assyrian sources as early as the twelfth century. Their ethnic affiliation and ancestry are not known to us, but the main outlines of their history can be reconstructed from Assyrian reports. Presumably the Assyrian identification of the Muški with the Phrygians was based on the fact that the Phrygian-Assyrian border area along the Halys River was settled on the Phrygian side by Muški who had fallen under Phrygian rule. But there currently exist different views regarding this complex problem.

With respect to its historical importance as well as on the basis of the current state of research, the Phrygian city of Gordion stands out. Its ruins lie not far west of Ankara, in the valley of the Sakarya River, near a ford. There the east-west road intersected an important north-south road. In the Hittite age this place was of only minimal significance, but in the Phrygian kingdom Gordion rose to become the capital and emerged as a center of material culture as well. The settlement consisted of three parts—a citadel, a lower city, and a suburb. The citadel was fortified. It was reached by a ramp that led to a monumental gate that still exists at a height of up to ten meters (Figure 23). The central buildings consisted of several rectangular *megara* with an anteroom and a main room; it is fairly certain that they were palaces and temples. Terrace buildings on the edge of the complexes served to supply the palaces. The lower city and suburb are more recent; the latter was unfortified. The city was destroyed by a catastrophic fire, and that is the most important fact in its older history. Until recently, the fire has been connected with the Cimmerian invasion that occurred ca. 700 BCE. Recent research dates the fire to the ninth century (ca. 830–800) and suggests that it was not the result of war. That would mean that the expansion of the citadel began in the tenth century. After its destruction, the city was rebuilt to be about the same size and on the same plan. In addition to these structures, there are more than eighty tumulus graves, some of them very high, in the area around Gordion, in which rulers or nobles were apparently buried. The oldest graves are supposed to date (in modern chronology) from the ninth and eighth centuries; the most recent come from the Hellenistic period. In some mounds burial chambers constructed of wood were found. In the chamber of one large tumulus that was built around 740, the body of the deceased had been preserved along with all its precious furnishings. This is probably a royal tomb, and is often attributed to the famous King Midas.

23. Ruins of Gordion.

With its palaces and temples, the city obviously was the center of a governmental, probably monocratic, organization; it was something like a headquarters for an imperial structure. What historical elements led to this empire and were associated with it, we do not know. The empire seems to have included all of central Anatolia, from the bend of the Halys River westward to the edge of the Anatolian upland. The political extent of this empire has been correctly equated with that of the Phrygian culture proven by archaeological discoveries. This culture presumably arose in Gordion and its vicinity and spread from there.

The first proof of the empire's existence dates from the eighth century BCE and is based on Assyrian sources. At the end of the eighth century (in the years from 718 to 710/709, under Sargon II), there were conflicts between the Assyrians and a King Mita of Muški, who is generally identified with the King Midas attested by the Greek tradition. The name Mita/Midas has its ancestry in Asia Minor; how it became a Phrygian royal name we do not know. Sargon's predecessors apparently already knew of Midas; therefore, the latter's rule had begun around the middle of the century. The Greek sources say that a King Midas also maintained connections with Greek cities. He married the daughter of King Agamemnon of Kyme. He is supposed to have been the first non-Greek to have sent a donation—a throne—to Delphi. Today, it is often maintained that there were several different persons who bore the same name and to whom various acts handed down by tradition have been attributed; but all these reflections are no more than hypotheses. To be sure, a second ruler named Midas is found in Assyrian sources between 680 and 669 (the period of Asarhaddon's reign)—though only in a not very informative context. The Greek sources convey a few more stories that deal with the legendary figure of King Midas and almost turn him into a myth;[51] but their origin is unclear, and their reliability difficult to assess. In any case, "wealth" is an essential element in these tales, and it seems that wealth was an important criterion in the Greeks' evaluation of the Phrygian Empire. In their view, wealth led to bad consequences; the gift given Midas by the god Dionysos, the ability to turn everything he touched into gold, brought Midas to the brink of death by starvation and thirst. In Phokaia and Kyme the story of the ass-eared Midas was told. In a musical competition between the gods in which Apollo played the cithara and Pan the flute, the king favored the latter, which led Apollo to punish him for his mistake in judgment by giving him ass's ears. The form of the Phrygian cap was invented, according to this story, to conceal this disfigurement, but everyone soon knew about it. The story was so popular that an image of this Midas was struck on coins; the oldest Greek vase paintings of Midas date from the sixth century BCE. Moreover, the Greeks were familiar with another, older Phrygian ruler named Gordios or Gordias, but his existence was probably only inferred or reconstructed from the name of the city.[52] Similarly, a legend concerning the foundation of the monarchy was told about Gordios—but also about Midas and Gordios together. After the Phrygians had made him king, he or his son Midas is supposed to have dedicated the legendary ox cart in the temple and attached its shaft with a "Gordian" knot that could not be untied. The man who was able to undo the knot was to rule over Asia. Later on, Alexander the Great, who in one version of the legend sliced through the knot with his sword, used the story for his propaganda.

The conflicts with the Assyrians may have arisen form the Phrygians' need for security: they may have wanted to prevent the Assyrians from invading their territory, even though the Assyrians did not make any attempt to do so. At the end of the eighth century, the Phrygian kingdom seems to have succumbed to the Cimmerian invasion that convulsed all Asia Minor (p. 110). The Greeks said that after the defeat Midas committed suicide by drinking oxblood (Strabo 1, 3, 21). Assyrian sources report the death of the king of Urartu in the war against the Cimmerians, but say nothing about the Phrygians in this connection. In any event, the city of Gordion survived. However, we have no later indications that an independent Phrygian kingdom continued to exist. Small principalities were probably formed again; for instance, a Greek testimony seems to prove the existence of Phrygian kings ca. 550 BCE (Herodotus 1, 35; compare 41–45). In the course of the sixth century, the Phrygians in the west fell under the control of the Lydians and in the east perhaps also of the Medes, and they were later subdued by the Persians. But we have no detailed knowledge concerning the course of these developments.

The Greeks had a rather negative opinion of the Phrygians and told inimical stories about them. The area in which the two peoples came in direct contact must have been in northwest Asia Minor, in the Troad and around the Propontis, the modern Sea of Marmara. Later people spoke of "Hellespontic Phrygia."

The Phrygians produced a rich culture that was marked by various influences. For example, they responded to the cultural stimulation of their neighbors in Asia

24. Old Phrygian inscription.

Minor and combined it with what they had brought with them from the Balkans. The forms of tombs, in particular the tumulus, and certain decorative motifs on ceramics provide particularly clear proof of this. Greek influences on Phrygian culture are also unmistakable. When they began remains an open question. An essential field where this influence is clear is ceramics. The forms of vessels and the nature of their decoration are obviously shaped by Greek models. Among the Phrygians' borrowings from the Greek sphere is the script (Figure 24), attested as early as the eighth century BCE—though there are also other opinions about this; the connection between letters and sounds is almost completely the same as in Greek (p. 132 f.).

However, there is no lack of Phrygian influences on the Greek cultural world. Phrygian farming was famous, especially their horse breeding. Phrygian achievements in the arts are remarkable as well; I have already mentioned them on several occasions. They also cultivated monumental sculpture: the statue of the goddess from the gate at Boğazköy, the former Hittite capital, is particularly noteworthy (Figure 25). The reliefs on the rock monuments found in the west between the present cities of Afyon and Eskişehir are among the most important Old Phrygian relics in Anatolia. They are difficult to date, but they were probably produced between the seventh and the fifth centuries BCE. Façades cut into the rock represent temples and houses, and images of gods sometimes appear in niches (Figure 26). These functioned as places of worship that may also occasionally have been connected with burial chambers. The complex known as "Midas City," near the village of Yazılıkaya (not to be confused with the place of the same name near Boğazkale) deserves spe-

25. Kybele of Boğazköy, Museum of Anatolian Civilizations, Ankara.

cial mention; it includes a whole series of rock-cut monuments around an elongated rocky height. Clues to Phrygian architecture have been provided in particular by American excavations at Gordion. The gate complex and the foundations of palaces show the Phrygians' sense of monumentality.

As already noted, the Phrygians also made significant achievements in the arts and crafts. Remains of wall paintings have been found in Gordion. Their pottery has characteristic traits, especially geometric decoration with representations of animals, that give Phrygian vases a distinctive appearance. Bronze casting as well as textiles in the Phrygian mode survived in the Greco-Roman world, for which etymology provides an example. The Latin adjective *phrygium* means "gilt edging" (and has survived down to the present day in the word "frieze"), whereas *phrygio* means "goldsmith." The Phrygian religion was also influential. They worshipped their gods in temples. Their supreme divinity was a mother goddess named Kybele (Phrygian

26. Midas City: rock-cut façade with cult niche.

matar kubeleja—or something like that—perhaps meaning "mountain mother"?), whose worship was shaped by various influences.[53] This cult spread far and wide; the Ionians took this divinity as far as their colonies in the west, to Lokroi in southern Italy and Massalia (now Marseille) in southern France. The conception of the lion as a sacred animal originated in ancient Asia Minor—and so did the adoration of the mural crown and holy stone in the cult of Pessinus, where this stone was venerated along with the goddess. The myth of Agdistis is connected with the cult of this site some 130 kilometers west of Ankara; one version dating from ca. 310 CE is still extant in a work by the Christian writer Arnobius of Sicca, *Adversus nationes*: Jupiter is said to have desired the sleeping Great Mother goddess, but could not reach her and spilled his semen on a stone; ten months later the stone gave birth to Agdistis, who became a fierce rebel against the gods, until the latter caused him, by means of a devious plot, to castrate himself. In this context some scholars have seen a connection with a Hurrian myth of the stone monster Ullikummi.[54] The Agdistis story is continued by that of Attis, which is handed down by Ovid (*Fasti* 4, 223 ff.) and other authors: the goddess's beloved was driven mad to punish him for breaking his promise to remain chaste, and castrated himself. His blood is said to have given its red color to the marble of Dokimeion (Statius, *silv.* 1, 5, 38). In the rite that was later seen as typical of the cult of Kybele in general and was practiced in various places, this story found its counterpart in the self-castration of the priests, who put themselves into a trance by means of shrill music. In the second century CE the writer Lucian described in detail the cult of a "Syrian goddess" in Hierapolis-Bambyke. Her priests (*galloi*) castrated themselves in ecstasy.[55] Priestesses of Artemis Perasia in Hierapolis-Kastabala limited themselves to walking barefoot over red-hot coals. One assumption even goes so far as to suggest that such ideas survived in the institution of the whirling dervishes founded in Turkish times by Jalāl ad-Dīn Muhammad Rūmī (1207–1272 CE) in Konya, the ancient Ikonion. Music was an especially important feature of Phrygian religious practices. The fact that the Phrygian influence on music proved fruitful may be connected with these religious customs: it is said that the double flute and other instruments were invented by the Phrygians, and the Phrygian mode is part of the musical theory of keys. How these cultural achievements of the Phrygians were handed down is not known to us.

The Phrygians obviously long maintained an awareness of having their own tradition. This is shown above all by the history of their language, which continued to be spoken far into the period of the Roman Empire and was sometimes also written (p. 399 f.). Moreover, some elements of the country's religious tradition may even have persisted in the Christian Montanist sect (p. 543).

The Cimmerian Invasion (ca. Eighth to Seventh Centuries BCE)

As in the case of the events that we seek to connect with the Kaska and the sea peoples, toward the end of the Phrygian Empire, Anatolia fell victim again to a movement of expansion; it is connected with the name of the Cimmerians.[56] This people belonged to a larger group of mounted nomadic tribes whose culture has been proven archaeologically by tomb discoveries, characteristic weapons, and parts of horse tack in an area stretching from the northern Caucasus to Thrace and Macedonia. Assyrian sources from the time of Sargon II (721–705 BCE) call them the Gumurru; later reports come from the Greeks, especially Herodotus and the Augustan geographer Strabo. According to them, the Greeks usually called the straits between the Sea of Azov and the Black Sea the Cimmerian Bosporus, on whose shores smaller groups settled in later times, according to Plutarch.

In his account, Herodotus (4, 11) says that the Massagetes beset the Scythians and drove them into the home of the Cimmerians, whereupon—after a deadly conflict among them in which many people died—the Cimmerians withdrew and made their way along the Pontic coast to Asia Minor and the peninsula where the Greeks founded Sinope. Excavations conducted in Sinope have up to this point not proven that any pre-Cimmerian city existed there. After 700, several waves of invasions by Cimmerians rolled through Asia Minor. The destruction in Gordion and the decline of the Phrygian Empire have been connected—wrongly, according to the results of recent excavations (p. 104)—with one of these invasions. One group seems to have invaded Anatolia from Thrace and to have been responsible for the threat to Lydia. Sardeis was finally plundered (652 BCE) by the Cimmerian chieftain Lygdamis—called Tugdammê in Assyrian sources—but the Lydians recovered from the shock. A good fifty years later their king Alyattes drove the last Cimmerians out of Asia Minor.

The Lydians and the Lydian Empire (ca. Seventh to Sixth Centuries BCE)

Everything we know about the culture and history of the Lydians that has not been learned from archaeology is derived from Assyrian and Greek sources (among the contemporaries, chiefly from poets like Archilochos, Sappho, Alkaios, and from the fifth-century prose writers, especially the historians Herodotus and Xanthos the Lydian). Over sixty inscriptions from Lydia (sixth to fourth centuries BCE) are known, including a Lydian-Aramaic bilingual one and a recently discovered twelve-line text on a fourth-century stele with a relief image of a sitting woman. They show the users of this language to have been relatives of the Hittite or Luwian population of Anatolia in the second millennium.[57]

Around 680 BCE, in the turbulent time when the Cimmerians were destroying and plundering the area, a noble named Gyges overthrew Candaules, the king of the Lydians. With this story we find ourselves on the terrain of Herodotus's delight in spinning tales, and the poet Archilochos of Paros, who lived during the time of Gyges, is supposed to have told it in iambic verse as well. The king is said to have sought to convince his trusted bodyguard Gyges of his wife's peerless beauty by having him see her naked. Candaules sweeps away his horrified friend's objections with a carefully thought-out plan:

> I will bring you into the chamber where she and I lie and set you behind the open door; and after I have entered, my wife too will come to her bed. There is a chair set near the entrance of the room: on this she will lay each part of her raiment as she takes it off, and you will be able to gaze upon her at your leisure. Then, when she goes from the chair to the bed, turning her back upon you, do you look to it that she does not see you going out through the doorway. (Herodotus 1, 9; trans. Godley)

But things do not go as planned; the queen notices the unwilling voyeur, and the next day she has him come to her and she gives him a choice between being put to death or killing the king and making her his wife. Gyges chooses to live.

In the extant poems of Archilochos we find only one brief reference to Gyges; in contrast, he appears in the royal inscriptions of the Assyrian Assurbanipal, where he is called Gugu of Luddu. The Cimmerian threat and probably also the desire for the great powers' recognition of him as a legitimate ruler led him, in the years between 668 and 665, to seek diplomatic contact with Assur; a dream is said to have moved him to do this. The emissary to the court of the Assyrian king had great difficulty making himself understood in Lydian. Assurbanipal, who regarded Gyges as a vassal living far way, wrote that the latter had come in order to "lay hold at [his] royal feet."[58] It makes sense that the version of the Lydian kinglist whose divine starting point is Ninos and the god Belos, the god of Assyrian Nineveh, was constructed or revived at precisely this time.[59] Later the relationship became cooler, and Gyges formed a new one with the Egyptian Pharaoh Psammetichus I (656–610).

Gyges already undertook campaigns against the Greek cities on the west coast; he is reported to have won a battle against the Smyrnaeans (Mimnermos FGrHist 578 F 5). It is of a certain historical import that the Lydian kings who descended from the noble family of the Mermnades began to orient themselves toward the west. As a result of this orientation, for the first time the Aegean coast was connected with the interior by the main trade routes through the valleys of the Hermos and Maeander rivers and was incorporated into the hegemonic realm of an Anatolian great power. However, this process was probably not completed until the reign of the Lydian king Croesus in the sixth century. In the meantime, Gyges had been killed during the Cimmerian king Tugdammê's (Lygdamis) attack on his capital in 644 BCE.

The Lydian capital Sardeis is located less than 100 kilometers from the Aegean coast, in the valley of the Hermos, at a point where the small river Paktolos, which flows down from the Tmolos mountains, joins the Hermos. Excavations have uncovered but little of the Old Lydian period. Hardly anything remains of the palace of the Mermnad kings, which presumably stood on the acropolis. The brickwork of the latter's walls, with a gate, is Lydian. The nearby tumuli (burial mounds), the largest in all Anatolia, were also constructed in the age of the Lydian Empire; Herodotus's attribution of them to individual kings has not been confirmed. The stepped base of a further tomb from the sixth century apparently supported a chamber and could have been a model for Cyrus the Great's tomb in Pasargadae.[60] The silver vessels, jewelry, and other objects that have become known as the "Lydian treasure" (sixth century BCE)[61] came from other tumuli farther inland, on the border with Phrygia. Last but not least, the precious metal ores found near Sardeis helped the dynasty rise and flourish.

Gyges was succeeded by his son Ardys and his grandson Sadyattes. The latter's successor, Alyattes, continued a successful policy of expansion. He was unable to incorporate the Greek city of Miletus and instead made a treaty with it. In Anatolia, he extended his sphere of power far into the former territory of the Phrygian Empire and there collided with the Medes, an Iranian mountain people whose land, Mada, is first mentioned in the annals of the Assyrian king Salmanasser III (835). Two centuries later these Medes apparently played a major role in the fall of the Assyrian Empire and seem to have expanded considerably in various directions, even if the nature and extent of a "Median Empire" remain unclear. In Herodotus's account the hostile conflicts between Alyattes and the Median leader Kyaxares culminated in the famous battle in which day suddenly turned into night—the solar eclipse of 585 BCE, which Thales of Miletus is said to have predicted. The military action was finally brought to an end by a treaty. The historical truth of the Thales anecdote, and even more importantly, that of Herodotus's claim that the Halys was then the border between the Lydian and Median empires, has been challenged by modern research. Exactly where a battle between Lydians and Medes took place and which of the two advanced far to the east or the west has not become sufficiently clear. Archaeological investigations on Kerkenes Dağ near Yozgat (east of the Halys) have proven that there was on this site an unusually large Iron Age settlement ringed by walls, where some researchers now seek to locate—taking up again an old hypothesis—the Pteria destroyed by Croesus, a city built by the Medes after 585. But what possibilities of comparison do we have that would allow us to recognize a Median mode of settlement on the basis of architectonic discoveries? The most recent, and so far the only, written texts that have been discovered are an Old Phrygian inscription on stone and Phrygian graffiti. At least we can say that the population thus seems to have been Phrygian.[62]

The Greek narrative tradition described the last Lydian king, Croesus, still more colorfully than it did Midas the Phrygian. In contrast to Gyges, who tried to connect the mythical origins of the Lydian kingdom with the Assyrian tradition, the "western" genealogy of the Lydian kings sought, at the behest of Croesus, to trace their ancestry back to Herakles. This construction of a Lydian line of Heraklidean-Mermnad rulers must have been known in some form to the historian Herodotus, since he based on it the distance in years between the beginning of the later dynasty and the beginning of the earlier one.[63] In any case, Croesus maintained close relations with Greece, and like his predecessors he used violence in an attempt to make the Greeks of Asia submissive and seems to have been quite successful in doing so. Finally, according to Herodotus, he ruled over the following peoples: Lydians, Phrygians, Mysians, Mariandynoi, Chalybes, Paphlagonians, Thynian and Bithnyian Thracians, Carians, Ionians, Dorians, Aiolians, and Pamphylians. But the Lydian and his kingdom fell victim to a greater force that seized the whole Middle Eastern and Mediterranean system of states: the sudden conquests made by the Persian who came to be known as Cyrus the Great (Kyros of Anšān). Croesus was allegedly the aggressor, since he crossed the Halys, conquered Pteria, and enslaved its inhabitants. Once again, Thales of Miletus plays a role in this story; to allow the army to cross the river, he is supposed to have diverted its course. But the campaign failed; the Persians counterattacked, drove as far as Sardeis, and surrounded the last Mermnad in his city. The date conventionally accepted by scholars, 547/546 BCE, must be questioned in view of recent research on the Nabonid chronicle carried out by Joachim Oelsner, an orientalist from the University of Jena, Germany: the event occurred in the period between 547 and 530 BCE, and thus Sardeis might have fallen only after Babylon (536 BCE). However, Herodotus (1, 153) assumes the opposite sequence when he says of Cyrus: "Babylon stood in his way." The consequences were grave. For more than two hundred years, Anatolia fell under the control of a power that at its highpoint was to stretch from modern-day Pakistan to the Aegean: the Persian Empire.

Croesus was probably killed, but he may also have been spared. His abrupt fall lent Greek imagination wings even more than did that of Midas. Herodotus sees in him the oriental despot who initiated the hostilities against the Greeks. For the Greek historian, Croesus's misfortunes, which he recounts with relish one after the other, were predetermined and ultimately the atonement for his ancestor Gyges's regicide. Deception is inherent in each of Croesus's actions and decisions, and currying the favor of the gods with lavish sacrifices is to no avail. He donated the golden oxen in the Ephesian Artemision and most of the pillars in the temple. It was possible to reconstruct his dedicatory inscription, "King Croesus erected this" from the fragments found (ca. 550 BCE). He also made extravagant donations to Greek sanctuaries outside Asia Minor, including Delphi. When the Lacedaemonians wanted to buy gold from him, he gave it to them free of charge. His subjects and secret admirers of his pomp and power felt a certain satisfaction at his sudden fall that comes through in the pejorative evaluations of his deeds.

The scene of his end on the pyre is depicted on the vase from Vulci, the amphora of Myson, which was painted around 490 BCE (Figure 27). However, his personal innocence was recognized, and miraculous rescues were frequently imagined. Thus for example, in the first half of the fifth century the poet Bakchylides wrote in one of his victory songs:

> witness the lord of horse-taming Lydia; when Sardis fulfilled the sentence delivered her by Zeus and was taken by the host of the Persians, Croesus was saved by Apollo of the golden bow. Aye, when he had come to that unlooked-for day, he would not await so woeful a lot as servitude, but had them build a pyre before his brazen-walled court and went up upon it with his trusty wife and his fair-tressed daughters wailing incessantly; and raised his hands towards high heaven and cried: "Almighty Spirit, where is the gratitude of the Gods? where is the Lord that Leto bare? Fallen is the palace of Alyattes, and I have no requital of the thousand gifts I gave; rather is the ancient city of Lydus aflame, the gold-eddied Pactolus empurpled with blood, the women reft unseemly from the well-built houses. What was hateful once is welcome now; sweetest it is to die." So speaking he bade one of his soft-stepping men kindle the wooden pile. Whereat the maidens shrieked and threw up their hands to their mother; for death foreseen is the hatefullest death to man. Nevertheless when the shining strength of that awful fire rushed over them, then sent Zeus a black veil of cloud and quenched the yellow flame. (3, 23; trans. Edmonds, text partly restored)]

With the Lydians at the latest we have entered into the age of a culture in western Anatolia that can be seen as actually a mixed culture of different peoples, mainly Lydians and Greeks, but also Carians and Greeks. The Lydian and Ionian cultures existed in a close symbiosis that Herodotus (1, 94) confirms when he says that the Lydians' mores were very similar to those of the Greeks. The depiction of the Phrygians' wealth and power was based on tradition, whereas contemporary Greek poetry's depiction of the wealth and power of the Lydians was based on direct experience: Archilochos (fr. 19, 1 f. West; trans. Edmonds) scorns the Lydians the way the fox scorns the grapes beyond his reach: "I care not for the the wealth of golden Gyges, nor ever have envied him." The word "tyrannis," first attested in these verses,

27. Croesus on the pyre. Vase from Vulci, now in the Louvre in Paris.

seems to have been of Lydian origin. Sappho of Lesbos (fr. 152 Diehl, trans. Campbell) writes: "I have a beautiful child who looks like golden flowers, my darling Cleis, for whom I would not take all Lydia." However, fashionable clothing such as Cleis wishes for herself is to be found only in Lydian Sardeis.

The Lydians' supreme god was apparently female: Kybebe. The name "Bakkhos" for a wine god is probably Old Lydian; just as Kybebe was equated with Artemis, Bakkhos was equated with Dionysos. The Ephesian Artemis was worshipped in Sardeis, and Lydian maidens served in the shrine of Artemis at Ephesos. When Herodotus attributes indecent behavior to Lydian girls—in significant contrast to Greek girls—because they earn their dowries by prostitution before getting married, this seems to refer to the old oriental custom of temple prostitution, which still existed in Asia Minor centuries later, in the time of Strabo.

Lydian ceramic inscriptions found in Old Smyrna allow us to presume that part of the city's population was Lydian. Lydian ceramics, so-called black-on-red and marbled ware, is found in Ephesos and Smyrna, and "Ephesian ware," which combines Lydian and Ionian elements, was in any case produced partly in Sardeis. Statuettes of silver and ivory found in a tumulus near Elmalı and similar ivory figures from Ephesos, which come from the seventh and early sixth centuries—depicting women and men in long robes and large headgear resembling bearskin caps—are part of a non-Greek Anatolian tradition (Figure 28).

28. Ivory statuettes from the Artemision in Ephesos. Photo courtesy Archaeological Museum, İzmir.

Metalworking flourished among the Lydians. The Greeks must have learned many crafts from them, especially in the areas of goldsmithing and silversmithing. They themselves attributed to the Lydians the invention of coined money (Xenophanes, Fr. 4 Diels and Kranz; cf. Herodotus 1, 94), which they immediately began to mint in their cities. This Lydian-Greek "birth of money" (Le Rider)[64] ca. 600 BCE is an event of extraordinary importance. Precious metals in the form of bars or lumps had long served as a means of payment. We recall the numerous, very precise "price data" in the commercial texts of the Assyrian Kārum Kaneš of the early second millennium. In Syria, the practice of sealing (i.e., indicating ownership, authority, or responsibility by means of a stamp), goes back to the late Neolithic and found manifold uses in ancient oriental cultures. The fact that in Lydia weights and measures were authorized by the king is suggested by the expression "king's ell" used in a verse by the Greek poet Alkaios. However, both stamping and the use of handy lumps of metal first appear together in this remarkable invention in Lydia, and experts seek an enlightening explanation for this advance. It is striking that the oldest Lydian lumps of metal stamped with lions' heads are made exclusively of electrum, an alloy of gold and silver that is found in nature, and precisely in the area around Sardeis. The dating of the first examples depends on that of a buried hoard that David George Hogarth found in the Artemision at Ephesos in 1904 and varies between 650 and 600 BCE.[65] One of these lumps of metal bears an incomprehensible Lydian inscription. The earliest municipal mintings, which followed soon thereafter, are also in electrum; they come from Sardeis, Kyzikos, Phokaia, Ephesos, Miletus, and Samos. Since the proportion of gold in natural electrum varies, some lumps were alloyed with copper to bring their appearance into line with the standard. The numismatist Robert W. Wallace[66] has interpreted this phenomenon as indicating that the institution issuing the metal sought thereby to guarantee that its assessed value could be immediately confirmed by glancing at the size and color of the lump, and to prevent lumps with a higher proportion of gold from being melted down. And this function of guaranteeing an approximately standard value measured by a certain size and weight was provided by the stamped seal. Minting coins was thus invented because in comparison to gold, silver, and copper, the true metal value of the electrum used as a means of exchange could be less easily determined by weighing and inspection, and to circulate successfully as a means of payment, it needed a visible "guarantee." The principle of this guarantee-stamp was soon transferred to pure silver and gold.[67] Coinage was a gift made by Lydian-Ionian Asia Minor to the ancient world: in the course of the sixth century, it was already widespread in the Greek motherland, in the colonies, and in the western part of the Persian Empire. The first Lycian coin with an image of Athena was minted in the last quarter of the sixth century BCE; a sharp increase in the domain of the Greek *poleis* on the coasts of Asia Minor began as early as the fourth century BCE.

Greeks, ca. Eleventh Century to 550 BCE

When the Lydians pushed their conquest to the coast, they encountered there, among other peoples, the Greeks, who lived in a series of harbor cities favorable to commerce and on the islands lying off the mainland. The archaeological findings that tell us most about the earliest phase of their presence there, especially protogeometric ceramics, reach from the Bodrum peninsula in the south to Phokaia in the north. Starting ca. 1100 BCE, various groups had emigrated from Greece to Asia. Experts disagree regarding how that happened, and whether and to what extent we can credit the relevant written sources that begin to appear in the seventh century.[68] Successive waves of immigration by Greeks from the motherland to Asia, resettlements, the rounding out of occupied territories and the growth of new towns, further emigrations, and secondary settlements took place over a long time until about 500 BCE. What these have in common is essentially a choice of a place on the seacoast—the Aegean and Mediterranean coasts for the earliest migrations, the coasts of the Sea of Marmara and the Black Sea for the later ones. The Hellenization of the interior begins with a similar intensity only after Alexander the Great.

AIOLIANS, DORIANS, AND IONIANS

Opinions differ as to whether at the outset these were closed tribal groups that retained the identity, institutions, mores and customs they had brought with them from their homeland, or whether we must understand the Asiatic Aiolians, Ionians, and Dorians as communities that first developed in Asia Minor. Such elements as hereditary kingship, the council, and the shrine common to all Ionians, could be old remains of a tribal organization that had lost its political significance and retained only a sacred meaning in the new homeland.

The first peoples who arrived there seem to have been the Aiolians, who were related by their language to the Thessalians. They settled Tenedos, Lesbos, and the mainland across from the latter, as far south as Smyrna.[69] On the hill of Bayraklı (Old Smyrna), in the urban area of the modern city of İzmir, the oldest post-Mycenaean Greek architecture was excavated: the earliest building in an oval shape was dated to the period between 925 and 900 BCE,[70] and the beginnings of the Temple of Athena to about 200 years later. The artful capitals of the pillars in this temple, which are ornamented with volutes and wreathed in leaves, are dated to ca. 600 BCE. The style, seldom found elsewhere (similar forms occur in the sixth century, e.g., in Phokaia, Neandria, and Larisa; outside Asia Minor, they also occur on Thasos[71]), is regarded as Aeolian, but the stimulus for this architectural decoration seems to have been small art objects in ivory and bronze from Syria (Figure 29).[72]

The Aiolians founded an alliance but were nonetheless driven out of some of their southern settlements by other groups, the later Ionians. The Ionians deprived them of Smyrna (Herodotus 1, 149), so that only eleven of the original twelve members of the alliance remained: Kyme, Larisa, Neonteichos, Temnos, Killa, Notion, Aigiroessa, Pitane, Aigaiai, Myrina, and Gryneion, which was the religious center, with its Temple of Apollo and its oracle. Other Aeolian groups settled farther north, in the Troad and as far as the shores of the Hellespont, for example in Ilion; however, this area was not part of Asiatic Aiolis in the strict sense. Later Aeolian settlements include both the cities named Magnesia, one on the Sipylos, northeast of Smyrna, and the other on the Maeander, southeast of Ephesos.

The migrations of "Dorian" groups over the islands led to settlements on the southernmost part of the west coast. The Dorian six-state alliance (*Hexapolis*) had, in addition to the *poleis* of Kos, Ialysos, Kamiros, and Lindos on the islands of Kos and Rhodes, two members on the mainland: Knidos and Halikarnassos. The latter was subsequently expelled from the alliance, allegedly because of the frivolity of one of its citizens who, after winning a tripod as a prize in the common games, had not dedicated it to the god, in accord with the religious requirement, but instead took it home with him (Herodotos 1, 144). The Triopion, the alliance's shrine dedicated to Apollo, was located on Knidos's territory, no doubt on the tip of the Carian peninsula, across from the island of Kos. The location of the oldest city is still a controversial question. Some researchers attribute the ruins excavated on the western tip of the

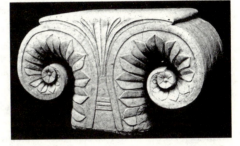

29. Base of a column and capital (re-construction) from the Temple of Athena in Old Smyrna, ca. 600 BCE. Photo courtesy Archaeological Museum, İstanbul.

peninsula to a later resettlement of the fourth century BCE, while the older village is supposed to be located near Datça, close to a shrine of Apollo Karneios proven to have been there.[73] In any case, the two cities were oriented toward the sea, and access to them from the hinterland, which was actually Carian, was not eased by broad river valleys. In the fifth century BCE, Halikarnassos (modern-day Bodrum) was still inhabited by a mixed population of Carians and Greeks.

The Ionians established themselves in the places where the best climate prevailed (Herodotus 1, 142), and particularly on the middle part of the west coast and on the islands lying across from it; the tradition of their Mycenaean predecessors may have provided them with a certain knowledge of the area that was their goal. The only passage in Homer's *Iliad* (13, 685) in which the *Iaones helkechitones* ("long-mantled Ionians") appear probably refers to Euboeans. The oldest proof of the same name of a people in an Assyrian cuneiform text from ca. 735 BCE, *Jamnaja*, has no precise connection with an ancestral area in the strict sense. Under Tiglatpilesar III, and also under Sargon II, who defeated them in a naval battle in the eastern Mediterranean, the Assyrians gave these names to peoples from the far west, whom they regarded as brigands: Greeks (perhaps together with non-Greeks) from the Aegean realm whose base for looting attacks on the coasts of Cilicia and Phoenicia was probably Cyprus.

The later Greek sources identify the northern Peloponnese as the Asiatic Ionians' ancestral home, out of which the Achaeans are said to have driven them.[74] Athens had a special claim to be the mother of the Ionian colonies. According to the myth, because of a quarrel between Kodros's sons over succession in Athens, the losers emigrated along with numerous followers. The names of the subunits of the citizenry (*phylae*) and a common festival called *Apaturia* may only apparently prove the old relationship with Athens, since a post facto construction of such correspondences cannot be excluded; the leading power of the fifth century BCE, Athens, had a special interest in them. According to Herodotus (1, 146), most of the emigrants had mixed with all the other tribes of central Greece; only a minority of the "most noble" Ionians who had come over directly from Athens brought with them no wives but instead married Carian women, whose men they had killed. "For this slaughter, these women made a custom and bound themselves by oath (and enjoined the same on their daughters) that none would sit at meat with her husband nor call him by his name, because the men had married them after slaying their fathers and husbands and sons" (trans. Godley). To be sure, the later "Ionian" area was settled by mixed groups, among which modern research has identified, on the basis of various indicators, a Boeotian one.[75]

The first contacts between the Greeks and the native peoples must not have been peaceful. In addition to the Carians, the people the Greeks called "Leleges" lived in the coastal area, but it has not been possible to find archaeological remains that are unambiguously Lelegian. In any event, the "Ionians" must have driven the Leleges and Carians away from the coast. Farthest to the south, in the Carian area, they founded Miletus, an old settlement that had already once been inhabited by Mycenaean Greeks and probably had also for a time been in the possession of the Carians (compare *Iliad* 2, 868), and that may be identical with the Hittite Millawanda. On one part of the Milesian territory, tombs and herdsmen's enclosures (so-called compounds) prove that there were native settlement centers there even after the Greeks took over the land. The pottery in these tombs is Greek. A long process of acculturation must have taken place in the Milesia from the Archaic down into the Hellenistic period. This territory, which was later about 270 square kilometers in extent, has recently been intensively investigated using the methods of the natural sciences, so that the outlines of ecological changes, the development of the settlement, and economic uses can be discerned.[76] In the sixth century, smaller communities, such as Assesos and Teichiussa, emerged in the Milesian hinterland, along with small scattered settlements and more individual farmsteads, a type of settlement that goes back to the Mycenaean age. The agricultural use of the land advanced slowly. In archaic times the religious site of Didyma in the south, though twenty kilometers from the city, was already considered the major shrine, and it was connected with Miletus by a sacred way.[77] In the archaic period the *chora* (city-territory) of the Pearl of Ionia thus had a differentiated pattern of settlement. The enormous economic boom of this *polis* was, however, decisively shaped by the city's outstanding harbor facilities and its connections overseas and in the interior.

North of Miletus lay Myus and Priene, and then Ephesos, Kolophon, Lebedos, Teos, Erythrai, Klazomenai, Smyrna, and, already in Aiolis, Phokaia (Map 4). Most of their sites have been archaeologically verified, but old Priene, which was called Kadme by the Boeotian immigrants (Strabo 14, 1, 12), remains a riddle. The exca-

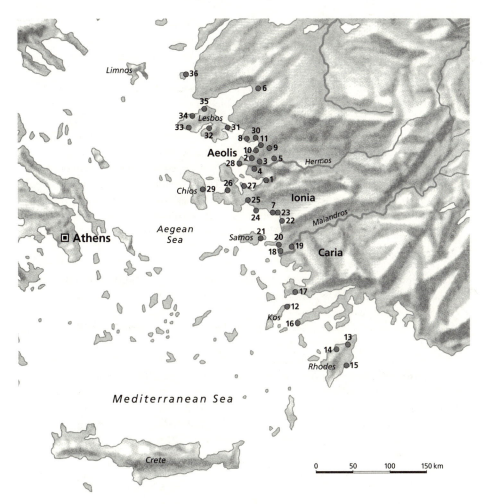

Map 4. Early Greek settlement in Asia Minor. Map drawn by Peter Palm, Berlin.

vated ruins are part of a rebuilt complex from the fourth century BCE. An earlier settlement of archaic Ephesos may have been identical with the place called Apasa (p. 89) in the time of the Hittites. The Greek legend of the foundation of the city of Ephesos again names Athens as it starting point. The Greeks are asserted to have driven out the Carians and Leleges and to have erected a shrine to Athena immediately after their arrival. At the time of Croesus's siege of the city (ca. 560 BCE), they tried to connect the city wall with the shrine of Artemis by means of a rope 1.5 kilometers long, to insinuate the city's inviolability. But Croesus nonetheless captured it and resettled its inhabitants elsewhere. Neither the site of the oldest Greek settlement nor the city of Croesus has been archaeologically proven; the latter may lie under meters of alluvial deposits on the plains south of the Artemision. The large ruin farther to the west, on Panayırdağ and Bülbüldağ, is the Hellenistic-Roman city; at its earliest stage this city was newly planned by the Diadochan Lysimachos.

In archaic times these Ionian cities, together with Chios and Samos, also constituted an alliance of twelve member cities around a sacred center called the *Panionion*, where oxen were sacrificed to Poseidon Helikonios. The emissaries of the members, called *basileis* (kings), assembled regularly. They are supposed to have waged in common a war against a city called Melia; the territory of the defeated party was divided between Samos and Priene. It may be that such a war led to the establishment of the alliance itself—in opposition to the ancient interpretation given on the Parian Marble, according to which the alliance was already founded at the time of the migration to Asia Minor (FGrHist 239 A 27). All this cannot be dated with precision. In any case, the prominent philologist Wilamowitz attributed to the Ionian alliance of the archaic period the decisive power of integration in the construction of an identity for the "Ionians" of Asia Minor.[78]

Like the older Priene and Ephesos, the situation of the archaic Panionion is a problem. It is to be sought on the Mykale peninsula, with the "lofty head" (*Iliad* 2, 869) of its tip pointing westward toward Samos and sloping down gently toward the north, abruptly toward the south, to the valley of the Maeander. For a long time it was believed that it could be identified with the remains near Güzelçamlı discovered and later excavated in 1898 by Theodor Wiegand, the German excavator of Miletus, Priene, and Didyma. These remains are located at the northern foot of the high ridge, on a hill named Otomatik-Tepe after a Turkish machine gun position established there during the First World War. A few years ago the Bochum archaeologist Hans Lohmann discovered, in the mountains right above Priene, the ruins of a very old structure that also included an archaic religious building. In his opinion, this is the site of Melia and also of the oldest Panionion, which the Persians destroyed, whereas the other site near Güzelçamlı goes back to a late classical refoundation. This assertion has not been proven.[79]

In the eighth century BCE powerful, insular *poleis* like Mytilene on Lesbos and Samos—followed in the sixth century by Chios, and by Tenedos and Klazomenai in the classical period—expanded their territories to include a strip on the mainland across the way; down into the Hellenistic period, conflicts over possessions of this kind repeatedly arose between the states on the mainland and those on the islands (see especially Rhodes, p. 226).[80]

SHRINES

The Greeks' ancestral shrines in Asia—Gryneion, Triopion, and Panionion—acquired far less significance than a few other very ancient religious sites devoted to foreign, Anatolian deities, of which the Greek immigrants had taken possession here and there and syncretically transformed. Over the following centuries, these sites developed into first-order religious centers with a broad power of attraction, even if not all at the same time. In addition to the Artemis of Ephesos, which we will discuss in a moment, the Apollo of Didyma (Branchidai) is an early example of this. Other, later examples are the Artemis with "white eyebrows" (*leukophryene*) in Magnesia on the Maeander, the Apollo of Klaros, and the Dionysos of Teos.

The origins of the religious site of Didyma (ca. 700 BCE) are bound up with the enclosure of two springs. About a hundred years later a hall with an earthen roof and a round, roofless building were built, and then, in the course of the sixth century, the archaic *peripteros*, a temple with a single row of columns all round it, the *naos* (inner chamber) of which was erected over a spring (Temple II). These were supplemented only after the middle of the sixth century by the sacred way leading to them from Miletus. What the earlier building (cf. Herodotus 6, 19, 3), which is now buried under the restored ruin of the Hellenistic temple and known only through a few architectural remains and discoveries, looked like has not been definitively clarified.[81] By analogy with its east Ionian sister buildings, the Heraion in Samos and the Artemision in Ephesos, it is conceived as a *dipteros*, a temple with a double row of columns. The Greeks saw the Didymaion as the place where Zeus and Leto engendered the twins Apollo and Artemis, and they worshipped a laurel tree next to one of the springs. Didyma was the seat of the oracle and already had an international reputation in the seventh century. The Egyptian Pharaoh Necho dedicated to it a piece of his armor after his victory over Josiah of Judah at Meggido (ca. 608 BCE; Herodotus 2, 159).[82]

Among these sacred sites on the west coast of Asia Minor, in the area inhabited by the Ionians, one deserves to be described in greater detail: the Artemision at Ephesos. Its precise location at the western foot of the hill of Ayasoluk near Selçuk was first determined in 1869 by the Englishman John Turtle Wood. The subsequent English and Austrian excavations revealed various religious sites and construction phases. It is likely that there is a Mycenaean prehistory here; the oldest post-Mycenaean votive offerings, gold and ivory statuettes, come from the late eighth or seventh centuries BCE. Several female divinities were apparently worshipped in the area; to one of them, who was interpreted by the Greeks as Artemis, a small *peripteros* with wooden pillars was built in the second half of the eighth century. This was also where the Lydian king Croesus dedicated, around 560 BCE, the construction of a marble *dipteros*, with whose quality and dimensions he wanted to surpass the large edifices that the free Ionians in Samos and Didyma near Miletus had recently begun building. This temple was destroyed in 356 BCE by a fire set by the fanatic Herostratos, who wanted to immortalize himself by committing this act of madness ("Herostratic fame")—and succeeded in doing so. On the site of the old temple a new structure rose that was considered one of the seven wonders of the world during the Hellenistic period. In the course of late antiquity and the Middle Ages, this structure almost completely vanished from the surface, and today only a few of its remains can still be seen in the marshy area.[83]

Archaeological evidence allows us to form an idea of the Ephesian Artemis (Figure 30). Therein we find a peculiar shaping of the history of religion in Anatolia—an especially vivid example of Greco-Asiatic syncretism on Ionian territory. The two

30. Artemis of Ephesos,
Museum Selçuk.

marble statues of the goddess were found not in the Artemision but in the city of
Ephesos that flourished in the time of the Roman Empire. These Roman copies
probably go back to the religious image of the earlier temple of the fourth century
BCE; the standing Artemis is flanked by does, and her gown is decorated with small
animal busts. The cone-shaped forms hanging from the upper body were long interpreted as breasts symbolizing fertility; in antiquity, the Church Father Jerome al-

ready referred to the "many-breasted" (*multimammia*) Diana. The Swiss scholar Gérard Seiterle saw in them a striking similarity to bull scrotums,[84] but so far there is no consensus in favor of this or other suggestions.

Iconographically, the Ephesian goddess seems close to the Phrygian Kybele, or to the woman venerated by the Lydians under the name of Kybebe. A statue 1.26 meters high depicting the half-naked goddess of Boğazköy, wearing a skirt and an enormous decorative headdress, is flanked by a harpist and a flutist who hardly reach her hip (see Figure 25). Numerous representations of these Anatolian goddesses show them with various attributes, sitting or standing between or next to animals: birds, lions, oxen, fish. We have already seen statues of women flanked by animals that were found at the Neolithic site of Çatal Höyük (see Figure 12). Shrines of Anatolian goddesses important beyond their region were located in Cappadocian and in Pontic Komana, as well as in Phrygian Pessinus. Numerous Anatolian and Syrian goddesses known as Artemis, such as the Artemis Perasia in Hierapolis-Kastabala and the Tar'tā (Greek: *Atargatis*) of Hierapolis-Bambyke, belong to this group (p. 110).[85]

A late shrine in Xanthos in Lycia that was probably Hellenized (i.e., connected with the names of Greek divinities) in the sixth or fifth century BCE was dedicated to the mother Leto and her twins Apollo and Artemis. Epigraphic sources in the native Lycian language prove that in pre-Greek times, in the sacred precinct later developed as a *Letoon*, a divine "mother" (Lycian: *ēni*) and her children were worshiped along with water goddesses (*elijāna*). A story told by Ovid (*met.* 6, 317–381) that certainly originated in Asia Minor is of exemplary significance for the syncretism that began with the Greek takeover of this and many other shrines. In the story, Lycian peasants pitilessly refuse to allow Leto and her children, who are tortured by heat and thirst, to drink from the small, reed-bordered pond, whereupon the goddess turns them into frogs. If it is correctly interpreted, this legend reflects a case of the native inhabitants' resistance to the identification of their "mother" and children with the Greek triad. Thus the natives opposed the syncretism transferred to the shrine by the settlers and their cult—probably in vain, because their own people's elite was absolutely open to Hellenization.[86]

PAMPHYLIA AND CILICIA

Turning from the Aegean coast toward the south, two very early Greek settlements on the Mediterranean coast of Anatolia dating from the Late Bonze Age and the Iron Age deserve our attention. In the case of Pamphylia, only the mythical tradition still reflects the memory of Greek settlements in the foreign environment: Aspendos is supposed to have been founded by Argives, Selge by Lacedaemonians, Side by Aiolians from Kyme, whereas Perge was founded by the seer Mopsos (after he participated in the Trojan War), the seer Kalchas, or the seer Amphilochos; Mopsos is said to have had a daughter named Pamphylia (Theopompos, FGrHist 115 F 103, 15). The Bronze Age city of Parḫa on the Kastariya River has been identified with Perge (p. 89). The first noteworthy occupation of this site that can be proven by ceramics occurred in the early seventh century, and in this phase everything suggests a settlement by Rhodians from Lindos, who are supposed to have founded Phaselis on the Lycian coast at about the same time.[87] Up to this point we still have no proof of Mycenaean settlement in other parts of Pamphylia. Greek settlement in Pamphylia can be dated archaeologically no earlier than the seventh century BCE; at that time Phoenicians were still living in the far eastern part of the country. A Phoenician inscription mentions a governor who gave his followers vineyards.[88] It has been thought that a further indication of Mycenaean settlement in Pamphylia could be found in the language. In later times there is a dialect that points to connections with Mycenaean Greek, but it is attested by only a few inscriptions and coins. Thus, for example, a legend on a coin names the Artemis of Perge *wanassa Preiia* (Mycenaean: "mistress," compare to *wanax/anax*—"master"). In addition to Phaselis, farther to the west, in the area on the border between Pamphylia and Lycia, there were more Rhodian colonies (e.g., Melanippion, Korydalla, Gagai, and Rhodiapolis) and Aeolian colonies (e.g., Thebes, Lyrnessos, Tenedos, and Kyme).[89]

Mopsos is also supposed to have traveled to Cilicia and founded there a city not far from Adana, Mophsuhestia (hearth or house of Mopsos). Here a historical person of this name seems actually to have ruled, though probably significantly later than the seer from Thebes: the eighth-century Luwian-Phoenician bilingual text from Karatepe mentions a *bt Mpš*. This was wrongly interpreted as the Phoenician equivalent of Mopsuhestia, whereas in fact it does not denote a building ("house" or "hearth") but a dynasty.[90] In several places on the plains of Cilicia and opposite them, on the north Syrian coast at Al Mina, archaeological evidence suggests the presence of Greeks in the eighth century—that is, at just the time when these coasts were being attacked by pirates known as "Ionians."

INTERNAL RELATIONSHIPS

We know little about the internal relationships of the Aeolian, Ionian, and Dorian communities during the oldest phase of settlement. I have already mentioned the problem of a tribal structure brought with them or first developed in Asia. But we can say that the Greeks' *poleis* in Asia differed from the states that we have come to know among the Hittites, the Phrygians, and the Lydians. The archaic *poleis* were small, separate structures comparable to the city-kingdoms of the Phoenicians, Aramaeans, or late Hittites in Taurus, Cilicia, and the Levant. Despite being organized into alliances, they remained independent and even divided. A permanent political union did not occur. They did not develop full-scale monarchies with titles, insignia, palaces, and royal households. Of course, at first there were "kings" (*basilees*), though they gradually disappeared. However, the king was *primus inter pares*; the claim to leadership was shared by collectives—the heads of the old, established clans and families. In Erythrai and Ephesos the aristocratic families were still called *basilidai* (royals), probably because the hereditary right to nominate the king had once been reserved to them. The aristocrats regularly met in council and were the spokesmen in meetings of the *politai* (citizens). All adult male members of the *polis* represented the community of the *politai*, from which the foreign inhabitants or cohabitants (*meta-nastai, paroikoi*) were sharply distinguished.[91] From a socioeconomic point of view, the majority of the *politai* must have been landowners who were engaged primarily in agriculture on *polis* territory, with the powerful aristocrats being the leaders in the political and religious life of the community and in campaigns and raiding forays, as well as being the richest and having the most land and livestock. On their estates there were not only male and female slaves—acquired primarily as war booty—but also free people who accompanied and served them. The great lords owned horses or ships (or both); traveled by cart to war or to the hunt; hoarded treasures from trade and war booty; joined in *hetairiai* (associations of companions) that often engaged in rivalries; and ate while lying on couches (a custom that came from the Assyrians) with music, recitations, and dances. They appeared as leaders at festivals and in processions, and hired and paid specialists, most of whom were itinerant: physicians, seers, singers, leather and metal workers, and craftsmen, such as ivory carvers and gold and silver smiths. Naturally, they also cultivated friendships and marital relationships with important families outside their *polis*. We know little about their residences and their architecture: in Larisa on the Hermos two sixth-century "palaces," rectangular buildings with projecting *antae* (side walls that extend to form a porch at the front) and Aeolian pillars between them have been excavated; they were probably manor houses.[92] An important work of the Anatolian-Greek stonecutter's art in the last third of the sixth century BCE is the marble Gümüşçay sarcophagus from the Troad, on which we find represented a scene from mythology: Neoptolemos's sacrifice of Polyxena on the grave of Achilles. This sarcophagus presumably came from a local princess's tomb.[93]

In the seventh century BCE we already hear of tyrants in Ionia.[94] The poet Archilochos connects, as we have seen, the word *tyrannis* with the violently acquired power of the Lydian Gyges. Greek texts written centuries later (Nikolaos of Damascus, Konon) report Greek tyrants in Miletus. The aristocrats were fighting one another. A certain Amphitres killed the respected Leodamas and had his followers occupy the city; the sons of the murdered man fled to take refuge with a friend in Assesos, and there the resistance continued. Leodamas's sons were finally able to avenge their father's murder by killing Amphitres. Among the Milesians, the office of *aisymnetes* (ruler and leader of the army), which was particularly precarious because of its power and status, was later filled by election. But in the war with the Lydians, another tyrant, Thrasybulos, appeared and not only succeeded in repelling the Lydian assault but was even recognized as an ally and a friend by the Lydian king Alyattes. Such personal relationships helped the Lydians—and later on, the Persian kings—to bind the Greek *poleis* to them.

Overthrows also occurred in Ephesos. The *basilidai* did not remain uncontested. Against them rose up a certain Pythagoras, whom the sources describe as a cruel tyrant. It is not clear whether he had the predecessor of the temple of Croesus built in the Artemision. The clan that had been deprived of power struck back, and Melas and his son Pindaros successively ruled the city. After Croesus took (and moved)

Ephesos, an Athenian arbitrator took steps to restore order, but it did not last long; soon further tyrants took over. The aristocratic parties in Erythrai were involved in a similar long-term struggle. The names of three leading members of a *hetairia* who picked a fight with the prominent *basilidai* in this city and came to power through murder and killing were Ortyges, Iros, and Echaros.

COLONIZATION

An event of far-reaching importance is the so-called great Greek colonization, which began in the eighth century BCE and continued until ca. 500 BCE. In Asia, two port cities played a decisive role as points of departure for emigration by sea: Miletus and Phokaia.

In the case of Miletus, modern research has counted nearly fifty colonies (Map 5).[95] Among the earliest and most important areas targeted by the Milesians were the Hellespont and the Propontis (Sea of Marmara). Starting ca. 700 BCE, Milesian groups settled on the western and southern coasts of the Propontis, in Abydos, Kyzikos, Prokonnesos, and Kios, not far from the major Megarian colonies (*apoikiai*, literally: settlements far from home) on the northern and eastern coasts: Byzantion, Kalchedon, Olbia, and Astakos. After an interruption from ca. 680 to 650, other groups pushed farther, through the Bosporus and toward the north. The Greek settlements on the Black Sea (seventh and sixth centuries BCE) are mainly Milesian, on the southern coast, and all are on the territory of modern-day Turkey: Tieion (Hisarönü), Sesamos (Amasra), and Kromna (Tekkeönü). The most important and probably also the earliest city is Sinope (Sinop), with secondary settlements, such as Kytoros (Gideruz), Kotyora (Ordu), Kerasus (Giresun), and Trapezus (Trabzon), whereas the origins of Amisos, the modern city of Samsun, may go back to both Milesians and Phokaians.[96] On the western shore of the Black Sea the Milesians founded, among other cities, Apollonia (Sozopol), Odessos (Varna), and Dionysopolis (Balcik) in modern Bulgaria, Tomis (Constanţa), and—at the mouth of the Danube—Istria (Histria) in Romania. They settled the north coast with Tyras on the Dniester, the island of Berezan and Olbia on the Dnieper (Porutino), Pantikpaion (Kerch), and Theodosia (Feodosiya) in Crimea, all of which are now in Ukraine. On the eastern coast they founded Dioskurias (Suchumi in Abkhasia) and Phasis (Poti, in Georgia). They may have had a part in founding the early trading settlements of Naukratis in the Nile Delta and Posideion (Al Mina) at the mouth of the Orontes River in northern Syria.

Almost nothing remains of Phokaia (Foça), which was in the Aeolian area and was the second most important Ionian mother-city. Excavations have uncovered a *megaron* and parts of an oval building dating from the oldest phase. Starting in ca. 600 BCE colonists sailed from this city's port as far as the western Mediterranean. Elea (Velia) in southern Italy and Massalia (Marseille) in southern France, along with the secondary colonies Alalia (Aleria) on Corsica and Emporiae (Ampurias) in Spain, and perhaps Monoikos (Monaco), Nikaia (Nice), and Antipolis (Antibes) on the Côte d'Azur, owe their existence to the Phokaians' daring. Another wave of emi-

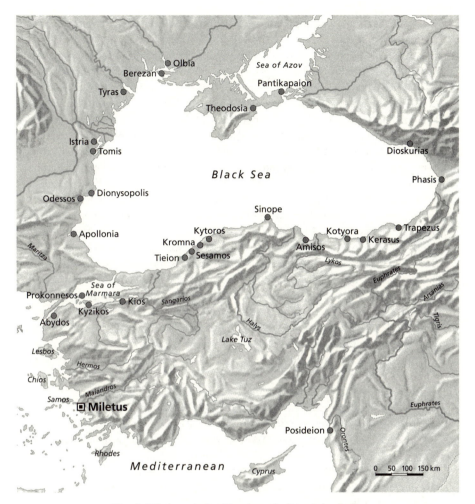

Map 5. Milesian colonies. Map drawn by Peter Palm, Berlin.

gration arrived in the already existing colonies when the Persians threatened Phokaia (after 545 BCE).

The reasons for these emigrations have been discussed extensively. According to the sources, the Lydian kings issued permission for a few of them, and it has been asked whether Gyges, Alyattes, and others played an active part in this and what their motives were. The rapid succession of new Milesian colonies has given rise to the notion that they might be the result of a plan worked out by state authorities. With regard to particular areas, trade interests and the desire to acquire valuable goods cannot be dismissed as important motives. However, as a rule the Milesian colonies were not really mere transfer points; their populations subsisted on farming, fishing, and cattle raising, and they constituted a new community of landowners. However, at least in the case of the Milesia (the city's territory) there is not enough proof to conclude that the emigrations were mainly a way of relieving the pressure of overpopulation and a lack of land in the home country. Above all, the internal tensions (*staseis*) that are attested at this time must have encouraged the decision made by large groups of people to follow the "pioneers" and leave the homeland for a place they already knew about. The followers of aristocrats were naturally drawn into the battles between the hostile houses (*oikoi*). Since in contrast to modern colonial movements, we cannot explain these events by reference to statistical data, we are reduced to suppositions. A disproportional increase in young men inclined to engage in conflicts and take risks, such as we see in many places in Europe between the sixteenth and the nineteenth centuries, cannot be excluded as a driving force.[97] The migrants doubtless did not consist of Milesians alone, but were joined by natives, especially Carians, and here and there also by groups from neighboring cities. The name of a *phyle* (subdivison of the citizenry, compare p. 423) in the Black Sea city of Sesamos that still existed in the time of the Roman Empire, *Halikarnassis* provides clear evidence of this. It testifies to a group of migrants from Halikarnassos joining the Milesians. Still another reason for people to leave their homeland in western Asia Minor can be seen in the system of mercenary soldiers that was flourishing at that time. Serving the wealthy oriental great powers promised a better future than the conflicts at home. The pharaoh's state in Egypt hired numerous Greeks, Carians, and Lydians and settled them. More Carian inscriptions from this time have been found in Egypt than in the homeland (p. 102). Graffiti with the names of mercenaries from Teos and Kolophon were found in Abu Simbel. A man from Priene, evidently a superior officer, was given valuable gifts by Psammetichus I in gratitude for his services, as he proudly recorded—engraved on a cubical stone stool ([195] SEG 37, 994; cf. 39, 1266). Antimeneidas, the brother of the poet Alkaios of Lesbos, was a mercenary in Babylon (Fr. 50 Diehl).

The memory of the long-past dispatch of a colony from its mother-city has found a wealth of expression in later records and in ancient literature. For example, in the second century BCE, in the city of Abdera on the coast of Thrace, it was officially announced that the citizens of Teos in Ionia were the "fathers" of the city ([195] SEG 47, 1646). Of course, many later genealogies were fabricated. Modern research tries to test these kinship relations by comparing the epigraphic and literary testimonies from offices, religious cults and festivals, calendars, and names of phylae and individuals. So far as their institutions are concerned, the many Milesian colonies were very conservative; they copied their mother-city in almost every respect, and for that reason in most cases they can be clearly proven to be of Milesian descent.

ALPHABETIC SCRIPT AND HOMER

If we look back at the oldest culture of the Greeks in Asia Minor, in terms of sources we find a dividing line running through approximately the middle of the seventh century BCE. Anything that precedes this line almost always has to be explained on the basis of later sources if archaeology does not provide the information we need. Afterward, the epigraphic and literary sources begin and steadily increase in number. Homer is a special case. In its extant form, the *Iliad* seems to have originated in Asia Minor. Most books say it was written down in the eighth century, but that date has also been cast in doubt, with good arguments, in favor of a later one. The English philologist Martin West has put the case in a striking and provocative way: "I suspect that most of those who subscribe to an eighth-century dating do so because most other people do."[98] In any case, the use of alphabetic script has to be considered as determining the earliest possible date for its completed form. But the Greek adoption of this script is itself problematic: When, from where, how, and by what means did it reach the Greeks? When we study Homer's text, we immediately encounter, along with questions about the transmission of the script, a multitude of other cultural influences from the east in the areas of language, literature, arts and crafts, and other historical phenomena mentioned in the *Iliad*; and this holds not only for this epic. The archaic epic of the Boeotian Hesiod is in this respect just as rich a creation. Direct models in the classics of cuneiform literatures have long been proven—for Hesiod's *Theogony* the succession myth of Hurrian-Hittite provenance; for the *Iliad* and *Odyssey* such canonical epics as *Gilgamesh*, *Atraḫasis*, and *Enūma Eliš*, which in ancient oriental cultures were school texts.

The cultural and geographical context of this problem exceeds the limits of our subject,[99] and yet Asia Minor moves to the center of attention—indeed the metaphor of the peninsula as a bridge over which the cultural transfer took place, imposes itself on us. It is interesting to consider the share in this that the Anatolian cultures of the Bronze Age and their descendants might be able to claim, and in particular how much of the culture of the Hittite age might in the following centuries have passed into early Greek culture via the Luwians of western and southern Anatolia and a Luwian cultural community—the so-called *koine*—that permeated the whole Anatolian realm between the Dardanelles and the Euphrates. Early Greek contains words that could have been borrowed from the Anatolian linguistic fund, for example, *kyanos* ("Lapis lazuli, dark blue," Hittite: *kuwanna*), or *kymbachos* ("helmet," Hittite: *kubahi*). Against the notion that the *Iliad* also describes on the Asiatic stage an essentially Greek world, scholars have sought to use the mores, clothing, and institutions of the Trojans as depicted by Homer to prove that the text contains "Anatolianisms," but the results are controversial. Finally it can be asked whether the Semitic alphabetic script might not have reached the Greeks, for instance via an Anatolian mediator (e.g., the Phrygians). These questions are not new; they were already raised by Ernst Loewy's "Typenwanderung" (1909) and Santo Mazzarino's opposition (1947) between the *via del mare* (sea route) and the *via di terra* (land route).[100]

The lion's share of oriental aspects in early Greek culture is Semitic. There are more than a hundred loanwords of Semitic origin in the Mycenaean and archaic Greek languages. The narrative material in literary, written form on which the poets of the *Theogony*, the *Iliad*, and the *Odyssey* drew could not have reached the Greeks

31. Nestor's cup, from Pithekussai (island of Ischia, Italy). Image from M. Guarducci, *L'Epigrafia greca dalle origini al tardo impero*, Rome 1987, table X.

of the Bronze Age from the cuneiform libraries of the Hittites. However, the conditions under which poets could make such borrowings from literatures in other languages were present in the heyday of the Neo-Assyrian Empire, that is, in the eighth and seventh centuries BCE. At that time the classics could have been translated into Aramaic, written in alphabetic script, and made accessible in various places to Greeks who were bilingual. Bilingual milieus must have existed at that time on Cyprus, in Cilicia, and on the Levantine coast. The Assyrians' deportations might even have taken Greek individuals or groups into the interior of Mesopotamia.

Among the ideas, skills, habits, and material goods moving from east to west, communication through writing has to be considered a touchstone of particular importance where contacts between givers and takers were intensive. Objects and craft skills pass easily from one country to another, but learning to write the Semitic signs with the help of the Semitic mnemonic device—ox (ʾāleph), house (bēt), and so forth, that is, precisely the alphabet—presupposes, beyond the reception and reshaping of poetry, living with people who have already long ago mastered this art.

The archaeological discoveries relating to users of the archaic Greek alphabetic script in Asia Minor that have been published up to this point are at least a hundred years more recent than the oldest examples from Greece and Italy—the Dipylon *oinochoe* (jug for pouring wine into cups) and Nestor's cup (750–720 BCE) (Figure 31). A jar with a few letters on it, taken from a tomb in Gabii (Osteria dell'Osa, Italy), is at least two decades older than the latter if the dating in accord with archaeological discoveries is correct.[101]

In Anatolia, the letter forms, very similar to Greek, of Old Phrygian inscriptions on a handful of shards from Gordion are dated to approximately the same period. Thus the question arises whether the Phrygians might have been the transmitters of alphabetic writing to the Greeks. Both alphabets have (with exceptions insignificant in this context) the Semitic set of letters. And both of them have a conspicuous special feature: the addition of a doublet from the Semitic semi-vowel *wāw*. This sign resembles an *ypsilon* (Y), and in its place in the Greek set is employed (later in the form of "F"–*digamma*; cf. *wanax, wanassa* "master," "mistress") to represent the semi-vowel *vau*. Its doublet is used to express the pure U-vowel and is placed at a different position. Since this invention is not likely to have been made independently, but either the Greeks introduced it and the Phrygians adopted it, or vice versa, the alphabet of either side must be considered as dependent on the other.

However, given the current state of research, particularly in regard to the dating of the Gordion inscriptions, the (previously mentioned) theory that the alphabet was communicated to the Greeks of Asia Minor via the Phrygians remains improbable.[102] We have to wait for the scientific publication of recent investigations carried out in Gordion. Other regional alphabets used in Asia Minor that must be of old age are Lydian, Carian, Lycian, and Sidetic, even if the extant inscriptions are later than the oldest Phrygian ones. But these systems of signs were (with the exception of Lydian) less close to Greek; they could have been adopted from other alphabets independently and influenced by the Greeks only secondarily. As in the case of poetry, so for the art of writing: the Greeks who lived in a Semitic milieu seem to have learned the alphabet directly from the Aramaeans or Phoenicians in the Levant, Cilicia, or on Cyprus ca. 800 BCE and quickly transmitted it to the Aegean world, especially to Euboea and Italy.

The royal road of cultural transfer to the west in the orientalizing epoch was certainly the sea route, and not the land route via Anatolia. Whatever one might imagine as a "royal way" in Gyges's time, the long and difficult road over the arid high plains was made for emissaries and soldiers and probably did not lead from one densely settled place to the next (on the Persian royal road, see p. 158). This would be so even if one wanted to attribute to traders a leading role in this transfer: transporting commodities by land over such distances would be avoided for reasons of cost alone. Strabo says that *miltos* (the "Sinopian" red chalk) was designated by this term because the merchants were accustomed to bring it from the Cappadocian mountains to the harbor at Sinope before the Ephesians' trade (by land) came into any contact with the inhabitants of Cappadocia (Strabo 12, 2, 10). In the seventh century, a road network connecting cities in Anatolia was still far in the future.

ASIA MINOR AND THE BEGINNINGS OF GREEK LITERATURE AND SCIENCE

Many of the great minds of early Greek literature taught, wrote, researched, and philosophized on the margins of the Lydian Empire.[103] Power struggles among the nobility, along with the Persian conquests, drove some of them to leave their Ionian homeland, and they also spread their influence far outside Asia. Anatolia and the islands off the coast enjoyed cultural leadership with regard to the motherland from the seventh century until well into the sixth century BCE. Even during the growing dominance of Athens in the fifth and fourth centuries, this tradition remained fully alive. Anticipating Chapter 5, we will therefore expand our discussion to deal with the Persian period.

These days it is hardly necessary to emphasize that modern research has liberated the "Greek miracle" from its centuries-long isolation from the oriental intellectual world. Yet with regard to Ionia, we must note in particular special achievements that were probably owed in considerable measure to a rare permeability of and free access to ideas coming from abroad, and in this case to cultures that were in contact and converging. In addition, at the same time Milesian and Phokaian colonization, advancing into unknown regions with an exchange of goods and reverse migrations, had increased the influx of foreign experiences. Finally, economic factors cannot be dismissed out of hand, because for the moment, the courts of the Lydian kings, the satraps and dynasties under the Persians, and a few tyrants in Asia and on the islands offered (along with the aura of oriental power and splendor) a better prospect of money, status, and fame in the arts and sciences than did the nobility and tyrants in Greece—for the time being. People went east the way Europeans now go to America. The east was simply richer, and wealth not only attracts people, but its possessors also like to adorn themselves with excellence. Polycrates of Samos received the Persian satraps' emissaries as he lay listening to the poet Anakreon (Herodotus 3, 121). In large areas of the empire, the great king and the satraps adopted the Lydian-Ionian invention of minting coins, and they brought scientists and specialists into their service. At Darius's behest, Skylax of Karyanda, a Greek from Caria, undertook an exploration of the coasts in wide areas of the Persian Empire and wrote a report in Greek about it. Scholars like Hekataios were as prized as bridge-builders and generals, admirals, and diplomats.

Because of their language, the *Iliad* and *Odyssey* are seen as works composed by an Ionian. Herodotus's uncle, Panyassis of Halikarnassos, who died in battle against the tyrant Lygdamis in 460 BCE, stands for post-Homeric epic poetry in Ionia—or more precisely, in the southern approaches to Ionia. His *Ionika* deals with Ionian colonization. The Milesian Phokylides is supposed to have put his aphorisms into epic hexameters on Hesiod's model much earlier, perhaps in the first half of the sixth century. A prominent outsider, Aristeas, came from the Propontis island of Prokennesos (if he was a historical person at all), far from Ionia. It is assumed that he lived under Croesus and Cyrus, and his name is associated with the fabulous narrative composed in hexameters about the peoples of the north, Issedonians, Arimaspians, and Hyperboreans.

The beginnings of the dark, much-discussed prehistory of other Greek literary genres—for instance, the lyric—also seem to lie in Anatolia. The role of music among the Phrygians has already been mentioned (p. 110). The elegy, and its special instrument, the flute, may have Asiatic roots, and the iamb may also be "a genuinely Ionian product."[104] Of the nine Greek lyric poets that the Alexandrians gathered into a canon, four came from Asia: Alkman, Sappho, Alkaios, and Anakreon. The earliest known names with fragmentary extant texts go back to the seventh century BCE. Kallinos of Ephesos, whose poems may have reflected the danger the Cimmerians posed to his homeland, and Mimnermos of Kolophon, whose book of elegies was named after a flute-player called Nanno, appear to be the oldest elegists in Ionia.

Semonides, who wrote iambic verse, moved from Samos to Amorgos, while Alkman of Sardeis (Fr. 16 Page), who may have been an Ionian, moved to Sparta, where he became famous with his "songs about girls" (*partheneia*). In the sixth century BCE, Hipponax of Ephesos wrote erotic poems and invective verses in iambs, in which Lydian and Phrygian loanwords appear. His sarcasm is supposed to have destroyed the sculptor Bupalos, whom he hated because of a quarrel over a woman. In the battles over the tyrants, Hipponax was driven out of Ephesos to Klazomenai, where he lived in abject poverty (*Suda-Lexikon* s.v.).

Aiolis played a key role. As early as the twenty-sixth Olympiad (676–673 BCE) a certain Terpander from Antissa on Lesbos is attested to have won the contest for Apollo Karneios in Sparta. According to the sources, Arion of Methymna took the decisive step in the development of the dithyramb into choral song. The world of the Aeolian upper aristocracy on Lesbos, off the coast of the Troad, is a milieu we can glimpse through the fragments of a large proportion of Lesbian lyric poetry. This is particularly true of the poems of Alkaios of Mytilene, through which we come to know the tyrants Melanchros, Myrsilos, and Pittakos, but also of the songs of the great Sappho, who was probably born in Eresos but lived in Mytilene. In the expression of the personal experience of happiness, pain, loneliness, erotic tension, and jealousy, her verses constitute a high point in psychology that had never before been achieved.

> For when I look at you for a moment, then it is no longer possible for me to speak; my tongue has snapped, at once a subtle fire has stolen beneath my flesh, I see nothing with my eyes, my ears hum, sweat pours from me, a trembling seizes me all over, I am greener than grass, and it seems to me that I am little short of dying. (Fr. 2 Diehl; trans. Campbell)

Ionia immediately caught up with Aiolis in regard to the lyric. Anakreon, who was from Teos, a harbor city south of Smyrna famed for its shrine to Dionysos, is one of those who fled Asia when the Persians arrived there (546–530 BCE). From Teos's colony Abdera, on the coast of Thrace, he moved first to the court of Polykrates, on Samos, and after the latter's death to the court of Hipparchos in Athens. The Athenians erected a statue of the master on the acropolis (Pausanias, 1, 25, 1); there are also vase paintings of him. As the lyrical poet of Ionia, he had an enormous influence. In the late fourth century CE Synesios of Kyrene still begins his ninth hymn with an echo of the great dialect groups of the lyric art language: Ionian, Aeolian, and Dorian, in which the "song of Teos" represents Ionian lyric.

Apart from Homeric poetry, tradition has preserved verses by the early Greek poets only in the form of a few quotations and fragments on papyrus, and yet these few remains have had a long-term influence that has helped shape Western literature and now world literature, literary theory, and aesthetics.

The beginnings of Greek science in Ionia are of world-historical importance. The name of the city of Miletus overshadows all others. We can still hardly form an idea of what it was like in the seventh and sixth centuries, but its harbors, buildings, and shrines must have befitted a center of the civilization of the oriental West. People and goods from the countries of the Mediterranean and the Black Sea converged on the city by sea; on the land side, the valley of the Maeander provided access to the long-distance roads of Anatolia. If we may speak of a Lydian-Ionian and a Carian-Ionian mixed culture in western Asia Minor, the city of Miletus itself was international and multicultural to an even higher degree. A tradition says that Thales came from a Phoenician family on his mother's side. He and others are supposed to have made long journeys abroad, with sojourns and even settlement outside Ionia: he is said to have visited Egypt and measured the height of the pyramids by measuring the length of the shadows they cast. Anaximandros is supposed to have been involved in the colonization of Apollonia on the Black Sea. Xenophanes of Kolophon fled Harpagos and reached Elea in southern Italy. He wrote about the "foundation" (*ktisis*) of his home town and about the colonization (*apoikismos*) of Elea. Pythagoras, who may have coined the term *philosophos*,[105] left Samos under the tyranny of Polycrates, and lived and worked in Kroton. In contrast, Heraclitus, who was from Ephesos, died at home.

On the basis of what materials, by what means of transmission, and to what extent thinkers like Thales, Anaximandros, and Anaximenes of Miletus became familiar with Oriental literature, we do not know. By their time, cuneiform classics had long since been transcribed onto animal skins and papyrus, and were certainly also available in translation. "Books" composed of this material were not available solely in the residences of kings and satraps, but were also in the possession of tyrants, nobles, and other individuals in the cities. It was demonstrated long ago that the ideas of the Ionian philosophers had quite precise counterparts in older Mesopotamian and also Iranian literature. Babylonian science anticipated knowledge of the theorem of Pythagoras of Samos by almost a millennium. Divine primordial substances (e.g., water) and the parts and levels of the cosmos, with upper, middle, and lower levels (the earth floating on water, with the underworld beneath it and one or more heavens above it, as in Anaximandros's three superimposed heavens) were all found in the oriental mythology of earlier and contemporary times. In Assyrian texts we can already discern efforts to harmonize the mythical-religious world-picture with the observed properties of nature. In the extant mythical narratives, ideas and images about the structure of the reality in which these stories take place intervene to explain and correct: "Working within this background of thought the ancient philosophers endeavoured to find ways of making existing theology accord more precisely with the facts of the natural world."[106] The step toward a view of a self-enclosed, autonomous cosmos was, however, made in Ionia. "The true foundation for Greek natural philosophy [becomes] visible in Anaximandros."[107] As the Zurich scholar Walter Burkert has shown, Iranian ideas about the "infinite light" also seem to have reached this Milesian, as they are present in the tradition of the Yašts. His *apeiron* ("unlimited-indefinite") is both the origin and the whole of the world. Anaximandros is the only one of the Ionian cosmologists of the archaic age from whom a quotation has been handed down verbatim—in the work of Simplikios, a sixth-century CE commentator on Aristotle:

> The indefinite (*to apeiron*) is both principle (*archē*) and element (*stoicheion*) of the things that are, and he was the first to introduce this name of the principle. He says that it is neither water nor any other of the so-called elements, but some other indefinite (*apeiron*) nature, from which come to be all the heavens and the worlds in them; and those things, from which there is coming-to-be for the things that are, are also those into which is their passing-away, in accordance with what must be. For they give penalty (*dikē*) and recompense to one another for their injustice (*adikia*) in accordance with the ordering of time. (Fr. 1, Diels; trans. Curd, http://plato.stanford. edu/archives/win2012/entries/ presocratics)

Just as the cosmologists simply developed the malleable form of nature partly empirically and partly speculatively—by inquiry and by reshaping the mythical framework—so other thinkers reorganized the structure and content of the old narratives regarding the distant past to lend it spatiotemporal order and credibility. For this latter enterprise, *historie*, the key name is that of the Milesian Hekataios. In his work, mythical monsters become real people or animals, enormous distances are reduced to reasonable proportions, and a man is not said to have fifty but at most twenty sons. His reductionism, his way of stripping mythical material down to a core of allegedly realistic, credible information, has to be regarded as naive from a modern point of view. And yet his work is based on the same striving that we find in the natural scientists of his time—namely, to harmonize each and every phenomenon found in the tales with the world as experienced, not for the sake of practical ends, but rather for that of an increase in knowledge. He was interested not only in genealogies (the sequence of the races of gods, demigods, and humans of ages long past) but also in the countries, towns, and peoples of the inhabited world. Like his contemporary and fellow Milesian Anaximandros, he boldly attempted to draw a map of the world. His successors concentrated on certain peoples: Xanthos the Lydian, who presumably came from Sardeis, wrote in Greek about his own people. He attributed to the Lydian kings atrocities like those that myths attributed to distant races of gods and heroes. One of these kings, he said, hacked his wife into pieces, ate her in a fit of gluttony, and then killed himself, while another had been the first to "emasculate" women and use them instead of male eunuchs. Ion of Chios, who also composed tragedies, comedies, dithyrambs, paeans, hymns, epigrams, and drinking songs, wrote in prose a history of the foundation of his city and a work with the title *epidemiai* ("presence in different places"), which apparently dealt with important contemporaries of the author, and above all with the Athenian politician and military leader Kimon.

We have only fragments of the works of all these writers. One work by an Ionian that has been almost completely preserved is still seen as the real beginning of historiography: the *historiai* of Herodotus of Halikarnassos. He came from a mixed

Carian-Greek family in this old community once belonging to the Dorian six-city league, which in his time had long been "Ionianized," and in which his uncle had already won literary fame. The family's flight from the tyrant and Herodotus's return, his extended journeys, a sojourn in Athens, and emigration to Thurioi in southern Italy are the most important stages in his life. Numerous streams of literary and scientific thought from the Greek and Middle Eastern world merge in his work. As a researcher following in the footsteps of Hekataios, he combines a knowledge of the peoples and lands of the contemporary Persian Empire with the history of the monumental battle between Persians and Greeks. The artistic means used in his account are manifold: a broad epic narrative; trenchant, witty short stories; monologues; dialogues; and scenes.[108] The art and power of his narrative are extraordinary and still fascinate readers today. Various colors gleam in the colossal historical picture that is hard to overlook from close up and comprises manifold themes, ranging from the fantastic borders of the known world to the splendor of cities and palaces; peoples and persons, their mores, religions, eating habits, tools, and clothing; animals and plants; to people's characters and ways of life, their skill, achievement, success, rise, arrogance, fall, and annihilation. Later writers—for instance, the author of a long Hellenistic verse inscription from Salmakis (Kaplan Kalesi) on the mythical beginnings of the city of Halikarnassos and its great sons—remember him as a "Homer" of history ([146] MS I 39). Herodotus seems not to have known any oriental languages, with the possible exception of Carian. Even with all the critical distance of the modern scientist regarding Herodotus's reliability in matters of detail, we still find in his work an enormously valuable and in many respects accurate body of information about the world of the eighth to the fifth centuries BCE. In it he devoted a substantial portion to the history and contexts of Asia Minor.

CHAPTER 5

The Western Persian Empire and the World of the Greeks in Asia Minor (547/546 BCE to 333 BCE)

Strabo, a Greek with Iranian relatives from Amaseia, wrote shortly after the turn of the eras:

> The Persians, of all the barbarians, became the most famous among the Greeks, be-
> cause none of the other barbarians who ruled Asia ruled Greeks; neither were these
> people acquainted with the Greeks nor yet the Greeks with the barbarians, except for
> a short time by distant hearsay. Homer, at any rate, knows nothing of either the empire
> of the Syrians nor that of the Medes. . . . The Persians were the first people to rule over
> Greeks. The Lydians had indeed ruled over Greeks, but not also over the whole of
> Asia—only over a small part of it. (Strabo 15, 3, 23; trans. Jones)

Since the age of the Hittites—about whom Strabo knew nothing—no other people had in fact ruled so large a part of the Asia Minor peninsula for such a long time, but in contrast to the Hittites, the new masters were outsiders. The centers of their empire were far away. Delegates of subject peoples from all countries traveled long distances to get there and joined an exotic parade of tribute bearers before the king (Figure 32). In the middle of the sixth century, all of Asia Minor was for the first time in the possession of a foreign power, as was later to happen again and again—from then until the time when Constantine's *Imperium Romanum* (330 CE) moved its capital to the threshold of the continent, on the European shore (!) of the Bosporus. I first sketch the sequence of events, and then examine the structure and character of Persian rule in Asia Minor.

Political History from Cyrus's Conquest to Alexander's Campaign

From Cyrus to Darius: The Subjection of Asia Minor

The original land of the new power was Iran. At the time of the Lydian Empire the Iranian Medes must have had a considerable reputation far to the west, so that the name of their people was simply transferred to the Persians who followed as conquerors and invaders. The homeland of the tribe that produced the Persian rulers of the world (for a list, see the Appendix) lay in the old empire of Elam, whose political

32. The "tribute bearers' relief" from the stairway of the great king's audience hall in Persepolis. In the middle zone, to the right, an Armenian delegation; below them, an Ionian (?) delegation.

power had been broken in 639 (the destruction of Susa), just as shortly afterward that of the Assyrians was broken in neighboring Mesopotamia, so that room for maneuver had emerged not only for the Median Empire and the new Babylonian Empire, but also for other expanding powers in the region. A certain Cyrus of Anšan rebelled against the Median king Astyages, overthrew him, and occupied Ekbatana (554/553 or 550/540 BCE). Other countries then fell like dominos. In the ninth year of the reign of King Nabonidos (547/546), Cyrus marched into the east Anatolian highlands and conquered Urartu (?), and Babylon surrendered to him without a fight in 539 BCE. The war against Croesus of Lydia and the fall of the city of Sardeis cannot be dated with certainty (p. 113). When they were urged to reject Croesus, the Greek cities of western Asia Minor saw themselves confronted by a choice. But only Miletus agreed, supported the Persians, and was rewarded. After the Persian success the others were coldly sent away when they tried to negotiate modest conditions. In the Panionion the Ionians held a council (without the Milesians) and decided to seek the help of Sparta, the strongest power in the motherland. But the Spartans merely warned Cyrus not to destroy any Greek cities.

After his victory over Croesus, the conqueror Cyrus himself did not remain much longer in Anatolia; he handed Sardeis over to a Persian governor, while the royal treasury was entrusted to a certain Paktyas. The latter was a Lydian and was apparently considered knowledgeable about financial matters. But behind the back of the withdrawing king, he used the resources to foment rebellion. Two Median generals, Mazares and Harpagos, conquered successively the west and the south, and put down the revolts everywhere, including in Priene, Phokaia, and Teos, whose inhabitants fled to the daughter-city of Abdera on the Thracian coast. Paktyas's flight ended in Chios, which handed him over. The Greeks and Carians in the south surrendered to Harpagos's invading forces; only the Kaunians and Lycians of Xanthos stubbornly resisted and preferred collective suicide to subjection (according to Herodotus 1, 176).

Cyrus's son Kambyses II, who conquered Egypt, was apparently never in Asia Minor. His successor Darius I, who designated himself, according to the genealogy of the forefather Haxamaniš (Achaimenes), as an "Achaimenid," not only extended Persian rule to the region of modern Pakistan and Cyrenaica but also led expeditions as far as the islands off the coast of Asia Minor, Thrace, and the lower Danube. The river was crossed by a bridge of boats. Personnel and logistical resources were provided in large measure by the heads of noble families living in the Greek cities of Asia and around the Straits, who were personally obligated to the king; the sources describe them as "tyrants" (though they did not describe themselves that way). In Histiaios, Miletus had a man who was devoted to the king and was trusted by him. During the campaign against the Scythians in the Danubian area, he is supposed to have dissuaded the Greeks from adopting the Athenian Miltiades's plan to betray the king and free Ionia from Persian rule. Describing the debates on this issue, Herodotus names (4, 138) a whole series of tyrants who ruled on the Sea of Marmara; the Bosporus; and the Hellespont in Abydos, Lampsakos, Parion, Prokonnesos, Kyzikos, and Byzantion; in Aiolis in Kyme; and in Ionia in Chios, Samos, Phokaia, and Miletus. The bridge over the Bosporus was built by the architect Mandrokles of Samos at a point halfway between Byzantion and the northern exit from the Straits, probably at the site of the modern fortress of Rumeli Hisarı (see Figure 1).

When Herodotus writes that the Greek cities in Asia Minor under Darius would have preferred to be ruled "democratically" rather than "tyrannically" (4, 137), he was certainly seeing this antithesis in the perspective of the experiences of his own time, predating it a good eighty years back, into the late sixth century BCE. Compare, for instance, his claim that at the beginning of the Ionian resistance, democracy had been introduced in Miletus, and after its end, throughout the whole of Ionia (5, 37; 6, 43). Nonetheless, even though there were no democracies in Greek cities, there were already at that time community constitutions that limited the power of the nobility, and in Chios, off the Ionian coast, a second council, a *bule demosie*, had been created some fifty years before (575–550 BCE). In the first half of the following century, the citizenry of Teos's desire to prohibit a governing office notorious for its power was expressed in a formal state document.[1] In any case, there were constant tensions within the *poleis*, and from the Persian point of view loyalty to the king and the reliability of the tyrants varied from one case to the next, probably particularly when they had come to power with Persian help and were under pressure at home. Byzantion freed itself of its own tyrant, Ariston, while the latter was fulfilling his military obligations in the land of the Scythians; thus Darius was forced to avoid retreating via the Bosporus and crossed the Hellespont instead. His general Otanes soon thereafter put down the anti-Persian resistance in the city. This was only a prelude. The king and his satraps must have been distrustful and had sharp ears. Darius took the Milesian Histiaios with him back to his court in Susa, and in Miletus a certain Aristagoras replaced him.

From the Ionian Resistance to the Athenian Empire

In Herodotus, the history of the Ionians' uprising against Persian rule in 500/499 BCE reads like a drama of greed, rage, and jealousy that involved prominent antagonists and was played out against the background of a dreadful quarrel among factions in and between cities. Deeper reasons for the uprising's general spread are not clear; whether people in the harbor cities of the Aegean and near the Straits really suffered or were justified in fearing that the expansion of the enormous empire to Egypt and Europe would interfere with trade by sea and result in economic setbacks cannot be determined. Miletus was still a flourishing and wealthy city, with a huge hoard of valuable votive offerings in the Didymaion.

It all began, naturally, with a group of political exiles. Coming to Miletus from Naxos, an island in the Cyclades, they were accepted as friends of Histiaios, and urged their hosts to join them in an attack on their adversaries in their homeland Naxos to win booty. Aristagoras aroused the interest of the satrap in Sardeis, Artaphernes, and received his military support. But the enterprise failed, not least because of bickering among the members of the attacking coalition. Aristagoras thereupon suddenly decided to agitate against the Persians in Ionia—it is alleged that Histiaios secretly encouraged him from Susa—and found a hearing. The empire's size and military strength was known, and the respected Milesian scholar Hekataios issued a warning. But the hope of success won out: one *polis* after another dared to resist and seized the opportunity to bring down the Persians' supporters in their own communities. The prospect of help from the motherland, and especially from the Spartans, whom they had already tried to mobilize against Cyrus, also played a role. Being only slightly acquainted with the Asian situation, the Spartans may have believed the Ionians when the latter scornfully suggested that the Persians went to war in trousers and with hats on their heads. But the Spartans were startled to learn that it took three months to get from the coast of the Aegean to the center of the Persian Empire. The Spartan king refused. Sparta had other concerns. Things did not go much better with the Athenians: their support for the Ionians with just twenty ships (with five more from Eretria) was a disappointment, and after the first military setback in Asia they sailed home.

The satrap in Sardeis was unprepared when a Greek army marched up the Kaystros from the coast near Ephesos, crossed the Tmolos Mountain, and attacked his city from the south. Taking refuge in the castle, he watched the houses and the shrine to Kybebe go up in flames. Counterattacks on the part of the Lydians and Persians forced the Ionians to retreat. But the Carians, Kaunians, and Cyprian kings joined the uprising, and the insurgents managed to take cities on the Hellespont and the Bosporus, including Byzantion. The war continued for four years. Around Cyprus, there was intense fighting on land and at sea; the excavations carried out in Old Paphos by Franz Georg Maier, an ancient historian from Zurich, made it possible to reconstruct the Persians' siege ramp.[2] The Persian troops hastily assembled in Asia Minor west of the Halys were led by three of the great king's sons-in-law. They pursued the Ionian land army and defeated it near Ephesos (498 BCE). Their operations on the Straits in the north and against the Carians in the south were only partly successful, and two of the Persian generals died. The third, Otanes, and the satrap of Sardeis, Artaphernes, marched into the heart of Ionia and undertook a large, combined attack on Miletus by sea and by land.

Neither Aristagoras nor Histiaios took part in the Ionians' final battle. The former had absconded to Thrace and fell there in a campaign in the interior. The latter, who had managed to get from Susa to Sardeis, was not given a friendly welcome by Artaphernes, but was instead subject to suspicion and called to account. He was able to escape to the coast in time, but in Ionia he met with rejection, especially in his Milesian homeland. Mytilene finally provided him with ships, which he used to engage in piracy on the Bosporus. After the fall of Miletus he was able to conquer Chios again, but while attempting to forage in the valley of the Kaikos on the mainland, he fell into the hands of the Persians and was killed.

In the Panionion the assembled Ionians decided to protect Miletus on the sea side. The Phokaian Dionysios led the supreme command. With 353 ships, including contingents from Miletus itself, Priene, Samos, Myus, Teos, Erythrai, Chios, Phokaia, and Lesbos, the Ionian fleet was still only little more than half as large as the Persian, whose crews consisted mainly of Phoenicians. The Greeks' crushing defeat (496 BCE) off Miletus, near the island of Lade, which can be seen today as low hills rising from the alluvial plain, resulted in a bitter fate for the most flourishing Ionian city. Women and children were enslaved, most of the men were killed, and some of them were deported to Mesopotamia. According to Herodotus (6, 19, 3), the Didymaion was plundered and reduced to ashes in revenge for the burning of Sardeis. Archaeological discoveries, however, argue against subjecting his account to an "extensive interpretation," and they also do not suggest that the Didymaion was sacked at the same time as Miletus.[3] The booty carried off included a bronze *astragalos* (gaming die), a votive offering that two men named Aristolochos and Thrason made to Apollo, and that was found during excavations in Susa ([109] Syll.[3] 3g). The Persians gradually reconquered the rest of the cities, and at first treated them just as harshly. Hekataios, who was respected by the Persians, is supposed to have interceded on behalf of the Ionians, asking that they be granted mercy. A general increase in the tribute to be paid did not occur. The tyrants who had been driven out and had sided with the Persians in the campaign against Miletus were not all reappointed.

In Greece, the catastrophe left an enduring impression. In Athens, the playwright Phrynichos staged "The Conquest of Miletus," the first play that represented contemporary events, and thereby produced a theatrical scandal: the audience wept, a repeat performance was prohibited, and the author was fined. But in retrospect, the rise and fall of the Ionians in the years between 499 and 494 BCE appear to be merely a prelude to the far greater conflict between the Persians and the Greeks that culminated in the attack on Greece made by Darius's successor Xerxes. A Persian expeditionary force under the command of Datis and Artaphernes had been defeated before at Marathon in 490 by the combined armies of Athens and Plataiai under Militiades; ten years later, the king himself led the Persian army from a large assembly area in Cappadocia via Kelainai in Phrygia to Sardeis. He wintered there and the following June crossed the Hellespont between Abydos and Sestos. The builder of the boat-bridge was again a Greek.

The completely unexpected collapse of this invasion in Greece, at Salamis and Plataiai, followed by the devastating attack on the Persian navy near the promontory of Mykale (479), abruptly changed the situation of the Greeks in Asia Minor. The Ionian cities detached themselves from the Persians once again. This time they found an active, aggressive leader in the vibrant, victorious Athenian power, which subsequently carried on the war at sea and put the Persian forces on the defensive all along the coast of Asia Minor in the west and in the south, until finally the Athenian Kallias negotiated a peace treaty around the middle of the century. Continuing bilateral negotiations with Ionian cities, the Athenians had already created the naval alliance later known as the Delian League (478/477 BCE). When in the early 460s a large Phoenician fleet from Pamphylia was supposed to take the initiative, the Athenian Kimon destroyed both the fleet and the troops on land with a surprise attack at the mouth of the Eurymedon in Pamphylia (near modern-day Serik, Turkey).

The leading power, Athens, developed the naval alliance step by step. It controlled ca. forty cities on the Straits, ca. thirty-five on the Aegean coast, and ca. sixty-five in parts of Caria, Lycia, and Pamphylia, including the city of Aspendos. At the outset, members of the alliance met in Delos to make decisions, in which each of them had an equal voice, and contributions to the continuation of the war were a matter of agreement. But this soon ceased to be the case. Athens transformed the financing system of a confederation into a system of taxing subjects, and in 454 it took over all power of decision. When Samos withdrew from the alliance in 440/439 BCE, this led to the secession of numerous cities in Caria. The overall tribute set at 460 talents by Aristeides was at first rather moderate; it was the total of contributions estimated differently for each member of the alliance, depending on its economic resources. For example, for the small Carian coastal city of Kaunos, it amounted to half a talent; in contrast, the nearby city of Telandros paid (in 443/442) 600 drachmas more, Halikarnassos paid almost two talents, and Lindos on Rhodes paid six talents. The drastic increase resulting from the reassessment made by the Athenian statesman Kleon in 425/424 brought in on average two to three times as much. For Kaunos this meant an increase in the levy from one half of a talent to ten talents. The final collapse of the naval alliance came in the last third of the Peloponnesian War (431–404). Dynasts and cities in Caria and Lycia went over to the Persian side, whose supreme commander, Tissaphernes, called on Sparta's military aid. A combined attack on Iasos put an end to the rule of the dynast Amorges, who had rebelled against the great king. From 412/411 BCE on, the Persians were once again able to demand tribute from the cities of Ionia (Thucydides 8, 5, 5).

For the great king and his satraps in Asia Minor, toward the end of the Peloponnesian War the perspective shifted from Athens to Sparta. For decades Athens had been the enemy that had caused them painful losses on the western periphery of the empire. They had supported Sparta, which in return left it to the Persians to reestablish their supremacy over Greek cities in Asia Minor even before the war was over (Thucydides, 8, 5 f.). The negotiations were led by the *karanos* (supreme commander) of Asia Minor, Tissaphernes. But he began to suspect Sparta, and only a few years later the winner of the Peloponnesian War turned into the new enemy. In the last years of the war one of the most prominent figures in Athenian history, Alkibiades, who had changed sides several times, perished. Like Histiaios of Miletus, he died a gruesome death in the interior of Asia Minor. On the orders of the satrap Pharnabazos, in Daskyleion, he was killed in the small village of Melissa in Phrygia (not far from modern-day Kütahya, Turkey).

March of the Ten Thousand through Anatolia

Cyrus the Younger (a brother of Artaxerxes II, the Persian king enthroned in 404 BCE) ousted Tissaphernes from his position and ruled as *karanos* in Asia Minor from 408 on, whereas Tissaphernes had to be content with Caria. However, Tissaphernes retained control over Miletus, which led Cyrus to besiege the city and to make extensive preparations for war, already in truth (according to Xenophon) with the intention of seizing his brother's throne in far-off Susa. Many Greek soldiers were hired, and Sparta sent reinforcements to Cilicia for the drive into Mesopotamia. In the first decisive battle near Kunaxa (not far from Baghdad), the army gained the upper hand, but Cyrus himself was killed. The expedition collapsed, and the Greeks struggled through hostile territory back to the Black Sea. They made a march almost 1,500 kilometers long across eastern Anatolia and down to the coast near the Milesian secondary colony of Trapezus (Map 6).

The Athenian Xenophon, one of the leaders, has left us an authentic eyewitness account that offers a wealth of information about the otherwise little-known area of eastern and northern Anatolia in this time.[4] Not far from Hasankeyf (Figure 33), the army left the valley of the Tigris River and climbed up to the plateau west of Lake Van. Western Armenia was ruled by the satrap Tiribazos, eastern Armenia by Orontes (Aroandes), a Bactrian and the great king's son-in-law. We will encounter him again later in Mysia. When the Greek army marched through his territory, he ruled over an area that was known above all for horse raising. The natives raised selected foals for tribute to the king, and according to Strabo (11, 14, 9) the satrap of Armenia sent his lord 2,000 foals every year. The Greeks were traveling there through a foreign world in which village and nomadic life was predominant. This perilous march had to be reconnoitered and safeguarded in advance: every time they first

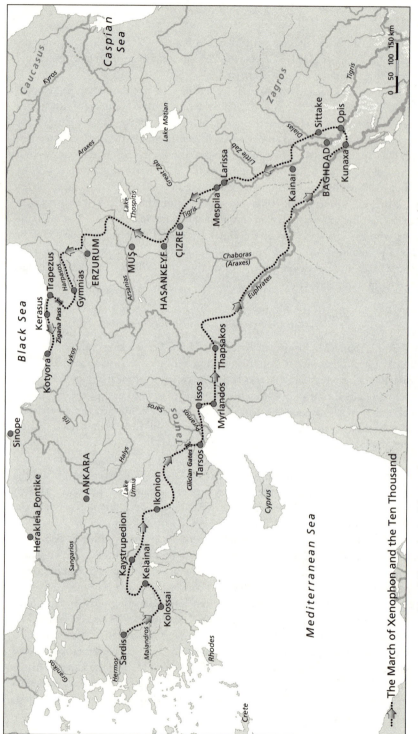

Map 6. The Anabasis of the Ten Thousand (approximate route of the march). Map drawn by Peter Palm, Berlin.

33. The Tigris near the town of Hasankeyf, Turkey.

entered into contact with a larger village-like settlement, they tried to take the local *komarches* (village chief) prisoner. Xenophon argued for adopting the gentle method: for guidance as far as the border of the next tribe, he promised the prisoner that he would be rewarded and treated well. Other officers let their men plunder, made reprisals, and took natives with them in irons.

Xenophon also describes the appearance of the villages:

> The houses here were underground, with a mouth like that of a well, but spacious below; and while entrances were tunneled down for the beasts of burden, the human inhabitants descended by a ladder. In the houses were goats, sheep, cattle, fowls, and their young; and all the animals were reared and took their fodder there in the houses. Here were also wheat, barley, and beans, and barley-wine in large bowls. (*An.* 4, 5, 25 f.; trans. Brownson)

The ancient reports regarding these underground or half-underground houses (cf. Diodorus 14, 28, 5) can be supplemented by those of nineteenth-century travelers. The living area was dug out and divided into rooms by means of tree trunks, and the hole was covered with beams, branches, and brush, on which earth was then spread and sealed with sod. Children playing on the roof or grazing sheep occasionally fell through the chimney; Carl Friedrich Lehmann-Haupt reports that the leg of one of the horses of his party suddenly broke through a roof, and the appearance of the horse's hoof inside the dwelling had horrified its occupants (Figure 34a).[5]

Engaging in heavy fighting with the mountain peoples, the Greeks finally climbed the coastal range of east Pontos. The most savage opponents were the Chalybes,

34. (a) Earth houses in a village near Ardahan, northeast Turkey. (b) Landscape in Armenia.

who sang and danced when they caught sight of the enemy and carried with them as they marched the hacked-off heads of their victims. At a mountain crest not far from the Zigana Pass (south of Trabzon) a moving scene occurred: The shouts of the men in the van were echoed in increasing numbers by those behind them until all of them reached the crest and threw their arms around one another and wept, not only the foot soldiers but also the generals and officers. What they saw in the distance before them was—the sea. Heinrich Heine's verse was still lent wings by the Greeks' shouts:

> Thalatta! Thalatta!
> Hail to thee, oh Sea, ageless and eternal!
> Hail to thee, from a jubilant heart
> Ten thousand times hail!
> Hail, as you were hailed by
> Ten thousand Grecian hearts.[6]

Modern travelers have made an intensive search for the stone cairns erected by the soldiers on the spot, but have been unable to determine its exact position with certainty.

On the north side of the coastal range the Greeks entered the land of the Makrones (Hekataios calls them the "Sanni") and of the larger group of the Colchians, who had settled the whole coast and the mountains east of Trapezus. The climate and vegetation were different from those of the lands from which most of the Greeks came. Many of Xenophon's soldiers poisoned themselves by eating the honey made from the nectar of an orange-flowered azalea (*Azalea pontica*), becoming intoxicated and suffering from diarrhea and vomiting. The same thing happened to Pompey's legionnaires three hundred years later, and even happens occasionally today when people consume this honey.[7] In Trapezus the Greek soldiers had not yet reached their goal, but they were safe; the majority of them made their way home by sea. Of 13,000, about 8,000 had survived.

Xenophon's march through Asia Minor did not come to an end there. Starting from Herakleia Pontike, the army crossed Bithynia as far as the Bosporus and sojourned in Byzantion. After constant shortages, mutinies, and a Thracian adventure in the service of King Seuthes, the army, much reduced in size, set out to cross the Propontis to Lampsakos and marched through the Troad as far as Pergamon, there to hand over the army to the Spartan Thibron. Pergamon later moved into the center of the history of Asia Minor. At that time it was ruled by a woman named Hellas, the widow of a Greek named Gongylos, the son of a man of the same name from Eretria. The elder Gongylos had been exiled from his homeland because of his *medismos* (partiality to the Persians)—after the Persian War this was an infamous crime in Greece. However, the great king had given him the cities of Gambrion, Palaigambrion, Gryneion, and Myrina in Asia. Hellas took the opportunity to use the army to rid herself of a bothersome Persian competitor in the valley of the Kaikos, and this last plundering expedition brought the Greek soldiers another rich haul of booty.

The King's Peace (387/386 BCE)

Tissaphernes returned to his former position as *karanos* in Sardeis, and even married one of the king's daughters (Diodorus 14, 26, 4). He waged war against the Spartans, who had now gone on the offensive. On the Spartan side, the supreme commander in Asia was Agesilaos, a Eurypontid king to whom Xenophon devoted a eulogy and Plutarch a biography. Between 396 and 394, he invaded the interior of Asia Minor several times, first feigning an attack on Caria and then descending on Phrygia. When in the following season he announced that he would attack Lydia, Tissaphernes believed it was another trick and waited for him in Caria, but when he recognized his mistake, he had to set out in great haste for Sardeis. In 395 there was a battle at the Paktolos River, which the Spartans won. After the defeat, Tissaphernes fell victim to the intrigues of his opponents and was executed in Kolossai (Xenophon, *HG* 3, 4, 24f.).

Agesilaos then marched through the land of Pharnabazos, the satrap of Daskyleion, who fearfully avoided a battle with him. Spithridates, a Persian general who had already fought against Xenophon's Ten Thousand, came into his camp and persuaded him to march toward Paphlagonia, to make its people secede. Agesilaos gave Spithridates's beautiful daughter—he himself cast an eye on the equally handsome son Megabates—to the Paphlagonian dynast, Kotys (Xenophon, *HG* 4, 1, 3 Otys) in marriage, to reinforce his troops with the latter's horsemen and shield bearers. On their return from Paphlagonia the Spartans enjoyed themselves in the hunting and fishing grounds of the satrap's residence in Daskyleion. A careless foraging brigade was attacked by Pharnabazos's cavalry and put to flight. In retaliation, the Greeks invaded the satrap's camp and took rich booty, but the conflicts over its division were so violent that Spithridates and the Paphlagonians went over to the Persian side. A Kyzikene mediator arranged a meeting between Agesilaos and the satrap: the Persian came with his entourage and with pillows and carpets, while the Spartan waited for him sitting on the grass. At the end of the discussion Agesilaos is supposed to have announced that he would withdraw from the country—which he did, in view of the situation in Greece (Xenophon, *HG* 4, 1, 38).

Before and after the battle at the Paktolos River the Lacedaemonians suffered defeats on the southern and western coasts of Asia Minor. The Persian naval formations in the eastern Mediterranean were under the command of a man from Athens who at the end of the Peloponnesian War had fled to Cyprus and entered the service of Persia: Konon, "the Great King's Instrument."[8] After the Spartans had been driven out of Rhodes, and Damagetos, the king of Ialysos, had been murdered, Konon took a position on the island and traveled back and forth between Rhodes and the mainland on several occasions. A Lacedaemonian attack on Kaunos was repelled (396 BCE). Only two years later he had his greatest success in the historically important naval battle near Knidos; it was the decisive victory over Sparta. He was awarded the highest honors. Erythrai made him an honorary citizen and put up a gilt bronze statue of him in the city. In the central shrine of the Carian city of Kaunos, his statue was set on a marble base bearing an inscription in Greek. The Athenians erected his statue and that of his friend Euagoras in the Agora; the Ephesians put his statue in the Artemision, and the Samians in the Heraion.

A chill was thus cast on Spartan ambitions with regard to the Greek cities in Asia. A new satrap, Tiribazos, moved into Tissaphernes's residence in Sardeis. At the peace negotiations held there, Tiribazos initially failed to convince the Greeks in the homeland to sacrifice their relatives in Asia, a step the Spartans were now prepared to take, but which the Athenians absolutely rejected. Konon, who in the meantime had been agitating against Sparta in his home town of Athens, with Persian support, accompanied a four-man delegation of his compatriots to Asia (Xenophon, *HG* 4, 8, 12 f.). There Tiribazos, who was favorable to Sparta, had the prominent Athenian arrested on pretexts. Konon died in Cyprus during his escape. Meanwhile, Tiribazos was recalled by the great king (autumn of 392). The latter appointed Struthas as the new satrap of Ionia, which had up to that point been co-administered by Tiribazos. Struthas changed the policy, favoring the Athenians again. A Spartan advance toward Ionia ended with a painful defeat in the valley of the Maeander. The Athenian Thrasybulos showed his abilities as a "new Konon" by carrying out successful naval operations all along the western and southern coasts between Byzantion and Aspendos. Extensive plundering of cities that did not obey him in every respect was part of the logistics of his way of waging war. The furious Aspendians attacked his camp and killed him.

The tables were turned on the Asiatic Greeks once again when Struthas was recalled and Tiribazos reappointed. With the latter's agreement, the Spartan Antialkidas now finally prevailed after he had negotiated an agreement with the great king in Susa. Xenophon (*HG* 5, 1, 31) tells us that at the decisive meeting in Sardeis in 387/386 BCE it was announced that

> King Artaxerxes thinks it just that the cities in Asia should belong to him, as well as Clazomenae and Cyprus among the islands, and that the other Greek cities, both small and great, should be left independent, except Lemnos, Imbros, and Scyros; and these should belong, as of old, to the Athenians. But whichever of the two parties does not accept this peace, upon them I will make war, in company with those who desire this arrangement, both by land and by sea, with ships and with money. (Trans. Brownson)

Historians commonly call this treaty the "King's Peace" or "Antialkidas's Peace."

This put an end to a struggle that see-sawed back and forth both in diplomacy and on the battlefield that was fought in Asia over the shattered Athenian empire after the defeat in the Peloponnesian War (404 BCE). For the countries of western and southern Asia Minor, the Persian Wars and the following decades-long period of Athenian supremacy had meant more than a temporary change in rulers. The inhabitants—even those who had no close connections with the victors—had been deeply marked by the gigantic triumph of the united mother country and by the opposition, deliberately stylized for the first time, between Hellenes and barbarians. In particular, in the *poleis* of Asia Minor and their hinterlands, the powerful Athenians had provided the model for constitutions, institutions, and mores, for Hellenic art and literature, and for Hellenic language and ways of writing. The Hellenization of the Lydians, Carians, and Lycians now really began.

However, in their political and military collaboration against the great power Persia, the Greeks of Asia and the mother country did not provide an edifying model. The Greek antithesis between freedom and slavery, in accord with which this conflict has still been conceived in modern historical works, does not correspond to reality: the Greeks enslaved one another. Power struggles within the *poleis* and among them too often impeded common actions. The fates of prominent individuals—such as Histiaios and Aristagoras of Miletus; Dionysios of Phokaia; Alkibiades, Konon, and Thrasybulos of Athens—mirror the internal conflicts among the Greeks in which powerful actors fell into freebooting private wars and also sometimes changed sides. Since the days when the Greeks raided the coasts of the Assyrian Empire, the seafaring nobility seems never to have lost a certain corsair mentality. Thus many a city on the coast of Asia Minor settled by Greeks, natives, or a mixture of the two must have preferred the satraps' government in their own country to the violence, plundering, and occupations of "liberators" from Greece. But the idea of resuming the war against the Persian Empire and "liberating" the *poleis* in Asia continued to be harbored in Greece until another man translated it into action a little more than half a century later.

The Satraps' Revolt

After the King's Peace, the most decisive event for all of Asia Minor is the so-called Satraps' Revolt that began ca. 368 BCE and ended ca. 362. Our knowledge of the details of this event remains sketchy, however, and the sources seem to exaggerate the dimensions of the revolt insofar as they suggest that there was concerted action, whereas on closer inspection we see that particular, distinct, and only sporadically related rebellions took place at different times. The two main sources are Cornelius Nepos's *vita* of the satrap Datames and a passage in Diodorus (15, 90, 1–3). The person who initiated the open revolt against the great king was a colorful figure, Datames: his father was a Carian or an Iranian living in Caria, and his mother was a Paphlagonian. As young man he initially served in the great king's palace guard and was then granted as a fief the part of Cilicia bordering on Cappadocia. From this base he pursued activities over a broad surrounding area. The sequence of events, which is difficult to date in detail, took place between ca. 390 and 360 BCE. While Datames was conducting campaigns against Thys, the rebellious dynast of the Paphlagonians, during which he took the city of Sinope in his vicinity, and another victorious campaign against Aspis, the dynast of Kataonia, his opponents plotted against him and aroused suspicions about him at the court in Susa. Thereupon he broke with the great king and formed a secret alliance with Ariobarzanes, who had been ruling as satrap of Phrygia in Daskyleion since 387 BCE. A second attack on Sinope was launched.

Reliefs on the Nemrud Dağ representing the Persian ancestors of King Antiochus of Commagene (first century BCE) show a man whom the inscriptions on the base call "Aroandes, son of Artasuras, married to Princess Rhodogune, the daughter of Artaxerxes."[9] We know this Aroandes or Orontes from Xenophon's *Anabasis* as the satrap of Armenia at the time of the March of the Ten Thousand. Another Orontes who later ruled the coastal satrapy of Mysia (Diodorus 15, 90, 3) and is supposed to have resided on the acropolis of Pergamon—this satrapy was newly formed in place of Yauna (with Magnesia on the Maeander as the satrap's residence)—is probably the same man. He also broke with the great king and put himself at the head of the rebellion. In contrast, the satrap of Sardeis, Autophradates, and the powerful prince Maussollos, who had ruled in Caria since 377, seem to have been hardly more than sympathizers and usufructuaries.

Orontes quickly switched sides: the great king promised the Armenian satrap the new satrapy on the west coast and in this way obtained the delivery of money, cities, and soldiers. The allies Datames and Ariobarzanes now stood alone. Datames defended his position at the Cilician Gates and in Cappadocia with great skill when the central power sent troops against him under Autophradates and then Artabazos. He was finally brought down by assassination. Ariobarzanes was also killed. The king pardoned all the rest. A few years later Orontes rebelled against the succeeding great king, Artaxerxes III (see [106] OGIS 264a) and was engaged in battle by Autophradates (Polyainos 7, 14, 2–4), but once again he yielded and retained his position in Pergamon.

Age of the Persians in Asia Minor

The structure and nature of Persian rule in Asia Minor shaped the country and founded a tradition that remained influential long after the Achaemenid Empire ceased to exist. A great diaspora of Iranians took up residence in the land, and they are mentioned in the written sources down into the time of the Roman Empire.[10] Aramaic was written in the chancelleries of the satrapies. However, in the fifth century BCE Greek was already gaining ground, and not only as a literary language: educated Lycians, Carians, and Lydians wrote Greek, for instance, the epic poet Panyassis of Halikarnassos and the historian Xanthos the Lydian, as well as the Lycian dynasts Xeriga and Arbinas. In the fourth century BCE, under the Carians Maussollos and Pixodaros, Greek became the official common language, used in preference to the local languages.[11] The municipal decree from the Letoon of Xanthos regarding the establishment of a state cult is written in three languages: the translation in Imperial Aramaic, which omits certain details, ends with the satrap's authorization. This language represents Persian sovereignty. However, the Greek in the parallel version of the Lycian actually has the function of a *lingua franca* that is prevalent far beyond the domain of the local language.

Long before the Greeks and Romans undertook to bring such enormous areas under their supervision, to develop them and manage their resources, the Iranians had created an administration and infrastructure in Asia Minor and set up a system of relationships of loyalty and possession that served as a guide down into the Hellenistic and Roman periods. In the early Roman Empire Persian measures of distance, *schoinos* or *parasang*, were still used in Pisidia.[12] Persian authority allowed the peoples, tribes, and cities of Asia Minor to retain much of their independence in matters of religion, economics, and politics. Setting aside the harsh measures taken against rebellions, there were no mass deportations, such as those that occurred under the Assyrians. The social structures in the regions remained intact, and the local religions were more encouraged than oppressed. It is true that Greek influence grew steadily greater in the arts and crafts, but it was mixed with local and Persian influences. In the spiritual domain, Zarathustrian ideas may have been transmitted to the Greeks, especially through the influence of Iranian *magoi* (p. 163) in the West.

The Satrapy System

The old way of supervising and administering conquered territories, which was already usual before the reign of Darius, consisted of establishing a kind of subordinate king over regions that were in some cases enormously large. In Old Persian, the word for this official is *xšaçapāvā*, meaning "protector of sovereignty." But the Greek word *satrapes* (first attested in Isokrates, whereas the word referring to a satrap's domain of sovereignty, *satrapeie*, is already found in Herodotus) has no direct etymological link to the term *xšaçapāvā*; a Median form may stand behind it that was itself transmitted to Greek via a language of Asia Minor.[13] Satraps are also occasionally designated by other expressions, such as the Greek *hyparchos* or *χñtawata* (king) in Lycian texts.[14] A chronological table of the names of satraps known to scholarship up to now is given in the Appendix.

Scholarly disagreements regarding the question of what the empire's satrapy system was like in the time of the Persians are rife; almost everything is in dispute. We do not have a single original list of satrapies dating from the Achaemenid epoch. The provenance and composition of Herodotus's (3, 89–97) list of twenty *archai* or *nomoi*—administrative districts—"which the Persians called 'satrapies'" and in which several neighboring tribes were included, remains controversial, and there is no general agreement that the "countries" or "peoples" mentioned in Darius's great rock inscription at Behistun and in other inscriptions correspond to satrapies. They do not, however, coincide exactly with Herodotus's list. The solution that consists in "rejecting Herodotus as a historical source"[15] is too simple. We need not pursue the question further here; we will limit our discussion to statements concerning Asia Minor.[16] In the Behistun inscription Asia Minor is represented only by Sparda (Lydia), Yauna (Ionia), Katpatuka (northern and central Anatolia), and Armina (earlier Urartu). In the case of Yauna, the inscriptions on the south façade of the Persepolis terrace, from the tomb of Darius in Naqš-i-Rustem, and from Susa distinguish among the Ionians of the plain, of the coast, and of the islands (or "shield-bearing" Ionians) and also mention the Carians. Recently, the question has been raised whether the people of Skudra mentioned in the inscriptions from Persepolis and Susa at the time of Darius I should be sought in Asia Minor, but sufficient proof of this has not been given.[17]

Herodotus (3, 90–94) includes in the first satrapy peoples of western and southwestern Anatolia: Ionians, Magnesians of Asia, Aiolians, Carians, Lycians, Milyans,[18] and Pamphylians. They paid a tribute of 400 talents of silver. The second satrapy includes the Mysians, Lydians, Lasonians, Cabalians,[19] and Hytennians (in southern Pisidia, between Lake Beyşehir and the coast). Tribute: 500 talents. In the third satrapy were combined the Hellespontians, Phrygians, Thracians, Paphlagonians, Mariandynoi,[20] and Syrians.[21] Tribute: 360 talents. The fourth satrapy consisted solely of the Cilicians, who paid a tribute of 500 talents and 360 horses. In the thirteenth satrapy were the Armenians and their neighbors as far as Pontos Euxeinos; their relation to the Alarodians around Lake Van mentioned in the eighteenth satrapy is not entirely clear. The nineteenth satrapy consisted of the northwestern neighbors of the Armenians, the mountain tribes above Trapezus: the Moschoi, Tibarenoi, Makrones, Mossynoikoi, and Mardians; they paid 300 talents in tribute.

Comparisons can be drawn not only with the previously mentioned Persian versions of the names of peoples or countries in inscriptions on stone but also with particular statements on clay tablets from Persepolis written between 509 and 494 BCE. These texts refer to persons who had been granted royal permission to use Persian imperial roads and stations (a kind of predecessor of the Roman *cursus publicus*, p. 380 f.). For example, a certain Dauma, traveling on an official mission from Sardeis to Persepolis, is mentioned in the Persepolis Fortification Tablet (PF) 1404.[22] He is said to have been carrying a sealed document from Irdapirna. The latter's name corresponds to the Greek Artaphernes and probably refers to the well-known stepbrother of Darius and satrap of Sardeis (Herodotus 5, 25, 1).

It is certain that during the two centuries of Persian rule over Asia Minor expansions, divisions and realignments of satrapies took place. We will not discuss them in detail here.[23] Because of its location, Sardeis (Sparda) was probably of preeminent importance, and at the end of the fifth century it was the headquarters of the *karanos* (supreme commander), whom the great king had endowed with special responsibilities for large parts of western and central Anatolia. In the fourth century BCE the satrapy of Caria had been ruled from Halikarnassos since the days of Maussollos. Cilicia was a satrapy with its seat in Tarsos. Cappadocia was divided into a southern part near the Taurus Mountains and a northern part on the Black Sea. A satrap in Kelainai (near Dinar) ruled over Greater Phrygia, whereas Hellespontic or Lesser Phrygia was ruled from Daskyleion.

The sources mention both Iranian and non-Iranian officials who performed various tasks under the satraps. Toward the end of the fifth century, the satrap of Sardeis probably had Lycia governed by two commanders, Artembares and Mithrapates, and when in the fourth century Pixodaros became the satrap of Lycia (p. 157), he appointed two Greeks as *archontes* (commissioners) of the country and a Lycian as the overseer of Xanthos. The Greek titles of these rulers are used in an ambivalent way, and the details of the hierarchies are not always clear. However, primarily native dynasts often ruled vast regions under Persian supervision, and on the coasts Greek tyrants were in command of one or several cities. Their loyalty was manifested in certain duties and ceremonies; there was a close personal connection with the satraps. Women could also hold such positions. A clear example of this is found in Xenophon (*HG* 3, 1, 10 ff.): the story of the Greek woman Mania. She had married Zenis of Dardanos, and after his death the satrap Pharnabazos recognized her as regent over parts of Aiolis. Like her late husband, she was allowed to exploit the area's resources and to generate her own revenues, and she enjoyed the satrap's trust and protection. In return, the satrap expected the punctual payment of levies, the presentation of gifts, special deference, and a ceremonial reception when he visited. When the satrap went on campaign against rebellious tribes in the interior, Mania had to provide soldiers, but she also undertook independent military operations against coastal cities that had not yet been subjected (Larisa, Hamaxitos, and Kolonai) to bring them under the satrap's control. This example of loyal vassalage contrasts with others that show disloyalty and betrayal. Atarneus, not far from Mania's domicile, was later ruled by the notorious tyrant Hermeias, who had studied with Plato alongside Aristotle, whom he brought to his court and to whom he gave his niece Pythias in marriage. His conspiratorial relationship with Philip II of Macedonia aroused suspicions, and he was arrested and executed.[24]

Persian rule characteristically varied in intensity depending on the time and place. Such peoples as the Thynians, Bebryces, Mariandynoi, Caucones, and Paphlagonian Henetoi (Strabo 12, 3, 3 ff.) served in the cavalry units. Mountain peoples in eastern Pontos, such as the Moschoi, Mossynoikoi, Chalybes, Makrones, and Sannoi for the most part escaped the control of the great power, but others, dynasts and cities, also occasionally tried to do the same. Some cities were allowed to stipulate alliances with one another. In the middle of the fourth century the Ionians revived their old alliance (Strabo 8,7, 2). A stone found in Sinope a few years ago contains a record in Greek of a treaty of alliance between this city and the family of the tyrants of Herakleia Pontike. The parties to the treaty committed themselves to support one another against aggressors by sending an army to help the party under attack. However, an exception was made in the event that the great king himself attacked one of the cities. If someone attacked in the name of the king, the symmachy came into force if the attacker refused to send a common delegation to the great king and to leave the territory until a decision was handed down from the highest authority. The Sinopians' experiences with Datames's unauthorized attacks on their city may have been the basis for this arrangement. In any case, the fact that the great king allowed such alliances represents a remarkable concession on his part with regard to the communities under his rule. Later on, the Romans did not allow any comparable treaties among free cities in their Anatolian provinces. One more detail deserves to be noted: the alliance also covered attacks from within; in Herakleia this was synonymous with an attempt to overthrow the tyrants' rule, but in Sinope it meant the dissolution of the people (the *katalysis* of the *demos*). The wording suggests that in the Sinope of that time there can have been nothing other than a democracy.

The political relations in the Lycia of the Persian era have been most fully investigated, because in this case the literary sources can be connected with relatively rich epigraphic sources, coins, and archaeological discoveries. For the minting of coins by the dynasts, a hoard buried in the fourth century and discovered in 1957 on the banks of the Avlan Gölü is of special importance.[25] The Athenian Isocrates thinks (4, 161 f.) that the Persians had never ruled Lycia. A prince named Kuprlli had played a supraregional role between 485 and 440,[26] but since the end of the fifth century local rulers had competed in various parts of the country: in the far west on the Gulf of Fethiye (Telmessos); in the valley of the Xanthos (Patara, Xanthos, Pinara, and Tlos), where the descendants of Harpagos, Xeriga, Xerēi, and Erbbina ruled; in the central area in Tymnessos, Kandyba, Phellos, Zagaba and Myra; and in the east in Limyra (Lycian: Zemuri, which may be identical with Zumarri, already existent in the Hittite age), Rhodiapolis, and Korydalla.[27] Around 380 BCE a χñtawata (king) appeared in Zemuri who bore the same name as the fifth-century Athenian statesman Perikles. He got involved in conflicts with the Iranian commanders over his land, was able to repel an attack by the west Lycian dynast Artembares (who obeyed the Persians), and on his campaigns expanded his domain as far as Telmessos in the west. Dynasts who had risen to prominence in this way were naturally dangerous, threatening to outshine the Iranian representatives of the great king's power in Asia Minor.

The best-known example of a native dynasty that ruled for an extended period of time is that of the Hekatomnids in neighboring Caria (see also p. 166).[28] The country is named as a unit "Karka" in Persian sources as early as the tomb of Darius in Naqš-i-Rustem. The Hekatomnid's capital was Mylasa (Milas), where they resided in castles. The patriarch Hyssaldomos was succeeded by his son Hekatomnos (392/391–377/376 BCE). The latter's five children replaced one another. First came Maussollos (377/376–353/352) and his wife and sister Artemisia (353/352–351/350), Idrieus (351/350–344/343) and his wife and sister Ada (344/343–341/340), followed by Pixodaros (341/340–336/335), who married a Cappadocian princess named Aphneis, and then his daughter Ada (the Younger) and her husband the Iranian Orontobates (336/335–334), whom Alexander the Great replaced by the elder Ada, Maussollos's sister. Pixodaros officially bore the title of satrap. According to Greek inscriptions from Mylasa, Hekatomnos and Maussollos already bore this title, but modern research suggests that the Hekatomnids who preceded Pixodaros were not satraps. The outstanding figure in this family history is Maussollos. Diodorus calls him a "dynast," while later writers, including Strabo, call him a "king." At a time when Pericles has disappeared from our records, Maussollos extended his rule to parts or even to the whole of Lycia, and research on the country considers this the end of the "Dynastic Period" and the beginning of the "Carian domination" that lasted until Alexander's arrival. After Pericles's reign there was no longer any Lycian dynastic coinage. The Carian Maussollos introduced Greek institutions and communicated in the Greeks' diplomatic forms: thus he granted *proxenia* (a distinction awarded foreigners comparable to honorary citizenship) to members of the Cretan community of Knossos, presumably a troop of mercenaries in his service. Before 362

BCE he moved his capital from Mylasa to the coast—to Halikarnassos—expanded the city, and hired Greek artists and architects.

The Royal Road

Since the loyalty of the various ethnic groups and individual regents of Anatolia with regard to the central power was constantly being put to the test, much depended on the efficient and rapid transmission of information between the Persian authorities and the distant parts of the empire in the west. The supposed route of the Royal Road from Sardeis to Susa, which was nearly 3,000 kilometers long and only part of a ramified road system in the whole empire, has been thoroughly investigated. Indeed, a precise knowledge of its exact route would provide information concerning the oldest known long-distance communication network across the whole Anatolian land bridge. To form an idea of it, we have to draw once again on the historian Herodotus of Halikarnassos (5, 52 f.), who seems to be using an official document. He speaks of 111 stations over a total distance of 450 parasangs. In addition to the number of days' march and measures of distance within each segment of the route, his description gives as a geographic reference system only the names of countries—Lydia, Phrygia, Cappadocia, Cilicia, and Armenia—and also mentions two river crossings, the Halys and the Euphrates. The measurements in parasangs (5–6 kilometers) do not allow us to calculate any precise distances, and the figures provided in Herodotus's text are probably corrupt in more than one passage. The sums of the individually named stations and the distances between them do not correspond to the overall figures: they fall thirty stations and 137 parasangs short.

Various routes between Sardeis and the valley of the Tigris are up for discussion (Map 7). Because of the crossing of the Halys, the road must have passed north of Lake Tuz. Afterward it ran through "Cappadocia" and "Cilicia" to the Euphrates. But what precisely does that mean? Did it negotiate the "Cilician Gates," cross the plains near Tarsos, climb over the Amanos, and reach the Euphrates near Zeugma, and then push on beyond the river, across the plains of northern Mesopotamia toward the Tigris? Or did it continue from Cappadocia on the plateau, presumably following the Assyrians' old trade route to Kārum Kaneš, leading down to the plains of Melitene, crossing the Euphrates near Tomisa, and finally reaching the Tigris near Amida (Diyarbakır)? If we prefer the latter route, that amounts to expanding Herodotus's geographical concept of "Cilicia" to include the country northeast of the Cilician Gates. The fact that Herodotus positions the border between "Cilicia" and "Armenia" at the passage over the Euphrates speaks against the alternative. However, the area of northern Mesopotamia between Zeugma and Nisibis was never called "Armenia."[29] Fundamental uncertainties prevent us from going into further detail regarding individual sections of the road. For instance, it is not at all certain that Persian emissaries must have traveled through cities such as Gordion and old central places such as Ḫattusa, or even past important religious sites such as the rock monuments of Midas City.

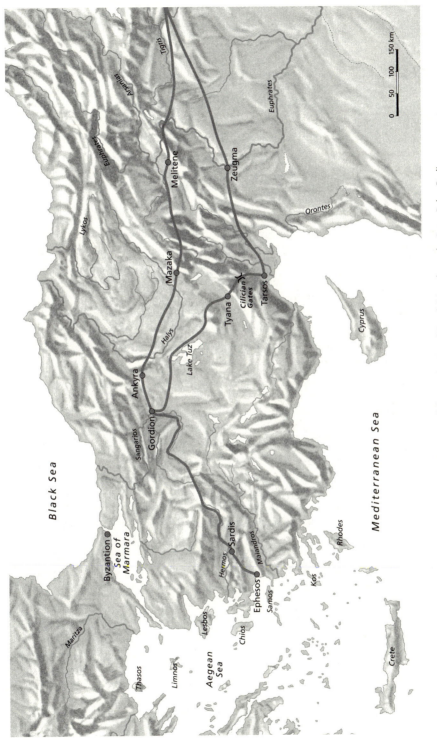

Map 7. Possible approximate routes of the Persian Royal Road. Map drawn by Peter Palm, Berlin.

Land Ownership and Tribute

The land the Persians conquered in Asia Minor was divided up among various owners, some of whom had to pay tribute, while others did not.[30] Opinions vary regarding the structure of ownership.[31] The problem is conveyed in a single text, Darius's
letter to the satrap Gadatas, but the authenticity of this document is in doubt.[32] The
king confirms that the priests ("sacred gardeners") of a shrine to Apollo are allowed
to draw revenues from a district but also speaks of "my land." What does he mean by
that? A modern theory assumes that all land—that is, all of Asia Minor—was the
great king's possession. Persian nobles, native priests, kings, dynasts, tyrants, and
tribal or municipal communities were simply allowed to receive the revenues and
had to pay the tribute, but the king could have intervened in this possession at any
time to grant it in fief to other favorites, foreign or Iranian. Cyrus had already given
seven cities to Pytharchos of Kyzikos, his liegeman. A prominent recipient of a *dorea*
(gift) of several cities was Themistokles, the victor of Salamis who was later banned
from Athens, fled to the Persians, and took up residence in Magnesia on the Maeander.[33] This has been interpreted as a kind of appanage system that probably was
stepped further down according to relationships on a regional and local basis. Recall
similar feudal relationships under the name of *isḫiul* among the Hittites (p. 78).

In contrast, there is the view that the Persians respected the land ownership of
local subjects. The great king is supposed to have not been the owner of all the land,
and the expression "my land" in Darius's letter would refer to the—numerous—seigneuries and estates that had passed into the personal possession of his predecessors
or himself through conquest or confiscation. *Doreai* (gifts) to favorites of all kinds
are assumed to have been taken solely from this personal property. Only these lands
were free of tribute.[34] The beneficiary could derive his own income from agriculture,
fishing, hunting, logging, and crafts. Tribute had to be paid on all other land.

Which of the two models is the right one is difficult to determine. In this case,
the difference is, however, largely theoretical. Whether exemption from paying tribute resulted from the fact that the king's land was once given to the local god Apollo,
or whether the district had always remained in the possession of the god and as such
was privileged, amounts here to much the same thing.

The problem proves to be especially in need of solution with regard to the Greek
poleis, since the theory of a royal claim to own the whole of Asia Minor is not in accord with the classic Greek conception of the autonomy of the *polis*. Regarding their
integration into the king's realm, the Greek *poleis* under the Persians were doubtless
not an exception—in contrast to the situation later under the Diadochi and Epigones. They had no legal claim to *chora* (territory) of their own. The distinctions between *poleis* and *chora basileos* (royal land) made by Greek historians do not represent the Achaemenids' conception of their empire, and statements reflecting the
latter's view of things are perfectly clear.[35] Herodotus (6, 42, 2) reports that in
493/492 BCE the satrap Artaphernes had the territories of the Ionian *poleis* measured to assess their tribute on that basis. That would mean that in the satraps' chan-

celleries there were cadastres that provided an individual basis for assessing local taxes.

The author of the pseudo-Aristotelian *Oikonomika*, who wrote in the Persian epoch, sketched out six categories of revenue source in the satraps' administration. The first and by far the most important and largest is the levy on agricultural products, the tithe or *ekphorion*. The second is the income from specific mineral resources: gold, silver, copper, and so forth. The third consists of the revenues from the *emporia* (exchange of goods), market taxes, custom duties, and tolls. The fourth is real estate and sales taxes. The fifth is taxes on livestock. The sixth includes all other kinds of revenue.[36] Up to this point, the most precise specification of individual levies in pre-Roman Asia Minor is provided by a document from Aigai in Aiolis that very probably dates from the time of the Persians.[37] Individuals who "take" and "give" are named in the singular and in the plural. Persons performing unpaid horse and cart work and other compulsory manual labor (or their slaves) were to be fed at the king's expense. High up on the list of what was "taken" was the tithe—apparently paid in grain. The levy amounted to one-eighth of the harvest of fruit and probably also grape vines, two of every hundred sheep and goats, along with a lamb and a goat kid, and one-eighth of the beehives. Of every wild boar and deer taken by hunting, one haunch had to be handed over. The "taker" was undoubtedly a royal official collecting taxes locally.

Minting Coins

In the sixth century BCE the Persian kings had already become acquainted with the Lydian-Ionian practice of minting coins and imitated it, using Lydian die-cutters. The silver and gold coins minted under Darius (*darics*) bear on the obverse full- or half-body images of the king with a bow; in contrast to Greek coins, on the reverse there is only a mark. Sardeis was probably the city where *darics* were minted. Under the Achaemenids, the Greek *poleis* independently minted their own coins.[38] However, in the Persian Empire the mintage of coins remained limited to western regions most proximate to Greek influences. In addition to the numerous dynasts, like Perikles or Maussollos (p. 157), individual satraps issued their own silver coins bearing images of the gods, portraits, or figures on the obverse. It is questionable, however, whether the persons represented with Persian headdress or attire represent these rulers themselves. On the reverse we find, alongside images of Persian, local, or Greek divinities and heroes, mixed motifs of Greco-Persian or local provenance as well as legends in Lycian, Greek, and Aramaic.[39]

Minted gold or silver was probably accumulated primarily for deposit in temples and in hoards at the residences of the satraps. It is difficult to form an idea of how it circulated as a means of payment. At the lowest level of the system of tribute, payments made by local peasants to landowners were probably in kind, not in money. According to Pseudo-Aristotle (*Oec.* 2, 2-1345 b 21), the coin (*nomisma*) is classified as one of four areas of the royal *oikonomia*, the other three being imports, exports (as sources of revenue), and expenditures. In addition to "small change" in the municipal domain, exchange in currency seems to have extended especially to borrowing from temples by notables, composition payments to the king, or royal donations to courtiers and favorites of all kinds, as well as to cities, and certainly also to the costs of hiring and paying soldiers.[40]

Religion, Art, and Culture

The historian Eduard Meyer attests to religious tolerance to the Persians: "'Everywhere, they tried to base their rule on the religion of their subjects, and made extensive concessions to it and to its representatives, the priests.'"[41] On closer inspection, a mixed picture emerges in Asia Minor. Xerxes destroyed all the temples in Ionia with the exception of the prominent Artemision in Ephesos. It enjoyed special protection after the Ephesians gave the priest an Iranian title as a sign of their bond: "Megabyxos." In this title we can recognize the Iranian word *bagabuxša*, which means "freed by God" or "pleasing God."

The conquerors brought their religion and their gods with them when they entered the country; Zoroastrianism goes back to the founder of a dualistic doctrine of Good and Evil, the Iranian Zarathustra, whose dates are hard to determine, but who in any case lived before the fifth century BCE. In the rock inscription at Behistun, Darius I refers to the Zoroastrian supreme god Ahura Mazdā. Another very ancient divinity named Mithras—in Persian, this name means "covenant"—was also worshipped by the Achaemenids and was widely revered as a sun-god in the Hellenistic and Roman periods.[42] In Asia Minor, Iranians also sacrificed to the gods traditionally worshipped in the given locality. The immigrants seem to have shown particular interest in Greek or local divinities called Zeus, Artemis, and Men, who most closely resembled their gods Ahura Mazdā, Anāhitā, and Māh, respectively.[43] In several places in Lydia—Hierakome, Hypaipa, and Philadelpheia—we find in the postclassical period shrines to a Persian Artemis, to whom sacred competitions were dedicated in the Roman Imperial period, and these shrines were of more than just regional importance.[44] An Iranian named Baradates founded the cult of a god who was equated with Zeus and worshipped as "Baradates's Zeus" by the satraps in Sardeis during the fifth or fourth centuries BCE. Similarly, a "Pharnakes's Men" presumably goes back to the foundation of a cult by a satrap of the same name residing in Daskyleion toward the end of the fifth century BCE. In 321 BCE, at the suggestion of the satrap Asandros, an Iranian named Bagadates was made *neokoros* (temple guardian) of the local shrine to Artemis in Amyzon in Caria.[45] We will return to the Iranian shrines in Pontos in Chapter 6. In all these cases a syncretic combination of imported religious ideas with related native or Greek ones could easily have taken place. Nevertheless, in the Baradates inscription in Sardeis, the satrap forbade temple servants entering the shrine to take part in the mysteries of Sabazios, Angdistis, and Ma, because in doing so they would pollute themselves. Thus from an Iranian point of view, the attitude toward the native cults was not a matter of complete indifference.

The Iranians' religion not only established itself with shrines in Anatolia but also exercised influence on the Greeks via Asia Minor. The routes and processes of change through which this body of ideas was transmitted are not easy to grasp in the literary tradition. It has been noted that the idea of the soul (*psyche*) that "goes to heaven" after a human's death, and may even gradually rise to the stars, then the moon, the sun, and finally the eternal lights, the seat of Ahura Mazdā, must underlie Anaximandros of Miletus's model of the heavenly wheels, and that in fact the soul's ascent to heaven became part of the Greeks' conception of the beyond as early as the fifth century. The Lycian composite creatures represented on the pillar tomb in Xanthos, winged women who are flying away with small children in their arms (wrongly described as "harpies" by Charles Fellows) appear to indicate this. In addition, Walter Burkert pointed to the important role played by the *magoi*.[46] The Iranian word *maguš*, which was incorporated into several ancient languages as a loanword, probably designates high-ranking priest-theologians. In the Greek sources we find another meaning that refers to itinerant specialists, conjurors, healers, and magicians. The Zoroastrians' well-known burial ritual, which involved exposing the corpse on elevated surfaces, can be proven to have been practiced only in a very small number of places in Asia Minor.[47]

In the remains of the ancient architecture and art of Asia Minor in the Persian period, traces of Persian dominance are mixed with the native tradition and Greek influence. It is characteristic of Persian rule, which in some ways resembled feudal structures, that we have testimonies through representational art chiefly from the seats of the satraps and dynasts down to the local nobility, though they are rather scarce and not well preserved. When images and figures show Persian ceremonies, Persian clothing, or Persian objects, this does not exclude the possibility that they were made by Greek or Lydian craftsmen. It is difficult to locate purely Persian elements in the art and crafts of Anatolia. Thus we are concerned not with Persian art, but rather with certain aspects of artistic works in the Asia Minor of the fifth and fourth centuries BCE. In addition, the small number of testimonies in the epichoric languages of Asia Minor have to be understood in their regional, cultural context.

Let us look first at the northern regions. The so-called Greco-Persian relief steles with Aramaic inscriptions are prominent among the discoveries at Daskyleion.[48] They were also found in Sinope and in the interior of Paphlagonia.[49] The multi-tiered steles structured by several "registers" represent individual scenes from the lives of the deceased. The clothing and objects are Persian or oriental, but there are also elements of Greek style. This also holds for the stele found in the valley of the Kaystros (Küçük Menderes) that has a Lydian inscription in which the dating in accord with a king Artaxerxes and the reference to a satrap named Rasakaś (Rhoisakes?) point to the year 342/341 BCE; beneath the anthemion decoration with volutes and palmettos also found on other Lydian funeral monuments, we see, in a single image field a sitting woman and a boy who is handing her an object; they are dressed in native garb.

Moving from the places settled by Greeks on the south coast of the Black Sea to the interior of the country, discoveries of pottery and the natives' use of Greek-type roof tiles in the region of the Cappadocian coast provide archaeological proof of cultural exchange as early as the late archaic period.[50] The Paphlagonian rock-cut tombs in the gorges of the Halys, Amnias, and Billaios river valleys are noteworthy.[51] The Paphlagonian type (which is also found outside Paphlagonia) is defined by spaces cut entirely from the rock, with one or more burial chambers behind an open antechamber ornamented with pillars. The bases of these pillars, decorated with *tori* (stone beading) are typical. They are found not only cut into the rock but also separately, as the remains of large structures from the Persian period. Cubical or rectangular capitals top the massive, unfluted pillars. The burial chambers in the rear—sometimes with imitations in stone of lantern or tent roofs—are placed parallel to one another or in a cloverlike arrangement around the antechamber. House forms with gables, roof beams, and cornices point to a native tradition of construction in wood that is imitated in the rock art, as in Lycia. At the same time, the influence of Greek temples is noticeable in the tomb façades with more than two pillars.

No doubt the most representative complexes in all of Paphlagonia are the tombs near Salarköy and Donalarköy in the valley of the Amnias. Both of them combined in their architecture and their pictorial decoration elements from various traditions—native, Phrygian, Persian, and Greek. At the rock-cut tomb at Donalar, "Kalekapı," the outline of a house-shaped façade with a gabled roof seventeen meters high and fifteen meters wide is cut into the smoothed rock (Figure 35). On both sides of and above the opening to the antechamber there are flat reliefs of exceptional quality that once again point to models taken from both Greek and Persian art. On the lowest level, to the right and left of the opening, are three framed reliefs clearly distinguished from the others, cut free from the surface: on the left is a charging bull, on the right a crouching lion, and under the lion a remarkable "unicorn." The latter—unique in visual art of antiquity—is either a mythical creature (cf. Ktesias, FGrHist 688 F 45 f.; Pliny the Elder, nat. 8, 76) or a failed attempt to represent a rhinoceros. In the pendentive under the peak of the gable an eagle spreads its wings, while under it two panthers lunge at each other. Below the two animal figures is another relief of approximately the same size whose left half has been largely destroyed, but in the right half the hindquarters of a lion can be clearly discerned. To judge by the contours, the naked hero might be represented here (as at Salarköy) wrestling down a lion. Together with the two enormous horned and winged lions on each side of the battle scene, the upper image group has a function closely related to that of the *potnia theron* motif (the representation of a goddess of animals): the animals surrounding the tomb should be understood as its guardians. In the same way, the lion sculptures found in great numbers in Paphlagonia guard tumulus graves.

Rock-cut tombs from the Persian period are rare in western Anatolia. The so-called stone tower (*taş kule*) near Phokaia (Foca), which has been dated to the sixth century BCE (though this has been challenged) is enigmatic. The upper part of this massive rock monument, with its cubical block on a tiered platform, faintly recalls

35. Rock-cut tomb near Donalar-Suleymanköy.

the shape of Cyrus's tomb in Pasargardae. Otherwise, the few simple examples of rock-cut tombs on the Paktolos River near Sardeis have no comparable architectonic elements. The chambers in tumuli familiar from old Anatolian cultures contain the burial places of notables and members of dynasts' families. Intact discoveries of their interior furnishings are valuable rarities: princely representational art in the otherwise largely lost genre of wall painting has been found in only a few places. For example, there are very well-preserved fifth-century frescos in the grave of a noble in Elmalı (Karaburun II, northern Lycia); a painting on the north wall of the burial chamber built of large, carefully clamped blocks of limestone depicts a battle between Greeks (?) and (victorious) Persians. On the south wall of the chamber is a representation of a procession with the owner of the tomb on a wagon, whereas the painting over the stone *kline* (a kind of couch) shows the same man at a banquet. Painting on wood, which has less often been preserved because of its perishability, comes from a tumulus grave in Tatarlı near Kelainai (Dinar), whose burial chamber was completely lined with planed and painted cedar wood.[52] The paintings depict on the one hand a funeral procession, and on the other Persians fighting Scythians wearing pointed caps. The middle depicts a duel: the Persian leader, wearing a *kidaris* (cylindrical crown) and richly decorated Persian-Elamite garb seizes with his left hand the Scythian by his goatee and with his right hand thrusts a dagger into his opponent's abdomen. The motif of the battle with Scythians also appears in small craftwork. It is historically noteworthy in Asia Minor, because in it the predecessor of a topos of "the barbarian" is represented that finds counterparts in depictions of Greeks fighting Persians and later in those of Greeks fighting Galatians.

A no less precious individual discovery of painted masonry art comes from the illicit excavation of a tumulus near Çan, in the Troad, not too far west of the satrap's seat at Daskyleion: on two sides of the marble sarcophagus found there reliefs have been partially preserved that have almost completely retained their bright colors. They show the owner of the grave riding a horse—on the long side of the sarcophagus he is hunting, brandishing a spear as he gallops toward a boar caught by dogs, and on the short side he appears, again on horseback, in a battle scene in which he is thrusting his spear into the right eye of a shield-bearing foot soldier who is already collapsing to the ground. His clothing and equipment show that the hunter and warrior is a local dynast, while the style and iconography suggest a dating to the early fourth century BCE, about the time when the satrap of Daskyleion, Pharnabazos, was battling Agesilaos's Spartans in the area.

The most spectacular discovery of the recent past was made in the town of Milas (the ancient city of Mylasa);[53] it is the substructure of a monumental mausoleum with a richly painted tomb chamber underneath that contains a marble sarcophagus carved with reliefs on all sides. Certainly one or more members of the Hekatomnid family, vassal kings and queens of the Persians (pp. 157, 170), were buried here; the architectural design resembles that of the famous "Maussolleion" in the nearby city of Halikarnassos (see p. 170), which was built for and named after the most prominent of them, Maussollos (ruled 377–352 BCE). What has been excavated at the site of the tomb in Milas is in a much better state of preservation. Research on the architecture, art, and a Greek metrical inscription of 123 verses—one of the longest known from antiquity—is in progress. The hymn, written on a stele in the Hellenistic period, was composed by a hitherto unknown poet, "Hyssaldomos" (a Carian name), in an extremely rare meter that had been invented probably by the archaic Ionian poet Hipponax of Ephesos (p. 135). The poem contains a long narrative of the fates of an individual named "Pytheas," who escaped the persecutions of "enemies" with divine help. Referring to a distant past, it may recall historical events in the time of the Hekatomnids when Mylasa was founded as a city.

A considerable concentration of dynastic monuments can be noted in Caria and even more in Lycia, where the evidence preserved has already been the object of long and intensive investigation (Map 8). The power and splendor of the noble Lycian clans is displayed here chiefly in funeral art, in text, image, and form.[54] The native tradition is unmistakable in the forms found in Lycia: in the numerous rock-cut tombs there the design of the façades is dominated by the half-timbered mode of construction, with a framework of vertical and horizontal beams, web-bracing with smooth walls or stepped coffers, and (usually) a flat roof on a base of round logs (imitated in stone). Half-timbered construction is also imitated in the multitiered sarcophagus monuments and block-shaped mausoleums that are sometimes cut completely out of the rock and sometimes pieced together. The characteristic pillars, found as early as the sixth century BCE, appear in the representative architecture of Lycia and eastern Caria down into the Roman Imperial period. All these stone monuments were originally painted. Other forms are less typical of the area and betray particularly strong Greek influence, without that providing by itself a reliable crite-

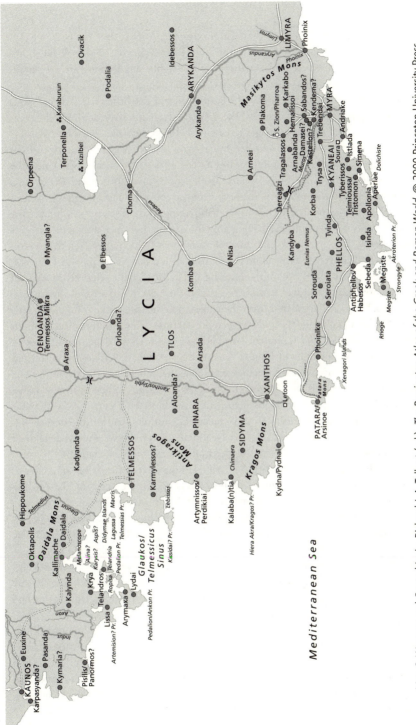

Map 8. Western and Central Lycia. Richard J. A. Talbert (ed.), *The Barrington Atlas of the Greek and Roman World.* © 2000 Princeton University Press.

rion for determining its place in a temporal order. A great deal has been written about the Greek models. Not only in the heroa but also in groups of rock-cut tombs like those in Telmessos and still farther west in neighboring Kaunos, architecture is found that imitates the façades of Greek temples.

Greek classicism, particularly in the Parthenon and Erechtheion in Athens, seems to have inspired those who designed the friezes and structural decorations. The commissioners caused narrative images to be chiseled into the stone of the external surfaces. The many images known from Lycia—and in a few cases the inscriptions as well—reflect an indigenous nobility's point of view on its own world, which must be understood in the context of a Lycian-Greek process of acculturation. The dynasts often represented themselves in ideal-typical royal contexts: engaging in war (scenes of battle, arming, and parades), hunting, banqueting, granting audiences, interacting with family and servants, and having a mythical past. I go into only a few aspects more deeply. The greatest Lycian funeral monument (which was taken to London and was built in Xanthos by an unknown dynast) is a temple tomb with Ionic columns whose pictorial decoration—hunting and battle scenes, including the siege of a city—are distributed over two frieze areas on the base, another on the architrave, and a fourth in a triangular area on the gable, while marble statues of dancing girls with fish, turtles, and birds stand between the columns. This structure owes its modern name—the Nereid Monument—to a comparison with the daughters of Nereus, the mythical sea nymphs in Homer. In Limyra, the dynast Perikles immortalized himself with a heroon in the form of a temple that has relief friezes on the walls of its cella (inner chamber). They represent a military procession, led by a carriage drawn by four horses and bearing the owner of the tomb himself, directly followed by his entourage, and then by horsemen and a phalanx. Another large, fourth-century heroon stood in Trysa in central Lycia. The elaborate pictorial program was developed on the internal and external sides of the wall that surrounded the family tomb, a two-tiered sarcophagus. The wall frieze, divided into two zones, is full of scenes of battle, all taken from the thematic fund of Greek myth: the deeds of Theseus, the centaurs against the Lapiths, the Greeks against the Amazons (a theme that was also developed on the relief friezes that ran around the base of the Maussolleion in Halikarnassos, now in the British Museum), Bellerophon riding the winged horse Pegasus and battling the Chimera. The Payava sarcophagus, transported from Xanthos to London, has scenes showing battles and audiences on the pediment covings and the base ([105] TAM I 40). On the outside of the burial chamber of the "Harpy Tomb" in Xanthos, men and women receiving gifts are represented sitting enthroned between winged women (Figure 36).

In the seaside necropolis at Myra an artistically significant relief combines different scenes. The deceased is represented lying on a *kline* during a meal, surrounded by male and female servants, with his wife sitting on a chair at the head end of the couch. Next to them on the left stand two naked warriors, the right-hand one leaning on a lance, and a warrior in armor to whom a squire is handing a shield and helmet (Figure 37).

36. Relief from the "Harpy Tomb" in Xanthos, Lycia. Now in the British Museum.

37. Rock relief in the necropolis at Myra.

A few monuments address the observer. For example, the dynast Xeriga decorated the pillar on the "Lycian acropolis" at Xanthos—which is simultaneously a funeral monument and a *tropaion*—with a record of his deeds written on three sides in his native Lycian language.[55] However, on the north side of the stone he had inscribed Greek verses singing the immortal fame of his military feats and victories in competitions. Here, in the Greek language he refers to the vantage point of the pillar as the *temenos* (sanctuary) of the twelve gods, which is part of an *agora* (main city square), and he speaks of his own rule as a *basileia* (royal dominion). Around 400 BCE the dynast Arbinas (Erbbina) also uses the Greek language in dedicatory inscriptions to Artemis and Leto, in which he boasts about his conquests in western

Lycia. And the owner of a rock-cut tomb near Olympos, represented lying on a couch with a drinking horn, next to a sitting woman, adds to the princely self-representation a noteworthy element of recollection in the Greek verse epigram inscribed on the stone: "Here lie I, the deceased Apollonios, son of Hellaphilos. I have acted justly, [and] in life have always taken pleasure in eating, drinking, and joking. But now pass on with a cheerful heart!" The name Apollonios, and even more his father's name, Hellaphilos (up to this point unique) already evoke this Lycian's evident fascination with the Greeks. Whether the reference to the triad of earthly delights in his life was inspired by Greek classical poetry—for instance, Herakles's speech in Euripides's *Alkestis* (788–791)—or by oriental tradition, cannot be determined. The words "eating, drinking, joking" remind us of the figure of the Assyrian Sardanapallos; his epigram was read by Alexander the Great's companions "in Assyrian writing" on the stone statue of his funeral monument in Cilicia, communicated to the educated Greek elite, and subsequently commented on repeatedly. It was often translated discreetly as "eat, drink, and be merry" (*paize*), but the phrase was also rebuked for the sexual connotation of the third element of the triad and for the statue's gesture—Sardanapallos is snapping his fingers—interpreted as a kind of "dirty dancing" on the part of an oriental weakling and libertine. The tradition of such maxims regarding life uttered at death's threshold is found in tomb epigrams down into the Roman Imperial period in various regions of Asia Minor.[56]

Whereas none of these Lycian monuments is mentioned by an ancient writer, the sepulcher of the Carian dynast Maussollos, from whose name the term "mausoleum" was derived as early as the fourth century BCE, was already world famous in antiquity. The original tomb was built in the new dynastic residence of Halikarnassos on the Aegean coast. Begun by Maussolos, it was completed only after his death, during the reign of his brother Idrieus. The Maussolleion remained intact down to the Middle Ages, until the Knights of St. John dismantled it in the fifteenth and sixteenth centuries and used it to construct their fortifications. In the nineteenth century, relief plaques retrieved from these fortifications were taken to the British Museum, and during his excavations Charles Newton found marble statues that may represent Maussollos and Artemisia. The names of the Greek sculptors and the description of the structure, including its measurements, are reported in a passage by the Roman writer Pliny the Elder (*nat.* 36, 30), but some of the numbers handed down cannot be right, and modern reconstructions remain problematic in detail. Ancient buildings of a similar type in Asia Minor that were constructed later, but are better preserved, deserve special attention. Good examples are the Hellenistic mausoleum of Belevi near Selçuk and a smaller tomb from the Roman Imperial period called "Gümüşkesen" (Turkish: "silver casket"), located east of the city center of Milas in Caria.

Dynastic representational art is not limited to tomb architecture and decoration: it finds manifold expression in numerous small objects such as seals, but especially in the mintage of coins. We cannot go into this subject here; instead, moving beyond aspects of individual architectural and pictorial works, let us glance at a relatively recent field of research that examines the structure of settlements beyond the Greek *polis* in the Persian period.

Except for those conducted in Sardeis and Halikarnassos, the only excavation of a genuine satrap's residence in Asia Minor has been carried out at Daskyleion (near modern Hisartepe/Ergili, Turkey), where the classic satrap residence has been located on the basis of terrace walls and marble architectural elements. The *paradeisoi* mentioned by Xenophon (*HG* 4, 1, 15 f.) are also to be found on the eastern shore of *Kuş Gölü* ("Bird Lake"; more than 250 species of birds are supposed to live there).[57] The *paradeisos* is a type of cultivated landscape brought into Asia Minor by the Persians; it consisted of both fenced, extensive wild game reserves maintained for hunting purposes and large, park-like gardens.

We still know very little about settlement types in the interior of Achaemenid Asia Minor. It would certainly be an error to imagine, for instance, that in the fourth century BCE the interior of northern, southern, central, and eastern Anatolia was covered solely by village-type settlements or marked by nomadic life. There must have been larger settlements not only near shrines but also at nodal points favorable to trade and productive agricultural lands long before Greek and Roman sources mention their old or new names. Places like Mylasa in Caria, Etenna, Laranda, and Isaura in the Taurus Mountains, Gaziura, Mazaka, Tyana, Ankyra, Gangra on the plateau, and many others were doubtless already incipient cities from the point of view of the typology of settlements.[58] However, the most fully investigated structures are in the dynastic seats of western and central Lycia—and these are also relatively near the coast and therefore only to a limited extent representative of Anatolia as a whole.[59]

In short, in the Lycian hinterland the transition from the castle settlement to the *polis* is already looming in the late classical epoch. Regarding the location of settlements, the lack of a strong interest in harbors had been characteristic of the early dynastic age. For the central seats of the dynasties in the highlands, flat-topped hills that had rock terraces and were surrounded by strong fortifications were preferred. There was no room for monumental palaces. The royal residential district was usually located in an elevated area bordering on or at the highest point of a castle complex. It was closed in on itself and separated from the rest of the settlement by a wall and was usually small. In a few reliefs, city layouts are represented, certainly in an ideal-typical way, with parts of walls, flat-roofed houses, and tall towers.[60] Religious structures and heroa like those in Trysa, Phellos, Limyra, and elsewhere were located in the immediate or proximate neighborhood of the residence, and in any case in the center of the settlement: just as Maussollos had erected his tomb in the polis of Halikarnassos, in the fifth century Xeriga erected his in the agora on the "Lycian acropolis" of Xanthos. The concentration of extravagant funeral architecture and inscriptions is an indication of dynastic seats. More or less extensive residential and economic complexes were connected with the latter. In addition, the area surrounding them was densely built up. Village settlements, small castle complexes, farmsteads, and individual residential towers, freestanding and fortified, were distributed all over the highlands of central Lycia.

No residences have been proven to have existed on the "Lycian acropolis," which developed from the seventh century BCE to the Byzantine age; within the classical fortifications, only religious and funeral architecture from this time has been preserved. The enceinte encloses an area of about twenty-five hectares, about the same as that of the walled settlement of Zemuri (Limyra) in the fourth century, with its agglutinating terraces. Hisarlık (walled) had a built-up area of about fifteen to twenty hectares, while Avaşar-Tepesi in the Yavu uplands of central Lycia, about eight kilometers north of the coast near Aperlai, had about sixteen hectares. Here it was possible to investigate a discovery undisturbed by later structures built over it, since the settlement was abandoned as early as the fourth century BCE: more than half the built-up area lay within the perimeter wall. The acropolis at the summit of the hill, which is also enclosed by a wall and is divided by elaborate terracing, did not serve as a residence but instead had religious and lordly representational functions. It also served as a storage area, with water reservoirs and several spaces interpreted as arsenals and storerooms along the curtain walls. Below the castle complex spread row after row of buildings that surrounded, in the southwestern part, a public space with a large *agora*. This square, about 2,000 square meters in area, was occupied by the long, rectangular podium of a religious building (?), the foundations of other buildings interpreted as having religious functions, and two pillar tombs. In addition to the residential architecture located on the slope of the hill, spaces used for commerce and a pen for livestock have been identified on the periphery. In all, an extensive, quite densely built-up area is outlined, on the basis of which the population has been estimated to have been between 800 and 1,000 people.[61]

Even before the transition to the Hellenistic period, Kyaneai, which was located a few kilometers northeast of Avşar Tepesi in the highlands of central Lycia, assumed the role of a *polis*-center. The surrounding castles and settlements, insofar as they had not been abandoned, as Avşar Tepesi had, were communities politically subordinate to Kyaneai. Important relocations had already taken place in the time of the dynasts: Hisarlık in the interior was abandoned in favor of Telmessos on the coast. Phellos acquired a port, Antiphellos, while the port of Teimiusa arose on the territory of Tyberissos, and the port Aperlai on that of Apollonia. In Xanthos, the trilingual state document from the age of the Hekatomnids allows us to infer the existence of a competent community on the model of the Greek *polis*, with "Xanthians" and "inhabitants of the surrounding vicinity" apparently being groups with equal political status.

✦ ✦ ✦

If we survey the Persian epoch in Asia Minor from the sixth to the fourth centuries BCE, we can speak only to a limited extent of a Persian culture in this land. The number of soldiers and landlords of Iranian descent who settled in Anatolia was certainly not small, but the religion, architecture, art, and ways of life of the old indigenous population were only minimally influenced by these immigrants. To be sure, the Persian ways of holding court and displaying splendor that came into the country fascinated the local potentates. And yet, especially after the Athenians' victories, the west, Ionia and Lydia, and the south, especially Lycia, fell increasingly under the sway of the *polis* culture on the coasts. In its wake Greek mythology, literature, crafts, and science entered Anatolia—if they did not already have their roots and traditions there. The Persians and their vassals were far from wanting to prevent this transfer, and benefitted in various ways from it, bringing a good deal of knowledge and skills back to their distant centers in Babylon, Susa, and Persepolis. Conversely, individual Persian religious ideas were widespread, as we have seen. Above all, what survived long after the time of Persian rule in Asia Minor was the pyramidally structured system of land ownership and the economic forms it entailed, the system of tributes and gifts, fiefs, and military service. It was practiced in the grand style from the Diadochi and Epigones down to the triumvir Mark Antony of the Roman republic.

The End of Persian Rule

While Artaxerxes III reigned on the throne of the great king for a good twenty years (359–338 BCE), upheavals of far-reaching significance were taking place in Europe. A new great power established its supremacy over Greece. It was the energetic king of Macedonia, Philip II, who succeeded in forming a Hellenic alliance under his leadership—after the victory he won at Charioneia (338), which amounted to the defeat of his strongest opponent, Athens. The Athenians were of two minds as to what their attitude toward him should be. As the raison d'être of this symmachy, a war on the Persians was declared to avenge the sacrilegious destruction of Greek temples (Diodorus 16, 89, 1).

Everything suggests that the king of Macedonia and the hegemon of the so-called Corinthian League sought only to create a system of states on both sides of the Aegean. But things turned out otherwise. After his assassination (336), Philip II's son, Alexandros III (Alexander the Great), went to war—at first, in accord with his father's plans. Over the following ten years he unleashed a process of conquest that exceeded all measure, expanding from goal to goal, rolling over all of Asia Minor and as far as the frontiers of the known world, until it finally stopped in Punjab. The Achaemenid Empire that Darius III had ruled since 338 collapsed under the blows struck by the bold Macedonians. Alexander's early death in Babylon in 323 BCE, in the course of ongoing campaign preparations, leaves historians unsure as to how he would have organized an empire stretching from the Indus to the Adriatic. While he was operating in Asia, he left the structures of the Achaemenid Empire mostly intact.[62] The fact that he "orientalized" himself in the choice of his personal resources as well as in the court ceremonies surrounding his person has led Pierre Briant to speak of Alexander as the last Achaemenid.[63] I now examine somewhat more closely what was happening in Asia Minor at that time.

Alexander in Asia Minor

From the time of Philip's offensive, the Macedonians had maintained a bridgehead on Asian soil at the Hellespont: Abydos, opposite Sestos. The army landed there in the spring of 334 BCE, with more than 30,000 foot soldiers and over 5,000 cavalry. Alexander himself crossed the strait at the southern tip of the peninsula, between Elaius and "the Achaeans' harbor." He dedicated his arms to Athena of Ilion, visited the "grave of Achilles," and made a point of giving the city of Ilion, which presented itself to him as the successor of Homeric Troy, its freedom.

On the Persian side, the satraps mobilized their troops, in whose ranks Greek mercenaries under the command of the Rhodian Memnon were the largest element. Daskyleion was the satrap's seat nearest the point where the Macedonian army entered Asian territory. Arsites, the satrap of Hellespontic Phrygia, and Spithridates, the satrap of Lydia and Ionia, assembled their troops not far from Zeleia, east of the little Granikos River. Out of a sense of superiority, the Persians did not accept Memnon's advice to avoid battle. On the banks of the Granikos, Alexander won his first battle against the Persians on the soil of Asia Minor. Thus western Asia Minor was laid open to the invaders. Parmenion, one of the old Macedonian generals, advanced eastward, toward the satrap's seat at Daskyleion. The Macedonian Kalas was made the new satrap, and was supposed to levy and pay the same tribute as his predecessor. Alexander himself marched toward Sardeis, where the castle and its treasure were handed over to him without a battle. He guaranteed the Lydians their autonomy and freedom, but left occupying forces in the castle, named a new tax collector, and also appointed another Macedonian (Asandros, the son of Philotas) as the regent of Spithridates's satrapy.

He took the royal road westward to Ephesos, after Ilion the first large *polis* of the Greeks in Asia Minor, whose "liberation" was cleverly chosen as the propagandistic goal of the campaign. The garrison serving the Persians was too weak to engage the invaders and fled. The oligarchy newly installed by Memnon was destroyed in a popular uprising. Genuine and suspected allies of the Persians were stoned to death until Alexander put a stop to the murders. He ordered the repatriation of the exiles and proclaimed a stipulation that was soon thereafter voiced before delegations from other cities and disseminated generally in Aiolis and Ionia, to the effect that "the oligarchies [are] everywhere to be overthrown and democracies to be established; he restored its own laws to each city and remitted the tribute they used to pay to the barbarians" (Arrian, *An.* 1, 18, 2, trans. Brunt). His preference for democracy seems paradoxical, if we think about his own experiences with Athens and those of his father. But it was carefully considered with regard to the situation in the *poleis*, since there was hardly a general jubilation about the invaders' arrival, spreading from city to city. In the notoriously brawling communities the proclamation mobilized those who were currently downtrodden, disadvantaged, or exiled.

In this part of Asia there were about forty Greek cities that were pledged by the treaty of 387/386 BCE to be loyal subjects of the Persian great king (p. 151). Alex-

38. Alexander the Great. Detail of the mosaic from Pompeii now in the Naples Museum.

ander's plans for their future political existence are unclear. In the debate over the continuity or discontinuity from Achaemenid to Diadochan rule, one text occupies a key position: Alexander's provisions concerning land ownership near Priene, recorded in the stone inscription on a projecting wall (*ante*) at the Temple of Athena in Priene. They are part of a body of regulations that were chiseled into stone only after Alexander's death, during the rule of the Diadochus Lysimachos.[64] The question whether they were issued in 334 or more than a year later[65] will not concern us here. Neither will we deal with the problem of the inscription—"King Alexander built the *naos* for Athena Polias" ([162] *IK* Priene 149)—on the temple itself, which was completed only much later. Alexander guaranteed the citizens of Priene who lived in the city itself or in the port, Naulochos, not only freedom, autonomy, and the possession of land, but also exemption from the *syntaxis* (contribution). The exemption from *phoros* (tribute) announced for all of Ionia, which must have applied to Priene as well, suggests that *syntaxis* was not covered by "tribute" but was a special tax. The following passage is of great importance: "I have decided that the land of the Myrseloi and the Pedieis will be my land, and that the inhabitants of these two villages are to pay tribute" ([162] *IK* Priene 1). It is the same term, "my land," that Darius used in the Gadatas inscription, and in this context, where it refers to the villages near Priene apparently inhabited by native Carians, it can only mean that Alexander is adopting for his own benefit the Achaenemids' claim to land and tribute. However, in contrast to the time of the Persians, in this text produced on the eve of the Hellenistic period the distinction between the *chora* (city territory) and land that has to pay tribute is already clear, and was in fact implied by the declaration of freedom. The key expressions "freedom," "exemption from tribute," "autonomy," and "democracy," which were taken up again and renewed, retained their appeal so long as cities and kings continued to be related to one another.[66]

From Ephesos, Alexander presumably marched directly to Miletus, while his general Antigonos Monophthalmos ("the One-Eyed") was ordered to go to Priene. A fierce struggle raged around the old Ionian metropolis of Miletus. It was held by Greek mercenaries who were awaiting the arrival of the Persian fleet of about 400 ships manned by Phoenicians and Cyprians. Three days before the fleet appeared near Mykale, 160 Greek triremes under Nikanor had arrived from Lesbos and Chios to block the entry to the harbor and occupy the island of Lade. Contrary to Parmenion's view, Alexander did not want to risk a defeat by the superior Persian fleet that might have destroyed the victor's aura he had enjoyed since the battle on the Granikos. The city did not long resist the siege from the land side, which was conducted with heavy equipment. The victor was lenient with the Milesians, granting them freedom as well and incorporating the defeated soldiers into his army.

Having arrived at the Hekatomnid capital of Halikarnassos on its way south by land, the army met with stiff resistance; Memnon of Rhodes, who had now become the official supreme commander of Persian forces in western Asia Minor, was personally present, along with the satrap of Caria, Orontobates. This Iranian was married to the Hekatomnid Pixodaros's daughter Ada the Younger, and had ruled Caria since 336/335 BCE, whereas the elder Ada (the sister of Pixodaros, Idrieus, Maussollos, and Artemisia) had been deposed.

After a major siege, the city and its harbor fell into the Macedonians' hands, but the satrap Orontobates held on in the harbor fortress of Salmakis for another whole year, while Memnon escaped to Kos with the fleet. To prove that he was treating the Carian people at least as leniently as he had the Lydians, the young Macedonian king had an unusual idea: he had himself symbolically adopted by the elder Ada and made the displaced territorial princess the satrap of Caria once again, though not in Halikarnassos, but rather in Alinda, in the interior.

With his vehicles and the alliance's army, Parmenion headed for Sardeis, where he prepared to march into inner Anatolia by the Royal road. During its winter campaign in southwest Asia Minor, Alexander's main army sought to counter the enemy fleet's superiority step by step by occupying the coastal strongpoints. This was a well-considered decision that had probably already been made in Miletus, where Alexander had even ordered the complete dispersal of his fleet to avoid any losses in a battle at sea. He corrected this mistake a few months later, but up to that point the Persian navy had been able to draw hardly any benefit from it. On the Aegean islands, Memnon even had to force Mytilene on Lesbos and Tenedos to ally themselves with the Persians and overturn the steles on which their treaties with Alexander had been engraved. But Alexander's army, instead of letting the winter go by without action, advanced through Xanthos, Patara, and Milyas in the interior down to the east Lycian coast near Phaselis, and from there into the Pamphylian plains toward Perge,

Aspendos, and Side. This strategy had achieved a significant partial success. The remainder of the Persian garrisons still holed up in Myndos, Halikarnassos, and Kaunos did not control the harbors. Among the coasts that had good road connections with Anatolia, the Persians now had easy access only to Cilicia.

After he had subdued the refractory Aspendians, Alexander united Lycia and Pamphylia in a satrapy that he entrusted to his boyhood friend and subsequent fleet commander Nearchos. Alexander then marched north from the Pamphylian coast up the difficult road through the Pisidian highlands, where he met with resistance. He had to abandon the siege of the fortified stronghold of Termessos, but he took by storm the Pisidian barbarians' blocking position near Sagalassos. During excavations there, a marble head of Alexander was found in an Augustan heroon; it may be an early Roman Imperial period copy of a bronze sculpture that was part of a victory monument.

When the army passed Lake Askanios and reached the Phrygian satrapy's capital of Kelainai, the satrap, Atizyes, who was defending the castle with 1,000 Carian and one hundred Greek mercenaries, still hoped that help would arrive. They agreed on a deadline for surrender (according to Curtius, 3, 1, 8, sixty days). Alexander did not wait, but instead entrusted the siege to the man he had put in charge of Phrygia, Antigonos Monophthalmos—about whom I shall later have much to say—and went on toward Gordion. There, some eighty kilometers west of Ankara, in the spring of 333 BCE Alexander's and Parmenion's army groups joined with significant reinforcements from Macedonia.

Before the departure from Gordion, Arrian (*An.* 2, 3) describes in great detail the story of the Gordian Knot (p. 106). The legend of the origins of the Phrygian royal family, which goes back to Gordios and his son Midas, developed around the simple farmer's wagon placed in the city's main shrine. According to this legend, the person who was able to untie the intricately woven knot of raffia that attached the wagon's yoke to the shaft was to rule over Asia. The historians of the Roman Imperial period offer differing accounts of how Alexander detached the wagon: rather cleverly, by simply pulling out the cherrywood peg that was inserted into the shaft, or more crudely by cutting it with his sword. Once again we see his sense of public relations, which led him to exclude the possibility of failure under any circumstances.

Alexander advanced via Ankyra to southern Cappadocia, where he installed the native Sabiktas as ruler.[67] After Memnon's sudden death in the early summer of 333 CE, the naval threat to the Macedonians' bases in Asia Minor dissipated entirely. The Great King Darius III still resided in Susa (Plutarch, *Alex.*, 18, 6) and set about assembling an army near Babylon to advance against the Macedonians and seek a decisive battle on land.

To Greeks or Persians who knew about history, the overall military situation at the time must have seemed grotesque. With the fleet of their League, the Athenians had once ruled the whole gamut of cities on the coasts of Asia Minor, and for decades maintained their control against the satraps of the interior; now the Macedonians and Greeks were established in the satraps' castles in Daskyleion and Sardeis, they were besieging the castle of Kelainai, and controlled the roads through Anatolia, whereas the Persians' ships cruised the Aegean and the eastern Mediterranean without being able to have any lasting effect. To be sure, Anatolia was still not firmly in the invaders' grip. Paphlagonians and Cappadocians who fought in the great king's army at Issos (333 BCE) continued to try, even after the battle, to reconquer terrain in Anatolia by armed force (Curtius 4, 1, 34; 5, 13). For the time being, the power of the new Macedonian satrap Kalas did not extend to Paphlagonia, to which Alexander had promised freedom from taxes (Curtius 3, 1, 23) while demanding obedience to Kalas—Sinope continued to mint coins with Aramaic legends.[68] Unrest persisted in southern Cappadocia, and in northern Cappadocia the prince Ariarathes continued to rule unchallenged even after Alexander's death,[69] as did the prince Orontes still further east, in Armenia. But the Macedonians Kalas and especially the later Diadochus Antigonos not only maintained their positions but subjected one area after another. Antigonos Monophthalmos, to whom the castle at Kelainai finally had to surrender, soon thereafter conquered Lycaonia, and was able, after Nearchos's recall, to extend his satrapy to Lycia, Pamphylia, and Pisidia (331 BCE?). Thus he laid the foundation for his later position of power in the battles among the Diadochi. Alexander had already descended into the Cilician plain when he learned that the fortresses of Myndos, Halikarnassos, and Kaunos had finally been conquered.

From the Hittites to the Crusaders, the Cilician plain was a key position for armies advancing toward Syria, Egypt, or Mesopotamia. Alexander's army moved toward the pass through the Taurus Mountains, the so-called Cilician Gates (see Figure 69). This defile was only guarded, not occupied, and the advance down toward Tarsos was quickly made. The Persian Arsames left the city in great haste and fled to Darius. When Alexander shortly thereafter fell ill, there was a necessary pause in his operations. After he recovered, he undertook an expedition against the insubordinate inhabitants of the Cilician Taurus. The Cilician *poleis* were basically of Greek origin, and only a little effort was required to bring them over to the Macedonian side. In Soloi the army held a great celebration. Alexander had installed the Macedonian Balakros as satrap of Cilicia only in late 333, after the battle at Issos.

Darius, who had in the interim moved his baggage, harem, and treasure to Damascus and marched toward northern Syria, must have been informed about these protracted delays. Against a turncoat's advice, he decided to leave the area, where he had planned to wage a defensive battle, and set out for Cilicia.

The coastal plain on the east side of the Gulf of İskenderun is bounded by the high, north-south ridge of the Amanos Mountains. Here the Macedonian army was moving south toward the Belen Pass, which Parmenion had already occupied, when it was learned that the Persians had crossed the Amanos in the opposite direction farther north and descended into the plain. Thus the fronts were inverted, with Alexander in the south and Darius in the north on the narrow strip of land between the coast and the Amanos, and it was there that the famous battle of Issos was fought, which decided the fate of Asia Minor. In the center of the battle order, the Macedonian phalanx was opposed on the Persian side by 30,000 Greek mercenaries, "the largest contingent of Greek infantry that had ever fought in a single battle."[70] Modern estimates indicate an overall force of 100,000 men on the Persian side, against a Macedonian army of about 30,000. Darius suffered a disastrous defeat but managed to escape over the Euphrates.

✦ ✦ ✦

Two hundred years after the Iranian Cyrus conquered Asia Minor from east to west, the same feat was achieved in the opposite direction by a wild warrior king from the Balkans at the head of Macedonian peasant-soldiers and allied Greeks. What long-term consequences this victorious campaign might have, no one could then guess. The change was not new: in the *staseis* (a state of unrest similar to civil war) of the "liberated" Greek *poleis*, the side that had previously not been favored by the Persian masters now had the upper hand once again. And in the interior? The Persian kings' dismissal and reestablishment of regents was over, and the threads of power no longer joined in Susa. However, the satrapies continued to exist and with them the pyramidal system of government by satraps and vassals, foreign lords and representatives of the native nobility, as well as Persian and indigenous institutions. And yet a barrier had been broken through that allowed the continuation in the interior of Asia Minor of a development that had begun with the Greek settlements on the coast more than seven centuries earlier. Increasing numbers of Greek-speaking settlers, first of all soldiers, arrived there. New communities were established that soon sought autonomy and became centers of gravity for Hellenization. It is certainly not true that Alexander's conquest of Asia Minor destroyed the Achaemenid traditions and implanted genuinely Macedonian ones in their stead.[71] But under the Macedonians the element of the *polis* gradually grew and achieved an extent that Persian Asia Minor had never experienced.

CHAPTER 6

Monarchies, Vassals, and Cities from Alexander's Empire to the Pax Romana (331 BCE to 31 BCE)

Here a brief presentation of the sources seems appropriate. For the contexts of Hellenistic history in general and the history of Asia Minor in particular, we lack a Herodotus, a Thucydides, or a Xenophon. However, comprehensive accounts definitely existed, but they have been preserved only in fragments. Hieronymus of Kardia produced a history of the Diadochi as seen by a contemporary, most of which is lost. The Bithynian Arrian, from Nikomedeia, a senator and provincial governor in Cappadocia from 132 to 137 CE, wrote ten books on events after Alexander.[1] Among Plutarch's biographies, his lives of two Diadochi are of special interest for Asia Minor, that of Eumenes and that of Demetrios, the son of the previously mentioned Antigonos Monophthalmos (the "One-Eyed"; see Chapter 5). And since the Diadochi were warlike, some supplementary details are found in the military handbooks of Frontin (first century CE) and Polyainos (second century CE). Pompeius Trogus, a contemporary of the Augustan historian Livy, wrote a *Historiae Philippicae* in forty-four books, of which—except for the *prologi* (information about the book's contents)—only Justin's *epitome* (abstract) has been preserved. For the history of the Epigoni—the generation of rulers that followed the Diadochi in the former Alexandrian Empire—the loss of Phylarchos of Athens's *Historiai*, on which both Polybius and Plutarch drew, is particularly unfortunate. The Achaean writer Polybius's *Historiai*, about one-third of which is extant, deals with events in Asia Minor in alternation with those in other regions in the second century BCE. In Sallust's books 2–4, and in many letters and a few speeches by Cicero (especially those addressed to Murena and to Flaccus), who had himself governed the province of Cilicia, there are valuable testimonies regarding the Mithridatic Wars and the period immediately following them. Strabo's *Geographica* is a first-rate source for our knowledge of the ancient geography of Asia Minor; it is full of historical excurses on events down to the early first century CE. In his biographies of Sulla, Lucullus, Pompey, and Mark Antony, Plutarch draws attention to late Hellenistic Asia Minor. Numerous other writers of the Roman Imperial period may be cited here, including the Alexandrine Appian (especially on Mithridates) and the Nicaean Cassius Dio.

The large fragment of a text by another writer from Asia Minor, Memnon, occupies an exceptional position. We know almost nothing about Memnon, other than that he was a citizen of Herakleia Pontike and lived there for a long time. His chronicle, which he based on the (lost) writings of chroniclers of his home town named Nymphis, Promathidas, and Domitius Kallistratos, begins with the early history of Herakleia and then discusses the heyday and decline of the tyrants, the Diadochan Wars, and the city's changing relationships with the greater and lesser powers of the Hellenistic period—with excurses on Bithynian history (FGrHist 434 F, 1, 12) and on the Romans (FGrHist 434 F, 1, 18, 1–5)—down to the Mithridatic Wars. It breaks off at 47 BCE (Caesar's return from the Orient). In Memnon's work, world history is interwoven with local history.

The construction and renovation of cities with stone architecture, temples, altars, funeral monuments, and sarcophagi with structural and sculptural ornamentation, rock-cut reliefs, statuary, ceramics, objects, and coins, provide a broad trail of relics from the Hellenistic period that leads straight through Asia Minor as far as eastern Anatolia. The Didymaion is undoubtedly on the highest level of the architectural remains on the west coast from this period. Complexes of Hellenistic urban architecture that are relatively little reshaped or overbuilt by later structures, including residential buildings, are found above all in Priene. More strongly marked by later Roman construction is a place that can nevertheless be considered archaeologically as the center for the period: what the ruins of Ḫattusa were for the Anatolian empire of the second millennium BCE and what the ruins of Ephesos were for the Roman Empire's province of Asia, Pergamon is for Hellenistic Asia Minor. Pergamon's architectural and art works on the western edge of Anatolia stand for a successful politics of power and culture with a simultaneous integration of Asia into the West, whereas far to the east the mountain shrines of Antiochos I of Commagene epitomize the peculiar connection between Hellenic gods and the Iranian religion (p. 514).

Inscriptions on stone are of special importance for the historian of Asia Minor in the Hellenistic and early Roman Imperial periods. In contrast, the number of Greek and Latin inscriptions on bronze tablets is small: a Hellenistic decree from Cappadocia that found its way to the antiques market in the nineteenth century is exceeded in length only by the treaty between Rome and the Lycians, which also appeared on the market not long ago; the most recent discoveries come from Sagalassos in Pisidia and Amasya. In general, neither classical Athens nor the great shrines at Delphi and Delos, with their thousands of Greek inscriptions, have produced a treasure of epigraphic sources as dazzling as Asia Minor's. The range of genres, the length of the texts, the differentiated multiplicity of the information they provide, and the continuing influx of discoveries are unparalleled. Mommsen called Augustus's record of his deeds on the temple walls in Ankara the "queen of inscriptions." Epicurus's doctrine is chiseled on a wall in the Lycian town of Oinoanda. In Aphrodisias, the wall of the *parodos* in the theater is decorated with a series of state documents. Julius Caesar's treaty with the Lycian League probably comes from a shrine in Lycia. Countless steles with royal epistles and community decisions report on the fate of the cities and their citizens, the goals and deeds of kings and dynasts, gods and festivals, and so forth. From crude lists of events to a refined chronology, these stones support reconstructions of political history where there are gaps in ancient historiography. And the spread of the "epigraphic habit" provides the basis for the study of the Hellenization and Romanization of the Middle East.

The Persian system of satrapies was adopted (with modifications) by the Macedonians, and prefigured, with its own gravity, the decline of imperial structures that embraced all of Anatolia. This decline ultimately led to the regional kingdoms that Rome gradually reduced to obedience and finally turned into provinces. In Alexander's collapsing empire, the Anatolian land mass was at first only one of several large fragments, along with Europe, Egypt, Babylonia, and Iran. Because of its central location and function as a geographical bridge, of course, but also because of its reservoir of human resources for military and civilian tasks, the key administrative and cultural role of the cities, and the economic wealth of the country, Asia Minor was more attractive to the contending powers than other parts of the world. The Seleucid Dynasty first emerged from this struggle as the master of Asia—even if never of all of Asia. This is not the place to enter into the debate over the structural weaknesses or the duration and coherence of the Seleucid Empire.[2] Whereas the Seleucids largely retained possession of Iran for 183 years (from 312 to 129 BCE) and of northern Syria for almost 250 years (until 63 BCE), most of Anatolia was lost after only ninety-two years (281–189 BCE). In the enormous conglomerate of countries that the first two kings ruled, the emancipation of local and regional rulers spread quite early in the area of modern-day Turkey, as in the cases of Eumenes I of Pergamon, Nikomedes in Bithynia, Mithridates in Pontos, and Ariaramnes in Cappadocia. Moreover, in the age of the Diadochi and afterward, some of the minor, ephemeral dynasts and tyrants—such as the sons of Klearchos in Herakleia Pontike, Eupolemos, Pleistarchos, Olympichos in southwest Asia Minor, Lysias in Phrygia, the Teucrids in Cilicia, and the tribal leaders of the Galatians west and east of Ankyra—were also already acting with their own troops, founding cities, and minting coins.[3]

Asia Minor and the Diadochi

For four decades, individuals are the focal point of historiography as they are in almost no other period; the number of biographies of such figures as Eumenes, Lysimachos, Antigonos, and Seleukos is constantly growing. Evaluations of their acts differ, depending on the actor from whose perspective the events are presented. The kaleidoscopic changes in the scenes of action—along with the rapid changes in control over whole countries and cities and the vagaries of the acquisition of power, conquests, defeats, mutinies, betrayals, and intrigues—is confusing and distracts attention from regulative and constructive measures within domains (for individuals and their careers, see the Appendix). To begin, I sketch the outlines of the military history of the area, glancing at events outside Asia Minor only insofar as it is absolutely necessary to do so. Afterward, the beginnings of long-term developments in Asia Minor that can be discerned in the age of the Diadochi will be discussed.

The Battle for Anatolia

After ending his campaign of conquest through the Persian Empire, Alexander returned to Babylon and died there in June 323 BCE. He had not designated a successor. At first, the generals made compromises with one another. The two-king solution with Philip Arrhidaios, Alexander's mentally handicapped brother, and the newborn son of Roxane, Alexander's wife, meant that formally, a single Macedonian empire was retained, of which Asia Minor would be a part. Carian communities in the interior, such as the Koarendeis, Amyzon, and Mylasa, continued to date their documents as they had under the Persian Empire, now counting the years of King Philip's reign. But neither Philip Arrhidaios (killed in 317) nor Alexander's and Roxane's child named Alexander (murdered in Macedonia in 310) played a notable role in Asia Minor. Alexander's sisters Kynane and Kleopatra in Sardeis, as well as an illegitimate son of Alexander, Herakles, in Pergamon, lost their lives when they were brought into play for political ends and became dangers to opponents.

The point of departure for the development of power relationships in Anatolia was the division of the satrapies undertaken in Babylon.[4] Lydia and Caria had already changed possessors; in Lydia, Asandros was replaced by Menandros, and in Caria Ada was initially replaced by a certain Philoxenos, who was also responsible for the financial and supply systems in all of Asia Minor,[5] and then by Asandros. Likewise, in Cilicia Philotas—not the trusted confidant who was accused of conspiracy and executed, but an otherwise unknown troop leader of Alexander's—had replaced Balakros, who had been killed on an expedition in Isauria, while in Phrygia at the Hellespont, an officer named Demarchos had replaced Kalas, who had also been killed. The enormous satrapy of Lycia-Pamphylia-Greater Phrygia continued to be ruled by Antigonos the "One-Eyed." Newcomers took over only in the north: Leonnatos—who was also one of Alexander's former generals—replaced Demarchos in Daskyleion, and the Greek Eumenes received the still-to-be-conquered countries of Paphlagonia and Cappadocia by the Sea.

The shifts in power in Asia Minor quickly led to a confrontation between two entirely different figures, Antigonos and Eumenes. Antigonos, who was going on sixty and now ruled the strongest satrapy in Alexander's empire in Anatolia, was not happy about the arrangements regarding Asia Minor that had been made in Babylon by the keeper of Alexander's signet ring and "regent of the kingdom," Perdikkas.[6] Eumenes, who came from Kardia (like his friend, the historian Hieronymos), and who as a very young man had already risen to become a secretary under Philip and a head of chancellery under Alexander, was then in his late thirties.[7] When he moved into his satrapy, equipped with money and Perdikkas's troops, the "One-Eyed" refused to support the "desk jockey."[8] But soon thereafter Eumenes received support from Perdikkas himself. His military power put an end to the still-existent rule of the Iranian Ariarathes in the northern part of Cappadocia. Eumenes was then able to establish himself on a firm foundation and build up his own army out of native Cappadocians. Perdikkas advanced into the Cilician plain and moved on to the northern edge of the Taurus Mountains, where he destroyed the cities of Laranda and Isaura (Diodorus 18, 22, 1). When the leader of the imperial army held Antigonos to account, the soil of Asia became too hot for the "One-Eyed." With his son Demetrios, he left for Greece on Athenian ships. But while Eumenes was still in Sardeis seeking to persuade Alexander's sister Kleopatra to marry Perdikkas (to increase the regent's authority among Macedonians as the custodian of Alexander's heritage), Antigonos landed with fresh troops from Europe, got the Ionian cities and the satraps of Lydia (Menandros) and Caria (Asandros) to side with him, and marched on Sardeis. Eumenes escaped just in time. He and his protector Perdikkas suddenly found themselves caught in the pincers of a European-Egyptian community of interest. Neither of the strong men in Europe at this time, Antipatros and Krateros, were content to divide up the ancestral land of Macedonia among themselves. Instead, they sought to win for Krateros a part of Asia they hoped to take from Perdikkas's supporters with Antigonos's welcome help. Egypt was ruled by another Diadochus from the narrow group of the deceased ruler's entourage: Ptolemaios, the son of Lagos, the founder of the most long-lived Hellenistic dynasty, which was to die out only with the suicide of Queen Cleopatra in 30 BCE. By stealing Alexander's corpse from the custody of Perdikkas's army, Ptolemaios had aroused the wrath of the supreme commander. When Perdikkas set out to invade Egypt, Eumenes assumed personal command in Asia Minor, but he had to recognize that in the meantime, Philoxenos (presumably the previously mentioned satrap of Caria), who had also just recently been established by Perdikkas as satrap of Cilicia, had changed sides. Things continued to go against Eumenes, because as the European potentates Antipatros and Krateros crossed over the Hellespont, the commander who had been installed in Armenia, Neoptolemos, also betrayed the supporters of Perdikkas. But Eumenes stood the test. Near Ankara he routed Neoptolemos, and when the latter accompanied Krateros, who was advancing into central Anatolia, he met the opposing army at the border of his satrapy. Krateros fell in the battle, and Neoptolemos, a Macedonian elite soldier (who had once been the first to scale the walls of Gaza), was killed by Eumenes in a duel. However, with Perdikkas's death in Egypt at about the same time, the tide turned against Eumenes again. The Macedonian military assembly in Egypt condemned him to death as Krateros's murderer. In Triparadeisos, in the autumn of 321,[9] his satrapy of Cappadocia was assigned to a certain Nikanor, Lydia to Kleitos (a successful naval commander), and Hellespontic Phrygia to Arrhidaios (not Alexander's brother of the same name). But Antigonos Monophthalmos was given supreme command as the "*Strategos* of Asia for combating Eumenes." This time the "One-Eyed" was able to develop his forces in Anatolia effectively. Eumenes was defeated in Cappadocia at a place named Orkynia[10] and was besieged for months in the fortress at Nora (presumably southeast of Lake Tuz, between Aksaray and Niğde). Antigonos hastened by forced marches to Pisidia and

39. Relief at the so-called Tomb of Alketas in Termessos, Pisidia.

neutralized Perdikkas's last partisans. The inhabitants of Termessos, the mountain town that Alexander had not been able to reduce, decided to hand over Alketas, Perdikkas's brother, but he took his own life before they could do so. The relief at the Macedonian rock-cut tomb at Termessos, although seriously damaged, still preserves a high quality work of art that depicts an attacking cavalryman in full armor (Figure 39). The tomb may well be Alketas's burial place.

While Eumenes was still under siege at Nora, Antigonos, considering the situation outside Asia, offered him a deal and let him go. However, the Greek chose to swear an oath of allegiance not to the *strategos* of Asia but rather to Alexander's mother Olympias and the (underage) kings, declining loyalty to anyone other than Alexander's "legitimate" heirs. He received support from Europe—from Antipatros's successor Polyperchon and from Olympias, whom the latter had brought back from Epirus to Pella. Along with the Macedonian royal hoard in the *gazophylakion* (a fortress serving as a treasury) at Kyinda in Cilicia and the elite troops of the *argyraspides* ("silver shield-bearers"), money was made available to him to hire mercenaries and reinforcements. But his later campaigns outside Asia Minor ended, after he had lost his treasure and his fleet, with a march on Babylon and Iran, where he was defeated and handed over to Antigonos, who had him immediately executed.

Antigonos was then at the zenith of his career, the most powerful man between Europe, Mesopotamia, and Egypt. Seleukos, who in Triparadeisos had been entrusted with Babylonia, was driven out of his satrapy by Antigonos and fled to Ptolemaios (315 BCE). The "One-Eyed" now had control over the gigantic financial resources of Alexander's trans-Euphrates empire. His son Demetrios was defeated in the battle against the allies Seleukos and Ptolemaios near Gaza in the winter of 312 BCE, but in the peace treaty of late summer, 311, the dynasts in Europe and Ptolemaios confirmed once again the status quo of the distribution of the empire until Alexander IV came of age and the Antigonids' rule over "Asia." Seleukos was not a party to the treaty and at that time apparently had no choice but to accept their claims to sovereignty.

In the person of the Macedonian Seleukos, who had also been one of Alexander's companions (*hetairoi*) and was just as important as a founder of a dynasty as Antigonos and Ptolemaios were, the masters of Asia Minor were to find their last and greatest opponent, who within the following decade established his strong position in the eastern parts of the empire, as far as Afghanistan, and once again even advanced as far as India, into the empire of King Chandragupta. Seleukos had already reconquered Babylon in the spring of 311, and his successes allowed Ptolemaios to break the peace treaty and seize Antigonos's garrisons in Rough Cilicia. Demetrios quickly took these back and drove deep into his opponent's territories. However, his expedition to southern Mesopotamia and another made by his father produced no longlasting consequences. When he returned to Asia Minor in 309, Demetrios found himself confronted by Ptolemaic bridgeheads on the south and west coasts. With his fleet, Ptolemaios had taken Phaselis, Xanthos, Kaunos, Myndos, and Iasos, before he had to abandon the siege of Halikarnassos and go back to Kos, and then to Egypt.

When Ptolemaios sought, as Perdikkas had done before him, to establish contact with Alexander's sister Kleopatra in Sardeis, Antigonos had her killed. The positions of the Antigonids in Asia were strengthened by founding cities at the Propontis, in the Troad, and on the Orontes in Syria, and Antigonos's son Demetrios made up for the losses in Caria and Lycia. Then the Ptolemaic external possession of Cyprus, a burdensome troublemaker on the threshold of Cilicia, was targeted. The brilliant naval victory won by Demetrios at Salamis in 306 BCE motivated the Antigonids to be the first to add the title of king to their names, and their example was followed soon thereafter (304) by the dynasts in the east, Ptolemaios and Seleukos, as well as by Lysimachos and Kassandros in the west. Antigonos's and Demetrios's combined attack on Egypt by sea and by land failed, as did the son's siege of Rhodes (305/304). Demetrios was henceforth given the byname of *poliorketes* (besieger of cities). Alarmed by his subsequent activities in Greece, Kassandros and Lysimachos entered into an alliance and ultimately formed the decisive coalition with Ptolemaios and Seleukos against the "One-Eyed" and the "Besieger of Cities" in Asia.

The events up to a point shortly before the decisive battle are described in the twentieth book of Diodorus. Armies were invading Asia Minor from three different directions. Lysimachos, the king of Thrace, crossed the Hellespont in the spring of 302. He divided his army into two columns, one of which captured the cities on the west coast (as Alexander had in his time), while the other, under the king's leadership, was to attack the Antigonids' heavily garrisoned fortresses in Phrygia. Sardeis resisted the first column, whereas Synnada opened its gates to the second column.

When he learned of this invasion, Antigonos broke off a major celebration in his newly founded city on the Orontes, crossed the Taurus Mountains and entered central Phrygia from the south, where Lysimachos's columns had united again. Seleukos had left Mesopotamia with 480 Indian elephants, 12,000 horsemen, and 20,000 foot soldiers. Ptolemaios, deceived by rumors of a victory by Antigonos, preferred to remain in Egypt.

The octogenerian's forces cut Lysimachos off from his ally in the east, but Antigonos was not able to force Lysimachos to fight a battle. The king of Thrace turned north and took up a defensive position in Herakleia Pontike, where he married the Iranian Amastris, the widow of the tyrant Dionysios. In the same year, Demetrios crossed over to Ephesos and returned the cities as far as the Hellespont and the Bosporus to the possession of the kings of Asia. The attempt made by Kassandros's brother Pleistarchos to bring reinforcements over the Black Sea to Herakleia was a disastrous failure, and mutinies threatened to spread in Lysimachos's army.

In the spring of 301, Antigonos and Demetrios united their troops in Hellespontic Phrygia. Farther east, perhaps in the area around Ankyra, Lysimachos and Seleukos finally managed to unite their forces and marched on the Royal Road toward the southwest. The decisive battle took place at Ipsos, about ten kilometers north of Afyon in Phrygia. The old Antigonos Monophthalmos fell in a hail of missiles, and the victors divided the spoils.

It was the first major breaking point in the history of the Diadochi and led to a new partition of the "world." Lysimachos claimed the Antigonids' satrapies in Asia Minor north of the Taurus Mountains, Seleukos the eastern part of Alexander's empire from the Syrian coast to the Indus, as well as southern Cappadocia and Armenia in Anatolia.[11] Pleistarchos received Cilicia, but could not hold it for long. So far as the land mass of Asia Minor is concerned, some possessions were merely verbal, while others were quickly lost. Demetrios had escaped alive from the battlefield at Ipsos, and Antigonid bases still existed in the coastal cities or were reconquered by him. In addition, the coalition of the victors at Ipsos immediately fell apart again. When Seleukos learned of the alliance between Ptolemaios and Lysimachos, who had married the Lagid's eldest daughter, Arsinoe, he came to terms with Demetrios and married the latter's daughter Stratonike. With the death of Antigonos, whose "kingdom" had grown from a conglomerate of satrapies in central Anatolia and who had conquered Anatolia from the inside out, the forces that were acting on Asia Minor began to shift toward the exterior. The growing importance of the Syrian-Palestinian theater on the one hand, and the European theater on the other, was accompanied by the fact that new centers were emerging on the Orontes and in Thrace. At the same time, Alexandria's influence on events in Asia Minor was growing steadily stronger.

Lysimachos's kingdom in Asia Minor remained a porous affair: its center of gravity lay opposite the European part of the kingdom in the north, on the Hellespont, and in Herakleia Pontike. He founded his residence, Lysimacheia, on the Thracian Chersonnesos, in immediate proximity to Kardia, Eumenes's home town. He cultivated a special relationship with Ilion, because for purposes of propaganda he styled himself the successor of Alexander and concerned himself with the reconstruction of the Temple of Athena. After the battle of Ipsos, Abydos and Parion minted his coins with the portrait of Alexander, and the supporters of Demetrios were probably not able to maintain themselves in Lampsakos, either. Lysimachos's ex-wife Amastris, whom he had divorced in Sardeis ca. 300 BCE, ruled on the Black Sea as his vassal. After her own sons murdered her, Lysimachos handed over part of her possessions to a man named Eumenes. The latter was the older brother of his officer and commander in Pergamon, named Philetairos, and the family's homeland was the city Tieion on the Black Sea, east of Herakleia. When Lysimachos's new wife Arsinoe—a quintessential Hellenistic femme fatale—demanded for herself the Black Sea cities ruled by Amastris and the king yielded to her, this certainly did not help maintain these brothers' loyalty. The inhabitants of Herakleia successfully resisted Arsinoe, and Eumenes ruled the city of Amastris even after Lysimachos's death.

In the regions on the Black Sea farther to the east, in Paphlagonia and in Cappadocia by the Sea, where one of Antigonos's Iranian officers had founded a dynasty, power relationships entirely escaped the supervision of Lysimachos (Diodorus 20, 111, 4; Appian, *Mith*. 9 [28]). Around 300, there was a tyranny in Sinope. Bithynia was divided de facto into two parts. The king had to subdue Kios in 289. Near the coast he could rely on cities whose network he strengthened. But nearby, the mountains east of the Sangarios River were hostile territory. There a Thracian princely family ruled; the dynast Zipoites could make so bold as to venture onto the plains as far as Astakos Bay and even to occupy the city of Astakos. This was the germ of an independent kingdom.

Mysia (along with the *gazophylakion* in Pergamon under Philetairos), Lydia (with the satrap's seat in Sardeis), and the interior of western Asia Minor (with the extensive Phrygian satrapies on the Hellespont and in Greater Phrygia) seem to have been loyal subjects of Lysimachos.[12] In contrast, the situations in the Ionian cities were not all the same. Lysimachos's competitors, Kings Demetrios and Ptolemaios, went on challenging him there and sought to establish relations by sea with the *poleis* on the Aegean wherever the opportunity to do so presented itself. Particularly in the first years after Ipsos, where Lysimachos maintained his position of power and where he lost it depended on the success or failure of his rival, the "Sea King" Demetrios. On the coast, Smyrna, and on the Ionian peninsula, Erythrai, Teos, and Lebedos were under Lysimachos's control, but Klazomenai was not, which belonged to Demetrios after 301 BCE ([106] OGIS 9). At first, Demetrios also held Ephesos, until it had to submit to Lysimachos in 294 BCE.

The Ephesians had been through a difficult period. A decision of the people (ca. 300 BCE) set the conditions under which citizens who had mortgaged their land because they were in financial difficulties caused by the war had to repay their creditors ([109] *Syll*.³ 364).[13] Now the whole community was being resettled against its will. Their neighbors, the residents of Kolophon, had it even harder. They had resisted, but the Macedonians had subdued them by bloody repression. The city was destroyed, and when the survivors were resettled in Arsinoeia-Ephesos, its political existence was completely annihilated. But not long afterward Prepelaos, Lysimachos's general, caused the people of Kolophon to be pardoned and allowed them to rebuild their city. They venerated their benefactor in a shrine called the "Prepelaion."

Unlike Priene,[14] where a royal cult was also established, after 301 Miletus could not at first be described as one of Lysimachos's allies, otherwise in 295/294 the Milesians would not have included Demetrios in their list of *stephanephoroi* (wreath-bearers) ([167] Miletus I 3, 123 l. 22). The latter, the city's top government officials, came from the financially powerful citizen elite, and their names were engraved on a large marble stele in the Temple of Apollo Delphinios. It was an extravagant gesture of devotion to appoint a foreign ruler to this annual office to honor him. Moreover, in some years this office was symbolically held by the god Apollo—whenever the community had to draw on the temple treasury to pay the associated financial expenditures.[15] Demetrios was not the first king to be on the list: in 334/333 Alexander had adorned it. When he invaded Asia again (p. 190), Demetrios the "besieger of cities" married in Miletus Ptolemais, a daughter of the Lagid ruler born from his marriage with Eurydike. However, at the same time Miletus was cultivating relationships with Seleukos; the latter made votive offerings to Apollo, and the community erected a bronze statue of him in the city. Seleukos's son Antiochos promised to build a large hall. His wife Apame helped Milesian soldiers who were fighting for the Seleucids far off in the east, and showed her concern regarding the progress of the work on the Didymaion ([171] I. Didyma 479.480). A short phase in which Miletus was allied with Ptolemaios seems to have begun after 294, to which Ptolemaios II refers later in his epistle to Miletus ([111] Welles, RC 14). But in 289/288 not only the Milesians but also the thirteen cities of the new Ionian League were under the supervision of a *strategos* in the service of Lysimachos ([109] Syll.³ 368).

In Caria, Lysimachos's claim collided with Ptolemaios's actual control of several strongpoints, on the one hand, and with Demetrios's reconquests, on the other. Halikarnassos adhered to Lysimachos, but Myndos and Iasos did not. Together with parts of inner Caria (certainly including Amyzon), the latter obeyed Ptolemaios. A royal epistle to Kaunos proves that since Ptolemaios's fleet had sailed to the harbor city in 309 the latter had been disloyal and gone over to Demetrios's side again. In the interior of the country, the appearance of two *dynastai* had made the situation unclear. One of these dynasts was Pleistarchos, Kassandros's brother, who had fled his satrapy of Cilicia when Demetrios arrived. He ruled for at least seven years in Caria. The community at the foot of Mt. Latmos called its city "Pleistarcheia," and the officials in the sanctuary of Sinuri, in Hyllarima, and Euromos dated their documents according to the years of Pleistarchos's reign. Another Macedonian who was one of Kassandros's officers, Eupolemos, ruled in Mylasa and had coins minted as a sign of his sovereignty.[16] The chronological relation between the two men is not clear. Experts also disagree concerning the original extent of the territory claimed by Pleistarchos, and especially as to whether after the Battle of Ipsos he was accorded not only Cilicia but also Caria.[17] In Lycia, Lissa may have belonged to Ptolemaios, and Limyra certainly did, as early as 288 BCE (p. 211). We have no real knowledge about the Lysimachan period in Pamphylia.[18]

After Kassandros's death (May 297) Demetrios the "besieger of cities" had mounted the throne in Macedonia in 294 and defended his dominion in Greece against Lysimachos, Ptolemaios, and Pyrrhos; in 287 he sought once again to take control of Asia. But his campaign straight across Anatolia, which he had begun with high hopes by taking Sardeis, ended in disaster. After crossing the Taurus and Amanos Mountains, in the spring of 285 he suffered a defeat near Kyrrhos in northern Syria. He was taken prisoner and interned by his ex-son-in-law Seleukos,[19] and died two years later at the age of fifty-four, after having lapsed into lethargy, gluttony, and drunkenness, spending most of his time playing dice (Plutarch, *Demetr.* 52).

Now Alexander's aged generals, Lysimachos and Seleukos, began to fight each other for control of Asia Minor. First came the dynastic intrigue at Lysimachos's court, which culminated in the murder of his eldest son, Agathokles. As the crown prince, Agathokles had had an energetic opponent in Arsinoe, his father's new wife. She succeeded in making the king suspect him of treachery. Among other moves away from Lysimachos, indignation about this behavior probably also led Philetairos to change sides again in the fortress at Pergamon and favor Seleukos. He occupied the place from now on in the interest of his future masters Seleukos and the latter's son Antiochos, minting coins bearing the king's image and having his chancellery date documents according to the years of the Seleucid king's reign. However, Seleukos's fate—he was soon thereafter assassinated—benefited Philetairos, making it possible for him to be in fact his own master and define his own domain undisturbed.

The Diadochi's decisive battle took place on the Korupedion, a plain near Magnesia on the Sipylos (now Manisa); it ended with the death of King Lysimachos and the fall of his empire. The Bithynian cities, including Nikaia, which he had founded but which had already seceded before the battle, celebrated the outcome, proclaiming an era of liberation. Seleukos "the Victor" (*nikator*) had defeated the great masters of Anatolia one after the other. For a time his empire seemed to coincide with that of the Achaemenids, with the exception of Egypt. Now seventy-seven years old, Seleukos had not seen his homeland of Macedonia in fifty-three years, and struck out to cross over into Europe. In his camp near Lysimacheia one of Ptolemaios's sons stabbed him.

The Structure of Diadochan Rule

In Asia Minor, the Diadochi were foreign rulers as the Persians had been before them. They adopted the system of satrapies. But at the same time the special title given Antigonos, *strategos tes Asias* (supreme commander of Asia), already implied a dominion that extended beyond satrapies to a kind of kingdom in the Middle East. Antigonos did not limit himself to Anatolia, either, and the center of gravity shifted from Kelainai, the seat of his satrapy in Phrygia to the new residence in Antigoneia on the Orontes (from 306 BCE on), close to the front with his opponents Seleukos and Ptolemaios. The satrapies in Asia Minor included Hellespontic Phrygia,[20] Greater Phrygia (*Phrygia megale*, also *ano Phrygia*),[21] Lydia, Caria, Lycia, Pamphylia, Pisidike, Cilicia, Cappadocia by the Taurus (Appian, Syr. 55 [281]: so-called Seleukis), Cappadocia by the Sea, and Paphlagonia. The satrapy system was partly supplemented or replaced by *strategiai*; the Greek title of *strategos* (literally, "leader of an army") can be used in place of that of satrap.[22] Levying taxes to establish and supply armies, along with making fortresses, cities, and harbors secure, were the primary tasks in the departments of the leadership personnel: Macedonian and Greek *philoi* (literally, "friends"); *strategoi*; and officials with simple titles, such as "prefect of" (*tetagmenos epi*) or "superintendent" (*epistates*), which defined a local jurisdiction of military and civilian authorities. The army was the center of power. The core army consisting of Macedonians had to be reinforced by hiring mercenaries. The recruiting of troops extended to natives, as we have seen particularly in the case of Eumenes in Cappadocia. All concepts of order and tax policy were subordinated to the primacy of the military. Thus, for example, part of the income received by Mnesimachos, one of Antigonos's followers to whom he had given land near Sardeis, was directly paid over to *chiliarchiai*, obviously military command centers in the area ([168] I. Sardis 1). On the coasts it was the cities with fortified acropolises and harbors, and in Anatolia the fortresses (Kelainai, Synnada, Ankyra, and Gaziura) that safeguarded the communication routes for troop movements, the backbone of military might. In a few of these castles the generals stored gold and silver to be used to finance their military campaigns; they were called *gazophylakia* (guarded treasure depots). One of the earliest and most important of them—which was also, of course, one of those most fought over—was the *gazophylakion* Kyinda, in Cilicia, where part of the booty from Alexander's campaigns in the east was stored and closely guarded (Diodorus 18, 62, 2; Strabo 14, 5, 10). Only a few years ago a previously unknown large fortified complex covering an area of a square kilometer was discovered twelve kilometers northeast of the provincial city of Kozan in the Taurus Mountains above the Cilician plain.[23] On the east side is preserved a polygonal structure as high as ten meters, with several chambers on the inside. Over a gate, a relief showing an Indian elephant can be seen—a clear allusion to the Seleucid army. The fortress is located high over the valley, guarding the passage from the eastern Cilician plain to the Cappadocian plateau. Pergamon has gone down in the history of the Diadochi as a *gazophylakion*, because it was the guardian of Lysimachos's treasure who got rid of his masters and laid the foundations for his successors' independent dominion. This inglorious origin of Pergamon's monarchy was well known even much later, at a time when the royal house had long since established the ideology of a heroic royal race of Greek descent. Attalos III had the grammarian Daphidas of Telmessos crucified on Mt. Thorax near Magnesia on the Maeander for having written a couplet that insulted the kings of Pergamon: "Purpled with stripes, mere filings of the treasure of Lysimachus, ye rule the Lydians and Phrygia" (Strabo 14, 1, 39; trans. Jones).

In large parts of the Anatolian interior the quasi-feudal system of land ownership continued to function as it had under the satraps. The Diadochi rewarded and obligated their followers by giving them land. A vivid example of both the social components and the legal situation is provided by the previously mentioned Mnesimachos inscription.[24] The Temple of Artemis in Sardeis had a temple deposit from which this Mnesimachos, who was a favorite of Antigonos Monophthalmos, received a payment for safekeeping (*parakatatheke*). When he could not pay back the money, he had to mortgage the land the king had given him (*ge en dorea*), but certain property relations not underlying the mortgage were excepted and specified. In any case, this involved several extensive estates to which belonged villages and individual farmsteads, houses, and gardens, the peasants working these same lands, their equipment, and all their possessions, including their slaves and their labor for the landlord.

In Asia, the period of the Hellenistic kingdoms was anything but a time of decadence of the *polis*.[25] If we take into account the fact that the wars of the Diadochi were waged on three continents, we can see that the Greek *poleis*, because of their geographical location on the coasts of Asia Minor, were in an increasingly crucial strategic position that was clearly distinct from their position on the periphery of the Persian Empire. This gave the *poleis* political weight. However, they were not only the point where military lines of communication by water and by land intersected, and where there were garrisons and harbors for warships. Gaining access to the *poleis* and promoting their internal stability was in the vital interest of the Greek-speaking Diadochi in other ways as well. There they found—so to speak—first-class "human capital" in the form of experts in the areas of construction technology, administration, finance, cults, and festivals. Money and natural produce were also deposited there, and invested and managed by civic authorities. There were also trading centers, famed religious sites that spread the prestige of the deities' powerful donors and devotees. And—not least—there were sites for the temples, altars, and festivals of the kings' own cults, which were visited by many people and were well suited to get the residents to show their loyalty and good will for the royal masters. Alexander came to Asia to liberate the Greek cities. He brought with him the fundamental distinction between *polis* and royal territory. His successors also adhered to this distinction. The Diadochi repeated, for the purposes of propaganda, Alexander's declaration that the cities were free. Already Antigonos the "One-Eyed" knew that he could use this weapon to threaten in two directions. Paradoxical as it may sound, for the Greeks it was a gift that promoted their readiness to let themselves be ruled by their benefactor, and at the same time it branded as illegitimate his opponents' attempts to force cities to support them.

The transition from primarily native settlement units to organized communities on the Greek model had long been under way in various regions. We have seen that before Alexander's arrival in the fourth century BCE, communities like Kaunos in Caria and Laranda in the Taurus—no doubt encouraged by their symbiosis with or proximity to the Greeks—had already adapted or imitated the institutions of the *polis*. In Lycia, *polis* territories were established in the areas formerly ruled by the dynasts; here the process has been extensively investigated, since epigraphic sources can be coordinated with the development of the settlements shown by intensive archaeological surveys: the Xanthians appeared as a community in the fourth century and made decisions with their *perioikoi* (inhabitants of the surrounding vicinity). The latter are also attested in Telmessos and Limyra.[26] Small and middle-sized estates, whose location in the classical period was determined chiefly by their defensibility, subordinated themselves to new *polis* centers emerging on the plains and appear in (later) Hellenistic inscriptions as different subdivisions of the polis territory: *demoi, komai,* and *peripolia.* However, they gradually expanded into the plains and developed vibrant communal activities with their own decisionmaking assemblies, officials, festivals, and public buildings. To the multipolar, decentered settlement structures in the city territories corresponded a clear hierarchy of local communities in a group held together by citizenship in the *polis,* in which an opposition between city and country could not prevail.[27]

In the age of the Diadochi, the *poleis hellenides* ("Greek cities"), most of which were on the coast, do not offer a unified image so far as their internal constitution, age, size, reputation, and the composition of their populations are concerned. Nonetheless, they constitute a distinct group whose spectrum was only gradually extended as new cities were founded farther into the interior. It was in the rulers' interest to establish order in the present cities and to win their allegiance. They went so far as to merge smaller Greek cities with one another or with larger ones to form a single new state, with or without resettling the citizens (*synoikismos*);[28] we can give the examples of the merging of Kebren, Skepsis, Larisa, Kolonai, Hamaxitos, and Neandreia in the Troad; the (unrealized) merging of Teos and Lebedos in Ionia under Antigonos; that of Tieion, Sesamos, Kromna, and Kytoros on the Black Sea; and that of Ephesos, Kolophon, and Lebedos on the Aegean under Lysimachos.

Antigonos's letter to Teos, preserved in an inscription on stone ([[111] Welles, RC 3) allows us to see a royal plan for *synoikismos* in all its details. Two cities, a large and a small one, were to be merged with each other. Antigonos decreed a transitional solution and a final regulation. Thus the citizens of the smaller city of Lebedos were to be provisionally housed in Teos, but after a maximum of three years, they had to have built houses on plots of land assigned to them that were at least as large as the ones they had owned in Lebedos. Lawsuits were to be judged according to a short-term agreement until an electoral college formed on an equal basis (a committee composed of citizens elected from each city, three from Teos and three from Lebedos) had drafted a new body of laws that was to be submitted to the king for his approval. The intended application of the laws of a third, foreign city, Kos, during the transitional period is noteworthy. Both parties had agreed to this after Antigonos, rejecting Teos's suggestion that its laws continue in force during the transition, decided in favor of Lebedos's desire to resort to Kos's body of laws instead. In many ways, this *synoikismos* resembles an earlier one carried out in Caria the decade following Alexander's death, under the satrap Asandros, which is also documented by inscriptions. Moreover, we find in this text the oldest (with the alleged exception of Ilion and Alexander[29]) case in Asia Minor in which an urban *phyle* (a subdivision of the citizenry) was named after a ruler—the satrap Asandros. Subsequently, many communities expressed their devotion to their *ktistai* (founders) in this way, until

40. Lysimachos's wall in Ephesos.

the naming of *phylae* after Roman emperors came into general use. The synoikismos under Asandros also aimed at the physical resettlement and incorporation of a small community, Pidasa, into a larger one named Latmos—temporarily called Pleistarcheia, and then renamed Herakleia—and the organization of the transition: the merging of revenues, debt redemption, and the provisional housing of citizens of Pidasa in Latmos. The following provision is unprecedented in historical records: for six years, daughters of families from each community could be married only to men from the other one.

The relocation that had the most far-reaching consequences for individual urban development, with new and expanded construction, the building of walls, and a founder's cult, was the Artemis city of Ephesos under Lysimachos.[30] The total area of about 280 hectares is supposed to have been surrounded by perimeter wall of massive ashlar blocks running over the top of the nearby hills, about nine kilometers long and defended by more than fifty rectangular towers. Its ruins are still to be seen there (Figure 40). The Roman metropolis later flourished on its Hellenistic site.

Behind this elaborate procedure stood various specific goals aimed at advantages that were both general and specific to the locality concerned: depending on the topography, relocation benefited communication and transportation, as well as the military infrastructure, and this becomes particularly clear in the case of Ephesos. From the governors' point of view, small states on small territories were a notorious source of unrest, for example in border conflicts, and they complicated legal and fiscal administration. Protracted legal proceedings between citizens of a city or between the latter and citizens of a neighboring city could cripple a community. Where it was possible, a *synoikismos* offered an opportunity to reform the legal system from the ground up. Antigonos Monophthalmos probably was the first to cope with this budding problem by appointing judges brought in from a different city.

Disregarding later dissolutions, the regional decreases in the numbers of *poleis* that accompanied the *synoikismoi* were more than compensated by the foundation of new ones (Map 9).[31] Providing soldiers with land and getting them to settle where they could be used promised to have advantages, and the choice of location was once again made based on similar considerations. Research on this category of settlements speaks of "military colonies." A strong Macedonian element can also be seen later, in names and other indicators, in many places in the interior of Anatolia, for example, communities in places like Dokimeion and Peltai in Phrygia, which called themselves "Dokimeian Macedonians" or "Peltenian Macedonians." Though at first the Macedonians or Greeks remained apart from the predominantly native population, they soon entered into a community with them, and Hellenistic cities were formed out of islands of mixed settlements (*katoikiai*). Unlike the cities founded by Alexander in the far east, which were not viable, many of those founded by the Diadochi in Anatolia flourished, and that permanently changed the political map of Asia Minor. I mention here the most important events: under Antigonos, Smyrna is supposed to have been refounded on the basis of a combination of village settlements. In addition to the city founded in the Troad by the *synoikismos* of six towns, other Antigoneiai named after him were founded near Kyzikos, Daskyleion (probably the harbor, not the satrap's capital), on Lake Ascania in Bithynia, and perhaps also Dorylaion in Phrygia. His general, Dokimos, who went over to Lysimachos in 302 BCE, founded the city of Dokimeion in Phrygia, later known for its production of marble. Lysimachos gave the Bithynian Antigoneia the name of his first wife, Nikaia; the city flourished and was to make (Church) history six hundred years later as the site of the ecumenical council. His second wife, Amastris, was allowed to give her name to the aforementioned *synoikismos* on the Black Sea. Lysimachos changed the name Antigoneia in the Troad to Alexandria. In Mysia there was an Agathokleia named after his eldest son. He renamed Smyrna Eurydikeia, after his daughter, but it retained its new name no longer than Ephesos did, which had been renamed Arsinoeia, after his third wife.

Seleukos the "Victor" had less time to found cities in Anatolia than the predecessors he had vanquished. The city of Stratonikeia on the Kaikos certainly was founded by his son, and Seleukeia on the Maeander (Tralleis), Seleukeia in Pamphylia, and Seleukeia in Pisidia were probably founded by the latter as well. The same is true of other new settlements, even if it is not completely out of the question that they might have been founded by Seleukos. These include the resettlement of the old Lydian city of Thyateira with Macedonian officers and soldiers, as well as Nysa (previously Athymbra) and Apollonia Salbake in Caria, Laodikeia Katakekaumene in Pisidia (which was named after Seleukos's mother Laodike), and Apameia (near Kelainai) in Phrygia, which was named after Apama, who came from Bactria and was

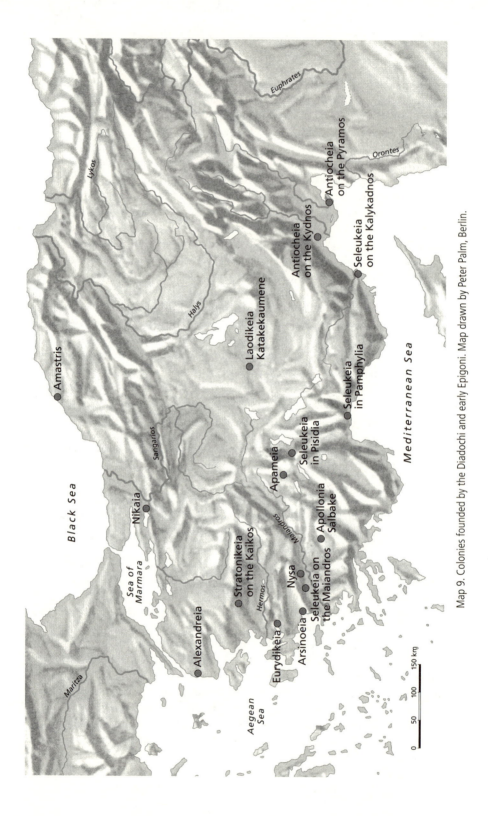

Map 9. Colonies founded by the Diadochi and early Epigoni. Map drawn by Peter Palm, Berlin.

married to Seleukos in the mass wedding in Susa in 324. In any case, of the cities founded by the Seleucids in Cilicia, which he conquered in 295 BCE, two—Antiocheia on the Pyramos (Magarsos) and Antiocheia on the Kydnos (Tarsos)[32]—may go back to him, while Seleukeia on the Kalykadnos, modern-day Silifke, is explicitly attributed to him (Ammianus 14, 8, 2; Stephanos of Byzantion, p. 560, 3–9 s. v.). The Ptolemaic rulers first made their appearance in Asia Minor as founders of cities during the reign of their second dynast, who bore the byname of Philadelphos and ruled from 282 to 246 BCE.

Many areas in Anatolia were not too far from a zone of already viable cities and were available for new settlements. We know little about the immediate effects of such processes on the property relations of established residents. The land designated for the new settlers must not have been ownerless everywhere. *Synoikismoi* certainly encountered tenacious resistance, and not a few were doomed to fail. In view of that fact, these measures have been quite negatively assessed by modern research as crude attempts to overcome the "introverted sense of community identity." The epigraphers Robert and Wörrle (who speaks of the "autocratic, brutal Diadochan manner"[33]) have argued against praising the increase in urban development. But after reviewing the various examples, no sweeping judgment is possible. Despite individual cases of hardship, such as Lysimachos's treatment of Kolophon, the rulers' plans and the steps they took did not approach the brutality of the Assyrian mass deportations, for example. Instead, we find thorough and differentiated consideration of the citizens' wishes and recommendations, as well as efforts to take existing institutions and traditions as a basis and to make use of them. Where resistance and discontent were involved, the local groups' animosity was probably not always directed against the ruler, but also against one another. On the part of the *poleis* there was still the larger community's latent desire to absorb a smaller one, and the monarch sometimes had to protect the weaker party.

In the age of the Diadochi, along with structural and constitutional changes some city centers also took on a new outward appearance. An architectural renaissance that had begun in a few cities during the time of Alexander continued well into the phase of *synoikismoi* and new settlements, especially in the form of new temples built of marble. The relocation and complete rebuilding of Priene—our sources say nothing about its initiators and founders—was undertaken in the second half of the fourth century but continued into the early Hellenistic age. The whole residential area, extending over a slope, was divided into rectangular lots of the same size, in accord with a general checkerboard plan. The Temple of Athena designed by Pytheos (one of the two architects of the Maussolleion) had been undergoing expansion since the late classical period, and at the same time work on the new Artemision near Ephesos was progressing, even before Lysimachos laid out the new city. In the time of Alexander the marble temple of Athena was built on the acropolis of Pergamon, and under Lysimachos the *peripteros* in the Doric order was built in Ilion. Around 300 BCE, construction of the enormous Artemision in Sardeis began, and at about the same time the shrine of Apollo of Didyma near Miletus, an entirely new struc-

41. Restored Temple of Apollo of Didyma near Miletus, staircase leading to the Two Columns Hall.

ture in the Ionic tradition, was designed and built (but never fully completed); it can be described as unique in various respects. The building that has now been excavated and restored is the largest temple ruin in Asia Minor (Figure 41). On the *stylobate*, the top step (51 by 109 meters) of a seven-level *krepis* (foundation), rise the *pronaos* (porch) and double ring-hall with 120 columns in all, each of them 19.7 meters high and 2 meters in diameter. The passage from the *pronaos* into the interior of the building led through two tunnels with barrel vaults on both sides of a rectangular room, the Two Columns Hall. The great "door" in the middle lay over a high threshold that could not be climbed from the outside, and which could be reached from the inside of the building only by the monumental broad open staircase. The innermost part—an area (*adyton*) inaccessible to the public—was a long, rectangular courtyard open to the sky (*hypaithral*), 21.7 by 53.6 meters in size, where the holy spring of the god's oracle and a small shrine containing his sacred image were located. The floor of this inner courtyard was considerably lower than that of the temple podium built around it; the courtyard was surrounded by a smooth, marble base wall, on which the scratched-in construction drawings have been found, and over it was a wall area articulated by pilasters as far up as the roof of the ring-hall.

The Age of the Epigoni

With Lysimachos's death in 281 BCE and the murder of Seleukos, which occurred shortly thereafter, the weightiest claim to dominion over Anatolia was still to be made by Seleukos's heirs, and first of all his son Antiochos I. For a family tree and a list of successors ruling in Asia Minor see Figure 42 and the Appendix. After 290 BCE Antiochos was elevated to the post of coregent and sent to the upper (i.e., the eastern) satrapies. Antiochos, we read in Memnon of Herakleia, "had through many wars recovered his father's kingdom with difficulty and even so not completely" (*FGrHist* 434 F 1, 9, 1; trans. Smith, http://www.attalus.org/translate/memnon1 .html). A coherent dominion over the whole country was not achieved, however, until it was subjugated by Rome. While the Seleucid Empire still continued to exist, the political map disintegrated into constantly changing fields of action and separate dominions, small and large, temporary or enduring, ruled by kings, usurpers, dynasts, confederations, and cities. (This held all the more after the Romans forced the empire's dissolution in most of Asia Minor in 189 BCE.) For this reason it is not always easy to maintain an overview of the development in Asia Minor during the age of the Epigoni. In the following, I examine the main lines of development and also the regional centers where important changes took place.

The Seleucid Empire in Anatolia

In the gigantic empire reaching from Afghanistan to the Aegean, the Anatolian possessions—seen, naturally, from the point of view of the central lands of Babylonia and Syria—were called the country "beyond" (*he epekeina*) the Taurus. They were later, under Antiochos III, entrusted as a whole to a regent, whose position amounted to that of a viceroy. Under Antiochos an "archpriest of all the sanctuaries in the land beyond the Taurus" also appeared. He was at the same time the archpriest of the cult of the ruler in the whole trans-Taurine area, and on this model Antiochus III ordered in 193 BCE the empire-wide appointment of *archiereiai* (archpriests) for the cult of Queen Laodike.[34] The kings apparently also continued to make use of the office of imperial finance minister, such as it already existed in the time of Alexander—the *hemiolios* ("one and a half").[35]

The most important Seleucid seat in Anatolia became Sardeis, where the kings resided when they were "beyond" the Taurus. However, tarrying there was seldom possible, since they moved from land to land in ongoing multifront wars, less to conquer new territories than to maintain or restore the existing system of relationships. The Seleucids were half Iranian in descent (Antiochos's mother was the Iranian Apama). Of all the kings in Asia Minor in the time of the Epigoni, they may have come closest to exercising the kind of territorial rule prefigured by the Achaemenid Empire and adopted by Alexander. With the exception of the added satrapy of Lycaonia, the system of satrapies of the Diadochi, outlined in the preceding section, continued in Asia Minor. The fortresses and *gazophylakia* retained their status in the strategic network and were certainly further expanded. The system of the subdivision of the satrapies is a difficult subject that I cannot expand on here. Under the Seleucids, it seems that a strict, unified order never existed over all of Asia Minor, which is hardly surprising, given the great geographical and historical variations.

Under the regents of a satrapy stood commissioners called *hyparchoi* ([111] Welles, *RC* 20 line 5, cf. 37 line. 1). The title of a royal representative from the time of Antiochos I, *epimeletes tu topu* (caretaker of the place) has given rise to the idea that in Anatolia as in Ptolemaic Egypt, the so-called toparchy was widespread as an administrative unit governed by a civil official. This *epimeletes* would then correspond to the *toparchai* known to us from Egypt and Syria.[36] The administrative work done by royal *dioiketai* (custodians) extended to the level of the satrapies; that of the *oikonomoi* (stewards) and *eklogistai* (tax accountants) extended also to the lower departments of the satrapy. Both designations, *dioiketai* and *oikonomoi*, were also used to refer to the stewards of private estates owned by the king and by courtiers—a conceptual ambivalence that later found a counterpart in the Roman *procuratores*, the imperial proctors for domains and taxes (p. 368).

The empire was "won by the spear," and it was royal land (*basileia, he tu basileos*). The settlement of Macedonians and Greeks on *kleroi* (parcels of land) alongside natives continued during the Seleucid period.[37] Beyond the coastal areas, in the open spaces of Anatolia, except for castles and imperial residences there were still only a few places that had an urban character with public buildings constructed of stone. Various levels of village-type settlements prevailed, inhabited by *laoi* (peasants) who had to pay tribute.[38] Apart from village or clan groups that were usually assembled around a religious center, the largest unit was the village (*kome*), which represented not only a type of settlement but also an association of people capable of making decisions. Various terms whose meaning often vacillates refer to still smaller settlement units, such as hamlets and farms (*chorion, topos, baris,* and *epaulia*).[39] Their dispersion must be conceived quite differently, depending on the kind of territory concerned. Archaeological surveys in the Lycian Yavu uplands showed a relatively high density of individual farms. For example, the fertile high basins of Cappadocia Pontica seem to have had thousands of villages, as the name of the region, *Chiliokomon*, suggests.

This royal land must be distinguished from the state territory of a Greek *polis* (*politike chora*) and the temple land that—as was already the case in earlier periods—was considered the divinity's property and was administered and exploited by a priesthood. So far as we know, these two categories of land were not considered to

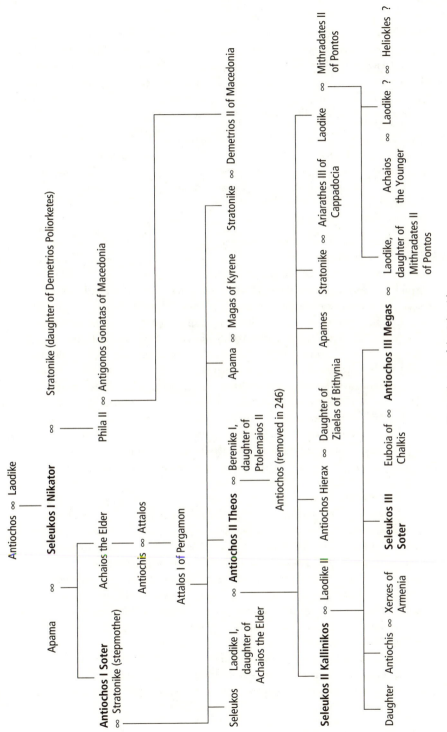

42. Family tree of the Seleucids.

have a duty to pay tribute, but this does not mean that no taxes (*syntaxeis*) were levied on *poleis*. The correspondence conducted between Antiochos I, his satrap Meleagros in Hellespontic Phrygia, and the city of Ilion ([111] Welles, RC 10–12) is instructive in this regard.[40] It was published in stone inscriptions that Heinrich Schliemann discovered in Troy in 1873. It concerns a gift of land to Aristodikides, the king's favorite and an illustrious citizen of the city of Assos in the Troad:

> King Antiochus to Meleager, greeting. We have given to Aristodicides of Assus two thousand plethra [a measure of area, about twenty-seven to thirty-five square meters] of cultivable land to join to the city of Ilium or Scepsis. Do you therefore give orders to convey to Aristodicides from the land adjacent to that of Gergis or of Scepsis, wherever you think best, the two thousand plethra of our land, and to add them to the boundaries of the land of Ilium or of Scepsis. (no. 10; trans. Welles)

The integration of lands into a city territory, that is, their exclusion from the *basileia* and incorporation into the category of the *ge politike* (the *polis*'s territory) was awarded to Aristodikides as a privilege, in accord with an earlier letter. Depending on the topographic conditions of the neighboring areas, different adjacent *poleis* could be chosen to attach the gift of royal land to one of them. However, after other cities had also applied to him and had sent him presents, Aristodikides selected Ilion. A similar operation was Antiochos II's gift—or rather, sale—of land to his ex-wife Laodike recorded in a collection of royal correspondence from 254/253 BCE ([111] Welles, RC 18–20). Laodike bought the lands in question, which bordered on the cities of Zeleia and Kyzikos, together with a large village and small hamlets or farms (*topoi*) and also the peasants living there and their possessions. She also received permission to incorporate the land into the city territory of her choice. Future buyers of Laodike's land would be allowed to add it to a city's territory if she herself had not already done so. In the wide-ranging discussion of this testimony, there are various competing views regarding property rights to land. I have already mentioned this question in discussing the concept of "my land" in the Persian king Darius's letter to Gadatas: was all the land of the *basileia* essentially the king's property? (see p. 160). Did the monarch retain, despite all relations of ownership, the sole power of disposal? That is, did he simply concede ownership of the land to others subject to revocation? Or did the king respect other individuals' property rights to land? Was the concept "royal land" (*basilike chora*) therefore limited, insofar as property law was concerned, to the king's private land (which was, to be sure, very extensive)?

This much is certain: the king respected not only clearly delimited units of land like Ilion's *politike chora*, which definitely lay, as a "*polis* in our *symmachia*," outside the royal domain, but also the manifold property relationships that had grown up within the *basileia* itself, including the parcels of land on which he had founded new settlements. As the historian Christof Schuler has convincingly shown, any attempt to use this land as a reservoir that could be arbitrarily reallocated at any time would have been doomed to fail and would not have been in the king's interest.[41] However, the rulers' interventions show that they associated ownership with good conduct and considered themselves justified in punishing disloyalty with confiscations of property (IG XII 6, 1, 11). Land that the king had "given" (*ge en dorea*) to private individuals, thereby founding a special relationship of loyalty on a territorial basis, he could also take back.[42] In individual cases monarchs did not even hesitate to "give away" whole *poleis*: from the second book of Maccabees (4, 30 f.) we learn that rebellions broke out in the Cilician cites of Tarsos and Mallos when Antiochos IV tried to give them to his beloved as a gift. His predecessor Antiochos III offered Eumenes of Pergamon his daughter's hand in marriage along with the cities he had earlier taken away from him. Eumenes himself gave Tieion on the Black Sea to Prusias of Bithynia after he had received it from Pharnakes (Polybius 25, 2, 7). And in 165/164 BCE the Rhodian emissary Astymedes petitioned the Roman Senate for permission to exclude certain cities from the liberation of his country's continental possessions, on the following grounds: "But as for Caunus, you will confess that we bought it from Ptolemy's generals for two hundred talents, and that Stratoniceia was given us as a great favor by Antiochus and Seleucus" (Polybius 30, 31, 3–8; trans. Paton).

Back to the gift to Aristodikides of land in the Troad. What is especially noteworthy is this: the transfer of the property to the domain of the city, that is, to the *politike chora*, must have been an advantage not only for the *polis* whose territory was thereby enlarged, but also for Aristodikides (and in the other case, for Laodike) as a landowner—and certainly not primarily because of homage paid them by the favored city and the additional presents given. In my view, the advantage must have involved a different practice of taxation that took into account the clear distinction between the *polis*'s land and the king's land. Just as in the case of the gift received by Mnesimachos in Sardeis, Aristodikides must also have remained subject to the royal tax authorities so long as his land continued to be part of the *basileia*. As part of a city territory it was presumably also not completely free of taxes,[43] but it was apparently assessed at a lower rate.

Arrival and Settlement of the Galatians in Asia Minor, and the Early Attalids of Pergamon

In the northwest of Asia Minor, in Bithynia, events of far-reaching significance were in the offing in the aftermath of the battle of Korupedion, fought in 281 BCE. The power vacuum left there by Lysimachos was exploited by Zipoites, who had fought on Seleukos's side, assumed the title of king, and founded the city of Zipoition. He deprived the *polis* of Herakleia Pontike of parts of its territory: Kieros—the later Prusias on the Hypios—Tieion, and the island of Thynias. For their part, the citizens of Herakleia were also trying to free themselves from Seleucid sovereignty. Antiochos I—whose residence was in Syria—first dispatched an army to Asia Minor, but the officer operating in Bithynia, Hermogenes of Aspendos, was ambushed by the Bithynians and killed. Thereupon the king decided to march on Bithynia himself.[44] In the meantime, Zipoites had been succeeded by his eldest son Nikomedes I. The latter acquired Herakleia as an ally in exchange for the assurance that he would return the areas taken away from it, but at the same time he was under pressure from his rebellious younger brother Zipoites II. Nikomedes thereupon invited the Celts to enter Asia Minor and to ally themselves with him against both Zipoites and Antiochos I.

The Celts, who advanced as far as the Thracian side of the Bosporus, consisted of two groups. Since the Byzantians initially opposed their embarkation, both groups marched to the Hellespont, where a detachment under the leadership of Lutatios was able to cross over during the winter of 278/277 BCE, while Leonnorios led his part of the army back to the Bosporus. There Nikomedes helped him make the crossing, and both groups were reunited on Asian soil in the same year, whereas a third group followed a year later. The overall number of Celts has been estimated at 30,000–35,000 men. The sequence of events is very incompletely documented. In any case, with their help Nikomedes was able to rid himself of his brother Zipoites. The Celts probably later took the initiative themselves, and some of them moved farther south. In 277/276 BCE they attacked the sanctuary at Didyma, plundered the temple treasury, and rampaged through Miletus's territory. In Priene, a courageous citizen organized forces to defend his country. Other places followed his example. Philetairos of Pergamon, who a few years earlier had gone over from Lysimachos to Seleukos and was now relatively independent, and above all very rich, gave the citizens of Kyzikos money and grain to help them defend their territory. When the community of Kyme in Aiolis asked him to provide it with weapons, he sent 600 shields ([195] SEG 50, 1195). Decrees issued by the people of Erythrai speak of "many horrors and dangers," hostage takings and tribute payments, and a votive stele in Thyateira in Lydia mentions the rescue of a man from Celtic captivity. Individual groups of Celts penetrated as far as the border area between Phrygia and Pisidia, Sagalassos, and even Tlos in Lycia. A decade after they entered Asia, in the year 268/267 BCE, the villagers of Neonteichos and Kiddiukome in Phrygia, where the city of Laodikeia on the Lykos later grew up, thanked two officials of the Seleucid government for having ransomed a large number of prisoners.[45]

Antiochos I won a victory that was important for his reputation throughout Asia Minor when he defeated the Celts somewhere in the area around Ankyra in the so-called Elephant Battle. The sight of elephants must have given the Celts a shock such as only seeing modern art can otherwise produce—this parallel is made, however, by the writer Lucian when he compares the effect made by Antiochos's elephant battle with that made on a contemporary observer by the female Hippocentaur in a painting by the famed artist Zeuxis:

> Neither the Galatians themselves nor their horses had previously seen an elephant and they were so confused by the unexpected sight that, while the beasts were still a long way off and they could only hear the trumpeting and see their tusks gleaming all the more brightly against their bodies dark all over and their trunks raised like hooks, they turned and fled in a disorderly rout before they were within bowshot. (Lucian, *Zeux.* 8–11; trans. Kilburn)

The victory monument erected by Antiochos is supposed to have represented an elephant trampling a Celtic warrior.

The exact date when this important change took place remains uncertain. Between 276/275 and 274, Antiochos I resided in Sardeis (cuneiform tablet B. M. 62689). The success must have been celebrated during the 260s, because in documents from the years between 267 and 262 we learn of the establishment of a cult of Antiochos Soter (the "Savior") in the cities of the Ionian League. Probably shortly thereafter the king exempted Erythrai from the Galatian *syntaxis*, a tax that all cities apparently had to pay for the war against the Celts. Furthermore, we must take into account the fact that between 274 and 271 Antiochos had to wage a war outside Asia Minor, the First Syrian War, against Ptolemaios II Philadelphos.[46]

THE GALATIANS IN ASIA MINOR

A short time after the extensive campaigns of war and plunder—Leonnorios had made a name for himself as the main leader—the Celts settled in central Anatolia in accord with three main tribes (see the Appendix). Those called Tolistoagii (in the inscriptions in Pergamon) or Tolistobogii settled in the West around an Old Phrygian shrine in Pessinus (not far from Gordion) that developed into an important trading center. Their dwelling area in the bend of the Sangarios River covered part of Greater Phrygia and probably also the mountainous southern edge of Bithynia. Fortresses named Blukion and Peion later protected the land.[47] The second, geographically more central group, the Tektosages, settled around the castle and the Men shrine of Ankyra. The third, eastern tribe, the Trokmoi, settled beyond the Halys River, around Tavium (Büyük Nefes Köy near Yozgat), where a shrine existed and an *emporion* (trading post) also developed. In this country, which already belonged to Cappadocia Pontica, further fortresses were built, to which the Galatians later added the castles of Mithridation and Danala. It is probable that the settlement of the western group took place soon after the crossing of the Bosporus and in agreement with Nikomedes. The central and eastern settlement areas may have been allotted by Antiochus to the Tektosages and Trokmoi after the Elephant Battle. The official version in Pergamon, according to which the settlement took place after Attalos I's victory (p. 214) is less credible (Pausanias 1, 4, 5; 1, 8, 1). The Byzantine writer Stephanos of Byzantion cites a Hellenistic author, Apollonios of Aphrodisias, according to whom the name of the city of Ankyra (Greek for "anchor") is connected in the following way with the city's founding by the Celts: in alliance with Mithridates and Ariobarzanes, the Celts had repelled an army of invasion sent by Ptolemaios of Egypt and pursued it as far as the coast. The fleeing troops had left behind the anchors of their ships, and the Celts are supposed to have taken them back to their settlement and named it after their prize. But Ankyra was certainly not founded by Celts. The invasion of a Ptolemaic fleet on the coast of the Black Sea at this time is also uncorroborated in other sources.[48]

Strabo sketches the organization of the Galatians, which solidified only later, as follows:

The three tribes spoke the same language and differed from each other in no respect; and each was divided into four portions which were called tetrarchies, each tetrarchy having its own tetrarch, and also one judge and one military commander, both subject to the tetrarch, and two subordinate commanders. The Council of the twelve tetrarchs consisted of three hundred men, who assembled at Drynemetum, as it was called. Now the Council passed judgement upon murder cases, but the tetrarchs and the judges upon all others. (12, 5, 1; trans. Jones)

The title of tetrarch is not attested in inscriptions or by authors before the first century BCE, and it has been suggested that the tetrarchy was first established by Pompey.[49]

To the old Anatolian, Thracian-Balkan, Greek, Iranian, and Semitic elements of the population of Asia Minor, the Galatians added one permanent one that was not scattered but remained in a relatively well-defined area of central Anatolia. At the beginning of the first century CE Strabo noted that the whole land settled by the Celts was called "Galatia" or "Gallograikia."[50] In his time, there was a Roman province with this name, to which many areas outside the heartland inhabited by the Celts were annexed. In the modern history of (Western) reception, the most familiar association with "Galatians," the name given the Celts in Asia Minor, is undoubtedly the letter of the Apostle Paul, and there is an old controversy over who the intended addressees really were—the people settled around Ankyra or the inhabitants of the parts of the province farther to the south. Tribal state institutions and aristocratic traditions still existed in the time of the Roman Empire, when individuals proud of their descent from tetrarchs referred to them in inscriptions. The Galatians' language remained alive down into late antiquity, even if nothing in writing is extant. Now only scattered evidence survives in the form of names and loanwords. The priest Alexandros (p. 521), who lived in neighboring Paphlagonia in the second century CE and issued oracular pronouncements—he is known to us from a malicious pamphlet by his contemporary Lucian—accepted questions in Celtic, but could not answer them himself and had to get translations made by these customers' compatriots (*homoethneis*) (Lucian, *Alex*. 51). In the fourth century CE St. Jerome remarked that the Galatians in the area around Ankyra spoke almost the same language as the residents of Trier (*in Gal.*, *PL* 26 382c). When writers of the Imperial period and late antiquity still speak of the Galatians with scorn, regarding them as stupid and crude barbarians, this is not a matter of anti-Celtism but rather part of their negative image of all the indigenous, un-Hellenized or insufficiently Hellenized and educated peoples of Anatolia. Nonetheless, already in the Hellenistic period, especially when it emanated from Pergamon, the specific image of a plundering and murdering mob of barbarians, on whose appearance *kindynos* (danger) and *phobos* (horror) break out, was attached to the Galatians and influenced iconography from Hellenistic sculptural art down to modern history books. Other armies in Hellenistic Asia Minor were no less involved in murder and plunder than the Galatians. It is interesting to see how Polybius evaluates the fact that after a victory over the Galatians at the Hellespont, King Prusias of Bithynia invaded their camp and butchered nearly all the women and children and had their possessions plundered: "By this exploit he freed the cities on the Hellespont from a serious menace and danger, and gave a good lesson to the barbarians from Europe in future not to be over ready to cross to Asia" (Polybius 5, 111; trans. Paton).

There is evidence that the Galatians in Asia Minor practiced human sacrifice. Despite some modern attempts to rebut such statements as relying on a stereotype of barbarians, they are no doubt historical. Diodorus speaks (31, 13) with revulsion of the practice of choosing the most handsome prisoners of war in their best years and sacrificing them to the gods, "if there is a god who accepts such honors," and having the rest killed with spears. Referring to the year 187 BCE, Livy (38, 47, 12) has the Roman general Gnaeus Manlius Vulso (p. 225) say in his apologia, that the cities of Asia owe to him their liberation from the affliction of the Galatians, who brought with them the custom of slaughtering their children as human sacrifices: *mactatas humanas hostias immolatosque liberos suos*. Excavations of Gordion, in the area where the Tektosages lived, uncovered skeletons of women and children who had been killed; they had probably been sacrifices.[51]

To a certain extent, the positive side of the image of the Galatians in ancient texts is their proficiency in war, their toughness, and their honesty. Among the Galatian women whom Plutarch (*mor.* 257e–258c; 258e–f) mentions in his work "On Virtues of Women" are Kamma and Chiomara. One of them, a priestess of Kybele, the wife of a tetrarch, and the object of another tetrarch's desire, resisted the latter's advances. After he had assassinated her husband, she did not rest until she had poisoned him and herself. The other woman, who was also the wife of a chieftain, had been taken prisoner during Manlius's expedition, raped by a Roman officer, and then offered to her tribe in exchange for ransom. She arranged for the Roman to be killed during the exchange and brought his head to her husband, saying that even finer than fidelity was the certainty that of the men who had ever touched her, only one was still alive. Plutarch adds that Polybius conversed with this woman in Sardeis and admired her intelligence and finesse.

DEVELOPMENT OF THE ATTALIDS' POWER IN PERGAMON

The weaknesses of Seleucid rule in Asia Minor were soon to be profoundly revealed by other than the Bithynians and Galatians. The dynasty of Pergamon ceased to be a vassal and became an opponent (for a family tree and list of rulers, see Figure 43 and the Appendix). The steep slopes of the hill over the valley of the Kaikos in southern Mysia (Figure 44)—where the officer Philetairos had been installed by Lysimachos with a treasure of about 9,000 talents and confirmed in his position by Seleukos— lies in far western Anatolia, near the Greek cities on the Aegean coast. Here was the city we already saw in the early fourth century BCE as being ruled by vassals of the Persian king, the family of Gongylos: Greek nobles and masters over what was probably a largely non-Greek population.

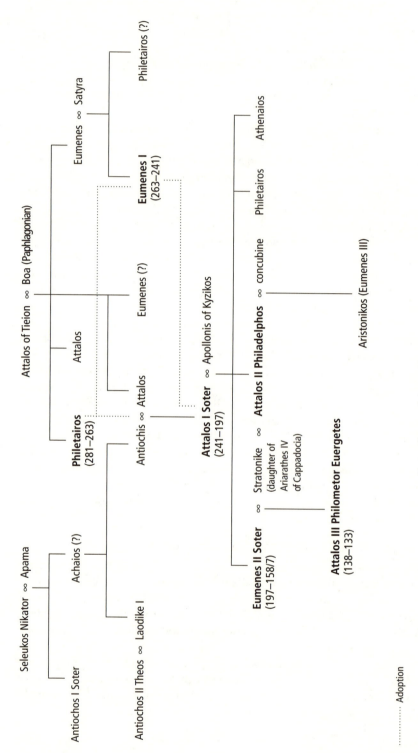

43. Family tree of the Attalids of Pergamon.

Seleukos Nikator ∞ Apama

Antiochos I Soter

Achaios (?)

Antiochos II Theos ∞ Laodike I

Attalos of Tieion ∞ Boa (Paphlagonian)

Philetairos (281–263)

Attalos

Eumenes (?)

Eumenes ∞ Satyra

Philetairos (?)

Antiochis ∞ Attalos

Eumenes I (263–241)

Attalos I Soter (241–197) ∞ Apollonis of Kyzikos

Attalos II Philadelphos ∞ concubine

Philetairos

Athenaios

Aristonikos (Eumenes III)

Eumenes II Soter (197–158/7) ∞ Stratonike (daughter of Ariarathes IV of Cappadocia)

Attalos III Philometor Euergetes (138–133)

· · · · · · · · · Adoption

44. Pergamon, Acropolis.

Philetairos's reign until the succession of his nephew Eumenes in 263 BCE remains obscure and can be illuminated by recent epigraphic and archaeological discoveries only on certain points. Strabo (13, 4, 1 f.) describes Philetairos as a eunuch from childhood on:

> for it came to pass at a certain burial, when a spectacle was being given at which many people were present, that the nurse who was carrying Philetaerus, still an infant, was caught in the crowd and pressed so hard that the child was incapacitated. He was a eunuch, therefore. . . . During these disorders the eunuch continued to be in charge of the fortress and to manage things through promises and courtesies in general, always catering to any man who was powerful or near at hand. At any rate, he continued lord of the stronghold and the treasure for twenty years. He had two brothers, the elder of whom was Eumenes, the younger Attalus. Eumenes had a son of the same name, who succeeded to the rule of Pergamum. (trans. Jones)

In the early third century, Pergamon appeared as a Greek *polis* with the usual institutions, which we will discuss in detail later on (p. 244). The dynast used his wealth to establish his popularity and authority in other cities of western Asia Minor. The Temple of Demeter, which was then still outside the city walls, was donated by him and apparently built on the site of an ancient Anatolian cult of a mother goddess. The approximately contemporary expansion of the temple of Meter Aspordene at Mamurt Kale on Jünd Dağ, thirty miles from the city, shows that Phi-

45. Portrait of Philetairos on a coin.

letairos encouraged the native, already long-established worship of the female divinities. A new perimeter wall surrounded the upper city, which was presumably named Philetaireia. A gymnasium cult for him in Pergamon probably also had its origin in his own lifetime, and in any case since Eumenes I the city's *prytanis* (title of the chief magistrate) held, along with his office, the priesthood at the head of a state cult of Philetairos.

Outside Pergamon, the dynast helped Pitane, an adjacent city, cope with its financial difficulties. The communities of Kyme in Aiolis and Kyzikos at the Propontis, which he had aided in the Galatian wars, honored him by celebrating a Philetaireia festival. He cultivated relationships with Thespiai in Boeotia, for whose shrines to the muses of Helikon and Hermes he gave "sacred" land, as well as with the great shrines in Delos (which also celebrated Philetaireia) and Delphi (which granted *proxenia*—a kind of honorary citizenship—to him, his brother Eumenes, and his nephew Attalos). But his "kingdom" was still narrowly limited to the middle valley of the Kaikos, and he did not dare break with King Antiochos.

His nephew Eumenes, who succeeded him in 263, did exactly that. The reasons are not known to us. He was probably not in the position of a defender, since he marched on the Seleucid and defeated him in a battle near Sardeis. His victory and the dedication of his statue to Athena Polias is celebrated by a verse inscription in Pergamon ([163] I. Pergamon 15). From that point on, coins replaced the portrait of Seleukos with a heroic image of Philetairos (Figure 45). Eumenes seems to have been under pressure by his own mercenaries precisely because of his gains. The troops in the fortress of Philetaireia at the foot of Mt. Ida and Attaleia mutinied. A compact guaranteed them improvements with regard to pay, terms of service, and maintenance; inscriptions recording the agreements were to be set up not only in Pergamon and Gryneion but also in Delos and Mytilene.

Egypt's Attempt to Gain Ground in Asia Minor

Before and during Eumenes's expansion of Pergamon, a strong competitor arose to challenge the Seleucid Antiochos I in Asia Minor: Ptolemaios II Philadelphos, who was active chiefly on the coasts, in Caria, and also deep in the interior. The Lagid—so called after his ancestor Lagos—continued with undiminished energy his father's policy directed against the claims made by the Antigonids and by Lysimachos, to gain ground in Asia Minor. Some of the bases that his father's fleet had conquered on the south and west coasts in 309 BCE had been lost again. But it can be shown that since the early 280s there had been a Ptolemaic presence in Lycia and Caria, and since the early 270s in Pamphylia, where Philadelphos had founded a city, Arsinoe, and installed a chief administrator to govern Pamphylia (a *pamphyliarches*). Between Side and Korakesion a military base, Ptolemais, had been set up. However, Side itself remained a thorn in the side of Ptolemaic territorial policy, because it remained loyal to the Seleucids, and the latter established the base Seleukeia between the city and the mouth of the Eurymedon River.[52] Over the following two decades two more cities were founded: another Arsinoe in Rough Cilicia near Nagidos (named after Ptolemaios II's wife and sister) and a city named after the king's daughter Berenike.

The chain of Ptolemaic bases now reached from the Cilician Taurus to the promontories of the west coast. The sovereignty of Ptolemaios Philadelphos is proven by evidence from Aspendos, Limyra and Arykanda, Araxa, Tlos, Xanthos and Patara, Telmessos, Lissa, Kaunos, Mylasa, Amyzon, Kildara, Halikarnassos, Theangela, Myndos, Bargylia, Iasos, Euromos, and Herakleia by Latmos. In Caria *strategoi epi Karias* (supreme commanders of Caria) and *oikonomoi* were active as royal officials.[53] For a time, an Athenian named Kallias had served as a Ptolemaic officer in Halikarnassos. Royal officials alleviated economic emergencies, as they did in Theangela, or they were assigned to handle gifts of land, as they did in Telmessos; Ptolemaios II granted the latter's request that its territory not be given away. But later on his successor gave it to a son of Lysimachos. However, the community owed to the latter a reduction of the apparently rather heavy taxes that had been levied on it under direct royal administration. The neighboring city of Kaunos founded a cult of queen Arsinoe and—perhaps already established at that time—a cult of the king with an *agon* (competition) named after him. It also gave the name Ptolemais to one of its *demoi*. A Sarapis-Isis shrine was built in the city center. From his extensive correspondence on papyrus, we learn about the activities of the administrative official Zenon of Kaunos at the Lagid court and his connections to his home city. Philokles, the king of the city of Sidon and a high-ranking *philos* (liegeman) of the king, ordered judges from Halikarnassos to go to Samos ([195] SEG 1, 363), and Iasos sent, at the king's written command, judges to Kalymna. After Philadelphos's father had incorporated it and firmly bound it to him by treaties, Iasos seems to have remained constantly loyal to the Lagid court.[54]

The relationships between the first two Ptolemaic rulers and the old Ionian pearl among the Greek cities—Miletus—are of special importance.[55] The city had at first abandoned an alliance with Ptolemaios I Soter, which was probably made after 294 and had gone over to Lysimachos in 289/288; in 280/279 Antiochos I was entered in the list of *stephanephoroi* (cf. p. 189). But immediately thereafter a donation of land made by Ptolemaios II Philadelphos to the community is registered. With the letter from the second Ptolemaios to the Milesians, we find ourselves in a time in which war was raging on water and on land between him and the powerful king of the Macedonians in Europe, Antigonos Gonatas, and there was a threat of naval attacks on the city (ca. 262?). The Milesians replied to King Ptolemaios with a decree of the council and popular assembly:

> when the demos had even previously chosen friendship and alliance with the god and savior (*theos kai soter*) Ptolemy, it happened that the city became prosperous and renowned and that the demos was judged worthy of many great goods, for which reasons the demos honored him with the greatest and most noble honors, and (whereas) his son, King Ptolemy, having succeeded to the throne, and having renewed the friendship and alliance with the city, has shown all zeal in promoting the interests of all the Milesians, giving land and arranging the peace for the demos and being responsible for other good things as well for the city, and now, when many great wars overtook us by land and sea and the enemy attacked our city by sea, the king, having learned that the city had stood honorably by its friendship and alliance with him, dispatched letters and the ambassador Hegestratos and praises the demos for its policy and promises to take all care for the city and to requite it even more with benefactions and calls upon the demos to maintain its friendship toward him for the future as well, and (whereas) the ambassador Hegestratos made similar declarations about the good-will which the king holds toward the city. (trans. Bagnall)[56]

The Seleucid roll-back took place under Antiochos II, who ruled from 261 to 246—at approximately the same time as Eumenes I of Pergamon. Ptolemaios "the son" (coregent with Ptolemaios II Philadelphos between 267/266 and 259) rebelled against his father shortly after the outbreak of the so-called Second Syrian War (Pompeius Trogus, prol. 26).[57] Antiochos exploited this situation to make rapid advances in southwest Asia Minor. It is certain that with Antiochos's help, Miletus rid itself of a tyrant named Timarchos in 260. Antiochos granted the city democracy and freedom, and it venerated him as a *theos* (Appian, *Syr.* 65 [344]; [106] OGIS 226). Furthermore, the Macedonian king Antigonos Gonatas won "the naval victory of his lifetime" over the Ptolemaic fleet in 255/254 BCE, off Kos.[58] It is certain that Lagid dominance also suffered painful losses in the interior of Caria, where Antiochos II already may have employed the *strategos* named Olympichos, who is attested there later. In the Marsyas valley Antiochos founded Stratonikeia and also, by amalgamating several villages, Laodikeia (named after his wife) on the Lykos River in Phrygia, both of which later became flourishing cities.[59] Egypt's possessions in Pamphylia and Cilicia may have been lost as well, since they are no longer mentioned in the catalog of the lands bequeathed by Philadelphos to his son and successor Ptolemaios III Euergetes ([106] OGIS 54).

The War between the Ptolemaic and Seleucid Empires (the Laodicean War)

The bitter struggle for the Mediterranean coasts of Anatolia entered its next phase with the Laodicean War (also called the "Third Syrian War") that broke out after the death of Antiochos II in the summer of 246 BCE. The late king's ex-wife, Laodike, who resided with the king's elder son Seleukos in Ephesos, acted with lightning speed, ordering the death of Antiochos's second wife Berenike and his younger son Antiochos, who stayed in Seleukeia, the harbor of the capital city Antiocheia on the Orontes. Berenike's brother, the recently enthroned Ptolemaios III Euergetes ("Benefactor"), hastened there with his fleet (his report has come down to us on a papyrus fragment) but arrived too late. Thereupon he went on the offensive. In one inscription dating from his reign—a sixth-century copy of which was made by Kosmas, a traveler to India, while he was in Adulis, Eritrea ([106] OGIS 54)—Ptolemaios Euergetes announces wide-ranging military campaigns to "Asia" with ships and also with infantry, cavalry, and elephants from southern Libya and Ethiopia. He also claims that the whole area this side of the Euphrates (Cilicia, Pamphylia, Ionia, the Hellespont, and Thrace) has been won, and that his troops have even advanced as far as Persis, Media, and Bactria (cf. Polyb. 5, 34, 7). However, the actual extent and duration of the campaign are unclear. Laodike's son Seleukos, after having received a wreath from Milesian emissaries and reminding them of the city's loyalty, departed from Asia Minor and is attested as king in Babylonia by July 245 BCE. In Ionia, not all the cities went over to Ptolemaios, contrary to what the formulation in the inscription found in Adulis implies. An interesting document shows us that Smyrna actively sided with Seleukos, obliging the mercenaries in the neighboring town of Magnesia on the Sipylos and the civilians living there to agree to remain loyal in exchange for the granting of citizenship. In 246 BCE a Seleucid garrison under Sophron held out in Ephesos (Phylarchos, *FGrHist* 81 F 24). We have no certain knowledge regarding the stances taken by Miletus and Priene (cf. [162] *IK Priene* 132).

The Seleucids in Crisis

Whereas Seleukos II quickly reconquered the eastern satrapies, his prospects were less bright on the far side of the Taurus, that is, in Anatolia. There, his younger brother Antiochos Hierax, who had been installed as viceroy over that area, did the same thing to him that Ptolemaios "the son" had done to his father Philadelphos: he made himself independent. In a battle between the two brothers fought near Ankyra, with the help of Galatian troops Antiochos Hierax got the upper hand and established his own independent kingdom. The cities of Sardeis in Lydia; Alexandria and Ilion in the Troad; and Abydos, Lampsakos, Parion, and Lysimacheia on the Straits minted coins bearing his portrait. The chronology of this war between brothers and the war against Pergamon discussed below, and their temporal relation to one another, are not clear.

Attalos of Pergamon's Successes against the Galatians, the Usurper Antiochos Hierax, and Seleukos III

Antiochos Hierax and his Galatian allies attacked the most powerful dynast in the area around Sardeis: Attalos of Pergamon. The latter bore the same name as his father (the nephew and adopted son of Philetairos, founder of the empire) and had succeeded the childless Eumenes in 241 BCE. He gave himself the title of king and added the byname *soter* (savior), because shortly after he came to power he had won a battle against the Tolistoagii near the sources of the Kaikos River, thereby relieving the inhabitants of western Asia Minor of a heavy burden, since

> they [the Galatians] exacted tribute from all Asia on this side of the Taurus, but established their own dwellings along the river Halys. And so great was the terror of their name, their numbers being also enlarged by great natural increase, that in the end even the kings of Syria did not refuse to pay them tribute. Attalus, the father of king Eumenes, was the first of the inhabitants of Asia to refuse. (Livy, 38, 16, 12–14; trans. Sage. Cf. Polybius, 18, 41, 7–8; Strabo 13, 4, 2)

Hierax and bands of Tolistoagii and Tektosages (i.e., members of Celtic tribes in western and central Anatolia) were in any case unable to accomplish anything against Attalos. According to the victory monuments erected in Pergamon, over a period of about ten years his armies fought several battles against them near Pergamon itself (Aphrodision), in Hellespontic Phrygia, near Sardeis in Lydia (near Lake Koloe), and in Caria. The location of these battlefields itself makes it clear that although Attalos was on the defensive near Pergamon, he went on the offensive after his victory in Hellespontic Phrygia at the latest and pursued Antiochos Hierax as far as the capital city of Sardeis and on into the south. The question as to why Antiochos headed for Caria is interesting, since there, in Mylasa, the Seleucid vassal Olympichos did more or less as he pleased. We know nothing about his stance regarding this war.

Antiochos Hierax left Asia Minor and was slain in 227 BCE; his brother Seleukos died the following year. The successor to the Seleucid throne, Seleukos III, began by sending several *strategoi* and his vassal Lysias (who resided in Phrygia) against Pergamon and then marched on Anatolia himself (223 BCE). But these attacks also failed: both their names are inscribed in the victorious Attalos's battle monument— a votive offering to the city's goddess Athena.

The precise reconstruction of the multipart victory monuments in Pergamon is problematic. On the newly reconstructed terrace of the Temple of Athena on the acropolis stood a round monument bearing the inscription "King Attalos who defeated the Galatian Tolistoagii near the sources of the river Kaikos has devoted this thank-offering to Athena"([163] I. Pergamon 20; trans. Marek). As it is clear from the extant remains, the votive offering erected there was not a sculpture of a Gaul, but a colossal statue of Athena Promachos.[60]

Fragments of a base and related remains of a foundation in front of the south *stoa* (covered walk) were apparently part of another multipart monument to Attalos's

46. "Ludovisi Gaul Killing Himself and His Wife." Museo Nazionale di Roma, Palazzo Altemps, Rome. Photo courtesy Gianni Dagli Orti / The Art Archive at Art Resource, NY.

victory over the Galatians and over Antiochos Hierax. The donors of the votive offerings to Zeus and Athena were the king, a general named Epigenes, and his officers and soldiers; a signature identifies the artist who cast the bronze as a man named Epigonos ([163] I. Pergamon 29). What the bronzes placed on the bases represented is uncertain. They have been connected with the artworks we know in Roman marble copies as the "Dying Gaul" (Capitoline Museums, Rome) and the "Ludovisi Gaul Killing Himself and His Wife" (now in the Museo Nazionale di Roma, Palazzo Altemps in Rome; Figure 46). However, these works may have stood on a third, rectangular monument in front of the south wall of the sanctuary of Athena ([163] I. Pergamon 21–28). The royal votive offerings to Athena that stood here were inscribed with thanks for victories on various battlefields, with the oldest victory at the sources of the Kaikos again decorating this base as well. In addition, there are monuments outside Pergamon: two battle monuments in front of the south hall of the Apollonion in Delos as well as a hall, sculptures, and a pillar monument in Delphi.

Much has been written about the interpretation of the victory monuments.[61] Whether already Attalos himself wanted to exploit the glory of these successes—to present himself as a protector of civilization who freed the Greeks from a barbarian people—remains an open question. The word *barbaroi* does not appear in the inscriptions. In any case, like his opponent Antiochos Hierax, Attalos of Pergamon, whose great-grandmother was from Paphlagonia, gladly accepted Celts in his army. For a time the result of these campaigns was that the dynast in the valley of the Kaikos gained control of an area that extended over the whole western plateau. It was no wonder that the cities on the Straits and the west coast proved loyal to him.

The Usurper Achaios

The younger Achaios, the son of Andromachos, was part of Seleukos III's army. After the king was assassinated, he assumed command of the troops. The successor to the throne, Antiochos III, a younger brother of Seleukos and Achaios's cousin, appointed him governor of Asia beyond the Taurus (223 BCE).

Achaios won respect by mounting a rapid invasion of Pergamon's territory and driving Attalos back to his home area. Encouraged by his success, he betrayed Antiochos III and had himself proclaimed king in Laodikeia on the Lykos, probably on his grandfather's lands (221 BCE).[62] But in the following five years he was not able to use the absence of the legitimate Seleucid ruler to eliminate Attalos entirely and bring Anatolia firmly under his control. Attalos may have been supported by the court in Alexandria.[63] The former enemies even joined in supporting Byzantion when the island republic of Rhodes allied itself with Prusias—who had been king of Bithynia since about 230—to wage war on the city, because it had levied tolls for passage through the Bosporus to finance the tribute it was paying to the Celts. However, resuming the hostilities, Attalos and Achaios tried to outmaneuver each other, the former with expeditions in Aiolis and Mysia, the latter with campaigns in Pisidia and Milyas, until finally in the spring of 216 the Seleucid Antiochos III marched into Anatolia with an army and advanced on his renegade kinsman Achaios. He concluded an agreement with Attalos (Polybius 5, 107, 4). The content of the treaty, which has not come down to us, seems to have included a concession made by the Seleucid that Attalos might add to his kingdom the Phrygian region bordering on Mysia as far as the valley of the Tembris.[64] In a flash, the Anatolian anti-king Achaios found himself isolated: after the siege and capture of Sardeis in 214, Antiochos had his cousin cruelly mutilated and killed in accord with the Achaemenid ritual for traitors to the king. The city of Sardeis was plundered. The excesses committed by the soldiers were so terrible that Antiochos himself soon decided to take steps to rebuild the city (deliveries of timber) and to reduce the heavy penalties that had been decreed in a letter from the king. Instructions to this effect were received by an officer named Zeuxis, whom the king trusted so much that despite all his bad experiences he made the officer governor of the area beyond the Taurus.

Emancipation of New Kingdoms from the Seleucid Empire

When in the winter of 213/212 Antiochos departed for the upper satrapies in the east, on a campaign that has gone down in history as the *anabasis*, he renewed and extended Seleucid rule (212–205 BCE). He left behind him an Asia Minor large parts of which were controlled by sovereigns who were in fact independent: Armenia was ruled by a king from the Orontid dynasty, probably Xerxes. In Cappadocia, Ariaramnes, a grandson of the Ariarathes executed by the Diadoch Perdikkas (p. 183 f.), had conquered in the 260s the southern part of the country, the area around Tyana. His son, Ariarathes III, drove out the Seleucid occupying forces and took the title of king at about the same time as Attalos did in the west. Since ca. 220 BCE the diadem had been worn by his son Ariarathes IV Eusebes (the "pious"). To the north, the Pontic dynasty of the Mithridatids had established itself, and to the northwest Prusias of Bithynia was consolidating his rule by founding cities. On the south coast, Seleucid power extended only as far as the plains of Cilicia and Pamphylia. There were also problems in the areas of central Anatolia governed by Zeuxis. Uprisings must have broken out while Antiochos was campaigning in the east. In the letter to his governor handed down to us by Flavius Josephos, he ordered a resettlement of Babylonian Jews to Anatolia that is interesting in its particulars:

> Learning that the people in Lydia and Phrygia are revolting, I have come to consider this as requiring very serious attention on my part, and, on taking counsel with my friends as to what should be done, I determined to transport two thousand Jewish families with their effects from Mesopotamia and Babylonia to the fortresses and most important places. For I am convinced that they will be loyal guardians of our interests because of their piety to God, and I know that they have had the testimony of my forefathers to their good faith and eagerness to do as they are asked. It is my will, therefore—though it may be a troublesome matter—that they should be transported and, since I have promised it, use their own laws. And when you have brought them to the places mentioned, you shall give each of them a place to build a house and land to cultivate and plant with vines, and shall exempt them from payment of taxes on the produce of the soil for ten years. And also, until they get produce from the soil, let them have grain measured out to them for feeding their servants, and let there be given also to those engaged in public service sufficient for their needs in order that through receiving kind treatment from us they may show themselves the more eager in our cause. And take as much thought for their nation as possible, that it may not be molested by anyone. (Josephos, AJ 12, 147–153; trans. Marcus)

Caria, Rhodes, Pergamon, and the Aegean

In the last quarter of the third century BCE the history of Asia Minor focuses on Caria, the land in the southwest, in two respects. First, because of the comparatively large number of epigraphic sources, we have a deeper insight into local events and circumstances here than we do elsewhere, though it is difficult to correlate them in detail with the chronology of the great events in royal history. Second, here we find ourselves in a zone of conflict between the great powers, in which important decisions are made whose significance extends far beyond the region.

Macedonian Ambitions in Caria and the Dynast Olympichos

The Ptolemaic hegemony over Caria that had continued for almost a hundred years was melting away. Rhodes had long possessed land on the nearby Carian Chersonnesos (its *peraia*).[65] Now the island state was able to extend this possession to the north, beyond the Gulf of Keramos. Seleukos II assigned to the Rhodians the city founded by the Seleucids in the Marsyas valley, Stratonikeia.[66] But other foreign powers were also interested in the region. In 227 BCE the Macedonian king Antigonos III Doson sent a fleet to Caria. The sources remain silent about his motives, alliances, and goals. Among the local dynasts in Asia Minor at that time was, according to Polybius, the aforementioned Olympichos. It may already have been Antiochos II who assigned him to Caria as a *strategos*, but in any case it has been proven that he was employed in this position under Seleukos II. He functioned as a mediator between the king and the city of Mylasa in the conflict over the Temple of Zeus in Labraunda. At the time of the Seleucid brothers' war, and that between Antiochos Hierax and Attalos, Olympichos must have made himself independent; in his correspondence we find no reference to a position subordinate to the king. Around the beginning of the 220s, an official document from Alinda proves that the *strategos* had a chancellery in that town. In 227 he appears to have seen in Antigonos Doson a welcome ally against troublemakers in his area, namely, Rhodes and the king of Pergamon.[67] The expedition of the Antagonid's fleet seems to have remained a single-season episode, but it apparently opened a door to the ambitions of his successor, Philip, who wanted to establish himself in Caria as well. Around 220, we see Olympichos corresponding with Philip because of the old conflict over Mylasa and Labraunda, and in an inscription from Iasos we read that this city on the Carian coast had been under pressure from one of his subordinates and had turned to Rhodes for help. In this phase, the community of Euromos might have already adopted the name Philippeis, after the Macedonian king. After 220, Olympichos disappears from our sources. In his legacy lies the germ of the opposition in Caria between Philip V and Rhodes. But that was only the southern flank of a far more significant opposition to Philip, into which Attalos of Pergamon entered, followed by the Rhodians as his allies.

Attalos of Pergamon Becomes Rome's Ally

The young Macedonian king Philip V, who had ruled since 221, found himself at war with the Aetolian League, which at that time had reached the apex of its power. Attalos of Pergamon made up his mind to help the Aetolians—their native territory lies in Greece, west of Delphi—expand a fortress (Polybius 4, 65, 6). What moved him to do that, or to take an interest in events in Greece at all, is unclear, but in any case he felt he had to acquire a battle fleet. When in 215 BCE King Philip made an alliance with Hannibal, who was operating successfully in Italy during the Second Punic War (218–201), the Romans reacted by forming an alliance with Macedonia's enemies in 212. Their treaty with the Aetolians contained a supplementary clause providing that

> if so disposed and willing, the Eleans and Lacedaimonians and Attalus and Pleuratus and Scerdilaedus should have the same rights of friendship [*amicitia*], Attalus being king of Asia and the last mentioned kings of the Thracians and Illyrians. (StV 536; Livy 26, 24, 9 f.; trans. Moore)

(Livy is wrong here, both kings are Illyrians). The designation of Attalos as the "king of Asia" is noteworthy, if it is really in the original text of the treaty of alliance and is not a formulation by Livy adapted to the later circumstances.

Attalos did not intervene personally, instead sending troops to support the coalition. After the latter had succeeded in taking the island of Aigina and handing it over to the Aetolians in accord with the division of spoils foreseen by the treaty, Attalos bought the island for a sum of thirty talents to use it as a base for his fleet. Right to the end, it remained the dynasty's most important naval base outside Asia. There, in the winter of 209/208, Publius Sulpicius Galba and the king met and apparently made an agreement regarding the division of the spoils similar to that between the Romans and the Aetolians. After operations on the north shore of the island Euboea, Attalos had to withdraw, because war was looming at home. Philip had not remained inactive but had used the same device that was employed earlier against him: he was mobilizing the enemies of his enemies, namely, his brother-in-law Prusias, the king of Bithynia. The peace treaty of Phoinike concluded in 205 BCE (StV 543) put an end to the First Macedonian War and also to the conflict between Attalos and Prusias. However, several other serious struggles between the two kingdoms were to follow.

Rome's First Entry into Asia

Shortly thereafter a five-man Roman delegation was received in Pergamon. After consulting the Sibylline books and the Oracle of Delphi, it had been assigned to bring the cult of the Magna Mater (Greek: *meter*)—in Asia Minor, various female divinities were worshipped as "Great Mothers"—to Rome. According to the version found in Livy, Attalos is supposed to have taken the delegation, after it had disembarked from the quinqueremes (warships), to the shrine of Meter at Pessinus in Galatia, and there handed over to them the sacred black stone:

> In Asia the Roman people had as yet no allied states. They bore in mind, however, that Aesculapius also had been summoned once upon a time from Greece on account of an epidemic, while there was as yet no treaty of alliance; that at present on account of a joint war against Philip they had already entered into friendly relations with king Attalus. (Livy, 29, 10-11; trans. Moore)

If this really involved a visit to the Great Mother Kybele in Pessinus and not to a shrine near Pergamon, we have to assume that the Celtic Tolistoagii were at that time on a friendly footing with the king of Pergamon, and such an undertaking could thus easily be arranged.

According to a version recited by the writer Herodian (1, 11, 3), on this occasion the Romans claimed that they were related to the Phrygians. This is not very credible. However, at that time there was another legend regarding Rome's relationship to Asia that was certainly already current among the Roman elite: the Romans' descent from the Trojans. Exactly when and how it arose, we do not know. Various references to such a genealogy go back as far as the third century BCE, but they are suspected of being later additions to their context. Thus for example the Roman historian of the Imperial period, Tacitus, doubted the authenticity of the "old letter" in Greek read by the young Nero before the Senate, in which the Senate and the Roman people had promised King Seleukos II friendship and alliance on the condition that he grant their Trojan relatives exemption from levies (Suetonius, *Claud.* 25, 3; Tacitus, *ann.* 12, 58, 1). Similarly, it is doubtful whether in the third century BCE the Acarnanians seemed to the Romans worthy of protection, because they "alone, of all the people of Greece, had not contributed aid to the Greeks against the Trojans, the authors of the Roman race" (Justin 28, 1, 5 f.; trans. Watson). Also, the predictions of a seer, Marcius, in which he is supposed to have warned of the catastrophe at Cannae during the Second Punic War (216 BCE), were probably written in verse long after the fact, in the second century BCE: "Flee the river Canna, thou descendant of Troy, that foreigners may not compel thee to do battle in the Plain of Diomed" (Livy 25, 12, 5; trans. Moore). However, the numerous discoveries of terra cotta objects depicting the Trojan hero Aeneas carrying his father Anchises on his shoulders suffice to show that as early as the fifth century there was already a cult of Aeneas in central Italy. In whatever form, the legend must have led an unobtrusive life in the west for a long time. But with Rome's first entrance into Asia in our period, it understandably gained wider influence and suddenly acquired political weight.

PERGAMON AND RHODES AGAINST PHILIP V OF MACEDONIA AND ANTIOCHOS III

Around the same time, in the year 204 BCE, Antiochos III (who now bore the byname "the Great" because of his victorious expedition to the east) crossed the Taurus and moved toward Sardeis. From that area conquests in Caria were undertaken, at first by Zeuxis, at the king's behest. Zeuxis marched into the Marsyas valley, took Alabanda, Alinda, and Amyzon, and came to an agreement with Mylasa. Because of the name of the religious association of the *Chrysaoreis* around the Temple of Sinuri near Mylasa, to which these cities belonged, the historian John Ma speaks of a Seleucid "Chrysaorian Caria."[68]

At the same time, Philip of Macedonia was cruising off the coasts of Asia. After making the Rhodians nervous with his activities in the Aegean and on Crete, in 202 he carried out successful operations on the Straits against allies of the Aetolians: Lysimacheia and Chalkedon were captured; Kios on the Propontis, which had just been besieged by his brother-in-law, Prusias of Bithynia, was stormed, plundered, and destroyed, and its inhabitants were sold into slavery (Polybius 15, 23, 1 ff.). This infamous action was too much for the Rhodians. After Philip attacked the Ptolemaic naval base at Samos in 201, they opened hostilities against him near the island of Lade, off Miletus, where Ionian resistance to the Persians had once collapsed in a great sea battle. The Rhodians were defeated, and in this emergency Attalos of Pergamon joined with them in the naval war against Philip. The result was a great, indecisive sea battle in the strait between Chios and the mainland, in the course of which Attalos was nearly taken prisoner by Philip. Having landed in the harbor of Miletus, Philip received the good wishes of the Milesians, but thanked them by giving Myus and its territory to their hostile northern neighbor, Magnesia.[69] Then he marched north, laid waste to the area around Pergamon (he did not even attempt to besiege the acropolis), and then turned south again. Abandoning the siege of Knidos, he attacked the Rhodian possessions on the mainland. Stratonikeia fell, Euromos was recaptured (from Rhodian possession?), and Herakleia by Latmos was taken. Farther south, he conquered the coastal cities of Iasos and Bargylia, and then Theangela, which he handed over to Antiochos.[70] However, Philip was having increasing supply problems, since his opponents' squadrons now controlled the coasts almost completely.

In the fall of 201 the fateful emissaries of Rhodes and Pergamon appeared before the Roman Senate to complain about Philip. The reference to the Macedonian's connections with Antiochos the Great and the two kings' intention to divide Egypt between them is supposed to have helped produce the Senate's decision to go to war. This decision led, as soon became evident, to a "turning point in the history of Greco-Roman antiquity"[71]—and thus also in that of Asia Minor.

Antiochos III and Rome

Antiochos III is the best-documented king in Asia Minor. The extant works of writers who discuss the rise of Rome to world power—Polybius, Livy, and others—deal with him at length. More than forty inscriptions have been found that directly or indirectly allude to his rule in Anatolia: royal epistles to cities, officials, and soldiers, city decrees, dedications, and religious regulations. By far the majority of these stone inscriptions were found in Caria, in Amyzon, Kildara, Iasos, Euromos, and Herakleia by Latmos. In temporal terms, these documents are concentrated in the period after 203 BCE and testify to Antiochos's effort to draw the cities to him during his great western offensive. By means of the latter, which extended over some seven years, the Seleucid succeeded in re-establishing, with a few limitations, his rule over Asia Minor in a form that had not been seen since Antigonos Monophthalmos and, for a short time, Seleukos Nikator. In the concert of the contemporary great powers, the rapidity and extent of his operations—both military and diplomatic—must have seemed broadly disturbing. For Antiochos himself, they were at first nothing more than the successful execution of the long-neglected Seleucid claims to possession that he took for granted. An extensively documented diplomatic offensive in 203 is to be found in the royal privilege granted to the city of Teos that was reputed to be the custodian of the internationally important Temple of Dionysos: the sanctuary's status of *hiera kai asylos* (sacred and inviolable) was conferred on the city as well.[72]

When in the spring of 200 Philip escaped his enemies' naval blockade and began to wage war in Thrace, the Seleucid king launched a combined attack, by sea and by land, on Ptolemaic possessions on the southern coast of Asia Minor. Before long, he extended his control in Cilicia beyond a few *castella* to the cities of Mallos, Zephyrion, Soloi, Aphrodisias, Korykos, Anemurion, Selinus, and Korakesion; only the latter put up any notable resistance (Livy 33, 20, 4 f.). After Philip's departure, the Rhodians attempted to pursue the reconquest of their possessions in Caria. The situation there was complicated by a war that was being fought by the Milesians, in alliance with Herakleia, against Magnesia on the Maeander and Priene; at issue was the border with the territory of neighboring Myus, which Philip had taken away from Miletus and given to Magnesia. The local conflict mirrored the turmoil in the broader one, insofar as it took place in the context of a Macedonian Caria that was coming apart. With Philip's defeat by the Romans at Kynoskephalai (a place in Greece) in June 197 BCE, this process was completed, and a new distribution of power prevailed. Attalos did not live to see his opponent's catastrophe; he died shortly before this battle.

In vain the Rhodians had warned Antiochos to continue his fleet's voyage west of Pamphylia beyond the Chelidonian Islands. One after another, Andriake, Limyra, Patara, Xanthos, and Telmessos, and then finally Iasos, Herakleia by Latmos, and Euromos fell under Seleucid control. In the same area, however, Kaunos and the coastal cities of Halikarnassos and Myndos, located at the promontories of western Caria, remained Ptolemaic allies under the protection of Rhodes, which also retained its mainland possession (*peraia*). In the interior, an arrangement was made: the Rhodians gratefully received from Antiochos Stratonikeia—which Seleukos had once given them, but which Philip had taken away shortly before. Antiochos spent the winter of 197/196 in Ephesos. The Ionian cities were already on his side, with the (soon to be very disturbing) exception of Smyrna. The latter city resisted him and successfully applied for diplomatic backing from Rome. As the first city in Asia Minor, the Smyrnans soon thereafter established at home a cult of the goddess Roma (Tacitus, *ann.* 4, 56, 1). The Milesians regained possession of Myus and concluded a peace treaty, presumably at this time, with Magnesia. During the following spring, Antiochos's ships were operating at the Hellespont and in the Propontis. Here, too, a city resisted: Lampsakos. Its delegation asking for Rome's help appealed to the ancient history of Asia: since their community was a member of the league of cities in the Troad, the people of Lampsakos were related to the Romans.

In 196 the Seleucid made his first advances deep into Thrace, and these were repeated several times over the following years. Otherwise, in 195/194 the ring of cities on the Mediterranean coast of Asia Minor was almost completely in Antiochos's hands. In the interior, only the Pergamene Kingdom's core area remained untouched;

all across Lydia, Greater Phrygia, and beyond the Taurus the Seleucid garrisons were dominant. In addition, alliances with the Galatians and the kings of Cappadocia and Pontos stiffened the backbone of Antiochos the "Great."[73] Prusias of Bithynia was courted by him but remained neutral. Meanwhile, his son and co-regent Antiochos received in Daphne a prominent refugee: the Carthaginian Hannibal (195).

After 140 years of captivity by the foreign great power Macedonia, since 197 BCE Greece had found itself in a frenzy of enthusiasm over the declaration of freedom issued by Titus Quinctius Flamininus, who had defeated Philip V. The Roman Senate's decision of 196 (Polybius 18, 44) assured the *poleis* of Asia that they would be freed from Philip V of Macedon; however, that promise was made at a time when some of them had long since gone over into the possession of Antiochos. As a consequence, Antiochos's emissaries in Corinth had to listen to Flamininus's demand that the king vacate these cities and moreover stay out of Europe. In the negotiations between the Romans and Antiochos that had been conducted since then in various places, in addition to the Roman demand that the king immediately withdraw from Europe, the *libertas* (freedom) of the Greek cities in Asia was also initially on the agenda. Special emphasis was placed on Lampsakos and Smyrna as examples. The king protested against the meddling in what was in his view a traditionally Seleucid sphere. However, the Roman guarantee of freedom was qualified in a remarkable way in the Senate's reply to Greek emissaries in 193 BCE: their freedom would be guaranteed not only against Philip but also against Antiochos, *nisi decedat Europa* ("if he did not retire from Europe," Livy 34, 59, 4 f.).[74] If this correctly represents the Roman standpoint, the senators cared little about freedom for the Greeks in Asia. In diplomatic dealings unusually brusque formulas were used—at least in the Greek translations of the Latin originals: when one of Antiochos's emissaries to the Senate solicited the recognition of Teos's status as *asylos* (inviolable), the Teians received a positive reply from the praetor Marcus Valerius Messala and a promise of friendly treatment on the condition that "in the future you also act loyally with regard to us" (Sherk, RDGE 34 line. 23 f.). In fact, the area of Teos was plundered by Roman soldiers shortly thereafter (Livy 37, 28, 4 f.).

In 192 BCE Attalos, the brother of the new king Eumenes II of Pergamon, was residing in Rome. He reported

> that king Antiochus had crossed the Hellespont with his army and that the Aetolians were making such preparations that they would be in arms at his arrival. Both Eumenes who was absent and Attalus who was present were thanked, and a free lodging was given Attalus, a place of entertainment and gifts were presented to him. (Livy 35, 23, 10; trans. Moore)

Antiochos landed in Demetrias, Thessaly, in the same year and advanced toward Lamia, where the Aetolians' assembly appointed him supreme commander with unlimited powers (*strategos autokrator*). In late autumn, Rome's first war against an Asian king began.

On Greek soil, at Thermopylae (see [297] Barrington Atlas 55), the king suffered a defeat and had to retreat into Asia Minor. Eumenes of Pergamon had been active in the war against Antiochos, operating from his naval base at Aigina. Rhodes entered the war. A second defeat at sea, near the Korykos promontory at the southern tip of Erythraean Chersonnesos, followed in the fall of 191. The following year, the Romans built a headquarters for their fleet in Samos. On the mainland, Antiochos bottled up the king of Pergamon in his capital city, while Galatian mercenaries plundered the surrounding area and at sea a fleet fitted out by Hannibal posed a threat to the Rhodians. But in the summer the allies annihilated the Seleucid naval forces in two sea battles near Side and Myonnesos. Antiochos was limited to defending himself on land when the Roman consul Lucius Cornelius Scipio advanced into the Thracian Chersonnesos with two Roman legions and Italian allies. One member of his staff was Publius Scipio Africanus, who had defeated Hannibal at Zama. Lysimacheia, which was well-stocked with food, was abandoned by the Seleucids—an inconceivable strategic error. Using vehicles provided by Eumenes, the Roman army was then able to cross the Hellespont unhindered. For the first time in history Roman legions stood on Asian soil. A royal emissary brought to their camp the king's offer to grant wide-ranging concessions: he was prepared to forgo Europe, would leave the cities of Ionia and Aiolis, whose freedom was desired by the Romans, and also pay half the costs of the war. But now the Roman side demanded not only that the Seleucids pay all the war costs but also that they retreat beyond the Taurus Mountains. By chance, the son of Scipio Africanus had fallen into the enemy's hands, and the negotiator sought to capitalize on this, but Scipio rebuffed them. The Roman legions marched through Dardanos, Rhoiteion, and Ilion to the mouth of the Kaikos and there united with Eumenes. As Publius Scipio lay ill in Elaius, Antiochos generously sent him the son. The king moved his army from Thyateira farther south and fortified a large camp near Magnesia on the Sipylos.

Toward the end of December, 190 BCE, a battle was fought there between two unequal armies. The Roman troops, reinforced by Eumenes, consisted of about 15,000 infantrymen, 3,000 cavalry, and sixteen African elephants (Livy 37, 39, 7–13). On the other side, around the core of the Macedonian phalanx and the King's guard (the silver shield-bearers), everything the Orient had to offer was assembled in far greater numbers: Iranians from Elymais, Medes, Syrians, Pisidians, Phrygians, Lydians, Cilicians and Carians, Cappadocians and Galatians, Mysians and Cretans. Lightly armed troops stood beside *kataphraktoi* (armored horsemen), scythed chariots drawn by four horses, and camels ridden by Arab archers, along with fifty-four Indian elephants with wooden towers on their backs, each of which contained four armed men.

The battle ended in disaster for Antiochos. On the Seleucid side 53,000 men are supposed to have fallen, but only about 350 on the Roman side. Eumenes's cavalry played a decisive role in the victory. Antiochos escaped via Sardeis to his family in Apameia; from there he retired over the Taurus. Almost a century and a half after the

Macedonians had marched into Asia and defeated a satrap's army on the Granikos, they had lost Anatolia north of the Taurus forever.

After a truce and negotiations conducted in early 189, a peace conference was held in the early summer of 188 in Apameia in Phrygia—not far from Antigonos Monophthalmos's old capital of Kelainai.

Gnaeus Manlius Vulso's Expedition and the Peace of Apameia

The future of Asia Minor was negotiated partly in the country and partly in Rome. For Antiochos, the conditions imposed by the Scipios were maintained: in addition to accepting a graduated payment model, he had to clear out of Asia Minor north of the Taurus Mountains. The condition for the truce requested a few weeks after the battle was that Antiochos supply the Roman army with food. The victorious commanders left Asia Minor, and sometime around March the new consul, Gnaeus Manlius Vulso, to whom the supreme command in Asia had been assigned by lot, arrived in Ephesos. While King Eumenes of Pergamon considered Rome the place where his presence was most urgently needed, his brothers Attalos and Athenaios were reinforcing the consul with their troops.

Experts disagree regarding the motives and goals of Gnaeus Manlius's expedition into the interior of Asia Minor.[75] Hannibal wrote a book in Greek about Manlius's misdeeds in Asia, dedicating it to the Rhodians (Cornelius Nepos, *Hann.* 13, 2). Many scholars take as their point of departure the traces of Livy's negative assessment of the consul as a looter. From Manlius's actions in the year 189 BCE, the English historian John Grainger has tried to extract a strategic rationale intended to strengthen the Roman army's position in Asia and to keep the still-threatening Seleucid power in check. Manlius first marched up the valley of the Maeander into northern Caria (see [297] Barrington, Atlas 61), in the direction of Antiocheia, where he met the co-regent Seleukos and forced him to provide food supplies not only for the Roman army but also for Pergamon's army. Having reached Termessos by way of Kibyratis, he extorted protection money and then turned toward Sagalassos, to whose territory he laid waste. A newly found inscription proves that Kibyra at that time stipulated a treaty with Rome (cf. [106] OGIS 762 = [162] *IK* Kibyra 1). Passing through Apameia (where he again met with Seleukos) and Synnada, Manlius pushed on into the area of the Tolistoagii and fought, near Gordion and near Ankyra, two battles against the Galatians, who were supported by troops provided by the Paphlagonian dynast Morzios and king Ariarathes of Cappadocia. In the spring of 188, his second expedition led from Ephesos to Perge, where he received the installment payment of 2,500 talents demanded from Antiochos.

In the meantime, a ten-man commission of the Roman Senate had arrived, and the provisions of the peace treaty were worked out. In addition to the clear Roman demands on Antiochos, there was the question of what to do with the areas of Asia Minor the Seleucids were to evacuate. In a closed-door hearing held the preceding summer in Rome, Eumenes had already urged the senators not to adopt the Rhodians' slogans regarding the freedom of the Greek cities. Offering to serve as the advocate for Roman interests in Asia, he recommended that the cities be handed over to him. The result was that Eumenes emerged from the negotiations as a clear victor. He rose from the status of a regional dynast to become the strongest ruler in Asia Minor. Every part of Asia that had earlier been under Seleucid control in the area north and west of the Taurus Mountains as far as the Halys River, which marked the western border of Cappadocia, was assigned to Pergamon: Lycaonia, Greater Phrygia, Phrygia on the Hellespont, Mysia, Lydia, and Ionia, but not Caria and Lycia south of the Maeander (see below). In the south, Eumenes also received Milyas and Telmessos (the latter without Ptolemaios's land gift of part of its territory to a son of Lysimachos). Pamphylia (which in his view was also on his side of the Taurus Mountains) was initially denied him, but two years later Scipio decided to grant him its western portion, although the cities of Aspendos and Side retained their independence.[76] Cilicia remained under Seleucid control. As for the other Greek cities in the Attalid Empire, the following formula was found: those that were free on the day of the battle were to remain free. The subordinate cities that already paid tribute to Attalos I (until 197) were in the future to pay it to Eumenes; those that Antiochos had forced to pay tribute in 197, but were previously free, were no longer required to pay it.

Naturally, Lampsakos was granted freedom. Of the members of the confederation of cities in the Troad, Alexandria, Dardanos, and Ilion were also liberated, and in addition Ilion was rewarded with Rhoiteion and Gergitha, less because of its behavior than because of its skillfully publicized kinship with the Romans. In contrast, Priapos, Parion, Skepsis, and Abydos were made subordinate to Eumenes; that is, they had to pay him tribute. Farther south, Phokaia, Smyrna, Erythrai, and Notion were jubilant, but not Magnesia on the Sipylos, Teos, Lebedos, Ephesos, or Tralleis. Scipio seems to have given Magnesia on the Maeander its liberty ([109] Syll.³ 679 line 54; Tacitus, *ann.* 3, 62, 1).

Rhodes, Lycia, and the Anatolian Kingdoms after the Peace of Apameia

The land south of the Maeander was divided up, though here, too, some cities retained their freedom. In Caria, these included—in addition to Mylasa and Alabanda, which gratefully introduced the worship of the goddess Roma—the *poleis* of Miletus and Herakleia by Latmos. Between 186 and 181 BCE, the latter two fought over a mountainous border region, but the conflict was ended by an agreement. It is unclear what happened to Knidos, Halikarnassos, Myndos, and Iasos. Up to that point, the Rhodian possessions on the mainland had included essentially the Carian Chersonnesos and Stratonikeia, which had been given to the Rhodians by Antiochos. Henceforth, Rhodian Caria consisted of three large parts. The old *peraia* ("the mainland and Physkos and the Chersonnesos"), which was under the control of a *strategos*, was given an additional supervisory official who bore the title of *hagemon*. Another *hagemon* oversaw the part of Caria to the north of the old *peraia*, while a third governed the extensive territory of Kaunos, which was geographically and also linguistically and culturally distinct from the rest of Caria and represented a unit of its own. If the information provided by Appian is correct, the Rhodians' previously mentioned purchase of Kaunos occurred immediately after the battle at Magnesia, but still before the Peace of Apameia (Appian, *Mith.* 23 [89]). In addition, the Rhodians appointed civilian and military officials serving as *epistatai* (overseers) for individual cities.

LYCIA

With regard to the status of Lycia, things developed in ways that greatly irritated the Rhodians. To understand the genesis and nature of political conditions in Lycia, which was incorporated into the Roman Empire only under the emperor Claudius (41–54 CE), it is helpful to begin by examining this situation more closely. First of all, as recent research has made increasingly clear, as in Herakleia and Miletus in Caria, in Lycia too individual cities were given preference, becoming autonomous and making bilateral agreements with the Rhodians. That was true of Xanthos, a city in a favorable position not least on the grounds of its "ancient historical" kinship with the Trojans (and thereby with the Romans) to which Homer testifies, and which now, in Apameia, was confirmed by the warmest recommendation made by a delegation from Ilion. Epigraphic sources suggest that Phaselis also had a partnership with Rhodes, and they clearly indicate one for the small east Lycian city of Melanippion, which through the intercession of a man from Phaselis was accepted into alliance and friendship with the Rhodians and was allowed to manage its own revenues.[77] However, these cities were not allies on equal terms with Rhodes. To the request made by Ilion's delegation in Apameia that the Lycians be generally pardoned for the fact that a series of their cities had gone over to Antiochos's side, the Roman commissioners replied evasively that they would do what they could. In fact, during the negotiations in Rome, Lycia had already been promised to the Rhodians, and in Apameia it was assigned to them. As they were going about organizing their new possession in their own way, there was a conflict with the Lycian delegates, who envisaged no direct rule by Rhodian executive officials in cities or districts, but rather autonomy, friendship, and alliance. The Lycians acted as a group, not as delegations from individual *poleis*. The result of the Rhodians' abrupt rejection of such conceptions was an expensive guerrilla war. When the free city of Xanthos entered the war on the side of the distressed Lycians, and Lycian emissaries in Rome reported their servitude, the Senate reacted with a decision that aroused sound and fury in Rhodes: there had never been any question of a gift, but only of an alliance. Scholars still disagree concerning the alleged contradictions in the accounts given by Polybius and by Livy.[78] In describing the attribution of Lycia to Rhodes, Polybius uses the expression *en dorea* (as a gift), familiar from royal donations of the Persian and Hellenistic periods.[79] Polybius's use of *en dorea* probably reflects a conception of the Rhodians cultivated in pro-Rhodian historical writing, whereas the Senate's version is expressed by Livy (41, 6, 12): "the Lycians had been placed under the administrative control and at the same time the protection of the Rhodians on the same conditions as the allied states enjoyed under the guardianship of the Roman people" (trans. Moore). The Romans probably conceived the relationship between the Rhodians and the Lycians on the model of their own relationship to their Italian confederates. But for the Rhodians, such a conception was more appropriate to individual alliances on the model of Melanippion, whereas regarding Lycia in fact they had in mind a form of donation traditional in the East, but foreign to the Roman view.

The beginnings of the Lycian League seem to lie in the common action and coalition against Rhodes. In research on the subject two different bits of evidence are adduced in support of the thesis that such an alliance or a predecessor already existed in the third century BCE, under the Ptolemaic rulers—for example in analogy with the league of the *Nesiotai* ("Islanders"), a group of island cities in the Cyclades.[80] But as yet there is no unambiguous proof of this. The oldest certain reference to the Lycian League is the honor granted a Ptolemaic diplomat ca. 182/180 BCE, the background of which may indicate that the Lycians were supported in their position by the Lagid court ([106] OGIS 99). Other references to it are uncertain and controversial regarding chronology: a long decree issued by the city of Araxa (in the northern Xanthos valley) for a citizen Orthagoras that presupposes the existence of the league, as well as the foundation of a kind of imitation of it, the tetrapolis of Bubon, Balbura, Oinoanda, and Kibrya—cities part of whose population was Pisidian.[81]

After 178 BCE a second uprising of the Lycians followed the first one. Whereas in the first, Eumenes of Pergamon still sided with Rhodes, in the second he supported the Lycians. Various irritations had soured the relationship between the two leading powers in western Asia Minor, to the point that a delegation of Rhodian judges decided that the Achaean League should revoke all the honors it had conferred on the king of Pergamon, creating a diplomatic scandal (Polybius 28, 7, 8). After the victory, the political interests of Rome's two Asian allies in the *bellum Antiochicum* diverged, and not only because of frictions on their own continent. Whereas Eumenes, with an eye to possible gains in Thrace, stood firm and positively urged the Romans to make war on the Macedonian king Perseus, the Rhodians, disappointed at the Roman "donation" of Lycia, triggered an internal debate over their position with regard to Macedonia. In the process, it may have occurred to them to ask whether their own claims to hegemony over the Aegean islands would not necessarily be destroyed if the Romans achieved an unlimited dominance in Greece. When, in the heat of Rome's preparations for war against Perseus, a pro-Macedonian faction became so influential in Rhodes that it adopted—contrary to Rome's expectation that it would be obedient—the role of a mediator, catastrophe was inevitable. Death sentences imposed on their own politicians after the Roman victory at Pydna (June 168 BCE) and several embassies sent to make extraordinary gestures of subordination did not prevent the Senate from declaring the freedom of all parts of Caria and Lycia, which had been assigned to Rhodes at the time of the War with Antiochos (Polybius 30, 5, 12). Shortly before, the Rhodians had put down rebellions by Kaunos and warded off an attack by Mylasa on the Euromos area. Kibyra and Alabanda joined the rebellion against Rhodes. A further decree from Rome ordered the

Rhodians to leave Stratonikeia and Kaunos. The twenty-year-long Rhodian inter-
lude as a power on the Asian continent was over. In many parts of Asia Minor a wave
of honors for Rome burst forth.[82]

If the late dating accepted in research on the question is correct, the Lycian
League also introduced the cult of Roma with a festival connected with it and dedicated a statue of the goddess Roma on the Capitol. Fragments of a treaty of alliance
with Rome, found in Tyberissos, might be from this time (however, see p. 277).[83]
The Kaunians erected on the edge of their *agora* a tall pillar monument with a statue
of the *populus Romanus*, and they founded a quadrennial competition in honor of
Leto and the goddess Roma. The worship of Roma, an unmistakable sign of gratitude for benefits, has also been proven in the time after 167 BCE in Antiocheia on
the Maeander, Plarasa/Aphrodisias, Tabai, and Kibyra. In the liberated territories,
new regional formations immediately emerged—apparently under Roman auspices:
Antiocheia on the Maeander was able to incorporate a neighboring community, and
from the *synoikismos* (the union of the communities) of Plarasa and Aphrodisias
proceeded a new *polis* that later flourished. Kaunos extended its area by incorporating numerous rural communities (*demoi*) but had to bow to a Roman decision and
give up part of the territory of the rebellious Kalyndians.

Thus after 167 an entirely unusual situation developed in southern Asia Minor.
For the first time since Cyrus the Great, a foreign ruler was not represented in the
area itself: no satrap, no *strategos*, no *dioiketes* or *oikonomos*, no *hagemon* or *epistates*.
Now everything depended on maintaining good bilateral relations with the far-off
city on the Tiber, and the *poleis* competed in their efforts to establish treaties or at
least a patronage relationship with a Roman senator. Lycia, the only federal state organization in Asia Minor, flourished after it was freed. Montesquieu still celebrated
it in his work *De l'Esprit des lois* (Bk. IX, chap. 3) as a model of a federal republic.
The federation minted silver drachmas on the Rhodian model, *plinthophoroi* (coins
bearing an image of a brick).[84] The most detailed description of the internal organization of the federation is given by Strabo, who refers to Artemidoros of Ephesos, an
author who wrote at the end of the second century BCE:

> There are twenty-three cities that share in the vote. They come together from each city
> to a general congress, after choosing whatever city they approve of. The largest of the
> cities control three votes each, the medium-sized two, and the rest one. In the same
> proportion, also, they make contributions and discharge other liturgies. Artemidorus
> said that the six largest were Xanthus, Patara, Pinara, Olympus, Myra, and Tlos, the
> last-named being situated near the pass that leads over into Cibyra. At the congress
> they first choose a "Lyciarch" [supreme magistrate of all Lycia], and then other officials
> of the League; and general courts of justice are designated. In earlier times they would
> deliberate about war and peace and alliances, but now they naturally do not do so,
> since these matters necessarily lie in the power of the Romans, except, perhaps when
> the Romans should give them permission or it should be for their benefit. (Strabo 14,
> 3, 3; trans. Jones)

In addition to the six cities named here, we know of at least nine more members by the coins they minted: Antiphellos, Apollonia, Arykanda, Kyaneai, Gagai, Limyra, Phellos, Rhodiapolis, and Sidyma. Not only politically but also economically, Lycia experienced an enormous boom that archaeology can also document for rural areas.

Competing Kingdoms

King Eumenes II, ruler of Pergamon since 197 BCE, consistently oriented toward the west a kingdom that had been significantly enlarged in the wake of Rome's wars against Philip of Macedonia and Antiochos of Asia. During his thirty-seven-year reign, he followed the policy of his predecessor Attalos I, who had himself ruled for forty-four years, by integrating his dynasty and his city into the Greek world by means of foundations and votive offerings, buildings and festivals, myths, and victories on the field of battle and in the hippodrome. His statues stood in Athens, Olympia, and Miletus; visitors from Greece came to Pergamon to take part in festivals, and Pergamon sent participants to the *poleis*'s great religious festivals. From a Roman point of view, Asia and the kingdom (*regnum*) of Pergamon were nearly the same thing. Therein lay the germ of a danger, since Pergamon could, even without making a faux pas like that of Rhodes, become suspect to the Senate, the new *hegemon* of the whole Mediterranean world. The danger was all the more serious because Asia Minor did not lack for rivals and envious rulers, of which the fiercest were the kings of Bithynia (see the Appendix).

Prusias I of Bithynia had expanded his kingdom by pursuing an aggressive policy of conquest and consolidated it by founding cities.[85] He had taken away from the Herakleians Tieion by the sea and Kieros in the interior, and founded his own city Prusias on the Hypios. Herakleia continued to be a thorn in his side. At some time after the battle at Magnesia, probably in the 180s BCE, the city made an alliance with Rome. After Kios (a city on the southern gulf of the Sea of Marmara that had been destroyed by Philip V) was rebuilt, the king named it "Prusias on the Sea"; similarly, he rebuilt the ruined Myrleia, some twenty kilometers west of Kios, and named it Apameia. For two sites that he had newly settled, we know no earlier names: Bithynion in Bolu Ovası, and Prusa, below the 2,543-meter-high Mt. Olympos (Ulu Dağ), present-day Bursa.

The new cities served primarily military ends. The older Greek cities and more recent Diadochan colonies were probably filled up with natives and mercenaries. The cities had no coinage of their own and apparently no territory. A Hellenistic decree from Prusa proves that it had the institutions of a *polis*. Even under the Roman Empire, one of the *phylae* of Prusias on the Hypios retained its name after the founder, and the king was venerated religiously as *Heros Ktistes*. Prusias must have appropriated a special piece of land as booty for himself about the time that Eumenes II became king: the part of Phrygia bordering on Mysia, which Antiochos had once given to Attalos I (p. 216).

Prusias had been dissuaded just in time by the Scipios from going over to Antiochos's side; in exchange for an assurance of territorial integrity he remained neutral, but after the Roman victory "Mysia" (which must have meant the northwest part of Phrygia) was taken away from him and given back to the king of Pergamon as the latter's legal possession. Prusias opposed this decision, and Eumenes had to wage war to obtain what had been promised to him. Herakleia and Kyzikos, the homeland of Eumenes's mother Apollonis, entered the war on his side. However, Prusias had received the refugee Hannibal at his court—a provocation for the Romans. After his flight, Hannibal had found at the Propontis his third consecutive asylum with Asian rulers: from Antiocheia in Syria he had gone to Artaxias of Armenia before arriving at Prusias's court. Several times he played an active role not only as a commander in the war on land and at sea, but also as an advisor and founder of cities: the royal foundations of the cities of Artaxata on the Araxes (Strabo 11, 14, 6) and Prusa on Olympos are supposed to go back to him (Pliny the Elder, *nat.* 5, 148).

However, despite Hannibal's successful maneuvers against his ships, Eumenes, the king of Pergamon, gained the upper hand militarily. An inscription in Telmessos dating from December 184 BCE, the earliest mention of the byname *soter* (savior) given to Eumenes, celebrates a great victory won by the king over Prusias and his Galatian allies.[86] As was to happen repeatedly, the Asian combatants turned to Rome, blaming each other. In 183 BCE the Senate sent no less a personage than Titus Quinctius Flamininus, whose most urgent task was to make peace between the kings. He demanded that Hannibal be turned over, but the latter anticipated him by committing suicide. Eumenes got back the disputed area of Phrygia *epiktetos* ("the acquired").

In the same year a conflict emerged with the king of Pontos, Pharnakes. It is high time that we turn our attention to this dynasty of the Mithridatids on the Black Sea (see the Appendix). First, let us glance back at the time of the Diadochi. If we can believe the historian Hieronymos of Kardia (Diodorus 19, 40, 2; cf. Polybius 5, 43, 2), Mithridates, the founding father of this dynasty, came from a family whose—probably fictitious—ancestor was one of the six co-conspirators who put the Persian king Darius I (549–486 BCE) on the throne, and whose descendants are supposed to have held the highest positions at the court and in the royal administration. Mithridates was a follower of Eumenes of Kardia, but then went over to the latter's opponent, the Diadoch Antigonos Monophthalmos, who assigned to him the city of Kios on the Propontis. When he tried to change sides again ca. 302 BCE, his treachery was discovered; Antigonos had him executed in his city. But his son of the same name, who had been a childhood friend of Monophthalmos's son Demetrios, escaped to Paphlagonia—an event that Théodore Reinach called the "hejira" of the history of the Mithridatids. He became the *ktistes* (founder) of a dynasty.[87] Somewhere in the Olgassys Mountains (Ilgaz Dağları) he established a base for raiding and highway robbery.[88] When Lysimachos died on the battlefield of Korupedion in 281, Mithridates controlled the Amnias valley in central Paphlagonia and the Iris basin east of it, both of which were easily accessible fertile areas. The situation seemed to him a good one for assuming the title of king. His kingdom gradually grew to become a unit clearly distinguished from the Cappadocian kingdom of the younger Ariarathes. As a result, about that time the part of Cappadocia that had earlier been called "Cappadocia by the *Pontos Euxeinos*" (Polybius 5, 43, 1) came to be called simply "Pontos." The coastal city of Amastris fell into Mithridates's possession as early as 279, and a few years later so did Amisos (Memnon, FGrHist 434 F 1, 16). According to Diodorus (20, 111, 4) the "Founder" reigned for thirty-six years (that is—counting from 302, not 281!—until 266, the date of his death). The order and chronology of his successors is not certain. Appian (*Mith.* 112 [540]) once counts eight Mithridates, as does Plutarch (*Demetr.* 4, 4), but in another passage (9 [29]) only six, while Synkellos (*Ecloga chronographica* p. 523 CSHB) counts ten; confusions with rulers of the same name belonging to the Arsakidian dynasty or the dynasty of Commagene are not impossible.

Around 220 BCE, the second of Mithridates' successors, Mithridates II, threatened to carry out an attack on the Greeks' most important coastal city, Sinope, which prepared to defend itself with Rhodian help (Polybius 4, 56). He was able to make an arrangement with the eastern Galatians and also make a firm alliance with the Seleucids: he married one daughter named Laodike to Antiochos Hierax (and after his death to Achaios), and another, also named Laodike, to Antiochos III; later on, Pharnakes I and Mithridates V also married Seleucid princesses.

When the Seleucids were driven out of Anatolia, the aforementioned Pharnakes was ruling Pontos (Figure 47). Recent research dates his reign earlier, between about 195 and 171 BCE.[89] His offensive, indeed aggressive, policies aroused disapproval: Polybius denounces him as the most unlawful of all kings up to that time. In late 183 he made a successful surprise attack on Sinope, to which the royal residence may already have been moved. With this conquest all the Greek coastal cities east of Tieion were in the possession of Pontos, and two years later Tieion was also attacked by Pharnakes's general Leokritos and fell. By means of *synoikismos* the king founded Pharnakeia (earlier the Milesian secondary colony Kerasus, now Giresun) east of Amisos.

His devastation and plundering in Cappadocia finally led to the formation of a coalition against him. Led by Eumenes, Ariarathes of Cappadocia, Morzios of Gangra, and the Galatian Gezatorix acted in concert, and Prusias II joined them as well. On behalf of Sinope, its great trading partner, Rhodes filed complaints with the Roman Senate. One after the other, several senatorial commissions traveled to Asia. When Eumenes blocked the Hellespont to cut Pharnakes off from sea transportation, he aroused the Rhodians against him. But in the end Pharnakes seems gotten into dire straits, because in the peace treaty of 179 he had to make painful concessions. Polybius tells us what the conditions were:

> There shall be peace between Eumenes, Prusias, and Ariarathes on the one hand and Pharnaces and Mithridates [the king of Lesser Armenia—C.M.] on the other for all time: Pharnaces shall not invade Galatia on any pretext: all treaties previously made between Pharnaces and the Galatians are revoked: he shall likewise retire from Paphlagonia, restoring to their homes those of the inhabitants whom he had formerly de-

47. Pharnakes I of Pontos. Photo
courtesy Hirmer Verlag, Munich.

ported, and restoring at the same time all weapons, missiles, and material of war. He
shall give up to Ariarathes all the places of which he robbed him in the same condition
as he found them, and he shall return the hostages: he shall also give up Tium on the
Pontus—this city was shortly afterwards very gladly presented by Eumenes to Prusias
who begged for it. Pharnaces shall return all prisoners of war without ransom and all
deserters. Likewise out of the money and treasure he carried off from Morzius and
Ariarathes, he shall repay to the above kings nine hundred talents, paying in addition
to Eumenes three hundred talents towards the expenses of the war. (Polybius 25, 2,
3–10; trans. Paton)[90]

The Roman-Attalid Ice Age

In the early phase of the war, in 182, Eumenes had used military successes as an occasion for founding quadrennial games dedicated to the goddess Athena: the Nikephoria. The sanctuary of Athena outside the city, the Nikephorion, was expanded
and declared to be sacred and inviolable—though this protection was to prove of
little avail. Decrees extant on stone regarding international recognition were issued
by the religious federation organized by several states around the shrine at Delphi
(the Delphic amphictyony), by the Aetolian League, Kos, and by an unknown city
in Caria. Moreover, during the 170s, after peace was made with Pharnakes, Pergamon was on good terms with Athens. In the intellectual capital of the Greek
world, Eumenes and his brothers possessed citizenship, were enrolled as members of
the *phyle* named "Attalis" after their father, and received public honors as benefactors of the state. But in general Greece was not well disposed toward Eumenes and,
hardly two decades after the joyful celebration of Flamininus—the victor over Macedonia and the liberator of Greece—it was enthusiastic about Perseus, the son of

Philip and the new king of Macedonia. In addition, Pergamon's relationship with the Rhodians was, as we have seen, at its nadir. In their view, as in Perseus's, Eumenes's reign in Asia was more tyrannical than that of Antiochos ever was.

In 172 BCE an attempt on Eumenes's life was made in Greece. On arriving in Rome as an agitator against Perseus, the king of Pergamon had been received favorably by the senators—with the exception of Cato the Elder, who did not like him. On his way home, he wanted to visit the Temple of Apollo at Delphi, but at a narrow place in the road leading up to the *temenos*, stones were thrown at him. Seriously wounded, he was carried back to his ship and taken to Aigina. A false report of his death spread quick as the wind to Rome and Pergamon. Thereupon his brother Attalos took steps in the capital to put the diadem on his own head and to marry the "widow" Stratonike.[91] However, this did not result in a break between the two brothers when the mistake was realized.

In the war on Perseus, the brothers from Pergamon took an active part on Rome's side. Eumenes directed the fleet, while Attalos and Athenaios participated in Aemilius Paullus's decisive battle at Pydna (168 BCE). Officers from Pergamon seem to have served as advisors on the staff of the victor during his tour through Greece, in the course of which the weal or woe of many *poleis* was negotiated.[92] But after the victory at Pydna, Eumenes had to reap the bitter harvest of his western policy: the Senate no longer needed him and began to humiliate him. The declaration that the Thracian cities of Ainos and Maroneia were to be free, even though they had been promised to Eumenes, constituted an affront to him. Asked for mediation and help in the battle against the restless Galatians on the kingdom's eastern border, the Roman diplomats played a delaying game. The apex of the irritations came when the old king himself landed in Italy to travel to the city on the Tiber and appear before the Senate. A quaestor coolly explained to him that no king was allowed to enter Rome, and asked him whether he wanted something from the Senate; if not, he should leave the country as soon as possible. Eumenes replied that he wanted nothing, and turned his back on Italy.

While Eumenes was in Greece, about the time of the outbreak of the war against Perseus, there had been further battles with the Galatians. The Pisidian city of Amlada joined the insurgents, but it was quickly reconquered and had to pay a high tribute and provide hostages. Eumenes, after his return, repelled the Galatians so successfully that Sardeis and Tralleis instituted games in his honor, the Panathenaia and Eumeneia, and in Pergamon itself the Soteria and Herakleia games were established on the basis of royal grants.[93] His arch-enemy Bithynia joined the chorus of complaints against him that the Galatians presented in Rome. With regard to Eumenes, Prusias II now played a role before the Romans that Eumenes himself had once played with regard to Antiochos and Perseus. The brothers Attalos and Athenaios were received in Rome to defend themselves, but suffered another discouragement when a commission under C. Sulpicius announced from Sardeis that anyone who wished might bring complaints against Eumenes to him.

THE LAST ATTALIDS

King Eumenes died in 159 BCE. Polybius treats him with great respect, especially because the king was able to make three of his brothers loyal companions, a feat with few parallels in history. As planned and without frictions, Attalos succeeded his brother and married, at the age of 61, Queen Stratonike. During Eumenes's last years and the transfer of power to his brother, there had been uprisings in Cappadocia. Around 163, Ariarathes IV died. His son and successor Ariarathes V cultivated, like his father, exceptionally good relations with the Romans.[94] He disapproved of his cousin Demetrios, a Seleucid who had escaped Roman captivity and come to power in Antiocheia in Syria, and declined the cousin's offer to marry his sister. Demetrios took revenge for this humiliation by marching against him, overthrowing him, and replacing him as king with one of his older brothers, Orophernes, who had grown up in Priene. When he fled to Rome, the Cappadocian *amicus* did not receive the support he had hoped for, and even had to see emissaries sent by his opponents Orophernes and Demetrios allowed to appear before the Senate.

The Senate made a decision that it would have preferred to also make for Pergamon if the occasion arose: it divided the kingdom between Orophernes and Ariarathes (158 BCE), which only led to further conflicts between them. After surviving failed assassination attempts, Ariarathes had to flee again—this time to Pergamon.

Attalos II flouted Rome's decree of separation and put his brother-in-law and childhood friend back on the throne as sole ruler in Cappadocia. Orophernes, whose rule had not been popular with the country's inhabitants, could not maintain his position and had to leave the land in 156/155. In the Temple of Athena in Priene he had a deposit of 400 talents that Ariarathes now demanded as the legal king. But the city refused to disburse the money to anyone other than Orophernes and endured the occupation and plundering of its territory by Attalos and Ariarathes until the Senate declared in its favor. A letter from Orophernes gratefully recognizing Priene's loyal behavior has been preserved in an inscription. Orophernes sought refuge with Demetrios in Syria, where, instead of receiving a friendly welcome, he was interned. He no longer played any role. Pergamon plotted against Demetrios's Syrian throne by presenting an ordinary resident of Smyrna as the son of King Antiochos IV, whom he resembled. With Rome's blessing and Egypt's help, he was to become in fact a king, under the name Alexander Balas, in 150 BCE.

Attalos, whom Rome preferred even during Eumenes's lifetime, was not humiliated by the masters on the Tiber as his brother had been. Nonetheless, he was probably aware that as a ruler of the largest kingdom in Asia Minor, his relation to the Romans required him to walk a tightrope. One of the most interesting documents of the ancient world as a whole guides us into this context. It is part of a multipart collection of letters that were sent by Eumenes and Attalos to the priest Attis in Pessinus between 163 and 156 BCE. The letters were chiseled into blocks of stone, which presumably were made part of the wall of the Temple of Kybele in Pessinus only in the late first century BCE, more than a hundred years after the events. Attalos had met with Attis in Apameia to discuss common action against an unnamed enemy; after he returned to Pergamon, he wrote to the priest:

> When we came to Pergamum and I assembled not only Athenaeus and Sosander and Menogenes but many others also of my "relatives," and when I laid before them what we discussed in Apamea and told them our decision, there was a very long discussion, and at first all inclined to the same opinion with us, but Chlorus vehemently held forth the Roman power and counseled us in no way to do anything without them [the Romans]. In this at first few concurred, but afterwards, as day after day we kept considering, it appealed more and more, and to launch an undertaking without their participation began to seem fraught with great danger; if we were successful the attempt promised to bring us envy and detraction and baneful suspicion—that which they felt also toward my brother [Eumenes]—while if we failed we should meet certain destruction. For they would not, it seemed to us, regard our disaster with sympathy but would rather be delighted to see it, because we had undertaken such projects without them. As things are now, however, if—which God forbid—we were worsted in any matters, having acted entirely with their approval we would receive help and might recover our losses, if the gods favored. I decided, therefore, to send to Rome on every occasion men to make constant report of cases where we are in doubt, while [we] ourselves make [thorough] preparation [so that if it is necessary] we may protect ourselves. ([111] Welles, RC 61; trans. Welles)

Even in the archived memoranda from modern history there are few comparable examples of an insider's description of debates in the innermost circle of political decisionmakers. The originally secret character of this correspondence can hardly be doubted. One wonders why and in what way it was published at all. For the ancient contemporaries who were interested in history and read this text with attention, Rome must have appeared in an unfavorable light. The letter shows the royal advisor's clear insight into the true behavior of the Romans with regard to their Asian allies, and in this he is in accord with modern historians' judgment based on other observations. Beyond destroying its great opponents in the East, up to this point the Roman Senate had not found its way to a constructive policy with regard to Asia, at least not from the point of view of Pergamon. The Roman practice of repeatedly playing off kings and cities against one another—along with solely reactive measures and positions that were often taken after long delays—led to aversion and mistrust of Rome that had to be discharged sooner or later.

In the summer of 156, Prusias II invaded the kingdom of Pergamon. The same king who had appeared before the Romans a decade earlier, after Perseus's death, wearing Italic clothing and on his head a *pilleus*—a cap that was usually worn by slaves and freedmen—and said to them in Latin: "I am the *libertus* of the Romans " (Appian *Mith.* 2 [5]), now paid no attention at all to Rome's objections. Attalos turned to Rome, and a three-man commission decided that the two kings, accompanied by only 1,000 horsemen, should meet and negotiate a peace treaty. The Bithynian pretended to agree and then advanced with his whole army. With great difficulty, Attalos escaped and was surrounded in his capital, along with the Roman mediators. Prusias, who according to Polybius (32, 15, 13) violated all bounds because he made war not only on people but also on gods, went about burning and robbing the shrines of Pergamon outside the city walls—the Nikephorion and Asklepieion. He also besieged Elaia in vain, laid waste to the territories of Aigai and Kyme, and then turned inland, where he plundered the Persian Temple of Artemis of Hierakome, the area of Temnos, and a small city named Herakleia. Prusias then finally retreated to Prusa. That was too much even for the Senate, and it stepped in unambiguously on Pergamon's side. Prusias was judged to be the aggressor and obliged to make high payments for damages to several communities. In an incredible plot, Prusias threatened his own son Nikomedes with death if he did not manage to get the punitive payments annulled in Rome; the son went over to the other side and allied himself with Attalos to seize the throne in Nikomedeia. The two men marched into Bithynia and besieged the city. In desperation, Prusias once again turned to the Senate, but the delegation it appointed—derided by Cato the Elder as lame, leaderless, and stupid—was a long time in arriving. By treachery, Nikomedes and Attalos were able to enter the city, and Prusias was stabbed to death in the Temple of Zeus. His rampage had made a great impression on the public, and his demise was seen as divine punishment. The inscribed marble base of the victory monument dedicated to Athena Nikephoros in Pergamon has been preserved ([106] OGIS 327).

In the last decade of his reign, Attalos II proved to be a loyal ally of Rome. He helped fight Andriskos, a usurper who gained a following in Macedonia after he falsely claimed to be "Philip" the son of Perseus; his hometown was Adramyttion in the kingdom of Pergamon. Attalos's fleet also helped Mummius capture Corinth. A visit made by the Scipio Africanus the Younger to Pergamon confirmed his good relations with Rome shortly before he died in 139 BCE, at the age of eighty-two.

We know little about his successor, Attalos III. In modern research the suspicion has arisen that he was not the son of Eumenes and Stratonike but rather a son born of the union begun between Attalos and Stratonike after the former received the false report of his brother's death.[95] Diodorus (34, 3) describes him as a cruel and distrustful person. Centuries later, his experiments with *pharmaka* (poisons), whose effects he is said to have tested on prisoners, interested his countryman, the famous physician Galen. He is also supposed to have written a treatise on agriculture. Inscriptions declare that he was a benefactor of various shrines in Pergamon's hinterland. When he died after reigning only six years, he left behind a will that bequeathed his heritage to the Romans. This was to prove an act of world-historical significance. Rome's opponents later suspected that this will was a counterfeit (Sallust, *epist. Mithr.* 8), but discoveries of inscriptions have proven its certain existence. So far as the exact provisions of the will and the Romans' interpretation and execution of them are concerned, there is a complex problem in our sources. I examine it more closely later on (p. 251).

Pergamon: Capital, Kingdom, and Cities

Under Eumenes II and Attalos II the city of Pergamon underwent extensive expansion and rebuilding about which Strabo says: "He [Eumenes II] built up the city and planted the Nicephorium with a grove, and additional embellishment of the settlement of Pergamum with sacred buildings and libraries, raised to what it now is, goes back to him" (13, 4, 2; trans. Marek). The discoveries made during excavations confirm that in the first half of the second century BCE the whole upper city was rebuilt, and its appearance changed again only under the Roman Empire. Characteristic of the appearance of the city, which was surrounded by a new wall, four kilometers long (the Eumenian Wall), was the cascade of terraces on the acropolis (Map 10). On the latter's eastern edge there grew up a narrow settlement belt, while on the southwestern and western edges a wider belt emerged that reached as far as the river Selinos and is called the Eumenian New City. Particularly luxurious residences were built around the lower *agora*. Above them, spread over four terraces, were the Temple of Demeter and the multipart gymnasium, which was probably begun in the second century (before 146/145 BCE), and towering over both, the Temple of Hera, Zeus's wife. The remains still visible on the terraces go back to a Roman construction phase of additions to and conversions of existing buildings, in which the splendid marble features were first introduced. Nonetheless, the original structure is already one of the largest gymnasium buildings known from the Hellenistic period. The whole complex covers an area of 210 by 150 meters. Of this area, the lowest terrace, which is triangle-shaped, occupies the least space. The middle terrace is bordered on its northern side by a long hall and occupies a space of about 150 by 36 meters, while the uppermost terrace, which is surrounded on three sides by two-story halls, occupies a space of about 210 by 80 meters. Complexes of rooms intended for changing clothes, applying oil, and bathing, as well as for various exercises (for instance, a *sphairisterion*—a room for playing ball) were located on three sides of the *palaistra*. The terraces were ornamented by small temples, numerous votive offerings, and statues—including a whole series depicting the *gymnasiarchoi* (superintendents of the gymnasium)—and lists of the *epheboi* (young men liable for military service) were inscribed on the walls.

The "upper city" comprised a no less bold set of terraces with elaborate supporting walls on the steeply sloping land. The precipitous western rim of the hill is dominated by the enlongated theater terrace with the temple of the theater god Dionysos, and over it, a theater structure unusual in the Greek world that was presumably also built in the time of Eumenes II. Nearby was an Attaleion, donated by the founder of an association of Attalistai, a Pergamon variant of the *Dionysostechnitai* (Dionysian artists' association), where drinking bouts were probably regularly held.

The central square in the upper city, north of the gymnasium complex, included the Temple of Athena. Only in the time of the Attalids did the worship of the goddess Athena become the main cult in Pergamon, outshining all others. Various indications suggest that in the fifth and fourth centuries BCE an Apollo Pasparios was

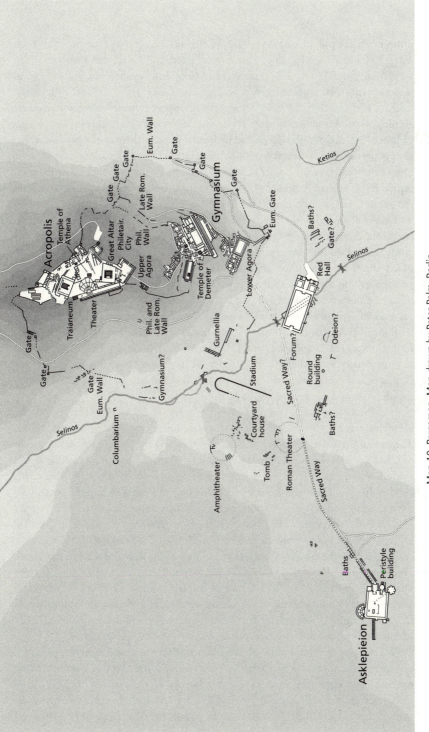

Map 10. Pergamon. Map drawn by Peter Palm, Berlin.

prominent. The oldest temple of Athena Polias on the acropolis was probably built when Alexander's son Herakles, then a small child, and his mother Barsine were in Pergamon, from 330 to 325. Architectural form and construction technology, as well as numismatic arguments, support this conjecture. The numismatic argument refers to Pergamon's oldest gold staters with an image of the Palladion, the standing goddess, viewed from the front.[96] The earliest dedicatory inscription ([163] I. Pergamon 1) is written in the Greek and Lydian languages. There can be no doubt that the goddess of Athens, whose temple was also located on the acropolis, provided the model and that Eumenes and Attalos I were flirting with the idea of turning their capital into a second Athens. There may also have been a Panathenaic Festival from the outset ([163] I. Pergamon 18 l. 17).

On the plains below the city a dynast had erected a second Temple of Athena and had given this goddess the byname of Nikephoros (bringer of victory), which certainly makes us think first of all of Attalos I as builder, since he is generally thought of as styling himself as victor and savior. The byname was then also transferred to the goddess on the acropolis, so that in many a written testimony we can hardly tell which temple is being referred to. The Nikephorion outside the city walls, which had several temples and altars as well as a sacred grove and a *temenos* wall, was destroyed by Philip V and again by Prusias II, and rebuilt each time. So far it has not been found in the area. Dedications in the Temple of Athena in the upper city also often refer to Zeus, the goddess's father. Attalos III made Zeus Sabazios, the god of the Cappadocian ruling house whom his mother had introduced in Pergamon, into a *synnaos* ("co-lord of the temple") of Athena.

In the time of Eumenes, not far below the Temple of Athena in the upper city, the great altar was built on a newly expanded terrace aligned with the Temple of Athena. The base of this altar, ten meters high, measures 35.64 by 33.4 meters. As the group of principal gods represented on the frieze suggests, it was dedicated to Athena and her father Zeus. Its marble components were transported to Berlin in the nineteenth century (p. 28). The frieze showing the battle between the gods and the giants (Gigantomachy), which is important from an art-historical point of view, is 120 meters long by 2.30 meters high and constitutes the base area over the orthostats (vertical ashlars). The sun god is represented with his sister Eos, followed by Selene, Nyx, Eris, and the *moirai* (fates), Poseidon and Amphitrite, Okeanos and Tethys, Zeus with Herakles, Athena, Nike, Ares, Hera, Leto, Artemis, Apollo, and Hekate. On the altar platform over them stands a hall with Ionic columns, between which stood statues. A wall running all the way to the ceiling divides the inside of the altar, where the actual sacrificial altar was located, from the outside columned hall. On the inside of this wall was another narrative sequence of images, the *Telephos* frieze.

We can only speculate as to what ultimately gave rise to this structure, which is one of Asia Minor's most important art works. In addition to that question, many others remain open. The archaeologist Wolfgang Radt's evaluation of the ceramics discovered in the foundations of the altar allows us to conclude that construction on the altar began ca. 170 BCE—that is, at the later of the times discussed in the litera-

48. The Pergamon Altar, showing Athena. Now in Berlin.

ture (as opposed to ca. 190–180 BCE).[97] The abundance and quality of the sculptural decoration would undoubtedly have led the observer to compare it with that of the Parthenon in Athens and to associate Pergamon, as the new site of a model of Greek culture, with *tes hellados paideusis*. In the theme of the Gigantomachy, a high point in Hesiod's *Theogony* is translated into a new pictorial language: the younger generation of gods headed by Zeus, the son of the Titan Kronos, overpowers the demons of the Underworld with their snake-like legs (Figure 48). The power of the massive sculptures inspired a writer of our own time:

> These faces just created, then expiring again, these powerful, hacked-up hands, these widespread wings drowning in the brute rock, this stony look, these lips opened wide to scream, this striding, stamping, these blows dealt with heavy weapons . . . this trampling, this rearing up and collapsing, this endless striving to emerge from the granular blocks.[98]

Researchers seek to discern in this elaboration of the mythical material an encrypted self-representation of the role in history played by the Attalids, the most recent of the old Hellenistic families of monarchs that came to power by conquering the barbarians, who by freeing the Greeks from these barbarians, made their city the home of art and culture. While there is a broad consensus regarding the historical connection between the Gigantomachy and the Attalids' victories over the Galatians,[99] allusions to other enemies of Pergamon in the images are not recognized by consensus. Even if a direct connection cannot be established, the topos of the barbarian in general (as well as the act of founding a shrine in connection with the myth of a victory over barbarians) nonetheless has precedents, especially in Asia Minor. Strabo (11, 8, 4) tells us the story of the foundation of the shrine in Zela, one of the three largest in Pontos: after the Saka, a nomadic Asian people, had penetrated deep into what was then Cappadocian territory, they celebrated their spoils one night. While they were doing so, the Persians attacked and completely destroyed them. At the site of the Persians' victory, over a rock on the plain, their military leader had an artificial hill mounded up—in another passage, Strabo (12, 3, 37) calls it the "Hill of Semiramis"—a wall built around it, and a shrine erected on top of it for the community of the gods Anāhitā, Anadatos, and Omanos. The Persians founded an annual festival, the Sakaia, which was still celebrated in Strabo's time.

The *telephos* frieze has another theme: it recounts the life of the mythical founder of the city, a son of Herakles and Auge, the priestess of Athena Alea at Tegea in Arcadia. It is one of the numerous myths in which the intertwined fates of demigods and humans take them from Greece to Asia, where they finally found on Asian soil a family and a city, often after participating in the voyage of the Argonauts or the Trojan War. Local families—in this case that of the mythical King Teuthras—were factored in, so that a twofold rootedness in the country itself and in the original Greek homeland was secured. These interrelations with Greek mythology are older than the Hellenistic period, but more and more communities on Asian soil now began to provide themselves with a place in this network by means of sophisticated literary versions disseminated in writing (p. 474). For the writers of the Roman Imperial period, the people of Pergamon were still *telephidai* (descendants of Telephos) and inhabited Teuthras's land. It has been pointed out that Herakles—and not, for example, his father Zeus—plays a prominent role in the foundation myth, both in words and in images, because this hero was known as the "destroyer or tamer of monsters" par excellence.[100]

Except for a brief mention by an author writing under the Roman Empire,[101] in ancient literature there is no clear reference to this altar and its pictorial program. The biblical Book of Revelation, composed near the end of the first century CE, may contain an allusion to this structure as "Satan's throne":

> And to the angel of the church in Pergamum write: "The words of him who has the sharp two-edged sword. I know where you dwell, where Satan's throne is; you hold fast my name and you did not deny my faith even in the days of Antipas my witness, my faithful one, who was killed among you, where Satan dwells." (Revelation 2:12 f.; Revised Standard Version)[102]

The library in Pergamon was presumably also built in the course of the construction planned under Eumenes II. A royal center of erudition and knowledge was in tune with the Attalids' intention to present their capital as the Greek cultural metropolis in Asia, known to us from the altar's pictorial program. The immediate model is naturally the Egyptian Alexandria, but Athens was also a mediate model.

Pergamon competed with both of them. However, the tradition of the royal library is much older and finds its archetype in the library of the neo-Assyrian king Assurbanipal, in the seventh century BCE. The Attalids, like the Ptolemies before them, proceeded rather ruthlessly to acquire as many books as possible. The library of Theophrastus, a friend and successor of Aristotle who lived from 371/370 to 287/286 BCE, had been brought to Skepsis and bequeathed to his descendants by Neleus, a pupil of Aristotle and Theophrastus. It included the works of Aristotle, and Neleus's heirs buried the books in their city to prevent them from being seized by Pergamon (Strabo 13, 1, 54). We know that when Mark Antony gave it to Cleopatra in 41/40 BCE, the library of Pergamon had 200,000 scrolls, less than half as many as the library in Alexandria before it was burned. Such scrolls were made of papyrus. In Pergamon another support for writing had become important: parchment. According to the account given by the Roman scholar Varro (who lived 116–27 BCE) (Pliny the Elder, *nat.* 13, 70), Eumenes II began producing this writing material from animal skins after the Ptolemies cut off the supply of papyrus because they were no longer willing to tolerate competition from the library in Pergamon. The great scholar at the library, Krates of Mallos, the author of comprehensive commentaries on Homer, is supposed to have initiated the export of parchment to Rome, where it became known under the name of *membrana Pergamena.*[103]

We know next to nothing about the library's organization as a school for scholars analogous to the Museion in Alexandria. Not a single work of the more or less prominent intellectual lights proven to have been active in Pergamon besides Krates of Mallos has survived intact. Antigonos of Karystos wrote a book about artists that Pliny the Elder later excerpted for his *naturalis historia*. Polemon of Ilion wrote descriptions of his travels; he had visited many regions of Greece and also collected inscriptions. Musaios and Leschides composed epics, and Apollodoros wrote a chronicle from the destruction of Troy up to the year 144 BCE. Biton, Sudines, and Apollonios of Perge were engineers, astronomers, and mathematicians, while Neanthes of Kyzikos wrote biographies of philosophers. One of Krates of Mallos's pupils, Panaitios of Rhodes, was a very important figure; he introduced the Roman aristocracy to Greek philosophy.

Archaeology has thus far been unable to give an uncontested answer to the question of the library's exact location. The starting point for most theories is the architectural remains immediately behind the north hall of the Temple of Athena, where Alexander Conze had already conjectured the library was.[104] The Temple of Athena also had a royal art collection with older works from Greece, including archaic and classical sculptures by Bupalos of Chios, Onatas of Aigina, Theron of Boiotia, and Silanion of Athens that had been brought to Pergamon by Attalos I, Eumenes II, and his brother Attalos II, the last from Corinth, which Mummius had destroyed. A smaller marble copy of the Athena Parthenos from Pergamon now stands in the Pergamon Museum in Berlin. The Attalid collection included among its treasures selected paintings from the fifth and fourth centuries BCE. As in the case of books, here the agents were not always able to acquire everything they wanted. Mummius snatched Aristeides's panel painting of Dionysos from under Attalos's nose when the latter offered 100 talents for it (Strabo 8, 6, 23; Pliny the Elder, *nat*. 35, 24). But when Pergamon had become powerful, it attracted artists who worked in the city itself, such as Epigonos, Nikeratos, and Phyromachos.

Although the great altar is hardly mentioned at all in ancient literature (as already noted), another complex of buildings in ancient Pergamon is illuminated by numerous testimonies: the Asklepieion. The origins of this place of worship, located about two kilometers southwest of the city and connected with it by a road, go back far beyond the time of the Attalids. On the rocky subsoil around several water holes, a shrine to the god of healing was erected. In the sources, its foundation is connected with a man from Pergamon named Archias. Pausanias (2, 26, 8) says Archias brought the worship of Asklepios from Epidauros to Pergamon out of gratitude to the god for healing him after a hunting accident. This origin is certified by a decree from Epidauros honoring the priest of Asklepios in Pergamon on the ground that his ancestors had introduced the cult to Pergamon (IG IV 1² 60). Unfortunately, we are unable to say when this Archias lived. Whether he is the same as the Archias in the chronicle of the city of Pergamon who allegedly introduced the high state office of the *prytany* in the first half of the fourth century, and was its first holder (*prytanis*), remains uncertain.

RESIDENCE AND POLIS

Exactly like Alexandria on the Nile, the city of Pergamon combined the organizational form of a *polis* with that of a royal residence. On the east side of the upper city, between the quarter where the guards of the acropolis' gate lived and the barracks and magazines in which grain supplies and military materiel were stored, a series of rooms of varying size were each grouped around an inner courtyard with a portico on all sides of it. It has been interpreted as the residence of the kings during the period between 281 and 160 BCE. Today, only foundations remain; most of the relics belong to the so-called "Palace V." The rooms had high-quality floor mosaics as well as walls that were made partly of marble and were partly stuccoed and painted.

Around the king gathered a small group of advisors, to which his brothers, other close relatives, and selected courtiers—usually called *philoi* (friends)—belonged. According to the Macedonian custom, young men (pages) were chosen from the noble families in the king's entourage and brought up along with his sons (*syntrophoi*). The royal correspondence was conducted by a chancellery, but we have no direct testimony about its personnel. In addition, there were bodyguards, a keeper of the seals, and a "guardian" of the king's private property (*rhiskophylax*). An official responsible "for sacred revenues" probably occupied an office in the city. Finally, a royal official bearing the simple title of *epi tes poleos* (city prefect) apparently supervised the administration of the capital city.[105] Otherwise, the king exercised his influence directly on the decisions made by municipal bodies, by means of royal ordinances and letters: thus Attalos III had his *prostagmata* (orders) included in the religious laws ([111] Welles, RC 67 l. 15 f.).

The polis administered its own revenues, which were divided into sacred and profane. The eponymous official who gave his name to the year was the *prytanis* and priest of Philetairos, who led the city's cult of the ruler. The popular assembly's decisions could be made with or without previous deliberation in the council (*probuleuma*). However, often (but not always) they were preceded by a vote by the five *strategoi*. This board of magistrates was long assumed to have been not elected by the people but rather—since Eumenes I—appointed by the dynast or king. But Helmut Müller, an ancient historian, has deprived this assumption of its foundation and shown that the council of the *strategoi* in Pergamon consisted of officials appointed in the usual way by the people, though this did not preclude royal interventions in the process. These officials seem to have divided among themselves certain responsibilities, one of which concerned the "city."

The citizenry was divided into twelve *phylae*, of which a few were named after kings: Philetairis, Eumenis, Attalis. An unusually rich trove of information about the everyday problems of the densely built city is provided by the so-called *astynomoi* inscription, a document that was published on stone under the Roman Empire, but whose legal provisions go back to the time of the kings, presumably toward the end of that period. The council of the *astynomoi* and the law enforcement officials under them were responsible for the maintenance and cleaning of the streets, public and private walls, springs, and so forth, and punished any offense against the laws with heavy fines. One interesting provision, also proven in other places during the Imperial period, is that the owners of each adjacent property had to see to it that their section of a public street was cleaned ([106] OGIS 483 l. 29 ff.).

After the battle at Magnesia, a significant amount of wealth in the form of tributes, taxes, and duties flowed into this capital of the largest kingdom in Asia Minor. Horace still considered "what a King Attalos could offer" (*carm.* 1, 1, 12: *Attalici condiciones*; trans. Marek) to be synonymous with alluring splendor, just as the Lydians' gold once was for Archilochos. Under Eumenes, the taxes (the *phoros* and the *telesma*) paid by a small, distant city in Phrygia—Amlada—that subsisted mainly on wine production (Strabo 12, 7, 2) amounted to two talents a year; in extreme emergencies, Attalos II remitted half a talent to the community. The royal domains, the temple grounds, and the tribal and city communities (which were obliged to pay tribute) produced grain, wine, and olives in great quantities. In certain regions like the Troad and Laodikeia in Phrygia, pastoral farming played a major role; from here came the particularly valuable black wool produced by a well-known sheep-raising operation. Wood for ship building came from the slopes of the Mysian Mt. Olympos and Mt. Ida. The connection between Pergamon and the world overseas was the harbor city of Elaia at the mouth of the Kaikos, which has recently been subjected to more precise investigation. Attalos II sought in vain to do something about the silting up of the harbor in Ephesos. There were lead mines in Pericharaxis, east of the Gulf of Adramyttion, copper mines near Perperene and Trarion northwest of Pergamon, and gold mines in the Tmolos and Sipylos mountains. There were also marble quarries near Synnada in Phrygia, between Parion and Priapos in the Troad, and

49. A *cistophorus* minted by the Attalids.

in the mountains north of the Kaikos near Pergamon. The capital was a center for pottery production; its products were distributed as far away as the western Mediterranean and north of the Black Sea. The dynast or king had craft industries, such as weaving and weapons factories, in which an army of his slaves worked.

The kingdom and the city of Pergamon were very active in minting coins, and this was surely connected with the country's economic boom. As in the coastal cities, in the capital Pergamon civic coinage had long preceded the period of Attalid rule and continued during it, supplementing the regal issue of coins, even if from then on solely in bronze. The dominant motif appearing on the coins is the head of the city's goddess, Athena. After Philetairos, royal coins minted in silver and bronze almost always bear the brawny image of the founder of the dynasty (see Figure 45), with the exception of one coin issued under Eumenes II. The reverse sides of the coins are usually decorated with the image of a sitting Athena. Both free and tribute-paying cities minted their own coins, also in silver, and in the second century BCE a few rural communities followed suit, such as the Abbaitai or Kaystrianoi. One issue produced by the Attalids in accord with an Ephesian standard and minted throughout the kingdom is of special importance. These coins were called *cistophori* (*cista*-bearers) after the Dionysian pictorial motif of the *cista* (casket) from which a snake is emerging (Figure 49). Only markings on these coins indicate the various cities as the sites where they were minted. They turned out to be one of the ancient world's most successful currencies.

The kings spent their wealth on numerous buildings, foundations, and benefits in the Greek world. To mention only a few: Attalos I's dedications of monuments and buildings in Delphi and on Delos, the naming of an Attic *phyle* after him and the display of his likeness on the monument to the heroic founders of *phylae* in the Athenian *agora*; the temple in Kyzikos built by the brothers Eumenes II and Attalos in their mother's home town; Eumenes II's hall in Athens near the Dionysos theater, the Temple of Poseidon on Kalaureia, and the gymnasium in Miletus; and Attalos

II's hall in Termessos, and especially the great, two-story hall on the east side of the *agora* in Athens.

KINGDOM

Just how the Attalids changed the Seleucids' organization of the kingdom is still not clear in detail. The ancient historian Hermann Bengston assumed that the administrative subdivisions were largely taken over as they were under the Seleucids and put under the control of the respective royal *strategoi*. The areas of competence of these *strategoi* apparently included the *polis* territories: thus we know of a *strategos* responsible for Ephesos and its surroundings, the valley of the Kaystros, and the Kilbianoi region ([162] *IK* Ephesos 201 + Add. p. 6).

As is shown by the written correspondence of various officials in the area of the ancient Lake Gygaia in Lydia, the Attalids continued not only the practice of appointing local *oikonomoi* (managers) but also the system of archpriests and the supervision of all "sacred" income throughout the kingdom. In addition, the title of *epi ton pragmaton* (master of affairs) used in Pergamon reminds us of the title of the "viceroy" used by the Seleucids in cis-Taurine Anatolia (*epi ton epitade tou Taurou pragmaton*), which can thus be understood as indicating a kind of royal chancellor. The position of an official who was responsible for the kingdom's tax revenues and bore the title of *hemiolios* (one and a half) seems to have come down to the Pergamon monarchy from the time of Alexander through the Seleucids. We have yet to discuss the *dioiketes* and *eklogistes*. Both of these officials are mentioned in a recently published inscription from the time of Eumenes II that provides a hierarchical ranking of members of the royal family and royal officials in precisely the places where they would also belong in the Seleucid official hierarchy: the *dioiketes* had a regional jurisdiction that corresponded to that of a satrap or *strategos*. It has long been suspected that the *dioikeseis* of the Roman province of Asia (p. 260), that is, the later assize districts of the proconsuls (Latin: *conventus*) go back to these Attalid administrative units.[106] Immediately after the *dioiketai* in the hierarchy came—not (yet) attested under the Seleucids, but in Cappadocia—an *archeklogistes*, and beneath the *oikonomos* an *eklogistes*, both of them officials entrusted with setting and calculating taxes. It becomes increasingly clear that at least in Attalid western Anatolia there was a stringent and differentiated administration for which we can find parallels only in the papyri of Ptolemaic Egypt.

As it had been under the earlier rulers of Anatolia, the military security network was connected with garrisons in the cities and castles in rural areas along major lines of communication and was expanded by colonies of soldiers settled throughout the country (Map 11). Significant numbers of citizens of Pergamon served in the Attalid army alongside Macedonians and mercenaries from all over the world. A document of the city of Lilaia, which granted *proxenia* to a collective of soldiers from Pergamon who had defended the small Phokian city against Philip V's forces in 209 BCE, provides an interesting cross-section of the composition of that troop (FD 4, 132–135): alongside soldiers from Asia Minor—Cilicia, Lycia, Caria, Ionia, Mysia,

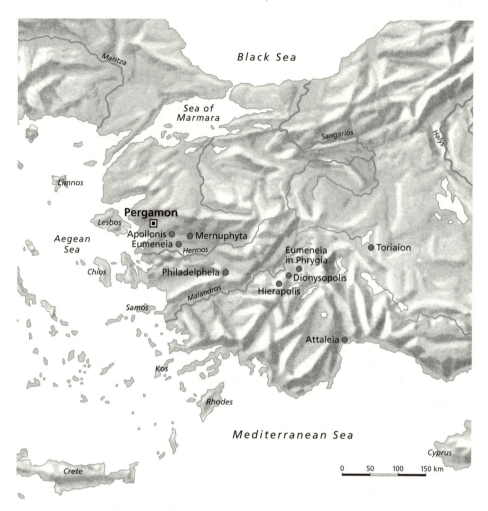

Map 11. Attalid colonization. Map drawn by Peter Palm, Berlin.

and Aiolis—there were also mercenaries from cities as distant as Massalia. Crete was of course a major area for the Attalids' recruitment of mercenaries, and groups of Galatians also constituted an important part of the army.

After the Peace of Apameia, the *poleis* were divided into those that were subject to tribute and garrisoned and those that were not. Royal prefects, *epi tes poleos*, are found in Pergamon as well as in other cities. They were civilian officials with administrative responsibilities. The country consisted not only of city territories and royal domains but also of temple lands, lands occupied by military colonies, and lands occupied by tribal or clan groups (which often formed around native shrines, as did for example the Mokkadenoi, Kilbianoi, Milatai, Moxeanoi, and Poimanenoi).

The continuation of the *synoikismoi* and urbanization of the interior of Anatolia begun by the Diadochs and Epigones is of great historical importance. One outstanding example here is Attaleia, on the extreme western edge of the Pamphylian plain, whose foundation we cannot, unfortunately, date. There Pergamon tried to build a harbor for warships and trade, which was supposed to offset the denial of Aspendos and Side after Apameia. There was also Philadelpheia, which lay on the northern slopes of the Tmolos Mountains, not far from the Kogamos River, on a long-distance road connecting the capital with southern Asia Minor. The founder of this city was Attalos II Philadelphos. Strabo (12, 8, 18) reports that despite the repeated earthquakes that had put many of its inhabitants in a state of constant alarm, an important urban *polis* had developed there. The colonists whom Attalos I and Eumenes II had settled in Mernuphyta near Thyateira named themselves Herakleastai, after Herakles, the father of the founding hero Telephos. Apollonis, named by one of Eumenes's brothers after their mother, emerged between Pergamon and Sardeis from a *synoikismos* of native settlements and new settlements of Macedonians. To remain in Lydia: north of the middle stretch of the Hermos River, on the plain that was called Hyrkania after the country on the Caspian Sea and had once been settled by Persian colonists, Eumenes II (?) founded the city of Eumeneia in Hyrkania (Stephanos of Byzantion, p. 286, 1–3 Meineke s. v.). Another Eumeneia lay in Phrygia. It was laid out by Attalos II and named after his brother. Not far to the west lay Dionysopolis, which is supposed to have owed its foundation to the fact that the brothers, Attalos and Eumenes, found a wooden statue of Dionysos on the site. Under Eumenes II, Hierapolis (which may have been named after Hiera, the wife of Telephos, the mythical founder of Pergamon) is supposed to have been refounded in the same area. However, its name may go back to an older "sacred city" that already owed its status as a *polis* to a Seleucid ruler.[107] This city, which flourished under the Roman Empire, has now become a magnet for tourists in western Anatolia because of its impressive ruins on the edge of picturesque travertine terraces known today by the Turkish name of Pamukkale ("Cotton Castle").

In cases the sources allow us to make a comparison, the process of founding such *poleis* did not differ in any essential way from that under earlier kings. The combination of Macedonian and/or Greek settlers (or Hellenized local residents) with native inhabitants to form a new state is typical, but it occasionally happened that native residents were driven out, as for example in the case of a new settlement founded near Sardeis under Eumenes II ([159] Herrmann and Malay, 2007, no. 32).

A document rare in its detail provides an insight into the urbanization of a rural community in Phrygia Paroreios, an area on the border between Phrygia and Lycaonia that had come into the possession of Eumenes II immediately after the Peace of Apameia. Emissaries from the Toriaitai, who lived in a settlement that had already been mentioned by Xenophon and during the Hellenistic period had been filled with Macedonian or Greek soldiers, appeared before Eumenes, drew his attention to proofs of their loyalty, and asked that in return he grant them the status of a *politeia* (citizen community) with its own laws, a gymnasium, and everything else that went along with it. The king did so, but not without noting that this was no small concession on his part and that his generosity had more reliability and endurance than any other because he had received their land from the victorious Romans. The Greeks were allowed to constitute themselves, along with the natives living alongside them, as a citizenry, establish a council and offices, subdivide the citizenry into *phylae*, organize a gymnasium, and pay for the anointing oil for young men that would be necessary there, everything else depending on the legal foundation to be created. These new laws could be chosen or drafted by the Toriaitai, but the king reserved for himself the right to look over them to be sure that they contained nothing harmful. However, should there be differences of opinion regarding the laws to be submitted, the king offered to provide the laws himself. In a second letter to the already existing *polis* community, the urgent need of financing for the supply of oil for the gymnasium was filled by a provision that the control over the market taxes would be temporarily ceded to the city until the royal *hemiolios* had established a more appropriate basis for paying the cost.[108] This monarchical interventionism exercised on a community that had been raised to the status of a *polis* raises an old, much-discussed question: were all "cities" free, or did they differ in the degree of freedom granted them? Is it possible to classify them into different groups depending on their claims to freedom?

To distinguish newly founded cities like Toriaion from the old, established free Greek cities, modern research draws on the former's classification as "subordinate or subject cities" (*villes sujettes*).[109] However, this is a fluctuating category. Having the distinctive status of a genuine Greek *polis* (*polis hellenis*) could not *per definitionem* ensure a city's freedom or make it fundamentally more immune to royal intervention than a newly founded *polis* was. There is no absolute criterion of freedom in abstraction from the relevant relation between city and ruler. Where power relationships allowed it, royal intervention could generally be exercised in every domain, even matters internal to the city (finances, law). Nonetheless, the initiative and mechanisms of the cities' politics remained unbroken. The kings did not abolish and replace them with something else or essentially alter them. They never incorporated civic decrees and laws into an imperial or royal body of law. Neither did they systematically hinder cities' activities in foreign affairs and diplomacy. The process of encouraging the *polis* is best explained on the basis of its attractiveness for the ruler and the ruled alike. The model quickly developed its appeal outside the exclusive relations between Greeks and the monarchs, and first of all among the mixed groups of settlers that the settlement policies pursued by the Diadochs and Epigones necessarily produced. On the part of these subjects thrown together or of communities existing in other forms, grouped around village centers or temples, the concepts of freedom and autonomy founded a new identity. They were allowed to organize, define themselves territorially, regard themselves as privileged, and deal with the ruler and his representatives as a state, not as slaves (cf. p. 192).

From Roman Hegemony to the Roman Empire

One of the questions debated in recent research, in regard to Asia Minor as well as to other parts of the world under Roman control, is when a consistently stabilizing, systematically ordered, constructive long-term governance came into being and superseded the earlier Roman policy that sought essentially just to weaken whatever autonomous states were currently strongest and to absorb the needed or available riches from the subjected area. In other words: when did Asia become part of the Roman Empire? The answer that immediately suggests itself is: when it acquired the heritage of Pergamon and decided to make of it a Roman *provincia* on Asian soil.[110] But this answer is not universally accepted. It has been argued that the change took place in the age of the Mithridatic Wars.[111] In itself, the fact that immediately after 133 BCE the Romans had already transferred the kingdom to the legal framework of a province of the Roman people is not decisive evidence against this view. Whether the new province of Asia was more than what an overseas colony was in the nineteenth century can be determined by examining the relevant individual measures and developments. Some researchers are interested in defining a Roman Eastern policy and seek to work out its principles and mechanisms.[112] We cannot discuss the problem in this context and will limit ourselves to the viewpoint of Asia Minor. From that viewpoint, however, the early stages of Roman activities in Anatolia do not appear in a favorable light.

From the Kingdom of Pergamon to the Roman Provinces of Asia, Lycaonia, and Cilicia

The date of Attalos III's death probably falls in May 133 BCE. Immediately thereafter the people of Pergamon passed a decree in the capital ([106] OGIS 338). According to this decree, Attalos had left his native city (*patris*) "free" after his death and also added to it state territory (*politike chora*) to a certain extent. It was considered as necessary that the Romans certify the will. In regard to the general security situation, it was then decreed that loyal inhabitants of the country and the soldiers and military personnel who had settled or were stationed in the city, the country, or the fortress, would be granted citizenship, while freedmen and royal slaves would be granted the status of residents of the country. In addition, those who had left the country after the king's death, or might leave it in the future, would be punished. This is a clear reflex reaction to an immediately looming situation of conflict, in which people were probably already going over to the other side (not named in the document).

The attention of the people of Pergamon was now focused on drafting a constitution for a *polis* that—stripped of the superstructure of the royal supervisory bureaucracy—can only be called a *demokratia*. The hopes for such a future had models in the past, for example, in the Carian and Lycian cities after 167 BCE. Here, however, they were not to be fulfilled in the same way.

It is well known that in Rome the news of the testament from Pergamon was immediately incorporated into the plans of the people's tribune, Tiberius Gracchus, who wanted to secure, by means of popular decisions, the royal treasury and the expected tax revenues for his agrarian reforms. However, he encountered resistance on the part of the senators. At the same time, with the rebellion of a certain Aristonikos, civil war broke out in Pergamon.[113] Aristonikos was an illegitimate son of Attalos II who apparently rebelled against the application of Attalos III's will and immediately claimed the throne for himself by legitimate succession. According to Strabo (14, 1, 38), the kingdom's cities and the kings of Bithynia and Cappadocia instantly reacted and mobilized against him.

Only in the winter of 133/132 BCE did a five-member commission from Rome arrive in Pergamon; it included Cornelius Scipio Nasica, who died there shortly afterward. The commissioners introduced an activity perceived as "Roman legislation"; it was dealt with by the *buleuterion*, a kind of special council operating as a new municipal commission. It appears that differences of opinion now arose between the Romans and Pergamon's delegates that required the latter to show a talent for cautious and circumspect negotiation. From the retrospective point of view of our source texts, these difficulties are always only implied. The results of the Roman commission went into the *senatus consultum Popillianum* (Sherk, RDGE 11), which, thanks to a reading of the stone inscription by the epigraphist Michael Wörrle, can now be dated with certainty to the fall or winter of 132 BCE. Unfortunately, this inscription is extant only in very fragmentary form, in copies from Pergamon and Synnada. In any case, it refers to the whole Attalid heritage and the situation in Asia, and in particular it enables us to understand the injunction that the Roman commanders going to Asia must not overstep their jurisdictions and must respect the provisions of the will.[114]

Another document reflects the same situation in Asia (the situation in the aftermath of the decree of the Roman Senate of 132 BCE, which acknowledged the provisions of the will). This time it came not from the city of Pergamon, but rather from one of the kingdom's subservient cities, Metropolis. The decree honoring a citizen named Apollonios adds a new element to our information: Aristonikos is said to have acted to strip Metropolis of the freedom that the Senate had guaranteed, because the Romans had restored freedom to everyone who had earlier been subjects in Attalos's kingdom. Thus the Romans had gone beyond the king's gift of freedom to the *patris* Pergamon as stated in the decree of Pergamon ([106] OGIS 338), apparently in accord with declarations of freedom for the other cities as well, one of which was Metropolis (these declarations have not come down to us). Beyond that, the exact meaning of the phrase "all earlier subjects of Attalos" is for the time being difficult to determine. In addition to the cities, there were other communities in the kingdom, so that even in the broadest possible interpretation of this text only the royal domains were included in the bequest ([195] SEG 53, 1312).

At the beginning of the war, the cities alone were not able to command the situation, and it is unclear just when the troops of King Nikomedes II of Bithynia, Pylaimenes of Paphlagonia, Ariarathes V of Cappadocia, and Mithridates V of Pontos arrived to help. Aristonikos managed to acquire a fleet, made Leukai (near Smyrna) its base, and began to seize places on the west coast, including Kolophon, Samos, and Myndos. Smyrna resisted, despite a siege. The insurgent received support from Phokaia, for which the Roman Senate later wanted to retaliate by destroying this city, but refrained from doing so after mediation by its daughter city Massalia. Near Kyme Aristonikos suffered a defeat in a battle against the Ephesian ships and thereupon withdrew into the interior, where he gathered the poorer rural people and slaves around him to fight for freedom and proclaimed a community of *heliopolitai*. The Romans were a long time coming. The city of Kyzikos on the Propontis was in danger; in this emergency the city turned to the governor of Macedonia and then to the Senate.

In 131 BCE the consul Publius Licinius Crassus took over the supreme command. The allied cities and the kings' troops took part in the following military operations. In an offensive against Thyateira, which was under siege by Aristonikos, Ariarathes V and the previously mentioned Apollonios from Metropolis fell on the Roman side, after Apollonios had led a contingent of young citizens into battle. Aristonikos took Apollonis, a few other fortresses, and Stratonikeia on the Kaikos. In these cities of Mysia he had *cistophori* with the royal name Eumenes (III) struck. In early 130, he inflicted a catastrophic defeat on the Roman forces near Leukai, in the course of which the consul was killed. His successor, Marcus Perperna, was able to end the war in the summer of that year, when he surrounded Aristonikos and took him prisoner near Stratonikeia on the Kaikos. The prisoner and the royal treasure of Pergamon were transported to Italy. Aristonikos ended up in a dungeon in Rome. In the fall, during the preparations for the victory celebration in Pergamon, Perperna died. The following year, 129 BCE, a ten-member commission under the new consul, Manius Aquillius, finally began to settle matters on the spot.

THE PROVINCE OF ASIA

In Pergamon, differences over the "Roman legislation" must have immediately arisen at that time; a Pergamenian citizen, Menodoros, appeared with bold candor before the Romans to present arguments in favor of his *patris*. The *polis* believed it had the law on its side. What the conflict was about, we do not know. Documents from other cities also report problems, and quite a few give specific indications. In the war, cities had already undergone hardships and encroachments by the Romans: billeting, impressment, and levies of contributions. The citizens of the coastal city of Bargylia were forced by a Roman officer to provide auxiliary troops, which put them under heavy pressure. The community was threatened with the loss of its *autonomia*. Citizens of other free cities were sentenced to death by Roman verdicts, and regulations issued by Roman officers ran counter to city laws. The Senate had to deal with such complaints over and over. We usually learn about them only when things turned out well for the city concerned, because that was followed by decrees honoring the successful negotiators. Here the Greek citizen elite proved its rhetorical and philosophical education in a critical situation. It was a matter of convincing the Romans that their representatives on site were not acting properly. Among all these texts, two long hymns of praise inscribed on stone in the sanctuary of Apollo in Klaros in honor of Polemaios and Menippos, the benefactors of the city of Kolophon, stand out.[115] They describe the latter's lives as youths and citizens who held various offices and positions, and not only as emissaries. In courageous negotiations with the Roman Senate, Polemaios won compensations for the plundering of his city by Roman troops and obtained a senatorial decree (*epitagma*, probably *mandatum* in Latin) to the effect that the Romans active in the country must not inflict any injustice on the city. He had paid out of his own pocket for the lodging and maintenance of Romans who were billeted in the city, and made those with whom he cultivated good contacts *patroni* of the city. These too were phenomena that appeared in Asia for the first time and continued to develop into institutional forms until the early Imperial period: they established a relationship, which resembled patronage in Roman society, between Roman officials and authorities on the one hand and on the other, the Greek *poleis* and especially—representing the *poleis*, as it were, and to their benefit—their rich, respected, and highly educated elites.[116]

Menippos's diplomatic career comes across as even more imposing. It had already begun under the kings. During the process of creating a Roman *provincia*, he negotiated not only with the Senate in Rome but also with officials in the province. In all, he appeared before the Senate on five occasions between ca. 129 and 120 BCE. Much was at stake, first of all the status of the *polis*, and then, after its freedom and autonomy were guaranteed, the boundaries of its territory. The legal and jurisdictional competence of the *polis* seems precarious and must have been repeatedly disregarded or violated. Nevertheless, the text, like no other from this early phase of the province, leaves not the slightest doubt that *polis* (*civitas libera*) and province (*eparcheia*) are two strictly different domains. The provincial governor's accusations against citizens and the collection of bail money on the basis of these accusations were condemned by the Senate as encroachments on the sphere of the *polis* and its force of law; outside the domain of the province, the proconsul was not allowed to exercise any judicial activity (*krinein*) or make any regulations not within his purview (*polypragmonein*). The city's laws and the jurisdiction of its courts were also valid when citizens of the *polis* were accused by Romans or when Romans were accused by citizens of the *polis*. The case of a man from Kolophon who as an accuser (or judge) had obtained (or imposed) a death sentence against a Roman citizen apparently led once again to a strident controversy over juristic competencies, in the course of which the Greek was arrested, and the city itself was indicted.[117] Once again, Menippos appeared before the Senate and obtained a favorable decision.

It can be safely assumed that such events were hardly unique in the first years of the province and did not lead everywhere to a solution that was favorable to the

50. Honorary plaque for the citizen Menippos at a column near the Temple of Apollo in Klaros: "The people [honor] Menippus, [son] of Apollonides [by adoption], according to nature [son] of Eumedes, who is a benefactor and in the interests of the body of citizens zealous and devoted to [their] good and at the head of the fatherland in times of necessity" ([195] SEG 37, 957; J. R. Harrison (trans.), "Times of Necessity," in: S. R. Llewelyn (ed.), *New Documents Illustrating Early Christianity: A Review of the Greek Inscriptions and Papyri Published in 1986–1987*, vol. 9, Grand Rapids, MI 2002, 7.)

community. The epigraphists Jeanne and Louis Robert aptly describe these conflicts as "resistance" to the abuses of power committed by the first Roman commanders in Asia.[118] The grateful communities rewarded the courage of their protagonists in the conflict with the new masters of Asia with monuments erected in prominent places in the city (Figure 50).

Manius Aquillius remained in Asia for two more years. Later on, Pergamon itself honored him with religious veneration as an exceptional benefactor (IGR IV 292 l. 39; 293 col. II l. 23). One of the eleven milestones bearing his name that was found five kilometers west of Side shows that the Romans not only repaired the road passing through Thyateira, Sardeis, Philadelpheia, Laodikeia, and Termessos, but also immediately laid claim to the harbor of Attaleia in western Pamphylia as part of the Attalid heritage. Even if the road led on through the Pamphylian plain as far as Side, it is not at all clear that the latter city was also annexed. At the time of Attalos's death it was a free city in a part of Pamphylia that still belonged to the Seleucids: Antiochos VII had sojourned there for a long time before mounting the throne in 138 BCE.[119] Aquillius's repair and protection of the kingdoms' roads marked the beginning of the Romans' centuries-long development of paved highways and connecting roads through Anatolia (p. 372).[120] Under Aquillius, Pergamon and Ephesos were the starting points for the distances given on the milestones in the province.

Not all parts of Anatolia ruled by the Attalids were incorporated into the new province. Allegedly as the result of a bribe, the Romans left the eastern portion of Greater Phrygia under the control of their ally Mithridates V of Pontos.[121] The sons of the Ariarathes of Cappadocia, who had fallen in battle, were rewarded with part of Lycaonia. Furthermore, the Attalids' European possessions in Thrace and the island of Aigina were not included in the new province. The area south of the Maeander, which had been declared free in 168/167 BCE and—with the exception of the acknowledged exclaves—did not belong to Pergamon, remained outside the province.[122] For governors of the province under the Republic, see the Appendix.

TAXES

Research on taxation in the early province of Asia is a minefield. Nonetheless, I will give what seems to me a probable account, being well aware that it could be invalidated by the discovery of new inscriptions. Certainly the royal land received from Attalos's legacy was immediately taxed. It was made part of the Romans' state property (*ager publicus*). This almost necessarily raised boundary questions, because cities that had been privileged as free and not subject to tribute payments under the kings were supposed to retain this status, and in any case the *ager publicus* bordered on city territory. It is obvious that the new masters of the province were not always inclined to let the Greeks define the precise borders of the property they had just acquired. We do not know exactly how the former royal land was taxed in the early years of the province. It seems *a priori* plausible that the Romans simply adopted from the Attalids an existing and functioning system of taxation, as they also did in Sicily after the death of King Hieron (275–214 BCE). One indication of this is found in a customs law for the province of Asia dating from the time of the Roman Empire and depending in substance on an earlier law that was passed in 75 BCE and subsequently amended several times: a few of Attalos's customs stations were to be taken over.

Customs duties were received in coin, and the revenue transported to Italy. In contrast, farmers paid land taxes on the *ager publicus* in kind and to the proconsul. Nineteenth-century *voyageurs* in the interior of Ottoman Anatolia still observed similar practices, as First Lieutenant von Flottwell wrote:

> In Jalym we had an opportunity to witness an instance of Turkish tax collection. The collection of the tithe, the most important Turkish tax, is generally farmed out and exacted, with great rigor, in kind. The farmer is not allowed to harvest crops from his fields until the tax officials have been in the village and assessed the yield. Since these officials have an easy life in the villages, they are in no hurry to make their rounds.[123]

Under Manius and even later, part of the grain exacted was used for supply of regular troops in the province; the other part would probably have been sold in the market there. Italic tax farmers (*publicani*) might already have been active, but that is not certain, because the dating of an important document that mentions them presumably comes from a later phase. I examine this document briefly here.

The decision made by the Senate regarding the land of Pergamon (*senatus consultum de agro Pergameno*, [162] *IK* Smyrna 589), exists in three versions coming from Adramytteion, Smyrna, and Ephesos. Their date is the subject of scholarly controversy. Arguments have been made for dating them to the years 129 or 101 BCE. The partly preserved name of a consul, Aquillius, limits the possibilities to these two years; the reference is either to the organizer of the province of Asia or the younger Manius Aquillius, who was consul together with Gaius Marius. The extant parts of the text speak of a dispute between the citizens of Pergamon and the Roman tax farmers over which land is subject to levies. It was up to a Roman magistrate and his fifty-seven-member advisory board to decide exactly where the boundaries of the land were. If the date 129 BCE is correct, this would be the earliest evidence of *publicani* in Asia. An initial tax assessment would then have been made immediately after the establishment of the province. However, the date of an individual mentioned in the text as one of the commissioners offers an argument, though not a conclusive one, for the year 101. The question raised by this date is why almost thirty years after the Romans took possession of the Attalid heritage, problems regarding the boundaries between land that was subject to tribute and land that was free could still arise.

Only six years after the end of the War of Aristonikos, in 123 BCE, Asian taxes were being farmed out by the censors in Rome (*censoria locatio*; Cicero, *Verr.* II 3, 12) in accord with the younger Gracchus's *lex Sempronia*. In any case, of the kinds of taxes levied in Asia, the right to collect the *decuma* (land tax) and possibly already at that time, pasture taxes and customs duties, was periodically—that is, every five years (*quinquennium*)—sold to the highest bidder in auctions held by the censors. Here the large publican companies came into play.[124] In Cicero's time we even find the province of Asia's pasture taxes (*scriptura*) and customs duties (*portoria*) in the hands of a single company, which also owned, moreover, the province of Bithynia's *scriptura* (Cicero, *fam.* 13, 65, 1; *Att.* 11, 10, 1). At this time the revenues from the province of Asia constituted the majority of Rome's state revenues in general. The income from the most recent years may have provided the estimated standard value for the minimum bid for tax-farming leases in Rome. It was the duty of the official (*pro magistro*) who acted for the master (*magister*) on site—the headquarters was Ephesos—to pay the contractually agreed installments to the quaestor of the province on time. He and his agents made contracts with cities and communities on a yearly basis. In this way the rates were established in accord with the publican company's expected profits, and naturally the Roman businessmen tried to set them as high as possible. There were legally determined maximums. Thus the land tax could not be more than the tithe (10 percent), and customs duties that had to be paid on goods crossing borders could not be more than the usual 2.5 percent of their value. But neither the unlawful violation of these limits nor the ingenious introduction of various new fees was consistently halted by governors, even less so after the latter, having returned home from the province, could, in accord with Gracchian legislation, be brought before a court over which the *publicani*'s equestrian peers presided. But then *publicani* were sometimes cheated of the revenues they had expected when communities exercised, in the middle of the leasing period, the privilege of freedom from taxes.[125] Numerous testimonies regarding the conflicts between the communities and the *publicani* are extant, particularly from the first century BCE: in Priene, where it was a question of the revenues from salt works; in Ephesos and Ilion, whose shrines to Artemis and Athena, respectively, were robbed of large revenues; in Mytilene, and, outside Asia, in Herakleia Pontike in 73 BCE.[126] Behind the enforcement of demands recognized as being in accord with the law stood the power of the state. If the communities were not able to pay on time, they had to take out loans, and it is known that in such cases Roman bankers stood ready to transform this need into another source of profits. According to the ancient historian Ernst Badian, the goal of this centralized tax farming was to organize the levying of land taxes more effectively and independently of the provincial governor by leasing the task to tax-collection companies, since these *societates* had at their disposal far greater resources in personnel, transportation, and storage than did the governor's staff. For the cities, it must have brought with it a dramatic deterioration of their initial situation, and Mark Antony was probably referring to this ninety years later when he reminded the Greeks of the province of Asia that: "Your king Attalus, O Greeks, left you to us in his will, and straightway we proved better to you than Attalus had been, for we released you from the taxes that you had been paying to him, until the action of popular agitators also among us made these taxes necessary" (Appian, *BC*, 5, 1, 4; trans. White). This has always been dismissed as a misunderstanding. But the sources available do not prove that the cities were taxed before 123/122 BCE, the year of the law proposed by Gaius Gracchus (to whom the expression "popular agitators" alludes here). And in fact it seems likely that with the arrival of the big tax-collection companies after this date, the border problems and especially the status problems began all over again and could be repeated precisely at the beginning of each tax-collection *quinquennium*. In the wars of the first century BCE the extortion with special and en-bloc levies was to increase even further. A lasting change in the system was finally introduced by Caesar in 49 or 48 BCE, when he deprived the tax-collection companies of the proceeds of the land tax, the tithe.[127]

The Romans not only allowed the silver *cistophori* introduced under the kings of Pergamon to circulate in Asia, they also continued to mint them for their own use. The triumvir Mark Antony had them coined in large numbers. They were struck in Ephesos, Pergamon, Tralleis, Laodikeia, and Apameia (CIL I² pp. 761–764), but this money also went to Rome. However, a letter from Cicero to Atticus in April 59 BCE makes it clear that people were not entirely confident that they could be converted into Roman denarii without loss: "But to come to business, I have written to the City Quaestors about Quintus' affair. See what they have to say, whether there is any hope of denarii or whether we must let ourselves be foisted off with Pompey's cistophores."[128] In Asia, the radical break that would have resulted from the abolition of the cistophorus would have raised various problems: for one thing, how immediately to provide enough silver money to supply such a large region with many cities, and for another, how to force people to accept the denarius.

Asia was normally ruled by praetors appointed annually, except at the outset, when it was governed by Manius Aquillius, and during the Mithridatic Wars, when it was ruled by Cornelius Sulla (87–84 BCE), Lucius Valerius Flaccus, and Lucius Licinius Lucullus, who were consuls.[129] In inscriptions, they are abbreviated as *anthypatos* (Latin: *pro consule*). After the departure of Aquillius in 126, in 125 Asia may have been governed by Cornelius Lentulus (who was honored on Delos), in 122/121 certainly by Gaius Atinius Labeo (this can be proven by his minting of *cistophori*), who was perhaps followed by Valerius Messala, and (ca. 120) by the elder Quintus

Mucius Scaevola. The presence of military tribunes during several of the latter's sojourns in Kolophon, which were financed by the citizen Menippos (p. 254), can be
seen as an indication that the governor was provided with a legion, contrary to the
later practice under the empire.[130] From the outset, his staff probably consisted of a
quaestor responsible for taxation and three legates, each of whom could represent
him on site.

The governors' most important tasks were to preside over lawsuits in the province
and to supervise tax collection. As judges, they functioned simply as a court of appeal
in all civil suits involving *peregrini* (foreigners) and minor infractions; the everyday
judicial system continued to function in the subject cities and communities as it had
under the kings. Some governors, such as Mucius Scaevola and, following his example, Cicero, avoided any involvement in this sphere. However, whether death sentences might also be imposed by the city courts after the province's earliest phase
(p. 254), or whether this "right of the sword" (*ius gladii*) was soon reserved for the
governor, even when non-Romans were concerned, remains an open question. As we
have seen, Romans who were citizens and/or residents of free Greek *poleis* fell under
the jurisdiction of the *polis*. As citizens, they could, naturally, be elected to city offices; we know of *polis* officeholders with Roman names in Priene in the first century
BCE. Romans living in the province were subject to the jurisdiction of the proconsul.
A Roman citizen accused of a capital crime had to be transferred to Rome to appear
before the consuls. Other jurisdictional responsibilities at first remained with magistrates in Rome and were only gradually transferred to the provincial governors.[131]

Lycaonia, Cilicia

After the assassination of Mithridates V of Pontos, who left behind him under-age
sons, Greater Phrygia was declared in 119 or 116 BCE to be an autonomous region,
but de facto it was added to the province of Asia. Furthermore, even before the turn
of the century a new province of Lycaonia was to become an annex of Asia that could
be ruled in conjunction with the latter by the governor of Asia. This region, which
since 129 had been left to the Cappadocians, was taken away from them now after
the death of Ariarathes VI (111 BCE?).

Since 102 BCE there had been another Roman province on the soil of Asia: Cilicia. It owed its establishment to the assignment of the area to a special command that
was exercised by the praetor Marcus Antonius (the grandfather of the later triumvir)
in that year; he had been put in charge of combating pirates on the south coast of
Asia Minor. A law of 100 BCE regarding the provinces of the praetors (*lex de provinciis praetoriis*), written in Greek and known from copies found in Knidos and Delphi,
expressly stipulates that the people of Rome had made Cilicia a praetorian province.[132] After his year of office as praetor in Rome (97 BCE), Sulla ruled this province
and in this capacity put Ariobarzanes I on the throne of Cappadocia (p. 271). The
extent of the area that was called "Cilicia" at the time remains unclear and a matter of
debate. According to Jean-Louis Ferrary's argument, which we are following here,
Lycaonia, which was initially co-governed by the proconsul along with Asia, became

a separate province and together with Pamphylia was put under Antony's control first in 102, and then repeatedly under his successors, until much later in 64/63 BCE Pompey organized an entirely new, geographically quite differently situated province of Cilicia.[133] Now, under Antony's command, additionally the non-Attalid Pamphylia may have become a provincial region. However, Caria and part of the Kibyratis remained outside and were attatched to the province of Asia only later (p. 277).

Roman Dioceses, Provincial Koinon

On the basis of this system of three provinces in Asia Minor (Asia, Lycaonia, and Cilicia) as it existed ca. 80 BCE, we know a system of subdividing the provincial area into districts, called *dioikeseis* in Greek or *conventus* in Latin.[134] Its earliest attestation is in 62 BCE. However, there is consensus regarding an earlier date of its introduction. At the beginning of the Imperial period, Strabo writes in one passage (14, 1, 38) that Manius Aquillius had organized the province in a form of government that was still valid in his own time, and in another (13, 4, 12) that the Roman principle of organization was determined not by where the tribes (*kata phyla*) lived, but rather by the location of the *dioikeseis* where their assemblies and legal proceedings were held. We should not interpret these passages as suggesting that the Romans had invented something entirely new. I have already noted the striking relationship between the idea of *dioikesis* and the Seleucid and Attalid official title of *dioiketes*. For the time being, however, their precise connections remain hidden to us. We can count eighteen such districts in all, but three of them appear only in the Imperial period (Thyateira, Philadelpheia, and Aizanoi), and the other fifteen did not all exist at the same time: some, like Halikarnassos, were formed only later on, while others, like Mylasa and Tralleis, were subsequently abolished. Random evidence of complete findings at a given time shows eleven or twelve such districts. Most of these are named after their main cities: Adramyttion, Pergamon, Smyrna, Sardeis, Ephesos, Miletus, Tralleis, Alabanda, Mylasa, Halikarnassos, Apameia, and Synnada. An exception to this rule is the district at the Hellespont (*dioikesis Hellespontia*), whose main city is Kyzikos. This, too, is a striking indication of recourse to something older. However, if the *dioikesis* Kibyratike has as its main city not just Kibyra, but rather Laodikeia on Lykos, that is for purely practical reasons—the latter city was located much more conveniently for the governors' journey on the main road. A third exception, a district with the city of Philomelion as its main city, was not originally a *dioikesis* at all. It was a province, Lycaonia (*eparcheia Lycaonia*), which was subject to the governor of Asia and over time assumed the function of a single *dioikesis* (Map 12).

Whereas the Seleucid and Attalid administrators (*dioiketai*) surely were involved in the taxation of the districts assigned to them, we cannot say that the Roman system was essentially fiscal, at least at first.[135] So far as we know, such a fiscal system was added to the already existing context only under Sulla, when the eleven *dioikeseis* were each divided into four regions for purposes of taxation, thus comprising forty-four fiscal regions altogether. But at the outset, the chief goal of the *dioikeseis* was, as is made particularly clear by the Latin term used to designate them, *conventus* (*conve-*

Map 12. *Conventus Asiae* (assize districts). Map drawn by Peter Palm, Berlin.

nire—come together), obviously to create assize districts in whose main cities the governors could regularly sit in judgment. These cities had to be easily accessible for the governors and also for their subjects in the surrounding smaller localities.

By studying the main roads already attested under Manius Aquillius, it has been possible to reconstruct the circuits traveled by the magistrates for their court sessions. A northern circuit went from Ephesos via Pergamon to Adramyttion and on to Kyzikos, while a southern circuit went from Ephesos via Miletus, Halikarnassos, and Alabanda back to the harbor city on the Kaystros. Cities that were located on the main road to Philomelion through Sardeis, Laodikeia, Apameia, and Synnada were visited by the governor of Cilicia on his way to the province. Even without this enormously long route through the interior of Asia Minor, the proconsul of Asia still had to cover a considerable distance during his year in office, and it is questionable whether every *conventus* capital was visited by every governor, or whether there was a specific cycle apart from such important cities as Ephesos, Smyrna, and Pergamon. Official buildings for the governors, quaestors, or legates have not been found, not even in the presumed headquarters in Ephesos. The magistrates were provided with suitable lodging and meals by the communities or by rich citizens. However, the subjects' obligations were limited in this respect as well (Cicero, *Verr.* II 1, 65).

In addition to their most important function as judicial centers, there is no lack of evidence indicating that these nodal points served other purposes as well. Proclamations by the Roman authorities, senatorial decisions, and edicts issued by the governors were made public there. In addition, they were the sites where the Romans continued to mint *cistophori*. Recruiting may also have been carried out in these cities. For their part, the inhabitants made use of the system for province-wide projects, as when the Jews collected gold for the construction of the Temple in Jerusalem (Cicero, *Flacc.* 68 f.).

In 94 BCE the governance of Quintus Mucius Scaevola the Younger benefited the province, so that his rule was represented as exemplary (Valerius Maximus 8, 15, 16). For example, he mediated a bitter dispute between Ephesos and Sardeis ([106] OGIS 437). In these cities, games named "Mucia," which included dramatic performances and athletic events, were established in his honor. A council (*synedrion*) acting in this context was certainly not connected with the gathering of the provincials, the so-called Commonalty (*koinon*). The latter institution, however, also existed as early as the Hellenistic period. Its earliest testimonies date from around the middle of the first century BCE. At that time a Roman governor wrote to the *koinon* "of the Hellenes" (Sherk, RDGE 52 l. 42 f.), while the *koinon* "of the Hellenes of Asia" honored two citizens of Aphrodisias ([179] Reynolds, *Aphrodisias*, 1982, Doc. 5). The official titles here make it clear, as do similar titles in other provinces later on, that this gathering did not represent all inhabitants of the province, but only the Greeks (i.e., the citizens of the *poleis*), even if their envoys to the Roman authorities sought results beneficial to the cities and peoples (*ethne*). The *koinon* that awarded golden crowns to the two citizens of Aphrodisias—both were also citizens of Tralleis—met in Ephesos. As a reason for these high honors the decree refers in great detail to the two men's willingness to carry out embassies to the Senate and the magistrates and endure many dangers to secure the most important interests of the people in Asia, after the tax collectors had once again plagued cities and communities throughout the province. The rhetorician Diodoros from Sardeis who is mentioned in Strabo (13, 4, 9) may have also been a representative at this earliest *koinon* we know about. He was a man who was also active in many conflicts "for the interest of Asia." For the time being, however, it cannot be determined whether the *koinon* of the Hellenes in Asia owes its origin to the ongoing conflicts with the tax collectors. The representa-

51. The city of Amasya, Turkey.

tion of the provincials' interests before the Senate and later before the emperor remained one of its chief tasks.

✦ ✦ ✦

This was the condition of Roman rule in Asia Minor when it was attacked there and challenged by a conflict that lasted decades. The Romans' great opponent was a king from the house of the Mithridatic dynasty of Pontos, which had already been involved in conflicts with Pergamon and Rhodes. To combat their foe, the Romans drove deep into the interior of the country, and their invasion was as fateful for the future of Asia Minor as those of the Persian king Cyrus and the Macedonian Alexander had once been. We now turn to the internal situations in the kingdoms.

The Kingdoms of Pontos and Cappadocia

The evidence provided by archaeology and epigraphy regarding Pontos is slim compared with that regarding the kingdom of Pergamon. The general overviews of the history of this kingdom produced in the nineteenth century on the basis of the literary tradition have been superseded only in part by more recent works (see the list of kings in the Appendix). Important advances have been made primarily by numismatics.[136] Much of what we know about the conditions in Hellenistic Pontos we owe to Strabo, who came from Amaseia in Pontos and left us a precise description of his native city, including the palace and the monuments of the kings (Figure 51):

My city is situated in a large deep valley, through which flows the Iris River. Both by human foresight and by nature it is an admirably devised city, since it can at the same time afford the advantage of both a city and a fortress; for it is a high and precipitous rock, which descends abruptly to the river, and has on one side the wall on the edge of the river where the city is settled and on the other the wall that runs up on either side to the peaks. These peaks are two in number, are united with one another by nature, and are magnificently towered. Within this circuit are both the palaces and monuments of the kings. The peaks are connected by a neck which is altogether narrow, and is five of six stadia in height on either side as one goes up from the river-banks and the suburbs. (Strabo 12, 3, 39; trans. Jones)

A more precise investigation of the monuments of the kings has recently been undertaken by the Austrian archaeologist Robert Fleischer.[137] In contrast to the numerous rock-cut tombs of the Paphlagonian type (p. 164), few of those of the Pontic type are known—in addition to a few small tombs, there are six monumental ones from Amaseia and another, the largest, in a gorge near Lâçin, between Çorum and Osmancık. It is characteristic of these that they are in the form of buildings cut on all sides wholly or almost wholly out of the rock. In the absence of clear criteria, it is difficult to date them.

No inscriptions identify the owners at the five caverns in the castle rock in Amaseia that Strabo describes as tombs of the kings—a group of three to the east (A–C) and another group of two to the west (D, E). Immediately below the fortress on the peak of the castle rock, a commander of the garrison, Metrodoros, had an altar and a terrace with a flowerbed made for King Pharnakes I. Since this king had probably already moved to Sinope, Fleischer conjectures that the latest, uncompleted tomb E, on the left of the western group, belonged to him. In the cases of both the neighboring tomb and two of the older group of three tombs directly above the ruins of the palace complex, visible traces left on the stone allow us to see that their façades mimicked those of Greek temples, with four and six Ionic columns, respectively.

Tombs deviating from this type include, in addition to the one attributed to Pharnakes and tomb C (the one on the left of the group of three), the tomb of the archpriest Tes, which lies on the northern edge of the city of Amasya and was later occupied by a certain Egatheos, Menandros's son, and the enormous tomb near Lâçin that bears the owner's inscription "Hikesios." Fleischer considers these latter two later forms; according to him, the typological development diverges from the Greek path toward an unmistakable Pontic form. The Hikesios tomb is not only higher (thirteen meters) than the royal tombs and the priest's tomb in Amaseia but is also distinguished by an unusually extensive set of terraces with stairways leading to it, suggesting that it was used for religious ceremonies.

With the exception of the royal residence of Amaseia, in the interior of Pontos only the old shrines had larger settlements. Two of these had been founded by the Persians (pp. 242, 516): the temple of the goddess Anāhitā in Zela and the temple of the moon god (Men) with the "village city" (komopolis) Ameria, where at the time of Mithridates Eupator a royal palace; a water mill; a zoo; and, nearby, the royal hunting grounds and mines were located. The name of this royal estate (*basileion*), "Kabeira," apparently goes back to a Hellenistic sanctuary of the Cabeiri, a group of chthonic deities. The moon god enjoyed the monarchy's greatest veneration; the royal oath was sworn by Men and by the king's *tyche* ("Luck," "Fate"). His shrine included that of the moon goddess Selene. A priest managed the revenues from the temple's land; the temple servants (*hieroduloi*) who worked it constituted part of Ameria's resident population. This Kabeira, along with its temples, may have been located on the site of the later city of Neokaisareia and modern-day Niksar, but this is not entirely certain.[138] Information provided by Strabo (11, 8, 4) allows us to localize the Anāhitā temple in Zela on the castle hill of Zile. Pilgrims from all over Pontos went there to worship Anāhitā along with Anadatos and Omanos (presumably the Persian Vahu-manah, "good spirit"). Anāhitā, "the pure," is a goddess who was revered by the Iranians, on the model of the Semitic Ištar, with the appearance of the planet Venus; the Greeks saw in her the "Persian Artemis." In contrast, no Greek counterparts have come down to us for Anadatos and Omanos, about whom we otherwise know little. Strabo himself witnessed one of the most sacred processions in which the wooden image of Omanos was carried out of the temple. The site of what was probably the oldest of the great Pontic shrines, Komana, near the village of Gümenek, a few kilometers northeast of Tokat, has also been determined and is now being excavated. The worship of the mother-goddess Ma-Enyo had a site with the same name in Kataonia, the Kumani of Hittite times. Twice a year there were "excursions" of the goddess, and on these occasions the priests were allowed to wear a diadem. Like Kabeira and Zela, Komana's land in the green, fertile Iris valley was managed like a temple-state and cultivated by a large number of *hieroduloi*; wine-growing was of special importance. Women prostituted themselves in the service of the divinity.

Strabo locates another of the Mithridatids' *basileia* in Gaziura, modern-day Turhal. On the basis of the evidence provided by coins minted under Datames (ca. 362 BCE) and Ariarathes I (before 322 BCE), in the fourth century, Gaziura, with its castle-hill, was already a royal seat and the place of a sanctuary of Baal-Gazur ([199] Head, HN² 749). Nothing more detailed regarding the beginnings of this shrine can be said. "Baal" is the Semitic term, widely used, especially in Syria and Phoenicia, meaning "master," "ruler," or "owner," for the local divinity dominating a place. After Alexander's death, the diadoch Eumenes of Kardia established his military power base here in Gaziura. There are two Hellenistic rock inscriptions in Greek; one, whose poor condition makes it difficult to read, says that in this place there had been a Greek *agon* and a gymnasium, and this has been interpreted as indicating that the Hellenization of the kingdom of Pontos at that time had become rather advanced.[139]

Noble landlords resided on the many castle-hills in the interior of Pontos; they ruled over dependent farmers, shepherds, craftsmen, and merchants belonging to various native ethnic groups who lived in villages and farmsteads. It is said that in the kingdom of Mithridates VI, as many as twenty-seven languages were spoken, and the king must have known most of them. The Mithridatids' kingdom included very fertile areas of land. The royal house drew its income from large domains and monopolies, such as mining, customs, and war booty. Regular tributes (in contrast to taxes exacted on the occasion of war) seem to have been levied only on the non-Pontic parts of the kingdom that had been conquered under Eupator; we know nothing about tributes paid by cities on the coast of the Black Sea. Nonetheless, Strabo (12, 3, 11) chooses the word *duleuein* ("to be a slave") when describing Sinope's relationship to Pharnakes and all his successors down to Eupator.

Of the more than seventy castles in the kingdom (we know the names of about ten of them), many served as treasuries (*gazophylakia*) where equipment, bars of precious metals, and coins were stored, closely guarded by garrisons under the command of the *phrurarchoi*. Under Mithridates Eupator the most valuable hoard was located on a steep-sided, impregnable rock near Kabeira called "Kainon Chorion" (Strabo 12, 3, 31). The royal coinage in gold, silver, and bronze served chiefly to pay garrison soldiers and mercenaries in wars. We know of no less than twelve mints in the area of the kingdom in Asia Minor: Amastris, Sinope, Amisos, and Pharnakeia on the coast; and Amaseia, Kabeira, Chabakta, Komana, Gaziura, Taulara, Laodikeia, and Pimolisa in the interior.[140] However, coinage tells us nothing about the *polis* status or "autonomy" of these places. Apart from Pharnakeia's *synoikismos*, Pontic kings did not pursue a policy of urbanization, and certainly not a policy of founding *poleis* like Toriaion in Phrygia under Eumenes II. A few renamed places, such as "Eupatoria" and "Laodikeia" in Pontos, should not mislead us about this.[141]

It is not surprising that the royal court, the kingdom, and the military, insofar as they are known to us, bear the traits of Hellenistic monarchies as we have seen them in the case of the Seleucids and Attalids. Greek or Hellenized personnel were dominant in the king's entourage and in offices of various kinds. At the court his relatives (*syngeneis*) and "closest friends" (*protoi philoi*), along with the prefects (*tetagmenoi*), dominated departments such as the judicial system (*epi tes dikaiodosias*) and the secret service (*epi tu aporrhetu*), while the *phrurarchoi* and *strategoi* controlled fortresses and towns.[142] The Greeks did not always remain loyal to the Iranian royal house. Strabo (12, 3, 33) refers with pride to the dissidents in his own family and contritely remarks that Pompey's hostility to Lucullus prevented the Senate from recognizing them as pro-Roman insurgents.

Much remains unclear regarding the organization of the kingdom. The title of "archpriest," given to the Tes whose tomb in Amaseia is comparable in size to the royal tombs, reminds us of the establishment of such an office by the Seleucid king Antiochos III and its continuation by the Attalids. Seleucid traditions are also reflected in the titles of satraps: *hyparchoi*, *strategoi*, and *dioiketai*. As in the interior of the kingdom of Pergamon, in the broad basins of Paphlagonia and Pontos we find many names ending in "–ene" and "–itis," such as Pimolisene, Gazakene, Kulupene, Kamisene, Saramene, Domanitis, Karanitis, Dazimonitis, and Gadilonitis. Were these subdivisions of the Pontic kingdom? Strabo's use of the term *eparcheia* is ambivalent. Sometimes it designates the Roman province, sometimes an area or district of which Pompey allocated "a great number" to the territory of Zela (Strabo 12, 3, 37). Before Eupator's conquests expanded the kingdom, it consisted of the coast as far as Amastris (that is, as far as the Parthenios River) in the west and Kerasus-Pharnakeia in the east, and in the interior west of the Halys, only a strip of northern Paphlagonia. East of the river, the Pontic heartland was bounded by the Trokmoi tribal centers and the kingdoms of Cappadocia and Lesser Armenia. The term "satrapy" was first used for the lands conquered under Eupator beyond these bounds, such as Colchis in the east, and Phrygia and Bithynia in west.

The craft of war, siege techniques, and the buildup of naval fleets were developed in particular by Mithridates V's supreme commander, a Greek from Amisos named Dorylaos. Up to that point the army had consisted almost exclusively of mercenaries: Thracians, Galatians, and Greeks. Eupator added a standing royal army, whose infantry was organized on the Macedonian model, with a phalanx of hoplites bearing *sarissai* (pikes) and swords, as well as light infantry with leather helmets, daggers, and javelins. In the war against Lucullus, the king switched over to Roman-style maniple tactics, that is, operations with small combat units. The line was supplemented by archers and slingers, a small unit with scythed chariots, and the lightly armed cavalry. In the Pontic army there was no armored cavalry (*kataphraktoi*) as in the armies of the Armenians and Parthians.[143]

The monarchy's foreign relations[144] and self-representation made use of Hellenistic forms and media, but the series of coins issued by Mithridates VI Eupator did not forgo reference to his Persian descent. Mithridates II was already intent on not taking a back seat in the Greek public sphere when it was a matter of helping the city of Rhodes after it had been hard hit by the earthquake of 227/226 BCE (Polybius 5, 90, 1). In the spring of 195 BCE the Athenians honored Pharnakes I for his generous promises by erecting statues of him and his wife Nysa in Delos. Mithridates IV might have been the king with the bynames Philopator and Philadelphos who dedicated a statue to the *populus Romanus* on the Capitol in Rome (Moretti, IGUR 9). Greek beneficiaries erected statues to the "benefactor" Mithridates V in Delos. And an Athenian priest had the good relations between Mithridates VI Eupator and Athens in mind when he added a small temple to the front of the shrine of the Cabeiri that he had built and devoted this *naiskos* to the gods and the king of Pontos. The edifice was richly decorated with relief busts of this king and his neighbors Ariarathes VII and Antiochos VIII Grypos, as well as of notables at his court and at other courts.[145] He himself, whose statue also stood in Rhodes "in the most frequented part of their city" (*in celeberrimo urbis loco*; Cicero, *Verr.* II 2, 159), dedicated his arms in Nemea and Delphi (Appian, *Mith.* 112 [549]).

Eupator (see Figure 52) bore as a second byname: that of the god Dionysos. At the court in Sinope he appointed Greek savants, such as the Academician Diodoros of Adramyttion and Metrodoros the younger (the "Roman-hater"), to positions of trust. Science, art, and crafts of the highest level were found at his court. If we had archaeological evidence in Sinope or other cities on the south coast of the Black Sea

52. Portrait of Mithridates Eupator on a coin. Münzkabinett Winterthur.

comparable to that found in Pergamon, we would not be limited to admiring the images on coins and individual testimonies to masterpieces in Pontos Euxeinos, such as Pliny the Elder's comment (*nat.* 37, 11) on the best collection of gems and Strabo's reference (12, 3, 11) to Sthennis's statue of Autolykos and Billaros of Sinope's *sphaira*. We know nothing about Billaros, but his *sphaira* must have been a kind of globe like that of Archimedes, which Marcellus brought to Rome after the conquest of Syracuse. All the evidence suggests that part of this work from Sinope was found in the early twentieth century near Antikythera, in a shipwreck dating from between 80 and 70 BCE: a complicated device consisting of thirty-one interlocking cogwheels that served to calculate the movements of heavenly bodies.[146]

According to Strabo (12, 1–2), under the kings (see the Appendix), Cappadocia, the broad central Anatolian highland on Pontos's southern border, was subdivided into ten *strategiai* (prefectures), five in the north and five in the south.[147] Garsauritis, the westernmost *strategia* in the southern region, bordered on Lake Tuz, while Tyanitis (near Niğde), Cilicia, Kataonia, and Melitene extended to the east. Starting from the northeast shore of Lake Tuz lay, west to east, the *strategiai* of Morimene, Chamanene, Saravene, Sargarausene, and Laviasene (south of Sivas).

Here, as in Pontos, there were important temple-states: to them belonged the lands around the shrine of Zeus in Venasa in Morimene and those around the temple of Enyo in Komana in Kataonia, which in Strabo's time were still cultivated by 6,000 *hieroduloi*; in the remote mountain site near the modern-day village of Şarköy all that remains standing is the façade of a Roman tomb. The two centers of the kingdom were Tyana, which since Ariarathes V Eusebes Philopator had been called Eusebeia by the Taurus, and the royal residence of Mazaka, on the heavily wooded northern slope of the 4,000-meter-high, snow-capped Mt. Argaios (Erciyes Dağ); from that time on, Mazaka was also called Eusebeia.[148] This place in the *strategia* of Cilicia is only a few kilometers west of the old Assyrian commercial center of Kārum Kaneš. It has no archaeological remains from the time of the Ariarathids, but the previously mentioned bronze plaque with a decree of the community of Hanisa comes from Kaneš itself.[149] In this document, composed in perfect Greek chancellery style, Hanisa presents itself as a Hellenized citizenry with a council, popular assembly, and festivals for Greek gods (Zeus, Soter, and Herakles; the main shrine of the city, however, belongs to the old Oriental goddess of war and love, Astarte). It thus provides clear evidence of a *polis* constitution of a local community under the monarchy—moreover, a *polis* that apparently did not emerge from a former settlement of Macedonian or Greek (or both) military colonists. In that respect it distinguishes the Cappadocian kingdom from the neighboring one of the Mithridatids, where such a constitution is not attested, though in other regards of course—kingship, populations of indigenous and Iranian ethnic origin, and settlement structure in general—Cappadocia closely resembled the kingdom of Pontos. For its part, the Iranian ruling family adapted Hellenistic forms, and Greek was spoken at the court. In particular, it seems that Ariarathes V, the friend of Attalos II, encouraged Hellenization. An inscription from the time of Ariarathes VI indicates that Tyana had a gymnasium and an *agon* in honor of Hermes and Herakles ([162] *IK* Tyana 29). The kingdom was obviously also organized by this dynasty on the Seleucid model (compare the *archidioiketes* in Mazaka-Eusebeia). Its coins, which had a portrait of the king wearing a diadem on the obverse side and (for the most part) an image of the standing Athena "the victory-bearer" (*nikephoros*) on the reverse, bore legends in Greek from King Ariarathes III on. In addition to the usual bynames—Philopator, Philometor, Eusebes—with Orophernes we find "victory-bearer" (*nikephoros*), and with Ariobarzanes, put on the throne by Sulla (p. 271), "friend of the Romans" (*philorhomaios*). Greek crafts and Greek culture spread; ca. 100 BCE a Cappadocian sculptor signed a marble statue on the *agora* in Samos, and a rhetorician from Mazaka received citizenship in Athens and honors in Delphi for his contributions to education and the art of oratory. The advanced Hellenism in the Cappadocia of the kings contradicts the scorn of some intellectuals of the Second Sophistic (see Chapter 9) for the alleged provincialism of this country.[150]

The Rise of Mithridates Eupator and the Conquest of Asia Minor

Our conception of Mithridates Eupator's youth has been distorted by legends. He must have been born toward the end of the 130s BCE, and had just turned eleven when his father was murdered by courtiers in Sinope. His mother, who took the reins of government in hand, seems to have favored his younger brother. The boy rid himself of both by poisoning them (Sallust, *hist.* fr. 2, 75 f. Maurenbrecher). In a first bitter experience with Rome, the region of Phrygia that Manius Aquillius had promised his father after the War of Aristonikos was taken away from him again by the Senate in 119 or 116 BCE (p. 255).

In the following years he extended his rule toward the north and east, and for the first time in the history of the dynasty he set up a dominion that made the Pontos the most powerful kingdom of the Middle East this side of the Euphrates. First, Antipatros, the ruler of the highlands of Armenia Minor in the upper reaches of the river Lykos (between Mt. Paryadres and the Euphrates) submitted to him. Then he subjugated the smaller dynasties along the southeastern coast of the Black Sea and annexed the Trapezusia, the legendary Colchis on the lower Phasis, and the east coast as far north as beyond the Caucasus. Of eminent importance, however, was the additional conquest of territory on the northern coast by the deployment of the fleet. The opportunity was provided by the notorious pressure the Scythians of the hinterland were putting on the Greek cities in that region. With the support of the citizens of Chersonnesos, Diophantos of Sinope, Mithridates Eupator's military commander, conducted several campaigns that gave him control over the whole area in and around Crimea. The community honored Diophantos with a bronze statue on the acropolis ([109] Syll.³ 709). This newly acquired territory paid tribute in silver and grain to the crown. The tribes were obligated to recruit soldiers for service in the royal army. At the king's command, deserving mercenaries received citizenship in Greek cities, such as Phanagoreia.[151]

It may be doubted whether Mithridates Eupator's successes could already have prompted the idea of subjecting the whole of Asia Minor. He is supposed to have made an extended inspection tour of the country, incognito and in the company of a few trusted advisors. However, his first acts sought to gain the upper hand in the conflict, inherited from his father, with the neighboring dynasties, namely the Bithynian and Cappadocian royal houses. In the struggle between Orophernes and Ariarathes V to supersede each other, we have already seen the violent rancor in the family of the heirs to the Cappadocian throne. However, the widow of this Ariarathes (who fell in the War of Aristonikos), surpassed all previous crimes in magnitude: to ensure that Ariarathes VI Epiphanes Philopator would succeed to the throne, she had no fewer than five of his older brothers murdered. Mithridates V, who was still ruling in Pontos, gave him the hand of his daughter Laodike, Eupator's sister, in marriage, and she bore him three sons. Mithridates Eupator seems to have wanted to improve the prospects of a takeover by having Ariarathes VI assassinated by an agent named Gordios. But King Nikomedes III of Bithynia, the only other monarchy of about the same stature in the Asia Minor of that time, refused to accept this. After Gordios was banished, Nikomedes marched into Cappadocia and married Laodike. The reaction was not long in coming: the king of Pontos drove his opponent Nikomedes and his own sister out of the country. He put her oldest son on the throne as Ariarathes VII—the king whose bust adorns the Mithridates monument on Delos. However, the young Ariarathes defied paternalism and above all, he opposed his uncle's intention to bring Gordios, his father's murderer, back from exile. Mithridates summarily overthrew him (ca. 100 BCE) and replaced him with his own eight-year-old son, as Ariarathes IX, with Gordios as his guardian.

In the meantime, Nikomedes was establishing his power on a second front, in Paphlagonia. However, the simultaneous usurpation of the two rivals in 108/107 BCE was condemned by the Senate. But while Mithridates tried to assert a hereditary claim before the Roman emissaries, Nikomedes renounced his claim as part of a clever deception: he put forward as the legitimate king a young man with the familiar dynastic name of Pylaimenes—who turned out to be his own son. However, faced with this *fait accompli*, the Senate declined to intervene. People were mesmerized by the wars against Jugurtha in North Africa and against the Cimbrians and Teutons in northern Italy, and by the conflicts in their own ranks over the laws proposed by the partisans of Gaius Marius. Consequently Rome once again limited itself to supporting the apparently weaker of the two opponents at the expense of the stronger. And this must have been perceived by the Pontic Mithridates as another humiliation—following that of the seizure of Phrygia.

A short time after Gaius Marius (the victor over the Cimbrians and Teutons) had visited the shrine of Meter in Pessinus and then Cappadocia, and also had met with Mithridates (ca. 99/98 BCE), resistance to the foreign rule of the son of Mithridates broke out in the Cappadocian kingdom (Justin, 38, 2, 1–3, 4). The goal was to bring back from exile a brother of Ariarathes VII, a son of Laodike, and to restore the rule of the Ariarathids. But Mithridates of Pontos and Gordios were victorious in a battle. Meanwhile, Nikomedes located the third son of Ariarathes VI and Laodike. He sent Laodike to Rome to claim the legitimate succession to the throne for her child. There she went around groveling, as did Gordios and a third party of Cappadocian aristocrats. The Senate rejected both the Bithynians' claim and that of the king of Pontos, and declared Cappadocia free. It then granted the aristocrats' wish to be allowed to choose a king for themselves. A man named Ariobarzanes was selected.

There are differing views regarding the chronology of subsequent events.[152] This is probably what happened: under the protection of the propraetor of Cilicia, Lucius Cornelius Sulla, Rome put this Ariobarzanes on the throne of Cappadocia in 96/95 BCE. Mithridates yielded and took his son back to Pontos with him. At that time, a memorable scene took place in eastern Anatolia: the first meeting between the antipodes of the future, the Mediterranean world power and the Parthian Empire. On the west bank of the Euphrates near Melitene, the Roman Sulla met with Orobazes, the emissary of the Arsakid king Mithridates II. Ariobarzanes was also present. Sulla arranged the seating so that he was placed between the two oriental representatives as the giver of the audience, dominating the scene.[153]

Mithridates Eupator was on the lookout for a chance to strike back. He sought an ally in the Artaxiad King Tigranes II, who had just mounted the throne in the kingdom of Armenia, and gave Tigranes his young daughter Kleopatra's hand in marriage. When Nikomedes III died in Bithynia in 94 BCE, the opportunity to meddle arose again: to oust the king's son, Nikomedes IV, Mithridates used the latter's half-brother, Sokrates Chrestos. Almost simultaneously, Tigranes's agents, with Gordios's help, drove Ariobarzanes out of Mazaka (Justin, 38, 3, 2) and reinstalled Eupator's son, Ariarathes IX.

The Senate's reaction—Rome was then engaged in the Italian War—was in accord with its usual behavior. In 91 or 90 BCE a commission under the leadership of Manius Aquillius the Younger arrived in Asia Minor charged with the task of reestablishing the two legitimate kings, Nikomedes and Ariobarzanes, on their thrones. Once again, Mithridates backed off. His son was withdrawn from Mazaka,

Ariobarzanes returned, and Sokrates Chrestos was killed. But the Roman emissaries exceeded their mandate by urging Nikomedes, who was in debt to Italian creditors, to plunder the Pontic cities on the Black Sea coast of Paphlagonia. When Mithridates complained and insisted that he had a right to defend himself, the commissioners replied to the effect that they did not wish Mithridates to suffer any injustice at the hands of Nikomedes, but neither did they wish a war against Nikomedes to be started, since it was not in Rome's interest for him to be damaged. The conflict grew more intense when Mithridates drove the Cappadocian Ariobarzanes out of the country anew and made his own son king again as Ariarathes IX.

The Roman emissaries reacted with an ultimatum, refusing any contact before their conditions were met. At the same time they made preparations for war, which later caused Manius Aquillius to be accused of having triggered a war without the authorization of the Senate and the people of Rome. The proconsul of Asia, Gaius Cassius, did not have enough troops to attack the kingdom of Pontos. But Nikomedes IV marched through the Amnias valley with a large army of mercenaries headed for Pontos. The Roman contingents were posted behind the Bithynian troops, with one division under Cassius (on the border between Bithynia and Galatia) and another under Manius Aquillius still farther forward (probably in the Karabük basin). Near Byzantion a Roman fleet guarded the Bosporus. The governor of Cilicia, Quintus Oppius, was assigned the task reinstating Ariobarzanes on the throne in Mazaka. What the Bithynian king's army was supposed to do—whether an invasion of Pontos was envisaged or only an attempt to draw Mithridates away from Cappadocia—is not clear. Mithridates's fleet—Sinope was its most important harbor—consisted of about 300 ships. Three divisions of the main army were commanded by the king himself along with the two Greek generals, Neoptolemos and Archelaos. The Greek Dorylaos commanded the phalanx of heavy infantry, while a certain Krateros (a Macedonian?) led 130 war chariots into the field. The cavalry was provided by the allied clan princes from Armenia Minor.

In early 89 BCE the opening battle of the Mithridatic Wars was fought on the banks of the Amnias (in modern-day Vilayet Kastamonu). According to Appian (*Mith.* 18 [66 f.]) the terrifying effects of the Pontic scythed chariots achieved the decisive breakthrough. These chariots were driven into the Bithynian troops at high speed, cutting some men in half and others in small pieces when they got stuck on the sickles. Behind the fully exhausted army, the Roman divisions quickly abandoned their position. Mithridates advanced into the river plain near Karabük, climbed Skorobas (presumably Mt. Keltepe), and pursued his opponents toward the south. Cassius and Nikomedes withdrew to the Phrygian fortress on top of a rock known as "Lion's Head"—no doubt the 226-meter-high rock in the modern city of Afyon, near which the Royal Road from the Hermos valley intersected the road to Apameia. Farther south the main route branched off from the latter, leading through the valleys of the Lykos and Maeander toward Ephesos on the coast. Cassius continued his retreat as far as Apameia. Here a wealthy citizen of the city of Nysa, Chairemon, son of Pythodoros, offered to supply grain and help. Chairemon and his son were so successful as collaborators with the Romans that Mithridates himself issued instructions for their arrest. We later find Chairemon agitating against the Pontic king from his asylum in the Artemision in Ephesos before the former disappears from the records.

Mithridates arrived for the siege of Laodikeia. The city was held by Quintus Oppius, who had hurried there from the east with his remaining troops, for a short time, while Cassius was retreating toward Rhodes, and Manius Aquillius and the Bithynian king Nikomedes toward Pergamon. From the pursuit of the defeated enemy, which was reforming, the Pontic forces moved on to attack the heart of the Roman province of Asia, which Mithridates now clearly intended to conquer. Could he count on being received with open arms when he advanced as a conquering monarch on a country rich in cities, including many citizens of Greek *poleis*? In retrospect, it seemed to the Romans that the Greeks of Asia had been perfidious almost without exception. Almost: the famous exception was—in addition to Rhodes, where the Romans and their loyalists took refuge—the city of Magnesia on the Sipylos, about whose precise role we know nothing further. However, the general reproach of faithlessness can be made only against the *provincia* of Asia, not against the cities of western and southern Asia Minor as a whole. Inscriptions have been discovered that indicate a series of cases of pro-Roman resistance to Mithridates. The center of this resistance was the interior of Caria—which was at that time not yet part of the Roman province. One of the first communities to send Quintus Oppius an offer of military aid was Plarasa/Aphrodisias.[154] Later on, Sulla acknowledged that the communities of Tabai and Stratonikeia had also provided military aid in a similar way. Against the latter city, which had signed a treaty of alliance with Rome, the king himself undertook a punitive expedition from Ionia and put down its resistance. In addition, a decree from Alabanda allows us to divine that this *polis* also provided services for the Roman army and that a few of its citizens had been made prisoners of war.[155] When later in the war the Pontic fleet attacked Rhodes, the Lycian League mobilized its forces under a *strategos* with plenipotentiary authority and came to the aid of the island republic, while in eastern Lycia the Pontic forces, apparently collaborating with pirates, had to be battled on water and on land at the same time ([106] OGIS 552–554).[156] There is nothing mysterious about the motivation for the resistance in this area: Caria and Lycia, which had been free from Rhodes since 167 and did not have to pay Roman taxes, had no reason to embrace a new Hellenistic ruler.

Things were otherwise in the Roman province: the king was already enthusiastically welcomed when he marched into the Maeander valley, that is, in Tralleis and Magnesia on the Maeander. In a burst of anticipatory obedience, the Ephesians hastened to pull down the statues of the Roman proconsuls. By sea, the king visited the cities on the coasts and islands; Mytilene on Lesbos handed over to him Manius Aquillius, who had fled there from Pergamon. The Pontic king put this senator to a gruesome death, apparently considering him not an opponent but rather a corrupt traitor. It may be that the way Manius Aquillius was killed, according to Appian (*Mith*. 21 [80])—molten gold is supposed to have been poured down his throat— corresponded to a Persian ritual of execution that was used particularly in cases of bribery and avarice. Among the atrocious modes of execution that Plutarch's life of Artaxerxes communicates to us from Ktesias, we may recall this one: the mother of the great king had the Carian punished who claimed to have killed the rebellious usurper Cyrus the Younger, because the man declined to be fobbed off with what he was offered as a reward. She ordered that molten iron be poured in his ears (Plutarch, *Art.* 14, 5).

Soon thereafter, in 88 BCE, the event that has gone down in history as the "Ephesian Vespers" took place in the Province and also in isolated cases outside it.[157] Mithridates sent by secret emissaries to the satraps and commissioners in the cities written orders to have all Romans and Italians, along with their wives, children, and freedmen, killed on a certain day (Appian, *Mith.* 22 f. [85–91]). Anyone providing aid to the enemies was to be punished, while denunciations or murders committed by their slaves were to be rewarded with emancipation, and if their debtors committed the same, they were to receive cancellation of half of the debt. In Ephesos, Tralleis, Pergamon, Adramyttion, and especially the port city of Kaunos, scenes of indescribable cruelty occurred. A philosopher named Demetrios—otherwise of negligible importance—had the whole municipal council of his home town of Adramyttion executed. The estimates of the number killed vary between 80,000 and 150,000. At an international colloquium held in 2007, the question as to whether this should be considered genocide was discussed. In fact, Appian states that the people to be persecuted came from the *genos Italikon*, and were thus not merely holders of Roman civil rights. These men, who were for the most part active as tax collectors, agents, traders, merchants, or creditors, lived with their families in the Asian cities in communities that separated themselves from those of the citizens of the *polis*.[158] They were therefore more easily localizable, and were also identifiable by their clothing (they were called *tebennophoruntes*: "toga-wearers") and their appearance—not necessarily immediately by their language. The incitement to murder fell on the fertile soil of latent hatred that had accumulated over the three decades since the establishment of the province of Asia and now broke out everywhere. At least the inhabitants of Kos later emphasized that they had sheltered Roman citizens in the Asklepieion outside the city (Tacitus, *ann.* 4, 14, 2). Exactly what the king's goal was in ordering this massacre, if indeed he had any rational goal, is not uncontroversial. His modern biographer Théodore Reinach implies that Mithridates must have seen in these inhabitants of Asia dangerous groups of spies, traitors, and conspirators in the service of the enemy, and that he knew how to channel the irresistible flow of popular hatred to fill his coffers. However, according to Reinach the true driving force was avarice and the little people's hatred of the rich:

> Asian democracy would only too willingly have included in the death of the Italians all the rich people whose wealth it coveted; and only Mithridates's intervention kept the killing limited to Roman citizens. Who can deny that in comparison to a social bloodbath whose only goal is robbery and plundering, the crimes of racial fanaticism are not devoid of a certain greatness?[159]

This judgment, which was written in 1895 and is disturbing against the background of the experiences of the twentieth century, clearly distinguishes itself from that of the historian Theodor Mommsen insofar as it negates his stereotype of oriental barbarism. For Mommsen, this Iranian king embodied the "sultanism" expressed in the massacre insofar as it inflates to colossal proportions a pointless act of blind, brutal revenge.[160]

The operations against Rhodes conducted by Mithridates's fleet began with the voyage to Kos. Its inhabitants opened their gates to him and handed over the son of Ptolemaios IX, who was staying there, along with a rich treasure that had been deposited on the island by his mother, Kleopatra III. The enemy had long been expected in Rhodes: though inferior in numbers, the Rhodians were experienced in naval warfare. After the debacle with the *sambyke*, a giant ladder brought up to the city wall by ship, Mithridates gave up the attempt and withdrew his forces from the siege. An attack on the Lycian port city of Patara also failed. Despite these setbacks, the king expanded his offensive. He did not intervene actively to support Rome's opponents in the Italian War. Instead, following in Antiochos III's footsteps, he saw his mission outside Asia as the re-establishment of a Hellenistic monarchy in Greece. There the general mood, and especially the internal condition of the first and richest city in Hellas, Athens, was grist for his mill.[161] In Athens, incredible illusions regarding the true power relationships and the irretrievability of the Athenians' past greatness abruptly broke the dam that had held for more than a hundred years, since the invasion of the Seleucid Antiochos III. Though Athenian documents from the 90s had still described the Romans as benefactors of the people, the "people" now fell prey to the agitation of a philosopher of the Aristotelian school, Athenion, who, returning from an embassy to the king, triumphed with window-dressing and promises (Poseidonios, FGrHist 87 F 36). The friends of the Romans left the city, and the philosopher was elected as the *strategos* of the hoplites. In 88/87 BCE Mithridates himself figured as the eponymous *archon* of the proud city—later corrected in the stone chronicle by the addition: "anarchy."[162]

Delos, the little island community in the center of the Cyclades that had been in Athenian possession since 166 BCE, decided the time had come to declare itself against Athens and for Rome. In the hope of winning its freedom? Or did the numerous Italics, who may in addition have already heard about the Ephesian Vespers, tip the balance? After the expedition sent by Athenion against Delos had dismally failed, Archelaos conquered the island of Apollo with the Pontic fleet, had all the Italics killed, and sent the temple's treasure to Athens by ship. When he arrived there, he overthrew Athenion and installed a philosopher of the Epicurean school, Aristion, as tyrant. Thereupon Archelaos and his general Metrophanes set out from their headquarters in Piraeus and undertook to win large parts of Greece for the king. The Peloponnese, Euboia, and Boeotia, where only Thespiai resisted, went over to his side. The Roman presence was not able to mobilize any military resistance. The governor of Macedonia, Sentius Saturninus, was kept in the north by Thracian advances.

Mithridates was at the height of his power. He had his son of the same name rule over the Pontic kingdom's homeland, Colchis, and Crimea; his son named Ariarathes ruled over neighboring Cappadocia and Lesser Armenia. The rest of Anatolia was ruled by his satraps and officers, while he himself resided—significantly—in Pergamon. There he married a Greek woman, Monime, from Stratonikeia, who was to achieve a prominent position among the numerous wives in his harem. Mithridates assigned to her father, Philopoimen, the supervision of Ephesos.

As a contemporary, one had to have an incorruptible eye to resist the blinding power of the almost complete Roman loss of what had been gained since the beginning of the second century BCE by the campaigns of the likes of Titus Quinctius Flamininus, Aemilius Paullus, Cornelius Scipio, and Manius Aquillius. At the time it would have taken remarkable insight to recognize that the Romans would no longer be kept out of the Hellenistic world and that their ability to reply militarily to the Pontic conquests was present even if inhibited, not least by internal discord regarding the question as to who was to implement it.

In 87 BCE Cornelius Sulla arrived in Greece at the head of five legions. Athens became the focal point of the operation. With the fall of the city, the evacuation of Piraeus, and the defeat of the Pontic forces at Chaironeia and Orchomenos, the tables were turned, even if Sulla still lacked the ships urgently needed to push the opponent back onto Asian soil.

In Asia the fascination with Mithridates had long since faded, and opposition and conspiracy were countered with terrorism and gifts. The first thing the king did was to violently do away with all the Galatian "tetrarchs," except for three who escaped him, and replace them with a satrap; a punitive expedition against Chios escalated into the deportation of the whole citizenry. After revolts were put down in Ephesos, Tralleis, Hypaipa, and Metropolis (Appian, *Mith.* 48 [189 f.]), tensions in the cities were supposed to be allayed by means of a general declaration of freedom, debt relief, the naturalization of metics, and the emancipation of slaves.

Sulla, who before departing Italy had been forced to seize the disputed supreme command by marching on Rome, was outlawed under the rule of the consul Cinna (a companion of Marius), his command was taken away from him, and his house burned down. While Sulla was negotiating with Archelaos near Delion, the consul Lucius Valerius Flaccus, who had been assigned to conduct the war against Mithridates in his place, arrived at the Bosporus to have his army ferried over the strait to Asian soil by the Byzantians and take the field against the king. But a mutiny under the leadership of his legate Gaius Flavius Fimbria cost him his life. Fimbria took assumed command of both legions and took Roman arms back to Asia, from which they had been expelled almost five years earlier. His actions became a serious danger to Sulla, not only because he threatened to defeat the king before he (Sulla) did, but also because Mithridates intended to use him as a trump card in the negotiation of a peace treaty. After Fimbria had subjected Bithynia to murder and plundering, he drove the king himself out of Pergamon to Pitane and defeated the king's son in

Mysia. Lucullus, whose fleet was operating off the west coast and who might have been able, in concert with Fimbria's land army, to overthrow the king in Pitane, gave the mutineers the cold shoulder. Thus Mithridates was able to escape to Mytilene on Lesbos.

While Fimbria was rampaging through the Troad and burning down Ilion, Sulla's army reached the Hellespont and met Lucullus's ships there. The scales tipped in Sulla's favor at just the right moment: now he was the strongest Roman military power on Asian soil. However, the situation in Rome demanded that he bring the war to an end as soon as possible and return to Italy. In the summer of 85 BCE Sulla and Mithridates met in Dardanos in the Troad. The Roman stood by the demands he had already made in the negotiations with Archelaos, and when the king said nothing he retorted: "But surely it is the part of suppliants to speak first, while victors need only to be silent" (Plutarch, *Sull.* 24, 1; trans. Perrin). Mithridates agreed to give up all the conquests he had made in Europe and Asia since the beginning of 89 BCE, to pay war damages in the amount of 2,000 talents, to hand over seventy armored warships with their crews and 500 archers, and to release prisoners of war. In exchange he was to retain possession of his ancestral kingdom, including the areas north and southeast of the Black Sea he had conquered before 89, and he was once again counted among the Romans' friends and allies. Fimbria committed suicide when Sulla advanced on his camp near Thyateira in Lydia, and many of Fimbria's soldiers went over to Sulla.

Asia lay at the victor's feet. Amnesty and declarations of freedom could not conceal the fact that most of the cities whose numerous emissaries were hastening to him in Ephesos were severely punished. Sulla forced them to pay tribute for five years and an additional payment of 20,000 talents. The Roman soldiers billeted there received, at the expense of the citizens, a daily wage of 16 drachmas (forty times their usual pay), the centurions received fifty drachmas, and food and clothing had also to be provided. Asia was divided into forty-four tax districts (Cassiodorus, *chron.* II, p. 132, 484 Mommsen), each of the existing eleven *dioikeseis* into four. Sulla or Licinius Murena, who soon thereafter also annexed part of Kibyratis and attached the cities of Oinoanda, Balbura, and Bubon to the Lycian league of cities, may have included Caria in the Roman province.[163] On-site negotiations with Sulla followed numerous missions to Rome made by city envoys. As he promised Ilion, Chios, Magnesia, and Rhodes freedom and Rome's friendship for their loyalty (Appian, *Mith.* 61 [250]), so he rewarded Tabai, Stratonikeia, and the Lycians.[164] The fragments of a *senatus consultum* found in a small community in eastern Lycia (Sherk, RDGE 19) and the previously mentioned treaty between Rome and the Lycian League from Tyberissos (p. 229) may also be part of this historical context. Once again it is prominent citizens who boldly acted on behalf of their community, some to moderate harsh provisions, others to file complaints about violations of the conditions they had been promised. Diodoros Pasparos of Pergamon is to be counted among these; he traveled to Rome, probably between 85 and 73 BCE, to appear before the Senate. A series of honors for him has been preserved—unfortunately, in very fragmentary form—on stone; they show a man who was outstanding among the benefactors of Asia Minor and who was awarded religious honors during his own lifetime. Archaeologists have discovered a heroon that was built in the city of Pergamon after his death.[165]

Insofar as he could lay hands on them, Sulla had those responsible for the "Ephesian Vespers" executed. Mytilene, which had handed over Manius Aquillius, continued to resist until 79 BCE, when the Roman fleet made a successful attack and completely destroyed the city. Sulla gave Kaunos, where many Italics had been killed, back to Rhodes. But the inhabitants of Kaunos were apparently able to persuade the propraetor Lucius Licinius Murena, who succeeded Sulla in command over Asia, to let them pay taxes to the Romans rather than to the Rhodians. On the edge of their *agora* they erected an equestrian statue of him as their "savior and benefactor."[166] When the Rhodians protested in Rome, Sulla probably reversed this decision, but by the early 60s at the latest Kaunos belonged to the province of Asia, not to Rhodes.

The peace concluded at Dardanos, the end of Mithridates's rule, and Sulla's reorganization of the province was felt by many cities to be a profound break. Until late in the Imperial period, inscriptions and coins issued by Asian communities date in accord with an era—the so-called Sullan era—whose starting point can be determined as 85/84 BCE.[167]

From the Second Mithridatic War to the Death of Mithridates

The so-called Second Mithridatic War was an extended campaign conducted by Licinius Murena that in many respects resembled that of Gnaeus Manlius Vulso following the Roman victory over Antiochos III. After the Pontic general Archelaos had fallen out with his king and had fled from Sinope to Murena, the latter took warnings provided by the defector as an occasion to advance with his legions on Cappadocia and Pontos and to plunder the sanctuary of Komana (83 BCE). Against the Senate's instructions, the following year he began an attack on Sinope but was driven back by the king's troops and thrown out of Cappadocia. On Sulla's orders, he ceased to engage in further military actions.

Mithridates was not inclined to go to war. On returning from western Asia Minor to his ancestral kingdom, he had found conditions there and in Crimea unstable. The governor of his dominion at the Cimmerian Bosporus was threatening to make himself independent and had to be subjugated by a military campaign, whereupon Mithridates installed his son Machares as king in that place; his other son, Mithridates, who was supposed to reign in Colchis, became suspect to him, was arrested, and died shortly thereafter. In Colchis, satraps moved in again. The king still owed the clearing of certain areas to Ariobarzanes in Mazaka, to whose son he married an under-age daughter. When Ariobarzanes complained in Rome, Sulla refused to execute the written peace treaty until Mithridates had completely withdrawn from Cappadocia. Although the king finally complied with this demand, his wish to receive the written treaty remained unfulfilled. Sulla died in 78 BCE, and the Senate did not take up the matter.

Whereas in post-Sulla Rome the kingdom of Pontos was increasingly seen as a threat to the province of Asia, in the far east of Anatolia another power of disturbing magnitude arose and moved into the vacuum that the shrunken and desolate remains of the Seleucid Empire had left behind it. Within a decade Tigranes II reconquered not only the parts of Armenia the Parthians had annexed, but also established his authority over neighboring small kingdoms in the area between Georgia, Azerbaijan, and northern Mesopotamia. Thereupon he invaded northern Syria and seized control of the capital, Antiocheia, where he had his coins minted. The Seleucid Philippos II fled to Cilicia, but there too he was not beyond Tigranes's reach. Finally Tigranes attacked Cappadocia again and occupied Mazaka. Like the Assyrians, from his campaigns in the Cilician lowlands and Cappadocia the Armenian king took thousands of local inhabitants with him to settle them in his kingdom. His chief goal was to populate a newly founded capital, Tigranokerta. Of this city, which continued to exist far down into late antiquity, nothing remains that could provide information about its exact location, and the written testimonies contradict one another. The most likely site is near modern-day Silvan (northeast of Diyarbakır).[168] In the early 70s BCE an alliance between the king of Pontos and Armenia led to the emergence of a power bloc in the east that overshadowed the Hellenistic monarchies in Egypt and Syria established by Alexander's successors. However, Tigranes pursued his own ambitions, and from the outset the alliance lacked cohesiveness.

Under Murena and his successors the economic problems of the Asian cities did not decrease. The return of the tax collectors drove the communities to the brink of ruin. The Roman magistrates' interest in regulatory measures was extremely slim; they still considered Asia mainly as an opportunity for self-enrichment. The praetor Aulus Terentius Varro went so far in that line that the inhabitants of the province sued him for their claims to restitution of unjustifiably imposed levies (*de repetundis*) (Broughton, MRR II 97). Arrogance and contempt for the provincials are mentioned in connection with an event that occurred in Lampsakos in 80/79 BCE. This city in Thracian Chersonnesos was then administered by the governor of Macedonia, Gnaeus Dolabella, whose legate Verres had taken up residence there with his entourage. Verres and his men had designs on the beautiful young daughter of a respected Greek, Philodamos, and to the latter's, their host's, dismay they baldly presented their demands. When they resorted to violence, furious residents of Lampsakos hastened to the house and killed a lictor. The situation did not calm down after Verres and his men went away. The next morning, people would have invaded the legate's quarters with stones, iron bars, and firebrands, had Roman merchants not pacified the crowd and thus spared the city a great danger: "[they] collected hastily on the spot, and began to urge the people of the town to let their respect for Verres' official position outweigh their resentment of his outrageous conduct, admitting that the man was a dirty villain" (Cicero, *Verr*. II 1, 64–69; trans. Greenwood).

Piracy

Given the Romans' prevailing style of rule, it is no wonder that a problem well known from earlier times, piracy, spread freely and established bases in the mountainous areas of eastern Lycia and in Rough Cilicia. The fact that this meant heavy losses for many coastal cities was nothing new and can be seen in detail in inscriptions from earlier periods, such as the third and second centuries BCE.[169] After the province of Asia was established more than a few Italics settled in the cities. Rome was responsible for their protection,[170] and a threat to sea communications was necessarily extremely disturbing for their trade. At the end of the second century piracy had grown so prevalent on the south coast of Asia Minor that a special province of Cilicia had been set up to combat it (p. 259). But in the time of the Mithridatic Wars the corsairs' haunts had acquired a menacing new power through the influx of uprooted groups. After Murena had neutralized a certain Moaphernes in Kibyratis, the pirate prince Zeniketes, who used the nearby Olympos as his base for attack and retreat, controlled the east Lycian cities of Korykos and Phaselis (Strabo 14, 5, 7) as well as various places in the plains of Pamphylia, the center of the new Roman province. Here Roman officeholders like the legate Verres ruthlessly plundered Perge and Aspendos alike. In desperation, the small city of Syedra on the border of eastern Pamphylia sent emissaries to the oracle of Apollo in Klaros, and the reply in thirteen verses they received advised them not only to carry out an apotropaic ritual but also: "you yourselves together put your hand to the hard toil, and either chase these men away or bind them in unloosable bonds; do not delay the terrible vengeance on the plunderers, for thus you will escape from impairment."[171] In a campaign conducted between 78 and 75 BCE the praetor Publius Servilius Vatia Isauricus was able to conquer numerous strongholds and also Zeniketes's main fortress on Olympos.[172] Shortly thereafter, probably in 75/74 BCE, a young Roman fell into the hands of pirates on the island of Pharmakusa off the west coast of Asia Minor, south of Didyma, and was able to regain his freedom only by paying ransom. His name was Gaius Julius Caesar. Although a private individual, he had no rest until he had captured most of these pirates by force of arms and had them crucified (Velleius 2, 41, 3–42, 3).

The Third Mithridatic War had long been under way when in 67 BCE the *lex Gabinia* established a special command to fight piracy in the whole Mediterranean world and assigned it to Gnaeus Pompeius. It included a three-year proconsular *imperium aequum in omnibus provinciis usque ad quinquagesimum miliarium* (Velleius 2, 31, 2), that is, supreme command on all coasts and as far as fifty miles inland. Pompeius was equipped with twenty-four legates, 120,000 infantrymen, 5,000 cavalrymen, 500 ships, and 36 million denarii, the greatest power that Rome until then had ever put in the hands of a single individual. In only forty days the general carried out his task in the west, and then turned to the Cilician coast, where his crackdown was no less successful. Fortresses were taken, ships confiscated, building materials burned. Many of those whom war and poverty had driven into piracy were resettled in some of the places that Tigranes had depopulated. Piracy in the eastern Mediterranean realm never recovered from this blow. For the coastal cities, a period of flourishing trade could now—once the war was over—begin in Asia Minor, a period that lasted until the end of the Roman Empire.

The Third Mithridatic War

The outbreak of the Third Mithridatic War in 73 BCE resembled, in the constellation of political interests in Asia, the outbreak of Aristonikos's rebellion sixty years earlier. The Senate claimed the kingdom of Bithynia as the legacy of Nikomedes IV, who had died in late 75 or 74 BCE.[173] Mithridates VI of Pontos made his own the cause of a king's son who had been passed over. He knew that a Roman Bithynia would deprive his kingdom on the Black Sea of any future, and he immediately reacted by going to war. The two consuls for the year 74—Sulla's legate, the abovementioned Lucius Licinius Lucullus, and Marcus Aurelius Cotta—were given command in the theater of operations: Lucullus as proconsul of Asia and Cilicia, Cotta as proconsul over Bithynia, which was to be occupied.

The king of Pontos was heavily armed, having at his disposition infantry, cavalry, scythed chariots, and a fleet with several hundred ships. He maintained relations with the pirates and with the Roman dissident Quintus Sertorius in Spain. Sertorius—an exceptional man to whom Plutarch devoted a parallel biography with Eumenes of Kardia—refused to promise Mithridates control over all of Asia Minor in the event that they defeated their common opponent. For the Roman, giving up the Asiatic provinces of Asia and Cilicia was out of the question, no matter who was to rule them. So Mithridates accepted a treaty that guaranteed him Bithynia, Paphlagonia, and Cappadocia, and obligated him to provide money and ships for the battle in Spain.[174] But the Spanish insurrection quickly collapsed when Sertorius was killed in 72 BCE, one year after the war began in Asia Minor.

Mithridates went on the offensive. A Pontic army group attacked Cappadocia and once again drove out the luckless Ariobarzanes, while the king himself led the army and the fleet against Bithynia. The Roman high command there was led by Cotta, who was, however, sick during most of the fighting. A battle flared up over Chalkedon, which the fleet prefect Publius Rutilius Nudus was not able to hold. Thereupon the Pontic forces moved against Kyzikos, while Lucullus advanced into Bithynia from the south, where he had been in the middle Sangarios valley. Lucullus's skill and energy quickly transformed Mithridates from the besieger into the besieged. During the winter, the legionaires completely wore down the Pontic army. The king escaped to Lampsakos on the Hellespont. Only part of his fleet in the Propontis remained to him. His confidant, the philosopher Metrodoros of Skepsis, went to Artaxata to get help from Tigranes. He is supposed to have told the Armenian that as an emissary he had to ask for his aid, but as a friend he advised him to refuse it (Plutarch, *Luc.* 29; Strabo 13, 1, 55).

Lucullus now faced the task of subduing the Black Sea coast to the east, city by city. Herakleia Pontike, which Cotta put under siege, was not really on Mithridates's side, but the *strategos* Lamachos had opened the gates to the Pontic forces and allowed a garrison of 4,000 mercenaries under the Celt Konnakorex to enter the city. Lucullus himself sailed with the fleet against Amisos, and then, in the spring of 71 BCE, dared to advance into the interior of Pontos. He was completely successful: the defense of the religious center Kabeira and the "new castle" with the royal treasury, the archive, and the harem, collapsed. Mithridates had many women killed, and he himself escaped by the skin of his teeth only because the legionnaires, instead of concerning themselves with him, devoted their attention to pack animals loaded with gold. In Armenia, his son-in-law Tigranes had the refugee interned. He remained out of action for a year and a half (autumn of 71 to spring of 69). Tigranes had no intention of doing the Romans any favors, and he refused a request to hand Mithridates over to them. He wanted to retain the option of ruling Pontos himself.

In 70 BCE the cities on the coast of the Black Sea fell: Cotta had Herakleia plundered and burned to the ground. Amastris was taken by the legate C. Valerius Triarius; Sinope finally surrendered to Lucullus himself. In the spring of 69 the latter invaded the interior again with 20,000 men, marching through the valley of the Lykos and Lesser Armenia to the headwaters of the Euphrates near Erzincan. This extremely daring expedition against Armenia, comparable to Xenophon's March of the Ten Thousand, passed through the eastern Anatolian highland on the upper Tigris to Tigranokerta, where the king was waiting for him with a large army. In October 79 the Roman legions won a complete victory, and Lucullus took as booty a large sum of money and the whole inventory of the royal residence. Many of the Greeks Tigranes deported were sent back to their homeland (Plutarch, *Luc.* 29). The Armenian was now deserted by lesser vassals, including Antiochos of Commagene. Mithridates was released and reconciled with his son-in-law.

While the two kings hastened to raise armies, which Mithridates equipped and trained in the Roman fashion, in 68 Lucullus led the legions east through the valley of the Arsanias toward the old royal residence of Artaxata in the valley of the Araxes, at the foot of Mt. Ararat (see Figure 3). The enormous distances and the autumnal weather conditions exhausted the soldiers' energies, and they finally refused to continue the march. A retreat to the Black Sea during the winter was out of the question. Lucullus headed south, toward warmer regions, descended from the highland into the valley of the Tigris (see Figure 33) and reached Nisibis in northern Mesopotamia—now Nusaybin on the Turkish-Syrian border—which he seized after a brief siege. In the meantime, his command had been taken away from him at the instigation of his enemies in Rome. In the capital, what counted against him was not so much the reports on the military situation as the steps that Lucullus had already taken earlier in the province of Asia contrary to the interests of the tax collectors and for the benefit of the inhabitants.

The Senate appointed the praetor Publius Cornelius Dolabella as the new governor of Asia, immediately after his year in office in Rome, and thus demoted Asia to the status of a praetorian province (68 BCE). In 67 he was succeeded by the nephew of the dictator Sulla, Publius Cornelius Sulla.[175] Quintus Marcius Rex took over the governorship of Cilicia and Manius Acilius Glabrio became proconsul of Bithynia with a claim to supreme command in the war against Mithridates. Glabrio meanwhile remained inactive in Bithynia. The troops stationed in Pontos under Lucullus's legate Triarius proved too weak to resist the royal army; they were annihilated near Zela in the spring of 67. Lucullus himself was too far away to be able to intervene, and he was denied the two legions he had requested from Marcius Rex as reinforcements. When a ten-man senatorial commission arrived to set up a province of Pontus, it was forced to recognize that the country was to a large extent in enemy hands. However, at the same time—while Lucullus was in the middle Halys valley—Pompey replaced *de facto* Marcius Rex in Cilicia and consolidated his forces there.

Despite the painful setbacks, conspiracies, and mutinies among the troops and among the officers, Lucullus left behind him a military situation that a successor with far greater resources could build on. Lucullus's operations, being different in kind from the haphazard campaigns of such leaders as Manlius Vulso and Licinius Murena, laid the foundation for the complete Roman domination of Asia Minor. Bithynia was conquered, both straits came under Roman control, and the Pontic port cities were in the Romans' grip. By his skilful march on Tigranokerta and Nisibis he had forced the Armenian king, who at that time was at the height of his power, to withdraw from northern Mesopotamia, northern Syria, and the Cilician plains. In Antiocheia, Antiochos XIII Asiatikos, who was in Lucullus's entourage, mounted the throne as the last Seleucid king. The whole of central Anatolia was thus easily accessible from two sections of the coast, and the rear of future Roman advances into the interior was thus much better protected.

In 66 BCE, on the basis of the *lex Manilia*, Gnaeus Pompeius became governor of Cilicia, Bithynia, and Pontus and supreme commander against Mithridates. He met with Lucullus in Danala, a fortress in the area of the Galatian Trokmoi. They quarreled. The new governor declared all his predecessor's regulations invalid and put his troops under his own command. Lucullus set out for home with only about 1,000 men. Pompey immediately undertook the reconquest of Pontos.

Mithridates escaped to the east, into the high basin of Lesser Armenia. After Pompey had received two legions as reinforcements from Cilicia, he followed Mithridates and surrounded him with a twenty-two-kilometer-long siege line of walls and palisades, but once again Mithridates escaped. The legions demonstrated their rapidity and discipline, so that not far away, in the upper valley of the Lykos near the modern town of Suşehri, Pompey was able to catch his opponent and destroy his army. In the highlands near the battlefield the victor later had the city of Nikopolis founded. Since ancient building materials were discovered there, its site is presumed to be near the village of Yeşilyayla (earlier Pürk).

From that point on, the king's fate took on adventurous traits: he escaped with a small number of friends, and in the end he must have managed to get away accompanied only by his beloved Hypsikrateia. So long as there were in the country guarded storehouses with money and precious objects, all of which the Romans had presumably not discovered, and in any case could not seize in the wink of an eye, Mithridates could draw on resources with which he bought support and shelter for himself. Furthermore, he was familiar with the country, the people, and the language. The prospects of tracking him down seemed slim.

For Pompey, the immediate goal was to prevent Mithridates from making his way to the king of Armenia again. At the latter's court, complications had arisen that pushed Pompey even more to go there: the old Tigranes, deeply estranged from his son of the same name at the Arsakid court, who was a son-in-law of the Parthian king Phraates, found himself facing an unexpected threat. The young man had not hesitated to advance, along with the Parthians, on the paternal capital of Artaxata, but an attempted siege failed and Phraates withdrew again.

Seeking an ally, the refractory king's son made contact with Pompey, went to see him, and escorted the legions toward Artaxata. Fifteen miles from the city, Tigranes, advancing to meet them, entered the Roman camp and threw himself at Pompey's feet. Pompey instinctively favored the opposing party of an Armenian-Parthian alliance, that is, the old Tigranes, and thus anticipated a basic position of Roman oriental policy over the coming centuries. He had already entered into contact with the Parthian king through emissaries he had sent from Cilicia, and the old agreement with Sulla (to the effect that the Euphrates was to be the border between the two spheres of interest) was renewed. What was on Sulla's part hardly assertive and on that of the Parthians more a careless act of courtesy—which later cost the negotiator his head (Plutarch, *Sull.* 5, 5)—emerged thirty years later as a reality. With the foreseeable demise of the Pontic kingdom, there was no longer an organized great state in the realm of Anatolia, Syria, and northern Mesopotamia.

Neighboring Armenia was closely intertwined ethnically, linguistically, and culturally with Iran, and remained for centuries (until the Middle Ages) an outpost from which Iranian culture radiated into the area. If Rome wanted to dominate that region, Armenia itself could not be abandoned, and especially not to the Parthians (or later, the Sasanids). Pompey, who could at most have glimpsed this problem, confirmed the king of Armenia's rule over his ancestral kingdom but ordered him to give up his conquests in Mesopotamia, Syria, and Cilicia and pay damages in the amount of 60,000 talents. The young Tigranes received only one part, Sophene, a country at the junction of the Arsanias and the Euphrates rivers. His reaction to this seemed so surly that Pompey had him arrested. He was later to be paraded, along with his whole family, in a triumphal procession through Rome. The Roman camp subsequently became the center of attraction for a series of embassies from Parthian vassals, such as the kings of Elymais and Media, who hoped with Roman help to extricate themselves from the supremacy of the Arsakid throne. Pompey's legates undertook reconnaissance campaigns to Mesopotamia. On the threshold of the *Oriens Romanus*, Roman policy proved to be what it was to remain for the next 600 years: offensive and even aggressive.

In the meantime, it was learned that Mithridates, on whose head the old Tigranes had put a price, had gone to the area of modern-day Erzurum, descended into the valley of the Çoruh River, and reached the mouth of the Phasis in Colchis. From

53. Mzcheta at the confluence of the rivers Kura and Aragwi, where the ancient sites of Harmozika and Seusamora are located.

there he went to Dioskurias (now Suchumi). The Roman fleet controlled the southeast part of the Black Sea but was unable to land any troops that could have pursued Mithridates. That was no doubt Pompey's goal when he turned north up the valley of the Araxes, and from there descended into the valley of the river Kyros (Kura), into modern-day Georgia. The king of Albania, Oroizes, and the king of Iberia, Artoces (the ancient names of their kingdoms are not to be confused with modern Albania and Spain), promised to allow the Romans to pass through their lands, but an attack soon revealed their true intentions. In the summer of 65 BCE the army arrived at a place where the Kyros and Aragos (Kura and Aragwi) rivers merged and where the center of the Iberian kingdom was located. Artoces now intended to defend his capital. Above the city were two fortresses, which Strabo calls Harmozika and Seusamora (Figure 53).

On the conical mountain overlooking the river there was presumably a religious site dedicated to the supreme Persian divinity, Ahura Mazdā, from whose name the Greek form *Harmozika* is derived. On the plain on the other side of the river the most important religious site in Christian Georgia (Sweti Zchoweli) grew up in the Middle Ages. Only a short distance upstream excavations have uncovered the remains of a palace and bath, a rampart, and tombs from the first century BCE. The fortress was later repaired under Vespasian (69–79 CE), as is indicated by a building inscription ([195] SEG 20, 112).

Pompey's legions managed to take the fortress. The Iberian king withdrew to the west, crossing river after river by means of wooden bridges. The Roman army marched through the valley of the Phasis to the coast of Colchis and made contact with the fleet, which was presumably near modern-day Batumi. However, just as Lucullus had been unable to prevent Mithridates from fleeing to Armenia, Pompey was now unable to thwart this flight to the north. The kingdom of the Cimmerian Bosporus ruled by the king's son Machares had long since gone over to the victor's side. But to control the situation in the Crimea and in the surrounding cities, an invasion by Roman land troops would have been necessary. Pompey did not dare transport troops to the other side of the Black Sea, and in any event that would also probably have proved impossible. The land route along the east coast of the Black Sea, by which the king escaped, passed through difficult terrain and was rejected as too dangerous. Mithridates had made his way—by means of violence and gifts—through this foreign tribal area where the thickly wooded southern slopes of the Caucasus sometimes fell vertically down to the sea and provided passage only on narrow paths (Appian, *Mith*. 102 [469]). Once again he succeeded in mobilizing the population of the Bosphoran viceroyalty behind him and drove his son Machares out of Phanagoreia to Pantikapaion, in the Crimea. The rebellion in support of the king even spread to the other shore. Mithridates pursued Machares and was able to storm Pantikapaion, whereupon his son committed suicide.

The events south of the Caucasus cannot be unambiguously organized temporally and spatially on the basis of our narrative sources. Pompey is supposed to have marched again from the Black Sea to the banks of the Kura to put down a rebellion by the Albanians. The accounts reporting another *anabasis* in the direction of the Caspian Sea, which are surely inspired by a desire to imitate that of Alexander the Great, veer into the fantastic.[176] A more realistic view is that in Pontos and Lesser Armenia the Romans set about systematically using boulders to block wells in fortresses. In the spring of 64 BCE, legates, the army, client-kings, and delegations of the cities gathered in the city of Amisos, where Pompey undertook to reorganize Pontos (see p. 289). Again at this time he distanced himself from the adventurous notion of attacking the Cimmerian Bosporus, ordering a naval blockade instead. While his legates Gabinius and Afranius were already operating south of the Taurus Mountains, he himself turned south to set in order the areas of Syria that had been evacuated by Tigranes, with the clear intention of consolidating Roman control over these rich and fertile lands on the eastern Mediterranean coast, which were also located in a key position for trade and communication. First he marched from the coast of the Black Sea into the interior of the Pontos to the battlefield near Gaziura (Dio 36, 12 f.) where Triarius perished. Going on, Pompey crossed eastern Cappadocia and presumably took this opportunity to invade the kingdom of Commagene between the Taurus Mountains and the Euphrates, where the ruler was the Antiochos I (Appian, *Mith*. 106 [497], cf. 117 [576]) whose enormous tomb-sanctuaries can still be seen in the mountains (see p. 514 and Figures 101, 102). However their meeting went, Pompey extended the kingdom as far as Seleukeia, which lay on the Euphrates (Strabo 16, 2, 3), and a few years later Antiochos was already considered an ally of Rome (Cicero, *ad Q*. fr. 2, 11 (10), 2).

After Pompey had put an end to the rule of the last Seleucid ruler (Antiochos XIII Asiaticus, who had been enthroned by Lucullus) in Syria and annexed the country, he marched on toward Palestine. Before he arrived in Jericho, or perhaps on the road from Damascus to Petra, the unexpected news of Mithridates's death reached him (Plutarch, *Pomp.* 41, 3–5). The king of Pontos had so firmly established his authority in Pantikapaion that he had been able to consider equipping another large army and a fleet. With a view to this possibility such Roman writers as Appian, Plutarch, and Cassius Dio engage in speculations regarding his plans and goals: a march up the Danube, over the Alps into Italy. The historian and biographer of Mithridates, Théodore Reinach, offers this reflection: "Who can say whether at that time Rome would not have already suffered the fate that Alaric, Geiseric, and Totila were to impose on it five hundred years later."[177] Instead, treachery in his own family and the calculations of individuals adept at saving their own skins brought Mithridates to a sudden end. Unlike the people, the elites at the court and in the cities of the Bosphoran kingdom may have reacted to the seizure of power by the old ruler of Pontos with more fear than enthusiasm, since many of them in positions of trust were in danger of being replaced. In addition, the prospect of keeping one's position in a Roman client-kingdom was tempting. In Phanagoreia an uprising broke out, and Theodosia, Nymphaion, and Chersonnesos gradually fell away.

Mithridates' daughter Kleopatra and his sons Dareios, Xerxes, Oxathres, and Artaphernes fell into the hands of the rebels and were handed over to officers of the Roman fleet. His son Pharnakes, who was later to become a well-known opponent of Caesar, was prepared to betray his father and allowed himself to be proclaimed king. His soldiers forced their way into the residence of the almost seventy-year-old Mithridates; the latter ordered his bodyguard, the Celt Bitokos, to run him through with his sword. On hearing the news of Mithridates's death, Pompey wrote to the Senate that the war was over. The consul Marcus Tullius Cicero ordered a ten-day celebration in thanks. Emissaries from Pharnakes brought the corpse of his father to Amisos, where Pompey, who had returned from Palestine, set up his headquarters again in 63 BCE. Pharnakes was confirmed as a client-king ruling the kingdom on the Bosporus. The burial of Rome's great opponent took place in Sinope or Amaseia. His tomb has still not been discovered.[178]

Mithridates' achievements are impressive. He held out for twenty-six years against the greatest power of the ancient Mediterranean world: six generals of consular rank—Cassius, Sulla, Murena, Cotta, Lucullus, and Pompey—campaigned against him. He absorbed a series of heavy defeats from Rhodes to Chaironeia, Orchomenos, Kyzikos, Kabeira, and Nikopolis; survived a twenty-month internment in Armenia; and in his late sixties still possessed, after apparently being definitively beaten, the tenacity to march several hundred kilometers through difficult terrain and build up a new front.

✦ ✦ ✦

There is no ancient biography of Mithridates, any more than of a Seleucid or Attalid king. It is hard to form a biographical image of him, even though he is described in detail in Greek and Roman sources. From their point of view, he is primarily an opponent, described with hostile intention as the very model of despotism and cruelty. Accordingly, modern evaluations of him are guided less by his achievements than by their effects. For instance, in the third volume of his history of Rome, Mommsen writes:

> He became still more significant through the position in which history had placed him than through his individual character. As the forerunner of the national reaction of the Orientals against the Occidentals, he opened the new conflict of the east against the west; and the feeling remained with the vanquished as with the victors, that his death was not so much the end as the beginning.[179]

At the end of the second century BCE a threshold still appears at the forefront of the new Roman province of Asia: on one side is the Hellenistic culture of the *polis*, on the other that of the lands thoroughly imbued with the older Eastern high cultures of Mesopotamia, Syria, and Iran. The cities founded by the Diadochi, the Epigones, the kings of Bithynia, and the Attalids had pushed this threshold from the coastal areas deeper into the interior and considerably farther to the east, as far as the bend in the Halys River. But the Anatolian kingdoms of Cappadocia, Pontos, and Armenia remained on the other side, despite their Hellenized courtiers, Greek *philoi*, officers, and soldiers, and the titles given their kings—"Friend of the Greeks" (*philhellen*) and "Friend of the Romans" (*philorhomaios*). Before Mithridates appeared, the Senate in Rome did not seem inclined to cross this threshold. Mithridates was no Hannibal or anti-Alexander driven by a desire to conquer Italy and the West. The motive that led him to repeatedly go on the offensive is probably better described as a desire to resist Roman domination over Asia.[180] However, his actions had the opposite effect insofar as his victories made it immediately and brutally clear to the Romans that with the efforts committed up to that point, they could not even be sure of holding Greece. At the latest, the setbacks suffered during Lucullus's campaigns confirmed the view that Asia Minor would either have to be abandoned or organized and ruled at considerably greater expense. The decisive step in this direction was to be taken by Pompey, who thereby laid the foundations of the *Oriens Romanus*.

Centuries later, the fate of the old man of Pontos still fascinated Europe.[181] In 1770, the fourteen-year-old Mozart composed his first serious opera for Milan; it was called "Mitridate, Re di Ponto." The subject was traditional, and Mozart's elaboration of a varied, dramatic love story involving Mithridates, his sons, and his fiancée built on the most famous literary version to date, a tragedy titled "Mithridate" in five acts by Jean-Baptiste Racine (1639–1699) originally performed at the Hôtel de Bourgogne in Paris on January 12, 1673. In the foreword to the play, Racine claims to have faithfully followed the historical tradition and lists his sources—Florus, Plutarch, Cassius Dio, and Appian. The play draws its energy from the four-way relationship among its main characters. Old Mithridates, an enemy of Rome full of hate, gifted with subtlety and the art of disguise, and driven by passion and love for his slave Monime, has two sons, Pharnace (the bad son who makes common cause with the Romans) and Xipharès (an upright, courageous, loyal youth—a model for the young aristocracy of the age of Louis XIV). Monime is desired not only by the king but also by his two sons, while she is passionately in love with the noble Xipharès. Mithridates, who believes he has been defeated in the last battle with the Romans, falls on his sword. Dying, he overcomes his jealousy and gives his blessing to the lovers' union.

Pompey's Reorganization of Asia Minor

The reorganization of the area of Asia Minor dominated by Rome was carried out between 67 and 63 BCE. Early on, when he was put in command of forces to combat piracy, Pompey completed Lucullus's project of repopulating the impoverished cities of the Cilician plain by settling some of the resocialized corsairs in Soloi, Adana, Epiphaneia, and Mallos (Plutarch, *Pomp.* 28; Appian, *Mith.* 96 [444]). The city of Soloi, which later celebrated him as its founder (*ktistes*) and patron (IGR III 869), was named Pompeiopolis after him; this is the earliest proven example of a *polis* founded in Asia Minor by a Roman. As in Soloi-Pompeiopolis (founded in 66/65 BCE), the cities of Epiphaneia (67), and Mallos (67/66), Mopsuhestia (67), and Alexandria on the Issos (67) documented the beginning of their eras between 67 and 65 BCE by their coinage, and thus they viewed their birth as *poleis* as having occurred under Pompey's *imperia* against the pirates and Mithridates ([199] Head, HN² 716, 724 f.).[182] At that time the *de facto* incorporation of Plain Cilicia into the Roman sphere of domination was already being carried out, and the legal reorganization of the *provincia Cilicia* was soon to follow.

After Pompey had deposed the Seleucid Antiochos XIII in Syria and thus eliminated a Seleucid authority over the Cilician plain that still formally existed, this area became part of the significantly enlarged province of Cilicia on the south coast of Asia Minor. The new province now included, beyond Pamphylia, the shores of Rough Cilicia and the great alluvial plain of the Pyramos and Kydnos rivers, as well as the east coast of the Gulf of Issus (now called the Gulf of İskenderun), but it probably extended no farther inland than the fifty-mile zone defined by the *lex Gabinia*. Pompey allowed dynasties in the interior to continue to exist as small vassal-states—as apparently did the Teucrids' temple-state in the west above Seleukeia on the Kalykadnos River, with its shrine to Zeus Olbios (Uzuncaburc). He handed over Hierapolis-Kastabala in eastern Cilicia (and perhaps also other cities, such as Elaiussa and Korykos in the west, and Anazarbos and Aigai in the east?) to a former pirate named Tarkondimotos, whom Antony soon thereafter made a king. Tarsos became a provincial assize (*conventus*) for the provincial governor's court hearings (Cicero, *Att.* 5, 16, 4).

The situation at the end of the war in northern Asia Minor was more complicated. Three regional complexes differing in their histories, situations, and coherence were to be divided up: first, the kingdom of Bithynia, which Rome claimed as the legacy of Nikomedes IV; second, the core of the Pontic kingdom, without the areas conquered by Mithridates in the west, east, and north; and third, the lands subjugated by Mithridates Eupator. The latter Pompey transferred to client-rulers. The possessions in the Crimea and on the Cimmerian Bosporus—with the exception of the city of Phanagoreia, which was the first to abandon Mithridates and was rewarded with its freedom—remained in the hands of Mithridates's son Pharnakes. Colchis was promised to a certain Aristarchos. In Cappadocia Ariobarzanes, as a loyal "Friend of the Romans," once again mounted the throne in Mazaka from which he had so often been deposed and ruled there until 62 BCE. Parts of Lycaonia in the west and Armenia in the east—such as Sophene, which had been intended for the young Tigranes—were annexed to his kingdom. The most richly endowed potentate was to be the Galatian Deiotaros. Pompey made him tetrarch over the Tolistoagii; it is unclear and debated whether in Galatia a council of tetrarchs existing at that time was abolished, whether one ruler was named for each of the three tribal groups, or four tetrarchs were confirmed (Appian, *Syr.* 50 [254]).[183] But Deiotaros also received the coast east of the territory of the city of Amisos as far as Colchis—thus including the cities of Pharnakeia (Kerasus) and Trapezus—as well as large parts of Lesser Armenia. Nor was that all; in addition, he received an area in the middle of the Pontic kingdom, namely, a part of the alluvial plain called Gadilonitis, between the mouth of the Halys and Amisos. This was still not enough. Soon thereafter the prince gained ascendancy over the tribal chieftains in other parts of Galatia, so that he controlled, along with the areas inhabited by the Tolistoagii, the Tektosages, and the Trokmoi, enormous regions of central Anatolia.[184] Only Paphlagonia south of the Olgassys (Ilgaz Dağları), with the old royal stronghold of Gangra as its center, came into the possession of a scion of the Pylaemenid dynasty named Attalos (see the Appendix).

As in Cilicia, Pompey reserved the most fertile areas, such as the valley of the Amnias and the Halys, Iris, and Lykos river basins, and especially the coast itself, for a provincial organization based on cities. The Greek cities of Amastris, Sinope, and Amisos—all on the Black Sea coast—belonged to the Pontic kingdom. *Polis* status was now granted to them, and probably also to Abonuteichos (between Amastris and Sinope). Only the temple land around Komana in Pontos was, like Gadilonitis, to remain an enclave. Pompey had not only not touched, but had even enlarged this oldest—even pre-Iranian—of the three great sanctuaries. Archelaos was made the high priest. The other two sanctuaries were transformed into cities in the new province: Zela, considerably enlarged by the reassignment of regions (presumably including Amaseia), and Kabeira, which as a *polis* was thenceforth called "Zeus city" (*Diospolis*). The names of four cities founded in the interior were supposed to remind people of Pompey "the Great" and his victory over Mithridates: Nikopolis in the basin of the upper Lykos, which was taken away from Deiotaros's possessions in Lesser Armenia and added to the province of Pontus; Megalopolis on the upper reaches of the Halys; Magnopolis near the fortress of Eupatoria at the confluence of the Iris and the Lykos rivers; and, after the city in Cilicia, a second Pompeiopolis in the fertile valley of the Amnias in central Paphlagonia, north of the Olgassys. The main city of the Phazemonitis country, which still belonged to Paphlagonia and lay on the right bank of the Halys River, was organized as a *polis* with the name Neapolis ("new city," now Vezirköprü). It is almost certain that Pompey settled Roman legionnaires in Nikopolis and Pompeiopolis; the other newly founded cities were probably settled by natives and Greeks. What is of exceptional importance here is that a Roman undertook, for the first time, to subdivide the whole province into city territories—in the case of the core Pontic Kingdom plus Nikopolis, eleven of them.

That is how the province of Pontus was created. It was expanded by the inclusion of two coastal cities that lay in Bithynia: Tieion and Herakleia Pontike. We know nothing about the measures Pompey took in Bithynia, which also had *poleis* in the interior. Bithynian cities dated their coins according to an era, the starting point of which corresponds to 282/281 BCE—apparently coinciding with their liberation from Lysimachos. Remarkably, the use of this era did not immediately disappear when royal rule ended in Bithynia and the Roman province was established. Under two Roman governors who ruled the province between 61 and 58 and in 46 BCE, the coins minted in Nikaia, Nikomedeia, Tieion, Prusa, Bithynion, and Apameia were stamped with these governors' names and the number of years that had elapsed since 282/281 BCE, which means that the era of liberation from Lysimachos continued into this period. But during the Imperial period these same cities no longer used this or any other era. In contrast, the *poleis* in neighboring Paphlagonia and Pontos that had been founded or liberated during the Mithridatic War or later and had adopted a new system of eras, each starting from the individual city's fateful political turn that its incorporation into a Roman province constituted, continued these eras into the Imperial period. The use of that system here lasted down into late antiquity. This suggests that the Bithynian cities wanted to distinguish themselves from these other cities in Paphlagonia and Pontos with respect to their past, because they claimed to have already possessed *polis* status under the Bithynian kings or even earlier, not as late as most of their eastern neighbors. They saw no reason to connect the establishment of the Roman province with a new beginning of their political existence—any more than Miletus, Smyrna, or Ephesos in Asia did. In this respect Herakleia and Tieion, even though Pompey had added them to the province of Pontus, did as the Bithynian *poleis* had done: since they believed that they had existed as *poleis* long before Nikomedes IV left his kingdom to Rome, and—apart from a short occupation during the war—had never belonged to Mithridates's kingdom, they did not adopt an era-dating of their coins starting from any Roman liberation.

Pompey added the two areas divided into city territories between the Sea of Marmara and Lesser Armenia to the double province of Pontus et Bithynia. It was probably he who gave the cities permission to form a Commonalty (koinon) and elect a chief official to preside over it. A *lex provinciae* bearing his name is mentioned a few times in later literature; it was still in force in the third century CE. It defined the role of the municipal councils in accord with the Western model of the *ordines decu-*

rionum, the lifelong council membership of a citizen elite constituted on the basis of a census of minimum assets. It eased the incorporation of the rural population but prohibited double citizenship.[185]

Thus before the middle of the first century BCE a process of revitalizing or refounding urban cells on the Hellenic model got underway in both the northern and southern parts of Asia Minor. Nothing like it had been seen on such a scale since the Attalids. The organization on the basis of the *polis* territories turned out to be particularly important for the future—the principle was later employed in many stages of the expansion and rounding out of the provinces of Anatolia. No doubt Pompey brought from Spain experience and sensitivity regarding how to secure areas conquered in war and to win over the inhabitants by means of leniency and benefits. The prominent Greeks in his immediate entourage probably encouraged him in his Graecophilia on the model of the Diadochi and Epigones. From Mytilene on Lesbos, which had been severely punished by Rome, came a man who—as *prytanis* of his home town, he belonged to the Greek citizen elite—entered into friendly relations with Pompey and accompanied him as a historian on his campaigns in the East. His city was given its freedom for his sake, and he himself acquired Roman citizenship. He is known to us from many inscriptions as Gnaeus Pompeius, son of Hieroitas, Theophanes.[186] Like him, the freedman Demetrios, from Gadara in Syria, was surely among Pompey's most trusted advisors.

On his way home Pompey crossed Asia Minor as if in a festive procession, "very panegyric," as Plutarch puts it (*Pomp.* 42, 4).[187] When he reached the west coast he embarked from Ephesos for the voyage to Greece. In Rome, the celebration of his triumph began on September 28, 61 BCE. The tablets on which the names of the nations he had subjugated were written listed Pontos, Armenia, Cappadocia, Paphlagonia, Media, Colchis, Iberia, Albania, Syria, Cilicia, Mesopotamia, the lands of Phoenicia and Palestine, Judea, Arabia, and all the pirate entities on water and on land; a thousand conquered fortresses, no fewer than 900 cities, 800 pirate ships seized, and 39 cities founded. Enormous sums were distributed to the soldiers or ended up in the state treasury. Among the prisoners, the young Tigranes was paraded along with his wife and daughter, Zosime, one of the elder Tigranes's wives, a sister and five children of Mithridates, Scythian women, and hostages who had been sent by the kings of Iberia, Albania, and Commagene. The city of Rome had never before witnessed such a display of the Orient. Pompey, although he was already in his forties, allowed himself to be compared with Alexander (Plutarch, *Pomp.* 46, 1). But the Senate did not recognize the arrangements he had made, and so Pompey formed with Caesar and Crassus—ambitious, wealthy politicians—the first triumvirate. His *acta* were confirmed only in 59 BCE.

Asia Minor after Pompey

With the end of the Mithridatic Wars and its exceptional commands, the three large provinces of Asia Minor—Asia, Pontus et Bithynia, and Cilicia—made the transition to a regulated administration. One of its bases was Sulla's legislation (*leges Corneliae*) of 81 BCE, according to which the two consuls and (for the first time) eight praetors were to rule a province not during but only after their year in office in Rome.[188] In 52 BCE this provision was changed at Pompey's initiative (*lex Pompeia de provinciis*), to the effect that magistrates could not be chosen for a governorship immediately after their year in office but only at least five years afterward. The allocation of governorships was made by drawing lots (*sortitio*) or by arrangement (*comparatio*), and the normal one-year term of office could be prolonged (*prorogatum*), which was often done in the subsequent period.[189]

After Lucullus was replaced in Asia by Publius Dolabella, and the latter was succeeded by five other ex-praetors until 63 BCE, Lucius Valerius Flaccus took control of the province the following year. We know him both from correspondence and from the speech given by Cicero in his defense in August/September 59. Flaccus had been accused of extortion, the penalty for which was full restitution (*de repetundis*). Although Cicero's defense was successful, the testimony given by his speech suggests that Flaccus's rule had indeed increased poverty in the province. Among other things, the governor drew exceptionally large sums of money from the cities to assemble a pirate-fighting fleet that was never put in action. His successor was Cicero's brother Quintus, whose first term in office was prolonged two additional years, and who did not leave the province until the spring of 58. Cicero feared that he would also be indicted. For determining the precise chronology of the following governors, the *cistophori* issued in the cities of Asia are an important source. The first, Titus Ampius, moved from Asia to Cilicia; among his successors, the third, C. Claudius (55–53), was accused of extortion and condemned (*de repetundis*) after he returned to Rome in 51 BCE. Q. Minucius Thermus governed Asia during Cicero's governorship in Cilicia.

The first well-known governor of Cilicia after Pompey was Marcus Porcius Cato, in 58 BCE. The province had originally been assigned to the higher-ranking proconsul Aulus Gabinius. But this former legate of Pompey the Great made sure he would get the governorship of Syria. In Cilicia Cato, who was assigned the task of annexing Cyprus, was subsequently replaced by Titus Ampius. During the four-year term in office of the latter's successor, P. Cornelius Lentulus Spinther (56–53), not only Cyprus but also Phrygia, with the dioceses of Synnada, Apameia, and Laodikeia, were put under the governor of Cilicia. The next one was Appius Claudius Pulcher (53–51). Before we come to Cicero, who succeeded Claudius Pulcher as governor, I must mention an event whose consequences, seen from Rome's point of view, were to trouble Anatolia. In May 53 Licinius Crassus had invaded northern Mesopotamia with an army of more than 40,000 men and had been completely routed near Carrhae by the Parthian cavalry. Crassus himself fell in the battle. Artaxata, the Armenian capital on the Araxes, was the scene of a gruesome sequel: the Armenian king Artavasdes was hosting the Parthian king Orodes II in his palace when a messenger brought in Crassus's head. At that moment, Euripides's play *The Bacchae* was being performed before the court, and an actor named Iason of Tralleis slipped into the role of Agaue, took the head in his hands and spoke the verse: "We bring from the mountain a tendril fresh-cut to the palace, a wonderful prey." Plutarch adds that "This delighted everybody" (Plutarch, *Crass.* 33, 3 f.; trans. Perrin). Encouraged by their victory, under the leadership of the king's son Pakoros the Parthians soon thereafter crossed the Euphrates and threatened Antiocheia. For the first time, the Iranian great power used force to stem the eastern expansion of the developing Roman hegemony.

Cicero's Governorship in the Province of Cilicia

Marcus Tullius Cicero's voluminous writings made him one of the best-known persons of antiquity. Elected consul in 63 BCE, he was subsequently exiled but was rehabilitated after his return to Rome; he served as governor of the province of Cilicia from July 31, 51 BCE to the late autumn of the following year. From this time alone, we have more than a hundred of his letters. To this correspondence, as to Pliny the Younger's later correspondence with Trajan, we owe a deep insight into the situation in Asia Minor under Rome's rule. Cicero (*fam.* 2, 7, 4, etc.) constantly worried that this burdensome governorship might be prolonged, and as soon as he arrived in Anatolia he began to long for his return to "*lux, forum, urbs, domus*" (*Att.* 5, 15, 1; "the world, the Forum, Rome, my house") in Italy.[190] The fifty-five-year-old Cicero's itinerary during the few months in his enormous area of jurisdiction in southern Asia Minor is impressive. He disembarked in Ephesos, where he was received by a great crowd, including a delegation of tax collectors; he was greeted as though he had come with an army behind him (Cicero, *Att.* 5, 13, 1). His actual headquarters and the first destination in his own province was Laodikeia on the Lykos (Figure 54). Here his staff was waiting for him: legates, tribunes, prefects (the quaestor was absent), and two legions warmly welcomed him (*Att.* 5, 15, 1). On several occasions he spent extended periods in Laodikeia, where he wrote most of his letters; games involving gladiators were also arranged there (*Att.* 6, 3, 9). He wanted to have panthers from the Lycian Taurus Mountains caught for the aedile who organized games in Rome. These rare animals, he wrote, alluding to the leniency of his rule, were the only living beings in his province that were not left undisturbed (Cicero, *fam.* 2, 11, 2).

Military duties were imposed on this governor who was—as he acknowledges with self-irony—not very military: battling robbers in the Taurus and protecting the province behind the front against the Parthians, which at that time ran through Syria. When he arrived, Cicero intended to devote the summer months to the military campaign and the winter months to jurisdictional matters. After sojourning in Apameia, Synnada, and Philomelion, he went in the high summer of 51 BCE to Ikonion (Konya). An embassy from the king of Commagene arrived in his camp and reported that the Parthians had crossed the border into Syria. While his quaestor Appius was holding court in Tarsos, Cicero himself fought the robber baron Moiragenes in the Lycaonian Taurus, and then pitched his camp near Kybistra, on the

54. Laodikeia on the Lykos.

northern edge of the range (west of Konya-Ereğli). The constant exchange of letters with his correspondents in Rome was not broken off even while he was on campaign; a letter from the capital reached Kybistra in the record time of 46 days (Cicero, *Att.* 5, 19, 1)—while today a letter from Germany sometimes takes nine days to reach Switzerland. He was concerned about the threat posed by the Parthians, because he knew the weakness of his forces and longed for the support of the prince Deiotaros, whom the Senate had in the meantime elevated to the rank of king, while Cicero himself was still having Roman citizens conscripted and grain stored up in secure warehouses (*Att.* 5, 18). Emissaries from Deiotaros promised that the king would join him with his entire army. Then the arrival of Ariobarzanes III, whom the Senate saw as the legitimate heir to the throne in Cappadocia, was announced. Cicero heard that a rebellion against the king was afoot, which was openly supported by the priest of the Cappadocian Komana. Cicero issued statements that made Rome's backing for the heir to the throne perfectly clear and had the priest of Komana expelled from the country. He claimed to have saved the king's life.

Other reports led him to cross the Taurus through the Cilician Gates. He visited Tarsos and Mopsuhestia, and marched to the Amanos, the mountain range that separated his own province from the that of Syria and on whose eastern slope the governor of Syria, Bibulus, was waiting for the Parthians, who had marched into the Kyrrhestike. "For a few days we encamped near Issus in the very spot where Alexander (a considerably better general than either you or I), pitched his camp against Darius."[191] Cicero conducted plundering campaigns in the Amanos, from which he returned victorious and—having been proclaimed *imperator* in Issus—full of pride: "*erat in Syria nostrum nomen in gratia.*"[192] He gloated when Bibulus tried to imitate him and suffered losses. The relationship between the two men was less than warm. When the Parthians appeared for a short time before the gates of the Syrian capital Antiocheia and people were counting on Cicero's army for reinforcement, Bibulus is said to have several times declared that he would endure anything rather than leave the impression that he needed Cicero's help (Cicero, *fam.* 2, 17, 6). The next stopping point was Pindenissos, a mountain fortress outside the provincial boundaries of Cilicia. After an eight-week siege, Cicero's soldiers stormed it; it was plundered and its inhabitants were sold into slavery. While his brother Quintus took over command in the army's winter quarters in Cilicia, the governor recrossed the Taurus to Laodikeia. After sojourns in Synnada and Pamphylia, in the spring of the following year he returned to Cilicia, where he took up residence in Tarsos on June 5.

The centers of Cicero's nonmilitary activities were the cities. His main tasks concerned the supervision of accounting, finance, contracts made by the communities, tax revenues, matters of inheritance, and the purchase and sale of goods. He picked no quarrels with the tax collectors: "I dote upon them, defer to them, butter them up with compliments—and arrange so that they harm nobody."[193] Making an effort to pay down communal debts, he discovered the malversations committed by city officials. He practiced self-denial for himself and his staff (*Att.* 6, 2, 4); in the six months of his governorship the dioceses of Asia had received no payment order from him and never had to accept even billeting—a burden that prosperous communities were prepared to pay large bribes to avoid. In fact, he was profoundly impressed by the wretched condition of the province in the period after the Mithridatic Wars, and his attitude seems sincere. Soon after his arrival he wrote:

> I stayed three days in Laodicea, three in Apamea, and as many at Synnada. I have heard of nothing but inability to pay the poll taxes imposed, universal sales of taxes, groans and moans from the communities, appalling excesses as of some savage beast rather than a human being. In a phrase, these people are absolutely tired of their lives. However it is some relief to the wretched communities that no expense is incurred on my account or that of my Legates or my Quaestor or anyone whosoever. I may tell you that besides hay or what is customarily given under the lex Julia we even decline wood; and except for four couches and a roof no one takes anything—in many places not even a roof; they usually sleep under canvas. So the way the people flock in from every country district, village, and town is hardly to be believed. Upon my word the mere fact of my arrival brings them back to life, knowing as they do the justice, the abstinence, and the clemency of your friend Cicero, which has surpassed all expectations.[194]

When he put a stop to the communities' paying heavy expenses for embassies to Rome, he incurred the wrath of his predecessor, Claudius Pulcher, who had ordered them to do so (Cicero, *fam.* 3, 7, 2). We can gain an idea of the extent of municipal indebtedness outside the province from the case of Titus Pinnius, to whom the city of Nikaia in Bithynia owed 8 million sestertii (*fam.* 13, 61). The Roman magistrates themselves, and the members of their entourages, were often those who lent the money and collected the interest, or were on friendly terms with those who did. Thus Cicero also represented the interests of Roman moneylenders, for example, of his friend Cluvius, a banker in Puteoli, to whom citizens of Bargylia, Herakleia, Mylasa, Alabanda, and Kaunos in Caria owed money (*fam.* 13, 56). After he had—like Lucullus before him in Asia—issued an edict that set the interest rate at 12 percent per year, he was badgered by a Roman businessman who was a creditor of the community of Salamis on Cyprus: this Marcus Scaptius demanded that force be used to compel Salamis to repay the debt. But the community was prepared to pay back the money at the set rate of 12 percent; it said it was, thanks to Cicero's generous offer to forgo the otherwise usual honorary payments made to the praetors, completely able to pay its debt! But Scaptius shamelessly demanded 48 percent interest. In their greed, the "bankers" of that time seem not to have been very different from some of their modern counterparts. Cicero was proud of his leniency and thoughtfulness with regard to the Greek communities, and he sometimes overpraises himself. In his jurisdiction he took as his model the earlier benefactor of Asia, Mucius Scaevola, and allowed the Greeks not only to proceed among themselves in accord with their own law, but also, if this interpretation is correct, to call on foreign judges—"babblers, you may call them," as he writes, anticipating Atticus's thoughts.[195]

His fear that his governorship would be prolonged turned out to be groundless. Already feverishly anticipating his return home, he had to appoint a representative, in accord with the Senate's decision. He thought first of his brother Quintus, but then decided instead to choose the quaestor Coelius Calvus. From Side, perhaps while watching a summer sunset at the beach, he wrote: "*Amicorum litterae me ad triumphum vocant*" ("My friends' letters beckon me to a Triumph").[196] In the fall, he sailed home, via Rhodes, Ephesos, and Athens.

Caesar in Asia Minor

We know little about the governors of the new province of Pontus et Bithynia after Pompey returned to Rome.[197] Gaius Papirius Carbo, who had served as quaestor in Bithynia under Aurelius Cotta, was the first regular officeholder among them. He remained there three to four years (ca. 61–58). His successor, Gaius Memmius, the patron of the famous poets Lucretius and Catullus, left the province after one year. For an unknown period of time he was followed by a governor, Gaius Caecilius Cornutus, known by coins from Amisos; then, during Cicero's term of office in Cilicia, these northern provinces were governed by a certain Publius Silius, followed by the supporter of Pompey Aulus Plautius (Cicero, *fam.* 13, 29, 4) and the well-known Gaius Vibius Pansa (47/46 BCE), who later (after Caesar's death) was to hold the office of consul in Rome, along with Aulus Hirtius. Each of these men was sent to the province after completing his year of office as praetor in Rome.

Dark clouds gathered again on the horizon of Asia Minor's cities and dynasties when in 49 BCE civil war broke out between Pompey, who had many friends and clients in Asia, and Caesar, the conqueror of Gaul. Pompey now merged Pamphylia and the dioceses of Phrygia that had until then been administered—as still under Cicero—by the governor of Cilicia, with the province of Asia.[198] While Pompey himself remained in Greece, his father-in-law Quintus Caecilius Metellus Scipio Nasica oppressed the cities of Asia, just as Sulla had before him and the murderers of Caesar were to do afterward: he demanded a poll tax on each slave and taxes on pillars (*columnaria*) and doors (*ostiaria*), and grain, soldiers, weapons, oarsmen, catapults, and work with draft animals. The Roman officers and their agents coolly explained to the Greeks that they had been driven out of their homeland and lacked the necessities. In addition, forced loans were demanded from cities, Roman businessmen, and tax collectors. Only the sudden invasion of Greece by Caesar's troops prevented Scipio from plundering the temple treasury of the Artemision of Ephesos (Caesar, *civ.* 3, 33, 1).

King Deiotaros was to prove a skilful survivor who repeatedly changed sides at just the right time. On August 9 of the following year Pompey the Great, his patron, was defeated in the battle near Pharsalos in Thessaly. Pompey fled to Alexandria and was murdered there. Pursuing him, the victor, Julius Caesar, traversed Thrace, crossed the Hellespont, visited Ilion and granted the city privileges (Strabo 13, 1, 27), and then marched on Pergamon (IGR IV 1677). Here a certain Mithridates, son of Menodotos, gained his trust and obtained favorable treatment for his city. An embassy led by Potamon, son of Lesbonax, also came over from Lesbos to request that the citizens of Mytilene be considered Rome's friends and allies.[199] In addition, honors were bestowed by the Phokaians, Chians, and Samians.[200] Fragments of bases that held statues of Caesar have been discovered in several places in Pergamon's upper city. Finally, the victor of Pharsalos stopped in Ephesos and Rhodes. The league of Ionian cities hastened to praise him as a "god incarnate, descended from Ares and Aphrodite" and the "savior of human life" ([109] Syll.³ 760) and was not alone in doing so. The Ephesians inaugurated a new era that took Caesar's victory at Pharsalos as its starting point ([195] SEG 26, 1241).[201] Delegations from Stratonikeia, Aphrodisias, and Miletus went home with assurances of "inviolability" (*asylia*) for their cities.[202]

It was doubtless on this trip, probably in Rhodes, that the treaty with the Lycian League was made. The recently published text from a copy in cast bronze is one of the rare bronze inscriptions in Asia Minor. The tablet was taken from unauthorized excavations in Turkey and ended up in private possession. It is apparently a Greek version based on the Latin original on the Capitol in Rome, a duplicate of which had been preserved in a Lycian shrine. The text of this treaty, which was sworn to on July 24, 46 BCE, is the longest of any treaty between Rome and a community in the East that has become known so far.[203] As the states in southern Asia Minor that were independent of Roman administration and militarily powerful, the Lycian League and Rhodes were of great importance for a civil war that might be pursued further in the eastern Mediterranean. Given their experience, especially in the First Mithridatic War, the Romans must have been able to appreciate the value of a Lycian commitment to their cause. On the basis of the promise of eternal friendship, a stipulation emphasized that neither the Romans nor the Lycians would give their respective foes any support and would help each other in the event of an attack on either of them. Further agreements concerned prohibitions and procedures to be followed if individual Lycians or Romans violated the treaty, to which both parties expressly committed themselves, and the obligation to release and hand over to the other partner to the treaty prisoners and enslaved Lycians or Romans, along with stolen horses and ships. A series of places is listed, classified into cities (*poleis*), villages (*komai*), fortresses, territories, and harbors within the boundaries of Lycia, that Caesar assured the Lycians in addition. This latter assurance was obviously made in exchange for the duty to provide assistance, which was certainly invoked on the current battlefields in the East. In any case, five of the Lycians' ships then took part in the battle at Alexandria (Caesar, *Bellum Alexandrinum* 13, 5).

Caesar had left his legate Gnaeus Domitius Calvinus in Asia with three legions, of which two were put on the march to Egypt to support him there. Domitius now received disturbing news from king Deiotaros: Pharnakes, the son of Mithridates Eupator, whom Pompey had installed as king of the Bosphoran kingdom, was threatening not only his possession of Lesser Armenia but also the neighboring Cappadocia, where Ariobarzanes III Eusebes Philorhomaios ruled. He was even said to have subjugated cities in the area of the Roman province of Pontus. This was a clear affront to Pompey's Roman order in the Orient, to whose ratification Caesar himself had contributed; but still more disturbing, given the state of things, must have been Deiotaros's warning that if he lost his possession of Lesser Armenia, he would not be in a position to contribute to Caesar's war. Domitius acted. He reinforced the legion that remained to him by two further legions that Deiotaros had trained in the Roman manner and assembled these forces in the Pontic city of Komana. Pharnakes, with whom he had established contact, proved unwilling, for the time being, at least to give up Lesser Armenia: he now saw himself as the legitimate heir of the king of Pontos, his father, whom he had betrayed and overthrown. Domitius did not engage in any negotiations but instead advanced on Nikopolis, the city founded by Pompey on the western edge of Lesser Armenia, and forced his opponent to do battle. The battle ended with his defeat, in which Deiotaros's legions in particular apparently played a less than worthy role. (Caesar, *Bellum Alexandrinum* 40). A stone altar bearing an inscription dedicating it to "Calvinus, the god" has been found in Zela ([108] *Studia Pontica* 260); on the whole the Roman seems to have done extraordinary good deeds for the community or the land, but we have no further details regarding them. He retreated to the province of Asia and the following year took part in the African campaign.[204] Pharnakes triumphed. Aware of Caesar's highly precarious situation far outside Asia Minor, he now imagined himself safe enough to occupy his father's ancestral land, the Roman province of Pontus. Amisos resisted; it was plundered, and its men fit to bear arms were murdered. He broke off the following attack on Bithynia and Asia when he learned of Asandros's rebellion on the Cimmerian Bosporus (Dio 42, 45 f.).

In May or June 47, Caesar left Egypt and passing through Syria, went first to Tarsos in Cilicia, where he held court and settled the cities' affairs. The city of Aigai made its era on coins begin in the year 47/46 BCE, and this is certainly connected with Caesar's benefactions; perhaps the dictator had freed it from Tarkondimotos's dominion. Then he crossed back over the Taurus through Cappadocia and on to Komana in Pontus, where he met with Deiotaros in person and issued the first regulations. The Galatian's attitude and clothing were humble, and he offered convoluted explanations as to why he had not been able to support Caesar against Pompey (at Pharsalos, he had reinforced Pompey's side). Caesar coolly reminded him of his contribution to the confirmation of his possessions. Deiotaros, who had met with hostility from the other Galatian princes because of his privileged status, now had to share Lesser Armenia with Ariobarzanes (see the Appendix). Shortly afterward he also lost the east Galatian tetrarchy of the Trokmoi (around the modern city of Yozgat), but he probably retained the Gadilonitis in Pontos—the alluvial plain on the lower Halys River. Caesar deposed Archelaos as the priest of Komana and replaced him with a certain Lykomedes (Appendix). Then he moved with his army against Pharnakes, who was waiting for him in the hills above Zela. In addition to Deiotaros's single legion, Caesar had two more that had not proven themselves in battle. Only the Sixth Legion brought from Alexandria was battle hardened, but enormous losses had reduced its normal numbers to about one-fifth. Nevertheless, Caesar won at Zela—precisely where Mithridates had routed Triarius's Roman army two decades earlier—the famous battle that he reported to his friend Matius in Rome in the following words: *veni, vidi, vici* (Plutarch, *Caes.* 50, 2; Suetonius, *Iul.* 37, 2). The familiar quotation is now familiar to (almost) every resident of the small city of Zile and the surrounding villages.

Before Caesar left Asia Minor, he issued further regulations in Nikaia. The previously mentioned Mithridates of Pergamon replaced Pharnakes as king of the Bosphoran kingdom and was given the region of the Galatian Trokmoi in Anatolia. Probably in or on the way to Nikaia Caesar also arranged for Italic settlers to be sent to Herakleia Pontike, Sinope, and Apameia;[205] apart from Pompey's settlements, these were the first Roman colonies in Asia. In Sinope, the era of the newly founded colony Julia Felix known from coins commences in 46/45 BCE; the colony in Strabo's time still shared the city and the territory with the Greek community. The same remarkable sharing is also mentioned regarding Herakleia (on Herakleia, Sinope, and Apameia, see Strabo 12, 3, 6.11; 4, 3), and later emerged in Ikonion in Lycaonia (now Konya), under Augustus. Caesar guaranteed tax reductions for the communities of the province of Asia; but above all he took the "tithe" (*decuma*) away from the tax collection companies and had the provincials themselves henceforth levy the tax to be paid on the crop yield (*tributum soli*) (Appian, *BC* 5, 1, 4; cf. Plutarch, *Caes.* 48, 1; Dio 42, 6, 3).[206]

In November 45 BCE Deiotaros and Caesar were supposed to see each other again—in Caesar's house in Rome, where the dictator presided in person and behind closed doors over the lawsuit filed against Deiotaros by Kastor, one of the king's grandsons, along with his slave and physician. Deiotaros was accused of having planned to kill Caesar. The speech given by the defender, Marcus Tullius Cicero, is extant *in toto*. Deiotaros must have had little affection for the Roman who had painfully amputated his possessions in Asia Minor. But the claim that he had planned to murder Caesar was certainly false. We do not know Caesar's decision. A few months after the dictator's murder on the Ides of March, 44 BCE, Deiotaros seized once again the tetrarchy of the Trokmoi, which he had been forced to give up; Mithridates of Pergamon had fallen in battle and could not contest his repossession of the country. But Mark Antony hastened to draw the old dynast of Anatolia to his side and recognized his territorial claims—his wife Fulvia is said to have been bribed (Cicero, *Att.* 14, 12, 1). Deiotaros thanked him by immediately switching his allegiance to the side of Caesar's murderers; but when the latter were defeated at Philippi in 42 BCE, he once again went over to the victors. He died peacefully in bed in 40 BCE.

Under Caesar's Murderers and Mark Antony

The fleeing murderers of Caesar, Brutus and Cassius, sought in the East a platform from which to conquer Italy. What the defeated Pompey had already envisaged before he turned toward Alexandria, these two now tried to achieve: an alliance with the Parthians. Cassius sent to the Arsakid court Quintus Labienus, the son of Caesar's legate who had gone over to Pompey and had ultimately fallen in battle against the dictator near Munda.

Everything in Asia Minor was going haywire. Partisans of the conspirators ruled in the provinces of Pontus and Bithynia in northern Asia Minor—first the proconsul Marcius Crispus, followed by Lucius Tillius Cimber. Brutus had fitted out a fleet in Nikomedeia and Kyzikos and marched into Ionia. Asia was given as governor a proconsul who had already been appointed by Caesar, but who belonged to the group of conspirators and provided resources for Caesar's murderers as soon as he arrived there: Gaius Trebonius. However, in the same year he was executed in Smyrna by Publius Cornelius Dolabella, who was on the way to his province of Syria. After Dolabella went on to Syria, where Cassius fought against him, Trebonius's quaestor, Publius Cornelius Lentulus Spinther, took over the governorship. The province of Asia suffered, as it already had under Sulla: it had to pay ten years' tribute in advance. Brutus and Cassius, who were anything but hand in glove when they met in Smyrna and Sardeis, shared the task of militarily subjecting the southwest coast of Asia Minor, and especially the free states of Rhodes and the Lycian League, which were so important for the control of the seaways, and whose support Caesar had also sought in the civil war after Pharsalos and in the *Bellum Alexandrinum*. It is hardly surprising that they were not received with open arms. Cassius took Rhodes after a short siege. When a few people in the city addressed him as "lord" and "king," he replied sarcastically: " Neither lord nor king, but chastiser and slayer of your lord and king!" (Plutarch, *Brut.* 30, 3; trans. Perrin). He had the Rhodians pay out of the community treasury a sum of 8,000 talents plus a 500-talent punitive fine. Meanwhile, Brutus undertook to break the Lycians' resistance. The correspondence between him and the Kaunians and Lycians that has come down to us has been declared—not necessarily convincingly—at least partly inauthentic.[207] The Lycians were supposed to have preserved in Kaunos old siege machinery, and Brutus demanded it for use in the battle against Rhodes. Kaunos declared its loyalty, but regretted that it could not provide any material help, and thus was the object of threats. Plutarch (*Brut.* 31, 7) gives a colorful description of the fate of Xanthos, no doubt inspired by Herodotus's report (1, 176) of the Xanthians' collective suicide during Harpagos's attack. Their descendants, contrary to the besiegers' will, set fire to their city and put women, children, and themselves to death. On the other hand, Patara opened its gates to Brutus. Caesar's murderers—specifically, Cassius—also soon gained access to the provinces in the southeast. It seems that Lucius Statius Murcus, after declaring himself for the conspirators while still in Rome (Appian, *BC* 2, 17, 119), took over the province of Syria. His successor Dolabella was besieged by Cassius in Laodikeia (Lattakia) and committed suicide. Cassius accepted an *imperium maius*, in which Cilicia was probably also included. The last known governor of the province of Cilicia created by Pompey was Lucius Volcatius Tullus, in 45 BCE, still under Caesar; according to the historian Ronald Syme, the province ceased to exist and was restored only under Vespasian.[208] The continued use of the eras starting from the years of Pompey's organization (p. 289), however, suggests that the cities in the Cilician plain at least were not subjected to a new dynastic dominion, for if this were the case, one would expect new eras referring to a further, more recent liberation as a starting point for counting their years.

The decisive event that led to the deaths of both Caesar's murderers at the battle of Philippi in Thrace in 42 BCE marks a turning point for Asia Minor as well. For almost a decade the Orient was to be ruled by Caesar's former cavalry officer, Mark Antony, the triumvir and victor of Philippi. He moved away from the provincial regulations and clienteles that had been founded by Pompey and wove for himself a network of relationships with numerous regional and local dynasts that was entirely centered on his person. They provided him with military service under his personal command or under that of his numerous legates and prefects, who operated in various theaters of the Orient, on water and on land, and also went on diplomatic missions. These included, for example, Decidius Saxa, who was killed by the Parthians in Cilicia, Ventidius Bassus, who defeated the Parthians, the historian Quintus Dellius, and Marcus Titius. The last besieged Sextus Pompeius, who had been defeated at Naulochos and fled to Asia Minor, took him prisoner, had him executed in Miletus, and put his army in the service of Mark Antony. Many others are also known to us from coins and inscriptions in Asia Minor, such as the *quaestor pro praetore* Marcus Barbatius Pollio; the *legatus pro praetore* Fonteius Capito; and the fleet prefects Lucius Caninius Gallus, Lucius Sempronius Atratinus, Marcus Oppius Capito, Lucius Bibulus, and Marcus Aeficius Calvinus.[209] Before describing this network in greater detail, I must briefly outline the historical context of Antony's activities in the East, with special attention to Asia Minor. He had two basic goals: one was to carry out a planned campaign against the Parthians, and the other was to develop and assert his oriental dominion in the looming conflict with the young Octavian, the great-nephew and heir of the murdered Caesar.

Antony first trod Asian soil after the battle at Philippi, initially in Bithynia in the spring of 41 BCE. Herod, the later king of the Jews, hastened there to justify himself. In Ephesos, Antony gave the speech to the delegations of the Asiatic *poleis* in which he demanded—how could it be otherwise?—ten years' tribute from them. After the Greeks had fallen at his feet, moaning and complaining, he eased that demand only a little, even though, as he wrote to Hyrkanos (Josephos, *AJ* 14, 312), it would ulti-mately be up to him to put the diseased body of Asia on its feet again. It didn't help to celebrate him as the "god" Dionysos. Even kings, dynasts, and free cities had to pay. However, in recognition of the position the Lycians had taken with respect to Brutus, he completely exempted them from tribute and took an interest in the re-construction of Xanthos.

After making the rounds of Phrygia, Mysia, Galatia, and Cappadocia, he went down to the Cilician plain, where he awaited the arrival of the queen of Egypt. He had instructed his legate, Quintus Dellius, to summon her to this meeting. The little city of Tarsos has perhaps never seen such a festivity—with the possible exception of a boozy archaeological conference in 1998—like the one that accompanied the ar-rival of Queen Cleopatra VII in 41 BCE. Antony was holding court in the city cen-ter when all at once everyone ran off and left him sitting there. Coming up the Kyd-nos River was a boat with a gilt poopdeck and crimson sails; its silver-plated oars struck the water in time with the music of flutes, drums, harps, and lutes. The queen, dressed as Aphrodite, lay lasciviously in the shade of a canopy, surrounded by boys cooling her with fans. The whole scene was enveloped in a cloud of exotic perfumes. The people ran along both banks of the river, some following the boat upstream, oth-ers streaming out of the city to meet it.

The story of Antony and Cleopatra's love, so often told (and filmed), began here and ended with their death in Alexandria after the Battle of Actium in 31 BCE. Antony boarded her ship with her in Tarsos and spent the autumn and winter of 41/40 in her capital city on the Nile, while the Parthians, under Labienus and the king's son Pakoros, began a major attack on Syria. When the news arrived that Labi-enus had invaded Asia Minor and advanced as far as Caria, Lydia, and Ionia, Antony sailed to Tyros. But when he learned that his wife Fulvia and his brother Lucius were under siege by Octavian in Perusia, he broke off his preparations for war and hurried back to Italy via Athens. Reconciled with Octavian, he was assigned, by the Treaty of Brundisium, the eastern provinces and the task of leading the war against the Parthians.

This plan went back to Caesar, who had already intended to depart for the Orient on March 18, 44 BCE. Antony now sent the legate Ventidius Bassus to Asia on ahead of him. This capable officer defeated the Parthians at the Cilician Gates, on the Amanos, and near Gindaros in Syria (38 BCE) and drove them out of Anatolia;

55. Antiochos I of Commagene shaking hands with Herakles-Artagnes. Relief at the ancient site of Arsameia on the river Nymphaios.

they were never again to penetrate so far into the Roman Empire. Labienus and Pakoros were killed. Antony passed the winter of 39/38 BCE in Athens and then set out for Asia again. He met his legate near Samosata on the Euphrates, where he was besieging King Antiochos of Commagene, who had sided with the Parthians and taken in their refugees (Dio 49, 20 ff.).

The situation of the kingdom on the Euphrates, like that of the many small principalities in the area of northern Syria and Mesopotamia, was exposed to direct Parthian pressure. Antiochos also had family connections with the Arsakid royal house; his daughter was married to Orodes II, who was at that time still on the throne. Thus the fidelity to Rome he had sworn first to Pompey and then to Cicero had not lasted long. Now he found himself in an extremely dangerous position, from which he tried to extricate himself by offering to pay large sums of money. On the Roman side, a pretender to the throne stood ready. But an agreement was made, probably also because Antony did not have time for a long siege: in return for a payment of 300 talents, the dynast was guaranteed peace. Ventidius was allowed go home and celebrate a triumph over the Parthians. In his inscriptions in Commagene Antiochos himself refers to "struggles" and "great dangers" and had himself represented on various reliefs shaking hands (*dexiosis*) with a god, to show that the helping hand of the gods allowed him to survive all dangers and struggles (*agones*) (Figure 55).[210] This very probably referred primarily to his survival of the siege laid to the city by Ventidius and Antony.

The real Parthian campaign, which Antony himself was leading, took place only in 36 BCE, after another stay in Italy. Modern scholars are uncertain regarding the strategic goals of the enterprise, which we know in detail from an eye-witness report by Quintus Dellius used by Plutarch. Even in the later history of Rome we find hardly any other campaign of such dimensions. Apparently adopting Caesar's plan to attack the Parthians in the north, from Armenia (instead of through flat Mesopotamia, as Crassus had), in 37 BCE Antony had already sent Publius Canidius Crassus to the Caucasus to gain the support of the kings of Iberia and Albania. At first, encouraged by the turncoat Monaises, Antony marched up the middle of the Euphrates Valley, but then spontaneously accepted King Artavasdes of Armenia's invitation to join in a common attack on the neighboring realm of the king of Media. With no less than sixteen legions and additional auxiliary troops, Antony proceeded at top speed up the Euphrates through the eastern Anatolian highlands. Hurrying on ahead of one part of his army that was moving more slowly because it was transporting siege equipment, he attacked the Median fortress of Phraata east of Lake Urmia. What was his goal? Was the advance from the north through Media Atropatene supposed to continue as far as the Parthians' heartland?[211] The Romans suffered a fiasco almost as disastrous as the one that had befallen Crassus in 53 BCE. The fortress of Phraata stood firm, and the legions in Antony's rear were routed; Artavasdes the Armenian had betrayed him. During the 3,000-kilometer retreat, more than a third of the whole army perished: over 1,000 legionnaires died of hunger, exhaustion, and cold, and 20,000 died in attritional battles. With the exception of Cannae, these were the greatest losses cited by ancient writers for any Roman army.

A second campaign to eastern Anatolia in 34 BCE took revenge on Artavasdes, whom Antony finally took back to Alexandria in chains and there displayed him in a triumphal procession. The following year he went with Cleopatra to Ephesos, where his forces were assembled for the war with the western empire; auxiliary troops, relief supplies, and gifts from vassals all over the Orient were received there. Finally, on the island of Samos, he married Queen Cleopatra, who had in the interim borne him two children. In Ephesos he received two officials of the association of victors in games, who asked him to exempt its members from the burdens of military duty, billeting, and other service obligations imposed on ordinary citizens, and to guarantee them protection and other privileges; he granted these requests. Before leaving Asia Minor he gave the actors' guild (*Dionysostechnitai*) Priene as its main residence.

Pompey's organization of northern Asia Minor was particularly affected by the changes in territorial domains in Anatolia that go back to Antony's rule.[212] Not even Bithynia remained intact. Antony gave the city of Prusias on the Sea to a granddaughter of Mithridates Eupator, who minted coins there as "Queen Muse." The part of the city of Herakleia Pontike that was inhabited by the Greeks he gave to the

Galatian Adiatorix, and allegedly even allowed the latter shortly afterward to attack the Roman colony in the immediate neighborhood and murder the Italics. The valley of the Amnias and to the east the Phazemonitis, areas of inner Paphlagonia, where the *poleis* founded as Pompeiopolis and Neapolis were located and which Pompey had included in the province of Pontus, he gave to the dynast Kastor II, who lost it to Deiotaros Philadelphos in the 30s BCE. The triumvir also forwent a Roman administration of the heartland of the former Pontic kingdom, including Pompey's new *poleis*. He returned Zela to its status as a temple-state. A certain Ateporix received part of the territory of the former city of Megalopolis on the upper Halys River. The rest of the interior of Pontos, and possibly also Amisos on the coast, he assigned to Mithridates's grandson Dareios. The Roman province of Pontus was thus *de facto* obliterated. Only a narrow strip running east along the coast as far as the Halys was added to the still-existing provincial territory of Bithynia, over which Antony made Gnaeus Domitius Ahenobarbus governor. The latter's rule lasted several years, and the Roman *gens*-name of a series of Domitii among later provincials seems to go back to him.

When in 37/36 Dareios fell into disfavor with the triumvir, the latter gave his Pontic possessions and also Lesser Armenia to a Greek named Polemon, the son of the rhetorician Zenon, from Laodikeia on the Lykos. This man's family background is interesting: he was married to Pythodoris, the daughter of Pythodoros of Tralleis and his wife Antonia, whom Theodor Mommsen regarded, probably incorrectly, as Mark Antony's daughter.[213] And this Pythodoros, Polemon's father-in-law, seems in all likelihood to be no other than the son or grandson of Chairemon, son of Pythodoros of Nysa, whom I have already mentioned, while discussing Mithridates' attack on the Roman province of Asia in 89 BCE, as a friend of the beset Romans (p. 272 f.). For Antony, Polemon had already distinguished himself in Ventidius Bassus's war against the Parthians, and Ikonion and part of Cilicia were given to him as a reward, even before he was made ruler of Pontos. This Greek from a provincial, Roman-friendly urban elite had no relation whatever with the Pontic royal family of the Mithridatids or any other royal or noble family in the Anatolian client-kingdoms. It may have been for precisely that reason that his reign stood the test of time. Along with his wife Pythodoris, who succeeded him as regent, he founded a reliable dynasty at the forefront of the Roman provinces in Anatolia that endured almost exactly a century (see the Appendix). Since Polemon's case was not unique, it might be asked whether there was method in Antony's choice of a ruler foreign to the country, instead of allowing merely accidental personal friendships and sympathies to come into play. In Cappadocia, when in the wake of preparations for war against Caesar's supporters it was a question of mobilizing the client-princes, Caesar's assassin Cassius had Ariobarzanes III Philorhomaios murdered. Thereupon the younger Ariarathes seized the throne in Mazaka. But Antony once again favored over him a man who stood outside the royal family and the country, Archelaos Sisinnes. The latter was the son of the priest of Komana in Pontos whom Caesar had deposed, and he was made king in 37/36.

Table 1. Mark Antony's Vassalages

Territory	Vassal
Prusias	Muse
Herakleia	Adiatorix
Inner Paphlagonia	Kastor, Deiotaros Philadelphos
Pontos	Dareios, Polemon
Galatia Pamphylia	Kastor, Amyntas
Cappadocia	Ariarathes, Archelaos Sisinnes
Lesser Armenia	Polemon
Cilicia	Cleopatra, Tarkondimotos
Cyprus	Kleopatra

After Deiotaros's death (40 BCE), his grandson Kastor continued to reign for a while in Galatia, and following him, here too a foreigner to the country, Amyntas, received dominion over the whole kingdom—probably at the same time as Archelaos received Cappadocia and Deiotaros Philadelphos was made ruler of Paphlagonia. This former secretary to Deiotaros—he had defected to Antony's side shortly before the Battle of Philippi—was from the Phrygian-Pisidian border area of the province of Asia and had been installed as king of Pisidia by Antony in 39 BCE (Strabo, 12, 6, 3; Appian, *BC* 5, 8, 75). He had to fight for recognition in the rebellious mountain country and was supported in this by the Termessians.[214] In addition to the Galatian tribal area (in which he was officially called not "king" but "tetrarch"), he was now to have parts of Lycaonia and, with the eastern part of the Pamphylian alluvial plain, including the cities of Aspendos and Side, a territory that had previously been under Roman administration (Dio 49, 32, 3). This strip of land stretching across central Anatolia as a coherent dominion anticipated a Roman provincial formation of the Imperial period largely coextensive with it: the Roman province of Galatia (see p. 320 and Map 14).

Antony cut out from Cilicia other areas for his vassals, first and foremost the heavily wooded slopes of the Taurus in Rough Cilicia, which he assigned as a reservoir to provide ship-building wood for the queen of Egypt. At this point at the latest, Cleopatra received from him (if she had not already taken it from Caesar) the island of Cyprus, which under her ancestors had been a traditional Ptolemaic area.[215] He made the previously mentioned dynast, Tarkondimotos of Hierapolis-Kastabala, king over a domain in East Cilicia that cannot be precisely defined. In addition to Anazarbos in the interior, Tarkondimotos may have also held the cities of Elaiussa and Korykos at the coast further west, which his son lost under Augustus.[216] Coins identify him by the title *basileus Tarkondimotos philantonios*. What now remained of the province organized by Pompey thirty years earlier was under the control of the governor of Syria—between 38 and 36 BCE that governor was Gaius Sosius (Dio, 49, 22, 3).[217] After the second campaign against the Parthians in 34 BCE, Antony is supposed to have allotted Armenia, Media, and Parthia to his son Alexandros by

Cleopatra, but Phoenicia, Syria, and Cilicia to Ptolemaios (Plutarch, *Ant.* 54, 4) (Table 1).

The war and post-war propaganda of the victor at Actium imprinted the stigma of an un-Roman monarchy on this delicate organization of vassal kingdoms, representing Antony as a weakling who left this dominion wholly in the hands of a woman. However, on closer inspection it can be seen as the sole attempt made by a Roman after Pompey to put the whole region in a carefully thought out order on principles guided by the necessities of current tasks, to be sure, but also by the long-term structures of Hellenistic rule. The British historian of the Roman revolution, Ronald Syme, has offered a positive assessment: "Antonius, wise and courageous in his generosity, gave over to the vassals of Rome many regions that were difficult to police or unproductive to exploit."[218] It was not, however, the model for the future. Pompey's urbanization, which the historian Buchheim wrongly sees as a failure in his study on Antony's eastern policy, survived.

In 31 BCE the decisive battle with the young Caesar loomed on the horizon. As it once had at Magnesia on the Sipylos, the East marched against the West in Greece; and this was to be the last such advance for a long time. From Asia Minor, the kings Tarkondimotos of Cilicia, Archelaos of Cappadocia, Deiotaros Philadelphos of Paphlagonia, and Mithridates (the son of Antiochos) of Commagene were present in Antony's army; Polemon of Pontos and Lesser Armenia and Amyntas of Galatia had sent troop contingents. Amyntas and Deiotaros went over to Octavian before the battle. The West won, and the East was no longer able to counterpose against the victor any strong kingdom that could have challenged it.

Modern historical writing sees the outcome of the Battle of Actium as marking the end of the Hellenistic period. It is true that for Asia Minor as a whole, this event constitutes a break, since the repeated attacks of the foreign armies and fleets of the Persians, Greeks, Macedonians, and Romans that had gone on for centuries came to an end, and the perpetual struggles for a share of the peninsula died down. In the existing and new provinces the juridification of Roman power spread and established frameworks and limits for the peoples and communities there that also influenced their internal structure. But in essence what in the Hellenistic period had begun developed further: the Hellenization of Anatolia. "Greece is one, but its cities are several," said the comic dramatist Poseidippos of Kassandreia.[219] The homogeneity of the universal Greek model of the autonomous *polis* seems, paradoxically, to be opposed to the increasing parceling into *polis* territories. Despite all their differences, people were fixated on this in all decisionmaking, in Toriaion as in Ephesos, in Lycian Tyberissos as in Paphlagonian Pompeiopolis.[220] The model benefited even more broadly from the West's victory at Actium than it had before. The long-since successful convergence in a unified political culture eased the incorporation of Anatolia and other parts of the Middle East into the Roman Empire.

CHAPTER 7

Imperium Romanum: The Provinces
from Augustus to Aurelian

Before discussing the Imperial period, I must first add a few remarks about the sources that supplement those presented at the beginning of Chapter 6. The country, its inhabitants, and the political, cultural, and economic conditions under the emperors are referred to in a multitude of statements in the Greek and Latin poetry and prose of writers of the Imperial, Late Antique, and Byzantine periods, and to a lesser extent in works by Syrian and Arab writers as well. Although they were written in the early years of the empire, Books 11–14 of Strabo's *Geographica* provide not only the sole coherent geography but also the bases for understanding conditions in the region of Asia Minor during the Imperial period.[1]

Additional materials are found in the works of scientific writers and scholars, such as Pliny the Elder, Galen, and Athenaios, also Plutarch and Pausanias. Our knowledge of spatial and political geography and topography is gained from the lists of cities in Pliny the Elder's *Naturalis historia*, the descriptions of the coastal areas, such as Arrian's *Periplus Ponti Euxini* and Claudius Ptolemaios's *Geography*, the materials on places and people collected in Stephanos of Byzantion's *Ethnica*, information about places given by other early and middle-era Byzantine and Arab writers, and finally the "itineraries" (late-Antique route descriptions), the *Itinerarium provinciarum Antonini Augusti* (originally from the time of Caracalla), the *Itinerarium Burdigalense* (a description of a pilgrimage from Bordeaux to Jerusalem and back, 333 CE), as well as the *Tabula Peutingeriana*, a road map of the Roman Empire named after Konrad Peutinger, the Augsburg town clerk (1465–1547), the only one of its kind extant.

Book 10 of Pliny the Younger's collection of letters should be mentioned as an unusual, indeed unique, document for provincial history.[2] Pliny the Younger was a senator from Comum and served as governor of the province of Pontus-Bithynia under Trajan (98–117). In only two years he wrote sixty-one letters to the emperor and received forty-eight replies. These deal with particular decisions that were to be made by the governor, but regarding which he nonetheless wanted the emperor's opinion. Unlike Cicero's letters from the province of Asia, they constitute official documents. The sophist and rhetorician Dion of Prusa (ca. 40–120 CE), who was later given the byname Chrysostomos ("Golden-mouth"), discusses municipal matters as well. In addition to smaller works and fragments, eighty speeches bearing his name are extant, including fourteen (38–51) on affairs in the cities of Bithynia—

Prusa, Nikomedeia, Nikaia, and Apameia—in which he was himself partly involved, as well as in Kelainai and Tarsos.[3] The fifty-five speeches of his later colleague, the sophist and "concert orator" Aelius Aristeides, from Hadrianoi in Mysia (ca. 117–187 CE), contain an ample treasury of contemporary impressions from western Asia Minor in the Imperial period. The Syrian writer Lucian of Samosata lived in the age of the Antonines (138–192); his wide-ranging works provide satirical glimpses—occasionally making a mockery—of the religion, philosophy, sophistics, and rhetoric of the time. Like Dion, Aristeides, and Lucian, in his lives of the sophists written in the third century CE Philostratos records not only a chapter of intellectual history but also touches on many aspects of daily life in the provinces.

In contrast, historical writing dealing with the whole period remains marginal, especially since in times of peace there is little to recount from large parts of the area. These works contain more or less detailed reports on Asia Minor as the scene of events in the conflict between Rome and Persia and in the war of the pretenders to the imperial throne, and little on the invasions by northern peoples and by the Palmyrenes in the third century. The most prominent of these works is the history of Rome written by a writer from Asia Minor, Cassius Dio, a senator from Nikaia in Bithynia. Of its eighty books, which recount events up to the year 229 CE (the year of his second [ordinary] consulate), the fifty-second begins with the age of the Principate, and thus with the rule of Augustus (27 BCE to 14 CE). He is the only contemporary historian whose work guides modern historical scholarship more or less continuously through the history of provincialization of Anatolia. Although the majority of these books have come down to us in an abbreviated and fragmentary form, some of the gaps are filled by the epitomes given by Johannes Xiphilinos (eleventh century CE). Tacitus's main extant works repeatedly refer to Anatolia and focus on Roman magistrates, client-kings, provinces, and military history; the books of the *Annals* (1–4, beginning of 5, 6, 11–16) go as far as Nero (37–68); the extant part of the *Histories* reaches from the year of the four emperors (69 CE) to 70 CE.

Only scattered details are provided by the Roman history of Velleius Paterculus (first century) regarding the period up to 30 CE, that of Eutropius (fourth century) for the period ending with the death of Jovian in 364 CE, and the eight books of Herodian's history of the emperors (third century) on the period from the death of Marcus Aurelius to Gordian III (180–238 CE). The same is true for the accounts of the Lives of the Caesars, beginning with those of Suetonius, which deal with Julius Caesar and all the emperors down to Domitian, followed by the biographies of the so-called *Historia Augusta* (which, however, has gaps) on the period from Hadrian to Numerianus (117–285 CE), and finally the short biographies of the emperors by Sextus Aurelius Victor (fourth century), from Augustus to Theodosius. *The Jewish War* and *Jewish Antiquities* by Flavius Josephos (from 37/38 to after 100 CE) are occasionally informative on conditions and events in Anatolia in the Julio-Claudian and Flavian periods.

The time of crisis in late Antiquity is reflected in historical works by Byzantine authors. The *Historia Nova* by the court officer and staunch pagan Zosimos (com-

56. Ivory relief from the terrace houses of Ephesos. Selçuk Museum.

posed ca. 500 CE) deals with the time from Augustus to shortly before Alaric's sack of Rome in 410; the general history of the monk Georgios Synkellos (ninth century) goes as far as Diocletian; and the general chronicle of the official and monk Zonaras (twelfth century) continues up to his own time.

On the rise of Christianity and its consequences in Asia Minor, Eusebius of Caesarea's *Ecclesiastical History* (written in the age of Constantine the Great) contains wide-ranging material, supplemented by the extant writings of other Christian authors, and in particular Tertullian (ca. 160–after 220); Lactantius's *De Mortibus Persecutorum* ("On the Deaths of the Persecutors"), written ca. 313–316; the *Martyrium Pionii* (p. 539); the correspondence of the Carthaginian Cyprian; and a letter of Gregory Thaumaturgus (p. 357). From the fourth century on, Christian writing becomes much more voluminous and offers numerous descriptions of the lives of local martyrs and saints (with valuable material on historical reality, especially geography and topography), tractates, hymns, and the like. With the Church Fathers known as the "three great Cappadocians"—Basileios of Caesarea, Gregory of Nazianzus, and Gregory of Nyssa—Asia Minor contributed three monuments to the history of Christian literature.

Here we cannot examine in detail the archaeological sources on the Imperial period (see Figure 56); the construction boom that occurred during this period is discussed later on (p. 437). Modern excavations and surveys, notably those conducted in western and southern Asia Minor, have uncovered a material heritage of Antiquity, most of which proceeds from the Roman Imperial period. This is especially true for monumental stone architecture. The only cities comparable in that respect to Ephesos, Aphrodisias, Sagalassos, Hierapolis, and Perge in other provinces are a few North African or Syrian cities. In Turkey in particular there are many middle-sized and small complexes of ruins from the Roman period that testify to the lavish facilities in second-tier, even humble towns. Asia Minor has also preserved unsurpassable testimonies to the art of sculpture in stone, both freestanding and in relief: this art proves that in the time of the Principate, the people's prosperity extended even into rural regions, and it is a source for the study of provincial society, its ways of life, views, and ways of thinking.

We have already discussed the wealth of inscriptions on stone (see the start of Chapter 6). The Imperial period is initially not inferior in this respect to the Hellenistic period, and with the age of Hadrian the number of such inscriptions reached its highest sustained level. Around the middle of the third century the inscriptions become less numerous and poorer, with regard to both the quality of their craftsmanship and their content. After another increase in the first half of the fourth century, they steadily decline in every respect. They do not completely disappear in the Byzantine period, but we can no longer speak of an "epigraphic habit."

The high point of civic coinage in Asia Minor was attained during the Principate.[4] We will look into the economic aspects of the monetary economy in Chapter 9. The types of coins and the legends on them offer a source of information—still unexhausted—on a broad range of subjects: gods and heroes, the founders of cities, local myths and festivals, representations of structures, names of communities, proper names, and dates of eras, along with geography and topography, political titles, and ideals. The image programs are representative of the civic pride,[5] religion, and public propaganda of a *polis*, as well as the elites' scholarship and understanding of history. These programs communicate with those of their neighbors, tell us something about the friendly relationships, rivalries, or even enmities between cities while at the same time vividly portraying the provincial inhabitants' identification with the emperor and the Roman Empire.[6] The resultant evidence illustrates, from point to point, from city to city, and often over long periods of time, aspects of ancient life in the provinces. And in them lies—precisely because of the large quantity of relatively evenly distributed "miniatures"—a potential testimony that writers and inscriptions cannot offer in such density.[7] Here I should mention a claim made by the historian and numismatist Konrad Kraft,[8] which, if it is correct, seems to strictly limit the individual cities' freedom of design in this respect. According to him, the types of coins in the Imperial period were determined less by the individual creative will of individual communities (or of their officials) than by specialized workshops that used their stocks of types to serve several different cities at the same time.[9]

✦ ✦ ✦

In the first three centuries after the Battle of Actium (31 BCE), Asia Minor passed through a time of peace that was disturbed only in a few places and for short periods.

I report phenomena that suggest a prosperity unparalleled in the subsequent pre-modern history of the area. This claim is, like most blanket judgments, not uncontroversial; there are researchers who emphasize the existence of hunger, poverty, exploitation, and forced labor, especially in rural Anatolia. These cannot be disregarded, but I believe that they are not characteristic of the area as a whole.

The history of events is determined primarily by the antagonism between the two great empires of the Occident and the Orient, the Roman Empire and the Arsakid or Sasanid Empires, whose respective peripheries collided in eastern Anatolia and Syria. As a result of this antagonism, the border region between Trapezus and the upper reaches of the Tigris gradually developed into a heavily occupied and fortified military border, the "Anatolian *limes*." The heaviest fighting in Asia Minor took place during Nero's reign, under the commands of Caesennius Paetus and Domitius Corbulo. In the Parthian Wars waged by the emperors Trajan and Lucius Verus (161–166 CE), eastern Anatolia also suffered from the military actions conducted under the commands of M. Sedatius Severianus and M. Statius Priscus. It should be noted that in these wars the whole peninsula became a conduit for large troop movements from west to east and from east to west. The civil war between Pescennius Niger and Septimius Severus (196–211) over the emperor's throne was fought on the Bosporus, in Bithynia, and in Cilicia before it ended in northern Syria. Further hard fighting struck Asia Minor in the third century with the invasions of the Goths and Sasanids.

The New Beginning under Augustus

In 9 BCE a gubernatorial edict introduced in the province of Asia the official Asian calendar, according to which the year began on Augustus's birthday, September 23.[10] The first month was to bear the name of Caesar, and in the numbering of their days all the months were to be adapted to and synchronized with the Roman calendar. The Bithynian cities also adopted the Roman calendar. However, it was not adopted everywhere; large cities such as Miletus, which led the way by adding Augustus to the list of *stephanephoroi*,[11] and also Ephesos and Smyrna in Asia, continued to use their respective old calendars. Amaseia in Pontos changed its calendar by introducing into it the new month-names of Agrippeios and Sebastos.

To express their loyalty, the communities had from the outset made use of traditional means; these gestures were not made all at once everywhere, even though Augustus's sojourn in Asia during the summer of 20 BCE provided an additional opportunity for them. Throughout Asia Minor, coinage, decrees, and statues, the names of cities, phylae, and months, festivals and ceremonies, cults, and eras reflect the beginning of a new age. In the early Principate a cult of the ruler grew up in Asia. The religious veneration of the ruler and benefactor was, however, nothing new in Anatolia. Not only had shrines to the goddess Roma long existed in several places, but cults of living Romans were also practiced in earlier times. Thus in Pergamon a priesthood for Manius Aquillius was created (IGR IV 292.293), and in Ephesos the cult of Roma was combined with the veneration of Publius Servilius Isauricus. This cult of the individual even continued, alongside the additional cult of the emperor, into the age of the first princeps, in which cults of governors such as M. Vinicius, Fabius Maximus, and Marcius Censorinus have been proven.[12]

In 29 BCE Octavian gave permission to establish a *temenos* (sacred precinct) for the goddess Roma and the heroized Julius Caesar in Nikaia and in Ephesos, and he instructed the Italics resident there to take part in their veneration. In accord with the requests of the Greeks organized in the *koina* (commonalties) of both provinces, Pontus-Bithynia and Asia, he allowed the provincials to found shrines to himself in Nikomedeia and Pergamon (Dio 51, 20, 7). In another place, fourteen years later, the remarkable separation between the shrines of the *Rhomaioi* resident in Asia Minor and those of the Asians no longer appears: on March 6 of the year 3 BCE, inhabitants of Paphlagonia and Romans dwelling in the country gathered in Gangra to solemnly swear a common oath of loyalty to Augustus:

> I swear by Zeus, the Earth, the Sun, all the gods and goddesses and by the Augustus himself that I will be loyal towards Caesar Augustus and his children and descendants throughout [my life] in word, deed and intention, regarding as friends those whom they might regard as friends and considering as enemies those whom they might judge to be enemies. And for the furtherance of their interests I will spare neither body, nor soul, nor life, nor children, but by any means defending what befits them will take any risk necessary. Whatever I might perceive or hear being said, planned or done against them, I will disclose, and I will be an adversary of anyone who says, plans or does any of this. And those they themselves judge to be enemies, on land and at sea I will pursue them and retaliate with weapons and with an iron fist. If I should do anything against this oath or not precisely as I have sworn, I myself shall call down upon myself, my own body, soul and life, my children, all of my family and my possessions, destruction and utter ruin extending to all those that succeed me and all my descendants. And the land and the sea shall neither receive the bodies of my family or my descendants, nor shall they bear them fruit. ([106] OGIS 532; trans. Marek)

This oath of loyalty to the emperor was sworn not only here but also in the other cities of the recently established province of Paphlagonia, at the altars of the *Sebasteia* (shrines to the Augustus).[13] Solemn vows (*vota sollemnia*) continued to be a ceremony regularly celebrated at the beginning of the year, under the leadership of the governor and with the participation of *commilitones cum provincialibus* (soldiers and civilians; Pliny the Younger, *ep.* 10, 100).

The cult of the emperor provided provincials with an occasion for erecting temples. According to the lists of the donations and services of the imperial priests in the province of Galatia under Tiberius (14–37 CE) that were engraved on its *antae*, the temple dedicated to the divine (*divus*) Augustus and the goddess Roma still standing in Ankara was called the *Sebasteion*. The building seems to date from the Augustan age (Figure 57).[14] After Augustus's death a copy of the *res gestae*, a record of the first princeps's deeds, was engraved on its wall, probably at the behest of a governor; the

57. Monumentum Ancyranum: the temple of Roma and Augustus in the Ankara city center (at right, next to the minaret).

original was written on a bronze pillar in the mausoleum of Augustus in Rome.[15] In Pisidia, for which the same governor was responsible, additional fragments of this text were found in the nineteenth and first half of the twentieth centuries in Apollonia (a broken base with statues of Augustus and his family) and in Antiocheia (the ruins of a gate through which the temple precinct was entered). The *Sebasteion* in Aphrodisias in Caria was not built until the period of Tiberius and Nero. But the imposing, three-story halls with statues of the gods and the emperors between the columns of their façades, and mythical scenes and representations of peoples (especially of the barbarians who lived on the margins of the empire) epitomize the new world power of the princeps in the sites of his veneration in association with the Julian city goddess and ancestress, Aphrodite. On Lesbos, statues representing Augustus's daughter Julia as Venus Genetrix were erected (IGR IV 9); these may be compared with the statues on Samos of M. Livius Drusus and Alfidia, the parents of Augustus's wife Livia, who was herself venerated as a goddess.[16]

In addition to the practice of eras based on the date of the acquisition of freedom, in Cilicia (Anazarbos), Paphlagonia, and Pontus, the practice of numbering years from the victory at Actium (September 2, 31 BCE), which was for the most part introduced retroactively a few years after this event, spread in the cities of the province of Asia.[17] A whole series of cities were named after Caesar Augustus, and not only ones that were constituted as *poleis* in the time of his reign, as, for example, all three of the main cities in the Galatian tribal area: Sebastenoi Tolistobogioi Pessinuntioi, Sebastenoi Tektosagoi Ankyranoi, and Sebastenoi Trokmoi Tavianoi. Tralleis in the province of Asia and Anazarbos in Cilicia were allowed to take the name of Kaisareia. A town called Sebaste was established in Phrygia and another called Kaisareia (later Germanike) in extreme southwest Bithynia. And not far away in the mountains that separate eastern Bithynia from the Tembris valley was Juliopolis, which the robber chieftain Kleon founded on the site of his native village. A community in western Paphlagonia took the name of Kaisareis *Proseilemmenitai* ("the added"); the inhabitants of the Karanitis region in Pontos celebrated their city's *polis* status under the name Sebastopolis, while the capital of the neighboring dynasty— once raised by Pompey to Diospolis—was now renamed Sebaste, and still farther east, Pompey's Megalopolis was renamed Sebasteia (today Sivas). Similarly, the royal residence of Archelaos I Philopatris Ktistes in Elaiussa, Cilicia (Strabo 12, 2, 7; 14, 5, 6) was named Sebaste. A rarity is Liviopolis, a little city on the Pontic coast of the Black Sea between Kerasus/Pharnakeia and Trapezus, which may have been named after Augustus's wife Livia (Pliny the Elder, *nat.* 6, 4, 11).[18] The new imperial city names are not typical of Asia Minor alone, but were widespread, especially in the East. Names of phylae, such as Sebaste, Sebastene, and Sebasteis, also appeared—for instance in Ephesos; in Nysa, Laodikeia Katakekaumene, Kyzikos, and Dorylaion; in Prusias, Nikaia, Bithynion, Amisos, Ankyra, Pessinus, and Vasada.[19]

This sort of thing was not imposed from on high: the turn toward peace and order elicited gratitude and devotion all over the country. The decision made by the "Hellenes in Asia"[20] to introduce the calendar put into words what looking back on two decades of the Principate had pounded into them:

> Since Providence, which has divinely disposed our lives, having employed zeal and ardor, has arranged the most perfect (culmination) for life by producing Augustus, whom for the benefit of mankind she has filled with excellence, as if [she had granted him as a savior] for us and our descendants, (a savior) who brought war to an end and set [all things] in order; [and (since) with his appearance] Caesar exceeded the hopes of [all] those who had received [glad tidings] before us, not only surpassing those who had been [benefactors] before him, but not even [leaving any] hope [of surpassing him] for those who are to come in the future.[21]

The forty-four years of Octavian/Augustus's autocracy had brought significant changes in the regional organization of Asia. They began by following the paths Antony had laid out. After Actium, Octavian was confronted by a part of the Roman Empire that he himself had never seen, and in which—even in lower positions than those of high authority and leadership that we discuss in a moment—a dense net of clienteles woven by the two generals of the East, Pompey and Antony, remained intact. High-ranking Romans with experience in the East were available, including individuals who had received or inherited from their fathers patronage over communities in Asia Minor.

Antony's system had left only two governorships in Anatolia, that of Asia and that of Bithynia (Map 13). Neither province was among those whose leadership was handed over to the princeps on the basis of the new principle introduced in 27 BCE, and which he had transferred to his delegates (*legati Augusti*). Instead, following the traditional method, both Bithynia and Asia were assigned by lot—normally for one year—to senators, the lower-ranking Bithynia to a senator of praetorian rank, while Asia, the oldest and largest province on Asian soil, to a senator of consular rank. We know the names of nineteen proconsuls of Asia between 27 BCE and 14 CE, and one of the first was Marcus Tullius Cicero, the son of the great orator, philosopher, and statesman who had been proscribed and then murdered. When Augustus was sojourning in Asia and Bithynia in 21/20 BCE, he intervened to set things in order, gave money to needy communities, and arranged general debt relief (Dion of Prusa *or.* 31, 66), but he also imposed punitive payments on some of them in addition to the tribute they owed (Dio 54, 7, 6). An incident in Kyzikos, where resident Italics had been lynched during a popular uprising, induced him to withdraw the city's right to freedom; but the latter was restored by Agrippa only five years later. From 27 BCE on, Bithynia once again regularly had proconsuls as governors. It has been shown that under Augustus and Tiberius there were five or perhaps six such officeholders.

Beyond these provinces the kings who had survived Actium, or their sons, were waiting to see what the new world leader would do. Octavian's behavior with regard to the dynasts—deposing or confirming, punishing or rewarding them—was not at all directed merely by whether they had been for or against him before the decisive battle.[22] Across from Egypt, in Cilicia, there was a patchwork of Cleopatra's possessions, smaller dynasties, and autonomous cities. The Galatian king Amyntas was the first to benefit from the end of the Ptolemaic outposts in Cilicia. After his death in 25 BCE the fate of these territories is unclear; perhaps they were co-administered from Ankyra until Augustus gave them to Archelaos of Cappadocia in 20 BCE. Tarkondimotos *philantonios* had died at Antony's side in the Battle of Actium. Octavian initially denied the king's dynastic possessions to his son,[23] but ten years later (20 BCE) he transferred them to him in full, though with the subtraction of the coastal cities assigned to Archelaos of Cappadocia (Dio 54, 9, 2; cf. Strabo 14, 5, 6). It is not without irony that as a Roman citizen the son of the "Friend of Antony," who himself bore the byname *philopator* ("father-loving"), now adopted the name Gaius Julius—representative of Antony's enemy and the victorious new dynasty.[24] The Teucrids' priesthood also continued to exist in Olba, even if the tyrant Aba, who had married into the family and had been tolerated by Antony and Cleopatra after her coup d'état, was forced to abdicate and make room for her descendants (Strabo 14, 5, 10). There is no mention of a governor, but in any case the autonomous *poleis*—some of which continued to calculate their years according to the Pompeian era, while others calculated according to the Julian era down into the Imperial period—regarded themselves as free from dynastic rule and may have been overseen by the governor of Syria.

Strabo provides us with an interesting insight into the situation in Tarsos, the former provincial assize (14, 5, 14). There a poet and rhetorician named Boethos had made himself beloved of the people by favors and of Antony by flattery, but then

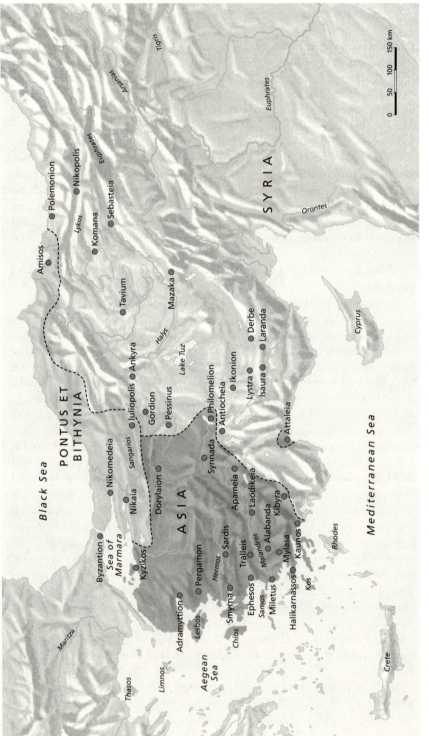

Map 13. The provinces of Asia Minor, ca. 27 BCE. Map drawn by Peter Palm, Berlin.

so shamelessly enriched himself and his family that he angered the Roman. He managed to calm Antony, but when after Antony's death Octavian's rhetoric teacher, the aged Stoic Athenodoros, returned to his home city to put everything in order, Boethos's machinations came to an end. However, his corrupt supporters refused to accept his exile and painted on the walls the following words against the old man: "Work for young men, counsels for the middle-aged, and flatulence for old men." Athenodoros had this "corrected" to read "thunder for old men!" (trans. Jones) Driven out of Tarsos, the scoundrel Boethos may have ended up going to Telmessos in Lycia, where an inscription on a sarcophagus refers to a man of this name who lies in it embalmed in sweet honey, as an "outflowing of the art of poetry" ([146] MS IV 12). According to Strabo (14, 5, 15), many educated people from Tarsos lived in Rome at that time, and one of them, the Academician Nestor, teacher of Marcellus, succeeded Athenodoros as regent of the city. Such members of the Greek intellectual aristocracy were also active elsewhere on behalf of the new princeps. Strabo (13, 2, 3) says that at some point Augustus appointed the son of Pompey's friend Theophanes of Mytilene, Pompeius Macer, as procurator in Asia.

On the Black Sea, there was urgent need to set things in order. The Galatian Adiatorix, who had had the Italic settlers in Herakleia Pontike murdered, did not escape punishment. But his son Dyteutos so impressed Augustus that the latter gave him the priesthood in Komana Pontike which he had previously given Kleon, the former brigand from Bithynia (p. 316) whom he had protected but who had suddenly died. Shortly after Actium, the city of Amisos on the coast of the former Mithridatic kingdom got rid of a tyrant named Straton and was granted freedom. One of Antony's most important supporters in Asia Minor, Polemon of Pontos, went over to the side of the victor and was accepted. Lesser Armenia was taken away from him and transferred to Artavasdes, but the "king of Pontos" presumably received a compensation for this, namely the territory of Zela, which therefore ceased to exist as a temple state. In this city, Polemon erected a statue to his new patron; remarkably, he bears no royal title in the inscription on its base.[25] Following the example of the Diadochi and Epigones, he wanted to create a monument to himself by founding a city named "Polemonion" on the coast east of Amisos. When uprisings broke out in the Bosporan kingdom—where Asandros, a client-king married to one of Pharnakes's daughters, had been killed and Agrippa was trying to reestablish Roman authority—Polemon enjoyed enough confidence to be put in charge of the Crimea as well (14 BCE). For the first time since Mithridates VI, both sides of the Black Sea were under a single ruler. But only briefly. Polemon could not overcome the resistance in this area and died in the tribal area of the Aspurgianoi in 8/7 BCE. What then happened to the Crimea is unclear. The Romans later tolerated the rule of a dynast named Aspurgos on the Cimmerian Bosporus. In Pontos, Polemon was immediately succeeded by his wife Pythodoris, who married Archelaos. Strabo (12, 3, 29) grants her the stature of a wise stateswoman.

Archelaos of Cappadocia, who had fought at Antony's side at Actium, retained his kingdom, which was further expanded to include Lesser Armenia and places on the coast of Rough Cilicia. However, his reign encountered difficulties. His own people revolted against him and would probably have deposed him had Tiberius not defended him. In addition, there was a conflict with Titius, the governor of Syria, which Herod of Judea helped resolve. Because of his support for Antony, Mithridates of Commagene—the mountainous country on the Middle Euphrates—had to abdicate, and the kingdom was entrusted to his brother Antiochos II. However, shortly afterward the latter was summoned to Rome by Octavian and brought before the Senate: accused of having treacherously murdered an emissary whom his brother Mithridates had sent to Rome, Antiochos was condemned and executed (Dio 52, 43, 1). His successor, whose name is not known, sought to secure the throne for himself by having Mithridates assassinated, only to be himself replaced on Augustus's demand by the still youthful son of the murdered man (Dio 54, 9, 3).

The most important decision was made in central Anatolia in 25 BCE: initially, Amyntas was also confirmed here. His advances from Lycaonia and Isauria—where he built royal residence for himself on the site of the old city of Isaura, which he had destroyed—into the high Taurus Mountains cost him his life during a battle with the Homonadeis (Strabo 12, 6, 3). Augustus sent a *legatus pro praetore*, Marcus Lollius, who put the Roman annexation of the area in movement: the province of Galatia with its capital at Ankyra in central Anatolia was to become a kind of hinge that joined with subsequent Augustan annexations to form a provincial territory in Asia Minor that far exceeded the republican one. Amyntas's enormous possessions, which stretched from the Pamphylian plain to the central Anatolian Galatia of the tetrarchs and in the southeast as far as the border of the Cilician Taurus Mountains, were for the most part completely incorporated into the new large province, though not all of them from the outset (Map 14).

So far as the border areas are concerned, many things are still unclear—for example, the assignment of Pamphylia and of the sites in Rough Cilicia. In any case, Amyntas's share of Pamphylia had included Side; it now became a provincial area.[26] The unification of all of Pamphylia with Galatia certainly took place before the year 69 CE, when it is proven to have existed under Galba (Tacitus, *hist.* 2, 9, 1). The eastern area of the tetrarchs' land around the town of Tavium, with a *polis* community of the Sebastenoi Trokmoi, apparently remained for a short time outside the province of Galatia. There, in contrast to Pessinus and Ankyra, the local era was calculated as beginning not in 25 but only in 20 BCE.[27] Part of Lycaonia that was probably also included only later on (Dio 49, 32, 3) was called "the added [land]." And with Amyntas's land possessions in Rough Cilicia, Augustus thought of King Archelaos only in 20 BCE. Here in the Taurus were retreats and nests of resistance for a rebellious mountain population. The consul Sulpicius Quirinius's action against the Homonadeis was so successful that he was awarded the insignia of triumph (Tacitus, *ann.* 3, 48, 2; cf. Strabo 12, 6, 3).[28]

Galatia was never subjected to a long-term occupation by Roman legions; the legion that had once been recruited by Deiotaros and later called the Deiotariana soon left for Egypt; another legion may have remained in the country for a certain

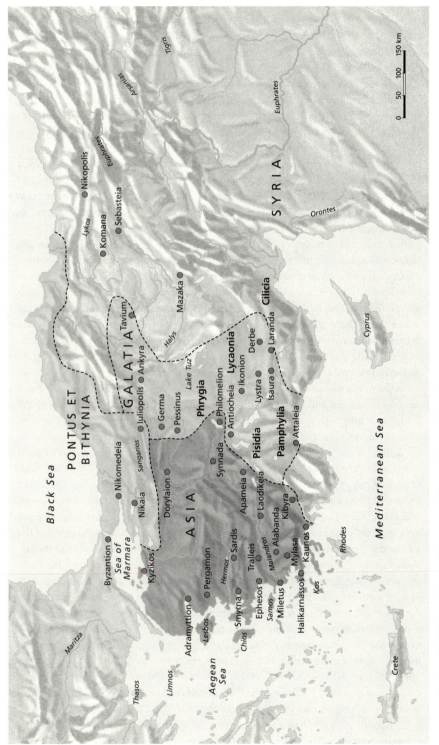

Black Sea

Sea of
Marmara

Byzantion

Kyzikos

Nikomedeia

Nikaia

PONTUS ET
BITHYNIA

Sangarios

Dorylaion

GALATIA

Juliopolis Ankyra

Germa

Pessinus

Tavium

Halys

Lake Tuz

Mazaka

Lykos

Komana

Sebasteia

Nikopolis

Axsinius

Euphrates

Euphrates

Tigris

SYRIA

Orontes

Cyprus

Phrygia

Philomelion

Antiocheia

Ikonion

Lystra

Isaura

Lycaonia

Derbe

Laranda

Cilicia

Adramyttion

Pergamon

Lesbos

Smyrna

Chios

Ephesos

Samos

Miletus

Hermos

Sardis

Tralleis

Maiandros

ASIA

Synnada

Apameia

Laodikeia

Alabanda

Kibyra

Mylasa

Halikarnassos

Kaunos

Pisidia

Pamphylia

Attaleia

Kos

Rhodes

Aegean
Sea

Limnos

Thasos

Maritza

Crete

Mediterranean Sea

0   50   100   150 km

Map 14. Galatia between 25 and 6 BCE. Map drawn by Peter Palm, Berlin.

time but had no successor there.[29] A whole nest of newly set-up Roman *coloniae* in Pisidia—Olbasa, Komama, Kremna, Parlais, and the most important, Antiocheia[30]—was supposed to safeguard the connecting roads between the valley of the Maeander, Pamphylia, and Lycaonia in the south of the great province. It was the most massive Roman colonization in Asia Minor,[31] and it was supplemented by individual Augustan colonies in other areas: Germa in the area of the Tolistoagii, Lystra and Ikonion in Lycaonia, and Alexandria Troas on the Aegean coast.[32] The country of the great shrine of Men Askaenos near Antiocheia[33] passed into the possession of the veterans who had settled there. Perhaps on the model of the seven hills of Rome, the Romans established *vici* (villages) to which they gave names taken from the city of Rome,[34] and they called the broad main street Augustea platea. The structure of the community led by a *duovirate* (two-man commission) must have been guided, as it was elsewhere, by *lex coloniae* (the law of a Roman colony). A certain Greek way of life, as represented by the gymnasium, was not forgone here; likewise, the citizenry was subdivided into *tribus* on the model of Greek *phylae*. The colonies served primarily to secure major communication routes and coasts. Given the location and number of these colonies, a "Romanization" emanating from them into the rest of the country cannot have been intended, nor did anything of the kind occur, in even a rudimentary form. On the contrary, Hellenic language and lifestyles partly took possession of them after a relatively short time, though Antiocheia long remained an exception to this rule.

In the north and northeast, the province of Galatia bordered on areas that Pompey had urbanized and subjected to Roman rule. In these former *eparchiai* of the Mithridatic kingdom, such as Domanitis and Phazemonitis, urban centers had been established. As potential *polis* territories, they were almost preprogrammed, so to speak, to be included in the Galatian great province when the occasion arose, even if it was still twenty years before the next step was taken. Strabo (12, 3, 41) mentions as the last ruler of Inner Paphlagonia, which had once been part of the Pompeian province of Pontus et Bithynia, the son of Antony's liegeman Kastor. On coins he appears as "King Deiotaros Philadelphos." After his death in 5 BCE, Rome annexed his kingdom; Paphlagonia became a provincial territory, and the princeps put the area under the control of his legate in Ankyra. In the fertile land along the middle stretch of the Amnias River lay the city founded by Pompey the Great. Like Pompeiopolis, Gangra and Neapolis also celebrated the implementation or final recovery of their status as *poleis* by establishing eras. As in Lycaonia, in the southwest part of the country there was an area still completely untouched by the process of urbanization that was incorporated into Paphlagonia, and was—as already mentioned—named Kaisareis Proseilemmenitai. Finally, in 2 BCE Augustus annexed parts of the former Pontic homeland that were on the eastern border of Galatia: the valley of the upper Skylax River—the region of Karanitis with its central city Karana-Herakleopolis, which had been called Sebastopolis since the provincialization—and the fertile country of Amaseia, Strabo's homeland (Map 15).

A Roman Anatolia had grown out of a conglomerate of client-kingdoms that covered about two-thirds of modern-day Turkey (for the lists of rulers, see the Ap-

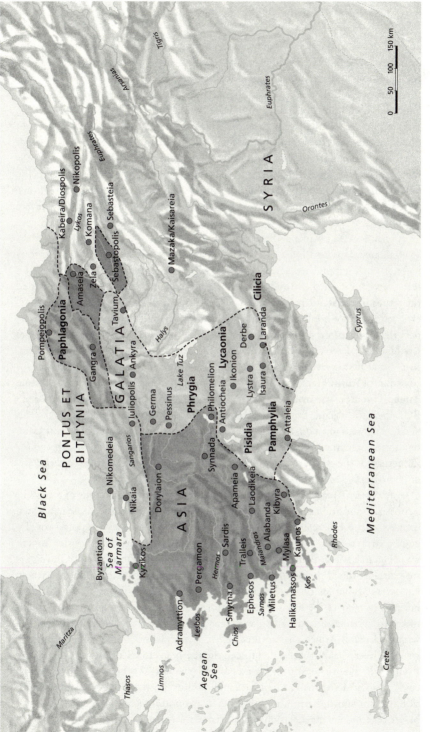

Map 15. Expansion of Galatia to include Paphlagonia (6/5 BCE.), Amaseia, and Sebastopolis (2 BCE). Map drawn by Peter Palm, Berlin.

pendix). It left to the kings loyal to Rome only the high plateau countries of Commagene, Cappadocia by the Taurus, and Cappadocia by the Sea, where there were few cities, as a buffer zone against the Iranian vassal-kingdoms. Farther on, between the Caucasus and the Kurdish Taurus, on the Arsanias River, in the valleys of the Kura and Araxes, and on Lake Van and Lake Urmia lay countries that were under the influence of the Parthians (for the list of kings, see the Appendix). We have not yet discussed the relations between Rome and the Parthians under Augustus, though they are just as important for the Augustan development of the Roman *provinciae* as for that under the succeeding emperors. Licinius Crassus's catastrophe, as well as the failed campaign against the Parthians planned by Caesar and carried out by Antony, were for Augustus among of the most irksome problems he inherited from the late Republic.[35]

Augustus certainly planned no campaign in Parthian Mesopotamia or, *per Armeniam minorem*, toward Ekbatana. But the humiliation of Crassus and then Antony had remained unpunished, and the Roman *signa* (standards) taken during these defeats were still in the hands of the enemy. Antony had already officially demanded the return of the standards lost in 53 BCE. The general elation over the end of the civil war must not be allowed to drown out the voices of prominent writers that reflect the expectations of part of the senatorial leadership class that the *dux* (leader) would undertake to resolve this problem.[36] Octavian/Augustus did not remain inactive. But at first everything went wrong: negotiations in late 30 BCE with the ambassadors of King Phraates in Syria failed. Rome supported a pretender to the throne named Tiridates, who managed to seize the throne for a short time; his coins (26/25 BCE) bear the legend "Friend of the Romans." But Phraates returned, and Tiridates fled to Augustus in Spain, accompanied by Phraates's son. In 25 BCE, the year Galatia was annexed, the Arabian campaign failed.[37] In new negotiations the demand for the return of the standards was not met, and the royal son was freed without any quid pro quo.

A few years later a diplomatic success was won that developed out of a crisis in Armenia. Opposition to the anti-Roman king of Armenia, Artaxias, arose in his own country and a call resounded—probably not without Rome's support—for Tigranes, Artaxias's brother, to become king (for the Armenian kings, see the Appendix). Tigranes was at that time detained in the city on the Tiber. In 20 BCE Augustus sent Tiberius with an army to eastern Anatolia, where the rebellious party now had Artaxias murdered. Tiberius managed not only to put Tigranes on the throne but also to recover the lost standards from the Parthians.[38] To buttress the diplomatic arrangement, the Parthian king sent sons to Rome as hostages. There coins with the legend "Armenia is captured" (*Armenia capta*) were minted, and Augustus wrote in his *res gestae* that he had forced the Parthians to seek the friendship of the Romans. If the princeps in the same passage (chapter 27) further claimed that he could have made Armenia a *provincia* and did not do so only on grounds of tradition, we can conclude from this that different options were discussed at this time before the fundamental decision announced in the Senate was made. Augustus alleg-

58. Island in the Euphrates near Zeugma, the presumed site of the meeting between Gaius
Caesar and the Parthian king Phraatakes.

edly wanted neither to expand the provinces in the East nor to extend the indirectly
ruled area, but rather to declare himself content with the present possessions (Dio
54, 9, 1). Finally, the erection of a large arch in the Forum depicting Augustus driving a team of horses in triumph suggests that at that time he thought he had found a
satisfactory and long-lasting order for the political situation in the East.

Rome's relationship to Armenia remains of far-reaching importance. Rome's
right to determine succession to the throne was henceforth claimed as a prerogative.
However, the Parthians opposed this idea, and in the country itself the monarchy
proved to be notoriously unstable. The reign of Tigranes III, who died before 6
BCE, was initially followed by the joint rule of his son Tigranes IV and his sister
Erato. Augustus refused to recognize them and tried to install, under military protection, a certain Artavasdes, but was thwarted by the recalcitrance of the country's
inhabitants. Tigranes then won the support of the Parthian troops, which threw
Roman-Parthian relations into a new crisis.

This development prompted the princeps to dispatch another armed mission to
eastern Anatolia in the year 1 BCE.[39] It was led by his grandson Gaius Caesar, accompanied as a *comes* and *rector* by the experienced consul Marcus Lollius, the first
governor of Galatia, until he fell into disfavor and committed suicide.[40] He was replaced by Sulpicius Quirinius, the victor over the Homonadeis. Before he came to
Armenia, Gaius had met on an island in the Euphrates (probably near Zeugma; Figure 58) with the Parthian king Phraatakes, who had just come to power by violent
means, and who made Gaius concessions and promised that his troops would leave

Armenia. Tigranes now sought to make his own arrangements with the Romans. Shortly thereafter he was killed in a battle against rebels (Dio 55, 10, 20 f.; 10 a, 5). A series of mishaps followed. A new Roman candidate, the former Median king Ariobarzanes, met with rejection. During military operations in Armenia that were intended to put him on the throne, an assassination attempt on Gaius was made. Wounded, he set out for home and died on the way in Limrya, Lycia, where the ruins of his monumental cenotaph can still be seen today. Ariobarzanes died shortly afterward, and his son Artavasdes IV, who mounted the throne ca. 4 CE, was murdered only two years later. The same happened to his successor chosen by Rome, Tigranes V, so that around the time of Augustus's death the widow Erato was ruling once again. Finally, a son of the Parthian king, Vonones, seized the throne when Tiberius was already ruling in Rome. The Roman prerogative that Tiberius himself had established thirty-four years earlier broke down, and Armenia immediately presented the new princeps with a problem.

Provincialization in the Julio-Claudian Epoch (27 BCE–68 CE)

In the Augustan epoch the whole country as far as the Euphrates and the Phasis rivers, including the client-kingdoms, was seen as part of the *Imperium Romanum*, and not only from the Roman perspective. Since Augustus, the Roman emperor reserved the right to intervene in the succession to the throne in client-kingdoms. In this sense, at that time Armenia was probably considered part of the *Imperium Romanum* in Rome as well.

In 17 CE Tiberius transformed the kingdom of Cappadocia into a Roman province (Map 16).[41] Archelaos, who was in his seventies, was indicted and summoned to Rome to justify himself before the Senate (Tacitus, *ann.* 2, 42, 2 f.; Suetonius, *Tib.* 37, 4; Dio 57, 17, 3 f.). The exact nature of the accusations against Archelaos is not known; he died in Rome. To carry out the measures connected with the process of provincialization, Tiberius sent a legate of praetorian rank, Quintus Veranius, who was not, however, followed by a governor of senatorial rank. Instead the early province was administered by a "knight" (Dio 57, 17, 7; cf. Tacitus, *ann.* 12, 49), which in this context can only mean a prefect or procurator.[42] At first, the province received only cohorts and *alae* (cavalry units), not a legion. These (*auxilia*) were units that had been recruited under Augustus in Galatia, Bithynia, and Crimea; two additional cohorts came from Spain.[43]

Polis status was enjoyed by Tyana and Mazaka (which had already been renamed *Kaisareia* under Augustus) and perhaps also by the city bearing the dynastic name of Archelais—which was previously called Garsaura and soon thereafter became a Roman colony (Pliny the Elder, *nat.* 6, 8), as well as Komana. Outside the province the Cilician Taurus Mountains remained with the king's son, Archelaos II (Tacitus, *ann.* 6, 41), with the exception of the temple state of Olba; in the latter Aias, son of Teukros, now ruled as priest and district governor (*toparches*) over the tribes of the

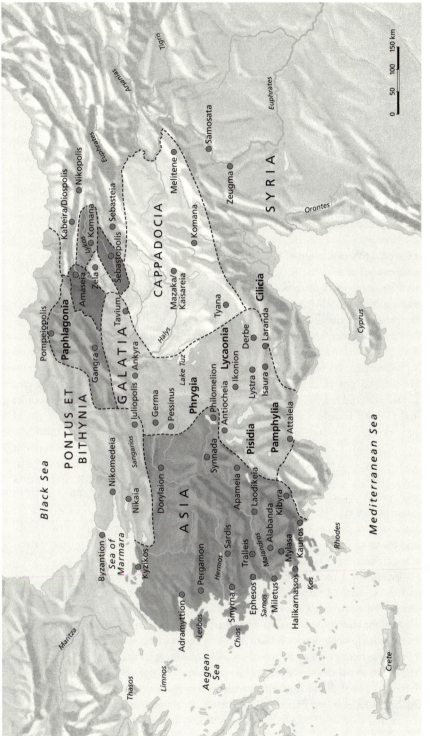

Map 16. Organization of the provinces under Tiberius: Cappadocia in 17 CE and Komana Pontica in 34 CE. Map drawn by Peter Palm, Berlin.

Kennatai and Lalasseis. Archelaos II was later to have, like others before him, problems with the tribes in the Taurus, and in 36 CE these led him to ask Rome for help. It was granted him. With 4,000 legionaries, Trebellius, a legate of the governor of Syria, put down the uprising by the rebellious highlanders entrenched in fortifications. In the meantime, at the northeastern end of the kingdom, Lesser Armenia, which had until recently been ruled by Archelaos I, also came under Roman control in connection with the establishment of the province of Cappadocia, probably with the inclusion of the Black Sea cities of Kerasus and Trapezus.[44] In the same year Antiochos III, the son of Mithridates, died in Commagene. After spokespersons for various parties in the country had been heard, the desire of Antiochos's children to continue to rule as kings was rejected, and Commagene was annexed and put under the control of the governor of Syria (Tacitus, *ann.* 2, 56). As in the case of the country bordering Syria on the south, Judea, Commagene was governed by a prefect.[45] However, this expansion of the province in both the north and the south was only temporary. For the time being, of the territory under client kings in Anatolia west of the Euphrates, there remained in the north only the dominions of Pythodoris and in the south, those of Archelaos the son (Archelaos II), together with temple land of the priest from the Teucrid dynasty.

After the Parthian king Vonones had also failed as king of Armenia and fled to Syria,[46] his rival, Artabanos II, installed one of his sons in Armenia. Tiberius reacted with Germanicus's mission in 18 CE; the latter was given an authority that put him above all governors. On his wide tour through various parts of Asia Minor the emperor's adopted son left many traces: Kaisareia in Bithynia was named Germanike and Germanikopolis was founded near Gangra in Paphlagonia. Various grants of honors suggest visits to Sinope, Eumeneia in Phrygia, Notion, Klaros, Priene, Iasos, and Alabanda. The honorary arch with a quadriga in the Amanos range not far from Issos was erected after Germanicus's death and was doubtless a deliberate allusion to the battle Alexander once won there.[47] The Parthians did not resist his intervention in Armenia. A son of Polemon, Zenon, was crowned in Artaxata; he took the throne name of Artaxias. He was chosen because he had been "an imitator from earliest infancy of Armenian institutions and dress, had endeared himself equally to the higher and the lower orders by his affection for the chase, the banquet, and the other favourite pastimes of barbarians" (Tacitus, *ann.* 2, 56; trans. Jackson).

In 34/35 CE the temple state Komana Pontica, over which Augustus had finally put the Galatian Dyteutos as priest—we know of no successor—was annexed by Rome and constituted itself as a *polis*. It took the name Hierokaisareia only later on.[48] In the same year Zenon-Artaxias died in Armenia, and the Parthian king Artabanos III, knowing that in Rome only an aging and withdrawn princeps governed, felt he was strong enough to make his son Arsakes king on the Araxes. He demanded the return of the treasure Vonones had carried off to Syria: "At the same time, he referred in boastful and menacing terms to the old boundaries of the Persian and Macedonian empires, and to his intention of seizing the territories held first by Cyrus and afterwards by Alexander" (Tacitus, *ann.* 6, 31; trans. Jackson).

In the country an aristocratic opposition once again rose up against Artabanos, and this encouraged Rome to send Prince Phraates to Ctesiphon as the pretender to the throne. When Phraates died en route, another pretender named Tiridates was sent, and he managed to reach Vitellius, the governor of Syria, who escorted him as far as the Euphrates. Mithridates, the brother of the Iberian king Pharasmanes, was to become king in Armenia.

The invasion of Armenia begun by the Iberians led to the murder of the ruling Arsakes in Artaxata, and the great king's army, which was bringing in still another Parthian king's son, lost the battle. The coup ended in complete success: Roman client-kings resided both on the Araxes and in Ctesiphon, though in the latter only briefly. The Parthian nobility again drove Tiridates out, and Artabanos III returned from Hyrcania. In the meantime, he had abandoned his ambition to rule Armenia, and in a meeting with Vitellius on the Euphrates in 37 CE he recognized the status quo.

Far away, in western Asia Minor, imperial rule continued to be generally regarded as a blessing.[49] Only Kyzikos suffered the loss of its "freedom" because of a murky affair—Romans are said to have been imprisoned, and the Temple of Augustus that had been begun was not completed (Tacitus, *ann.* 4, 36; Suetonius, *Tib.* 37; Dio 57, 24, 6). The cities of Asia and Bithynia flourished. Sardeis took the name Kaisareia, Philadelpheia that of Neokaisareia—a name that the regent of Pontos, Antonia Tryphaina, also gave to the residence on the Lykos that her mother had already renamed Sebaste (now Niksar). In northwest Phrygia, on the border with Mysia, a Tiberiopolis emerged. The town Pappa in the region of the Oroandeis tribes on the eastern edge of the Pisidian highland took the name Tiberiopolitai Pappenoi Orondeis.[50]

Emperor Gaius (Caligula) was celebrated in Asia as a "new Helios" ([109] Syll.[3] 798); he commanded the Milesians to dedicate the Didymaion to him (Dio 59, 28, 1). Under his rule, the misfortune of expropriation befell the Iberian Mithridates, but we do not know the reasons for it. Summoned to Rome and there interned, he had to abandon Armenia to its fate. Eastern Anatolia once again experienced a renaissance of dynastic rule. Antiochos IV received Commagene, which had been annexed by Tiberius, but he soon fell into disfavor and lost it again. But he retained two other gifts in Anatolia: on the one hand, the possessions in Rough Cilicia that Archelaos II had inherited from his father and that were now transferred to him (including the coastal cities of Selinus, Anemurion, Kelenderis, and Korykos), and on the other hand areas north of the Taurus with the cities of Derbe and Laranda. But these were not necessarily, as has been suggested,[51] Archelaos's former dynastic land, but rather (more probably) part of the province of Galatia, which Caligula was just as prepared to give away as he was Commagene and the Pontic and Lesser Armenian territories. Later on it bore the name *Antiocheiane* (Ptolemaios, *Geog.* 5, 6, 17).

The date of Pythodoris of Pontos's death is not certain, but it probably occurred under Tiberius, ca. 22 CE.[52] During her lifetime, her daughter, Antonia Tryphaina, was married to the Thracian king Kotys, and bore him three sons: Rhoimetalkes, Kotys, and Polemon. After she had the murderer of her spouse condemned in Rome

59. Polemon II (left), head of the young Nero (right). Silver drachma, 57/58 CE. Münzkabinett Winterthur.

in 21 CE, she went to Asia and resided for a time in Kyzikos, where she became priestess of the cult of Livia and Drusilla (Caligula's sister). After Pythodoris's death she apparently ruled Pontos for her still under-age son; at that time she did not yet bear the title of queen. The emperor then gave the adult sons the kingdoms that "were due to them." Rhoimetalkes received Thrace, Kotys Lesser Armenia, and Polemon II Pontos ([109] Syll.[3] 798), which he ruled as king (see Figure 59) starting in 38/39 CE, sometimes with his mother "Queen Tryphaina."[53] The part of the Black Sea coast annexed by Tiberius—Kerasus and Trapezus—was returned to the possession of the dynasty; in addition, it ruled over territories on the Cimmerian Bosporus. However, a few years later (41 CE) Claudius transferred the area on the north coast of the Black Sea to a native dynast (Dio 60, 8, 2); just as Augustus had once done for Polemon I, he now provided the grandson with a compensation for the loss with "a certain territorial possession" in Cilicia. The reference is apparently to the enlarged territory of the Teucrids, since a Polemon, probably the same one, figures on coins as the "archpriest and dynast of the holy land of Olba and (of the tribes) of the Kennatai and Lalasseis." Josephos (*AJ* 20, 145) calls him the "king of Cilicia."[54]

Claudius revoked the deposition of the dynasts of Commagene and Armenia. Antiochos IV got his kingdom of Commagene back and thus advanced to become the ruler over two dominions separated by the province of Syria: Commagene and the whole area of Rough Cilicia, along with the part of Lycaonia called *Antiocheiane*, ceded to Archelaos II during the provincialization of Cappadocia. I examine the Iberian Mithridates' return home to Armenia in the following section. But first let us discuss a step taken by the emperor that fits into the context of his expansionist imperial policy: the provincialization of Lycia.

Like Rhodes, the great federal state in southwestern Asia Minor could point to a proud succession of close federal partnership relations with the great power Rome, even in times of serious danger, and was therefore one of the very few countries on the Mediterranean that had retained its freedom into the Imperial period.[55] This freedom was withdrawn from it in 43 CE, allegedly because of internal unrest and the murder of Romans. Diplomatic activities, in which a pro-Lycian Roman woman in Corinth distinguished herself as an assistant and mediator, seem to have preceded the event or accompanied it.[56] The task of establishing order was entrusted to a praetorian legate, Quintus Veranius the Younger; he was a son of the senator to whom Tiberius had assigned the setting up of Cappadocia. Three years later the Lycians erected a monumental pillar in Patara dedicated to the emperor as the "savior of the *ethnos*." On it is inscribed the network of road connections "created" by Veranius between the Lycian *poleis* (see the section on roads in Chapter 8).[57] As it was being founded, the province was probably already expanded to include the quite extensive territory of Kaunos, at the expense of the province of Asia.[58]

The administration of Lycia long posed a difficult problem for research, since literary testimonies seemed to contradict one another. The view that Claudius already formed a new double province of Lycia et Pamphylia was based on a formulation found in Cassius Dio (60, 17, 3–4). The problem has now been solved by further discoveries of inscriptions from Patara.[59] Under Claudius, Lycia was constituted as a province of its own and never again escaped the supervision of a Roman governor. It was last ruled, for eight years (ca. 63–70 CE), by Marcius Priscus. The double province of Lycia and Pamphylia was created only under Vespasian.

One year after the provincialization of Lycia (44 CE), the emperor also took away the freedom of the island state of Rhodes. During the course of the Imperial period, Rhodes' freedom was repeatedly restored and withdrawn; but this was connected with nothing more than the recognition or withdrawal of certain privileges, especially since free cities could be very differently privileged.

In the time of Claudius as well, individual communities expected to receive something in return for renaming themselves after the emperor. Neapolis, a rather unimaginatively named Paphlagonian city in the Phazemonitis country, took the name *Neoclaudiopolis* (New Claudius City), perhaps just after Bithynion had beat it to the punch with Klaudiupolis. A settlement with the name of Claudius emerged in the far east of Cappadocia (Pliny the Elder, *nat.* 5, 85), and Laodikeia Katakekaumene, Ikonion and Seleukeia in North Pisidia added an honorary prefix to their names: Claudiolaodicea, Claudiconium, and Claudioseleucia, while Tralleis named its city council the Klaudiabule.[60] Outside the provinces dynasts founded, as they had done in the past, *poleis* in honor of themselves or their *patroni*. This occurred in various places and is recognizable in the striving to centrally organize and pacify rebellious mountain tribes or scattered rural communities. Thus Polemon added a Claudiopolis (the modern town of Mut) in the area he ruled northwest of Olba, where the Lalasseis tribe had its home. Antiochos IV chose for a city he founded in Commagene the byname of his *patronus* (Gaius, Claudius, or Nero): Germanikeia, as well as that of the Germanikopolis in the Cilician part of his dominions. There he founded not only Claudiopolis Ninica and Eirenopolis in the interior but also cities on the coast that bore his and his daughter's name: Iotape and Antiocheia on the Kragos. The location of another Philadelpheia (after Iotape Philadelphos) is unknown.[61] Under these dynasts the unruly tribes of Rough Cilicia took a considerable step toward the urbanization of the area in which they lived.

War in Armenia

When Claudius sent the Iberian Mithridates to Armenia with a military escort, there was only moderate resistance in that country; the Parthians were tied down by a rebellion in Seleukeia in their homeland, and a "governor" in Armenia named Demonax could be quickly eliminated. Antonia Tryphainas's son Kotys, who ruled in Lesser Armenia, made claims to Armenia, but withdrew them because of a letter from the emperor. However, Iberian troops and a Roman garrison in Gorneae (Tacitus, *ann.* 12, 45; modern Garni, twenty kilometers east of Jerevan) were able to support Mithridates's monarchy for only a short time. A new, serious conflict arose because the Iberian king Pharasmanes considered it more important that instead of his brother, his son Rhadamistos mount the throne in Armenia (Tacitus, *ann.* 12, 44–51). Feigning a rift with his father, Rhadamistos fled to his uncle's court to reconnoiter the situation there himself and then returned to Iberia on the pretext of a reconciliation with his father. Pharasmanes and Rhadamistos then together carried out an armed invasion of Armenia. The king fled and entrenched himself with the Romans in Gorneae. There the prefect Caelius Pollio and the centurion Casperius quarreled over what to do.[62] Mithridates was finally forced to leave the fortress. Contrary to their promises, the Iberians murdered him along with his wife and children. The procurator Julius Paelignus, hastening there from Cappadocia with auxiliary troops, achieved nothing and even allowed himself to be bribed into recognizing Rhadamistos. The legate of one of the Syrian legions, Helvidius Priscus, also thought it better to make an arrangement and after he arrived did nothing against the new power-holder (Tacitus, *ann.* 12, 49, 2).

In the meantime, a new successor to the throne had emerged from the power struggles in the Arsakid court: Vologaises I (autumn of 51 CE), who immediately renewed the claim to Armenia as part of his vassal system. Of his brothers, to whom he planned to give various parts of the kingdom as fiefs, he planned to put Tiridates on the throne on the Araxes and marched into the country. Helvidius Priscus did not risk war with the Parthians and withdrew from Armenia along with his legion. King Rhadamistos fled. But the Parthian army could not endure the winter. Lack of provisions and sickness forced it to retreat to warmer regions, and the Iberian came back. Before long, his tyranny provoked an uprising that drove him out of the country for good (Tacitus, *ann.* 12, 50). His own father later had him killed to please the Romans (Tacitus, *ann.* 13, 37, 3). What happened between that time and the beginning of Nero's reign remains obscure.[63] In late 54 CE, at about the same time that Nero became emperor (October 13), the Parthians were back in Armenia.[64] The new government on the Tiber was unwilling to accept this. This time it meant war.

Although western Asia Minor was hardly affected by Nero's war against the Parthians, for the country as a whole the conflict was of exceptional importance. For the first time since Antony's campaign in 36 BCE, a massive Roman military capability got into serious difficulties. The initial goal was not achieved. Each side had to recognize that it was too weak to force the other to accept a diktat. In fact the Romans had to shelve their prerogative of determining the succession to the throne in Armenia, though they never formally renounced it, and Hadrian still " allowed " (*permisit*) the Armenians to have a king (HA *Hadr*. 21, 11). A long-term occupation of this restive country was beyond the Romans' power. Thus they arrived at a compromise on Armenia. But the part of Anatolia immediately west of Armenia was no longer unoccupied. The earliest fixed quarters of the Roman legions in Asia Minor were established on the Euphrates. The true genesis of the Anatolian *limes* (fortified border) began after Nero.

Nero's advisers Seneca and Burrus immediately urged the princeps to reinforce the army in the Orient; for that purpose Domitius Corbulo was sent to Syria as a new legate of the unified provinces of Galatia and Cappadocia, with the assignment of winning back Armenia (*retinendae Armeniae*). Corbulo, a tall, powerfully built man with iron discipline, incorruptible and intelligent, had been suffect consul and legate in lower Germania during the reign of Claudius and had ruled Asia as a proconsul. The four Syrian legions were commanded by the *legatus pro praetore* of Syria, Ummidius Quadratus. But he was forced to relinquish two legions to Corbulo, the III Gallica and VI Ferrata, and naturally he was not happy about that. To avoid the transfer in the middle of his province itself, he went to Cilicia to see Corbulo. Auxiliary troops were provided by Antiochos IV of Commagene and the Jew Agrippa II, ruler in Galilee and in the *peraia* (east of the Jordan). Aristobulos (a descendant of Herod) took the place of the insecure, unreliable Kotys in Lesser Armenia.

According to Tacitus, in his eastern Anatolian winter quarters Corbulo devoted his time to disciplining these disorderly Syrian legions:

> It was a well-known fact that his army included veterans who had never served on a picket or a watch, who viewed the rampart and fosse as novel and curious objects, and who owned neither helmets nor breastplates—polished and prosperous warriors, who had served their time in the towns.[65]

Galatians and Cappadocians were conscripted to replace old and sick legionaries. In the end, Ummidius had to march one more of the two remaining Syrian legions, the X Fretensis, to Corbulo. In return, the IV Scythica was brought in from Moesia, and was replaced by a legion from Dalmatia. Winter duty in Cappadocia was hard, and the bone-chilling cold killed some of the men. Finally in early 58 CE, Corbulo moved into Armenia, where Tiridates also found himself attacked by the Moschoi mountain people from the Paryadres in the north and by Pharasmanes's troops from Iberia and those of Antiochos from Commagene. Some of the supplies came through the Black Sea harbor of Trapezus. The Parthian could not hope for his brother's support just at that moment, because Vologaises was busy dealing with a rebellion of the Hyrcanians.

An agreed-on meeting did not take place, and the armies camped distrustfully within sight of one another. Thereupon the divided Roman forces seized the initiative by conquering one fortress after another. The Parthians were unable to stop the advance of the main army toward Artaxata. Their swarming mounted archers could do nothing against the well-protected march formation and skilled use of the terrain, though a decurio who ventured too far forward died pierced by arrows.

Artaxata was taken without a fight in 58 CE and razed to the ground. This astonishing deed was probably based on the recognition that unless it was occupied by a significant number of troops, the capital would immediately be retaken by Armenians favorable to the Parthians, who presumably constituted a majority in the country. The legions made a forced march against Tigranokerta; on the way, their commander narrowly escaped being assassinated by an Armenian. The Armenians' second capital also mounted no resistance (59 CE). As a result of operations led by the legionary legate Verulanus, Tiridates was driven out of Armenia. Tigranes, the great-grandson of Herod of Judea on his father's side and of Archelaos of Cappadocia on his mother's side (Josephos, *AJ* 18, 139), whom Nero planned to put on the throne, arrived in Armenia from Rome. Corbulo left in the country a protective force of 1,000 legionaries, three auxiliary cohorts, and two cavalry units (*alae*). However, he cut a few border areas off the extensive kingdom and put them under the control of the neighboring client-kings, Polemon of Pontos, Aristobulos of Lesser Armenia, and Antiochos of Commagene. Corbulo's assignment seems to have been successfully completed. Some scholars argue that from the outset the general did not intend to enforce the Roman prerogative, insisting only on an investiture of Tiridates by the emperor at Rome, while the Parthians resisted this imposition to the bitter end, but this view has been rejected for good reasons. Unlike its predecessors, Nero's government was prepared to go all the way. Construction of a triumphal arch on the Capitol was begun.[66]

When Ummidius died in 60 CE, Corbulo took over the governorship of Syria in addition to that of Galatia/Cappadocia, and assembled five legions under his command. Bad news led him to write to Rome; Tigranes had nothing better to do than rashly attack and plunder Adiabene, thereby increasing the determination of the Parthians and their vassals to go to war over Armenia.[67] But a withdrawal from Syria of the forces necessary to defend the highlands appeared too risky. Corbulo advised the transfer of the East Anatolian provinces to a new Imperial legate. Nonetheless, the two legions that were still in Anatolia under the command of Verulanus Severus and Vettius Bolanus hastened to help Tigranes, who had been attacked by the Parthian commander Monaises and thrown back on Tigranokerta. Except for the latter, the whole country suddenly seemed to favor the Parthian cause. How long the city held out is unknown, and so is Tigranes's later fate.

Meanwhile in Nisibis one of Corbulo's officers, the centurion Casperius, had been negotiating, not without success, with the Parthian king, who was prepared to send emissaries to Rome. What these emissaries suggested to Nero has not come down to us. The Parthians may have sought to compensate for their demand that

60. The valley of the Arsanias (Murad Su).

Tiridates be made king of Armenia by conceding the necessity of his investiture by the emperor. But the emissaries returned empty-handed, and Vologaises himself made the decision to invade Armenia (62 CE).

The princeps appointed Caesennius Paetus, one of the ordinary consuls in 61 CE, as legate of Galatia/Cappadocia. Paetus took over command of the IV Scythica and XII Fulminata legions and received another legion from Moesia, the V Macedonica, for which the governor of this province (Plautius Silvanus) received no replacement. The new legate had nothing but scorn for what Corbulo had achieved: the enemy had not suffered any real defeat, and cities were only nominally under Roman control. Paetus boasted that he would impose on Armenia not a shadow-king but levies and Roman laws.[68] In actuality, however, he proved incapable. Underestimating distances and difficulties of supply, after a campaign in the autumn of 61 CE he withdrew, exhausted, to winter quarters in Cappadocia. When the following spring he advanced again—one of the three legions remained in Pontos, far from the theater of war—with divided army groups, he suffered defeats at the hands of the large Parthian contingent under Vologaises that now appeared in the country. The situation came to a dramatic head—the legions, one worn down, the other bottled up in Randeia on the Arsanias (Figure 60), had to capitulate. Paetus reluctantly agreed to ask Corbulo for help. To humiliate his opponent, the Parthian also ordered him to have a bridge built over the Arsanias. In exchange for handing over all fortresses and supplies, and a complete withdrawal from Armenia, the defeated troops that remained to Paetus were allowed to escape and join Corbulo, who was only three days' march away in Tomisa, on the east bank of the Euphrates.

Corbulo coolly refused to use his forces without orders from the emperor. His demand that the Parthian king also withdraw from Armenia was complied with only in appearance: in early 63 CE emissaries brought to Rome itself the news of the Arsakid's decision to finally convey Armenia to his brother Tiridates. The latter allegedly could not come to Rome because of his duties as priest; at most, he could appear at his formal investiture in front of images and symbols of the emperor: *ad signa et effigies principis* (Tacitus, *ann.* 15, 24). In Rome it was debated whether a risky war or a humiliating peace should be chosen. The princeps had nothing but contempt for Caesennius Paetus, who had returned to Rome. Nero ultimately reacted by appointing Domitius Corbulo supreme commander of all the Oriental legions. Tacitus compares the legate's superior position with the authority granted Pompey in the war against the pirates. The two decimated legions in Cappadocia were filled out by means of conscription and transferred to Syria. The three unused Syrian legions (III Gallica, VI Ferrata, and X Fretensis) were sent to Anatolia, where the V Macedonica (which had been withdrawn from Pontos) joined them, and the XV Apollinaris set out from Carnuntum in Pannonia to do the same. Reinforcements by task forces (*vexillationes*) dispatched from Illyria and Egypt were also added. With his seven legions (two in Syria, five in Cappadocia) and special units, Corbulo had under his command more than a quarter of the Roman Empire's military might—exceeded in the Imperial period up to that time only by Tiberius's campaign against Marbod in 6 CE with twelve legions (Tacitus, *ann.* 2, 46).

From Melitene (Malatya), the five Cappadocian legions invaded Armenia in the summer of 63 CE. However, it was no longer a question of putting a Roman candidate on the throne; the only goal was to ensure that Tiridates could receive the crown only from the emperor, and only in Rome itself (Dio 62, 22, 3). Once again making camp on the Arsanias, Corbulo invited Tiridates to negotiate, and he imposed the Roman conditions on him: in exchange for the prospect of receiving them in Rome as a petitioner, the great king's brother had to solemnly lay the royal regalia before the image of the emperor in the military camp in Randeia. This compromise signaled the end of the Armenian dynasty of the Artaxiads; from then on the Arsakids had a claim to the land's throne, but they needed to be confirmed by the Roman emperor. Shortly thereafter, Tiridates set out for Rome.

At first, Corbulo's forces did not leave Armenia. Rome felt itself impelled to reply to the Armenian compromise by strengthening its position west of the Euphrates.[69] In 64 CE Polemon II's reign, which had lasted more than a quarter of a century, came to an end, and his kingdom was incorporated as a *provincia* (Map 17). It was constituted by six *poleis*: the *polis* territories in the interior, Neokaisareia, Zela, and Sebasteia, together with the territories of Polemonion, Kerasus, and Trapezus on the Black Sea coast. The unit was designated, in the Roman nomenclature, as *Pontus Polemoniacus* or *Polemonianus*. The annexed name element (recalling the kingdom's last ruler) distinguished the new province from those existing in its neighborhood: the one named in *Pontus et Bithynia* and another unit called *Pontus Galaticus*. Whereas the latter, constituted by the territories of Amaseia and Karana in 2 BCE,

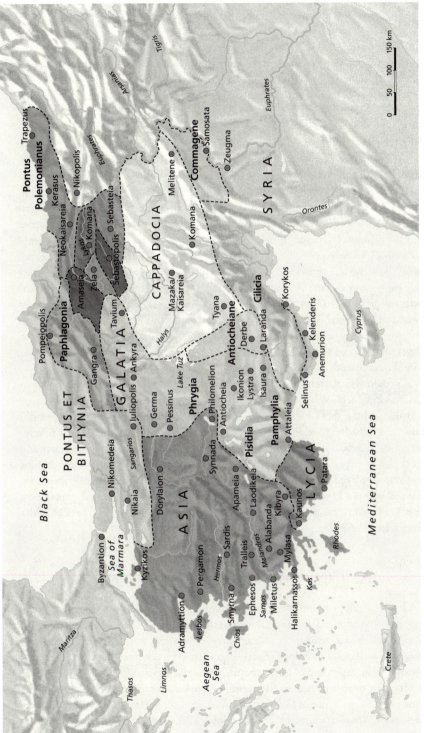

Map 17. The provinces after the annexation of the Kingdom of Polemon, 64 CE. Map drawn by Peter Palm, Berlin.

and Komana in 34/35 CE, had been merged with Galatia, the Pontus Polemonianus was attached to Cappadocia and ruled by the governor of this province. The royal guard was established as a Roman auxiliary cohort, and Polemon's fleet provided the heart of the later *classis Pontica* (Tacitus, *hist*. 3, 47, 1–2). Polemon retained his possessions in Cilicia (p. 330).

In 65 CE Tiridates left for Rome. A strange drama of the meeting between two different cultures was played out in the Parthian's trip to Italy: he rode on horseback alongside his wife, who wore, instead of the prescribed veil, a golden helmet, and he brought with him his own sons, those of his brothers, and those of the great king. Escorted by the whole of his court and 3,000 Parthian cavalrymen, for nine long months he traveled west through the splendidly decorated cities. In 66 CE Nero made of Tiridates' reception and coronation a great festival in Naples and in the forum in Rome. The descriptions in Suetonius (*Nero* 13) and Dio (63, 4 f.) provide indications of Nero's conception of the future status of Armenia and its king, because the scene was consciously designed to intimidate Tiridates with Roman military power and victoriousness. The ceremonies and *spectacula* that were presented before the Arsakid in Rome and in the cities of Asia during the return trip alternately awed and horrified him. Back in his homeland, he rebuilt Artaxata, which was temporarily given the name Neroneia. Great King Vologaises rejected an invitation to travel to Rome; he refused to consider making such a long voyage by sea, but said he would be prepared to arrange a meeting somewhere in Asia (Dio 62 [63], 1–7).

Corbulo was withdrawn from the Orient and summoned to the emperor in Corinth in Greece. While the emperor was getting ready to listen to a cithara player, he told Corbulo that he should commit suicide. The sources favorable to Corbulo find an explanation for this in the depraved emperor's hatred for the noble war hero. It cannot be determined whether the motive was a well-founded doubt concerning Corbulo's loyalty to the emperor. It is known that Corbulo's son-in-law, Annius Vinicianus, played a leading role in the conspiracy instigated in Benevento in 66 CE.[70] We do not know the rank or the identity of the official who ruled Cappadocia after Corbulo's death. Perhaps it was returned to the supervision of a prefect under the governor of Syria.

The Flavian Province and Frontier System

Under Vespasian, who had emerged from the Jewish War and the Civil War as the new emperor, three major annexations and the beginning of the "Anatolian *limes*" in Cappadocia had a lasting influence on the development of the peninsula. Modern research based on archaeological and epigraphic evidence documents with increasing clarity the expansion of infrastructure under the Flavians.[71]

The new double province of Lycia et Pamphylia was created and enlarged at the expense of the province of Galatia: Pamphylia and the southern half of Pisidia, perhaps as far as Sagalassos,[72] were absorbed into the new province. The enormous central Anatolian conglomerate of Galatia was thus deprived of its southern part, which had the most cities, and the major tasks of administering them were transferred to another governor. From the point of view of communications and geography, henceforth the province of Galatia was oriented more than ever toward its eastern neighbor, Cappadocia. Shortly afterward, in 75 CE, Vespasian merged them again and put them under a legate of consular rank.

In the same year as Lycia and Pamphylia, Lesser Armenia and Commagene were annexed and affiliated with different provinces (Map 18). Aristobolus's kingdom, where the descendants of the veterans whom Pompey had once settled in Nikopolis had founded a new *polis* and began their era from the year 72, was completely absorbed into the province of Cappadocia. In the case of King Antiochos IV, things were more complicated; he ruled over two kingdoms, Commagene and large parts of Rough Cilicia. The latter were combined with the east Cilician alluvial plain (Cilicia *campestris*), which had up to that time been co-administered by the governor of Syria—the rebirth of a province of Cilicia after more than 130 years! Antiochos's daughter Iotape is supposed to have later held a small part of the country (cf. Josephos, *AJ* 18, 140: kingdom in Ketis).

The expansion of the new province of Cilicia, which was formed under Vespasian and ruled from Tarsos,[73] is particularly problematic with regard to its western part. We cannot determine with precision the frontiers of the dynastic rule of Archelaos, Archelaos II, Antiochos IV, and Polemon II. Much later, under Antoninus Pius (138–161), the legate Gaius Etrilius Regillus Laberius Priscus[74] ruled over the *tres eparchiae* of the province of Cilicia: Cilicia, Isauria, and Lycaonia. It is not impossible that Vespasian combined these three territories into a single province as early as ca. 72 CE and thus expanded its domain—in a way completely analogous to what was done in forming the province of Lycia et Pamphylia at the same time—to include, beyond Cilicia proper, the plain on the northern edge of the Taurus.[75] However, this complex must have been dissolved again by Domitian (81–96 CE) and remained divided among other formations at least until the time of Hadrian (117–138), because in the interim gubernatorial inscriptions put Lycaonia and Isauria under the legates of the great province of Galatia-Cappadocia.[76]

The kingdom of Commagene—a mountainous land with few larger settlements and many mountain sanctuaries, divided into so-called *strategiai*—is supposed to have been taken away from King Antiochos on grounds of disloyalty. Although he acquiesced, his sons, Epiphanes and Kallinikos, decided to resist in Samosata but could not hold the capital against the legate of Syria, Caesennius Paetus—no other than the loser in Armenia—who arrived with the VI Ferrata legion. For a short time they fled under Parthian protection. In 73 CE one of the Syrian legions, the III Gallica withdrawn from Rhaphaneai, occupied Samosata, the royal capital (Figure 61). As it had been in the past, Commagene again became part of the province of Syria (Josephos, *BJ* 7, 219–243).

Down to Nero's time, Syria had been the only province occupied by a large legionary force, which protected the middle Euphrates against the Parthian area on

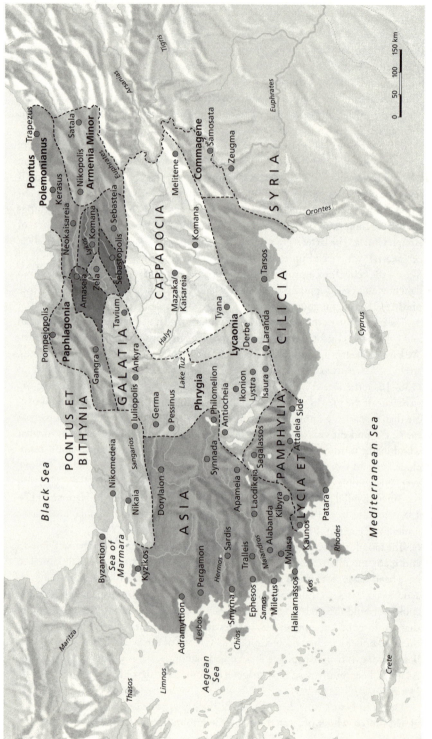

Map 18. The provinces under Vespasian, 72 CE. Map drawn by Peter Palm, Berlin.

61. Samosata on the Euphrates (1987). Remains of a Roman building using the masonry technique known as *opus reticulatum* ("network").

the north Mesopotamian plain. Its four legions were well supplied and posted not far from the Mediterranean and the metropolis of Antiocheia on the Orontes, which was developing into a major world city. Vespasian no longer left it to these permanent camps to provide security for Anatolia as well. Under Corbulo's command in the Orient, it had become clear that the border area of the empire between Commagene and Trapezus, which was about 340 kilometers long (as the crow flies) and more than 800 kilometers long by road, required its own *exercitus*. Moreover, the division of the Euphrates legions between two legates reflected the emperor's care not to concentrate power in the provinces in one hand. As early as 70/71 CE, Vespasian's son Titus withdrew the XII Fulminata legion from Syria and stationed it in Melitene (Malatya). Five years later, another newly conscripted legion, the XVI Flavia Firma, was quartered far to the north, in a town named Satala that may have been already used by Corbulo. Until the early 90s, several auxiliary cohorts from Syria, as well as a I Raetorum cohort from Moesia Inferior were transferred to Cappadocia. Securing the zone of the whole right bank of the Euphrates in Anatolia began with the building of the road network and forts (p. 381).

The sources give as the reason for Vespasian's initiative the then looming danger of an attack by the Alani from the Caucasus area (Josephos, *BJ* 7, 244–251; cf. Suetonius, *Vesp.* 8, 7). In 72 CE this equestrian people had invaded Armenia, and in 75, in view of the threat posed to his region, the Parthian king sought Roman help, but in vain (Suetonius, *Dom.* 2; Dio 65, 15, 3). A Flavian presence in Iberia, a kingdom located south of the Caucasus whose ruler then bore the titles of *philokaisar* and *philorhomaios*, has been proven. According to a Greek inscription (ILS 8795), Vespasian restored the castle complex at Harmozika, where the Aragwi River descends from the mountains and debouches onto the Kura floodplain (see Figure 53). However, it was not the Alani alone, but also the first Flavian's longer-term and spatially wide-ranging conception that may have been responsible for the deployment of the two legions and auxiliaries as well as for the combination of the provinces of Galatia and Cappadocia. In the second century CE the Iberian court was romanized, though its strong Iranian tradition persisted. In 1940 an Aramaic-Greek bilingual inscription was found in a tomb:

> Serapītis, daughter of Zewaḥ the younger, *pitiax*, wife of the son of *pitiax* Publicius Agrippa, Yodmangan, he who has gained many victories as steward (*epitropos*) of the great king of the Iberians, Xepharnūg—she died too young, [being] twenty-one years [of age], she who had inimitable beauty.[77]

Shielded by the armies on the frontiers, Flavian Asia Minor enjoyed lasting peace and prosperity. Now for the first time numerous members of the Anatolian upper classes became senators. The urban notables cultivated an exuberant philanthropy (euergetism), including the financing of many construction projects in Pergamon, Smyrna, Ephesos, Miletus, Laodikeia, and Aphrodisias.[78] The measures taken by Domitian to limit wine production, for which we have literary evidence, were not intended, as Philostratus claims, to free inhabitants of the province from the craving for revolution conceived under the influence of alcohol, but rather to increase the provinces' production of grain to a level sufficient to meet their own needs. However, these measures met with indignation: at the behest of the Asian Commonalty, the sophist Skopelianos gave in Rome a speech opposing them (VS 520; compare Suetonius, *Dom.* 7), and the emperor abandoned the plan. New cities were founded, and existing cities changed or added to their names. In Bithynia Flaviopolis was constituted on the site of the settlement Kreteia. A city of the same name grew up in the Cilician plain at about the same time that Diokaisareia was founded in the immediate vicinity of Olba in Rough Cilicia. In Lydia, the communities of Daldis and Temenuthyrai named themselves Flaviopolitai, the cities of Philadelpheia and Grimenothyrai both took the name Flavia, and Sala (on the Phrygian border) became Domitianopolis, presumably after receiving the emperor's permission.

✦ ✦ ✦

With the Flavian epoch the provincialization of Asia Minor essentially came to an end. All the coasts and the whole Anatolian plateau beyond the isthmus, the narrow part of the peninsula between the Black Sea and the Mediterranean on either side, were under Roman administration. This process lasted two centuries, about as long as the whole reign of the Achaemenids over Asia Minor, and more than half a century longer than the reign of the Seleucids, the heirs to Alexander's conquests. However, in the history of Roman expansion, the provincialization of similarly large land masses in the West, Gaul, and Spain[79] proceeded much more rapidly. The main reason for this is surely that in Hellenistic and early Imperial Asia Minor, for a long time, even after the country had been conquered and the accumulations of power had been broken up, the relatively highly developed structures already in place long made it more advantageous to govern indirectly. But then, on the one hand, the "failure" (as seen from the Roman point of view) of local rulers gradually led to direct Roman control—as early as 17 CE in Cappadocia, then in Lycia and also in Commagene. According to Josephos (*BJ* 7, 219–223) that was in fact the official reason given for the invasion of Commagene in 72 CE. On the other hand, constantly increasing military demands were also a reason for the transition to direct rule. Under Pompey the Euphrates border had already attracted Rome's attention, and Strabo (6, 4, 2; cf. 16, 1, 28) described the Euphrates and Phasis as the frontiers of the empire. But it was only in the Flavian age that it became—no doubt because of Corbulo's experiences and the new assessment of Armenia's status—a carefully developed and secured line of defense for the Roman Empire.

The Parthian Wars and Imperial Visits: The Near Side and the Far Side of the Euphrates

During the first decades of the second century CE, under Nerva and Trajan, general prosperity continued to grow in Asia Minor. In the cities, profligacy, bickering, mismanagement, and corruption became a problem. On the border between Lydia and Phrygia (at Grimenothyrai) and in Cilicia (Epiphaneia), new communities named themselves Traianopolis. Between about 107 and 113 CE Trajan had the united provinces of Galatia and Cappadocia divided again, and probably around the same time the *eparchiae* in Pontus were reorganized: the cities of Pontus Galaticus, Amaseia, Komana, and Sebastopolis, along with those of Pontus Polemoniacus, Neokaisareia, Zela, and Sebasteia, were incorporated into the new entity of Pontus Mediterraneus; the coasts, with Kerasus and Trapezus, constituted an *eparchia* of its own.[80] The whole of Pontus (not to be confused with the western, coastal area of the same name that had been joined with Bithynia) was henceforth under the control of the governor of Cappadocia. Whether this was a measure connected with the planned war against the Parthians cannot be determined with certainty.

On the Far Side of the Euphrates: Trajan's Parthian War

The eastern frontier had long remained quiet. The energetic Parthian king Vologaises I had been dead for almost two decades, and Vologaises II and the brothers Pakoros II and Osroes I were fighting an acrimonious war over his succession. An Armenian king accepted by Rome was abruptly overthrown on Osroes's initiative (between ca. 110 and 112 CE) to make room for the latter's nephew Parthamasiris. Trajan took this—out of a thirst for glory, as Dio says (68, 17, 1)—as a *casus belli* and headed for the east in October 113 CE. As in the case of the Armenian campaigns under Nero, our sources are incomplete; the most coherent major report is provided by Cassius Dio (68, 17–31). Among the various motives for the war debated among researchers, one of the more convincing is that Trajan wanted to put an end to the notorious insecurity regarding power relationships in Armenia, and in addition to erect a bulwark against the Parthians in northern Mesopotamia.[81] But the motive of his own fame must certainly have also played a significant role in the case of an emperor who bore so many victorious bynames (Germanicus, Dacicus, Parthicus).

Pliny the Younger's governorship in Pontus et Bithynia, which his correspondence with the emperor made famous, immediately preceded this eastern campaign. Presumably it occurred between September 110 and 112 CE; Trajan suspended the normal procedure, according to which the governorship would be assigned by lot in the Senate, and sent Pliny to Bithynia as his delegate (*legatus Augusti pro praetore*)—but not without having this decision approved by a resolution in the Senate. Pliny's rank, as it appears in an inscription from Como, was officially *leg(atus) pro pr(aetore) provinciae Pon[ti et Bithyniae pro]consulari potestate*, which may be translated as "Praetorian representative (of the emperor) for the government of the province of Pontus et Bithynia, endowed with an authority corresponding to that of a proconsul."[82] After Pliny's death the consul C. Julius Cornutus Tertullus, also acting as a delegate of the emperor, provided supervision in the province. It has often been suggested that preparations for war were a deeper reason for the temporary special regulation, but there is no convincing proof of this. The troop movements, however, must also have passed through northern Anatolia, so that imperial supervision was required there as well. Under Hadrian posts were once again filled by selecting praetorian proconsuls.

Since Augustus, no Roman emperor had set foot in Asia, with the exception of a short landing made by Vespasian on his way back from Alexandria to Rome. Now the princeps in person, coming from Athens, arrived on the west coast and crossed part of the country (by what roads we do not know) and then boarded a ship for Syria, probably in Patara.[83] Meanwhile, task forces (*vexillationes*) detached from the legions on the Rhine and Danube crossed the Bosporus and advanced through northern Anatolia to the Euphrates; auxiliaries were conscripted in Paphlagonia and Galatia. Trajan led the imperial army through Commagene to the XII Fulminata legion's garrison in Melitene and on to Satala, where the XVI Flavia Firma was replaced by the XV Apollinaris.[84] From there he entered Armenia to meet with Parthamasiris. An exchange of letters preceded the meeting. The fact that the king first requested communication via the legate of Cappadocia, Marcus Junius Homullus, allows us to infer that a personal, perhaps even friendly relationship with this "neighbor" already existed; the princeps sent him not Junius himself, but his son (Dio 68, 19, 1). However, the emperor was not interested in establishing genuine communication; the meeting in Elegeia turned into a humiliating tribunal. Parthamasiris's proposal to renew Nero's compromise and receive the diadem from Trajan met with a brusque rejection, both in the princeps's tent and before the eyes and ears of the soldiers in the camp: Armenia now belongs to the Romans! The Parthian was murdered during a scuffle as he left the camp; in a letter to Osroes Trajan denied the accusation that he had ordered this done.[85]

Struggling with wintry conditions, the emperor led the legionaries across the west Armenian highlands and down into northern Mesopotamia, where he took Nisibis and Batnai.[86] The tomb epigram of Amazaspos, an Iberian prince who died in Nisibis and who had accompanied the emperor with his troops, was discovered in Rome in the seventeenth century ([146] MS V 47). In Edessa Trajan held an audience and accepted the apologies of Abgar and other Arab sheiks for not having attended upon him earlier and assuring him of their absolute loyalty. Finally, he established his winter quarters in Antiocheia. There he narrowly escaped death when a powerful earthquake that lasted for several days and nights struck the city brimming over with natives and outsiders, civilians and soldiers; he managed to escape through a window of the collapsing building he was in. One of the incumbent consuls, Pedo, lost his life. The emperor's staff set up its headquarters outside, in the hippodrome (Dio 68, 24 f.).

The following spring the powerful Roman war machine moved east, via Zeugma and Nisibis to the Tigris. The river was crossed by means of a bridge made of boats that had been brought along on wagons. The army was divided into units that advanced into southern Mesopotamia. After closer inspection by his specialists, Trajan abandoned the project of connecting the Euphrates and the Tigris by a canal at the "bottleneck." Once again, boats were transported by land to the Tigris, which the main army unit crossed in January 116 and took Ctesiphon, the Arsakid capital, without encountering resistance (Dio 68, 28, 2–4). Ostensibly, this was a dazzling success that Rome had been able only to dream about since the disastrous defeats of Crassus, Antony, and Caesennius Paetus. Dio (68, 29, 1) tells us that after the march to the Gulf near Spasinu Charax, the sixty-three-year-old emperor stood on the shore musing as he watched an Indian traveler, and wished he were younger and could advance, like Alexander, farther toward India and beyond.

This was the culmination of the territorial extent of the Roman Orient and of the whole Roman Empire. All of Armenia from the Araxes to the Euphrates was a province united with Lesser Armenia and Cappadocia under a senatorial legate with an equestrian procurator (ILS 1041.1338). It has been shown that the Roman army did construction work in Artaxata in 116 CE (AE 1968, 510). Whether the occupied areas in Mesopotamia were incorporated into a new province of Assyria (Eutropius 8, 3, 2; Rufius Festus 14, 20), and how far the latter extended toward the south, is uncertain. In any case, the Anatolian peninsula was flanked on the east and the south by large areas under Roman control; the frontier had shifted farther east, and the region was no longer the edge but rather the middle. After the annexation of the Nabataean kingdom ten years earlier, Rome found itself in possession of both coasts of the Arabian Peninsula on the gulfs of the Erythraean Sea. For the time being Trajan's conquests seemed excessive, but they provided the framework that later advances and long-term occupations filled out. Under Antoninus Pius, the Egyptian II Traiana Fortis legion maintained an outpost on the island of Farasan off the southwestern coast of Arabia, near Jizan; this island had probably already been occupied under Trajan by soldiers of the VI Ferrata legion.[87] A province of Mesopotamia became a lasting institution under the Severan dynasty.

Within months, a series of calamities that ended with the death of the emperor forced the Romans to abandon most of the positions they had won. In the legions' rear Jewish uprisings had broken out in many places as far away as Cyrenaica (Dio 68, 30, 1 ff.; Eusebius, *h. e.* 4, 2, 3; Orosius, *hist.* 7, 12, 6 f.). Vologaises, the son of Sanatrukes, invaded Armenia. When the governor, Catilius Severus, was unable to cope with him, emissaries sent by the emperor to the Parthians guaranteed them part of Armenia).[88] After establishing a prince friendly to Rome, Parthamaspates (a son of Osroes), in Ctesiphon, Trajan undertook the siege of Hatra. Meanwhile several generals and officers attacked the rebels in Cyrenaica, Egypt, and Mesopotamia. Although they were partly successful, conquering Seleukeia, Nisibis, and Edessa, which was now destroyed by Lusius Quietus after it had changed sides again, the imperial army withdrew from Hatra without achieving anything, and after Trajan fell seriously ill it retreated to Syria (Dio 68, 33, 1–3). Partially lamed by a stroke, Trajan left Publius Aelius Hadrianus with the army and sailed back to Italy. In August, 117 CE Trajan died in Selinus, a small harbor on the coast of Rough Cilicia. The town was later given the name Traianopolis (today Gazi Paşa, about forty kilometers southeast of Alanya). On Cyprus, in Cyrene, and in Egypt, where Greeks and Jews had massacred each other with indescribable cruelty, the Romans were gradually able to gain control of the situation by means of a frightful bloodletting. The flourishing cities of Asia Minor seemed to have been spared unrest.

On hearing of the princeps's death, Hadrian hurried to Selinus and from there returned to Syria. He did nothing about the loss of Armenia and Mesopotamia, where Parthamaspates could not maintain his position and Osroes returned to Ctesiphon. In the following winter of 117/18 CE he crossed Asia Minor, passing through Tarsos, Tyana, Ankyra, and Juliopolis, as far as the Bosporus. He returned five years later—though not, like his predecessor, under arms.

The Near Side: Hadrian

Under the reign of this greatest Philhellene among the Roman emperors, which lasted more than twenty years, Asia Minor reached the apex of its economic prosperity and cultural splendor.[89] It is no accident that from this period we have an especially rich documentation regarding endowments and festivals, municipal coinage—including precious silver coins (*cistophori*) and medallions—construction projects, inscriptions, and the erection of monuments, as well as the increasing competition among cities over titles and predicates indicative of their rank. Hadrian displayed himself to his subjects, provided help and spent money, regulated and moderated, and everywhere he was venerated as "Zeus Olympios," "Founder" (*ktistes*), "Restorer" (*restitutor*), and "Savior" (*soter*), while his wife was revered as a "new Hera." Erythrai celebrated his arrival with a "landing festival." On its coins, the little city of Saittai in Lydia showed the personified city shaking the emperor's hand, bursting with pride over the ruler of the world's visit. The residents of Sagalassos, a city in the Pisidian mountain country, erected a finely sculpted, larger-than-life statue of

Hadrian, which has recently been excavated. Kyzikos and Parion were allowed to add the byname "Hadriane" to their names, and Stratonikeia on the Kaikos added the byname "Hadrianopolis." In the interior of Mysia, a city named Hadrianutherai was founded on the site where the emperor had killed a bear, as well as Hadrianoi below Mt. Olympos and Hadrianeia; in Paphlagonia Hadrianopolis (previously Kaisareis) was founded. In Cilicia another city bearing this name was founded with Zephyrion, while other cities in this province also added "Hadriane" to their names, as did Nikopolis, Neokaisareia, and Amaseia in Pontos and Lesser Armenia. Oresta in Thrace was also given the name "Hadrianopolis"; later it was known as Adrianople (it is the modern Edirne).

In addition to the consolidation of the territories in the interior of Pontus to form Pontus Mediterraneus (that had taken place probably under the reign of Trajan, but in any event no later than that of Hadrian), in southern Asia Minor a further new entity was formed: Isauria and part of Lycaonia (the eastern part, which until 72 CE had been ruled by Antiochos IV of Commagene) were combined with Cilicia; together, they constituted the *tres eparchiae* (Map 19).[90]

Hadrian's first two trips through Asia Minor began in Syria, in 117 and 123 CE.[91] During a (presumed) meeting with Osroes before the latter date, the Euphrates was once again mutually recognized as the border, and the trans-Euphrates area was given up. The Parthian, who was at this time competing with Vologaises III to be the sole ruler, was given back his daughter, who had been taken from Ctesiphon as a prisoner by Trajan, but not the royal throne stolen from that same city, which Antoninus Pius was also to refuse his successor (HA *Hadr.* 13, 8; *Pius* 9, 7). Starting from Syria, the emperor moved north along the Cappadocian *limes*, crossed the Pontic mountains at the place where Xenophon's Ten Thousand had looked down on the Black Sea, and descended into Trapezus, where he ordered the expansion of the harbor. He made a short detour to the east to visit the military posts on the Pontic *limes*. He probably traveled by sea to farther Pontic harbors in the west and finally to Bithynia, where he spent the winter of 123/124 in Nikomedeia and Nikaia.

At that time he may have made the acquaintance and become fond of the young Antinoos, who came from a small village near Bithynion-Klaudiupolis (Figure 62). The beloved youth's premature death at the age of twenty in Egypt only a few years later (October 130 CE) triggered various forms of cult worship of the deceased as god or hero throughout the Empire that have left many traces in literary, epigraphic, numismatic, and archaeological evidence. The homosexual relationship between emperor and teenager became a paradigm that aroused the resentment of Christian writers (Eusebius, *p. e.* 2, 6, 9, compare Athanasius, *contra gentes* 9, 43) and appears in modern European literature (e.g., Oscar Wilde).

We know little about the route Hadrian took for further travels in the province of Asia in 124. The version given in the sophist Polemon's *Physiognomika*, according to which the emperor came to Asia with his entourage by way of Thrace, is controversial.[92] The first large city in the province where he sojourned was Kyzikos, where he had the construction of the enormous temple completed. After stays in Ilion, Per-

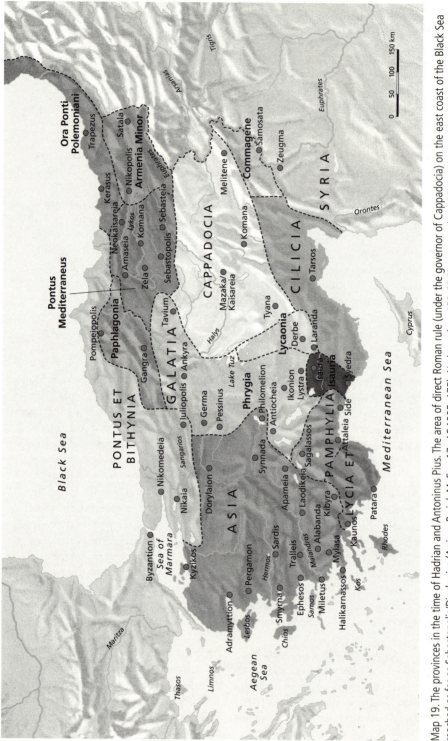

Map 19. The provinces in the time of Hadrian and Antoninus Pius. The area of direct Roman rule (under the governor of Cappadocia) on the east coast of the Black Sea reached as far as Sebastopolis/Dioskurias (Arrian, *Peripl. M. Eux.* 17; *AE* 1905, 175). No later than 152 CE Pityus was also added to this area (M. P. Speidel, Roman Army Studies II [1992] 209 ff.). Map drawn by Peter Palm, Berlin.

62. *Antinoos.* Rome, Capitoline Museum.

gamon, and Stratonikeia on the Kaikos, Hadrian visited the interior of Mysia, where the emperor and his entourage went hunting. Having returned to the coast, Hadrian honored Polemon's adopted home, Smyrna, crossed by ship to Erythrai, and made, of course, a visit to the pearl of Asia, Ephesos (August 124 CE).

Five years later he returned there from Eleusis. The text of an edict that he issued in Asia has been fully preserved; it will be discussed later (p. 381). This time his route passed through Caria (Miletus and Tralleis), Phrygia (Laodikeia on the Lykos, Apameia, and Melissa), and Ikonion to reach Cappadocia. It is not known how far east he went here. In Cappadocia he may have made contact with the king of the Iberians, Pharasmanes (HA *Hadr.* 17, 11 f.).[93] Afterward Hadrian crossed the Taurus through the Cilician Gates and traveled to Antiocheia, where he climbed Mons

Casius, which towered over the city on the south (autumn of 129 CE). Once again, during his voyage back from Alexandria in 131 CE, he made stops on the south and west coasts, certainly in Phaselis, and perhaps also again in Ephesos.

On the Far Side: Antonines and Severans

In the age of the Antonines a bleaker wind began to blow in Asia Minor. Under Antoninus Pius (138–161) relations between the Romans and the Parthians deteriorated. Vologaises IV mounted the Arsakid throne in 147/148 CE, and the crisis became so intense that the emperor prepared for war (HA *Aur.* 8, 6; *Pius* 9, 6).[94] Troops were shifted to Syria and Cappadocia. The latter probably received another legion, the VIIII Hispana, which was transferred there from Nijmegen in Lower Germania.[95] The preparations also included, no later than 159 CE, the transformation of Pontus et Bithynia from a senatorial to an imperial province. In compensation for this the status of Lycia et Pamphylia was changed to the reverse, so that it was henceforth governed by proconsuls.[96] At the beginning of Marcus Aurelius's reign a further step was taken: the territories of the port cities of Abonuteichos, Sinope, and Amisos on the Black Sea were put under the supervision of the legate for Galatia, through the northern part of which ran both of the main west-east communication routes connecting Juliopolis, Ankyra, and Sebastopolis, on the one hand, and Bithynion, Pompeiopolis, and Neapolis on the other.[97]

Vologaises IV took advantage of the change of government in Rome in 161 CE to make an overt attack on Armenia. The legate of Cappadocia, Marcus Sedatius Severianus, the "silly Celt," as Lucian (*Alex.* 27) calls him because of his naive belief in oracles, had been trapped with the VIIII Hispana in a pocket near Elegeia and annihilated by the numerically superior Parthian forces (Dio 71, 2). The legate of Syria, Lucius Attidius Cornelianus, proved unable to counter the subsequent threat of Syria, and in early 162 the co-emperor Lucius Verus set out for the East to wage a new war against the Parthians. On the way he lingered in several cities on the western and southern coasts of Asia Minor.[98] Cappadocia's troops were reinforced by *vexillationes* that were drawn from the Danube legions and commanded by the legionary legate P. Julius Geminius Marcianus (ILS 1102). The militarily experienced M. Statius Priscus was hurriedly transferred from Britain to the Euphrates—clearly an emergency measure, since Britain was a province that normally ranked much higher than Cappadocia. In 163 CE he conquered Armenia, occupied Artaxata, and established near the capital a standing garrison, Kainepolis. In Sohaimos the country received, this time for a long period, a new ruler who was loyal to Rome.

After a long stay in Antiocheia, from which he sailed back to Ephesos to marry Lucilla (HA *Ver.* 7, 7; cf. *Aur.* 9, 4) in 163, Verus advanced downstream along the Euphrates with the large Roman expeditionary force, and Seleukeia and Ctesiphon fell once again into Roman hands. By 165 CE the victory over the Parthians was complete. Nevertheless, Marcus and Verus did not attempt to set up provinces on the far side of the Euphrates, though here (as in Kainepolis) several garrisons were estab-

63. Parthian monument of Ephesos. Vienna, Ephesos Museum.

lished. Subsequently, coins bearing the images of Lucius Verus, Marcus Aurelius, and Commodus were struck in Carrhae, while in Edessa coins bearing the images of Lucius Verus, Lucilla, Marcus Aurelius, Faustina II, and Commodus were struck.

So far as we know, the emperor did not sojourn in Asia Minor on his way home, though in Ephesos the sophist Damianos hosted the troops returning from the war ([162] *IK* Ephesos 672 l. 7–10; 3080 l. 7–10). A victory monument was erected in that city (Figure 63). But the exhausted troops were carrying with them a dreadful booty—probably smallpox, which spread to epidemic proportions (Dio 71, 2, 4) and swept through western Asia Minor (Aristeides, *or.* 33, 6; 48, 38 f.; 51, 25). Signs of general economic distress were subsequently observable in the country.[99]

A first sign of another unfolding disaster was the migration into the empire of the Alani, an unknown people from the north. They were followed by other peoples whose widespread raids on the coasts of the western Black Sea and the Aegean as far as Attica also unsettled the Greeks of Asia and prompted the introduction of special taxes, though these peoples did not yet invade Asia Minor itself. One of these groups was the Costoboci.[100] They attacked places on the coasts of the Black Sea and the Propontis, in Macedonia and Thrace, and plundered Elatea in Phocis and Eleusis in

Attica. Under the immediate impact of the catastrophe reported from Greece, the prominent sophist Aelius Aristeides gave a speech about Eleusis before the council of the city of Smyrna. A gravestone in Pompeiopolis in Paphlagonia (the province of Galatia) praises two men who fell in "a great battle" during the war against the Costoboci, and who were clearly not Roman soldiers. Since there is no other indication that this city was attacked, the two men's involvement must have taken place outside their homeland; they may have been volunteers who had joined a militia deployed in Greece.

In the spring of 175 CE, after Marcus had entrusted him with the supervision of the whole of the Orient, one of the generals in the Parthian War, the native-born Syrian Avidius Cassius, declared himself emperor (Dio 71, 3, cf. VS 563).[101] To put down the uprising, Marcus left the theater of war on the Danube and went to the Orient, where the usurper had in the meantime been killed. In the spring of 176, he traveled back from Antiocheia through Asia Minor. He heard an oration by the sophist Hermogenes in Tarsos and another by the sophist Aelius Aristeides in Smyrna (VS 577–583; Aristeides, *or.* 19, 1; 42, 14). En route, his wife Faustina died in Halala, north of the Cilician Gates (HA *Aur.* 26, 4.9). Just as decades earlier the small coastal city of Selinus had taken the name of Traianopolis to commemorate the death of the great emperor there, so Halala was renamed Faustinopolis in memory of the empress.

Under Marcus Aurelius's successor Commodus (180–192) a change in the provincial structure of the Taurus area seems to have taken place, since it appears that a proconsul named M. Flavius Carminius Athenagoras governed Lycia et Pamphylia and Isauria at this time—that is, the *eparchia* of Isauria was temporarily detached from the great province of Cilicia and added to the province adjoining it on the west. Whether and how long this arrangement existed, we do not know.[102]

For the first time in more than 200 years a major war waged using all available forces was fought on the soil of western Asia Minor. After Avidius Cassius, another governor of Syria, Pescennius Niger, had declared himself emperor in Antiocheia and received support in the East, for example from the proconsul of Asia, Asellius Aemilianus. On the opposing side stood Septimius Severus (193–211), who was favored by the legions of the Rhine and Danube, and who had seized Rome and secured the Senate's recognition. Severus's generals attacked the proconsul near Kyzikos; in January 194 CE they met Niger himself near Lake Ascania in Bithynia (Dio 75, 6 f.; Herodian 3, 2; HA *Sept. Sev.* 8, 6 ff.; *Pesc.* 5, 3 ff.). The two most important Bithynian cities took opposing sides: Nikomedeia chose Severus, Nikaia chose Niger—the loser. Niger retreated over the Taurus toward Syria, but not without occupying the Taurus passes. In Bithynia (where inscriptions from Prusias on the Hypios in particular suggest that the provincials had to endure billeting of troops and forced purchases of grain to supply the armies)[103] and also south of the Cilician Taurus, cities were drawn directly into the conflict. An inscription now preserved in the Museum of Alanya, a letter from Septimius Severus to Syedra in Isauria, praises the resistance of the residents of that little community, who had been driven out of their city by Niger's officers.[104] Tarsos seems to have supported Niger, while Anazarbos did not.

Severus's generals advanced from Bithynia through Galatia to Cappadocia and were forced to besiege their opponents' fortresses at the Cilician Gates. When with the onset of the winter rains and floods Niger's troops, who had occupied the passes, withdrew from their positions, the way to Cilicia and Syria lay open. At Issos, where Alexander had defeated Dareios, and Cicero (and later Germanicus) had associated themselves in different ways with the victory won by the glorious Macedonian, the army finally annihilated its enemy. Leaving Perinthos, Severus himself marched through Bithynia and farther by way of Ankyra toward the southeast.

Presumably only after the decisive battle did the emperor reach Syria, where he distributed praise and punishment. Nikaia in Bithynia lost its rank titles and predicates (p. 479). The metropolis Antiocheia was especially hard hit; it was demoted to a village (*kome*) of its harbor, Laodikeia (today Lattakia), which was raised to the status of a *polis*. It also lost its Olympic games, which were renamed Severeia Olympia Epinikia and moved to Cilicia, to a place close to the battlefield at Issos, where a monument with a quadriga had been erected in honor of Germanicus.[105] The historical choice of the site for the games further exalted the victories won against the Parthians after Issos and before the first celebration of the games took place.

Two Parthian Wars are distinguished. In the spring of 195, Severus invaded the trans-Euphrates area to punish the local princes who had supported Niger (Dio 75, 2; Aurelius Victor 20, 14 f.). This campaign came to an end with the occupation of Nisibis and an expedition to Adiabene made by Severus's generals. Then Severus marched straight across Asia Minor and back to Europe by way of the Bosporus to battle the next pretender, Clodius Albinus. He won a victory at Lugdunum in early 197 CE. In the summer of that year, the army returned to the Orient (Dio 76, 9–12; Herodian 3, 9; HA *Sept. Sev.* 15 f.). Trajan's successes were repeated: Seleukeia and Ctesiphon were conquered, though Hatra once again resisted two sieges. But this time the Roman armies remained on the other side of the Euphrates.

Severus's First Parthian War led to the creation of the province of Mesopotamia. Before the fourth century Osrhoena, an area in northern Mesopotamia immediately south of Commagene, was never an independent province; it was put under the supervision of a procurator, assigned to the province of Coele-Syria, and later incorporated into Mesopotamia. In Osrhoena, the city of Edessa (today Urfa) and its territory were held by the prince Abgar, the son of Ma'nu, who ruled for thirty-five years, from 177/178 to 212. He was a devoted client and friend of the emperor, was received in Rome with ceremonial splendor, and bore the title "the Great."[106] He developed his city magnificently. For example, the remains of columns with inscriptions from the citadel in modern day Urfa date from about his time,[107] and so do the very high-quality mosaics with family scenes of the nobility of Edessa (Figure 64) and representations taken from Greek mythology.[108] His son and his successors had shorter and less successful reigns.[109] In the year 248 CE, the kingdom was finally abolished, and Edessa was incorporated into the Roman province of Mesopotamia.

64. Muqimu, son of Abdnahay, with his daughters, daughter-in-law, and sons. Drawing by Seton Lloyd, after a mosaic in Urfa that is no longer extant. Image from J. B. Segal, *Edessa: The Blessed City*, Oxford 1970, Plate 1.

The splendor and wealth of the age of Severus declined during the subsequent, unending wars, whereas Edessa's literary-theological importance in the Christian empire expanded.

Under Caracalla (211–217), with certain reservations all free adults in the empire received, through the "Constitutio Antoniana," Roman citizenship. A few years after Severus's oriental campaigns, the provinces and cities of Asia Minor that lay alongside the great military routes saw the imperial army once again moving: in 214 CE Caracalla crossed the Hellespont with the intention of waging another Parthian War (Dio 77, 16, 7; Herodian 4, 8, 3–6; HA *Carac.* 5, 8 f.). Beforehand, he had deposed the son and successor of Abgar "the Great" in Edessa as well as the king (his name is not known) in Armenia, whereupon that country fell into anarchy. It has been proven that in the province of Asia Caracalla visited Ilion, Pergamon, and Thyateira, which he made an assize town (*conventus iuridicus*) ([106] OGIS 517), and then sojourned in Bithynia. His march continued through Ankyra and Tyana to Tarsos and Antiocheia in Syria. Once again the inscriptions at Prusias on the Hypios in Bithynia tell us that the notables of the little city had to provide food and lodging for the imperial entourage and the "holy" army.

Thus we are in a time in which the burdens imposed on provincials were in no way limited to the army's passage alone. The campaigns were preceded and accompanied by hectic movements of soldiers and imperial officers on the primary and secondary roads of Anatolia; a series of documents from the Lydian-Phrygian area that date from the Severan age and later tells us about the hardships endured by the *coloni* (tenants on imperial or senatorial estates) and peasants on the plains and their desperate attempts to gain a hearing from the emperor by means of petitions:

> We are being harassed to the extent of the unaccountable and extorted by those who ought to be protecting the public. . . . Living in the open countryside and not near military camps we nevertheless suffer affliction alien to the golden age of your reign. Traversing the territory of the Appians and leaving the main roads, soldiers, leading men from the town of Appia, and your agents are coming to us and are leaving the main roads and they are taking us away from our work, requisitioning our draft animals and extorting that to which they have no right. (trans. Marek) [110]

The new element in the situation that can be inferred from these testimonies is not the individual abuse. Whereas before people had been able to rely on legal regulations and the governor's supervision, henceforth the certainty of law was clearly weaker, and in certain transit zones people were prompted to seize the initiative against the increasing "military anarchy." [111]

After wintering in Edessa (Dio 78, 5, 4; HA *Carac.* 6, 6–7, 1), Caracalla was murdered while on his way to Carrhae, on April 8, 217. Macrinus, who was made emperor, never made it to either Asia Minor or Rome, but was, after concluding a peace treaty with the Parthian Artabanos IV, defeated by the troops of his Roman opponents near his "capital" of Antiocheia (Dio 78, 39, 1). These troops were raised on the initiative of a woman: Julia Maesa. She was Septimius Severus's sister-in-law and was married to the senator Julius Avitus Alexianus from Emesa, who came from Syria. The marriages of the daughters of this pair, Julia Sohaemias and Julia Avita Mamaea, produced the Syrian emperors Elagabalus (218–222) and Severus Alexander (222–235).

Under Severus Alexander a reorganization of certain provinces in Asia Minor was begun (ca. 230–235 CE), the evidence for which is almost exclusively drawn from an abundant series of milestones stretching from the second quarter of the third century to the second half of the fourth century CE. It is significant for the crisis in the East that governors' names, previously rather rare, show up frequently on these stones. The *eparchiae* Pontus Mediterraneus and Paphlagonia were no longer under the supervision of legates of Cappadocia and Galatia but are joined together under that of an equestrian procurator who acted as governor with the title *praeses Ponti Paflagoniae* (or either *eparchia* might be named *pars pro toto*). Various lists have been compiled in scholarly literature, all of them outdated. At present we know the names of twenty *praesides* from seventy-eight milestones. Later, under Decius (249–251), Phrygia and Caria were detached from the province of Asia. These new provinces were not led, as in Pontos, by equestrians, but rather by consular legates.[112]

In this period, starting ca. 220 CE, the Parthian kingdom declined, while the Sasanids, a Persian clan that traced its ancestry back to Sāsān, ascended (for a list of rulers of this new dynasty, see the Appendix). As had once happened among the Achaemenids, in Persis there arose from a small local dominion a powerful prince named Ardashir (perhaps Sāsān's grandson). This Ardashir had defeated Artabanos IV in battle and taken the title "King of Kings."[113] The last known Parthian coin was struck in 228 CE. The 300-year-old opposition between Rome and the Parthian kingdom, whose influence on the situation in Asia Minor had become increasingly strong, thus came to an end. However, peace did not return on the Euphrates and the Tigris. On the contrary, wars on several fronts in the country and on its borders threw the empire into its most serious crisis since the beginning of the Imperial period.

Crisis and Transition

Around the middle of the third century CE the Roman Orient fell into a crisis that the historian Alfred Heuss characterized as "the collapse of the empire."[114] Today, this event is viewed in a more subtle and complex way. Internal weaknesses and invasions of the empire from the outside were intertwined. Asia Minor was attacked by various external enemies. Between ca. 255 and 276 CE several major intrusions from the north took place as Goths, Borani, and Heruli landed in Asia Minor and devastated parts of the peninsula.[115] The chronology of the individual waves of invaders is difficult to determine and cannot be discussed here. They attacked and plundered Trapezus, advanced along the coast as far as Herakleia, and also penetrated the interior of Cappadocia, Paphlagonia, and Galatia. One wave passed through the Bosporus to reach the cities of Bithynia: Nikomedeia, Nikaia, Kios, Apameia, and Prusa were pillaged. Further waves struck the west and south coasts. Ilion, Ephesos, and the Artemision did not escape the invader's destructive fury (HA *Gall.* 6, 2), though it was still possible to defend Miletus and the Didymaion. The citizens of Miletus, under siege by the barbarians, were saved from dying of thirst by a freshly discovered water source, which the proconsul Flavius Festus later had architecturally decorated ([146] MS I 108). The circumstances resembled those during the invasions of the Galatians more than half a millennium earlier, especially in that once again local and regional authorities had to seize the initiative to defend themselves, as did the Asiarch Makarios in Miletus ([146] MS I 132) and the citizens of Side during the attacks on the coast of Pamphylia (Dexippos, FGrHist 100 F 29). I have already mentioned the obvious "military anarchy" that occurred in these circumstances. One of the authorities that undertook to provide order, at least within its religious community, was the Christian church. This is vividly described in an authentic letter of Gregory Thaumaturgus to a neighboring bishop:[116]

Canon V.

But others deceive themselves by fancying that they can retain the property of others which they may have found as an equivalent for their own property which they have lost. In this way verily, just as the Borani and Goths brought the havoc of war on them, they make themselves Boradi and Goths to others. Accordingly we have sent to you our brother and comrade in old age, Euphrosynus, with this view, that he may deal with you in accordance with our model here, and teach you against whom you ought to admit accusations, and whom you ought to exclude from your prayers.

Canon VI.

Concerning those who forcibly detain captives (who have escaped) from the barbarians. Moreover, it has been reported to us that a thing has happened in your country which is surely incredible, and which, if done at all, is altogether the work of unbelievers, and impious men, and men who know not the very name of the Lord; to wit, that some have gone to such a pitch of cruelty and inhumanity, as to be detaining by force certain captives who have made their escape. Dispatch ye commissioners into the country, lest the thunderbolts of heaven fall all too surely upon those who perpetrate such deeds.

Canon VII.

Concerning those who have been enrolled among the barbarians, and who have dared to do certain monstrous things against those of the same race with themselves. Now, as regards those who have been enrolled among the barbarians, and have accompanied them in their irruption in a state of captivity, and who, forgetting that they were from Pontus, and Christians, have become such thorough barbarians, as even to put those of their own race to death by the gibbet (ξύλῳ) or strangulation, and to show their roads or houses to the barbarians, who else would have been ignorant of them, it is necessary for you to debar such persons even from being auditors in the public congregations (ἀκροάσεως), until some common decision about them is come to by the saints assembled in council, and by the Holy Spirit antecedently to them.[117]

The emperor Tacitus died in 275/276 CE during a campaign against the Heruli, who had once again attacked Cappadocia out of the north (Zosimos 1, 63; HA *Tac.* 13, 2–5).

Around the same time, an even greater storm was gathering in the east.[118] Ardashir's son Shapur had invaded Nisibis and Carrhae after 235 CE. The cities were temporarily reconquered by the army brought straight across Asia Minor by Emperor Gordian III (238–244) and the praetorian prefect Timesitheos[119] (Zonaras 12, 18; Zosimos 1, 18; HA *Gord.* 26, 6–27, 3), but the army was defeated in the battle near Misiche in Mesopotamia in 244 CE. The succeeding emperor, Philippus Arabs, was able to purchase peace with Shapur by paying him a large sum of money (Figure 65). But in the years following 250 CE the Sasanids invaded Armenia, which Shapur conquered and had his son Hormizd rule. When farther to the north Iberia also fell under Sasanid control, only enemy territory remained beyond the middle

65. Naqš-i-Rustem, Iran, Fars province. The Roman emperors Valerian and Philippus Arabs as inferiors before the Sasanid king Shapur.

Euphrates. Worse was on its way. After a further Roman defeat near Barbalissos in northern Syria in 253, the Sasanids carried out a pincer movement on the province of Coele-Syria. The last time a Parthian army had managed to enter Antiocheia had been almost 300 years earlier, in 40 BCE. Now it happened again: according to the account given by the historian Ammianus Marcellinus, the people of Antiocheia were sitting in the theater—the audience had its back to Mons Silpius—and were enjoying the performance of a mime and his wife when the latter suddenly saw armed men appear on the crest of the mountain and shouted: "Unless I am dreaming, here are the Persians!" (Ammianus 23, 5, 3).[120]

While conducting a third campaign, the Roman emperor Valerian (253–260) was taken prisoner near Edessa (see Figure 65). Shapur obviously could not take this city itself, but ca. 260 CE several of his army groups invaded Cappadocia and marched along the Cilician coast as far as Traianopolis. Such major cities as Tarsos in Cilicia and Kaisareia below Mt. Argaios in Cappadocia were plundered and their citizens taken prisoner and hauled off.

While on the Roman side the usurpation carried out by Macrianus and Quietus against Gallienus, Valerian's son, pinned down forces and weakened the defense, Shapur encountered a dangerous opponent in the Syrian caravan city of Palmyra. A certain Hairan came from one of the leading families of wealthy merchants in this city. Under Severus this family had received Roman citizenship, and around the middle of the third century Hairan had achieved senatorial rank and gave himself the Palmyrene title of *reš Tadmôr* ("supreme head of Tadmor"—that is, the older,

66. Ruins of the city founded by Zenobia on the Euphrates ca. 270 CE.

Semitic name of the city). In a Greek inscription from 258 CE his son Septimius Odainathos is given the additional name of *hypatikos* (Latin: *consularis*), a usual designation for the governor of a Roman province. But it is not clear whether Odainathos was actually the governor of Syria Phoinike. In any case, he distinguished himself with two victories that must have seemed brilliant from the Roman perspective of the ruling emperor Gallienus: first he got rid of the usurper Fulvius Quietus in Emesa (today Homs). Then he attacked Sasanid Mesopotamia, conquered Carrhae and Nisibis, and advanced as far as Ctesiphon, but without taking it (ca. 261/262 CE). The Palmyrene empire emerged, a remarkable hybrid between an oriental kingdom and a Roman governorship. Odainathos and his son Vaballathus now called themselves "king of kings," "leader of the Romans" (*dux Romanorum*), and "restorer of the whole Orient" (*corrector totius Orientis*).

Odainathos was assassinated in 267/268 CE, and his widow Batzabbai, better known under the Greek name Zenobia (ca. 240–ca. 272) seized control (Figure 66). She created what was in effect a splinter empire, since she no longer acted with the agreement of or on behalf of Rome. A Palmyrene army under her general Zabdas occupied Egypt. Finally, the Palmyrenes took Antiocheia, drove over the Taurus into Asia Minor as far as Ankyra, and even on to the Bosporus: Chalkedon closed its gates when the "Syrians " arrived (Zosimos 1, 44). Zenobia had coins minted in Antiocheia showing the emperor Aurelian on the obverse and her son L. Julius Aurelius Septimius Vaballathus Athenodorus, *rex, consul, imperator, dux Romanorum*, on the reverse. The continued use of names and symbols of the Roman power[121] is an important sign of how membership in the Roman Empire seems to have become, even in this marginal region and despite all the power of local traditions, the only conceivable or desirable lifeworld.

Emperor Aurelian's expedition to the Orient in 271/272 CE, which once again passed through Asia Minor on the main road via Ankara, Tyana, and the Cilician Gates, put an end to the Palmyrene splinter empire. Zenobia appears to have died in Roman captivity. What must be remembered is that the Palmyrenes' conquests at no time established their rule north of the Taurus. There was no "splinter empire" in Anatolia. Only in the phase of direct confrontation with the emperor did the Arab queen and her son emerge as counter-emperors, Zenobia calling herself "Augusta" (Sebaste) and her son styling himself Imperator Caesar L. Julius Aurelius Septimius Vaballathus Athenodorus Persicus Maximus Arabicus Maximus Adiabenicus Maximus Pius Felix Augustus. From the Anatolian point of view, there had been another power struggle in the imperial military under which parts of the country had been made to suffer.

Sasanid Armenia first became a Roman protectorate again in 297, when the Caesar Galerius (293–311; after 305 Augustus) defeated Shapur's son Narseh in eastern Anatolia. It was the final chord that put an end to a cacophony of war and chaos. Late in the same century fundamental changes loomed on the horizon, and the coming century was once again to bring a new order in the provinces.

CHAPTER 8

Asia Minor and Imperial Administration under the Principate

Provincia and Eparchia

The term *provincia* in the Asia Minor of the Imperial period raises a problem.[1] In Roman inscriptions, the word's meaning is ambivalent. Sometimes it refers to the great provinces ruled by a senatorial governor—Asia, Pontus et Bithynia, and Cilicia since the time of the republic, and under the Principate also Galatia, Cappadocia, Lycia et Pamphylia, and a newly formed province of Cilicia. However, the same documents use the term for smaller units that were part of one of these great provinces and were occasionally transferred from one of them to another. In particular, the provinces of Galatia and Cappadocia consisted of formations that retained their respective names, even in official documents, well into the Imperial period: Pisidia, Phrygia, Lycaonia, Pamphylia, Paphlagonia, and Pontus Galaticus, as well as Pontus Polemonianus, Pontus Mediterraneus, and Armenia Minor. The same goes for the coastal provinces of Lycia, which was enlarged by the addition of Pamphylia, and for Cilicia, to which Isauria and part of Lycaonia were joined.

The official title of a governor of a great province generally listed all its constituent parts, one after another. For example, in the time of Trajan, Lucius Caesennius Sospes bore the title *legatus Augusti pro praetore provinciae Galatiae, Pisidiae, Phrygiae, Lycaoniae, Isauriae, Paphlagoniae, Ponti Galatici, Ponti Polemoniani, Armeniae* (ILS 1017).[2] The governor's dominion as a whole is represented by the name at the head of the queue. Research has not been able to fully explain the significance of such lists from the Roman point of view. It has been suggested that they may refer to assize districts (*dioikeseis*, or in Latin, *conventus*)[3] or that the governor sought to preserve the identity of the different regions in a province, perhaps out of consideration for the subject population or to display before his subjects the range of his area of activity.[4] However, it may be asked why in inscriptions regarding their careers, Asia's proconsuls list neither an assize, nor—as rulers of a province comparable in size to the other "great" provinces—the names of the geographic areas corresponding to the various ethnic groups and regions of Asia, such as Troas, Aiolis, Mysia, Lydia, Ionia, Caria, or Phrygia.

Galatia, Cappadocia, and Cilicia, in contrast to Asia or Bithynia, may be characterized as provincial conglomerates that were gradually put together: the governor did not see himself as the ruler of just the core area (whose name, as just mentioned, may sometimes stand for the whole) but instead listed the regional units that complemented and enlarged the core area. His title gives us a genetic model, so to speak, of his great province, even if the correct chronological sequence is not respected. At the time when it was annexed, each additional unit was inscribed into the *forma* or *formula provinciae*, the register of the cities and other communities subject to the Romans under a governor. We do not know whether each unit received from the Romans its own framework legislation or was referred to an existing one. Thus for instance we do not know whether Pompey's *lex* of the province of Pontus et Bithynia, to which in his time the northern part of Paphlagonia belonged, still remained in force in Paphlagonia after that regional unit was newly established as *provincia* in 5 BCE. It may have been put under a new law—whether its own or a (not proven) law of Galatia. [5]

If one studies the emergence and shifting of these units, it becomes clear that almost every one of them has a past as part of a dynastic possession that in some cases is also reflected in the nomenclature: *Pontus Polemonianus, Lycaonia Antiochiana, tetrarchia ex Lycaonia*. To be sure, several of these formations might have been united in one kingdom as early as the Hellenistic period (e.g., under the dynast Amyntas), but they did not lose their original identity even later in the Roman provincial system. The history and geography of the provincialization of Paphlagonia, the two Pontic entities (*Pontus Galaticus, Pontus Polemonianus*), and Lesser Armenia (*Armenia Minor*) , between 6/5 BCE and 72 CE are clear. That is not the case for Pisidia, Phrygia, Lycaonia, and Pamphylia.

As regards Pisidia, the former possession of Amyntas was absorbed into the early form of the great province of Galatia. The legate of Ankyra had to relinquish part of it to the newly founded double province of Lycia et Pamphylia (ca. 72 CE), but this part was never written out in the enlarged province's official name. In the inscriptions of the post-Flavian period, "Pisidia" refers only to the northern part of Pisidia that remained part of Galatia.

The whole, extensive region of Phrygia was not part of the nucleus of the province of Asia established in 129 BCE. The same holds for Caria. Both areas were added to this province in the time of the Roman Republic, but Phrygia was never entirely absorbed into it. The easternmost part of this country was incorporated, as the eparchy of Phrygia (mentioned among the governor's titles in the time of the Flavians and Trajan), into the Imperial period province of Galatia, while the eparchy of Caria was separated from Asia as a distinct unit only in the middle of the third century CE.

Like "Phrygia," "Lycaonia" designates a country that was considerably larger than the *provincia* constituted out of it. Its history is complicated. An annexed province of Lycaonia was first joined with Asia toward the end of the second century BCE and then integrated, as an independent assize district with its center in Philomelion (p. 259), into the province's administration. This Asian assize district continued to exist until at least 40 CE ([171] I. Didyma 148). From it must be distinguished the separate units known as the "tetrarchy from Lycaonia," on the one hand, and "Lycaonia proper," on the other, which lay between Lake Tuz and the Taurus (Pliny the

Elder, *nat.* 5, 95). According to Strabo (12, 6, 1; cf. 12, 5, 4), both were held by Amnytas, the former apparently he held as as tetrarch and the latter as king, together with the conquest of his new residence in Isaura farther to the south. Probably as soon as at the date of his death, in 25 BCE, both were incorporated into Galatia. After "Lycaonia proper"—that is, the southeastern part of the steppe near the Taurus Mountains—had been ceded to Antiochos IV Ephiphanes of Commagene between 38 and 72 CE, under Vespasian this part, known as *Antiocheiane*, was absorbed into the Galatia-Cappadocia conglomerate. It was presumably Hadrian who first added it to Cilicia; but Prifernius Paetus, the governor of Cappadocia ca. 129 CE, still counts Lycaonia among the eparchies he ruled. However, the earliest stage of the *tres eparchiae* of Cilicia—Cilicia, Isauria, and Lycaonia—is uncertain; we cannot prove this formation's existence before Antoninus Pius.

Finally, there are also questions about the genesis of the eparchy of Pamphylia. Whereas Amnytas held only an eastern section of the Pamphylian coast with the city of Side, the larger western part of this country with Attaleia remained part of the province of Asia. Both of them had first been united when Pamphylia was absorbed into the conglomerate of Galatia (cf. Pliny the Elder, *nat.* 5, 146 f.), that is, the province of Asia was diminished to the advantage of the new formation.

From the known sources we cannot infer that anywhere Roman magistrates specifically responsible for them stood at the head of these eparchies. However, procurators seem to have been responsible for one or more of them. As mentioned earlier, these units cannot be equated with *conventus*. And yet they were in no way insignificant in the administrative pyramid: as in the oldest provinces established under the republic, during the Imperial period so-called provincial commonalties (see p. 415) were set up in eparchies. So far as we know, these were organizations that were more tolerated by the Romans than created by them. However, they were nowhere constituted independently of the Roman system, but rather always on the basis of a *provincia*. We can observe the almost complete congruence of the provincial commonalties and the eparchies. With the exception of Pisidia and Isauria, there is testimony for all the eparchies showing that they had provincial commonalties: Phrygia, Galatia, Paphlagonia, Pontus, Cappadocia, Lesser Armenia, Lycia, Pamphylia, Lycaonia, and Cilicia. Once they had founded their provincial commonalties after being annexed, the eparchies retained them unchanged during the shift from one great province to another. Where, as in the case of Cilicia as a part of Syria, one provincial commonalty was formed of several eparchies, after a shift the old affiliation might persist for a time across the new provincial boundaries. In contrast, when territories in Anatolia that had been provincialized and then given back to dynasts were provincialized again, they never went back to the older provincial commonalties but always formed new ones. As a result, we see that when organizing themselves, the subjects constantly strove to achieve a structural adaptation to the Roman units. The reason for this can only lie in the administrative functions they had to perform for the governors and, as the example of Lycia may show, first of all in the fiscal domain.

Roman Administrative Organization

How Rome's rule over Asia Minor during the *pax Romana* was organized cannot be determined on the basis of a coherent body of laws or regulations, but only on that of the kind of people it employed and what they did. This personnel included proconsuls assigned by lot in the Senate, legates sent to the country by the emperor, procurators, freedmen, and slaves, as well as the soldiers stationed there, in contrast to the personnel appointed by the provincial commonalties, cities, and communities themselves in accord with traditional rules and in part in accord with Roman guidelines (p. 426). On the basis of the sources, the scope, density, and nature of such an imperial "administration"—the justification for using this term is already questionable—can be grasped only with difficulty, and remain highly controversial.[6] As we shall see, there are also great differences within Asia Minor regarding the conditions under which Rome's personnel ruled. However, we can hardly go wrong in making the general observation that the formation of *poleis* begun during the Hellenistic period (which had advanced significantly in some areas) provided decisive support for the Roman mode of government. Where it was possible, Rome pushed still further this way of penetrating the country.

Governors

The praetorian and consular governors had advanced to their posts in accord with a system of promotion well established since Augustus; they ruled areas that were sometimes of enormous extent (for a list of governors, see the Appendix). Although Roman policy allowed the inhabitants of the provinces to file complaints with the Senate against governors after the conclusion of the latter's term in office, from the point of view of the subjects we can say that these rulers had an almost monarchical status. At first, under Augustus, governors still received cult-like reverence, and cities were allowed to honor them by putting their portraits on coins along with the image of the emperor, or even alone. However, these portraits soon yielded everywhere to that of the emperor, though the last known examples still date from the early reign of Claudius.[7]

The governor himself was, as Aelius Aristeides (*or.* 26, 31 f.) put it in his encomium to the Roman Empire, both ruler and ruled—and as such was on an equal footing with the governors of other provinces. They turned to their master, like a chorus to its director, whenever they had the slightest doubt.[8] As far as governors and their senatorial and equestrian subordinates with leadership functions are concerned, a considerable number of individuals is known to us by name from the provinces of Asia Minor during the period from Augustus to Diocletian. We probably know more than 80 percent of the proconsuls of Asia from Augustus to the end of the third century. The percentage is lower for other provinces, and only a small number of the personnel at the lower levels have been recorded. Nevertheless prosopographic research has informed us about parts of a three-century-long intact system of Roman government in Asia Minor to an extent unmatched by our knowledge of any other system of government in the ancient history of the land. To be sure, the personnel lists—year by year and province by province—remain incomplete, and the fine points of their chronology are problematic. They cannot be examined in detail here.[9]

From the islands of the eastern Aegean Sea to the middle Euphrates, at any given time five or six governors ruled, depending on whether Galatia-Cappadocia was united or divided. The short-term gubernatorial functions of the so-called praesidial procurators mentioned above can be left out of consideration here.

Every governor was fundamentally limited to his province; he was not allowed to interfere in the affairs of a colleague in a neighboring province; indeed, he was not allowed even to cross the border of another province in an official function. Depending on rank, function, and other characteristics, there were differences among individual officeholders. The rulers of Asia and Cappadocia stand out in various respects. The *proconsul Asiae* was, like his colleague in Africa, generally at the apex of his senatorial career, and in the early Imperial period he had usually been a consul at least five years back before becoming governor; from the Flavians on, this period rose to fifteen years and sometimes even more. As the provost of the most civilized province with the largest population, the densest network of cities, and the greatest economic power, an older, highly-decorated senator was usually chosen—for example, Sextus Appuleius (a nephew of Augustus) or Boionius Arrius Antoninus (who later became Emperor Antoninus Pius). Most of these "mandarins" had experience in the administration of other provinces also in Asia Minor: C. Antius Julius Quadratus had been active in three Anatolian provinces over nearly thirty years (from ca. 80 to 110 CE), as a judge (*juridicus*) under the governor in Galatia-Cappadocia, as governor in Lycia et Pamphylia and in Asia, and also in Commagene (as part of Syria). They also had experience in dealing with troops; one need think only of Domitius Corbulo, Ulpius Traianus (the father of the emperor, who as Syria's legate had earned *ornamenta triumphalia*), or Pompeius Falco (who had commanded legions in Judea, Moesia Inferior, and Britain). In the second century the *proconsul Asiae* was paid a million sesterces for one year's service in office (Dio 79, 22, 5).

The emperors also usually entrusted Cappadocia, the sole Anatolian province with legionary garrison, only to an ex-consul. The province required a man with a general's mantle who was, even in times of peace, familiar with military camps and staff quarters in a rough and harsh country and spent less time than others at the theater, in the agora, or in the colonnaded house of a philosopher friend. Most legates appear to have matched this profile; I mention here only C. Julius Quadratus Bassus, previously legate of Judea and Trajan's army commander (*dux*) and companion (*comes*) in the Dacian War, where he was awarded the *ornamenta triumphalia*.

In contrast to Cappadocia and Asia, Cilicia, Lycia et Pamphylia, and Pontus et Bithynia remained rungs fairly far down the career ladder, which were usually reached at least five years after the praetorship and the consulate. Most of their governors were still quite young, between 35 and 45 years old, whereas the few older ones did not have exactly brilliant careers behind them. For the majority of them, this was the first province in which they served; they did not bring with them much experience in governing other provinces. When they did have experience in governing, it tended to be nonmilitary—for example, men who had been proconsuls of Achaia, like Valerius Severus before he led Lycia et Pamphylia (ca. 120–123 CE), Pactumeius Clemens before he led Cilicia (ca. 138), or Julius Scapula before he governed Galatia at about the same time. Pliny's successor in Pontus et Bithynia, Tertullus, knew the Narbonensis as the proconsul's legate, as did its Severan governor, Fabius Cilo, who had also worked as quaestor in Crete and Cyrene, served as governor of Galatia, before becoming governor of Pontus et Bithynia, and so forth. Years of service as a subordinate frequently preceded a governorship in Asia Minor, often as a proconsular legate in the same or another province.

The princeps determined the term of office for imperial delegates (*legati Augusti pro praetore*, p. 316 f.), but as a rule it was two to three years.[10] Marcius Priscus served in turbulent times as legate of Lycia for eight years under Nero, Galba, Otho, Vitellius, and Vespasian. The proconsuls served for one year, but among them there were also exceptions. Information gleaned from coins minted in Pergamon indicates that under Tiberius, P. Petronius's proconsulate in Asia lasted six years (ca. 29–35 CE). The proconsul Egnatius Victor Lollianus governed the same province for three years under Gordian III and Philippus Arabs.

Many of the governors had literary and intellectual interests. In fact, some of the proconsuls were particularly prominent men of letters. Under the Flavians Asia was governed by the poet and Stoic philosopher Silius Italicus, the author of *Punica*, an epic in seventeen books, and under Domitian by Julius Frontinus, who wrote technical treatises on aqueducts and military matters, and after his governorship became head of the water supply system (*curator aquarum*) in Rome. Under Trajan, the historian Cornelius Tacitus (ca. 58–ca. 116) held the office. Hardly half a century later Cornelius Fronto, a celebrated orator and the tutor of Marcus Aurelius and Lucius Verus, had to decline the post because he was ill.[11] In Pontus et Bithynia we find a Petronius—who is very probably the author of the *Satyricon* and the "expert in matters of refined ways of living" (*elegantiae arbiter*) who committed suicide under Nero—and also the writer Pliny the Younger. Cappadocia could claim Flavius Arrianus, a philosopher, scientist, and historian of Alexander the Great's campaigns.

So far as their ancestry is concerned, natives are in the minority among the governors of the Anatolian provinces. People from Italy or the western provinces are predominant; and even among those who came from the regions of Asia Minor, we find not a few who have a "western migration background" (e.g., citizens of the *coloniae* of Alexandria Troas or Antiocheia in Pisidia). In Pontus et Bithynia, Plancius Varus is the first who we are sure came from a family that had taken root in Asia Minor, in Perge. Perge is also the homeland of the family of Cornutus Tertullus, who administered the same province after Pliny. Otherwise, only Antiocheia in Pisidia, Pergamon, and Ankyra can be proven to have produced several provincial governors. All the others of gubernatorial rank came without exception from cities in western

Anatolia, Nikomedeia and Nikaia, Alexandria Troas, Mytilene, Sardeis, Nysa, and Side.[12]

Personnel

Naturally, each governor brought with him a small number of officials and companions, and found in the legions, auxiliaries, and naval units of the fleet (*classis Pontica* on the Black Sea) a reservoir of soldiers who could be commandeered to perform specific tasks in his surroundings. We cannot determine with precision the number of personnel available in any province at any given time. It is estimated that for the province of Asia the total, from senatorial officeholders down to subordinate service personnel, remained far fewer than a hundred, but for the rest it may have been entirely different from one province to another. If we conservatively assume that there were a few hundred Roman officials in the five Anatolian great provinces—excluding the standing army troops—we have an astonishingly small body of personnel, which helps us understand how much Roman rule depended on the stratum of Hellenized dignitaries in the cities. The Cambridge historian Keith Hopkins contrasted the slender presence of Roman "elite administrators" (senators and knights) in the provinces with the conditions in southern China in the twelfth century: "The Chinese government had twenty-five times as many élite administrators at work in the provinces as the Roman government."[13]

The personnel can be divided into senators, knights, and subaltern officeholders, along with a few special commissioners. Let us examine first the so-called senatorial provinces. The task of the proconsul's legates consisted entirely of representing and supporting the governor. Unlike the proconsul of Asia, who had three legates, each of the other proconsuls had only one to assist him. The task of the quaestors (who were under the proconsul's authority) was to supervise the collection of taxes. As advisors in legal, military, and technical matters, the proconsuls were allowed to bring with them to the province a set number (*Digest* 27, 1, 41, 2), for example six to ten, of *comites* or a "group of friends" (*cohors amicorum*), as well as an undetermined number, for example twelve to twenty, of slaves. There were also a number of *apparitores* brought along from Rome: attendants for the proconsul and his quaestor, along with *scribae* and *tabularii* working in the secretariat and the archives, and other officials, among them also the lictors who preceded the proconsuls during public appearances, carrying a bundle of rods (*fasces*) with a projecting axe-blade. At some point, despite his theoretical claim to twelve lictors, the proconsul of Asia limited himself, like his colleague in Africa, to six, the number due to other proconsuls.[14] The lictors were not purely a status symbol, but also a means of exercising jurisdiction. In contrast to the other *apparitores*, five lictors were also assigned to the *legati Augusti pro praetore* in the so-called *provinciae Caesaris*. Any further service in support of the latter was covered by commandeered soldiers on their staffs (*officia*), and we know a whole range of their various functions. At the top of the hierarchy was the *cornicularius*, a kind of head of personnel and organizer, then came the *librarii* under a *princeps* or *optio praetorii* ("office manager"), then staff members and orderlies who had executive and supervising functions, such as the *beneficiarii*, and also specialists who wrote up the official diaries (*commentarienses*), kept the minutes (*exceptores*), cared for the horses (*stratores*), performed police duties (*frumentarii*),[15] served as executioners (*speculatores*) and torturers (*quaestionarii*), attended religious rites (*haruspices*). In addition, there were the governor's bodyguards (*pedites* and *equites singulares*).[16]

The emperor's private property, the *patrimonium*, was administered in all provinces by patrimonial procurators appointed directly by the princeps (when these were associated with landed estates, they are distinguished in modern scholarly literature as "domanial procurators"). The tasks performed by quaestors in senatorial provinces were performed in the imperial provinces by financial or fiscal procurators, who always came from the equestrian order. They were responsible to the emperor for tax revenues and also handled payment of the troops. In inscriptions from the Imperial period, the responsibilities of the procurators in Asia Minor were defined titularly by a declaration of territories and/or specific tasks, such as the administration of the *patrimonium*, the carrying out of tax assessments (*census*), the levying of the inheritance tax, and the administration of gladiator schools. We know the names of about eighty of these officials. In the vast majority of cases their areas of responsibility corresponded to territories of provinces, such as Asia, Galatia, Bithynia, Paphlagonia, and Phrygia; exceptions include the procurators assigned to collect the inheritance tax: *vicesima hereditatium regionis Cariae et insularum Cycladum* or *per insulas Cycladas*, and subprocurators who were responsible for certain regions in Lycia or Asia. For their part, procurators had a staff composed of commandeered soldiers (*officiales*).

Since the time of Trajan there had been special categories of officials who were not part of the gubernatorial personnel but were also not really municipal officials—although they were often responsible for individual cities: the *curatores rei publicae*[17] and the *correctores rei publicae*. The latter were imperial special commissioners, appointed temporarily at the provincial level, whose task was "to set in order the constitution of free cities" (*ad ordinandum statum liberarum civitatum*) (Pliny the Younger, *ep.* 8, 24; trans. Radice). The *curatores*, who were also appointed by the emperor on a temporary basis, were responsible for the stabilization and supervision of municipal finances in general or in specific sectors, such as public works; at first, as a rule they did not come from the city concerned but were instead recruited mainly from the class of notables in their home provinces. Only later on were they chosen from residents of the cities themselves. An imperial epistle to the city of Ephesos ([162] *IK* Ephesos 15–16) shows that the *curatores'* supervisory authority over the financial conduct of municipal bureaucracies, even concerning years lying far in the past, could be extremely rigorous.[18]

Activities

Governors' travel to their posts, their arrival, administrative activity, and return home took place in firmly established ways and were accompanied by certain ceremonies. The threshold through which many Romans entered and left the Asian continent was the splendid metropolis of Ephesos. Thus Pliny the Younger (*ep.* 10, 17) did not head directly for his province of Pontus et Bithynia, either by sea or by land, but rather sailed to Ephesos, from which he traveled north by carriage—suffering from the oppressive heat—as far as Pergamon and its harbor Elaia, whence he boarded coastal vessels that took him through the Dardanelles and on to Bithynia.

As a rule, the first destination must have been the governor's residence. The Roman term for this is *caput provinciae*, "provincial capital" (*Digest* 1, 16, 7), whereas there is—remarkably—no corresponding word in Greek. We are not sure of the assignment of every capital city in all the Anatolian provinces, as we are in the cases of Ephesos for Asia and Ankyra for Galatia.[19] For the others, Nikomedeia (Pontus et Bithynia), Kaisareia below Mt. Argaios (Cappadocia), Tarsos (Cilicia), and Patara (Lycia et Pamphylia), can be considered more or less certain. Archaeologists have not found remains of an actual government building in any of the places named, not even in Ephesos. Naturally, the *capita provinciarum* benefited from their proximity to the governor. The burden this proximity may have imposed on them, as on other cities on the occasion of a governor's visit (particularly the requirement that they provide lodging for officials' entourages) is hard to assess.

No doubt the cities were also keen to welcome the governor within their walls. Thus the genre of the oration of invitation and greeting developed in the rhetorical textbooks of the Imperial period (Menandros 3, 378–382; 14, 424–430), and a fine example of this kind of text is offered by a speech that was delivered in Smyrna by Aelius Aristeides (*or.* 17). It is refreshingly short; obviously the virtuoso's artistic prose was not supposed to strain the Roman's patience or spoil his mood. But Ephesians who were there must have been annoyed, because in this speech Smyrna, a competitor of the capital and the orator's adopted home, is wreathed in a dazzling light outshining all other cities. The account of the various phases of its founding and settlement culminates, as in a carefully revised artwork, in perfect harmony. And the verbal tour of the present-day city offers the sympathetic listener such a compelling idyll that once he has left it, his mind's eye cannot help turning back to it again. He is as shocked by its beauty as he would be by a snake bite. The Bay of Hermios offers itself as a "breast" (*kolpos*, the Greek word for "bay" and "breast"): soft, beautiful, well-formed, and—useful! The speaker has no need to tell the governor anything more about the people: "For you yourself will judge them and will make them better still by prescribing for them in the best way."[20] In Menandros's handbook, the examination of the situation of the subjects is an established part of the welcoming speech (*peri ton hypekoon logos*).

The governor did not merely stand at the top of the civilian administration of the whole province. He was also in command of the Roman troops stationed there.[21] In that respect there was in theory no difference between proconsuls of senatorial provinces or *legati Augusti* of imperial provinces, even if the active role these governors played as military leaders could diverge considerably. He administered justice to the soldiers and was responsible to the emperor for the enforcement of *disciplina militaris*. Recruitment, pay, promotion, and dismissal took place on his responsibility. At specific times governors had to take the initiative for developing the military and civilian infrastructure (in particular the roads) on the provincial level. In addition, they had to direct central religious activities in which soldiers, Roman citizens, and provincials participated.[22] The governor was apparently not usually present at meetings of the *concilium provinciae* (p. 314), but he did sometimes attend them.[23]

In forming a judgment regarding the mode of government and the degree of governmental control,[24] we have to keep in mind that the primarily urban epigraphic evidence provides us with a superficial and regionally one-sided knowledge of these subjects. In general, our documentation shows that the governors reacted to numerous petitions directed to them by their subjects, individuals and communities; replying to these petitions must have represented a considerable share of their routine activity.

Most of the monuments honoring governors, legates, quaestors, and procurators arose from decrees made by the communities.[25] The large, prominent *poleis* in the western parts of the country are predominant in our sources. The same goes for patronage relationships.[26] Although a term of office was not particularly long, even in the imperial provinces, it was primarily in these places where networks of relationships with urban notables developed. In second place after the provincial capital (*caput provinciae*), the *conventus* cities, the places where the governor regularly held court every year or every two years, were privileged. Dion of Prusa (*or.* 35, 15) told the citizens of Kelainai in Phrygia, a city on the main road through the southwest plateau:

> The courts are in session every other year in Celaenae, and they bring together an un-numbered throng of people—litigants, jurymen, orators, princes, attendants, slaves, pimps, muleteers, hucksters, harlots, and artisans. Consequently not only can those who have goods to sell obtain the highest prices, but also nothing in the city is out of work, neither the teams nor the houses nor the women. (trans. Cohoon and Crosby)

Just as small animals penned up make lots of manure, so in cities large numbers of humans make lots of revenue. The "free cities" (*civitates liberae*), which the governor usually did not enter, were excepted from the *formula provinciae*; when one of them, Aphrodisias, invited the governor to visit it, he politely replied that he would accept the invitation "if no law of your city or decree of the Senate or instruction or letter from the emperor prevents the proconsul from making a stay in [your] city."[27]

We know that from the time of the republic governors made various tours through their provinces. Our best information comes from the province of Asia, where the governor had to visit nine dioceses in a regular monthly cycle to dispense justice there;[28] senatorial legates were allowed to represent the proconsul. We know of few such tours in other provinces, and in some, such as Cappadocia, of none at all, but we must assume they occurred everywhere. Pliny presumably made shorter or longer stays in at least nine of the nineteen cities of his province of Pontus et Bithynia (see especially Pliny the Younger, *ep.* 10, 33).

In the judicial system the governor served simply as the higher court. The *ius gladii*, the right to impose death sentences on Roman citizens (since Hadrian with the exception of members of the city council) as well as provincials, lay with him alone. However, the municipal courts and authorities had already done most of the work before he got involved, including the preliminary investigations and preliminary negotiations in the case of capital crimes. Trials conducted before him often took place in the presence of a large audience in the agora, the theater, or the hippodrome. But he never judged alone; instead, he had to consult his *consilium*, of which jurors (*judices*) recruited on the spot might be members; a secretary kept a record in Latin on wax tablets. Transcripts of the court records—the best source for some Christian acts of the martyrs—were preserved. However, in contrast to the documentation on papyrus in Egypt, we have little certain information about genuine state archives in the Anatolian provinces; there was probably something of the kind in Bithynia when Pliny ruled there.[29]

During his visits, the governor was also concerned with the supervision of the account books and assets of the *civitates* of the *formula provinciae*. This regular activity can be described as simply "administration." In Pliny's collection of letters we have a valuable testimony to this; since his correspondence with the emperor is a complete dossier on his gubernatorial activity, it allows us to determine the relative extent of the topics he had to deal with. In addition to dispensing justice, legislation, and military and police tasks, according to this dossier the cities' internal finance and construction projects were the hotspots where mismanagement and waste on the provincials' part might prevail. The conditions in other provinces with a high proportion of cities were probably not fundamentally different. The proconsul Fabius Persicus limited the granting of loans from public treasuries in Ephesos, instituted cost-cutting measures, and made decisions regarding the employment plan for municipal personnel.[30] A decree issued by Quintus Veranius in the province of Lycia regulated and normalized the municipal system of documentation.[31] Gubernatorial stipulations, such as the granting of market rights, descended to the level of village communities on the city's territory, whereas questions concerning villages located on imperial domains were settled by the patrimonial procurator responsible for them.[32] Certain decisions, including those concerning the cities—for instance, their status as free or subject to tribute, the foundation of high-level festivals, and the granting of civil rights—exceeded the competence of the provincial administrator and were to be made by the emperor or the Senate alone. In addition, rules and guidelines were set for a governor's activity: thus both proconsuls and imperial legates brought a kind of instruction sheet (*mandata*, Greek: *entolai*) with them when they arrived in the province. Because his *mandata* prohibited the formation of clubs (*hetairiai*), Pliny could not grant the community of Nikomedeia permission to set up a fire-fighting team (Pliny the Younger, *ep.* 10, 33 f.; cf. 96, 7). Similarly, he was not allowed to pardon persons he himself or his predecessors had expelled (Pliny the Younger, *ep.* 10, 56, 3). Cities, including free ones like Amisos, did not have the right to make gifts to private individuals paid for by communal treasuries or the like (Pliny the Younger, *ep.*

10, 110 f.). Excerpts, at least, from these *mandata* were generally known, and inhabitants of the province referred to them (Pliny the Younger, *ep.* 10, 96, 7; 110, 1).

Naturally, in each case the edicts and rescripts, the "divine writings" (*theia grammata*) of earlier emperors, also had to be considered. Transcriptions were available in the provinces, not only in the governor's residence[33] but also in individual municipal archives, and in queries addressed to the emperor, the governor included extracts from the relevant documents that had been submitted to him by petitioners. Private individuals, such as the philosopher Archippos in Prusa, could also submit to the governor copies of official documents that they possessed (Pliny the Younger, *ep.* 10, 58, 4).

Roman Infrastructure, Roads, Imperial Boundaries, and the Military

We limit our discussion here to the imperial government's actions concerning infrastructure. But we have to keep in mind that there was a whole range of tasks of this kind on the level of the cities, in which the emperor and Roman officials repeatedly intervened with the intention of fostering and regulating activities. These tasks include above all advancing urbanization, and especially developing communication routes and water supplies, which the government considered particularly worthy of support. Every inhabitant of modern-day Turkey knows the abbreviation YSE (*yol, su, elektrik*, "road/street, water, electricity"), which stands for a government program to provide basic services all over the country. So far as we know, the Roman government did not envisage providing roads and water for every village. But it is no accident that the emperor and the governor appropriated substantial funds for the construction and maintenance of water systems that supplied not only cities but also on occasion even villages.[34] The imperial leadership was also aware of the economic importance of good communication routes and well-developed harbors. Pliny, for instance, by recommending to the emperor a canal project intended to link Lake Sapanca (east of Nikomedeia) with the Sea of Marmara by means of a navigable waterway, emphasized the project's economic significance for the transport of commodities (*ep.* 10, 41 f., 61 f.).

Roads

Long before the Romans arrived, a long-distance road system had been maintained in Asia Minor; the best proven is the Persian Royal Road from Sardeis to Susa (p. 158).[35] An old south-north road led from Cilicia all the way across Cappadocia to the Black Sea near Amisos. Road building and maintenance activities by the Hellenistic kings have still been little studied. Not a single pre-Roman road outside settlements and necropolises has been proven to have been paved in stone. With provincialization from 129 BCE on, development began little by little, and in the Imperial period the Roman road network in Anatolia attained a density and quality that was

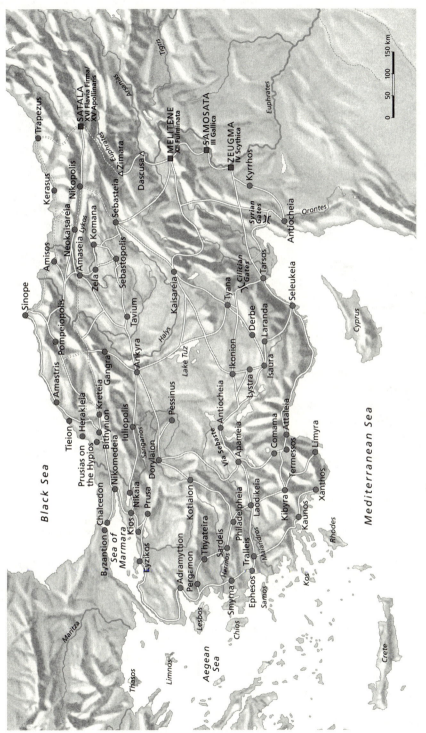

Map 20. Roman main roads in the Imperial period. Map drawn by Peter Palm, Berlin.

67. Paved Roman road in the mountains of Pisidia.

unique in the history of the country until the end of the nineteenth century; it re-mained intact until at least the seventh century CE. For long distances, the caravan routes of Ottoman Turkey and even the asphalt roads of the modern republic still followed Roman roads, and on the site of many a *han* (caravansary) and many a Turkish town, there must have been a stopping point in antiquity (Map 20).

Our knowledge is based on sources of very different kinds. In not a few places the paving stones of imperial highways and connecting roads[36] are still visible above ground (Figure 67), and in addition numerous bridges or foundations for bridges indicate where roads used to be. A Roman long-distance road had a pavement about eight meters wide, which was supported on both sides by a border of rectangular blocks; the surface sloped slightly down from the center line to allow water to run off. However, not all long-distance roads were paved.

Little remains of the stations (*mansiones, mutationes*) that were part of the facili-ties, or of construction inscriptions relating to the roads. In contrast, about 1,100 milestones have been found in Asia Minor (more have been discovered only in North Africa).[37] With their help we can form a picture—even if it remains fragmen-tary—of the routes of at least the long-distance roads in the various parts of the country.

The cylindrical milestones were set up at regular intervals, usually under the re-sponsibility of the provincial governor, less often of a quaestor, procurator, or (still less often) city magistrate. Since today they are usually found not far from their origi-nal locations, from which they have been carried off by the local people for reuse, the concentration of findings in an area can indicate the approximate route taken by a road. The texts engraved on the stones mention the emperor and only occasionally the governor or other magistrates: the name of the governor appears on less than 10 percent of the milestones in Asia Minor. The reason for this is presumed to be a decline in gubernatorial initiative as soon as a development or restoration plan was completed and the maintenance of the road was taken over by the local authorities.[38] The predicate in the formulas of milestone inscriptions refers to the new construction or repair of the road. Unlike the milestones erected under the republic in the province of Asia with the sole *caput viae* Ephesos, those erected under the Principate sometimes mention at the end of the inscription the main city of any municipal territory on which they stand as the starting point of the mile count. Thus for example the formula "From Nicomedeia to the borders XXIII" (*a Nicomedia ad fines XXIII*) means that the stone marks the twenty-third mile of the road from the city on the gulf of the Sea of Marmara (İsmit) to the border of the city's territory (Figure 68). Beyond the border the mile count refers to the main city of the neighboring territory. The archaeological and epigraphic evidence is supplemented by literary evidence, in particular late Antique itineraries and the Tabula Peutingeriana (mentioned near the start of Chapter 7), which also gives us the names of the very numerous stations connected with the long-distance roads (Map 21). However, by far the majority of these cannot be localized with certainty.

Since Hellenistic times, the road network had been densest in western Asia Minor. Under the Attalids, there was even a forerunner of the Roman milestones, the *dekastadion*, which indicated distances from Ephesos and Sardeis in *stadia*.[39] Here I cannot examine in detail the ramified road system in the province of Asia.[40] Of special importance are the north-south route that runs near the coast between the Hellespont and the Lycian peninsula, and, branching off from it, the roads that run through the valleys of the Hermos and Maeander rivers toward inner Anatolia. Also significant is the transverse road running over the plateau from Pergamon through Thyateira, Sardeis, Philadelpheia, Laodikeia, and Termessos down to Attaleia, which Manius Aquillius (the governor at the time the province was founded) had already planned. Augustus then saw to it that two main roads, both of which were called *via Sebaste*, were built at the eastern exit from the province of Asia to connect it with the *coloniae* founded in Pisidia. They started from Antiocheia in Pisidia. One of them led west, continued via Apollonia and, after a bend toward the south, passed through Comama to join up with Manius Aquillius's road near Termessos. The other ran southeast and forked, with one branch going to Ikonion (Konya) and the other to Lystra.

The main roads went around Lycia. The few known milestones from that country, the majority of which date from the late Antique period, stood on the two most important north-south roads, which passed through the valleys of the Xanthos and the Arykandos. Yet it was precisely in Lycia that a unique document on the roads of a province—indeed even of the empire—came to light a few years ago: the base of an equestrian statue of the emperor Claudius in Patara, a harbor city and *caput provinciae*. Claudius had established the province, and the statue was put in place in 46 CE,

68. Milestone from the time of
Gordian III. Now in the İzmit
Museum.

toward the end of the term of office of Lycia's first governor, Quintus Veranius. It
presents the complete road network: seventy connections between all the cities are
listed, along with information on distances given in *stadia*.[41] The emperor, it says,
had the roads built by his governor. It can be assumed that there were already roads
on the Lycian peninsula before Claudius, and a comprehensive new construction of
them under Veranius is improbable, if only for reasons of time. The fact that the
distances are given in *stadia* rather than miles indicates that this infrastructure must
be distinguished from that of the Roman long-distance roads in Anatolia. The Kyaneai project conducted in the Yavu mountain country of central Lycia under the
auspices of the University of Tübingen allows us to see still another level deeper; one
of the west-east connecting roads listed in the Claudian *stadiasmos* runs through this
area, from Phellos via Kyaneai to Myra. In addition to this main road, this intensive
survey identified a dense ancient route network by the terracing, rock cutting (stairs
in some cases), and occasional paving, and by its orientation toward ancient settlement sites. The breadth and quality of the roadway suggest vehicle traffic only in a
few cases; thus the network served chiefly regional economic needs. In Pergamon,
the maintenance of the roads belonging to the community (*leophoroi*) on the city's

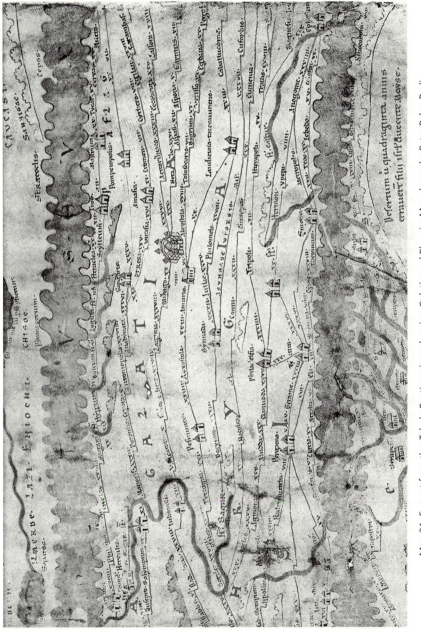

Map 21. Excerpt from the *Tabula Peutingeriana* showing Galatia and Phrygia. Map drawn by Peter Palm, Berlin.

territory—the larger ones were twenty ells wide, the rest at least eight ells wide—was legally regulated ([106] OGIS 483).

Beyond Lycia, the continuation of Manius Aquillius's road coming out of inner Anatolia crossed the Pamphylian plain. Milestones prove its route farther eastward on the steep Mediterranean coast of Rough Cilicia, over the bridges on the Saros and Pyramos, and through the alluvial land of the Cilician plain. Eastern Cilicia remained the communication hub that it had been in earlier periods. Whereas the direct route to the Euphrates near Zeugma went around the Amanos Mountains on the north, several branches turned off toward the south, leading down to the Syrian metropolis of Antiocheia. The westernmost branch followed the shore of the Gulf of Issos and climbed the mountains to the Belen Pass, which was known as the "Syrian Gates" in ancient times. The roads toward Antiocheia that branched off the main road on the east side of the ridge ran along the foot of the mountains through Nikopolis on the one hand, and on the other through Kyrrhos—where again Roman bridges have survived—and Gindaros.

Long-distance roads in northern, central, and eastern Anatolia were built chiefly for military purposes. This began under Augustus and culminated under the Flavians. The construction carried out under Aulus Caesennius Gallus, the legate of the double province of Galatia-Cappadocia from 80 to 82 CE, extended to the eparchies of Galatia, Cappadocia, Pontus, Pisidia, Paphlagonia, Lycaonia, and Lesser Armenia. Later new construction programs have not been proven, but repeated repairs have: the concentration of milestones dating from the times of Trajan's and Severus's great oriental wars, along with the new order introduced by Diocletian and Constantine, provides clear evidence of this. The length of this road system alone has been estimated at 9,000 kilometers (5,600 Roman miles).

Until the beginning of the Imperial period the Pontic port cities on the Black Sea from Herakleia to Trapezus were probably still connected only by sea, since over long stretches the steep coast made travel by land difficult. The earliest testimony to Imperial period road-building in the province of Pontus et Bithynia is Julius Aquila's monument (45 CE) above Amastris, where the road coming from Tieion had to be cut into the rock.[42] Remains of pavement and milestones near Çatalzeytin (west of Abonuteichos) prove that in the Imperial period the coast road continued on as far as Sinope, though they date from the third century.

The two most important long-distance roads in the interior of northern Asia Minor led from Nikomedeia and Nikaia inland. In Trajan's time, at least, the northern one ran from the Bosporus to Bithynion-Klaudiupolis (today Bolu) in the east Bithynian highland. In the green Bithynian plain, not far from Adapazari, it had to cross the lower reaches of the Sangarios, which was in flood in the springtime. Its continuation on the plateau probably ran north of Gangra in the valley of the Devrez Çay to the bend in the Halys River and from there into Pontus as far as Amaseia. Near Bithynion-Klaudiupolis a road branched off from it, following the heavily forested valley of the Ladon River down to Tieion on the coast; it had existed since Vespasian's time and was repeatedly repaired up into the third century. North of the high Olgassys mountain range a parallel road ran through the Amnias valley via Pompeiopolis; it has been proven that its eastern section passing through Phazemon-Neoclaudiopolis to Amaseia existed under Nerva, while a road over the pass and down to Sinope on the coast has been shown to exist already under Vespasian.

The southern route, one of the empire's most important military roads, climbed east from Nikaia into the mountains, where it continued through the middle Sangarios valley via Juliopolis and straight on to Ankyra, and from there to Amaseia in Pontus. It was repeatedly repaired from the time of Trajan to that of the tetrarchs. Near Juliopolis on the Sangarios it was joined by a road from the province of Asia. Because of the heavy transit traffic over the provincial border, Pliny the Younger (*ep.* 10, 77) vainly sought to get the emperor to station a legionary centurion there—*in capite Bithyniae.*

The earliest evidence of the Pontic road system in the Imperial period comes from the region of Erzincan on the upper Euphrates: a milestone from Domitian's reign that suggests a connection between Satala and central Pontos through the valley of the Lykos (via Nikopolis). In Pontos, the remains of bridges are more numerous than in the west, but without closer investigation it cannot be determined with certainty that they are Roman constructions. They cross the Halys, the Iris, the Lykos, and the Skylax, as well as their tributaries.[43]

The most important of the central Anatolian arteries of communication led from Dorylaion (Eskişehir) out of the province of Asia and through the gentle hills of Galatia toward Ankyra, where it branches. One branch links the Galatian metropolis with Tavium[44] and Sebasteia (Sivas) on the upper Halys, and there forks again toward Nikopolis and Satala on the one hand and toward Melitene (Malatya) on the other. A second branch led to Lake Tuz and then turned east to Kaisareia, where it joined the road coming from the Euphrates border near Melitene. Not far from the eastern shore of Lake Tuz a third road branched off from the second and led south; it is known, because of its use since the Middle Ages, as the "Pilgrim's Road"; it went to Tarsos, which it reached via the Cilician Gates (Figure 69).

It was up to local communities to build and maintain the main and secondary roads. In response to an inquiry made by Pliny the Younger (*ep.* 10, 32), Trajan implies that offenders sentenced to forced labor who were getting old and were no longer capable of hard work could be used in building roads and streets (perhaps within cities). The provincial population was called on for construction work on imperial roads section by section, in the framework of the so-called *munera*, not only from nearby communities but also sometimes from far distant ones. Services, about which we are well informed by inscriptions, also had to be provided in connection with the roads. These special contributions, distinct from other taxes and liturgies, included furnishing means of transport and draft animals, and room and board for government authorized travelers: slaves, freedmen, officials, and soldiers on the different levels of the administration and the army. The beneficiaries had to justify their claims by means of a special permit, a *diploma*. In addition, the communities and also individuals had to see to the supervision and maintenance of the stations, their equip-

69. The "Cilician Gates" with an inscription dating from the reign of Caracalla ([283] Hild and Hellenkemper, TIB 5, 1990, 387).

ment and the complete inventories. However, all this did not have to be provided free of cost; the compensation for the corresponding expenses was fixed though probably not always adequate. A similar procedure goes back at least as far as the organization of message transmission during the Persian period; Herodotus (8, 98) uses the word *angareion* to designate it.[45]

Under Augustus, the development of a specific system called first *vehiculatio*, and later *cursus publicus* ("state route," sometimes also translated as "state post"; the Latin term first appears in legal sources from the fourth century CE) began. This system existed into late Antiquity and was even continued by the Romans' Germanic successors in the West and the Arabs in the East.[46] One of the most important Imperial period testimonies to the system is Suetonius's short report (*Aug.* 49, 3) on its introduction. Another is a Latin-Greek inscription containing an edict ordered by the governor of Galatia, Sextus Sotidius Strabo Libuscidianus; it dates from the beginning of the first century CE ([195] SEG 26, 1392) and was found near Sagalassos in Pisidia. In the introduction the legate criticizes certain people for having disregarded the clear rules set by two emperors, Augustus and Tiberius, concerning compensation for services and orders the written publication of the rates on steles, one of which has come down to us. The inhabitants of Sagalassos were required to provide ten wagons and the same number of mules—or, as a substitute, twice as many asses—on a specific stretch of the road, as far as Cormasa and Conana. Set prices were to be paid for these, but meals and lodging for state officials had to be provided without compensation. The inhabitants of Sagalassos were allowed to pay a neighboring community, city or village, to take over their obligation. Another document that has been published recently deepens our understanding of this subject.[47] During his stay in the province of Asia in the summer of 129, the emperor Hadrian was prompted to issue an edict clarifying the modalities of making claims, which makes it obvious that the latter were commonly excessive. For instance, since soldiers were to march only on the main roads, they were henceforth ordered to refrain from hiring unnecessary guides—with an interesting exception: in winter, when the road was no longer visible under the snow. So far as uncompensated meals and lodging were concerned, some people had probably become used to receiving them even when they were not traveling on official business—in particular, transporting state funds, prisoners, or wild animals (intended for exhibition battles in large cities)—but privately; today similar abuses occur when state employees use official vehicles to go on vacations.

There is no doubt that from the outset this arrangement put a constant burden on provincials. However, the economic advantage that the infrastructure brought the population has to be taken into account. This advantage is virtually impossible to assess, but it must have been considerable at times. But times change: before long, complaints began to pile up—complaints not about traffic jams but about the excesses of official users. Regarding the *cursus publicus*, Aurelius Victor (13, 6; trans. Marek) wrote: "This institution, initially of profound benefit, turned into a plague of the Roman world because of the avarice and insolence of the later emperors." The susceptibility to abuse of the *angareia* is evident, and the rulers' occasional interventions remained patchy.[48] For instance, a clear deterioration is shown by the comprehensive dossier from Takina/Phrygia in the time of Caracalla. There is no longer any mention of *diplomas* and payment. The tenant farmers of the domain complained to the emperor about naked violence ([195] SEG 37, 1186, cf. p. 355). The chaos grew as soldiers, officials, and private individuals put increasingly great demands on the infrastructure. In the fourth and fifth centuries, bishops' travels in connection with councils occasionally led to a kind of collapse of the *cursus publicus*. As a result the latter had to be expanded and equipped, and a distinction between *cursus velox* (for quicker travel) and *cursus clavularis* (for less urgent and slower heavy transport) was made.

The Imperial Border and the Military

The military infrastructure on the Roman Empire's Anatolian eastern border deserves special attention. As we have already seen (p. 338), its development into a genuine line of defense was first pursued on a large scale in conjunction with Rome's new assessment of Armenia in the aftermath of Corbulo's war under Nero.

In connection with the Flavian road construction program on the Euphrates border, military bases far from any settlement were built of stone and thus made to last. Whereas the Roman frontier on the Syrian steppe and in modern-day Jordan has remained clearly visible thanks to a dense series of architectural remains and discoveries, and has been intensively investigated, the border system in Commagene, Cappadocia, and Pontus has not left any comparable wealth of archaeological traces.

Older research found itself forced to conclude that there was no Anatolian *limes* beyond the legionary bases.[49] But we have to recognize that settlement and agricultural activities since the Middle Ages, the theft of building stones, and catastrophic earthquakes have caused the disappearance of most of what nineteenth-century *voyageurs* were looking for. In addition, this area, which remained difficult to access until well into the twentieth century, long escaped thorough investigation, and the great Turkish dam projects ultimately put whole areas of archaeologically significant land under water—for example, the legionary base at Samosata. Nevertheless, intensive research using modern methods would still be able to make important discoveries. In Zeugma, which is also now partly submerged, the most recent geophysical investigations undertaken by the Swiss mission in cooperation with the Gaziantep Museum were not able to trace the true camp of the IV Scythica legion, but did discover—on *At Meydanı* ("horse ground"), a plateau northwest of Belkis Tepe—architectural remains, inscriptions, and bricks that suggest a "stage or transition camp."[50] In the 1960s and 1970s, before the dam reservoirs were filled, the British researcher Timothy Mitford searched nearly the complete course of the Anatolian Euphrates border for ancient relics.[51] As a result, we now know that there was a network of military installations and roads connecting them over the whole distance.

For long stretches, the Roman border follows the right bank of the Euphrates, partly accompanied by the so-called Sultan Murat or Baghdad road.[52] But whereas in some places the latter prefers the valley bottom, the Roman road runs for the most part on higher land along the edge of the valley. The routes of Ottoman roads are marked by the remains of caravansaries.

Two roads led out of northern Commagene—the western one over the superbly maintained Chabinas bridge (Figure 70), through the Taurus Mountains and into the plain of Malatya. Over this plain, near the crossing of the Euphrates west of Tomisa, the main road ran west, passed through the Anti-Taurus Mountains, and continued to Kaisareia (*Kayseri*). Modern development of Eski Malatya has left nothing remaining of the XII Fulminata legion's camp or the ancient city, where in the sixth century Procopius (*Aed.* 3, 4, 18 f.) still saw temples, an agora, halls, baths, and theaters. Farther to the north, the border ran close to the bank of the Euphrates again. Pağnik, which is now submerged in the western part of the Keban reservoir, is the only Roman fort that was excavated (by the British archaeologist Richard Harper). Here lay the ancient Dascusa. Its existence as early as Flavian times is confirmed by an inscription for Aulus Caesennius Gallus, legate from 80 to 82 CE (AE 1975, 809), that was reused in a new building constructed in the fourth century. Between two western tributaries of the Euphrates (the Çit Çay and the Arabkir Çay), the border road climbed over the Anti-Taurus Mountains and came out not far west of Divriği in the valley of the Çaltı Çay, shortly before the latter flows into the Euphrates. Nearby lay Zimara, a military base, which certainly also went back to the Flavian period. Regarding the further course of the border as far as Satala, there are two possibilities that cannot be discussed here. Flavian milestones were found east of Refayihe, and an inscription of the I Thracum Syriaca cohort (second century CE) was discovered in a village near Kemah.

70. Roman bridge over the Chabinas.

From the point of view of traffic, the locality of Satala is a key position no less important than Melitene. It controls the entrance into the upper valley of the Lykos, which leads down into Phanarhoia, the Pontic heartland. It is the only military camp in Asia Minor that remains visible above ground. Unlike Samosata, Zeugma, and Melitene, the Flavian camp was not connected with an existing civilian settlement. Such a settlement grew up only later on the western and southern edges of the camp, where vestigial remains of a late Antique basilica still stand.[53] The rectangular fortress wall, now reduced to rubble, dates from the sixth century CE (the period of Justinian). The Swiss archaeologist Martin Hartmann has recently cast new doubts on whether the relatively small walled-in area, consisting of eight built-up hectares (not including a rocky rib), was truly the XVI Flavia Firma legion's permanent base—in the time of Trajan this legion was replaced by the XV Apollinaris—and suggested that it was a smaller camp established much later. However, discoveries of bricks and ceramics on the ground indicate that in the high Imperial period the site of the camp was on the broad, flat expanse extending from the eastern side of the fortifications. Wherever the quarters for the legionaries were, the soldiers of this garrison must have suffered severe hardships in the winter, with meter-high snows.[54] North of Satala the military road climbed—not via the Zigana Pass but somewhat farther east of it—the east Pontic coastal range, where it reached an elevation of more than 2,500 meters at the pass. It ran down the valley and joined near Macka the route of the modern road that leads down to the sea at Trabzon. Trapezus, through whose harbor the grain supplies for the castles and military camps along the northern section of the eastern border were trans-shipped, received a legion in late antiquity, under Diocletian (284–305): the I Pontica. Over the course of the Imperial period, a series of small military posts was established from here to the east: Ysiportus, Rhizus (Rize), Apsarus, Petra, Phasis, Sebastopolis (Suchumi) and Pityus—the so-called Pontic *limes*.[55]

In a sense, the north coast of Asia Minor was also an imperial border, for whose security along its whole length not only the troops in Pontus et Bithynia and Cappadocia but also the Black Sea fleet were responsible.[56] Josephos (*BJ* 2, 366–368) names forty Roman warships for the middle of the 60s of the first century—ships that kept in check the peoples on the Black Sea outside the provincial area. The *classis Pontica* had as its bases, in addition to Trapezus, certainly the harbors of Sinope, where there was a hamlet (*vicus*) of veterans of this military branch;[57] Amastris; and Kyzikos on the southern shore of the Propontis (Dio 79, 7, 3). From the latter city comes a tomb epigram for a prefect named Crispinus ([146] MS II 49). Whether the prefect of the coast of Pontus (*praefectus orae Ponticae maritimae*), M. Gavius Bassus, who asked Pliny for more soldiers, was the commander of the "Pontic Fleet" (proven only later) or only of a kind of coast guard cannot be determined (Pliny the Younger, *ep.* 10, 21).

The forces occupying Cappadocia did not consist solely of the legions; before the latter arrived in the Flavian period, auxiliary units were already stationed in the country. Our best source for this is Arrian's work "*Ektaxis* (deployment of the army) against the Alani," which dates from late in Hadrian's reign. In it, four cavalry units (*alae*) and ten cohorts are mentioned. The picture is filled out by stone inscriptions and recently also military diplomas, as well as by a papyrus from Fayoum in Egypt. The oldest of the military diplomas, which preserves the numbers of three *alae* and fourteen cohorts, comes from the time of Domitian, while another diploma from the early reign of Trajan mentions four *alae* and thirteen cohorts.[58] In his description of the coast of the Black Sea, Arrian says (*Peripl. M. Eux.* 6) that five cohorts were stationed in Apsaros (near Batumi) alone. As we can infer from their names, most of these units originally came from the west.

To be sure, the other provinces in Asia Minor, where no legions were deployed, also had *auxilia* as occupying forces, and sometimes units detached from legions stationed in Cappadocia or on the Danube, but our knowledge about these is sketchy. Tacitus (*ann.* 4, 5) noted that it was hard to enumerate the auxiliary troops in the provinces, because they were shifted about from time to time and their numbers were sometimes increased, sometimes diminished.[59] However, the number of auxiliary troops stationed in any other province was considerably less than in Cappadocia. In Pontus et Bithynia Pliny the Younger (*ep.* 10, 21.106) had a mounted unit, the *cohors VI equestris*, which is also proven by epigraphic evidence as late as the third century. Soldiers who belonged to it served in a post on the main road that ran along the shore of the Sea of Marmara to Nikomedeia. Moreover, cohorts known as "Cyprian," "Thracian" (*cohors I Thracum*), and "Campestrian" (*cohors Campestris*) were very probably also constantly in the province.

Information from the provinces on the south coast is sparser. For Cilicia, Tacitus (*ann.* 2, 68) mentions the cavalry prefect Vibius Fronto as the commander of an *ala*.

We know of no cohorts. Before it was transformed from an imperial to a pr(
province, Lycia et Pamphylia hosted at least four cohorts; the earliest, *coh(*
served there in the first century CE, and the three others served under the
Trajan, Hadrian, and Antoninus Pius, respectively. Military diplomas ((
128; RMD I 67 and later) testify to another cohort, *cohors I Flavia Nu(*
being present there into the first half of the third century CE. Nothing is
any garrison site. No doubt the great granaries (*horrea*) of Hadrian's time,
and Andriake, were under military guard.[60]

Apart from the possibly short-term legionary occupation under Augu(
were certainly more units in the enormous central Anatolian province (
than the ones currently known to us. Three cohorts were among these.[61]
ince of Asia hosted at least one cohort continuously, probably not more at
The *cohors Apula* dates from the Augustan period; from 148 CE on, th
Raetorum still mentioned in Arrian's *Ektaxis* (1) as a Cappadocian unit w
nently stationed in Asia at least down to the time of Caracalla. In the se
third centuries, a castle in Aulutrene near Apameia in Phrygia was one of
important staging areas for the armies' transit marches toward the East. /
was occupied by soldiers temporarily detached from the armies on the Da(
are mentioned in dedicatory and tomb inscriptions from the region;[62] here
the *via Sebaste*. Not at all far to the northwest lies the sole garrison site in
ince of Asia that we are sure of: Eumeneia.

Military groups of differing strengths, from Imperial armies to deta
forces, were regularly received and supplied on their way to the eastern b
back: an agent for the army's grain supply "on the transit march to the
probably in the third century, called Nikomedeia his home (([105] TAM I
In the third century the city of Termessus Minor in northern Lycia than(
its most prominent citizens for having freed the community's officials of t
of paying for a freshly recruited Roman unit moving to the Orient.[63] In th
period, dignitaries in the small city of Prusias on the Hypios used stereo
mulas to refer to their merits for having accompanied, entertained, fed, a
the "holy" Roman army and the emperor in their region.

Another subject of interest is Asia Minor as a recruiting ground and ho
soldiers in the legions and the *auxilia* who served not only here but al
world: from upper Egypt to Britain, from Mauretania to Bostra in Arabia.
atic study of this remains desirable.[64] In addition to their importance for th
history of the *Imperium Romanum* in general, the tomb, dedicatory, and
inscriptions of soldiers, sometimes with outlines of their careers, offer us
into an important segment of the social structure of the Anatolian provin

We can discuss only briefly here the recruitment of Asians for the legic
began with the inclusion of Deiotaros's Galatians in the Roman army as
Deiotariana, along with recruitment for the auxiliary troops during the In
riod.[65] In the latter period, the native population contingent continued
important role, as the names of whole units raised in Asia Minor indica(

Phrygum, cohortes Ulpiae Galatarum, cohortes Ulpiae Paflagonum, cohors I Cilicum,
cohors I Flavia Cilicum equitata. In addition, there were two *alae* whose names, *colo-*
norum or *Antiochiensium,* refer to citizens of the Augustan colonies.[66] In some places
we find a conspicuous accumulation of tombstones with the names of deceased soldiers who had served in one and the same unit, as in Amaseia the legion V Macedonica (stationed in Moesia inferior, modern Bulgaria). However, overall Asia
Minor came in behind other recruiting areas, for example, the Danube region. Of
the slightly more than 700 military diplomas currently known, fewer than 5 percent
are accounted for by Anatolians.

Honorably discharged soldiers earned, along with Roman citizenship, at least
prestige, which they could increase, if they were well off, by means of munificence
and offices ranging from village priest to councilman for life, and more than a few
communities could even point proudly to fellow citizens in high positions in the
military command. For instance, Priscus, a Paphlagonian who had been recruited as
a young man along with other men from his country for Trajan's wars, owed his promotion to standard-bearer to having caught the attention of the emperor himself.[67]
His tombstone proudly explains in verse the contribution to victory made by the
standard, the "imperial symbol," which he was allowed to carry before the troops
(presumably the cohort) when they went into battle. He apparently participated in
the Parthian campaign. Having gone home as a Roman citizen, he managed an estate
"as Hesiod taught us to do," grew old in prosperity and wisdom, and looked back on
a life whose fulfillment was based on the two pillars of his existence: soldiering and
farming. During their long absence from their homeland, provincials gained additional education and knowledge of the wider world. The global, more than twenty-
year-long tour of one of Diocletian's soldiers, a member of the *Legio VIII Augusta*
with its main base in Strasbourg, is unsurpassed. This man came from a small village
in Phrygia, and he was constantly on the march (*kykleusas*). In the order given in his
list—though it is interrupted by lacunae in the inscription—he went to Asia (he
means the province), Caria, Lydia, Lycaonia, Cilicia, Phoenicia, Syria, Arabia, Palestine, Egypt, Alexandria, India (he means Ethiopia), Mesopotamia, Cappadocia, Galatia, Bithynia, Thrace, Mysia, Carpia, Sarmatia, Viminacium (a legionary camp on
the Mlava near Kostolac in the province of *Moesia Superior*), Gothia, Germania,
Dardania, Dalmatia, Pannonia, Gallia, Spain, and Mauretania.[68]

Many men from all the provinces of Asia Minor, most of them from the province
of Asia,[69] served as equestrian officers, and some of them glittered with military
medals. Sextus Vibius Gallus, who came from Amastris, belonged to the XIII Gemina legion, which was transferred to Dacia under Trajan. He had his medals depicted
on stone and identified by inscriptions; the comparatively extravagant pictorial program on three sides of the base may have been inspired by the pictorial splendor of
the 40-meter-high column in Trajan's forum in Rome (Figure 71).[70] A Cappadocian
who fell in Severus Alexander's Parthian War held a position in the leadership of the
Legio IV Scythica. Gnaeus Claudius Severus, who hailed from Pompeiopolis in
Paphlagonia, held an even higher rank; he was the legionary legate of the *III Cyre-*

71. Different views of a statue base with reliefs and inscription honoring Sextus Vibius Gallus. Now in the Archeological Museum of Istanbul.

naica, which was already stationed in Bostra, Arabia, at that time. This young senator is probably the same person as the grandson of the first governor of Trajan's province of Arabia; he later married Marcus Aurelius's daughter.

Taxes and Customs

During the Imperial period, Roman taxation of subjects in the provinces changed from that in the period of the republic.[71] On the whole, the tax burden at first diminished, after limits were put on abuses. Later on, especially from the third century on, the number of taxes grew and so did the amount of the burden. In this period there was a further, more fundamental shift to levies in kind (*annona*) as the main tax, which was concentrated on supplying the troops, the administration, and the large cities. Here the discussion is limited to the first two centuries CE.

What was new was not only the poll tax (*tributum capitis*) on males over the age of fourteen and females over twelve; it was introduced by Augustus and can be proved to have been imposed in Asia as well. The same holds for the taxes on the manumission of slaves (*vicesima libertatis*) and on inheritances (*vicesima hereditatium*); these were assessed as percentages and were collected irregularly. However, the tax on inheritances affected only Roman citizens, and next of kin and the poor were exempted, so that before 212 CE most people did not have to pay it.[72] Additional smaller taxes and revenues, such as taxes on sales, the *aurum coronarium* (gold crowns), the *fiscus judaicus* ("Jewish tax"), and a tax on iron,[73] along with gifts, confiscations, and fines for violating tombs, can be only mentioned in passing.

Since Caesar, Roman taxes on crop yields (*tributum soli* or *agri*), which were a burden on landowners with and without Roman citizenship in the provinces, had been freed from the leases granted to tax collection companies (*societates publicanorum*) in Rome and were now managed by cities and communities in the provinces (p. 300). In the cities there were registers of the units of land in the territory. A landowner had to pay to the city a fixed sum that was determined by the size of his or her property, not hand over a tenth of his or her crop yield.[74] Since agriculture was the most productive use of land, this tax, together with the pasture tax (*scriptura*) must have brought in the highest revenue for the Roman state, especially from the enormous provinces on the Anatolian peninsula, which were immeasurably rich agriculturally. For ancient history, we lack the statistics available to historians of the modern period, so that we cannot quantify the real tax burden. It is estimated to have been moderate in the early Imperial period.[75] After Cappadocia became a Roman province, rates were relatively low compared to the earlier royal taxes (Tacitus, *ann.* 2, 56). Nonetheless, peoples that had settled in remote areas first had to become accustomed to paying regular taxes: the Kietai, who lived on the edge of the Taurus, resisted when Archelaos II introduced in 36 CE a property assessment on the Roman model, and they withdrew into the mountains (Tacitus, *ann.* 6, 41). Peoples like these must have found it strange to be forced to hand over part of their produce. In contrast, in the civilized regions of Bithynia, Asia, Lycia, and Pamphylia not only could the emperor resort to well-established mechanisms that had to some extent already been in operation under the Hellenistic kings and free states, but also the population had already long since had to adjust their economic productivity to yield a surplus that would allow them to pay taxes.

It was the responsibility of the governor to conduct a census at various intervals for the purpose of assessing wealth. Special assessments were led by officials, such as the *procurator ad censum agendum* Aemilius Bassus in Pontus et Bithynia in the time of Hadrian (AE 1915, 58). After Caesar's reform, a fixed lump sum based on an estimate of the productivity was presumably levied in Asia, though of course it had to be regularly reset. The assessment was ultimately based on information supplied by property owners and their neighbors. These had provided tax officials with a written declaration of the name, location, size, ownership or leasing, kind of revenue, and extent of the property (cf. *Digest* 50, 15, 4).

The actual tax assessors and collectors were the councilors in the cities. Among them, the tax liability for the sum to be raised by the city was borne by the "ten first" (*dekaprotoi*) in several provinces, and in Lycia after 124 CE by the "twenty first" (*eikosaprotoi*). Just how the city went about amassing this sum is less clear and may have differed from province to province. The lowest-level authorities with the most precise knowledge of local real property relationships were probably village officials.[76] Moreover, at least for Lycia, a collaboration of the *koinon* at the provincial level can be proven: The "arch-guardian" (*archiphylax*)[77] advanced the money to the cities to be transferred to the *koinon* and passed on to the Roman fiscal authorities, whereby he assumed, backed by his private assets, the liability for the province's whole tax payment. It has been suggested that no such ex officio function existed, and that instead this was an exceptional good deed performed by the super-rich Lycian Opramoas of Rhodiapolis,[78] whose inscription repeatedly emphasizes that he held this office.[79] Wrongly! The obligation is exactly paralleled by the similar guarantee of revenues from customs duties made by the *koinon* (p. 390 f.).[80]

The payment was made in money or in kind and against receipt. Interim storage required storehouses and depots in individual cities, including the one in which the governor, quaestor, or financial procurator resided. The cost of transporting payments in kind was the responsibility of the taxpayers. How much and in what form money from the tax revenues flowed from the provinces to Rome cannot be determined; presumably it was mainly in the form of gold or in any case silver coins, that is, primarily in denarii or *cistophori*.

In antiquity, a customs tariff (*portoria*, Greek: *tele*) was a levy that was imposed on merchandise when it crossed certain borders. Basically, it was a source of state revenue, not an instrument for protecting the domestic economy or for directing the flow of goods, although in individual cases such intentions cannot be excluded. For example, it was made more expensive to bring slaves into Asia than to take them out of the province, apparently to help cope with a shortage of slaves on the markets in other provinces.[81] The customs system in Asia Minor is better known than anywhere else in the *Imperium Romanum*, thanks to an unusually detailed documentation that came to light only in recent decades. We owe two documents to a step taken by Nero in 58 CE henceforth to make public the relevant legal situation, which up to that point had not been generally accessible (Tacitus, *ann.* 13, 50). These documents include not only the customs law of Asia, the *lex portoria Asiae* (*nomos telonikos*), which became known through a 1989 discovery in the Church of St. John in Ephesos, but also a recently discovered customs law for the province of Lycia (*nomos demosionikos*).[82] This subject is also dealt with in a gubernatorial edict from Myra and the detailed endowment inscription in Kaunos, both of which refer to the Lycian customs law, so that other regulations become clear.

The customs inscription of Ephesos begins with a law from the time of the republic, which over time was complemented step by step by addenda and finally passed by the Senate in 62 CE, under Nero, whereafter it was summarized and published in a Greek translation in the provincial capital of Ephesos. The regulations it contains, in accord with which the Roman Senate leased the collection of customs duties to the *publicani*, refer to the whole province of Asia, although the customs district, for purely practical reasons, is not coextensive with the provincial boundaries. These regulations define, among other things, customs boundaries, the construction and location of customs stations, special customs duties and exemption from customs duties, obligations to declare goods, and the right of confiscation.

A list of the main customs stations along the coast between the Bosporus and Side in Pamphylia is given in §9 (modern arrangement) of the document; however, because of damage to the stone, this list has lacunae, so that we can assume there were even more stations than the twenty-nine that can still be read in it (Map 22). Customs stations were also located at certain distances along the eastern border, far inland. The Romans had found some of these stations already there when the kingdom of Pergamon was annexed and simply took them over, while others had to be set up after the acquisition of territories. As in customs districts of the Western Empire (*quadragesima Galliarum*), here too a customs duty of 2.5 percent on the value of commodities had to be paid on crossing a customs boundary; however, there were exceptions to this rule, for example, a set payment of five denarii per capita for young slaves, or a certain amount for mineral-rich earth that was acquired by mining and transported to Rome (§34). All goods transported for state officials and military men (and also *publicani*), goods "for private use," such as slaves and animals that people brought with them from home, minted bronze and silver coins, books, writing tablets and documents, footwear, water, and anything unusable (e.g., stones or earth), as well as ships and naval equipment, and finally things that might be taken along out of fear of enemies, were classified as not having the character of commodities and thus exempted from customs duties.

The texts that were found in Ephesos and Andriake go into particular detail regarding the modalities of declaration (by the number of items, by weight, etc.), customs fraud, and the institution of the *commissum*: commodities that were undeclared or falsely declared were confiscated by the customs officer. During the Hellenistic period the proceeds were to be transferred, after the final decision of the court, to the state, whereas the customs officer was only partially remunerated. According to Roman customs law the confiscation was accompanied by the customs officer's immediate acquisition of ownership of the object of the fraud. If he had no access to it, because the item in question had already been sold or was otherwise inaccessible, he could demand a pledge (*pignoris capio*).[83] However, as is elucidated in particular by the customs law of Lycia, the limits of these rigorous, independent means of coercion exercised by the *publicani* were defined by certain legal rights guaranteed to the persons subject to customs duties in defending against the claims.

The customs organization of Lycia differs in essential ways from that of Asia.[84] Here, too, the Romans probably took over an older system developed by the Hellenistic Lycian league of cities. The period of the lease was, as in Asia, five years. On the top level, the high priest and the secretary of the *koinon* were liable for the whole of the Lycian customs. The customs leaseholders guaranteed them the payment of the duties with 5,000 denarii each in the form of mortgages on land. Here I must emphasize especially the peculiar distribution of the management of customs between

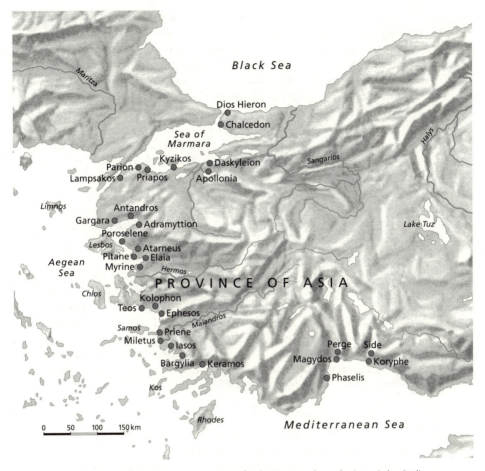

Map 22. Harbors listed in the customs law of Ephesos. Map drawn by Peter Palm, Berlin.

the league and the cities: the latter were allowed to levy the import duty on commodities that were sold on their territory, but had to make a fixed annual payment to the Lycian league out of these revenues. Through its tax leaseholders, the Lycian league imposed on unsold goods taken out of the country or in transit to an inland city a double customs duty, import and export duties of 5 percent. The Lycian league thus administered two separate customs accounts, one consisting of the revenues of its customs officers and another consisting of the revenues from municipal lump-sum payments. Under Nero, Rome expected from Lycia an annual payment to the *fiscus Caesaris* of 100,000 denarii.

Nothing is known about other customs districts in Asia Minor. The Cilician coast must have been brought in somewhere. So far as Pontus et Bithynia and the trade in goods from and to the Black Sea are concerned, this may have been tariffed at the Bosporus customs stations, Dios Hieron and Chalkedon. Zeugma, the bridge over the Euphrates that connected Syria with Mesopotamia, had a customs station. Asked by the customs officer what he was carrying with him, the nomadic philosopher and miracle-worker Apollonios of Tyana (p. 523) is supposed to have answered: "I am taking with me temperance, justice, virtue, continence, valour, discipline." The officer demanded that he declare in writing these slave girls of his as export goods. "Impossible," Apollonios replied, "for they are not female slaves that I am taking out with me, but mistresses" (Philostratos, VA 1, 20; trans. Conybeare).

The levying of taxes, customs duties, and tributes was a concrete expression of Rome's direct rule. In any case, it was justified by the cost of maintaining the army, which also benefited the subjects (cf. Tacitus, *hist.* 4, 74); the word *tributum* was explained by reference to a false etymology as meaning "what is paid to soldiers."[85] The tax authorities did not usually forgo income, but definitely gave the communities room for maneuver so long as the tax revenues were forwarded to them. Cities' market taxes and customs duties could be reduced or canceled on the occasion of and during local festivals, though the governor's agreement to this was required.[86] The moderate taxation that was long practiced in general, the privileges and alleviations granted by the Roman authorities in particular cases, and the government assistance that was especially visible in construction projects (p. 438) doubtless had a broad effect on the prosperity of large parts of Asia Minor. But we cannot speak of a genuine economic policy with respect to the provinces. That Imperial policy (as has been alleged for instance in the case of Asia) had a "structural-programmatic character," or that in this context labor market policy considerations even played a role, is not only unproven but is also highly unlikely.[87]

✦ ✦ ✦

Emperors and governors sought primarily, in addition to tax revenues, solid order and peace (Pliny the Younger, *ep.* 10, 117: *perpetua quies*; cf. *Digest* 1, 18, 13: *curare, ut pacata atque quieta provincia sit quam regit*). Where abuses and conflicts arose, the governors intervened with commands and prohibitions, and they granted privileges to petitioners when the latter were not making unreasonable requests. But they also did not merely react, but instead oversaw, assisted, and ordered, insofar as the *Imperium* was concerned with the welfare of the cities (*civitates*). Their ability to "manage" themselves long allowed Rome not to even think about creating a special governmental apparatus for the cities.

Gubernatorial rule functioned well for about 200 years. There is no conclusive evidence that it was experienced as oppressive foreign rule or that the Italic masters exercising it were lumped together as oppressors. For a long time most inhabitants of this enormous land never or seldom saw a military man face to face.[88] Uprisings like those in Gaul or Judea were unknown in Imperial period Asia Minor west of the Euphrates. The Jewish author Josephos (*BJ* 2, 365 f.; trans. Thackeray) had Agrippa II warn his rebellious people: "It is hard to serve, you will tell me. How much harder for Greeks. . . . And then the five hundred cities of Asia: do they not, without a garrison, bow before a single governor and the consular fasces?" To be sure, the hundreds of Roman officials here included some who made themselves conspicuous by their cruelty or greed. Nonetheless, the threat of being denounced hovered over them (p. 421). Only at the end of the second century CE did the wind begin to change: it seems that an affliction returned in the form of the Roman soldier that resembled the hardships inflicted by the Roman tax collectors at the beginnings of the province of Asia more than two hundred years earlier. Uncontrolled military violence replaced the certainty of law; undermined the discipline that behooved the governed; and left them powerless or indifferent before the abuse, injustice, and violence of a growing number of armed men and imperial agents (*caesariani, frumentarii, stationarii*, etc.). The *belle époque* of the familiar civilian rule came to an end.[89]

Diocletian's New Order

The system of the provinces was transformed throughout the empire by Diocletian, who during the "rule of four" (Tetrarchy, 284–305 CE) resided chiefly in the East and made Nikomedeia in Bithynia the center of this part of the empire. The reorganization initiated by him and further developed by Constantine in the Orient remained in place until the Arab conquest. However, within the broad frontiers of the empire's large subdivisions there were displacements and new formations of smaller provinces after Diocletian as well. Our sources provide even fewer details on this than they do on the first three centuries of the empire. A precise reconstruction of the provinces from the Tetrarchy to Justinian is not possible. We must also keep in mind that the changes introduced at the end of the third century were completed only in the course of the fourth.[90]

Diocletian began by reducing the size of the provinces (Lactantius, *mort. pers.* 7, 4), and these were eventually combined into dioceses that were then—certainly only after Diocletian—assigned to three prefectures, each under the supervision of a *praefectus praetorio*. The *praefectus praetorio per orientem* was responsible for the East, with at first three dioceses: Oriens, with Egypt and the Levant as far as the Taurus, including Cilicia and Isauria; Pontica, with northern and eastern Anatolia; and Asiana, with southern and western Anatolia (Map 23). In 395 CE the dioceses under the *praefectus praetorio per orientem* were expanded to five by separating off Aegyptus and also putting Thracia under his supervision. The dioceses were led by deputies of the prefects with the title of *vicarius*. Like the *praefecti praetorio*, they had no military but only civilian functions. The provosts of the provinces, who also had no military competence, were the *praesides* (Greek: *hegemones*), who at first came mainly from the equestrian order. The military command was organized supraprovincially by the prefecture or the emperor; since Constantine, "masters of the army" (*magistri militum* or *equitum*) had held overall command, whereas the troops, mostly from two provinces, were commanded by "leaders" (*duces*).

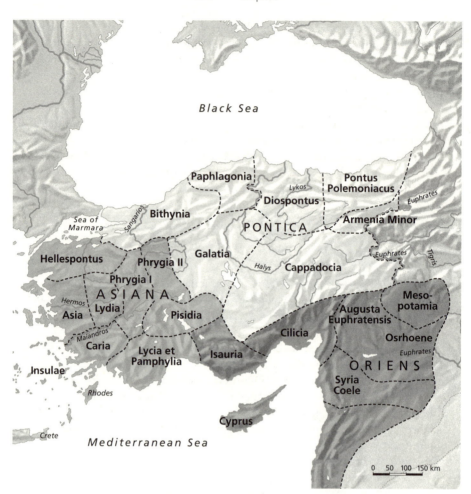

Map 23. The dioceses (Asiana, Pontica, and Oriens) and provinces after the reorganization carried out under Diocletian and Constantine. Map drawn by Peter Palm, Berlin.

In the fiscal domain, the reorganization of the *annona*, which had already been made the main tax, and other monetary levies resulted in greater burdens for provincials that were accompanied by stricter controls. The tighter squeeze was overseen by a growing army of imperial officials (*officiales*), a bureaucracy that had slowly grown and left the autonomous *polis* only a little remaining elbow room. The voluntary communal contributions made by the urban elites did not disappear but diminished in the measure that these elites were systematically counted on as liable for state revenues. The coined money that the cities had issued into the second half of the third century was abolished, and under Diocletian and Constantine the imperial currency was also clearly redenominated. The reason given for the Edict on Maximum Prices

Diocletian issued in 301 CE was to protect soldiers against exorbitant prices on local markets. The attribution of other motives is controversial, but the edict may also have been connected with monetary reform. Records from the great catalog of goods and services for which the edict set maximum prices have been found in stone inscriptions in Aphrodisias and Aizanoi.[91] When Diocletian's and Constantine's new order was completed, the imperial province system of Asia Minor was a thing of the past. The centuries-old privilege enjoyed by senators allowing them act as the military, juridical, and administrative representatives of the emperor disappeared. In addition, territories, personnel, the chain of command of the imperial government, and taxation were reorganized.

CHAPTER 9

Economic, Socio-Political, and Cultural Conditions in the Provinces of the Imperial Period

Population

Demography

When people talk about population figures in Antiquity, they still draw on the pioneering work of Karl Julius Beloch.[1] Whereas the demography of the ancient world has since become a discipline using sophisticated methods applied in particular to Roman Egypt, Italy, and the Latin West,[2] the demography of Asia Minor as a whole remains largely uninvestigated. Only the American historian Thomas R. S. Broughton has ventured to follow in Beloch's footsteps.[3]

Beloch took his data almost exclusively from literary sources across the different periods. He calculated population on the basis of the contingents of armed men: the Paphlagonians in the time of Xenophon and the Galatians during their war against Manlius Vulso. Among various ancient data regarding the numbers of citizens or inhabitants in cities—according to Memnon (FGrHist 434 F 1, 40, 2) Herakleia Pontike had 8,000 inhabitants; according to Strabo, Selge in Pisidia had "at some time" 20,000 men, while according to Beloch's projection of the chiliastys (i.e., the subdivisions of citizens by thousands), Ephesos had 225,000 inhabitants, and according to Zonaras (12, 23) Kaisareia-Mazaka in Cappadocia had 400,000 inhabitants—the physician Galen's estimate regarding Pergamon toward the middle of the second century deserves the most attention: "If, then, our fellow citizens number about forty thousand and if you add to these the women and slaves, you will find that you are not satisfied with being richer than one hundred and twenty thousand."[4] In his estimations Broughton took into account the capacity of theater buildings and figures of municipal councils. Beloch estimated the population density of the province of Asia at an average of 44 inhabitants per square kilometer (6 million inhabitants on a territory of 135,000 square kilometers), and that of Galatia at 10–12.5 inhabitants per square kilometer (on a territory of 40,000 square kilometers). According to Beloch, the total ran to 4–4.5 million inhabitants for the densely populated west, 5–6.5 million for Anatolia north of the Taurus, and 2 million for the coastal region south of the Taurus, or altogether 11.5–13 million. Broughton adds for comparison a Turkish census conducted in 1935: 13,657,661 inhabitants, without European Turkey and Armenia (in July 2014 the population of Turkey was

75,837,020). Regardless of whether these estimates approach the real numbers in the Imperial period, their bases are much too tenuous for them to be considered reliable. The data base for Asia Minor cannot compare with that for Egypt, from which we have information from various kinds of sources in much larger quantities. Because of the great differences in topography, studies on individual regions and aspects cannot be used to form an overall picture, but they do register methodological advances and interesting insights. The Tübingen survey on the *polis* territory of Kyaneai in the Yavu mountain country of central Lycia covered a surface of 106 square kilometers and found, for the period from the sixth century BCE to 1300 CE, about 3,800 settlement sites (the whole urban area of Kyaneai, including the necropolis, being counted as a single site), that is, thirty-five settlements per square kilometer. For the Imperial period, Frank Kolb found fifty-five rural settlements in this area and calculated about fifteen to one hundred inhabitants for each of them. He estimates that in this period, the whole territory, including the city of Kyaneai (about 1,000 inhabitants) had about 6,000 inhabitants.[5] That is, especially given the rural conditions, a relatively high density of about five inhabitants per square kilometer, which confirms that Lycia was a province with great agricultural productivity. The territory of Sagalassos in Pisidia, with 1,800 square kilometers, is incomparably larger. For the Imperial period, researchers have found a little more than 300 settlements in this area, thus a still higher density, but are reluctant to estimate population figures.[6] In other regions, for instance the interior of Paphlagonia and the Pontos area, Lycaonia, or Cappadocia, the density of rural settlement cannot have been nearly so high. Therefore it makes no sense to try to convert our information into an estimate of the population density of Asia Minor as a whole.

Ethnic Groups and Languages

If we look back on the history of Asia Minor in the pre-Imperial period, we recall a series of settlement waves that added to or expelled the existing populations on the coasts and in the interior: the Greeks in the Archaic period, the Iranians in the Classical period, and then more Greeks and Iranians, along with Macedonians, Celts, Semites, and finally Italics in the Hellenistic period. Naturally, by the Imperial period these settlers had themselves been resident there for generations. But we tend for the most part to call "natives" the population elements that were already settled in the country in the second and early first millenia BCE, in contrast to the Semitic, Iranian, Celtic, Italic, and Greek elements that came later.

The large population groups include in the northwest the Bithynians, with their subgroups, such as the Mariandynoi and Kaukonians (in Herakleia's hinterland as far as the Parthenios River). Along the north coast, toward the east, lived the Paphlagonians and Cappadocians, and in eastern Anatolia, the Armenians. On the western plateau Mysians, Lydians, Phrygians, and Pisidians had settled; in the south, Carians, Lycians, Pamphylians, Lycaonians, Isaurians, and Cilicians. On the local level, the sources mention a number of less numerous peoples and tribes, such as the Homonadeis and Kietai in the Taurus; the Mokkadenoi in Lydia; the Moschoi, Mossynoikoi, and Sannoi in the mountains of eastern Pontos.

Apart from the terms for population groups used by Greek and Roman writers (which are not always reliable), the linguistic heritage in the texts that have come down to us, and in particular the names of deities, persons, and places that abound in our epigraphic sources, allows us to distinguish the indigenous elements from one another.[7] Although almost all the names attested in the Imperial period are traditionally written in Greek or (more rarely) in Latin spellings, a non-Greek or non-Roman origin usually remains discernible behind these spellings and can provide hints as to the peoples from which they stem. In any case, names have their own laws determined by social and cultural history that have to be taken into account above and beyond their etymology. In the case of personal names in particular, the body of Latin names in Asia Minor in the Imperial period does not indicate that the people concerned were of Italic or western origin, and Greek names provide only minimal evidence of Greek origin. Many social climbers of various backgrounds "lurk" behind names of both kinds, to which the prestige of the upper class was in general attached (but not everywhere in the same way), and especially behind Greek names, which were associated with the dominant culture. The sources mentioning indigenous names would presumably be more numerous if even in the lowest strata of society, every family had put up a tombstone. But in the case of Iranian and even native names as well, we have to consider secondary phenomena of adaptation and fashion. A well-known example is Midas, the mythical royal name from Phrygia, which does not necessarily belong to any indigenous Phrygian but may instead mirror a connection with tradition similar to that of the names derived from Christian saints' names in our own time.[8] The *Lallnamen* ("short names with repetitive phonemes probably deriving from baby-talk" [R. Parker]) common all over Asia Minor—for instance, Apphe, Lala, Mama, Nana, Papa—are another phenomenon that cannot be associated with any particular linguistic group.[9]

In Roman times, such Iranian names as Artapates, Aribazos, Ariarathes, Mithridates, and Pharnakes were widespread all over Anatolia, and especially in Cappadocia and Lycia. They testify to the continuity of Iranian culture in families of the Persian diaspora or among Iranized inhabitants of the former Achaemenid Empire.[10] A mixture of non-Greek and Greek name-elements in a single family was not rare. In the inscription on a rock tomb in Pontos that probably still dates from the Hellenistic period, the wife Theophile bears a Greek name, while her father Zabdes has a Semitic name, and his father (her grandfather) again has a Greek name: Bias. Her husband with the Greek name Philochares calls himself the son of a Maiphates, an Iranian name that means "protected by the moon goddess (Māh)."[11]

Like the Iranian diaspora, the Semitic diaspora in Asia Minor continued uninterrupted from the Hellenistic period into the Imperial period. The Jews, isolated in the country since the advent of Persian rule, greatly increased their numbers under the Seleucids by the resettlement of 2,000 Jewish families from Babylonia and Mesopotamia to Phrygia and Lydia under Antiochos III (p. 217). According to Philo (*Legat.*

33 [245]), they had become numerous in every city in Asia and Syria. Literary evidence, the architectural remains of synagogues, and also small discoveries (lampstands), and above all inscriptions provide evidence of this; in inscriptions, they can only occasionally still be recognized by their names: Benjamin, Joshua, Samuel, Deborah, Rebekah, Sarah, and so forth.[12]

The Celtic population element that became indigenous in the early Hellenistic period preserved a rich fund of names within and outside the true settlement areas of the Tolistobogii, Tektosages, and Trokmoi. According to Strabo (12, 3, 41), a whole area was known as the "Land of Gezatorix."

Most of the names recognized as Anatolian in the narrower sense can be understood as characteristic of one or more regions ("isoglosses" and "interglosses").[13] Strabo (12, 3, 25) writes that in the whole land on the Halys, the border region between Cappadocia and Paphlagonia, two native languages were spoken, Cappadocian and Paphlagonian, and that "Paphlagonian" names were common there. A few of these names, Maes, Sasas, Atotes, Tibios, and also place and river names in northern Anatolia (e.g., Amasia, Kinolis, and Sangarios) occur as personal names in the northern Black Sea area; thus there seems to have been a relationship between population elements on both sides of the Black Sea that is now discernible only in these traces. In epigraphic name material the Paphlagonian, Pontic, and Cappadocian regions are relatively little represented, but—not surprisingly—in these same regions the preparation and erection of inscriptions on stone is less common than in the west. Of the small number of "Cappadocian" names that we know, four are found in a late Hellenistic decree, recorded on a metal tablet, by the city of Hanisa, which in the Imperial period was presumably absorbed into Kaisareia-Mazaka: Anoptenes, Balasopos (or Balasopes), Sindenos, and Teires.[14] Northwestern Asia Minor has handed down names that can be traced back to a Thracian linguistic heritage, names such as Mokazis (or Mokasios), Ziaelas, Ziailis, Turigos, and Dorosinthos. The southern belt from Cilicia to Lycia and the western plateau is much more productive quantitatively: conservative peoples, such as the Phrygians, Pisidians, and Lycians, are prominently represented in the body of names used in the Imperial period, and the Lydians and Carians are hardly less well represented.[15]

Beyond the names and the religious traditions to be discussed later in the chapter, our grip on indigenous identities in the Imperial period remains limited. Although almost the whole written heritage from the time when Asia Minor was part of the Roman Empire was written in Greek or Latin, indigenous languages were certainly still spoken in Rome's Anatolian provinces. That does not take into account the Celtic idiom that first established itself in the Hellenistic period, and which Saint Jerome (in Gal. PL 26, 382c) nonetheless still heard spoken there more than six hundred years later.[16] But Lycaonian (Acts 14:11) and Paphlagonian seem in fact also to have been spoken there during the Imperial period (Lucian, Pseudol. 14), and in two other cases we even have a small number of linguistic testimonies in inscriptions: after a pause of several centuries, during the high Imperial period people in rural Phrygia began to write short formulas on tombstones in neo-Phrygian, below a

Greek text on most stones, but only in that language on a few.[17] In addition, there are indigenous linguistic testimonies in Pisidia; new discoveries come from the small city of Timbriada.[18] There as in Selge, where after 212 CE members of the urban elite still bore indigenous names, Pisidian continued to be spoken far into the Imperial period.

Regular "errors" in Greek in tomb inscriptions, especially in central Anatolia, which were unhesitatingly "corrected" by earlier editors, are now recognized to be *faits de langue*: an indication of the penetration of Greek by native linguistic forms. Nonetheless, the degree of "linguistic Hellenization" even among the rural population is astonishing.[19] Like the English historian Stephen Mitchell, we have to assume bilingualism in large areas of rural Anatolia in the Imperial period.[20] In the very lowest strata of society the native language might even have been the only one people really knew, but in any case many people's Greek must have been rather weak. Greek tomb inscriptions that betray a faulty knowledge of the language seem to confirm this.[21] The survival of indigenous languages clearly was concentrated in inland Anatolia, where they did not disappear until the Christian age or even after the arrival of Islam.[22]

Economic Bases

"Asia is so rich and fertile as easily to surpass all other countries in the productiveness of her soil, the variety of her crops, the extent of her pastures and the volume of her exports" (Cicero, *Manil.* 14; trans. Hodge). This view was expressed in a time when the country was still laboring under the heaviest burdens. Contemporaries of the *pax Romana* since Augustus, such as Strabo in particular, confirm the favorable state of the resources to which the peninsula had access. As is reflected in the public and private wealth of the Imperial period, the age must have produced an economic power that was elevated compared to preceding times. The underlying conditions under which production, distribution, exchange, and consumption took place may have been primarily constitutive for this power: in addition to the continuing peace, other factors included the improved infrastructure, monetarization, the maneuvering room provided by urban autonomy, and last but not least the opportunities offered by a "globalized world" in the whole Mediterranean region that the *pax Romana* had made possible.[23]

Agriculture, Hunting, and Fishing

Broad basins with fertile soil framed by rocky mountain ranges are characteristic of many parts of Asia Minor, whereas extremely high plains and the surrounding mountains are used primarily as pastures, hunting grounds, and wood sources. Up to this point, only individual research projects in western and southern Asia Minor have been able to estimate the percentage of intensively cultivated areas in a particular region investigated as a whole. Strabo (12, 2, 7) notes the presence of expanses of fallow land in the territory of Mazaka in Cappadocia: " the districts all round are utterly barren and untilled, although they are level; but they are sandy and are rocky underneath" (trans. Jones). In northern, central, and eastern Anatolia there must have been quite a few areas where the land was basically arable but was left fallow because of low population density, the enormous distances between settlements, and other adverse factors.

The Mediterranean triad of grain, wine, and olive oil was primary in Asia Minor as well. Mixed crops were grown in many areas, with grain cultivated between sparse stands of olive trees, wine grapes between fig, fruit, and olive trees. Grain varieties of varying quality—wheat, barley, oats, and millet—were grown in most regions, but great granaries like Egypt, North Africa, Sicily, and the area north of the Black Sea did not exist on the peninsula, even if Lydia and Phrygia could be considered centers of wheat production.

Olive trees provided food, medical and body care products, and fuel for lamps, and were thus a universal resource for everyday life. There were olive plantations even on the steep slopes of the north coast and in flatter areas in the interior (Strabo 12, 3, 12; 8, 14); in Sagalassos they were present at elevations as high as 1,300 meters,[24] but they were probably most extensive on the west and south coasts. Grape vines were cultivated not only on slopes but also on the plains and yielded, in addition to wine, table grapes, raisins, vinegar, perfume, and medicine. Apart from specialties like those produced in Phrygia (Pliny the Elder, *nat.* 14, 75. 113), we find focal points for vineyards near the Sea of Marmara, on the Aegean coast and the offshore islands, and on the south coast.[25] Grapevine tendrils and grape clusters have been frequent pictorial motifs in Asia Minor since the age of the Hittites. The site of the city of Nikaia is supposed to have earlier been a place called Helikore ("rich in vines"), and Wiyanawanda-Oinoanda, a small city in the Lycian highlands, has had the word "wine" (*oinos*) in its name since earliest times. Strabo (12, 3, 30) found the best wine in Pontos in Phanarhoia, the country at the confluence of the Iris and the Lykos Rivers, in the area around Amaseia.

To meet nutritional needs through these products, the horticulture widely practiced in Asia Minor provided not only a supplement but also manifold alternatives: various kinds of vegetables, salad greens, nuts, fruit, figs, mushrooms, and spices. The northern part of the country produced high quality fruit. Apples from Gangra were supposed to have been equaled only by a variety grown near Aquileia in the Alps (Athenaios 3, 82 c). On the plains around Themiskyra there was such a superabundance of apple trees that only some of them were cared for and their fruit harvested (Strabo 12, 3, 15). The name of the town of Kerasus, which goes back to Greek settlers on the coast of the Black Sea, means "rich in cherries." Lucullus brought the grafted sweet cherries cultivated on the coast of East Pontos to Europe. They have completely disappeared from this area. Kaunos on the south coast exported figs to Italy. Saffron was bought in the interior of Lycia and exported through one of the harbors. And in Smyrna, someone seems to have loved the wild marjoram produced there so much that he was nicknamed "Origanion" ([162] *IK* Smyrna 210). In various regions, apiculture and the cultivation of plants for textiles and medicines also sought to produce surpluses for export.

Since the time of the kings, eastern and central Anatolia had been the domains of livestock raising: horses were raised in Armenia and Cappadocia, and cattle and sheep pastures were extensive, especially in Lycaonia, Galatia, Pisidia, and Phrygia, which according to Pliny the Elder (*nat.* 8, 190) produced the finest wool, but there were also complaints about the browsing damage done by flocks of sheep in the vineyards.[26] Almost all parts of the country produced milk, cheese, wool, leather, and meat and also used oxen as draft animals. Goats and swine did not require large pastures, and as producers of milk, cheese, and meat, they were also commonly part of the peasant's household economy. The analysis of animal bones found in Limyra in Lycia showed a 9:1 predominance of goats over sheep.[27] Some inhabitants of Anatolia—not only the Jews—considered pigs unclean; swine were not allowed on the territory of Pontic Komana, and eating their flesh was forbidden (Strabo 12, 8, 9).

The basic sources of food also included hunting as well as fishing in rivers and lakes and along the seacoasts. Wild game in Asia Minor must have been ample and varied: in addition to small animals and birds, there were also deer, roe deer, antelopes, gazelles, and large numbers of wild boars. Big cats and bears were also native in the country. A comprehensive investigation of hunting in ancient Asia Minor has never been carried out. Its economic significance is difficult to estimate. From the time of Persian rule into the Imperial period, hunting appears as a pictorial motif on monuments, and kings and nobles are depicted hunting big game. On the territory of Hadrian's hunting grounds in the interior of Mysia, cities emerged: Hadrianutherai and others.[28] A modern study of wild boar hunting in Lycia focuses on the Persian period; it defends the thesis—also regarding the Imperial period—that in the countryside the threat posed by wild boars required hunting to reduce their numbers.[29] In contrast to the present-day situation, in which these animals are hunted less for their meat than to protect crops, ancient hunters generally consumed the meat. In Bithynia, Paphlagonia, Lycia, and elsewhere, the terms used to designate hunters— *theragrotai*, *kynegoi* (hunters using hounds), or *oresidromoi* (mountaineers)—are supplemented by depictions of hunting (especially boar hunting) on tombstones. For example, a young man in Mysia died as a result of a hunting accident ([146] MS II 94). Hunting with falcons was already practiced in the Cilicia of late Antiquity ([110] MAMA III 17.79).

Commercial fishing is also a wide-ranging topic. Pickled fish and fish sauce (garum) were exported overseas (Pliny the Elder, *nat.* 31, 94). Various species of freshwater fish were caught in Lake Ascania (modern-day Lake İznik) near Nikaia, including a fish up to two meters in length and weighing as much as sixty pounds known as the *kestreus*, which was apparently a kind of catfish.[30] Lake Stephane in Pontos was full of fish (Strabo 12, 3, 38). Fish were also caught in the Sangarios River (Livy 38, 18, 8 f.). Commercial fishing was practiced on all the coasts, with observation posts, fishing fleets, salting houses, and garum factories. In Iasos, which lived chiefly on fishing and had hardly any arable land, a cithara singer's audience, except a man who was hard of hearing, deserted him when bells announced the opening of the fish market (Strabo 14, 2, 21). The straits at the Hellespont and the Bosporus offered especially rich fishing grounds, where schools of fish moving between the Mediterranean and Pontos Euxeinos were easy to find. Strabo describes in detail the *pelamydes* (Turkish: *palamut*; English: Atlantic bonito), *Sarda sarda*, a kind of mackerel up to a meter long and weighing as much as twenty-two kilograms that is found in the Mediterranean and the Black Sea (Strabo 7, 6, 2; 12, 3, 11.19; Aelian, *Natura Animalium* 15, 5).[31]

Logging, resin-tapping, and pitch production played a significant role in the Pontic and Taurus Mountains along the north and south coasts—especially in Rough Cilicia (Strabo 14, 5, 3.6)—and on the slopes of Mt. Ida and Mt. Olympus. The west had little timber good enough for construction, as was also true in parts of the central Anatolian plateau. However, Cicero's witticism (*Flacc.* 41) about a Phrygian who had never seen a tree is far off the mark.[32] Many coastal towns near logging areas had facilities for shipbuilding and repair. In Kyzikos, Strabo (12, 8, 11) found more than 200 ship sheds; Side in Pamphylia had wharfs that were already used by the Cilician pirates (Strabo 14, 3, 2), and that is also true of Korykos farther to the east ([110] MAMA III 502.535). The area east of Amastris also had a reputation as a supplier of prized, hard boxwood. In Sinope, walnut planks were made into table-tops (Strabo 12, 3, 12). References to the vocation of people in the woodworking industry and depictions of their tools are found in many tomb inscriptions.

Texts and pictures on stones found in many parts of Asia Minor illustrate the rural milieu: vows made for good harvests, and for the protection of "children and livestock," sacrifices of cattle and wine to the gods, and verses on the right kind of agriculture, suited to the season, as Hesiod teaches it. The images depicted yoked oxen pulling plows (Figure 72), the heads of cattle, grapevine tendrils, and the pruning knife—the symbol for the prestigious activities of growing olive trees and wine grapes. Coins also depict the outstanding products of a city's territory. This evidence, in addition to the literary testimonies, must not be neglected when we seek to form an image of agricultural prosperity. But we also have to take into account statements about problems. When whole armies that were engaged in wars made requisitions on the soil of Asia Minor, they left behind them supply crises in the cities. But even in times of peace famines were reported. Galen (ca. 129–ca. 216 CE), the great physician from Pergamon, refers to several successive years of rampant food shortages during the Antonine period that were surely among the most severe of the Imperial period:

> Those dwelling in the cities took the total wheat harvest from the fields—as they normally do when during the summer they lay in stock sufficient amounts of grain for the following year—together with barley, beans, and lentils. To those living in the countryside they left the other products of Demeter: field crops that are called pulses and vegetables, after they had taken away and brought to the city a significant proportion even of them. The villagers then consuming the remainder during the winter fell on hard

72. Relief depiciting a plowman from Prusa. Museum of Bursa.

times, being forced to eat unwholesome food throughout the spring season, boughs and leaves from the trees and bushes as well as purse-tassels and roots of unwholesome plants, and to fill up and satisfy themselves with wild herbs wherever available ; they also cooked yellow weed, which they previously had not even attempted to taste. (trans. Marek)[33]

From such serious crises striking both urban and rural regions, we must distinguish the bottlenecks restricting grain supply in the cities that are occasionally recorded in inscriptions. In view of the limited farmland around precisely the heavily populated cities near the coasts, and also of the dominant use of land for the more profitable production of olives and wine, these areas seldom produced enough grain to meet their needs, and most were dependent to a greater or lesser degree on imports. The giants among the grain producers—especially Egypt and North Africa—did not make regular deliveries to Asia, as they did to Italy and Rome. Accordingly, only in exceptional cases such cities as Ephesos or Tralleis were allowed to import Egyptian grain.[34] The normal additional demand had to be met by an interurban grain trade that was certainly volatile, especially when market prices were driven up by disruptive factors, such as poor harvests caused by bad weather and attacks by pests. The speculations of wheat dealers and large landowners added to the problem. Communities tried to protect themselves by creating grain stockpiles (*sitonia*),[35] and in emergencies Roman officials intervened, even if not in every case effectively:[36] in Aspendos, a governor was in danger of being lynched by an excited mob; only when the speculators relented did the situation become less tense (Philostratos, VA 1, 15).

However, considering the body of source material, we cannot speak of frequent, serious, or persistent food supply crises in Asia Minor during the Imperial period, in either the cities or the countryside, and in view of the multiplicity of agricultural products, such conditions were not likely. If, as in Sagalassos in Pisidia, settlements in the rural *chora* multiplied exponentially during the high Imperial period, especially on the plains, we have to assume that there was a sustained abundance of agricultural resources at this time.

Mining and Marble Quarrying

Reports on mining in Anatolia go as far back as our written sources. Paphlagonian mines in the Sandarakurgion ("Realgar") Mountains lay abandoned there at the beginning of the Imperial period. Formerly run by leaseholders who used enslaved criminals as labor, they had become unprofitable because of the high mortality rates (Strabo 12, 3, 40). Emperor Tiberius appropriated the large mines from private or urban possession (Suetonius, *Tib.* 49, 2). Strabo (12, 3, 19.30) mentions *metalla* near Pharnakeia (Kerasus) on the Pontic coast, near Kabeira (Neokaisareia) in the hinterland, and gold and iron ore mines in Colchis and Armenia (Strabo 11, 2, 19; 11, 14, 9). The old gold deposits at Paktolos near Sardeis no longer existed in the Imperial period. Silver mines supposedly existed in the east Pontic highlands, but in Strabo's time (12, 3, 19) there remained only iron mines. The iron content in these mountain ranges, the Paryadres (Giresun Dağları) can still be recognized by the reddish color of the soil. Here, as in Cappadocia, *miltos* was presumably mined; it was known as "Sinopian earth," because it was exported through the important Black Sea port of Sinope. *Miltos* was used for medical purposes, as a thickener, and as a dye-stuff—a less expensive alternative to vermilion. Salt was extracted from rock in Cappadocia (Strabo 12, 3, 37.39), from Lake Tuz in central Anatolia (Strabo 12, 5, 4; cf. Pliny the Elder, *nat.* 31, 84), and from sea water in many places. The salt from Kaunos, where archaeologists have recently discovered saltworks (Figure 73),[37] was especially prized (Pliny the Elder, *nat.* 31, 99; cf. also [162] *IK* Priene 67).

The splendid development of imperial, municipal, and private stonework and architecture cannot be conceived without marble. Many cities had their own quarries producing stone of good quality, such as Miletus on the southern edge of Lake Bafa, Aphrodisias in Caria, Hierapolis in Phrygia, or Sagalassos in Pisidia. In Sagalassos, the last lines of an epigram on stone proudly note that "Concerning this monument, if it wrongly impresses to be carved in Phrygian stone, it misleads you. The stone originates locally."[38] However, the Roman emperors secured the exploitation of the best deposits, as they did in the case of mining.[39] Two Anatolian quarries enjoyed worldwide fame and supplied construction projects throughout the empire: Dokimeion in Phrygia, on the territory of Synnada, and the island of Prokonnesos in the Propontis (Sea of Marmara region), which was part of the territory of Kyzikos. In both places, semifinished products were made to order under the guidance of imperial officials—bases for columns, capitals, column sections and pilasters, entabla-

73. Saltworks near Kaunos.

tures, sarcophagi, and so forth—which were carefully marked with the date, the name of the foreman, the origin, and the destination ([110] MAMA IV 7). Transported to the ultimate buyer by water, overland, or both, the blocks were partly further finished by craftsmen who came from the region of origin.

Trades and Services

The range of trades and services, up to the upper levels of physicians, jurists, and teachers, impresses us by its multiplicity and testifies to a differentiated distribution of labor that presupposes a high degree of urbanization in large parts of the country. Not all words that appear in the sources as the names of occupations can be interpreted,[40] and it is frequently unclear whether the activities mentioned should be seen as belonging to the domain of production or to that of sales. Moreover, in urban and rural areas of Asia Minor in the Imperial period the name of an activity does not always refer to a long-term occupation. Food production, and the production and finishing of clothing, wood, clay, stone, and metal can be distinguished as the major trades.

By far the most common "trade," that of the farmer (*georgos*) is seldom mentioned in inscriptions, probably because it applied to most people and was too vague to distinguish an individual or group. Things were otherwise in the case of trades in the cities, where baking was one of the most important activities, and where such specialists as flour sifters, dough kneaders, confectioners, and cake bakers were represented (cf. esp. [162] *IK* Side 30) much more frequently than butchers. Wool and flax workers, linen weavers, embroiderers, sack makers, felt and hat makers, tailors, cobblers, tanners, dyers, wreath makers, and so on represented the textile trades, whose great strongholds were Miletus, Sardeis in Lydia, Hierapolis and Laodikeia in Phrygia, and Tarsos in Cilicia. Smaller cities, such as Thyateira and Saittai in Lydia, were also prominent sites in this line of work. The dyeing industry on the west and south coasts and in Pontos (Vitruvius 7, 13, 2), along with fishing for the sea snails from which *purpura* dye is made, were closely connected with textile finishing. We find pottery-making centers in Pergamon and Sagalassos in Pisidia (*terra sigillata*), and large-scale amphora production in Rhodes, Knidos, Chios, and Sinope. Pottery workshops must have been everywhere, right down to the village level. *Quam bene caelatis, tam bene fictilibus*—"Drinking from plain earthenware is as great a pleasure as drinking from decoratively painted cups" says a graffito in Ephesos ([146] MS I 330; trans. Marek). There was an inexhaustible demand not only for roof tiles, pipes, clay lamps, jars, and everyday utensils of all kinds, but also for terra cotta figurines. The latter had a religious function as votive offerings in sanctuaries and in small shrines and niches in people's houses. Since the early Hellenistic age figurines had gradually become detached from a purely religious function, apparently increasingly acquiring representative and decorative goals as well, especially in connection with the *symposion*.[41]

A glassblower (*hyeliarios*) in Seleukeia on Kalykadnos ([110] MAMA III 10) and gem cutters (*kabidarios, daktylokoiloglyphos*) in Korasion, Cilicia ([110] MAMA III 118), Sardeis ([146] MS I 482), and Philadelpheia ([105] TAM V 3, 1901) provide us with some of the seldom attested names of trades. Archaeological evidence has also proven that glass was produced, for example, in the village center Hoyran on the territory of the Lycian city of Kyaneai.[42] Metalworkers range from the simple village blacksmith to the highly specialized urban fine craftsmen, of whom the silversmiths of the Artemision in Ephesos are the best known to us, from the New Testament; we will return later to their conflict with the Apostle Paul (p. 529 f.). A late Hellenistic center of bronze-working in Cappadocia probably drew its raw materials from mines in Pontos and eastern Paphlagonia.[43] Various terms in great numbers prove the range of metalworking and stone cutting, whose practitioners produced many sarcophagi and tombstones with figurative and decorative reliefs, along with wood production and processing. The sarcophagus of a certain M. Aurelius Ammianus from Hierapolis in Phrygia deserves special attention; the owner of the tomb describes himself as the producer of a machine depicted in the relief, in which we can recognize a water-powered stone sawmill. The remains of such a machine have been found in the terrace houses of Ephesos.[44]

Many skilled craftsmen did not stay at home: among the craftsmen mentioned in Asia Minor's inscriptions there are foreigners, and conversely Anatolians are to be found far outside the peninsula. In view of the marble deposits in and around Bithynia, it is striking that signatures and dedicatory and tomb inscriptions repeatedly prove the existence of stone-cutters from Nikomedeia in Italy and North Africa as well. The beautifully ornamented pilasters of the basilica in Leptis Magna—native city of the African emperor Septimius Severus (193–211)—are of Prokonnesian marble, and inscriptions of that city mention a mason from Nikomedeia. Finally, the important school at Aphrodisias, where statues of exceptional quality were made and where competitions among stone cutters were part of the agonistic program, also benefited from the nearby marble deposits.[45]

In the services sector, more often than in other lines of work, occupational designations appear that can be connected with slaves: property and storehouse managers, stewards, secretaries, and agents worked for private individuals, while gravediggers, bath attendants, and guards at sports areas in the cities probably worked for communities. Painters (*zographoi*), cooks, hairdressers, astrologists, occasional poets, musicians, and many others worked for wages, as did most physicians and veterinarians, jurists, construction experts, and individuals employed in the educational system, from elementary teachers to itinerant rhetors.

Craftsmen and merchants were organized into guilds, and so were, for instance, physicians, blacksmiths, greengrocers, and shipowners.[46] However, it has often been doubted that these corporations pursued economic goals and thus exercised an influence on economic events: no mention is made anywhere of trade union negotiations or cartels, or regulations and standards with regard to the products made or marketed by their members. Instead, in our sources these guilds are presented as social confraternities taking part in religious life and making decisions to honor benefactors. When in individual cases it is a question of good deeds from which the members' specific trade might also indirectly benefit, this connection remains too vague to allow us to conclude that a permanent representation of the trade's interests is involved. The Roman officials feared that some corporations might transform themselves into locally active political clubs (*hetairiai*) that would form cells and cause trouble (Pliny the Younger, *ep.* 10, 33 f.). In the oft-cited "baker's strike" in Ephesos ([162] *IK* Ephesos 215), the proconsul intervened with these words:

> I therefore order the bakers not to gather together as an association (*hetairia*) nor to boldly act as leaders. Rather they are to obey completely the regulations established for the common welfare and to supply the city with the necessary production of bread without fail.[47]

Depending on the tradition and importance of the local industry, in some communities trade groups constituted a significant proportion of the population.

Commerce

As a producer and consumer, Asia Minor participated intensively in the Empire's inter-regional commerce. If in the case of crafts the widespread urban milieu favored a high degree of division of labor, at the same time it offered the consumer a hitherto unparalleled wealth of varied commodities, and not only in the major centers.[48] Modern research has dissociated itself from the view that any amount of sustained commerce in goods that met sophisticated needs (not including foodstuffs) failed to reach out beyond the elites in the major cities due to the lack of money and high transportation costs. Most evidence runs counter to this view. The Empire imported luxury goods, silk, gemstones, perfume, and spices from Arabia, East Africa, India, and China—and not solely for Rome. In the provinces there were enough super-rich individuals to ensure sales for these items. If proper names such as Malabathrine, Kinnamos, Zmaragdos, and Sardonyx appear in tomb inscriptions in Lycia, Bithynia, and Paphlagonia, this mirrors the familiarity of wealthy households with exotic wares from the long-distance trade that flourished in the Imperial period: wares such as malabathron, cinnamon, smaragd, and sardonyx.[49] By itself, the already noted number of customs stations on the borders of the province of Asia shows at how many places goods were transshipped and reached or left Anatolia by sea. We have recently acquired more information regarding the Lycian customs stations at Kaunos, Kalynda, and Andriake,[50] but the customs situation in the port cities of Cilicia and on the south coast of the Black Sea remains unknown. The Pontos Euxeinos lay as far away from the maritime routes of the ancient Mediterranean world as did the Erythra Thalassa (the Red Sea and the Indian Ocean), and yet via both these seas goods were shipped from the infinitely distant *terra incognita* to the Nile and the Bosporus.

Port cities were the headquarters for great trading companies (*emporoi* and *ergastai*) that chartered entire ships or freight space, for shipowners and/or captains (*naukleroi*), and for money-lenders in the business of insuring ships and their freight. In the Imperial period, among them were many important merchants of Italic descent (*negotiatores*).[51] In the commentary on Dionysius Periegeta's (second-century) geography that Eusthathios wrote in the twelfth century, the Bithynians are described as a seafaring nation.[52] In fact, Nikomedeia was prominent as the homeland of shipowners, sailors, and bankers. The metropolis on the east coast of the Propontis, which had a guild hall and shrine built by a shipowner's guild, and which decorated its Imperial period coins with images of ships and ship's prows, was undoubtedly one of Asia's gates to the world. Trade in marble seems to have enjoyed the lion's share of the export business through Nikomedeia.[53] As in the case of stone cutters working with marble, dealers in marble (*lithemporoi*) from Bithynia appear far outside their homeland, namely in Italy (Rome and Terni). Let us consider only commercial cities in the north: among the more than forty people from Sinope who are mentioned in inscriptions outside their city were businessmen resident in the northern and western Black Sea ports, in Athens, Rhodes, and Rome, and much the same was true of the distribution of people from Herakleia, one of whom was a shipowner in Alexandria. The relatively high number of citizens from the little city of Prusias (eighteen) is astonishing; they include merchants in Tomis on the Romanian coast and in Latium. A man from Tieion ended up doing business with Mainz on the Rhine, and a woman from Pisidia is supposed to have visited Italy and many other lands—perhaps at the side of a merchant ([195] SEG 19, 840).

Beyond the harbors, land transport began or ended. River transport into the hinterland was possible only over short stretches; the Sangarios, for instance, was navigable only as far as the mouth of the Gallus River. The longest river in Anatolia, the Halys, is not an important watercourse for anything beyond small boat traffic either on the high plains or in the area around its mouth. Depending on the nature of the land, inter-regional transport within Asia Minor must have required travel on roads and paths over hundreds of kilometers. Strabo (12, 8, 15) mentions Apameia in Phrygia as one of the most important inland emporia; it imported commodities from Italy and all of Greece. Asia Minor exported high-value marble, whose transportation to Rome is proven by the freight found in several shipwrecks off the Peloponnese, Sicily, and lower Italy, as well as by marble blocks at the Marmorata wharf in Rome itself. But in addition it exported various agricultural products, especially wine and oil, and also, above all, textiles. Miletus had a reputation as a supplier of the finest wool and dyed fabrics.[54] Minerals and metals, leather items (parchment), and ceramics of all kinds also played a role. In the Imperial period, the slave trade, though in steep decline with respect to Hellenistic times, had not yet ended. Several inscriptions use the term *statarium* ("slave market"),[55] and the customs regulations of the province of Asia took the slave trade into consideration with special tariffs.

Even with an abundance of information regarding Asia Minor's exports and imports, we lack the bases for determining any kind of balance of trade and cannot answer questions regarding the relation between Roman tax revenues and Italic imports, on the one hand, and the profits made by exports to Italy, on the other, with anything more than rough guesses.[56]

In magnitude and intensity, retail trade over short distances, in which merchant and producer were often identical, far exceeded inter-regional wholesale trade. Wherever surpluses were produced in the largest sector, the agricultural one, they usually found their way to the nearest market. But this was not a one-way street: craft products and also some imported commodities moved not only from city to city (for a market place in the city, see Figure 74), but also from cities to rural markets. The distances overland that a farmer had to cover on foot or mounted, transporting his wares with pack or draft animals, must have been for the most part the equivalent of a day's journey, that is, about twenty-five to thirty kilometers in all. He did not always go to the market in the central city of the territory in which he worked, but instead to the nearest towns or rural markets. These markets have recently been much discussed on the basis of a few documents from the province of Asia. In each case, upon application the proconsul granted a village community the right to hold a market on one to three given days a month or, in a case in which a Zeus festival was celebrated, on seven consecutive days a year. The scheduling of the markets thus authorized was worked out with the neighboring villages that already had this right, and with the central city, and took into consideration the routes of itinerant merchants.[57] Major market activities were concentrated around festivals in the cities and in the countryside. If one goes to a harvest festival in modern Turkey, such as the Sarımsak festival (a thanksgiving celebration for the garlic harvest) in Taşköprü (the ancient Pompeiopolis), one can gain an idea of what such local market festivals might have been like in Antiquity.

74. Ephesos, *agora* with market halls.

Monetary Economy

The minting of coins was invented in Asia Minor (p. 116 f.). Of course, "money" did not achieve the economic importance in any period of Antiquity that it now has: the number of people in Asia Minor—especially in rural areas—who regularly participated in the circulation of money remained small. On the whole, a barter economy prevailed. However, despite this reservation, in the Imperial period Asia Minor played, with regard to a monetary economy, a singular role in ancient history (and beyond). In no other part of the Roman Empire did a frequent output of such large quantities of money ever cover a comparably extensive area. After the Hellenizing policies of the Seleucids and Attalids had spread the minting of money far beyond the belt of old Greek *poleis* into the interior of the country, it reached its maximum extent under the emperors. Research has established that not every city with *polis* status minted money;[58] however, even tiny mountain towns in the Taurus and on the plateau took the initiative at some time or other. In Phrygia, coins were issued by fifty-two cities between the first and third centuries CE—a sixth of all coin types in Asia Minor, and more than in any other area.[59]

In the East, the main denomination of imperial money, the denarius, was considered equivalent to the drachma. In general the striking of gold and silver coins was limited to imperial mints. Gold was never minted by communities in the Asia Minor of the Imperial period. Apart from the fact that here and there a city might be allowed to mint silver on festive occasions, as did Amisos, Aphrodisias, Perge, Side, and Tarsos, client-kings continued to issue money in Asia Minor to the time of Ves-

75. Coin issued by the city of Neokaisareiain Pontos. Obverse: portrait of Emperor Geta; reverse: one sitting and five standing city goddesses representing Neokaisareia as a metropolis and the five member cities of the Pontic commonalty. Cast in the Winterthur Münzkabinett.

pasian: Amyntas in Side, the Polemonids in Neokaisareia, Archelaos of Cappadocia, dynasts in Cilicia, and the Lycian League. In addition, there was the drachmas from Kaisareia Mazaka and the often-mentioned *cistophori* (see Figure 49). The emperors not only accepted the *cistophorus*, which was introduced by the Attalids and minted in several cities, but continued to mint it themselves—with an altered image program—in fifteen different places, the *cistophorus* being equivalent to three denarii. Until the time of Caracalla, varying quantities of new and reminted *cistophori* were issued under some emperors, and none at all under others. Here the leader was Hadrian, during whose reign *cistophori* were minted not only in Asia but even in the name of the provincial commonalty of Bithynia.

Below the imperial and so-called special currencies in silver, provincial commonalties and cities issued bronze coins (Figure 75). With a few exceptions, municipal coins were not stamped with any value before the third century CE. Although they also varied in size and weight, the denominations of the monetary systems used by cities and provincial commonalties were adjusted to mesh with the system of Roman imperial money, so that conversion posed no problems. The most important basis for calculation was the *assarion*—which was equivalent to the Roman *as* of imperial currency. However, we know from inscriptions (IGR IV 352), that the actual exchange of municipal coins for imperial ones as compared to the reverse exchange involved a loss: for one silver denarius (sixteen Roman *asses*, one had to hand over seventeen or eighteen *assaria*. The *assarion* of municipal bronze coins dominated retail sales all the way down to everyday shopping. The fact alone that outside the provincial commonalties and the *poleis* there was no other authority issuing coins (e.g., villages or associations) suggests that Rome did not give the provinces in the East free rein in this regard: the right to mint money must have been somehow limited, even if there is no direct evidence for this. However, the cities' autonomy was manifested in an apparently far-reaching freedom of decision as to when and in what quantities they wanted to mint their money. The minting took place on the basis of a decision made by the *polis*'s council. The responsibility did not lie exclusively with special officials accountable for the monetary system but was assumed by *strategoi*, *archontes*, secretaries, *agoranomoi*, and others whose names were also stamped on the coins.[60]

For a long time the emperors had a stake in the cities' right to mint money. This right—granted both to communities that had already minted coins during the Hellenistic period and to a multiplicity of others—guaranteed the supply of metal money to the subordinate regions without the imperial government's direct involvement. Municipal coinage was not continuously issued, but rather episodically, from place to place, at irregular intervals. The triggers were above all visits by the emperor and the troops, as well as major festivals, insofar as the influx of visitors increased the need for local and regional small change.

Apart from that, however, the quantities of money available and the continuity of minting varied greatly from city to city. Small coins issued by cities circulated primarily in their own provinces, and they were usually issued by the larger cities. Kyzikos and Pergamon dominated Mysia. In Bithynia, for instance, Nikaia held the record for the greatest amount of money, followed by Nikomedeia. Of the twelve cities in Bithynia, these two were the only ones that minted coins almost continuously. It is estimated that in all Nikaia issued 40 percent of Bithynian money, and Nikomedeia only about half that amount, whereas the remaining 40 percent was shared by the other cities. As a rule, imperial money or foreign coins appear only in small numbers. Coins issued by the cities or the provincial commonalties of Asia Minor are sometimes found in hoards discovered far outside the peninsula—for instance, on the Euphrates and also on the Rhine; the most likely explanation for this is the mobility of Roman troops.

One phenomenon that is interpreted differently by researchers is the abrupt end of municipal coinage in the time of the emperor Gallienus (253–268)—more or less simultaneously with the invasions of the Goths—apart from isolated exceptions that occur up to the end of the third century. The most plausible explanation is probably the one proposed by the numismatist Wolfram Weiser, that this resulted from an imperial prohibition.[61] During the Severan dynasty, the emperors had already gradually decreased the precious metal content of the imperial silver coins to increase revenues. They were led to do this because of the costs of wars. From a silver content that was first still 50 percent, the content of the double denarius (also known as the *antoninianus*, introduced by Caracalla in 215 CE) fell to 3 percent. The silver content of the *cistophorus* was decreased in corresponding stages. The result was an imbalance in relation to the metal value of the provincial coins (brass and bronze) that was so great that when people attempted to exchange imperial coins for the latter, rate problems arose or the imperial coins were simply rejected. In addition, older coins were hoarded, and a black market in currency was established, as we know from Mylasa in Caria (cf. [106] OGIS 515). To counteract this, officials adopted the practice of increasing the value of provincial money in circulation by restamping it and marking new coins with the corresponding symbols of value.[62] In some places, upvaluation more rapidly mounted as the silver content of the imperial currency declined.

The abrupt end of provincial coinage marked a deep caesura in the economy of Asia Minor. After Aurelian's monetary reform,[63] the new start under Diocletian also had a monetary economy that, like the earlier one in the West, had nothing but the imperial currency, which did not allow it to build on the prosperity under the Principate.

City and Country: Internal Organization of the Provinces

From the point of view of the great majority of the inhabitants of Asia Minor's provinces in the high Imperial period, the *polis,* the father-city (*patris*), was everywhere equally primary; it was the foundation for the consciousness of political community and togetherness.[64] The superstructure of the Roman Empire was conceived by intellectual urban dwellers as a *hyper-polis*: Strabo (17, 3, 24) regarded the successful governance exercised by the Roman masters of the world as a "civilized rule" (*politikos archein*).[65] In his speech to Rome (or. 26, 61), Aelius Aristeides saw the relation of the city on the Tiber to the empire as analogous to that between the *polis* and the *chora*: "What a city is to its boundaries and its territories, so this city is to the whole inhabited world, as if it had been its common town. You would say that the *perioeci* of all the people settled in different places *deme* by *deme* assemble at this one acropolis."[66] The rhetor describes the emperor's rule in terms of the "office" of the *prytanis* (ibid. 31), under whose leadership the state can be conceived as nothing less than a "general democracy" in which all citizens with equal rights assemble "as in a common *agora*" (ibid. 60).

In late Antiquity, Asia Minor had more than 600 cities.[67] In the early Imperial period, the west, north, south, and a large part of the center were already based on an urban structure that gradually advanced into the border province of Cappadocia. Bithynia had twelve cities. Pontus, the coastal section on the Black Sea, which alongside Bithynia was co-administered from Nikomedeia or Nikaia, was divided among six cities. The province of Asia was divided into at least thirteen *conventus* (assize districts), the *conventus* of Pergamon had twenty-two cities, about as many as the Lycian League had in the time of Strabo. In the early Imperial period, the province of Asia as a whole officially had 282 cities. According to modern estimates, the remote region of Pisidia, which extended about 120 kilometers from north to south and 170 kilometers from east to west and was divided between Asia and Lycia et Pamphylia, had fifty-four cities; we know the names and locations of forty-seven of them.[68] The location of about half of the fifty-two Phrygian cities in the eastern part of the province of Asia[69] that are known to us through their coinages still cannot be determined with certainty. Around 140 CE Lycia had at least thirty cities; the Byzantine author Hierokles lists forty cities. Under the Flavians, coins were issued by six cities in Pamphylia proper and by seventeen in the province of Cilicia, which was constituted at this same time. In the core area of Galatia, the predominant cities were, in addition to the *colonia Julia Augusta Felix Germa*, the old tribal centers Pessinus, Ankyra, and Tavium as *poleis*. In the north and east, the eparchies of Paphlagonia and Pontus Galaticus, which had been added to Galatia, consisted of seven city territories, while those in the south—Lycaonia, Isauria, Pisidia, and Pamphylia—had 191 of them.[70] Cappadocia, where at the beginning of the Principate there was not even a handful of *poleis*, flourished in late Antiquity; in the lists of bishops fifteen cities are mentioned—not including the five cities in the former kingdom of the Polemonids in East Pontus and the six cities in Lesser Armenia, the province divided off from Imperial period Cappadocia, "First Armenia" or *Armenia I.*

From the historical relationship to Rome that evolved there resulted differences in status that were not always and everywhere of practical importance. Since the time of Julius Caesar, colonies of Italics had been established in Asia Minor at Apameia on the Sea of Marmara, in Herakleia and Sinope on the Black Sea, Alexandria and Parion in the Troad, Antiocheia and other places in Pisidia, in Lycaonia, and in Cilicia. They enjoyed the privilege of being considered, along with their territories, as being on Italic soil, and thus not being subject to the same supervision as the provincials. However, the citizens of Apameia told Pliny the Younger (*ep.* 10, 47) that before him no Roman proconsul had ever audited the city's accounts, thereby indirectly referring to their right, as a *colonia*, to supervise themselves, but Trajan nonetheless insisted that his governor inspect them. Old bilateral agreements with Rome guaranteeing "freedom" and "tax-free status," to which Amisos or the little city of Tyberissos in Lycia, for example, could look back, were formally respected into the Imperial period: thus Amisos, which had the status of a *civitas libera et foederata* (ibid. 92) claimed the proud title of "contractual partner of the Romans." Trajan also allowed the people of Amisos to do what he denied other cities in the province: create a fund for the relief of the poor. Hadrian confirmed Aphrodisias's exemption from the tax on iron. However, no later than the Imperial period these statuses—*foederata, libera,* and *immunis*—became privileges that could be granted to communities or withdrawn from them.

The cities of a province in Asia Minor were not unconnected units. They joined together for certain common activities and functions, as they already had in Hellenistic times and continued to do in the Imperial period. Before going deeper into the cosmos of the individual cities, I have to briefly examine this organization on the provincial level.

Commonalties

In the documents, the institution known as a "commonalty" in English is called a *koinon* ("league").[71] We must keep in mind that this word also designates various other kinds of political and religious associations and communities.[72] The commonalty has to be distinguished from them—and this has not always been achieved without misunderstandings. Thus for example the Ionian League continued to exist and to cultivate its traditions in the Imperial and Late Antique periods (into the third century CE). It organized the Panionia festival and decreed honors for many individuals.[73] But the Ionian League was not a commonalty, since there was never a province of Ionia. The same goes for the religious groups that gathered around a sanctuary or affiliations of settlers in a rural area that continued from the Hellenistic period to the Imperial period, such as the *koinon* of the plain of the Hyrgalians in Phrygia ([110] MAMA IV 315). The decisive characteristic of the rising commonalties in Asia Minor under the Romans is a fundamental connection with a *provincia*. For that reason the official name of a provincial commonalty usually contained a reference to a provincial area—for example, *koinon Galatias* (sometimes also "*koinon* of the Galatians") or "*koinon* of the cities in Pontus"—that was usually coextensive with it.[74] The name of the area is also present in the titles of the chief magistrates of the *koinon*. With the exception of Asia, the areas dealt with here do not refer to the great provinces ruled by a governor but rather to the units combined into a conglomerate or a double province; to distinguish them I have used the Greek term "eparchy," but the Latin inscriptions make no distinction, as they refer to these smaller units as *provinciae* as well as to the great ones (p. 361).

Despite independent initiatives in constituting them, commonalties were not originally autonomous federations like the sympolitical federal state of Lycia founded in the second century BCE. The latter's autonomy was already strictly limited in Strabo's time, and after Lycia was annexed by Claudius, the league was reformed into an organization that resembled a commonalty.[75] The earliest commonalties, those of Asia and Pontus et Bithynia, go back to the time of the republic. A new Bithynian *koinon* appeared in the early Augustan period. According to the account given by the historian Cassius Dio (51, 20, 7), the indigenous peoples, so far as they were subjects of the Romans, followed the Greeks' example. From the great list of the Galatian provincial priests' expenses in the temple of Ankyra, we can infer that the early form of the province of Galatia already had (from 25 BCE on) a commonalty. As Dio understands it, the basis for such a self-organization was ethnic; that also holds for Asia, whose *koinon* was originally considered an affair of the "Hellenes," that is, the Hellenized citizens of *poleis*. In Bithynia and Galatia, the distinction between the "Hellenic" and the non-Hellenic part of the organization was still expressed in the titles of chief magistrates: *helladarches, hellenarches,* and *bithyniarches*,[76] whereas—significantly—this distinction is lacking in Lycia and in other later commonalties, and the superior officials represent a people's name: *lykiarches, galatarches, pamphyliarches,* or the like. In Lycia, *ethnos* was used almost as a technical term for *koinon*.

Every further acquisition of territory added to an already existing province was at the same time an act of founding *poleis*. And we know of most of the annexed territories that they were the basis for the formation of *koina*—from the outset or only after a certain time. Only three years after Augustus's annexation of Paphlagonia (5 BCE) a countrywide cult of the emperor began; the existence of the *koinon* of

Paphlagonia is proven by a coin dating from Domitian's reign at the earliest, and an inscription from the late Imperial period mentions the *paphlagoniarches*. Cappadocia had a commonalty already under Tiberius, as is indicated by the *koinos Kappadokias*, games organized in Kaisareia (Moretti, IAG 62 lines 7 f.). The person in charge was called *kappadokarches* (*Digest* 27, 1, 6, 14). An *armeniarches* (IGR III 132) presided over a *koinon* of Lesser Armenia, which was organized as an eparchy in 72 CE and incorporated into Cappadocia.

The bewildering multiplication and transformation of *koina* with the name *Pontos*—in addition to various *koina* bearing this name in Asia Minor, there is another outside it, consisting of six cities on the western shore of the Black Sea—can be understood only on the basis of the genesis of these eparchies. The Pontic *koinon* of the age of the republic had covered the province of Pontus formed under Pompey from the area of the Mithridatic kingdom plus Herakleia and Tieion, but after the dissolution of that province under Mark Antony it was never reestablished in this form.[77] Coins and inscriptions allow us to recognize a new *koinon* of Pontos that existed from 64 CE; its area must be distinguished from the province of Pontus united with Bithynia. This new Pontic *koinon* that combined the cities of Polemonion, Kerasus, Trapezus, Neokaisareia, Zela, and Sebasteia was coextensive with the eparchy of Pontus Polemonianus that was formed out of the former kingdom of Polemon and added to Cappadocia; it corresponded another new *koinon* of the Galatian Pontos in its western neighborhood: Pontus Galaticus with the cities of Amaseia, Komana, and Sebastopolis that had been formed presumably no later than this. Then, under Hadrian or a little earlier, an "interior" Pontos was formed whose *koinon* combined Neokaisareia, Zela, Sebasteia, Amaseia, Sebastopolis, and Komana. The coast may have formed its own *koinon* with Kerasus and Trapezus.

The cities of Pamphylia were not absorbed into the Lycian League when the province was combined with Lycia under Vespasian. The widespread opinion that there was no *koinon* in Pamphylia, but only a "loose" affiliation of cities—whatever that may mean—is certainly wrong.[78] In any case, the Pamphylian cities, which also included Termessos, elected a *pamphyliarches* to lead them.[79] Inscriptions in the city of Perge referring to a *synagogeus* ("assembler") of the *ethnos pamphylon* prove the existence of another official of this commonalty ([162] *IK* Perge 294.321).

The genesis of such commonalties east of Pamphylia is complicated and somewhat obscure. When Vespasian detached the Cilician plains from Syria and put all of Cilicia under its own governor, its eastern part's internal connection with Syria initially remained intact—at least in one respect: in the late Flavian period joint games among the three eparchies of Syria, Cilicia, and Phoenicia were held in Antiocheia (Moretti, IAG 67 line 15).[80] Cilicia's own *koinon* in Tarsos—which organized the *Hadrianeia Olympia* games, bore the title of *neokoros* (temple guardian) on its coins, and was presided over by the *kilikarches* mentioned in inscriptions and on coins (IGR III 883.912; [199] Head, HN² 733)—appeared from the time of Hadrian on.[81]

The reconstitution of Cilicia out of three eparchies—Cilicia, Isauria, and Lycaonia—is first proven by the legate Gaius Etrilius Regillus Laberius Priscus's inscription from the time of Antoninus Pius. Although Lycaonia was a dynastic land that Vespasian had annexed long before (72/73 CE) and that had been added as an eparchy to the great province of Galatia-Cappadocia, and finally transferred to Cilicia, the earliest coins bearing the legend "koinon of Lycaonia" were minted under Pius.[82] In the time of Trajan, Isauria also already figured as an eparchy of Galatia-Cappadocia.[83] We know nothing about a separate *koinon* of Isauria, but the community of Isaura stamped the title "metropolis of the Isaurians" on its coins (SNG Levante 259; BMC 6), and a *provincia Isauria* appears as the dedicator in an inscription for Gordian III (CIL III 6783).

We cannot with certainty exclude the possibility that there was already a *koinon* of Cilicia before Hadrian, or a *koinon* of Lycaonia (and perhaps Isauria) before Antoninus Pius. Precisely how the Lycaonian *koinon* might be related to the "*koinon* of the three eparchies of the Tarsians" mentioned on coins from the age of the Severans is unknown. No doubt Tarsos, as an old *conventus* city and the bearer of the title of *metropolis* since Augustus, claimed a superordinate rank. But in the same period Anazarbos called itself the "presiding metropolis of the three eparchies of Cilicia, Isauria, and Lycaonia." However, it can hardly be right to infer from the relatively sparse numismatic evidence that Lycaonia was merely a subdivision of the Cilician commonalty and to deny it its own functions.[84]

The conditions in central Anatolia are still more obscure. Like Pisidia, Phrygia is described as an eparchy ruled by the governor in Ankyra. Up to now, no clear evidence of a provincial commonalty in Pisidia has been found. Sagalassos claimed to be the "first [city] of Pisidia" (IGR III 350–352; [203] SNG Aulock 5200). Coins from Apameia Kibotos bearing the formula "the Apameians [organize] the common [games] of Phrygia" dating from the time of Nero (54–68 CE) to that of Philippus Arabs (244–249) suggest that Phrygia had its own provincial cult of the emperor. However, Apameia was part of the province of Asia before the third century. Thus, as in the case of Cilicia, a Phrygian commonalty seems to have extended beyond provincial boundaries and to have also met in Apameia.

In the commonalty all cities of an eparchy were represented, and at least a few of them had more than one representative. The communities may have elected their delegates (*synedroi*), perhaps annually. We know little regarding the way in which delegates were elected. In 4 BCE 150 delegates met in Asia ([168] I. Sardeis 8 line 76 f.). In any case, Smyrna sent several *synedroi* to the commonalty (Aristeides, *or.* 50, 103). In the Hellenistic Lycian League, votes were weighted in accord with the size of the city (as described by Artemidoros in Strabo, 14, 3, 3), but it is uncertain whether this practice was continued in the Imperial period. At that time the league had, in addition to the federal assembly, a council whose members (presumably elected for life) were chosen from "the best"; in addition, it even had law courts, whose exact function we do not know. It is presumed, on the basis of various clues, that one meeting place of the Lycian assembly of delegates, in which all members of the council and officials of the *koinon* participated, was the recently discovered assembly hall in Patara.[85]

To judge by the most important ceremonial function of the commonalties—the cult of the emperor—in most cases the highest office coincided with that of a priest. Modestin (*Digest* 27, 1, 6, 14) defines the Asiarchy, Bithyniarchy, and Cappadociarchy as the "priesthood" (*hierosyne*) of a people (*ethnos*). The Roman authorities did not meddle in the election of this superior official of the *koina*. The election took place in the commonalty. The inscriptions prove that wealthy dignitaries were generally chosen for this office, and we have further knowledge about more than a few prominent persons among them. It very rarely happened and was therefore not really foreseen that one and the same person was elected successively in different provinces.[86] An exception to this rule is the usual tenure of the Bithyniarchy and Pontarchy in the double province of Pontus et Bithynia, whereas there was nothing comparable in the double province of Lycia et Pamphylia.

In the republic, the *koinon* of Asia was represented by an "archpriest of the Roma," whose title was changed to "archpriest of Asia" in the early Principate. Only from the late first century CE on does one find alongside this title that of "leader of Asia" (*asiarches*). Since the beginning of the twentieth century, a scholarly controversy has developed regarding the identity or nonidentity of the two offices. The evidence for identity is stronger, as it is in other provinces.[87] The bearers of both titles exercised the same functions, and in particular organized gladiator battles; the wives both of archpriests and asiarchs bore the title *archiereiai* (archpriestesses). Both titles appear on the provincial as well as on the municipal level; *archiereus Asias/asiarches* of the "father city" or of "the temples in Ephesos," of the "temples in Smyrna." Acts (19:31) speaks of "some officials [*asiarchs*]" in Ephesos, and Strabo (14, 1, 42) speaks of a number of citizens of the city of Tralleis who belong to the nomenklatura of the province and are called "asiarchs." Thus several asiarchs lived at the same time in one city, but this shows only that the officials retained the title after their term of office was over. Today we know of more than 140 asiarchs and 212 archpriests of Asia,[88] fourteen bithyniarchs, thirteen pontarchs (of different provinces with the name "Pontus"), ten persons bearing the title of "archpriest" of Bithynia or Pontus,[89] more than seventy archpriests of Lycia (or lyciarchs),[90] and more than forty archpriests of Galatia (or galatarchs), to mention only the provinces in which both titles occur. Archpriestesses (*archiereiai*) appear in considerable numbers in Asia (more than thirty), less often in Lycia, where a few women also bore the title of *lykiarchissa*.[91] Contrary to a view according to which these noble ladies were independent, elected officials,[92] they were the wives or mothers of archpriests, asiarchs, or lykiarchs who were concurrently in office. In Asia special emphasis was put on "the inclusion of family into the most representative (double) office that Asia had to offer its prominence."[93]

In the beginning, a single archpriest was at the head of the province of Asia. As the larger cities in this province built one or several temples dedicated to the emperor, each of them received an archpriest. The epigraphic source material suggests that in Pontus et Bithynia as well, there were several archpriests simultaneously in the sites for the worship of the emperor in the individual cities, and it may even be that each city had a priest of the cult of the emperor. When it was a city's turn to organize the province's festival, an elected official or volunteer assumed the function of high priest, often along with the presidency of the provincial games (*agonothetes*). The same individual derived from this activity the honor of bearing the title of bithyniarch. Thus this institution was not constantly present and permanent in a certain place, but rather a function that was assumed on occasion, here or there, by this or that wealthy provincial. In contrast, Lycia never had more than one provincial archpriest at the same time, although in the individual cities there were priests of the cult of the emperor—who must be distinguished from the archpriests—and also special priesthoods for Roma and Tiberius. This is also seen in the fact that only in Lycia did the official in question give his name to the year, and from the early Imperial period on it became routine to date official documents by naming him. The self-administration of a large commonalty like Asia's also employed secretaries and officials concerned with finances.[94]

The center of activities was the expensive organization of religious festivals paying homage to the emperor. These celebrations brought together in a sort of provincial congress not only the *koinobulion* (the assembly of elected representatives of the cities) but also a great number of other citizens and inhabitants of the country. The cult of the emperor did not remain limited to the provincial sanctuaries in Nikomedeia and Pergamon that Augustus had authorized. In 26 CE the competition among cities of Asia to be the site of another sanctuary was decided by Rome in favor of Smyrna (Tacitus, *ann.* 4, 55, 3; 56, 1). Under Hadrian, a whole series of cities in this province had several provincial temples—not only Pergamon and Smyrna but also Ephesos and Sardeis, and Kyzikos and Tralleis each had one. The same is true for the provinces of Bithynia, Lycia, and Cilicia. A city expressed the elevation in status formally by adding the predicate "temple guardian" (*neokoros*) to its name, and if it had several provincial temples, by adding the formula "twice, thrice temple guardian."[95]

In Asia, Bithynia, the Pontic provinces, Lycia, and Cilicia, the *koinon*'s assemblies and festivals did not always take place at the same site in the province, even if early on there were cities that claimed to be the true "capital." The status predicate that could be used only with the emperor's permission was "mother city" (*metropolis*). The American ancient historian Glen Bowersock pointed out that until the time of Hadrian, this title was generally allotted to only one city in a province, though Syria was an exception to this rule.[96] In Asia, Ephesos was the first to bear this title, followed by Pergamon, Smyrna, Sardeis, Laodikeia, Tralleis, and Philadelpheia. Permission to use the title had been withdrawn from Philadelpheia at a time in the third century when the commonalty sought to compel that city to make the usual monetary contribution to the *metropoleis* for the offices of imperial priest and panegyriarch. Thereupon the Philadelphians complained to the emperor, arguing that as an ex-metropolis it was exempt from making this payment ([105] TAM V 3, 1421). In Lycia, Xanthos was allotted the title, but it was soon also borne by Patara, Telmessos, and Tlos, and in the Severan period by Limyra. In Pamphylia, Perge gained it as late as 275/276 CE, under the emperor Tacitus. Shortly thereafter Side was also permitted to bear it, and in Cilicia, as already mentioned, Tarsos and Anazarbos. In

Bithynia Nikomedeia and Nikaia bore the title; the province of Pontus that was combined with Bithynia had *metropoleis* in Herakleia and Amastris, though these are attested only under Trajan. The mother-cities in Paphlagonia and Galatia were Pompeiopolis and Ankyra; in Pontus Galaticus and Pontus Polemoniacus, Amaseia and Neokaisareia; in Cappadocia, Kaisareia below Mt. Argaios; in Lycaonia, Laranda; and in Isauria, Isaura.

The same word was often transferred to other contexts: like Miletus, which called itself the metropolis of Ionia, and even referred back to its ancient role as the mother-city of cities in Pontos Euxeinos and Egypt,[97] other cities styled themselves the "capital" of a larger or smaller region; for instance, Sardeis as "Lydian" (BMC 89), Stratonikeia as "Carian" ([162] *IK* Stratonikeia 15), Temenuthyrai and Silandos as "capitals" of the region of Mokkadene (IGR IV 618; [105] TAM V 1, 47), Elaiussa-Sebaste as of the region "on the coast" (SNG Levante 844.847), Koropissos as of "Kietis" (SNG Levante 583; BMC 4), Diokaisareia as of "Kennatis,"[98] Lamos as of "Lamotis" (SNG Levante 480.482), and so on.

In addition to the regular organization of religious ceremonies, festivals, and games in honor of the emperor, the political representation of the provincials with respect to the emperor was a duty that had to be fulfilled. Complaints or petitions filed by the cities with the governor or the emperor did not require the mediation of the *koina*, and conversely, for the most part the emperor and the governors also communicated directly with individual cities. Nevertheless, debates on this subject must have occupied whole sessions of the *koina*. The latter sent numerous envoys to appear on their behalf before the emperor and the Senate, and usually selected rhetorically polished intellectuals. However, legal specialists were also brought into the negotiations; they are recognizable by the designations of their function: *ekdikos, syndikos* (lawyer).

Complaints about the governor constantly recurred. The earliest case from Asia for which we have detailed proof dates from between 5 and 1 BCE and is documented by nine decrees, two of them issued by the commonalty, and three letters, including one from the princeps ([168] I. Sardeis 8). Already in the Julio-Claudian period, complaints about gubernatorial malversations led to condemnations of proconsuls of Asia, like that of Lucius Valerius Messala Volesus, who held office from ca. 9 to 13 CE, and Gaius Iunius Silanus, who held office in 20/21 CE and who was accused not only by his own legate and quaestor but also by "the most silver-tongued men in all of Asia" (Tacitus, *ann.* 3, 67 f.). Procurators also ended up in the dock; for instance, in 23 CE the patrimonial procurator Gnaeus Lucilius Capito, who had deployed soldiers and administered justice during his term in office. In Rome, the Bithynians had earned a name as notorious grousers. Pliny the Younger (especially *ep.* 4, 9) discusses at length the case of the Bithynian governor C. Julius Bassus. When the following governor was also accused, people in Rome gradually got weary of it—"The Bithynians again" (Pliny the Younger, *ep.* 5, 20, 1)—and in addition the provincials had been quarrelling about it: an envoy who arrived after the fact wanted to let the matter drop, but the old delegation refused.

In addition to extortion, robbery, and theft, the complaint also alleged occasional cruelty. In Asia, Messalla Volesus had had more than a hundred men decapitated in a single day. Gaius Arrius Antoninus was accused after his return from Asia in 189, because he had had the son of the sophist Polemon, Attalos, condemned to death; this condemnation was asserted by a favorite of the emperor Commodus (180–192) named Cleander, who, like Polemon's family, came from Laodikeia in Phrygia (HA *Comm.* 7, 1). When in the Severan period the governor ruling in Bithynia, the sophist Aelius Antipater (from Hieropolis in Phrygia), had people executed without hesitation, he was recalled. Threats must also have been made against local assemblies that tried to make complaints: a rescript—a reply from the emperor to clarify a legal matter, in this case, from Severus Alexander to the *koinon* of the Hellenes in the province of Bithynia—stipulated that appeals made by the provincials to the emperor were allowed and that procurators and provincial governors were strictly forbidden to make reprisals and use violence against the plaintiffs (*Digest* 49, 1, 25).

Naturally, there were also acquittals. The impressive series of complaints should definitely not lead to an overall judgment that the provinces were generally misgoverned. Probably even more often than they complained, Rome's subjects sang the praises of the governor, in any case so often that the practice, already limited by Augustus, was flatly forbidden by Nero—though entirely without success (Tacitus, *ann.* 15, 22). Moreover, many tributes to the governor took place in the provinces themselves. In addition, provincials did not always agree about the complaints, since governors were situated in networks of relationships to individual *poleis* and their dignitaries, so that their government could benefit some more and others less.

Several *koina* issued coins irregularly and at differing intervals.[99] The silver *cistophori* with the legends ROM(AE) ET AVGUST(O) and COM(MVNE) ASIAE date from Augustus to Trajan; those with the legend COM(MVNE) BIT(HYNIAE) appear only under Hadrian. However, the determination of who actually authorized minting these coins is controversial.[100] Copper coins issued by the *koinon* of Asia from ca. 23 to 26 CE are known.[101] The Bithynian *koinon* issued coins from the time of Claudius down to that of Hadrian, the *koinon* of the Pontic heartland from the period of the Antonines to that of Gallienus, the Galatian *koinon* from Nero to Trajan,[102] the Cilician *koinon* from Hadrian into the time of Caracalla, the Lycaonian *koinon* from Antoninus Pius to Philippus Arabs. In contrast, in the case of the Paphlagonian *koinon* we know of minting solely under Domitian, and in that of Lesser Armenia only one minting under Trajan. Masters of mints (*monetarii*) at the provincial level are not known to us. The *koina* seem to have had the power not only to authorize the minting of coins in the name of the league, but also to set or recommend certain standards for the *poleis*'s coinage. Thus when in the third century the cities of Pontus et Bithynia gradually increased the value of their money with respect to the imperial currency, this took place within the partial province of Bithynia in a coordinated process, with which the cities of the partial province of Pontus did not at first keep up.

This exhausts our knowledge of the competencies and activities of most of the *koina*, but we cannot exclude the possibility that others existed that have left no trace in our sources. The collaboration of the league with the Roman tax authorities' levying of taxes and customs duties is known to us from Lycia. Whether Lycia should be considered a special case must for the time being remain an open question.

Municipal Institutions, Offices and Services, and Finances

If we could examine the microcosm of the Imperial period *polis* under a magnifying glass, we would see between Mykale and the Euphrates a complex order that is generally similar everywhere but definitely differs in its nuances. References to a legal framework valid for all the cities in an Anatolian province, which in research (but not anywhere in ancient sources) is usually called the *lex provinciae*, are rare. Thus in the Menodoros decree from Pergamon there is a reference to a body of "Roman legislation" that was introduced at the beginning of Asia's provincialization.[103] Moreover, the particular provisions of a *lex Pompeia* for Pontus et Bithynia, which were still in force during the Imperial period, are known, and the epigraphist Michael Wörrle has postulated, using the example of Oinoanda, a similar body of laws for Lycia.[104] This is not the place to go into details. What is clear is that essential components of the internal order were taken over from the Classical-Hellenistic tradition of the *poleis*.

PHYLAE

In the Imperial period the adaptation and assimilation of the institutions of the Greek *polis*, that spread across the interior of Anatolia over centuries, led to different ways of classifying the citizenry.[105] The term *phyle* ("tribe") implies in general a part of the citizenry in the sense of a personal association, but in some areas of Asia Minor it has been shown also to connote a territorial unit. We will discuss this latter aspect later; here we limit ourselves to the personal association. In some cities we find subdivisions of the *phylae*, such as "thousand" and "hundred" (*chiliastys* and *hekatostys*), and in addition, as in Athens, a cantonal division of the city's territory into *demes* that underlies divisions of the citizenry. In Lydia particular phylae are named after craft groups—for example, the wool and linen weavers in Philadelpheia and Saittai. Whether these are part of a system of *phylae* based on craft associations—consider the role of the guilds in the cities of early modern Europe—or simply an association's specific adaptation of the name *phyle* cannot be determined.

Complete systems of *phylae* are known to us from only a few cities—Miletus, Bithynion, Prusias on Hypios, and Ankyra. Differences are identifiable in a chronological and regional respect, the Greek cities on the west coast (and in the hinterland Sardeis) not only having the oldest systems, but also—not surprisingly—appearing to be the most conservative and resistant to reform: Miletus retained down into the Imperial period the ten Kleisthenian *phylae* it had once taken over from

Athens and simply added two more to them at some later time. At the time of their foundation or soon thereafter, the *poleis* that were initially founded in the Hellenistic and Imperial periods usually adopted a system of *phylae* that was supposed to look "genuinely" Greek, but in some places is recognizable as one that has been adapted to the specific conditions of the indigenous population. Even the Roman *coloniae* preferred a system of subdivisions into "tribes" (*tribus*) based on the Greek model.

As they grew, many communities increased the number of their *phylae* from time to time, giving them archaizing or new names. The step moving from names of gods and monarchs to those of other prominent persons—like Sulla in Sardeis (Pompey has not yet been attested) or the benefactor Diodoros Pasparos in Pergamon—is not a particularly big one; in Imperial period Ankyra the seventh *phyle* gave itself the name of a benefactress, Klaudia Athenaia. However, personal names in Kibyra probably have to be understood as eponyms (p. 427) changing in accord with the annual leaders of the *phylae*. Finally, sometimes *phylae* are simply listed by their numbers, as in Ankyra. From the time of Augustus on, in many cities the names of emperors, empresses, and other members of the imperial household make their way into the lists of *phylae*. The cities on the west coast, as well as those of Lycia and Pamphylia, maintained a striking reserve in this regard, with the significant exception of Ephesos. The most common emperors' names used by the *phylae* in other parts of Asia Minor came from Augustus and Hadrian, and the names of some emperors, like Nero's, are completely lacking; Claudius's name does not appear even in Klaudiupolis, where we know all the *phylae* from the Severan period. This practice came to an end in the time of the Antonines: *phylae* named after Severans, tetrarchs, Constantine, or later emperors do not appear, even though systems of *phylae* persisted far into late Antiquity—evidence from Side proves the existence of phylarchs (heads of *phylae*) in the fifth century CE.

The functions of the *phylae* that can be gleaned from inscriptions show that in the Imperial period they still played an active role in the organism of the *polis*. A bureaucratic apparatus and a separate financial administration required regular assemblies. Ceremonial activities in the religious and festival system, as well as tributes to benefactors, occurred both in isolation and in coordination with the whole *phylae* network and the *polis*. Individual examples of the principle of rotation between phylae in the council, the *prytany*, and in the occupation of offices, well known from classical Athens, are still found in Imperial period Asia Minor.

City Councils and Citizens' Assemblies

The councilors (*decuriones*) were a select minority among individuals holding full citizenship. A member of the city council, which was the decisionmaking body in every respect, belonged to the *polis*'s social elite. In official documents, this body claimed for itself extravagant epithets such as "devoted to the Romans" (*philorhomaios*), "loyal to the emperor" (*philokaisar*), "most splendid" (*lamprotate*), "most powerful" (*kratiste*), and "preserving the community" (*demosostike*). Since the time of Hadrian, among the privileges of the councilors who had Roman citizenship was that they were not subject to the governor's right to impose capital punishment—except in cases of patricide or matricide (*Digest* 48, 19, 15). One did not have to be a Roman citizen, but citizenship in the *polis* was indispensable, and in addition to this condition and the age limit, the minimal presupposition for membership in the council was the possession of a certain wealth. The system was a copy of the Roman Senate, including the censors who made decisions regarding acceptance or rejection. Anyone who was accepted remained a member for life, unless he was expelled. Though there might be several hundred of them, the number of members was limited even if the great press of people could lead an emperor to allow a city to exceed it (Pliny the Younger, *ep.* 10, 112; cf. Dion of Prusa, *or.* 45, 7). The claims made by long-serving officials had to be taken into account, so that many a young aristocrat obviously did not get his chance at the earliest possible time.

The size of the councils varied.[106] It has been shown that Thyateira and Oinoanda had 500 or more councilors, Ephesos 450, and at the other end of the scale, Knidos had only sixty. A community that wanted to achieve the status (*ius et dignitas*) of a *polis* had to have at least fifty councilors. Promising to surpass this limit in the future, the citizens of Tymandos in Pisidia applied to the (unknown) emperor (ILS 6090).

The city council regularly met in the city hall under the chairmanship of presidents. *Prytaneis* acting as an executive committee, as in the Kyzikos of Hadrian's time,[107] and apparently also in Stratonikeia, Kaunos, and Myra, are to be distinguished from the annually elected officials of the same name proven to have existed in many cities (p. 427). A specific committee of the council responsible chiefly for levying taxes and known as "the first ten" (*dekaprotoi*) has been found in several provinces; the "first twenty" (*eikosaprotoi*) in Lycia after 124 CE.[108] As a rule, the council had a secretariat and a herald, and it chose censors from its own ranks. The council's secretaries, like those of the popular assembly, held key positions for various duties.[109] Naturally, there were municipal archives, in Miletus and Kolophon, for example,[110] presided over by officials. Apparently both private and public documents were preserved—from dowry and marriage contracts to letters from the emperor. Urban communities liked to have major government documents—especially correspondence with rulers, even if it dated from the distant past—chiseled in stone on public squares; the *parodos* wall of the theater in Aphrodisias offers a genuine extract from the archives (Figure 76).[111]

In the Imperial period citizens no doubt still regularly gathered and made decisions, preferably in theaters, observing a certain seating order (depending on *phylae* in Saittai, Hierapolis, Kibyra, and Ephesos). They may also have elected officials and carried out an important preselection for the city council. Although these popular assemblies often routinely confirmed by acclamation what the council had already advised, they were not at all reduced to a chorus with a purely ceremonial function. Conflict is a sign of commitment. Political strife took place among citizens even under the *pax Romana*; in their provisions, wealthy donors expressed concern that

76. Excerpts from state documents of the city archives inscribed into the parodos-wall of the theater in Aphrodisias.

popular decisions might prevent their gifts from achieving the desired goals.[112] Dion of Prusa reproached the citizens of Tarsos for their internal differences when the council and the popular assembly, the old and the young, acted at cross purposes. If someone were to go through the whole list of citizens, Dion said (*or.* 34, 16.20 f.), he would not find two men who were of the same opinion. The particular contentiousness of the elderly seems to have been assumed in a city where there was a "priest of concord among the old" ([106] OGIS 479), just as the medal for concord (*homonoia*) must have had another side that remains almost entirely hidden to us, given the character of our documentation. That municipal affairs might even lead to tumultuous altercations is shown by the case of Prusa, where the governor, Varenus Rufus, banned public meetings on this account (Dion of Prusa *or.* 48, 1). Decisions made by the council and popular assembly had to be certified by the governor ([162] *IK* Smyrna 713).

OFFICES AND SERVICES

Among the individual city offices, only a few of which we can present here, the lower level ones that had to be held before entering the city council must be distinguished from the higher ones; an inscription from Xanthos ([105] TAM II 1, 301) speaks of "council offices" (*archai buleutikai*) and "community offices" (*archai demotikai*). The total inventory of the Lycian town of Oinoanda, though small, nonetheless had ten different titles for twenty-two officials.[113]

The superior officials, after whose first chairman the calendar years were usually named (eponymous offices), did not bear the same title everywhere. In most cities there were colleges of *strategoi* or *archontes*, generally five in number, including the presiding "first *archon*" or the one "together with whom" the others exercised their official functions. In accord with tradition, they were known as "wreath-bearers" in Miletus, Magnesia on Maeander, and Smyrna, and also in the imperial communities of Aphrodisias, Nysa, Tralleis, Stratonikeia, and Kaunos. Priests (*hiereis*) or *prytaneis* (these must be distinguished from the previously mentioned monthly committees of the council) were also often named as members of a board[114] or as individual officials. The *strategoi* and also, for instance, the "cavalry leaders" (as in Kyzikos, IGR IV 117), bore titles of former offices in the military leadership but performed exclusively civilian functions. *Strategoi* who were authorized to make use of weapons, as in Smyrna,[115] were not superior officials but rather police forces. In Smyrna such a *strategos* was responsible for seeing to it that public assemblies and the distributions of bread made at them took place in an orderly manner.[116]

Where assemblies of citizens occurred officially as communities, as during religious ceremonies in sanctuaries or in the theater, they sat in tiers in accord with subdivisions, usually with one or several officials at their head. In many cities the *phylarchoi* presided over the *phylae*. About the details of their tasks we can say little. *Phylae* inscriptions with the names of the presidents were always meant to honor or thank. In Bithynia, in any case, the organization of the *phylae* also included secretaries and treasurers; in the city of Bithynion each *phylarch* was aided by a *strategos*. Since the equable distribution or rotation of rights and duties (e.g., reception of gifts of grain or money, liturgies), and the constitution of colleges of *prytaneis* probably took place through the city *phylae* system, we can assume that administrative duties were involved.

The important office of *agoranomos* corresponded to some extent to the Roman *aedilis*. It extended to the administration of the grain supply and public buildings—insofar as this was not done by special officials—and included a kind of market supervision, particularly regarding prices and weights and measures. A series of well-preserved lead weights from Bithynia is signed not only with the names of the emperor and the governor, but also with that of the *agoranomos* (Figure 77), and scales are depicted on the *agoranomoi*'s altars (Figure 78).[117] They probably supervised special agencies responsible for guaranteeing measures of capacity by means of stone blocks with one or several cavities, not a few examples of which have been found during excavations in Asia Minor (Figure 79).[118] Their term of office seems to have usually been less than a year, at least in Side, Perge, in the cities of Lycia,[119] and in Tralleis, where an *agoranomos* boasted of being the first and only one to have assumed this office for the whole year ([162] *IK* Tralleis 90). A *polis*'s local and regional trade network required special officials at transshipment points—*limenarchai* in the harbors, *emporiarchai* in the larger market towns in the interior.[120]

The importance of the gymnasium as an identity-producing institution at the center of the *polis* elite can hardly be overestimated. When young citizens were first

77. Lead weight with the name of the *agoranomos*. From Nikomedeia. Now in the J. Paul Getty Museum, Malibu, California.

78. Altar with the inscription *agoranomikos*. From Tieion.

79. Stone blocks with cavities for measuring volumes: *hemihekton, hemimedimnon, medimnos*. From Kaunos.

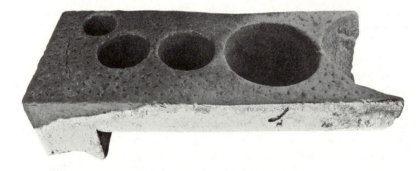

allowed to enter the gymnasium, with its marble splendor and awe-inspiring statues of the "greats" of their own community, it must have had somewhat the same effect on them as the venerable colleges of Oxford and Cambridge have on modern-day undergraduates. It was not only the place where the education of the young was organized; groups of citizens of differing ages and public functions also met there to exercise and train their bodies, to rehearse performances, and to socialize. It is not surprising that in the later Hellenistic period the office of gymnasiarch became almost the quintessential model of leadership in civic virtues. It was open only to the most respectable and, of course, wealthiest citizens, most of them already advanced in age.[121] They surely paid for part of the oil used for personal care and for lighting; communities had a special fund to pay for the rest (Pliny the Younger, *ep.* 10, 23; [162] *IK* Prusias 1; [105] TAM II 1, 145). The size of the establishment required subordinate officials and special functionaries under this directorship. Kios, Tlos, and Arykanda had sub-gymnasiarchs, while Patara had a *palaistrophylax* (supervisor of the sports area). Some cities divided the office of gymnasiarch among the different gymnasiums and the groups using them, old and young, ephebes and—in the case of Dorylaion—even women ([106] OGIS 479).

The *gerusia*, the council of elders, is a constitutive part of the *polis* or community (in communities without *polis* status), not a private association, even if its public functions cannot be precisely determined. It often appears as a committee that can make decisions. It is led (in Prusias on Hypios) by an *archigerusiastes*, and a financial supervisor (*curator*) of the "sacred *gerusia*" refers to the fact that here, in any case, it had access to a communal fund. Pliny the Younger (*ep.* 10, 33) mentions an official building in Nikomedeia. Special conditions can be detected in the city of Side in Pamphylia: there was more than one *gerusia*, each distinguished by its name (e.g., "the *gerusia* of those of the great altar" and "at the great gate") and associated with a certain part of the city ([162] *IK* Side 105–112). Some evidence suggests that the elderly were entertained with common meals and received allowances.

The education of the youth in the gymnasium distinguished two age groups, the young (*neoi*), that is, young adults, and the "ephebes," young men who were just making the transition to adulthood, whose leaders, the *ephebarchai*, have been described by the epigraphist Michael Wörrle as being a kind of "class representatives."[122] Teachers or trainers (*paidonomoi, paidotribai*) were employed for educating the young, and for instruction in reading and writing—for girls as well in Hellenistic Teos ([109] Syll.³ 578, lines 9 f.)—*grammatodidaskaloi*.

Religious personnel in the city's temples to the gods also played a role. The number and titles of these priestesses and priests varied greatly: *hiereis, hierophantai, hierothytai, stephanephoroi, chrysophoroi, neokoroi, prophetai*, and so forth. Urban community life was dominated by religious festivals whose organization, financing, and supervision was provided by festival leaders and, when it was a matter of athletic and musical competitions, presidents of the games (*agonothetai*). *Agonothesia* might be connected with the office of the priest in the cult of the emperor, which required expenditures for sacrifices, banquets, and processions, as well as for animal hunts and gladiator combats.

In most communities, the supervision of the city's finances was carried out by the treasurer, whose other titles were "superintendent of revenues" and *oikonomos* of the city (Olympos, [105] TAM II 3, 1151); large communities like Pergamon, Smyrna, and Miletus had a college of these officials. We will discuss later the role of state banks and city special agents in the finance sector.

Various tasks in the domains of the council, of the *agoranomia*, and the *gymnasiarchia* in particular demanded an administration of finances separate from the one by the office of the city's treasurer. The council members' entrance fees were recorded separately. The basic supply of oil and grain was a delicate problem for which specific reserves were established: city grain stocks were managed by *sitonai* (Nikomedeia),[123] *sitologoi* (Nikaia), *eutheniarchai* (Amastris), oil funds by *argyrotamiai ton elaionikon chrematon* or *elaiones* (Aphrodisias). In the case of grain and public works projects the finances were supervised by *curatores annonae* (Greek *logistai ton sitonikon chrematon*) and by the *curatores operum publicorum* (cf. *ergepistatai*, etc.) appointed on the basis of an imperial directive. The municipal water supply was also supervised by special officials, as in Hadrianoi (IGR IV 242).

Communal officials, from whom expertise, time, and physical exertion were demanded more than wealth, included legal advisors or lawyers and notaries, judges, community physicians, and the group that was concerned with policing tasks in the widest sense.[124] As guardians of order in the domain of city facilities (e.g., streets, walls, and springs), we know of the *astynomoi* from Pergamon, Ankyra, and other places; there were avenue supervisors (*platearchai*) in Amastris.[125] Simple security duties, as well as work cleaning public facilities, might be done by community slaves (Pliny the Younger, *ep.* 10, 31 f.) or imposed on residents.

Military matters were fundamentally the concern of the Roman Empire, and the cities of the Imperial period maintained no military forces or institutions. However, policing tasks fell on the communities. Only in the Imperial period did the "peace-keeper" or "peace representative" (*eirenarches* or *prostates eirenes*), a kind of police chief, appear in many places in Asia Minor.[126] We learn about his recruiting in Asia from one of the "sacred tales" of Aelius Aristeides (*or.* 50, 72) from the year 153 CE. Every year, the proconsul C. Julius Severus received from each city in his province a list with ten names of leading citizens from which he chose one for each city. These municipal eirenarchs belonged to an elite, performed leading functions, and had henchmen (*diogmitai*); others, especially in Pisidia, Pamphylia, and Cilicia, probably occupied a lower social level and carried out policing operations themselves.[127] In several communities the *paraphylax*[128] performed a similar function, apparently for rural areas, aided by the mountain guards (*orophylakes*),[129] and in rural Paphlagonia the counterpart of this "sheriff" could be an *agriopiastes* (the word is attested only there): someone who "pursues wild men."[130]

Robbers seem to have been the chief problem in the extensive rural territories.[131] The ex-brigand Kleon, the founder of Juliopolis in Bithynia who was entrusted with the office of priest of Komana under Octavian, and a certain Tilliboros (or Tilloboros) who operated in Mysia and on Mt. Ida, on whom Arrian is said to have written a work (Lucian, *Alex.* 2), were prominent. Both a (police?) prefect in Prusa on Olympos ([162] *IK* Prusa 1008) and a field guard in Hadrianupolis/Lycaonia lost their lives for the fatherland in combat missions against robbers.[132] The communal authorities' arrest and interrogation of bandits were regulated by an edict issued by the proconsul Antoninus (*Digest* 48, 3, 6, 1), the later emperor. The *paraphylakes* and their escorts seem to have made regular rounds through the villages. Like Roman soldiers and officials, they occasionally succumbed to the temptation to abuse their power. Some of these ancient policemen demanded that the farmers not only provide firewood, forage, and housing, but also protection money or other services ([106] OGIS 527).

The Roman military men stationed in the provinces did not get involved in ensuring everyday security. It would certainly be a mistake to think that the police were generally an instrument in the hands of a cultural elite in the cities that sought to extort and oppress the countryside and its uncultivated underdogs.[133]

EUERGETISM AND LITURGIES

Depending on the point of view, there are various possible ways of systematically classifying all these names for offices and functions that have come down to us.[134] They have little to do with the bureaucratic apparatus of modern communities and countries. "The politicians of that time were true amateurs."[135] According to Roman jurists, a major difference was that a few offices required the holder to make payments in money or kind that were sometimes considerable, while others did not. The technical term for such payments imposed on a certain group of persons is *leiturgiai* ("liturgies"), and they could be associated with a certain office or have to be made without an office. As such, they are an ancient component of the Greek *polis*. Fixed sums to be paid before entering office, similar to those paid on taking a seat on the city council (an institution that we know in the West as *summa honoraria*)[136] can hardly be distinguished conceptually from the *leiturgiai* firmly connected with the office. Examples of the regular purchase of offices by well-off notables for themselves, their wives, or their sons[137] show the prestige value of these *archai*.[138]

The liturgies put minimal demands on the officeholder, just as in American restaurants leaving a tip that is a set percentage of the bill is almost obligatory. And just as waiters and taxi drivers consider worthy of thanks only the amount of a tip that exceeds the set percentage, honorary inscriptions for individual officeholders note only what goes beyond the usual, and sometimes quantify it, while the usual is dispatched with formulas such as "he also provided the customary *leiturgiai* and *archai*." Naturally, continuity in office was of special importance.[139] The normal procedure for selecting amateur politicians does not seem to have been capable of guaranteeing this continuity always and everywhere, so that voluntary repetition of terms of office and extensions were praised as exceptional services: a citizen of Limyra residing in the country was a member of the *dekaproteia* (ten-man committee of the council) for twenty-five years, and another Lycian served in the same capacity from the age of eighteen until he was an old man.[140] Where lifelong priestly offices could not be filled and vacancies appeared, resort was made to exceptional takeovers by the god himself, that is, to financing from the temple treasury—in Amisos, Apollo was a *prytanis* sixty-three times ([106] OGIS 530). It was not only in Lycia that individual rich men held offices in several *poleis* in the province ([105] TAM II 3, 773.774; cf. Dion of Prusa, *or.* 38, 41).

A multitude of monuments in the public space honor benefactors (*euergetai*). With them the *polis* offered the person honored an eternal medium in which he could stage and represent himself and his family. The most common forms ranged from bronze or marble statues on a pedestal to elaborate structures, each of which had appropriate display surfaces on which the inscription could be chiseled. Thus whole clans (e.g., in Kremna in Pisidia) were able to immortalize themselves with their names as donors in a central place, where the divinations by lot beloved and much visited by the people were engraved (p. 520 f.);[141] others erected groups of statues on stone benches (*exedrae*) or in wall niches of large buildings on city squares that provided the best publicity. Among them are the longest inscriptions that have been found in Imperial period Asia Minor.

The tendency toward increasingly more expansive praise for individuals using an extravagant rhetoric begins in the Hellenistic period. In addition to the actual services, the worthy citizen was associated with a bundle of colorful and varied virtues. Over and above all that the state granted—acting in a way not unknown today—formal honorary titles: "Nourisher of the community," "donor of wealth," "benefactor," "caregiver," "protector," "founder," "father," and "mother" of the home city, and even "king," "queen," "hero," and "heroine."

For contemporaries, these were not empty words.[142] In these texts we can find the astonishing political morals and public engagement of a patriotic elite that long constituted the backbone of Roman provincial rule. Many wealthy people also distinguished themselves as benefactors beyond official activities. The benefactor's will with regard to the goal of the donated capital or goods and the way it was to be used was generally announced (*epangelia*) in writing, and usually it was certified (*kyrosis*) by the Roman (the emperor, the governor, or both) and by the municipal authorities. In the epigraphic sources, buildings appear as the dominant goal of donations,[143] followed by expenditures related to festivals, and then by the distribution of money and grain to the citizens, meals, and so forth. Serving meals to a segment of the citizenship defined by law or by custom, or even to all the residents of a city, regular popular banquets, was undertaken chiefly by religious officials in the framework of communal festivals.[144] Well into Christian late Antiquity, this institution continued to be a key element of community life in the cities; on holidays rich Christians were expected to invite the poor to public banquets after church.[145]

In small cities, such as Lunda in Phrygia, benefactors financed the minting of money (IGR IV 769), and they got express permission to do so in a decision made by the council.[146] An original goal of donations is revealed by the great customs inscription on the spring house in Kaunos. Here two wealthy citizens had the idea of suspending the import duties the state levied on merchants and subsidizing the communal loss of revenues. This donation insured the city against the risk that suspension of import duties would result in a loss of revenues and thus difficulties in paying taxes to the league and indirectly to the Roman tax authorities. At the same time, it promised an increase in commodity imports.[147] In inscriptions in Asia Minor during the Imperial period, a frequent topic is expenditures that helped overcome an emergency that arose "in an urgent crisis" connected with "a grain shortage," and contributed to "saving the citizens."

No chapter on the benefactors of the cities of Asia Minor, indeed of the Roman Empire as a whole, can ignore the record set by Opramoas of Rhodiapolis. According to the testimonies referring to him (not all of which are entirely certain) he spent more than 2.1 million denarii out of his own pocket—for the construction of new theaters and baths, the repair of buildings in Lycian cities after a devastating earthquake in 141 CE, the distribution of money and food to councilors and citizens, festivals, the maintenance of children, dowries for the daughters of poor families, and burial expenses. The man was neither a senator nor a Roman knight. As a citizen of all the Lycian cities, he undertook offices and liturgies in several of them. Xanthos erected statues to him. Wearing a gold wreath and a purple gown, he had an honored seat at league festivals and listened to the litany of his public honors read out loud. The inscription on the walls of the heroon (now in ruins) in his home city is the longest Greek inscription found anywhere.[148] There are twelve imperial letters from Antoninus Pius alone, as well as twenty-six letters from Roman governors and procurators and thirty-two decrees issued by the Lycian League. It is not surprising that the governor, as we can infer from the documentation itself, sought to brake the escalating iteration of Opramoas's honors; he failed because of the emperor's intervention, which was brought about by a delegation sent to Rome by the Lycian League.[149]

The urban elite's readiness to make donations presupposes a certain balance. It inevitably became overburdened in the course of time. The earliest reference to this is provided by a passage in the correspondence between Pliny and Trajan: admission charges to be paid by those joining the city council were originally not stipulated by legislation. When Trajan allowed a few cities to exceed the legal maximum number of council members, it became the custom to take in between 1,000 and 2,000 denarii from the surplus members. Moreover, a proconsul ordered that in some cities new members elected by the censors to the regular seats also had a duty to pay. Trajan recommended that the laws continue to be observed but wanted voluntary payers to be given precedence over citizens appointed by the censors against their will (Pliny the Younger, *ep.* 10, 112 f.).

As ordered by the emperor, certain occupational groups enjoyed, in addition to other privileges, that of being exempt from liturgies. A decision of the Senate from the time of the Triumvirate already anticipated the exceptional status of grammarians, rhetors, and physicians ([162] *IK* Ephesos 4101).[150] Augustus favored physicians, Vespasian extended the exemption to grammarians (i.e., teachers) and rhetors,[151] and Hadrian added philosophers (*Digest* 27, 1, 6, 8). The latter's successor Antoninus Pius was the first to set strict limits: in small cities at most five exempted physicians, three sophists or rhetors, and three grammarians; in middle-sized cities seven physicians, four rhetors, and four grammarians; and in large cities ten physicians, five rhetors, and five grammarians. About philosophers he said:

> The number of philosophers was not fixed since those who study philosophy are few. I suppose the very wealthy will voluntarily give the benefits of their studies to their countries, but if they direct their arguments to their own ends, they will immediately be revealed not to be philosophers.[152]

However, philosophers who did not teach in their home cities and those who were recognized (especially by the emperor) to be superstars (*agan epistemones*) were exempted. Things were not always settled smoothly by volunteering. We know of sophists who insisted on their privileges. The most prominent case in Asia is Aelius Aristeides, who certainly claimed to be a superstar. After much discussion back and forth, the emperor assured him that he was exempt, and had the next governor confirm the exemption on taking office.

FINANCES

If we consider the nature of the system of municipal offices, with its liturgies, expenditures, donations, and distinctive euergetism, we could easily get the impression that a genuine communal financial budget did not exist at all and that cities essentially depended on a steady flow of gifts made by rich citizens. In fact, such views have been defended;[153] they forgo any proof and seem to apply inappropriately to Asia and other oriental provinces the results of research done on the Western Empire.[154] First of all, we have to take into account the fact that inscriptions on stone were not a medium for the state system of accounting, whose documentation on impermanent writing material certainly existed but has been entirely lost, whereas the stone monuments that have been preserved put disproportionate emphasis precisely on euergetism. Even in times in which the latter reached its greatest extent and continuity (probably in the second century CE), we cannot assume that the state budget had entirely atrophied. On the contrary, a great deal of epigraphic evidence can be adduced from which we can infer regular state budget items along with financial and political standards and regulations.[155] Just as misleading is the view proposed by older and some more recent research, which depicts in gloomy tones a financial poverty of the city and speaks of a chronic lack of funds, finally seeing this as causally related to the introduction of state commissioners (the *curatores* and *correctores*) from the time of Trajan on. More probing analyses of the source material throw a different light on these measures, and especially on the problems with which Pliny (who as governor of Pontus et Bithynia concentrated his attention on state finances) had to struggle: not scarcity and impoverishment, but rather excess, waste, corruption, and malversations, apparently as a consequence of increasing revenues.

There can be no serious doubt that for more than 200 years the *poleis* were generally successfully managed financially. To explain this success, it has been rightly pointed out that many Greek cities had had budgeting systems for centuries.[156] To be sure, the privileges increasingly granted to groups and individuals diminished the potential in sectors in which the liturgies were part of the system, but not until late Antiquity were cities affected by a regular flight of the contributors on whom they usually drew.

Sanctuaries must be seen as a special focus of municipal financial management. But it would be misleading to suppose that they had a separate "economy of the sacred."[157] In contrast to the older temple states in Anatolia and in the Near East, in the Imperial period it was characteristic of the *poleis*'s sanctuaries that their administration was closely interwoven with that of the city. The leadership personnel occupied city offices and was accountable to the community; in no case can a closed management of the budget be proven in which, for example, expenditures for religious purposes could be financed by using religious revenues only. Conversely, a *polis* like Hierapolis-Kastabala had free access to the revenues of Artemis Perasia (IGR III 904). The income from sanctuaries represented a significant item in the state budget, especially when profit was sought from banking transactions, in addition to that derived from the leasing or renting of extensive real estate (which was officially the divinity's property).[158] The role of the Artemision of Ephesos as a bank of supraregional importance is well known.[159] In addition to its function as trustee of *deposita* of various articles of value and money (for which it was attractive chiefly on grounds of security, as are its counterparts in modern-day Switzerland), the sanctuary was favored as the inheritor of private wealth and also generated interest income on the loans it granted, preferably in exchange for security in the form of real estate. A gubernatorial edict from the time of Claudius stipulates that priests of Artemis and annual officeholders were allowed to grant only as many loans from public funds as could be financed by the same year's revenues ([162] *IK* Ephesos 17 lines 48 f.). The budget management of villages on a *polis*'s territory was also not entirely independent, but they had their own revenues.[160] In a few rural areas (Lydia) traditional forms of temple economy survived,[161] as did the *hierodulia* (p. 516), far into the Imperial period.

It is well known that on the revenue side, the cities largely abstained from direct taxation of their citizens (except in emergencies). However, such taxation must be distinguished from the tributes that can in some cases be proven and that were demanded from native rural inhabitants who had inferior civil rights (p. 453). Otherwise direct taxation was something for the Roman fiscal authorities. An important source of the cities' revenues was, as in the case of the sanctuaries, communal real property and monopolies of various kinds (e.g., money-changing: [106] OGIS 515). Communities could own land even on the territory of other communities. Large seigneuries that were leased were reflected in the budget, as were the rent from shops in the *agora*, the income from baths, the rent from observation posts for fish catches on the coast,[162] and the leasing of ferry services[163] or fishing rights. The *polis* also participated in market activity as a creditor and carried on its own banking business—currency exchange, *deposita*, and loans—directly or indirectly through lessees who held a monopoly on currency exchange. It was concerned not to leave money in its treasury as idle capital—"*pecuniae . . . ne otiosae iaceant*" (Pliny the Younger, *ep.* 10, 54)—and invested preferably in land, though the market was not always and everywhere able to meet the demand. In Bithynia, under Trajan it was necessary, because of the lack of supply on the real estate market, to resort to the capital market. But here the search for borrowers remained unsuccessful, because private lenders offered more favorable interest rates (12 percent per year). Permission to force councilors to borrow from the community was not granted.

Various other kinds of state revenues are known, first of all customs duties, market or sales taxes, and diverse fees, and then come fines. That not only the Roman tax authorities but also cities sought revenues from customs duties we have already discussed for Lycia, but it has long been presumed that the same was true for Asia and Bithynia as well (cf. Dion of Prusa, *or.* 38, 32).[164] Fines have been amply proven by Pergamon's *astynomoi* law, and indeed fines for various kinds of offenses in the municipal domain ([106] OGIS 483). Tomb inscriptions warn of penalties to be paid to the city community, for instance, in the case of unauthorized use and damaging of tombs.[165]

So far as the expenditure side is concerned, the most striking difference with modern communal budgets and their personnel costs must have been that in the ancient *polis* officials did not receive any salary worth mentioning. However, the personnel sector did not function entirely without state expenditures. Compensation was received by quite a few employees and wage earners, such as community slaves for the municipal guard and police, sanitation workers for the streets, squares, and baths, and scribes in offices (Pliny the Younger, *ep.* 10, 31 f.). In any case, state-owned slaves seem to have been cheaper than free wage earners, since the proconsul Paulus Fabius Persicus forbade Ephesos, as a cost-cutting measure, to replace the former with the latter ([162] *IK* Ephesos 18c lines 13–18). In the healthcare and education system—where in contrast to the modern situation, financing by a mixture of public expenditures, donations, and liturgies prevailed—communities paid physicians and elementary teachers. There were also architects paid by the community ([167] Miletus VI 2, 569). The lawyers the city brought in for legal disputes and complaints received honoraria. Municipal embassies, which sometimes covered great distances, going even to the emperor in Rome, incurred considerable travel costs. Each year, Byzantion sent a well-wisher to the emperor, at a cost of 3,000 denarii; another was sent, for a quarter of that amount, to Moesia, to pay his respects to the governor there (Pliny the Younger, *ep.* 10, 43). The Roman authorities did not demand that this be done, on the contrary.[166] But in the Imperial period cities seem to have thought it worthwhile to network with rulers and notables in and outside the province. Expenditures for housing and feeding the emperor, the army, and Roman magistrates were partly imposed on officeholders; that much is made clear in an inscription in the small Lycian city of Termessos Minor.[167]

The most important fields of communal investment, which had to be regularly managed, were first, the *polis*'s food supply, which was guaranteed even in emergencies by stocks of grain and oil, followed by the provision of personnel for the religious services and festivals, equipment, and money (including contributions to the provincial cult of the emperor). In third place was financing the construction and maintenance of public buildings and institutions—the most expensive probably being the gymnasiums: in Apameia in Phrygia, expenditures for the oil used in the city's gymnasiums are supposed to have run to 34,000 denarii (IGR IV 788).

The Imperial period construction boom, indeed the rage to build, has been the subject of numerous recent investigations.[168] One of the most valuable and productive testimonies to approximately simultaneous construction activities and the costs, tensions, and inadequacies associated with them in a province under the Roman Empire is provided by the correspondence between Pliny the Younger and the emperor

Trajan. Municipal construction projects had to be authorized and supervised by the Roman authorities. The task of the *curatores* was to put a project out to bid, award it cost-effectively, and supervise its execution within the time and cost limits. Given the sums that were involved, such a position must have been susceptible to corruption and exposed to pressure from various sides. The *curatores* were not experts in construction; in many places, the latter were evidently in short supply (Pliny the Younger, *ep.* 10, 17b.37.39.41).[169] For Pliny, abysses yawned in the two large cities of Bithynia: when Nikaia wanted to build a new, larger gymnasium and also a theater with a gallery above the auditorium and *basilicae* (large public buildings) on either side but received only unfinished buildings with serious defects, this failed investment amounted to 10 million sesterces (Pliny the Younger, *ep.* 10, 39). The reason for such abuses was less incompetent construction work than manipulation, malversations, and a craving for status. In the construction trade, the notorious receivables were particularly likely to contribute to shortages of public funds (Pliny the Younger, *ep.* 10, 17a). Since the community, as the creditor of bankrupt construction entrepreneurs, indebted lessees, or buyers incapable of paying, had to compete with private creditors when it came to liquidation (Pliny the Younger, *ep.* 10, 108), it sought to secure for itself the right of precedence for execution. The office of the *praktor* of state finances, that is, the "executor" or "court executor," in Kios ([162] *IK* Kios 16 A. line 13) seems to have been connected with these conditions; and the term "*anapraktes*" probably designated the same function in Tlos (ZPE 24, 1977, 265 no. 1, cf. [195] SEG 27, 938]). On the whole, however, such failed construction projects were less frequent than successful ones, even for imposing, massive expansions and reconstructions of city centers.

City Centers and Building Stock

In the fifth volume of his *Roman History*, for which he was awarded the Nobel Prize in literature, Theodor Mommsen wrote:

> Wherever a corner of the country, neglected under the desolation of the fifteen hundred years which seperate us from that time, is opened up to investigation, there the first and most powerful feeling is that of astonishment, one might almost say of shame, at the contrast of the wretched and pitiful present with the happiness and splendour of the past Roman age.[170]

This sentence may—even from the perspective of the nineteenth century—distort the whole reality of the *Imperium romanum*. Nonetheless, today someone standing before the architectural remains of the Imperial period can easily admit to the same feeling, and all the more because many a structure reconstructed by modern science and partly or wholly rebuilt surpasses even our imagination. Experienced travelers in the Mediterranean world are aware of Asia Minor's wealth in relics from that period. It is also due to the once-unparalleled density of urban centers that large parts of this region attained under the Principate, whose superb, even extravagant development did not remain limited to "great cities" but also made middle-sized and small cities seem "elegant and beautiful" (*elegans et ornata*) even in the eyes of a resident of Rome (Pliny the Younger, *ep.* 10, 98). What is striking is less the sheer monumentality than a structure and composition in brick, marble, mosaics, reliefs, and statuary, elaborately worked out in decorative detail to form a whole whose aesthetics and functionality are in perfect harmony with its spatial surroundings.

Hundreds of inscriptions, dozens of pictorial motifs on coins issued by the city, and many statements made by writers testify to the pride taken by citizens in the display of their architectural splendor, representing themselves through it, being distinctive and yet belonging to the great family. To that extent the efforts made even by small cities to convey an impression of their identity through architecture and pictorial decoration are identical with the contemporary constructs of their ancient history, the revival of their archaic cults and institutions, and the founding of their festivals (pp. 473, 498). In addition, the cities were provided with an unprecedented infrastructure—proudly honored by writers as a domain of specifically Roman architecture—for a cultivated, urbane way of life, with baths and gymnasiums, covered walks, libraries, schools with lecture halls (*museia*), water pipes, spring houses, cisterns, latrines, storehouses, market halls, and paved streets, some of them lighted at night.

It must be noted that grand buildings in Asia Minor also looked back on a long tradition. I have already mentioned the wave of urbanization and the architectonic flourishing in the Hellenistic period. But there is no doubt that the age of the Principate raised the construction industry of ancient Asia Minor to a new level—the highest in its history. In addition to new buildings, the reconstruction and expansion of many structures dating from the Hellenistic age was undertaken, so that modern research on them is almost always confronted by a complex architecture of consecutive construction phases. Imperial period architects included the whole ensemble of Hellenistic buildings in their spatial conception, in which structural levels and visible sides were coordinated. Very strong Western cultural influences are to be seen in the arrangement of space, architecture, construction technique, and ornamentation.[171]

The construction boom culminated in the Augustan age and in the time of Trajan and Hadrian, declined markedly in the third century, and then bloomed again in the fourth century. Although it was expansionary over the long term, the development was uneven, depending on the time and the region. Some cities faded early, others bloomed late. A particular achievement was the successful connection between the initiatives of urban elites and imperial engagement: the reshaping of the cities served both to represent monarchical power and generosity (*liberalitas*) and increasingly to lend the provinces the glitter of a coherent, Roman world civilization.[172] The emperor promoted the construction not only of religious buildings but also of profane architecture.

By modern standards, the urban centers were not extensive, even in the Imperial period. At the beginning of that period, Strabo reckoned the enceinte of Nikaia, a middle-sized provincial metropolis, at sixteen *stadia*, that is, given the square layout, sides 714.4 meters long and an area inside the walls of somewhat more than half a square kilometer. The mountain town of Sagalassos in Pisidia did not have more space available to it. In contrast, already under Lysimachos the area of the city of Ephesos, which lay between the hills Pion and Koressos and was surrounded by a sweeping perimeter wall, covered 2.8 square kilometers. Gradually built up, in the Imperial period it developed into the sophisticated gateway to the East.[173] The cosmopolitan city of Alexandria was almost five times as great in area.

Here I briefly digress to discuss a selection of the typical elements of the architecture of cities in the Imperial period. Significant remains of the perimeter walls that already surrounded them in pre-Roman times have been preserved in countless places. They were equipped with towers and tower-flanked gates of various forms. We repeatedly find structures that were rebuilt and repaired in late Antiquity, at a time when there was suddenly a need for them again. During the period of peace from the first to the third centuries, little was invested in maintaining the fortifying efficiency of these enclosures; instead, richly decorated, magnificent gates dedicated to the emperor and other eminent individuals, such as the East Gate in Attaleia (Antalya) for Hadrian or the South Gate of Anazarbos for Macrinus, were built. Also, multipart arches not integrated into the city walls are still standing, for example, the one for Domitian in Hierapolis in front of the North Gate, or the one in Patara, which is decorated with busts of the governor's family.

Within the walls of most cities we find layouts conceived in regular grids of streets crossing each other at right angles, a typical ideal Greek city plan that was adopted even by cities founded on steep slopes, sometimes almost fully, like Priene, and sometimes partially, like Pergamon. In Amastris, the blocks of buildings that were the basic units into which the main streets usually divided the built-up surface of the city were called *amphoda*. In some places they were named—for instance, after important buildings in their neighborhood. Foreign quarters or Jewish quarters like those in Alexandria have not been proven.

An element that decisively shaped urban space in many cities of Asia Minor in the Imperial period found its model in the Syrian metropolis Antiocheia, after it was introduced there by Herod and Tiberius: the broad *platea* (avenue) lined with colonnades as the central artery. There are several imposing examples on the plains of Cilicia, not far from Antiocheia: Soloi-Pompeiopolis, Anazarbos, and Hierapolis-Kastabala. Let me mention a few more. In Ephesos, one of these axes crossed the area that had been filled in to gain new building space that extended the harbor farther west: the "Arcadiane" developed under Arcadius (395–408), was eleven meters wide, paved with marble, flanked on both sides by halls of five meters' depth, and lit at night by fifty lanterns (Figure 80). It led past the harbor gymnasium directly to the theater, whose southern side entrance was connected with an older main street running north and south. This borders on the great *agora* (110 meters on a side) and turns off immediately in front of the Celsus library into a stately street that runs across the rectangular grid and is called Embolos; it leads to the upper *agora* with the

80. The Arcadiane, Ephesos.

Prytaneion and the Odeion. Today, one can walk the whole length of the *platea* in Perge in Pamphylia. This avenue, twenty meters wide and lined by halls, begins at the city gate with the inner courtyard enlarged by Plancia Magna, and after taking an S-shaped course ends in front of the hill of the acropolis at a grandiose two-story gate, with projecting side wings and two passageways, that was at the same time a nymphaeum. From the spring at its center water flowed into a stone-built canal that divided the twenty-meter wide *platea* into two halves. The *platea* in Phaselis in eastern Lycia, which runs across a peninsula and connects two harbors, is exceptionally broad (twenty to twenty-four meters). The city of Hierapolis, located on a plateau over travertine terraces (*pamukkale*), is also transected by a broad *platea* that divides the side of the city on the northeast slope from the side that extends to the southwest as far as the edge of the plateau.

So far as the build-up of centers with residential housing is concerned, in all of Asia Minor there are two outstanding excavation sites where research on this topic has advanced the farthest. In Priene, large contiguous parts of the stone foundations on which walls of mudbrick were built can be reconstructed. In the Hellenistic and Imperial periods the blocks consisting of eight houses each and nearly equal in size that were built during the foundation of the city underwent several reconstructions, in the course of which neighboring buildings were combined to form larger units, but large units were also sometimes divided into smaller ones. The rectangular house layout comprised an antechamber (*prostas*), an unroofed peristyle, a large living space (*oikos*), a banquet room (*andron*), and smaller rooms surrounding the central courtyard. A natural catastrophe in the second century BCE, during which stones

81. Terrace house with floor mosaics and painted walls, residential unit 3, Ephesos.

falling from the acropolis demolished buildings in the western part of the city, left behind it in one place, buried under the rubble of pieces of the roof and walls and a burned layer, a large amount of household goods, including bronze couch feet, kettles, pots, hand-mills, lamps, and terracotta figurines. From the archaeologist's point of view, the find is a stroke of luck comparable to many discoveries made in Pompeii after it was buried by an eruption of Vesuvius.

Still more favorable conditions for archaeology were left behind by an earthquake in Ephesos in late antiquity: recent research and excavation have shown that what long lay buried under the rubble provides a glimpse of aristocratic life during the high Imperial period (Figure 81). The extensive restoration presents two blocks of residences built on the slope south of the Embolos, on whose sides lanes with steps led up to individual houses. Block 2 has seven residential units, some of which have several stories and are furnished with extravagant luxury. Here too a central peristyle courtyard is a fixed component, with around it reception rooms, living rooms, dining rooms, kitchens, baths, bedchambers, servants' rooms, and storerooms. The house is equipped with mosaic floors in some places and is rich with decorative and figured scenes in wall paintings, statues in wall niches, and the like. One of the private baths consists of three heated rooms with a water supply. A room in residential unit 6 was completely sheathed with colorful marble plaques and had a fountain inside the room and another in a wall niche.

The community centers, the gymnasiums (which were already lavishly equipped in the Hellenistic age, as in particular in royal Pergamon), were transformed during the Imperial period through reconstructions and additions into large complexes with grandiose two-story façades—restored in an especially impressive way in Sardeis—columned halls, libraries, and lecture halls, club and banquet rooms, restaurants, boutiques, bodycare salons, athletic fields, gymnastics rooms, indoor pools, and open-air baths. The enormous Vedius gymnasium from the Antonine age in Ephesos was entered through a forecourt on the south side, from which one came into an "Imperial hall" surrounded by a two-story portico. The bath wing, which consisted of rooms with cold water, lukewarm water, and hot water, as well as sweatrooms, required an elaborate heating system. Here, as in other *thermae*, the hypocaust system developed in the first century BCE was used: hot air from heating chambers fired by enormous amounts of wood passed through hollow spaces under a floor supported by small brick pillars (*suspensurae*) and up through hollow bricks (*tubulatio*) in the walls. *Thermae* that are partly still standing, with visible room divisions, can be admired in Miletus and Perge, for example; at the Caracalla *thermae* in Ankyra only the foundation walls are still standing, as they are in many places. On the *palaistra*, which is seventy meters square, there is now an open-air museum with stone inscriptions. In the Phrygian city of Aizanoi remains of one of the largest complexes anywhere have been found; it was completely sheathed in marble. Many cities first received their *thermae* in the middle and late Imperial period. In the time of Trajan, Prusa in Bithynia needed a new bath; the old one was old-fashioned and dilapidated, and the governor considered tearing down a derelict peristyle building to make room for an elegant, grandiose building with *exedra* and covered walks, to be dedicated to the emperor (Pliny the Younger, *ep.* 10, 23.70). After Herod Atticus, the sophist and friend of the emperor, had taken note of the poor facilities in the *colonia Alexandria* during a visit there, he persuaded the emperor to build a new bath with its own long-distance water supply, and helped finance it himself (VS 548). In the Imperial period, the baths, which promoted health, bodycare, and pleasure, ripened into the essence of an urbane lifestyle. In the cities of late Antiquity there were—in addition to those that were part of private homes—several baths of differing size, both publicly and privately operated, open to the people in exchange for an entrance fee, and segregated by sex or open to both sexes. Ephesos had at least six. A sophisticated *therma* in the countryside that was visited by Aelius Aristeides lies somewhat more than twenty kilometers inland from Pergamon.[174] The baths were the greatest consumers of water and were accompanied by the construction of more and more short- and long-distance water supply lines.

The expertly built aqueducts are masterpieces of Roman engineering. The execution of the work nonetheless sometimes went wrong because of incompetence, as in Nikomedeia under Trajan (Pliny the Younger, *ep.* 10, 37). Pergamon already had a long-distance water supply dating from the Hellenistic period, and in the Imperial period it received seven supply lines. Thick metal or stone pipes ran under the ground or over it in stone jackets, crossed valley bottoms on aqueducts, following a steady decline to their endpoint, or passed over hills in the area through pressure lines using the principle of communicating vessels, as in the case of the splendidly

82. The Celsus library, Ephesos.

preserved system of Aspendos in Pamphylia. Such expenditures did not have to be made everywhere—nor could they be—and people often made do with the water supply from springs and cisterns in the city area. To the water supply corresponded the water discharge system, which was also carefully constructed, using covered canals that made use of inclines. As in Ephesos, enormous amounts of water from the baths flowed through these canals down to the sea, along with wastewater from households and from the great latrines.

The bustling centers of the Roman cities of Asia Minor were the lavish squares intended for meetings and trade: the *agorai*. Many cities had several such squares—as did Ephesos, Priene, and Miletus, where the largest, the South Market, which measured 127 by 161 meters, was entered through a two-story ornamental gate with several arches and projecting side wings. Access to the great *agora* of Ephesos was provided by a small door on the north and two monumental gate structures on the west and south. The triple-arched south gate, erected by two of Agrippa's freedmen in honor of him and of Augustus, delimited at the same time the forecourt of a Roman structure that modern mass tourism has made the best known in Asia Minor—the Celsus Library built between ca. 110 and 135 CE. Intended as a donation and tomb of the proconsul Tiberius Julius Celsus Polemaeanus, who governed the province from 105 to 107, it was completed by his descendants (Figure 82).

The abundance of the original construction parts found on the site allowed the Roman building to be understood and restored down to the refinements of incon-

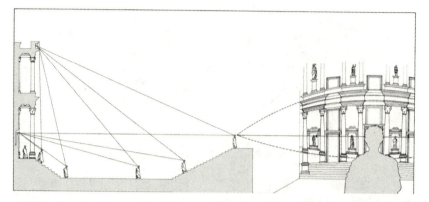

83. Drawing taken from Friedmund Hueber, *Ephesos. Gebaute Geschichte*, Mainz 1997, 83.

spicuous details. The inside contained the burial chamber and, in the wall niches of the main room, the bookshelves. The ground floor of the two-story façade is divided, in alternation with wall niches containing statues, by three doors between four projecting *aediculae* with two columns topped by composite capitals (i.e., capitals in which ornamental elements originally of different styles are combined). The entablature supporting the upper story that rises over the vine-tendril frieze shifts its cornice in such a way that here the *aediculae* are not over those of the lower story, but over those of the intermediate rooms. The stylobate supporting the row of columns and the entablature both have a concave curvature,[175] which is intensified by the increasing height of the pillars from the sides to the middle. This is counteracted by a convex curvature that is achieved by increasing the height of the bases of the pillars from the middle to the sides. This optical effect makes the façade seems broader than it really is (Figure 83).

When we look at the market halls surrounding the squares in many cities, a few of them are well preserved, as are the ones in Aigai (Aiolis), Alinda (Caria), and Lyrbe (Pamphylia). In Alinda, they were built into the slope in such a way that the double-bay hall with its pillared façade constituting the upper story was at ground level on the market square. On the back of the buildings the lower story was entered through doors (and also had windows beside the doors); in the middle story, which was windowless, there was a series of storerooms. A ruin that is still called the *bedesten* (market) stood at the edge of the *agora* in Amastris: 118.1 by 42.8 meters in size, it was divided into fourteen rooms. The elegant façade of this brick building, which was completely sheathed in marble, was punctuated by half-round and rectangular wall niches for statues.

On the squares and on the sides and intersections of the grand streets stood the monuments, benches (*exedrae*) and bronze and marble statues of dignitaries, standing, sitting, and mounted on horses. Inscriptions and also certain details of the furnishing allow us to identify smaller complexes as food, meat, or fish markets (or

84. The lighthouse of Patara.

some combination thereof), as for example in Priene or (presumably) in Aizanoi. Among the buildings constructed for specific purposes during the economically prosperous centuries were the enormous granaries of Andriake and Patara, both near the coast (p. 669 n. 60) and the still little-investigated harbor facilities with jetties, breakwaters, quay walls, shipyards, and lighthouses. An excellent example of the latter has recently been excavated in Patara, the provincial capital of Lycia (Figure 84). It was a structure that clearly emulates the celebrated Pharos of Alexandria.[176]

Municipal government buildings, in particular the council hall and the *prytaneion*, were also incorporated into the squares used for citizen assemblies, as in Assos, Priene, and Ephesos. In Priene one entered, through a door in the back wall of the market hall built later, a corridor with the two front entrances to the council hall. In contrast to the otherwise usually half-circular rows of seats in the council buildings, the tiers of seats on the back and side walls of this almost square building intersect conically and are divided by diagonal stairways. In the middle of the small auditorium stood an altar. The immediately adjacent *prytaneion* had the form of a peristyle building; on three sides of its courtyard, behind the covered walkway, was a series of eight rooms, one of which contained the state hearth.

Of the large structures being built in the cities of Asia Minor, theaters were among the most prominent. A city was not a city if it did not have a theater. A few cities even had two of them, as in Laodikeia on Lykos or in Kibyra. The spectator galleries (*koila*) generally held 10,000 to 15,000 people. These *koila* were cut into slopes or built on vaulted substructures and took a somewhat more than semicircular form, subdivided into two or three tiers by horizontal aisles and into wedges by narrow vertical stairways. The theater in Ephesos was one of the largest; with sixty-six rows in three tiers, it had as many as 24,000 seats. The best preserved ancient theater in Turkey, in Aspendos, could hold almost as many, about 20,000: its semicircular auditorium is divided by the "girdle" (*diazoma*) into two parts, the upper nineteen rows and the lower twenty rows. On the sharply articulated façade of the two-story stage house, the *aediculae* are supported by forty columns, those on the lower level with Ionic capitals, those on the upper level with Corinthian. At the top, there are seventeen openings for the beams of a wooden roof. Builders were fond of decorating friezes on stage houses and prosceniums with figured reliefs that depicted masks, mythological scenes, and especially Dionysian themes.

In addition to the theaters, many *poleis* built a *stadion*. Most of these were located on the edge of the city center, took up a great deal of space, and held as many as 30,000 spectators (e.g., Aphrodisias). Aizanoi in Phrygia offers an unusual complex. The rectangle of the *stadion*, whose long sides with the spectators' rows were slightly concave, was open on its south side (with a view of the temple) and closed on the north by the stage house of the theater. The latter was sheathed in marble and faced both ways, being oriented toward the theater and toward the *stadion*. Recent research indicates that this complex was constructed in the first century CE. The amphitheaters found throughout the west of the Empire are largely lacking in Asia Minor, except for one example in Anazarbos.

The enormous sacred precincts outside the city walls, such as the Artemision of Ephesos, the Didymaion in Miletus, or the Asklepieion in Pergamon were reached in part by covered processional avenues. But the city centers were dominated not only by theaters but also by halls and baths, and usually by several temples of varying size and form. The architectural history of many of them goes far back in time. Among the new structures of the Imperial period, the prostyle—a temple with freestanding columns on the front side only—stands out; the Corinthian established itself as the favorite order. Temples on the Italic model were also situated on high podiums accessible only by an exterior staircase on one side.[177] The sacred precincts in the city were often but not always integrated into the rectangular architectonic context, and subsequent construction projects were oriented by the axes of the sanctuaries that had already existed in pre-Roman times. In Ephesos, a double temple dedicated to the *divus Julius* and the goddess Roma was built on a common podium as early as the first century BCE. Since the time of Augustus the cult of the emperor had moved into existing or newly constructed temples that were dedicated to the ruler, alone or with a divinity. Of the Roma-Augustus temple in Ankyra, which was presumably a *pseudodipteros*, only the walls of the *cella* remain standing.

The Sebasteion of Aphrodisias is a square surrounded by halls, with a small podium temple inside it. The Sebasteion of the *colonia Antiocheia* in Pisidia was entered through a three-arched gate. Here there was also a podium temple in the semicircular courtyard surrounded by two-story *porticus* (covered walkways). In Ephesos, in addition to the Temple of Augustus, at least two other neocorate temples, one for Domitian and one for the Nerva-Antonine dynasty, the Olympieion, have been lo-

85. The Traianeum, Pergamon.

cated, although only a few ruins remain after their destruction during the Christian period. In contrast, the Traianeum on the acropolis of Pergamon dedicated to both Trajan and Zeus Philios can be viewed by the modern-day observer in a partially reconstructed form (Figure 85). It is also a Roman podium temple with six Corinthian columns on its short sides and ten on its long sides that was built on a square surrounded by halls. In front of the wall of Eumenes the old quarter of Bergama surrounds the splendidly preserved Sarapieion, a massive brick structure from the time of Trajan and Hadrian; and in Euromos the *peripteros* dedicated to the Carian Zeus Lepsynos, with six columns on its short sides and eleven on its long sides, stands erect as far as the roof area.

However, the best-preserved Roman temple ruin in Asia Minor has pride of place on the artificially leveled flat hill in the middle of the city of Aizanoi. It is built on the foundation of a terrace constructed of massive blocks, on which the *pseudodipteros*,[178] with fifteen columns on its long sides and eight on its short sides, rises over a seven-tiered substructure (*krepis*). Enormous architrave blocks bridge the distance between the cella wall and the ring of columns, and in the middle of the frieze over the *pronaos* and *opistodom* sat massive busts of women entwined with vine tendrils. According to a lost dedicatory inscription in the *pronaos*, which it has been possible to reconstruct with the help of pinholes in the stone, the building was dedicated to Zeus and the emperor Domitian (Figure 86).

Not many of the synagogues that probably existed in most cities are archaeologically identifiable, with the exception of the one in Sardeis (third century CE), which has been splendidly restored with mosaics, colored marble, and inscriptions. The

86. Temple of Zeus in Aizanoi, Phrygia.

basilica, a type of structure not often found in Asia Minor—there are examples in Patara, Aphrodisias, Smyrna, and Tieion—is a forerunner of Late Antique church architecture, as is shown by the architectural history of the Church of Mary in Ephesos. Churches, sometimes with bishops' palaces (Aphrodisias, Miletus, and Limyra) do not appear before the fourth century; most of them are from the fifth and sixth centuries and belong to a time in which the image of urban architecture in Asia Minor had already permanently changed.

Structure of Rural Settlement and Territorial Units

In the Imperial period, a multipart organization of the whole country from legal, administrative, and economic points of view was developed, in which traditional elements partly persisted and partly disappeared, and new ones appeared.[179] Estates held by kings, aristocratic landlords, and priests were gradually incorporated into city territories. The fate of temple states and royal domains can be traced only in part. Broughton hypothesized that the Seuleucid colonial foundations were carried out mainly at the expense of temple possessions.[180] By the middle of the first century CE, Anatolia no longer had any genuine temple states with large territories.[181] However, even in the Imperial period not all provinces were subdivided into completely coherent city territories. Between city territories great imperial, senatorial, and private domains were established. Information about them can be gleaned not only from a few direct testimonies but also and especially from the concentration of Italic families that supplied knights and senators. Thus the *gens Catilia* from Apameia in Bithynia owned extensive lands in the interior of Bithynia as far as the border with Galatia. On the central Anatolian plateau, the early senatorial families of Antiocheia in Pisidia, and of Attaleia and Perge in Pamphylia owned large properties. These were seigneuries in which villages and rural communities with a certain degree of self-administration also developed; for example, the *demos* of the *Moiteanoi* and *Soenoi* in Phrygia. The inhabitants raised crops mainly as tenant farmers under the supervision of the landlord's staff; in the emperor's case, the latter consisted of imperial slaves, freedmen, and procurators. The tenant farmers were not bound to the soil and could even threaten to switch over to private land.[182] On senatorial and other large domains, "property managers" (*oikonomoi*) were used; they are often mentioned in tomb and dedicatory inscriptions. It is certain that this kind of property ownership increased in Anatolia and reached enormous dimensions in Late Antiquity and the early Byzantine period.

Apart from the private domains there also existed, until well into the Imperial period, territories of rural communities that did not belong to a *polis*. But the most widespread type of legal-administrative regional unit in the Imperial period in general was the *polis*. Within its precisely defined borders were private land, temple land, and community land, also of villages belonging to the *polis*. Some city territories were extensive, especially in northern and eastern Anatolia. Areas of more than 10,000 square kilometers have been proven.

A deeper analysis of the *polis* territory leads us to a relational structure that presents numerous problems. Within this cosmos we also find, especially in the epigraphic documentation, references to phylae, demes and districts, village associations, villages, *katoikiai* (settlements), trade centers (*emporia*), "neighborhoods," "localities" (*choria*), hamlets, and farms. The meanings of these terms are multifaceted and partly ambivalent, insofar as they can stand for localities and settlements as well as groups of people. The subject of the typological integration into the whole raises the question of a hierarchy within the *polis*. Did the *polis* govern even the most remote corners of its territory, and conversely, did the inhabitants of the rural areas participate in the full range of urban community life—for example, in festivals, cults, and elections for the city council and offices?

A widespread characteristic of the post-Classical, Hellenistic, or Imperial period foundations are adapted systems with phylae as "territorial units." These are most clearly recognized in declarations according to which someone "lives in this or that phyle" ([105] TAM IV 1, 60). In such cities the phyle system could be explained genetically and structurally as a joint organization of inhabitants of different regions whose names, possibly derived from that of a main town or village, were transferred to the subdivisions of the citizens. We do not know whether these systems included the whole territory or only a part of it; the city itself appears as a special category *extra ordinem*, in which the city dwellers (*astikoi*) reside. A complete set of this kind seems to have been preserved in an inscription honoring Septimius Severus that was found in Bithynion-Klaudiupolis.[183] The system used in Side in Pamphylia is striking as a unique case that turns this model of "territorial units" on its head: the traditional names refer exclusively to quarters of the city. Structural changes must have accompanied the gain or loss of land: in some places, such as Stratonikeia and Kaunos in Caria, older, surrounding *polis* communities, and larger settlements or villages (or both) could be integrated into a tiered system of demes and phylae on the Athenian model; in other areas, for example in northern Asia Minor, villages or groups of villages might be subsumed under territorial phylae.

The term *demos*, insofar as it does not refer to the whole citizenry of a *polis*, stands in a similarly genetic and structural context for previously independent communities formed out of "people who live around" a specific locality that gives them its name and who continue to administer themselves as corporations after their integration into a *polis*. In the epigraphic formula they are quite often presented as decisionmaking bodies formed of delegates from several villages. A specialty of southwestern Asia Minor that still appears in the Imperial period is the *peripolion*. It presumably derives a privileged status superior to the village from its older role as an independent unit. As opposed to the purely personal unions of the demes and village associations, the superior status of the *peripolion* also seems to manifest itself in a more urban type of settlement, particularly in the local garb of perimeter walls, stone architecture, and the like.

From another point of view, settlement units designated as trade centers (*emporia*) represent a special category. They were not located solely on the coasts; for instance, Tataion, in Nikaia's hinterland, was a major *emporion*. Here officiated an *emporiarches*, C. Cassius Publianus, who (to judge by his name) belonged to a rich family in the metropolis ([162] *IK* Nikaia 1071). An inscription in an *emporion* located on the Bithynian coast of the Black Sea makes the *polis*'s official supervision of these places on its territory clear: Marcus Aurelius Chrysenius Demetrius, formerly Bithyniarch and Pontarch, and now the city's financial overseer (*curator civitatis*), has "without harming any individual [resident], increased the *emporion*'s income, and also finished up the *emporion* for the city by carrying out construction work, and all that in his term of office as *curator*" ([162] *IK* Prusias ad Hypium 29; trans. Marek).

We have already noted the regional subdivision of kingdoms into districts in the northeastern and eastern areas of Anatolia, where the *polis* got a foothold later (p. 266). This principle of division seems in some cases to have also been used in newly founded *poleis*, such as Zela (according to Strabo 12, 3, 37), whose territory Pompey had formed out of several districts, and Amaseia (according to epigraphic evidence). On the territory of Amaseia lay the sacred district of a Zeus Stratios that was the *polis*'s main cult in the Severan period; there several inscribed stone markers were found bearing the names of localities and the associated district names that allowed delegates who were streaming in from towns and villages of various districts on festive occasions to use "their" locality's marker to situate themselves.

We come finally to the village, for which our sources usually use the word *kome*. In all areas of Anatolia, villages are more or less densely distributed. It is difficult to define them in terms of their appearance alone, because a few of them definitely had a building stock comparable to that of a city, even if they did not have perimeter walls: spring houses (*nymphaea*), water pipes, baths, marketplaces with halls, workshops, shops, and of course temples have been proven.

In terms of the typology of settlements, the village is not on the lowest level. Just as in modern Turkey, the term "village" (*köy*) often designates only a conglomerate of scattered individual settlements (*mahalle*), so the settlement pattern in an area may have consisted of tiny hamlets without a genuine village center. And as the field research conducted by the Tübingen Lycian project has shown, over broad stretches of land, especially on the south coast of Lycia as far as Cilicia, individual farms (*oikia*, *aule*, *tyrsis*, and other terms), together with the "tower-farm" (which still had a defensive function in Hellenistic times), continued to play an important role even in the Imperial period. The archaeological research that investigates the traces of these smallest settlement units far from urban centers finds them with the help of architectural remains of residential and commercial buildings; terrace walls; cisterns; grape and olive presses; hearths; tombs; sarcophagi; dedicatory, honorary, and tomb inscriptions; ceramics; jewelry; coins, and so forth. The scattered settlements making inroads in central Lycia during the Imperial period included on average five, and at most fifteen, houses. Up to 200 farms that were still being worked during the Imperial period were distributed over about 5,000 hectares of arable land. With a territorial area of 106 square kilometers and about fifty-five rural settlements, this comes to an average of about two settlements per square kilometer. A rural territory that has been subjected to similarly intensive investigation, that of Sagalassos, shows an enormous increase in the number of rural settlements in the Imperial period, with about five to six per square kilometer.[184]

However, with respect to legal and administrative matters the village is the lowest level of the hierarchy. The word "village" is strikingly rare in epigraphs from Paphlagonia, Pontos, and Cappadocia. This could indicate that the way in which the rural population was organized here differed from that in other provinces and was not based on villages or village associations, even though there were, of course, great numbers of village settlements in that region as well, as can be inferred from a name like "Thousand Villages" (*chiliokomon*). Most testimonies suggesting that villages were communities come from Bithynia, Phrygia, and Lydia. They prove that inhabitants of several villages appeared as associations and formed "two-villages," *dikomia*, (Nikaia), "three-villages," *trikomia* (Nikomedeia), and up to "five-villages," *pentakomia* (Balbura in northern Lycia). Village assemblies of both village associations and individual villages were called demes, for instance "the *Dablenoi* and *Pronnaeitai*, the *demos* of the *dikomia*."[185] Moreover, it has been documented that the villages had precisely defined boundaries; acted as corporations capable of making decisions; elected eponymous annual officials as village chiefs, financial officers, market supervisors, village priests, and other religious personnel; controlled their own revenues from common land, pasture fees, fines (for desecrating tombs), endowments, and private donations; organized their own cults, festivals, and markets, and carried out construction projects. In addition, there were village *gerusiai* (corporations of the elderly), written records of administrative actions, and a village archive. Not a single village established a council (*bule*)—an unmistakable sign of the *polis*.

In this system the village provided the lowest level of communal supervision of landed property and the burdensome duties connected with it. When the city of Oinoanda in Lycia organized a *polis* festival and demanded that the rural communities provide one or several sacrificial animals, depending on their differing capabilities, it drew up a complete inventory of the villages and the boundaries of their territories.[186] There were thirty-five of them. That villages also maintained a cadastre of all landed properties within their boundaries is shown by an inscription from northern Lycia that is in this respect unique and provides details such as are otherwise found only in papyruses about conditions in Egypt. Here, too, it is a question of ensuring a fair distribution of the burdens of cultivating a rural cult of Zeus, with periodic sacrifices, banquets, and games. The burdens were not calculated per capita but rather by the unit of land (*chorion*), and for this purpose a complete inventory of land ownership was drawn up for the whole village territory of fifty-four units. The names of female or male owners, or of the property-owning community, denote either an individual plot of land (x or y's *chorion*) or several, not necessarily contiguous, plots (x or y's *choria*). Larger or more productive and smaller or less productive plots of land are combined into five neighborhoods (*homuriai*) in such a way that each of them was expected to make the same, precisely calculated contribution. The scattered holdings of individual landowners in different neighborhoods and the fluctuation produced by inheritance, sale, and leasing are striking.[187]

The villager's participation in the *polis* can be recognized by several criteria. Prosopographic research shows that prominent village families were not only present in the urban elite, with offices, donations, and honors, but also appear on the provincial level and in the imperial service. The rural population attended the *polis*'s festivals, and a few city theaters permanently reserved seats with the names of villages. Village communities described themselves as belonging to a *polis*, dated events according to the *polis*'s superior officials or honored them with statues and inscriptions (or both), followed the city's calendar, and obligated themselves to coordinate their market days with those of the *polis*.

The assimilation of rural communities into the city in political, administrative, economic, and cultural respects, of which I have given only a rough sketch here, was, as the ancient historian Christof Schuler rightly noted, a sign of the advanced process of Hellenization in the Imperial period.[188] It is an error to imagine that developments in the countryside and in the cities of Asia Minor were separate, describing like two differently set clocks the dynamics of civilization on the one hand, and persistence in archaic conditions on the other. Instead, we have to assume complex mutual influences. Research on the rural territories of Kyaneai in the central Lycian uplands and of Sagalassos in Pisidia show that the wave of urbanization and the growing concentration on the central town did not lead to demographic, economic, and architectonic atrophy in the countryside—on the contrary.

Society

Incorporation and Exclusion

In the Imperial period, not all inhabitants of Asia Minor were citizens of a *polis*. In principle, we should expect that autochthonous, free-born adults on the territory of a *polis* were also citizens. In any case, that was the goal of Roman legislation, as we can infer from the example of the *lex Pompeia* for the province of Pontus et Bithynia: the more citizens, the more contributors to communal activities and human resources for the Imperial service.[189]

Greeks always regarded citizenship in a *polis* as an exclusive prerogative. We know of not a few places in different parts of Asia Minor where groups of inhabitants were excluded. In the Imperial period, indeed even Late Antiquity, a distinction can be drawn in Asia Minor between the dominant citizens who were Hellenized or proved their Hellenic descent, on the one hand, and the "inhabitants" (*ethne*) or "residents" (*paroikoi*) who did not speak Greek or spoke it badly on the other hand. This distinction corresponded more or less to a dividing line between rich and poor, even if it was permeable and gradually disappeared in the course of the Imperial period.[190] For Dion of Prusa (*or.* 38, 26), "Bithynians" were a class incompatible with the citizens of a *polis*. In making donations, the Bithynian city of Prusias on Hypios distinguished between two groups of recipients: people who were "entitled" (citizens) and people who "lived in the hinterland" ([162] *IK* Prusias 17). A way of expressing the same phenomenon is found in the cities of Lycia, where inhabitants of the countryside were also citizens, though the right to receive grain to be distributed was reserved for an elite of citizens: *sitometrumenoi*.[191] In Sillyon and also in other cities of the Pisidian-Pamphylian region, to participate in the assembly (*ekklesia*), it seems not yet to have sufficed to be a citizen (*polites*); one had to belong to the group called *ekklesiastai* (IGR III 800.801). Thus we are dealing with two classes of citizens.[192]

A particular variant of the same dichotomy appears in a speech given by Dion to the inhabitants of Tarsos. The numerically significant group of them who were usually called "linen weavers" (*linurgoi*) stood, Dion said, "outside the constitution, so to speak." Although they were born in Tarsos and grew up there, they were sometimes seen as scum who were to blame for every kind of unrest and disorder, while at other times they were accepted as members of the community and allowed to participate in the popular assembly (Dion of Prusa, *or.* 34, 21). The example is noteworthy in light of the fact that in other places, in Philadelpheia and Saittai in Lydia, the organization of the citizenry was actually based on such craft groups.[193]

In this juxtaposition and mixture of Hellenic and Hellenized citizens, partly excluded and partly integrated natives, and foreigners (*xenoi*), another particular group—in addition to the Italics, to whom we shall return—should be singled out. Most of its members certainly had civil rights in the *polis*, but they nonetheless represented a community that differed in essential ways from the Greeks, insofar as they had no images of the gods, had a synagogue and Sabbath instead of the *polis*'s temple and festivals, lived in accord with their own rules (e.g., practiced circumcision and prohibited the eating of pork), and paid taxes to Jerusalem: the Jews. We have already noted that they were a major presence in the cities of the Imperial period. On Jewish holidays the entire cityscape of Smyrna is said to have looked different.[194] It is well known that such communities within communities did not exist without tensions; and the Jewish diaspora, like the Christians, is of first-rate importance for the religious and social history of Asia Minor.[195]

Tombs, Death, and Dying

Archaeology offers us a glimpse of the housing conditions of the living in only a few places. In contrast, research on the stone remains of the dwellings of the dead can draw on a rich inventory.[196] The architecture, pictorial decoration, and inscriptions of tombs in cities and in the countryside are a source of information on social relationships that has not yet been systematically analyzed by historians. It is true that of the erstwhile splendor, abundance, and multitude of tombs, only ruins still remain. But their types and forms can tell us, as they do elsewhere in the ancient world, something about the social rank and affluence of their owners. The tumulus—a large hill of earth with a burial chamber inside it, an ancient form of tomb in Anatolia—is also widespread in the Imperial period (Figure 87). Illicit excavations in Paphlagonia have uncovered large burial chambers built of stone blocks and covered with barrel vaults. Monumental rock-cut tombs also served to bury wealthy burgher families. Representative complexes with reliefs cut out of the rock are to be found in Cilicia (Adamkayalar, Kanytela). In the Imperial period, rock-cut tombs in northern Asia Minor are for the most part much smaller than their Hellenistic and Classical predecessors—inside them are simple chambers with stone benches cut into the rock, rectangular chests, or niches for urns.

Freestanding house forms (*heroon, oikos*) vary greatly (Figure 88). They, too, are tombs for the wealthy upper classes. The tradition of the mausoleums continued in Caria, as we have seen in the case of the Roman tomb "Gümüşkesen" (p. 170). On the Lycian coast stand two-story *heroa*, with space for a tomb guardian on the lower floor, and on the Cilician coast, near Seleukeia on Kalykadnos, one- and two-story temple-graves with richly decorated entablatures and Corinthian and Ionic columns contain sarcophagi on their upper floors.

Peculiar forms appear from region to region, for instance, a tomb described as a pyramid in Bithynia or the obelisk of C. Cassius Chrestos in Nikaia. In eastern Bithynia and western Paphlagonia we find rectangular or octagonal blocks cut from a single piece of stone that, in the form of a small temple (*naiskos*) or with a sculpture of a lion reposing on them, crowned the tomb complex. Here sculpted stone lions, serving as guardians, had been part of the tomb furnishings since pre-Roman times.

No doubt the most widespread type is the sarcophagus (Figure 89); countless examples have been preserved, not only where they were originally placed (*in situ*); they were also carried off and re-used or transported to museums all over the world.

87. Tumulus in Paphlagonia.

88. Mausoleum in the necropolis of Hierapolis, Phrygia.

89. Sarcophagus from Ephesos. Selçuk Museum.

In the Anatolian regions, they are rarer farther to the east, and in inner Paphlagonia, Pontos (in Amaseia and Neokaisareia), and Cappadocia, only isolated examples appear. For sarcophagi, the inscriptions themselves use words like *skaphe*, *pyelos*, and *enbate*, which are derived from the basic meaning of "trough" or "bathtub." Well-preserved, top-quality products of Imperial period stone-cutting compete in their decoration on both the long and short sides of the sarcophagi: architecture with pilasters, columns, figured entablatures, frames and medallions, flat reliefs or sculptures carved out to the point of becoming statuary, decorative elements (e.g., frequent garlands, vine tendrils, rosettes, leaves, wreathes, and spiral ribbons), figured images in favorite thematic contexts, Cupids, Gorgon's heads, masks, animals, whole scenes from mythology, but also images of the owners of the tombs and the world they lived in. The stone lids represent gabled roofs with decorated corner acroteria, sometimes also with statuary (e.g., lions) on the roof, or instead, couches with a recumbent married couple (Figure 90). In the necropolises, they stand at ground level, on pedestals or altar-shaped plinths, or on basements (*hyposorion*) that served, like the sarcophagi themselves, as burial chambers. Sarcophagi cut into the rock and closed with a lid are also found. Diliporis's sarcophagus in Bithynia towered up to six meters high and had a massive, finely worked, and inscribed altar as its base. A family sarcophagus from Nikomedeia formed, with its underlying altar base, a monument 4.18 meters high. Many of the Lycian sarcophagi still stand at their original sites; for example, impressive ensembles from the Imperial period are offered by Apollonia, Sidyma, and Kyaneai.[197] The smaller *larnax* (an urn for bones) and the *ostotheke* (a chest for bones or ashes) are related to the sarcophagus in their form and decoration.

90. Sarcophagus lid from a necropolis in Phrygia. Afyon Museum.

The poorer segment of the population buried their dead in the earth in simple caskets or clay urns.

In their wealth of forms and colors, the pillar-shaped and round altars (*bomoi*) and the mostly flat stone monuments are in no way inferior to the actual burial place, the mausoleums, chambers, and sarcophagi. Among the words used for them the most common is *stele*. The forms of *steles* also vary from one area to another, and in fact some types seem to have been favored in a given city territory, which allows us to conclude that certain workshops were dominant there. Rarer forms are the tomb cylinders in the Bithynian highland and in neighboring western Paphlagonia, or a phalloid tombstone from Daskyleion in Phrygia ([241] Pfuhl and Möbius 893). The shaft and tympanum offer surfaces for decorative or pictorial images and inscriptions; both could be chiseled in the stone by the stonemason or, less often, simply painted on. One or several story-like image fields (one over the other) and also borders and profiles show scenes, figures, objects, and decorative elements. Fixed in place by an inset stone anchor, the steles were erected in front of the tombs or, like the tomb cylinder, set atop the tumuli.

Elaborate tomb complexes had large, walled precincts where, in addition to the mausoleum and sarcophagi, altars (*bomoi*, *telamones*) with chests for bones or ashes, steles, statues, and benches (*exedrai*) could be erected. In isolated cases we even find tomb complexes belonging to wealthy landowners that included arable plots of land and gardens along with utility buildings.[198]

In the prosperous classes of society, people constructed and financed their tombs while they were still alive. Tomb inscriptions frequently describe precisely who had the right to be buried in them—relatives, foster children (*threptoi*), slaves, or friends—and in what part of the tomb they might be buried. In two-story mausoleums or in the sarcophagi with basements (*hyposorion*) typical of Lycia, the best places were on the upper level, whereas distant relatives and/or especially slaves and foster children were buried on the lower level. In several cases these regulations go back to explicit testamentary directions, and the owner reserved the right to make written changes.[199] Common ownership of *one* sarcophagus occurred as well, and ownership of tombs also could be shared by people not related to one another. Sites where extensive Imperial period necropolises can be studied in relation to the social differentiation documented by their arrangement and construction include Hierapolis in Phrygia and Anemurion in Cilicia. In Hierapolis monuments of most of the types already mentioned stand close by one another. The necropolis of Anemurion, which dates primarily from Late Antiquity, includes more than 300 tomb structures, ranging from simple barrel-arched chambers to two-story mausoleums whose interiors are decorated with mosaics and frescoes. Moreover, extensive city cemeteries are found in Termessos, Patara, Perge, and Elaiussa-Sebaste, where inscriptions with references to occupations allow us to record a broad spectrum of the urban middle class. Sagalassos has recently also been more intensively investigated.[200]

A particular characteristic of many Anatolian tombs that is relevant to the study of social history is the curses and formulas protecting against desecration of the tombs. Once built, tomb complexes were in danger of being usurped by outsiders or sold by impious descendants. The curse inscribed on a large plaque at the family tomb of a rhetor in Neokaisareia is unusually long. It makes this threat, among others:

> Whoever moves one of the bodies lying in this tomb or modifies any part of the monument by damaging it, breaking it into pieces, hammering something off or chiseling out any part of the inscription, he shall not dwell in his fatherland, the land shall bear him no fruit, he shall not sail the seas, women shall bear him no children in good physical health, himself being a violator he shall perish violently, being utterly eradicated himself, along with his children and grandchildren, his whole family, his name, the hearth of his house and the graves of his ancestors (trans. Marek).[201]

Unlike this one, many owners of tombs threatened monetary penalties that were in accord with the law concerning the crime of unauthorized use. The fine usually had to be paid to the Roman tax authorities, or occasionally also or solely to the city, and more rarely to the village community. The record fine in all of Asia Minor is demanded by an inscription on the territory of Nikaia: 130,000 denarii to be paid to the tax authorities plus 5,000 to the village community; the next-highest sum, 50,000 denarii, is found in an inscription from Aphrodisias in Caria. In Nikomedeia, a fine of 110 gold pieces is threatened; the epigram of the Christian Aberkios in Hierapolis, Phrygia, sets the sum at 2,000 gold pieces to be paid to the tax authorities and another 1,000 to the city. These are obviously particularly rich tomb complexes, but the amount demanded probably corresponds to their value. A standard measure, the most often set sum, is 2,500 denarii.[202]

People at the biological age limit of more than a hundred years are sometimes proven in ancient Asia Minor ([146] MS II 117), but there can be no doubt that the mortality rate was high among the young and middle-aged: "death is not an evil [in itself]—for this is what destiny designed—but [death] before maturity and earlier than one's parents is [an evil]."[203] What is hard to endure is the reversal of the natural succession, and reproaches are directed against the divinities of destiny, the Fates or *moirai*, and often even against the prematurely deceased themselves. The stones express mourning and ideas about death and the beyond in a conventional language borrowed from classical poetry, often in poignant detail:

> This stone barrier, traveler, already confines the handsome son of Zeno, Zenobios. At twenty-five he descended to the house of Acheron, leaving here Lamo[s?] his careworn [?] wife. This man Persephone led down to the house of Hades, loving him for his beauty and handsomeness. But he left twin [?] grief's to his dear sisters, and to his unhappy mother tears and groans. Near [?] [to his mother, *sc.*] did his brothers lay him, a great grief, and bringing no small mourning to his city. But stop your journeying, stranger, moisten your eyes with tears, and speak a greeting to those below earth.[204]

The residence of the dead, according to most epigrams, was Hades, where long night, darkness, and silence prevailed. Chthonian symbols, such as Hermes and riders, decorated many grave steles. The door steles particularly common in Phrygia are conceived as a symbol of the entry into the eternal residence of the dead (Figure 91). In his or her image, the deceased has "become stone" ([146] MS I 462; cf. III 70), but is almost always shown alive; *prothesis*—the representation of the dead as dead— is extremely rare. The chiseled inscription was recognized as serving as the deceased's voice. The deceased maintains contact with the loved ones who are still alive, and also addresses the unknown passerby, seeking to attract latter's attention to the tomb, to make him or her tarry a while and read it out loud, and sometimes make a libation. It was very popular to construct verse and prose as a dialogue between the deceased and the observer of the tombstone or others left behind.

For their part, the living, especially relatives and friends, sought at the tomb a connection with ancestors and with the recently deceased. Depictions show them mourning, sitting or standing with their left hands supporting their heads, or else raising their hands. Pulling out hair at the tomb was common, and daughters sheared their heads after their mother's death. Relatives venerated their dead as heroes, with sacrifices and offerings. The *rosalia* or *rosatio* festival, which was widespread in the western Empire, and to which, in addition to sacrifices and a banquet, the decoration of tombs with roses was central, exercised an influence on the cult of the dead in the Imperial period, especially in Bithynia. With the help of donations to associations and local communities, the regular decoration of one's own tomb or one's family tomb with roses or other flowers on certain days (e.g., on the birthday of the de-

91. Door stele. Afyon Museum ([255] Waelkens, *Türsteine*, 1986, no. 440).

ceased) was also ensured for the future. The Christian martyr cult is merely a continuation of these older customs.

Among the causes of death, illness (*nosos*) is—not surprisingly—especially often mentioned;[205] it is a theme in the "propitiatory inscriptions" discussed later (pp. 523–525), as well as in the questions the city asked the Imperial period oracle sites, after epidemics broke out. All too often birth pangs ended up being fatal for both mother and child, and lamentations over the wife who died during her confinement entered into the epigrammatic poetry of high literature (*Anthologia Palatina*, 7, 465).

There is no lack of references even to homicide and rape, though the few inscriptions do not allow us to draw conclusions regarding the general security situation.[206] Various perils on water and on land threatened to put a sudden end to life. Tombstones of sailors from Alexandria and from Bithynia who drowned at sea stand in Kyzikos and Kerkyra ([162] *IK* Kyzikos 492; IG IX 1, 884). The spectacle of animal hunts popular in the provinces led to deaths not only among the condemned victims but also among the staff: thus in Akmonia, in Phrygia, a man who cared for predators (*therotrophos*) was killed "not in the showdown in the arena, but in splendid rehearsals."[207]

Accidents killed especially children: falling out of trees, choking on a grape, poisoning, fatal injuries caused by a horse passing at a gallop or an operation by a physician.[208] A tragic report was written on a three-year-old's grave in Kolophon: a care-

92. Tombstone from Nikomedeia. Now in the Louvre.

less uncle took a child along to the water hole at the spring, where the toddler fell in. After the mother and nurse had run up and plaintively got the uncle to jump in to save the child, he was able to recover only the lifeless body ([146] MS I 365).

Regularly recurring kinds of violence included conflagrations, and especially earthquakes, which still kill people in Asia Minor today.[209] This misfortune was amply manifested in reports and references to the fate of cities and individuals in ancient literature and epigraphy. In İzmit (Nikomedeia), where one of the most severe recent quakes occurred in 1999, the tombstone of three victims once stood to recall with word and image to their shocking fate (Figure 92): the young tutor of Dexiphanes, five, and Thrason, three, had held the two children in his arms as the collapsing walls killed them all ([105] TAM IV 1, 134). Precisely this region has been struck over and over, especially hard in 358 CE, a disaster to which the orator Libanios's monody for Nikomedeia testifies.

Land Ownership, Families, Wives, Children, Foster Children, and Slaves

As elsewhere in the ancient world, in the Asia Minor of the Hellenistic and Imperial periods social status and prosperity were based chiefly on land ownership. The agricultural milieu is reflected in images and ornaments on tombstones and dedications. A beautiful image comes from Phrygia or Lydia: it shows the deceased young son of a landowner wearing a tunic and standing, with a riding whip in his hand, in front of his horse; in the panel beneath him four drinking cattle are depicted ([146] MS III 191). A stele from Kotiaion drips with agricultural opulence; we see grape tendrils, vine knives, and a servant carrying fruit in the lap of his robe; below, two round-backed oxen pull a plow with a dog standing on the shaft ([241] Pfuhl and Möbius 1136). Horses and cattle indicate membership in the upper class. Cattle were included in prayers, and stone sculptures of them were dedicated to the gods in rural shrines: after his cattle had survived an epidemic unharmed, the Phrygian landowner Sagaris erected a pair of marble oxen for Zeus ([146] MS III 413).

Most of the evidence for private ownership of large tracts of land comes from inner Anatolia: Bithynia, Lydia, Phrygia, and Pisidia. Many peasant families farmed there as tenants, most of them for generations. The landowners called them "my peasants"; in verses that two landlords in southern Cappadocia had chiseled on a rock at the boundary between their domains to celebrate their friendship, they called themselves "lords of the villages" ([146] MS III 33). In both Lycia and Mysia, the villagers seem to have systematically differentiated between simple residents and landowners.[210]

The rent or income from the surpluses produced and sold at the market allowed the lords and ladies to live like rentiers. Above a certain income level, people preferred to buy—but not always and everywhere—a residence in the city, and had themselves elected to office, as the Lycaonian Zotikos was elected a councilor in Ikonion, "proud of the number of his teams of animals and slaves" ([146] MS III 103). One level higher were the super-rich landowners: knights, senators, people prominent in public life, as we would now call them, who often had the rank of senators—for example, the stars among the sophists: Aelius Aristeides owned extensive lands in Mysia; his pupil Damianos of Ephesos also owned land, some of which bordered on the sea and was developed with artificial islands and dug-out harbor facilities that allowed freighters to sail in and out (VS 606).

A lower stratum was occupied by the numerous landowners who worked the land themselves: "To draw the rich furrows with polished ploughs, and to set up the soft fruitful cluster of the sweet vine of Bromius beneath the reedy wood."[211] The farmers' tomb inscriptions often say how arduous their daily work was. For some of them, it was hard to make ends meet.

For the great majority of people in this social stratum who lived in Asia Minor's countryside, families—the married couple with their sons, unmarried daughters, daughters-in-law, foster children, slaves, cattle, sheep, or goats, house, and land—were the center of life. Source material unique in its kind is offered for some aspects of rural life by the "propitiatory inscriptions" found in Lydia and parts of Mysia and Phrygia—especially so far as the inhabitants' "sins" are concerned. In the villages, there were conflicts between private property owners and the custodians of the countless shrines; people cursed, lied, and perjured themselves, borrowed money from their neighbors and did not pay it back, and sometimes concealed hogs that had come over from a neighbor's land, took advantage of opportunities for theft, or—as in a case in which the community (*katoikia*) intervened—broke into the house of orphaned heirs to seize documents. A slave constantly propositioned women, both married and unmarried. At that time already mothers-in-law were con-

sidered wicked, and one probably really was, because she gave her daughter's husband poison—at least according to the rumor making the rounds of the village! A
former slave freed from temple service whose son had fallen ill thought in economic
terms: she promised that if her boy got well again she would put up a stele in honor
of the moon-god, but only if there were no additional medical costs. The boy recovered, but she did not keep her promise. The divine punishment for this failure fell on
her husband and father.[212]

For farming families, marriage and children were the highest good; living single
was out of the question. Dying unmarried and without children was considered the
worst possible fate, for men as well as for women. The married happiness of a young
couple in Philadelpheia, Lydia, was destroyed by the untimely death of the twenty-
three-year-old wife before she could have children, so that the marriage chamber was
only "half finished" ([105] TAM V 3, 1896). Parents chose marriage partners for
both their daughters and their sons ([146] MS III 148). They were often sought
within a narrow circle of relatives; marriages between siblings occurred, for example,
in Cappadocia and Lycia.[213] Young men usually married in their early twenties,
whereas girls between twelve and fifteen years old were given in marriage. More than
a few inscriptions speak of remarriage for both men and women; in most cases—and
this is hardly surprising, given the high mortality rate—the first marriage had been
ended by the death of one of the partners. Adultery and divorce are seldom mentioned, but no doubt occurred: a Lycian gave his daughter-in-law the right to be
buried in the family tomb "so long as she stays with my son" ([105] TAM II 1, 53;
trans. Marek). Single mothers are to be found in urban milieus, where the verse inscription of a deceased child laments that the mother "has bestowed much more care
upon my upbringing than my father did; he left me an orphan in our home while I
was still little" ([146] MS II 53); trans. Marek).

The particular characteristics of a woman's role that are typical of the time in the
rural and urban society of Asia Minor remain largely unknown to us. Pictorial material and texts are numerous, but they conceal part of the reality in favor of idealized
archetypes borrowed from mythological and literary tradition.[214] These presented
the image required by propriety and morals. For the *communis opinio*, the marriage
bed and motherhood were the highest purpose and center of a woman's life. The
terms most often used for a wife, apart from *symbios* (life-partner) contain the word
"bed": *alochos, akoitis, parakoite, syneunos, synhomeunos*. Only Christian martyrs "ab-
horred the marriage bed" ([162] *IK* Tyana 100).

The image of woman from Homer's *Odyssey* adorns, as usual, the tombstones in
Imperial age Asia Minor. A Bithynian, Severa ([162] *IK* Nikaia 89 line 36), compares herself with Penelope, and so does a Cilician, Berus ([146] MS IV 229).[215] If
spindle, skirt, trousseau, and wool basket are depicted, and the woman is praised as
"first-rate in housework" or "leading a life that befits the mistress of the household
(*oikodespotikos bios*)," we should not conclude that in the Imperial period women
were relegated to the domain of the household. A vivid example of how things
changed in this respect can be found in Plutarch's views regarding marriage and a

woman's role.[216] The question as to why women's household utensils are far more often represented on tombstones in Asia Minor than elsewhere in the Greco-Roman world cannot be answered in gender-specific terms. In this we see once again the effort to demonstrate visible signs of membership in a Hellenized stratum of society, to "de-barbarize" oneself.

Women's names such as Euphemia ("of good reputation"), Eupraxia ("well-behaved"), Kallilogia ("elegance of language"), Tyrannis or Basilissa ("queen"), Zotike ("life-giving"), Anthusa ("blooming"), Empeiria ("experience"), Agathetyche ("good luck"), and others mirror the socially favored qualities of the daughter. In reliefs on tombstones we find depictions of jewelry and jewel-boxes, perfume bottles and make-up containers (often proffered by servant girls), combs and mirrors, carefully dressed hair in the fashion of Roman ladies, and pomegranates and/or doves as attributes of Aphrodite, symbolizing beauty, grace, and neatness. The culmination of the eternally recurring individual virtues is the perfect harmony symbolized by the wreath that the husband holds out to his wife. This wreath symbolism is combined with the metaphorics of competition (*agon stephanites*): the woman receiving the wreath is the victor in the *agon* for virtue, she wins the prize.

Unlike what happens in isolated cases in the West, where an epigram occasionally celebrates breasts and thighs,[217] no reference to the erotic or sexuality is found on women's tombstones in Asia Minor. Praise of beauty remains for the most part abstract, and similes such as "eyes like those of a cow" ([146] MS III 96) are rarely used. Women are never anywhere represented naked, but always wrapped in gowns.[218] However, erotic scenes were depicted on the tomb of a certain Menekrates in Kyzikos, which probably still dates from the Hellenistic period; the owner of the tomb excuses himself to some degree by referring to a nearby temple of Aphrodite with a statue of the famous poet Anakreon, who "knew longing" ([162] *IK* Kyzikos 520). The same epigram also expresses indirectly the social scorn for pederasty. Adages about how to live—"rejoice in the soft beds of Aphrodite!" or "Drink! Eat! Carouse! Fuck!"—are part of a long literary tradition and demonstrate both education and permissiveness (p. 170). In an entirely different context, the propitiatory inscriptions in Lydia occasionally reveal sexual transgressions committed by the "sacred slaves" (*hierodules*) in the temple precinct or of which temple slaves were the victims. Presumably these women were particularly exposed to sexual abuse.[219]

In the urban elites of the Imperial period education for women was taken for granted.[220] As already mentioned (p. 429), in Hellenistic Teos the community provided for the instruction of girls, and the Imperial period gymnasium of Dorylaion had a headmistress of the women (OGIS 479). In certain functions in which we encounter women other than those of the upper classes, the ability to read and write is presupposed. In the area of Nikaia and Prusa, Bithynian women took over the management of extensive tracts of land. These *oikonomissai* were slaves or freedwomen of the domain's owner, but enjoyed considerable prosperity themselves. Otherwise, real occupational titles are rare. From the inscriptions we know of few female physicians and philosophers.[221] However, traveling female artists repeatedly appear in the sources. The trade of "muses" is to be interpreted in the narrower sense connected with drama, dancing, and music. Female roles might be played on stage by women. A female flute player in Isauria interred by her daughter greets the audience joined to her in commemoration, "the best men" ([146] MS III 118).

The social and legal position of women in the upper classes seems to have been strong in Asia Minor. The pictorial representations do not disparage them in relation to men. Lycian women are testators and heirs, owners of plots of land, tombs, and slaves, and guardians of freed slaves. The epigraphic tradition repeatedly offers examples of wives who were superior to their husbands in wealth and status. A woman also sometimes married her *threptos* or slave.[222] We know of women who owned racing stables in Kyme; they are listed as winners in horse races ([162] *IK* Kyme 46; IG VII 417). Naturally, women also had citizenship in the polis, and a few of them were citizens of several cities. They were not members of city councils anywhere but were allowed to describe themselves as belonging to that status. They also appeared as officeholders, in accord with the general tendency among dignitaries in the *Imperium Romanum*, and even held eponymous offices:[223] being a priestess had long been one of women's roles in the public sphere of the polis. Among the numerous representatives of the female social elite in Imperial period Asia Minor, one of the most prominent is Plancia Magna of Perge in Pamphylia, the daughter of the proconsul of Pontus et Bithynia under the Flavians, a priestess of Artemis, and a benefactor of her city.[224] On the provincial level, imperial priestesses were the wives or mothers of men holding office at the same time; at this level, public display was preferably undertaken by the couple.[225] More as an honor than as an official title, Jewish women in Smyrna and Cappadocia bore the title of head of the synagogue: archisynagogos or archisynagogisa ([162] *IK* Smyrna 295 = *Inscriptiones Judaicae Orientis* II 43; ibid. 255). We will discuss the role of women in the Christian Montanist sect later (p. 544). But women took part not only in religious but also in other communal tasks. They could not be elected to the offices of *gymnasiarchos* or *agonothetes*, but rich female donors were allowed to bear the official title as an honorific in these male domains as well. For these offices' most important function—defraying costs—such women were not distinguished from the male gymnasiarchs and presidents of the games. The munificence of female donors, such as the illustrious Lalla of Tlos, was publicly praised. Women also received honorary titles (e.g., *philopolis*), gold crowns, statues, and state funerals.[226] For women active in the political arena the prosecutrix Furia Prima in Prusa may stand as an example; she indicted a philosopher named Archippos, and presented a memorandum against him to the governor (Pliny the Younger, *ep.* 10, 60).

Bringing up children (*trophe*) was considered "labor" ([146] MS II 56). Hence parents were entitled to receive compensation: people expected their children to care for them later on and to prepare a tomb for them—out of piety and dutiful reverence (*eusebeias heneken*). When there were several sons, this duty fell to the eldest. It was not always heeded, even in wealthy families, since in Bithynia a father felt it necessary to have inscribed on his tombstone, for all to see, a threat to disinherit his son if he did not bury him in the marble tomb as planned ([162] *IK* Prusias 86). To us today, some formulas seem disconcerting—for instance, when parents have their deceased four-year-old child lament: "I have disappointed my parents' benefactions" ([146] MS II 104), or when they wrote on the child's tomb: "If only Hades had carried you away from your mother right after birth and brought you to the damp demons, Hermokrates; now your mother suffers threefold pain, first the rearing, the trouble, and at present the lamentation about your death" ([146] MS II 56; trans. Marek). This does not imply any disdain for a child's life, but rather the moral duty of giving and taking firmly attached to a person's age and place in the family. The same tomb inscriptions contain numerous, occasionally gripping testimonies of parents' love for their children; thus after the loss of a child one mother sees herself transformed in other people's eyes into "stone tears" like Niobe, and begs the daemon of the underworld to return her daughter to her, at least for a short time in a dream ([146] MS I 539). Perhaps the most notable poem, from Dorylaion in Phrygia, has the moribund thirteen-year-old boy Gaianos write words of consolation to his parents on a wax tablet ([146] MS III 314).

But we also have the phenomenon of infanticide and child exposure.[227] There are many tales of exposed rediscovered children in Greek mythology and literature. Given the lack of explicit references to it in inscriptions, it is difficult to tell whether it was frequent, indeed almost common, in Asia Minor or how widespread it really was. The great number of so-called foster children, adopted children, and half-siblings, orphans, emancipated slaves, and slaves does not allow us to infer child exposure directly, even if it is clear that family members recruited these specific groups from foundlings. A religious commandment in verse, perhaps from Smyrna, forbids entry into the temple during "a waiting period of forty days after exposing a newborn" ([146] MS I 502).

Certain testimonies suggest that married couples gave one or more of their freeborn children to friends or relatives who had fewer children or none at all, and apparently not always because they were too poor to care for them, as is shown by an inscription—unusually informative in this respect—from Nikaia: a couple had seven sons, four of whom it brought up, and these are named: Alexandros, Chrestos, Musikos, and Gelasios. Three more, not named, were given away. The mother was proud to have given birth to all seven, and it was known that the three who had been given away also survived. Further references can be interpreted as indicating that this practice of giving children to relatives or family friends was not unusual: on her father's tombstone, a daughter emphasizes that he was her natural father and had also brought her up. Other inscriptions offer analogous clues: two brothers are "true sons" ([146] MS III 265); someone emphasizes that he is the father *and* progenitor ([146] MS III 271); an uncle has adopted as his daughter a girl whose parents are still alive ([146] MS III 293).

The institution of foster children (*threptoi or syntrophoi*, also *trophimoi*, Latin: *alumni*) existed throughout the country and is virtually characteristic of Asia Minor.[228] Such children can also be recognized by their names alone: Epiktesis ("acquisition," "gain"), Trophimos, Trophime, Syntrophion, Threptos, Threpte ("foster child"). In any case, *threptoi* seem to have constituted the great majority of serfs, especially in the interior of the peninsula. This serfdom is connected with old Anatolian family traditions and the forms of sacred and profane relationships of dependency. The situation cannot be understood with precision solely on the basis of the words used in our sources. For instance, we cannot always distinguish between free-born stepchildren or adopted children on the one hand, and slaves and manumitted slaves born in the house on the other. Even in the case of persons who are clearly not free in the legal sense, it is not easy to draw a dividing line between traditional Anatolian forms of serfdom and the chattel slavery customary throughout Asia Minor.[229] The terms *dulos, duleuein,* or *oiketes,* and also *apeleutheros* (manumitted slave) are established in both spheres: when Dion of Prusa (*or.* 31, 113) speaks of slaves (*duleuontes*) in inner Phrygia, he is hardly referring to chattel slaves; inscriptions from Pisidia repeatedly relate the term "emancipated slave" to "non-citizen resident" (*paroikos*) and thus suggest a connection with the legal category of the un-free with a class of the resident rural population.

Foster children, even freeborn ones, were clearly disadvantaged by their foster parents in comparison with *homogastrioi* ("born from the same belly") and could not inherit property. However, numerous statements indicate that foster children who died were not only loved and mourned but also buried in the family tomb or received from the head of the family, in some cases from their step-siblings, their own tombs. That foster children were buried in family tombs is shown by two-thirds of the inscriptions found both in the city necropolis of Kyaneai and in the highlands of central Lycia. Grown-up *threptoi* remained connected with the home of their foster parents. They worked the land as slaves or freedmen, as is made clear by the verses on the tomb of the soldier and farmer Priscus from Paphlagonia, who gave instructions to his "serfs brought up as foster children" (*threptoi georgoi*). They founded their own families, cultivated their own property, owned their own slaves, and could sometimes manage to bury their foster fathers or mothers or inter them in their own family tombs.

The dependency of farming families' activities on the "serfs" who cultivated the land may be proven by an exceptional document from Acem Höyük in Cappadocia,[230] if it is rightly interpreted. The owner of a tomb had testamentary instructions inscribed on it in which, to prevent the family from dying out, he/she forbade his/her own emancipated slaves to expose their children. The inscription threatens the worst consequences for anyone who does the former slaves and their children an injustice or harms them, offends against them, or takes away from them something the master or mistress gave them. The concern was apparently to ensure the maintenance of the lord's lands, whose future cultivation for his heirs also depended on the continued existence of the freed slave families. In contrast, the comparable testament of a landlord in Nakrason, Lydia, refers only to the care to be given his son's tomb, which he wants to ensure will be provided by his freedmen in exchange for the usufruct of plots of land that were part of his extensive estate.[231]

Threptoi were neither bought nor sold, but chattel slaves were even exported from Asia Minor. During the Imperial period, chattel slavery was widespread in both the cities and the countryside of Asia Minor. The omnipresence of male and female servants in the households of prosperous families is reflected in countless tomb reliefs, where they are represented by figures significantly smaller than those of their mistresses and masters or their children, serving or simply appearing as companions. In Asia Minor as well, people liked to name slaves after the countries they came from: "Arabios," "Persis," "Phrygis," "Syrios," and so forth. Eunuchs were a special group. Imperial law forbade castration in the provinces, but many eunuchs were imported into the empire.[232]

The Middle and Upper Strata of Society

Up to this point we have been concerned chiefly with landowners and those working in agriculture. However, in Imperial period Asia Minor there were people of all social strata below the Roman senators and knights in both the countryside and the city, whose occupation was not primarily concerned with farming. Property relationships and occupational activities were combined both in and outside agriculture. Among Anatolians living partly or exclusively from trade, crafts, and industry, people with the status of city council members were not unusual. Individuals got rich in the banking and credit systems and in inter-regional trade, especially shipowners (*naukleroi*) and merchants (*emporoi*).[233] Some of those working in the educational system, and also experts in the construction trade, law, and especially medicine belonged to the urban upper class. Artists and athletes who rise to become super-rich high-flyers are not an exclusively modern phenomenon. Among the city councilors and burghers of several cities there were men who had reached the pinnacle of society by winning victories on the worldwide circuit of athletic or staged contests (p. 498).

Like farmers, craftsmen, merchants, and tradesmen had sarcophagi and tombstones with reliefs and inscriptions made for them. But unlike farmers, they seldom chose decoration with scenes, objects, or symbols referring to their occupations. They preferred to represent themselves in the circle of the family, as citizens, spouses, and parents. Only in isolated cases do we see smiths hammering ([241] Pfuhl and Möbius 1168–1171), fishermen with tridents harpooning fish (ibid. 1129), hunters with spears cornering boars, and drivers with mule-teams drawing four-wheeled wagons. In contrast, fighting gladiators appear particularly often (ibid., plates 181–189). Pictorial elements that more or less explicitly allude to occupations are also rare, pigs referring to the pig-dealer (ibid. 1165); cobbler's knives and awls to the cobbler (ibid. 1504); compass and square to the carpenter; and chisels, cutters, and saws to the woodworker.[234]

In addition to prosperity or even wealth, education was also a means and an indication of social ascent. The capability through which the social stratum that has its say in the sources sought to distinguish itself was the art of speaking, reading, and writing Greek. A tombstone in Phrygia addresses passersby this way: "If you're educated, read on this monument for whom the memory has been engraved in letters" (trans. Marek), thus presupposing that not everyone can read ([146] MS III 250). In the homes of the wealthy, slaves supplied private elementary instruction.[235] The place where the education of youthful citizens truly crystallized was the city gymnasiums. There, girls were also educated, at least in some cities (p. 429). A small city in Mysia was able to send its sons to study with an expert on Homer ([146] MS II 92). But then as now, study did not suit all boys whose parents could afford it: a thirteen-year-old, also in Mysia, found this work with the muses difficult, so he excelled in sports instead ([146] MS II 121).

How great the proportion of illiterates was is hard to determine and probably differed from region to region. But to limit the art of reading and writing in general to the urban notables would be to disregard historical reality. The system of offices and archives in villages and rural communities speaks against such a limitation,[236] and so does the linguistic and contextual evidence of the numerous propitiatory inscriptions in the rural areas of eastern Lydia (pp. 523–525).[237] In the countryside as in the cities, we find tombstones of teachers: *paideutai, grammatikoi, didaskaloi, kathegetai*, and similarly. The *diptychon*, the scroll, and the writing case and stylus are pictorial motifs that are repeated everywhere on the tombstones of both men and boys, and sometimes of women as well, to draw attention to their education. Adults are shown reading, as in Chalkedon, where we find a twenty-five-year-old sitting in front of his servant, or in a tomb relief in Daskyleion by the Sea depicting Midias, son of Glykon, standing in front of shelves full of scrolls (Figure 93).

To be sure, the middle stratum of small farmers, like that of the craftsmen and tradesmen in the cities, straddles the dividing line so far as the ability to read and write goes. Only some of them had a knowledge of literature and could express themselves in writing. The inscriptions—even if they were (especially in the case of verse epigrams) commissioned from professionals who offered a flexible formal repertory—were nonetheless for the most part conceived by the owners of the tombs themselves or by their relatives. People knew about Homer, Hesiod, and Euripides and took pleasure in poetic attempts to use the elevated language of the classics to adorn their own milieu, virtues and standards of value, and mourning and joy. Priscus, who returned home to his paternal estate in Paphlagonia after years of military service in the Roman *auxilia*, borrowed from Homer and Hesiod to put into verse his career as a soldier and farmer, as did a merchant from Herakleia on Salbake (in inner Caria), who naturally represented his travel experiences with the third verse of the *Odyssey*: "Many were the men whose cities he saw and whose mind he learned" ([146] MS I 274; trans. Murray). This tendency is reflected, for instance, in the names fashionable in rural Lydia: "Briseis," "Chryseis," "Andromeda," "Admetos," "Alkinoos."[238] In Synnada, Phrygia, we find a man named "Aischylos" ([146] MS III 377), and a Bithynian woman was adorned by the name of the poetess Sappho ([162] *IK* Klaudiupolis 86). The display of education led to some bizarre results—for example, someone in Hadrianeia in Mysia named his cock "Plato" because he was the best singer ([146] MS II 113).

ΜΙΔΙΑ ΓΛΥΚΩΝΟΣ ΧΑΙΡΕ

93. Grave stele from Daskyleion by the Sea.
Image from Th. Corsten, *Caesarea Germanice.*
Epigraphica Anatolica 15, 1990, Tafel 5,2.

The process of Hellenization advancing in large segments of the population can be generally seen in the names given in successive generations, where the tendency is normally to move from native to Greek names. It does not always end up irreversibly in Greek, and the same goes for the relation between Greek and Latin names. Preferences can be observed from region to region, but I cannot pursue them here. For example, when men are named "Prusias," "Nikomedes," "Eupator," "Philopator," "Lucullus," and "Pompeius" or "Pompeianus" in the north, this corresponds to the fashion in Lycia of naming women "Ptolemais," "Berenike," or "Arsinoe." Since ancient times, people had been named after familiar places, rivers, and regions: Sinopis, Maiandros (or the nominal element *–mandros*),[239] Pontikos, and so forth. Nicknames were popular; in Lydian villages, for example, "Skollos" and "Kikinnas," which play on the names for hair styles that looked like cockscombs, the kind that we now call "Mohawks."[240]

In the Imperial period, the general trend in the upper classes was to readily adapt Roman nominal forms—admittedly also in families in small cities and among those who did not have the status of a Roman citizen (*civis Romanus*). This can be clearly shown, for instance, by the extensive lists of officials in the Bithynian cities of Klaudiupolis and Prusias on Hypos, the majority of whom bear names that combine Greek with Latin elements or annex the Latin suffix *-ianus* to the former (e.g., "Socratianus").

In a military career and at a certain level in civilian life (probably a fairly high level), a knowledge of Latin must have been indispensable. But was knowing "the ruling language of the world" (Themistios, *or*. 6, 71c Harduin) also a must for Greeks and Hellenized natives, Mysians, Phrygians, Galatians, Lycians, and the rest who sought social advancement? Did a cultural Romanization correspond to Hellenization at the next higher level? We do not know how widespread fluently spoken Latin was in the urban upper classes.[241] In Thyteira, in Lydia, parents put a Latin epigram on their two sons' tomb, and they buried the boys' deceased Latin teacher (*rhomaikos grammatikos*) with them. Not far away, in the Lydian metropolis of Sardeis, a marble bust of Cicero, "the most excellent of Latinists," was erected by a certain Polybios, who was probably a writer known from other sources, a high dignitary and an official ([146] MS I 403). The epigram is written in Greek. In Imperial period Anatolia, Latin as a native language was certainly spoken in numerous linguistic enclaves, but the citizens of the *coloniae* and *cives Romani* in the Greek *poleis* adapted and spoke and wrote Greek. Latin is encountered in the milieu of the imperial administration and the military, on milestones and monuments to procurators, on the tombs of Roman magistrates and their subordinate staff, and on imperial domains, in the families of their managers. Publically displayed Latin could be all the more impressive, as Theodor Mommsen once put it, because it was for the most part not understood. There are examples of Greeks using Latin as a status symbol in private inscriptions, to show that they are closely related to Roman citizens or married to Roman women, without themselves being Romans.[242] In the urban sphere, the bases of statues of the emperor, dedications to Jupiter Optimus Maximus, and tributes to the *populus Romanus* bear inscriptions in Latin or in both languages as an expression of special devotion. However, on the whole the circles and milieus in which the language of the rulers of the world dominated were limited. Even the use of Latin loanwords remained—outside the terminology of certain institutions, such as gladiator battles—less extensive than the use of Greek words by Roman magistrates.

In the eyes of other Anatolians, both Greeks and natives, the inhabitants of Italic descent formed distinct groups of "Romans." They were respected and revered, and yet even Greeks who had Roman citizenship had not completely assimilated themselves to them, but remained "Greeks." The latter, proud of their status and happy about their privileges, identified with the *Imperium Romanum* but not necessarily with Romans.[243] This was manifested especially in matters of cultural identities. An educated orator frowned on the use of Latin words, and in a decree issued by the Ionian League there was no place for a Latin word or Latin name, even if it was the name of a genuine Ionian (Philostratos, VA 4, 5). In the Imperial period, people felt connected above all to the ancient Hellenic cultural dominance over the West. However, that did not in any way signify a latent hostility to Rome, for which we have virtually no evidence.

Generally speaking, the desire to rise to the privileged status of a Roman citizen spread in the urban upper classes, but not everywhere to the same degree. Lycian notables seem to have developed little ambition to become Romans. In contrast, Anatolians were rising even to the highest positions. Pergamon had the most senators, but not the earliest ones.[244] In the early Imperial period, first generation of Anatolian senators was recruited from the aforementioned rather large group of immigrant Italics who brought with them part of their connections with Rome. Here the Augustan colony of Antiocheia in Pisidia stands out, presumably also because of its situation, which seemed predestined for extensive landed estates. Members of the Roman gens of the Sergii from this city were the first to receive, under Tiberius, "the broad stripe" (*latus clavus*)—the insignia of the senator worn on the toga—followed by other Italics under the Flavians. In the Julio-Claudian period, Akmonia in Phrygia was already the residence of a senatorial family, the Servenii. Italic clans that owned huge estates in central Anatolia were apparently concentrated in Pamphylia. Under Tiberius, the Calpurnia *gens* in Attaleia were able to supply the Senate, and under Nero the Plancii in Perge did the same. The first senators from Alexandria Troas and Apameia in Bithynia came under the Flavians. But some colonies, such as Ikonion or Kremna, lagged far behind. Future epigraphic discoveries may still surprise us; in this respect the city of Pompeiopolis in Paphlagonia, where Pompey settled veterans, would be interesting to explore. In theory, Anatolians with an Italic immigrant background had an initial advantage. But as the Hamburg ancient historian Helmut Halfmann notes, no national prejudices that would have worked against the genuine Greek upper class and favored those of Italic descent stood in the way of ascent to the highest levels of Imperial society. The decisive factors were the social, economic, and cultural presuppositions that long favored not only Italics over Greeks, but also Greeks over other Anatolians. The few families that emphasized their descent "from a princely family" (*ek basileion, ek tetrarchon*) represented to some extent an exception to this rule. C. Julius Antiochus Ephiphanes Philopappus, who came from the royal house of Commagene and was the son of the prince that Vespasian had long before driven out of the country, became a member of the Senate under Trajan. The first person from Ankyra who wore the broad purple stripe on his toga, Gaius Julius Severus, came from a connection between the royal family of Pergamon and the Galatian tetrarchs. The very first Greek who made it into the Senate, Q. Pompeius Macer, was a descendant of Theophanes of Mytilene, a friend of Pompey's.

With the broadening stream of aspirants to a seat in the Senate, an overload from the large cities in the west loomed. Small cities, such as Kibyra, Amastris, or Lydai in western Lycia, got a chance less often.[245] Not all of them were equally ambitious. The Lycians, who were rather resistant to the desire for advancement in the Empire, did not acquire their first senator, M. Arruntius Claudianus, until the end of the first century CE. From eastern Anatolia we know of only one senator, from Tyana in Cappadocia, Tiberius Claudius Gordianus, in the age of the Antonines. It was worthwhile for both small and large cities to have produced knights or even senators. The benefit gained by the town of Tripolis on the Maeander in Lydia—which attained this honor later than any of those mentioned above (in the third century CE)—took the form of beautiful buildings ([146] MS I 257). And the small city of Pompeiopolis on Amnias outdid itself in honoring the Claudii Severi: after Gnaeus's marriage to the daughter of the emperor, Annia Galeria Faustina in 162/163 CE, the archons decorated the city center with a series of statues of him. In the Artemision in Ephesos, the sophist Hadrianos of Tyros had erected a statue of Gnaeus, "for whom Harmonia herself built an imperial nuptial chamber [dedicated] to happy marriage" ([146] MS I 314). Worldly places like Ephesos, Smyrna, and Pergamon must have occasionally almost teemed with senators and celebrities. In the high Imperial period the Asklepieion in Pergamon resembled a Swiss sanatorium for the wealthy; there the sophist Aelius Aristeides met the jurist Salvius Julianus, the consuls Tullius Maximus and Cuspius Rufinus, the senators Sedatius Theophilus and Antoninus, and many other major figures in society.[246]

Through their literary work, two Bithynians became probably the most prominent senators from Asia Minor: Flavius Arrianus of Nikomedeia and Cassius Dio of Nikaia. Dio's father, Marcus Cassius Apronianus, was provincial governor of Lycia et Pamphylia and Cilicia ca. 180 CE. He himself wore the broad stripe under Commodus, later held the office of Consul, ruled several provinces (Africa, Dalmatia, and Pannonia Superior), and finally left Severus Alexander's service to return to his homeland. Disgusted by the intrigues at the court of the soldier-emperor, he wanted to complete his historical work at home, and ended it with the Homeric verse: "Hector anon did Zeus lead forth out of range of the missiles, out of the dust and the slaying of men and the blood and the uproar (Dio 80, 5, 3; trans. Cary).

Harmonies and Dissonances

By 26 CE the eleven competitors for permission to erect a temple to the emperor had been reduced to two: the ultimate victor, Smyrna, and Sardeis. The latter's emissaries in Rome presented a clever argument: they were, after all, related by blood. Of course, they could not adduce the myth of Aeneas, which was reserved for Ilion. So they resorted to the Etruscans: they claimed that sons of the Lydian king Atys, Tyrrhenos and Lydos, had divided up the once numerous people. Lydos stayed at home. But Tyrrhenos emigrated, founded new dwelling places, and thus became the ancestral father of the Italic Tyrrhenians, the Etruscans. Smyrna riposted by proposing three ancestors for debate: Tantalos, Theseus,[247] or an Amazon (Tacitus, *ann*. 4, 55, 3; 56, 1).

Two hundred years earlier in the Greek world, residents of Magnesia on the Maeander had sought the recognition of the festival for Artemis Leukophryene and sacred protection (*asylia*), and in so doing used the founding story of a certain Possis (Athenaios 7, 296 c; 12, 533 d). It can be roughly sketched, chiefly with help of inscriptions: men from the country of Magnesia in Thessaly who had gone to war against Troy (*Iliad* 2, 756–759) and had been shipwrecked on their way home, founded, at the behest of oracles, the Cretan Magnesia and then, years later under the leadership of a certain Leukippos, Magnesia on the Maeander in Asia Minor.[248] In reliefs and on the city's coins, Leukippos is depicted on horseback (his name means "white horse"), and on a coin from the third century CE he is shown standing on the prow of a ship.

Here we are dealing with a phenomenon that pertains to the society of Asia Minor as a whole. In it we find perhaps the clearest manifestation of what is usually called, on several levels, "Hellenization." Numerous Anatolian writers on local history, particularly in the fourth and third centuries BCE , constructed stories about the founding of their cities—in addition to Possis in Magnesia (*FGrHist* 480 F 1), Hermogenes in Smyrna ([162] *IK* Smyrna 536), Andron in Halikarnassos (*FGrHist* 10), and Polycharmos in Lycia (*FGrHist* 770 F 5). They proceeded in two ways: they explained the foundation of their city by weaving their ancestors into the acts of the heroes and gods in general Greek (and best of all, Homeric) mythology, or they claimed that their ancestors immigrated from Greece—and sometimes they combined these two strategies.[249] In many a theory of immigration there may be a grain of truth, whereas others are demonstrably invented. To create a myth of origin, relatively recent historical giants, such as Alexander, were also enlisted instead of heroic and divine founder-figures—proof of a conception that did not distinguish between "myth" and "history."[250]

For its recognition before the emperor and the world, a city's "good birth" (*eugeneia*), its ancestry, and the history of its establishment still had an existential significance in the Imperial period.[251] Enormous regions still had to cope with the problem of their non-Greek origin. This was particularly true of the towns, most of them in the interior, that had been settled by populations a considerable part of which was native—Mysians, Phrygians, Paphlagonians, Carians, Lycians, Galatians, and others. Although at first the emperors still avoided getting involved in these crises of self-discovery, by the time of Hadrian at the latest they began to show a strong interest in this quest for distinction, and the feverish striving that accompanied it seized almost every city throughout the country, even the Roman colonies.[252] Membership in the Athenian *Panhellenion*—which was founded in 132 CE, probably at Hadrian's behest,[253] and at whose festive ceremonies delegates from cities of genuinely Greek origin had to assemble—was connected with proof of *eugeneia*.[254]

The writings of local historians and mythographers from the Hellenistic period and also poems and verse oracles were preserved in the municipal archives. They were used by Imperial period scholars[255] and were even taken as models by Late Antique epic poets like Claudianus and Quintus of Smyrna. The jungle of diverse mythical narrative threads that led over to Asia—the Greeks versus Troy, battles with the Amazons, the voyage of the Argonauts—offered an ample choice of appropriate founding figures (*ktistai*) among the heroes vouched for by literature. Naturally, preferences were determined by geographical locations, for example on the Black Sea coast: Amisos, whose territory included Themiskyra and the Thermodon River, stamped images of warlike women (the Amazons) on its coins. The people of Sinope related themselves to the Argonaut hero Autolykos (Strabo 12, 3, 11). Others had to rely on more far-fetched connections. The Phrygian town of Otros represented Aeneas fleeing Troy with his father and son, the latter wearing Phrygian caps ([210] von Aulock, *Phrygien* I no. 787–789). Some founding figures were invented as late as the Imperial period.[256] Over time, several variants and versions that circulated simultaneously overlapped, and thus it often happens that the same hero was claimed by more than one city. Nikaia, which had a large wine-growing industry, alluded to the fact that the god of wine had seduced the nymph Nikaia, calling itself "the [city] descended from Dionysos and Herakles" (on coins from 54 CE). But Nikaia also wanted to trace its origin back to Theseus, whom Smyrna also claimed for itself (Plutarch, *Thes.* 26). The warriors Kibyras, Marsyas, and Kidramos supposedly founded cities named after them in the Pisidian-Carian-Lycian border area.[257] Synnada, Dorylaion, and Metropolis in Phrygia regarded Akamas as their founder, and Dorylaion also claimed a founder named "Dorylaios" descended from Herakles. Akmoneia was founded by Akmon, one of the Korybantes in the work of the epic poet Nonnos of Panopolis (13, 135 ff.; 28, 309 ff.); the noise of their war dance was said to have drowned out that made by the child Zeus and thus protected him from Kronos, the father of the gods, who strove to devour the child as he had his siblings.[258] The hero Dokimos founded Dokimeion, and the Lycian cities of Tlos, Xanthos, and Pinara were supposedly founded by the like-named sons of Tremiles and the nymph Praxidike (Panyassis, fr. 23 Bernabé). The hero Miletos founded Miletus, and the foundation of several other cities was connected with his family; one strand leads to Kaunos: Miletos had a son and daughter with Tragasie, Kaunos and Byblis. When the latter fell in love with her brother and confessed to him, Kaunos, shocked by her approach, emigrated and founded the town named after him.

A special form of etiology consists of etymological interpretation of the place-name in the context of myth. For instance, Tarsos is named after the sole of the foot (*tarsos*) of Perseus, Ikonion after the representation (*eikon*) of the head of the Gorgon with which Perseus petrified the Lycaonians,[259] and Temnos in Aiolis is named after an oracle according to which Malaos was to found a city where the axles of his wagon broke (*diatmethe*). Lykos is the Greek word for "wolf." The Lycaonians are named after Lykaon. On the coins of Laranda in Lycaonia, we see a wolf holding a human hand in its mouth ([208] von Aulock, *Lykaonien* no. 133). A passage in Eustathios (twelfth century) explains this by quoting an epic verse: no later than the third century CE, local poets had reworked the myth according to which the oracle spoken by Apollo to a certain Lykaon instructed him to found a city where a roaming wolf met him with a human hand in its fangs.[260]

Attica and the Peloponnese were favored by Anatolians as the homes of their ancestral fathers. Whereas the Ionian cities of Teos, Ephesos, and Priene naturally invoked Athens, other Asiatic dwellers allegedly originated from Achaeans, from the people of Argos, the Arcadians, and Spartans. Argos, Perseus's homeland, dominated the southern coast, in Cilicia (Soloi, Mallos) and Lycaonia. Alexander the Great himself is supposed to have regarded Mallos as Argive, and therefore rewarded it (Arrian, *An.* 2, 5, 9). The history of Lyrkos is woven into the legend of Kaunos to produce a connection with Argos. This is certainly based on something having to do with Rhodes,[261] because the Rhodians themselves came from Argos. Eumeneia, Akmoneia, Sebaste, and (perhaps) also Kidyessos, all of which lay close to one another in Phrygia,[262] constructed Achaean origins. A Lacedaemonian origin is also claimed in Pisidia and Kibyratis. The genealogy of Arcadian ancestors—as it is manifest in the Telephos myth in Asia Minor that became a trademark of Pergamon—was also adapted by Aizanoi in Phrygia and in eastern Bithynia by Bithynion-Klaudiupolis, where people thought they were connected with the town of Mantineia in the Peloponnese.

A Hellenistic rock inscription near Halikarnassos in Caria ([146] MS I 39) contains an unusual construct that refers both to the mythical origins of that city and the great "sons" to whom it gave birth. In the poetic narrative, part of which has unfortunately been destroyed, the Halikarnassians boldly drew on the past by locating on their territory the birth of Zeus and at the same time the emergence of the first humans. Hermaphroditos, who was born of the divinities Hermes and Aphrodite and who invented the nuptial bond between man and woman, was also brought up here by the nymph Salmakis. And there is more: visitors to this place included Bellerophontes (a Homeric hero on his way to Lycia), Kranaos (one of the original kings of Athens), and Endymion of Elis (a young man who was venerated as the founder of Herakleia by Latmos and who sank into an eternal sleep in a grotto, where Selene visited him at night). Halikarnassos also produced the "Homer of history," Herodotus; the epic poet Panyassis; and the Kyprias, who was considered the author of the first poem (in the narrative sequence) of the epic cycle; and also a series of poets listed by name.

This proud identification with great figures in literary history has numerous parallels. The Greek cities on the coast could boast philosophers, scientists, and poets of ancient times, whether they had remained in their homeland or spent their lives abroad. Sinope put up statues of the cynic Diogenes. Under Antoninus Pius (138–161 CE), Nikaia stamped the bust of the great astronomer and geographer Hipparchos on its coins. The noblest of them by far, Homer, was fought over: "Smyrna, Chios, Kolophon, Kyme, the whole of Pelasgian Hellas and the cities of the islands and of the land of Troy, all of them quarrel . . . but Zeus alone knows the place of your birth, and they are all barking up the wrong tree" ([146] MS I 598; trans. Marek), says a stone epigram in Pergamon. In the Imperial period, the small city of Amastris on the coast of the Black Sea dared to claim Homer as well in the propaganda on its coins, because the poet's homeland was alleged to be the tiny port town of Kromna on its territory.

Wherever they could, Hellenistic and Imperial period cities publicly indicated and memorably conveyed their membership in the Hellenic *koine* by means of monuments, inscriptions, and coins. Regarding *eugeneia*, a prevailing unanimity allowed the microcosms of the *poleis* to be absorbed in the cultural macrocosm of a large "family." This is repeatedly manifested by the acclaim for kinship. Particularly informative in this respect is a letter written by the *prytaneis*, the council, and the people of the Lycian city of Tlos to the community of Sidyma recommending the scholar Hieron of Tlos ([146] MS IV 26). He had given a long speech about the kinship and concord between the Lycian cities, in which he naturally delved deeply into the treasury of ancient history, where he found among other things a 129-year-old oracle of Apollo of Patara. He speaks of "the unity and concord with the people of Sidyma that has endured ever since it was created by the gods and the indigenous founders, unbroken under every circumstance, like that between children and parents, and also maintained up to the present time by marriages between inhabitants of the two cities" (trans. Marek).

Harmony among the *poleis* of the provinces was exactly what the rulers of the world wanted. The stars among the orators, Dion of Prusa and Aelius Aristeides, never tired of preaching it before city councils. But the medal of familiar concord had another side: *acerrima proximorum odia*—"all the bitter hatred that frequently exists between the closest relatives."[263] Plutarch reminded his readers that the Hellas of old, when *poleis* battled *poleis*, offered young men opportunities to distinguish themselves in war, diplomacy, or the overthrow of tyrants that were no longer available to them (*Praecepta gerendae rei publicae* 10 = *mor*. 805 a–b). In contrast to the past wars and border conflicts between cities, in the period of the Principate the Roman authorities were able to put an end to armed conflicts, and war against foreign enemies, against barbarians, was a matter for the emperor (Aristeides, *or*. 23, 3). But the craving for recognition sought a substitute.[264]

By the Flavian age at the latest, cities competed vigorously for the right to be considered a center for assemblies and religious activities standing above other cities in the same province. Status predicates expressing this claim, such as *metropolis* ("mother city") and *neokoros* ("temple guardian"), along with the permission to organize high-ranking games (*agones*), were bitterly fought over. In the province of Asia, Ephesos, Smyrna, and Pergamon were at the top. The order in which Aelius Aristeides (*or*. 23, 23) commemorated them in a eulogy was already seen by malicious listeners as a hierarchy and gave rise to complaints. Ephesos certainly stood at the pinnacle, but it was constantly concerned to ensure that the others paid this fact due respect. Ephesos complained to the emperor that the Smyrnans had omitted the title of their partner city in a decree regarding common sacrifices, and between ca. 140 and 144 CE Antoninus Pius had to appease the Ephesians by assuring them, in a letter to the officials, the council, and the people, that this had probably happened only "accidentally," and that both cities should use the correct titles of address in their future intercourse with each other.[265] In the dispute over the rights of its temple, Smyrna was able to win a victory, thanks to the emperor's high opinion of the greatly revered, recently deceased sophist Polemon, whose plea the emissaries were allowed to read out loud before the tribunal in Rome (VS 540). The Ephesians' ostentatious clarification to the effect that it was "the first and largest metropolis in

Asia" annoyed the Smyrnans, and they countered with "the first city of Asia—in beauty and in size!" In the third century the Ephesians went them one better, claiming to be "the only first ones of Asia." ([203] SNG Aulock 1909).

To the dismay of both Ephesos and Smyrna, Pergamon succeeded in receiving from Trajan a second neocorate—the custody of a second provincial temple dedicated to the cult of the emperor, for himself and for Zeus Philios, in addition to the one dedicated to Roma and Augustus—with all the associated privileges. Yielding to the complaints of the other two cities, Hadrian awarded each of them a second neocorate, and toward the end of his reign he had to reject Pergamon's request to be allowed to built a third temple for the cult of the emperor in the city.[266] Nevertheless, under Caracalla Pergamon pulled ahead of Ephesos with a third neocorate—though not for long. The coin legend pulls out all the stops: "the [city] of the Pergamenes, the first of Asia and the first metropolis and the emperor's first triple temple guardian" (BMC 318). The great province had long had other *metropoleis* in addition to these three. In fact, in the late Imperial period there was an official hierarchy in several provinces: in Asia, Magnesia on the Maeander ranked seventh ([199] Head, HN² 583); Aspendos in Pamphylia ranked third (Philostratos, VA 1, 15).

Being clearly subordinate or just second rate made cities inventive: thus Sardeis and Stratonikeia crowed about being "autochthonous." To its chagrin, the old royal seat of Gangra in Paphlagonia was forced to cede the rank of metropolis to its much younger, northern neighbor Pompeiopolis, but countered with a coin legend that read "oldest city in Paphlagonia." A stalemate could produce the same effect, as we see particularly in Pamphylia: an age-old enmity between Aspendos and Side, neighboring cities, appears to have been resolved in the Imperial period—simply to make room for a new one between Side and Perge. Rome's absurd decision to allow both of them to call themselves "the first in Pamphylia" required more subtle forms of expression. They were found in images on coins: Side had its sitting municipal goddess Athena shown being crowned by the standing Artemis Pergaia, while the Pergaians turned the relationship around on their coins: Athena crowns Artemis with a wreath.[267] Moreover, the two cities were neck and neck in the race to accumulate neocorates. Compared with the result, even the big cities of the province of Asia pale: when under Elagabal the city of Ephesos proudly announced that it was "the only one of all" to have a fourth neocorate ([199] Head, HN² 577), Perge in Pamphylia matched it, yet was still defeated: by Side, which with six neocorates held the record for the whole empire. In the second half of the third century the citizens of Perge erected a stele listing the privileges they had received from Rome, all of which were introduced by trite laudations of the city (*auxe Perge!*).[268]

In Cilicia, Tarsos, which had been the dominant "metropolis" since Augustus, was quite unpopular with the other cities, such as Mallos, Soloi, and Adana, which accused it of being overbearing and denigrating smaller municipalities (Dion of Prusa, *or.* 34, 14). Finally, Anazarbos, rewarded for its timely loyalty to Severus, managed to rise and catch up in titles. Tarsos immediately responded.[269] In the third century, both communities put on their coins—in abbreviated form, because there was not enough room for the accumulations of titles—claims to be "the first, most beautiful, biggest metropolis" and to have such and such a number of neocorates.[270]

Nowhere did this phenomenon flourish as it did in Bithynia. Since Claudius we are confronted by the paradox we found in Pamphylia: two cities, Nikaia and Nikomedeia, were "the first in Bithynia and Pontos." When under Hadrian Nikaia was also allowed to claim the title of metropolis and thus caught up with its rival, its proud citizens wrote it on the east gate of the city, with the addition "by edict of the emperor." Then the competition shifted to neocorates and games: under Commodus, Nikomedeia came to the fore when it was awarded a second neocorate and permission to organize a sacred *agon* (cf. Dio 72, 12, 2), but the same emperor withdrew both these privileges and gave the games to Nikaia, where coins were immediately struck with the legend: "Under Commodus the world is fortunate!" The good fortune did not last, because in the power struggle between the soldier-emperors, Nikaia chose the wrong side—Pescennius Niger instead of Septimius Severus—and it lost all its titles and epithets; the chisel marks erasing them from the city gate can still be seen. The victors gleefully celebrated with the malicious reply: "Under Severus the world is fortunate, and blessed are even the Nikomedeians, twice temple guardians!" In addition to these two cities, the province had two more squabblers: Prusa and Apameia (Dion of Prusa, *or.* 40, 16 f.; 41, 7 f.), which seem to have annoyed each other not with titles but with trading fees and blockades. As early as the first century, Dion of Prusa (*or.* 38, 37) perceived the pointlessness of this rivalry. He told the Nikomedeians that in Rome people laughed at all this, and that it suited the Romans just fine to pay off such fools with toys, as one would children. He tried to persuade the Tarsians that their claim to be the provincial assize city and the site of common sacrifices for the *poleis* of Cilicia had nothing to do with "domination" and that they were fighting over "an ass's shadow" (Dion of Prusa, *or.* 34, 48; trans. Cohoon and Crosby). There was also no lack of attempts on the part of the cities themselves to achieve and cultivate concord (*homonoia*). Pointed references to their union found expression in monuments, and especially on numerous bronze coins minted in common with the names of two or three cities (so-called *homonoia* mintings).[271]

In judging this phenomenon, one cannot avoid the conclusion that in general the sophists were right. Although holding judicial hearings, provincial festivals, and games might have economic advantages—we do not have a precise cost-benefit analysis for any city—the obsession with titles and prestige clearly goes far beyond the pursuit of material goals alone. We seek in vain for a merciless battle for existence behind all this,[272] because even small cities participated in the general prosperity precisely at the time when the large ones were fighting most bitterly. Wealth was not concentrated in the *metropoleis* or in the cities that had six neocorates. The Lycian "Rockefeller" par excellence, Opramoas, was a citizen of the completely backwoods town of Rhodiapolis.

Cultural Heritage and the Second Sophistic

More than half a millennium before the beginning of the Roman Imperial period, there had been a heyday of science and art in Ionia that produced great intellectual achievements unprecedented in Asia Minor (p. 133). In the following periods leadership in the Mediterranean world shifted toward Athens and Alexandria. Attalid Pergamon developed but did not catch up. Since the second century BCE, men of letters, artists, and scientists from the East (including slaves taken as prisoners of war) had been accumulating in Rome, although the capital of the rulers of the world was still unable to erode the prestige of the previously mentioned centers. With the exception of Athens, in the time after Alexander the importance of the Greek motherland declined, a tendency that grew still stronger under the Principate. The East built on its ancient cultural supremacy, even if its intellectual production in various fields never again achieved the heights occupied by its ancestors, especially the Ionians. One distinction between the orientalizing period of the seventh and sixth centuries BCE and the Hellenistic-Roman age is that henceforth the oriental part of the cultural world was primarily on the receiving end. Greek classicism relentlessly penetrated the educated classes of the cities, even in the interior. At first, in the Hellenistic and early Imperial periods, the preponderance of the Aegean coastal regions is obvious; at most, the Troad and the Propontis area were able to join in, but Lycia is strikingly poor. The countries of inner Anatolia apparently first began to gain influence with the spread of Christianity, a development that culminated in the great Cappadocians of the fourth century: the Church Father Basileios of Caesarea, Gregory of Nazianzus, and Gregory of Nyssa. For this period, Cappadocia is the best-documented country in Asia Minor. When we speak of Lycians, Milesians, or Nikaians, we must remember that the homelands or birthplaces of precisely those who became famous were seldom also the sites of their intellectual activity. Among the latter, Athens, Rhodes, Alexandria, and Rome were prominent. Without wishing to write a chapter on literary history here, I do want to call to mind a selected few of the more important Anatolians or persons with a background of Anatolian migration who appear in our sources. Because of their special status, I also examine more closely Imperial period philosophy, rhetoric, and sophistic.

Poets and Prose Authors from Asia Minor

Little of importance was created in the domain of the epic in the more than six centuries separating the Hellenistic poet of the *Argonautika*, Apollonios "of Rhodes," who actually came from Egypt, from the "continuation of Homer" (i.e., of the *Iliad*) by the late antique author Quintus "of Smyrna," whose ancestry is uncertain.[273] Noteworthy in this regard is the curious output of a certain Nestor of Laranda, who in the time of the emperor Septimius Severus (193–211) composed, among other works, a lipogrammatic *Iliad*. Statues of him on Cyprus, in Ephesos, Kyzikos, and

94. Tombstone of a "biologist" from Patara
(Lycia).

Rome testify to his fame.[274] Toward the end of the first or the beginning of the second century, the sophist Skopelianos wrote a gigantomachy (*gigantia*). Dramatists of the stature of Diphilos of Sinope, who belongs, together with the Athenians Menander and Philemon, to the outstanding trio of New Comedy in the Hellenistic age, had no successors in Asia Minor under the Principate, although new plays as well as revivals of old ones were very much in demand for the cities' periodic festivals. Mime and pantomime enjoyed great popularity in the Imperial period.[275] In the Hellenistic period, the Milesian Pyres (Athenaios 14, 620e) was one of the creators of a kind of mimed poetry in Ionic form, *ionikologoi*—verse with lascivious content that was sung by a soloist. A well-known mime of the Augustan age was Philistion,[276] who came from Nikaia or Prusa in Bithynia, and whose jokes were collected under the title "The Friend of Laughter" (*philogelos*). Martial knew him, and a bald-headed "biologist," (a stage performer, literally: one who represents to the life) Eucharistos, whose tomb epigram was found in Patara (Figure 94; [146] MS IV 37), presented his adages at festivals.[277]

Erotic poetry in various genres and with various characteristics had protagonists in Hellenistic Asia Minor, as in the case of the Ionian novella, especially the "Milesian Stories" (*milesiaka*) of a certain Aristeides of Miletus (second century BCE?), which L. Cornelius Sisenna, a Roman historian of the first century BCE, translated into Latin.[278] However, whether Aristeides was its creator or simply a collector remains an open question. An idea of its content is given by a story told in Petronius (111 f.), the "Widow of Ephesos": in her mourning for her deceased husband, a very beautiful woman with a reputation for virtue insists on following his body into the burial vault, sitting by it all day long, weeping and stubbornly refusing to eat, so that everyone in the city extols her as a model of inextinguishable conjugal love. Meanwhile, not far from the tomb, a soldier is guarding the bodies of executed thieves that are still hanging on the cross; he will pay with his life if anyone takes down one of the bodies and buries it. Having grown curious, the soldier nonetheless leaves his post to investigate a light coming from one of the tombs within sight, and finds the beautiful mourner. Using all imaginable arts of persuasion, which the widow resists for a long time until her own slave-girl—who has weakened—begins to badger her, the soldier finally gets her to eat something. Once one of the body's needs are met, it is no longer so difficult to awaken another one: the widow finally yields to the soldier, who visits her again and again in the tomb—until his self-authorized, periodic "leave" from his guard duty is noticed and exploited: one of the thieves' parents take their son down from the cross and carry him to a tomb. On seeing the empty cross, the soldier who has neglected his duty at once sees the certain prospect of his punishment by death, but the woman has an idea that saves him: it is better to give up her dead husband than to get her living lover killed; so she has the body of her husband hung on the cross.

A certain Parthenios from Nikaia or Myrleia in Bithynia, the author of a number of poems, was taken prisoner during the Third Mithridatic War and sent to Rome, where he wrote the work that has come down to us as the "Of the Sorrows of Love" (*erotika pathemata*) and dedicated it to the elegiac poet and first prefect of the province of *Aegyptus*, Cornelius Gallus. The latter probably was supposed to transform into elegant poetry these brief summaries of myths in prose excerpted from handbooks. Parthenios made a great impression in Rome; he was said to be Virgil's model, and was still widely read even in Hadrian's time.[279] The subject of love is also central to a literary genre whose disputed origins are closely connected with the name of Chariton of Aphrodisias: the novel.[280] We know little more about Chariton than that he was a rhetor's secretary; it is difficult to date him. However, his birthplace had become a flourishing city of inner Caria in the early Imperial period. Just as Chariton begins his work with the adventures of his Romeo-and-Juliet pair of lovers, Chaireas and Kallirhoe, in the Syracuse of the fifth century BCE and interweaves them with a pseudo-historical background, so Xenophon of Ephesos's novel *Ephesiaka* makes a procession in the temple of Artemis the prelude to the encounter between Habrokomes and Antheia, and the happy ending takes place on Rhodes. This Xenophon is as hard to date as Chariton is; he may have lived in the high Imperial period.[281]

Several renowned writers of the Hellenistic period came from Ionian Kolophon: the elegiac poet Hermesianax; the choliambic poet Phoinix, who produced a reworking of the already mentioned Sardanapallos epigram (p. 170);[282] and Nikandros, who dedicated a hymn to King Attalos (I or III) of Pergamon. More important are Nikandros's numerous so-called didactic poems, in which encyclopedic knowledge is presented with a claim to aesthetic form—poems on poisonous animals, agriculture, bee-keeping, *alexipharmaka* (remedies for poisoning), and other topics.[283] The work of this genre's true founder, Hesiod of Askra (ca. 700 BCE), who was also supposed to have come from Asia Minor, was an established part of a general education. Even before Nikandros, the genre had an important representative in Aratos, who came from the little town of Soloi in Cilicia (ca. end of the fourth century–middle of the third century BCE). Aratos, a many-faceted scholar and poet, went to Athens to study in the school of the Stoa, then to the court of Antigonos Gonatas in the venerable Macedonian city of Pella. Among various didactic poems, some of which deal with medicine, the ones on the stars and weather, under the title *phainomena kai diosemeia* won the greatest posthumous fame.[284] The tradition of didactic poetry was continued in Imperial period Asia Minor by Markellos of Side (on cures: *iatrika*)[285] and Oppianos of Korykos (on fishing: *halieutika*).[286]

At the beginning of the Hellenistic age, around the end of the fourth century BCE and the beginning of the third, Samos produced one of the greatest writers of epigrams: Asklepiades, the poet of the "Serenade" of the lover languishing outside his beloved's closed door (*paraklausithyron*). More than thirty epigrams deal with erotic themes.[287] Like Asklepiades, Herakleitos of Halikarnassos—a friend of the great librarian, scholar, and poet Kallimachos, who came from Cyrene and was at the court of the Ptolemies—found his place in the famed anthology "The Garland of Meleager" with a splendid poem that takes as its theme the mourning over the young woman who died in childbed (*Anthologia Palatina*, 7, 465).[288] The Augustan author of epigrams Krinagoras of Mytilene knew how to ingratiate himself in Rome by paying poetic homage in court circles.[289] A Bithynian named Demetrios wrote poems about Myron's cow (*Anthologia Palatina* 9, 730 f.), and the subject of the high Imperial period author Straton of Sardeis (Books 11–12 of the *Anthologia Palatina*) is pederasty: "What delight, Heliodorus, is there in kisses, if thou dost not kiss me, pressing against me with greedy lips, but on the tips of mine with thine closed and motionless, as a wax image at home kisses me even without thee?"[290]

We may also mention as a peculiarity from Asia Minor the Imperial period Orphic hymnbook that collects eighty-seven poems to various divinities, including the *meter Hipta* (nurse of Dionysos) so prominent in Lydian propitiatory inscriptions, and Mise, Hellenized old Anatolian goddesses from the group around Kybele. The author is not known, but it may be from a community's "songbook."[291] In the land of the father of history, Herodotus, Hellenistic and Imperial period historiography can boast a series of evocative names: Duris of Samos (*FGrHist* 76) and Hieronymos of Kardia (*FGrHist* 154), who wrote their works in the time of the Diadochi, and the Cnidian Agatharchides, from the second century BCE (*FGrHist* 86). The Anatolian Greeks Theophanes of Mytilene (*FGrHist* 188) and Metrodoros of Skepsis (*FGrHist* 184) wrote respectively about the deeds of Pompey and those of the kings of Pontos and Armenia, Mithridates and Tigranes. In the age of Augustus and Tiberius, Strabo, who came from Amaseia in Pontos and is known to us through his *Geography*, also attempted a large work of history in forty-seven books that was supposed to continue the work of Polybius (*FGrHist* 91).

Out of the veritable flood of regional and city histories, mythographies, and miscellanies that streamed from Anatolians' literary production into the Hellenistic and the Imperial ages, I mention here only a few. In the fourth century BCE Menekrates of Xanthos wrote about Lycia (*FGrHist* 769); Eratosthenes's pupil Menandros of Ephesos (ca. 200 BCE) translated the old records of the Tyrians in Phoenicia (*FGrHist* 783); and Demetrios of Skepsis (second century BCE) framed the history of his homeland, the Troad, as a commentary on the catalog of the Trojans in the *Iliad* (2, 816–877). Demetrios's rejection of the idea that ancient Ilios was located near the city of Ilion of his own time and his denial of the origin of Rome in Troy are remarkable: Aeneas, he says, did not survive the Trojan War.[292] From Ilion itself came Polemon, a learned and prolific author of the first half of the second century BCE. He was an antiquary and a collector of inscriptions who wrote about the foundation of cities, religiously significant places and objects, "marvels," and much more.[293] Alexandros the "polymath" (*polyhistor*) from Miletus wrote about everything imaginable, especially the peoples and regions of the Near East (among others, the Jews). Like Parthenios, he had been enslaved during the Third Mithridatic War; manumitted in Rome, he won renown there (*FGrHist* 273). The fifty narratives of the mythographer Konon, including some about the founding of cities, were dedicated to Archelaos Philopator of Cappadocia (36 BCE–17 CE). Konon may have come from Asia Minor. The homeland of Pausanias, the author of the famous Imperial period "travel guide" from the third quarter of the second century CE—ten books describing Greece, with mythological, geographical, and historical excurses— is not entirely certain; presumably it was Magnesia on Sipylos.[294] The miscellany compiled by Hadrian's freed slave, Phlegon of Tralleis, was the source of a collection of "marvels," including discussions of "wonderful things and long-lived people" (*FGrHist* 257) that became famous.[295]

Imperial period historiography in Asia Minor did not lag behind its Hellenistic predecessors, such as Dionysios of Halikarnassos (ca. 60–8/7 BCE), who wrote about older Roman history. It is represented by two great figures from Bithynia, the Roman senators Flavius Arrianus from Nikomedeia and Cassius Dio from Nikaia. Arrian's literary work was not limited to his famous history of Alexander and the Diadochi. Specialized treatises on tactics and hunting; a *periplus* (sailor's handbook) of the Black Sea coast; the *ektaxis* (deployment of the army) against the Alans; Bithynian and Parthian history and geography; and biographies of Timoleon, Dion, and the brigand Tillorobos reveal this officer as a many-sided researcher. Between 131 and 137 CE he spent several years in Cappadocia as governor and had a main residence not only in Rome but also in Athens, where he was a citizen. For ten years his compatriot Cassius Dio (ca. 164–after 229 CE), who came from an aristocratic family of Nikaia,[296] collected materials for his Roman history from the beginnings down to his own time, and then spent twelve years writing it. He too spent most of his life in Rome.

Grammarians—today, we would call them linguists—can already be found in the milieu of philosophers, such as the Stoic Antipatros of Tarsos (second century BCE).[297] Strabo considered Krates of Mallos, a philosopher at the court of Pergamon in the second century BCE, to be one of the greatest.[298] Other Anatolians of this ilk are Aristodemos of Nysa (second century BCE); Asklepiades of Myrleia (second/first century BCE); and Tyrannion, who came from Amisos, studied with the famous Dionysios Thrax, and was Strabo's teacher. Enslaved in his homeland in the year 71/70 BCE, he came to Rome and met Caesar and Cicero, whose nephew he tutored. In the family of Aristodemos—another of Strabo's teachers—there were several grammarians, and his cousin taught Pompey. He himself taught in Nysa and on Rhodes, supposedly rhetoric in the morning and grammar in the evenings (Strabo 14, 1, 48). Under the Principate we may name two Nikaians: Apollonides, who dedicated to the emperor Tiberius his commentary on the mocking/acerbic sayings of the skeptic Timon of Phlius, and Epitherses, who wrote, at about the same time, a study "On Comic and Tragic Figures of Speech in Attic."

In the sciences, Anatolians shone in the fields of mathematics, astronomy, geography, and medicine. Theodosios of Nikaia (second/first century BCE) composed the oldest Greek work on the geometry of the sphere (*sphairika*) and is considered the inventor of the sundial.[299] The city of Amisos on the Black Sea can boast two important mathematicians of the Hellenistic period, Dionysodoros and Demetrios, son of Rhatenos.[300] The astronomer Apollonides (ca. 200 BCE), the founder of the so-called epicycle theory of the orbits of the moon, sun, and planets, came from Perge in Pamphylia. The achievement of Aristarch of Samos (ca. 310–230 BCE), a pupil of the Peripatetic Straton of Lampsakos, can hardly be overestimated: he taught heliocentrism centuries before Nicolaus Copernicus established this theory in early modern Europe.[301] We know about this only through Archimedes (*Aren.* 1). Aristarch's only known work is titled "On the Sizes and Distances of the Sun and Moon." His compatriot Konon, a friend of Archimedes, was active in Alexandria as an astronomer and mathematician, and famous chiefly because he claimed to have found the lost "lock of hair belonging to Berenike," the wife of King Ptolemaios III Euergetes, in a heavenly constellation.[302] In the time of the Antonines, Nikaia, the home town of the illustrious astronomer and geographer Hipparchos (second century BCE)— who had quite accurately calculated the distance of the moon (33-2/3 diameters of the Earth)—was still proud of him.[303] In these fields, the Imperial period has less to offer. Under Hadrian, the Smyrnan Theon was a mathematician who left us a textbook titled "Introduction to the Mathematical Understanding of Plato."[304]

Geography as an exact science was the strength of neither the (lost) *geographumena* of Artemidoros of Ephesos (ca. 200 BCE) nor the geography of Strabo of Amaseia. The latter's work counts, along with those of Herodotus, Dion of Prusa, Pausanias, Galen, and Cassius Dio, as among the most wide-ranging extant works by Imperial period writers. Strabo, a Greek with Iranian relatives, had studied rhetoric and grammar with Aristodemos and Tyrannion, and had also been introduced to Stoic philosophy. His travels were punctuated by lengthy stays in Rome and Alexandria; we owe to his friendship with the prefect Aelius Gallus, whose campaign from Egypt to southern Arabia in 25 BCE failed, the most detailed ancient description of that distant land (today's Yemen) in the sixteenth book of his *Geography*.

Chalkedon on the Propontis was the birthplace of Herophilos (ca. 330/320–260/250 BCE), who was probably the greatest physician of the Hellenistic period.

His teaching remained influential down to the Renaissance. He was the first to locate the center of the nervous system in the brain rather than in the heart, like Aristotle. He is supposed to have dissected not only corpses but also living people (convicts). Herophiles probably spent most of his life outside his homeland, in Alexandria.[305] The physician Asklepiades, who influenced the science of medicine throughout Antiquity, and especially the "Methodic school," was born in Kios (Prusias on the Sea) on the eastern end of the Propontis. He lived in the second and early first century BCE and achieved success in Rome;[306] his pupils were Themison from Laodikeia and Thessalos from Tralleis.[307] Athenaios of Attaleia (first century BCE) is considered the founder of the "Pneumatic" school, which taught that the true bearer of life was a warm breath, *pneuma*, that resided in the heart.[308] His sphere of activity also lay in Rome. In contrast, Rufus of Ephesos appears to have practiced in his homeland; in the first century CE he wrote, among other works, a treatise on kidney and bladder problems.[309] Tertullian (*anim.* 6, 6) names Soranos of Ephesos as "the best-informed writer of the Methodic school of medicine." After studying in Alexandria, this important physician also came to Rome in the early second century CE, and there made a name for himself. His main area was gynecology. From his work "On Women's Diseases" a manual for midwives in question form (*gynaikeia kat' eperotesin*) was probably extracted only later.[310] That some doctors could lose their reputations as healers in wealthy circles and then have to find a new field of activity in the provinces is shown by the example of the unfortunate Pergamene Philiston, who lived ca. 170 CE: A woman for whom he had prescribed hot squid as a remedy for infertility, fell unconscious as a result of this therapy.[311] Philiston's compatriot Galen (ca. 129–200) became one the most outstanding physicians of the Imperial period. He began his study in his homeland, where the widely esteemed "sanatorium" of the Asklepieion was located, and continued it in Smyrna and Alexandria. Having returned to Pergamon, he practiced for several years as a physician at the school for gladiators run by the archpriest of Asia before going to Rome in 162 CE. He returned once more from Rome to Asia Minor, supposedly to escape the plague that was raging in Italy, but soon thereafter went back to Italy again to serve as the personal physician of Prince Commodus and the Emperor Marcus Aurelius. He wrote more than 150 works, carried out studies in other areas, and was particularly interested in philosophy in connection with medicine.[312] An extensive body of his texts is extant. Galen's influence was concentrated in Late Antique Alexandria. The connection between medicine and philosophy also appears in the work of the Lycian Herakleitos of Rhodiapolis (first-second century CE), who was frequently honored not only in his home town but also in Alexandria, Rhodes, and Athens. He was respected as a physician and a philosopher, and the philosophers of the Epicurean school in Athens called him a "Homer in the area of medical writing" ([105] TAM II 3, 910).

Outside the circle of these disciplines and also of medicine stands the Imperial period author Artemidoros of Daldis in Lydia (second century CE?). Daldis was his mother's birthplace; he himself was born in Ephesos.[313] His book on dreams (*oneirokritikon*) was conceived as an introduction to professional interpretation and is based on a systematic analysis of dreams. Superficially, he might be seen as an antique Freud; in any case, he saw himself as a scientist.

Philosophy, Rhetoric, and Sophistic

The writer Lucian of Samosata (ca. 115–190 CE), a Syrian who had traveled widely, an expert on Asia Minor, and an acute observer of his time, projected the wedding celebration in mythology that eventuates in a battle between Centaurs and Lapiths (*Odyssey*, 21, 295–303) into a burlesque setting in the Imperial period: the *Symposium, or the Lapiths*. There are philosophers everywhere, fighting with one another, but no philosophy. A normal, clear-thinking, reserved man—this is the story's moral—puts himself in peril when he sups with philosophers. The dialogic framework at first suggests an association with Plato's *Republic*—we are ultimately referred to a certain Lykinos (in whom Lucian is, as in other works, not difficult to discern) as a witness to an unheard-of event—so unheard of, that he hesitates a while before telling us about it.

In the house of the noble Aristainetos, the wedding of his daughter Kleanthis is being celebrated. The girl's name suggests, as does that of her brother Zeno, her father's philosophical training. It is a marriage of education with wealth, because the young groom is the son of a banker. The whole spectrum of academic philosophy appears at the banquet, and first of all the illustrious Stoic Zenothemis, and then Diphilos, called "the Labyrinth," the teacher of Aristainetos's son Zeno, as well as Ion, a Platonist and the groom's teacher, known as "Canon"; when he arrives, everyone rises as a sign of deep respect. The Peripatetic Kleodemos, nicknamed "Butcher Knife," also enters, followed by Hermon the Epicurean, from whom the Stoics immediately turn as if from one accursed, and finally Histiaios and Dionysodoros, a grammarian and a rhetor. The women, including the bride, take their place at the right of the entrance, opposite the father and the father-in-law. The seating plan is at the same time a pecking order: conflict immediately breaks out, but finally the old Stoic takes the best seat; at the bottom end of the table sit the rhetor and the grammarian.

As soon as the starters are brought in, the Stoic's greed becomes evident—he also serves his slaves who stand behind him. Then another, uninvited guest comes in: Alkidamas, an adherent of that school of Cynics that others generally regard as grubby urchins: they stand on streetcorners, at the gates to temples, and so forth and address themselves to rowdies, sailors, and other scum and impress people with gossip, vulgar mockeries, and rhetorical illusions (Dion of Prusa, *or.* 32, 9). Alkidamas excuses his impudence in inviting himself to the party with a quotation from Homer: "Menelaos comes of his own accord" (cf. Plato, *Smp.* 174c). He rejects as an impertinence the seat the host assigns him, at the bottom of the scale of value, and shrewdly chooses to wander about, "like nomads on the lush pasture ground," scooping up the delicacies the servants are bringing round. As he does so, he repeatedly condemns the luxury of the table, until the others, annoyed, shut him up with a big cup of wine,

with which he sinks down to the floor. One of the servants, a pretty slave boy, has to
be replaced after it has been noticed that Kleodemos, the Peripatetic, is trying to se-
duce him. The rhetor Dionysodoros's declamations are applauded only by the servants, and the grammarian Histiaios also seems ludicrous when he sings a pot-pourri
of verses from Pindar, Hesiod, and Anakreon. The party grows lively only gradually.
A clown (*gelotopoios*) brought in by the host imitates the Egyptian language.[314] But
then a certain fretfulness unexpectedly seeps in that reminds us of Eris, the goddess
of discord who in her anger at not being invited to the wedding of the goddess Thetis
and the hero Peleus, initiated the Trojan war. The uninvited Stoic and neighbor He-
toimokles has a messenger read out his complaint: that he has been disdainfully
overlooked, whereas in his place the table is ornamented by such "wonderful" Stoics
as Zenothemis or "the Labyrinth," whose big mouths he could stop with a single syl-
logism, and this is proof of the host's poor judgment. As a sign of apology, he should
be given roast pork and cakes: not that he would take them, for that could make it
look like he had sent the slave for that reason alone! Whereas the host, Aristainetos,
is painfully moved, a few guests are still laughing. Only the Peripatetic Kleodemos
explodes with anger: "Butcher Knife" hurls nasty abuse not only against the author
of the letter, but also against the asshole-philosophers of the Stoa in general. This is
too much for Zenothemis; he and Kleodemos exchange invectives, and when it escalates to spitting and throwing punches, Aristainetos intervenes. The Platonist Ion
offers to lure the group back to the dispassionate sphere of philosophical dialectic.
He does not want to overstrain the representatives of other schools, and chooses a
light but suitable theme: marriage. It is better, he proposes, to forgo marriage and
give preference to pederasty. But if women are needed, then they should not be mo-
nogamous, but rather "fair game" for all! Amusement returns—except for the
women, presumably—but only for a short time, because the rhetor ventures to criti-
cize the lofty Platonist's use of words. When the main course arrives, the seating arrangement proves fatal: each pair of guests has to share the portion on a single tray.
The old Stoic Zenothemis and his neighbor Hermon, the Epicurean, get into a battle
over the fatter of two chops, and the other guests, taking sides, join in. It begins with
the philosophers pulling each other's beards and escalates to serious physical assault
when the groom is hit on the head by a bottle meant for Hermon, and Kleodemos
gouges out one of Zenothemis's eyes and bites off a piece of his nose. The Stoic's
howls contradict his alleged indifference to pain. The women run around screaming.
After urinating in front of everyone, Alkidamas the Cynic brings the brawl to its
peak, hitting out at each and all until the lamp-stands are knocked over and everything goes completely dark. When the lamps are relighted, the room reveals an em-
barrassing scene: a bottle falls out of Dionysodoros's cloak, and Alkidamas is un-
dressing a flute-player. The party ends with the wounded being carried off, and only
the Cynic, Alkidamas, remains behind, stretched out on a couch sound asleep.

These outrageous caricatures are certainly not to be interpreted on intertextual
levels alone; the narrator presents us with a distorted image of the performance of
philosophy in the large and small cities of the Imperial East. Naturally, the philo-

sophical schools with the leading professorships had many little offshoots and emulators in the provinces. What went on in the schools and learned circles of the cities contained no less potential for pointless conflict than the battles over titles, imperial temples, and noble descent. Lucian may have been moved to compose his malicious tales by pent-up scorn for what he had personally experienced and observed on the contemporary scene. In his dialogue *Hermotimos* he once more pursues *ad absurdum* the aspirations of an adept of elite academic philosophy.[315]

Once again, stones offer valuable testimony. Among their relief depictions is the memorable, unsurpassed image of a sitting philosopher in Smyrna pointing with his staff to a skull ([241] Pfuhl and Möbius 847). All up and down the country Platonists, Peripatetics, Stoics, Epicureans, Cynics, and Neo-Pythagoreans taught the young in exchange for pay, held offices, founded schools, and networked. Cities were "nests" of one or another school, and in the larger cities several schools competed. Teaching focused on moral philosophy; the mathematical and scientific skills of the school founders in classical Athens or of a Eudoxos of Knidos in Asia Minor had receded into the background. Everything suggests that the Stoics were the largest faction. They could boast important men who came from Asia Minor: Kleanthes of Assos (ca. 331/330–230/229 BCE), the second head of the school, and Chrysippos from Soloi in Cilicia (third century BCE), of whom Galen said that he first really learned Greek in Athens (SVF 2, 24.894), or Epictetus from Hierapolis in Phrygia (ca. 50–125 CE). In the Imperial period, Stoics were dominant, for example, in Prusa in Bithynia: here Dion was born, and Publius Avianius Valerius was honored by the council and the people. His relative, the philosopher Avianius Apollonios, erected a statue of another member of the family, the Stoic Titus Avianius Bassus Polyainos, and still another, Claudius Polyainos, bequeathed his house to the emperor Claudius. More remote parts of the country did not lag behind. A philosopher whose gilt statue was put up in the mountain town of Kremna in Pisidia can be recognized as a Stoic by his surname, Chrysippos ([146] MS IV 112 f.). In an eighteen-verse rock epigram another Pisidian teaches passersby that true freedom comes from inside, from one's character, not from one's ancestry. The proof: Epictetus, who was born a slave and was physically handicapped, became a "godlike man" (*theios*) ([146] MS IV 121).

To show that Epicureanism remained alive in the Imperial period, the example of Diogenes of Oinoanda is often adduced. In the little mountain town of Oinoanda this Epicurean—his lifetime probably bridged the first two centuries of the Imperial period—had the master's doctrine inscribed on a large building or wall to make it literally closer to his fellow citizens.[316] Another Lycian, Herakleitos of Rhodiapolis (first-second century CE), the previously mentioned "Homer of medical writing" and philosopher, appears to have been an Epicurean. A high priest of the commonalty, Tiberius Claudius Lepidus (second century CE), taught Epicureanism in the Pontic town of Amastris on the Black Sea and drew together there a large number of followers. He was deeply odious to one of his contemporaries in nearby Abonuteichos, the Pythagorean Alexandros (p. 521). A personal friend of the Platonists and

Stoics, Alexandros persecuted the neighboring city's school of philosophy so rabidly that he had the scrolls with the *kyriai doxai*, the philosopher's main teachings, burned in the *agora*. If this philosophy had not still had a strong influence deep in the provinces in the time of the Antonines, this sort of thing could hardly be explained. Epitaphs like that of a certain Menogenes from Apameia Kibotos testify to the vitality of Epicurean thought in Anatolian cities ([146] MS III 172).

Of course, the realms of the philosophical Diadochi and Epigones did not have sharp borderlines. Doctrinal contents sometimes mixed or overlapped, precisely in the Imperial period. In any case, Plato was a "father figure" for philosophy, and neo-Pythagoreanism was really a kind of neo-Platonism.[317] In Ephesos, on the base of a statue of Ofellius Laetus, a Platonist who is also mentioned in Plutarch, we read that in him, Plato lived again ([146] MS I 315), and on the bust of the aforementioned mathematician, Theon of Smyrna, we find the inscription: "Platonic philosopher" (Figure 95). The neo-Pythagoreans referred to apocryphal texts falsely attributed to the old Pythagoras of Samos. The most prominent figure active under this banner in Asia Minor is no doubt Apollonios of Tyana, a guru, preacher, and wonder worker of the first century CE who tried to relive the legendary master's life. In what he did and what was imputed to him, we can see many parallels to Jesus Christ (p. 523). The young Alexandros of Abonuteichos—the famous neo-Pythagorean to whom we shall turn below—was close to a pupil of Apollonios. Having become famous as the founder and priest of the oracle on the Black Sea, in nocturnal processions Alexandros displayed his golden thigh in the torchlight, and presented himself as the reincarnation of the divine sage Pythagoras. Individual followers of the master are also recognizable in inscriptions. In the Lydian Philadelpheia, the symbol of the Pythagorean way of life adorned the tombstone of a man of "innate wisdom" who was also named Pythagoras ([105] TAM V 3, 1895). And a provincial philosopher in Kyzikos claimed that by using the Pythagorean doctrine, he could calculate the date of his own death ([146] MS II 47).

The basic discipline for all higher education was, as everywhere in the empire, rhetoric. Philosophy and rhetoric "claimed the whole of culture for themselves,"[318] and the latter was even more successful than the former. The Hellenistic author Hegesias of Magnesia (*FGrHist* 142) is considered the founder of the so-called Asiatic style—scorned as bombastic and overly ornate. Regarding him, Cicero (*orat.* 226)— who was himself trained in the late Hellenistic school of rhetoric on Rhodes—says that one needs to search no further for an example of a lapse in taste. He criticized two qualities of Asianism in particular—and he names a whole series of Asiatics— first, its vain, superficial play with ideas, and second its pathos:

> Of the Asiatic style there are two types, the one sententious and studied, less characterized by weight of thought than by the charm of balance and symmetry. Such was Timaeus the historian; in oratory Hierocles of Alabanda in my boyhood, and even more so his brother Menecles, both of whose speeches are masterpieces in this Asiatic style. The other type is not so notable for wealth of sententious phrase, as for swiftness and

95. Theon of Smyrna, Platonic philosopher. Capitoline Museums, Rome.

impetuosity—a general trait of Asia at the present time—combining with this rapid flow of speech a choice of words refined and ornate. This is the manner of which Aeschylus of Cnidus and my contemporary Aeschines of Miletus were representatives. (Cicero, *Brut.* 325; trans. Hendrickson)[319]

Caecilius of Caleacte (born ca. 50 BCE), who came from Sicily, the birthplace of rhetoric, and whose teacher, Apollodoros of Pergamon also taught Augustus, attacked the Asiatic style in a work titled "Against the Phrygians. How the Attic Style Differs from the Asiatic Style." The slogan was: "Back to the old models and masters of Attica." Rigorous form and purism won the prize. The great Atticist of the second century CE, Herodes, called the style of an Asiatic writer "drunken." Handbooks with lists of words and expressions that were proven to be Attic and recommended for use (Athenaios 1, 1e), were brought out, along with treatises on style and content. In the time of Hadrian, the Halikarnassian Aelius Dionysios collected Attic glosses. Hermogenes of Tarsos (born ca. 160 CE) published a manual of style and wrote on the use of the forceful style (*peri methodu deinotetos*). In the late third century CE the rhetor Menandros, from Phrygian Laodikeia, wrote treatises on exemplary speeches of various types and on various themes.

Since the "pure" model of such an idiom was as much as 700 years old, it had to be learned like a foreign language. One can imagine the efforts this demanded: the sophist Polemon astounded a governor who was reflecting on choice methods of torture for a felon by advising him to make the criminal learn something archaic by heart (VS 541). The training of sons began early, at about the age of fifteen. A student from Germania died in Ephesos at the age of twenty after studying for five years

([146] MS I 342). In contrast, the sophist Hermogenes of Tarsos is said to have been so respected at the age of fifteen that Emperor Marcus Aurelius wanted to hear him (VS 577). People left their homelands to get an education and liked to go to the great schools—thus students from Nikaia and Prusias on Hypios went to Ephesos and Athens—or, depending on their financial resources, only to nearby schools, like a young man from the town of Agrippeia who went to Klaudiupolis in Bithynia.

In the provinces, the widespread cultivation of the art of speaking was nourished by the competition in everyday political life particularly in the city councils.[320] The numerous judges, notaries, and lawyers had to be trained in rhetoric before they focused on their particular disciplines.[321] They were employed everywhere, from the municipal administration to the staffs of the provincial and the imperial administrations. Careers begun in rhetoric could lead to legal scholarship and politics. The sophist Quirinus, who came from a middle-class family in Nikomedeia, worked his way up to become an *advocatus fisci* of the imperial administration and exercised great power. A young man from the mountain town of Kolybrassos in Isauria advanced first to a position on the procurator's staff in Palestine, took a (presumably higher) one in the north Syrian metropolis of Antiocheia, and then "the splendid metropolis of the Bithynians received me," which means that we have to imagine him holding there a post at the seat of a Roman magistrate, presumably the governor. Later he went to work as assessor for a prefect in Thebes, Egypt ([195] SEG 26, 1456).

The interior of the country, and especially the east—Galatia, Pontos, Cappadocia, and Cilicia—were ridiculed as backward. In the third century CE, Philostratus said that the Cappadocians spoke Greek badly, mixed up consonants, and made long vowels short and short vowels long (VS 594). The sophist Pausanias's accent was so rebarbative that people called him a cook who spoiled the most precious delicacies by the way he prepared them. It was precisely the fanatical purists from the provinces where barbarian languages were spoken who were eagerly on the watch for a false note, a poorly chosen word, a slip in Attic. The greatest sensitivity erupts in lampoons like Lucian's *Pseudologista* (14), in which the Syrian insults his critic by telling him that apparently only a barbarian language like Cappadocian, Paphlagonian, or Bactrian is really understandable to him and pleasing to his ear.[322]

Above the professional rhetors a few masters, who were called sophists, played in a special league. They could be called star speakers, the kind the German philologist Ludwig Radermacher called "concert orators" (*Konzertredner*). As a rule, the sophists and rhetors—in contrast to professors at philosophical schools—went on lecture tours. They taught in exchange for money, and some of them adjusted their fees in accord with the financial means of their pupils. Chrestos of Byzantion had one hundred pupils who paid him for their lessons. The professorships of rhetoric sponsored by the emperor in Athens and Rome were coveted; the annual salary for the one in Athens was 10,000 drachmas (VS 591). But sophists were also called "philosophers" (*philosophoi*); they adhered to philosophical schools, and their oratorical art naturally made use of philosophical themes.

Although in the Imperial period an intellectual trend in this field consolidated precisely in Asia Minor, the so-called Second Sophistic, its significance lay less in its literary production than in the social and political role its representatives played.[323] Regarding the question of the role of the intellectual in society, which can be raised for all periods, the sophistic of the Imperial period imposes itself as a domain where the prerogative of interpretation ruled, where terms and conceptual models circulated that served to justify public and private behavior. To that extent the sophists' teachings and speeches were anything but art for art's sake. The famous figures represent only the highest level of a deep movement. Their names stand for the rise to status, office, power, and privileges by means of education. As professors and writers at the *museia*, as orators and teachers of the youth in the cities and as the tutors of princes at the court, as emissaries of their communities, and as advisors and friends of governors and emperors, they influenced the policies of councils right up to the monarchs in Rome.[324]

This phenomenon was in no way limited to Asia Minor, and not even to the eastern part of the Empire, and yet with regard to the motherland the cities of Anatolia had a significantly greater influence that could not be matched by the Egyptian metropolis of Alexandria or the Syrian metropolis of Antiocheia, but only by Athens. Various cities, both large and small, are presented as the birthplace of the sophists: Phokaia and Klazomenai in Ionia, Hadrianoi in Mysia, Hierapolis and Laodikeia in Phrygia, Perge in Pamphylia, Seleukeia on Kalykadnos, Aigai and Tarsos in Cilicia, as well as others. Among the places where they resided Athens, Smyrna, and Ephesos clearly stand out; in the third century, Nikomedeia, Nikaia, and finally Byzantion acquire importance.

There is no doubt as to which city in Asia Minor stood at the top: "Smyrna, which more than any other city sacrificed to the sophistic Muses" (VS 613, cf. 516; trans. Wright). The Klazomenian Skopelianos went to Smyrna, refusing his home town's request that he not leave it, saying that a nightingale needed not a cage but a grove (VS 516). The Lycian Herakleides also moved to Smyrna when an intrigue drove him out of a professorship in rhetoric at Athens that he had held from ca. 193 to 209. If one came to Smyrna by ship, as did the Thessalian Hippodromos of Larisa (end of the second/beginning of the third century), went to the agora and looked around, he saw in front of the temple of the Museion a line of book-carrying *paidagogoi* who were taking their boys to be instructed by an illustrious master (VS 618). A few stars attracted to Smyrna youths not only from Ionia, Lydia, Phrygia, and Caria but also Cappadocians, Syrians, Phoenicians, and Egyptians; indeed, even "Hellenes" from Greece. The fact that the eyes of half the world were on it, Philostratos said (VS 613), obligated the city to behave well and maintain a beautiful appearance. The sophists Polemon and Aristeides also obtained generous investments: Hadrian gave Polemon a whopping 10 million drachmas, which he used to build a grain market, a gymnasium, and a temple (VS 531), while Marcus Aurelius was so moved by Aristeides's speech (*or.* 18) lamenting an earthquake's destruction of

Smyrna in 178 CE that he promised to provide the means to rebuild the city (VS 582).

The great majority of the sophists came from the urban upper classes, and most of them had Roman citizenship. We can trace the ancestors of Polemon of Smyrna through the kings of Pontos back to Chairemon, the friend of the Romans who helped organize the resistance to the Asian army during the First Mithridatic War. Few of the sophists held offices. The philosopher C. Aurelius Flavianus Sulpicius was a galatarch in Ankyra. In addition to the *advoctus fisci* Quirinus, Alexandros of Seleukeia and Antipatros of Hierapolis are also mentioned as holders of imperial posts; both were secretaries of the imperial chancellery *ab epistulis Graecis*. Antipatros also served as governor of Bithynia until he was recalled because of his excessive imposition of capital punishment. Many of these men were so rich that they could delight their hometowns with magnificent buildings and other gifts and even act to benefit the poor. Niketes of Smyrna (second half of the first century CE) donated a gateway, Damianos of Ephesos (second half of the second century; inscriptions honoring him and remains of his extravagant tomb have been found in Ephesos) donated a columned hall in marble some 200 meters long, between the city gate and the Artemision (VS 605), and the previously mentioned Herakleides the Lycian had an oil fountain with a golden roof built in the Asklepios gymnasium of Smyrna (VS 613).

A sophist's speech might not have attracted as many people as pantomimes, athletes, or gladiators; nonetheless, the sophists' public visibility in the cities of Asia Minor should not be underestimated.[325] Wherever these stars went, they were sure to be noticed and admired. When addressed, they had to display a ready wit.[326] Their public appearances became events, often in the context of great festivals, and not solely when the emperor or governor was present with his entourage. In addition to the acoustic performance, the visual aspect also contributed to a "concert" that mesmerized the audience: the cloak, hair style, beard, and stature. Sound and rhythm were meticulously polished. Herodes Atticus (101/113–177) attested to the power and elegance of Polemon's discourse by citing Homer (VS 539): "My ears ring with the din of drumming hoofs" (*Iliad* 10, 535; trans. Fagles). Alexandros of Seleukeia (second century CE) might be imagined as like a prominent modern fashion designer: wrapped in exquisite cloth, with combed hair, gleaming teeth, and polished nails—he was considered simply beautiful. The ideal tended toward a decidedly feminine appearance.[327]

Menandros's tractates introduce the current genres: eulogies of the gods, lands, or cities, of the emperor and other dignitaries and benefactors, as well as speeches for specific occasions, each with obligatory components. A special challenge was the improvised declamation (*autoschedios logos*): the audience or an individual proposed to the speaker a theme or a thesis to be proved, and he had to speak on it *ex tempore*. A second speech arguing the exact contrary could be added to the first, or the orator might repeat his first speech with a different tone, rhythm, and diction. Aristeides did not like to improvise in public, opposing it to the polish of a carefully revised discourse (VS 583): he was one of those, he said, who "improve" (*akribunton*) rather than "vomit" (*emunton*). Polemon told a gladiator dripping with sweat before a fight for his life: "you are in as great an agony as though you were going to declaim" (VS 541; trans. Wright). In fact, many an outlandish theme required the speaker to quickly come up with something. For example, the Athenians asked Alexandros of Seleukeia to persuade the Scythians to resume their earlier nomadic life, because life in the city made them sick (VS 572). In Smyrna, the Thessalian Hippodromos was given this theme: the magician who wanted to die because he was unable to kill a magician who was an adulterer (VS 619). Naturally, historical subjects had to be taken from the classical period or the age of Alexander; Skopelianos's specialty was the Persians—Dareios and Xerxes. The emperor himself gave one sophist this subject: The fourth century BCE Athenian rhetor and politician Demosthenes, having fallen on his knees before Philip, king of Macedonia, defends himself against the accusation of cowardice (VS 626).

Airs and graces are part of being a star. According to Philostratos at least, Aristeides took the liberty of not appearing when the emperor visited Smyrna, and excused himself by saying that he had had to think about something so deeply that he could not get away from it. A choleric orator boxed the ears of one of his listeners who had fallen asleep during his speech (VS 578). Polemon of Smyrna rose to the height of arrogance: he communicated with cities as if they were his subjects, with emperors as if they were not his superiors, and with gods as if they were on an equal footing. An often-told story is that of the visit made to Smyrna by Arrius Antoninus, Hadrian's adopted son and later emperor, while he was governor of Asia. Antoninus had taken up quarters in the home of the absent sophist because it was the best house in the city and belonged to the most prominent citizen. But when the owner returned one night, he took offense, made a loud scene in front of the house, and forced Antoninus to seek lodging elsewhere. The proconsul graciously forgave him. When Polemon later visited Rome after Antoninus had become emperor, the latter embraced him, provided him with lodging, and commanded "that no one throw him out of there." And when a tragedian complained that as president of the festival, Polemon had dismissed him, Antoninus asked at what time he had been forced to leave the theater. The actor answered: "It was noon." The emperor thereupon replied: "But it was midnight when he expelled *me* from his house, and I did not prosecute him" (VS 534 f.; trans. Wright).

Jealousy, quarrels, and intrigue must have been everyday phenomena. Conflicts between cities and conflicts between sophists went hand in hand; in Ionia, Favorin the Gaul sided with Ephesos against Polemon of Smyrna. A disparaging judgment regarding competitors sometimes emerged from the group of the pupils; asked by the master for his opinion of Alexandros of Seleukeia, the "clay Plato," one of Herodes's people said: "lots of clay, little Plato" (VS 573). Philostratos himself is clearly biased; for example, his life of Skopelianos begins with a tirade against the critics and detractors of this sophist (VS 514), whereas he rejects the sophist Varus of Laodikeia just as strongly. Philagros the Cilician was *persona non grata* in Athens. He had offended by including in his tribute to the city of Athens a eulogy for his

96. Aelius Aristeides, sophist.
Vatican Museums.

wife, who had died in Ionia. The Athenians tricked him by giving him for an *ex tempore* speech a subject on which they knew he had already published a speech in Asia. When Philagros, assuming that this speech was unknown in Athens and could pass for improvised, began to speak, the audience declaimed the text out loud and laughed him off the podium.

In the case of two of the Anatolian sophists, such a large part of their legacy is extant that we can form a precise picture of their personalities and achievements: Dion of Prusa in Bithynia and Aelius Aristeides of Hadrianoi in Mysia (Figure 96). Dion was a sophist, philosopher, and historian.[328] He had studied with Musonius Rufus (ca. 30–100) and was probably introduced by him into court circles in the capital before he displeased the emperor Domitian and was forced to go into exile. Under Nerva, Dion was able to return to the city of his birth. In the time of Trajan the Bithynian stood at the zenith of his success and enjoyed the friendship and admiration of the emperor; Dion was even allowed to drive with him in his triumphal carriage at the end of the Second Dacian War. Philostratos thought highly of him, and at the end of the fourth century Synesios of Cyrene, a philosopher and bishop, dedicated a work to him as a great model.

Aristeides was born under Hadrian, ca. 129 CE. His travels to Egypt, through the Greek world, and to Rome were complemented by long sojourns in his adopted hometown of Smyrna and in Pergamon, where he treated his chronic physical ailments with cures and incubation in the Asklepieion; part of the cure consisted in blood-letting, vomiting, and eating partridges that had been spiced with crushed incense (VS 611). Among the fifty-three extant speeches, the "sacred" ones constitute a special group: in a diary-like structure the sophist reflects on his condition and his experiences, and communicates with the god of healing. Aristeides was a convinced Atticist and rose to become, along with Polemon and Herodes, one of the great star-sophists for his contemporaries.

The art of speaking and debating practiced by sophists and rhetors traveling from city to city found its direct continuation in the disputes among bishops, heretics, and pagans on the public squares in the cities and in the treatises of the Apologists and Church Fathers. In the time of the Second Sophistic, not only Cynic and Neo-Pythagorean itinerant preachers but also Christian apostles, prophets, and teachers traveled through the land, speaking on their "philosophy." These can hardly be distinguished, at least from an external, contemporary perspective, from the pagan "philosophers," and Christian writers complained that they were unjustifiably denied privileges that were granted the latter.[329] Aristeides's diatribes (*or.* 3, 664 ff., esp. 671) against "completely worthless people" can be applied to Christians, even if they were not his intended targets. Alexandros of Abonuteichos hated both Christians and Epicureans. So far as we know, the intellectual elite in the cities of Asia Minor generally still had for Christianity little respect, which might have found expression in writing. Only the works directed against Christians by authors named Celsus and Hierokles—the former still in the time of Marcus Aurelius, the latter around 300 CE—are known through the refutation composed by Origen, *contra Celsum*, and Lactantius (*inst.* 5, 2 f. 11). Apart from the texts of the New Testament that are published under the name of the Ephesian presbyter John, the earliest Christian work from Asia Minor that we know of goes back to John's pupil Papias of Hierapolis; a few sentences from his *Exposition of the Sayings of the Lord* are cited by later writers.[330] In the age of the Antonines a kind of Christian writing that has almost entirely been lost was already flourishing in Asia; according to Lucian, the itinerant preacher and guru Peregrinos Proteus of Parion (ca. 100–165) contributed to it. He not only commented on Christian books, but also is supposed to have written some himself (Lucian, *Pereg.* 11).[331] It is claimed that the philosopher Justin Martyr[332] who conducted a debate with Tryphon, then "the most important Hebrew," in Ephesos, had been converted there (Eusebius, *h. e.* 4, 18). Meliton, bishop of Sardeis, and Apolinarios of Hierapolis wrote somewhat earlier than Celsus and were cited by Eusebius. Among Meliton's extensive works (Eusebius, *h.e.* 4, 26), in addition to the letter to Marcus Aurelius, recently discovered papyri have provided more precise knowledge of his Easter sermon. The oldest list of the books of the Old Testament compiled by a Christian is his. It is certain that he had a great influence on ecclesiastical and theological debate in Asia.[333] Apolinarios wrote books titled *To the Hellenes* (i.e., pagans) and *To the Jews*, as well as a work attacking the Phrygian sect of Montanism (p. 543), all of which are lost.[334] Irenaeus (*Eirenaios*), the bishop Lugdunum, was a Greek who was born between 130 and 140, grew up in Smyrna, where he heard the bishop Polycarp speak. He wrote his main work in Gaul, in the Greek language. His well-known attack on Gnosticism was first translated into Latin in the fourth century under the title *adversus haereses*.[335]

Spectacula

In the Hellenistic-Imperial period cities of Asia Minor, festivals flourished as never before or since.[336] We know of about 300–400 different games, primarily in the eastern provinces of the empire, and by far the majority of them are in Asia Minor. Our main sources are inscriptions on stone—mainly lists of victors, but also deeds of foundation for festivals or edicts issued by the emperors and governors, epitaphs to competitors, and coins. Cities used their right to mint money to make propaganda by stamping the names and symbols of their large festivals on the reverse sides of their coins. However, all these sources of information do not produce a complete picture. An estimated number of unknown cases must be taken into consideration.

In the Greek world these events had a three-tiered hierarchy that had developed over centuries. Down to late antiquity, the ancient festivals in Olympia, Delphi, the Nemea valley, and the isthmus of Corinth, through their widely recognized rank, stood on the highest level. At first, only the Panathenaic Games in Athens and the athletic contests for Hera in Argos with the ancient ceremonial of the Shield (as victors' prize) followed to establish a second level. Then Ptolemaios Philadelphos started things off with the example of the isolympian *Ptolemaieia* in the city where he resided (Alexandria), joining that level with more contests. Cities and leagues of states in Greece and Asia Minor followed his lead by founding a "sacred" or "crown" competition (*hieros* or *stephanites agon*) that was modeled on one of these games with regard to periodicity, the classification of age groups, and honors for victors (olive, laurel, pine, or celeriac wreaths), and seeking to have it recognized by the international community.

The festival calendar of the Hellenistic world was gradually filled with sacred games, isolympian games, isopythian contests, and so on. Rhodes introduced *Heliaia* for the god Helios, Kos introduced *Asklepieia* for the god of healing. The citizens of Magnesia on the Maeander proudly claimed to be the first on the Asian mainland to have founded a "sacred *agon*."[337] Teos presented its *Dionysia*, Ephesos its *Epheseia*, Miletus its *Didymaia*; little Priene had its *Athenaia* announced in Athens and Samothrace, in Caria the city of Tralleis founded *Olympia* and *Pythia*, its neighbor Nysa founded *Theogamia*, Kaunos *Ptolemaieia*, and in the highlands north of Lycia the community of Kibyra founded *Rhomaia*. Sardeis decided on *Panathenaia* and

Eumeneia, and *Chrysanthina* to celebrate Kore, Demeter's daughter who was carried off by the god of the underworld, Pluto, as she was picking flowers; the winner's wreath was adorned with "golden flowers." In 182 BCE, after Eumenes II's victory over Prusias I and the Galatians, *Nikephoria* were organized at the royal residence of Pergamon; this was an isopythian contest of stage artists combined with an isolympian contest in which the athletic disciplines and horse races were central. First organized in 181 BCE, it was held every four years. *Soteria* and *Herakleia* were first celebrated in 165 on the occasion of Eumenes II's victory over the Galatians.

During the Imperial period, the classical circuit (*periodos*) of the first-rate festivals in the motherland was extended to include competitions in Nikopolis, Naples, and Rome. The *Rhomaia Sebasta* of Asia were later called the *koina* of Asia; as the *koina* of Bithynia and other *koina* these games were held by the provincial commonalties in various cities of the provinces. In Asia, the three major events in Pergamon, Ephesos, and Smyrna seem to have been distinguished by rank from several smaller ones, for example those of Kyzikos, Philadelpheia, Sardeis, and Tralleis. To found these and other new games—*Sebasteia, Kaisareia, Tibereia, Claudieia*, and later also *Augusteia*—permission was obtained from the emperor. As a rule, the initiative came from the communities themselves, more rarely from the emperor—or from client-kings, who organized such celebrations in their capital cities, such as Polemon II at Neokaisareia in Pontos, and Antiochos IV at Samosata in Commagene under Claudius. The names of emperors were in no way dominant; they competed or were coupled with *Olympia, Pythia*, the names of city gods, heroes, or even prominent individual mortals. In Ephesos, under Vespasian, an astrologer named Balbillus donated an *agon* that henceforth bore his name, *Balbilleia*. Over the centuries, the names of major *agones* were changed: the *Ptolemaieia* in Kaunos became *Letoa Rhomaia* (167 BCE?), later *Letoa Kaisareia*, and later still may have been called *Hadrianeia Olympia*. In Ephesos, a not entirely clear distinction was drawn between the *Balbilleia* and the newly founded *Hadrianeia*. More than fifteen cities in the eastern part of the empire announced *Hadrianeia* in inscriptions and on their coins. In the second half of the third century, *Antonineia, Commodeia, Severeia,* and *Philadelpheia* (celebrating the concord between the brothers Caracalla and Geta) followed.[338]

Recognized and attended by delegations from "the whole world," the great festivals were also called ecumenical. In 211 CE Ephesos had the honor of receiving a delegation from the African metropolis of Carthage. Anazarbos in Cilicia described its *agon* on its coins as "the common liturgy of the world" (*synthesia oikumenes*). Vying for a reputation as a festival site, more and more cities did not limit themselves to a single event. Imperial period Pergamon could boast at least five, not including the provincial commonalty's *agon*. Nonetheless Ankyra, the residence of the governor of the province of Galatia on the Anatolian plateau, whose population was predominantly Celtic and Phrygian-Paphlagonian, celebrated four.

This dance reached its high point in the second century CE, and by that time scheduling had become completely chaotic. The philhellene Hadrian, who delighted the Greeks by founding the Panhellenion and the *agon* of the same name in Athens, set out to adjust the schedule of the circuit in such a way that the latter would once again allow the itinerant professional competitors to appear punctually at the greatest possible number of large festivals. Not every city was prepared to adjust to the new system. To the emperor's dismay, Nikomedeia stubbornly adhered to its own tradition.[339]

In the cases of both the sacred *agones* and those of the third and lowest level (the ones with monetary prizes), the range of official competitive disciplines was divided into the categories of athletic, hippic, and stage performance competitions. Each discipline had a firmly established place in the rank order and in the sequence of the overall program. Far exceeding the classical disciplines in number, a multitude of sporting events was established, including horse and foal races, music, dance, drama, lectures, and crafts, divided into different age groups. Our knowledge of these events is for the most part fragmentary. Each "crown" competition sponsored by the Asian provincial commonalty in Pergamon, Smyrna, and Ephesos lasted forty days. The complete program of the monetary prize competition in the small city of Oinoanda in Lycia—which is classified as "thymelic," that is, involving stage presentations in the widest sense—lasted twenty-two days. Twelve days were devoted to regular competitions, four to the accompanying program, and six for council and community meetings, markets, and religious ceremonies. It began with the competition of trumpeters and heralds. Then the prose eulogists appeared; they delivered speeches praising the municipal gods, cities, the emperor, or a benevolent *patronus*, in accord with a precise set of rules laid down in a handbook. The poet's hymns of praise had a similar content but made use of epic meter. Flute players with choruses seem to have performed songs and music of the classic Greek choral lyric tradition. In the competition between comedic and tragic actors, there were restagings of the classics—Menander, Sophocles, and Euripides; the prize was given both for the direction and for the actors' performance. New plays were also performed. The most valued and, in the Greek competitions of the Imperial period, the most popular competitive discipline of a nonathletic kind was that for singers playing the cithara. The conclusion of the regular program consisted of elimination heats for the winners in all disciplines, *dia panton*, also called in other places *agonismata*.

Then came the accompanying program with mimes and clowns, along with the so-called *homeristai*. The latter mimed scenes from the Homeric epics; their props included specially made spears that telescoped when used. A *homeristes* from Lampsakos left us his wisdom in verses on his tombstone in Pompeiopolis:

> Hail, wanderer! So long as you can see dawn's light, delight your mind at the festival, have a good time eating and dancing, and enjoy the sweet charms of Kypris's [Aphrodite's] bed, for you should be very clear about this: when you are dead, you'll have forgotten everything. But if you want to know my house and name: my name is Kyros, my homeland is Lampsakos; I lie here in the earth of Pompeius and have left this light after often gracefully performing the divine Homer on stage. ([182] Marek, *Stadt, Ära*, 1993, 144, no. 28)

A relief on a stele from Lycian Patara (see Figure 94) immortalized the bald-headed mime Eucharistos, and he is lauded as follows:

> The mouthpiece of the muses, the flower of Hellas for eulogy, a treat for the ears of Asia, the most exquisite, famous, tasteful Lycian, a delightful, clever person, outstanding mime! He alone represented on the stage what life writes, and on the public scene and through his voice in theaters surpassed all others. Eucharistos for Eucharistos, his son, as a reminder. When I performed Philistion's pithy witticism, I often said: "The play is over." From now on I hold my peace; I am at the end of life. ([195] SEG 43, 982)

Many questions with regard to the disciplines remain open. What should we understand by *sphairismata* (ball playing?) or *eurythmia*? How did a competition of the *agalmatopoioi* (sculptors) go in Aphrodisias? What did an *agon* among physicians in Ephesos, in which it was a question of capabilities such as *cheirurgia*, consist of? The rules, which differed from place to place, were put in writing, and their observance was enforceable. The relevant model of an *agon* of the period was strictly copied; thus the victors in the Imperial period *Pythia* received an apple, as they did in Delphi, and an olive branch at the *Olympia*, and so forth. In Ephesos the presidents of the *agon* were called *hellanodikai*, as in Olympia, and it was also there that a married woman with the title *theoros* was present during the competitions, as the priestess of Demeter was present in Olympia. The *hellanodikai* (elsewhere called *agonothetes*) were assisted by *alytarchai*, officials responsible for maintaining order, on the model of Olympia. Men bearing rods and whips (*rhabduchoi, mastigophoroi*) intervened against rowdy behavior and rule violations not only by athletes but also by musicians and actors, sometimes striking so hard that an Imperial instruction commanded them to be more moderate, acting so "that people are not struck by several at once, and exclusively on the legs, and that no one is either maimed or suffers any other harm that would hinder the exercise [of his occupation]."[340] In Miletus white-garbed young boys whose parents were both still alive (*amphithaleis*) were allowed to lead the competitors ceremonially as they made their entry (*eisagein eis meson*).

Peace and prosperity provided the basis for the upward trend in the growth of the contests. It is obvious that this was accompanied by enormous changes in the sociocultural and economic sphere. The amount of effort absorbed by the festival system—in the education of the young in municipal gymnasiums, intellectual, artistic, and technical production, legal expertise, bureaucracy, and financial expenditure—can hardly be overestimated.

Games were one of the most important factors in mobility. Victors carried glamour and glory from one contest to another and drew behind them emulators who left their hometowns and spent years on the road. This is shown, for example, by the name of the great association that received privileges from Claudius, Vespasian, and later emperors: the *hiera peripolistike synodos* (holy synod of itinerant competitors moving from city to city). From a tradition of initially separate associations, a governing body apparently emerged. Since Hadrian, its main seat had been in Rome. It had gradually incorporated various synods of athletes and stage artists as well as victors in sacred contests. However, these synods could make their own decisions and also had local branches. Epithets such as "great" and "sacred" (*megale, hiera*) were introduced into the names of the associations. The latest evidence for this from Asia Minor comes from Pompeiopolis in Paphlagonia and dates from the Severan age; still later evidence is found on papyruses from Egypt.[341] In the time of the first tetrarchy (293–305), this was one such title: "The sacred music itinerant ecumenical Diocletian-Maximian great synod." Members who had retired or inactive officials had titular status as a group; an honorary inscription in Kaunos speaks of "Brothers, fathers, trainers, and young men" as bodies with decisionmaking powers, though the technical meaning of this is not entirely clear.[342] The major sections of the membership of these synods, athletics and stage art, are specified with adjectives: *xystike* and/ or *thymelike*, or *musike synodos*.

In tomb inscriptions from Asia Minor the itinerant life of both male and female competitors also appears as one of the most frequent reasons they died abroad. They had "performed in many theaters" and "had made many journeys." Of eighty-six people from Nikomedeia who we know were outside their homelands in the Imperial period, twenty-six have been identified as contestants. Among the victors, two Sinopians were the record holders. In the time of Trajan, there was the boxer Marcianus Rufus, who could boast forty-nine victories in twenty-seven sacred games: not only in Italy and Greece but also in the contests sponsored by the provincial commonalties of Bithynia and Asia in the cities of Nikomedeia, Nikaia, Smyrna, Pergamon, Ephesos, Sardeis, Philadelpheia, Tralleis, Hierapolis, Laodikeia, Thyateira, and Mytilene, and in the Anatolian provinces, in the contests of the *koina* of Pontus, Galatia, and Cappadocia. In addition, he won 110 other contests that offered a prize of half a talent ([162] *IK* Sinope 105). But this boxer was surpassed by his compatriot Valerios Eklektos, whose victor's inscription displayed in Athens dates from the third century CE: seventy-nine victories as herald in sacred games held in thirty cities of Italy, Greece, Macedonia, Thrace, Bithynia, Asia, and Syria (IG II/III³ 4, 1, 629).

The main economic burden involved in conducting the contests lay on the cities and was borne partly by communal funds, partly by private donations made by wealthy citizens, and partly by the liturgies provided by *agonothetai* and other officials. The looming excessive expenditures were a source of concern for the emperors and governors. Under Claudius, a proconsul of Asia already tried to cap the city's expenses for a contest in Ephesos ([162] *IK* Ephesos 18d lines 2–4). The details of the modalities of financing remain unclear. The best information we have is provided by two long documents chiseled on stone from the time of Hadrian.

The first, a ninety-line inscription, was excavated in Alexandria Troas in 2003 and consists of three letters from the emperor to the synod of Dionysian artists and victors in sacred contests from the year 133/134 CE.[343] The complaints the association's emissaries presented to Hadrian in Naples related to abuses in various places; therefore the emperor's directives are exceptionally informative concerning the worldwide competitive circuit. Organizers (i.e., city communities and their *agono-*

thetai) seem to have repeatedly canceled competitions, not paid the victor his or her prize money, and spent the appropriated funds for other purposes—for instance, construction projects or emergency purchases of grain. Hadrian responded by making any cancellation, refusal to pay, or use of funds for different purposes—and even payment of competitors in kind rather than in cash—contingent on his permission, and he put the finances under the supervision of Roman magistrates. How much of the organizers' overall budget was to be reserved for prize money had to be determined in advance. However, the victors also had to pay a 1 percent fee to cover the imperial officials' compensation. The city of Ephesos, where statues to victorious trumpeters and heralds were customarily erected, sought to shift their cost to the persons honored.

The second document is 117 lines long and also dates from the time of Hadrian (124 CE). It concerns the funds for the aforementioned monetary prize contest donated by a citizen named Julius Demosthenes in Oinoanda, Lycia. The financial requirements were set at 4,450 denarii in all, as follows: the installment of 1,000 denarii to be paid in the month of Dios (January) was to be immediately lent at interest. The annual yield was reckoned at 7.5 percent. The 1,000 denarii lent in the first year were to bring in, before the festival was organized, three annual returns, that is, 225 denarii; the 1,000 denarii lent in the second year two annual returns, 150 denarii; and the 1,000 denarii lent in the third year one annual return, 75 denarii. No interest was earned on the 1,000 denarii instalment paid in the year of the festival itself. Thus we arrive at the sum of 4,450 denarii. The largest part, 1,900 denarii, was allotted for the prizes for the victors. The rest was mainly spent on the judges' honoraria (1,500 denarii) and handed out to citizens, freedmen, and inhabitants with lesser rights (*paroikoi*).[344] More than a hundred years later, another donor for a monetary prize *agon*, Euarestos, appeared in the same city ([146] MS IV 20–24).

Organizing festivals was not the only financial burden on cities. By issuing decrees recognizing the Panhellenic status of a new *agon*, cities as early as in the Hellensitic age assumed the obligation to provide the victors among their citizens with honors and privileges as well as regular payments. In particular, these *obsonia, syntaxeis,* or *iselastica* were regulated by law, apparently at the level of the provincial commonalties; gradations were made depending on the rank of the *agon* and the discipline in which the victory was won.[345] A letter from Pliny to his emperor, Trajan, reads:

> The athletes, Sir, think that they ought to receive the grants you have decreed for victors in "Triumphal Entry Games" (*iselastica certamina*)[346] at once from the day they were crowned for victory. They argue that the actual date of their triumphal entry into their native towns is irrelevant; the date which matters is that of the victory which entitled them to the triumphal entry. On the other hand, I point out that the name refers to "triumphal entry" and so I am very much inclined to think that their date of entry is the one we should consider. They also claim awards for previous victories won in games which you have subsequently upgraded to "Triumphal Entry Games," arguing that if they receive nothing in games which have lost that rank after their victories it is only

fair that they should receive something for games which afterwards acquire it. Here, too, I very much doubt whether any retrospective claim should be allowed and feel that they should not be given anything to which they were not entitled at the time of victory. (Pliny the Younger, *ep.* 10, 118; trans. Radice, slightly corrected)

Trajan flatly rejected the demand made by the victors in Pontus et Bithynia, namely that their privileges be made retroactive to contests that were made "iselastic" after their victories; he pointed out that the victors were not asked to give up anything when an iselastic *agon* was later demoted. However, Hadrian yielded to the same demand made by the international association. In addition to payments there were such privileges as tax breaks and exemption from the obligation to provide services (liturgies). Third-century Amastris had an *amphodon hieroneikon*, a block of houses for victors in sacred *agones*; and under the Flavians exactly the same thing already existed in the Syrian metropolis of Antiocheia on Orontes: *plintheion stephaneiton*. These cities probably provided rent-free housing in certain neighborhoods that were known as "victors' housing blocks." Burial costs for competitors who died in a city while on tour also had to be paid from its public coffers.

The only genuinely Roman import in the world of Greek agones were the *munera gladiatoria*.[347] These cruel spectacles on the dark side of the *Imperium Romanum*'s culture stand side by side with *agones* in frequency and pervasiveness. In this respect, the residents of Greek *poleis* in the primarily urban and culturally Hellenized zones showed no less taste for such butchery than their counterparts in the Roman colonies or cities in the interior with larger proportions of other populations, such as Ankyra, Philadelpheia, or Sagalassos.

The gladiator battles and their accompanying programs were not sponsored by cities but rather were "given"—that is, they were organized and financed—by individuals and were called donations (*munera*). Their festive context was the cult of the emperor, and this kind of munificence was part of the liturgies regularly provided by the priests of the emperor, both provincial and municipal. The officeholders (and often their wives, who certainly attended the events) donated them for public entertainment. For a certain time, they maintained gladiators' schools, *familiae*, which were attended by slaves and hired free men. Such a group, including service personnel and physicians, could be sold to the next holder of the office. Where we have numbers from Asian cities, most of the gladiators of a troop were free men. Among them we even find Roman citizens, Greeks with municipal civil rights, but very seldom men with native names. However, the usual battle names conceal the gladiator's ancestry and status. Free gladiators were often married, and their wives mourned them on their tombstones. Victors and favorite fighters were highly respected, received citizenship in foreign cities just like prominent athletes and artists, and their tombs were ultimately cared for by the city.

Tomb inscriptions and other monuments with relief depictions of individual gladiators and individual scenes of battle often give, along with the gladiator's name, the number of his victories and crowns (not every victory entailed the right to receive a crown). An *essedarius* (a gladiator who fought from a battle-wagon) listed seventy-five victories on the gladiator monument in Klaudiupolis, Bithynia ([146] MS II 237 f.). The "serious battles" (*apotoma*) for life or death are particularly emphasized in the hymns of praise for the donors of the spectacle, as in the case of the priest Tertullus in Sagalassos ([146] MS IV 114): "He struck down a virtual army of Ares-loving fighters in the arena. He killed bears, panthers and lions, deeming his fatherland more important than his private property" (trans. Marek). In the same city there were duels every day for four days in a row—with two opponents each and with a fatal outcome.[348] In Klaudiupolis twelve gladiators died in three days. Also among the attractions were women as fighting opponents, as in Halikarnassos, where an "Amazon" battled an "Achillea," though neither was killed.[349]

The accompanying program consisted of several parts, in which an animal manager (*therotrophos*) continually led wild beasts into the arena and there let them loose to do battle with condemned criminals or professional hunters or animal fighters. The more exotic the animals, the more attractive the program. For instance, Ephesos saw *zoa Libyka* (African beasts); in Prusa, Aizanoi, and Synnada, lions were standard. Among the most feared beasts was the bear, which appeared in several places. A specialty was the *Taurokathapsia*, a kind of bullfight, which was particularly popular in Thessaly and was first displayed in Rome under Caesar.

Though fictitious, Lucian's account in his dialogue "Toxaris, or on Friendship" provides us with information about the reality of such events, precisely in many smaller cities as well. The scene is Amastris, a port city on the south coast of the Black Sea. The Scythian Toxaris wants show the Greek Menippos how greatly friendship is respected among his people, assuring him: "That, Menippos, did not happen either in Machlyene or among the Alans, so as to be unattested and possible to disbelieve; there are many Amastrians here who remember the fight of Sisinnes" (trans. Harmon). Toxaris once went on a sea voyage with his boyhood friend Sisinnes, sailing from their Scythian homeland to Athens. On the way, the ship stopped at Amastris. After the two men had found lodging, they went shopping. When they got back, they found that someone had broken into their room and stolen everything they had—cash, valuable carpets (apparently to sell in Athens), and clothing. Naturally, no one had heard or seen anything, and it seemed pointless to blame the host or the people in neighboring rooms. In a world without travel insurance or credit cards, the prospect of dying of hunger and thirst made Toxaris so desperate that he was already thinking of committing suicide. But his friend held him back and promised to find a way out of their dilemma. First Sisinnes found a job as a wood hauler, and kept their heads above water with his wages. One morning, as he was on his way to the agora, he saw young men parading with weapons. They told him that they had registered for a prize to be given for exhibition fights two days hence, and he perceived in this an opportunity to free himself and his friend from their unfortunate situation. On the prescribed day he took Toxaris with him to the theater. His friend was expecting a show of the usual "Greek" kind—*Homeristai*, pantomimes, dancers, and the like—but it began with wild animals being chased by dogs and killed with spears, and then others were let loose to attack fettered convicts. Finally the prize-fighters came in. The herald led a man strong as a bear into the middle of the arena and offered 10,000 drachmas to anyone who dared to fight him. Sisinnes advanced, asked for weapons, and brought Toxaris the money, asking his friend to bury him and return to their homeland in the event that he was killed. Toxaris was appalled, but his objections failed to prevent Sisinnes from buckling on the armor and descending into the arena. His opponent attacked with a scimitar, and his first blow struck Sisinnes in the back of the knee and cut the tendons, so that he doubled over, bleeding profusely. Sitting on the spectators' bench, Toxaris, half dead with fear, thought all was lost. But when the giant too brashly came at him again, Sisinnes struck him a fatal blow in the breast. Grievously wounded, Sisinnes sank down on the corpse of his opponent. He almost bled to death, but Toxaris carried him out of the theater as the acknowledged victor and took him back to their lodging, where he cared for him so that he survived—though he was permanently crippled.[350]

Even with all the diversity in the background of the disciplines—the variety of venues, stages, arenas, stadiums, and hippodromes, with the extreme contrast between music, dance, and oratory on the one hand, and on the other the blood orgies of the gladiators, the dust and sweat of boxing matches and horse races—from the second century on at the latest the whole affair was seen by contemporaries as a unified phenomenon. It was summed up by Tertullian in the word *spectacula* and perceived by Tatian as thoroughly Hellenic—that is, "pagan." Christian agitators preached the strongest conceivable opposition to its ideology.

Precisely where the boundaries of this urban culture of pleasure in the Imperial period and Late Antiquity should be drawn—geographically, ethnically, socially, religiously, and psychologically—remains an open question. The rather casual modern assessments contradict one another. Emphasis is put on barriers separating city and country, separating a small urbanized coastal zone from inner Anatolia. One scholar suggests that the *spectacula* remained alien to Jews and Christians, and especially to the majority of the rural population of Asia Minor and the Fertile Crescent, which did not have full urban civil rights and did not speak Greek.[351] But in Kolophon's Hellenistic decree for its citizen Menippos we read that the festival was attended by Hellenes and barbarians alike.[352] Whole rows of seats were reserved for rural communities, as in Seleukeia on Kalykadnos.[353] Villages organized their own *agones*, some of them making significant expenditures for the purpose.[354] What about Jews and Christians? In his "Speech to the Greeks" (22–24), the Syrian Christian Tatian subjects theater to a hail of invective: actors are blowhards and lechers, raving madmen in clay masks, nasally declaiming smut, they play matricides, maniacs, and adulterers, while the athletes are fattened ruffians. Such polemics and the prohibition on taking part in anything of the kind run throughout early Christian literature.[355] However, the majority of Tatian's coreligionists seem to have attended the theaters and arenas, which explains the vehemence of the diatribes against these events, as well as the fact that Tertullian (*spect.* 30) holds out the prospect of heavenly games on the occasion of the Last Judgment that will far surpass all earthly ones. Refractory

97. Theater in Aphrodisias.

Christians pointed out that the prohibition on drama is nowhere to be found in the Scriptures, and that charioteers, dance, and music appear in the Old Testament (Novatian, *spect*. 2). This resistance continued until far into the Christian *imperium*, as we can see in Jacob of Serugh's homily from the second half of the fifth century.[356] What the bishops feared was the deeply rooted culture of pleasure that prevailed in the urban and rural population's communal experience, in both large and small towns; this was mass entertainment par excellence whose international character was almost unparalleled until the advent of the American Way of Life in our own time.

Visible traces of ancient mass entertainment in the cities of Asia Minor are preserved by the virtually countless theater buildings (Figure 97). Information about the significance of the *agon* can also be provided by linguistic analysis: in literature, inscriptions, and papyruses, the use of agonistic terminology is omnipresent, especially in Late Antiquity. Men of letters educated in Greek, such as the Jew Philo of Alexandria, the Syrians Tatian, and Lucian of Samosata were all completely familiar with the technical expressions of *agones*. With regard to the theatrical offerings in Edessa, the entry of Greek and Latin loanwords into the Syrian literary language is noteworthy: *theatron, agon, agonistes, ludus, arena*. How deeply the culture of the *agon* permeated people's thought and language in the Imperial period and Late Antiquity is shown by metaphors in the formula of a multitude of inscriptions of ordinary inhabitants of the provinces: the poem on a three-year-old boy's tombstone from Kolophon takes the wrestling ring as a metaphor for the age of life beyond childhood, education and training in the gymnasium, which he never reached ([146] MS I 365). The tombstone of a wife in rural Bithynia praises her virtue by using the expression *brabeion aretes*, which refers to a metal crown awarded as a prize in the *agon*.[357] These agonistic images were unhesitatingly used even by the most vehement opponent of the games, Christianity; Paul wrote: "Henceforth there is laid up for me the crown of righteousness, which the Lord, the righteous judge, will award to me on that Day, and not only to me but also to all who have loved his appearing" (2 Timothy 4:8; Revised Standard Version). This runs through the literature down to the Church Fathers.[358] The affinities between the symbolism of the *agon* and Christian symbolism are obvious: the *virtus* of the competitor, the gladiator's askesis and blood, stand in direct connection with the passion of Christ, the scourging and the crown of thorns, with suffering and death and at the same time with the victory and triumph of the martyrs.[359] The Christian philosopher Clement of Alexandria (ca. 150–before 221) equates Christian life with the *agon*:

> For the *agonothetes* is the Almighty God, and the *brabeutes* (He who awards the prize) is the only-begotten Son of God. Angels and gods are spectators; and the contest, embracing all the varied exercises, is "not against flesh and blood," but against the spiritual powers of inordinate passions that work through the flesh. (*Strom.* 7, 3, 20, 4; trans. Wilson)

Religion

The religious history of Asia Minor bridges the millennia separating the T-top pillars of Göbekli Tepe from the dancing dervishes of the Mevlana cloister. This part of the world absorbed nearly everything that was believed, thought, prayed to, venerated, and prophesied between Iran, Mesopotamia, Egypt, and the Mediterranean world. It is the land of syncretism as such; in the dense, multicolored fabric of Hellenistic-Imperial age religion in Asia Minor, individual threads can be traced back to their origins only to a certain extent. In a noteworthy article on the cults of Lydia,[360] the Austrian ancient historian and epigraphist Josef Keil has spoken of the historical strata of the religion practiced in the Roman period, primarily in rural areas, overlying one another; he distinguished an oldest, "Anatolian" stratum from later "Phrygian," "Persian," "Greek," "Syrian and Egyptian," and "Jewish influenced" strata, following one after the other. In addition to the diachronic stratigraphy there is the synchronic distribution differentiating according to geographical areas. The religious landscape of Asia Minor was at no time unified. Thus for example, Mithras played no role in western Asia Minor, where gods like Men or "the pious and righteous" (*hosios kai dikaios*) were concentrated.

In the Imperial period, there was a turning point in the religious history of the Roman provinces of Asia Minor. In most provinces of the Asian *Imperium romanum*, the *poleis* celebrated with increasing extravagance and in peace and prosperity the official cults of gods and the emperor, sacrifices, processions, and community festivals. But more and more people sought their personal salvation at the sites of oracles, magicians, and visionaries, in sanatoria at religious sites, or in the simple but strict rules of life of small, deviant communities of belief. The ancient, pre-Greek tradition of rural religiousness was reawakened by the search for security, health, and protection by so-called highest, all-powerful gods. Sacred books, oracles, divine laws, and theological-philosophical treatises spoke not only to Jews and Greeks but also to Phrygians, Galatians, and Cappadocians in a single language, Greek; and even the simple farmer in the countryside gave his prayer to his god the consecration of the same language.

Gods, Cults, and Shrines

The varied, multileveled world of gods in Imperial period Asia Minor is reflected not only in hundreds of pictorial themes and legends on city coinages but also by religious laws, oracular pronouncements, and decrees recorded on stone, votive objects in the city and in the country, religious buildings and stone altars, and reliefs and statues (including terra cotta figurines that can be held in the palm of one's hand). Many of these objects bear their donor's inscriptions with votive formulas, addresses to the divinity or divinities, vows, requests for prosperity and protection, salvation from danger, the health and growth of animals and fruits of the field for themselves, their children, their wives, their cherished parents, their slaves, and their *polis* or village (e.g., [195] SEG 38, 1089). In addition, in the epigraphic sources for certain localities we find a striking concentration of theophoric proper names, a kind of naming cultivated out of piety from which we can infer the prominence of a certain divinity. To speak of a cult, we have to distinguish merely occasional worship unrelated to a place from regular worship at a specific place.[361] Literary sources—written by contemporaries who sometimes are worshippers (Aelius Aristeides), sometimes distanced observers and critics (Lucian), but mostly copy older literature—describe not a few of the temples and also the cult's personnel, rites, and myths. Finally, the ruins of shrines have survived in great numbers throughout the land and are focal points for archaeological research and religious studies.

The names and surnames of the gods that appear in our sources are of exceptional importance for the religious history of Asia Minor. In many places an Artemis or Zeus was not brought in by Greeks but was instead an indigenous divinity. Non-Greek names that were still in use, surnames (*epikleses*), or the qualities that are attributed to them or can be inferred from images reveal their non-Greek character and indicate the level to which they should be assigned. Names derived from a people, such as Pratomysios, Lydios, or Karios, and Greek epithets such as "fatherly" (*patroos*) or "ancestral" (*progonikos*) represent old tribal gods. Most of all the *epikleses* point to the name of a place that was the cult's home and to which it was in many cases limited. Zeus Syrgastes, a Thracian-Bithynian god, appears only in Tieion on the Black Sea, while Zeus Poarinos appears only in Abonuteichos. Bithynia, Mysia,

Lydia, and especially Phrygia are full of gods' names that can be connected with villages—such as Bonita, Agrostea, Zburea, and Petara.[362] In this small-celled cult landscape there are, of course, also branches of foreign, super-regional, even worldwide gods, such as the Ephesian Artemis, the Epidauran and Pergamene Asklepios, and Kybele of Pessinus. Under the name of Jupiter Dolichenus, soldiers carried the god of Doliche in Commagene far into the Latin West.

Plutarch gives us a Lydian name for the double-headed axe (*labrys*) that is at the same time attached to the Zeus of Labraunda in Caria, who also carries it: Labrandeus (Plutarch, *Quaestiones Graecae* 45 = *mor.* 301 f–302 a).[363] The Celtic surname of a Zeus Bussurigios is translated by "who rules with his mouth."[364] Many Greek epithets attribute qualities and powers to the rural gods of Anatolia: one of the most important cults in western Asia Minor is that of the "thundering" Zeus (*bronton*). He is a god identified in some places in Phrygia with Zeus Bennios, whose name is derived from the Greco-Phrygian word *bennos* (league, association), referring to a religious community.[365] The additional name given him in some places, "harvest-giver" (*karpodotes*) identifies him as a farmers' harvest god—just as *epikarpios* indicates a Zeus "responsible for the harvest," *kallikarpos* a Dionysos of the "good harvest," *thallos* a Zeus of growth, and so forth. Protection, salvation, help, power, and fame are attested by such epithets as "savior" (*soter*), "best," "greatest," "most famous," "pious and righteous," "king," "tyrant," or "ruler of the world," as well as by personified abstractions, such as "happiness," "wealth," "health," "beauty," and "victory."

The sacred was seen in many natural places in Anatolia—cliffs, caves, groves, and above all waters—and this was expressed not only in the cults of nymphs at spring houses and water sources in the cities and the countryside but also in the popular representation of numerous river gods on coins. In prominent places, such as mountains (Zeus *oreites*), groves (Zeus or Apollo *alsenos*), or trees (Zeus of the twin oaks), people recognized the residences, birthplaces, or abodes of the immortals. One peculiarity is the proper names in the genitive attached to the name of a god; they refer, as for example in "Zeus of Baradates" (p. 162) and "Men of Pharnakes," to historical or fictitious founders of cults. In neither the cities nor the countryside are cults always connected with sacred architecture in stone: altars, cliffs, trees, springs, and other objects sometimes constituted the centers of equally important religious sanctuaries.

The "mother" must be emphasized as the Anatolian divinity par excellence, whose tradition can be traced through all levels back to the Hurrian-Hittite, and perhaps even prehistoric, religion (pp. 108 f., 125). Under the Principate, this goddess was still represented in both the east and the west of Anatolia, with widely famed shrines, even if in general her importance was beginning to wane at that time.[366] The Cappadocian Komana (*Kumani*) in the mountains of Kataonia accommodated the sanctuary of Ma that had been one of Asia Minor's religious centers since the time of the Hittites. The shrine of this goddess's twin sister was located in Pontos, a few kilometers northeast of Tokat (p. 265).

Rural western Anatolia owes a dense network of shrines that flourished in the Imperial period to the previously mentioned (pp. 108 f., 115) adoption of the "mother" by the Phrygians and Lydians. At the rock-cut shrines around Midas City, which were created between the eighth and the sixth centuries BCE, we find traces of the worship of Meter (Kybele) until the third century CE. "Christianity replaced her with the Queen of Heaven, Mary."[367] Alone or in association with other divinities, woman as Meter, *megale* Meter, or Meter *Hipta* received veneration proven by votive and expiatory inscriptions in many small towns and villages (Figure 98); Meter *Hipta* is mentioned in an Orphic hymnbook that presumably comes from Asia Minor. The old Anatolian Meter probably stood behind the name of many another rural goddesses, for example in the case of the "great" Hera with the local *epiklesis* Kandarene in one of the numerous mountain shrines in the area of Olgassys in Paphlagonia, which was equipped with rooms, a banquet hall, and a kitchen.

The mother-goddess's characteristic relation to cliffs and caves distinguishes an important religious site mentioned by Pausanias (10, 32, 3). It is the cave called *Steunos* near Aizanoi in Phrygia, in whose interior it has been possible to locate the main shrine of Meter *Steuene*.[368] Images on coins from Aizanoi show the goddess as Zeus's mother, and the Temple of Zeus erected in Flavian times has a vaulted cellar room beneath the stylobate that may have imitated the cult cavern, alluding to the birthplace of the divine child in Aizanitis. The Celtic Tolistobogii had taken possession of Pessinus, another prominent temple also located in Phrygia. We know it as the stronghold of a cult that interested the Romans as early as the republican period. There a religious community called *Attabokaioi* celebrated mysteries, and the head priest bore the title of Attis. The Greek coastal cities had no lack of *Metroa*: the governor of Pontus et Bithynia, Pliny, asked the emperor whether the citizens of Nikomedeia should be allowed to relocate an "ancient shrine of the Magna Mater" during the construction of a new forum (Pliny the Younger, *ep.* 10, 49), and Strabo (14, 1, 37; cf. Aristeides, *or.* 17, 10) knew of a temple of Meter not far from the harbor in Smyrna.

Smaller cult niches for the Mother cut into solid stone are found in several cities, for example on the Panayır Dağ at Ephesos, at the foot of the acropolis of Priene, and on a rocky ridge above Kaunos.

The frequency of stone inscriptions in the villages of inner Anatolia during the second and third centuries CE reflects an immense wealth of regional and local gods of Phrygia and the immediately adjacent high plains (Figure 99). Most of them are called Zeus. For the most part, the reliefs and statues, all of them executed primitively, represent these protectors of agriculture as bearded and curly haired, either as busts or as standing full-length figures, often with the farmers' most valuable possessions that they are to protect: horses, asses, oxen, and calves.[369] The god "Moon" (Men) was dominant in about the same areas between the bend of the Halys and the middle Hermos and Maiandros valleys, in the south as far down as Pamphylia.[370] In most representations, also as a rider, he appears in a Phrygian outfit: cap, mantle, trousers, and boots. The points of the crescent moon stick up behind his shoulders, and he holds a pinecone in his right hand, which may be a fertility and vegetation symbol. We encounter Men or Meis, carrying a scepter and called *tyrannos* and *kyrios,* in propitiatory inscriptions from the Lydian region of Maionia in the upper valley of the Hermos. Strabo mentions Men Karos, at whose temple a medical school based on the teachings of Herophilos was established, as well as the cult of Men

98. Altar for Meter in Aşağı-yakaköy, Paphlagonia.

99. Phrygian god. Afyon Museum.

Askaenos near Antiocheia in Pisidia. This cult was the center of a clerical state with extensive land holdings; the latter was abolished when the Augustan colony was founded (Strabo 12, 8, 14.20), but the cult itself continued to flourish. Temples of Men also existed in Ankyra, Sardeis, and Nysa. In which period the Anatolian Men originated cannot be definitively determined. The repeatedly demonstrated relation with Anāhitā and the high-ranking cult of Men Pharnaku of Kabeira under the Iranian dynasty of the Mithridatids are adduced by the American scholar Eugene Numa Lane in support of his supposition that the Anatolian Men was an Iranian god.[371]

The indigenous Carians' sanctuaries, with their banqueting halls and temples, are in southwestern Asia Minor: Kaunos, Sinuri, Mylasa, Euromos, Labraunda, Gerga, and others. A few of their gods bore *epikleses* derived from the local language, for example, Osogollis and Lepsynos. However, most of them were coopted through *interpretatio graeca* as Zeus, Hekate (Lagina), or Apollo (Kaunos). An equally fascinating ancient cult area preserved by Greek and indigenous linguistic monuments is neighboring Lycia. Here too only a few surnames of the gods in the local languages were still in use during the Imperial period: *Kakasbos, theoi Loandeis* (Hippukome), *Tobaloas* (Arneai), *Trosobios* (Limyra), and *Arbbazuma* (Kyaneai).[372] Lycian names for divinities taken over from Greek—*Ertēmi* (Artemis), and *Pedrita* (Aphrodite)—

100. The three adjacent temples of the Letoon at Xanthos.

testify to the early Hellenization of Lycia also observable in other respects. In the Hellenistic period, Apollo, whose Lycian name is *natri*, became the most revered divinity in that country.

Lycia's most important shrine, the Letoon at Xanthos, belongs to the Mother with Two Children, a triad that was worshipped, through *interpretatio graeca*, as Leto and the twins Apollo and Artemis (Figure 100). The sanctuary, constructed of stone during the classical period, was remodeled in the middle of the Imperial period; the remains of these buildings were uncovered by French excavators. Elsewhere, the triad appears chiefly in western Lycia, in Tlos, Pinara, and Sidyma. The celebratory speech published in Sidyma refers to the birth of twins or an epiphany: "God-bearing Earth has brought forth stone figures shaped like Leto's twins, celestial appearances of light born in Araxa, Apollo and Artemis" ([146] MS IV 29 lines 42–47; trans. Marek). The Greeks equated with Herakles a Lycian god, *Kakasbos* (Lycian *Chachakba*), whose main temple was located in Telmessos, and who is represented in numerous votive reliefs found in areas bordering on Lycia as mounted on a horse and swinging a mace.[373] He had a temple in Sagalassos.

Artemis of Perge, who was prominent in Pamphylia, was probably also originally an indigenous goddess. Her cult was less widespread than that of her Ephesian counterpart. Her shrine, which has not yet been localized with certainty, is to be sought on the heights around the Imperial period ruins of the city. In Cilicia, theophoric proper names, such as Tarkondimotos and Teukros, have been related to an indigenous god, *Tarhu(nt)*, who may stand behind the Zeus of Olba (*Olbios*). His sanctuary, which has a large Hellenistic temple, was the religious center of a dynasty estab-

101. Antiochos's religious inscription in Arsameia on the Nymphaios.

lished in the network of Seleucid vassal states whose successors ruled into the Flavian period.[374] The Perasia of Hierapolis-Kastabala, at whose temple, as Strabo (12, 2, 7) says, barefoot priestesses walked on hot coals without feeling pain, is once again related to the Anatolian Mother and the Syrian goddess.[375]

Now turning to the Iranian stratum of Imperial period religion in Anatolia, I must begin by examining Commagene, an eastern Anatolian land that in the late Hellenistic period was virtually covered with shrines; there an unparalleled discovery of archaeological and epigraphic sources allows us insight into the syncretic religion of an Iranian-Armenian dynast. It was its minor king Antiochos who in the middle of the first century BCE found himself confronting the powerful Roman commanders Pompey, Ventidius Bassus, and Mark Antony, and survived thanks to divine help (pp. 286, 304).[376] This syncretic religion is represented by several larger and smaller complexes, tomb-sanctuaries (*hierothesia*)—among which that of Antiochos himself on the peak of Nemrud Dağ, more than 2,000 meters high, stands out in every respect—and by cult precincts, some with remains of walled squares, rooms with mosaic floors, processional routes with rock stairways, smoothed stone walls, relief steles, and inscriptions.[377] Antiochos's religious law is spread over several sites; the longest extant passages come from Nemrud Dağ and from Arsameia on the Nymphaios (the Cendere River; Figure 101).[378]

On twenty-six holidays each year the nearby villages were supposed to make processions to the royal tomb on Nemrud Dağ and to other cult sites throughout the country, and to organize celebrations and feasts with music. Right at the foot of the tumulus made of piled-up gravel, fifty meters high and 150 meters in diameter, there

102. Nemrud Dağ, east terrace.

are three terraces, the one on the north left undeveloped, those on the west and east largely but not entirely completed. On its outer edges were rows of inscribed bases for relief steles and monumental sitting figures, each oriented toward the center (Figure 102), an unparalleled collection of images of gods and ancestors. The row of Antiochos's ancestors on his father's side, with fifteen bases, goes back as far as the Persian Great King Dareios; that of his ancestors on his mother's side, with seventeen bases, goes back to Alexander the Great. However, this is not merely a gallery of ancestors; at its lower end there were also images of the king's wife and daughter.[379]

The row of sitting figures flanked by pairs of eagles and lions, situated directly on the edge of the tumulus, presents the image of the king on the observer's left, with the local goddess of Commagene at his side, wearing a crown of fruit. Like the chief god towering in the center as Zeus-Oromasdes (*Ahura Mazda*), the two placed to the right of him are designated by Iranian-Greek combinations of names, Apollo-Mithras-Helios-Hermes and Herakles-Artagnes-Ares (the Iranian Vrthragna). At the same time, the appearance of a heavenly body is represented in each of the divine figures: Luna (Commagene), Jupiter, Sol, and Mars. A pictorially represented configuration on the lion relief found nearby (the "Lion Horoscope") has been dated to July 7, 62 or 61 BCE—perhaps the day of Antiochos's coronation, but in any case not the date of his birth or death. The person who conceived the whole complex doubtless intended to use the statues to express symbolically the notion that the soul of the deceased king had taken his place in the starry sky. The relationship with Platonic and Stoic ideas regarding the soul and *logos*, and the influence of a work by the early Hellenistic author Euhemeros of Messene (FGrHist 63), which is known to us only in extracts, is unmistakable: reference is made to a legendary sanctuary somewhere in the Indian Ocean, where the stories of Uranos, Kronos, Zeus, and others are written on golden steles. But these were not gods, but rather primeval human kings. Uranos ("sky") was so named because he knew the movements of the stars. His grandson Zeus traveled far and wide, to Babylon, to Mt. Kasios in Syria, to Cilicia, and so forth, erecting monuments to himself everywhere, until he died on Crete. The places where these human kings died became the main sites of their religious veneration.[380]

Several attempts to find a royal burial chamber inside the tumulus on Nemrud Dağ have been made, but so far none has been successful. A religious celebration may never have taken place on its terraces. There is no evidence indicating any kind of activity during the Roman period. Like the Pergamon altar, this colossal structure left virtually no trace in ancient literature. The verses directed against grave robbers by the Cappadocian Church Father Gregory of Nazianzus are the first to allude to a "Cappadocian" funerary monument just as admirable as the Carian *Maussolleion* of Halikarnassos; but it remains doubtful whether this refers to Antiochos's mountain sanctuary, which clearly was not robbed.[381]

In the 1990s, two caverns where Mithras, the "Hellenized" Iranian god in Commagene's pantheon, was worshipped were found near the shrine of Zeus Dolichenos.[382] His worship in Cappadocia is proven by a votive inscription near Tyana and another cult cavern near Pharasa (Ariaramneia), where someone wrote on stone that he had carried out the magic sacrificial rites.[383] Mithras's image appears on an Imperial period coin from Trapezus on the Black Sea. In the rest of Anatolia (apart from Armenia), testimonies to this mystery religion widespread in the Latin West of the empire are rare. The case is different for a female divinity of Iranian provenance: Anāhitā (Greek *Ana[e]itis*), who appears in the great Yašt of the *Avesta*. We have already discussed her oldest Anatolian shrine in Pontic Zela (pp. 242, 265), on the "hill of Semiramis" (Strabo 12, 3, 37). Her cult was observed in western Asia Minor even in the Imperial period, in some places along with that of Meter and Artemis. Around a hundred votive inscriptions are concentrated in Lydia, most of them in Maionia. She had urban shrines in Philadelpheia, Hypaipa, and Hierokaisareia, where an Imperial period dedication transferred slaves to her.[384]

The institution of sacred slaves, *hierodulia*, which already existed in the time of the Hittites, still existed at religious sites in the interior of Anatolia in the Imperial period, even after the great temple states ruled by priests had been annexed. Strabo still describes them: shortly before his time, there were supposed to be in Zela, Komana, and Venasa (Cappadocia) thousands of "sacred slaves" (*hieroduloi*) who, like the land and all other facilities, were the inalienable property of the divinity, and as such under the protection and guidance of the priest. The temple state was fed by their work in the fields and their services, and even produced surpluses. Unless they were manumitted, the *hieroduloi* remained in this bondage throughout their lives. Antiochos of Commagene tried to secure their services for his religious ceremonies:

The group of musicians whom I have chosen for the purpose and those who may later be consecrated, their sons and daughters, and also their descendants shall all learn the same art and be set free from the burden of every other responsibility; and they are to devote themselves to the observances which I have established to the end, and without any evasion are to continue their services as long as the assembly requests it.[385]

The sacred women of the Ma of Komana Pontike prostituted themselves. At temples for Anāhitā in Akilisene, an area in Greater Armenia (Strabo 11, 14, 16), there were not only both male and female *hieroduloi* in large numbers, but the custom, widespread among noble Armenian families, of dedicating sexually mature girls to sacred prostitution for an extended time before they were married was also observed. It is possible that this custom was still observed in isolated cases during the Imperial period. In any event, the existence of *hieroduloi* as late as the third century CE is proven by Lydian propitiatory inscriptions to Meter Hipta and Zeus Sabazios.[386]

A religious tradition somewhat later than the Iranian one, the Egyptian cults of Sarapis, Isis, and Osiris, had been in Asia Minor since the Hellenistic period. We do not need to examine them further. Their temples and sanctuaries were widespread. According to one tradition, the god Sarapis was brought from Sinope to Egypt under Ptolemaios I. In Ankyra, Sarapis was equated with Zeus-Helios, and in Lycia, Isis was equated with Leto.

On the coasts of Asia Minor the Greek stratum of Anatolian religious history is very old. We have already discussed individual sanctuaries and cities' foundation myths (pp. 122, 473). I cannot expand here on the Imperial period legacy of this 600- to 1000-year-long tradition of the *poleis*. Each city had its own little pantheon of first- and second-rate gods. The German ancient historian Johannes Nollé rightly speaks of a " religion of Greek cities " rather than of a "Greek religion."[387]

In a new environment the old gods—omnipresent in the Mediterranean world settled by the Greeks—required plausible constructions of their respective connections with specific places outside this world, which further required in particular that the genealogies and storylines in the Hesiodic, Homeric, and other Greek traditions familiar everywhere be adapted to the divinity worshipped at that cult site. Pausanias (4, 33, 1) groans that it is impossible to count up all the people who would like Zeus (born on Crete)[388] to have been born and raised in their country. In Asia Minor, that idea was propagated by Pergamon, Laodikeia on Lykos, Apameia, Aizanoi, and Tralleis, for example. Euripides (*Ba* 460–464) already knew that Dionysos had come into the world in the Tmolos Mountains above Sardeis in Lydia. After Dionysos's mother Semele had demanded that Zeus, his father, reveal himself to her in his true nature, he appeared to her as lighting bolts and fire. She was struck dead by his splendor, but Zeus saved his son and transplanted him in his thigh. Perge in Pamphylia claimed before all the world that Dionysos's birth from Zeus's thigh took place there, on the banks of the Kestros. This scene was proudly represented in a sequence of images on the frieze of the theater. The Ephesians located the birth of their Artemis on their own territory, of course, in the Ortygia grove. Amazons were supposed to have founded the temple and been the priestesses. The *polis* called itself the owner and guardian (*neokoros*) of the Temple of Artemis, and the goddess herself was the "head of the city," her feast-month (Artemision) was sacred, and during it profane business could not be conducted. Around 160 CE, a decree of the city council was delivered to the proconsul C. Popillius Carus Pedo, politely reminding him that his predecessors had respected the holidays, which he had apparently neglected ([109] Syll.³ 867).³⁸⁹ Even if they were not born in the place, Greek gods and heroes acted or suffered in them, and founded cities in Asia, such as Hermes Amaseia, and Dionysos Nikaia. One of the highest mountains in central Anatolia, Olgassys (*Ilgaz Dağ*), on the territory of Gangra-Germanikopolis, was regarded by the citizens of this Paphlagonian city as the Olympus where their ancestor Tantalos was present at the banquet at the "hearth of the gods."

On several grounds, a further place is worth noting here for its importance during the Imperial period: the Asklepieion of Pergamon. The god of healing, much revered in other places in Asia Minor—numismatic evidence allows us to identify 167 cult sites, most of them in Phrygia—was imported there from Epidauros long before. By the age of Hadrian and the Antonines his sanctuary had gone through a dozen construction phases in the Hellenistic period and six more in the early Roman period. One of Fronto's letters (*ep. ad. M. Caesarem*, 3, 10, 1 f.) and the "sacred" speeches of Aelius Aristeides show that it was a sanatorium of worldwide fame. Among the ruins that can be seen today is also the so-called *Kurhaus* (a public room at a health resort). The round structure with a central hall surrounded by semicircular exedras was probably the site of Aristeides's incubation; there the rhetor and sophist received the dreams through which the god showed him how to be healed (Figure 103).³⁹⁰

Oracles, Wonder Workers, and Rural Religiousness

Higher divination is connected with the shrines of Apollo, where in elaborate ceremonies divine advice was dispensed to delegations sent by cities or to prominent individuals. This had a long tradition and was continued unaltered during the Imperial period, when emperors, governors, and senators were among the clients. Communities took emergencies such as bad harvests or epidemics as occasions to send their delegates to one of the sites issuing advice, and they received the god's instruction to the citizens, for instance to conduct processions, sing hymns, or erect statues of the god at certain places. Oracles of the third century CE also contained "theological" information, in which the nature of the god was described in greater detail. The divine word, brought home in written form, consisted basically of verses, which were couched in an archaic, artificial language that sought to use rare coinages.

Here and there, at certain appointed times, the great oracular gods issued prophecies to ordinary private individuals as well, but in a less elaborate, rather routine way. This lower divination was not limited to their sanctuaries. Through various procedures, a person seeking advice might choose readymade pronouncements by lot. This

103. The Asklepieion in Pergamon: the "Kursaal" on the southeast corner of the temple.

practice could be compared with the modern-day horoscopes with which newspapers seek high circulations and professional seers seek income. Of course, ancient clients also had to pay in cash for advice.

The most important oracular god was Apollo.[391] He prophesied at many different places that had differing ceremonies. A few of his oracle sites were very old but had not maintained their activity continuously down to the Imperial period. Didyma and Klaros were considered by far the most powerful Imperial period oracles. Questions were generally submitted in writing. In the Didymaion located on Milesian territory, questioners registered in a *chresmographeion* (the oracle's secretariat) but were not allowed to enter the deepest level of the temple's interior. There a woman sat over the sacred spring, receiving the divine answers (as did the Pythia at Delphi) and transmitting them to prophets, who brought them up the great stairway leading from the inner sanctum to the threshold and announced them to the people waiting in the *pronaos* (Iamblichos, *Myst.* 3, 11, compare Figure 38). A sacred spring was the focal point in Klaros as well. It was located in the arched cellar room under the temple, which once again only the prophet receiving the oracle was allowed to enter, to drink the water (Figure 104). The prophet himself, or a specialized official (*thespiodos*), sang the augury, which was then put in writing by secretaries. The whole procedure took place by torchlight and lamplight on the previously announced nights.

Less is known about other Apollonian oracle sites in Asia Minor. In Chalkedon on the Propontis an Apollo Chresterios prophesied. On the west coast the Apollonion of Gryneion must have still been operating in the Imperial period. There was a sibylline oracle in Erythrai, and the god's oldest and most important Lycian oracle

104. Cellar room under the Temple of Apollo in Klaros.

was in Patara. The oracle of Apollo Sarpedonios in Cilicia may have emerged on the site of a heroon for Sarpedon that cannot be precisely located. It was questioned in 271 CE by the Palmyrenes.

Among the more important sites during the Imperial period we must count the Cilician oracle of Amphilochos in Mallos. According to Dio (72, 7, 1), this was a dream-oracle, that is, it was based on the interpretation of the incubant's dreams, as in the shrine of Apollo's son Asklepios in Pergamon. In contrast, Lucian (*Philops.* 38) has a questioner report that he submitted his question in writing to the prophet and received a plain, definite answer.

Johannes Nollé's research has thrown much light on the everyday "horoscopes" practiced in the city and in the countryside.[392] Nollé finds in Pisidia, Pamphylia, and the adjacent parts of Kibyratis, southern Phrygia, and western Cilicia a downright fashion of divination by lot. The procedure was simple: on central squares, tomb complexes, gates, walled precincts, cliffs, pillars, blocks of stone, tables, and the walls of buildings, collections of oracular pronouncements, some of them extensive, were written, also in verse, but in the simple, pithy language of adages. Anyone who wanted to know whether he should get married or lend money, whether he should go on a sea voyage or stay at home, whether he would get well, and so forth might go to consult them. The client had to determine, by casting dice or by some other method, the pronouncement that concerned him. Astragales (*Astragalorakel*)—usually knuckle bones from the hind legs of goats or sheep—were used as dice. These dice could fall on only four sides; each of them was assigned a number. Several throws of the dice, in Asia Minor five or seven, determined the pronouncement appropriate to the person seeking advice, which was identified by the same series of numbers. The case of alphabet oracles was different. Here one-line pronouncements were written one under another, each in an exact sequence depending on the letter of the alphabet with which it began. The process of drawing lots used to determine the appropriate pronouncement is not known. As in modern horoscopes, most of the advice was vague, for instance: "It is essential to make an effort: then the outcome will be good."[393]

In the second century CE on the north coast of Asia Minor, there occurred a meteoric rise of a new oracle whose reputation at the apex of its popularity was hardly inferior to that of the great oracles in Didyma, Klaros, and Mallos. It belonged to a speaking serpent that introduced itself as Apollo's son Glykon, and as a new Asklepios. While its published pronouncements have nowhere come down to us in inscriptions—with one exception—a pamphlet unique in its kind written by the contemporary eyewitness Lucian gives us information about its emergence and operation that is clearer than that regarding any other oracle. This work concerns the founder and head priest, the Paphlagonian Alexandros, from the town of Abonuteichos on the Black Sea.[394] In his youth he roamed about, but in Macedonia a dazzling idea came to him: in that place there were tamed snakes that were kept as house pets. He realized that by using one of these as a snake-oracle he could make money, preferably at home, because the people there were considered particularly gullible and superstitious. At the site of the oracle of Apollo Pythaios in Chalkedon, he buried metal tablets bearing the message that Apollo and his son Asklepios would soon move to Pontos and take up residence in Abonuteichos. These were found and, as he had planned, they elicited excitement in Abonuteichos, where the citizens immediately began building a temple.

When he got home, Alexandros cunningly staged the birth of the "new Asklepios" before an astonished crowd. Then the full-grown snake came into play (Figures 105 and 106). He took seat in a dimly lit sanctuary with the snake wound about his body. He concealed its actual head in his armpit while over his shoulder poked out a human-like figure made of linen, whose mouth could be opened like that of a marionette, using a very thin horsehair, and a long, black tongue could be moved. This clever arrangement escaped closer inspection, especially since the speaking serpent was subsequently not shown to just anyone: the customer had to pay a high price to enter the temple and hear the answer from the serpent's mouth. In the gradually refined and routinized oracle business, those seeking advice usually submitted their questions in writing, sealed; on the appointed day, their submission was returned to them with an apparently undamaged seal, along with Glykon's answer, at the cost of one drachma, two oboles—which was still four times as much as what people paid in Mallos (Cilicia).

The enterprise was enormously successful, and the number of visitors rapidly rose—probably also because its founder, taking into account with shrewd foresight the general boom in oracles, had chosen a huge, remote area largely free of other or-

106. Glykon coin from Ionopolis. Cabinet des médailles, Paris. Photo courtesy Bibliothèque nationale de France.

105. Glykon, the oracle-snake of Abonuteichos. Constanţa Museum.

acle sites. The oracle of Apollo in Chalkedon in Bithynia and that of the old Mysian god named Zeus Kersullos, near Hadrianoi in Mysia, lay far away. It is not known whether the oracle of Autolykos, the deified founder of the nearby city of Sinope, was still active there, as he had been earlier in Strabo's time. People streamed in, not only from Paphlagonia, but also from Bithynia, Galatia, and Thrace, and the oracle's fame finally reached senatorial circles. Alexandros had the good fortune to find in Publius Mummius Sisenna Rutilianus, the suffect consul and governor of the province of Upper Moesia (in the fifties of the second century CE), not only an interested prospective customer but also a son-in-law through whom he could establish relationships with influential Romans. Thus he had access to information with which he could foil opponents, since the oracle of Abonuteichos was not immune to the hostility of illustrious intellectuals and people who envied him. Lucian was one of these opponents, and he claimed that during his visit to Abonuteichos he narrowly escaped an attempt on his life fomented by the priest.

Lucian's pamphlet expresses, line by line, his loathing for a villainous fraud; his scorn is aimed at the person, but also at oracles in general, as in other passages in his writing. He was not alone in this. In one place, Pausanias (1, 34, 3) calls the oracle of Amphilochos in Mallos "the least mendacious." In the time of Hadrian, the Cynic Oinomaos of Gadara wrote a book about the inanity of oracles titled *Detection of Deceivers*, wherein he reports on an experience he had in Klaros. During one of the sacred nights he was given an utterance that basically amounted to nothing more than the Hesiodic proverb: The gods put sweat before success. And during the same night he learned that a businessman from Pontos had received the same answer as he did, word for word. Further test questions addressed to the god were answered vaguely or enigmatically: "A man throws stones from a long-whirled sling and with them kills enormously many geese feeding on the grass." Oinomaos comments bitterly that the god can just go hang himself with his long-whirled sling (Eusebius, *p. e.* 5, 23, 3).

After Lucian's Alexandros had been deemed incredible by older research, the French researcher on antiquity Louis Robert demonstrated the factual framework underlying the report. Lately, the critique of the critic is once again dominant.[395] It is argued that Lucian's view, darkened by hostility, misses the religious essence, and that his report is not free from assumptions and exaggerations. Oinomaos is also accused of being disingenuous in speaking of deception, since everyone must have known from the outset that the answers handed out to him were taken from collections of oracular utterances prepared in advance.[396] However, it can hardly be assumed that in the routine mass processing of the general fascination with oracles, prophets and priests were constantly in the grip of religious fervor and unaware of the workmanlike, commercial character of their activities.

It is surely no accident if in the same period itinerant preachers, Christian and pagan prophets who traveled through the land and gathered people around themselves, became famous.[397] Frauds were also found among them. The Cynic Peregrinos Proteus from Parion, who had himself been the target of a ferocious literary attack of Lucian's, collected, as a "new Socrates," a large group of followers, converted to Christianity, and even wrote Christian works. Finally he emulated Diogenes of Sinope and detached himself from Christianity again. In Olympia he staged, immediately after the games in 165 CE, his spectacular self-cremation. Apollonios of Tyana, a neo-Pythagorean in the time of Nerva, incurred criticisms no less harsh. A certain Moiragenes represented him as a magician. In contrast, the sophist Philostratos opposed this view with a biography of Apollonios written at the behest of the empress Julia Domna (ca. 170–217, Septimius Severus's wife since ca. 185). In it, the historical Apollonios is largely covered up by the image of a healing, demon-banishing wonder worker who could also awaken the dead and clearly had traits of the Christian Jesus. It is an image that presupposes the spread of Christianity and the controversy over it. In his *lararium* in Rome the Roman emperor Severus Alexander (222–235) erected, among other statues, that of the already widely venerated Apollonios of Tyana next to those of Jesus Christ, Abraham, and Orpheus (HA *Alex. Sev.* 29, 2). Around 300 CE, the legend of Apollonios was used by the writer Hierokles to play it off against Christianity and assert the superiority of the Pythagorean from Tyana over Christ.

A rare phenomenon that coincides temporally with the budding obsession with oracles, the belief in miracles, and the individual search for protection and salvation, is the so-called propitiatory inscriptions in Asia Minor. These appear only there in the Imperial period, from the middle of the first to the end of the third centuries, and are distributed over a coherent region focused on the upper and middle valley of the Hermos. As votive gifts to one or several divinities, they were erected in shrines near villages or towns. They are almost totally absent in urban centers; thus we can speak of a rural religiousness. What is striking from the outset is that the area where they are found is immediately adjacent to that where early evidence of Christian ruralists has been discovered; indeed, the former overlaps the latter. To form a clear idea of the procedure underlying a propitiatory inscription, it is helpful to reverse the order of events as reported on the stone:[398] A woman named Syntyche dedicates to the god Men a stele on which she has a twenty-five-line report chiseled under a crescent moon. She was moved to do this by an illness or accident suffered by her thirteen-year-old son. Since the boy had done nothing that deserved divine punishment, his mother sought and found the guilt in herself: she had allowed herself to be persuaded not to mention the pregnancy of the unmarried daughter of a neighbor. That her silence was a sin followed from her interpretation of the defloration as a punishment that the god wanted to see made public: the same girl had previously stolen from Syntyche's own house a valuable stone that her husband had earlier "found." Syntyche had herself been suspected by the owners or authorities who were searching for the stone, and had asked Men to prove her innocence. The girl did in fact return the stone, though damaged and half burned up (from use in magical practices?). Nonetheless the girl's punishment (defloration) followed on the thirty-first day after the theft.

This is one of the longest of these about 150 texts, which are always constructed in accord with the same schema: because of a catastrophe perceived as a punishment suffered by herself or someone connected with her, a person publicly displays a report on it. This is not a matter of "pillorying" or "publicly humiliating" someone, but rather part of a ritual of propitiation that restores balance to a relationship between god and humans that has been disturbed: the power of the all-seeing and all-hearing divinity must be made public (along with the sacrifices to be made, etc.) to arrive at a resolution. Resolution means the abolition of a persistent menacing condition, not for instance the healing or recovery of the person punished, which in no way has to accompany the resolution. Knowledge of the connection between a catastrophe and a misdeed—in the example cited above, a whole causal series—can be communicated to the person concerned through an epiphany, a dream, or a divine afflatus conveyed through messengers. The punishments, which are almost always physical, are represented in word and image and stand in no recognizably graduated relationship to the severity of the offense. Reliefs show breasts, eyes (very often), legs, buttocks, and genitalia, while the texts speak of killing, silencing, and the like. Among the transgressions, by far the majority are in the realm of the sacred; in the profane realm they are hardly relevant in either civil or criminal matters, such as entering the sanctuary in an impure state, misconduct during rituals, not fulfilling vows, or impiety. Even in the case of "worldly" sins it depends on whether the divinity is in some way involved, for example, when someone burdened with guilt enters a sanctuary ([105] TAM V 3, 1539), but it also occurs in other ways as well: Meter and Men punished a delinquent debtor by death because the creditor documented the loan to the gods.[399] The demand for payment remained intact and was paid by the debtor's daughter to the gods with additional interest, and resolution was not achieved until the inscribed stele was erected. Priests were not explicitly involved in the procedure of punishment, recognition, and resolution that followed the offense. Whether they played the role of gods—for example, when it was a matter of divine councils issuing judgments in which Zeus appeared as "legal counsel" to the accused—is an open question.[400] But it would certainly be a mistake to assume that in villages justice was predominantly dispensed by priests rather than by the secular system.

The language of these reports is anything but artificial and is very remote from the poetry enriched by Homeric formulas characteristic of many tomb inscriptions. In this we can recognize the unmediated handwriting of a simple rural population. However, its piety certainly had limits. People sometimes expressed themselves disrespectfully when speaking of a god or refused to donate some part of their property for religious purposes until they were made to do so under threat of punishment. We even know of a case of open revolt.[401] The whole procedure falls outside the framework of pagan religious practices in the Imperial period. It differs from Christian confession primarily in that the first reaction is to the infliction of punishment and that purification is brought about by public praise for power, not by a private reception of the grace of God. Oriental, Hittite, parallels have been noted; are we to suppose that here constantly practiced religious rites and procedures that remained silent for a millennium and a half speak and are made visible on stones?[402]

The people confessing were without exception worshippers of pagan divinities of the Anatolian or Iranian strata; divinities that "ruled" certain villages, cities, and regions. Not a single confession comes from a Christian. The custom of singing the praises of the divinity proven in several texts was recognized as borrowed from Jewish religious practice, and reminded scholars of the Jewish colonization of Lydia under Antiochos III.[403] The propitiatory inscriptions may reflect not only a linear extension of the old Anatolian religion but also a reaction to encroaching religious competitors, such as Christianity.

Convergence toward Monotheism

In the religious landscape, which varyied from city to city, a common element occupied a prominent place in the festive calendar of the provincials as well as in their religious structures as a whole: the cult of the emperor. We need not discuss this empire-wide institution in detail here.[404] In the Anatolian provinces its institutionalization took place on two levels: The first level was the already discussed provincial commonalty's temples of the emperor and their personnel, which might be distributed over several cities in a province that had the predicate of "temple guardian." The second level consisted of countless *poleis* that cultivated a municipal cult of the emperor with its own priests and priestesses. Provincial and especially local worship of the emperor was closely connected with the worship of the city's gods, in whose sanctuaries sacrifices were customarily made to the emperors as "cohabitants" (*syn-*

naoi theoi). After Hadrian founded the *Panhellenion* in Athens (132 CE), veneration of this emperor also penetrated provincials' private homes, where numerous altars of *Olympios* as "savior" and "founder" (*soter* and *ktistes*) were erected. Dedications and prayers were mostly addressed to the deceased emperors, who had officially become divine rulers, but also to members of the imperial family. In the festival calendar of the cities of Asia minor several dates were firmly connected with the cult of the emperor—as in the inscription from Pergamon concerning the hymn singers ([163] I Pergamon 374)—among them the several emperors' or empresses' birthdays, such as that of Augustus (September 23) and that of Livia (September 21). The program included various ceremonies, ceremonial processions, sacrifices, and competitions, one of the latter being gladiator battles.

The cult of the emperor was directed to a god whose veneration brought together different religious communities. Jews and Christians worshipped *one* god who stood over everything, who did not allow his people to have any other gods, and who was himself not visible in images. Both groups demarcated themselves from outsiders but were also not unified internally. In contrast, in the domain we call pagan, there was no fixed ruling pantheon with branches in various places, but rather a dynamic process in which a vast number of old and new gods from different parts of the world and cultures crowded in alongside and over one another. Their cults, rules, and beliefs competed in a limited space. Outsiders demanded an explanation of their ancestry, their nature. "Who are you?" a visitor to the newly founded sanctuary in Abonuteichos asked the prophesying serpent Glykon. "I am the latter-day Asclepius." "A different person from the one of former times? What do you mean?" "It is not permitted you to hear that" (Lucian, *Alex.* 43; trans. Harmon). Honorifics such as "the highest," "best," "greatest," "all-powerful," and "ruler of the cosmos" announced simultaneously differentiation and the lifting of barriers.

> God is one, who alone rules, immense, uncreated,
> Almighty, invisible, alone himself seeing all,
> Himself yet not viewed by any mortal flesh.
> For what flesh can see with eyes the heavenly
> And true immortal God, who dwells in heaven?[405]

That is how the bishop of Antiocheia, Theophilos, conceived the Christian God in the second century. At Apollo's behest, a man in Amastris on the Black Sea erected an altar for a "highest god," a god "who comprehends everything and is not seen, but sees all evil," and a man in Lydia called himself the "Priest of the one and only God."[406]

In Late Antique Christian sources references to "Messaliani" and "Hypsistarii" or "Hypsistiani" occur. They are said to be worshippers of *one* god, but not true Christians. In about 300 inscriptions, mostly from Asia Minor, the expression *theos hypsistos* ("highest god") appears as the sole mode of address for a god without a name. The British ancient historian Stephen Mitchell maintains—contrary to the conventional conception of an ambivalent term applicable to the Jewish, Christian, and pagan gods—that the worshippers of this god were a separate, unified group that was re-shaped by the Jewish diasporic religion and stood between paganism, Judaism, and Christianity. For Mitchell, the terms *Hypsistarii* and *Messaliani* refer precisely to this group. They are supposed to have called themselves "God-fearing" (*theosebeis*)—the same term that the New Testament uses to refer to a non-Jewish minority in the synagogues, a community interested in Jewish rules of life and belief and somehow close to the Jewish community. In Aphrodisias, they constituted a group distinct from proselytes and Jews, and in the theater at Miletus seats were reserved for them alongside the Jewish seats.[407]

In the third century CE two altars were chiseled out of blocks of the Hellenistic city wall of Oinoanda in the mountains of Lycia. They bear inscriptions indicating that they belong to the cult of a "highest god" ([146] MS IV 16–19). Six verses that are later reused almost verbatim in Christian writings (Lactantius, *inst.* 1, 7, 1; Tübingen theosophy) quote from a theological oracle in Klaros:

> Born to itself, untaught, without a mother, unshakeable, not contained in a name, known by many names, dwelling in fire, this is god. We, his angels, are a small part of god. To you who ask this question about god, what his essential nature is, he has pronounced that Aether is god who sees all, on whom you should gaze and pray at dawn, looking towards the sunrise.[408]

The expression "we, his angels" provides an astonishing definition of Apollo as an angel in the service of a higher god; the priests of Klaros are here clearly propagating monotheism. On many votive altars of the second and third centuries, mainly in the interior of western Anatolia, "angels" as mounted messengers are described as "pious and righteous" (*hosios kai dikaios*), this composite expression designating one person or two different persons, depending on the region. This pair also serves a higher-ranking god, in most cases Helios, as the bearer of the divine righteousness that watches over human behavior at all times.[409]

It is clear that in individual cases the expression *theos hypsistos* could also be used in addressing Jahweh, the Christian God, or a Zeus or Helios. But the limits of this kind of address seem in general indistinct: someone who dedicates something to a god with this name is not necessarily a pagan, a Jew, or a Christian. He or she may be committed to a form of monotheism that borrowed from pagan, Jewish, and Christian beliefs. It is understandable that such believers found it easy to join a Christianity that was steadily growing stronger, as did, for example, the father of Gregory of Nazianzus.

Asia Minor and Early Christianity

For centuries Asia Minor played a prominent role in the spread of Christianity. As almost nowhere else, the network of cities in this country—in which long since the Jewish diaspora had been established, a syncretism of very ancient and more recent cults and doctrines was present, and a deeply rooted religiousness had been rekindled, a single language prevailed, writing and culture reached the villages, and commerce and trade flourished—offered both the ideal spiritual breeding ground and the best infrastructure for its spread. The new sects found the model for their organization at home and in the world at their front door, so to speak, in the village associations, *thiasoi*, and religious communities and on through the provincial commonalties to the worldwide associations of the athletes' and artists' synods. It was probably only here that local groups could attain a kind of self-consciousness that pertained to seeing themselves as cells of an *oikumene*—not unlike the way Aelius Aristeides conceived the *poleis* and the empire together. The one new people, the "third race" (*triton genos*) after the pagans and Jews that was at the same time the oldest and first, that was higher, and into which the others were destined from the outset to be absorbed, had risen up precisely together with the Roman imperial world peace (*pax Augusta*). It was no accident that in a letter to Marcus Aurelius (in Eusebius, *h. e.* 4, 26) the bishop of Sardeis, Meliton, wrote:

> For our philosophy formerly flourished among the Barbarians; but having sprung up among the nations under thy rule, during the great reign of thy ancestor Augustus, it became to thine empire especially a blessing of auspicious omen. For from that time the power of the Romans has grown in greatness and splendor. To this power thou hast succeeded, as the desired possessor, and thus shalt thou continue with thy son, if thou guardest the philosophy which grew up with the empire and which came into existence with Augustus; that philosophy which thy ancestors also honored along with the other religions. And a most convincing proof that our doctrine flourished for the good of an empire happily begun, is this–that there has no evil happened since Augustus' reign, but that, on the contrary, all things have been splendid and glorious, in accordance with the prayers of all. (trans. McGifford)[410]

Beginnings

Tarsos, the birthplace of the tentmaker Paul, a Jew fluent in Greek, communicated over short distances with Cyprus and Syria. It was in the latter's metropolis of Antiocheia that those who acknowledged Christ, whether Jews or pagans, first received the name Christians (Acts 11:26). The Jewish assembly in Jerusalem still named itself "Nazarenes" after the place where Jesus grew up (Acts 24:5).[411] Paul received his early education in Jerusalem and was a Pharisee there (Acts 23:6; Phil. 3:5). We have no detailed knowledge of his time in his Cilician homeland. His companion Barnabas came from Salamis on Cyprus. The island was the first stop on their common missionary journey that began in Syria. From the reports on it modern research has put many things in question, not always on valid grounds. We cannot discuss the pros and cons here.[412]

Perhaps we might see precisely in a Roman proconsul, Cyprus's governor Sergius Paulus, the first prominent pagan Christian, and in Cyprus the first country to be ruled, temporarily, by a Christian.[413] Saul is supposed to have taken his name from him and henceforth called himself Paul[us] (Jerome, *vir. ill.* 5). Soon thereafter the traveling apostles chose Sergius's homeland, the *colonia Antiocheia* in Pisidia,[414] as their next destination. This goal was determined spontaneously by the meeting on Cyprus, and in any case their further journey did not stick to a plan established at the beginning. It cannot be determined whether it was on this journey that the very first steps of the Christian mission to Anatolia were taken. There were Jewish communities everywhere in the land, and the early message was surely carried forth by more persons than we can identify.

In the synagogue of Antiocheia in Pisidia, as later in other Anatolian cities, the word was heard not only by circumcised Jews, but also by the so-called God-fearing (*theosebeis*). The Jews did not fail to react, and in the innermost circle of the first listeners tensions broke out and escalated so far that the foreigners "shook off the dust from their feet" (Acts 13:50 f.). Strangely, they did not think of going down into the heavily populated province of Asia, but instead turned in the opposite direction on the *via Sebaste*, where other Augustan *coloniae* were to be found in the southeastern part of the province of Galatia, on the inland slopes of the Taurus Mountains. In the Julia Augusta Iconium *colonia* (modern-day Konya), the turmoil was repeated and forced them to move on once again. In the Julia Felix Gemina Lustra *colonia* (Lystra), the "miracle" Paul performed on a crippled man won him such respect among the people that to their dismay the missionaries found themselves called, in Lycaonian, epiphanies of Zeus and Hermes. "And the priest of Zeus, whose temple was in front of the city, brought oxen and garlands to the gate and wanted to offer sacrifice with the people" (Acts 14:13; all quotes are from the Revised Standard Edition). But an agitated crowd of Jews from Antiocheia and Ikonion came into the city and pelted Paul with stones. The missionaries fled eastward, toward Derbe. Nonetheless, they must have won some sympathizers in the *coloniae*, because after reaching Derbe they turned around and traveled back the long way, supposedly via the same cities through which they had passed before as far as Attaleia in Pamphylia, not taking a shortcut to the coast through the Kalykadnos valley or the Cilician Gates.

Otherwise, Acts mentions by name only a few of the places in Asia Minor that were stops on the two subsequent missionary journeys or that received epistles from the first generation of apostles. Paul moved through Cilicia, the Galatian country, Phrygia, and Mysia, passing through the cities of Derbe and Lystra, Alexandria Troas, Assos, Miletus, and Patara. In the Epistle to the Colossians (2:1; 4:13), not only Kolossai but also Laodikeia and Hierapolis are addressed as communities. His extended stay in Ephesos is of special interest, if only because it was the most important metropolis of the Roman Orient after Alexandria in Egypt and Antiocheia in Syria.[415] A Christian sect had been established there even before he arrived. The hostility simmering in the synagogue led Paul to reschedule his public appearance in the school of a private individual named Tyrannos, but anger was aroused in larger groups when the silversmiths at the Temple of Artemis took offense at a sermon in which Paul said that "gods made with hands are not gods," thereby denigrating their handmade devotional objects (Acts 19:26). The Ephesians were proud of the fact that their goddess was revered "throughout Asia and the world." The call "Great is the Ephesians' Artemis!" echoed through the city. The wrath of the people in the packed theater endangered the lives of two of Paul's collaborators, and the disturbance alarmed officials. Significantly, the officials refused to bend to the crowd's demands, and the silversmiths were advised to take legal action.

One of the presumed earliest letters of Paul is the Epistle to the Galatians. When and where it was written cannot be determined with certainty. Libraries could be filled with the commentaries on it. Regarding the question of to whom it was actually addressed,[416] I share the view that "Galatians" designates the inhabitants of the Roman province named "Galatia," and thus first of all the citizens of the previously mentioned cities that were visited several times, and not, for example, those of the Celts' old settlement areas around Ankyra and Tavium, which the apostle probably never saw. From the letters we can infer that in the first Christian communities founded by Paul on Anatolian soil, his teaching was not without competitors, but missionaries who arrived later pressured believers to adopt, with regard to circumcision and Jewish law, the opposing position of the "true" apostles in Jerusalem. Probably not all believers considered Paul the true apostle or, if they did, remained loyal to him. "If anyone is preaching to you a gospel contrary to that which we preached to you, let him be accursed" (Gal. 1:9).

In provinces like Pontus et Bithynia—in which two generations later the number of people of all ages, social classes, and both sexes accused of being Christians was already high, the faith had spread over the cities and the countryside, temples were neglected, ceremonial sacrifices had long been abandoned, and the sales of feed for sacrificial animals had decreased—an answer to the question of how and through whom Christianity reached them so early still completely eludes us. The same goes for large parts of the province of Asia as well as the countries of Galatia, Paphlagonia, and Cappadocia (cf. 1 Pet. 1). Not only the small, original communities that emerged in the places mentioned by name, but also encounters en route and beyond Asia Minor radiated out and spread the faith further. A purpura dealer from Thyateira whom Paul converted in Phillipoi (Thrace), along with Aquila and Priscilla, a tent-making couple from Pontos (Amastris?) who had been expelled from Rome,[417] whom Paul converted in Corinth, and who resided for a long time in Ephesos, may perhaps be considered transmitters in their respective homelands.

It is doubtful whether Peter played a role in Asia Minor. But in the time of the Apostles there were other efficacious missionaries in this country: Aristion, Andreas, Philippos and his daughters, and the greatest of all of them, John. He is just as important for the beginnings of Christianity in general as Paul is. John's name is connected with Ephesos, the "second base of Christianity after Antioch,"[418] where the

107. The basilica of St. John in Ephesos (photo: Max Gander).

enormous basilica on Ayasoluk hill, built under Justinian, still commemorates him (Figure 107). Ancient Christian writers are already divided regarding his identity. The bishops of Lyon, Irenaeus (*haer*. 3, 1, 1), and of Ephesos, Polykrates (in Eusebius, *h. e.* 3, 31; 5, 24, 3)—prominent contemporaries in the Easter controversy at the end of the second century—wrongly thought the Ephesian was Christ's favorite disciple of the same name (John 13:23), whereas Eusebius (*h. e.* 3, 39, 5 f.) distinguished the presbyter John from the apostle John, son of Zabadaeus, both of them supposedly buried in Ephesos.

And there is the question of who wrote the three New Testament texts that bear the name John: the Gospel, Revelations, and the Letters. Eusebius attributed (probably erroneously) the Gospel to the apostle and Revelations to the presbyter. According to a view widely held among researchers, Revelations, as the earlier work, was composed in the time of Domitian on the island of Patmos,[419] to which the exiled author had gone (Tertullian, *praescr.* 36, 3). Eusebius (*h. e.* 3, 20, 9) has him returning from Patmos to Ephesos. The original version of the probably repeatedly revised Gospel may stem from the same author. From the metropolis, the presbyter and evangelist governed the Asian communities until he died at an advanced age in the early years of Trajan's reign. Did a small group of his pupils, including Papias of Hierapolis, manage to publish and distribute the aforementioned writings there, and win recognition for them?

Spread

In the first and second centuries the Christian faith spread throughout Asia Minor, even if at the beginning of the fourth century Christians still constituted a minority in most places.[420] Christian writers tend to exaggerate the numbers of the faithful and their omnipresence. The John who composed the Apocalypse (7:9) already speaks, from an Anatolian point of view, of a large multitude that no one can count, from all nations and tribes and peoples and languages. In his province, Asia, Christian communities may in fact have been established early on, in city after city. The first of the seven epistles was received by Ephesos, where there was already a Christian sect, the Nicolaitans (cf. Acts 6:5), to be fought; the second by Smyrna, where Christians were oppressed by the large Jewish community; the third by Pergamon, where the Throne of Satan stood (the great Zeus altar, p. 240) and where the martyrdom of a certain Antipas is supposed to have occurred at about this time. Further letters were received by Thyateira, Sardeis, and Philadelpheia in Lydia, and finally by Laodikeia in Phrygia, where the brothers were apparently not easy to teach, but rather lukewarm, smug, rich, and satisfied with themselves; that is, they were numerous and lived in peace.[421] The same province seems also to have been the first to have rapidly solidifying groups of Christians in smaller cities and in the countryside; the sources suggest that by the second century a rural region like Phrygia was already full of nests of Christians.

However, pagan chroniclers seldom took notice of the Christian presence in the provinces. Even Herodian, who wrote (ca. 240 CE) a history of the age of the Antonines down to his own time, does not mention Christians anywhere. The exception is the Syrian Lucian (*Peregr.* 11–13), whose description of Christians a few decades earlier is probably based on his experiences in Asia Minor. He sees in them the followers of a "wondrous wisdom" who live in brotherly solidarity and are somewhat naive, both in their neglect of material goods and their "communism"—which moreover encouraged swindlers to trick them—and in their conviction that they would live forever, scorning death and voluntarily handing themselves over to their persecutors. These remarks are often wrongly interpreted as mocking and contemptuous. But the usual reproaches—blood and sex, "Thyestic meals" (eating children), and "Oedipal crimes" (incest)—are not found here or elsewhere in Lucian's work; instead, we find a mode of observation that is distanced but also based on astonishment and sympathy.[422] Although the groups separating themselves from the public in the *polis* repelled the general community precisely because they practiced a rigorous morality, they were popular because of their generosity, openness, and hospitality. After all, they gave alms to the needy; conducted funerals; supported teachers, widows[423] and orphans, the old, and the ill; and took care of prisoners, those condemned to work in mines, and slaves. In prison in Syria, Peregrinos discovered the solidarity of his Asian coreligionists, who had traveled there expressly to support him. Their groups included rich and poor alike.

By the end of the second century CE, in Anatolia there were increasing numbers of inscriptions made by Christians even before tolerance of their religion was decreed in the age of Constantine. In these inscriptions Christians make themselves known in different ways that are not always unambiguous and reliable.[424] The earliest epigraphic evidence of this kind comes from the area around Kadoi, Synaos, and Aizanoi in Phrygia. In northwestern Phrygia, especially around Kotiaion (now Kütahya), the owners of tombs often affirmed their Christian faith with the formula "Christians for Christians" (*christianoi christianois*).[425] Key words like *ichthys* (fish), *episkopos*, or *martys*, and symbols, such as crosses on the stele's tympanum or in a prominent place on the tombstone, are references just as clear as the *menorah* is among Jews. The letters *chi* (X) and *rho* (P) are less reliable signs that cannot always be interpreted as Christograms. We are always on slippery terrain when interpreting individual statements, expressions, and words. Even the way in which a god is addressed can be ambiguous in regard to the religion of the worshipper. Possible indicators are "resurrection," "Judgment Day,"([162] *IK* Nikaia 555 lines 17 f.), "disciple of the Holy Shepherd" ([142] Johnson 2.13; [146] MS III 182), "the seal" (*sphragis*) as a symbol of baptism ([142] Johnson 4.16 line 26), the designation of the tomb as a "place of sleep" (*koimeterion*; e.g., [142] Johnson 2.14), and, commonly in Phrygia, threats stating that those who profane graves will have "to deal with God" or "answer for it before God." The latter is the "Eumenian formula" (named after the Phrygian city of Eumeneia); however, it seems not to be exclusively Christian.[426] Some longer phrases allow us to attribute them to Christians. A text on a tomb from Phazemonitis in Paphlagonia can serve as an example:

> Here Earth enshrouded the man, Reglos, who has been adorned with all wisdom and virtue, together with his two children. The names of the Children are Olympion and Akylina, whose souls God the Begetter himself received, remembering the piety they duly engaged in. For their souls' salvation they filled beggars with good things, and they honored their friends, they watched over their family with great and inimitable affection, and they were eager to be hospitable to all men. (trans. [142] Johnson 4.15 with slight corrections by Marek)

The sects (p. 542) are also present in inscriptions on stone. The formula "filled with spirit" (*pneumatikos*) and persons named Montanos or Montane after the founder [427] allow us to recognize Montanists; Novatianists can be identified by the reference to their membership in the *ekklesia* of the Nauatianoi or the "pure" (*katharoi*).

If we search through the inscriptions on early tombstones that belonged to Christians, looking for indications of their occupations, we find a predominance of craftsmen and farmers.[428] Before the third century hardly any Asian Christians are known to have held municipal, provincial, or imperial offices; among the most noteworthy exceptions is Marcus Demetrianus in Klaudiupolis, the first *archon* and president of the contests, the latter being exactly the institution most scorned by Christian writers.[429] Tomb inscriptions from Phrygia—Eumeneia, Sebaste, and Laodikeia Katakekaumene—name councilmen ([142] Johnson 3.2–3.7); among them we also find the member of the *gerusia* on whose tombstone reliefs depicting wreaths with inscriptions and oil-scrapers (*strigiles*) allude to his victories in athletic competitions ([142] Johnson 3.4). The inscription on the sarcophagus of a certain Marcus Junius Eugenius was probably chiseled only ca. 340 CE. But the owner of this tomb looked back on his life before the Constantine Turning Point. His father was a councilman in the city of Kuessos, and he himself—being married to the daughter of an (otherwise unknown) senator named Gaius Nestorianus—was an official (*officialis*) on the staff of the governor of Pisidia. As a Christian, during the persecution under Maximinus Daia (ca. 311 CE) he had to undergo questioning by the governor and leave his post; he finally became bishop of Laodikeia and remained in that office for twenty-five years ([142] Johnson 3.5).

Women played a prominent role in the reception and spread of the faith, especially in Asia Minor.[430] The Anatolian Strabo (7, 3, 4) attributes to women in general a stronger religiousness than that of men. The Apostle Paul's letters are full of references to active Christian women in his entourage as well as in the communities. Although over time a tendency to deny women the right to teach and baptize, and to use them only as deaconesses in the service of the congregation, grew stronger in the Church, in both of the first two centuries we find examples of Christian women as apostles, teachers, and prophets. A line can be drawn from Priscilla (Acts 18:18), Junia (Rom. 16:7), and Thekla (Acts of Paul) through the prophesying daughters of Philippos (Acts 21:9) to the Montanist prophets Ammia, Quintilla, Maximilla, and Priscilla (p. 544). Christ appeared to Priscilla when she was sleeping in Pepuza—this is scandalous for the theology of the majority Church—in the guise of a woman (Epiphanios, *haer.* 49, 1, 3). A female Montanist communicated with angels, and also with God; she saw and heard secrets, saw into people's hearts, and gave curatives to those who asked for them (Tertullian, *anim.* 9, 4). Women also appear in clerical offices in the Phrygian sects: thus there were female bishops and presbyters.[431] Furthermore, Christian women are found earlier and in greater numbers in the upper strata of society than are Christian men. Wives and relatives of pagan officeholders confess their faith: Alke, the aunt of the police chief in Smyrna who arrested Polycarp, is apparently identical with the Christian woman who appears in Ignatius's letters (Ignatius to Polycarp 8, 3, and Ignatius to the Smyrnans 13, 2). Tavia (or Gavia), the prominent Smyrnan Christian woman mentioned by name in the same passage of Ignatius's letter to the Smyrnans, was perhaps the same as the woman Ignatius mentions in his letter to Polycarp only as the "procurator's wife."[432] In Cappadocia, the wife of a governor converted to Christianity in the Severan age (Tertullian, *Scap.* 3). That the cofounders of Montanism were rich and noble women can be inferred from the accusations that were made against them, and the Juliana in Cappadocian Kaisareia, with whom the Christian philosopher Origen stayed for several months, must have been a respected and prosperous citizen.

In none of the persecutions were female Christians spared. St. Thekla was and is revered as the earliest female martyr. In the *acta Pauli et Theclae* we find the story of

108. Church of St. Mary in Ephesos (photo: Emanuel Zingg).

the young Thekla, who heard the Apostle Paul speak in Ikonion (today Konya), was converted by him, and remained constantly at his side. Because of her steadfast faith, she was taken to be executed in Ikonion itself and again in Antiocheia in Pisidia, but both times she was miraculously saved, and ended up living for decades in a cave where she preached and baptized. This story goes back to the fanciful elaboration of a presbyter in Asia ca. 180 CE (Tertullian, *bapt*. 17). The legend became enormously popular. Alongside Ephesos, where the cult of Mary was celebrated (Figure 108), the most prominent Asian pilgrimage site of the new religion was the cavern near Seleukeia on Kalkadnos, where after an earlier building of the third century the three-aisled Basilica of St. Thekla was constructed ca. 375 CE. Among its earliest visitors were Gregory of Nazianzus and the Spanish (or Gallic) woman Egeria.

Persecution

Over the course of the first two centuries persecutions sporadically flared up in the cities of Asia Minor. At first, they were locally limited. The occasions were similar in that in them the population's pent-up resentment against those unwilling to adapt was discharged, whether this was spontaneous or instigated by interest groups like the Jews, the silversmiths, the merchants of meat for sacrifices, or the municipal and provincial imperial priesthood. With the growth of a new, parallel religious society, the leading classes in the communities as a whole must have been provoked, because most of the numerous officeholders were intimately involved in the rites of the traditional religion that were practiced everywhere and filled their calendars. They ranged from the asiarchs or galatarchs down to the leaders of *thiasoi* in the villages, and they enjoyed all the social and economic advantages associated with their offices.[433] Among them, and hence among the opinion makers in every gathering, the more specifically motivated anti-Christian forms of agitation immediately found a broad and deep response.

The authorities who represented the Roman world power in Asia Minor kept their distance from this sort of agitation. Death sentences and martyrdoms were at first exceptions to the rule. From the Roman point of view, however, the ultimately unavoidable criminal case involved the public rejection of the religious, ceremonial loyalty oath to the emperor that was usually made by the community of the provincials on the occasion of festivals. If a judge could recognize a genuine Christian only if the latter refused to take the oath, then for him, the judge, a constitutional link between being a Christian and sacrilege and lèse-majesté was immediately suggested. In any case, before the persecutions under the emperor Decius (249–251), the participation of every inhabitant of the province in the cult of the emperor in the cities of Asia Minor was neither required nor enforceable. Most Christians, who kept their distance, lived undisturbed by the Roman government so long as they were not overwhelmed by a wave of denunciations. A minority of this community of belief was endangered by its status and activity, which drew more public attention to its behavior. In it adaptation and compromise were probably the rule.

The Christian writers Lactantius, Eusebius, and Augustine count ten major persecutions: under Nero, Domitian, Trajan, Antoninus, Severus, Maximinus, Decius, Valerian, Aurelian and, the tenth, under Diocletian and Maximian. No estimate of the number of people killed in these persecutions can be given, either in general or only for Asia Minor. The reliable reports—primarily that of Eusebius, who collected them—give only excerpts, and the *Acta Martyrum* are late and wreathed in legends, and therefore problematic as sources. Not many people can have withstood the terrible tortures that are described in detail, and the number of those who renounced their faith must have far exceeded that of those executed in each of the waves of persecution. A special case is the self-incrimination first mentioned in relation to the martyrdom of Polycarp (p. 538) and judged in the same text to be unevangelical, because it made the martyr into a virtual suicide; this kind of behavior was attributed primarily to the Montanists. Thus the self-incriminators to whom the proconsul of Asia, Arrius Antoninus, called out that if they wanted to die, they should hang themselves or jump off a cliff, may have been Montanists (Tertullian, *Scap.* 5, 1).

It can be considered certain that Asia Minor was already caught up in the persecution under Domitian, even though we know hardly anything concrete about it.[434] In Pliny's letter (*ep.* 10, 96), we read that trials of Christians had already taken place (under Domitian? But he says nothing about the province!); the invectives in Revelation target the offensive religious policy of the emperor who was supposed to be addressed as "lord and god" (*dominus et deus*), describing him instead as a "beast" that opened its mouth only "to utter blasphemies against God" (Rev. 13:5 f.). The prospect of actual danger emerges from the epistle to Smyrna: "Do not fear what you are about to suffer. Behold, the devil is about to throw some of you into prison, that you may be tested, and for ten days you will have tribulation. Be faithful unto death, and I will give you the crown of life" (Rev. 2:10).

The correspondence between Pliny the Younger (*ep.* 10, 96–97) and the emperor Trajan ca. 111/112 CE must be considered the earliest authentic documentation we have from a non-Christian perspective regarding the conflict between Christians and Roman state power. As governor, Pliny reacted to the increasing numbers of reports from the people of the province of Pontus et Bithynia, including many anonymous ones, with a procedure that we find attested for the first time in this text—though he certainly did not invent it—and that was later generally practised: he called on those who denied being Christians to do ceremonial homage before the gods and the image of the emperor and to curse Christ. To him, what the deaconesses admitted to him under torture seemed a boundless superstition; his colleague Tacitus (*ann.* 15, 44, 10) held a similar opinion: *exitiabilis superstitio*! But uncertainty as to what was really punishable is mirrored in both his letter and the emperor's reply. Is it just being a Christian (*nomen ipsum*), even if the person has committed no punishable offense, or is it only crimes that are connected with being a Christian (*cohaerentia nomini*)? In the investigating magistrate's initial perplexity, the obstinacy manifest in the believer's heroism with regard to death, which even Stoics like Epictetus (Arrian, *Epict.* 4, 7, 6) and Marcus Aurelius (11, 3) scorned as absurd, could itself be seen as such a crime. For Trajan's answer—one should not ferret out the Christians, anonymous denunciations should not be considered, but those accused and handed over should nonetheless be punished unless they deny the charge and prove by the "test" that they are not Christians, though they remain suspect—the Christian apologist Tertullian (*apol.* 2, 8) has nothing but contempt: " Oh, perplexity between reasons of state and justice! He declares us to be innocent, by forbidding us to be searched after, and at the same time commands us to be punished as criminals" (trans. Reeve).[435]

What else happened in Pontus et Bithynia we do not know. A further legal measure is concerned with events in the province of Asia. A letter from Hadrian to the proconsul Minicius Fundanus, which is extant in Eusebius's Greek translation (*h.e.* 4, 9), takes up the subject again. With the stipulation that the crowd of those bringing accusations against Christians be referred to the courts, instead of giving in to their demands and screams, this document reminds us of the story of the silversmiths in Acts. When the emperor demands proof of a transgression of the law and threatens to punish mere slander, he seems to be strengthening the certainty of law for the Christians, in contrast to what Trajan decreed. The text was interpreted the same way by later Christian authors, though modern scholars have cast doubt on it as unhistorical.[436] However, there are no grounds for this doubt: Trajan's reply to Pliny need not be seen as a basis for all later trials; mutually contradictory instructions were certainly given by emperors. The jurist Ulpian (ca. 170–223) wrote a commentary on the many imperial decrees, precisely because such uncertainty prevailed as to what was to be considered legally valid.[437] Under Hadrian's government (117–138) there was, so far as we know, not a single martyrdom in Asia Minor.

One of the oldest reports on a Christian martyrdom describes in detail the violent death of Polycarp, the bishop of Smyrna who had been installed by John. Polycarp belonged to the small group of prominent theological opinion leaders in the post-Apostolic period whose sphere of influence was already the worldwide Church. The text reproduced by Eusebius (*h. e.* 4, 15), which is partly reproduced verbatim, partly paraphrased, and takes the form of a letter to the Phrygian community of Philomelion, was probably reworked but is basically historical. It contains both narrative and argumentative passages. Regarding the dating of the event there is still confusion in the literature. The term of office of the previously mentioned governing proconsul, "Quadratus," presumably L. Statius Quadratus (ca. 154/155), can serve as a starting point.[438]

It began with accusations against Christians who were citizens of Smyrna and Philadelpheia. Public hearings were held in the theater. Deeper causes of the repressions seem once again to have been resentments—with an especially strong Jewish component in Smyrna. The dissensions escalated to become pogrom-like outbreaks. Stubborn adherents to their faith were supposed to be forced by torture or the threat of death to renounce Christianity, whether they forswore it or carried out a pagan sacrifice. The proconsul himself attempted to persuade some individuals to do so. He was successful precisely in the case of a Phrygian who had incriminated himself and urged his coreligionists to do the same. The crowd, enraged by the imperturbability and contempt for death shown by another young Christian, demanded a manhunt for the bishop. Imprisonment and interrogation once again were accompanied by the urgent efforts to persuade made first by the police chief (*eirenarches*), and then by the proconsul, who, if they were historical and not invented to prove an exemplary power of resistance to temptation, again show that the Roman authorities were disinclined to impose capital punishment, or even a condemnation, on these people. However, in the case of twelve people, including Polycarp, their efforts were unsuccessful. But the asiarch (also known from [106] OGIS 498 f.) still did not yield to the crowd's desire to throw the Christians to the wild animals, because the warm-up program for the gladiator battles, the animal hunts (*venationes*), was already over. Polycarp was put on a pyre and received the coup de grâce in the fire. Foreseeing a practice of his coreligionists that was probably already well known at this time, religiously venerating the remains (relics) of the martyrs, the city authorities refused to give them up; only after the complete consumption of the body by fire could the bones, "more precious than gems and more valuable than gold" be collected and buried, "to celebrate the anniversary day of his martyrdom, both as a memorial for those who have already fought the contest and for the training and preparation of those who will do so one day."[439] This is the earliest testimony to the worship of the saints performed in countless places in Asia Minor.

In the same century, Asia Minor experienced several regional persecutions. The emperor Marcus Aurelius's instructions (*mandata*) to the provincial governors, who were to impose severe punishments on the sacrilegious (*sacrilegi*), were accused by Meliton, bishop of Sardeis (ca. 176–180), of triggering regular manhunts for the "God-fearing" in the province of Asia.[440] Karpos, Papylos, and Agathonike seem to have died at this time in Pergamon, and the bishops of Eumeneia and Laodikeia, Thraseas and Sagaris were put to death in Phrygia (Eusebius, *h. e.* 4, 15). A relatively quiet time followed. Locally limited conflicts flared up in eastern Anatolia. Around the turn of the third century, a governor in Cappadocia who was furious about his wife's conversion is supposed to have set a persecution in motion; mortally ill and already eaten up by worms, he repented and almost became a Christian himself (Tertullian, *Scap.* 3). The Cappadocian bishop Firmilianus's letter to Cyprian (75, 10)[441] recalls a governor of Cappadocia named Licinius Serenianus, a particularly avid and cruel persecutor. The occasion of his persecution seems to have been the people's anger after serious earthquakes in Pontos and Cappadocia; they were looking for scapegoats. Many threatened Christians fled to neighboring areas, where things remained peaceful.

As is well known, the empire-wide measures undertaken by the emperor Decius in 250 CE assumed a new quality insofar as the Roman authority no longer acted on denunciations but instead required everyone to provide sacrifices and eat sacrificial meat.[442] From Smyrna, the same city in which Polycarp's martyrdom took place, another, quite different testimony bears witness to this persecution—the seventh on the long list (Augustine, *civ.* 18, 52). It concerns the martyrdom of a man named Pionius.[443] The report is based on the original transcript of the governor's hearing. Pionius was a model citizen of Smyrna, admired by all. Eusebius, who incorrectly dates Pionius's martyrdom and also that of Polycarp to the reign of Marcus Aurelius, refers to a text on Pionius

> which contains a full account of his several confessions, and the boldness of his speech, and his apologies in behalf of the faith before the people and the rulers, and his instructive addresses and, moreover, his greetings to those who had yielded to temptation in the persecution, and the words of encouragement which he addresses to the brethren who came to visit him in prison, and the tortures which he endured in addition, and besides these the sufferings and the nailings, and his firmness on the pile, and his death after all the extraordinary trials.[444]

One of the three city temple guardians (*neokoroi*), accompanied by policemen (*diogmitai* and a *hipparchos*), went to find Pionius because he had refused to perform sacrifices. He was waiting for them in his house with the Christians Sabina and Asklepiades. The three had already put shackles around their necks to show that they were ready to go to prison. While efforts were made to persuade them to follow the example of others who had already performed the sacrifice, the three were led through the streets to the *agora*. In this case, unlike Polycarp's, the assembled crowd was not raging against the prisoners. After the people had listened to a long speech addressed to pagans and Jews by Pionius, it sought once again to persuade the beloved man to reconsider his refusal—in vain. Sabina was not intimidated by the threat of the punishment foreseen for Christian women, being put in a brothel. After an initial hearing conducted by the *neokoros*, the three were taken to prison. Learning that Euktemon—probably the bishop of the city—had performed a sacrifice, the *neokoros* undertook another attempt at persuasion before the prisoners were forcibly hauled off to the sanctuary. When this, too, proved useless, the only remaining option was to incarcerate them until the proconsul arrived. With his questions, this rhetorically trained man was trying to entice Pionius to adopt a common position when he noticed that the praying Christian's eyes were turned toward heaven, and said:

> "We reverence all the gods, we reverence the heavens and all the gods that are in heaven. What then, do you attend to the air? Then sacrifice to the air." "I do not attend to the air," answered Pionius, "but to him who made the air, the heavens, and all that is in them." The proconsul said: "Tell me, who did make them?" Pionius answered: "I cannot tell you." The proconsul said: "Surely it was the god, that is Zeus, who is in heaven; for he is the ruler of all the gods."[445]

Pionius did not allow himself to be persuaded and forced the proconsul to condemn him to death on the pyre.

Interesting coincidences have been noted by comparing the documents concerning the martyrdom of St. Ariadne with the epigram inscribed on stone by the imperial priest Tertullus of Sagalassos ([146] MS IV 114–117). The report, late, repeatedly reworked and embellished with legends, might contain a historical core if the Tertullus in Prymnessos is identical with the one in Sagalassos (about 120 kilometers away). The rich man from Prymnessos owned a Christian slave, Ariadne; this was denounced and led to a complaint against him being filed with the governor. In the speech his nephew delivered in his defense, tribute was paid his merits coinciding in content with those of the Sagalassian and praised in a style that resembles the eulogies on meritorious citizens of the Imperial period. He was acquitted, but his slave Ariadne was condemned. She escaped through a miracle, in view of which 3,000 people converted to Christianity. According to the *Acts of the Martyrs*, this event took place during the (unhistorical) combined rule of Hadrian and Antoninus Pius. The authentic passages could have been taken from an older martyrdom report, probably from the third century, unless they are modeled on copies of one or several earlier inscriptions for dignitaries.[446]

For the execution of those condemned *ad bestias*—including the Christians—both large and small cities usually planned animal hunts (*venationes*) for the program preceding or accompanying the gladiator battles. One of the most authentic detailed descriptions of such a spectacle recounts the martyrdom of two young women in Carthage: the *passio Perpetuae et Felicitatis*.[447] Most of it can be transferred to Anatolian venues. Relief depictions that have been preserved in various places allow us to put excerpts from such a program in context.

Before the victory of the Church under Constantine, the worst persecutions of all, those under Diocletian and Maximian, raged in Asia Minor. The main sources on this are Lactantius (*mort. pers.* 10 ff.) and Eusebius (*h. e.* 8, 2 ff.). The persecutions began in Nikomedeia in Bithynia, where many Christians already lived at that time (Eusebius, *h. e.* 9, 9), including also imperial personnel of the palace and court in what was then one of the central points of the empire. A role that was ominous from a Christian point of view was played not only by the current *Augustus*, Diocletian, and his *Caesar* Galerius, but also by a certain Hierokles, the *praeses* of Bithynia and the author of the work "To the Christians." First Diocletian brought in an oracle of Apollo from Didyma, in addition to advice of high-ranking officials and officers. Then, as a prelude, the emperors had a Christian church that could be seen from the palace destroyed. Several edicts valid throughout the empire followed, widening the groups of the oppressed and increasing the punishments with which they were threatened. The first edict, hung up on a favorite square in Nikomedeia, was torn down by a Christian in front of everyone, thus accepting martyrdom. When fire repeatedly broke out in the palace, Christians were charged with arson. The bishop of Anthimos died under the axe, and many men and women went "with indescribable eagerness" to the pyre (Eusebius, *h. e.* 8, 6). To prevent the burial and veneration of the martyrs' bones, other bodies, even some that had already been buried, were thrown from boats into the sea with millstones around their necks.

At that time there were martyrs in many other places in Asia Minor. The Augusti's special focus was considered to be the "cleansing" of the army, and the documents are full of *passiones* of soldiers, although some of these testimonies may be forgeries. Among the Anatolian legions, the Legio XII Fulminata stationed in Melitene on the Euphrates had been said since the days of Marcus Aurelius to have a large number of Christian members (Eusebius, *h. e.* 5, 5). Under Maximian, the recruit (*tiro*) Theodoros died in Amaseia; a pious woman transported his body to the little town of Euchaita and buried it there. The grave became, like many others, a pilgrimage site; Gregory of Nyssa (Thdr. PG 46, 737) describes the mosaics and paintings in the church erected there.

The persecutions in the diocese of Oriens continued until 311, under Maximinus Daia. Even after Galerius issued his edict of toleration (April 30, 311) this emperor remained an opponent of the new religion, which he fought by means of propaganda. He made use of the resentment felt by numerous citizens in many cities who, now as before, did not want to grant the Christians any freedom. Thus when he was sojourning in Nikomedeia, Galerius himself claimed to have received citizens who carried images of the gods before him and asked him not to allow the Christians to live in their city (Eusebius, *h. e.* 9, 9). Similar requests and parts of the emperor's answers have been preserved in inscriptions, including one found in the Lycian city of Arykanda—the Lycians' and Pamphylians' letter in Greek together with a few lines in Latin from the end of the rescript, as well as another reply from the emperor written in Latin in Sardeis and addressed to the Pisidian city of Kolbasa.[448] But under

Constantine's monocracy, a complete breakthrough was made, first to the tolerance and then to the privileging of Christianity. The Christians' steely resistance and at the same time the radical intolerance, so to speak, of their claim to exclusivity, which was completely foreign to most other religious cults, had won its first decisive victory. For the short span of three years (360–363), the emperor Julianus tried once again to favor paganism. However, persecutions did not occur, which led Gregory of Nazianzus and Theodoret of Kyrrhos to complain that the monarch was denying Christians even martyrdom. Under Theodosius I, in 381 CE, the Christianity guided by the Nicaean Creed (*Nicaena fides*) began to become something like a state religion; special churches were banned. The empire and the Church were henceforth closely connected with each other.

Heresy

The development of Christianity in Asia Minor during the second and third centuries CE reminds us in many respects of the sects in modern America. Interpreters, prophets, and visionaries followed various new paths and took many people along with them. What was established as "orthodoxy" after the councils of Nicaea (325) and Chalkedon (451) was still occasionally almost on the defensive in certain regions. By the second century we can already speak of a "majority church" that took possession of the apostolic tradition and intervened actively against deviations.

Very early, still in the time of the apostles, groups with their own doctrines and rules broke off, like the Nicolaitans mentioned in Revelations and the followers of a certain Kerinthos (Rev. 2, 6.15; Eusebius *h. e.* 3, 28 f); both groups are mentioned in Irenaeus's work refuting the Gnostics, in a series that includes Karpocrates, Kerdon, and Marcion. In Ephesos, John is supposed to have immediately left the *thermae* when he encountered Kerinthos there, which is not surprising if one has read the views attributed to this man: for him, the Kingdom of Christ consists of satisfying the stomach with food and drink and the organs lying still lower. We can say nothing more concerning the spread of these two sects in Asia Minor.

It came to pass in Rome that the respected bishop Polycarp of Smyrna met a rich shipowner from Sinope who had already spent a long time in the world metropolis and sought acceptance for his new ideas. His name was Marcion, and he advocated a complete exclusion from Christianity of all Jewish elements and the whole of the Old Testament. He maintained that the God of the Old Testament was not the Christian God, and that the latter was a new, previously unknown God.[449] The Roman community rejected this original theologian and the money he offered them. Polycarp's answer was: " I recognize you as the first-born of Satan" (Eusebius, *h. e.* 4, 14). We know only the general outline of his doctrine and a few isolated statements solely (as is the case for most heresies) from his opponents' ultimately prevailing books. Marcion's "heresy" provoked a flood of polemics, including some that have been lost—like those written by the Anatolians Rhodon, in Rome, and Meliton, in Sardeis—and the most famous of them, Tertullian's *Adversus Marcionem*, which dates from the first half of the third century. The anecdotes—Marcion is supposed to have seduced a virgin and been excommunicated by his own father, who was a bishop—reflect, as does the abuse of him as a "Pontic wolf" (Eusebius, *h. e.* 5, 13), a "self-castrator," and a "Pontic mouse" (Tertullian, *adv. Marc.* 1, 5), the rage over the success of this heresy. It was the oldest to come from Asia Minor and spread there as well as throughout the empire. The bishop of Corinth opposed it in letters to Nikomedeia and Amastris written ca. 180 CE. According to Basileios (*ep.* 199, 47), Marcionism produced several Anatolian heretical offshoots, including the sects of the Sakkophoroi, Enkratitai, and Apoktaktitai.[450] As late as the sixth century, an unknown poet in the West wrote a poem of 1,302 hexameters against the followers of the doctrine, the *carmen adversus Marcionitas*.

There is nothing specifically Anatolian in either Gnosticism or Marcionism, whose originators lived in a cosmopolitan milieu, whether at home or in Rome. The case is different for the sect of Montanism, which arose only a few years later and can be considered of first-rate importance for the Christian development of Asia Minor. It called itself the "New Prophecy" (Tertullian, *adv. Marc.* 3, 24, 4); the name Montanism, which is derived from that of its founder, Montanus, was attached to it only centuries later. In its exuberant willingness to believe in miracles and its prophetic enthusiasm, its expectation of an imminent end of the world, its readiness to undergo martyrdom, and its unusually rigorous rules of conduct, the movement shows the peculiar traits that are thought to be rooted in Phrygia. The church historian Sokrates (*h. e.* 4, 28) attributes to the Phrygians of his time a way of life averse to natural drives (*epithymetikon*); he said that they were not fascinated, like everyone else, by horse races and the theater, and were violently opposed to any kind of unchastity. The Phrygians shared an extreme asceticism with the offshoots of the Marcionist doctrine in Pisidia and around Laodikeia Katakekaumene, and also with Anatolian Novatianism. In any case, in the Imperial period rural Asia Minor was highly prone to believe in miracles; in his "Sacred Speeches," even a sophist like the Mysian Aelius Aristeides showed his credulity in this regard. In Paphlagonia, Pontos, and Cappadocia visions and magical beings were practically epidemic. The Paphlagonians rushed in great numbers to consult the aforementioned prophesying serpent Glykon (p. 521); in Pontos, Gregory "the wonder worker" drew attention to himself, and in Firmilianus's letter (*ep.* 75, 10) to Cyprian mention is made of a woman in Cappadocia who presented herself as a prophetess, fell into ecstasy, behaved "as if she were full of the Holy Spirit," attracted droves of followers, celebrated the Eucharist, and baptized people. A bishop in Pontos believed that the end was so near that he called on his coreligionists to abandon their homes and fields (Hippolytos, *Dan.* 4, 19).

More controversial is the rootedness of Montanism in the cult of Kybele characteristic of religion in Anatolia and in particular in the Lydian-Phrygian highlands. According to later sources, Montanus, whom St. Jerome (*epist.* 41, 4, 1 Hilberg: *abscisus et semivir*) ridiculed as a "castrated half-man," was a pagan priest—but of the god Apollo and not the oriental goddess whose worship still involved, in the Imperial age, the *galloi*'s ritual self-castration.[451] Certainly pagan origins may have been imputed to sects by later, mainly hostile writers, and it is hard to discern substantial differences with the majority Church in the few cases authenticated for the period of origin.[452] If the representatives of the majority Church nevertheless immediately rebelled against Montanist activities, that may have been because it involved above all their interpretive authority, which they saw as threatened by the supporters of the new prophecy. The strikingly prominent role played by women in the heretical movement of this time—the majority Church of the time tended to insist on the subordination of women—gives the modern debate a feminist aspect: "Proving the orthodoxy of the Montanist doctrine would make it possible to justify women teaching and holding office in the Church."[453]

The most important extant source with regard to Phrygian beginnings is Eusebius's *Church History* (*h. e.* 5, 14–19), in which older authors of polemics are cited, including an Apolinarios, an Apollonios, an Anonymus, and the apologist Miltiades. Further details are offered by a succession of oracular pronouncements quoted here and there, and by later writers—especially Tertullian, who was the only one who adhered to the new philosophy, and Epiphanios, with his *Panarion* opposing the heresies.[454] Montanus is supposed to have converted to the Christian faith in a Mysian village, Ardabau, and to have aroused respect when he fell into ecstasy, uttered strange noises, and said strange things. His prophetic inspiration was soon shared by two of his pupils, Priscilla and Maximilla, married women who left their husbands to follow Montanus. The latter predicted wars and uprisings that did not in fact occur. An early community formed in Philadelpheia and listened to the prophecies of a certain Ammia and one Quadratus. Montanus himself, who considered himself a medium conveying the Holy Spirit or the Spirit of Truth whom God had sent to men at Jesus's behest (John 14:16 f., 14:26), invoked, in accord with Revelation 21:10, the impending descent of the heavenly Jerusalem. The prophecy foresaw as the site of this imminent event and as *the* future holy place of Montanism a lonely stretch of Phrygia that could be surveyed, Biblical style, from a high mountain. Two towns are mentioned by name—Pepuza and Tymion (the latter only in Apollonios; Eusebius, *h. e.* 5, 18, 2). Generations of researchers have looked for it; one of the most zealous was the Scotsman William Ramsay (p. 24).[455] However, only an inscription found a few years ago has provided sufficient clarity regarding its precise location. The rescript of Severus and Caracalla, found engraved on a stone in Sarayçık south of Uşak, shows that Tymion was not a city but rather a settlement of tenant farmers on an imperial domain. About twelve kilometers farther south, near the village of Karayakuplu in the gorge of the Banaz-Çay, there is a rock cloister and traces of a settlement that is now thought to have been Pepuza.[456]

After its first investigations, the Church reacted to the spread of the Montanist doctrine with synods in Asia, exorcisms, and excommunications—but in vain. The community in Thyateira, which received one of the seven epistles, is supposed to have gone over to Montanism early on (Epiphanios, *haer.* 51, 32 f.). Apolinarios was forced to remark contritely that even the central Anatolian metropolis of Ankyra had become a stronghold of Montanism (Eusebius, *h. e.* 5, 16). The largest body of Montanist inscriptions is located in the area of Temenothyrai in the upper valley of the Tembris.[457] In Epiphanios's time (*haer.* 48, 14, 2) there were Montanists from Constantinople to Cilicia and Cappadocia. Like Marcionism, Montanism finally reached the West as well—Rome, Lyon, and Carthage. The letter from the Christian communities of Lugdunum (Lyon) and Vienna to their brothers "in Asia and Phrygia" that Eusebius (*h. e.* 5, 1–4) reproduces verbatim indicates that as early as ca. 177 CE, two years after Maximilla's death, there were already Montanists in Gaul. At the same time, the presbyter of Lugdunum, Irenaeus, traveled to see the Bishop of Rome to speak on behalf of the followers of the new prophecy coming from his homeland. The visions of Perpetua, who was martyred in Carthage ca. 203 CE, are apparently related to Montanist convictions, and in 207 CE the Carthaginian Church Father Tertullian became a Montanist and remained one to the end of his life. The town of Pepuza, which was destroyed, perhaps by an earthquake, in the fourth century (Epiphanios, *haer.* 48, 14, 1), disappears from the sources only in the ninth century. In the fifth century two churches dedicated to the prophetesses Priscilla and Quintilla still stood there as Montanism's religious center (*Liber Praedestinatus* 1, 27); not until the sixth century were the Montanists' relics destroyed, the shrines of their founder razed, and their books burned by John of Ephesos.[458]

Another fundamentalist heresy, to which many Montanists converted, came from outside Asia Minor in the middle of the third century CE and established itself in the interior of the country. It was originated by the Roman presbyter Novatus (also called Novatianus), who allegedly came from Phrygia (Philostorgios, *h. e.* fr. 8, 15 Winkelmann) and who refused to allow Christians who had apostatized during the persecutions (Eusebius *h. e.* 6, 43) to rejoin the Church. The mainline Church excommunicated him but could not prevent the sect calling itself "the pure" from continuing to spread throughout the empire. According to the inscriptions, Laodikeia Katakekaumene in Lycaonia was its stronghold in the center of Asia Minor.[459] In Paphlagonia and Bithynia there were uprisings and bloody clashes among Christians. In the first half of the fourth century, Novatian zealots killed Hypatios, the bishop of Gangra. When under Constantius II (337–361) the Church tried to take action against the Novatians in Mantineion, East Bithynia, they mounted a stubborn resistance that ended in a massacre.[460]

Clergy and Church

Before the third century, there seem to have been no consecrated places of Christian worship and altars in Asia Minor. People gathered in private homes or publicly accessible places. The apostles, prophets, and teachers were not attached to any specific location, and were nowhere "elected," but rather were respected and accepted as authorities appointed by the divine spirit. They did not always receive a friendly reception, as had already been the case for the author of the Third Letter of John: "Diotrephes, who likes to put himself first, does not acknowledge any authority ...

prating against me with evil words. And not content with that, he refuses himself to welcome the brethren, and also stops those who want to welcome them and puts them out of the church. (3 John 9–10).

With waning missionary activity and the growing veneration of the twelve apostles as an exceptional elect, the following generations of traveling "superintendents" lost some of their charisma; elected, locally based officeholders gained in importance insofar as they performed the same functions as the latter and became just as venerable (Didache 15, 1 f.). This process did not advance at the same pace everywhere. Initially, numerous elders and supervisors were at the head of the communities (collective episcopates) until the monarchical bishopric (monepiscopate) emerged. It is not clear when this took place in Asia Minor; in any case, it can be observed in the second century. The individual bishop functioned as a ruler and a teacher, and also conducted baptisms and celebrated the Eucharist. The "elders" (*presbyteroi*)—operating as a committee modeled on the city council (*bule*) of a *polis*—who had formerly held the same rank, assumed the functions of councilors, assistants, and even representatives of the bishops. The deacon performed manifold services in caring for and ministering to the members of the congregation in the celebration of the Eucharist, in baptism, and in the supervision of catechumens. Deaconesses were recruited from widows and virgins, and performed a corresponding range of tasks with respect to female members of the congregation. According to Pliny's letter (*ep.* 10, 96, 8: *quae ministrae dicebantur*), they already existed in the second century. Before the third century, testimonies to these offices in Anatolian inscriptions remain rare. A more differentiated hierarchy of clerical offices did not emerge until the eve of the Church's victory under Constantine.[461]

We do not know whether and how long congregations may have existed without a monepiscopacy. In the end, every reasonably numerous group of Christians in cities and villages seems to have put a bishop at its head.[462] The overall picture is dominated by the municipal bishopric, but there were also bishops in the countryside; not before the fourth century did their designation as "rural bishops" (*chorepiskopoi*) imply a lower rank.[463] In the case of the urban bishops, the model of the Roman organization of the provinces assigned metropolises a genuine priority.[464] When conventions of bishops at the provincial level were established in Asia in the second half of the second century, the metropolitans may have already been their main spokesmen; in the so-called Easter Controversy around the end of the second and the beginning of the third centuries, the bishop of Ephesos, Polycrates, emerged as the head of the bishops of Asia. He prided himself on being the eighth in a series of bishops of this city (Eusebius, *h. e.* 5, 24). At this time a serious dispute arose between Asia and Rome that was settled through Irenaeus's mediation:

> For the parishes of all Asia, as from an older tradition, held that the fourteenth day of the moon, on which day the Jews were commanded to sacrifice the lamb, should be observed as the feast of the Saviour's passover. It was therefore necessary to end their fast on that day, whatever day of the week it should happen to be. But it was not the

custom of the churches in the rest of the world to end it at this time, as they observed the practice which, from apostolic tradition, has prevailed to the present time, of terminating the fast on no other day than on that of the resurrection of our Saviour.[465]

In the 230s, great synods met in Ikonion and Synnada, where the largest congregations in Asia were located (Eusebius, *h. e.* 7, 7). In Kaisareia in Cappadocia annual synods of *seniores et praepositi* were held (Cyprian, *ep.* 75, 4). Starting in the third century, the work of prominent teachers of religious doctrine made eastern Anatolia increasingly important. Cappadocia became a stronghold of Christianity. Firmilianus (d. 268), whose correspondence with the Carthaginian Cyprian (*ep.* 75) tells us more about him, was the bishop of Kaisareia at about the time when the learned virgin Juliana was hosting the Christian philosopher Origen in the city. Firmilianus insisted that heretics who wanted to return to the fold of the mainline Church—in accord with the decision of the synods of Ikonion and Synnada—had to be rebaptized, because their first baptism had been nullified. He asserted his view with assurance and launched furious diatribes against the current Roman bishop, who was threatening him with excommunication. When the Goths attacked the country in the middle of the third century, they carried off numerous Christians as prisoners, including the grandparents of Wulfila, who later translated the Bible into Gothic. Cave settlements and churches were probably established in the extensive tuff terrain lying below Mt. Argaios (Erciyas Dağ) as early as the time of the invasions by the Sasanids, Goths, and Palmyrenes, as well as under the Diocletian persecutions that followed shortly thereafter.

Neokaisareia in eastern Pontos produced several Christian spiritual leaders. A certain Theodoros returned to his homeland there after he had traveled with his brother Athenodoros to Berytos (Beirut), met Origen in Palestine, and spent five years at Origen's school. Theodoros became the bishop Gregory, a successful missionary and highly respected "wonder worker" (*thaumaturgos*). His brother also held a bishop's see in Pontos (Eusebius, *h. e.* 6, 30).[466] Another Gregory and his brother Basil, the sons of a rhetor, also grew up in Neokaisareia; their writings and letters were to make them famous along with their friend Gregory of Nazianzus, as the three great Cappadocian Fathers and prove decisive for Christian theology in general.[467]

Special developments occurred on the eastern and southeastern periphery of Asia Minor. Edessa, the rich caravan city in Osrhoene (now Urfa), probably became temporarily Christian even before the ultimate victory of the Church in the fourth century under the pro-Roman prince Abgar the Great (177/178–212 CE). During the same period, Bardaisan, a philosopher from Edessa and author of the *Book of the Laws of the Countries*, converted to the Christian faith. He was later excluded from the majority Church as a gnostic heretic. Christianity became the catalytic factor for the literature in the Syrian language that flourished in this city. According to a legend whose beginnings go back to at least the second century CE, a forefather of Abgar the Great, Abgar the Black, corresponded with Jesus Christ; an emissary from the Holy Land named Addai healed the ailing king and brought the Christian message into the country. The correspondence, the earliest version of which has come down to us in Eusebius's history of the Church (*h. e.* 1, 13), soon circulated throughout the Christian world in several languages. Although a sixth-century papal decree had already declared it apocryphal, this legend became the most successful Christian heritage after the New Testament and remained an object of living belief until the beginnings of historical criticism in the nineteenth century, at a time when people in English country houses were still accustomed to put copies of the letters on the reverse side of picture frames to bring blessings on their homes.[468]

The Christianization of Armenia is almost entirely concealed under hagiography and legend, so that the task of "digging a historical kernel out of it is simply impossible."[469] Since the Middle Ages, the year 301 has been officially recognized as the date of the Armenian kingdom's conversion to Christianity. The country had become a Sasanid province as a result of Shapur's conquests around the middle of the third century; it was taken over first by Shapur's son Hormizd Ardashir (later Shapur's successor as great king), after the flight of an Armenian king named Tiridates (Zonaras 12, 21). In the 270s it was ruled by Narseh, another of Shapur's sons, who also became great king in 293. It is hard to determine and remains controversial exactly when Trdat (Tiridates), whom the legend of Christianization made famous, was enthroned as "king" of Armenia (or a part of the country), and whether he is identical with one of two Armenians of the same name, one being the aforementioned "king," who had been driven out decades earlier, the other a vassal under (or alongside?) Narseh during the latter's reign. Depending on the answer to that question, the restoration of a Trdat is attributed to the Emperor Probus in 279 or the Emperor Diocletian between the second and fifteenth years of his reign (i.e., between 283 and 298). That latter date coincides with that of the peace agreement between the Romans and the Persians that Narseh was forced to accept after his defeat at the hands of Galerius. By the end of the third century, there must have already been a certain number of followers of the Christian religion in the country; northern Armenia was evangelized from Lesser Armenia and Cappadocia, while southern Armenia was evangelized from Mesopotamia.

Various legends are connected with King Tiridates's persecution of Christians: Gregory, a nephew of the king—his father is supposed to have killed the latter's father—converted to Christianity, and after cruel torture was held prisoner in a pit full of vipers and scorpions for thirteen or fifteen years. When Tiridates had the beautiful Hripsime, who refused to join the royal harem, put to death along with her companions as martyrs, divine vengeance transformed him into a wild boar; but when Gregory was freed, the king was transformed back into a man. The king converted to Christianity and had all the Persian shrines in the country destroyed. Gregory "the Illuminator" was sent, accompanied by the Armenian nobility, to the Cappadocian Metropolitan Leontios, and was consecrated as bishop of Armenia in Kaisareia (or Neokaisareia). Opinions differ as to whether this consecration—attested as historical by the name Leontios—took place before or after the edict of toleration issued by Galerius in 311 in Nikomedeia. Could Tiridates really adopt a religion while it was still being so harshly persecuted by the Emperor Diocletian, to whom he owed his throne? The main mother-church of Armenia founded by Gregory on his return was located in Ashtishat in the country of Taron (near modern-day Muş).

The most valuable source for our knowledge of the spread of episcopal sees throughout Anatolia is the subscription lists of the Council of Nicaea in 325 CE. The arrangement found in the text that has come down to us was not written all at once, but rather emerged gradually in the course of the fourth century, and there are also interpolations; I cannot go into this problem here.[470] According to Eusebius (*v. C.* 3, 8), more than 250 bishops came to the Bithynian metropolis, only seven of them from the West (Bishop Silvester of Rome sent a representative). About one hundred came from Asia Minor, including a few bishops representing rural regions, mainly Isaurians and Cappadocians. Bishops of the Goths, Persians, and Arabs, as well as an Armenian bishop, also took part in the meetings at the imperial palace. At the center of the debates stood the Christology of the presbyter of Alexandria, Arius, according to which Christ was *homoiusios*, merely similar in nature to God; this conception was condemned. Among the other decisions (*kanones*) made—the best source is the ecclesiastical history written by an Anonymus of Cyzicus in the fifth century—the most important with regard to the clergy in Asia Minor are the following:

> On the appointment of bishops: It is very important that the appointment of a bishop be endorsed by all the bishops of the province. If that should prove difficult due to urgent necessities or the length of the journey, at least three of them shall come together, and those who are absent shall participate in the election and cast their votes by letter. The control over the procedure, however, shall rest with the Metropolitan in every province. (Anonymus of Cyzicus, *h. e.* 2, 32, 4; trans. Marek)

Bishops, presbyters, deacons, and other members of the clergy were not allowed to leave the parishes to which they were assigned and move to another city (Anonymus of Cyzicus, *h. e.* 2, 32, 15 f.). The doctrine formulated against Arius, the Nicaean Creed, made the name of the Bithynian city a landmark and memorial site for world Christianity. Since 330 Constantinople had been the capital of the Eastern Roman Empire. From there eastern Europe was Christianized and thus connected with the culture of the ancient Mediterranean world. Asia Minor became henceforth the heartland of a Christian world empire for about seven centuries.

CHAPTER 10

Epilogue and Outlook

A history of Asia Minor in Antiquity need not end with the new organization of the state introduced by Diocletian, or with the victory of the Church and the transfer of the capital to the Bosporus under Emperor Constantine. Depending on one's perspective, the following period can be considered early Byzantine as well as late Roman.[1] In addition, the arc we have followed in the preceding pages, ranging from prehistory to the Roman Imperial period is too broad to find in it a coherence any stronger than that between Late Antiquity and the Byzantine Age. Yet there are good reasons for seeing a break here and bringing this history to an end. The first is that the nature of our evidence changes dramatically in Late Antiquity, and the Christian period requires a very specific approach with regard to methodology and the evaluation of sources. The flood of thousands of documents on local and regional events and conditions that the epigraphic habit of the Imperial age cities sent down to us rapidly recedes; similarly, with the disappearance of provincial coinage, a rich source flowing from precisely these microcosms and their connections with one another dries up. However, literary sources increase to enormous dimensions, but at the same time Christian themes and contents prevail in these numerous and voluminous works. With Constantinople as its capital, the empire is more strongly centralized than ever; for the most part, substantial information regarding government, administration, economics, architecture, religion, and art can henceforth be acquired only from the headquarters. Power, wealth, and splendor seem to be concentrated in a few centers of political and religious influence. No expert on Asia Minor will underestimate the visible remains of Late Antique and Byzantine architectural phases in the many still-intact cities of Anatolia as mere signs of the decline of antique civilization. Nonetheless, regarding their abundance and quality, these remains are so clearly different from their predecessors that even architecture has to be studied in the context of a new period.

The transition from Roman to Byzantine Asia Minor took place gradually. The fourth century brought the country another decided boom in the material culture of the Imperial age. Although it was fading, this culture did not disappear altogether even in the fifth and sixth centuries; in Anatolia, its foundation—the network of focal points of urban settlement, urban building stock, and complex infrastructure—did not begin to crumble away broadly and permanently until the seventh century CE, the age of the Arab invasions. Part of ancient learning was absorbed and assimilated into Late Antique Christian and Byzantine intellectual culture. But pagan education and religion also persisted alongside and against Christianity, although it was increasingly limited to elite circles, whereas the majority of the population no longer took any significant part in it beyond education in the church. Meanwhile, pagan festivals and customs lived on for centuries in the lower strata of urban society and in the countryside.[2] The awareness of being "Roman" became stronger in the Byzantine Empire; the point around which the identity of regional communities crystallized shifted from the *polis* to the province, the administrative unit constituted by the emperors; and in the language of the Christian *Imperium* the Greek word for "people," *ethnos*, was increasingly used as a synonym for "province." However, old ethnic identities, so far as they survived the Hellenization process at all, finally disappeared, along with the epichoric languages that provided only weak support for them.[3] Even in the concrete process of the empire's contraction, the imperial idea remained vital and dominated the whole of Byzantine history. The name "Rome" as the bearer of this idea was usurped, as it was by the Palmyrenes Odainathos and Zenobia in the third century, by medieval opponents of Byzantion: the Bulgars Symeon (tenth century), Ivan Asen, and Ivan Alexander (thirteenth–fourteenth centuries) called themselves "Emperor of the Bulgars and the Romans," and in the thirteenth century the Seljuk sultanate around Konya, the homeland of Jalāl ad-Dīn Muhammad Rūmī, was called Rum. Cultural and political continuities can be traced down to the early modern and modern periods; the heritage of Antiquity did not break off with the Turks' conquest of Constantinople in 1453.

Under Justinian I (527–565), the Romans—as the Byzantine emperors called themselves—for a short time reestablished an empire that included almost all the coasts of the Mediterranean, including all of Asia Minor. Starting in the seventh century Arabs and Turkic peoples invaded (the latter first in the Balkans) and forced the rulers on the Bosporus to fight prolonged wars on several fronts. In 674 the Arabs appeared before the walls of the capital, but abandoned the siege four years later after heavy losses (Regarding the water supply of the capital, see Figure 109). In the second half of the tenth century there was a Byzantine "Reconquista," but in the eleventh century the Turks began to advance everywhere in Anatolia. An event that took place on the eastern frontier of the empire in August 1071 is a landmark for the permanent withdrawal of Byzantine rule from Asia Minor: not far from Manzikert (today Malazgirt, north of Lake Van), the Seljuk Alp Arslan defeated a large Byzantine army under Emperor Romanos IV Diogenes. By the end of the 1070s Nicaea was already the capital of the Seljuk Kilij Arslan Ibn Suleiman. The Islamic emirs ruled from cities, and nomadic tribes roamed through the surrounding areas. Armenians emigrated from their homeland toward the south, into the mountains of Cilicia, where Lesser Armenian principalities emerged as further enemies of the Byzantine Empire.

The Crusaders who entered Asia Minor in 1096 were aware of the outcome of the Battle of Manzikert; in their opinion, through that defeat Byzantion had forfeited its claim to be the protector of the Christians of the East. The Crusaders themselves were not able to halt the Turkification of Asia Minor. When in the spring of 1097

109. Cistern from the age of Justinian in the center of Constantinople.

the last army corps of the First Crusade under Robert of Normandy, Stephen of Blois, and Robert of Flanders entered Constantinople, the Crusader forces, marching further east on the Asiatic side, had already begun their siege of Seldjuk Nicaea. One of the first encounters between the Western knights and the Turks inspired an unknown author to write these lines:

> Verumtamen dicunt [scil. Turci] se esse de Francorum generatione, et quia nullus homo naturaliter debet esse miles nisi Franci et illi. Veritatem dicam quam nemo audebit prohibere. Certe, si in fide Christi et Christianitate sancta semper firmi fuissent, et unum Deum in Trinitate confiteri voluissent, Deique filium natum de Virgine Matre, passum, et resurrexisse a mortuis et in caelum ascendisse suis cernentibus discipulis, consolationemque Sancti Spiritus perfecte misisse, et eum in caelo et in terra regnantem recta mente et fide credidissent, ipsis potentiores et fortiores vel bellorum ingeniosissimos nullus invenire potuisset.

> Indeed, the Turks say that they are related to the Franks and that no man ought by nature to be a knight save the Franks and themselves. I speak the truth, which no one can deny. that if they had always been steadfast in Christ's faith and in Christianity, if they had wished to confess one triune Lord, and if they had honestly believed in good faith that the Son of God was born of the Virgin, that he suffered and rose from the dead and ascended into heaven in the presence of his disciples, that he has sent the perfect comfort of the Holy Spirit, and that he reigns in heaven and on earth; if they had believed all this, it would have been impossible to find a people more powerful, more courageous, or more skilled in the art of war.[4]

Appendix

Lists of Rulers

Hittites

	King	Relationship	Dates	King	King
	Pitḫana of Kussara			Pitḫana of Kussara	Pitḫana of Kussara
	Anitta			Anitta	Anitta
1	Ḫuzziya I				*Ḫuzziya I
2	Papaḫdilmaḫ				*Papaḫdilmaḫ
3	Labarna				*Labarna
4	Ḫattusili I	Nephew of 3 (?)	1565–1540 BCE	Ḫattusili I (=Labarna?)	Labarna II Ḫattusili
5	Mursili I	Grandson (?) of 4	1540–1530	Mursili I	Mursili I
	Sack of Babylon		High: 1659 Middle: 1595 Low: 1531 Ultra-Low a: 1499 Ultra-Low b: 1467		
6	Ḫantili I	Brother-in-law of 5		Ḫantili I	*Ḫantili I
7	Zidanta I	Son-in-law of 6		Zidanta I	Zidanta I
8	Ammuna	Son of 7		Ammuna	Ammuna
9	Ḫuzziya I			Ḫuzziya I	*Ḫuzziya II
10	Telipinu	Son of 8 (?), Brother-in-law of 9	ca. 1500	Telipinu	*Telipinu
11	Taḫurwaili			Taḫurwaili	Alluwamna
12	Alluwamna	Son-in-law of 10		Alluwamna	*Taḫurwaili
13	Ḫantili II	Son of 12		Ḫantili II	Ḫantili II
14	Zidanta II			Zidanta II	Zidanza II
15	Ḫuzziya II			Ḫuzziya II	*Ḫuzziya III
16	Muwatalli I			Muwatalli I	Muwatalli I
17	Kantuzzili (?)				*Kantuzzili*
18	Tudḫaliya I (= II)	Son of 17	ca. 1420–1400	Tudḫaliya I	Tudḫaliya I *Ḫattusili II* Tudḫaliya II
19	Arnuwanda I	(Adopted) Son, or Son-in-law of 18	ca. 1400–1375	Arnuwanda I	Arnuwanda I
20	Tudḫaliya II (= III)	Son of 19	ca. 1375–1355	Tudḫaliya II	Tudḫaliya III

	King	Relationship	Dates	King	King
21	Tudḫaliya III (?)	Son of 20			
22	Suppiluliuma I	Son of 20	ca. 1355–1320	Suppiluliuma I	Suppiluliuma I
	daḫamunzu episode: An Egyptian royal widow requests a Hittite prince as her new consort.		After the death of: Amenophis IV: 1341/1333, Smenḫkare: 1340/1332, or Tutankhamen: 1330/1322		
23	Arnuwanda II	Son of 22	ca. 1320–1318	Arnuwanda II	Arnuwanda II
24	Mursili II	Son of 22	ca. 1318–1290	Mursili II	Mursili II
	Omen of the Sun in Mursili's tenth year, if solar eclipse:		June 24, 1312 or April 13, 1308		
25	Muwatalli II	Son of 24	ca. 1290–1272	Muwatalli II	Muwatalli II
	Battle of Qadeš		1274		
26	Mursili III (Urḫi-Teššub)	Son of 25	ca. 1272–1265	Mursili III (Urḫi-Teššub)	Mursili III (Urḫi-Teššub) *Kurunta*
27	Ḫattusili "III"	Son of 24	ca. 1265–1240	Ḫattusili II (III)	Ḫattusili III
	Treaty with Egypt		1259		
28	Tudḫaliya IV	Son of 27	ca. 1240–1215	Tudḫaliya III (IV)	Tudḫaliya IV
29	Arnuwanda III	Son of 28	from ca. 1215	Arnuwanda III	*Arnuwanda III*
30	Suppiluliuma II	Son of 28	until ca. 1190	Suppiluliuma II	Suppiluliuma II

Sources: Columns 2 and 3: based on Gernot Wilhelm, "Generation Count in Hittite Chronology," in: H. Hunger et al. (eds.), *Mesopotamian Dark Age Revisited*, Vienna 2004, 71–80. Columns 4 and 5: Based on [321] Starke, *Chronologische Übersicht*, 2002, 310 ff. Column 6: Based on O. Carruba, *AoF* 32, 2005, 246–271.

Notes: Asterisk indicates a still unattested (or unclear) geneaological sequence. Names written in italics indicate persons whose status as great kings is uncertain.

Rulers of the Neo-Hittite States in Asia Minor and Northern Syria

Rulers in the Tabal region

Source	Date	Tabal	Ḫubušna	Kaska	Atuna	Tuwana	Ištunda	Sinuḫtu
A	836 BCE	Tuwatti						
A		Kikki*	Puhamme					
H						Saruwani		
H						Muwaharami		
H		Tuwati						
A	738	Wassurme*	Urimme	Dadilu	Ushitti	Urballa*	Tuhamme	
A	732	Wassurme	—	Dadilu	Ushitti	Urballa	Tuhamme	
A	ca. 730	Hulli						

Source	Date	Tabal	Ḫubušna	Kaska	Atuna	Tuwana	Ištunda	Sinuḫtu
A	ca. 730	Ambaris*						
H					(Ashwi)			
A	718	Ambaris			Kurti**			Kiakku
A	713	Ambaris deposed			Kurti			
A	709					Urballa?		
H						Muwaharami*		
A	ca. 679	Iskallu						
A	663	Mugallu						
A	651	Mugallu						
A	ca. 640	[. . .]ussi*						

Source: Based on [99] Hawkins, *Corpus of Hieroglyphic Luwian Inscriptions.*
Notes: A = Assyrian, H = Hieroglyphic Luwian.
* Proven sons of the above
** Possible sons of the above.

Rulers of Amuq/Patina

Source	Date	Ruler	Remarks
A	ca. 870	Luburna (Labarna)	
A	mentioned 858	Sapalulme (Suppiluliuma)	
A	at least 857–853	Qalparunda (Halparuntiya)	
A	?–829	Lubarna (Labarna) II?	
A		Surri	Usurper
A		Sasi	Assyrian vassal king
A	?–738	Tutammu	
A	738–?	Assyrian province	

Source: Based on [99] Hawkins, *Corpus of Hieroglyphic Luwian Inscriptions.*
Notes: A = Assyrian. Only Assyrian sources available; no utilizable hieroglyphic sources.

Rulers of Kummaha/Kummuh/Commagene

Source	Dates	Ruler	Remarks
A	at least 866–857 BCE	Qatazili (Hattusili) I	
A	mentioned 853	Kundašpi	
A	at least 805–773	Ušpilulume (Suppiluliuma)	Assyrian subject
H		Hattusili II	Son of preceding
U/A	at least 750–732	Kuštašpi	Urartian and Assyrian subject
A	at least 712–708	Mutallu (Muwatalli)	Installed by Assyrians
A	708–	Assyrian province	

Source: Based on [99] Hawkins, *Corpus of Hieroglyphic Luwian Inscriptions.*
Notes: A = Assyrian, H = Hieroglyphic Luwian, U = Urartian.

Rulers of Maraş/Gurgum

Source	Dates	Ruler	Remarks
H		Larama I	
H		Muwizi	Son of preceding
H		Halparuntiya I	Son of preceding
H/A	ca. 858	Muwatalli I	Son of preceding
H/A	ca. 853	Halparuntiya II	Son of preceding
H/A		Larama II	Son of preceding
H/A	at least 805–early seventh century	Halparuntiya III	Son of preceding
A	mentioned 743	Tarhulara	
A	?–711	Muwatalli II	
A	711–?	Assyrian province	

Source: Based on [99] Hawkins, *Corpus of Hieroglyphic Luwian Inscriptions*.
Notes: A = Assyrian, H = Hieroglyphic Luwian.

Rulers of Karkamiš

Source	Date	Ruler	Remarks
Hittite	thirteenth century BCE	Talmi-Teššub	
H	ca. 1200	Kuzi-Teššub	Son of preceding
A	ca. 1100	Ini-Teššub	
H		Sapaziti	
H		Ura-Tarhunza	Son of preceding
H		Tudhaliya	
H	according to archaeological	Suhi I	
H	criteria tenth–early	Astuwatamanza	Son of preceding
H	ninth century	Suhi II	Son of preceding
H		Katuwa	Son of preceding
A	at least 870–848	Sangara	
H		Astiruwa	
H		Yariri	"Subject of Astiruwa"
H		Kamani	Son of Astiruwa
H		Son of Sastura	Sastura was a "vizier" of Kamani
A	at least 738–717	Pisiri	

Source: Based on [99] Hawkins, *Corpus of Hieroglyphic Luwian Inscriptions*.
Notes: A = Assyrian, H = Hieroglyphic Luwian.

Rulers of Malida, Malatya

Source	Dates	Ruler	Remarks
H	ca. 1200 BCE	Kuzi-Teššub	= Kuzi-Teššub of Karkamiš
H		PUGNUS-mili I	Son of preceding
H		Runtiya I	Son of preceding
H		Arnuwanti I	Brother of preceding
H		PUGNUS-mili II	Son of preceding
H		Arnuwanti II	Son of preceding
H		CRUS + *RA/I*	
H		Wasu (?)-Runtiya	Son of preceding
H		Halpasulupi	
H		Suwarimi	
H		Mariti	Son of preceding
H		Sahwi	Position in genealogy unclear. Possibly = Sahu (father of Hilaruada)
H		Sati (?)-Runtiya	Son of preceding
A	at least 853–835	Lalli	
U		unknown king	paid tribute to Urartu
U	at least 780–760	Hilaruada	called "Son of Sahu"
A	at least 743–732	Sulumal	
A	ca. 720	Gunzianu	
A	?–712	Tarhunazi	Installed by the Assyrians instead of Gunzianu
A	?–708	Mutallu of Kummuh	Decreed by the Assyrians
A	708–?	Assyrian province	
A	at least 675–651	Mugallu	Independent king
A	mentioned ca. 640	[. . .]-ussi	Son of preceding

Source: Based on [99] Hawkins, *Corpus of Hieroglyphic Luwian Inscriptions.*
Notes: A = Assyrian, H = Hieroglyphic Luwian, U= Urartian.

Urartians

Ruler	Dates
Sarduri I (son of Lutipuri)	ca. 840–830 BCE
Išpuini (son of Sarduri)	ca. 830–820
Išpuini and Minua (co-rulers)	ca. 820–810
Minua (son of Išpuini)	ca. 810–785/780
Argišti I (son of Minua)	780/785– 756
Sarduri II (son of Argišti)	756– ca.730
Rusa I (son of Sarduri)	ca. 730–714/13
Argišti II (son of Rusa)	713–?
Rusa II (son of Argišti)	

Assyrian synchronisms: Mention of a King Rusa in 673/72 (Rusa II) and in 655/54 (Rusa II or Rusa III), as well as a King Sarduri in 643 (Sarduri III or Sarduri IV):

Rusa II (son of Argišti)		Rusa II (son of Argišti)
Sarduri III (son of Rusa)	or	*Erimena*
Sarduri IV (son of Sarduri)	or	Rusa III (son of Erimena)
Erimena	or	Sarduri III (son of Rusa)
Rusa III (son of Erimena)	or	Sarduri IV (son of Sarduri)

Sources: Based on [406] Salvini, *Urartäer*, 1995, and [403] Kroll, *Urartus Untergang*, 1984, 151–170.

Lydians

Name	Dates
Gyges	before 668–644 BCE
Ardys	644–?
Sadyattes	?–?
Alyattes	?–?
Kroisos	?–between 547 and 530 (later than 547/546)

Source: Based on Peter W. Haider, "Lydien," in: W. Eder and J. Renger (eds.), *Herrscherchronologien in der antiken Welt. Namen, Daten, Dynastien*, DNP Suppl. 1, Stuttgart and Weimar 2004, 83–87.

Persians (Achaemenids)

Name	Dates
Kyros (Kuruš) II (= Cyrus the Great)	ca. 558–530
Kambyses (Kambujiya) II	530–522
Smerdis (Gaumāta/ Br̥diya)	522
Dareios (Dārayavauš) I	522–486
Xerxes (Xšāyar̥šan) I	486–465
Artaxerxes (R̥taxšaça) I	465–424
Xerxes II; Sekyndianos	424–423
Dareios II	423–404
Artaxerxes II	404–359
Artaxerxes III	359–338
Arses	338–336
Dareios III	336–330

Source: Based on [486] Wiesehöfer, *Das antike Persien*, 2005.

Persian Satraps in Asia Minor

Lydia

Dates	Place	Ruler	Source
Second half of sixth century BCE	Sardeis including Ionia, at the time of Dareios, and also Daskyleion after the death of Mithrobates	Oroites	Debord 117
at least until 492	Sardeis	Artaphernes	Debord 117
at least 488-465	Sardeis	Artaphernes II	Debord 119
	*Sardeis	*Mithropaustes?	Debord 119
at least 440-420	Sardeis	Pissuthnes	Debord 119
ca. 413/12-407	Sardeis, Ionia, Aiolis, Caria, Lycia	Tissaphernes	Debord 122
407	Cyrus as Karanos and Satrap of Cappadocia, Greater Phrygia and Lydia		Debord 105, 122
401	Sardeis	Artimas (installed by Cyrus the Younger)	Debord 124
401/400–395	Lydia, Ionia, Caria	Tissaphernes	Debord 124
393/392	Sardeis	Tiribazos	Debord 128
392/391	Sardeis (with Lycia)	Autophradates	Debord 128
388	Sardeis (with Ionia?)	Tiribazos	Debord 129
ca. 380	Sardeis	Autophradates	Debord 129
ca. 344	Sardeis and Ionia	Rhoisakes	Debord 153
ca. 340?–334	Sardeis and Ionia	Spithridates	Debord 153; [479] Briant 721, 816, 838

Sources: Based on [480] Debord, *Asie mineure*, 1999; [479] Briant, *Empire Perse*, 1996, 721, 816, 838.
Note: * = uncertain rulers/place.

Ionia

Dates	Place	Ruler	Source
second half of sixth century BCE	Ionia part of the Satrapy of Sardeis	Oroites	Debord 117
Time of Dareios I	*Ionia?	*Gadatas?	Debord 118
ca. 413/412–407	Sardeis, Ionia, Aiolis, Caria, Lycia	Tissaphernes	Debord 122
401	Ionia-Aiolis	Tamos (installed by Cyrus the Younger)	Debord 124
401/400–395	Lydia-Ionia	Tissaphernes	Debord 124
392/391	Ionia	Struthas	Debord 129
388	Sardeis (with Ionia?)	Tiribazos	Debord 129

Source: Based on [480] Debord, *Asie mineure*, 1999.
Note: * = uncertain rulers/places.

Caria

Dates	Place	Ruler	Source
ca. 413/412–ca. 395 BCE	Sardeis, Ionia, Aiolis, Caria, Lycia (407–400 only Caria)	Tissaphernes	Debord 122, DNP
392/391–377/376	Caria	Hekatomnos	Debord 128, 135
377/376–353/352	Caria	Maussollos	Debord 135
353/352–351/350	Caria	Artemisia	Debord 135
351/350–344/343	Caria	Idrieus	Debord 135
344/343–341/340	Caria	Ada I	Debord 135
341/340–336/335	Caria	Pixodaros	Debord 135
336/335–334	Caria	Orontobates	Debord 135

Source: Based on [480] Debord, *Asie mineure*, 1999; DNP *Tissaphernes*.

Daskyleion

Dates	Place	Ruler	Source
523–	Daskyleion	Mitrobates	Debord 92
after Mitrobates	Daskyleion	Oroites	Debord 92
End of 6th Cent.	*Daskyleion	*Megabazos or Otanes?	Debord 92
ca. 493	Daskyleion	Oibares	Debord 92
	*Daskyleion	*Hydarnes ?	Debord 93
until 477	*Daskyleion	*Megabates?	Debord 93; DNP *Megabates* (Thucydides 1, 129, 1)
478–	Daskyleion	Artabazos (Son of Pharnakes)	Debord 93
ca. 430	Daskyleion	Pharnakes (Son of Pharnabazos)	Debord 93
414 or 412– ca.388	Daskyleion	Pharnabazos (Son of Pharnakes)	Debord 94
388–	Daskyleion	Ariobarzanes	Debord 96
362–	Daskyleion	Artabazos	Debord 104
ca. 340	Daskyleion	Arsites	Debord 104
	*Daskyleion	*Mithropastes	Debord 114

Sources: Based on [480] Debord, *Asie mineure*, 1999; DNP *Megabates*.
Note: * = uncertain rulers/place.

Cappadocia

Dates	Place	Ruler	Source
Time of Cyrus	Cappadocia	Pharnakes	Debord 89–90
ca. 521/ 520 BCE	Cappadocia	Otanes	Debord 89–90
ca. 515	Cappadocia	Ariaramnes	Debord 89–90
407	Cyrus as Karanos and Satrap of Cappadocia, Greater Phrygia and Lydia		Debord 105, 122
401–	Cappadocia (and Lycaonia)	Mithradates	Debord 105

Dates	Place	Ruler	Source
after 404	*pars Ciliciae iuxta Cappadociam*, southern Cappadocia	Kamisares	Corn. Nep. *Dat.* 1.1. he may have been only hyparchos
Shortly before 380	Cappadocia (and at times also parts of Cilicia, Kataonia, possibly parts of Pamphylia)	Datames	Debord 106
after 358	Southern Cappadocia	Successor of Datames	Debord 109
after 358–334	Pontic Cappadocia	Mithrobouzanes and possibly his predecessor	Debord 109
333–332	Cappadocia	Sabiktas	Debord 109
until 322	Cappadocia	Ariarathes	Debord 109

Source: Based on [480] Debord, *Asie mineure*, 1999.

Armenia

Dates	Place	Ruler	Source
Time of Cyrus	*Armenia	*Hydarnes	Balcer
after 401–361/360 BCE	Armenia	Orontes I	
until ca. 330	Armenia	Orontes II Tiribazos	

Source: Data from Jack Balcer, *A Prosopographical Study of the Ancient Persians Royal and Noble*, Lewiston, NY et al. 1993, 336.
Note: * = uncertain rulers/place.

Greater Phrygia

Date	Place	Ruler	Source
407	Cyrus as Karanos and Satrap of Cappadocia, Greater Phrygia and Lydia		Debord 105, 122
401	Phrygia	Artakamas (installed by Cyrus the Younger)	Debord 124
after 401	Greater Phrygia	Araios	Debord 105
ca. 350	Phrygia	Tithraustes	DNP *Tithraustes*, but cf. Debord 157
ca. 334	Phrygia	Atizyes	Diodorus 17, 21, 3; Arrian *An.* 1, 25, 3; 2, 11, 8

Source: Based on [480] Debord, *Asie mineure*, 1999.

Aiolis

Dates	Place	Ruler	Source
ca. 413/412–407 BCE	Sardeis, Ionia, Aiolis, Caria, Lycia	Tissaphernes	Debord 122
401	Ionia-Aiolis	Tamos (installed by Cyrus the Younger)	Debord 124
401/400–395	Lydien, Ionia	Tissaphernes	Debord 124
early fourth century	Aiolis (as sub-satraps of Pharnabazos of Daskyleion)	Zenis and Mania (later only Mania)	Briant 579, 614

Sources: Based on [480] Debord, *Asie mineure*, 1999; [479] Briant, *Empire Perse*, 1996, 579, 614.

Paphlagonia

Date	Place	Ruler	Source
ca. 400 BCE	Paphlagonia	Korylas	Xenophon. *An.* 7, 8, 25; Debord 112
ca. 395	Paphlagonia	Thys (= Thuys, Otys, Gyes)	Debord 113
380	Paphlagonia	Datames (as army commander)	
after 362	Paphlagonia integrated into the satrapy of Daskyleion		Debord 114

Source: Based on [480] Debord, *Asie mineure*, 1999.

Lycia

Dates	Place	Ruler	Source
ca. 413/412–407 BCE	Sardeis, Ionia, Aiolis, Caria, Lycia	Tissaphernes	Debord 122

Source: Based on [480] Debord, *Asie mineure*, 1999.

Cilicia

Date	Place	Ruler	Source
		?	A. Lemaire, *EpigrAnat* 21, 1993, 9–14
ca. 401	Cilicia	Syennesis	O. Casabonne, "Le syennésis cilicien et Cyrus", Pallas 43, 1995, 165
ca. 360–	Cilicia (military leader or satrap?)	Mazaios	Casabonne, *Pallas* 43, 1995, 165
ca. 333	*Cilician Gates (proven), probably a military leader	*Arsames?	Casabonne, *Pallas* 43, 1995, 165
333–	Cilicia	Balakros (installed by Alexander)	Debord 163

Source: Based on [480] Debord, *Asie mineure*, 1999.
Note: * = uncertain rulers

Diadochi in Asia Minor

ANTIGONOS MONOPHTHALMOS

Based on [509] Billows, *Antigonos the One-Eyed*, 1990.

from 333 Satrap of Greater Phrygia

321 Flight to Europe, to Antipatros and Krateros. Alliance with Krateros, Antipatros, Ptolemaios and Lysimachos in the First War of the Diadochi against Perdikkas

Autumn 321 after the conference at Triparadeisos: *strategos* of Asia for the Battle against Eumenes

319 Victory at the Battle of Orkynia against Eumenes

318–315 Alliance with Kassandros, Ptolemaios and Seleukos in the Second War of the Diadochi, another victory over Eumenes

314–311 Third War of the Diadochi against Ptolemaios, Kassandros and Seleukos

311 Peace with Kassandros and Lysimachos, later also with Ptolemaios. Antigonos is accepted as ruler of Asia

306 Assumption of the title of king

301 Defeat and death in the Battle of Ipsos against Lysimachos and Seleukos

EUMENES OF KARDIA

Based on Christoph Schäfer, *Eumenes von Kardia and der Kampf um die Macht im Alexanderreich*, Frankfurt am Main 2002; Edward M. Anson, *Eumenes of Cardia*, Leiden and Boston 2004.

from 323 Satrap of Cappadocia and Paphlagonia

from 321 *Strategos* of Asia (installed by Perdikkas)

Autumn 321 Condemned to death at the Triparadeisos conference

320 Battle against Krateros in the First War of the Diadochi

319 Defeat in the Battle of Orkynia

318 *Strategos autokrator* of Asia (installed by Polyperchon)

316 Victory in the Battle in the Paraitakene

End 316/beginning 315 Defeat in the Battle of Gabiene

January 315 Imprisonment and death

DEMETRIOS POLIORKETES

Based on Pat V. Wheatley, "The Lifespan of Demetrius Poliorcetes," *Historia* 46, 1997, 19–27; [509] Billows, *Antigonos the One-Eyed*, 1990.

From 317 Commander in the army of his father Antigonos

306 Assumption of the title of king alongside his father

301 Defeat at the Battle of Ipsos and flight

299 Connection with Seleukos, who marries his daughter Stratonike

295/254 Conquest of Athens
294 King of Macedonia
285 Taken prisoner by Seleukos
283/282 Death

Lysimachos

Based on Helen S. Land, *Lysimachus*, London and New York 1992; Hatto H. Schmitht, *Lysimachos*, *LdH*, 2005, 647–648.

323 Satrap of Thrace
305 Assumption of title of king
301 Victor, with Kassandros and Seleukos, in the Battle of Ipsos. Claims large parts of Asia Minor north of the Taurus Mountains
283/282 Murder of his son Agathokles, flight to Seleukos of the widow Arsinoe and many followers
281 Battle of Korupedion against Seleukos; Defeat and death

Seleukos

Based on Hatto H. Schmitt and Johannes Nollé, "Seleukiden(reich)," *LdH*, 2005, 956–984.

323 Chiliarchos
Autumn 321 Attribution of the Babylonian satrapy at the conference in Triparadeisos
318–315 Alliance with Kassandros, Ptolemaios and Antigonos in the Second War of the Diadochi
314–311 Alliance with Ptolemaios and Kassandros against Antigonos in the Third War of the Diadochi
ca. 310–308 Further military activities against Antigonos Monophthalmos
305 Assumption of the title of king
310–ca. 303 Conquest of the upper satrapies as far as the Indus
301 Victor, with Kassandros and Lysimachos, over Antiogonos Monophthalmos and Demetrios Poliorketes at the Battle of Ipsos
298 Marriage to Stratonike, the daughter of Demetrios Poliorketes
285 Capture of Demetrios
Early 281 Victory over Lysimachos at the Battle of Korupedion
Summer 281 Murdered by Ptolemaios Keraunos on the way back to Thrace and Macedonia

Seleucids up to Antiochos III

Ruler	Dates
Seleukos I Nikator	311–281 BCE (king from 305 on)
Antiochos I Soter	281–June 2, 261
Antiochos II Theos	261– summer 246
Seleukos II Kallinikos	246–226/225
Seleukos III Soter	226/225–223
Antiochos III (the Great)	223–187

Pergamon

Ruler	Dates
Philetairos	281–263 BCE
Eumenes I	263–241
Attalos I	241–197
Eumenes II	197–158/157
Attalos II	158/157–138 (or 139?)
Attalos III	138–133
Eumenes III	133–130

Sources: Based on Walter Eder, "Die Attaliden von Pergamon", in: W. Eder and J. Renger (eds.), *Herrscherchronologien in der antiken Welt. Namen, Daten, Dynastien, DNP* Suppl. 1, Stuttgart and Weimar 2004, 88–89; on Eumenes II's death: Georg Petzl, "Inschriften aus der Umgebung von Saittai I," *ZPE* 30, 1978, 263–267; Dominique Mulliez, "La chronologie de la prêtise IV (170/69–158/7) et la date de la mort d'Eumène II", *Topoi* 8, 1998, 231–241.

Bithynia

Ruler	Dates
Zipoites	ca. 315–280 BCE
Nikomedes I	ca. 280–245
Ziaelas	ca. 245–230
Prusias I	ca. 230–182
Prusias II	ca. 182–149
Nikomedes II	ca. 149–127
Nikomedes III	ca. 127–94
Nikomedes IV	ca. 94–74/73; –75: cf. R. Merkelbach, *ZPE* 81, 1990, 97–100.

Source: Based on [549] Marek, *Pontus et Bithynia*, 2003, 187.

Galatia

Tectosages

Ruler	Dates
Comboiomarus [or Trocmus]*	189 BCE
Gaizatorix	180
Kastor I	63/62 (?)–44
Deiotaros	44– ca. 40
Kastor II	ca. 40–36

Source: Based on Martin Schottky, "Galatia," in: W. Eder and J. Renger (eds.), *Herrscherchronologien in der antiken Welt. Namen, Daten, Dynastien*, *DNP* Suppl. 1, Stuttgart and Weimar 2004, 99–101.

*See Trocmi table below.

Tolistobogii

Ruler	Dates
Leonnorios	before 279–after 271 BCE
Eposognatus	189
Ortiagon	before 189–183
Paidopolites	second century
Sinatos	late second century
Sinorix	late second century
Deiotaros	86 (63/62) –ca. 40

Source: Based on Martin Schottky, "Galatia," in: W. Eder and J. Renger (eds.), *Herrscherchronologien in der antiken Welt. Namen, Daten, Dynastien*, *DNP* Suppl. 1, Stuttgart and Weimar 2004, 99–101.

Trocmi

Ruler	Dates
Lutarios	before 279– after 274
Comboiomarus [or Tectosage]*	189
Gaulotos	189
Brogitarus	63/62–55/52
Domnilaus (Domnekleios)	55/52–49
Mithridates	47
Deiotaros	44–ca. 40
Adiatorix	d. 29

Source: Based on Martin Schottky, "Galatia," in: W. Eder and J. Renger (eds.), *Herrscherchronologien in der antiken Welt. Namen, Daten, Dynastien*, *DNP* Suppl. 1, Stuttgart and Weimar 2004, 99–101.

*See Tectosages table above.

Galatia as a whole (not including foreign rulers)

Ruler	Dates
Ortiagon	189–183 BCE
Kassignatos	before 180–171
Solovettius	167

Source: Based on Martin Schottky, "Galatia," in: W. Eder and J. Renger (eds.), *Herrscherchronologien in der antiken Welt. Namen, Daten, Dynastien, DNP* Suppl. 1, Stuttgart and Weimar 2004, 99–101.

Paphlagonia

Ruler	Dates
Morzios	at least 189–179 BCE, briefly interrupted by Pharnakes of Pontos's invasion
Gezatorix	
Attalos	63–41
Kastor	40
Deiotaros Philadelphos, Deiotaros Philopator	before 36?
Became a province	6/5

Sources: Based on [182] Marek, *Stadt, Ära*, 1993, 60–61; Hatto H. Schmitt, "Paphlagonien," *LdH*, 2005, 754–755.

Pontos

Ruler	Dates	Literature
Mithridates I	ca. 302–266/265	
Ariobarzanes	ca. 265–255	
Mithridates II	ca. 255–220	Primo: before 246–before 196/195
Mithridates III	ca. 220–190	
Pharnakes I	ca. 190–160	Habicht: ca. 195–171/170 Højte: ca. 195–155 Primo: before 196/195–170/169
Mithridates IV Philopator, Philadelphos	ca. 160–150	Primo: 170/169–152/150
Mithridates V Euergetes	ca. 150–121	Primo: 152/150–121/120
Mithridates VI Eupator	ca. 120–64	Primo: 121/120–63
Pharnakes II	63–47	
Dareios	ca. 39–37	

Sources: [549] Marek, *Pontus et Bithynia*, 2003, 187; Christian Habicht, *Athen, die Geschichte der Stadt in hellenistischer Zeit*, Munich 1995, 228; Jakob M. Højte, "The Date of the Alliance between Chersonesos and Pharnakes (IOSPE I² 402) and Its Implications," in: V. F. Stolba and L. Hannestad (eds.), "Chronologies of the Black Sea Area in the Period C. 400-100 BC," *Black Sea Studies* 3, 2005, 137–152; Andrea Primo, "Mitridate III: Problemi di cronologia e identità nella dinastia Pontica," in: B. Virgilio, *Studi ellenistici* XIX, Pisa 2006, 307–329. J. T. Ramsay, "Mithridates, the Banner of Ch'ih-Yu, and the Comet Coin," *HSCP* 99, 1999, 197–253, dates the first regnal year of Mithridates VI to 123 BCE.

Polemonids

Ruler	Years	Events
Polemon I	39 BCE	Installation in the region of Ikonion by Mark Antony
	38/36	Exchange of *Dynasteia* over the region of Ikonion for rule over Pontos
	34/33	Installation in Lesser Armenia
	14	King of the Regnum Bosporanum
	ca. 8	Death
Pythodoris Philometor	ca. 8	Queen of Pontos, Colchis, and the Regnum Bosporanum, though soon forced to yield the latter to Dynamis
	3/2 BCE	Married to Archelaos of Cappadocia
	17 CE–34/35 (?)	Death of Archelaos, monocracy again.
Antonia Tryphaina	ca. 21–36 CE	Married to the Thracian king Kotys VIII; together with her son Polemon II she ruled in Thrace at least eighteen years, possibly until 39/40 CE
Polemon II	37–64	Installed as king of Pontos and the Regnum Bosporanum by Caligula
	41	Loss of the Regnum Bosporanum, granted part of Cilicia as compensation
	64	Loss of Pontos, which became the Roman province of *Pontus Polemonianus*
	until 68	Ruler of part of Cilicia

Source: Based on Richard D. Sullivan, "Dynasts in Pontus," *ANRW* II 7.2, 1980, 913–930; [182] Marek, *Stadt, Ära,* 1993, 60–61.

Komana

Ruler/ Event	Years
Dorylaos	before 63 BCE
Archelaos I	63–55
Archelaos II	55–47
Lykomedes	47– before 29
Kleon	ca. 29
Dyteutos	29–?
Comana Pontica/ Hierokaisareia attached to the province of Galatia	34/35 n. CE

Based on Martin Schottky, "Komana Pontika," in: W. Eder and J. Renger (eds.), *Herrscherchronologien in der antiken Welt. Namen, Daten, Dynastien, DNP* Suppl. 1, Stuttgart and Weimar 2004, 108; [182] Marek, *Stadt, Ära,* 1993, 60.

Lesser Armenia

Ruler/ Event	Years
Mithridates	attested 179 BCE
?	after 179 BCE
Mithridates Euergetes	133–129
Sisis (?)	
Antipatros	?–ca. 107
Mithridates Eupator	ca. 107–66 = Mithridates VI of Pontos
Deiotarus	63/62–47
Ariobarzanes	47-42 = Ariobarzanes III of Cappadocia
Polemon	34/33–after 31 = Polemon I of Pontos
Artavasdes	after 31–before 20 = Artavasdes III of Media Atropatene
Archelaos	20 BCE–17 CE = Archelaos Sisines of Cappadocia
became Roman	17–38 CE
Kotys	38– before 54
Aristobulos	54–71/72
province of Cappadocia	72 and later

Source: Based on Martin Schottky, "Klein-Armenien," in: W. Eder and J. Renger (eds.), *Herrscherchronologien in der antiken Welt. Namen, Daten, Dynastien*, *DNP* Suppl. 1, Stuttgart-Weimar 2004, 95.

Cappadocia

Ruler	Years
Ariarathes	ca. 350-322 BCE
Eumenes of Kardia	323–
Nikanor	320
Ariarathes II	ca. 280–ca. 255
Ariaramnes	ca. 255–225
Ariarathes III	co-ruler from 255, ca. 225–220
Ariarathes IV Eusebes	ca. 220–163
Ariarathes V Eusebes Philopator	ca. 163–130
Orophernes	ca. 160-155
Ariarathes VI Epiphanes Philopator	130–111 (116?)
Ariarathes VII Philometor	111(116?)–ca. 100
Ariarathes VIII	ca. 100– ca. 96
Gordios	ca. 100–93 with interruptions, regent for Ariarathes IX
Ariarathes IX Eusebes Philopator	ca. 101/100–88 with interruptions
Ariobarzanes I Philorhomaios	94/92 or 89–63/62
Ariobarzanes II Philometor	63/62–52/51
Ariobazanes III Eusebes Philorhomaios	52/51–42
Ariarathes IX/X Eusebes Philadelphos	42–41/36
Archelaos Sisines	41/36 BCE–17 CE
His son Archelaos II ruled parts of Cilicia Trachea until 38 CE	

Source: Based on Martin Schottky, "Randstaaten Kleinasiens in hellenistisch-römischer Zeit, VI.6 Kappadokia," in: W. Eder and J. Renger (eds.), *Herrscherchronologien in der antiken Welt. Namen, Daten, Dynastien*, *DNP* Suppl. 1, Stuttgart and Weimar 2004, 102–103; Sviatoslav Dmitriev, "Cappadocian Dynastic Rearrangements on the Eve of the First Mithridatic War," *Historia* 55, 2006, 285–297.

Commagene

Ruler	Facella	Schmitt
Orontes		
Samos I	ca. 260 (p. 172)	
Arsames	Middle of third century (p. 175)	
Ptolemaios	163/2–ca. 130 (pp. 199–202)	163/2–ca. 130
Samos II Theosebes Dikaios	ca. 130 (p. 172)	ca. 130–ca.100
Mithridates I Kallinikos	ca. 100–70	ca. 100–ca. 69
Antiochos I Theos	ca. 70– ca. 36 (–before 31)	ca. 69–36
Mithridates II	ca. 36– ca. 20	ca. 36–20
Mithridates III	ca. 20	ca. 20–12 (?)
Antiochos III	–20 (?) –17 CE (p. 315)	12 (?)–17 CE
Antiochos IV	38–72 CE	38–72 CE

Sources: Based on Margherita Facella, *La dinastia degli Orontidi nella Commagene ellenistico-romana*, Pisa 2006; Hatto H. Schmitt, "Kommagene", *LdH*, 2005, 573–574.

Armenia

Ruler/ Events	Dates
Orontes	220– before 190 BCE
Artaxias I	before190–ca. 160
Artavasdes I	ca. 160–ca. 120
Tigranes I	ca. 120–95
Tigranes II	95–ca. 55
Artavasdes II	ca. 55–34
Artaxias II	34–20
Tigranes III	20– before 6
Tigranes IV	before 6 BCE– ca. 1 CE
Erato	before 6 BCE–ca. 1 CE
Artavasdes III	ca. 5–2 BCE
Ariobarzanes	ca. 2–4 CE
Artavasdes IV	ca. 4–6 CE
Tigranes V	ca. 7–12 CE
Erato	ca. 13–15 CE
Vonones (king of the Parthians)	ca. 16–17 CE
Artaxias III	18–34 CE
Arsakes I	35 CE
Orodes	36 CE
Mithridates	35–38 CE
Demonax	38–42 CE
Mithridates	42–51 CE
Radamistus	51–54 CE
Tiridates I	52/3–60 CE
Tigranes VI	60/61 CE

Ruler/ Events	Dates
Tiridates I	61/66–ca. 75 CE
Sanatrukes	ca. 75– ca. 110 CE
Axidares	ca. 110– ca. 112 CE
Parthamasiris	ca. 112– ca. 114 CE
Roman province of Armenia	114–117 CE
Vologaises	116/7–after 136 CE
?	after 136–160 CE
Aurelius Pacorus	160–163 CE
Sohaimos	164–ca. 180 CE
Vologaises II	ca. 180–190 CE
Chosroes I	ca. 190–214/6 CE
Tiridates II	217–252

Based on Martin Schottky, "Armenien," in: W. Eder and J. Renger (eds.), *Herrscherchronologien in der antiken Welt. Namen, Daten, Dynastien*, *DNP* Suppl. 1, Stuttgart and Weimar 2004, 93–94.

Arsakids (Parthians)

Ruler	Dates
Arsakes I	247 (?) – after 217 BCE
Arsakes II	after 217– ca. 191
Phriapatios	ca. 191–176
Phraates I	ca. 176–171
Mithridates I	ca. 171–139/138
Phraates II	ca. 139/198–128/127
Artabanos I	ca. 127–124/123
Mithridates II	ca. 124/123–88/87
Gotarzes	91/90– ca. 80
Orodes I	ca. 80–78/77
Sinatrukes	78/77–71/70
Phraates III	71/70–58/57
Orodes II	58/57– ca. 39
Phraates IV	ca. 40–3/2
Tiridates	25
Phraates V	3/2–4 CE
Orodes III	4–6
Vonones	8/9
Artabanos II	10/11– ca. 38
Vardanes I	ca. 39–45
Gotarzes II	43/4–51
Vologaises I	ca. 51–76/80
Vologaises II	77/8–78/79
Pakoros II	77/8–86/87
Artabanos III	79/80–80/81

Ruler	Dates
Vologaises II	89/90
Osroes	89/90
Pakoros II	92/93–95/96
Osroes	108/09–127/28
Vologaises III	111/12–146/48
Pakoros II	113/14–114/115
Vologaises III	129–146/148
Vologaises IV	147/48–190/93
Vologaises V	190/201–206/207
Vologaises VI	207/08–221/222
Artabanos IV	213–222 (?)

Based on Klaus Schippmann, *Grundzüge der parthischen Geschichte*, Darmstadt 1980, 123 ff.

Sasanids up to the beginning of the fourth century CE

Ruler	Dates
Sāsān	ca. 200 CE
Papak	205/6 (?)
Ardashir	208–211 (?)
Artabanos IV (s.v. Arsakids)	ca. 213
Ardashir	224–239
Shapur I	239–270/3 (?)
Hormizd I	270/273–274
Bahram I	274–276
Bahram II	276–293
Bahram III	293
Narseh	293–302

Based on Klaus Schippmann, *Grundzüge der Geschichte des Sasanidischen Reiches*, Darmstadt 1990, 141 ff.

Governors of the Roman Provinces in the Time of the Republic

Date	Asia
131	P. Licinius Crassus Mucianus
130	M. Perperna
129	M'. Aquillius
128	M'. Aquillius
127	M'. Aquillius
126	M'. Aquillius
125	Cornelius Lentulus (?)
124	

Date	Asia
123	
122	C. Atinius Labeo Macerio
121	M'. (or M.) Valerius Messalla (?)
120	Q. Mucius Scaevola (?)
119	
118	
117	
116	Cn. Papirius Carbo (?)
115	L. (Calpurnius) Piso (Caesoninus) (?)
114	
113	praetor n.n.
112	Ser. Cornelius Ser. f. Lentulus (?)
111	
110	C. Rabirius (?)
109	
108	praetor n.n.
107	
106	
105	
104	
103	
102	C. Billienus (?)

Date	Asia	Cilicia
101		M. Antonius
100	M. (Plautius) Hypsaeus (?)	M. Antonius
99	C. Iulius Caesar	
98	C. Iulius Caesar	
97		
96	L. Lucilius (?)	L. Cornelius Sulla
95	C. Valerius Flaccus (?)	L. Cornelius Sulla
94	Q. Mucius Scaevola (?)	L. Cornelius Sulla (?)
93	L. Gellius (?)	L. Cornelius Sulla or L. Gellius
92		
91	L. Valerius Flaccus (?) C. Cassius (?)	
90	C. Cassius	
89	C. Cassius	Q. Oppius
88	C. Cassius	Q. Oppius
87	L. Cornelius Sulla	Q. Oppius

Date	Asia	Cilicia
86	L. Cornelius Sulla L. Valerius Flaccus	Q. Oppius
85	L. Cornelius Sulla L. Valerius Flaccus	Q. Oppius L. Cornelius Lentulus (?)
84	L. Cornelius Sulla	L. Cornelius Lentulus (?)
83	L. Licinius Murena	L. Cornelius Lentulus (?)
82	L. Licinius Murena	L. Cornelius Lentulus (?)
81	L. Licinius Murena M. Minucius Thermus	C. Valerius Flaccus
80	C. Claudius Nero	Cn. Cornelius Dolabella
79	C. Claudius Nero	Cn. Cornelius Dolabella
78		P. Servilius Vatia Isauricus
77	Terentius Varro (?)	P. Servilius Vatia Isauricus
76	M. Iunius Silanus (?) Murena (?)	P. Servilius Vatia Isauricus
75	M. Iunius Iuncus	P. Servilius Vatia Isauricus

Date	Asia	Cilicia	Bithynia
74	M. Iunius Iuncus (also Bithynia) L. Licinius Lucullus (?)	L. Octavius	M. Iunius Iuncus (also Asia) M. Aurelius Cotta (?)
73	L. Licinius Lucullus	L. Licinius Lucullus	M. Aurelius Cotta
72	L. Licinius Lucullus	L. Licinius Lucullus	M. Aurelius Cotta L. Licinius Lucullus
71	L. Licinius Lucullus	L. Licinius Lucullus	M. Aurelius Cotta L. Licinius Lucullus
70	L. Licinius Lucullus	L. Licinius Lucullus	L. Licinius Lucullus
69	L. Licinius Lucullus	L. Licinius Lucullus	L. Licinius Lucullus
68	P. Cornelius Dolabella	L. Licinius Lucullus	L. Licinius Lucullus
67	P. Cornelius Sulla*	Q. Marcius Rex	L. Licinius Lucullus M'. Acilius Glabrio
66	T. Aufidius (?)	Q. Marcius Rex Cn. Pompeius Magnus	M'. Acilius Glabrio Cn. Pompeius Magnus
65	P. Varinius (?)	Cn. Pompeius Magnus	Cn. Pompeius Magnus

Date	Asia	Cilicia	Pontus et Bithynia
64	P. Orbius (?)	Cn. Pompeius Magnus	Cn. Pompeius Magnus
63	P. Servilius Globulus (?)	Cn. Pompeius Magnus	Cn. Pompeius Magnus
62	L. Valerius Flaccus	Cn. Pompeius Magnus	Cn. Pompeius Magnus
61	Q. Tullius Cicero		C. Papirius Carbo (?)
60	Q. Tullius Cicero		C. Papirius Carbo
59	Q. Tullius Cicero		C. Papirius Carbo
58	T. Ampius Balbus	M. Porcius Cato	C. Papirius Carbo
57	C. Fabius (?) Hadrianus	(A. Gabinius → Syria) T. Ampius Balbus	C. Memmius

Date	Asia	Cilicia	Pontus et Bithynia
56	C. Septimius	P. Cornelius Lentulus Spinther	C. Caecilius Cornutus
55	C. Claudius Pulcher	P. Cornelius Lentulus Spinther	
54	C. Claudius Pulcher	P. Cornelius Lentulus Spinther	
53	C. Claudius Pulcher	P. Cornelius Lentulus Spinther (?)	
52		Ap. Claudius Pulcher	
51	Q. Minucius Thermus	Ap. Claudius Pulcher M. Tullius Cicero	P. Silius
50	Q. Minucius Thermus	M. Tullius Cicero	A. Plautius
49	C. Fannius		
48	C. Fannius Cn. Domitius Calvinus**		
47	Cn. Domitius Calvinus**	Q. Marcius Philippus (?)	C. Vibius Pansa
46	P. Servilius Isauricus	Q. Marcius Philippus (?) Q. Cornificius	C. Vibius Pansa R. Sulpicius Rufus
45	P. Servilius Isauricus	Q. Cornificius L. Volcatius Tullus	R. Sulpicius Rufus
44	P. Servilius Isauricus C. Trebonius	L. Volcatius Tullus Q. Marcius Crispus (?)	Q. Marcius Crispus
43	C. Trebonius M. Iunius Brutus		L. Tillius Cimber P. Cornelius Lentulus Spinther
42	M. Iunius Brutus M. Antonius		
41	M. Antonius		
40	L. Munatius Plancus M. Cocceius Nerva (?)		
39			
38			
37			
36	C. Furnius		
35	C. Furnius M. Titius (?) C. Norbanus Flaccus		
34			
33	M. Herennius Picens (?)		
32	M. Herennius Picens (?)		

Sources: Based on T. Corey Brennan, *The Praetorship in the Roman Republic*, vol. 2, Oxford 2000, 714 ff.; [490] Magie, *Roman Rule*, 1950, 1579 ff.; Gerd R. Stumpf, *Numismatische Studien zur Chronologie der römischen Statthalter in Kleinasien (122 v.Chr.-163 n. Chr.)*, Saarbrücken 1991, 306 ff.
Note: Minor corrections indicated by *.
*[183] Marek, *Kaunos*, 2006, 288–229.
**C. Habicht, *ZPE* 169, 2009, 158.

Governors of the Roman Provinces from Augustus to Diocletian

Year	ASIA	PONTUS-BITHYNIA
29 BCE	L. Volcatius Tullus (?) M. Tullius Cicero (?)	
28	L. Volcatius Tullus (?) M. Tullius Cicero (?) M. Potitus Valerius Messalla (?)	Thorius Flaccus (?) Ap. Pulcher (?)
27	L. Volcatius Tullus (?) M. Tullius Cicero (?) M. Potitus Valerius Messalla (?)	
26	L. Volcatius Tullus (?) M. Tullius Cicero (?) M. Potitus Valerius Messalla (?)	

Year	ASIA	PONTUS-BITHYNIA	GALATIA, Phrygia, Pisidia, Pamphylia, Lycaonia
25	M. Tullius Cicero (?) M. Potitus Valerius Messalla (?)		M. Lollius (?)
24	M. Tullius Cicero (?) M. Potitus Valerius Messalla (?)		M. Lollius (?)
23	M. Tullius Cicero (?) M. Potitus Valerius Messalla (?) Sex. Appuleius (?)		
22	Sex. Appuleius		

Year			
21	Sex. Appuleius (?)	M. Tullius Cicero (?)	M. Potitus Valerius Messalla (?)
20		M. Tullius Cicero (?)	M. Potitus Valerius Messalla (?)
19			
18			
17			
16	Q. Aemilius Lepidus (?)		L. Calpurnius Piso (pontifex) (?)
15	Q. Aemilius Lepidus (?)		L. Calpurnius Piso (pontifex) (?)
14	Q. Aemilius Lepidus (?)		L. Calpurnius Piso (pontifex) (?)
13	Q. Aemilius Lepidus (?)		
12	Q. Aemilius Lepidus (?)		
11	Q. Aemilius Lepidus (?)		
10	Q. Aemilius Lepidus (?)	Paullus Fabius Maximus	
9	Paullus Fabius Maximus	Iullus Antonius (?)	
8	P. Cornelius Scipio (?)	Iullus Antonius (?)	
7	P. Cornelius Scipio (?)	Iullus Antonius (?)	P. Cornelius Scipio (?)

Year	ASIA	PONTUS-BITHYNIA	GALATIA, Phrygia, Pisidia, Pamphylia, Lycaonia
6	Iullus Antonius (?)		Cornutus Aquila
	P. Cornelius Scipio (?)		
	C. Marcius Censorinus*		

Year	ASIA	PONTUS-BITHYNIA	GALATIA, Phrygia, Pisidia, Pamphylia, Lycaonia, Paphlagonia
5	C. Marcius Censorinus*		
	C. Asinius Gallus		
4	C. Asinius Gallus		
	Iullus Antonius (?)		
	P. Cornelius Scipio (?)		
	C. Antistius Vetus (?)		
3	Iullus Antonius (?)		
	P. Cornelius Scipio (?)		
	C. Antistius Vetus (?)		
2	C. Antistius Vetus (?)		
	Cn. Cornelius Lentulus (augur)		
1 BCE	Cn. Cornelius Lentulus (augur)		
	C. Antistius Vetus (?)		
1 CE	C. Antistius Vetus (?)		
2	C. Antistius Vetus (?)		
3	C. Antistius Vetus (?)		

4	C. Antistius Vetus (?)
	M. Plautius Silvanus (?)
5	C. Antistius Vetus (?)
	M. Plautius Silvanus (?)
	L. Calpurnius Piso (augur) (?)
6	C. Antistius Vetus (?)
	M. Plautius Silvanus (?)
	L. Calpurnius Piso (augur) (?)
7	M. Plautius Silvanus (?)
	L. Calpurnius Piso (augur) (?)
	P. Vinicius (?)
8	M. Plautius Silvanus (?)
	L. Calpurnius Piso (augur) (?)
	P. Vinicius (?)
	L. Volusius Saturninus (?)
9	M. Plautius Silvanus (?)
	L. Calpurnius Piso (augur) (?)
	P. Vinicius (?)
	L. Volusius Saturninus (?)
	L. Valerius Messalla Volesus (?)
10	M. Plautius Silvanus (?)
	L. Calpurnius Piso (augur) (?)
	P. Vinicius (?)
	L. Volusius Saturninus (?)
	L. Valerius Messalla Volesus (?)
	L. Licinius ... (?)

Year	ASIA	PONTUS-BITHYNIA	GALATIA, Phrygia, Pisidia, Pamphylia, Lycaonia, Paphlagonia
11	M. Plautius Silvanus (?) L. Calpurnius Piso (augur) (?) P. Vinicius (?) L. Volusius Saturninus (?) L. Valerius Messalla Volesus (?) C. Vibius Postumus (?)	L. Licinius . . . (?)	
12	M. Plautius Silvanus (?) L. Calpurnius Piso (augur) (?) P. Vinicius (?) L. Volusius Saturninus (?) L. Valerius Messalla Volesus (?) C. Vibius Postumus (?)	L. Licinius . . . (?)	Sex. Sotidius Strabo Libuscidianus (?)
13	M. Plautius Silvanus (?) L. Calpurnius Piso (augur) (?) P. Vinicius (?) L. Volusius Saturninus (?) L. Valerius Messalla Volesus (?) C. Vibius Postumus (?) C. Vibius Postumus (?)	L. Licinius . . . (?)	Sex. Sotidius Strabo Libuscidianus (?)
14		M. Granius Marcellus	Sex. Sotidius Strabo Libuscidianus (?)

Other governors under Augustus

M. Herennius Picens		M. Plautius Silvanus
Vinicius		Arr]enus (?)
C. Norbanus Flaccus		[. . . S]abinus
15	C. Vibius Postumus (?)	M. Granius Marcellus
		Sex. Sotidius Strabo Libuscidianus (?)
16	C. Vibius Postumus (?)	Sex. Sotidius Strabo Libuscidianus (?)

Year	ASIA	PONTUS-BITHYNIA	GALATIA, Phrygia, Pisidia, Pamphylia, Lycaonia, Paphlagonia	CAPPADOCIA
17	C. Iunius Silanus	P. Vitellius (?)		
18	C. Iunius Silanus	P. Vitellius (?)		
19	M'. Aemilius Lepidus	P. Vitellius (?)		
20	M'. Aemilius Lepidus			
21	C. Fonteius Capito (?) Sex. Pompeius (?)			
22	C. Fonteius Capito (?) Sex. Pompeius (?)			
23	C. Fonteius Capito (?) Sex. Pompeius (?)			Priscus
24	C. Fonteius Capito (?) Sex. Pompeius (?)			
25	M. Aurelius Cotta Maximus Messalinus (?) Sex. Pompeius (?)			

Year	ASIA	PONTUS-BITHYNIA	GALATIA, Phrygia, Pisidia, Pamphylia, Lycaonia, Paphlagonia	CAPPADOCIA
26	M. Aurelius Cotta Maximus Messalinus (?)			
	Sex. Pompeius (?)			
	Scribonius Libo*			
27	Scribonius Libo*			
	M. Aemilius Lepidus			
28	M. Aemilius Lepidus (?)			
29	C. Vibius Rufus Rufinus			
	P. Petronius			
30	P. Petronius			
31	P. Petronius			
32	P. Petronius			
33	P. Petronius			
34	P. Petronius			
35	P. Petronius			
	M. Aurelius Cotta Maximus Messalinus (?)			
36	M. Aurelius Cotta Maximus Messalinus (?)			
37	M. Aurelius Cotta Maximus Messalinus (?)			

Other governors under Tiberius

	ASIA		GALATIA	
	Favonius (?)		Metilius	
	Sex. Nonius Quinctilianus		Fronto	
	Q. Poppaeus Secundus		Silvanus	
			T. Helvius Basila	

38	C. Asinius Pollio (?) C. Calpurnius Aviola (?) M. Vinicius (?)
39	C. Asinius Pollio (?) C. Calpurnius Aviola (?) M. Vinicius (?)
40	C. Asinius Pollio (?) C. Calpurnius Aviola (?) M. Vinicius (?)
41	C. Cassius Longinus C. Cassius Longinus

Other governors under Gaius

Year	ASIA	PONTUS-BITHYNIA	GALATIA, Phrygia, Pisidia, Pamphylia, Lyca-onia, Paphlagonia	CAPPADOCIA	LYCIA
42	C. Sallustius Passienus Crispus		T. Helvius Basila		
43	C. Sallustius Passienus Crispus	C. Cadius Rufus (?)			Q. Veranius
44		C. Cadius Rufus (?)			Q. Veranius
45		C. Cadius Rufus (?)			Q. Veranius
46		C. Cadius Rufus (?)			Q. Veranius
47	P. Memmius Regulus (?)	C. Cadius Rufus (?)			Q. Veranius

Year	ASIA	PONTUS-BITHYNIA	GALATIA, Phrygia, Pisidia, Pamphylia, Lycaonia, Paphlagonia	CAPPADOCIA	LYCIA
48	P. Memmius Regulus (?)	C. Cadius Rufus (?)			Q. Veranius M. Calpurnius Rufus (?)
49	P. Memmius Regulus (?)		M. Annius Afrinus (?)		M. Calpurnius Rufus (?) Vilius Flaccus (?)
50	P. Memmius Regulus (?)	C. Sertorius Brocchus (?)	M. Annius Afrinus (?)		Vilius Flaccus (?) T. Clodius Eprius Marcellus
51	P. Memmius Regulus (?) L. Pedanius Secundus	C. Sertorius Brocchus (?)	M. Annius Afrinus (?)	Iulius Paelignus	T. Clodius Eprius Marcellus
52	P. Memmius Regulus (?) L. Pedanius Secundus	C. Sertorius Brocchus (?)	M. Annius Afrinus (?)		T. Clodius Eprius Marcellus
53	L. Pedanius Secundus	C. Sertorius Brocchus (?)	M. Annius Afrinus (?)		T. Clodius Eprius Marcellus
54	M. Iunius Silanus	C. Sertorius Brocchus (?) Attius Laco (?)	M. Annius Afrinus (?) Q. Petronius Umber (?)		T. Clodius Eprius Marcellus

Other governors under Claudius

P. Cornelius Lentulus Scipio
Paullus Fabius Persicus
Cn. Domitius Corbulo
P. Suillius Rufus

L. Mindius Pollio
L. Mindius Balbus
P. Pasidienus Firmus
L. Dunius Severus

55	M. Iunius Silanus Ti. Plautius Silvanus Aelianus (?) Marius Cordus (?)	Attius Laco (?)	Q. Petronius Umber (?)	Cn. Domitius Corbulo
56	Ti. Plautius Silvanus Aelianus (?) Marius Cordus (?)			Cn. Domitius Corbulo
57	Ti. Plautius Silvanus Aelianus (?) Marius Cordus (?) Q. Allius Maximus			Cn. Domitius Corbulo
58	Q. Allius Maximus L. Vipstanus Poplicola	M. Tarquitius Priscus (?)		Cn. Domitius Corbulo
59	L. Vipstanus Poplicola C. Messalla Vipstanus Gallus	M. Tarquitius Priscus (?)		Cn. Domitius Corbulo
60	C. Messalla Vipstanus Gallus M. Vettius Niger (?) Q. Marcius Barea Soranus (?)	M. Tarquitius Priscus (?)		Cn. Domitius Corbulo
61	M. Vettius Niger (?) Q. Marcius Barea Soranus (?)			Cn. Domitius Corbulo L. Iunius Caesennius Paetus
62	M. Vettius Niger (?) Q. Marcius Barea Soranus (?) P. Volasenna (?) L. Salvius Otho Titianus (?) L. Antistius Vetus (?)			L. Iunius Caesennius Paetus

Year	ASIA	PONTUS-BITHYNIA	GALATIA, Phrygia, Pisidia, Pamphylia, Lyca-onia, Paphlagonia	CAPPADOCIA	LYCIA
63	P. Volasenna (?) L. Salvius Otho Titianus (?) L. Antistius Vetus (?)			L. Iunius Caesennius Paetus Cn. Domitius Corbulo	Sex. Marcius Priscus
64	P. Volasenna (?) L. Salvius Otho Titianus (?) L. Antistius Vetus (?)			Cn. Domitius Corbulo	Sex. Marcius Priscus
65	P. Volasenna (?) L. Salvius Otho Titianus (?) L. Antistius Vetus (?) M'. Acilius Aviola				Sex. Marcius Priscus
66	M'. Acilius Aviola M. Aefulanus (?) (A. Ducenius?) Geminus (?)				Sex. Marcius Priscus
67	M. Aefulanus (?) (A. Ducenius?) Geminus (?)		L. Nonius Calpurnius Asprenas		Sex. Marcius Priscus
68	M. Aefulanus (?) (A. Ducenius?) Geminus (?) C. Fonteius Agrippa				Sex. Marcius Priscus

Other governors under Nero

	P. Petronius Niger, L. Montanus	C. Iulius Proculus (?)	C. Licinius Mucianus
69			Sex. Marcius Priscus
70			Sex. Marcius Priscus
71			Avidius Celer

Year	ASIA	PONTUS-BITHYNIA	GALATIA, Phrygia, Pisidia, Pamphylia, Lycaonia, Paphlagonia	CAPPADOCIA, Pontus, Armenia Minor	LYCIA-PAMPHYLIA	CILICIA
69	C. Fonteius Agrippa, M. Suillius Nerullinus (?)					
70	M. Suillius Nerullinus (?), T. Clodius Eprius Marcellus					
71	T. Clodius Eprius Marcellus					
72	T. Clodius Eprius Marcellus					
73	T. Clodius Eprius Marcellus, M. Vettrius Bolanus (?), M. Aponius Saturninus (?)					
74	M. Vettrius Bolanus (?), M. Aponius Saturninus (?)					
75	M. Vettrius Bolanus (?), M. Aponius Saturninus (?)					
76	M. Vettrius Bolanus (?), M. Aponius Saturninus (?)			Cn. Pompeius Collega, Ti. Iulius Celsus Polemaeanus (,,sublegatus") (?)	L. Luscius Ocrea	

Year	ASIA	PONTUS-BITHYNIA	GALATIA, Phrygia, Pisidia, Pamphylia, Lycaonia, Paphlagonia	CAPPADOCIA, Pontus, Armenia Minor	LYCIA-PAMPHYLIA	CILICIA
77	M. Aponius Saturninus (?) Ti. Catius Asconius Silius Italicus (?)			Ti. Iulius Celsus Polemaeanus („sublegatus") (?)		L. Octavius Memor (?)
78	Ti. Catius Asconius Silius Italicus (?) Arrius Antoninus (?)			Ti. Iulius Celsus Polemaeanus („sublegatus") (?)		L. Octavius Memor (?)
79	Arrius Antoninus (?) M. Ulpius Traianus			M. Hirrius Fronto Neratius Pansa L. Iulius Proculeianus („sublegatus") (?)	T. Aurelius Quietus	

Other governors under Vespasian

Year	ASIA	PONTUS-BITHYNIA	GALATIA, Phrygia, Pisidia, Pamphylia, Lycaonia, Paphlagonia	CAPPADOCIA, Pontus, Armenia Minor	LYCIA-PAMPHYLIA	CILICIA
		M. Maecius Rufus M. Salvidenus Proculus M. Salvidenus Asprenas M. Plancius Varus			M. Hirrius Fronto Neratius Pansa Cn. Avidius Celer Fiscillinus Firmus	
80	M. Ulpius Traianus C. Laecanius Bassus Caecina Paetus (?)			A. Caesennius Gallus L. Iulius Proculeianus („sublegatus") (?)	T. Aurelius Quietus (?)	M. Petronius Umbrinus

81	C. Laecanius Bassus Caecina Paetus (?) Q. Iulius Cordinus C. Rutilius Gallicus (?)	A. Bucius Lappius Maximus (?)	A. Caesennius Gallus L. Iulius Proculeianus („sublegatus") (?) C. Antius A. Iulius Quadratus („sublegatus") (?)	C. Caristanius Fronto
82	Q. Iulius Cordinus C. Rutilius Gallicus	A. Bucius Lappius Maximus (?) Velius Paulus (?)	A. Caesennius Gallus C. Antius A. Iulius Quadratus („sublegatus") (?)	
83	Q. Iulius Cordinus C. Rutilius Gallicus	A. Bucius Lappius Maximus (?) Velius Paulus (?)	C. Antius A. Iulius Quadratus („sublegatus") (?)	
84	Q. Iulius Cordinus C. Rutilius Gallicus (?)	A. Bucius Lappius Maximus (?) Velius Paulus (?)	C. Antius A. Iulius Quadratus („sublegatus") (?)	
85	Sex. Iulius Frontinus (?)	A. Bucius Lappius Maximus (?)	P. Baebius Italicus	
86	Sex. Iulius Frontinus (?) P. Nonius Asprenas Caesius Cassianus			
87	Sex. Iulius Frontinus (?) P. Nonius Asprenas Caesius Cassianus C. Vettulenus Civica Cerealis (?)			
88	C. Vettulenus Civica Cerealis (?) L. Mestrius Florus (?)			Ti. Iulius Celsus Polemaeanus (?)

Year	ASIA	PONTUS-BITHYNIA	GALATIA, Phrygia, Pisidia, Pamphylia, Lycaonia, Paphlagonia	CAPPADOCIA, Pontus, Armenia Minor	LYCIA-PAMPHYLIA	CILICIA
89	L. Mestrius Florus (?) M. Fulvius Gillo (?)			Ti. Iulius Candidus Marius Celsus (?)		Ti. Iulius Celsus Polemaeanus (?)
90	M. Fulvius Gillo (?) L. Luscius Oscrea (?)			Ti. Iulius Candidus Marius Celsus (?) L. Antistius Rusticus (?)		Ti. Iulius Celsus Polemaeanus (?)
91	L. Luscius Oscrea (?)			Ti. Iulius Candidus Marius Celsus (?) L. Antistius Rusticus (?)		Ti. Iulius Celsus Polemaeanus (?)
92	P. Calvisius Ruso Iulius Frontinus			Ti. Iulius Candidus Marius Celsus (?) L. Antistius Rusticus (?)		Q. Gellius Longus (?)
93	P. Calvisius Ruso Iulius Frontinus L. Iunius Caesennius Paetus (?)			Ti. Iulius Candidus Marius Celsus (?) L. Antistius Rusticus (?)		Q. Gellius Longus (?)
94	L. Iunius Caesennius Paetus (?) M. Atilius Postumius Bradua			L. Antistius Rusticus (?) T. Pomponius Bassus (?)		
95	M. Atilius Postumius Bradua			T. Pomponius Bassus		
96				T. Pomponius Bassus		

Other governors under Domitian

	M. Maecius Rufus	Ti. Iulius Celsus Polemaeanus / L. (Iulius Marinus?) / Tullius Iustus		C. Antius A. Iulius Quadratus / L. Domitius Apollinaris
97	Sex. Carminius Vetus		T. Pomponius Bassus	
98	Cn. Pedanius Fuscus Salinator (?) / Q. Vibius Secundus (?)	C. Iulius Bassus (?)	T. Pomponius Bassus	L. Iulius Marinus Caecilius Simplex (?)
99	Cn. Pedanius Fuscus Salinator (?) / Q. Vibius Secundus (?)	C. Iulius Bassus (?) / Varenus Rufus (?)	T. Pomponius Bassus	L. Iulius Marinus Caecilius Simplex (?)
100	Q. Iulius Balbus (?) / Cn. Pedanius Fuscus Salinator (?) / Q. Vibius Secundus (?) / Licinius Sura (?)	C. Iulius Bassus (?) / Varenus Rufus (?)	T. Pomponius Bassus	L. Iulius Marinus Caecilius Simplex (?)
101	Q. Iulius Balbus (?) / Cn. Pedanius Fuscus Salinator (?) / Q. Vibius Secundus (?) / Licinius Sura (?)	C. Iulius Bassus (?) / Varenus Rufus (?)	Q. Orfitasius Aufidius Umber	
102	Q. Iulius Balbus (?) / Cn. Pedanius Fuscus Salinator (?) / Q. Vibius Secundus (?)	C. Iulius Bassus (?) / Varenus Rufus (?)	Q. Orfitasius Aufidius Umber	C. Trebonius Proculus Mettius Modestus (?) / Q. Roscius Pompeius Falco (?)

Year	ASIA	PONTUS-BITHYNIA	GALATIA, Phrygia, Pisidia, Pamphylia, Lycaonia, Paphlagonia	CAPPADOCIA, Pontus, Armenia Minor	LYCIA-PAMPHYLIA	CILICIA
103	C. Aquillius Proculus	Varenus Rufus (?)			C. Trebonius Proculus Mettius Modestus (?) Q. Roscius Pompeius Falco (?)	
104	C. Aquillius Proculus L. Albius Pullaienus Pollio (?)	Varenus Rufus (?)			Q. Roscius Pompeius Falco (?)	
105	L. Albius Pullaienus Pollio (?) Ti. Iulius Celsus Polemaeanus (?)	Varenus Rufus (?)		P. Calvisius Ruso Iulius Frontinus	Q. Roscius Pompeius Falco (?)	
106	L. Albius Pullaienus Pollio (?) Ti. Iulius Celsus Polemaeanus (?) L. Nonius Calpurnius Asprenas Torquatus (?)	Varenus Rufus (?)		P. Calvisius Ruso Iulius Frontinus		
107	Ti. Iulius Celsus Polemaeanus (?) L. Nonius Calpurnius Asprenas Torquatus (?)	P. Servilius Calvus (?)		C. Iulius Quadratus Bassus (?)		
108	M. Lollius Paullinus D. Valerius Asiaticus Saturninus (?)	P. Servilius Calvus (?) C. Plinius Caecilius Secundus (?)		C. Iulius Quadratus Bassus (?)		

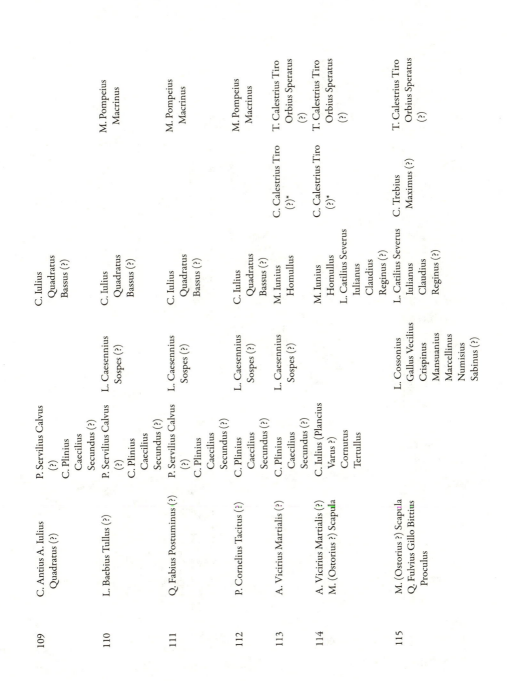

109	C. Antius A. Iulius Quadratus (?)	P. Servilius Calvus (?) C. Plinius Caecilius Secundus (?)		C. Iulius Quadratus Bassus (?)		
110	L. Baebius Tullus (?)	P. Servilius Calvus (?) C. Plinius Caecilius Secundus (?)	L. Caesennius Sospes (?)	C. Iulius Quadratus Bassus (?)		M. Pompeius Macrinus
111	Q. Fabius Postuminus (?)	P. Servilius Calvus (?) C. Plinius Caecilius Secundus (?)	L. Caesennius Sospes (?)	C. Iulius Quadratus Bassus (?)		M. Pompeius Macrinus
112	P. Cornelius Tacitus (?)	C. Plinius Caecilius Secundus (?)	L. Caesennius Sospes (?)	C. Iulius Quadratus Bassus (?)		M. Pompeius Macrinus
113	A. Vicirius Martialis (?)	C. Plinius Caecilius Secundus (?)	L. Caesennius Sospes (?)	M. Iunius Homullus	C. Calestrius Tiro (?)*	T. Calestrius Tiro Orbius Speratus (?)
114	A. Vicirius Martialis (?) M. (Ostorius ?) Scapula	C. Iulius (Plancius Varus ?) Cornutus Tertullus		M. Iunius Homullus L. Catilius Severus Iulianus Claudius Reginus (?)	C. Calestrius Tiro (?)*	T. Calestrius Tiro Orbius Speratus (?)
115	M. (Ostorius ?) Scapula Q. Fulvius Gillo Bittius Proculus	L. Cossonius Gallus Vecilius Crispinus Mansuanius Marcellinus Numisius Sabinus (?)		L. Catilius Severus Iulianus Claudius Reginus (?)	C. Trebius Maximus (?)	T. Calestrius Tiro Orbius Speratus (?)

Year	ASIA	PONTUS-BITHYNIA	GALATIA, Phrygia, Pisidia, Pamphylia, Lycaonia, Paphlagonia	CAPPADOCIA, Pontus, Armenia Minor	LYCIA-PAMPHYLIA	CILICIA
116	Q. Fulvius Gillo Bittius Proculus Ti. Iulius Ferox		L. Cossonius Gallus Vecilius Crispinus Mansuanius Marcellinus Numisius Sabinus (?)		C. Trebius Maximus (?)	T. Calestrius Tiro Orbius Speratus (?) C. Bruttius Praesens L. Fulvius Rusticus (?)
117	Ti. Iulius Ferox	C. Sertorius Brocchus (Q.) Servaeus Innocens (?)	L. Cossonius Gallus Vecilius Crispinus Mansuanius Marcellinus Numisius Sabinus (?)		C. Trebius Maximus (?) T. Pomponius Antistianus Funisulanus Vettonianus (?)	C. Bruttius Praesens L. Fulvius Rusticus (?)

Other governors under Trajan

Year	ASIA	PONTUS-BITHYNIA	GALATIA, Phrygia, Pisidia, Pamphylia, Lycaonia, Paphlagonia	CAPPADOCIA, Pontus, Armenia Minor	LYCIA-PAMPHYLIA	CILICIA
118	L. Dasumius [. . .] Hadrianus (fortasse unus idemque) Secundus	Anicius Maximus Iunius Kanus (?)			Iulius Frugi	
118	Galeo Tettienus Severus M. Eppuleius Proculus Ti. Caespio Hispo				C. Trebius Maximus (?) T. Pomponius Antistianus Funisulanus Vettonianus (?) C. Valerius Severus (?)	

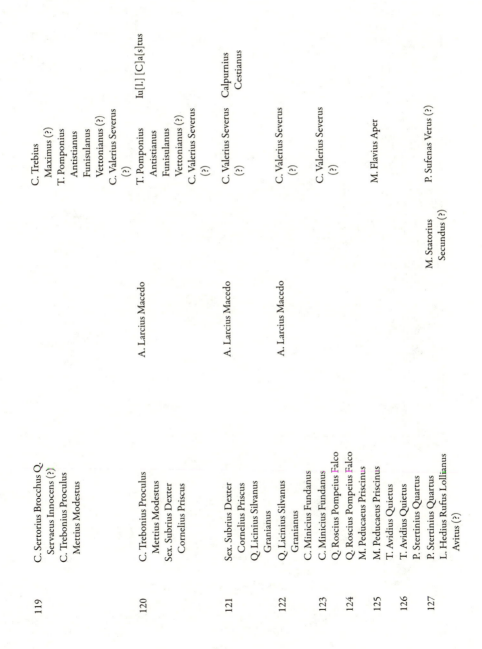

119	C. Sertorius Brocchus Q. Servaeus Innocens (?) C. Trebonius Proculus Metrius Modestus		C. Trebius Maximus (?) T. Pomponius Antistianus Funisulanus Vettonianus (?) C. Valerius Severus (?)	
120	C. Trebonius Proculus Metrius Modestus Sex. Subrius Dexter Cornelius Priscus	A. Larcius Macedo	T. Pomponius Antistianus Funisulanus Vettonianus (?) C. Valerius Severus (?)	Iu[l.] [C]a[s]tus
121	Sex. Subrius Dexter Cornelius Priscus Q. Licinius Silvanus Granianus	A. Larcius Macedo	C. Valerius Severus (?)	Calpurnius Cestianus
122	Q. Licinius Silvanus Granianus C. Minicius Fundanus	A. Larcius Macedo	C. Valerius Severus (?)	
123	C. Minicius Fundanus Q. Roscius Pompeius Falco		C. Valerius Severus (?)	
124	Q. Roscius Pompeius Falco M. Peducaeus Priscinus			
125	M. Peducaeus Priscinus T. Avidius Quietus		M. Flavius Aper	
126	T. Avidius Quietus P. Stertinius Quartus			
127	P. Stertinius Quartus L. Hedius Rufus Lollianus Avitus (?)	M. Statorius Secundus (?)	P. Sufenas Verus (?)	

Year	ASIA	PONTUS-BITHYNIA	GALATIA, Phrygia, Pisidia, Pamphylia, Lycaonia, Paphlagonia	CAPPADOCIA, Pontus, Armenia Minor	LYCIA-PAMPHYLIA	CILICIA
128	L. Hedius Rufus Lollianus Avitus (?)		C. Trebius Sergianus	M. Statorius Secundus (?)	P. Sufenas Verus (?)	
129	L. Hedius Rufus Lollianus Avitus (?) P. Iuventius Celsus T. Aufidius Hoenius Severianus			T. Prifernius Paetus Rosianus Geminus Laecanius Bassus [?Fron]to	P. Sufenas Verus (?)	
130	P. Iuventius Celsus T. Aufidius Hoenius Severianus P. Afranius Flavianus (?)				P. Sufenas Verus (?) Mettius Modestus	
131	P. Afranius Flavianus (?) L. Fundanius Lamia Aelianus			(L.?) Flavius Arrianus	Mettius Modestus (?)	T. Vibius Varus (?)
132	L. Fundanius Lamia Aelianus C. Iulius Alexander Berenicianus			(L.?) Flavius Arrianus	Mettius Modestus (?)	T. Vibius Varus (?)
133	C. Iulius Alexander Berenicianus T. Aurelius Fulvus Boionius Arrius Antoninus (?) Q. Coredius Gallus Gargillius Antiquus (?) P. Afranius Flavianus (?)	C. Iulius Severus (?)		(L.?) Flavius Arrianus	Mettius Modestus (?) [Domiti]us Seneca (?)	T. Vibius Varus (?)

134	T. Aurelius Fulvus Boionius Arrius Antoninus (?) Q. Coredius Gallus Gargillius Antiquus (?) P. Afranius Flavianus (?)	C. Iulius Severus (?)		(L.?) Flavius Arrianus	[Domiti]us Seneca (?)	
135	T. Aurelius Fulvus Boionius Arrius Antoninus (?) Q. Coredius Gallus Gargillius Antiquus (?) P. Afranius Flavianus (?)	C. Iulius Severus (?)		(L.?) Flavius Arrianus	[Domiti]us Seneca (?)	
136	Q. Pomponius Marcellus	C. Iulius Severus (?)		(L.?) Flavius Arrianus	[Domiti]us Seneca (?) T. Calestrius Tiro Iulius Maternus	
137	Q. Coredius Gallus Gargillius Antiquus (?) P. Afranius Flavianus (?) Cornelius Latinianus (?)	C. Iulius Severus (?)		(L. ?) Flavius Arrianus	T. Calestrius Tiro Iulius Maternus Curio Navus	
138	Cornelius Latinianus (?) L. Venuleius Apronianus Octavius Priscus	C. Iulius Severus (?)	C. Iulius Scapula…. [D]onatus [….] nus	L. Burbuleius Optatus Ligarianus	Curio Navus Cn. Arrius Cornelius Proculus	P. Pactumeius Clemens

Other governors under Hadrian

C. Bruttius Praesens L. Fulvius Rusticus

Year	ASIA	PONTUS-BITHYNIA	GALATIA, Phrygia, Pisidia, Pamphylia, Lyca-onia, Paphlagonia	CAPPADOCIA, Pontus, Armenia Minor	LYCIA-PAMPHYLIA	CILICIA
139	L. Venuleius Apronianus Octavius Priscus Cornelius Latinianus (?)			L. Burbuleius Optatus Ligarianus (?)	Cn. Arrius Cornelius Proculus	
140	Cornelius Latinianus (?)	Q. Voconius Saxa Fidus (?)			Cn. Arrius Cornelius Proculus	
141	Cornelius Latinianus (?)	Q. Voconius Saxa Fidus (?)			Iulius Aqui[lius ?] Q. Voconius Saxa Fidus (?)	
142		Q. Voconius Saxa Fidus (?)			Iunius Paetus (?) Q. Voconius Saxa Fidus (?)	
143		Q. Voconius Saxa Fidus (?)			Iunius Paetus (?) Q. Voconius Saxa Fidus (?)	
144					Q. Voconius Saxa Fidus	A. Claudius Charax (?)
145	[...I]ulianus	L. Coelius Festus (?)			Q. Voconius Saxa Fidus	A. Claudius Charax (?)
146		L. Coelius Festus (?)				A. Claudius Charax (?)
147	L. Antonius Albus	L. Coelius Festus (?)			C. Iulius Avitus (?)	
148	L. Antonius Albus T. Flavius Tertullus				C. Iulius Avitus (?)	

149	T. Flavius Tertullus Popillius Priscus		C. Iulius Avitus (?) D. Rupilius Severus	
150	Popillius Priscus L. Tutilius Lupercus Pontianus		D. Rupilius Severus	
151	L. Tutilius Lupercus Pontianus T. Vitrasius Pollio		D. Rupilius Severus	
152	T. Vitrasius Pollio C. Iulius Severus		[? Aeli]us Pro[culus ?]	
153	C. Iulius Severus T. Statilius Maximus (?)			
154	T. Statilius Maximus (?) L. Statius Quadratus			
155	L. Statius Quadratus T. Statilius Maximus (?)			
156	Gratus			Cornelius Dexter
157	T. Statilius Maximus (?)			
158				
159	P. Mummius Sisenna Rutilianus (?)	L. Hedius Rufus Lollianus Avitus (?)	P. Vigellius Raius Plarius Saturninus Atilius Braduanus Caucidius Tertullus (?)	

Year	ASIA	PONTUS-BITHYNIA	GALATIA, Phrygia, Pisidia, Pamphylia, Lyca-onia, Paphlagonia	CAPPADOCIA, Pontus, Armenia Minor	LYCIA-PAMPHYLIA	CILICIA
160	P. Mummius Sisenna Rutilianus (?)				P. Vigellius Raius Plarius Saturninus Atilius Braduanus Caucidius Tertullus (?)	
161	P. Mummius Sisenna Rutilianus (?) L. Stertinius Quintilianus Acilius Strabo Q. Cornelius Rusticus Apronius Senecio Proculus (?)		P. Iuventius Celsus (?)	M. Sedatius Severianus Iulius Acer Metilius Nepos Rufinus Ti. Rutilianus Censor	P. Vigellius Raius Plarius Saturninus Atilius Braduanus Caucidius Tertullus (?) Sal[vius ? an -lustius?] (?)	

Other governors under Antoninus Pius

	ASIA		GALATIA	CAPPADOCIA	LYCIA-PAMPHYLIA	CILICIA
	M[. . . .] [P. Cluvius Maximus Paullinus dest.] ? M. Peducaeus Stloga Priscinus		P. Alfius Maximus (?) L. Fulvius Rusticus Aemilianus (?)	L. Aemilius Carus	Fl(avius) Severinus (?)	C. Errilius Regillus Laberius Priscus

162	L. Stertinius Quintilianus Acilius Strabo Q. Cornelius Rusticus Apronius Senecio Proculus (?) C. Popilius Carus Pedo (?)	P. Iuventius Celsus (?)	P. Vigellius Raius Plarius Saturninus Atilius Braduanus Caucidius Tertullus (?) Sal[vius ? an -lustius?] (?) Ti. Iulius Frugi (?)
163	C. Popilius Carus Pedo (?)	P. Iuventius Celsus (?) L. Fufidius Pollio (?)	M. Statius Priscus Licinius Italicus Sal[vius ? an -lustius?] (?) Ti. Iulius Frugi (?)
164	Q. Pompeius Sosius Priscus (?)	L. Fufidius Pollio (?)	D. Fonteius Fronto Sal[vius ? an -lustius?] (?)
165	M. Gavius Squilla Gallicanus (?) L. Sergius Paullus (?)	L. Fufidius Pollio (?)	D. Fonteius Fronto (?) Iulius Modestus (?) Sal[vius ? an -lustius?] (?)
166	M. Gavius Squilla Gallicanus (?) L. Sergius Paullus (?)	C. Iulius Severus (?)	Iulius Modestus (?) Sal[vius ? an -lustius?] (?)
167	M. Gavius Squilla Gallicanus (?) L. Sergius Paullus (?)	C. Iulius Severus (?)	Sal[vius ? an -lustius?] (?)
168	M. Gavius Squilla Gallicanus (?)	C. Iulius Severus (?)	Sal[vius ? an -lustius?] (?)

Year	ASIA	PONTUS-BITHYNIA	GALATIA, Phrygia, Pisidia, Pamphylia, Lyca- onia, Paphlagonia	CAPPADOCIA, Pontus, Armenia Minor	LYCIA-PAMPHYLIA	CILICIA
169	Sex. Quintilius Valerius Maximus					
	A. Iunius Rufinus (?)					
170	A. Iunius Rufinus (?)					
	M. Nonius Macrinus					
171	M. Nonius Macrinus					
	A. Iunius Rufinus (?)					
	Sex. Sulpicius Tertullus (?)					
172	A. Iunius Rufinus (?)					
	Sex. Sulpicius Tertullus (?)					
173	A. Iunius Rufinus (?)	Ti. Oclatius Severus				
	Sex. Sulpicius Tertullus (?)					
	[M. Postumius Festus dest. (?)]					
174	Sex. Sulpicius Tertullus (?)	Ti. Oclatius Severus				
	[M. Postumius Festus dest. (?)]	P. Herennius Niger Atticianus				
175	Sex. Sulpicius Tertullus (?)	P. Herennius Niger Atticianus		P. Martius Verus		
	[M. Postumius Festus dest. (?)]			C. Arrius Antoninus		
176	[M. Postumius Festus dest. (?)]	Q. Aurelius Polus*		C. Arrius Antoninus		
177	[M. Postumius Festus dest. (?)]	Q. Aurelius Polus*	L. Licinnius Mucianus			

178				L. Licinnius Mucianus		Licinius Priscus		
179				L. Licinnius Mucianus			(M.?) Cassius Apronianus (?)	(M.?) Cassius Apronianus (?)
180	Novius P[riscus] (?)						(M.?) Cassius Apronianus (?)	(M.?) Cassius Apronianus (?)
Other governors under Marcus Aurelius								
	T. Pomponius Proculus Vitrasius Pollio (?)	L. Albinius Saturninus (?)		L. Saevinius Proculus (?)				L. Saevinius Proculus (?) / Caecilius Capella (?)
181	Novius P[riscus] (?)						(M.?) Cassius Apronianus (?)	(M.?) Cassius Apronianus (?)
182	Novius P[riscus] (?)						(M.?) Cassius Apronianus (?)	(M.?) Cassius Apronianus (?)
183	Novius P[riscus] (?)	Severus						
184			Caelius Calvinus					
185					C. Pomponius Bassus Terentianus (?)			
186					C. Pomponius Bassus Terentianus (?)			
187					C. Pomponius Bassus Terentianus (?)			

Year	ASIA	PONTUS-BITHYNIA	GALATIA, Phrygia, Pisidia, Pamphylia, Lycaonia, Paphlagonia	CAPPADOCIA, Pontus, Armenia Minor	LYCIA-PAMPHYLIA	CILICIA
188					C. Pomponius Bassus Terentianus (?)	
189			L. Fabius Cilo Septiminus Catinius Acilianus Lepidus Fulcinianus (?)		C. Pomponius Bassus Terentianus (?)	
190			L. Fabius Cilo Septiminus Catinius Acilianus Lepidus Fulcinianus (?)		C. Pomponius Bassus Terentianus (?)	
191			L. Fabius Cilo Septiminus Catinius Acilianus Lepidus Fulcinianus (?)		C. Pomponius Bassus Terentianus (?)	
192	Asellius Aemilianus		L. Fabius Cilo Septiminus Catinius Acilianus Lepidus Fulcinianus (?)		C. Pomponius Bassus Terentianus (?)	

Other governors under Commodus			
	P. Iulius Geminius Marcianus L. Aemilius Frontinus Q. Pompeius Senecio C. Arrius Antoninus T. Flavius Sulpicianus M. Sulpicius Crassus	M. Didius Severus Iulianus	M. Flaccus Carminius Athenagoras (?)
193	Asellius Aemilianus Aemilius Iuncus (?)	L. Fabius Cilo Septiminus Catinius Acilianus Lepidus Fulcinianus (?) M. Silius Messala (?)	Q. Venidius Rufus Marius Maximus L. Calvinianus (?)
194	Aemilius Iuncus (?)	L. Fabius Cilo Septiminus Catinius Acilianus Lepidus Fulcinianus (?) M. Silius Messala (?)	Q. Venidius Rufus Marius Maximus L. Calvinianus (?)
195		M. Silius Messala (?)	Q. Venidius Rufus Marius Maximus L. Calvinianus (?)

Year	ASIA	PONTUS-BITHYNIA	GALATIA, Phrygia, Pisidia, Pamphylia, Lycaonia, Paphlagonia	CAPPADOCIA, Pontus, Armenia Minor	LYCIA-PAMPHYLIA	CILICIA
196		M. Silius Messala (?)				Q. Venidius Rufus Marius Maximus L. Calvinianus (?)
197		M. Silius Messala (?)	?[Va]lerianu[s...]ninus (?)			Q. Venidius Rufus Marius Maximus L. Calvinianus (?)
198		Q. Tineius Sacerdos	?[Va]lerianu[s...]ninus (?) L. Petronius Verus C. Atricius Norbanus Strabo	C. Iulius Flaccus Aelianus	C. Sulpicius Iustus Dryantianus (?)	
199		Q. Tineius Sacerdos Ti. Claudius Callippianus Italicus (?)	C. Atricius Norbanus Strabo	L. M[...]ius (?)	C. Sulpicius Iustus Dryantianus (?)	
200		Ti. Claudius Callippianus Italicus (?)	C. Atricius Norbanus Strabo		C. Sulpicius Iustus Dryantianus (?)	
201	Q. Hedius Rufus Lollianus Gentianus		C. Atricius Norbanus Strabo		C. Sulpicius Iustus Dryantianus (?)	
202	Q. Hedius Rufus Lollianus Gentianus		C. Atricius Norbanus Strabo		Tarius Titianus (?)	Flavius Ulpianus

Year					
203			C. Atticius Norbanus Strabo		Tarius Titianus (?)
204					Tarius Titianus (?)
205	[P]opilius Pedo Apronianus	Ti. Claudius Callippianus Italicus (?)			Tarius Titianus (?)
206					
207					
208	Q. Caecilius Secundus Servilianus		P. Caecilius Urbicus Aemilianus		
209	Q. Caecilius Secundus Servilianus	Ti. Manilius Fuscus (?)			
210		Ti. Manilius Fuscus (?)		Gavius Tranquillus (?)	
211	T[---]	Ti. Manilius Fuscus (?)			
	C. Gabinius Barbarus Pompeianus (?)				
Other governors under Septimius Severus					
	Q. Aurelius Polus Terentianus [Aelius Aglaus proc.]	M. Claudius Demetrius Aelius Antipater			Antonius Balbus
	Q. Licinius Nepos				Antonius [....]lius
	Q. Tineius Sacerdos				
	[Sem]pronius Senecio				
212	Ti. Manilius Fuscus (?)	Iulius Proculus		Gavius Tranquillus (?)	
	C. Gabinius Barbarus Pompeianus (?)				

Year	ASIA	PONTUS-BITHYNIA	GALATIA, Phrygia, Pisidia, Pamphylia, Lycaonia, Paphlagonia	CAPPADOCIA, Pontus, Armenia Minor	LYCIA-PAMPHYLIA	CILICIA
213	Ti. Manilius Fuscus (?) C. Gabinius Barbarus Pompeianus (?) L. Marius Maximus Perpetuus Aurelianus	Iulius Proculus			Gavius Tranquillius (?) M. Iunius Concessus Aemilianus (?)	
214	L. Marius Maximus Perpetuus Aurelianus				M. Iunius Concessus Aemilianus (?)	
215	L. Marius Maximus Perpetuus Aurelianus C. Iulius Avitus Alexianus					
216	C. Iulius Avitus Alexianus					
217	C. Iulius Asper Q. Anicius Faustus			Catius Clemens vel Clement[inus]		
218	Q. Anicius Faustus M. Aufidius Fronto (?)	Caecilius Aristo Cl. Aelius Pollio	L. Egnatius Victor Lollianus (?)	Catius Clemens vel Clement[inus] M. Munatius Sulla Cerialis (?)		Claudius Nysius (?)
219	M. Aufidius Fronto (?)		L. Egnatius Victor Lollianus (?)	M. Munatius Sulla Cerialis (?) M. Ulp(ius) Ofellus Theodorus (?)		Claudius Nysius (?)
220	M. Aufidius Fronto (?) C. Aufidius Marcellus		L. Egnatius Victor Lollianus (?)	M. Ulp(ius) Ofellus Theodorus (?)		Claudius Nysius (?)

221	M. Aufidius Fronto (?) C. Aufidius Marcellus	L. Egnatius Victor Lollianus (?) Aurelius Basileus (?)	M. Ulp(ius) Ofellus Theodorus (?) Aurelius Basileus		Claudius Nysius (?)
222	M. Aufidius Fronto (?) C. Aufidius Marcellus	L. Egnatius Victor Lollianus (?) L. Iulius Apronius Maenius Pius Salamallianus (?)	Aurelius Basileus Asinius Lepidus (?)		Claudius Nysius (?)
223		P. Alfius Avitus	P. Alfius Avitus (?) L. Iulius Apronius Maenius Pius Salamallianus (?)	Asinius Lepidus (?)	
224		P. Alfius Avitus C. Pontius Pontianus Fuficius Maximus	P. Alfius Avitus (?) L. Iulius Apronius Maenius Pius Salamallianus (?)	Asinius Lepidus (?) P. Alfius Avitus (?)	
225		C. Pontius Pontianus Fuficius Maximus	L. Iulius Apronius Maenius Pius Salamallianus (?)	Asinius Lepidus (?) P. Alfius Avitus (?)	
226			L. Iulius Apronius Maenius Pius Salamallianus (?)		
227					
228			Q. Servaeus Fuscus Cornelianus (?)		
229			Q. Servaeus Fuscus Cornelianus (?)		

Year	ASIA	PONTUS-BITHYNIA	GALATIA, Phrygia, Pisidia, Pamphylia, Lycaonia, Paphlagonia	CAPPADOCIA, Pontus, Armenia Minor	LYCIA-PAMPHYLIA	CILICIA	PONTUS-PAPHLAGONIA ruled by governors of equestrian rank
230			Q. Servaeus Fuscus Cornelianus (?)				
231	Amicus (?)						
232				Aradius Paternus			
233			M. Domitius Valerianus (?)				
234			M. Domitius Valerianus (?)	Licinius Serenianus (?)			

Year	ASIA	PONTUS-BITHYNIA	GALATIA, Phrygia, Pisidia, Pamphylia, Lycaonia,	CAPPADOCIA, Armenia Minor	LYCIA-PAMPHYLIA	CILICIA	PONTUS-PAPHLAGONIA ruled by governors of equestrian rank
235	C. Furius Sabinius Aquila Timesitheus L. Ranius Optatus (?)	M. Domitius Valerianus (?)	M. Domitius Valerianus (?)	Licinius Serenianus (?)		M. Domitius Valerianus (?)	Q. Faltonius Restitutianus Claudianus

Other governors under Severus Alexander

	ASIA			CAPPADOCIA		CILICIA	
	M. Clodius Pupienus Maximus (?) Q. Virius Egnatius Sulpicius Priscus Q. (Hedius) Lollianus Plautius Avitus			Q. Iul(ius) Proculeianus		Ostorius Euhodianus	

236	Valerius Messala (?) Fl(avius) Balbus Diogenianus (?) [C. Furius Sabinus Aquila Timisitheus proc. (?)]	L. Ranius Optatus	M. Domitius Valerianus (?)	Licinius Serenianus (?) Sex. Catius Clementinus Priscillianus (?)		M. Domitius Valerianus (?)	Claudianus P. Aelius Vibianus
237	Valerius Messala (?) Fl(avius) Balbus Diogenianus (?) [C. Furius Sabinus Aquila Timisitheus proc. (?)]	L. Ranius Optatus	M. Domitius Valerianus (?)	Sex. Catius Clementinus Priscillianus (?)		M. Domitius Valerianus (?)	P. Aelius Vibianus
238	Valerius Messala (?) Fl(avius) Balbus Diogenianus (?) M. Triarius Rufinus Asinnius Sabinianus (?) [C. Furius Sabinus Aquila Timisitheus proc. (?)]	L. Ranius Optatus D. Simonius Proculus Iulianus (?)	M. Domitius Valerianus (?)	Claudianus Sex. Catius Clementinus Priscillianus (?) Cuspidius Flaminius Severus		M. Domitius Valerianus (?) L. Serg[ius . . .]us Zeno (?)	P. Aelius Vibianus (?) Cl. (?) Marcellus
239	M. Triarius Rufinus Asinnius Sabinianus (?) [C. Furius Sabinus Aquila Timisitheus proc. (?)]			Cuspidius Flaminius Severus	Ti. Pollenius Armenius Peregrinus (?)	L. Serg[ius . . .]us Zeno (?)	Cl. (?) Marcellus
240	M. Triarius Rufinus Asinnius Sabinianus (?)				Ti. Pollenius Armenius Peregrinus (?)	L. Serg[ius . . .]us Zeno (?)	Cl. (?) Marcellus
241	M. Triarius Rufinus Asinnius Sabinianus (?)				Ti. Pollenius Armenius Peregrinus (?)	L. Serg[ius . . .]us Zeno (?)	Cl. (?) Marcellus
242	M. Triarius Rufinus Asinnius Sabinianus (?) L. Egnatius Victor Lollianus				Ti. Pollenius Armenius Peregrinus (?)	L. Serg[ius . . .]us Zeno (?)	Cl. (?) Marcellus

Year	ASIA	PONTUS-BITHYNIA	GALATIA, Phrygia, Pisidia, Pamphylia, Lycaonia,	CAPPADOCIA, Armenia Minor	LYCIA-PAMPHYLIA	CILICIA	PONTUS-PAFLAGONIA ruled by governors of equestrian rank
243	L. Egnatius Victor Lollianus	Ti. Claudius Attalus Paterclianus (?)			Ti. Pollenius Armenius Peregrinus (?)	L. Serg[ius...]us Zeno (?)	
244	L. Egnatius Victor Lollianus	Ti. Claudius Attalus Paterclianus (?) M. Aurelius Artemidorus		Antonius Memmius Hiero (?) P. (?) Petronius Polianus (?)		L. Serg[ius...]us Zeno (?)	
245	L. Egnatius Victor Lollianus	Ti. Claudius Attalus Paterclianus (?) M. Aurelius Artemidorus		Antonius Memmius Hiero (?) P. (?) Petronius Polianus (?)			
246				Antonius Memmius Hiero (?) P. (?) Petronius Polianus (?)			
247				Antonius Memmius Hiero (?) P. (?) Petronius Polianus (?)			Cl. Aurelius Tiberius (?)
248				P. (?) Petronius Polianus (?)			Cl. Aurelius Tiberius (?)

Year	ASIA, CARIA ET PHRYGIA	PONTUS-BITHYNIA	GALATIA, Pisidia, Pamphylia, Lycaonia	CAPPADOCIA, Armenia Minor	LYCIA-PAMPHYLIA	CILICIA	PONTUS-PAFLAGONIA ruled by governors of equestrian rank
249	C. Iulius Fl(avius) Proculus Quintil(l)ianus Q. Fabius Clodius Agrippianus Celsinus [Caria et Phrygia]	L. Egnatius Victor Lollianus (?)		P. (?) Petronius Polianus (?) C. Valerius Tertullus (?)			Cl. Aurelius Tiberius (?)
250	C. Iulius Fl(avius) Proculus Quintil(l)ianus ?Optimus Q. Fabius Clodius Agrippianus Celsinus [Caria et Phrygia]	L. Egnatius Victor Lollianus (?) C. Sabucius Secundus Paulus Modestus (?)	M. Iunius Valerius Nepotianus	P. (?) Petronius Polianus (?) C. Valerius Tertullus (?)			M. Iunius Valerius Nepotianus
251	?Optimus	C. Sabucius Secundus Paulus Modestus (?)		C. Valerius Tertullus (?) A. Vergilius Maximus (?)			Aelius Decrianus (?)
Other governors under Decius							
		Q. Umbricius (?)					
252				A. Vergilius Maximus (?)			Aelius Decrianus (?)
253		C. Iulius Octavius Volusenna Rogatianus		A. Vergilius Maximus (?)			Aelius Decrianus (?)
254	C. Iulius Volusenna Rogatianus (?)						
255	M. Aurelius Diogenes [Caria et Phrygia]	M. Antonius Hiero					

Year	ASIA, CARIA ET PHRYGIA	PONTUS-BITHYNIA	GALATIA, Pisidia, Pamphylia, Lycaonia	CAPPADOCIA, Armenia Minor	LYCIA-PAMPHYLIA	CILICIA	PONTUS-PAFLAGONIA ruled by governors of equestrian rank
256		M. Antonius Hiero					
257							
258							
259		(C. Iulius ?) Senecio					
260		(C. Iulius ?) Senecio					
261							
262							
263							
264							
265							
266							
267							
268							

Other governors under Gallienus

	ASIA, CARIA ET PHRYGIA	PONTUS-BITHYNIA				CILICIA	
	P. Aelius Septimius Mannus [Caria et Phrygia] [an sub Valeriano?]					A. Voconius Zeno	
269		(C. Sedatius ?) Velleius Macrinus					

270				
271				
272				
273				
274	?Arellius Fuscus			
275	?Arellius Fuscus			
276	?Faltonius Probus			
277	?Faltonius Probus			
278	[Iul(ius) Proculus proc.]		Terentius Marcianus	
279		Ael. Casinus Atianus		Aelius Quintianus
280				Aelius Quintianus
281				
282				Claudius Longinus
283				Claudius Longinus
284				

Sources: Based on [560] Thomasson, *Laterculi praesidum*, vol. 2, 2, 1978, and the supplements on CDs sent by Thomasson. For governors of the province of Pontus-Paflagonia see: Christian Marek, "Epigraphy and the Provincial Organisation of Paphlagonian Cities," in: Kristina Winter-Jacobsen and Lâtife Summerer, *Landscape Dynamics and Settlement Patterns in Northern Anatolia during the Roman and Byzantine Period*, Stuttgart 2015, 316–328. A few additional supplements are indicated by *. I thank Werner Eck, Rudolph Haensch, and Georg Petzl for reference to recent scholarship.

Chronological Table

Paleolithic (Old Stone Age) (ca. 2,000,000–10,000 BCE)	
Starting ca. 20,000 BCE	Remains of earlier human beings in Anatolia
	Karain Cave near Antalya (Neanderthals)
	Yarımburgaz Cave near Istanbul
	Belbaşı and Beldibi cultures in Lycia

Neolithic (New Stone Age) and Chalcolithic (Copper Age) (tenth millenium to 3500 BCE)	
Pre-pottery Neolithic A (PPNA) ca. 9600–8800	Göbekli Tepe Level III: Sanctuary with stone pillars decorated with reliefs
Pre-pottery Neolithic B (PPNB) ca. 8800–6800	Göbekli Tepe Level II
ca. 8300–7600	First sedentary cultures in Asia Minor
Eighth millennium	Nevali Çori: Settlement with homes and agricultural buildings, sanctuary with monumental stone figures
	Çayönü: Settlement with various kinds of buildings. Ritual burial under the buildings' floors.
	Earliest evidence of copper working with hammers and annealing
ca. 7600–5000	Villages occupied year-round. Textile production, copper craftwork.
ca. 7000–5500	Çatal Höyük: Largest Neolithic settlement in Anatolia. Rich imagery on painted walls
ca. 5000–3700	Thousands of villages all over Anatolia. In the southeast, Halaf and Obed cultures (painted ceramics)

Bronze Age (ca. 3000–1200 BCE)	
Early Bronze Age (EB) ca. 3000–2000	Regional governmental and economic centers
From 3300	Early culture on the Arslantepe: temples, stockpiles, administration, seals made of clay
Second half of third millennium	Kültepe near Kayseri: center of Cappadocian polychrome pottery, ruler's seat—casternmost appearance of the *megaron*-type building
	Troy I–II: fortified castle hill. Pottery made on a wheel. "Priam's Treasure"; more than 8,800 individual items, including gold jewelry.
	Alaca Höyük: shaft graves, metal urns, gold jewelry.

Middle Bronze Age (MB) ca. 2000–1700	Beycesultan: large palace ("Burnt Palace").
	Oldest written documents in Anatolia: Kārum Kaneš (Kültepe). Assyrians' trade network in eastern Anatolia. Presence of Indo-European immigrants.
Late Bronze Age (LB) ca. 1700–1200	Rise and flourishing of Hittite Kingdom.
Eighteenth century	Kussara Dynasty, center at Nesa (Kaneš). Conquest and destruction of Ḫattusa.
Seventeenth–sixteenth centuries	Old Kingdom: capital Ḫattusa. Conquest of northern Syria (Aleppo).
Fifteenth–early fourteenth centuries	Middle Kingdom. Dark Age, period of external pressure. Rise of Arzawa Empire in the west, south, or southwest. In addition, Aḫḫiyawa Kingdom (Mycaenean Greeks?).
Middle of fourteenth century–1200	New Kingdom
	Consolidation of kingdom. Confrontation with Egypt in northern Syria, capital temporarily moved to Tarḫuntassa in the south. Balance of powers, treaties (first extant peace treaty in history, 1259, between Ramses II and Ḫattusili).
Second half of thirteenth century	Further pressure on the kingdom. In the east, Assyrians' strength grows.
ca. 1220–1200	Economic difficulties, internal disturbances, attacks by the Kaska from the north, destruction of Ḫattusa. Invasion of "Sea Peoples" on the coasts.
ca. 1190–1180	Troy VIIa [VIi] destroyed.

Small States, Peoples, and New Kingdoms (ca. 1000–550 BCE)	
Eleventh century–708	So-called Late Hittite monarchies in Cilicia and north Syria, including Karkamiš, Kummuh, Malida; at the end of the eighth century, they fall under domination of Neo-Assyrian Kingdom.
From ca. 1100	Immigration of Greeks to the west coast of Asia Minor. Immigration of Phrygians to inner Anatolia.
Tenth century	Gordion: oldest stone architecture, expansion of the citadel, several *megaron* structures.
	Oldest Greek house architecture in Klazomenai, Smyrna

856	First mention of a king of Urartu.
From end of ninth century	Rise of Urartian Kingdom around Lake Van.
From middle of eighth century	Rise of Phrygian Kingdom. Oldest appearance of alphabetic script in Anatolia.
Second half of eighth century	Repeated attacks by Cimmerians from the north, to which Phrygian Kingdom seems to succumb at the end of century.
ca. 700	First important early Greek sanctuaries: Didyma at Miletus and the Artemision at Ephesos.
Seventh century	Early Greek lyric, especially on Lesbos: Terpander, Sappho, Alkaios. Greek tyrants in Ionia.
ca. 700–680	Greek colonies around Sea of Marmara (*Propontis*).
Before 668	Gyges king of the Lydians in western Anatolia.
ca. 668–665	Diplomatic relations between the Lydian king Gyges (Gugu of Luddu) and the Assyrian king Assurbanipal.
From ca. 650	Greek colonies around the Black Sea; important role of the mother-city Miletus.
Late seventh century	Urartu disappears from history. Immigration of the Armenians?
Sixth century	Flourishing of Greek science in Ionia: Thales, Anaximandros, Anaximenes of Miletus, Hekataios of Miletus (considered first writer of *historie*, that is, "exploration") Heraclitus of Ephesos.

Asia Minor under the Persians (ca. 550–333 BCE)

547/546	Persian Cyrus II marches into eastern Anatolia. He conquers Kingdom of Lydia (probably only after the fall of Babylon in 539), and takes Sardeis.
499–494	Uprising by the Ionians against Persian rule. Destruction of Miletus.
481	Persian king Xerxes leads army through Anatolia to attack Greece.
479	Defeat of Persian fleet off Mykale promontory.
478/477	Foundation of the Delian League, which many Greek cities in Asia Minor joined over time.
ca. 469/468	Victory of the Athenian Kimon in double Battle of the Eurymedon against Persians.

Second half of fifth century	Herodotus of Halikarnassos, "father" of Greek historiography.
	Downfall of Athenian hegemony in Peloponnesian War (432–404); in 412, Persians resume exaction of tribute from Greek cities of Ionia.
399	March of "the Ten Thousand" through eastern Anatolia.
394	Konon, an Athenian admiral in service of Persia defeats Spartans near Knidos: a decisive weakening of Spartan influence in Asia Minor.
387/386	"King's Peace" (also called "Antialcidas's Peace"): Greeks of Asia Minor are, with few exceptions, guaranteed by treaty as subjects of Persian great king.
377/376–353/352	The Carian siblings, Maussollos and Artemisia, rule in southwestern Asia Minor.
368–362	So-called Satraps' Revolt: several satraps in Asia Minor rebel against great king but are defeated.
334	Alexander crosses into Asia Minor; Battle of the Granicus in Mysia.
333	Battle of Issos in Cilicia; Alexander defeats Persian great king Darius III and ends Persian domination over Asia Minor.

Age of the Diadochi (323–281 BCE)

323	Alexander's death in Babylon. New distribution of the satrapies among his generals
321–316	Confrontation between Antigonos Monophthalmos and Eumenes of Kardia. Antigonos *strategos* of Asia asigned the task to fight Eumenes. Defeat and death of Eumenes.
311	Antigonos and his son Demetrios confirmed in their rule over Asia.
309	Ptolemaios I's fleet operates at the south coast of Asia Minor.
306	Demetrios's naval victory at Salamis (Cyprus); shortly thereafter the Diadochi assume title of king.
302	The "hejira" of Mithridates, one of the Antigonids' liegemen, to Paphlagonia; later he founds Mithridatid Dynasty of Pontos.
301	Battle of Ipsos in western Asia Minor: Antigonos and Demetrios defeated by Seleukos and Lysimachos.

| 301–281 | Lysimachos rules most of western and central Anatolia. On the west and south coasts, the Ptolemies and Demetrios control individual cities. Southern Cappadocia and Armenia belong to Seleukos's kingdom. |
| 281 | Decisive battle on the Korupedion in western Asia Minor, between Lysmachos and Seleukos; the latter wins, but is murdered shortly afterward. End of Wars of the Diadochi. The strongest power in Asia Minor is the Seleucid Kingdom under the son and successor of Seleukos, Antiochos I. |

Age of the Epigones (281–189 BCE)

278/277	Nikomedes, king of Bithynia, helps Galatians move into Asia Minor.
	Galatians conduct plundering raids in western and southern Asia Minor.
ca. 270–268	Victory of Antiochos I over Galatians in "Battle of the Elephants."
263	Philetairos, former officer of Lysimachos and ruler of Pergamon, is succeeded by his nephew Eumenes; the latter defeats Antiochos I at Sardeis.
ca. 262	Diplomatic relations between Ptolemaios II and Miletus. Cities on the western and southern coasts as well as in the interior of Caria and Lycia are under Ptolemaic rule.
from 255	Ariarathes III co-ruler in Cappadocia; after driving out the Seuleucid occupying force, he assumes the title of king.
246–241	So-called War of Laodike between Ptolemaios III and Seleukos II. For a short time, Ptolemaios controls large parts of Asia Minor.
242–228/227	Antiochos Hierax, Seleukos II's younger brother, makes himself independent and establishes Anatolian kingdom.
241	Attalos I of Pergamon defeats Galatians and takes title of king; further victories over Antiochos Hierax, who leaves Asia Minor in 227 and is slain.
227	Macedonian king Antigonos Doson's fleet makes expedition to Caria.

227–223	Expansion of kingdom of Pergamon into Seleucid Anatolia; Seleucid governor Achaios is the first to repel Attalos.
221	Achaios declares himself king.
ca. 220	Mithridates II of Pontos attacks Sinope.
216–214	Antiochos III invades Anatolia, besieges and defeats Achaios in Sardeis.
212–205	Antiochos III's campaign ("Anabasis") in the upper satrapies (eastern parts of his kingdom).
212	Attalos of Pergamon included as *amicus* of Romans in alliance of several Greek states (the Aitolians leading) with Rome that is directed against Macedonian king Philip V.
ca. 204	Roman delegation in Pergamon. Returning from his Anabasis in the East, Antiochos III crosses the Taurus and advances toward Sardeis.
201	Rhodians and Attalos of Pergamon wage a naval war against Philip V; Rhodian-Pergamene mission presents complaints against Philip before Roman Senate.
June 197	Philipp V defeated by Romans in Greece.
196–192	Antiochos III solidifies rule in southern and western Asia Minor by bringing numerous cities under his control.
192–188	Romans wage war against Antiochos III: *Bellum Antiochicum*.
December 190	Antiochos III defeated by Romans under leadership of the brothers Lucius and Publius Cornelius Scipio near Magnesia on Sipylos.

From Roman Hegemony to the Roman Empire (188–30 BCE)

188	Peace of Apameia: Seleucid rule forced to withdraw to area beyond the Taurus and thus loses almost all of Asia Minor; the beneficiaries are Pergamon, gaining areas in central Anatolia, and Rhodes; Rhodes is promised areas of Caria and Lycia south of the Maeander.
183–179	War between Eumenes II of Pergamon and Pharnakes of Pontos, who may have already moved the residence of the Pontic kingdom to Sinope at this time.
ca. 182 to after 178	Conflicts between Rhodes and Lycians. Lycians found a league of cities.

ca. 170	Construction of Pergamon altar begins.
172	Unsuccessful attempt on Eumenes II of Pergamon's life, near Delphi.
167	Senate declares Caria and Lycia free; Rhodes loses most of its Anatolian possessions.
158–156/55	Senate divides Cappadocia between Ariarathes V and Orophernes; with Pergamene help, Ariarathes ousts Orophernes.
156	Prusias II of Bithynia attacks Kingdom of Pergamon.
149	In league with Prusias's son Nikomedes, Attalos II defeats king of Bithynia.
ca. May 133	Death of Attalos III, who bequeathes his kingdom to Rome.
131–129	Romans wage war against Aristonikos (Eumenes III); establishment of province of Asia.
123	Roman censors lease collection of Asia's taxes to tax-farming companies (*censoria locatio*) in Rome.
ca. 120	Mithridates VI Eupator king of Pontos.
119 or 116	Part of Phrygia is incorporated de facto into province of Asia.
102	Region of the south coast of Asia Minor designated as *Cilicia* is put under control of Roman magistrates, who wage war on pirates.
ca. 100–93	Government (with interruptions) of Gordios, an agent of Mithridates VI of Pontos, in Cappadocia.
96/95	Meeting between Sulla and delegate of king of the Parthians on the Euphrates, near Melitene.
94	Nikomedes IV king of Bithynia.
ca. 93	Senate recognizes Ariobarzanes as the legitimate king of Cappadocia, but he is subsequently ousted again by kings of Pontos and Armenia.
ca. 90	Reinstatement of previously ousted kings Nikomedes of Bithynia and Ariobarzanes of Cappadocia.
89	Outbreak of First Mithridatic War.
88	"Ephesian Vespers": murder of thousands of Italics in province of Asia on Mithridates VI's orders.
84	Treaty of Dardanos between Sulla and Mithridates.
83	Licinius Murena's campaign to Pontos and Cappadocia, the so-called Second Mithridatic War.

73–64	Third Mithridatic War.
72–70	Lucullus conquers cities on Anatolian coast of Black Sea.
67	Pompey in charge of combating piracy.
66	Pompey's supreme command in war against Mithridates and Tigranes.
64	Death of Mithridates. Pompey's reorganization of Asia Minor, with establishment of provinces of Pontus et Bithynia and Cilicia.
May 53	Crassus is defeated by the Parthians at Carrhae (Harran).
July 51–autumn 50	Cicero governor of Cilicia.
48	Caesar marches through western Asia Minor. Treaty with Lycian league of cities.
47/46	Caesar hastens to Pontos to bring down Pharnakes; Battle of Zela; *veni, vidi, vici.*
44–42	Disorganized situation in Asia Minor; Caesar's assassins put the squeeze on cities.
41	Mark Antony in Asia Minor; meets Cleopatra in Tarsos.
38	Antony and his legate Ventidius Bassus besiege Antiochos of Commagene in Samosata; in the realm of this king, who ruled from 70 to ca. 36, sanctuaries are built, including the *hierothesion*—royal tomb and cult site—on the Nemrud Dağ.
36	Failure of Antony's campaign against the Parthians, which passes through Armenia and Azerbaijan.
31	Battle of Actium in Greece; end of Civil War and beginning of a new epoch, in which Octavian/Augustus founds monarchy.

Asia Minor under the Pax Romana (30 BCE to the first half of the third century CE)

25 BCE	Death of Amyntas of Galatia; establishment of central Anatolian province of Galatia. Several Roman colonies are subsequently established in central and southern Asia Minor, including Antiocheia in Pisidia.
9 BCE	Introduction of Asian calendar with year beginning on Augustus's birthday (September 23).
6/5 BCE	Paphlagonia is incorporated into province of Galatia.

2 BCE	Annexation of Karanitis with city of Sebastopolis and area of Amaseia to province of Galatia (*Pontus Galaticus*).
1 BCE	Armed mission carried out in Armenia by Augustus's grandson Gaius; Rome claims prerogative of determining succession to throne in Armenia, which Parthians do not accept.

CE
Tiberius 14–37

17	Archelaos of Cappadocia dies in Rome; Tiberius makes his kingdom a Roman province, with inclusion of Lesser Armenia and coastal area of east Pontos, with the cities of Kerasus and Trapezus; Commagene is put under control of governor of Syria.
18	Germanicus's mission to the Orient.
23–25	Death of Strabo of Amaseia.
34/5	The temple-state of Komana in Pontos becomes a *polis*.

Caligula 37–41

37/38	King of Armenia, Mithridates, interned in Rome. In Commagene, Antiochos IV becomes king and is shortly thereafter deposed again; east Pontic coastal cities join kingdom of Polemon II of Pontos.

Claudius 41–54

42	Antiochos IV is reinstalled in Commagene and Mithridates in Armenia.
43	Lycia becomes Roman province.
44	Rhodes loses its freedom.
48/49	Apostle Paul's first journey to Asia Minor begins via Cyprus to Antiocheia in Pisidia, Derbe and Laranda in Lycaonia.
51	Parthian king Vologaises claims throne of Armenia for his brother Tiridates.
52–55/56	Paul's second journey through Asia Minor, lengthy stay in Ephesos.

Nero 54–68

54–63	Rome's war against Parthians for right to determine succession to throne of Armenia, mainly under command of Domitius Corbulo.

Corbulo's invasion of Armenia; destruction of Artaxata.

Capture of Tigranokerta.

As governor of Galatia-Cappadocia, Caesennius Paetus resumes the war in Armenia, but fails.

Corbulo receives the supreme command of army in the Orient (seven legions and auxiliary troops) and invades Armenia again. The Roman demand that Parthian pretender to the throne, Tiridates, must be confirmed in Rome, is accepted.

Polemon II's kingdom of Pontos becomes Roman province (Pontus Polemonianus).

In festive ceremony in Rome, Nero makes Tiridates king of Armenia.

Roman legions are stationed on the Euphrates, in Melitene, Samosata, Satala.

Formation of the double province of Lycia et Pamphylia; Lesser Armenia is added to province of Cappadocia, and Commagene to province of Syria, not without resistance on the part of sons of King Antiochos IV; reformation of a province of Cilicia between the Taurus and Amanos Mountains.

onstruction of Temple of Zeus in Aizanoi.

mperor wants to limit wine-grape growing in Asia nor, but withdraws this proposal.

secution of Christians in Asia Minor; activities of byter and evangelist John in Ephesos.

n separates governorship of Galatia from that of adocia; Pontic eparchies in the interior are com- (Pontus Mediterraneus).

ruction of Celsus Library in Ephesos.

he Younger governor of Pontus et Bithynia; cordence with Emperor Trajan, including the letter l proceedings against Christians.

f Dion of Prusa (born ca. 40).

113–117	Trajan's war against Parthians after nephew of Parthi[a] king Osroes, Parthamasiris, was elevated to throne of Armenia.
117	Trajan dies in Selinus on coast of Rough Cilicia.

Hadrian 117–138

117–131	Hadrian's travels through Asia Minor; reformation [o] province of Cilicia: *tres eparchiae* of Cilicia, Lycaoni[a] and Isauria.
124	Julius Demosthenes's donation in Oinoanda in Lyci[a]
131–137	Arrian of Nikomedeia governor of province of Cap[pa]docia; *ektaxis* against Alans.
133/134	Hadrian's letters to synod of competitors in games; form of system of contest circuits.

Antoninus Pius
138–161

ca. 141	Opramoas of Rhodiapolis active as a benefactor in homeland of Lycia.
ca. 140–145	Foundation of cult of new Asklepios, the prophes[y] serpent Glykon, by Alexandros in Abonuteichos [o]n Black Sea; oracle is international success.
ca. 144	Marcion of Sinope's activities in Rome.
150s	Beginnings of Phrygian sect (Montanism).
155/156 (?)	Martyrdom of Bishop Polycarp in Smyrna.
159	Tensions between Romans and Parthians intensi[fy] again; through an exchange with Lycia et Pamph[ylia,] Pontus et Bithynia is transformed from senatoria[l] perial province administered by *legati Augusti*, a[nd] eastern part is soon afterward put under control [of gov]ernor of Galatia ("Galatie maritime").

Marcus Aurelius
161–180

161–166	Marcus Aurelius's and Lucius Verus's Parthian [War]
161	Governor of Cappadocia, Sedatius Severianus, [de]feated in Armenia.
163	Conquest of Armenia by Statius Priscus; Rom[an garri]son at Kainepolis near Artaxata; marriage of L[ucius] Verus and Lucilla in Ephesos.
176	Marcus Aurelius's return journey from Syria th[rough] Cappadocia, by way of Tarsos; death of Fausti[na in] Halala.

Septimius Severus
193–211

after 177 | Death of the sophist and orator Aelius Aristeides of Hadrianutherai.

177–212 | Abgar "the Great" rules in Edessa; economic and cultural flourishing of that city; the prince probably converts to Christianity, as does the gnostic Bardaiṣan.

194 | War between generals of Septimius Severus and Pescennius Niger in Bithynia; the defeated Niger withdraws over the Taurus to Cilicia.

194/5 | Severus's First Parthian War: conquest of Osrhoene, establishment of province of Mesopotamia.

197–199 | Severus's Second Parthian War.

Caracalla 211–217

212 | *Constitutio Antoniniana*: all free, adult inhabitants of empire receive Roman citizenship.

214–217 | Caracalla's Parthian War.

ca. 216 | Death of physician Galen of Pergamon (b. 129).

Severus Alexander
222–235

After 229 | Death of historian, senator, and consul Cassius Dio of Nikaia.

230s | Christian synods in Ikonion and Synnada.

ca. 232–235 | Reorganization of the administration of Paphlagonia and Pontus Mediterraneus, which are ruled by *praesides* of equestrian rank.

ca. 234 | Persecution of Christians in Cappadocia.

Philippus Arabs
244–249

248 | End of client-kingdom of Edessa; city is incorporated into province of Mesopotamia.

Decius 249–251

249–251 | Phrygia and Caria are detached from province of Asia and made independent provinces under administration of senatorial legates.

250 | Widespread persecution of Christians: martyrdom of Pionius in Smyrna.

Time of Crisis and New Beginning (from the second half of the third century CE to 330 CE)

Gallienus 253–268

253	Sasanid Shapur I seizes Antiocheia in Syria.
255–276	Attacks on Asia Minor by Goths, Borani, and Heruli.
260	Army groups of Sasanid Shapur invade Cilicia and Cappadocia.
261–267/68	Odainathos of Palmyra fights Sasanids.
ca. 266–268	Cities in Asia Minore stop minting coins (isolated exceptions until end of third century).

Aurelian 270–275

270/271	Palmyrene separate kingdom led by widow of Odainathos, Zenobia; Palmyrene troops cross the Taurus and invade Asia Minor.
271/272	Aurelian's expedition to Orient; victory over Palmyrenes.

Diocletian 284–305

Galerius 293–311

February 303–311	Persecution of Christians under Diocletian, Maximian, and Maximinus Daia.
311	Galerius issues edict of toleration in Nikomedeia.

Constantine I 306–337

325	Council of Nikaia.
330	Constantinople becomes capital of empire.

Notes

Chapter 1. Introduction: Anatolia between East and West

1. Udo Steinbach, *Geschichte der Türkei*, fourth ed., Munich 2007.

2. Cf. Gernot Wilhelm, "Anatolien zwischen Ost und West," in: [327] *Die Hethiter*, 2002, 16 f.

3. [605] Keil, *Kulte*, 1923, esp. 239–241.

4. References in [467] Blum, *Anatolien*, 2002, 310 n. 270; most recently [1] Schwertheim, *Kleinasien*, 2005, 7.

5. Walter Burkert, *Die orientalisierende Epoche in der griechischen Religion und Literatur*, Heidelberg 1984, 118.

6. See Wolfgang Röllig, "Asia Minor as a Bridge between East and West. The Role of the Phoenicians and Aramaeans in the Transfer of Culture," in: *Greece between East and West, 10th–8th Centuries B.C., Papers of the Meeting at the Institute of Fine Arts, New York University, March 15–16th, 1990*, Mainz 1992, 93.

7. Quoted from Onofrio Carruba, "Beiträge zur mittelhethitischen Geschichte I. Die Tudḫilyas und die Arnuwandas," *SMEA* 18, 1977, 159 f. The Akkadian dedicatory inscription on a bronze sword found in Ḫattusa in 1991 is connected with the same King Tudḫaliya; on it, he also mentions the destruction of the land of Assuwa. Cf. Piotr Tracha, "Is Tudḫaliya's Sword Really Aegean?" in: [329] Beckman et al. (eds.), *Hittite Studies*, 2003, 367–376.

8. Jakob Wackernagel, *Sprachliche Untersuchungen zu Homer*, Göttingen 1916, 86. (The asterisk indicates a morpheme—a grammatical unit in language that can be reconstructed according to rules but is unattested in written language.)

9. Hesiod, Fr. 165 line 11 Merkelbach and West.

10. Ptolemaios, *Tetr.*, e.g., 2, 3, 62: ἡ μικρὰ Ἀσία.

11. [274] Hütteroth, *Türkei*, 1982, 21.

12. According to a Hittite text (KUB XXXI 79, 4–20), grain and bread were transported between places called Pitiyarik, Samuḫa, and Arziya. Samuḫa is probably the same as Kayalıpınar (suggestion made by A. Müller-Karpe).

13. [9] del Monte and Tischler, *Répertoire* 6, 1978, s. v.

14. [274] Hütteroth, *Türkei*, 1982, 45.

15. *Mandeville's Travels, Text and Translations* by Malcolm Letts, Nendeln/Liechtenstein 1967, 106. Isidore of Seville had already said that the remains of the Ark could still be seen on the mountain, orig. 14, 8, 5: *Ararat mons Armeniae, in quo arcam historici post diluvium sedisse testantur. Unde et usque hodie ibidem lignorum eius videntur vestigia.*

16. Friedrich Parrot, *Reise zum Ararat*, Berlin 1834.

17. Olivier Casabonne, "Brèves remarques à propos du Taurus cilicien, des Hittites aux Romains," in: [286] Bru, Kirbihler, and Lebreton, *L'Asie Mineure*, 2009, 205 ff.

Chapter 2. Modern Fieldwork in Asia Minor

1. *The Travels of Ibn Baṭṭūta, A.D. 1325–1354.* Translated with Revisions and Notes by H.A.R. Gibb, Millwood, NY 1986, esp. ch. VIII, 413 ff. It was Johann Ludwig Burckhardt, a

student of the Orient from Basel and the discoverer of Petra and Abu Simbel, who first drew attention to Ibn Baṭṭūta's report on his experiences.

2. [34a] Clive Foss, "Pilgrimage in Medieval Asia Minor," *DOP* 56, 2002, 129–151.

3. Eve Borsook, "The Travels of Bernardo Michelozzi and Bonsignore Bonsignori in the Levant," *JWCI* 36, 1973, 145–197.

4. *The Pilgrimage of Arnold von Harff, Knight from Cologne*, ed. with notes and an introduction by M. Letts, London 1946.

5. Thomas Smith, *Remarks upon the Manners, Religion and Governement of the Turks*, London 1678. Cf. J. Theodore Bent, "The English in the Levant," *EHR* 5 (20), 1890, 654–664.

6. Edmund Chishull, *Antiquitates Asiaticae Christianam Aeram antecedentes*, London 1728; id., *Travels in Turkey and back to England*, London 1747 (published posthumously by Dr. Mead).

7. Richard Pococke, *A Description of the East and Some Other Countries*, 2 vols., London 1743–1745.

8. Domenico Sestini, *Voyage de Constantinople à Bassora en 1781 par le Tigre et l'Euphrate et retour à Constantinople en 1782 par la désert et Alexandrie* (translated from the Italian), Paris 1797.

9. Francis V. J. Arundell, *Discoveries in Asia Minor*, 2 vols., London 1834.

10. Eugène Boré, *Correspondence et mémoires d'un voyageur en Orient* I, Paris 1840.

11. Guillaume de Jerphanion, *Une nouvelle province de l'art byzantin, les églises rupestres de Cappadoce*, 5 vols., Paris 1925–1942.

12. Ian Macpherson, "Six Inscriptions from Galatia," *AnSt* 22, 1972, 217.

13. Ruy Gonzales de Clavijo, *Historia del Gran Tamorlán e itinerario y ennarracion del viage, y relación de la embajada que Ruy Gonzales de Clavijo le hizo por mandado del muy poderoso señor Rey Don Henrique el Tercero de Castilla*, second ed., Madrid 1782 (*Chronica* vol. 3).

14. Ghiselin de Busbeck, *Vier Briefe aus der Türkei* (Legationis Turcicae Epistolae IV). Translated from the Latin, with an introduction and notes by W. von Steinen, Erlangen 1926.

15. Hans Dernschwam, *Tagebuch einer Reise nach Konstantinopel und Kleinasien (1553–1555)*, ed. von F. Babinger, Leipzig 1923.

16. Michael H. Crawford, "William Sherard and the Prices Edict," *RNum* 159, 2003, 83–107.

17. Pascal T. Fourcade, "Mémoire sur Pompeiopolis ou Tasch Kouprou, avec quelques rémarques sur Tovata ou Voyavat," in: *Maltebrun's annales des voyages* XIV, 1811, 30 ff.

18. Louis-Alexandre Corancez, *Itinéraire d'une partie peu connue de l'Asie Mineure, contenant: La description des régions septentrionales de la Syrie; celle des côtes méridionales de l'Asie Mineure et des régions adjacentes encore peu connues; l'examen des causes de l'abaissement du niveau à l'extrémité du bassin oriental de la Méditeranée, etc.*, Paris, 1816.

19. James Brant, "Journey through a Part of Armenia and Asia Minor, in the Year 1835," *Journal of the Royal Geographic Society* 6, 1836, 187–223; id., "Notes of a Journey through a Part of Kurdistan, in the Summer of 1838," ibid., vol. 10, 1841, 341–432.

20. Published by H. Kierpert in the extracts translated by R. Kayser, in: *Zeitschrift der Gesellschaft für Erdkunde zu Berlin* 1, 1866, 415 ff.

21. Terence B. Mitford, "Biliotti's Excavations at Satala," *AnSt* 24, 1974, 221–244.

22. Edward Bodnar and Clive Foss, *Cyriac of Ancona. Later Travels*, Cambridge, MA

2003; Edward Bodnar, *Cyriacus of Ancon's Journeys in the Propontis and the Northern Aegean, 1444–1445*, Philadelphia 1976; Paul Mackendrick, "A Renaissance Odyssey: The Life of Cyriac of Ancona," *ClMediaev* 13, 1951, 131–45.

23. Jean Baptiste Tavernier, *Les six voyages de Jean Baptiste Tavernier en Turquie, en Perse et aux Indes* 1, second ed., Paris 1677; cf. Heinrich Ritter von Srbik, "Zur Lebensgeschichte des Forschungsreisenden Jean-Baptiste Tavernier," *HZ* 167, 1943, 29–40.

24. Friedrich Gronovius, *Memoria Cossoniana. Hoc est Danieli Cossonii vita […] cui annexa est nova editio Monumenti Ancyrani*, Leiden 1695.

25. Jacques Spon and George Wheler, *Voyage d' Italie, de Dalmatie, de Grèce et du Levant, fait par Iacob Spon et Georges Wheler*, 1678; new edition by Henri Duchêne and Jean-Claude Mossière (eds.), Geneva 2004; Jacques Spon, *Recherches curieuses d' antiquités*, Lyon 1683. Also: Jean Baptiste Tavernier, *Les six voyages de Jean Baptiste Tavernier, écuyer baron d'Aubonne, qu'il a fait en Turquie, en Perse, et aux Indes, pendant l'espace de quarante ans, & par toutes les routes que l'on peut tenir: accompagnez d'observations particulieres sur la qualité, la religion, le gouvernement, les coutumes & le commerce de chaque païs; avec les figures, le poids, & la valeur de monnoyes qui y ont court*, Paris 1676.

26. Thomas Drew-Bear, Christian Naour, and Ronald Stroud, *Arthur Pullinger: An Early Traveler in Syria and Asia Minor*, Philadelphia 1985. Cf. Richard Pococke, *Inscriptionum antiquarum Graecarum et Latinarum liber*, London 1752.

27. C. A. Hutton, "The Travels of 'Palmyra' Wood in 1750–51," *JHS* 47, 1927, 102–128.

28. Philippe Le Bas and William H. Waddington, *Voyage archéologique en Grèce et en Asie Mineure*, 6 vols., Paris 1868–1877.

29. "Je quittai Mylasa, ayant pressé le citron jusqu'à la dernière goutte. Les voyageurs peuvent se dispenser de passer par là désormais, je ne leur ai point laissé le moindre petit épi à glaner." L. Le Bas (ed.), *Voyage archéologique de Philippe Le Bas en Grèce et Asie Mineure, du 1er janvier 1893 au 1er décembre 1899. Extraits de sa correspondance*, RA 1898 I, letter no. 45, 100.

30. Joseph Pitton de Tournefort, *A Voyage into the Levant […]*, 3 vols., London 1741.

31. Paul Lucas, *Voyage du sieur Paul Lucas au Levant*, Paris 1705; id., *Voyage du sieur P. Lucas fait par ordre du Roy dans la Grèce, l'Asie Mineure, la Macédoine et l'Afrique, tome I contenant la description de l'Anatolie, de la Caramanie et de la Macédoine*, Paris 1712.

32. *Carsten Niebuhrs Reisebeschreibung nach Arabien und andern umliegenden Ländern*, 2 vols., Copenhagen, 1774–1778, vol. 3. ed. J. N. Gloyer and J. Olshausen, Hamburg 1837; Barthold G. Niebuhr, *Carsten Niebuhr's Leben von B. G. Niebuhr. Aus den Kieler Blättern abgedruckt*, Kiel 1817 (reprint Munich 1921).

33. Richard Chandler, *Ionian Antiquities, Published with Permission of the Society of Dilettanti by R. Chandler, M.A.F.S.A., N. Revett, Architect, and W. Pars, Painter*, London 1769; R. Chandler, *Inscriptiones antiquae, pleraeque nondum editae, in Asia Minore et Graecia, praesertim Athenis collectae*, Oxford 1774; id., *Travels in Asia Minor; or an Account of a Tour Made at the Expence of the Society of Dilettanti*, Oxford 1775.

34. Marie-Gabriel-Florent-Auguste Comte de Choiseul-Gouffier, *Voyage pittoresque dans l'empire Ottoman, en Grèce, dans la Troade, les îles de l'archipel et sur les côtes de l'Asie Mineure*, Paris 1782.

35. Joseph von Hammer-Purgstall, *Topographische Ansichten, gesammelt auf einer Reise in die Levante*, Vienna 1811.

36. His notes were published in: William George Browne, *Travels in Various Countries of*

the East, Being a Continuation of Memoirs Relating to European and Asiatic Turkey etc., ed. R. Walpole, Rev. M.A., London 1820.

37. [409] Lehmann-Haupt, *Armenien* I, 1910, 6 f.

38. William M. Leake, *Journal of a Tour in Asia Minor, with Comparative Remarks on the Ancient and Modern Geography of that Country*, London 1824.

39. John MacDonald Kinneir, *Journey through Asia Minor, Armenia, and Koordistan in the years 1813 and 1814 : With Remarks on the Marches of Alexander and Retreat of the Ten Thousand*, London 1818.

40. Lucie Bonato, "Camille Callier: un officier instruit de l'armée française qui explora Chypre en 1832," *Thetis* 10, 2003, 113–142.

41. William J. Hamilton, *Researches in Asia Minor, Pontus, and Armenia: with some account of their antiquities and geology*, London 1842.

42. Charles Fellows, *A Journal Written during an Excursion in Asia Minor*, London 1839; id., *An Account of Discoveries in Lycia, Being a Journal Kept during a Second Excursion in Asia Minor*, London 1840; id., *Travels and Researches in Asia Minor, and More Particularly in the Province of Lycia*, London 1853.

43. Richard Hoskyn, *Journal of the Royal Geographical Society of London* 12, 1842, 143 ff.

44. T. A. B. Spratt and Edward Forbes, *Travels in Lycia, Milyas, and the Cibyratis*, 2 vols., London 1847.

45. Ludwig Ross, *Kleinasien und Deutschland*, Halle 1850; J. A. Schönborn, *Einige Bemerkungen über den Zug Alexanders durch Lycien und Pamphylien*, Posen 1849; cf. Otto Benndorf and Georg Niemann, *Das Heroon von Gjölbaschi-Trysa*, Vienna 1889; Fritz Eichler, *Die Reliefs des Heroon von Gjölbaschi-Trysa*, Vienna 1950; Wolfgang Oberleitner, *Das Heroon von Trysa. Ein lykisches Fürstengrab des 4. Jahrhunderts*, Mainz 1994.

46. Friedrich Fischer, "Geographische Notizen über Klein-Asien," in: *Memoir über die Construction der Karte von Kleinasien und Türkisch Armenien etc.*, revised by Dr. Heinrich Kiepert, Berlin 1854; *Reise in den cilicischen Taurus über Tarsus von Dr. Theodor Kotschy, K. K. Custosadjunct am botanischen Hofcabinet in Wien*. With a foreword by Carl Ritter, Gotha 1858.

47. On this [26] Robert, *Asie Mineure*, 1980, 48 f. Two works in particular should be mentioned here, that of Ludwig Ross, loc. cit., and that of Bernhard Schwarz, *Quer durch Bithynien. Ein Beitrag zur Kenntnis Kleinasiens*, Berlin 1889. Cf. the report by the cavalry captain Walther von Diest (see below note 51), who takes up these ideas.

48. Peter Tschichatschew, *Asie Mineure*, 8 vols. with atlas, Paris 1853–1868; id., *Lettres sur la Turquie*, Brussels 1859.; id., *Une page sur l'Orient*, second ed., Paris 1877; id., *Kleinasien*, Leipzig 1887; *Peter v. Tschihatscheff's Reisen in Kleinasien und Armenien 1847–1863 (mit Karte von Kleinasien), begleitet von Heinrich Kiepert*, Gotha 1867.

49. Xavier Hommaire de Hell, *Voyage en Turquie et en Perse*, Paris 1855–1860.

50. G. Maercker, "Beiträge zur Erforschung Klein-Asiens I. Das Stromgebiet des unteren Kyzyl Yrmak (Halys)," *Zeitschrift der Gesellschaft für Erdkunde zu Berlin* 34, 1899, 363 ff.; Hauptmann Schäffer, "Erkundungen und Routen-Aufnahmen im Gebiet des Kyzyl Yrmak und des Jeshil," ibid., 391–406; von Flottwell, "Aus dem Stromgebiet des Qyzyl-Yrmaq (Halys)," *Petermanns Geographische Mitteilungen*, Ergänzungsheft 114, Gotha 1895, 1–55. On them, [26] Robert, *Asie Mineure*, 1980, 31.

51. Walther von Diest, "Von Pergamon über den Dindymos zum Pontos," *Petermanns Geographische Mitteilungen*, Ergänzungsheft 94, Gotha 1889, 69; cf.. Walther von Diest and Max Anton, "Neue Forschungen im nordwestlichen Kleinasien, mit Beiträgen von Leutnant Graf Götzen, Dr. A. Körte und Dr. G. Türk," ibid., Ergänzungsheft 116, Gotha 1895.

52. Richard Leonhard, *Paphlagonia. Reisen und Forschungen im Nördlichen Kleinasien*, Berlin 1915, 128.

53. Von Flottwell, "Aus dem Stromgebiet des Qyzyl-Yrmaq (Halys)," *Petermanns Geographische Mitteilungen*, Ergänzungsheft 114, Gotha 1895, 29.

54. Von Flottwell, "Aus dem Stromgebiet des Qyzyl-Yrmaq (Halys)," *Petermanns Geographische Mitteilungen*, Ergänzungsheft 114, Gotha 1895, 35.

55. Charles Burney, "The Kingdom of Urartu (Van): Investigations in the Archaeology of the Early First Millennium BC within Eastern Anatolia (1956–1965)," in: [31] Matthews (ed.), *Fifty Years*, 1998, 146.

56. Sir William M. Ramsay and Gertrude Bell, *The Thousand and One Churches*, London 1909.

57. The *Historical Geography* does not contain what its title promises: cf. [279] Robert, *Villes*, second ed., 1962, 428: "ce livre confus, tumultueux, désordonnée, bâcle, n'est plus qu'une ruine, et d'abord grâce aux voyages de Ramsay lui-même pendant toute une vie."

58. [104] Sterrett, *Journey*, 1888.

59. John G. C. Anderson, "A Journey of Exploration in Pontus," *Studia Pontica* I, Brussels 1903; "Voyage d'exploration archéologique dans le Pont et la petite Arménie," *Studia Pontica* II, Brussels 1906; vol. III of *Studia Pontica*, published in 1910 by Anderson, Franz Cumont, and Grégoire, contains the inscriptions.

60. Henri Grégoire, "Rapport sur un voyage d'exploration dans le Pont et la Cappadoce," *BCH* 33, 1909, 3–169; *Recueil des inscriptions grecques-chrétiennes d'Asie Mineure*, Paris 1922 (reprint Amsterdam 1968).

61. [259] Wartke, *Urartu*, 1993, 14.

62. Alfred Philippson, "Reisen und Forschungen im westlichen Kleinasien," *Petermanns Geographische Mitteilungen*, Ergänzungsheft 1–5, Gotha 1910–1915.

63. Karl Buresch, *Aus Lydien. Epigraphisch-geographische Reisefrüchte, hinterlassen von Karl Buresch*, ed. O. Ribbeck, Leipzig 1898 (reprint Hildesheim 1977).

64. Josef Keil and Anton von Premerstein, "Bericht über eine Reise in Lydien und der südlichen Aiolis, ausgeführt 1906 im Auftrage der Kaiserlichen Akademie der Wissenschaften," *Kaiserliche Akademie der Wissenschaften, Phil.-hist. Klasse, Denkschriften* 53,2, Vienna 1908; id., "Bericht über eine zweite Reise in Lydien, ausgeführt 1908 im Auftrage des K. K. Österreichischen Archäologischen Instituts," loc. cit., 54,2, Vienna 1911; id., "Bericht über eine dritte Reise in Lydien und den angrenzenden Gebieten Ioniens, ausgeführt 1911 im Auftrage der Kaiserlichen Akademie der Wissenschaften," loc. cit., 57,1, Vienna 1914.

65. Matthias Recke, *In loco Murtana, ubi olim Perge sita fuit: der Beginn archäologischer Forschungen in Pamphylien und die Kleinasien-Expedition Gustav Hirschfelds 1874*, Antalya 2007.

66. Eugen Adolf Hermann Petersen and Felix von Luschan, *Reisen in Lykien, Milyas und Kibyratis*, Vienna 1889.

67. Otto Benndorf and Georg Niemann, *Reisen im südwestlichen Kleinasien*, vol. I, *Reisen in Lykien und Karien*, Vienna 1884; Theodore Bent, "A Journey in Cilicia Tracheia," *JHS* 12, 1891, 220–222; Rudolf Heberdey and Ernst Kalinka, *Bericht über zwei Reisen im südwestlichen Kleinasien, ausgeführt im Auftrage der Kaiserlichen Akademie der Wissenschaften*, Kaiserliche Akademie der Wissenschaften, Phil.-hist. Klasse, Vienna 1897; Rudolf Heberdey and Adolf Wilhelm, *Reisen in Kilikien*, loc. cit., 1896.

68. Sir Charles Newton, *Travels & Discoveries in the Levant*, London 1865.

69. [244] Bammer and Muss, *Artemision*, 1996, 15.

70. Wolfgang Müller-Wiener (ed.), *Milet 1899–1980. Ergebnisse, Probleme u. Perspektiven einer Ausgrabung. Kolloquium*, Frankfurt am Main 1980, Tübingen 1986.

71. Theodor Wiegand (ed.), *Didyma. Erster Teil: Die Baubeschreibung von H. Knackfuß*, Berlin 1941.

72. Manfred Flügge, *Heinrich Schliemanns Weg nach Troia. Die Geschichte eines Mythomanen*, Munich 2001; Justus Cobet, "Vom Text zur Ruine. Die Geschichte der Troia-Diskussion," in: Ch. Ulf (ed.), *Der Neue Streit um Troia*, Munich 2003, 19–38; id., Heinrich Schliemann. *Archäologe und Abenteurer*, Munich 1997.

73. [525] Radt, *Pergamon*, 1999, 309–330.

74. Hubert Szemethy, *Die Erwerbungsgeschichte des Heroons von Trysa. Ein Kapitel österreichisch-türkischer Kulturpolitik*, Vienna 2005.

75. Quoted from [244] Bammer and Muss, *Artemision*, 1996, 1.

76. Mustafa Cezar, *Müzeci ve ressam Hamdi Bey*, Istanbul 1987.

77. Andreas E. Furtwängler, "Felix von Luschan," in: *Neue Deutsche Biographie*, vol. 15, Berlin 1987, 528 f.

78. Letter from Hogarth to Flinders Petrie, July 10, 1911, cited in Jeremy Wilson, *Lawrence of Arabia*, London 1990, 85.

79. Letter from T. E. Lawrence to his family, May 23, 1911, cited in Jeremy Wilson, *Lawrence of Arabia*, London 1990, 88.

80. Richard D. Barnett, *Carchemish*, vol. 3, London 1952, 258.

81. Johannes Nollé and Sencer Şahin, "Ekrem Akurgal. Ein Leben für die Erforschung des antiken Anatoliens," *Antike Welt* 34, 2003, 99–100; Fahri Işik, "In Memoriam Ekrem Akurgal," *IstMitt* 53, 2003, 5–8.

82. Klaus Tuchelt, *Didyma. Ergebnisse der Ausgrabungen und Untersuchungen seit dem Jahre 1962*, Mainz 1996.

83. Frank Rumscheid, *Priene. Führer durch das "Pompeji Kleinasiens,"* Istanbul 1998.

84. Klaus Rheidt (ed.), *Aizanoi und Anatolien*, Mainz 2010.

85. Friedmund Hueber, *Ephesos. Gebaute Geschichte*, Mainz 1997, 19; [29] Wohlers-Scharf, Forschungsgeschichte, second ed., 1996.

86. Orhan Bingöl, "Magnesia," *Byzas* 3, 2006, 215–226.

87. [447] Hanfmann and Mierse, *Sardis*, 1983.

88. Kenan T. Erim, *Aphrodisias. City of Venus Aphrodite*, London 1986.

89. Francesco D'Andria, *Hierapolis in Phrygien (Pamukkale). Ein archäologischer Führer*, Istanbul 2003.

90. Daniela Baldoni, Carlo Franco, Paolo Belli, and Fede Berti, *Carian Iasos*, Istanbul 2004.

91. Cf. Hansgeorg Bankel, "Knidos. Der hellenistische Rundtempel und sein Altar. Vorbericht," *AA* 1997, 51–71.

92. Christine Bruns-Özgan, *Knidos. Ein Führer durch die Ruinen*, Konya 2002.

93. Pontus Hellström, *Labraunda. A Guide to the Karian Sanctuary of Zeus Labraundos*, Istanbul 2007.

94. Baki Öğün and Cengiz Işik, *Kaunos. Kbid. The Results of 35 Years of Research (1966–2001)*, İzmir 2003.

95. Jacques de Courtils, *Guide de Xanthos et du Létôon*, Istanbul 2003.

96. Fahri Işik, *Patara. The History and Ruins of the Capital City of Lycian League*, Antalya 2000.

97. Cevdet Bayburtluoğlu, *Arykanda. Anadolu'nun Aykiriçay'i*, Istanbul 2003.

98. Haluk Abbasoğlu, in: [34] Belli (ed.), *Contributions*, 2001, 206–210 (Side); 211–216 (Perga).

99. Haluk Abbasoğlu and Wolfram Martini, *Die Akropolis von Perge. Survey und Sondagen 1994–1997*, vol. 1, Mainz 2003, esp. 1–11.

100. Ümit Serdaroğlu, *Behramkale–Assos*, Istanbul 1995.

101. [16] Mitchell and McNicoll, *Archaeological Reports* no. 25 (1978/9) 61.

102. Stephen Mitchell, "The Aşvan Project," in: [31] Matthews (ed.), *Fifty Years*, 1998, 85–100.

103. Chris Lightfoot and Mucahide Lightfoot, *Amorion: A Byzantine City in Anatolia. An Archaeological Guide*, Istanbul 2007.

104. Sencer Şahin, "Forschungen in Kommagene I–II," *EpigrAnat* 18, 1991, 99–132; Jörg Wagner (ed.), *Gottkönige am Euphrat. Neue Ausgrabungen und Forschungen in Kommagene*, Mainz 2000.

105. Engelbert Winter (ed.), "Patris pantrophos Kommagene. Neue Funde und Forschungen zwischen Tauros und Euphrat," *AMS* 60, Bonn 2008.

106. Charles Burney, "The Kingdom of Urartu (Van): Investigations in the Archaeology of the Early First Millennium BC within Eastern Anatolia (1956–1965)," in: [31] Matthews (ed.), *Fifty Years*, 1998, 144.

107. Frank Kolb, in: [247] Kolb (ed.), *Chora*, 2004, IX–XV and esp. the literature mentioned in note 10.

108. John M. Cook, *The Troad. An Archaeological and Topographical Study*, Oxford 1973.

109. Hans Lohmann, "Milet und die Milesia," in: [247] Kolb (ed.), *Chora*, 2004, 325–360.

110. [180] Robert, *Amyzon*, 1983; [170] Robert, *Carie*, 1954.

111. George E. Bean, *Turkey Beyond the Maeander*, London 1971.

112. Paavo Roos, *The Rock Tombs of Caunus*, vol. 1: *The Architecture*, Jonsered, Sweden 1972; vol. 2: *The Finds*, Jonsered, Sweden 1974.

113. Wolfgang Radt, *Siedlungen und Bauten auf der Halbinsel von Halikarnassos*, Tübingen 1970.

114. [155] Debord and Varinlioğlu, *Hautes terres*, 2001.

115. [261] Peschlow-Bindokat, *Latmos*, 1996.

116. Hans Lohmann, "Zwischen Kaunos und Telmessos," *OrbTerr* 5, 1999, 43 ff.; id., "Zwischen Kaunos und Telmessos. Addenda et corrigenda," *OrbTerr* 7, 2001, 217 ff.; Werner Tietz, *Der Golf von Fethiye. Politische und kulturelle Strukturen einer Grenzregion vom Beginn der Besiedlung bis in die römische Kaiserzeit*, Bonn 2003.

117. George E. Bean, *Journeys in Northern Lycia 1965–1967*, Vienna 1971; id., *Lycian Turkey: An Archaeological Guide*, London 1978.

118. J. James Coulton, "Highland Cities in South-West Turkey: The Oinoanda and Balboura Surveys," in: [31] Matthews (ed.), *Fifty Years*, 1998, 225–236.

119. See preceding note; for futher research, see J. Hammerstaedt and M. F. Smith, "Diogenes of Oinoanda: The Discoveries of 2008 (NF 142–167)," *EpigrAnat* 41, 2008, 1–37.

120. Thomas Corsten, "Kibyratis in Antiquity," *AnatA* 11, 2005, 17.

121. [187] Wörrle, *Stadt und Fest*, 1988; A Bibliography of Wurster's und Wörrle's contributions to research on Lycia in: [415] Borchhardt and Dobesch (eds.), *Lykien-Symposion* vol. 2, 1993, 297 f.

122. [264] Kolb, *Burg-Polis-Bischofssitz*, 2008; Frank Kolb and Andreas Thomsen, "For-

schungen zu Zentralorten und Chora auf dem Gebiet von Kyaneai (Zentrallykien): Methoden, Ergebnisse, Probleme," in: [247] Kolb (ed.), *Chora*, 2004, 1–42.

123. Thomas Marksteiner, "Der Bonda-Survey: Archäologische Feldforschungen auf dem Territorium der ostlykischen Polis Limyra," in: [247] Kolb (ed.), *Chora*, 2004, 271–290; Mustafa Adak, "Lokalisierung von Olympos und Korykos in Ostlykien," *Gephyra* 1, 2004, 27–51.

124. Detailed critique in Louis Robert, *Hellenica* 13, 1965, esp. 236–238.

125. Stephen Mitchell, "The Pisidian Survey," in: [31] Matthews (ed.), *Fifty Years*, 1998, 237–253.

126. Stephen Mitchell, "The Pisidian Survey," in: [31] Matthews (ed.), *Fifty Years*, 1998, 238. Cf. also David French, "Isinda and Lagbe," in: id. (ed.), *Studies in the History and Topography of Lycia and Pisidia in Memoriam A.S. Hall*, Ankara 1994, 53–92.

127. [429] Brandt, *Pisidien und Pamphylien*, 1992; Bülent İplikçioğlu, "Ländliche Siedlungen und das Territorium von Termessos," in: [247] Kolb (ed.), *Chora*, 2004, 103–125; on Marc Waelkens, see the reports in the publication series Sagalassos V: *Report on the Survey & Excavation Campaigns of 1996 & 1997*, Leuven 2000.

128. [262] Berndt, *Midasstadt*, 2005.

129. [126] Drew-Bear, *Phrygie*, 1978; [177] Naour, *Tyriaion*, 1980. Cf. [609] Drew-Bear's introduction in: *ANRW* II 18.3, 1990, 191–194; [149] Drew-Bear, Thomas, and Yıldızturan, *Phrygian Votive Steles*, 1999.

130. [255] Waelkens, *Türsteine*, 1986.

131. Heinrich Swoboda, Josef Keil, and Fritz Knoll (eds.), *Denkmäler aus Lykaonien, Pamphylien, und Isaurien. Ergebnisse einer im Auftrage der Gesellschaft von Julius Jüthner, Fritz Knoll, Karl Patsch und Heinrich Swoboda durchgeführten Forschungsreise. Deutsche Gesellschaft der Wissenschaften und Künste für die Tschechoslowakische Republik in Prag*, Brünn and Vienna 1935.

132. Ernst Herzfeld and Samuel Guyer, *Meriamlik und Korykos. Zwei christliche Ruinenstätten des rauhen Kilikien*, *MAMA* II, Manchester 1930; Josef Keil and Adolf Wilhelm, *Denkmäler aus dem rauhen Kilikien. MAMA* III, Manchester 1931; George E. Bean and Terence Bruce Mitford, *Journeys in Rough Cilicia in 1962 and 1963*, Vienna 1965; id., *Journeys in Rough Cilicia 1964–1968*, Vienna 1970; [133] Dagron and Feissel, *Cilicie*, 1987. Cf. also [147] Tomaschitz, *Westkilikien*, 1998.

133. [162] *IK* Tyana, 2000.

134. Timothy Mitford, "Roman Frontier on the Upper Euphrates," in: [31] Matthews (ed.), *Fifty Years*, 1998, 255–272.

135. Chris Lightfoot, "Survey Work at Satala," in: [31] Matthews (ed.), *Fifty Years*, 1998, 273–284.

136. Anthony Bryer and David Winfield, *The Byzantine Monuments and Topography of the Pontos*, Washington 1985.

137. [565] French, *Milestones*, 1988, replaced by [161c] French, *Roman Roads and Milestones of Asia Minor*, 2012–2014; French, [162] *IK* Sinope, 2004.

138. F. Eray Dökü, *Paphlagonia bölgesi kaya mezarları ve kaya tapınakları*, Antalya 2008.

139. Giulio Jacopi, *Dalla Paflagonia alla Commagene. Relazione sulla prima campagna esplorativa (Settembre-Novembre 1935)*, Rome 1936; id., *Esplorazioni e studi in Paflagonia e Cappadocia. Relazione sulla seconda campagna esplorativa (Agosto-Ottobre 1936)*, Rome 1937.

140. Stephen Hill and James Crow, "The Byzantine Fortifications of Amastris in Paphlagonia," *AnSt* 45, 1995, 251 ff.

141. Cf. Friedrich Karl Dörner, *Bericht über eine Reise in Bithynien*, Vienna 1952; [113] Dörner, *Bithynien*, 1941.

142. Sencer Şahin, "Studien über die Probleme der historischen Geographie des nordwestlichen Kleinasiens" I: Strabon XII 3, 7 p. 543. "Der Fluß Gallos, die Stadt Mod<ren>e in Phrygia Epiktetos und die Schiffbarkeit des Sangarios," *EpigrAnat* 7, 1986, 125–152; id., "Studien über die Probleme der historischen Geographie des nordwestlichen Kleinasiens II: Malagina/Melagina am Sangarios," *EpigrAnat* 7, 1986, 153–167; on the inscriptions, see [162] *IK* Nikaia. A new collection of the inscriptions from this region is in print: [161e] Marek and Adak, *Forschungen*, 2016 (in print).

143. Above all, in the sections on Asia Minor of the [196] *Bulletin épigraphique* they publish annually in the journal *Revue des Études Grecques*, Jeanne and Louis Robert have commented on the advances in research up to 1984. John Ma, "The Epigraphy of Hellenistic Asia Minor: A Survey of Recent Research (1992–1999)," *AJA* 104, 2000, 95–121, offers a more recent overview that largely ignores, however, the regions beyond western and southern Asia Minor. See the individual volumes and series listed in the Bibliography under "Sources, Text Collections, and Translations."

144. Nesih Başgelen, Güler Çelgin, and A. Vedat Çelgin (eds.), *Anatolian & Thracian Studies in Honor of Zafer Taşlıklıoğlu*, Istanbul 1999, esp. XII–XIV, XVII f.

145. Johannes Nollé, "Zur neueren Forschungsgeschichte der kaiserzeitlichen Stadtprägungen Kleinasiens. Der schwierige Umgang mit einer historischen Quelle," in: [223] Nollé, Overbeck, and Weiß (eds.), *Münzprägung*, 1997, 11–26, quoted on p. 13. Cf. ibid., p. 27–35, Peter Weiß's article, "Kaiserzeitliche Städteprägung und Klassische Altertumswissenschaften."

146. Markus von Kaenel, "'ein wohl großartiges, aber ausführbares Unternehmen.' Theodor Mommsen, Friedrich Imhoof-Blumer und das Corpus Nummorum," *Klio* 73, 1991, 304–314.

147. [208] von Aulock, *Münzen und Städte Lykaoniens*, 1976; [209] *Münzen und Städte Pisidiens* 1–2, 1977–1979; [210] *Münzen und Städte Phrygiens* 1–2, 1980–1987.

148. Frank L. Kovacs and Henry C. Lindgren, *Ancient Bronze Coins of Asia Minor and the Levant from the Lindgren Collection*, San Mateo 1985; H. C. Lindgren, *Lindgren III, Ancient Bronze Coins from the Lindgren Collection*, San Mateo 1993; Edoardo Levante, *Sylloge Nummorum Graecorum Switzerland I, Levante-Cilicia*, Bern 1986; Supplement I, Zurich 1993; Ruprecht Ziegler, *Münzen Kilikiens aus kleineren deutschen Sammlungen*, Munich 1988; Johannes Nollé, *Sylloge Nummorum Graecorum, Pfälzer Privatsammlungen 4, Pamphylien*, Munich 1992.

149. [216] Klose, *Münzprägung Smyrna*, 1987. Also see Nollé, op. cit., p. 18, n. 141, and Wolfgang Leschhorn, "Die kaiserzeitliche Münzprägung in Phrygien," ibid. 49 f.

150. For example, [123] Lane, *Corpus Monumentorum Religionis Dei Menis 2. The Coins and Gems*, 1975.

151. [224] Franke and Nollé, *Homonoia-Münzen*, 1997.

152. William E. Metcalf, "The Cistophory of Hadrian," Numismatic Studies no. 15, American Numismatic Society, New York, 1980.

153. [225] *SNG Turkey 1: The Muharrem Kayhan Collection*, Istanbul-Bordeaux 2002. Vol. 2 (2007) is devoted to the Roman provincial coins in the Museum of Anamur, Cilicia.

154. Louis Robert, *OMS* IV, 1974, 400: "Il est anti-scientifique que chaque groupe professionnel, constitué d'ailleurs de hasard, veuille construire chacun sa cage à lapins avec un piège à loup devant la porte, veuille avoir chacun sa petite vitrine réservée; et puis on chanterait des

cantates en l'honneur des contacts 'multidisciplinaires.' Ce serait faire un fameux saut en arrière. Notre science ne fait pas en alignant des cubes les uns à côté des autres, chacun sa petite boîte marquée de beaux sigles, tamponnée, cachetée et stérilisée. C'est le cerveau de chacun qui fait la synthèse, et pour cela il faut travailler—travailler fort—en suivant les documents là ou ils nous entraînent."

Chapter 3. From Prehistory to the Oldest Written Culture

1. [305] Peschlow-Bindokat, *Antike Welt* 26, 1995, 114–117.

2. On chronology: [304] Yakar, *Prehistoric Anatolia*, 1991, 27–31. The abbreviation used below, PPN (A and B), stands for "pre-pottery Neolithic."

3. [300] Lichter (ed.), *Farming*.

4. Ceiridwen J. Edwards et al., "Mitochondrial DNA Analysis Shows a Near Eastern Neolithic Origin for Domestic Cattle and no Indication of Domestication of European Aurochs," *Proceedings Biological Sciences, The Royal Society* no. 274, June 2007, 1377–1385.

5. [308] Schmidt, *Sie bauten die ersten Tempel*, 2006; id., "Göbekli Tepe—the Stone Age Sanctuaries: New Results of Ongoing Excavations with a special focus on Sculptures and High Reliefs," *Documenta Praehistorica* 37, 2010, 239–256. Available at: http://arheologija.ff.uni-lj.si/documenta/authors37/37_21.pdf.

6. Harald Hauptmann, "The Urfa-Region," in: [306] Özdoğan and Başgelen, *The Neolithic in Turkey*, 1999, 65 ff.

7. [304] Yakar, *Prehistoric Anatolia*, 1991, 42–56.

8. Yakar, op. cit., 108–111.

9. Ian Hodder, Çatalhöyük: *The Leopard's Tale: Revealing the Mysteries of Turkey's Ancient "Town,"* London 2006; Heinrich Klotz, *Die Entdeckung von Çatal Höyük—Der archäologische Jahrhundertfund*, Munich 1997; James Mellaart, *Çatal Höyük—Stadt aus der Steinzeit*, Bergisch Gladbach, second ed., 1973.

10. Martin P. Nilsson, *Geschichte der griechischen Religion*, vol. 1, third ed., Munich 1967, 272 ff.

11. Walter Burkert, *Griechische Religion der archaischen und klassischen Epoche*, second ed., Stuttgart 2011, 65.

12. Wolf-Dietrich Niemeier, "Milet von den Anfängen menschlicher Besiedlung bis zur ionischen Wanderung," in: [372] Cobet et al. (eds.), *Frühes Ionien*, 2007, 6.

13. For an overview of the west: Wolf-Dietrich Niemeier, "Westkleinasien und Ägäis von den Anfängen bis zur ionischen Wanderung: Topographie, Geschichte und Beziehungen nach dem archäologischen Befund und den hethitischen Quellen," in: [372] Cobet et al. (eds.), *Frühes Ionien*, 2007, 37–96.

14. [315] Frangipane (ed.), *Arslantepe*, 2004.

15. [310] Lloyd and Mellaart, *Beycesultan I–III*, London 1962–1972.

16. Joan Goodnick Westenholz, *Legends of the Kings of Akkade. The Texts*, Winona Lake, IN 1997, 102–131 (Text 9 B); cf. Hans G. Güterbock, "Ein neues Bruchstück der Sargon-Erzählung "König der Schlacht," *MDOG* 101, 1969–1973, 14–26.

17. Since 1948, for more than five decades, the Turkish mission under the leadership of Tahsin Özgüç has been excavating at Kültepe; after Özgüç's death, the work was continued by Fikri Kulakoğlu.

18. The place name "Kaneš" persisted for more than three and half millennia, a record in Anatolia. Early Hellenistic bronze coins bear the city name "Hanisa," and a late Hellenistic

bronze plate from Kültepe contains a decree issued by this city. Finally, an Ottoman legal document from Kayseri mentions a village named "Kınış." [6] Robert, *Noms*, 1963, 466 f.

19. It is probable that there were tin deposits in Anatolia, but it is not clear whether they were of economic significance. Currently, evidence suggests that small amounts of tin were mined in the third millennium and led to the beginning of bronze technology. After these deposits were exhausted, importation of tin began (information supplied by Andreas Müller-Karpe).

20. [319] Veenhof, *Assyrian Merchants*, 1982, 151.

21. Tahsin Özgüç, *Kültepe-Kaniš/Neša, The Earliest International Trade Center and the Oldest Capital City of the Hittites*, Istanbul 2003.

22. [61] Dercksen, *Copper Trade*, 1996, no. 20, lines 24–26.

Chapter 4. The Late Bronze and Iron Age

1. Cf. Heinrich Otten, *Die hethitischen historischen Quellen und die altorientalische Chronologie*, Mainz 1968.

2. Silvia Alaura, "Archive und Bibliotheken in Hattusa," in: G. Wilhelm (ed.), *Akten des IV. Internationalen Kongresses für Hethitologie, Würzburg 4.–8. Oktober 1999*, Wiesbaden 2001.

3. Mitanni-Indian, as the source of a few names and loanwords, is not counted here; p. 70.

4. [82] Neu, *Der Anitta-Text*, 1974, 132–135; for a different opinion: [96] Haas, *Literatur*, 2006, 28 n. 28.

5. H.A. Hoffner, "Proclamation of Anitta of Kuššar," in: W. Hallo, and K. L. Younger Jr. (eds.), *The Context of Scripture*. vol. 1: *Canonical Compositions from the Biblical World*, Leiden 2003, 183 [Rev. lines 47-51].

6. Th. van den Hout, "The Proclamation of Telipinu," in: W. Hallo and K. L. Younger Jr. (eds.), op. cit., 196 [Obv. II lines 34 f.].

7. Alfonso Archi, "Middle Hittite—'Middle Kingdom,'" in: [329] Beckman et al. (ed.), *Hittite Studies*, 2003, 1–12.

8. Hans G. Güterbock, "The Deeds of Suppiluliuma as Told by His Son Mursili II," *JCS* 10, 1956, 93 ff. (fragment 28).

9. Treaty between Muwatalli II and Alaksandu of Wilusa (second decade of the thirteenth century?), § 14, III lines 10–12; cf. [69] Friedrich, *Staatsverträge* II, 1930, 69.

10. End of the so-called *Ten-Year Annals*, § 42, Rev. IV lines 44–48, quoted from R. Beal, "The Ten Year Annals of Great King Muršili of Ḫatti," in: W. Hallo and K. L. Younger Jr. (eds.), *The Context of Scripture*. vol. 2: *Monumental Inscriptions from the Biblical World*, Leiden 2003, 90.

11. § I lines 5–6, quoted from Th. van den Hout, "Apology of Ḫattušili III," in: W. Hallo and K. L. Younger Jr. (eds.), *The Context of Scripture*. vol. 1: *Canonical Compositions from the Biblical World*, Leiden 2003, 199.

12. Treaty between Ramses II. and Hattusili §18 (Obv. 60-64), quoted from: G. Beckman, *Hittite Diplomatic Texts*, second ed., Atlanta 1999, 99.

13. KUB XXIII 92 Obv. lines 9–12, trans. Max Gander; see also Heinrich Otten, "Ein Brief aus Ḫattuša an Bâbu-ahu-iddina, *AfO* 19, 1959–1960, 40.

14. Richard Haase, "Zur Stellung der Frau im Spiegel der hethitischen Rechtssammlung,

AoF 22,2, 1995, 277–281; Thomas Zehnder, *Die hethitischen Frauennamen: Katalog und Interpretation*, Wiesbaden 2010.

15. Instruction for temple officials, § 19 line 78, quoted from: Jared L. Miller, *Royal Hittite Instructions and Related Administrative Texts*, Atlanta 2013, 265.

16. Treaty with Manapa-Tarḫunta, A § 4 lines 60–62, quoted from G. Beckman, *Hittite Diplomatic Texts*, second ed., Atlanta 1999, 83.

17. Tablet I § 7, quoted from [89] Hoffner, *Laws*, 1997, 21.

18. Sausagamuwa-Treaty, Rev. IV lines 12–18, quoted from G. Beckman, op. cit., 106.

19. Treaty made by Suppiluliuma with King Ḫukkana of Hajasa, § 6 lines 38–59, quoted from G. Beckman, op. cit., 28–29.

20. Volkert Haas, *Hethitische Orakel, Vorzeichen und Abwehrstrategien. Ein Beitrag zur hethitischen Kulturgeschichte*, Berlin 2008.

21. [237] Ehringhaus, *Felsreliefs*, 2005, 50–56.

22. Mursili II's second Plague Prayer, § 9 lines 1–6, quoted from I. Singer, *Hittite Prayers*, Atlanta 2002, 60.

23. Ḫattusili II/III's Apology, § 4 lines 42–50, quoted from Th. van den Hout, "Apology of Ḫattušili III," in: W. Hallo, and K. L. Younger Jr. (eds.), *The Context of Scripture*. vol. 1: *Canonical Compositions from the Biblical World*, Leiden 2003, 200. A different translation of the last sentence: "I never did the evil thing of man," is given by [84] Otten, *Apologie*, 1981, 7.

24. [96] Haas, *Literatur*, 2006.

25. Harry A. Hoffner Jr., *Letters From the Hittite Kingdom*, Atlanta 2009.

26. Jörg Klinger, "Historiographie als Paradigma," in: G. Wilhelm (ed.), *Akten des IV. Internationalen Kongresses für Hethitologie*, Würzburg 4–8 October 1999, Wiesbaden 2001, 272–291; cf. Hubert Cancik, *Grundzüge der hethitischen und alttestamentlichen Geschichtsschreibung*, Wiesbaden 1976.

27. [237] Ehringhaus, *Felsreliefs*, 2005.

28. Among experts there is no consensus concerning an "Ionia" in Asia Minor during the Bronze Age: Peter Haider, "War ein 'Groß-Ionien' tatsächlich um 1360 v. Chr. in Westkleinasien existent? Eine kritische Analyse zu den Lesungen und Identifizierungen der jüngst entdeckten topographischen Namenlisten aus der Regierungszeit Amenophis III.," *Klio* 90, 2008, 291–306. On Hittite geography in general see: Lee Ullmann and Mark Weeden (eds.), *The Geography and Landscape of the Hittites* (forthcoming) Leiden.

29. Cf. Maciej Popko, "Zur Topographie von Ḫattuša: Tempel auf Büyükkale," in: [329] Beckman et al. (eds.), *Hittite Studies*, 2003, 315–323. For Ḫattusa in general see [351a] Schachner, *Hattuscha*, 2011.

30. However, a Bronze Age settlement was not found in Perge until recently: cf. Haluk Abbasoğlu and Wolfram Martini, *Die Akropolis von Perge*, vol. 1, Mainz 2003. (See below, note 87.)

31. [373a] Gander, *Die geographischen Beziehungen*, 2010.

32. Wolf-Dietrich Niemeier, "Milet von den Anfängen menschlicher Besiedlung bis zur ionischen Wanderung," in: [372] Cobet et al. (eds.), *Frühes Ionien*, 2007, 3–20; id., *Westkleinasien und Ägäis von den Anfängen bis zur ionischen Wanderung: Topographie, Geschichte und Beziehungen nach dem archäologischen Befund und den hethitischen Quellen*, ibid., 37–96.

33. Cf. Max Gander, *SMEA* 54, 2012, 281–309.

34. M. H. Kan, "Mycenaean Involvement on the Anatolian Coastline," in: Ç. Özkan Aygün (ed.), *SOMA 2007. Proceedings of the XI Symposium on Mediterranean Archaeology, Istanbul 24–29 April 2007*, Oxford 2009, 185–195.

35. For a different opinion see Niemeier, *Westkleinasien und Ägäis*, 86 f.

36. [451] Burkert, *Lydia*, 2001, 219.

37. Justus Cobet, "Vom Text zur Ruine," in: Ch. Ulf (ed.), *Der neue Streit um Troia*, Munich, second ed., 2004, 27.

38. [382] Kolb, *War Troia eine Stadt?*, 2003; [383] Kolb, *Traum und Wirklichkeit*, 2003.

39. On a few place names in Asia Minor found in the Linear-B tablets from Pylos, see p. 5 f.

40. Kenneth A. Kitchen, *Ramesside Inscriptions*, vol. 4, *Translations: Merenptah and the Late 19th Century*, Oxford 2003, p. 4, 5:3. Cf. [55] Breasted, *Records* 3, 1906, 244.

41. Jürgen Seeher, "Die Zerstörung der Stadt Hattusa," in: G. Wilhelm (ed.), *Akten des IV. Internationalen Kongresses für Hethitologie, Würzburg 4–8 October 1999*, Wiesbaden 2001, 623–634.

42. Wolfgang Helck, *Beziehungen Ägyptens und Vorderasiens zur Ägäis bis ins 7. Jh. v. Chr.*, second ed., Darmstadt 1995, 26–30.

43. Nonetheless, a few philologists think they can recognize the persistence of toponyms. Cf. Massimo Forlanini, "Am Mittleren Kizilirmak," in: H. Otten et al. (eds.), *Hittite and Other Anatolian and Near Eastern Studies in Honour of Sedat Alp*, Ankara 1992, 171–179.

44. Nicolò Marchetti (ed.), *Karkemish. An Ancient Capital on the Euphrates*, Bologna 2014. Various new epigraphic finds from Karkamiš have been published in *Orientalia* 83.2, 2014, 143–206.

45. J. David Hawkins, "Cilicia, the Amuq, and Aleppo: New Light in a Dark Age." *Near Eastern Archaeology* 72, 2009, 164–173; Gershon Galil, "A Concise History of Palistin/Patin/Unqi/'mq in the 11th–9th Centuries BC", *Semitica* 56, 2014, 75–104; Mark Weeden, "After the Hittites: The Kingdoms of Karkamish and Palistin in Northern Syria," *Bulletin of the Institute of Classical Studies* 56/2, 2015, 1–20; Belkis Dinçol, Ali Dinçol, J. David Hawkins, Hasan Pekerwith, A. Öztan, and O. Çelik, "Two New Inscribed Storm-God Stelae from Arsuz (İskenderun) ARSUZ 1 and 2," *AnSt* 65, 2015, 59–77.

46. Not to be confused with the term "Chaldeans," referring to a group of tribes who lived in southern Mesopotamia from the ninth century on.

47. Ivo Hajnal, "'Jungluwisch'—Eine Bestandsaufnahme," in: [418] Giorgieri et al. (eds.), *Licia e Lidia*, 2003, 187–205.

48. See Frank Kolb, "Aspekte der Akkulturation in Lykien in archaischer und klassischer Zeit," in: [418] Giorgieri et al. (eds.), *Licia e Lidia*, 2003, 207–237, esp. 207–209.

49. Craig Melchert, "Carian," in: R. D. Woodard (ed.), *The Cambridge Encyclopedia of the World's Ancient Languages*, 2004, 609 ff.

50. Claude Brixhe, "Du paléo- au néo-phrygien," *CRAI* 1993, 323–344. On Old Phrygian: Claude Brixhe and Michel Lejeune, *Corpus des inscriptions paléo-phrygiennes*, Paris 1984; Supplement I, *Kadmos* 41, 2002, 1102; Claude Brixhe and Taciser Tüfekçi Sivas, "Exploration de l'ouest de la Phrygie: Nouveau documents paléo-phrygiens, *Kadmos* 42, 2004, 65–76. Distribution map in Brixhe, *CRAI* 2004, 273. On alphabethical script, see p. 132 f.

51. Johannes Scherr, DNP s. v. Midas II. Griechisch-römische Literatur.

52. [402] Frei, *Wagen von Gordion*, 1972.

53. [253] Naumann, *Ikonographie,* 1983; [435] Roller, *God the Mother*, 1999.

54. Walter Burkert, "Von Ullikummi zum Kaukasus," in: M. L. Gemelli Marciano (ed.), *Kleine Schriften II: Orientalia*, Göttingen 2003, 87–95.

55. Patrick Taylor, "The GALA and the Gallos," in: [373] Collins, Bachvarova, and Rutherford (eds.), *Anatolian Interfaces*, 2008, 173–180.

56. Jan Bouzek, "Cimmerians and Scythians in Anatolia," in: C. Işik, Ç. Öğün, and B. Varkıvanç (eds.), *Calbis: Baki Öğün'e Armağan, Mélanges offerts à Baki Öğün*, Ankara 2007, 29–38.

57. Roberto Gusmani, *Lydisches Wörterbuch*, Heidelberg 1964, with a supplement 1980–86. Roberto Gusmani and Yilmaz Akkan, "Bericht über einen lydischen Neufund aus dem Kaystrostal," *Kadmos* 43, 2004, 139–150. A newly found Lydian inscription from Aphrodisias in Caria will be published by Angelos Chaniotis and Felipe Rojas.

58. Mordechai Cogan and Hayim Tadmor, "Gyges and Ashurbanipal," *Orientalia* 46, 1977, 65–85, for translation, see p. 73.

59. Herodotus 1, 7; cf. [451] Burkert, *Lydia*, 2001, 229 f.

60. Christopher Ratté, "The 'Pyramid Tomb' at Sardis," *IstMitt* 42, 1992, 135–161.

61. [16] Mitchell, *Archaeological Reports* no. 45 (1998/1989), 146.

62. Claude Brixhe and Geoffrey D. Summers, "Les inscriptions phrygiennes de Kerkenes Dağ," *Kadmos* 45, 2006, 93–135.

63. Burkert, op. cit., 224.

64. Georges Le Rider, *La naissance de la monnaie*, Paris 2001.

65. Stephan Karwiese, *Die Münzprägung von Ephesos*, Vienna 1995, 118 ff.

66. Robert W. Wallace, "The Origin of Electrum Coinage," *AJA* 91, 1987, 385–397.

67. Andrew Ramage, "King Croesus' Gold and the Coinage of Lydia," in: [418] Giorgieri et al. (eds.), *Licia e Lidia*, 2003, 285–290.

68. Irene S. Lemos, "The Migrations to the West Coast of Asia Minor: Tradition and Archaeology," in: [372] Cobet et al. (eds.), *Frühes Ionien*, 2007, 713–727; cf. Wolf-Dietrich Niemeier, "Westkleinasien und Ägäis von den Anfängen bis zur ionischen Wanderung: Topographie, Geschichte und Beziehungen nach dem archäologischen Befund und den hethitischen Quellen," ibid. 87–90. Alexander Herda, "Karkiša – Karien und die sogenannte Ionische Migration," in: [426a] Rumscheid (ed.), *Die Karer und die Anderen*, 2009, 27–108.

69. On ceramics (Aeolian Gray Ware): Dieter Hertel, "Der aiolische Siedlungsraum (Aiolis) am Übergang von der Bronze- zur Eisenzeit," in: [372] Cobet et al. (eds.), *Frühes Ionien*, 2007, 97–122. On Smyrna's architecture: Meral Akurgal, "Hellenic Architecture in Smyrna 650–546 B.C.," ibid., 125–136.

70. A building in Klazomenai may be even older: N. Aytaçlar, "The Early Iron Age at Klazomenai," in: A. Moustaka et al. (eds.), *Klazomenai, Teos and Abdera. Metropolis and Colony, Proceedings of the International Symposium held at the Archaeological Museum of Abdera, 20-21 October 2001*, 2004, 17–41.

71. Roland Martin, "L'architecture archaïque de Thasos et l'Anatolie," *Mélanges Mansel*, vol. I, Ankara 1974, 451–465.

72. [483] Boardman, *Perser*, 2003, 53 with n. 80.

73. The theory that in the time of Alexander the settlement was transferred from Datça to the tip of the peninsula goes back to George E. Bean and John M. Cook, "The Carian Coast," *BSA* 47, 1952, 171–212; cf. *BSA* 52, 1957, esp. 85–87. See now Alain Bresson, "Knidos: Topography for a Battle," in: [426b] Van Bremen and Carbon, Karia, 2010, 435–451.

74. Hesiod, Fr. 10a line 23 Merkelbach and West; Herodotus 1, 145. 7, 94; Strabo 8, 7, 1; Pausanias 7, 1, 1–6.

75. Alexander Herda, "Panionion-Melia, Mykalessos-Mykale, Perseus und Medusa," *Ist Mitt* 56, 2006, esp. 72–79.

76. Hans Lohmann, "Milet und die Milesia," in: [247] Kolb (ed.), *Chora*, 2004, 325–360, esp. 338–346.

77. Klaus Tuchelt, "Überlegungen zum archaischen Didyma," in: [372] Cobet et al. (eds.), *Frühes Ionien*, 2007, 393–412.

78. Ulrich von Wilamowitz-Moellendorff, "Über die ionische Wanderung," SBBerlin 1906, 59–79.

79. Hans Lohmann, "Melia, das Panionion und der Kult des Poseidon Helikonios" in: [470] Schwertheim and Winter (eds.), *Ionien*, 2005, 57–91. A detailed argument against Lohmann's thesis is found in Alexander Herda, "Panionion-Melia, Mykalessos-Mykale, Perseus und Medusa," *IstMitt* 56, 2006, 43–102.

80. [484] Carusi, *Isole e peree*, 2003.

81. Klaus Tuchelt, "Überlegungen zum archaischen Didyma," in: [372] Cobet et al. (eds.), *Frühes Ionien*, 2007, 393–412.

82. Tuchelt's doubts on this point, loc. cit., 408 and his explanation of this dedication by referring to Greek colonists in Egypt have not been accepted.

83. Michael Weißl, "Grundzüge der Bau- und Schichtenfolge im Artemision von Ephesos," *ÖJh* 71, 2002, 313–346.

84. Gérard Seiterle, "Artemis—Die Große Göttin von Ephesos," *AW* 10, 3, 1979, 3 ff.; on the various interpretations proposed, see [240] Fleischer, *Artemis* 1973, esp. 74–88.

85. Fleischer, loc. cit.

86. Peter Frei, "Konflikt und Synkretismus: Leto und die Frösche," in: *Le temple, lieu de conflit, Actes du colloque de Cartigny 1988*, Louvain 1995, 95–102.

87. Wolf-Dietrich Niemeier, "Ḫattusas Beziehungen zu West-Kleinasien und dem Mykenischen Griechenland (Aḫḫiyawa)," in: *Ḫattuša-Boğazköy. Das Hethiterreich im Spannungsfeld des Alten Orients. 6. Internationales Colloquium der Deutschen Orient-Gesellschaft 22.–24. März 2006*, Wiesbaden 2008, 298 with n. 67, mentions the recently proven Bronze Age settlement of the acropolis of Perge and the Mycenaean pottery among the discoveries made there. But whether these can prove a settlement by Mycenaean Greeks remains an open question. For a brief discussion, see Wolfram Martini, *Die Akropolis von Perge in Pamphylien. Vom Siedlungsplatz zur Akropolis, Sitzungsberichte der Wissenschaftlichen Gesellschaft an der Johann Wolfgang Goethe-Universität Frankfurt*, Stuttgart 2010 (information kindly provided by W. Martini).

88. Paul G. Mosca and James Russell, "Phoenician Inscription from Cebel Ihres Dağı in Rough Cilicia," *EpigrAnat* 9, 1987, 1–21. Wolfgang Röllig, "Zur phönizischen Inschrift von Cebel Ires Dağı," in: C. Roche (ed.), *D'Ougarit à Jérusalem: recueil d'études épigraphiques et archéologiques offert à Pierre Bordreuil*, Paris 2008, 51–56.

89. Mustafa Adak, "Die dorische und äolische Kolonisation des lykisch-pamphylischen Grenzraumes im Lichte der Epigraphik und der historischen Geographie," in: Ch. Schuler (ed.), *Griechische Epigraphik in Lykien. Eine Zwischenbilanz. Akten des Kolloquiums vom 24.–26. 2. 2005 in München*, Vienna 2007, 41–49.

90. Norbert Oettinger, "The Seer Mopsos as a Historical Figure," in: [373] Collins, Bachvarova, and Rutherford (eds.), *Anatolian Interfaces*, 2008, 63–66. Max Gander, "Aḫḫiyawa–Ḫiyawa–Que: Gibt es Evidenz für die Anwesenheit von Griechen in Kilikien am Übergang von der Bronze- zur Eisenzeit?," *SMEA* 54, 2012, 281–309, see esp. 298 note 112.

91. Cf. Jean-Marie Bertrand, "À propos des paroikoi dans les cités d'Asie Mineure," in: P. Fröhlich and C. Müller (eds.), *Citoyenneté et participation à la basse époque hellénistique*, Geneva 2005, 39–49.

92. Hans Lauter, "Die beiden älteren Tyrannenpaläste in Larisa am Hermos," *BJb* 175, 1975, 33–57.

93. Dirk Steurnagel, "Ein spätarchaischer Sarkophag aus Gümüşçay im Museum von

Çanakkale. Ikonographische Beobachtungen," in: R. Rolle, K. Schmidt, and R. Docter (eds.), *Archäologische Studien in Kontaktzonen der antiken Welt*, Hamburg 1998, 165–177.

94. Loretana de Libero, *Die archaische Tyrannis*, Stuttgart 1996, esp. 249 ff., with the important sources for the following.

95. [460] Ehrhardt, *Milet*, 1983. cf. [372] Cobet et al. (eds.), *Frühes Ionien*, 2007, Part 4: *Ionien am Pontos*, 465 ff.

96. Margret K. Nollé, "Koloniale und mythische Verwandtschaften der Stadt Amisos in Pontos," in: [223] Nollé, Overbeck, and Weiß (eds.), *Münzprägung*, 1997, 157–164.

97. Gunnar Heinsohn, *Söhne und Weltmacht*, fifth ed., Zürich 2006.

98. "The Date of the Iliad," *MusHelv* 52, 1995, 203. More recently, cf. Dieter Hertel, "Zur Datierung der homerischen Epen," in: R. Biering et al. (eds.), *Maiandros*, FS von Graeve, Munich 2006, 133–140.

99. The fundamental studies are Walter Burkert, *The Orientalizing Revolution*, Cambridge (MA) 1992; Martin West, *The East Face of Helicon. West Asiatic Elements in Greek Poetry and Myth*, Oxford 1997. Cf. Mary R. Bachvarova, "The Poet's Point of View and the Prehistory of the Iliad," in: [373] Collins, Bachvarova, and Rutherford (eds.), *Anatolian Interfaces*, 2008, 93–106.

100. Ernst Loewy, "Typenwanderung," *ÖJh* 12, 1909, 243–304; Santo Mazzarino, *Fra oriente e occidente. Ricerche di storia greca archaica*, Florence 1947.

101. Emilio Peruzzi, *Civiltà greca nel Lazio preromana*, Florence 1998.

102. For the date of the oldest Phrygian inscriptions from Gordion see Keith DeVries, Textual Evidence and the Destruction Level, in: C. B. Rose and G. Darbyshire, *The New Chronology of Iron-Age Gordion,* Philadelphia 2011, 49–57. The significance of another (possibly earlier) doublet of the Semitic sign for the *jod* and its appearance for /i/ and /j/ in the Phrygian alphabet (it also occurs in vase inscriptions in an indigenous language on the coast of Thrace and on Samothrace, c. sixth century BCE) remains unclear. Cf. Claude Brixhe, "Nouvelle chronologie anatolienne et date d'élaboration des alphabets grec et phrygien," *CRAI* 2004, 271–289; id., "Zôné et Samothrace: Lueurs sur la langue Thrace et nouveau chapitre de la grammaire comparée?" *CRAI* 2006, 121–146; id., "Les alphabets du Fayoum," I 46, 2007, 15–38.

103. Joachim Latacz, "Frühgriechische Epik und Lyrik in Ionien," in: [372] Cobet et al., *Frühes Ionien*, 2007, 681–700; Ernst Heitsch, "Ionien und die Anfänge der griechischen Philosophie," ibid. 701–712.

104. Latacz, op. cit., 695.

105. Christoph Riedweg, *Pythagoras*, Munich 2002, 120–128.

106. Alasdair Livingstone, *Mystical and Mythological Explanatory Works of Assyrian and Babylonian Scholars*, Oxford 1986, 71.

107. Walter Burkert, "Iranisches bei Anaximandros," in: M. L. Gemelli Marciano (ed.), *Kleine Schriften II: Orientalia*, Göttingen 2003, 195.

108. Cf. Walter Marg, "Herodot über die Folgen von Salamis," *Hermes* 81, 1953, 196–210; Kenneth H. Waters, "The Purpose of Dramatisation in Herodotus," *Historia* 15, 1966, 157–171: Papyrus with the remains of what was probably a Hellenistic Gyges tragedy elaborated on the basis of Herodotus.

Chapter 5. The Western Persian Empire and the World of the Greeks in Asia Minor (547/546 to 333 BCE)

1. Peter Herrmann, "Teos und Abdera im 5. Jahrhundert v. Chr. Ein neues Fragment der Teiorum Dirae," *Chiron* 11, 1981, 1–30.

2. Franz Georg Maier, *Nordost-Tor und persische Belagerungsrampe in Alt-Paphos*, Mainz 2008, 63 ff.

3. Klaus Tuchelt, "Überlegungen zum archaischen Didyma," in: [372] Cobet et al. (eds.), *Frühes Ionien*, 2007, 410.

4. Otto Lendle, *Kommentar zu Xenophons Anabasis* (Books 1–7), Darmstadt 1995.

5. [409] Lehmann-Haupt, *Armenien*, 1910, 266 f.

6. *Buch der Lieder*, "Die Nordsee," second cycle, I, "Meergruß." Trans. Louis Untermeyer, in: *Poems of Heinrich Heine*, New York: Harcourt Brace, 1916.

7. K. v. Malottki and H. W. Wiechmann, *Deutsche Medizinische Wochenschrift* 121, 1996, 936–938; cf. Erich Keller, ibid. 122, 1997, 1610 f.

8. Hermann Bengtson, *Griechische Geschichte*, Munich, fourth ed., 1969, 267.

9. Friedrich K. Dörner and John H. Young, "Sculpture and Inscription Catalogue," in: D. H. Sanders (ed.), *Nemrud Daği. The Hierothesion of Antiochus I of Commagene, 1,* Winona Lake, IN 1996, 261 ff., 293 ff.

10. Cf. [487] Briant, *Transition*, 2006, 328–330, who accords the phenomenon less importance than earlier researchers. Cf. id., "Les Iraniens d'Asie Mineure après la chute de l'empire achéménide," *DialHistAnc* 11, 1985, 167–195.

11. Chrstian Marek, "Political Institutions and the Lycian and Carian Language in the Process of Hellenization between the Achaemenids and the Early Diadochs," in: E. Stavrianopoulou (ed.), *Shifting Social Imaginaries in the Hellenistic Period. Narrations, Practices, and Images*, Leiden and Boston 2013, 233–251.

12. Stephen Mitchell, "Requisitioned Transport in the Roman Empire: A New Inscription from Pisidia," *JRS* 66, 1976, 121 f.

13. Rüdiger Schmitt, "Der Titel 'Satrap,'" in: A. Morpurgo Davies and W. Meid (eds.), *Studies in Greek, Italic, and Indo-European Linguistics*, Innsbruck 1976, 373–390. On the function of satraps, cf. Hilmar Klinkott, *Der Satrap. Ein achaimenidischer Amtsträger und seine Handlungsspielräume*, Frankfurt an der Oder 2005.

14. Autophradates, the satrap of Sparda in the fourth century BCE: χñtawata wataprddatehe (TAM I 61).

15. [476] Jacobs, *Satrapienverwaltung*, 1984, 94.

16. Christian Marek, "Zum Charakter der Hekatomnidenherrschaft im Kleinasien des 4. Jh. v. Chr.," in: [488b] Winter and Zimmermann, *Satrapen und Dynasten*, 2015, 1–20; Marek, "Local Administration: Asia Minor," in: B. Jacobs and R. Rollinger (eds.), *A Companion to the Achaemenid Persian Empire*, Oxford (in print).

17. Gerd Gropp, "Saßen die Skudra wirklich in Thrakien? Ein Problem der Satrapienverteilung in Kleinasien," in: [481] Bakır et al. (eds.), *Achaemenid Anatolia*, 2001, 37–42.

18. A people inhabiting the northern part of the Lycian peninsula.

19. These last two names refer to one and the same people related to the Lydians, who settled in northern Lycia, being the Milyans' western neighbors.

20. On the coast of the Black Sea, in the hinterland of Herakleia Pontike.

21. The name "Syrians" refers to the Cappadocians around Mazaka.

22. Richard T. Hallock (ed.), *Persepolis Fortification Tablets*. University of Chicago Oriental Institute Publications vol. XCII, Chicago 1969, 396 PF 1404.

23. Cf., esp. for the fourth century, [480] Debord, *Asie Mineure*, 1999; [476] Jacobs, *Satrapienverwaltung*, 1984, esp. 119–123.

24. The sources are found in Johannes Engels, *Hermias*, DNP [1]. Cf. Peter Green, "Politics, Philosophy, and Propaganda. Hermias of Atarneus and His Friendship with Aristotle," in:

W. Heckel and L. A. Tritle (eds.), *Crossroads of History: The Age of Alexander*, Claremont, CA 2003, 29–46.

25. Nekriman Olçay and Otto Mørkholm, "The Coin Hoard from Podalia," *NumChron* ser. 7.10, 1971, 1–29; cf. Frank Kolb and Werner Tietz, "Zagaba: Münzprägung und politische Geographie in Zentrallykien," *Chiron* 31, 2001, 347–416.

26. According to Michael Wörrle, "Epigraphische Forschungen zur Geschichte Lykiens IV," *Chiron* 21, 1991, 211, at this time eastern and western Lycia were unified politically.

27. [416] Keen, *Lycia*, 1998.

28. Hilmar Klinkott, "Zur politischen Akkulturation unter den Achaimeniden," in: [295] Blum et al. (eds.), *Brückenland*, 2002, 173–204.

29. The fact that in the first century BCE it belonged for a time to the Armenian empire of Tigranes the Great is irrelevant.

30. On tribute: [479] Briant, *Empire Perse*, 1996, 399–433. Raymond Descat, "Mnésimachos, Hérodote et le système tributaire achéménide," *REA* 87, 1985, 97–112. On the Mnesimachos inscription, cf. below, p. 191 f.

31. Discussion in Briant, op. cit., 430–433. Cf. esp. [499] Schuler, *Ländliche Siedlungen*, 1998, 137–145.

32. Skepticism has recently been expressed by Pierre Briant, "Histoire et archéologie d'une texte. La lettre de Darius à Gadatas entre Perses, Grecs et Romains," in: [418] Giorgieri et al. (eds.), *Licia e Lidia*, 2003, 107–144, with a detailed discussion of the research. Cf. Robin Lane Fox, "The Letter to Gadatas," in: G. E. Malouchou and A. P. Matthaiou (eds.), *Eis mnemen W. G. Forrest*, Athens 2006, 149–171.

33. Cf. Pierre Briant, "Dons de terres et de villes: l'Asie Mineure dans le contexte achéménide," *REA* 87, 1985, 53–71.

34. However, in the Hellenistic period this did not generally hold true for the *ge en dorea*. Owners had to pay royal taxes on their revenues.

35. [499] Schuler, *Ländliche Siedlungen*, 1998, 139, who refers esp. to Thucydides 8, 18. 37. 58.

36. Raymond Descat, "Qu'est-ce que l'économie royale?" In: F. Prost (ed.), *L'orient méditerranéen de la mort d'Alexandre aux campagnes de Pompée*, Rennes 2003, 149–168.

37. Hasan Malay, "A Royal Document from Aigai in Aiolis," *GrRomByzSt* 24, 1983, 349–353.

38. Leo Mildenberg, "Über das Münzwesen im Reich der Achämeniden," *AMI* 26, 1993, 55–79.

39. On the Lycian coin legends, see [211] Mørkholm and Neumann, *Münzlegenden*, 1978.

40. Oliver Casabonne (ed.), "Mécanismes et innovations monétaires dans l'Anatolie achéménide." *Numismatique et histoire, Actes de la table ronde internationale, Istanbul 22–23 mai 1997*, Istanbul 2000.

41. Eduard Meyer, *Geschichte des Altertums* IV, 1, third ed., Stuttgart 1939, 88.

42. Mary Boyce, *A History of Zoroastrianism*, [2] HdO VIII 1, 2, 2A, vol. 1, Leiden 1975, 192 ff. (Ahura Mazdā), vol. 2, Leiden 1982, esp. 119 (Darius and Ahura Mazdā); 28 (Mithras).

43. Boyce, op. cit., vol. 2, 15 (Ahura Mazdā); 18, 245 f. (Māh); 29–31, and cf. Mary Boyce and Frantz Grenet, ibid., vol. 3, 203 ff. (Anāhitā). Marijana Ricl, "The Cult of the Iranian Goddess Anāhitā in Anatolia before and after Alexander," *Živa Antika* 52, 2002, 197–210. On the association between Artemis and Anāhitā, see also: Lâtife Summerer, "Die Göttin am Skylax. Ein monumentales hellenistisches Felsrelief in Nordanatolien," *AA* 2006, 1, 17–30,

with further literature. Summerer interprets the monumental rock relief discovered in 1985 at the Çekerek Suyu, the ancient Skylax in Pontos, which shows a standing goddess, as a Hellenistic representation of Anāhitā. She also identifies as Anāhitā the bronze head excavated in Satala that is now in the British Museum.

44. Louis Robert, "Monnaies grecques de l'époque impériale," *RNum* 18, 1976, 25–56; Ricl, loc. cit.

45. Peter Frei, in: P. Frei and K. Koch, *Reichsidee und Reichsorganisation im Perserreich*, second ed., Fribourg-Göttingen 1996, 90–96. [152] de Hoz, *Kulte*, 1999, 77, thinks that the Baradateo on the stone at Sardeis is probably only a misspelling of Bagadateo. Cf. Stephen Mitchell, "Iranian Names and the Presence of Persians in the Religious Sanctuaries of Asia Minor," in: E. Matthews (ed.), *Old and New Worlds in Greek Onomastics*, Oxford 2007, 151–171, esp. 157 ff.: the Bagadates in Sardeis was, like the Bagadates in Amyzon, a temple guardian comparable to the *bagabuxša* in Ephesos. On the Baradates inscription, see [487] Briant, *Transition*, 2006, 329.

46. [468] Burkert, *Griechen und Orient*, 2003, esp. 118 f.

47. Adrian D.H. Bivar, "Magians and Zoroastrians. The Religions of the Iranians in Anatolia," in: [481] Bakır et al. (eds.), *Achaemenid Anatolia*, 2001, 91–99; Oric P.V. L'vov-Basirov, "Achaemenian Funerary Practices in Western Asia Minor," ibid. 101–107.

48. Margret Nollé, *Denkmäler vom Satrapensitz Daskyleion. Studien zur graeco-persischen Kunst*, Berlin 1992; André Lemaire, "Les inscriptions araméennes de Daskyleion," in: [481] Bakır et al. (eds.), *Achaemenid Anatolia*, 2001, 21–35.

49. Serra Durugönül, "Grabstele eines 'Adligen' aus Paphlagonien der dritten Satrapie," *AMS* 12, 1994, 1–14.

50. Lâtife Summerer, "Greeks and Natives on the Southern Black Sea Coast in Antiquity," in: G. Erkut and St. Mitchell (eds.), *The Black Sea. Past, Present and Future*, Ankara 2007, 27–36.

51. [252] von Gall, *Felsgräber*, 1966; F. Eray Dökü, *Paphlagonia bölgesi kaya mezarları ve kaya tapınakları*, Antalya 2008; Christian Marek, "Paphlagonie et Pont. Les tombes rupestres préromaines du nord de l'Anatolie," *Dossiers d'archéologie & sciences des origines*, no. 328, Juli/August 2008, 62–71; Lâtife Summerer and Alexander von Kienlin, "Achaemenid Impact in Paphlagonia: Rupestral Tombs in the Amnias Valley," in: J. Nieling and E. Rehm, *Achaemenid Impact in the Black Sea. Communication of Powers*, Aarhus, Denmark 2010, 195–221.

52. Lâtife Summerer, "From Tatarlı to Munich: The Recovery of a Painted Wooden Tomb Chamber in Phrygia," in: O. Casabonne et al. (eds.), *The Achaemenid Impact on Local Population and Cultures in Anatolia. Proceedings of the International Workshop Held in Istanbul (May 2005)*, Istanbul 2007, 131–158; id., "Picturing Persian Victory: The Painted Battle Scene on the Munich Wood," in: *AncCivScytSib* 13, 2007, 3–30. For Karaburun see Machteld J. Mellink, *Kizilbel: An Archaic Painted Tomb Chamber in Northern Lycia*, Bryn Mawr, PA 1998.

53. See: http://archive.archaeology.org/1101/topten/turkey.html. See also: http://whc.unesco.org/en/tentativelists/5729/, and for the inscription: http://www.hurriyetdailynews.com/longest-poem-of-classical-era-unearthed-in-western-turkey.aspx?pageID=238&nID=73190&NewsCatID=375.

54. [417] Schweyer, *Lyciens*, 2002; cf. Frank Kolb, "Aspekte der Akkulturation in Lykien in archaischer und klassischer Zeit," in: [418] Giorgieri et al. (eds.), *Licia e Lidia*, Rome 2003, 207–237; [249a] Mühlbauer, *Grabarchitektur*, 2007.

55. Marc Domingo Gygax and Werner Tietz, "'He who of all mankind set up the most

numerous trophies to Zeus.' The Inscribed Pillar of Xanthos Reconsidered," *AnSt* 55, 2005, 89–98, see the monument as having been worked in successive stages, so that the 138-line inscription on the south and east sides was not cut into the stone at the same time as the 105-line text on the west side.

56. Michael Wörrle, "Leben und Sterben wie ein Fürst," *Chiron* 28, 1998, 77–83. Sardanapallos: Strabon 14, 5, 9; Arrian, *An.* 2, 5, 2–4; Athenaios 12, 530b; Walter Burkert, "Sardanapal zwischen Mythos und Realität: Das Grab in Kilikien," in: U. Dill and Ch. Walde (eds.), *Antike Mythen*, Berlin and New York 2009, 502–515. On the Roman Imperial period, cf. the collection of evidence in [146] MS I 252, with additional literature; also [549] Marek, *Pontus et Bithynia*, 2003, 141; CIG Add. et Corr. 3846 l (Aizanoi).

57. Tomris Bakır, "Die Satrapie in Daskyleion," in: [481] id. et al. (eds.), *Achaemenid Anatolia*, 2001, 169–180. On the *paradeisos* cf. [499] Schuler, *Ländliche Siedlungen*, 1998, 123 ff.

58. Cf. [480] Debord, *Asie Mineure*, 1999, 164 f.

59. Frank Kolb, "Aspekte der Akkulturation in Lykien in archaischer und klassischer Zeit," in: [418] Giorgieri et al. (eds.), *Licia e Lidia*, 2003, 207–237; Thomas Marksteiner, "Städtische Strukturen im vorhellenistischen Lykien," in: M. H. Hansen (ed.), *A Comparative Study of Six City-State Cultures*, Copenhagen 2002, 57–72; Wolfgang Wurster, "Dynast ohne Palast. Überlegungen zum Wohnbereich lykischer Feudalherren," in: [415] Borchhardt and Dobesch (eds.), *Lykien-Symposion*, vol. 2, 1993, 7–30; id. "Antike Siedlungen in Lykien. Vorbericht über ein Survey-Unternehmen im Sommer 1974," *AA* 1976, 23–49; id., "Wohnbereiche antiker Siedlungen in Lykien," in: *Bericht über die 29. Tagung für Ausgrabungswissenschaft und Bauforschung vom 26.–30. Mai 1976 in Köln*, Karlsruhe 1978, 21–24.

60. Thomas Marksteiner, "Stadtdarstellungen und lykische Städte," in: Borchhardt and Dobesch (ed.), op. cit., 31–38.

61. A. Thomsen, *Die lykische Dynastensiedlung auf dem Avşar-Tepesi*, Bonn 2001.

62. Here I will not go into the question of the organization of the empire and the controversial interpretations of coinage, which would take us far beyound the bounds of Asia Minor. See esp. [487] Briant, *Transition*, 2006, esp. 312–317.

63. Pierre Briant, *Alexandre le Grand. De la Grèce à l'Inde*, second ed., Paris 2005, 126. Criticized by Hans-Ulrich Wiemer, "Alexander—der letzte Achaimenide? Eroberungspolitik, lokale Eliten und altorientalische Traditionen im Jahr 323," *HZ* 284, 2007, 283–309.

64. Susan Sherwin-White, "Ancient Archives: The Edict of Alexander to Priene, a Reappraisal," *JHS* 105, 1985, 69–89; [480] Debord, *Asie Mineure*, 1999, 439–445; cf. the discussion in [488] Briant, *Transition*, 2006, 330–336.

65. Ernst Badian, "Alexander and the Greeks of Asia," in: *Ancient Society and Institutions. Studies Presented to V. Ehrenberg*, Oxford 1966, 37–69.

66. Andrew J. Heisserer, *Alexander the Great and the Greeks*, Norman, OK 1981; Michele Faraguna, "Alexander and the Greeks," in: J. Roisman (ed.), *Brill's Companion to Alexander the Great*, Leiden 2003, 99–130; Krzysztof Nawotka, "Freedom of Greek Cities in Asia Minor in the Age of Alexander the Great," *Klio* 85, 2003, 15–41.

67. Arrian, *An.* 2, 4, 2; in Curtius 3, 4, 1 the manuscripts have *Abhistamenes*.

68. [480] Debord, *Asie Mineure*, 1999, 114 with literature in n. 242. However, this coinage does not allow us to infer that there was resistance on the part of forces loyal to the Persians.

69. In Gaziura? Cf. the coins with the Aramaic legend "Ariorat" and an image of a god with the inscription "Baal-Gazur," [199] Head, HN² 749.

70. [505] Wiemer, *Alexander*, 2005, 101.

71. On the debate regarding the continuity of Achaemenid institutions vs. a change with an *imperium macedonicum*, see [487] Briant, *Transition*, 2006, 336–342, with further literature.

Chapter 6. Monarchies, Vassals, and Cities from Alexander's Empire to the Pax Romana (331 BCE to 31 BCE)

1. To the papyrus discovered 1932 containing a fragment of Arrian's *History of the Diadochi* (PSI XII 1284) a palimpsest discovered 1977 in Göteborg, Sweden, must be added. See Boris Dreyer, "Zum ersten Diadochenkrieg. Der Göteborger Arrian Palimpsest," *ZPE* 125, 1999, 39-60. Both texts narrate in detail events in Asia Minor ca. 320/319 BCE.

2. [510] Kuhrt and Sherwin-White, *Seleucid Empire*, 1993, share the view that the empire was strong.

3. [511] Kobes, *Könige*, 1996.

4. Diodorus 18, 3; Curtius 10, 10, 1–6; Dexippos, *FGrHist* 100 F 8; Arrian, *FGrHist* 156 F 1. R. Malcolm Errington, "From Babylon to Triparadeisos," *JHS* 90, 1970, 49–77; id., "Diodorus Siculus and the Chronology of the Early Diadochoi, 320–311 B. C.," *Hermes* 105, 1977, 478–504; Ludwig Schober, *Untersuchungen zur Geschichte Babyloniens und der Oberen Satrapien von 323–303 v. Chr.*, Frankfurt am Main and Bern 1981; Hilmar Klinkott, *Die Satrapienregister der Alexander- und Diadochenzeit*, Stuttgart 2000.

5. On Philoxenos, see Helmut Müller's recent study, "Hemiolios. Eumenes II, Toriaion und die Finanzorganisation des Alexanderreiches," *Chiron* 35, 2005, 364 ff.

6. [509] Billows, *Antigonos*, 1990, 57.

7. On Eumenes: Christoph Schäfer, *Eumenes von Kardia und der Kampf um die Macht im Alexanderreich*, Frankfurt/M. 2002; Edward M. Anson, *Eumenes of Cardia. A Greek among Macedonians*, Leiden 2004.

8. Pierre Briant, *Antigone le Borgne. Les débuts de sa carrière et les problèmes de l'assemblée macédonienne*, Paris 1973, 157.

9. Brian Bosworth, "Plutarch's Eumenes 71–78," *Chiron* 22, 1992, 55–81.

10. The location given in Plutarch, *Eum.* 9, 2, cannot be verified on geographic grounds; cf. Wolfgang Orth, *Die Diadochenzeit im Spiegel der historischen Geographie*, Wiesbaden 1993, 56.

11. The relationship between the early Seleucids and the Iranian dynasties in Armenia and Commagene is not clear. Cf. [510] Kuhrt and Sherwin-White, *Seleucid Empire*, 1993, 14 f.

12. Appian's claim that after Ipsos Phrygia belonged to Seleukos (*Syr.* 55 [280]), is now recognized by most scholars to be mistaken.

13. Andreas Victor Walser, *Bauern und Zinsnehmer. Politik, Recht und Wirtschaft im frühhellenistischen Ephesos,* Munich 2008.

14. The neighboring cities of Magnesia on the Maeander and Priene were involved in a quarrel with one another, and Lysimachos intervened on Priene's behalf ([106] OGIS 11–12, [111] Welles, RC 6). However, in the later dispute with Samos over the Batinetis he decided against Priene.

15. See Louis Robert, *Hellenica 2*, 1946, 51–64.

16. Raymond Descat, "La carrière d'Eupolemos, stratège macédonien en Asie Mineure," *REA* 100, 1998, 167–190.

17. See [511] Kobes, *Könige*, 1996, 123–125. According to an older view, all of southern

Asia Minor, including Caria, Lycia, Pamphylia, and Cilicia, is supposed to have belonged to him.

18. Under Philadelphos a *pamphyliarches* is attested (278 BCE); before the Battle of Korupedion Pamphylia may have been ptolemaic: Aspendos received military support from troops under the command of [Phi]lokles and Leonides. [507] Bagnall, *Possessions*, 1976, 111.

19. Sick with love for her, Seleukos's son Antiochos had received Demetrios's daughter Stratonike as his wife.

20. Frédéric Maffre, "La Phrygie hellespontique: étude historique, I–IV," Université de Bordeaux II (unpublished; quoted from [487] Briant, *Transition*, 2006, 350).

21. In the time of the Epigoni, Lycaonia was not part of Greater Phrygia.

22. Hermann Bengtson, *Die Strategie in der hellenistischen Zeit*, 2 vols., Munich 1964.

23. Adolf Hoffmann and Mustafa H. Sayar et al., "Vorbericht zu den in den Jahren 2003 bis 2005 auf dem Berg Karasis (bei Kozan, Adana) und in seiner Umgebung durchgeführten Untersuchungen," *IstMitt* 57, 2007, 365–468.

24. Richard A. Billows, *Kings and Colonists. Aspects of Macedonian Imperialism*, Leiden 1995, 111–145. For a persuasive criticism of Billows's theory of the Macedonian origin of this kind of gift-giving in Asia Minor, see [487] Briant, *Transition*, 2006, 337–342. Cf. also Gerassimos G. Aperghis, *The Seleukid Royal Economy. The Finances and Financial Administration of the Seleukid Empire*, Cambridge 2004, 137–144; Georges Le Rider and François de Callataÿ, *Les Séleucides et les Ptolémées. L'héritage monétaire et financier d'Alexandre le Grand*, Paris 2006, 262–266; Raymond Descat, "Mnésimachos, Hérodote et le système tributaire achéménide," *REA* 87, 1985, 97–112.

25. [602] Robert, *Discours d'ouverture*, 1984, 41: "Dans l'étude de l'histoire sociale de l'époque hellénistique et romaine existent au moins deux fables convenues, deux mystifications. La première est la mort de la cité grecque à Chéronée et, désormais, le rôle exclusif des rois."

26. On the *perioikoi*, see Michael Wörrle, "Epigraphische Forschungen zur Geschichte Lykiens," *Chiron* 8, 1978, 236–242; Marc Domingo Gygax, "Los periecos licios (siglos IV–III a. C.)," *Gerión* 9, 1991, 111–130.

27. See esp. Martin Zimmermann, *Untersuchungen zur historischen Landeskunde Zentrallykiens*, Bonn 1992; Christof Schuler, "Politische Organisationsformen auf dem Territorium von Kyaneai," in: [247] Kolb (ed.), *Chora*, 2004, 87–102.

28. Andreas Victor Walser, "Sympolitien und Siedlungsentwicklung," in: A. Matthaei and M. Zimmermann, *Stadtbilder im Hellenismus*, Berlin 2009, 135–155.

29. [598] Kunnert, *Phylen*, 68. The name of the *phyle* refers to Alexander-Paris of the Trojan legend rather than to Alexander the Great.

30. Christian Habicht, *Gottmenschentum und griechische Städte*, second ed., Munich 1970, 40 f.; for Priene cf. also 38.

31. The fundamental works here are: [497] Cohen, *Hellenistic Settlements*, 1995; Christian Mileta, "Überlegungen zum Charakter und zur Entwicklung der Neuen Poleis im hellenistischen Kleinasien," in. A. Matthaei –M. Zimmermann, *Stadtbilder im Hellenismus*, Berlin 2009, 70–89.

32. Ina Savalli-Lestrade, "Antioche du Pyrame, Mallos et Tarse/Antioche du Kydnos à la lumière de SEG XII 511: histoire, géographie, épigraphie, societé," in: B. Virgilio (ed.), *Studi ellenistici* XIX, Pisa 2006, 119–247.

33. Michael Wörrle, "Der Synoikismos der Latmioi mit den Pidaseis," *Chiron* 33, 2003,

121–143, quoted on p. 133 and 140, with a quotation from Louis Robert, *Études de numismatique grecque*, Paris 1951, 1 ff.

34. Helmut Müller, "Der hellenistische Archiereus," *Chiron* 30, 2000, 519–542.

35. Helmut Müller, "Hemiolios. Eumenes II., Toriaion und die Finanzorganisation des Alexanderreiches," *Chiron* 35, 2005, 355–384. It has not been possible to assign a conclusive meaning to this official's title.

36. A title borne by the ruler of Edessa in the apocryphal correspondence between Jesus and Abgar reproduced five hundred years later by Eusebius (*h. e.* 1, 13).

37. Marcel Launey, *Recherches sur les armées hellénistiques* I, Paris 1949, 335 ff.

38. Pierre Briant, *Rois, tributs et paysans. Recherches sur les formations tributaires du Moyen-Orient ancien*, Paris 1982, 95–135; Fanoula Papazoglou, *Laoi et paroikoi. Recherches sur la structure de la société hellénistique*, Belgrad 1997.

39. [499] Schuler, *Ländliche Siedlungen*, 1998.

40. Alice Bencivenni, "Aristodikides di Asso, Antioco I e la scelta di Ilio," *Simblos* 4, 2004, 159–185.

41. Christof Schuler, "Landwirtschaft und königliche Verwaltung im hellenistischen Kleinasien," *Topoi* Suppl. 6, 2004, 509–543. Cf. Laurent Capdetrey, "Le basilikon et les cités grecques dans le royaume séleucide. Modalités de redistribution de la richesse royale et formes de dépendance des cités," ibid., 105–129. There is also a good summary of the scholarship on this question in Christophe Chandezon, "Les campagnes de l'ouest de l'Asie Mineure à l'époque hellénistique," in: F. Prost (ed.), *L'Orient méditerranéen de la mort d'Alexandre aux campagnes de Pompée. Cités et royaumes à l'époque hellénistique. Actes du colloque international de la SOPHAU, Rennes, 4–6 avril 2003*, Rennes 2003, 193–214. Finally, [487] Briant, *Transition*, 2006, 336–342.

42. With regard to the Diadochus Antigonos, this emerges very clearly from col. II, line 13 of the Mnesimachos inscription, [168] I. Sardeis 1.

43. Léopold Migeotte, "La situation fiscale des cités grecques dans le royaume séleucide," *Topoi* Suppl. 6, 2004, 213–228.

44. According to Memnon *FGrHist* 434 F 1, 10, an additional threat arose for Antiochos from Antigonos Gonatas.

45. For a thorough discussion of all the sources, see Michael Wörrle, "Antiochos I., Achaios der Ältere und die Galater," *Chiron* 5, 1975, 59–87.

46. [515] Strobel, *Galater* I, 1996, 257 f., dates the battle after the First Syrian War, in 268.

47. Stephen Mitchell, "Blucium and Peium. The Galatian Forts of King Deiotarus," *AnSt* 24, 1974, 61–75.

48. In opposition to this view, cf. Christian Habicht, *Gottmenschentum und griechische Städte*, second ed., Munich 1970, 116 f.

49. On this, see Altay Coşkun, "Die tetrarchische Verfassung der Galater und die Neuordnung des Ostens durch Pompeius (Strabon geogr. 12, 5, 1, App., Mithr. 560)" in: H. Heftner and K. Tomaschitz (eds.), *Ad Fontes! FS Dobesch*, Vienna 2004, 687–703.

50. On the Latin and Greek names of the Celts in Asia Minor, see the detailed discussion in [515] Strobel, *Galater* I, 1996, 123 ff.

51. Jeremiah R. Dandoy, Page Selinsky, and Mary M. Voigt, "Celtic Sacrifices in Gordion, Anatolia," *Archaeology* 55, 1, 2002, 44–49; cf. Karl Strobel, "Menschenopfer und Kannibalismus," *Antike Welt* 33, 2002, 487–491.

52. Johannes Nollé, "Die feindlichen Schwestern. Betrachtungen zur Rivalität der pam-

phylischen Städte," in: [43] Dobesch and Rehrenböck (eds.), *Hundert Jahre Kleinasiatische Kommission,* 1993, 304.

53. [507] Bagnall, Possessions, 1976, 93.

54. If the decree of Kaunos ([183] Marek, Kaunos, 2006, no. 4), which is dated to the fifteenth year of a King Antigonos's reign, refers to Gonatas rather than to Monophthalmos and accordingly dates to the year 268 BCE, then we must suppose that Antigonos Gonatas occupied Kaunos and briefly interrupted Ptolemaic sovereignty there.

55. Jakob Seibert, "Ptolemaios I. und Milet," *Chiron* 1, 1971, 159 ff.

56. [167] Milet I 3, 139 C lines 23 ff. Roger S. Bagnall et al. (eds. and trans.), *The Hellenistic Period: Historical Sources in Translation,* Oxford 2004, 42–44, no. 21.

57. He was later killed by mercenaries in Ephesos. On the controversy regarding the chronology of his appearance in Ionia, see Bagnall, op. cit., 170–172.

58. Kostas Buraselis, *Das hellenistische Makedonien und die Ägäis,* Munich 1982, 161.

59. [512] Ma, *Antiochos,* 1999, 42; on the other hand [497] Cohen, *Hellenistic Settlements* 1995, 269, thinks Stratonikeia was founded by Antiochos I.

60. [524] Schalles, *Kulturpolitik,* 1985, 53 ff.; [525] Radt, *Pergamon,* 1999, 162. The statue was probably removed in 20 BCE and replaced by a statue of Augustus, perhaps the bronze model for the famous statue of Prima Porta.

61. For details, see Schalles, op. cit., 53–104; cf. [520] Hansen, *Attalids,* second ed. 1971, 37 f.

62. Michael Wörrle, "Antiochos I., Achaios der Ältere und die Galater," *Chiron* 5, 1975, 77.

63. Werner Huß, *Ägypten in hellenistischer Zeit,* Munich 2001, 364.

64. *IGR* IV 571: inscription at the Temple of Zeus in Aizanoi from the time of Hadrian (125/6 CE); Hadrian returned to the temple and the city the land given "by kings." The reference must be to Attalos I and Prusias I.

65. Peter M. Fraser and George E. Bean, *The Rhodian Peraea and Islands,* Oxford 1954. Cf. [484] Carusi, *Isole e peree,* 2003, 219–224. Hans-Ulrich Wiemer, *Structure and Development of the Rhodian Peraia: Evidence and Models,* in: [462b] van Bremen and Carbon (eds.), *Hellenistic Karia,* 2010, 415-434.

66. On this question: [512] Ma, *Antiochos,* 1999, Appendix 5; Michael Wörrle, "Der Friede zwischen Milet und Magnesia. Methodische Probleme einer communis opinio," *Chiron* 34, 2004, 54 and n. 58; in contrast, [518] Wiemer, *Rhodos,* 2002, 182–184.

67. See Yann Le Bohec, *Antigone Dôsôn, roi de Macédoine,* Nancy 1993, 327–346.

68. [512] Ma, *Antiochos,* 1999, 69.

69. On Miletus's border conflicts with its neighbors at this time, cf. Michael Wörrle, "Der Friede zwischen Milet und Magnesia," *Chiron* 34, 2004, 45–57.

70. Hans-Ulrich Wiemer, "Karien am Vorabend des 2. Makedonischen Krieges," *EpigrAnat* 33, 2001, 1–14.

71. [518] Wiemer, *Rhodos,* 2002, 209. Wiemer is skeptical about the notion that the Romans had seen a threat in the rumors about a division of Egypt between Philip and Antiochos. On this, 208–218.

72. [512] Ma, *Antiochos,* 1999, 308 ff. The fundamental discussion: Peter Herrmann, "Antiochos der Große und Teos," *Anadolu* 9, 1965, 29-159.

73. Sources in [512] Ma, *Antiochos,* 1999, 92.

74. John Briscoe, "Flamininus and Roman Politics 200–189 B. C.," *Latomus* 31, 1972, 22–53.

75. John D. Grainger, "The Campaign of Cn. Manlius Vulso in Asia Minor," *AnSt* 45, 1995, 23–41. For a survey of research, see p. 23 f.

76. On this, see Johannes Nollé, "Die feindlichen Schwestern. Betrachtungen zur Rivalität der pamphylischen Städte," in: [43] Dobesch and Rehrenböck (eds.), *Hundert Jahre Kleinasiatische Kommission*, 1993, 307, with n. 60. Cf. [520] Hansen, *Attalids*, second ed. 1971, 96.

77. Mustafa Adak, "Die rhodische Herrschaft in Lykien und die rechtliche Stellung der Städte Xanthos, Phaselis und Melanippion," *Historia* 56,4, 2007, 251 ff.

78. For a detailed discussion with sources and literature, see [518] Wiemer, *Rhodos*, 2002, 277–288.

79. It makes no sense to distinguish here between a "fief" and a "gift in the proper sense" (see the discussion in Wiemer, op. cit.) with regard to either the older examples or these. Although, contrary to modern conceptions of property law, kings sometimes took back such gifts in cases where they felt they had to punish the donees, the Romans did exactly the same thing as late as 167 BCE, when they declared Lycia free.

80. [517] Behrwald, *Lykischer Bund*, 2000, with sources and literature.

81. Esp. R. Malcolm Errington, "Θεὰ Ῥώμη und römischer Einfluß südlich des Mäanders im 2. Jh. v. Chr.," *Chiron* 17, 1987, 97–118; Behrwald, op. cit., 89–105.

82. Errington, op. cit., 97 ff.; Ronald Mellor, "The Dedications on the Capitoline Hill," *Chiron* 8, 1978, 319–330.

83. Ed. pr., with extensive commentary: Christof Schuler, "Ein Vertrag zwischen Rom und den Lykiern aus Tyberissos," in: Ch. Schuler (ed.), *Griechische Epigraphik in Lykien. Eine Zwischenbilanz. Akten des Kolloquiums vom 24.–26. 2. 2005 in München*, Vienna 2007, 51–79. Another dating is proposed by Frank Kolb, "Lykiens Weg in die römische Provinzordnung," in: N. Ehrhardt and L.-M. Günther (eds.), *Widerstand, Anpassung, Integration. Die griechische Staatenwelt und Rom*, FS Deininger, Stuttgart 2002, 207–221.

84. Hyla A. Troxell, *The Coinage of the Lycian League*, New York 1982. On the Lycian League: Denis Knoepfler, "«Un modèle d'une belle république fédérative»? Montesquieu et le système politique des Lyciens, de la genèse de *l'Esprit des lois* aux découvertes épigraphiques les plus récentes en Asie Mineure méridionale," *Journal des Savants* 2013, 113–154.

85. Cf. [513] Michels, *Kulturtransfer*, 2009.

86. Mario Segre, "Due nuovi testi storici," *RFil* 60, 1932, 446–452.

87. [528] Reinach, *Mithradates*, 1895, 27.

88. The Kimiata fortress was presumably in the country of Kimistene, not far southeast of Eskipazar, cf. [182] Marek, *Stadt, Ära*, 1993, 123 f.

89. See Christian Habicht, *Athen. Die Geschichte der Stadt in hellenistischer Zeit*, Munich 1995, 228.

90. See Andrea Primo, "Il ruolo di Roma nella guerra Pontico-Pergamena del 183–179: Giustino XXXVIII, 6, 1," in: B. Virgilio (ed.), *Studi ellenistici* XIX, Pisa 2006, 617–628.

91. William S. Ferguson, "The Premature Deification of Eumenes II," *ClPhil* 1, 1906, 231–234.

92. Christian Marek, *Die Proxenie*, Frankfurt am Main and Bern 1984, 188 f.

93. [526] Wörrle, *Pergamon*, 2000, 561 f.

94. Helmut Müller, "Königin Stratonike, Tochter des Königs Ariarathes," *Chiron* 21, 1991, 411 ff.

95. F. Koepp, "De gigantomachiae in poeseos artisque monumentis usu," Diss. Bonn

1883, Sententia controversia IX. Cf. [522] Hopp, *Attaliden*, 1977; Helmut Müller, "Königin Stratonike, Tochter des Königs Ariarathes," *Chiron* 21, 1991, 400 ff.

96. [524] Schalles, *Kulturpolitik*, 1985.

97. After 166 BCE: Theun-Mathias Schmidt, "Der späte Beginn und der vorzeitige Abbruch der Arbeiten am Pergamonaltar," in: B. Andreae, G. de Luca, and N. Himmelmann (eds.), *Phyromachos-Probleme*, Mainz 1990, 141–162.

98. Peter Weiß, *Die Ästhetik des Widerstands. Roman*, vol. 1, Frankfurt am Main 1985.

99. Karl Strobel, "Keltensieg und Galatersieg. Die Funktionalisierung eines historischen Phänomens als politischer Mythos der hellenistischen Welt," *AMS* 12, 1994, 67–96.

100. Louis Robert, "Héraclès à Pergame et une épigramme de l'Anthologie XVI 91" *RPhil* 58, 1984, 7–18 = *OMS* VI 457–468.

101. Ampelius 8, 14.

102. Adela Yarbro Collins, "Satan's Throne. Revelations from Revelation," *Biblical Archaeology Review*, May/June 2006, 1–11, with further literature. For another view, [641] Witulski, *Johannesoffenbarung*, 2007, 262 ff.

103. Herodotus 5, 58 indicates that it was not invented in Pergamon, however.

104. Volker Michael Strocka, "Noch einmal zur Bibliothek von Pergamon," *AA* 1, 2000, 155–165.

105. A recent study of the officials of the Attalid royal house is Helmut Müller and Michael Wörrle, "Ein Verein im Hinterland Pergamons zur Zeit Eumenes' II," *Chiron* 32, 2002, 220 ff.

106. Walter Ameling, "Drei Studien zu den Gerichtsbezirken der Provinz Asia in Rep. Zeit," *EpigrAnat* 12, 1988, 17 f.; already conjectured by U. v. Wilamowitz-Moellendorff, cf. Adolf Schulten, *De conventibus civium Romanorum*, Berlin 1892, 129.

107. 106 [497] Cohen, *Hellenistic Settlements*, 1995, 305–308.

108. Ed. pr. Lloyd Jonnes and Marijana Ricl, "A New Royal Inscription from Phrygian Paroreios: Eumenes II Grants Tyriaion the Status of a Polis," *EpigrAnat* 29, 1997, 1 ff. Corrections in Helmut Müller, "Hemiolios. Eumenes II., Toriaion und die Finanzorganisation des Alexanderreiches," *Chiron* 35, 2005, 355–384, esp. 355–357 and n. 3 with references to the literature.

109. Robert, *Carie* 1954, 302; cf. Léopold Migeotte, "La situation fiscale des cités grecques dans le royaume séleucide," *Topoi* Suppl. 6, 2004, 213 with further literature in n. 1–2.

110. Ernst Badian, *Imperialism in the Roman Republic*, second ed., Oxford 1968, 44–59.

111. [533] Kallet-Marx, *Hegemony to Empire*, 1995.

112. Erich S. Gruen, *The Hellenistic World and the Coming of Rome*, Berkeley 1984, esp. II 529–610; [530] Sherwin-White, *East*, 1984.

113. Christian Habicht, "The Seleucids and Their Rivals," in: *CAH* VIII, second ed., Cambridge 1989, 378–380; Christian Mileta, "Eumenes III. und die Sklaven. Neue Überlegungen zum Charakter des Aristonikosaufstandes," *Klio* 80, 1998, 47–65. Cf. in general [527] Daubner, *Bellum Asiaticum*, second ed., 2006.

114. [526] Wörrle, *Pergamon*, 2000, 567: "probably only a short excerpt from a long series of Roman regulations that as a whole must have amounted to a context which, taking into account Kallet-Marx's warnings against anachronistic ideas of dominion, is nonetheless best described as the establishment of a Roman province."

115. [181] Robert, *Claros*, 1989.

116. Claude Eilers, *Roman Patrons of Greek Cities*, Oxford 2002.

117. That is Jean-Louis Ferrary's interpretation in "Le statut des cités libres de l'empire ro-

main à la lumière des inscriptions de Claros," *CRAI* 1991, 567–570. Objections are to be found in Stephen Mitchell, "The Treaty between Rome and Lycia of 46 BC," in: R. Pintaudi (ed.), *Papyri Graecae Schøyen*, Florence 2005, 200 f., but they are not conclusive. Cf. Gustav A. Lehmann, "Römischer Tod in Kolophon/Klaros. Neue Quellen zum Status der freien Polisstaaten an der Westküste Kleinasiens im späten 2. Jh. v. Chr.," *NAWG* 1988, no. 3.

118. [181] Robert, *Claros*, 1989, 86.

119. [430] Nollé, *Side I*, 1993, 65 f. and 164, *TLit* 30 (Eusebius, *Chronicon*, 160th Olympiad).

120. [551] Mitchell, *Administration*, 1999, 17–46; on p. 19, Mitchell gives a table of M. Aquillius's milestones.

121. According to [533] Kallet-Marx, *Hegemony to Empire*, 1995, 250, this happened later, in the 90s of the first century BCE.

122. Christian Marek, "Karien im ersten Mithradatischen Krieg," in: P. Kneissl and V. Losemann (eds.), *Alte Geschichte und Wissenschaftsgeschichte,* FS Christ, Darmstadt 1988, 283–308.

123. V. Flottwell, "Aus dem Stromgebiet des Qyzyl-Yrmaq (Halys)," *Petermanns Geographische Mitteilungen,* Ergänzungsheft 114, 1895, 4.

124. Ernst Badian, *Publicans and Sinners: Private Enterprise in the Service of the Roman Republic,* Ithaca, NY 1983. Cf. Ulrike Malmendier, *Societas publicanorum. Staatliche Wirtschaftsaktivitäten in den Händen privater Unternehmer,* Cologne and Vienna 2002.

125. Norbert Ehrhardt, "Strategien römischer Publicani gegenüber griechischen Städten in der Zeit der Republik," in: N. Ehrhardt and L.-M. Günther (eds.), *Widerstand–Anpassung–Integration. Die griechische Staatenwelt und Rom,* FS Deininger, Stuttgart 2002, 135–153.

126. Thomas Drew-Bear, "Deux décrets hellénistiques d'Asie Mineure," *BCH* 96, 1972, 450 f.

127. Giovanna D. Merola, "Il sistema tributario asiano tra Repubblica e Principato," *Mediterraneo Antico* 4, 2001, 459–472.

128. Cicero, *Att.* 2, 6, 2; *Cicero. Letters to Atticus,* vol. II, trans. D. R. Shackleton Bailey, Cambridge MA and London 1999, 151–153.

129. Jean-Louis Ferrary, "Les gouverneurs des provinces romaines d'Asie Mineure (Asie et Cilicie), depuis l'organisation de la province d'Asie jusqu'à la première guerre de Mithridate (126–88 av. J.-C.)," *Chiron* 30, 2000, 161–193, with a list of the governors up to 88 BCE, based on the current state of research. See also T. Corey Brennan, *The Praetorship in the Roman Republic,* 2 vols., Oxford 2000.

130. Cf. [533] Kallet-Marx, *Hegemony to Empire*, 1995, 120 f.

131. Jean-Louis Ferrary, "La création de la province d'Asie et la présence italienne en Asie Mineure," in: C. Müller and C. Hasenohr (eds.), *Les Italiens dans le monde grec, IIe siècle av. J. C.-Ier siècle ap. J. C. Circulation, activités, intégration, BCH* Supplément 41, 2002, 133–146. Cf. ibid., Alain Bresson, "Italiens et Romains à Rhodes et à Caunos, 147–162" and R. Malcolm Errington, "Aspects of Roman Acculturation in the East under the Republic," in: P. Kneissl and V. Losemann (eds.), *Alte Geschichte und Wissenschaftsgeschichte,* FS Christ, Darmstadt 1988, 140–157.

132. Michael H. Crawford, *Roman Statutes,* London 1996, I no. 12; [162] *IK* Knidos 31 col. III lines 28–37.

133. Bernd Kreiler, "Zur Verwaltung Kilikiens von 102 bis 78 v. Chr.," *Gephyra* 4, 2007,

117–126, opposes the conception traditional in research, namely that Cilicia had been an independent province since 102, arguing that it became one only at the end of the 80s.

134. [551] Mitchell, *Administration*, 1999, 22–29; [561] Haensch, *Capita*, 1997, 307 ff.

135. Cf. [574] Drexhage, *Wirtschaftspolitik*, 2007, 26 f.

136. [506] Meyer, *Pontos*, 1879; [528] Reinach, *Mithradates*, 1895; cf. recently [513] Michels, *Kulturtransfer*, 2009; François de Callataÿ, "Les Mithridates du Pont: un exemple périphérique de rapport entre cités et rois hellénistiques," in: O. Picard et al. (eds.), *Royaumes et cités hellénistiques de 323 à 55 av. J.-C.*, Lassay-les-Châteaux 2003, 218–234; cf. id., "The First Royal Coinages of Pontos (From Mithridates III to Mithridates V)," in: [534] Højte (ed.), *Mithridates*, 2009, 63–94.

137. Robert Fleischer, "Zwei pontische Felsgräber des hohen Hellenismus mit monumentalen Inschriften," *Chiron* 35, 2005, 273–284; id., "The Rock-tombs of the Pontic Kings in Amaseia (Amasya)," in: [534] Højte (ed.), *Mithridates*, 2009, 109–119; cf. Jakob Munk Højte, "The Death and Burial of Mithridates VI," ibid. 121–130.

138. [531] Olshausen and Biller, *Historisch-geographische Aspekte*, 1984, 45–54.

139. Louis Robert in: N. Fıratlı (ed.), *Les stèles funéraires de Byzance gréco-romaine*, Paris 1964, 154 f.

140. The *emporion* Dia, southwest of Herakleia, was not part of the kingdom, but it was briefly occupied by Eupator's troops. In Pergamon the king also had coins minted ([199] Head, HN² 501); cf. also the gold staters minted in Athens under Aristion (ibid. 385).

141. Jakob Munk Højte, "The Administrative Organisation of the Pontic Kingdom," in: [534] Højte (ed.), *Mithridates*, 2009, 95–107.

142. Ivana Savalli-Lestrade, *Les philoi royaux dans l'Asie hellénistique*, Geneva 1998.

143. Cf. Jean-Christophe Couvenhes, "L'armée de Mithridate VI Eupator d'après Plutarque, *Vie de Lucullus*, VII, 4–6," in: [286] Bru, Kirbihler, and Lebreton, *L'Asie Mineure*, 2009, 415 ff.

144. [532] McGing, *Mithridates VI*, 1986.

145. Walter H. Gross, "Die Mithridates-Kapelle auf Delos," *AuA* 4, 1955, 105–117; Patric-Alexander Kreuz, "Monuments for the King: Royal Presence in the Late Hellenistic World of Mithridates VI," in: [534] Højte (ed.), *Mithridates*, 2009, 131–144.

146. Attilio Mastrocinque, "The Antikythera Shipwreck and Sinope's Culture during the Mithridatic Wars," in: [534] Højte (ed.), *Mithridates*, 2009, 313–319; Giovanni Pastore, *Antikythera e i regoli calcolatori*, Rome 2006.

147. A. Sofou, "Strabo and the Historical Geography of Cappadocia," *MedAnt* 8, 2005, 739–766.

148. Who refounded Mazaka as Eusebeia, however, is a matter of debate, cf. [497] Cohen, *Hellenistic Settlements*, 1995, 377.

149. [6] Robert, *Noms*, 1963, 457–523.

150. Ibid., 490–499.

151. Juri G. Vinogradov-Michael Wörrle, "Die Söldner von Phanagoreia," *Chiron* 22, 1992, 159–170.

152. Sviatoslav Dmitriev, "Cappadocian Dynastic Rearrangements on the Eve of the First Mithridatic War," *Historia* 55, 2006, 285–297.

153. Karl-Heinz Ziegler, *Die Beziehungen zwischen Rom und dem Partherreich*, Wiesbaden 1964, 20 ff.

154. [179] Reynolds, *Aphrodisias and Rome*, 1982, Doc. 2.

155. Christian Marek, "Karien im Ersten Mithradatischen Krieg," in: P. Kneissl and V.

Losemann (eds.), *Alte Geschichte und Wissenschaftsgeschichte,* FS Christ, Darmstadt 1988, 285 ff.

156. On this, see Christian Marek, "Der lykische Bund, Rhodos, Kos und Mithradates," *Lykia* 2, 1995, 9–19; Patrick Baker and Gaétan Thériault, "Les Lyciens, Xanthos et Rome dans la première moitié du Ier s. a. C.: Nouvelles inscriptions," *REG* 118, 2005, 329–366.

157. On the model of the term "Sicilian Vespers" used to refer to the bloodbath of 1282 in Sicily, this expression came into use in the nineteenth century. In the second volume of his *Römische Geschichte,* fifth ed., Berlin 1869, 289, Theodore Mommsen speaks of "Ephesischen Mordbefehle(n)," and in the fifth volume, Berlin 1885, 164, he writes in connection with the British Boudicca Rebellion: "Es war eine nationale Vesper gleich jener mithradatischen." A few years later, Théodore Reinach, who knew Mommsen's work well, spoke in the first edition of his book on Mithridates, 1890, 131 of "Vêpres éphésiennes."

158. Jean Hatzfeld, *Les trafiquants italiens dans l'Orient hellénique,* Paris 1919; Christiane Delplace, "Publicains, trafiquants et financiers dans les provinces d'Asie Mineure sous la République," *Ktema* 2, 1977, 233–252; Christel Müller and Claire Hasenohr (eds.), *Les Italiens dans le monde grec, IIe siècle av. J. C.-Ier siècle ap. J. C. Circulation, activités, intégration, BCH* Supplément 41, 2002.

159. [528] Reinach, *Mithradates,* 1895, 124.

160. Th. Mommsen, *Römische Geschichte,* vol. 2, fifth ed., Berlin 1869, 289.

161. See esp. Christian Habicht, *Athen. Die Geschichte der Stadt in hellenistischer Zeit,* Munich 1995, 297–313.

162. Christian Habicht, "Die Geschichte Athens in der Zeit Mithridates' VI.," *Chiron* 6, 1976, 127 ff.

163. In 76 BCE the decree issued by a *phyle* in Mylasa ([162] *IK* Mylasa 109) still mentions that an emissary "went over to Asia" to ask the praetor Iunius Silanus, the city's patron, to visit it.

164. Cf. also the later of the two dedicatory inscriptions on the Capitol: Ronald Mellor, "The Dedications on the Capitoline Hill," *Chiron* 8, 1978, 319–330.

165. [525] Radt, *Pergamon,* 1999, 248–254.

166. [183] Marek, *Kaunos,* 2006, no. 103.

167. [496] Leschhorn, *Ären,* 1993, 214–221.

168. [281] Syme, *Anatolica,* 1995, 58–65.

169. Cf. IG XI 4, 1054; Reinhold Merkelbach, "Der Überfall der Piraten auf Teos," *Epigr-Anat* 32, 2000, 101–114.

170. Jean-Louis Ferrary, "La création de la province d'Asie et la présence italienne en Asie Mineure," in: C. Müller and C. Hasenohr (eds.), *Les Italiens dans le monde Grec, BCH* Supplément 41, 2002, 134 f.

171. [146] MS IV 168 f.; A. Chaniotis (trans.), *War in the Hellenistic World: A Social and Cultural History,* Malden, MA 2005, 163.

172. Egon Maróti, "Die Rolle der Seeräuber in der Zeit der Mithradatischen Kriege," in: L. de Rosa (ed.), *Ricerche storiche ed economiche in memoria di Corrado Barbagallo,* Neapel 1970, 481–493; [430] Nollé, *Side* I, 1993, p. 69 ff.

173. Ernst Badian, *Zöllner und Sünder* (trans. W. Will and S. Cox), Darmstadt 1997, 227–230.

174. The sources are found in [528] Reinach, *Mithradates,* 1895, 312 n. 1.

175. [183] Marek, *Kaunos,* 2006, no. 106.

176. [537] Dreher, *Pompeius,* 1996, 188–207.

177. [528] Reinach, *Mithradates*, 1895, 403.

178. Jakob Munk Højte, "The Death and Burial of Mithridates VI," in: [534] Højte (ed.), *Mithridates*, 2009, 121–130.

179. Th. Mommsen, *The History of Rome*, Vol. IV, trans. W.P. Dickson, rev. ed. London 1912.

180. Brian C. McGing, "Mithridates VI Eupator: Victim or Aggressor?," in: [534] Højte (ed.), *Mithridates*, 2009, 203–216.

181. Lâtife Summerer, "The Search for Mithridates. Reception of Mithridates VI between the 15th and the 20th Centuries," in: [534] Højte (ed.), *Mithridates*, 2009, 15–34.

182. [536] Ziegler, *Ären*, 1993, 203–219. Zephyrion ([199] Head, HN² 734) should be struck from the list.

183. Cf. Altay Coşkun, "Die tetrarchische Verfassung der Galater und die Neuordnung des Ostens durch Pompeius (Strab. *geogr.* 12, 5, 1. App. *Mithr.* 560)," in: H. Heftner and K. Tomaschitz (eds.), *Ad fontes!* FS Dobesch, Vienna 2004, 687–703.

184. Sources on Deiotaros in [539] Buchheim, *Orientpolitik*, 1960, 111 n. 130.

185. [182] Marek, *Stadt, Ära*, 1993, 42–46.

186. Vasilis I. Anastasiadis and George A. Souris, "Theophanes of Mytilene: A New Inscription Relating to His Early Career," *Chiron* 22, 1992, 377–383.

187. Luis Amela Valverde, "Inscripciones honoríficas dedicadas a Pompeyo Magno," *Faventia* 23, no. 1, 2001, 87–102.

188. T. Corey Brennan, *The Praetorship in the Roman Republic*, Oxford 2000, vol. 2, 588–596.

189. Brennan, ibid., vol. 2, 714–722.

190. D. R. Shackleton Bailey (trans.), *Cicero. Letters to Atticus*, vol. II, Cambridge, MA, and London 1999, 65.

191. Cicero, *Att.* 5, 20, 3; Shackleton Bailey (trans.), *Cicero. Letters to Atticus*, 81. This affinity connected with the same stopping place as that of Alexander the Great was later also mentioned by Germanicus and Septimus Severus, pp. 328, 353.

192. Cicero, *Att.* 5, 20, 3; "My name stood high in Syria," Shackleton Bailey (trans.), *Cicero. Letters to Atticus*, 81.

193. Cicero *Att.* 6, 1, 16; Shackleton Bailey, *Cicero. Letters to Atticus*, 121.

194. Cicero, *Att.* 5, 16, 2 f.; Shackleton Bailey, *Cicero. Letters to Atticus*, 67–69.

195. Cicero, *Att.* 6, 1, 15; Shackleton Bailey, *Cicero. Letters to Atticus*, 121. On the significance of *peregrini iudices* see [533] Kallet-Marx, *Hegemony to Empire*, 1995, 132–134 and Jean-Louis Ferrary, "La création de la province d'Asie et la présence italienne en Asie Mineure," in: C. Müller and C. Hasenohr (eds.), *Les Italiens dans le monde Grec, BCH* Supplément 41, 2002, 138.

196. Cicero, *Att.* 6, 6, 4; Shackleton Bailey, *Cicero. Letters to Atticus*, 167.

197. Brennan, ibid., vol. 2, 404–406.

198. Ronald Syme, "Observations on the Province of Cilicia," in: W. M. Calder and J. Keil (eds.), *Anatolian Studies Presented to Sir William Hepburn Buckler*, Manchester 1939, 324. On Pamphylia, which may also have first been incorporated into Asia under Caesar, cf. Cicero, *fam.* 12, 15, 5.

199. Robert K. Sherk, "Caesar and Mytilene," *GrRomByzSt* 4, 1963, 217–230.

200. Louis Robert, *Hellenica* 10, 1955, 257–260.

201. See [496] Leschhorn, *Ären*, 1993, 221–225. The era also appears in Apollonis.

202. Sources in Stephen Mitchell, "The Treaty between Rome and Lycia of 46 BC," in: R. Pintaudi (ed.), *Papyri Graecae Schøyen*, Florence 2005, 234.

203. Mitchell, op. cit. Cf. Christof Schuler, "Notizen zu dem Vertrag zwischen Lykien und Rom aus dem Jahr 46," in: Ch. Schuler (ed.), *Griechische Epigraphik in Lykien. Eine Zwischenbilanz. Akten des Kolloquiums vom 24.–26. 2. 2005 in München*, Vienna 2007, 74–79.

204. On this Roman, see Wolfgang Blümel, Christian Habicht, and T. Corey Brennan, "Ehren für Cn. Domitius Calvinus in Nysa," *ZPE* 169, 2009, 157–161. Pharnakes was not defeated by Caesar near "Zeleia" (as is mistakenly stated on p. 158), but rather near Zela, see p. 300.

205. Apameia might also have been founded as a colony first by Antony, not by Caesar. See Glen Bowersock, *Augustus and the Greek World*, Oxford 1965, 63–68; there were also settlements of Italics (not colonies) in Lampsakos, Parion, Kyzikos, and Amisos.

206. On taxation during the Imperial period, see below, chapter 8.

207. Luigi Torraca, *Marco Giunio Bruto: Epistole greche*, Neapel 1959.

208. Ronald Syme, "Observations on the Province of Cilicia," in: W. M. Calder and J. Keil (eds.), *Anatolian Studies Presented to Sir William Hepburn Buckler*, Manchester 1939, 324.

209. [183] Marek, *Kaunos*, 2006, no. 109–111.

210. Georg Petzl, "Antiochos I. von Kommagene im Handschlag mit den Göttern," *AMS* 49, 2003, 81–84. The widespread older interpretation that the *dexioseis* symbolized the apotheosis of Antiochos, has been proven false by a newly discovered text fragment from the religious inscription. On the chronology, see [539] Buchheim, *Orientpolitik*, 1960, 81.

211. That is the view suggested by Hermann Bengtson, "Zum Partherfeldzug des Antonius," SBMünchen 1974, no. 1, 1–48.

212. Cf. the maps in [549] Marek, *Pontus et Bithynia*, 2003, 182.

213. Peter J. Thonemann, "Polemo, Son of Polemo (Dio 59, 12, 2)," *EpigrAnat* 37, 2004, 144–150.

214. Stephen Mitchell, "Amyntas in Pisidien—der letzte Krieg der Galater," *AMS* 12, 1994, 97–103.

215. Ronald Syme, "Observations on the Province of Cilicia," in: W. M. Calder and J. Keil (eds.), *Anatolian Studies Presented to Sir William Hepburn Buckler*, Manchester 1939, 324.

216. [493] Jones, *Cities*, second ed. 1971, 204 f.; on the later development, see Hans Taeuber, "Die syrisch-kilikische Grenze während der Prinzipatszeit," *Tyche* 6, 1991, 201–210.

217. Syme, "Observations on the Province of Cilicia," 325.

218. Syme, "Observations on the Province of Cilicia," 325 f. Cf. [539] Buchheim, *Orientpolitik*, 1960, 92–97. See now [541a] Halfmann, *Marcus Antonius*, 2011, 139–176.

219. Fr. 30, PCG; Jeffrey Rusten (ed.), *Texts, Documents, and Art from Athenian Comic Competitions*, 486–280, Baltimore, MD 2011, 687.

220. [491] Tarn, *Kultur*, 1966, 87 and Peter Herrmann, "Die Selbstdarstellung der hellenistischen Stadt in den Inschriften: Ideal und Wirklichkeit," in: C. Pelekides, T. Peppa-Delmouzou, and B. Petrakos (ed.), ΠΡΑΚΤΙΚΑ ΤΟΥ Η ΔΙΕΘΝΟΥΣ ΣΥΝΕΔΡΙΟΥ ΕΛΛΗΝΙΚΗΣ ΚΑΙ ΛΑΤΙΝΙΚΗΣ ΕΠΙΓΡΑΦΙΚΗΣ, Athens 1984, 108–119 on the diplomatics of the Hellenistic *polis*, and in particular the inclusion in decrees (esp. in those for foreign judges) of long references to the documents of foreign communities. Furthermore: foreign judges had to proceed in accord with the laws of the city to which they were summoned, which required an exchange of juristic knowledge.

Chapter 7. Imperium Romanum: The Provinces from Augustus to Aurelian

1. [282] Biraschi and Salmeri, *Strabone*, 2000.

2. Adrian N. Sherwin-White, *The Letters of Pliny—A Historical and Social Commentary*, Oxford 1966.

3. Christian Marek, "Intellektuelle in Bithynien und ihre Feindschaften," *AMS* 69, 2012, 33–46.

4. Johannes Nollé, "Zur neueren Forschungsgeschichte der kaiserzeitlichen Stadtprägungen Kleinasiens. Der schwierige Umgang mit einer historischen Quelle," in: [223] Nollé, Overbeck, and Weiß (eds.), *Münzprägung*, 1997, 11–26.

5. Johannes Nollé, "Stadt und Bürgerstolz. Gedanken zu kleinasiatischen Stadtprägungen des Winterthurer Münzkabinetts," *MünzenRevue* 30, 1998, no. 11, 102 ff.

6. Wolfgang Leschhorn, "Die kaiserzeitliche Münzprägung in Phrygien," in: [223] Nollé, Overbeck, and Weiß (eds.), *Münzprägung*, 1997, 55 f.

7. Chris Howgego, Volker Heuchert, and Andrew Burnett (eds.), *Coinage and Identity in the Roman Provinces*, Oxford and New York 2005.

8. [207] Kraft, *Münzprägung*, 1972.

9. Louis Robert objected to that argument. Robert's most important statements are compiled by Johannes Nollé in "Zur neueren Forschungsgeschichte der kaiserzeitlichen Stadtprägungen Kleinasiens. Der schwierige Umgang mit einer historischen Quelle," in: [223] Nollé, Overbeck, and Weiß (eds.), *Münzprägung*, 1997, 24 n. 67.

10. [106] OGIS 458; see also [496] Leschhorn, *Ären*, 1993, 215.

11. [167] *Milet* I 3, 127 line 2; 17/16 BCE, cf. l. 13, 7/6 BCE. Peter Thonemann, "The Calendar of the Roman Province of Asia," *EpigrAnat* 196, 2015, 123–141.

12. Glen W. Bowersock, *Augustus and the Greek World*, Oxford 1965, Appendix I, 150 f.

13. Peter Herrmann, *Der römische Kaisereid. Untersuchungen zu seiner Herkunft und Entwicklung*, Göttingen 1968.

14. Helmut Halfmann, "Zur Datierung und Deutung der Priesterliste am Augustus-Roma-Tempel," *Chiron* 16, 1986, 35–42, esp. 40 ff.

15. The text is now available in [193] Scheid (ed.), *Res gestae*, 2007. Cf. [186a] Mitchell and French, *Ankyra* 1, 2012, no. 1.

16. IG XII 6, 1, 370.371; see also ILS 125. 125a; CIL II 1667 and *Epigrammata Bobiensia* 39, a poem of Domitius Marsus to Atia, Augustus's mother: *Ante omnes alias felix tamen hoc ego dicor sive hominem peperi femina sive deum*; Marion Lausberg, in: O. Brehm and S. Klie (eds.), *Mousikos aner*, FS Wegener, Bonn 1992, 259 ff. (Thanks to W. Eck for bringing this to my attention).

17. [496] Leschhorn, *Ären*, 1993.

18. My attention was kindly drawn to this passage by Anne Kolb.

19. [598] Kunnert, *Phylen*, 2012.

20. On the commonalties, see p. 415 ff.

21. [106] OGIS 458 II; Robert K. Sherk (ed.), *Rome and the Greek East to the Death of Augustus*, Cambridge 1984, 125 no. 101 VI.

22. Glen W. Bowersock, *Augustus and the Greek World*, Oxford 1965, esp. chaps. III and IV.

23. See [490] Magie, *Roman Rule*, 1950, 444 f.

24. Bowersock, op. cit., 47.

25. [549] Marek, *Pontus et Bithynia*, 2003, 44, figure 67.

26. The interpretation of the passage in Dio (53, 26, 3) is controversial. [549] Brandt and Kolb, *Lycia et Pamphylia*, 2005, 21, have recently interpreted it as indicating that this part of Pamphylia was now reunited with the other "district" (*nomós*), and that Pamphylia as a whole already at that time was attached to Galatia. See the older literature cited in id., p. 24, note 5. However, this passage has to be translated as "returned to its own law (*nómos*), which refers to Pamphylia's inclusion in the *formula provinciae*. Cf. Dio 60, 17, 3–4: "He [Claudius] had the Lycians included in the law of Pamphylia." See the first section of Chapter 8 in this book.

27. Wolfgang Leschhorn, "Die Anfänge der Provinz Galatia," *Chiron* 22, 1992, 315–336.

28. [281] Syme, *Anatolica*, 1995, 257–269.

29. Karl Strobel, "Die Legionen des Augustus. Probleme der römischen Heeresgeschichte nach dem Ende des Bürgerkrieges: die Truppengeschichte Galatiens und Moesiens bis in tiberische Zeit und das Problem der Legiones Quintae," in: P. Freeman, J. Bennett, Z. T. Fiema, and B. Hoffmann (eds.), *Limes XVIII. Proceedings of the International Congress of Roman Frontier Studies*, Oxford 2002, 51 ff.

30. Hadrien Bru, "L'origine des colons romains d'Antioche de Pisidie," in: [286] Bru, Kirbihler, and Lebreton, *L'Asie Mineure*, 2009, 263–287.

31. Barbara Levick, *Roman Colonies in Southern Asia Minor*, Oxford 1967. On Ikonion, and the double existence of a *colonia* and a *polis* down into the time of Hadrian, see Stephen Mitchell, "Iconium and Ninica. Two Double Communities in Roman Asia Minor," *Historia* 28, 1979, 409–438.

32. The site of an Augustan colony called Ninica is uncertain; see [490] Magie, *Roman Rule*, 1950, 1328 note 46.

33. [281] Syme, *Anatolica*, 1995, 344–347.

34. *Vici* also appear in the colony of Alexandria Troas.

35. André Oltramare, "Augustus und die Parther," in: W. Schmitthenner (ed.), *Augustus, Wege der Forschung*, Darmstadt 1969, 118–139; Dieter Timpe, "Zur augusteischen Partherpolitik zwischen 30 und 20 v. Chr.," *Würzburger Jahrbücher* new series 1, 1975, 155 ff.

36. Hans D. Meyer, *Die Außenpolitik des Augustus und die Augusteische Dichtung*, Köln-Graz 1961.

37. On the connection between the Roman-Parthian conflict and Aelius Gallus's Arabian campaign of 25 BCE, see Christian Marek, "Die Expedition des Aelius Gallus nach Arabien im Jahre 25 v. Chr.," *Chiron* 23, 1993, 121–156. Another view is proposed by Michael A. Speidel, "Außerhalb des Reiches? Zu neuen lateinischen Inschriften aus Saudi-Arabien und zur Ausdehnung der römischen Herrschaft am Roten Meer," *ZPE* 163, 2007, 301 ff.

38. Karl Kramer, "Zur Rückgabe der Feldzeichen im Jahre 20," *Historia* 22, 1973, 362.

39. [281] Syme, *Anatolica*, 1995, 317–334.

40. On Lollius, see Werner Eck and Semra Mägele, "Kolossalstatuen in Sagalassos. Marcus Lollius und seine politische Machtstellung im Osten als Begleiter des Gaius Caesar," in: E. Winter (ed.), *Vom Euphrat bis zum Bosporus. Kleinasien in der Antike,* FS Schwertheim, Bonn 2008, 177–186.

41. Michael A. Speidel, "Kappadokien—Vom Königreich zur Provinz. Zum Prozeß der strukturellen Integration unter Tiberius," in: I. Piso (ed.), *Die römischen Provinzen. Begriff und Gründung*, Cluj-Napoca 2008, 51–64.

42. See [553] Eck, *Struktur*, 2007, 193–195. The probability that it was a prefect is significantly increased since everything suggests that in the first decades of direct rule Cappadocia was assigned to the area under the command of the Syrian governor, and procurators presiding

over provinces are otherwise first attested only from Claudius on. Cf. Speidel, "Kappadokien—Vom Königreich zur Provinz."

43. Michael A. Speidel, "The Development of the Roman Forces in Northeastern Anatolia," in: A. S. Lewin et al. (eds.), *The Late Roman Army in the Near East from Diocletian to the Arab Conquest, Akten des Kolloquiums in Potenza, Acerenza und Matera, Mai 2005*, Oxford 2007, 73–90.

44. [182] Marek, *Stadt, Ära*, 1993, 62.

45. Michael A. Speidel, "Early Roman Rule in Commagene," *ScrClIsr* 24, 2005, 85–100.

46. On his later fate, see Tacitus, *ann.* 2, 68 and on the Senate's decision concerning Cn. Piso, Werner Eck, Antonio Caballos, and Fernando Fernández, *Das Senatus consultum de Cn. Pisone patre*, Munich 1996, 40–42 lines 37–45 and the commentary, p. 162–166.

47. Tassilo Schmitt, Die drei Bögen für Germanicus und die römische Politik in frühtiberischer Zeit," *RStorAnt* 27, 1997, 73–137.

48. [496] Leschhorn, *Ären*, 1993, 130.

49. On charges made against governors, see 421 f.

50. [493] Jones, *Cities*, second ed., 1971, 136 f.

51. [490] Magie, *Roman Rule*, 1950, 1368.

52. The connection of the date of death with that of the annexation of Komana is unfounded: [182] Marek, *Stadt, Ära*, 1993, 62 note 417; [496] Leschhorn, *Ären*, 1993, 29.

53. Leschhorn, *Ären*, 99–105.

54. [490] Magie, Roman Rule, 1950, 1407, note 26, assumed an error made by Dio and guessed that the ruler of Cilicia was a person different from Polemon II of Pontos. Cf. Theodora S. MacKay, "The Major Sanctuaries of Pamphylia and Cilicia," *ANRW* II 18. 3, 1990, 2082–2103; Ulrich Gotter, "Tempel und Großmacht: Olba und das Imperium Romanum," in: [367] Jean, Dinçol, and Durugönül (eds.), *La Cilicie*, 2001, 315 f. Matthäus Heil's opposing view in *Die orientalische Außenpolitik des Kaisers Nero*, Munich 1997, 146 f. note 9 is probably correct.

55. On the relationship that might have existed with Augustus here as well, and on the conception of his reign the inscription published by Christof Schuler, "Augustus, Gott und Herr über Land und Meer. Eine neue Inschrift aus Tyberissos im Kontext der späthellenistischen Herrscherverehrung," *Chiron* 37, 2007, 383 ff. offers important insights.

56. [195] SEG 18, 143; see [517] Behrwald, *Lykischer Bund*, 2000, 120–128; [187] Wörrle, *Stadt und Fest*, 1988, 97 f. note 100.

57. [194] Adak and Şahin, *Stadiasmus*, 2007; cf. Thomas Marksteiner and Michael Wörrle, "Ein Altar für Kaiser Claudius auf dem Bonda tepesi zwischen Myra und Limyra," *Chiron* 32, 2002, 545 ff. Cf. the inscription in Rome, CIL VI 41075.

58. [183] Marek, *Kaunos*, 2006, 101.

59. [553] Eck, *Struktur*, 2007, 197.

60. [490] Magie, *Roman Rule*, 1950, 1405 note 21; on Tralleis [112] Robert, *Études anatoliennes*, 1937, 413 f.

61. Magie, *Roman Rule*, 1407–1409; [493] Jones, *Cities*, second ed., 1971, 210–212.

62. The garrison at Gorneae presumably consisted of a divison of legionaries (from Syria) under the command of Casperius and a complete auxiliary unit under Caelius Pollio. ILS 394 and ILS 9117 can be compared here (even if from a later time, but still from Armenia). (Suggestion kindly supplied by Michael A. Speidel.)

63. Matthäus Heil, *Die orientalische Außenpolitik des Kaisers Nero*, Munich 1997, 60 f.

64. Heil, *Die orientalische Außenpolitik des Kaisers Nero*, with an extensive discussion of the sources, 28–57. Domitius Corbulo himself apparently wrote a work on the events (Tacitus, *ann.* 15, 16, 1), but it has been lost. The main source for the following events is Tacitus (*ann.* 13, 7–9. 34–41; 14, 23–26; 15, 1–7), along with a short passage in Cassius Dio (62, 19–23).

65. Tacitus, *ann.* 13, 35; trans. Jackson. Scholars consider this description greatly exaggerated, partly to glorify Corbulo's achievements. Cf. Everett Wheeler, "The Laxity of Syrian Legions (1st to 3rd c. A. D.)," in: D.L. Kennedy (ed.), *The Roman Army in the East*, JRA Suppl. 18, 1996, 229–276.

66. Heil, *Die orientalische Außenpolitik des Kaisers Nero*, 80–83. On Nero's triumphal arch, 92 f.

67. Heil, *Die orientalische Außenpolitik des Kaisers Nero*, 101 note 3 with the literature on this problem.

68. Whether the statements attributed to him by Tacitus (*ann.* 15, 6) give evidence for the plan for a province of Armenia is a matter of debate among experts, but the possibility cannot be excluded. Cf. [490] Magie, *Roman Rule*, 1950, 1416 note 54.

69. The reasons for the provincialization of the Kingdom of Pontos are discussed in detail in Heil, *Die orientalische Außenpolitik des Kaisers Nero*, 144–158, with older literature.

70. Heil, *Die orientalische Außenpolitik des Kaisers Nero*, 183 ff.

71. Ronald Syme, "Flavian Wars and Frontiers," *CAH* XI, 1936, 131–187; [542] Dabrowa, *Asie Mineure*, 1980; Jörg Wagner, "Die Römer an Euphrat und Tigris," *Antike Welt* special number, 1985, 42–51; Julian Bennett, "The Cappadocian Frontier: From the Julio-Claudians to Hadrian," in: P. Freeman, J. Bennett, Z. T. Fiema, and B. Hoffmann (eds.), *Limes XVIII. Proceedings of the International Congress of Roman Frontier Studies*, Oxford 2002, 301–312.

72. Michel Christol and Thomas Drew-Bear, "D. Fonteius Fronto, Proconsul de Lycie-Pamphylie," *GrRomByzSt* 32, 1991, 397–413; Werner Eck, "Der Anschluss der kleinasiatischen Provinzen an Vespasian und ihre Rekonstruierung unter den Flaviern," in: L. Capogrossi Colognesi and E. Tassi Scandone (eds.), *Vespasiano e l'impero dei Flavi*, Atti del Convegno, Roma, Palazzo Massimo, 18-20 novembre 2009, Rome 2012, 27ff.; id., "Die Dedikation des Apollo Klarios unter Proculus, *legatus Augusti pro praetore Lyciae-Pamphyliae* unter Antoninus Pius," in: J. Poblome (ed.), *Exempli Gratia*, FS Waelkens, Leuven 2013, 43-49.

73. [561] Haensch, *Capita*, 1997, 267–272.

74. [559] Rémy, *Carrières*, 1989, no. 306.

75. The fact that the formulae of the governor's inscriptions from the time preceding the age of Hadrian do not name all three of the *eparchiae* cannot serve as a criterion, since later inscriptions do the same: Rémy, *Carrières*, 347–349.

76. Rémy, *Carrières*, no. 108.157.159; Robert K. Sherk, "Roman Galatia. The Governors from 25 B. C. to A. D. 114," *ANRW* II 7.2, 1980, 1007–1011.

77. [195] SEG 16, 781; trans. B.M. Metzger, *JNES* 15, 1956, 18–26.

78. [490] Magie, *Roman Rule*, 1950, 582–587. Cf. [581] Dräger, *Städte*, 1993, 86 ff.

79. [553] Eck, *Struktur*, 2007, 190.

80. [182] Marek, *Stadt, Ära*, 1993, 79.

81. Michael A. Speidel, "Bellicosissimus Princeps. Traian und das Heer und Traians Eroberungspolitik," in: A. Nünnerich-Asmus (ed.), *Traian. Ein Kaiser der Superlative am Beginn einer Umbruchzeit?*, Mainz 2002, 23–40; esp. 36 ff.

82. On the interpretation and restoration of CIL V 5262 = ILS 2927, see Geza Alföldy, *Städte, Eliten und Gesellschaft in der Gallia Cisalpina: Epigraphisch-historische Untersuchungen*, Stuttgart 1999, 221–233.

83. Helmut Halfmann, *Itinera principum: Geschichte und Typologie der Kaiserreisen im Römischen Reich*, Stuttgart 1986, 187.

84. The precise date has not been determined, but it may have been only at the beginning of Hadrian's reign (reference kindly provided by Michael A. Speidel).

85. Arrian, *Parthika* fr. 40 Roos and Wirth; Fronto, *principia historiae* 18; Eutropius 8, 3, 1.

86. Arrian, *Parthika* fr. 85 Roos and Wirth; Themistios, *or.* 15, 205a Harduin.

87. Carl Philipps, François Villeneuve, and William Facey, *A Latin Inscription from South Arabia, Proceedings of the Seminar for Arabian Studies* 34, 2004, 239–250.

88. Dio 75, 9, 6, Boissevain places this after 68, 30, 3.

89. Anthony R. Birley, *Hadrian. The Restless Emperor*, New York, 1997.

90. [552] Ziegler, *Koinon*, 1999, 137–152.

91. Helmut Halfmann, *Itinera principum: Geschichte und Typologie der Kaiserreisen im Römischen Reich*, Stuttgart 1986, 188–210.

92. Halfmann, op. cit., 201 f.; cf. Peter Weiß, "Hadrian in Lydien," *Chiron* 25, 1995, 213–224, esp. 218.

93. This king was later accused by the Parthians of having encouraged the Alani to make further attacks on Albania and Media, which subsequently also affected Armenia and Cappadocia, until Flavius Arrianus's mission put an end to them in ca. 135 CE (Dio 69, 15).

94. Peter Weiß, "Militärdiplome und Reichsgeschichte: Der Konsulat des L. Neratius Proculus und die Vorgeschichte des Partherkriegs unter Marc Aurel und Lucius Verus," in: R. Haensch and J. Heinrichs (eds.), *Herrschen und Verwalten. Der Alltag der römischen Administration in der Hohen Kaiserzeit*, Cologne, Weimar, and Vienna 2007, 160–172.

95. Werner Eck, "Zum Ende der Legio IX Hispana," *Chiron* 2, 1972, 459–462. Michael A. Speidel, "The Development of the Roman Forces in Northeastern Anatolia," in: A. S. Lewin et al. (eds.), *The Late Roman Army in the Near East from Diocletian to the Arab Conquest*, Oxford 2007, 73–90.

96. [553] Eck, *Struktur*, 2007, 202 f.

97. [549] Marek, *Pontus et Bithynia*, 2003, 183, map V.

98. Helmut Halfmann, *Itinera principum: Geschichte und Typologie der Kaiserreisen im Römischen Reich*, Stuttgart 1986, 210–212.

99. [490] Magie, *Roman Rule*, 1950, 663.

100. Anton von Premerstein, "Untersuchungen zur Geschichte des Kaisers Marcus II," *Klio* 12, 1912, 139–178; id., "Kostoboken," *RE* XI, 1922, 1509; Walter Scheidel, "Probleme der Datierung des Costoboceneinfalls im Balkanraum unter Marcus Aurelius," *Historia* 39, 1990, 493–498; Achilles Humbel, *Ailios Aristeides, Klage über Eleusis*, Vienna 1994, 38–45.

101. However, inscriptions naming Cassius as the Syrian governor do not refer to any such superordinate position in the Orient.

102. [559] Rémy, *Carrières*, 1989, no. 268. For the family of Carminius Athenagoras see: Anne-Valérie Pont, "L'inscription en l'honneur de M. Ulpius Carminius Claudianus à Aphrodisias (CIG, 2782)," *Cahiers du Centre Glotz* 19, 2008, 219–245.

103. [549] Marek, *Pontus et Bithynia*, 2003, 88.

104. Mustafa H. Sayar, "Brief des Septimius Severus an die Stadt Syedra (194 n. Chr.)," in: J. Fischer and E. Trinkl (eds.), *Der Beitrag Kleinasiens zur Kultur- und Geistesgeschichte der Griechisch-Römischen Antike*. Akten des Internationalen Kolloquiums Wien, 3.-5. November

2010, Vienna 2014, 333–342; Christopher P. Jones, "A Letter of Septimius Severus to the City of Syedra," *ZPE* 195, 2015, 121–126.

105. [552] Ziegler, *Koinon*, 1999, 143–145.

106. Michael A. Speidel, "Ein Bollwerk für Syrien. Septimius Severus und die Provinzordnung Nordmesopotamiens im dritten Jahrhundert," *Chiron* 37, 2007, 405–433. On the chronology of the kings, see Andreas Luther, "Elias von Nisibis und die Chronologie der edessenischen Könige," *Klio* 81, 1999, 197.

107. Han J. W. Drijvers and John F. Healey, "The Old Syriac Inscriptions of Edessa and Osrhoene: Texts, Translations, and Commentary," *HdO* 1, 42, Leiden 1999, 45 no. As 1.

108. See esp. Judah B. Segal, *Edessa. The Blessed City*, Oxford 1970, tables 1–3; Jules Leroy, "Mosaiques funéraires d'Edesse," *Syria* 34, 1957, 306 ff.; Janine Balty, "La mosaique au Proche-Orient I," in: *ANRW* II 12.2, 1981, 369 ff.; Klaus Parlasca, "Neues zu den Mosaiken von Edessa und Seleukeia am Euphrat," in: R. F. Campanati (ed.), *III Colloquio internazionale sul mosaico antico (Ravenna, 6–10 settembre 1980)*, Ravenna 1984, 227 ff. Cf. the mosaic inscriptions in Drijvers and Healey, "The Old Syriac Inscriptions of Edessa and Osrhoene," marked in the numbering by "m."

109. Peter Herrmann, "Überlegungen zur Datierung der ‹Constitutio Antoniniana›," *Chiron* 2, 1972, 529.

110. [571] Herrmann, *Hilferufe*, 1990, no. 6 (= [106] OGIS 519, ca. 244–247 CE). Tor Hauken, *Petition and Response. An Epigraphic Study of Petitions to Roman Emperors, 181–249*, Bergen 1998. Cf. [195] SEG 53, 1517: harassment of the *coloni Tymiorum* (the center of the Montanists!) *et Simoentium*.

111. Herrmann, op. cit., 57. A persuasive case against the unjustified assumption that this phenomenon was general is made by Michael A. Speidel, *Heer und Herrschaft im Römischen Reich der Hohen Kaiserzeit*, Stuttgart 2009, 473–500, esp. 485 ff.

112. [553] Eck, *Struktur*, 2007, 202; Charlotte Roueché, "The Fasti. Governors of Caria and Phrygia," in: A. Chastagnol, S. Demougin, and C. Lepelley (eds.), *Splendidissima civitas. Études d'histoire romaine en hommage à François Jacques*, Paris 1996, 236–239; [135] Roueché, *Aphrodisias*, 1989, Appendix I, "Governors of Caria and Phrygia from the later 240s until shortly before 305," p. 319; David French and Charlotte Roueché, "Governors of Phrygia and Caria," *ZPE* 49, 1982, 159–160; Charlotte Roueché, "Rome, Asia and Aphrodisias in the Third Century," *JRS* 71, 1981, 103–120.

113. Klaus Schippmann, *Grundzüge der parthischen Geschichte*, Darmstadt 1980, 73 f.

114. Alfred Heuß, *Römische Geschichte*, Braunschweig 1971, chap. IX, 407 ff. On the debate over the concept of crisis, [571] Herrmann, *Hilferufe*, 1990, 3–11, and the critical remarks in Werner Eck, "Krise oder Nichtkrise—Das ist hier die Frage," in: O. Hekster, G. de Kleijn, and D. Slootjes (eds.), *Crises and the Roman Empire. Proceedings of the Seventh Workshop of the International Network Impact of Empire (Nijmegen, June 20–24, 2006)*, Leiden 2007, 23–43.

115. Goths: esp. Jordanes, *Get.* 107 f.; Zosimos 1, 28.31–35.46; Dexippos *FGrHist* 100 F 29; HA Claud. 12, 1. On Herakleia and Paphlagonia cf. Belke, *TIB* 9, 1996, 64 f. and in general Barbara Scardigli, "Die gotisch-römischen Beziehungen im 3. und 4. Jh. n. Chr. Ein Forschungsbericht 1950–1970. 1. Das 3. Jh.," in: *ANRW* II 5.1, 1976, esp. 241 ff.; Maciej Salamon, "The Chronology of the Gothic Incursions into Asia Minor in the IIIrd Century A. D.," *Eos* 59, 1971, 109 ff.; Jeanne and Louis Robert, *Hellenica* 6, 1948, 117–122.

116. [633] Guyot, *Chaos in Pontos*, 1998, 64 ff., quotation 67 (ep. can. § 5–7); cf. the tomb inscription for a girl presumably murdered by the barbarians: [146] MS II 293; [549] Marek, *Pontus et Bithynia*, 2003, 123.

117. Stewart D. F. Salmond, *The Works of Gregory Thaumaturgus, Dionysius of Alexandria, and Archelaus*, Edinburgh 1871, 33f. [online at www.archive.org].

118. Erich Kettenhofen, *Die römisch-persischen Kriege des 3. Jh. n. Chr. nach der Inschrift Šāhpurs I. an der Ka'be-ye Zartošt*, Wiesbaden 1982; Klaus Schippmann, *Grundzüge der Geschichte des sasanidischen Reiches*, Darmstadt 1990.

119. This is how the name is given in CIL XIII 1807.

120. See Glanville Downey, *A History of Antioch in Syria from Seleucus to the Arab Conquest*, Princeton 1961, 257.

121. Cf. also the Latin inscription ILS 8924.

Chapter 8. Asia Minor and Imperial Administration under the Principate

1. Cf. Colin J. Hemer, "Book of Acts in the Setting of Hellenistic History," *WUNT* 49, 1989, 296: "The practice of a similar listing of separate territories within the single provincial complex remains a difficulty." [182] Marek, *Stadt, Ära*, 1993, 51–61; 73–82; [552] Ziegler, *Koinon*, 1999, 139 f.; [553] Eck, *Struktur*, 2007, esp. 200. The subject is dealt with in detail in [568a] Vitale, *Eparchie und Koinon*, 2012.

2. [559] Rémy, *Carrières*, 1989, no. 108; ILS 1017.

3. [551] Mitchell, *Administration*, 1999, 28; [562] Meyer-Zwiffelhoffer, *Statthalter*, 2002, 224 note 3; Hans-Georg Pflaum, *Les fastes de la province de Narbonnaise*, Paris 1978, 37, even suggests a division of the province of Asia into three major dioceses (Ephesiaca, Pergamena, Sardiana), in analogy with the areas of competence assigned to proconsular legates in the province of Africa.

4. See Ronald Syme, *Roman Papers* I, Oxford 1979, 145; cf. Eck, op. cit., 200; Michael Rathmann, "Der Statthalter und die Verwaltung der Reichsstraßen in der Kaiserzeit," in: A. Kolb (ed.), *Herrschaftsstrukturen und Herrschaftspraxis. Konzepte, Prinzipien und Strategien der Administration im römischen Kaiserreich*, Berlin 2006, 208 note. 31.

5. On Galatia, see [544] Mitchell, *Anatolia* I, 1993, 63–69.

6. Recent assessments with secondary literature: [562] Meyer-Zwiffelhoffer, *Statthalter*, 2002; [574] Drexhage, *Wirtschaftspolitik*, 2007, 18 ff. (for Asia).

7. Dirk Erkelenz, "Das Porträt des Statthalters in der Lokalprägung der römischen Provinzen. Überlegungen zu Funktion und Verbreitung des Phänomens in Republik und Kaiserzeit," *SchwNumRu* 81, 2002, 65–91.

8. Cf. Werner Eck, *Die Verwaltung des Römischen Reiches in der Hohen Kaiserzeit: ausgewählte und erweiterte Beiträge II*, Basel 1998, 109.

9. [554] Kreiler, *Statthalter*, 1975; [556] Eck, *Jahres- und Provinzialfasten* 1982, 281–362; ibid. 1983, 147–237; [557] Rémy, *L'évolution*, 1986; [558] id., *Fastes*, 1988; [559] id., *Carrières*, 1989; [560] Thomasson, *Laterculi praesidum I–III*, 1984–1990.

10. See Werner Eck, *Die Verwaltung des Römischen Reiches in der Hohen Kaiserzeit: ausgewählte und erweiterte Beiträge II*, Basel 1998, 58 f.

11. Fronto, *ad Antoninum Pium* 8; cf. *ad M. Caesarem et invicem* 5, 51.

12. Evidence for individual cases in [555] Halfmann, *Senatoren*, 1979, no. 16 (Sardeis), 44 (Mytilene), 54 (Nysa), 56 (Nikomedeia), 75 (Alexandria Troas), 113 (Side), 123 (Nikaia).

13. Keith Hopkins, "Taxes and Trade in the Roman Empire," *JRS* 70, 1980, 121.

14. [561] Haensch, *Capita*, 1997, 710–713. Eck doubts this (personal letter).

15. On this problematic category, see Anne Kolb, *Transport und Nachrichtentransfer im römischen Reich*, Berlin 2000, 290 ff.

16. Haensch, op. cit., 713–724.

17. Graham P. Burton, "The Curator rei publicae: Towards a Reappraisal?," *Chiron* 9, 1979, 465–487.

18. [574] Drexhage, *Wirtschaftspolitik*, 2007, 118–122.

19. For an exhaustive account, see [561] Haensch, *Capita*, 1997.

20. Trans. Charles A. Behr, *P. Aelius Aristides. The Complete Works*, 2 vols., Leiden 1981–1986.

21. See Werner Eck, *Die Verwaltung des Römischen Reiches in der Hohen Kaiserzeit: ausgewählte und erweiterte Beiträge II*, Basel 1998, 187–202.

22. Eck, *Die Verwaltung des Römischen Reiches in der Hohen Kaiserzeit*, 203–217.

23. Eck, *Die Verwaltung des Römischen Reiches in der Hohen Kaiserzeit*, 215.

24. [562] Meyer-Zwiffelhoffer, *Statthalter*, 2002.

25. Dirk Erkelenz, *Optimo Praesidi. Untersuchungen zu den Ehrenmonumenten für Amtsträger der römischen Provinzen in Republik und Kaiserzeit*, Bonn 2003, see especially the lists of various officials, 235 ff.

26. Meyer-Zwiffelhoffer, *Statthalter*, Appendix III, 336–338.

27. Joyce Reynolds (trans.), *Aphrodisias and Rome*, London 1982, 175 no. 48; see [112] Robert, *Études anatoliennes*, 1937, 303.

28. [561] Haensch, *Capita*, 1997, 705–707. Cf. Graham P. Burton, "Proconsuls, Assizes and the Administration of Justice under the Empire," *JRS* 65, 1975, 92–106.

29. Rudolph Haensch, "Das Statthalterarchiv," *ZSav* 109, 1992, 209–317. Cf. Georgy Kantor, "Knowledge of Law in Roman Asia Minor," in: R. Haensch (ed.), *Selbstdarstellung und Kommunikation. Die Veröffenlichung staatlicher Urkunden auf Stein und Bronze in der römischen Welt*, Munich 2009, 249–265.

30. [574] Drexhage, *Wirtschaftspolitik*, 2007, 30.

31. [549] Brandt and Kolb, *Lycia et Pamphylia*, 2005, 32 f., with a reproduction of the inscription. Ed. pr. Michael Wörrle, "Maßnahmen des Quintus Veranius zur Reform des Urkundenwesens," in: J. Borchhardt (ed.), *Myra. Eine lykische Metropole in antiker und byzantinischer Zeit*, Berlin 1975, 254–286.

32. [551] Mitchell, *Administration*, 1999, 37 ff.

33. Rudolph Haensch, "Das Statthalterarchiv," *ZSav* 109, 1992, 209–317.

34. Examples in [574] Drexhage, *Wirtschaftspolitik*, 2007, 22. See esp. Werner Eck, "Roms Wassermanagment im Osten. Staatliche Steuerung des öffentlichen Lebens in den römischen Provinzen?," *Kasseler Universitätsreden* 17, Kassel 2008, with another emphasis: this happened because the cities turned to the emperor and because often more than one city's territory was included, which is why the higher level was brought in.

35. [563] Pekáry, *Reichsstraßen*, 1968; [564] French, *Road-System*, 1980, 698–729; [544] Mitchell, *Anatolia*, 1993, 124 f., Michael Rathmann, "Der Statthalter und die Verwaltung der Reichsstraßen in der Kaiserzeit," in: A. Kolb (ed.), *Herrschaftsstrukturen und Herrschaftspraxis. Konzepte, Prinzipien und Strategien der Administration im römischen Kaiserreich*, Berlin 2006, 201–259.

36. On the different terms, see Michael A. Speidel, "Heer und Straßen—*Militares Viae*," in: R. Frei-Stolba (ed.), *Siedlung und Verkehr im römischen Reich. Römerstraßen zwischen Herrschaftssicherung und Landschaftsprägung*, 2004, 331–344.

37. [565] French, *Milestones*, 1988; cf. Rathmann, "Der Statthalter und die Verwaltung der Reichsstraßen in der Kaiserzeit," 206.

38. Rathmann, "Der Statthalter und die Verwaltung der Reichsstraßen in der Kaiserzeit," 212.

39. Peter Thonemann, "Hellenistic Inscriptions from Lydia," *EpigrAnat* 36, 2003, 95 f.

40. Cf., for example, the recent research done on a city territory in Caria carried out by Anneliese Peschlow-Bindokat, "Das Straßennetz der Latmia. Pleistarch und die Erschließung des Territoriums von Herakleia am Latmos," in: E.-L. Schwandner and K. Rheidt (eds.), *Stadt und Umland. Neue Ergebnisse der archäologischen Bau- und Siedlungsforschung. Bauforschungskolloquium in Berlin vom 7. bis 10. Mai 1997,* Mainz 1999, 186–200. An overview is offered by the [287] Barrington Atlas, 2000, maps 51, 52, 56, 57, 61, 62; cf. [574] Drexhage, *Wirtschaftspolitik,* 2007, 222–224.

41. [194] Adak and Şahin, *Stadiasmus,* 2007. Cf. Denis Rousset, "Le stadiasme de Patara et la géographie historique de la Lycie: itinéraires et routes, localités et cités," in: P. Brun et al. (eds.), *Euploia. La Lycie et la Carie antiques. Dynamiques des territoires, échanges et identités.* Actes du Colloque de Bordeaux, 5, 6 et 7 novembre 2009, Bordeaux 2013, 63-75.

42. [549] Marek, *Pontus et Bithynia,* 2003, 56 f. and 48, with ill. 72.

43. Eckard Olshausen, "Pontica IV. Das römische Straßennetz in Pontos. Bilanz und Ausblick," *Orbis Terrarum* 5, 1999, 93 ff.; cf. in general Jochen Briegleb, "Brücken im Straßenverkehr der antiken Welt," in: E. Olshausen and H. Sonnabend (eds.), *Stuttgarter Kolloquium zur historischen Geographie des Altertums 7,* 1999, Stuttgart 2002, 105–108.

44. See esp. Karl Strobel, "Beiträge zur historischen Geographie Zentralanatoliens," in: U. Fellmeth, P. Guyot, and H. Sonnabend (ed.), *Historische Geographie der Alten Welt,* FS Olshausen, Hildesheim 2007, 309–351.

45. Michael Rostovtzeff, "Angariae," *Klio* 6, 1906, 249–258.

46. Anne Kolb, *Transport und Nachrichtentransfer im römischen Reich,* Berlin 2000.

47. Tor Hauken and Hasan Malay, "A New Edict of Hadrian from the Province of Asia Setting Regulations for Requisitioned Transport," in: R. Haensch (ed.), *Selbstdarstellung und Kommunikation. Die Veröffentlichung staatlicher Urkunden auf Stein und Bronze in der römischen Welt,* Munich 2009, 327–348.

48. [571] Herrmann, *Hilferufe,* 1990, esp. 38–49.

49. Franz Cumont, "Le gouvernement de la Cappadoce sous les Flaviens," *BullAcadBelgique, Classe des lettres,* 1905, 213. On the other hand, cf. Victor Chapot, *La frontière de l'Euphrate de Pompée à la conquête arabe,* Paris 1907.

50. Martin Hartmann and Michael A. Speidel, "The Roman Army at Zeugma, Recent Research Results," in: R. Early et al. (eds.), *Zeugma, Interim Reports,* JRA Supplementary Series 51, 2003, 100–126.

51. Timothy B. Mitford, "The Roman Frontier on the Upper Euphrates," in: [31] Matthews (ed.), *Fifty Years,* 1998, 255–272; id., "Cappadocia and Armenia Minor. Historical Setting of the Limes," *ANRW* II 7.2, 1980, 1169–1228; cf. also Friedrich Hild, *Das byzantinische Straßensystem in Kappadokien,* Vienna 1977.

52. Cf. Franz Taeschner, *Das anatolische Wegenetz nach osmanischen Quellen* 1–2, Leipzig 1924–1926.

53. These ruins have repeatedly been wrongly described as an aqueduct, for instance in Jörg Wagner, "Die Römer an Euphrat und Tigris," *Antike Welt* special number, 1985, 28 ill. 45, and most recently in Margot Klee, *Grenzen des Imperiums. Leben am römischen Limes,* Stuttgart 2006, 92. Against this view, see Lightfoot, in the following note.

54. Chris S. Lightfoot, "Survey Work at Satala: A Roman Legionary Fortress in North-East Turkey," in: [31] Matthews (ed.), *Fifty Years,* 1998, 273–284; inscriptions: Terence B. Mitford, "Some Inscriptions from the Cappadocian Limes," *JRS* 64, 1974, 164 ff.

55. Vadim A. Lekvinadze, "Pontijskij Limes," *VDI* 108, 1969, 75–93.

56. Dieter Kienast, *Untersuchungen zu den Kriegsflotten der römischen Kaiserzeit,* Bonn 1966, 105 ff.

57. If the abbreviations *vicus C(lassis) O(rae) P(onticae) D(- - -) Ve(teranorum)* in the inscription [162] *IK* Sinope 102 have been correctly interpreted.

58. Barbara Pferdehirt, *Römische Militärdiplome und Entlassungsurkunden in der Sammlung des Römisch-Germanischen Zentralmuseums*, 1, Mainz 2004, 18 f., with a reference to the still unpublished diploma; cf. Michael A. Speidel, "The Development of the Roman Forces in Northeastern Anatolia," in: A. S. Lewin et al. (eds.), *The Late Roman Army in the Near East from Diocletian to the Arab Conquest, Akten des Kolloquiums in Potenza, Acerenza und Matera*, May 2005, Oxford 2007, 73–90.

59. Michael P. Speidel, "The Roman Army in Asia Minor. Recent Epigraphical Discoveries and Research," in: St. Mitchell (ed.), *Armies and Frontiers in Roman and Byzantine Anatolia*, Oxford 1983, 7–34, with older literature on p. 25, note 20; cf. Werner Eck, "Prokonsuln und militärisches Kommando," in: id., *Die Verwaltung des Römischen Reiches in der Hohen Kaiserzeit: ausgewählte und erweiterte Beiträge* II, Basel 1998, 187–202.

60. Laurence Cavalier, "Horrea d'Andriakè et Patara. Un nouveau type d'édifice fonctionnel en Lycie à l'époque impériale," *REA* 109, 2007, 51–65.

61. Speidel, "The Roman Army in Asia Minor," 14.

62. Michael A. Speidel, "Auf kürzestem Weg und gut verpflegt an die Front. Zur Versorgung pannonischer Expeditionstruppen während der severischen Partherkriege," in: M.A. Speidel, *Heer und Herrschaft im römischen Reich der hohen Kaiserzeit*, Stuttgart 2009, 255-271.

63. Nicholas P. Milner, "Athletics, Army Recruitment and Heroisation: L. Sep. Fl. Flavillianus of Oinoanda," *AnSt* 61, 2011, 151-167.

64. On the contribution made to this subject by Roman military diplomas: Werner Eck, "Rekrutierung für das römische Heer in Kleinasien: Das Zeugnis der Militärdiplome," in: O. Tekin (ed.), *Ancient History, Numismatics and Epigraphy in the Mediterranean World. Studies in Honour of Clemens E. Bosch, Sabahat Atlan and Nezahat Baydur*, Istanbul 2009, 137–142.

65. Michael P. Speidel, "Legionaries from Asia Minor," *ANRW* II 7.2, 1980, 730–746.

66. Michael P. Speidel, "The Roman Army in Asia Minor. Recent Epigraphical Discoveries and Research," in: St. Mitchell (ed.), *Armies and Frontiers in Roman and Byzantine Anatolia*, Oxford 1983, 19 f.

67. Christian Marek, "Wer war der Paphlagonier Priscus?" in: E. Winter (ed.), *Vom Euphrat bis zum Bosporus. Kleinasien in der Antike*, FS Schwertheim, vol. 2, *AMS* 65, Bonn 2008, 423–430.

68. Thomas Drew-Bear, "Les voyages d'Aurélius Gaius, soldat de Dioclétien," in: T. Fahd (ed.), *La géographie administrative et politique d'Alexandre à Mahomet. Actes du Colloque de Strasbourg, 14–16 juin 1979*, Leiden 1981, 93–141; cf. Maurice Sartre, "Les voyages d'Aurélius Gaius, soldat de Dioclétien, et la nomenclature provinciale," *EpigrAnat* 2, 1983, 25–32.

69. Michael P. Speidel, op. cit., 20 f.

70. [549] Marek, *Pontus et Bithynia*, 2003, 57.

71. See in general Lutz Neesen, *Untersuchungen zu den direkten Staatsabgaben der römischen Kaiserzeit (27 v. Chr.–284 n. Chr.)*, Bonn 1980; Frank Ausbüttel, *Die Verwaltung des römischen Kaiserreiches*, Darmstadt 1998, 75–78; [574] Drexhage, *Wirtschaftspolitik*, 2007, 32 ff.

72. Werner Eck, *Die Verwaltung des Römischen Reiches in der Hohen Kaiserzeit: ausgewählte und erweiterte Beiträge* II, Basel 1998, esp. 132 ff.; Drexhage, op. cit., 34 f.

73. Joyce Reynolds, "New Letters from Hadrian to Aphrodisias," *JRA* 13, 2000, 5–20, esp. 16. The fabrication of items out of iron, such as nails, was taxed.

74. Cf. [121] Herrmann and Polatkan, *Epikrates*, 1969, 25 f.

75. Keith Hopkins, "Taxes and Trade in the Roman Empire," *JRS* 70, 1980, esp. 116–124.

76. Josef Keil and Anton von Premerstein, "Bericht über eine dritte Reise in Lydien und den angrenzenden Gebieten Ioniens, ausgeführt 1911 im Auftrage der Kaiserlichen Akademie der Wissenschaften," *Kaiserliche Akademie der Wissenschaften, Phil.-hist. Klasse, Denkschriften* 57,1, Vienna 1914, p. 67–71.

77. Cf. Martin Zimmermann, "Zwischen Polis und Koinon: zum *hypophylax* im lykischen Bund," *EpigrAnat* 21, 1993, 107–119.

78. [579] Deininger, *Provinziallandtage*, 1965, 79.

79. [191] Kokkinia, *Opramoas*, 2000, II E 6 ff.; III F 13 ff.; IV E 6 ff.

80. [183] Marek, *Kaunos*, 2006, 175–221.

81. [574] Drexhage, *Wirtschaftspolitik*, 2007, 38.

82. On the extensive literature see Marek, op. cit., 187 f. In addition: [568] Cottier, Crawford, et. al. (eds.), *The Customs Law of Asia,* Oxford 2009. The customs law of the province of Lycia, found in Andriake, will be published by Burak Takmer; provisionally, see Burak Takmer, "Lex Portorii Provinciae Lyciae. Ein Vorbericht über die Zollinschrift aus Andriake aus neronischer Zeit," *Gephyra* 4, 2007, 165–188.

83. Georg Klingenberg, *Commissum. Der Verfall nicht deklarierter Sachen im römischen Zollrecht,* Graz 1977, 94 ff.

84. [183] Marek, *Kaunos*, 2006, 175–222.

85. *Digest* 50, 16, 27; Theodor Mommsen, Paul Krueger, and Alan Watson, *The Digest of Justinian*, vol. 4, Philadelphia 1985, 935.

86. Lukas de Ligt, *Fairs and Markets in the Roman Empire. Economic and Social Aspects of Periodic Trade in a Pre-Industrial Society*, Amsterdam 1993, 65 f.

87. [574] Drexhage, *Wirtschaftspolitik*, 2007, 50 f.

88. Michael A. Speidel, *Heer und Herrschaft im Römischen Reich der Hohen Kaiserzeit*, Stuttgart 2009, 473–500.

89. [571] Herrmann, *Hilferufe*, 1990; Walter Scheidel, "Dokument und Kontext: Aspekte der historischen Interpretation epigraphischer Quellen am Beispiel der 'Krise des dritten Jahrhunderts,'" *RStorAnt* 21, 1991, 145–164. Cf. also Michael A. Speidel, op. cit.

90. Wolfgang Kuhoff , *Diokletian und die Epoche der Tetrarchie. Das römische Reich zwischen Krisenbewältigung und Neuaufbau (284–313 n. Chr.),* Frankfurt am Main. 2001; Alexander Demandt, Andreas Goltz, and Heinrich Schlange-Schöningen (eds.), *Diokletian und die Tetrarchie. Aspekte einer Zeitwende*, Berlin and New York 2004.

91. See Kuhoff, op. cit., 543–564 with sources and literature; Hartwin Brandt, "Erneute Überlegungen zum Preisedikt Diokletians," in: Demandt, Goltz, and Schlange-Schöningen, op. cit., 47–55.

Chapter 9. Economic, Socio-Political, and Cultural Conditions in the Provinces of the Imperial Period

1. Karl Julius Beloch, *Die Bevölkerung der griechisch-römischen Welt*, Leipzig 1886. Asia Minor is dealt with on p. 223 ff. On Beloch's contribution in general, see Glen W. Bowersock, "Beloch and the Birth of Demography," *TAPhA* 127, 1997, 373–379.

2. On the method of age-band statistics, Walter Scheidel (ed.), *Debating Roman Demography*, Leiden 2001; W. Scheidel, "Roman Age Structure: Evidence and Models," *JRS* 91,

2001, 1–26; Bruce W. Frier, "Demography," *CAH* XI 2, 2000, 787–816; on calculations based on census figures in Egypt, Roger S. Bagnall and Bruce W. Frier, *The Demography of Roman Egypt*, Cambridge 1994. In general, Pierre Salmon, *Population et dépopulation dans l'Empire Romain*, Brussels 1974 (here, too, Asia Minor is given practically no attention).

3. [569] Broughton, *Asia Minor*, 1938, 499–918. Critique of Beloch and Broughton: P. D. Warden and R. S. Bagnall, "The Forty Thousand Citizens of Ephesos," *CP* 83, 1988, 220-223.

4. Vol. 5 p. 49 Kühn; trans. Paul W. Harkins, *Galen On the Passions and Errors of the Soul*, 1963, 63.

5. [264] Kolb, *Burg-Polis-Bischofssitz*, 2008, 428.

6. Hannelore Vanhaverbeke and Marc Waelkens, *The Chora of Sagalassos. The Evolution of the Settlement Pattern from Prehistoric until Recent Times*, Turnhout 2003, esp. 199.336; id., "La genèse d'un territoire. Le cas de Sagalassos en Pisidie," in: [286] Bru, Kirbihler, and Lebreton, *L'Asie Mineure*, 2009, 243 ff.

7. [7] Zgusta, *PN*, 1964; [6] Robert, *Noms*, 1963. Place names: [10] Zgusta, *ON*, 1984. Cf. Günter Neumann, "Kleinasien," in: G. Neumann and J. Untermann (eds.), *Die Sprachen im römischen Reich der Kaiserzeit*, Bonn-Köln 1980, 167–185.

8. [7] Zgusta, *PN*, 1964, 9–19.

9. Jeanne and Louis Robert, *Hellenica* 6, 1948, 90. The quote is from [50a] Parker, *Names in Ancient Anatolia*, 2013, 5.

10. In general on Iranian elements (cults, names, etc.) in western Asia Minor in Hellenistic and Roman times: Mary Boyce and Frantz Grenet, *A History of Zoroastrianism. III. Zoroastrianism under Macedonian and Roman Rule*, [2] *HdO* VIII 1, 2, 2, vol. 3, Leiden 1991, 209–253.

11. [6] Robert, *Noms*, 1963, 517 note 2.

12. [157] Ameling, *Inscriptiones Judaicae* II, 2004; id., "Die jüdischen Gemeinden im antiken Kleinasien, in: R. Jütte and A. R. Kustermann (eds.), Jüdische Gemeinden und Organisationsformen von der Antike bis zur Gegenwart," Vienna-Köln-Weimar 1996, 29–55. Cf. in general [620] Trebilco, *Communities*, 1991. Interesting verse inscriptions: [146] MS I 472; III 344.414 (Debbora).

13. [7] Zgusta, *PN*, 1964, 539.

14. [6] Robert, *Noms*, 1963, 457–523.

15. Cf., in addition to [7] Zgusta, *PN*, 1964: Peter Frei, "Die epichorischen Namen im griechisch-römischen Inschriftenbestand der Region von Eskişehir, in: H. Otten et al. (eds.), *Hittite and other Anatolian and Near Eastern Studies,* FS Alp, Ankara 1992, 181–192; Wolfgang Blümel, "Einheimische Personennamen in griechischen Inschriften aus Karien," *EpigrAnat* 20, 1992, 7 ff.; [431] Doni, *Pisidians*, 2009.

16. A remark made by Strabo (14, 2, 3; trans. Jones) regarding the Kaunians—"it is said that they speak the same language as the Carians"—should not be taken as evidence for the vitality of this idiom at the beginning of the Imperial period; it is clearly a reference to Herodotus (1, 171 f.): [591] Stephan, *Honoratioren*, 2002, 270.

17. Claude Brixhe, "Interactions between Greek and Phrygian under the Roman Empire," in: J. N. Adams, M. Janse, and S.C.R. Swain (eds.), *Bilingualism in Ancient Society. Language Contact and the Written Text*, Oxford-New York 2002, 246–266.

18. Claude Brixhe, Thomas Drew-Bear, and Durmuş Kaya, "Nouveaux monuments de Pisidie," *Kadmos* 26, 1987, 122–170.

19. Claude Brixhe, "La langue comme critère d'acculturation: l'exemple du grec d'un dis-

trict phrygien," in: R. Lebrun (ed.), *Acta Anatolica E. Laroche oblata*, Löwen-Paris, 1987, 45–80; id., *Essai sur le grec anatolien au début de notre ère*, second ed., Nancy 1987.

20. [544] Mitchell, *Anatolia* I, 1993, 174 f.

21. [549] Marek, *Pontus et Bithynia*, 2003, 149; [146] *MS* I 465; III 69.265.

22. Karl Holl, "Das Fortleben der Volkssprachen in Kleinasien in nachchristlicher Zeit," *Hermes* 43, 1908, 240–254.

23. For the province of Asia, [574] Drexhage, *Wirtschaftspolitik*, 2007 is now fundamental. Cf. [573] Mitchell and Katsari (eds.), *Patterns*, 2005; Erik Gren, *Kleinasien und der Ostbalkan in der wirtschaftlichen Entwicklung der römischen Kaiserzeit*, Uppsala-Leipzig 1941; [569] Broughton, *Asia Minor*, 1938.

24. Marc Waelkens and Lieven Loots (eds.), *Sagalassos* V 1, Löwen 2000, 30.

25. Testimonies in [569] Broughton, *Asia Minor*, 1938, 609 ff.

26. [112] Robert, *Études anatoliennes*, 1937, 104; cf. [110] MAMA IV 297; [109] Syll.³ 1157 lines 73–83.

27. [264] Kolb, Burg-Polis-Bischofssitz, 2008, 337. This analysis refers to the period of the sixth to seventh centuries CE, but a similar relationship is assumed for the Imperial period.

28. [132] Robert, *Documents*, 1987, 133–148.

29. Johannes Nollé, *Die Abwehr der wilden Schweine. Schwarzwildjagden im antiken Lykien*, Munich 2001. Cf. Erika Bleibtreu and Jürgen Borchhardt, "Wildschweinjagd zwischen Ost und West," in: E. Winter (ed.), *Vom Euphrat bis zum Bosporus. Kleinasien in der Antike*, FS Schwertheim, vol. 1, AMS 65, Bonn 2008, 61–101.

30. [162] Museum Iznik II 3, T 16 with literature.

31. [549] Marek, *Pontus et Bithynia*, 2003, 162.

32. On the ancient abundance of timber in Phrygia, [614] Drew-Bear and Naour, "Divinités," *ANRW* II 18.3, 1990, 1924 f.

33. Text: Galen vol. 6, p. 749 Kühn [*De rebus boni malique suci* (CMG V. 4,2)].

34. Michael Wörrle, "Ägyptisches Getreide für Ephesos," *Chiron* 1, 1971, 325–340; cf. Jörn Kobes, "Fremdes Getreide. Beobachtungen zum Problem der Getreideversorgung in der kaiserzeitlichen Provinz Asia," *Laverna* 10, 1999, 81–98.

35. Johan Strubbe, "Sitonia in the Cities of Asia Minor under the Principate I," *EpigrAnat* 10, 1987, 45–82; II, *EpigrAnat* 13, 1989, 99–122.

36. Hans-Ulrich Wiemer, "Das Edikt des L. Antistius Rusticus: Eine Preisregulierung als Antwort auf eine überregionale Versorgungskrise?," *AnSt* 47, 1997, 195–215.

37. Sema Atik, "A New Discovery in Kaunos. Sal Caunitis," in: E. Winter (ed.), *Vom Euphrat bis zum Bosporus. Kleinasien in der Antike*, FS Schwertheim, vol. 1, AMS 65, Bonn 2008, 39–45.

38. Trans. Patrick Degryse, Tom Heldal, Elizabeth Bloxam, Per Storemyr, Marc Waelkens, and Philippe Muchez (trans.), "The Sagalassos Quarry Landscape: Bringing Quarries in Context," in: P. Degryse and M. Waelkens (eds.), *Sagalassos VI. Geo- and Bio-archaeology at Sagalassos and in Its Territory*, Leuven 2008, 261.

39. Literature in [574] Drexhage, *Wirtschaftspolitik*, 2007, 249 and note 840.

40. Examples in op. cit., 188.

41. Frank Rumscheid, *Die figürlichen Terrakotten von Priene. Fundkontexte, Ikonographie und Funktion in Wohnhäusern und Heiligtümern im Licht antiker Parallelbefunde*, Wiesbaden 2006.

42. [264] Kolb, *Burg-Polis-Bischofssitz*, 2008, 433.

43. [6] Robert, *Noms*, 1963, 471.

44. Tullia Ritti, Klaus Grewe, and Paul Kessener, "A Relief of a Water-Powered Stone Saw Mill on a Sarcophagus at Hierapolis and its Implications," *JRA* 20, 2007, 139–163.

45. Roland R. R. Smith, *Aphrodisias II: Roman Portrait Statuary from Aphrodisias*, Mainz 2006. Julie A. Van Voorhis, *The Sculptor's Workshop at Aphrodisias*. Unpublished Ph.D. Dissertation, New York University 1999.

46. [577] Zimmermann, *Handwerkervereine*, 2002; [576] Dittmann-Schöne, *Berufsvereine*, 2001; [575] van Nijf, *Associations*, 1997. Cf. Stefan Sommer, *Rom und die Vereinigungen im südwestlichen Kleinasien (133 v. Chr.–284 n. Chr.)*, Hennef 2006.

47. Ph. Harland (trans.), "Proconsular Edict Concerning Bakers (ca. 150–200 CE)," in: *Associations in the Greco-Roman World: A Companion to the Sourcebook*, http://www.philip harland.com/greco-roman-associations/?p=6299).

48. [574] Drexhage, *Wirtschaftspolitik*, 2007, esp. 197 ff.

49. Christian Marek, "Imperial Asia Minor: Economic Prosperity and Names," in: [50a] *Personal Names*, 2013, 175–194.

50. [183] Marek, *Kaunos*, 2006, 175 ff.

51. Bernard Holtheide, "Zum privaten Seehandel im östlichen Mittelmeer," *MünstBeitr* 1.2, 1982, 8. On a *naukleros* in the Lycian Olympus: Mustafa Adak and Orhan Atvur, "Das Grabhaus des Zosimas und der Schiffseigner Eudemos aus Olympos," *EpigrAnat* 28, 1997, 18 f. no. 3. A shipowner's name on a late Antique tombstone in Korasion, Cilicia: [110] MAMA III 179.

52. Karl Müller, *Geographi Graeci Minores*, vol. 2, Paris 1861, 153 line 793.

53. John B. Ward-Perkins, "Nicomedia and the Marble Trade," in: *BSR* 48, 1980, 23 ff.; id., "The Marble Trade and its Organization: Evidence from Nicomedia," in: J. H. D'Arms and E. C. Kopff (eds.), *The Seaborne Commerce of Ancient Rome. Studies in Archaeology and History*, Rome 1980, 325 ff.

54. Peter Herrmann, "Milesischer Purpur," *IstMitt* 25, 1975, 142–147.

55. Peter Herrmann, "Neues vom Sklavenmarkt in Sardeis," *ADerg* 4, 1996, 175 ff.

56. [569] Broughton, *Asia Minor*, 1938, 878.

57. Johannes Nollé, "Marktrechte außerhalb der Stadt: Lokale Autonomie zwischen Statthalter und Zentralort," in: W. Eck (ed.), *Lokale Autonomie und römische Ordnungsmacht in den kaiserzeitlichen Provinzen vom 1. bis 3. Jahrhundert*, Munich 1999, 93–113; [570] Nollé, *Nundinas*, 1982.

58. Johannes Nollé, "Münzen als Zeugnisse für die Geschichte der Hellenisierung Kleinasiens," in: U. Peter (ed.), *Stephanos nomismatikos*, FS Schönert-Geiss, Berlin 1998, 509.

59. Wolfgang Leschhorn, "Die kaiserzeitliche Münzprägung in Phrygien. Stand der Arbeiten und Probleme der Forschung," in: [223] Nollé, Overbeck, and Weiß (eds.), *Münzprägung*, 1997, 49–59.

60. Peter Weiß, "The Cities and their Money," in: Ch. Howgego, V. Heuchert, and A. Burnett (eds.), *Coinage and Identity in the Roman Provinces*, Oxford 2005, 57–68.

61. Wolfram Weiser, *Katalog der Bithynischen Münzen der Sammlung des Instituts für Altertumskunde der Universität zu Köln*, 1. *Nikaia*, Opladen 1983, 109 ff., esp. 182 f.

62. Cf. also Hans-Dietrich Schultz, "Das Ende der städtischen Münzprägung von Ephesos und Samos unter Gallienus (260–268 n. Chr.)," in: [223] Nollé, Overbeck, and Weiß (eds.), *Münzprägung*, 1997, 231–245.

63. Wolfram Weiser, "Die Münzreform des Aurelian," *ZPE* 53, 1983, 279–295.

64. [591] Stephan, *Honoratioren*, 2002, esp. 115–178; Henri-Louis Fernoux, "Frontières

civiques et maîtrise du territoire: un enjeu pour la cité grecque sous le Haut-Empire (Ier–IIIe siècle apr. J.-C.)," in: [286] Bru, Kirbihler, and Lebreton, *L'Asie Mineure*, 2009, 135 ff.

65. [562] Meyer-Zwiffelhoffer, *Statthalter*, 2002, esp. 8 ff.

66. Charles A. Behr (trans.), *P. Aelius Aristeides. The Complete Works*, 2 vols., Leiden 1981–1986.

67. Anthony D. Macro, "The Cities of Asia Minor under the Roman Imperium," *ANRW* II 7.2, 1980, 658–697.

68. Stephen Mitchell, "The Pisidian Survey," in: [31] Matthews (ed.), *Fifty Years*, 1998, 238.

69. Wolfgang Leschhorn, "Die kaiserzeitliche Münzprägung in Phrygien," in: [223] Nollé, Overbeck, and Weiß (eds.), *Münzprägung*, 1997, 51.

70. [493] Jones, *Cities*, second ed. ,1971, 134 f.

71. Cf. [568a] Vitale, *Eparchie und Koinon*, 2012.

72. Overview of the different meanings of the term on coins in [14] Franke and Leschhorn, *Lexikon*, 2002, 171–173.

73. Peter Herrmann, "Das *koinon ton Ionon* unter römischer Herrschaft," in: N. Ehrhardt and L. Günther (eds.), *Widerstand–Anpassung–Integration. Die griechische Staatenwelt und Rom*, FS Deininger, Stuttgart 2002, 223–240.

74. For a different view, see [591] Stephan, *Honoratioren*, 2002, 185.

75. [517] Behrwald, *Lykischer Bund*, 2000, 129.

76. [549] Marek, *Pontus et Bithynia*, 2003, 66. In Galatia: [186a] Mitchell and French, *Ankyra*, 2012, no. 72f.140.

77. For a detailed refutation of the opposite claim made in [579] Deininger, *Provinziallandtage*, 1965, see [182] Marek, *Stadt, Ära*, 1993, 73–82.

78. Deininger, *Provinziallandtage*, 81 f.; [549] Brandt and Kolb, *Lycia et Pamphylia*, 2005, 73. To the formula "Cities in Pamphylia" in [105] TAM II 2, 495 lines 16 f. corresponds "Cities in Pamphylia and Cities in Lycia and Cities in Asia" in [106] OGIS 567, and it is thus nothing more than a variant title.

79. IGR III 474 line 14; [105] TAM III 1, 127 line 6; 138 line 4; [184] İplikçioğlu, Çelgin, and Çelgin, *Termessos*, 2007, no. 13; cf. [581] Dräger, *Städte*, 1993, 250–255.

80. A new formation of the Syrian eparchies without Cilicia is first mentioned in inscriptions from the period of Trajan: Syria, Phoinike, and Commagene. Evidence in Dräger, op. cit., 257 note 5. It seems that even during the early reign of Hadrian, in 119/120 CE, Antiocheia claimed the proud title of "mother city" (*metropolis*) with respect not only to the three Syrian eparchies but also to a fourth, which is assumed to be Cilicia. Whether this meant that Syria's commonalty persisted up to forty years after Cilicia was separated from it or was simply an anachronistic continuation of the title cannot be determined.

81. [552] Ziegler, *Koinon*, 1999, esp. 153.

82. A coinage from Ilistra dating 138–140 CE: Marco Vitale, "Zwei neue Prägephasen des 'Koinon von Lycaonia,'" *SchwMBll* 240, 2010, 103-111.

83. [559] Rémy, *Carrières*, 1989, no. 163.

84. Ziegler, *Koinon*, 140 note 17.

85. [549] Brandt and Kolb, *Lycia et Pamphylia*, 2005, 29 and 27 ill. 26.

86. [579] Deininger, *Provinziallandtage*, 1965, 150 f.

87. Peter Weiß, "Asiarchen und Archiereis Asias," in: N. Ehrhardt and L. Günther (eds.), *Widerstand–Anpassung–Integration. Die griechische Staatenwelt und Rom*, FS Deininger, Stuttgart 2002, 241–254.

88. [584] Campanile, *Sacerdoti*, 1994; Maria D. Campanile, "Sommi sacerdoti, asiarchi e culto imperiale: un aggiornamento," in: B. Virgilio (ed.), *Studi ellenistici* XIX, Pisa 2006, 523–584.

89. [549] Marek, *Pontus et Bithynia*, 2003, 67.

90. Martin Zimmermann, "Die Archiereis des lykischen Bundes. Prosopographische Überlegungen zu den Bundespriestern," in: Ch. Schuler (ed.), *Griechische Epigraphik in Lykien. Eine Zwischenbilanz. Akten des Kolloquiums vom 24.–26. 2. 2005 in München*, Vienna 2007, 111–120.

91. Riet van Bremen, *The Limits of Participation. Women in Civic Life in the Greek East in the Hellenistic and Roman Periods*, Amsterdam 1996, 114–141. Cf. Campanile, op. cit., 22–25.

92. Rosalinde A. Kearsley in several studies, most recently: "Asiarchs, Archiereis and Archiereiai of Asia. New Evidence from Amorion in Phrygia," *EpigrAnat* 16, 1990, 69–80.

93. Michael Wörrle, "Neue Inschriftenfunde aus Aizanoi I," *Chiron* 22, 1992, 370.

94. [579] Deininger, *Provinziallandtage*, 1965, 51.

95. Barbara Burrell, *Neokoroi. Greek Cities and Roman Emperors*, Leiden 2004.

96. Glen W. Bowersock, "Hadrian and Metropolis," in: J. Straub (ed.), *Bonner Historia Augusta Colloquium 1982/3*, Bonn 1985, 75–88.

97. [112] Robert, *Études anatoliennes*, 1937, 245 f. Thus Pontic Herakleia also used the title "Mother of the emigrant cities," [200] Waddington, Babelon, and Reinach, *Recueil*, 1925, 357–376 no. 72.129.205.

98. Giovanni M. Staffieri, *La monetazione di Diocaesarea in Cilicia*, Lugano 1985, no. 13.

99. [14] Franke and Leschhorn, *Lexikon*, 2002, 172.

100. [579] Deininger, *Provinziallandtage*, 1965, 170 f.

101. Brooks Levy, "The Date of Asinius Pollio's Asian Proconsulship," *JNG* 44, 1994, 79 ff.

102. Deininger, op. cit., 69.

103. [526] Wörrle, *Pergamon*, 2000, 544 line 13.

104. [187] Wörrle, *Stadt und Fest*, 1988, 96 ff.

105. The following is based on [598] Kunnert, *Phylen*, 2012.

106. [569] Broughton, *Asia Minor*, 1938, 814.

107. Frederick W. Hasluck, *Cyzicus*, Cambridge 1910, 250 f.; Valerio Caldesi Valeri, "Le assemblee di Stratonicea in Caria," *MinEpigrP* 2, 1999, 185–233; [183] Marek, *Kaunos*, 2006, no. 34; [109] Syll.³ 1234.

108. On Lycia, [187] Wörrle, *Stadt und Fest*, 1988, 162.

109. [490] Magie, *Roman Rule*, 1950, 645.

110. [181] Robert, *Claros*, 1989, 43.

111. [179] Reynolds, *Aphrodisias and Rome*, 1982, 33 ff.

112. On the example of Aphrodisias: Angelos Chaniotis, "Macht und Volk in den kaiserzeitlichen Inschriften von Aphrodisias," in: G. Urso (ed.), *Popolo e potere nel mondo antico. Atti del convegno internazionale, 23–25 settembre 2004*, Pisa 2005, 47–61.

113. [187] Wörrle, *Stadt und Fest*, 1988, 100–123.

114. Wörrle, *Stadt und Fest*, 109–111.

115. [162] *IK* Smyrna 721; further evidence in ibid., vol. II 2, p. 439, Index s. v.

116. [631] Robert, *Pionios*, 1994, 67.

117. Cf. [162] *IK* Smyrna 781–798b and Peter Weiß, "Marktgewichte aus Kyzikos und Hipparchengewichte," in: E. Schwertheim (ed.), *Mysische Studien*, AMS 1, Bonn 1990, 135–

137; Rudolf Haensch and Peter Weiß, "'Statthaltergewichte' aus Pontus et Bithynia. Neue Exemplare und neue Erkenntnisse," *Chiron* 37, 2007, 183–218.

118. Victor Walser in [183] Marek, *Kaunos*, 2006, 332–335.

119. [549] Brandt and Kolb, *Lycia et Pamphylia*, 2005, 35.

120. Ibid.; cf. [549] Marek, *Pontus et Bithynia*, 2003, 78.

121. Michael Wörrle, "Zu Rang und Bedeutung von Gymnasium und Gymnasiarchie im hellenistischen Pergamon," *Chiron* 37, 2007, 502–516.

122. Michael Wörrle, Vom tugendsamen Jüngling zum <gestreßten> Euergeten, in: P. Zanker (ed.), *Stadtbild und Bürgerbild*, Munich 1995, 249.

123. Johan Strubbe, "Sitonia in the Cities of Asia Minor under the Principate I," *EpigrAnat* 10, 1987, 45–82; II, *EpigrAnat* 13, 1989, 99–122.

124. On the security aspect: Johannes Nollé, "Marktrechte außerhalb der Stadt: Lokale Autonomie zwischen Statthalter und Zentralort," in: W. Eck (ed.), *Lokale Autonomie und römische Ordnungsmacht in den kaiserzeitlichen Provinzen vom 1.–3. Jh.*, Munich 1999, 93–113; [593] Brélaz, *Sécurité*, 2005.

125. [106] OGIS 483; [186a] Mitchell and French, *Ankyra*, 2012, no. 127.129.132.; [182] Marek, *Stadt, Ära*, 1993, 172 no. 56.

126. Nikos Yannakopulos, "Preserving the Pax Romana: The Peace Functionaries in Roman East," *MedAnt* 6.2, 2003, 825–905 with a list of inscriptions and literary evidence 884-895.

127. Alessandro Zamai, "Gli irenarchi d'Asia Minore," *Patavium* 17, 2001, 53–73; id., "L'andreia degli irenarchi," *Patavium* 18, 2001, 63–83.

128. [112] Robert, *Études anatoliennes*, 1937, 101 f.

129. [180] Robert, *Amyzon*, 1983, 101–109.

130. [182] Marek, *Stadt, Ära*, 1993, 145 no. 32.

131. Martin Zimmermann, "Probus, Carus und die Räuber im Gebiet des pisidischen Termessos," *ZPE* 110, 1996, 265–277.

132. [104] Sterrett, *Journey*, 1888, 156.

133. A view rightly opposed by Michael Wörrle, "Ermandyberis von Limyra, ein prominenter Bürger aus der Chora," in: [247] Kolb (ed.), *Chora*, 2004, 299.

134. [597] Zuiderhoek, *Munificence*, 2009.

135. Wörrle, op. cit., 295.

136. [578] Liebenam, *Städteverwaltung*, 1900, 54–65.

137. [490] Magie, *Roman Rule*, 1950, 652.

138. E.g. [112] Robert, *Études anatoliennes*, 1937, 339 no. 1.

139. [495] Quaß, *Honoratiorenschicht*, 1993, 334–337.

140. Wörrle, op. cit., 295.

141. [160] Nollé, *Losorakel*, 2007.

142. [591] Stephan, *Honoratioren*, 2002, 85–113; Michael Wörrle, "Vom tugendsamen Jüngling zum 'gestreßten' Euergeten," in: P. Zanker (ed.), *Stadtbild und Bürgerbild*, Munich 1995, 241–250.

143. Lutgarde Vandeput and Christof Berns, "Private Freigebigkeit und die Verschönerung von Stadtbildern. Die Städte Kleinasiens in traianischer Zeit," in: A. Nünnerich-Asmus (ed.), *Traian*, Mainz 2002, 73–82.

144. Pauline Schmitt Pantel, *La cité au banquet. Histoire des repas publics dans les cités grecques*, Rome-Paris 1992, esp. 261 ff.

145. Christian Marek, "Der Dank der Stadt an einen comes in Amisos unter Theodosius II.," *Chiron* 30, 2000, 367–387, esp. 380 f.

146. Dazu Peter Weiß, "The Cities and Their Money," in: Ch. Howgego, V. Heuchert, and A. Burnett (eds.), *Coinage and Identity in the Roman Provinces*, Oxford 2005, 57–68.

147. [183] Marek, *Kaunos*, 2006, no. 35; Christian Marek, "Stadt, Bund und Reich in der Zollorganisation des kaiserzeitlichen Lykien. Eine neue Interpretation der Zollinschrift von Kaunos," in: H.-U. Wiemer (ed.), *Staatlichkeit und politisches Handeln in der römischen Kaiserzeit*, Berlin 2006, 115.

148. [191] Kokkinia, *Opramoas*, 2000.

149. [579] Deininger, *Provinziallandtage*, 1965, 79, connected the Opramoas phenomenon with a special sense of community that had been powerful only in Lycia since pre-Roman times.

150. See Klaus Bringmann, "Edikt der Triumvirn oder Senatsbeschluß? Zu einem Neufund aus Ephesos," *EpigrAnat* 2, 1983, 47–76.

151. Rudolph Herzog, *Urkunden zur Hochschulpolitik der römischen Kaiser*, Berlin 1935, 7.

152. *Digest* 27, 1, 6, 7; Theodor Mommsen, Paul Krueger, and Alan Watson (trans.), *The Digest of Justinian*, vol. 2, Philadelphia 1985, 783.

153. [543] Sartre, *Orient*, 1991, 133.

154. On research, see esp. [587] Schwarz, *Soll oder Haben*, 2001, 2–23.

155. [587] Schwarz, *Soll oder Haben,* 2001; cf. [574] Drexhage, *Wirtschaftspolitik*, 2007, 97–100.

156. [587] Schwarz, *Soll oder Haben*, 2001, 18–20.

157. [574] Drexhage, *Wirtschaftspolitk*, 2007, 93–97; cf. also [612] Dignas, *Economy*, 2002.

158. For Ephesos see Dieter Knibbe, Recep Meric, and Reinhold Merkelbach, "Grundbesitz der ephesischen Artemis im Kaystros-Tal," *ZPE* 33, 1979, 139–147. Cf. [569] Broughton, *Asia Minor*, 1938, 676 ff.

159. Strabo 14, 1, 22; Diogenes Laertios 2, 6, 7; Aristeides, *or.* 23, 24; Dion of Prusa, *or.* 31, 54 ff.

160. See Michael Wörrle, "Epigraphische Forschungen zur Geschichte Lykiens VI. Der Zeus von Dereköy: Die Reform eines ländlichen Kultes," *Chiron* 27, 1997, 452 f.

161. Peter Herrmann and Ender Varinlioğlu, "Theoi Pereudenoi. Eine Gruppe von Weihungen und Sühninschriften aus der Katakekaumene," *EpigrAnat* 3, 1984, 5 on a kind of religious "sales tax."

162. See [124] Schwertheim, *Meterverehrung*, 1978, 813 f., cf. [549] Marek, *Pontus et Bithynia*, 2003, 162.

163. [106] OGIS 572; [569] Broughton, *Asia Minor*, 1938, 801.

164. [587] Schwarz, *Soll oder Haben*, 2001, 404 f.; [183] Marek, *Kaunos*, 2006, 214 f.

165. [145] Strubbe, *Arai*, 1997.

166. [574] Drexhage, *Wirtschaftspolitik*, 2007, 117.

167. Nicolas P. Milner, "Athletics, Army Recruitment and Heroisation: L. Sep. Fl. Flavillianus of Oinoanda," *AnSt* 61, 2011, 151–167.

168. [586] Halfmann, *Städtebau*, 2001; [585] Winter, *Baupolitik*, 1996, cf. [569] Broughton, *Asia Minor*, 1938, 746 ff.

169. A few architects in Anatolian cities are listed in Broughton, op. cit., 850 f.

170. Th. Mommsen, *The History of Rome, The Provinces from Caesar to Diocletian*, Part I, trans. W. P. Dickson, New York 1899, 384.

171. Esp. [595] Meyer, *Neue Zeiten—Neue Sitten*, 2007; [595] Berns, Hesberg, Vandeput, and Waelkens, *Patris und Imperium*, 2002.

172. [585] Winter, *Baupolitik*, 1996.

173. Friedmund Hueber, *Ephesos. Gebaute Geschichte*, Mainz 1997, 41.

174. Helmut Müller, "Allianoi. Zur Identifizierung eines antiken Kurbades im Hinterland von Pergamon," *IstMitt* 54, 2004, 215–225.

175. This is an "optical correction" that involves "a slight upward arching of the stepped base and the entablature […] that is intended to counteract, in the case of long horizontals, the impression of sagging" (Wolfgang Müller-Wiener, *Griechisches Bauwesen in der Antike*, Munich 1988, 135, with the examples familiar from Greek temple construction in the Classical age).

176. Cf. Christopher P. Jones, "The Neronian Inscription on the Lighthouse of Patara," *ZPE* 166, 2008, 153 f.

177. [589] Pohl, *Tempel*, 2002.

178. A *dipteros* is equipped with a double colonnade on all four sides. A *pseudodipteros* is a type of temple which lacks the inner row of columns in its *peristasis*, but has double-width porches.

179. Fundamental: [499] Schuler, *Ländliche Siedlungen*, 1998.

180. [569] Broughton, *Asia Minor*, 1938, 643 f.

181. Cf. [612] Dignas, *Economy*, 2002, esp. 233–246.

182. [571] Herrmann, *Hilferufe*, 1990, no. 4 line 91 ff. (from Thrace); no. 8 lines 41–54 (Ağabey-Köy in Lydia) = [105] TAM V 3, 1418.

183. Christian Marek, "Die Phylen von Klaudiupolis, die Geschichte der Stadt und die Topographie Ostbithyniens," *MusHelv* 59, 2002, 31–50.

184. Hannelore Vanhaverbeke and Marc Waelkens, *The Chora of Sagalassos. The Evolution of the Settlement Pattern from Prehistoric until Recent Times*, Turnhout 2003, esp. 241 ff. and 336.

185. List in [499] Schuler, *Ländliche Siedlungen*, 1998, 291–297.

186. [187] Wörrle, *Stadt und Fest*, 1988, p. 12 f. lines 72–79.

187. Michael Wörrle and Wolfgang W. Wurster, "Dereköy: Eine befestigte Siedlung im nordwestlichen Lykien und die Reform ihres dörflichen Zentralkultes," *Chiron* 27, 1997, 393–469.

188. [499] Schuler, *Ländliche Siedlungen*, 1998, 263 with note 309.

189. [182] Marek, *Stadt, Ära*, 1993, 43 f.

190. Cf. [591] Stephan, *Honoratioren*, 2002, 261 ff.

191. [187] Wörrle, *Stadt und Fest*, 1988, 123–131.

192. [549] Brandt and Kolb, *Lycia et Pamphylia*, 2005, 38.

193. [575] van Nijf, *Associations*, 1997, 10.20.184 f. 233; [576] Dittmann-Schöne, *Berufsvereine*, 2001, 203.

194. *Martyrium Pionii* 3 according to [631] Robert, *Pionios*, 1994.

195. Walter Ameling, "Die jüdischen Gemeinden im antiken Kleinasien," in: R. Jütte and A. R. Kustermann (eds.), *Jüdische Gemeinden und Organisationsformen von der Antike bis zur Gegenwart*, Wien-Köln-Weimar 1996, 29–55; [620] Trebilco, *Communities*, 1991; [157] Ameling, *Inscriptiones Judaicae* II, 2004, 1–36.

196. [248] Cormack, *Space of Death*, 2004.

197. On the Lycian tomb landscape cf. Oliver Hülden, *Gräber und Grabtypen im Bergland von Yavu (Zentrallykien). Studien zur antiken Grabkultur in Lykien*, Bonn 2006.

198. [121] Herrmann and Polatkan, *Epikrates*, 1969, 7–36. Cf. IGR IV 661.

199. Op. cit., 22 with note 23.

200. Veli Köse, *Nekropolen und Grabdenkmäler von Sagalassos in Pisidien in hellenistischer und römischer Zeit*, Turnhout 2006. Lycia: [264] Kolb, *Burg-Polis-Bischofssitz*, 2008, 367–373.

201. [145] Strubbe, *Arai*, 1997, no. 155.

202. [145] Strubbe, *Arai*, 1997.

203. [186] Kokkinia (trans.), *Boubon,* 2008, 74 no. 38.

204. [146] MS I 253; C. P. Jones (trans.), "Two Inscribed Monuments of Aphrodisias," *Arch. Anz.* 1994, 458.

205. Bruce W. Frier, *Demography*, *CAH* XI 2, 2000, 791 ff.

206. [549] Marek, *Pontus et Bithynia*, 2003, 174 note 3.

207. [146] MS III 166; trans. Marek. Such a *therotrophos* is represented on a tombstone from Hierapolis, showing how he tamed a lion with a switch: [241] Pfuhl and Möbius 1194.

208. [146] MS I 524.542.644; II 296; [105] TAM IV 1, 367.

209. [132] Robert, *Documents*, 1987, 92 ff.

210. Michael Wörrle, "Epigraphische Forschungen zur Geschichte Lykiens VI. Der Zeus von Dereköy: Die Reform eines ländlichen Kultes," *Chiron* 27, 1997, 438 note 186. Kyzikos: CIG 3695 b.

211. [146] MS I 73; G. E. Bean and J. M. Cook (trans.), "The Carian Coast III," *ABSA* 52, 1957, 111 no. 2.

212. [141] Petzl, *Beichtinschriften*, 1994, 5.35.62.68.69.

213. *AnSt* 18, 1968, 115 no. 5,10; [105] TAM II 2, 593.636, II 3, 979.1122.1166.

214. In general: Anne-Marie Vérilhac, "L'image de la femme dans les épigrammes funéraires grecques," in: A.-M. Vérilhac (ed.), *La femme dans le monde méditerranéen* I, Lyon 1985, 85–112; Josef Pircher, *Das Lob der Frau im vorchristlichen Grabepigramm der Griechen*, Innsbruck 1979.

215. Cf. Vérilhac, op. cit., 108–112.

216. Hans-Ulrich Wiemer, "Die gute Ehefrau im Wandel der Zeiten—Von Xenophon zu Plutarch," *Hermes* 133,4, 2005, 424–446.

217. Helmut Häusle, *Das Denkmal als Garant des Nachruhms. Eine Studie zu einem Motiv in lateinischen Inschriften*, Munich 1980, 99 ff. no. 30; cf. Géza Alföldy, "Inschriften und Biographie in der römischen Welt," in: K. Vössing (ed.), *Biographie und Prosopographie. Internationales Kolloquium zum 65. Geburtstag von Anthony R. Birley*, Stuttgart 2005, 29–52, esp. 42 f.

218. A notable exception is a group of stone reliefs from central Paphlagonia that present a frontal view of a female bust with emphasis on the breasts. But they cannot be tombstones.

219. On temple prostitution, see p. 517.

220. See Wiemer, op. cit., 443.

221. [146] MS II 354; [162] *IK* Kios 52; [162] *IK* Herakleia 10; IGR IV 125. On women philosophers in general: Mario Meunier, *Femmes pythagoriciennes. Fragments et lettres*, second ed., Paris 1980.

222. [264] Kolb, *Burg-Polis-Bischofssitz*, 2008, 367–373.

223. Riet van Bremen, *The Limits of Participation. Women and Civic Life in the Greek East in the Hellenistic and Roman Periods*, Amsterdam 1996, esp. 303–357; François Kirbihler, "Les femmes magistrats et liturges en Asie Mineure (IIe s. av. J.-C.–IIIe s. ap. J.-C.)," *Ktema* 19, 1994, 51–75; [502] Dmitriev, *City Government*, 2005, 178 ff.

224. Stephen Mitchell, "The Plancii in Asia Minor," *JRS* 64, 1974, 27–39.

225. Van Bremen, op. cit., 114–141.

226. Van Bremen, op. cit., 180–190.

227. In general: William V. Harris, "Child-Exposure in the Roman Empire," *JRS* 84, 1994, 1–22; Pierre Brulé, "Infanticide et abandon d'enfants," *DialHistAnc* 18, 2, 1992, 53–90; Donald Engels, "The Problem of Female Infanticide in the Greco-Roman World," *ClPhil* 75, 2, 1980, 112–120.

228. Patricio Guinea, "La peculiaridad de los 'threptoi' en el Asia Menor," *DialHistAnc* 24, 1, 1998, 41–51; Barbara Levick and Stephen Mitchell, in: [110] MAMA IX, 1988, Introduction LXIV ff.; Teresa Giulia Nani, "ΘΡΕΠΤΟΙ," *Epigraphica* 5–6, 1943–1944, 45–84; Alan Cameron, "ΘΡΕΠΤΟΣ and the Related Terms in the Inscriptions of Asia Minor," in: W. M. Calder and J. Keil (eds.), *Anatolian Studies Presented to W. H. Buckler*, Manchester 1939, 27–62.

229. [572] Bussi, *Schiavitù*, 2001.

230. [195] SEG 52, 1464 ter.

231. [121] Herrmann and Polatkan, *Epikrates*, 1969, 7–36.

232. Thomas Drew-Bear, "Un eunuque arménien en Cappadoce," *EpigrAnat* 4, 1984, 139–150.

233. [241] Pfuhl and Möbius, Textband II, p. 290–292.

234. [549] Marek, *Pontus et Bithynia*, 2003, 167.

235. Harald Schulze, *Ammen und Pädagogen. Sklavinnen und Sklaven als Erzieher in der antiken Kunst und Gesellschaft*, Mainz 1998.

236. [499] Schuler, *Ländliche Siedlungen*, 1998, 231 ff., here p. 451.

237. Maria Paz de Hoz, "Literacy in Rural Anatolia: The Testimony of the Confession Inscriptions," *ZPE* 155, 2006, 139–144.

238. Georg Petzl, "Ländliche Religiosität in Lydien," *AMS* 17, Bonn 1995, 45.

239. Peter Thonemann, "Neilomandros. A Contribution to the History of Greek Personal Names," *Chiron* 36, 2006, 11–43.

240. [6] Robert, *Noms*, 1963, 268–270.

241. Cf. Werner Eck, "Latein als Sprache politischer Kommunikation in den Städten der östlichen Provinzen," *Chiron* 30, 2000, 641–660; Bruno Rochette, *Le latin dans le monde grec. Recherches sur la diffusion de la langue et des lettres latines dans les provinces hellénophones de l'Empire romain*, Brussels 1997.

242. Theodor Mommsen, AM 16, 1891, 281 f.

243. [591] Stephan, *Honoratioren*, 2002, 222–260.

244. On this and the following, see esp. Helmut Halfmann, "Die ersten römischen Senatoren aus Kleinasien," in: E. Winter (ed.), *Vom Euphrat bis zum Bosporus. Kleinasien in der Antike,* FS Schwertheim, vol. 1, AMS 65, Bonn 2008, 297–307.

245. [555] Halfmann, *Senatoren*, 1979, 78–81.

246. Charles A. Behr, P. Aelius Aristides. *The Complete Works* I, Leiden 1986, 2.

247. Louis Robert, *OMS* III, 1969, 1638.

248. The sources are collected in [146] MS I 180 ff.; cf. Hans-Joachim Gehrke, "Myth, History and Collective Identity: Uses of the Past in Ancient Greece and Beyond," in: N. Luraghi (ed.), *The Historian's Craft in the Age of Herodotus*, Oxford-New York 2001, 287–297.

249. See Peter Weiß, "Kaiserzeitliche Stadtprägung und Klassische Altertumswissenschaften," in: [223] Nollé, Overbeck, and Weiß (eds.), *Münzprägung*, 1997, 31.

250. Peter Weiß, "Alexandria Troas, Griechische Traditionen und Mythen in einer römischen Colonia," *AMS* 22, 1996, 157–173. The story of Alexander's dream about an oracle was also used to explain the refoundation of Smyrna (Pausanias 7, 5, 1–3; cf. the version in Strabo 14, 1, 37).

251. [591] Stephan, *Honoratioren*, 2002, 208–222; [583] Lindner, *Mythos*, 1994; [582] Scheer, *Mythische Vorväter*, 1993; [580] Leschhorn, *Gründer*, 1984; Johan H. M. Strubbe, "Gründer kleinasiatischer Städte. Fiktion und Realität," *AncSoc* 15–17, 1984–1986, 253–304.

252. Weiß, op. cit.

253. For another view, see Christopher P. Jones, "The Panhellenion," *Chiron* 26, 1996, 29–56.

254. We do not have a complete list of its members, but we know that among the participants were the Ionian cities of Samos, Miletus, Magnesia on the Maeander, Thyateira and Sardeis in Lydia, Aizanoi, Synnada, Eumeneia (?), and Apameia Kibotos in Phrygia, and also Kibyra and Rhodes, all of them cities in the province of Asia.

255. [105] TAM II 1, 174, cf. [146] MS IV 26–33. Osvalda Andrei, *A. Claudius Charax di Pergamo. Interessi antiquarie e antichità cittadine nell'età degli Antonini*, Bologna 1984.

256. See Peter Weiß, "Lebendiger Mythos. Gründerheroen und städtische Gründungstraditionen im griechisch-römischen Osten," *WürbJb* 10, 1984, 179–211.

257. [170] Robert, *Carie*, 1954, 73.87–91.

258. Johannes Nollé, "Vielerorts war Bethlehem—Göttergeburten im kaiserzeitlichen Kleinasien," *Antike Welt* 34, 2003, 635 f.

259. [132] Robert, *Documents*, 1987, 71.75.

260. Peter Weiß, "Mythen, Dichter und Münzen von Lykaonien," *Chiron* 20, 1990, 221–237.

261. On the descent of the Rhodians from Argos, [518] Wiemer, *Rhodos*, 2002, 215 f.

262. Peter Weiß, "Eumeneia und das Panhellenion," *Chiron* 30, 2000, 617–639.

263. Tacitus, *hist.* 4, 70; Clifford H. Moore (trans.), *Tacitus. The Histories*. Books IV–V, Cambridge, MA, and London 1931 [reprint 1992], 137.

264. [594] Heller, *Bêtises*, 2006.

265. James H. Oliver, *Greek Constitutions of Early Roman Emperors from Inscriptions and Papyri*, Philadelphia 1989, no. 135 AB; on the quarrel, cf. already Dion of Prusa, *or.* 34, 48. Reinhold Merkelbach, "Der Rangstreit der Städte Asiens," *ZPE* 32, 1978, 287–296.

266. Helmut Müller, "Hadrian an die Pergamener. Eine Fallstudie," in: R. Haensch (ed.), *Selbstdarstellung und Kommunikation. Die Veröffentlichung staatlicher Urkunden auf Stein und Bronze in der römischen Welt*, Munich 2009, 368–406.

267. Johannes Nollé, "Die feindlichen Schwestern. Betrachtungen zur Rivalität der pamphylischen Städte," in: [43] Dobesch and Rehrenböck (eds.), *Hundert Jahre Kleinasiatische Kommission*, 1993, 297–317.

268. Peter Weiß, "*Auxe Perge*. Beobachtungen zu einem bemerkenswerten städtischen Dokument des späten 3. Jh. n. Chr.," *Chiron* 21, 1991, 353–392.

269. [552] Ziegler, *Koinon*, 1999, 137–153.

270. Peter Weiß, "Kaiserzeitliche Stadtprägung und Klassische Altertumswissenschaft," in: [223] Nollé, Overbeck, and Weiß (eds.), *Münzprägung*, 1997, 28 f.

271. [224] Franke and Nollé, *Homonoia-Münzen*, 1997.

272. Nollé, op. cit., 313. With respect to the *conventus* cities, cf. [574] Drexhage, *Wirtschaftspolitik*, 2007, 27.

273. In Smyrna's case this may be a fictitious adaptation of the ancestry of Homer for whom this city had in general a strong preference. On the dating (probably third century) and the literary background: Manuel Baumbach and Silvio Bär, "An Introduction to Quintus Smyrnaeus' Posthomerica" in: M. Baumbach and S. Bär (eds.), *Quintus Smyrnaeus. Transforming Homer in Second Sophistic Epic*, Berlin and New York 2007, 1–26. On the stylization as Homer: Silvio Bär, "Quintus Smyrnaeus und die Tradition des epischen Musenanrufs," in: Baumbach and Bär (eds.), *Quintus Smyrnaeus*, 29–64.

274. Joachim Latacz, DNP [3].

275. Ismene Lada-Richards, *Silent Eloquence. Lucian and Pantomime Dancing*, London 2007.

276. Manuel Baumbach, DNP.

277. William D. Furley, DNP [3].

278. Massimo Fusillo and Lucia Galli, DNP [2].

279. Maria Sotera Fornaro, DNP [1].

280. Niklas Holzberg, *Der antike Roman. Eine Einführung*, third ed., Darmstadt 2006, esp. 60 ff.

281. Consuelo Ruiz Montero, "Chariton von Aphrodisias: Ein Überblick," *ANRW* II 34.2, 1994, 1006–1054; Ruiz Montero, "Xenophon von Ephesos: Ein Überblick," *ANRW* II 34.2, 1994, 1088–1138; Stefan Tilg, *Chariton of Aphrodisias and the Invention of the Greek Love Novel*, New York and Oxford 2010.

282. Massimo Di Marco, DNP [4].

283. Marco Fantuzzi, DNP [4].

284. Fantuzzi, DNP [4].

285. Fornaro, DNP [2].

286. Fornaro, DNP [1].

287. Enzo Degani, DNP [1].

288. Maria Grazia Albiani, DNP [3].

289. Albiani, DNP.

290. W. R. Paton (trans.), *The Greek Anthology*, vol. IV, Cambridge, MA, and London 1918 [reprint 1999], 375–377. Niklas Holzberg, *Applaus für Venus. Die 100 schönsten Liebesgedichte der Antike*, Munich 2004, 135.

291. Claude Calame, *Orphik*, DNP.

292. Franco Montanari, DNP [34].

293. Alice A. Donohue, DNP [2].

294. Christian Habicht, *Pausanias und seine "Beschreibung Griechenlands,"* Munich 1985.

295. Peter L. Schmidt, DNP.

296. [596] Bekker-Nielsen, *Urban Life*, 2008, 109 ff.

297. Karl-Heinz Hülser, DNP [10].

298. Maria Broggiato, DNP [5].

299. K. Ziegler, RE V a, 1934, 1930 ff.

300. F. Hultsch, RE IV 2, 1901, 2849 no. 17 and V 1, 1903, 1005 no. 19.

301. Menso Folkerts, DNP [3].

302. Wolfgang Hübner, DNP [3].

303. Hübner, DNP [6].

304. Folkerts, DNP [5].

305. Heinrich von Staden, *Herophilus: The Art of Medicine in Early Alexandria: Edition, Translation, and Essays*, Cambridge 1989.

306. Vivian Nutton, DNP [6].

307. Nutton, DNP [6], Themison [2], and Thessalos [6].

308. Nutton, DNP [6].

309. Nutton, DNP [5].

310. Werner A. Reuss, DNP.

311. Galen, commentary on Hippokrates, *Epid.* 2 (CMG V, 10, 1, p. 401–404).

312. Nutton, DNP. On physicians in honorary and tomb epigrams in Smyrna, [146] MS I 516.536.

313. Beat Näf, *Traum und Traumdeutung im Altertum*, Darmstadt 2004, 124–128; Michael Trapp, DNP [6].

314. At the time, people laughed at barbarian stammering, as we see especially in mime; cf. the Oxyrhynchos papyrus no. 413.

315. Peter von Möllendorff, *Lukian: Hermotimos, oder, Lohnt es sich, Philosophie zu studieren?*, Darmstadt 2000.

316. Jürgen Hammerstaedt and Martin Ferguson Smith, "The Inscriptions of Diogenes of Oinoanda: New Investigations and Discoveries (NF 137–141)," *EpigrAnat* 40, 2007, 1–11; id., "Diogenes of Oinoanda: The Discoveries of 2008 (NF 142–167)," *EpigrAnat* 41, 2008, 1–37.

317. Christoph Riedweg, *Pythagoras*, Munich 2002, 162 f.

318. Albin Lesky, *Geschichte der griechischen Literatur*, third ed., Bern and Munich 1971, 926.

319. The style of Antiochos of Commagene's great inscription was given as a model of pathos. Cf. Eduard Norden, *Die antike Kunstprosa* I, Leipzig 1898, 141; see also below, p. 514.

320. Cf. [604] Schmitz, *Sophistik*, 1997.

321. Georgy Kantor, "Knowledge of Law in Roman Asia Minor," in: R. Haensch (ed.), *Selbstdarstellung und Kommunikation. Die Veröffentlichung staatlicher Urkunden auf Stein und Bronze in der römischen Welt*, Munich 2009, 249–265.

322. On linguistic purism, see Schmitz, op. cit., 67–96.

323. [600] Bowersock, *Sophists*, 1969; [604] Schmitz, *Sophistik*, 1997. Tim Whitmarsh, *The Second Sophistic. Greece and Rome—New Surveys in the Classics*, Oxford 2005. On the controversy over the thesis advanced by Peter A. Brunt, "The Bubble of the Second Sophistic," *BICS* 39, 1994, 25–52; [591] Stephan, *Honoratioren*, 2002, 204 f.

324. Inscriptions: Bernadette Puech, *Orateurs et sophistes grecs dans les inscriptions d'époque imperiale*, Paris 2002.

325. Martin Korenjak, *Publikum und Redner. Ihre Interaktion in der sophistischen Rhetorik der Kaiserzeit*, Munich 2000.

326. The emperor forced Hermokrates of Phokaia to marry. Someone asked when he wanted to celebrate the unveiling of the bride, and he replied: "Say rather the veiling, when I am taking a wife like that!" (VS 611). Niketes of Smyrna silenced his opponent, who had shouted at him "Stop barking at me!," with the retort: "Stop biting me!" (VS 511). When Philagros of Cilicia borrowed an "impure" word and was asked "in what classic is that word to be found?" he replied: "In Philagros!" (VS 578; trans. Wright).

327. Lucian, *Rh. Pr.*, esp. 11 ff.; cf. Serena Zweimüller, *Lukian «Rhetorum praeceptor.» Einleitung, Text und Kommentar*, Göttingen 2008.

328. [596] Bekker-Nielsen, *Urban Life*, 2008, 119–145.

329. [624] von Harnack, *Mission*, third ed., 1915, 348 f.

330. Irenaeus, *haer.* 5, 33, 4; Eusebius, *h. e.* 2, 15, 2; 3, 36, 2; 3, 39. On Papias, Eva Schulz-Flügel, LACL.

331. [616] Pilhofer, Baumbach, Gerlach, and Hansen (eds.), *Peregrinos*, 2005.

332. Claus Peter Vetten, LACL.

333. Georg Röwekamp, LACL.

334. Roman Hanig, LACL.

335. Ulrich Hamm, LACL.

336. Still fundamental: [602] Robert, *Discours d'ouverture*, 1984; [187] Wörrle, *Stadt und Fest*, 1988; cf. Harry W. Pleket, "Mass-Sport and Local Infrastructure in the Greek Cities of Roman Asia Minor," *Stadion* 24, 1, 1998, 151–172.

337. Peter Thonemann, "Magnesia and the Greeks of Asia" (I. Magnesia 16.16), *GrRomByzSt* 47, 2007, 151–160.

338. Wolfgang Leschhorn, "Die Verbreitung von Agonen in den östlichen Provinzen des römischen Reiches," *Stadion* 24, 1, 1998, 31–57.

339. [192] Petzl and Schwertheim, Hadrian, 2006. See the commentaries of: Christopher P. Jones, "Three New Letters of the Emperor Hadrian," *ZPE* 161, 2007, 145–156; William J. Slater, "Hadrian's Letters to the Athletes and Dionysiac Artists Concerning Arrangements for the 'Circuit' of Games," *JRA* 21, 2008, 610–620. The debate continues.

340. Petzl and Schwertheim, op. cit., 11.

341. Peter Frisch, *Zehn agonistische Papyri*, Opladen 1986.

342. [183] Marek, *Kaunos*, 2006, no. 139, III C lines 12–14.

343. Petzl and Schwertheim, op. cit.

344. [187] Wörrle, *Stadt und Fest*, 1988.

345. [181] Robert, *Claros*, 1989, 20–23.

346. The name "iselastici" designated competitions whose victors received, along with other privileges, the right to enter their home cities in a carriage, *eiselaunein*. This ceremony was a popular spectacle in the cities. Abstracted from the ceremony, the word refers to the regular payments that cities were legally required to make to their residents who had won competitions classified in this way.

347. In general: [599] Robert, *Gladiateurs*, 1940.

348. [599] Robert, *Gladiateurs*, 1940, no. 97.

349. Ibid. no. 184.

350. Lucian, *Tox.*; cf. [549] Marek, *Pontus et Bithynia*, 2003, 99 f.

351. Peter Herz, "Herrscherverehrung und lokale Festkultur im Osten des römischen Reiches," in: H. Cancik and J. Rüpke (eds.), *Römische Reichsreligion und Provinzialreligion*, Tübingen 1997, 255 f.

352. [181] Robert, *Claros*, 1989, 65 II 31 f.

353. [499] Schuler, *Ländliche Siedlungen*, 1998, 276.

354. Schuler op. cit., 267–272; Michael Wörrle, "Epigraphische Forschungen zur Geschichte Lykiens VI. Der Zeus von Dereköy: Die Reform eines ländlichen Kultes," *Chiron* 27, 1997, 399–461.

355. [624] von Harnack, *Mission*, third ed., 1915, 288–290.

356. Jacob of Serugh, *Homilies on the Spectacles of the Theatre*, ed. Cyril Moss, *Le Muséon* 48, 1934–5, 87–112. Cf. Winfrid Cramer, "Irrtum und Lüge. Zum Urteil des Jakob von Sarug über Reste paganer Religion und Kultur," *JbAC* 23, 1980, 96–107.

357. SEG 57, 1288. On the expression, cf. Louis Robert, "Une vision de Perpétue martyre à Carthage," *CRAI* 1982, 263–266.

358. See Reinhold Merkelbach, *Hestia und Erigone. Vorträge und Aufsätze*, ed. W. Blümel et al., Leipzig 1997, 393–436.

359. Colin Eisler, "The Athlete of Virtue. The Iconography of Asceticism," in: M. Meiss (ed.), *De artibus opuscula XL, Essays in Honor of Erwin Panofsky*, New York 1961, 82 ff.; cf. Victor C. Pfitzner, *Paul and the Agon Motif. Traditional Athletic Imagery in the Pauline Literature*, Leiden 1967; Glen Bowersock, *Martyrdom and Rome*, Cambridge, MA 1995, 51–57.

360. [605] Keil, *Kulte*, 1923.

361. [609] Frei, "Götterkulte," *ANRW* II 18.3, 1990, 1731 f.

362. [609] Drew-Bear and Naour, "Divinités," *ANRW* II 18.3, 1990, 1907–2044; [149] Drew- Bear, Thomas, and Yildizturan, *Phrygian Votive Steles*, 1999.

363. On the Carian Zeus: Pierre Debord, "Sur quelques Zeus Cariens. Religion et politique," in: B. Virgilio (ed.), *Studi ellenistichi* XIII, 2001, 19–37.

364. Hans Schwabl, "Zum Kult des Zeus in Kleinasien," in: [43] Dobesch and Rehrenböck (eds.), *Hundert Jahre Kleinasiatische Kommission*, 1993, 329–338.

365. Cf. Hans Schwabl, "Zum Kult des Zeus in Kleinasien (II). Der Phrygische Zeus Bennios und Verwandtes," *ActaAntHung* 39, 1999, 345 ff.

366. [435] Roller, *God the Mother*, 1999.

367. Josef Keil, "ΧΑΡΙΣΜΑ, Artemis als Göttermutter und Himmelsgöttin," in: *Festgabe zur 25–jährigen Stiftungsfeier des Vereins klassischer Philologen in Wien*, Wien 1924, 26 (non vidi, reference provided by Georg Petzl).

368. Rudolf Naumann, "Das Heiligtum der Meter Steuene bei Aezani," *IstMitt* 17, 1967, 218–247.

369. [149] Drew-Bear, Thomas, and Yildizturan, *Phrygian Votive Steles*, 1999.

370. Guy Labarre, "Les origines et la diffusion du culte de Men," in: [286] Bru, Kirbihler, and Lebreton, *L'Asie Mineure*, 2009, 389 ff.

371. [609] Lane, "Men," *ANRW* II 18.3, 1990, 2161–2174.

372. [609] Frei, "Götterkulte," *ANRW* II 18.3, 1990, 1729–1864.

373. [151] Delemen, *Rider Gods*, tables 1–13.

374. [609] MacKay, "Sanctuaries," *ANRW* II 18.3, 1990, 2045–2129.

375. [146] MS IV 227. Louis Robert, *La déesse de Hiérapolis Castabala*, Paris 1964.

376. Jörg Wagner, "Dynastie und Herrscherkult in Kommagene. Forschungsgeschichte und neuere Funde," *IstMitt* 33, 1983; Jörg Wagner (ed.), *Gottkönige am Euphrat. Neue Ausgrabungen und Forschungen in Kommagene*, Mainz 2000. Margherita Facella, *La dinastia degli Orontidi nella Commagene ellenistico-romana*, Pisa 2006; [270a] Blömer and Winter, *Commagene*, 2011.

377. Anke Schütte-Maischatz, "Götter und Kulte Kommagenes. Religionsgeographische Aspekte einer antiken Landschaft," *AMS* 45, 2003, 103–113.

378. On the new Temenos-inscriptions, see [195] SEG 53, 1762–1777.

379. Bruno Jacobs, "Die Galerien der Ahnen des Königs Antiochos I. von Kommagene auf dem Nemrud Dağ," in: J. M. Højte (ed.), *Images of Ancestors*, Aarhus 2002, 75–88.

380. Reinhold Merkelbach, *Mithras*, Königstein 1984, 65–70.

381. Georg Petzl, "Die Epigramme des Gregor von Nazianzus über Grabräuberei und das Hierothesion des kommagenischen Königs Antiochos I.," *EpigrAnat* 10, 1987, 117–129.

382. Engelbert Winter (ed.), "Patris Pantrophos Kommagene. Neue Funde und Forschungen zwischen Taurus und Euphrat," *AMS* 60, Bonn 2008.

383. [162] *IK* Tyana 34; Henri Grégoire, "Note sur une inscription gréco-araméenne trouvée à Faraša (Ariaramneia-Rhodandos)," *CRAI* 1908, 434–447.

384. Marijana Ricl, "The Cult of the Iranian Goddess Anāhitā in Anatolia before and after Alexander," *ŽivaAnt* 52, 2002, 197–210.

385. [106] OGIS 383, lines 161 ff.; trans. Donald H. Sanders (ed.), *Nemrud Dağı: the "Hierothesion" of Antiochus I of Commagene. Results of the American Excavations*, vol. I: Text, Winona Lake, IN 1996, 216.

386. [141] Petzl, *Beichtinschriften*, 1994, 49.77.

387. Johannes Nollé, "Vielerorts war Bethlehem—Göttergeburten im kaiserzeitlichen Kleinasien," *AW* 34.6, 2003, 635–643.

388. Attilio Mastrocinque, "Zeus Kretagenès seleucidico: da Seleucia a Praenesta (e in Giudea)," *Klio* 84, 2002, 355–372, on the "Cretagenic Zeus" attested in Amyzon and Mylasa.

389. [609] Oster, "Ephesus," *ANRW* II 18.3, 1990, 1661–1728.

390. Jürgen W. Riethmüller, *Asklepios. Heiligtümer und Kulte*, Heidelberg 2005, vol. 2/1, 334–359, vol. 2/2, 352 ff. (catalog).

391. [608] Parke, *Oracles*, 1985.

392. [160] Nollé, *Losorakel*, 2007.

393. Ibid. 234.

394. Dorothee Elm, "'Alexander oder der Lügenprophet.' Ein religiöser Spezialist und ein Text zwischen Tradition und Innovation," in: H. Cancik and J. Rüpke (eds.), *Römische Reichsreligion und Provinzialreligion*, Erfurt 2003, 34 ff.; Angelos Chaniotis, "Old Wine in a New Skin. Tradition and Innovation in the Cult Foundation of Alexander of Abonuteichos," *Electrum* 6, 2002, 67 ff.

395. [26] Robert, *Asie Mineure*, 1980, 393–421; cf. esp. Ulrich Victor, *Lukian von Samosata. Alexandros oder der Lügenprophet*, Leiden 1997, 1–58.

396. Reinhold Merkelbach and Josef Stauber, "Die Orakel des Apollon von Klaros," *EpigrAnat* 27, 1996, 2.

397. [615] Anderson, *Holy Men*, 1994; [613] Dzielska, *Apollonius of Tyana*, 1986; [617] Demoen and Praet (eds.), *Theios Sophistes*, 2009; Roger Pack, "The Volatilization of Peregrinus Proteus," *AJPh* 67, 1946, 334 f.; [616] Pilhofer, Baumbach, Gerlach, and Hansen, *Peregrinos*, 2005.

398. Cf. esp. Angelos Chaniotis, "Drei kleinasiatische Inschriften zur griechischen Religion," *EpigrAnat* 15, 1990, 127–131. The inscription is interpreted differently by [141] Petzl, *Beichtinschriften*, 1994, commentary on no. 59.

399. [141] Petzl, *Beichtinschriften*, 1994, 54.

400. Ibid. 5 lines 18 ff.

401. [159] Herrmann and Malay, *New Documents from Lydia*, 2007, no. 84.

402. Raffaele Pettazoni, *La confessione dei peccati*, vol. II, Bologna 1935, 90 ff.; Alexander Sima, "Kleinasiatische Parallelen zu den altsüdarabischen Buß- und Sühneinschriften," *AoF* 26, 1999, 140-153.

403. [611] Mitchell, *Theos Hypsistos*, 1999, 112.114.

404. [619] Witulski, *Kaiserkult*, 2007.

405. Autol. 2, 36 lines 10–14; Robert M. Grant (trans.), *Theophilus of Antioch. Ad Autolycum*, Oxford 1970, 89.

406. Christian Marek, "Der höchste, beste, größte, allmächtige Gott," *EpigrAnat* 32, 2000, 129–146; cf. Wolfgang Wischmeyer, "Theos Hypsistos. Neues zu einer alten Debatte," *ZAntChr* 9, 2005, 149–168; Alfons Fürst, "Christentum im Trend. Monotheistische Tenden-

zen in der späten Antike," *ZAntChr* 9, 2005, 496–523. On the priest: [121] Herrmann and Polatkan, *Epikrates*, 1969, 51 ff. no. 9.

407. [611] Mitchell, *Theos Hypsistos*, 1999.

408. Mitchell, op. cit., 86.

409. Marijana Ricl, "Hosios kai Dikaios," *EpigrAnat* 18, 1991, 1–70; 19, 1992, 71–102; Vera Hirschmann, "Zwischen Menschen und Göttern. Die kleinasiatischen Engel," *EpigrAnat* 40, 2007, 135–146.

410. Cf. [166] I. Priene 105. The translation is available online at: www.ccel.org/ccel/schaff/npnf201.html.

411. On names and designations, see [624] von Harnack, *Mission*, third ed., 1915, 395, 403.

412. On this problem, cf. Simon Légasse, "Paulus und der christliche Universalismus," in: L. Pietri (ed.), *Die Geschichte des Christentums* I, Freiburg 2003, 105–113.

413. So argues Franz Georg Maier, *Cypern, Insel am Kreuzweg der Geschichte*, second ed., Munich 1982, 71.

414. Michel Christol and Thomas Drew-Bear, "Les Sergii Paulli et Antioch de Pisidie," in: Th. Drew-Bear, M. Taşlıalan, and Ch. Thomas (eds.), *Actes du Ier Congrès international sur Antioche de Pisidie*, Lyon 2002, 178–181. Cf. Alexander Weiß, "Sergius Paullus, Statthalter von Zypern," *ZPE* 169, 2009, 188 ff. This Roman was probably the senator known to us through inscriptions as the *curator riparum et alvei Tiberis* under Claudius.

415. [638] Trebilco, *Early Christians*, 2004, 53–196.

416. [634] Witulski, *Adressaten*, 2000.

417. On Aquila and Priscilla: Helga Botermann, *Das Judenedikt des Kaisers Claudius*, Stuttgart 1996, 45 ff.

418. [624] von Harnack, *Mission*, third ed., 1915, 186.

419. [641] Witulski, Johannesoffenbarung, 2007, takes a different view; he argues for a dating to the time of Hadrian.

420. Origen, comm. on Matthew 24:9 p. 75 lines 27 f. Klostermann: *multi enim non solum barbararum, sed etiam nostrarum gentium usque nunc non audierunt Christianitatis verbum.*

421. Johannes Lähnemann, Die sieben Sendschreiben der Johannesapokalypse. Dokumente für die Konfrontation des frühen Christentums mit hellenistisch-römischer Kultur und Religion in Kleinasien," in: S. Şahin, E. Schwertheim, and J. Wagner (eds.), *Studien zur Religion und Kultur Kleinasiens,* FS Dörner, Leiden 1978, 516–539.

422. Hans Dieter Betz, *Hellenismus und Urchristentum* I, Tübingen 1990, esp. 14 ff. On the suspicions directed against Christians: [632] Guyot and Klein, *Christentum*, vol. 2, 1994, esp. 216 ff.

423. Misuse: widows lent at interest the money given them (*Didascalia Apostolorum* 15). See [640] Hübner, *Klerus*, 2005, 177 f.

424. Cf. [627] Blanchetière, *Christianisme*, 1977, 491–516; [544] Mitchell, *Anatolia* II, 1993, 38.

425. 408 [628] Gibson, *The "Christians for Christians" Inscriptions*, 1978.

426. Paul Trebilco, "The Christian 'and' Jewish Eumeneian Formula," *MedAnt* 5, 2002, 63–97.

427. [144] Tabbernee, *Montanist Inscriptions*, 1997, 401–406 no. 63.

428. Examples in [142] Johnson, Index F, p. 160.

429. [162] *IK* Klaudiupolis 44; [142] Johnson 3.1; cf. [132] Robert, *Documents*, 1987, 109 ff.

430. [624] von Harnack, Mission II, third ed., 1915, 58–78. Cf. Anne Jensen, *Gottes Selbstbewußte Töchter*, second ed., Münster 2003.

431. Epiphanios, *haer*. 49, 2, 5; cf. the inscription from Uşak in Phrygia: [255] Waelkens, *Türsteine* no. 367. In general: Ute E. Eisen, *Amtsträgerinnen im frühen Christentum*, Göttingen 1996.

432. [638] Trebilco, *Early Christians*, 2004, 704 with note 60.

433. Emphasized by [160] Nollé, *Losorakel*, 2007, 289 f.

434. On the persecution of Christians under Domitian: Euseb, *h. e.* 3, 17 f.; Dio 67, 14, 2; Rev., esp. 2:13 (Antipas). Cf. Rudolf Freudenberger, *Das Verhalten der römischen Behörden gegen die Christen im 2. und 3. Jh.*, second ed., Munich 1969, 139 note 138.

435. On Pliny's letter, Christopher P. Jones, "A New Commentary on the Letters of Pliny," *Phoenix* 22, 1968, 111 ff.; Freudenberger, op. cit.; Òscar de La Cruz Palma, "L'epístola X 96 de Plini a la Ilum d'altres fonts del segle II., *Faventia* 20,2, 1998, 109 ff.

436. Cf. Richard Klein, in: [632] Guyot and Klein, *Christentum*, vol. 1, 1993, 326 note 34. In general: Gerd Buschmann, *Das Martyrium des Polycarp*, Göttingen 1998.

437. I owe this argument to Werner Eck (communicated in a personal letter).

438. Géza Alföldy, *Konsulat und Senatorenstand unter den Antoninen*, Bonn 1977, 214 f. For the literature, ibid. 329 f. note 20, and [639] Hirschmann, *Horrenda Secta*, 2005, 41 f.

439. *Martyrium Polycarpi* 18, 3; Herbert Musurillo (trans.), *The Acts of the Christian Martyrs*, Oxford 1972.

440. Sources in [632] Guyot and Klein, *Christentum*, vol. 1, 1993, 48 f.

441. Incorrectly dated in [549] Marek, *Pontus et Bithynia*, 2003, where Serenianus's persecution is inadvertently dated to the time of the correspondence itself, twenty-two years later.

442. James Boykin Rives, "The Decree of Decius and the Religion of Empire," *JRS* 89, 1999, 137.

443. [631] Robert, *Pionios*, 1994.

444. Trans. McGifford; Available at www.ccel.org/ccel/schaff/npnf201.html.

445. *Martyrium Pionii* 19, 10–13; Herbert Musurillo (trans.), *The Acts of the Christian Martyrs*, Oxford 1972.

446. [26] Robert, *Asie Mineure*, 1980, 250.

447. Louis Robert, "Une vision de Perpétue martyre à Carthage en 203," *CRAI* 1982, 229–276 (OMS V 791–839).

448. [162] *IK* Arykanda 12 (= [106] OGIS 569); Stephen Mitchell, "Maximinus and the Christians in A. D. 312: A New Latin Inscription," *JRS* 78, 1988, 104–124. Cf. the rescript to the city of Tyros reproduced in Euseb. *h.e.* 9, 7, 3-14.

449. [625] von Harnack, *Marcion*, second ed., 1924.

450. [544] Mitchell, *Anatolia* II, 1993, 102 f.

451. Didymos of Alexandria (fourth century CE), Trin. PG 39, 989 (Book III Chap. 41) calls Montanus a priest of an undetermined pagan divinity (*eidolon*); Apollo is mentioned in the Dialexis, a fourth-century disputation between a Montanist and an orthodox believer ([630] Heine, *Oracles and Testimonia*, 1989, 112–126). On the *galloi* see Lucian's work on the Syrian goddess; cf. Hans-Ulrich Wiemer and Daniel Kah, "Die Phrygische Mutter im Hellenistischen Priene," *EpigrAnat* 44, 2011, 30–32. Eunuchs were not rare in Imperial period Asia Minor (p. 468); Bishop Meliton of Sardeis was a eunuch (Eusebius, *h. e.* 5, 24).

452. Detailed discussion in [639] Hirschmann, *Horrenda Secta*, 2005.

453. Ibid. 19.

454. Cf. [630] Heine, *Oracles and Testimonia*, 1989.

455. William Ramsey, *The Cities and Bishoprics of Phrygia*, Oxford 1895.

456. [642] Tabbernee and Lampe, *Pepouza and Tymion*, 2008.

457. [544] Mitchell, *Anatolia* II, 1993, 39.

458. Pseudo-Dionysius of Tell-Mahrē (eighth century), *Chronicle of the Year 550*; Michael the Syrian, *Chronicle* 9, 33 lines 5–25.

459. [544] Mitchell, *Anatolia* II, 1993, 100–108.

460. [283] Belke, TIB 9, 1996, 104 f.

461. [640] Hübner, *Klerus*, 2005.

462. Claudia Rapp, *Holy Bishops in Late Antiquity*, Berkeley, CA 2005.

463. Ibid. 62–65.

464. [624] von Harnack, *Mission* II, third ed., 1915, 454. Metropolitan sees around 300 CE: Amaseia, Ankyra, Kaisareia in Cappadocia, Kyzikos, Ephesos, Gangra, Herakleia, Ikonion, Laodikeia in Phrygia, Neokaisareia, Nikomedeia, Patara, Perge, Sardeis, Tarsos, and perhaps also Amastris, but this is opposed by [283] Belke, TIB 9, 1996, 104. In the time of Justinian Asia Minor had 33 metropolitan sees; cf. [640] Hübner, *Klerus*, 2005, 217.

465. Eusebius, *h. e.* 5, 23; trans. McGifford, available at: www.ccel.org/ccel/schaff/npnf201.html.

466. On Gregory's life and work, see Richard Klein's introduction in: *Gregor der Wundertäter, Oratio Prosphonetica ac Panegyrica in Originem*, trans. P. Guyot, introduction by R. Klein, Freiburg, Basel, and Wien 1996, 7 ff.; [633] Guyot, *Chaos in Pontos*, 1998, 63 ff.

467. On the Christianization, culture, and society of Late Antique Cappadocia, see Raymond van Dam's three monographs, [637] *The Conversion*, 2003; [636] *Families and Friends*, 2003; [635] *Kingdom of Snow*, 2002.

468. Christian Marek, "Jesus und Abgar. Das Rätsel vom Beginn einer Legende," in: T. Fuhrer, P. Michel, and P. Stotz, *Geschichten und ihre Geschichte*, Basel 2004, 269–310.

469. Erich Kettenhofen, *Tirdad und die Inschrift von Paikuli. Eine Kritik der Quellen zur Geschichte Armeniens im späten 3. und frühen 4. Jh. n. Chr.*, Wiesbaden 1995, esp. 48–135.

470. [623] Gelzer, Hilgenfeld, and Cuntz, *Nomina*, 1898; Ernest Honigmann, "La liste originale des Pères de Nicée," *Byzantion* 14, 1939, 17–76.

Chapter 10. Epilogue and Outlook

1. Georg Ostrogorsky, *Geschichte des byzantinischen Staates*, Munich 1965, 3 (reprint 1980).

2. Frank R. Trombley, *Hellenic Religion and Christianization, c. 370–529*, 2 vols., Leiden 1993–1994.

3. Stephen Mitchell, "Ethnicity, Acculturation and Empire in Roman and Late Roman Asia Minor," in: St. Mitchell and G. Greatrex, *Ethnicity and Culture in Late Antiquity*, London 2000, 117–150.

4. *Gesta Francorum* 3, 9, 5, 50–52, trans. James Brundage. Available at: www.fordham.edu/halsall/source/gesta-cde.asp.

Bibliography

General Presentations

[1] Elmar Schwertheim, *Kleinasien in der Antike. Von den Hethitern bis Konstantin*, Munich 2005.

Handbooks

[2] *Handbuch der Orientalistik* (HdO), Leiden-Köln 1954 ff. (Ongoing; see individual volumes).

[3] Hermann Müller-Karpe, *Handbuch der Vorgeschichte*, Munich 1966–1980.

[4] *The Cambridge Ancient History* (CAH), Third Edition:

I.1: *Prolegomena and Prehistory*, Cambridge 1970.

I.2: *Early History of the Middle East*, Cambridge 1971.

II.1: *History of the Middle East and the Aegean Region c. 1800–1380 B.C.*, Cambridge 1973.

II.2: *History of the Middle East and the Aegean Region c. 1380–1000 B.C.*, Cambridge 1975.

Second Edition:

III.1: *The Prehistory of the Balkans and the Middle East and the Aegaean World. Tenth to Eighth Centuries B.C.*, Cambridge 1982.

III.3: *The Expansion of the Greek World. Eighth to Sixth Centuries B.C.*, Cambridge 1982.

Plates:

Plates to Volumes I and II, Cambridge 1977.

Plates to Volume III. The Middle East, the Greek World and the Balkans to the Sixth Century B.C., Cambridge 1984.

Reference Works

[5] *Paulys Realencyclopädie der classischen Altertumswissenschaft* (RE). New edition begun by Georg Wissowa, continued by Wilhelm Kroll and Karl Mittelhaus. With the collaboration of numerous experts, ed. by Konrat Ziegler et al. First series, A–Q, second series, R–Z. Supplemental volumes 1–15. Index of the additions and supplements by Hans Gärtner and Albert Wünsch, Stuttgart-Munich 1893–1980.

[6] Louis Robert, *Noms indigènes dans l'Asie Mineure gréco-romaine*, Paris 1963.

[7] Vladislav Zgusta, *Kleinasiatische Personennamen*, Prague 1964.

[8] Johannes Tischler, *Kleinasiatische Hydronomie*, Wiesbaden 1977.

[9] Giuseppe F. del Monte and Johannes Tischler, *Répertoire géographique des textes cunéiformes*, vol. 6, *Die Orts- und Gewässernamen der hethitischen Texte*, Wiesbaden 1978. Supplemental vol. 6/2, Wiesbaden 1992.

[10] Vladislav Zgusta, *Kleinasiatische Ortsnamen*, Heidelberg 1984.

[11] *The Oxford Dictionary of Byzantium*, ed. Alexander P. Kazhdan, 3 vols., Oxford 1991.

[12] *Der Neue Pauly. Enzyklopädie der Antike* (DNP), ed. Hubert Cancik and Helmuth Schneider, Stuttgart-Weimar 1996 ff. English edition: *Brill's New Pauly: Encyclopaedia of*

the Ancient World, ed. Hubert Cancik, Helmuth Schneider, Christine F. Salazar, and David E. Orton, Leiden and Boston 2002–2010.

[13] *The Oxford Encyclopedia of Archaeology in the Near East*, ed. Eric M. Meyers, 5 vols., Oxford and New York, 1997.

[14] Peter Robert Franke and Wolfgang Leschhorn, *Lexikon der Aufschriften auf griechischen Münzen*, Vienna, vol. 1, 2002; vol. 2, 2009.

[14a] *A Lexicon of Greek Personal Names*, vol. VA: *Coastal Asia Minor: Pontos to Ionia*, ed. Thomas Corsten, Oxford 2010.

[14b] *A Lexicon of Greek Personal Names*, vol. VB: *Coastal Asia Minor:Caria to Cilicia*, ed. Jean-Sébastien Balzat, Richard W. V. Catling, Édouard Chiricat, and Fabienne Marchand, Oxford 2013.

Bibliographies and Research Reports

General

[15] *L'année philologique*. Founded by Jean Marouzeau, published by Juliette Ernst, Paris 1928 ff.

[16] *Archaeological Reports* no. 17 (1970/1971): *Archaeology in Western Asia Minor 1965–1970*, by J. M. Cook and D. J. Blackman; no. 25 (1978/1979) 59–90: *Archaeology in Western and Southern Asia Minor 1971–1978*, by S. Mitchell and A. W. McNicoll; no. 31 (1984/1985) 70–105: *1979–1984*, by S. Mitchell; no. 36 (1989/1990) 83–131: *1985–1989*, by S. Mitchell; no. 45 (1998/1999) 125–192: *1989–1998*, by S. Mitchell.

[17] *Kazı/Araştırma Sonuçları Toplantısı*, ed. Ministry of Turkish Culture, Anıtlar ve Müzeler Genel Müdürlüğü, 1979 ff.

[18] Peter Rosumek, *Index des périodiques dépouillés dans la Collection de Bibliographie classique et Index de leurs sigles. Supplement à l'année philologique LI*, Paris 1982.

[19] *American Journal of Archaeology: Archaeology in Anatolia*, annual reports by Machteld J. Mellink up to 1993, by Marie Henriette Gates 1994–1997.

[20] *Anatolian Studies. Annual Report: Recent Archaeological Research in Turkey* (up to 1989).

[21] *Müze Kurtarma Kazıları Semineri*, ed. Anıtlar ve Müzeler Genel Müdürlüğü, 1989 ff.

[22] *Archiv für Orientforschung. Internationale Zeitschrift für die Wissenschaft vom Vorderen Orient*, 1923 ff. (Discoveries/collections/excavations).

[23] *Cuneiform e-Bibliography*, 1940 ff.: http://ancientworldonline.blogspot.ch/2012/03/online-keilschrift-bibliographie.html.

[24] *Online Bibliography Hittitology*: www.hethport.uni–wuerzburg.de/hethbib.

History of Geographical and Archaeological Research

[25] Dietmar Henze, *Enzyklopädie der Entdecker und Erforscher der Erde*, 5 vols., Graz, Austria 1973–2004.

[26] Louis Robert, *A travers l'Asie Mineure. Poètes et prosateurs, monnaies grecques, voyageurs et géographie*, Paris 1980.

[27] Reinhard Lullies and Wolfgang Schiering (eds.), *Archäologenbildnisse. Porträts und Kurzbiographien von klassischen Archäologen deutscher Sprache*, Mainz 1988.

[28] Stephane Yerasimos, *Les voyageurs dans l'empire Ottoman (14.–16. siècles),* Ankara 1991.

[29] Traute Wohlers-Scharf, *Die Forschungsgeschichte von Ephesos. Entdeckungen, Grabungen und Persönlichkeiten,* second ed., Frankfurt am Main 1996.

[30] Klaus Junker, *Das Archäologische Institut des Deutschen Reichs zwischen Forschung und Politik. Die Jahre 1929 bis 1945,* Mainz 1997.

[31] Roger Matthews (ed.), *Ancient Anatolia. Fifty Years' Work by the British Institute of Archaeology at Ankara,* Ankara 1998.

[32] *Archäologische Entdeckungen. Die Forschungen des Deutschen Archäologischen Instituts im 20. Jahrhundert,* ed. Deutsches Archäologisches Institut, 2 vols., Mainz 2000.

[33] Fatma Canpolat (ed.), *Boğazköy'den Karatepe'ye: Hititbilim ve Hitit Dünyasının Keşfi. From Boğazköy to Karatepe. Hittitology and the Discovery of the Hittite World,* Yapı Kredi Kültür Sanat Yayıncılık, İstanbul 2001.

[34] Oktay Belli (ed.), *Istanbul University's Contributions to Archaeology in Turkey, 1932–2000,* Istanbul 2001.

[34a] Clive Foss, "Pilgrimage in Medieval Asia Minor," in: Alice-Mary Talbot (ed.), *Dumbarton Oaks Papers* 56, 2002, Washington, DC, 2003, 129–151.

[35] Stephen L. Dyson, *In Pursuit of Ancient Pasts. A History of Classical Archaeology in the Nineteenth and Twentieth Centuries,* New Haven, CT 2006.

[35a] Ève Gran-Aymerich, *Les chercheurs de passé, 1798–1945,* Paris 2007.

[35b] Matthias Recke, *In loco Murtana, ubi olim Perge sita fuit. Der Beginn archäologischer Forschungen in Pamphylien und die Kleinasien-Expedition Gustav Hirschfelds 1874,* Antalya 2007.

Special Journals and Essay Collections (Alphabetical)[1]

[36] *Anadolu* (vols. 1–8: Anatolia), *Journal of the Institute for Research in Near Eastern and Mediterranean Civilisations of the Faculty of Letters of the University of Ankara,* Ankara 1956 ff.

[37] *Anatolian Archaeology, Annual Magazine of the British Institute at Ankara,* 1995 ff.

[38] *Anatolian Studies. Journal of the British Institute at Ankara,* London 1950 ff.

[39] *Anatolica. Annuaire international pour les civilisations de l'Asie anterieure, publié sous les auspices de l'Institut historique et archéologique néerlandais d'Istanbul,* Leiden 1967 ff.

[40] *Asia Minor Studien,* ed. Forschungsstelle Asia Minor im Seminar für Alte Geschichte der Westfälischen Wilhelms-Universität Münster, Bonn 1990 ff.

[41] *Belleten.* Türk Tarih Kurumu, İstanbul-Ankara 1937 ff.

[42] *Byzas,* ed. Deutsches Archäologisches Institut, Abteilung Istanbul, 2005 ff.

[43] Gerhard Dobesch and Georg Rehrenböck (eds.), *Die epigraphische und altertumskundliche Erforschung Kleinasiens: Hundert Jahre Kleinasiatische Kommission der Österreichischen Akademie der Wissenschaften, Akten des Symposiums 23.–25. 10. 1990 in Wien,* Vienna 1993.

[44] *Ege Üniversitesi Arkeoloji Dergisi,* Ege Üniversitesi İzmir 1993 ff.

[45] *Epigraphica Anatolica. Zeitschrift für Epigraphik und historische Geographie Anatoliens,* Bonn 1978 ff.

[46] *Gephyra. Zeitschrift für Geschichte und Kultur der Antike auf dem Gebiet der heutigen Türkei,* ed. Johannes Nollé and Sencer Şahin, Istanbul 2005 ff.

---

[1] Festschriften are not included.

[47] *Istanbuler Forschungen*, ed. Deutsches Archäologisches Institut, Abteilung Istanbul, Tübingen 1933 ff.

[48] *Istanbuler Mitteilungen*, ed. Deutsches Archäologisches Institut, Abteilung Istanbul, Tübingen 1933 ff.

[49] *Kadmos, Zeitschrift für vor- und frühgriechische Epigraphik*, ed. Wolfgang Blümel, Berlin 1962 ff.

[50] *Lykia, Anadolu–Akdeniz Kültürleri*, ed. Havva Işkan and Fahri Işık, Antalya 1994 ff.

[50a] *Personal Names in Ancient Anatolia*, ed. Robert Parker, Oxford 2013.

[50b] *Philia. International Journal of Ancient Mediterranean Studies*, ed. Mustafa Adak, Thomas Corsten, Koray Konuk, Konrad Stauner, Burak Takmer, and Peter Thonemann, Istanbul 2015 ff.

[51] *Revue Hittite et Asianique*, Paris 1930 ff.

[52] *Türk Arkeoloji Dergisi* (vols. 1–5: *Türk Tarih, Arkeologya ve Etnografya Dergisi*), Ankara 1933 ff.

[53] *Türkiye Bilimler Akademisi Arkeoloji Dergisi* (*Turkish Academy of Sciences Journal of Archaeology*), Ankara 1998 ff.

[54] *Yayla. Report of the Northern Society for Anatolian Archaeology*, Newcastle upon Tyne 1977 ff.

Sources, Collections of Texts, and Translations[2]

Cuneiform and Hieroglyphic

General

[55] James H. Breasted, *Ancient Records of Egypt*, 5 vols., Chicago 1906–1907.

[56] Daniel D. Luckenbill, *Ancient Records of Assyria and Babylonia*, 2 vols., Chicago 1926.

[57] Johannes Friedrich, *Kleinasiatische Sprachdenkmäler*, Berlin 1932.

[58] James B. Pritchard (ed.), *Ancient Near Eastern Texts Relating to the Old Testament* (*ANET*), third ed., Princeton, NJ 1969.

[59] Otto Kaiser et al. (eds.), *Texte aus der Umwelt des Alten Testaments* (*TUAT*), Gütersloh, Germany 1982 ff.

Kültepe

[60] Klaas R. Veenhof and Evelyn Klengel-Brandt, *Altassyrische Tontafeln aus Kültepe: Texte und Siegelabrollungen, Vorderasiatische Schriftdenkmäler der Staatlichen Museen zu Berlin 26*, Berlin 1992.

[61] Jan Gerrit Dercksen, *The Old Assyrian Copper Trade in Anatolia*, Istanbul 1996.

Hittites, Series

[62] *Keilschrifttexte aus Boghazköi* (*KBo*), Leipzig 1916–1923 (nos. 1–6), Berlin 1954– (nos. 7–).

[63] *Keilschrifturkunden aus Boghazköi* (*KUB*), since 1921 ed. by Staatliche Museen zu Berlin,

---

[2] See the individual chapters for editions of Urartian, Phrygian, Lydian, Carian, Sidetic, and Aramaic inscriptions.

from 1943 by Deutsche Orient-Gesellschaft zu Berlin, from vol. 35/1953 by Deutsche Akademie der Wissenschaften (of the GDR) zu Berlin; concluded with no. 60/1990.

[64] *Studien zu den Boghazköi-Texten (StBoT)*, Kommission für den Alten Orient der Akademie der Wissenschaften und der Literatur, Wiesbaden 1965 ff.

[65] *Studien zu den Boghazköi-Texten.* Supplements (*StBoT Beih.*), ed. Heinrich Otten. Kommission für den Alten Orient der Akademie der Wissenschaften und der Literatur, Wiesbaden 1988 ff.

[66] *Texte der Hethiter* [*TH(eth)*]. Annelies Kammenhuber (ed. 1971–1995), Gernot Wilhelm (ed. 1995–2004), Susanne Heinhold-Krahmer (ed. 2004–), Heidelberg 1971 ff.

[67] *Dresdner Beiträge zur Hethitologie (DBH)*, Dresden 2002–2004, Wiesbaden 2005 ff.

[68] *Hethitologie Portal Mainz–Materialien*, ed. Kommission für den Alten Orient der Akademie der Wissenschaften und der Literatur Mainz, Wiesbaden 2005 ff.

Hittites, Individual Editions (Selection)

[69] Johannes Friedrich, *Staatsverträge des Hatti-Reiches in hethitischer Sprache*, 2 vols., Leipzig 1926–1930.

[70] Albrecht Goetze, *Madduwattaš*, Leipzig 1928.

[71] Hans Ehelolf and Ferdinand Sommer, *Kleinasiatische Forschungen*, vol. 1, Weimar 1930.

[72] Ferdinand Sommer, *Die Ahhijava-Urkunden*, Munich 1932.

[73] Albrecht Goetze, *Die Annalen des Muršiliš, Mitteilungen der Vorderasiatisch-Aegyptischen Gesellschaft 38*, Leipzig 1933.

[74] Edgar Howard Sturtevant and George Bechtel, *A Hittite Chrestomathy*, Philadelphia 1935.

[75] Ferdinand Sommer and Adam Falkenstein, *Die hethitisch-akkadische Bilingue des Hattusili I*, Munich 1938.

[76] Hans Gustav Güterbock, *Siegel aus Boğazköy*, Part I: *Die Königssiegel der Grabungen bis 1938*, Berlin 1940.

[77] Hans Gustav Güterbock, *Siegel aus Boğazköy*, Part 2: *Die Königssiegel von 1939 und die übrigen Hieroglyphensiegel*, Berlin 1942.

[78] Hans Gustav Güterbock, *Kumarbi. Mythen vom churritischen Kronos aus den hethitischen Fragmenten zusammengestellt, übersetzt und erklärt*, Zürich and New York 1946.

[79] Emmanuel Laroche, *Textes mythologiques hittites en transcription*. I: *Mythologie anatolienne*, Paris 1965.

[80] Emmanuel Laroche, *Textes mythologiques hittites en transcription*. II: *Mythologie d'origine etrangère*, Paris 1969.

[81] Cord Kühne and Heinrich Otten, *Der Šaušgamuwa-Vertrag. Eine Untersuchung zu Sprache und Graphik*, Wiesbaden 1971.

[82] Erich Neu, *Der Anitta-Text*, Wiesbaden 1974.

[83] Trevor R. Bryce, *The Major Historical Texts of Early Hittite History*, Brisbane 1980.

[84] Heinrich Otten, *Die Apologie Hattusilis III. Das Bild der Überlieferung*, Wiesbaden 1981.

[85] Inge Hoffmann, *Der Erlaß Telipinus*, Heidelberg 1984.

[86] Alberto Bernabé, *Textos literarios hetitas. Traducción, introducción y notas*, Madrid 1987.

[87] Hans Gustav Güterbock and Theo P. J. van den Hout, *The Hittite Instruction for the Royal Bodyguard*, Chicago 1991.

[88] Elmar Edel, *Die ägyptisch-hethitische Korrespondenz aus Boghazköi in babylonischer und*

hethitischer Sprache, vol 1: *Umschriften und Übersetzungen*, vol. 2: *Kommentar*, Opladen, Germany 1994.

[89] Harry Angier Hoffner Jr., *The Laws of the Hittites. A Critical Edition*, Leiden, New York, and Cologne 1997.

[90] Harry Angier Hoffner Jr., *Hittite Myths*, trans. H. Hoffner, ed. Gary M. Beckman, second ed., Atlanta 1998.

[91] Ahmet Ünal, *Hittite and Hurrian Cuneiform Tablets from Ortaköy (Çorum), Central Turkey*, İstanbul 1998.

[92] Gary M. Beckman, *Hittite Diplomatic Texts*, ed. Harry A. Hoffner Jr., second ed., Atlanta 1999.

[93] José Virgilio García-Trabazo, *Textos religiosos hititas, mitos plegarias y rituales*, Madrid 2002.

[94] Itamar Singer, *Hittite Prayers*, ed. Harry A. Hoffner Jr., Atlanta 2002.

[95] Suzanne Herbordt and Peter Neve (eds.), *Die Prinzen- und Beamtensiegel der hethitischen Großreichszeit auf Tonbullen aus dem Nisantepe-Archiv in Hattusa. Mit Kommentaren zu den Siegelinschriften und Hieroglyphen von John David Hawkins*, Mainz 2005.

[96] Volkert Haas, *Die hethitische Literatur. Texte, Stilistik, Motive*, Berlin and New York 2006.

HATTIAN, HURRIAN, AND HIEROGLYPHIC LUWIAN

[97] Hans-Siegfried Schuster, *Die hattisch-hethitischen Bilinguen*, vol. 1, Leiden 1974.

[98] Erich Neu, *Das hurritische Epos der Freilassung. Untersuchungen zu einem hurritisch-hethitischen Textensemble aus Ḫattusa,* Wiesbaden 1996.

[99] *Corpus of Hieroglyphic Luwian Inscriptions*: vol. I 1–3 (*Inscriptions of the Iron Age*), ed. John D. Hawkins; vol. II (Karatepe-Aslantaş), ed. Halet Çambel, Berlin 1999–2000.

Lycian Inscriptions

[100] Ernst Kalinka, *Tituli Asiae Minoris* (TAM) I: *Tituli Lyciae Lingua Lycia Conscripti*, Vienna 1901.

[101] Günter Neumann, *Neufunde lykischer Inschriften seit 1901*, Vienna 1979.

[102] H. Craig Melchert, *Lycian Corpus*, http://www.linguistics.ucla.edu/people/Melchert/webpage/lyciancorpus.pdf [as of March 2009].

Greek and Latin Inscriptions

SUPERREGIONAL, REGIONAL, AND THEMATIC COLLECTIONS

[103] Philippe Le Bas and William Henry Waddington, *Inscriptions grecques et latines recueillés en Asie Mineure*, Paris 1870.

[104] John Robert Sitlington Sterrett, *An Epigraphical Journey in Asia Minor*, Boston 1888 (reprint Hildesheim 2007).

[105] *Tituli Asiae Minoris* (TAM), ed. Kleinasiatische Kommission der Österreichischen Akademie der Wissenschaften, 5 vols. to date, Vienna 1901–2007: *Lykien* [in the Lycian and Greek languages] (I–II); *Termessos in Pisidien* (III); *Bithynische Halbinsel und Nicomedia* (IV); *Lydien* (V).

[106] Wilhelm Dittenberger, *Orientis Graeci Inscriptiones Selectae* (OGIS), 2 vols., Leipzig 1903–1905.

[107] Hans Rott, *Kleinasiatische Denkmäler aus Pisidien, Pamphylien, Kappodokien und Lykien. Darstellender Teil.* With supplements by K. Michel, L. Messerschmitt, and W. Weber, Leipzig 1908 (Inscriptions 347–382).

[108] John G. C. Anderson, Franz Cumont, and Henri Grégoire, *Studia Pontica* III 1, Brussels 1910.

[109] Wilhelm Dittenberger, *Sylloge Inscriptionum Graecarum* (Syll.³), 4 vols., third ed., 1915–1924.

[110] *Monumenta Asiae Minoris Antiqua* (MAMA), 11 vols. to date, Manchester and London 1928–2013: *Eastern Phrygia* (I); *Meriamlik and Korykos* (II); *Rough Cilicia* (III); *Eastern Province of Asia and Western Galatia* (IV); *Dorylaeum and Nacolea* (V); *Western Phrygia and Northern Caria* (VI); *Eastern Phrygia* (VII); *Lycaonia, Pisido-Phrygian Borderland, Aphrodisias* (VIII); *Aezanitis* (IX); *Appia, Upper Tembris Valley, Cotiaeum, Cadi, Synaus, Ancyra Sidera and Tiberiopolis* (X). Southern Phrygia (XI).

[111] C. Bradford Welles, *Royal Correspondence in the Hellenistic Period* (RC), New Haven, CT 1934.

[112] Louis Robert, *Études anatoliennes. Recherches sur les inscriptions grecques de l'Asie Mineure*, Paris 1937.

[113] Friedrich Karl Dörner, *Inschriften und Denkmäler aus Bithynien*, Berlin 1941.

[114] Franciszek Sokolowski, *Lois sacrées de l'Asie Mineure*, Paris 1955.

[115] Peter Herrmann, *Neue Inschriften zur historischen Landeskunde von Lydien und angrenzenden Gebieten*, Vienna 1958.

[116] Maarten J. Vermaseren, *Corpus Inscriptionum et Monumentorum Religionis Mithriacae*, 2 vols., The Hague 1956–1960.

[117] George E. Bean, *Journeys in Rough Cilicia in 1962 and 1963*, Vienna 1965.

[118] Louis Robert, *Documents de l'Asie mineure méridionale. Inscriptions, monnaies et géographie*, Geneva and Paris 1966.

[119] Alois Machatschek, *Die Nekropolen und Grabmäler im Gebiet von Elaiussa Sebaste und Korykos im Rauhen Kilikien*, Vienna 1967.

[120] Hermann Bengtson, Robert Werner, and Hatto H. Schmitt, *Die Staatsverträge des Altertums* (StV) II–III, Munich 1962–1969.

[121] Peter Herrmann and Kemal Ziya Polatkan, *Das Testament des Epikrates und andere neue Inschriften aus dem Museum von Manisa*, Vienna 1969.

[122] C. H. Emilie Haspels, *The Highlands of Phrygia. Sites and Monuments*, vol. I, Appendix III: "Greco-Roman and Byzantine Inscriptions," Princeton, NJ 1971.

[123] Eugene N. Lane, *Corpus Monumentorum Religionis Dei Menis*, 4 vols., Leiden 1971–1978.

[124] Elmar Schwertheim, "Denkmäler zur Meterverehrung," in: Sencer Şahin, Elmar Schwertheim, and Jörg Wagner (eds.), *Studien zur Religion und Kultur Kleinasiens,* FS Dörner, Leiden 1978, 791–837.

[125] Sencer Şahin, *Bithynische Studien, IK 7*, Bonn 1978.

[126] Thomas Drew-Bear, *Nouvelles inscriptions de Phrygie*, Zutphen, The Netherlands 1978.

[127] Maarten J. Vermaseren, *Corpus Cultus Cybelae Attidisque*, vol. I, Leiden et al., 1987.

[128] *Regional Epigraphic Catalogues of Asia Minor* (RECAM), ed. British Institute of Archaeology at Ankara, 4 vols. to date, London 1982–2007: *Ankara Distrikt* (II); *Kibyra-Olbasa-Region* (III); *Museum Konya* (IV); *Museum Burdur* (V).

[129] Gertrud Laminger-Pascher, *Beiträge zu den griechischen Inschriften Lykaoniens*, Vienna 1984.

[130] Michel Christol and Thomas Drew-Bear, *Un castellum romain près d'Apamée de Phrygie*, Vienna 1987.

[131] Joyce Reynolds and Robert Tannenbaum, *Jews and God-fearers at Aphrodisias. Greek Inscriptions with Commentary*, Cambridge 1987.

[132] Louis Robert, *Documents d'Asie Mineure*, Paris 1987.

[133] Gilbert Dagron and Denis Feissel, *Inscriptions de Cilicie*, Paris 1987.

[134] Claude Brixhe and René Hodot, *L'Asie Mineure du nord au sud: inscriptions inédites*, Nancy 1988.

[135] Charlotte Roueché, *Aphrodisias in Late Antiquity*, London 1989.

[136] Alain Bresson, *Recueil des inscriptions de la Pérée Rhodienne*, Paris 1991.

[137] Wolfgang Blümel, *Die Inschriften der rhodischen Peraia*, IK 38, Bonn 1991.

[138] Bülent Iplikçioğlu, *Neue Inschriften aus Nord-Lykien* I, Vienna 1992.

[139] Gertrud Laminger-Pascher, *Die kaiserzeitlichen Inschriften Lykaoniens*, Fasc. 1, Öster-reichische Akademie der Wissenschaften, Philosophisch-historische Klasse, Denkschriften 232, Vienna 1992.

[140] Charlotte Roueché, *Performers and Partisans at Aphrodisias in the Roman and Late Roman Periods*, London 1993.

[141] Georg Petzl, *Die Beichtinschriften Westkleinasiens*, Bonn 1994.

[142] Gary J. Johnson, *Early Christian Epitaphs from Anatolia*, Atlanta 1995.

[143] Josef Stauber, *Die Bucht von Adramytteion*, 2 vols., IK 50.51, Bonn 1996.

[144] William Tabbernee, *Montanist Inscriptions and Testimonia. Epigraphic Sources Illustrating the History of Montanism*, Macon, GA 1997.

[145] Johan H. M. Strubbe, *Arai Epitymbioi. Imprecations against Desecrators of the Grave in the Greek Epitaphs of Asia Minor*, IK 52, Bonn 1997.

[146] Reinhold Merkelbach and Josef Stauber, *Steinepigramme aus dem griechischen Osten* (MS), 5 vols., Leipzig 1998–2002: *Die Westküste Kleinasiens von Knidos bis Ilion* (I); *Die Nordküste Kleinasiens* (II); *Der "ferne Osten" und das Landesinnere bis zum Tauros* (III); *Die Südküste Kleinasiens, Syrien und Palästina* (IV); *Addenda und Register* (V).[3]

[147] Kurt Tomaschitz, *Unpublizierte Inschriften Westkilikiens aus dem Nachlaß Terence B. Mitfords*, Vienna 1998.

[148] Stefan Hagel and Kurt Tomaschitz, *Repertorium der westkilikischen Inschriften*, Vienna 1998.

[149] Thomas Drew-Bear, Christine M. Thomas, and Melek Yıldızturan, *Phrygian Votive Steles*, Ankara 1999.

[150] Hasan Malay, *Researches in Lydia, Mysia and Aiolis*, Vienna 1999.

[151] İnci Delemen, *Anatolian Rider Gods*, Bonn 1999.

[152] María Paz de Hoz, *Die lydischen Kulte im Lichte der griechischen Inschriften*, Bonn 1999.

[153] Greg H. R. Horsley and Stephen Mitchell, *The Inscriptions of Central Pisidia*, IK 57, Bonn 2000.

[154] Rosalinde A. Kearsley, *Greeks and Romans in Imperial Asia*, IK 59, Bonn 2001.

[155] Alain Bresson, Patrice Brun, and Ender Varinlioğlu, "Les inscriptions grecques et latins," in: Pierre Debord and Ender Varinlioğlu (eds.), *Les hautes terres de Carie*, Bordeaux 2001, Chapter V.

[156] Lloyd Jonnes, *The Inscriptions of the Sultan Dağı* I, IK 62, Bonn 2002.

[3] Because of the impractical segmentation of the numbering system, I cite the inscriptions in this work only by volume and page number.

[157] Walter Ameling, *Inscriptiones Judaicae Orientis* II, *Kleinasien*, Tübingen 2004.

[158] Veronika Scheibelreiter, *Stifterinschriften auf Mosaiken Westkleinasiens*, Vienna 2006.

[159] Peter Herrmann and Hasan Malay, *New Documents from Lydia*, Vienna 2007.

[160] Johannes Nollé, *Kleinasiatische Losorakel*, Munich 2007.

[161] *Museo Archaeologico di Denizli-Hierapolis. Catalogo delle iscrizioni greche e latine: distretto di Denzili*, ed. Tullia Ritti, Napoli 2008.

[161a] Andreas Victor Walser, *Bauern und Zinsnehmer. Politik, Recht und Wirtschaft im frühhellenistischen Ephesos*, Munich 2008.

[161b] Pierre Debord and Ender Varinlioğlu, *Cités de Carie. Harpasa. Bargasa. Orthosia*, Rennes 2010.

[161c] David French, *Roman Roads and Milestones of Asia Minor*, vol. 3.1 Republican (2012), 3.2 Galatia (2012), 3.3 Cappadocia (2012), 3.4 Pontus et Bithynia (2013), 3.5 Asia (2014), British Institute of Archaeology at Ankara, Electronic Monograph. Ankara.

[161d] Jean-Louis Ferrary, *Les mémoriaux de délégations du sanctuaire oraculaire de Claros, d'après la documentation conservée dans le Fonds Louis Robert*, 2 vols., Paris 2014.

[161e] Christian Marek and Mustafa Adak, *Epigraphische Forschungen in Bithynien, Paphlagonien, Galatien und Pontos*, Philia Suppl. vol. 2, Istanbul 2016 (in print).

COLLECTIONS FROM INDIVIDUAL CITIES

[162] *Inschriften Griechischer Städte aus Kleinasien* (*IK*), ed. by Österreichische Akademie der Wissenschaften, Rheinisch-Westfälische Akademie der Wissenschaften, Bonn 1972 ff.,[4] 45 volumes to date on the following cities (in alphabetical order): Alexandria Troas (Marijana Ricl 1997), Anazarbos (Mustafa H. Sayar 2000), Antiocheia in Pisidia (Maurice A. Byrne, Guy Labarre 2006), Apameia und Pylai in Bithynia (Thomas Corsten 1987), Arykanda (Sencer Şahin 1994), Assos (Reinhold Merkelbach 1976), Bithynion-Klaudiupolis (Friedrich Becker-Bertau 1986), Byzantion (Adam Łajtar 2000), Ephesos (Hermann Wankel, Reinhold Merkelbach et al. 1979–1984), Erythrai und Klazomenai (Helmut Engelmann, Reinhold Merkelbach 1972–1973), Hadrianoi und Hadrianeia (Elmar Schwertheim 1987), Herakleia Pontike (Lloyd Jonnes 1994), Iasos (Wolfgang Blümel 1985), Ilion (Peter Frisch 1975), Chalkedon (Reinhold Merkelbach, Friedrich K. Dörner, Sencer Şahin 1980), Keramos (Ender Varinlioğlu 1986), Kibyra (Thomas Corsten 2002), Kios (Thomas Corsten 1985), Knidos (Wolfgang Blümel 1992), Kyme (Helmut Engelmann 1976), Kyzikos (Elmar Schwertheim 1980–1983), Lampsakos (Peter Frisch 1978), Laodikeia on Lykos (Thomas Corsten 1997), Magnesia on Sipylos (Thomas Ihnken 1978), Metropolis (Boris Dreyer, Helmut Engelmann 2003), Mylasa (Wolfgang Blümel 1987–1988), Nikaia (Museum İznik: Sencer Şahin 1979–1987), Parion (Peter Frisch 1983), Perge (Sencer Şahin 1999–2004), Pessinus (Johan Strubbe 2005), Priene (Wolfgang Blümel and Reinhold Merkelbach 2014), Prusa ad Olympum (Thomas Corsten 1991–1993), Prusias ad Hypium (Walter Ameling 1985), Selge (Johannes Nollé, Friedel Schindler 1991), Sestos (Johannes Krauss 1980), Side (Johannes Nollé 1993–2001), Sinope (David French 2004), Smyrna (Georg Petzl 1982–1990), Stratonikeia (M. Çetin Şahin 1981–2010), Tralleis and Nysa (Fjodor B. Poljakov 1989), Tyana (Dietrich Berges and Johannes Nollé 2000).

---

[4] The series contains collections that relate not to cities but to regions and themes [see under the header "Superregional, Regional, and Thematic Collections"]. It also contains regional collections outside Asia Minor (Filippo Canali De Rossi, *Iscrizioni dello estremo Oriente greco*, IK 65, 2004).

In addition to this series, collections on the following cities have appeared:

[163] *Altertümer von Pergamon* (AvP): Max Fränkel, *Die Inschriften von Pergamon,* AvP VIII 1–2, Berlin 1890–1895; Christian Habicht, *Die Inschriften des Asklepieions,* AvP VIII 3, Berlin 1969.

[164] Walther Judeich, in: Carl Humann, Conrad Cichorius, Walther Judeich, and Franz Winter, *Altertümer von Hierapolis, Jahrbuch des Kaiserlich Deutschen Archäologischen Instituts,* supplemental vol. 4, Berlin 1898 (Inscriptions 67–202).

[165] Otto Kern, *Die Inschriften von Magnesia am Maeander,* Berlin 1900.

[166] Friedrich Freiherr Hiller von Gaertringen, *Die Inschriften von Priene,* Berlin 1906.

[167] Georg Kawerau and Albert Rehm, *Das Delphinion, Milet* I 3, Berlin 1914; Albert Rehm, *Milet* VI 1, *Inschriften, Nachdruck mit Nachträgen und Übersetzungen von Peter Herrmann,* Berlin 1997; Peter Herrmann, *Milet* VI 2, *Inschriften,* Berlin 1998; Peter Herrmann, Wolfgang Günther, and Norbert Ehrhardt, *Milet* VI 3, *Inschriften,* Berlin 2006.

[168] William Hepburn Buckler and David M. Robinson, *Sardis* VII 1, Leiden 1932.

[169] Louis Robert, *Le sanctuaire de Sinuri près de Mylasa* I, Paris 1945.

[170] Jeanne Robert and Louis Robert, *La Carie* II: *Le plateau de Tabai et ses environs,* Paris 1954.

[171] Albert Rehm, *Die Inschriften von Didyma,* Berlin 1958.

[172] Louis Robert, *Nouvelles inscriptions de Sardes* I, Paris 1964.

[173] Clemens Emin Bosch, *Quellen zur Geschichte der Stadt Ankara,* Ankara 1967.

[174] Louis Robert, "Les inscriptions" in: Jean des Gagniers et al. (eds.), *Laodicée du Lycos, Le Nymphée,* Paris 1969, 248–389.

[175] Jonas Crampa, *Labraunda Swedish Excavations and Researches,* III: *The Greek Inscriptions* I–II, Lund 1969–1972.

[176] Friedrich Schindler, *Die Inschriften von Bubon, SBWien, Phil.-Hist. Kl. 278.3,* Vienna 1972.

[177] Christian Naour, *Tyriaion en Cabalide. Épigraphie et géographie historique,* Zutphen, The Netherlands 1980.

[178] André Balland, *Fouilles de Xanthos VIII. Inscriptions d'époque impériale du Letoon,* Paris 1981.

[179] Joyce Reynolds, *Aphrodisias and Rome,* London 1982.

[180] Jeanne Robert and Louis Robert, *Fouilles d'Amyzon en Carie* I, Paris 1983.

[181] Louis Robert and Jeanne Robert, *Claros* I. *Décrets hellénistiques,* Paris 1989.

[182] Christian Marek, *Stadt, Ära und Territorium in Pontus-Bithynia und Nord-Galatia,* appendixes 3–6: Kataloge der Inschriften von Pompeiopolis, Abonuteichos/Ionopolis, Amastris und Kaisareia/Hadrianopolis, Tübingen 1993.

[183] Christian Marek, *Die Inschriften von Kaunos,* Munich 2006.

[184] Bülent Iplikçioğlu, Güler Çelgin, and A. Vedat Çelgin, *Epigraphische Forschungen in Termessos und seinem Territorium* IV, Vienna 2007.

[185] Ferit Baz, *Die Inschriften von Komana (Hierapolis) in Kappadokien,* İstanbul 2007.

[186] Christina Kokkinia, *Boubon. The Inscriptions and Archaeological Remains. A Survey 2004–2006,* Athens 2008.

[186a] Stephen Mitchell and David French, *The Greek and Latin Inscriptions of Ankara (Ancyra). vol. I. From Augustus to the End of the Third Century A.D.,* Munich 2012.

[186b] Ergün Laflı and Eva Christof, *Hadrianopolis I. Inschriften aus Paphlagonia,* Oxford 2012. See also Eva Christof and Ergün Laflı, "Neue Transkriptions- und Übersetzungs-

vorschläge zu 43 Inschriften aus Hadrianopolis und seiner Chora in Paphlagonien," in: H. Bru and G. Labarre (eds.), *L'Anatolie des peuples, des cités et des cultures (IIe millénaire av. J.-C.–Ve siècle ap. J.-C.), Colloque international de Besançon, 26–27 novembre 2010, vol. 2: Approches locales et régionales*, Besançon, France, 2014.

[186c] Roberta Fabiani, I decreti onorari di Iasos. Cronologia e storia, Munich 2015.

[186d] Wolfgang Blümel, Riet van Bremen, and Jan-Mathieu Carbon, *A Guide to Inscriptions in Milas and its Museum*, Istanbul 2015.

EDITIONS OF PROMINENT INDIVIDUAL TEXTS, WITH COMMENTARY

[187] Michael Wörrle, *Stadt und Fest im kaiserzeitlichen Kleinasien. Studien zu einer agonistischen Stiftung aus Oinoanda*, Munich 1988.

[188] Helmut Engelmann and Dieter Knibbe, "Das Zollgesetz der Provinz Asia," *EpigrAnat* 14, Bonn 1989.

[189] Martin F. Smith, *Diogenes of Oinoanda: The Epicurean Inscription*, Oxford 1993.

[190] Ekkehard Weber, *Res gestae divi Augusti, nach dem Monumentum Ancyranum, Apolloniense und Antiochenum, lateinisch, griechisch und deutsch*, sixth ed., Düsseldorf and Zürich 1999.

[191] Christina Kokkinia, *Die Opramoas-Inschrift von Rhodiapolis. Euergetismus und soziale Elite in Lykien*, Bonn 2000.

[192] Georg Petzl and Elmar Schwertheim, *Hadrian und die dionysischen Künstler. Drei in Alexandria Troas neugefundene Briefe des Kaisers an die Künstler-Vereinigung*, Bonn 2006.

[193] John Scheid, *Res gestae divi Augusti. Hauts faits du divin Auguste*, Paris 2007.

[194] Mustafa Adak and Sencer Şahin, *Stadiasmus Patarensis. Itinera Provinciae Lyciae*, Istanbul 2007.

[194a] Denis Rousset, *De Lycie en Cabalide. La convention entre les Lyciens et Termessos près d'Oinoanda*, Paris 2010.

[194b] Peter Thonemann, "A Copy of Augustus' Res gestae at Sardis," *Historia* 61, 2012, 282–288.

SUPPLEMENTS

Every year, many inscriptions from Asia Minor, chiefly in Greek, appear or are published in improved form. An overview of these is offered by the following.

[195] *Supplementum Epigraphicum Graecum* (SEG), Leiden, later Amsterdam, since 1923 (currently appears with a few years' delay; last volume in 2010). The SEG publishes texts.

[196] *Bulletin épigraphique* published annually by Jeanne Robert and Louis Robert and their successors at the journal *Revue des Études Grecques*. In general, the *Bulletin* does not publish texts but only provides improvements and annotations.

Coins

[197] George Francis Hill, *Catalogue of the Greek Coins of Lycia, Pamphylia and Pisidia*, British Museum Coins (BMC), London 1897.

[198] Friedrich Imhoof-Blumer, *Kleinasiatische Münzen*, Vienna 1901–1902.

[199] Barclay V. Head, *Historia Numorum* (Head, HN²), second ed., Oxford 1911.

[200] William Henry Waddington, Ernest Babelon, and Théodore Reinach, *Recueil general des monnaies grecques d'Asie Mineure I (Pont et Paphlagonie)*, Paris 1925.

[201] Edward A. Sydenham, *The Coinage of Caesarea in Cappadocia*, London 1933 (reprint New York 1978).

[202] Clemens Emin Bosch, *Die kleinasiatischen Münzen der römischen Kaiserzeit* II 1, 1 (Bithynia), Stuttgart 1935.

[203] Kommission für Alte Geschichte und Epigraphik des Deutschen Archäologischen Institutes (ed.), *Sylloge Nummorum Graecorum, Deutschland, Sammlung Hans von Aulock (SNG Aulock)*, 19 vols., Berlin 1957–1981 (*Collection of Greek Coins from Asia Minor*, reprint in 4 vols., NJ 1987).

[204] Louis Robert, *Monnaies antiques en Troade*, Paris 1966.

[205] Louis Robert, *Monnaies grecques*, Paris 1967.

[206] Peter Robert Franke, *Kleinasien zur Römerzeit: Griechisches Leben im Spiegel der Münzen*, Munich 1968.

[207] Konrad Kraft, *Das System der kaiserzeitlichen Münzprägung in Kleinasien*, Berlin 1972.

[208] Hans von Aulock, *Münzen und Städte Lykaoniens*, Tübingen 1976.

[209] Hans von Aulock, *Münzen und Städte Pisidiens*, Part I, Tübingen 1977.

[210] Hans von Aulock, *Münzen und Städte Phrygiens* I, Tübingen 1980.

[211] Otto Mørkholm and Günter Neumann, *Die lykischen Münzlegenden*, Göttingen 1978.

[212] William E. Metcalf, *The Cistophory of Hadrian*, New York 1980.

[213] David R. Sear, *Greek Imperial Coins and Their Values. The Local Coinage of the Roman Empire*, London 1982.

[214] Wolfram Weiser, *Katalog der bithynischen Münzen der Sammlung des Instituts für Altertumskunde der Universität zu Köln.* vol. 1, *Nikaia. Mit einer Untersuchung der Prägesysteme und Gegenstempel*, Opladen, Germany 1983.

[215] Wolfgang Leschhorn, "Die kaiserzeitlichen Münzen Kleinasiens. Zu den Möglichkeiten und Schwierigkeiten ihrer statistischen Erfassung," *RNum* 27, 1985, 200–216.

[216] Dietrich O. A. Klose, *Die Münzprägung von Smyrna in der römischen Kaiserzeit*, Berlin 1987.

[216a] Alain Davesne and Georges Le Rider, *Gülnar II. Le trésor de Meydancıkkale (Cilicie trachée, 1980)*, Paris 1989.

[217] David MacDonald, *The Coinage of Aphrodisias*, London 1992.

[218] Gerd R. Stumpf, *Numismatische Studien zur Chronologie der römischen Statthalter in Kleinasien*, Saarbrücken 1991.

[219] Andrew Burnett, Michel Amandry, and Pere Pau Ripollès, *Roman Provincial Coinage*, 5 vols. to date and one supplemental volume, London 1992–2006.

[220] Oğuz Tekin, *Bibliography of Ancient Numismatics for Anatolia*, Istanbul 1993.

[221] Ruprecht Ziegler, *Kaiser, Heer und städtisches Geld. Untersuchungen zur Münzprägung von Anazarbos und anderer ostkilikischer Städte*, Vienna 1993.

[222] William E. Metcalf, *The Silver Coinage of Cappadocia, Vespasian–Commodus*, New York 1996.

[223] Johannes Nollé, Bernhard Overbeck, and Peter Weiß (eds.), *Internationales Kolloquium zur kaiserzeitlichen Münzprägung Kleinasiens, Nomismata* 1, Milan 1997.

[224] Peter Robert Franke and Margret K. Nollé, *Die Homonoia-Münzen Kleinasiens*, Saarbrücken, Germany 1997.

[225] Koray Konuk, *Sylloge Nummorum Graecorum* (SNG) *Turkey* 1: *The Muharrem Kayhan Collection*, Istanbul and Bordeaux 2002.

[226] Oğuz Tekin and Sencan Altınoluk, *Sylloge Nummorum Graecorum* (SNG) *Turkey* 2: *Anamur Museum* vol. 1, *Roman Provincial Coins*, Istanbul 2007.

Archaeology, Art, Illustrated Books, and Archaeological Guides[5]

General, Covering More than One Period

[227] Helmuth T. Bossert, *Altanatolien. Kunst und Handwerk in Kleinasien von den Anfängen bis zum völligen Aufgehen in die griechische Kultur*, Berlin 1942.
[228] U. Bahadır Alkım, *Anatolien I. Von den Anfängen bis zum Ende des 2. Jahrtausends v. Chr.*, Munich, Geneva, and Paris 1968.
[229] Henri Metzger, *Anatolien II. Vom Beginn des 1. Jahrtausends v. Chr. bis zum Ende der römischen Epoche*, Munich, Geneva, and Paris 1969.
[230] Ekrem Akurgal, *Ancient Civilisations and Ruins of Turkey. From Prehistoric Times until the End of the Roman Empire*, fourth ed., Istanbul 1978.
[231] Stephan W. E. Blum, Frank Schweizer, and Rüstem Aslan, *Luftbilder antiker Landschaften und Stätten der Türkei (mit Flugbildern von Hakan Öge)*, Mainz 2006.
[231a] Antonia Sagona and Paul Zimansky, *Ancient Turkey*, London and New York 2009.

From Prehistory to the Bronze Age

[232] Emmanuel Anati, "Anatolia's Earliest Art," *Archaeology* 21, 1966, 22 ff.
[233] Rudolf Naumann, *Architektur Kleinasiens von ihren Anfängen bis zum Ende der Hethiterzeit*, second ed., Tübingen 1971.
[233a] Bérengère Perello, *L'architecture domestique de l'Anatolie au IIIe millénaire av. J.-C.*, Paris 2011.

Hittites

[234] Ekrem Akurgal, *Die Kunst der Hethiter*, second ed., Munich 1976.
[235] Kurt Bittel, *Die Hethiter. Die Kunst der Hethiter vom Ende des 3. bis zum Anfang des 1. Jahrtausends v. Chr.*, Munich 1976.
[236] Wulf Schirmer, "Stadt, Palast, Tempel. Charakteristika hethitischer Architektur im 2. und 1. Jahrtausend v. Chr.," in: [327] *Die Hethiter*, 2002, 204–217.
[237] Horst Ehringhaus, *Götter, Herrscher, Inschriften. Die Felsreliefs der hethitischen Großreichszeit in der Türkei*, Mainz 2005.
[237a] Jürgen Seeher, *Götter in Stein gehauen. Das hethitische Felsheiligtum von Yazılıkaya*, İstanbul 2011.

Iranian, Greek, and Roman Periods

[238] Ekrem Akurgal, *Die Kunst Anatoliens von Homer bis Alexander*, Berlin 1961.
[239] George A. M. Hanfmann, *From Croesus to Constantine. The Cities of Western Asia Minor and Their Arts in Greek and Roman Times*, Ann Arbor, MI 1975.
[240] Robert Fleischer, *Artemis von Ephesos und verwandte Kultstatuen aus Anatolien und*

---

[5] For excavation reports, see the literature listed under "Bibliographies and Research Reports."

Syrien, Leiden 1973 [Supplement in: Sencer Şahin, Elmar Schwertheim, and Jörg Wagner (eds.), *Studien zur Religion und Kultur Kleinasiens*, FS Dörner I, Leiden 1978, 324–358].

[241] Ernst Pfuhl and Hans Möbius, *Die Ostgriechischen Grabreliefs*, 4 vols., Mainz 1977–1979.

[242] Ekrem Akurgal, *Griechische und Römische Kunst in der Türkei*, Munich 1987.

[243] Frank Rumscheid, *Untersuchungen zur kleinasiatischen Bauornamentik des Hellenismus*, Mainz 1994.

[244] Anton Bammer and Ulrike Muss, *Das Artemision von Ephesos*, Mainz 1996.

[245] Orhan Bingöl, *Malerei und Mosaik der Antike in der Türkei*, Mainz 1997.

[246] Daniela Pohl, *Kaiserzeitliche Tempel in Kleinasien unter besonderer Berücksichtigung der hellenistischen Vorläufer*, Bonn 2002.

[247] Frank Kolb (ed.), *Chora und Polis*, Munich 2004.

[248] Sarah Cormack, *The Space of Death in Roman Asia Minor*, Vienna 2004.

[248a] Dietrich Berges, *Knidos. Beiträge zur Geschichte der archaischen Stadt*, Mainz 2006.

[249] Askold Ivantchik and Vakhtang Licheli (eds.), *Achaemenid Culture and Local Traditions in Anatolia, Southern Caucasus and Iran: New Discoveries*, Leiden 2007.

[249a] Lore Mühlbauer, *Lykische Grabarchitektur. Vom Holz zum Stein*, Vienna 2007.

[250] Ulrike Muss, *Die Archäologie der ephesischen Artemis. Gestalt und Ritual eines Heiligtums,* Vienna 2008.

[250a] Guntram Koch, *Sarkophage der römischen Kaiserzeit in der Türkei*, Antalya, Turkey 2010.

[250b] Wolfram Hoepfner, *Halikarnassos und das Maussolleion*, Mainz 2013.

[250c] Takeko Harada and Fatih Cimok, *Roads of Ancient Anatolia*, 2 vols., İstanbul 2008.

[250d] Klaus Rheidt (ed.), *Aizanoi und Anatolien*, Mainz 2010.

Particular Regions

[251] Ekrem Akurgal, *Phrygische Kunst*, Ankara 1955.

[252] Hubertus von Gall, *Die paphlagonischen Felsgräber. Eine Studie zur kleinasiatischen Kunstgeschichte*, Tübingen 1966.

[253] Friederike Naumann, *Die Ikonographie der Kybele in der phrygischen und der griechischen Kunst*, Tübingen 1983.

[254] Thomas A. Sinclair, *Eastern Turkey. An Architectural and Archaeological Survey*, 4 vols., London 1985–1990.

[255] Marc Waelkens, *Die Kleinasiatischen Türsteine*, Mainz 1986.

[256] Friedrich K. Dörner, *Der Thron der Götter auf dem Nemrud Dağ*, Bergisch-Gladbach 1987.

[257] Jörg Wagner, *Kommagene. Heimat der Götter*, second ed., Dortmund 1988.

[258] Frank Kolb and Barbara Kupke, *Lykien*, Mainz 1992.

[259] Ralf-Bernhard Wartke, *Urartu, Das Reich am Ararat*, Mainz 1993.

[260] *Armenien. 5000 Jahre Kunst und Kultur von den Anfängen bis zur Gegenwart*, ed. Museum Bochum and Stiftung für Armenische Studien, Tübingen 1995.

[261] Anneliese Peschlow-Bindokat, *Der Latmos. Eine unbekannte Gebirgslandschaft an der türkischen Westküste*, Mainz 1996.

[262] Dietrich Berndt, *Midasstadt in Phrygien. Eine sagenumwobene Stätte im anatolischen Hochland*, Mainz 2005.

[263] Susanne Berndt-Ersöz, *Phrygian Rock-Cut Shrines. Structure, Function, and Cult Practice*, Leiden and Boston 2006.

[264] Frank Kolb, *Burg-Polis-Bischofssitz. Geschichte der Siedlungskammer von Kyaneai in der Südwesttürkei,* Mainz 2008.

[264a] Christopher Roosevelt, *The Archaeology of Lydia, from Gyges to Alexander,* Cambridge 2009.

[264b] Jürgen Borchhardt and Erika Bleibtreu, *Strukturen lykischer Residenzstädte im Vergleich zu älteren Städten des Vorderen Orients,* Antalya, Turkey 2013.

[264c] B. Beck-Brandt, S. Ladstätter, and B. Yener-Marksteiner (eds.), *Turm und Tor. Siedlungsstrukturen in Lykien und benachbarten Kulturlandschaften. Akten des Gedenkkolloquiums für Thomas Marksteiner,* Vienna 2015.

Guidebooks

[265] George E. Bean, *Kleinasien,* 1: *Die ägäische Türkei von Pergamon bis Didyma,* fourth ed., Stuttgart 1985; 2: *Die türkische Südküste von Antalya bis Alanya,* third ed., Stuttgart 1985; 3: *Jenseits des Mäander. Karien mit dem Vilayet Muğla,* Stuttgart 1974, 1–3 trans. J. Wiesner; 4: *Lykien,* Stuttgart 1980, trans. U. Pause-Dreyer. English edition: 1: *Aegean Turkey,* second ed., London 1984; 2: *Turkey's Southern Shore,* second ed., London 1979; 3: *Turkey. Beyond the Maeander,* London 1971; 4: *Lycian Turkey,* London 1978.

[266] Barbara Radt, *Anatolien* I, *Ankara und Hattuscha, Kappadokien, Konya, Phrygien,* Munich and Zürich 1993.

[267] Wolf Koenigs, *Westtürkei. Von Troia bis Knidos,* Munich and Zürich 1991.

[268] Jörg Wagner, *Südtürkei. Von Kaunos bis Issos,* second ed., Munich and Zürich 1997.

[269] Guide Bleu: *Turquie,* 2004.

[270] Baedeker Allianz Reiseführer, *Türkei,* seventh ed., Ostfildern, Germany 2005.

[270a] Michael Blömer and Engelbert Winter, *Commagene. An Archaeological Guide,* İstanbul 2011.

[270b] Mark Wilson, *Biblical Turkey. A Guide to the Jewish and Christian Sites of Asia Minor,* İstanbul 2010.

Geography

Physical Geography

[271] Herbert Louis, "Anadolu," in: Johannes H. Kramers, Hamilton A. R. Gibb, and Evariste Lévi-Provençal (eds.), *Encyclopédie de l'Islam* I, second ed., Leiden and Paris 1960, 475–479.

[272] Herbert Paschinger, "Türkei," in: Wolf Tietze and Ernst Weigt (eds.), *Westermann Lexikon der Geographie* 4, Braunschweig, Germany 1970, 716 ff.

[273] Werner Kündig et al., *Die Türkei. Raum und Mensch, Kultur und Wirtschaft in Gegenwart und Vergangenheit,* second ed., Tübingen 1977.

[274] Wolf-Dieter Hütteroth, *Die Türkei,* Darmstadt 1982.

[275] Oğuz Erol, *Die naturräumliche Gliederung der Türkei,* Wiesbaden 1983.

[276] John R. McNeill, *The Mountains of the Mediterranean World. An Environmental History,* Cambridge 1992.

Historical Geography and Topography

[277] Carl Ritter, *Die Erdkunde von Asien,* 19 vols., Berlin 1832–1859.

[278] William Mitchell Ramsay, *The Historical Geography of Asia Minor,* London 1890.

[279] Louis Robert, *Villes d'Asie Mineure,* second ed., Paris 1962.

[280] Jeanne Robert and Louis Robert, "La persistance de la toponymie antique dans l'Anatolie," in: *La toponymie antique. Actes du Colloque de Strasbourg 12–14 Juin 1975*, Leiden 1977, 11–63.

[26] Louis Robert, *A travers l'Asie Mineure. Poètes et prosateurs, monnaies grecques, voyageurs et géographie*, Paris 1980.

[281] Sir Ronald Syme, *Anatolica. Studies in Strabo*, ed. A. Birley, Oxford 1995.

[282] Anna Maria Biraschi and Giovanni Salmeri (eds.), *Strabone e l'Asia Minore, Incontri perugini di storia della storiografia antica e sul mondo antico 10, Perugia 25–28 maggio 1997*, Naples 2000.

[283] *Tabula Imperii Byzantini*, ed. Österreichische Akademie der Wissenschaften, Vienna. Volumes on Asia Minor are TIB 2: Friedrich Hild and Marcell Restle, *Kappadokien*, 1981; TIB 4: Klaus Belke and Marcell Restle, *Galatien und Lycaonien*, 1984; TIB 5: Friedrich Hild and Hansgerd Hellenkemper, *Kilikien und Isaurien*, 1990; TIB 7: Klaus Belke and Norbert Mersich, *Phrygien und Pisidien*, 1990; TIB 8, 1–3: Hansgerd Hellenkemper and Friedrich Hild, *Lykien und Pamphylien*, 2004; TIB 9: Klaus Belke, *Paphlagonien und Honorias*, 1996.

[284] Dietram Müller, *Topographischer Bildkommentar zu den Historien Herodots. Kleinasien*, Tübingen and Berlin 1997.

[285] Karl Strobel (ed.), *New Perspectives on the Historical Geography and Topography of Anatolia in the II and I Millennium B.C.*, Florence 2008.

[286] Hadrien Bru, François Kirbihler, and Stéphane Lebreton, *L'Asie Mineure dans l'Antiquité. Échanges, populations et territoires*, Rennes, France 2009.

[286a] Peter Thonemann, *The Maeander Valley. A Historical Geography from Antiquity to Byzantium*, Cambridge 2011.

[286b] Gojko Barjamovic, *A Historical Geography of Anatolia in the Old Assyrian Colony Period*, Copenhagen 2011.

Atlases and Maps

[287] *The Barrington Atlas of the Greek and Roman World*, ed. Richard Talbert, Princeton, NJ 2000.

[288] Heinz Gaube and Wolfgang Röllig (eds)., *Tübinger Atlas des Vorderen Orients* (TAVO), Wiesbaden 1969–2010.

[289] William M. Calder and George E. Bean, *A Classical Map of Asia Minor*, London 1958.

On the Names of Ancient Anatolia

[290] Demetrius J. Georgacas, "The name 'Asia' for the Continent: Its History and Origin," *Names* 17, 1969, 1 ff.

[291] Demetrius J. Georgacas, *The Name of the Asia Minor Peninsula and a Register of Surviving Anatolian Pre-Turkish Placenames*, Heidelberg 1971.

[292] Franz Taeschner, "Anadolu," in: Johannes H. Kramers, Hamilton A. R. Gibb, and Evariste Lévi-Provençal (eds.), *Encyclopédie de l'Islam* I, second ed., Leiden and Paris 1960, 475.

Cultural History and Ethnography

[293] Albrecht Goetze, *Kleinasien. Kulturgeschichte des Alten Orients*, second ed., Munich 1957.

[294] Jak Yakar, *Ethnoarchaeology of Anatolia. Rural Socio-Economy in the Bronze and Iron Ages*, Jerusalem 2000.

[295] Hartmut Blum, Bettina Faist, Peter Pfälzner, and Anna Maria Wittke (eds.), *Brücken-land Anatolien? Ursachen, Extensität und Modi des Kulturaustausches zwischen Anatolien und seinen Nachbarn*, Tübingen 2002.

Early Anatolia

General

[296] Robert J. Braidwood, *The Near East and the Foundations for Civilization*, Eugene, OR 1952.

[297] Barthel H. Hrouda, *Vorderasien* I, Munich 1971.

[298] Hans J. Nissen, *Grundzüge einer Geschichte der Frühzeit des Vorderen Orients*, Darmstadt 1983.

[299] Martha Sharp Joukowsky, *Early Turkey. An Introduction to the Archaeology of Anatolia from Prehistory through the Lydian Period*, Dubuque, IA 1996.

[300] Clemens Lichter (ed.), *How Did Farming Reach Europe? Anatolian-European Relations from the Second Half of the 7th through the First Half of the 6th Millennium cal. B. C.*, Istanbul 2005.

[231a] Antonio Sagona and Paul Zimansky, *Ancient Trukey*, New York 2009.

[300a] Piotr Taracha, *Religions of Second Millenium Anatolia*, Wiesbaden 2009.

[300b] Bleda S. Düring, *The Prehistory of Asia Minor. From Complex Hunter-Gatherers to Early Urban Societies*, Leiden 2010.

[300c] Jak Yakar, *Reflections of Ancient Anatolian Society in Archaeology From Neolithic Village Communities to EBA Towns and Polities*, Istanbul 2011.

[300d] Sharon R. Steadman and Gregory McMahon, *The Oxford Handbook of Ancient Anatolia, 10.000-323 B.C.E.*, Oxford 2011.

Neolithic and Chalcolithic

[301] James Mellaart, *The Neolithic of the Near East*, London 1975.

[302] Jak Yakar, *The Later Prehistory of Anatolia. The Late Chalcolithic and Early Bronze Age*, Oxford 1985.

[303] Robert J. Braidwood, "The First Great Change," in: Mario Liverani et al. (eds.), *Studi di paleoetnologia in onore di Salvatore M. Puglisi*, Rome 1985, 141 ff.

[304] Jak Yakar, *Prehistoric Anatolia. The Neolithic Transformation and the Early Chalcolithic Period*, Tel Aviv 1991, Suppl. vol. 1, 1994.

[305] Anneliese Peschlow-Bindokat, "Ziegenjagd und Kulttanz, Die ältesten prähistorischen Felsmalereien in Westkleinasien," *AW* 26, 1995, 114–117.

[306] Mehmet Özdoğan and Nezih Başgelen (eds.), *The Neolithic in Turkey. The Cradle of Civilization*, Istanbul 1999.

[307] Klaus Schmidt, "Animals in the Symbolic World of Pre-Pottery Neolithic Göbekli Tepe, South-Eastern Turkey: A Preliminary Assessment," *Anthropozoologica* 39 (1), 2004, 179 ff.

[300] Clemens Lichter (ed.), *How Did Farming Reach Europe? Anatolian-European Relations from the Second Half of the 7th through the First Half of the 6th Millennium cal. B.C.*, Istanbul 2005.

[308] Klaus Schmidt, *Sie bauten die ersten Tempel. Das rätselhafte Heiligtum der Steinzeitjäger*, second ed., Munich 2007.

[309] Michael Zick, *Türkei, Wiege der Zivilisation*, Stuttgart 2008.

[309a] Mehmet Özdoğan, Harald Hauptmann, and Nezih Başgelen (eds.), *The Neolithic in Turkey. New Excavations and New Research I—The Tigris Basin, II—The Euphrates Basin*, Istanbul 2011.

Early and Middle Bronze Age (3000–1700 CE)

[310] Seton Lloyd and James Mellaart, *Beycesultan*, 3 vols., London 1962–1972.

[311] Seton Lloyd, *Early Highland Peoples of Anatolia*, London 1967.

[312] James Mellaart, *Cambridge Ancient History*, I², 1971, 363 ff., 681 ff.

[313] Jak Yakar, *The Later Prehistory of Anatolia. The Late Chalcolithic and Early Bronze Age*, Oxford 1985.

[314] Tahsin Özgüç, *The Palaces and Temples of Kültepe-Kaniš/Neša*, Ankara 1999.

[315] Marcella Frangipane (ed.), *Arslantepe, la collina dei leoni*, Milan 2004.

[233a] Bérengère Perello, *L'architecture domestique de l'Anatolie au IIIe millénaire av. J.-C.*, Paris 2011.

Before the Assyrians (2000–1700 CE)

[316] Paul Garelli, *Les Assyriens en Cappadoce*, Paris 1963.

[317] Louis Lawrence Orlin, *Assyrian Colonies in Cappadocia*, The Hague and Paris 1970.

[318] Mogens T. Larsen, *The Old Assyrian City-State and Its Colonies*, Copenhagen 1976.

[319] Klaas R. Veenhof, "The Old Assyrian Merchants and Their Relations with the Native Population of Anatolia," in: Hartmut Kühne et al. (eds.), *Berliner Beiträge zum Vorderen Orient* 1, Berlin 1982, 147–160.

[320] Jan G. Dercksen, *The Old Assyrian Copper Trade in Anatolia*, Istanbul 1996.

Hittites

Chronology

[321] Frank Starke, "Chronologische Übersicht zur Geschichte," in: [327] *Die Hethiter*, 2002, 310–315.

General

[322] Margarete Riemschneider, *Die Welt der Hethiter*, second ed., Zürich 1955.

[323] Oliver R. Gurney, *The Hittites*, second ed., Harmondsworth, UK 1961.

[324] Heinrich Otten, "Das Hethiterreich," in: Hartmut Schmöckel (ed.), *Kulturgeschichte des Alten Orients*, Stuttgart 1961, 311–446.

[325] James G. Macqueen, *The Hittites and Their Contemporaries in Asia Minor*, second ed., London 1986.

[326] Horst Klengel, *Geschichte des Hethitischen Reiches. Unter Mitwirkung von Fiorella Imparati, Volkert Haas and Theo P. J. van den Hout*, HdO I 34, Leiden, Boston, and Cologne 1999.

[327] *Die Hethiter und ihr Reich. Das Volk der 1000 Götter*, ed. Kunst und Ausstellungshalle der Bundesrepublik Deutschland, Stuttgart 2002.

[328] Trevor Bryce, *Life and Society in the Hittite World*, Oxford 2002.

[329] Gary Beckman, Richard H. Beal, and J. Gregory McMahon (eds.), *Hittite Studies in Honor of Harry A. Hoffner Jr.*, Winona Lake, IN 2003.

[330] Charles Burney, *Historical Dictionary of the Hittites*, Lanham, MD, Toronto, and Oxford 2004.

[331] Trevor Bryce, *The Kingdom of the Hittites*, second ed., Oxford 2005.

[331a] Jörg Klinger, *Die Hethiter. Geschichte, Gesellschaft, Kultur*, Munich 2007.

Peoples and Languages in the Age of the Hittites
LANGUAGES AND WRITING

[332] *Altkleinasiatische Sprachen*, HdO 1. Abteilung, 2. Band, 1. und 2. Abschnitt, Lieferung 2, Leiden 1969.

[333] Annelies Kammenhuber, "Das Hattische," in: [332] Altkleinasiatische Sprachen, 1969, 428–546.

[334] Hans-Georg Güterbock, "Hethiter, Hethitisch," in: Erich Ebeling et al. (eds.), *Reallexikon der Assyriologie und vorderasiatischen Archäologie* 4, 1975, 372–375.

[335] Emmanuel Laroche, "Hieroglyphen, Hethitische," in: Erich Ebeling et al. (eds.), *Reallexikon der Assyriologie und vorderasiatischen Archäologie* 4, 1975, 394–399.

[336] Onofrio Carruba, "Das Palaische," StBoT 10, Wiesbaden 1970.

[337] Erich Neu, *Das Hurritische. Eine altorientalische Sprache in neuem Licht*, Wiesbaden 1988.

[338] Volkert Haas (ed.), *Hurriter und Hurritisch*, Konstanz 1988.

[339] Massimiliano Marazzi, *Il Geroglifico anatolico*, Rome 1990.

[340] Reinhold Plöchl, *Einführung in das Hieroglyphen-Luwische*, DBH 8, Dresden 2003.

[341] *The Cambridge Encyclopedia of the World's Ancient Languages*, ed. Roger D. Woodard, Cambridge 2004.

PEOPLES

[342] Einar von Schuler, *Die Kaškäer. Ein Beitrag zur Ethnographie des Alten Kleinasien*, Berlin 1965.

[343] Gernot Wilhelm, *Grundzüge der Geschichte und der Kultur der Hurriter*, Darmstadt 1982.

[344] Jacques Freu, *Histoire du Mitanni*, Paris 2003.

[345] H. Craig Melchert (ed.), *The Luwians*, HdO I 68, Leiden and Boston 2003.

Asia Minor in the Time of the Hittites
GENERAL

[346] John Garstang and Oliver R. Gurney, *The Geography of the Hittite Empire*, London 1959.

[347] Wolfgang Helck, *Die Beziehungen Ägyptens zu Vorderasien im 3. und 2. Jahrtausend v. Chr.*, second ed., Wiesbaden 1971.

[9] Giuseppe F. del Monte and Johannes Tischler, *Répertoire géographique des textes cunéiformes*, vol. 6, *Die Orts- und Gewässernamen der hethitischen Texte*, Wiesbaden 1978. Supplemental volume 6/2, Wiesbaden 1992 (by G. F. del Monte).

[347a] Francis Breyer, *Ägypten und Anatolien. Politische, kulturelle und sprachliche Kontakte zwischen dem Niltal und Kleinasien im 2. Jahrtausend v. Chr.*, Vienna 2011.

Capital

[348] Kurt Bittel, *Hattusha, The Capital of the Hittites*, New York 1970.

[349] Peter Neve, *Hattuscha Information*, Istanbul 1987.

[350] Peter Neve, *Hattuscha. Stadt der Götter und Tempel. Neue Ausgrabungen in der Hauptstadt der Hethiter*, second ed., Mainz 1996.

[351] Jürgen Seeher, *Hattuscha-Führer. Ein Tag in der hethitischen Hauptstadt*, third ed., Istanbul 2006.

[351a] Andreas Schachner, *Hattuscha. Auf der Suche nach dem sagenhaften Großreich der Hethiter*, Munich 2011.

[237a] Jürgen Seeher, *Götter in Stein gehauen. Das hethitische Felsheiligtum von Yazılıkaya*, Istanbul 2011.

Other Places

[352] Andreas Müller-Karpe, "Kuşaklı, Ausgrabungen in einer hethitischen Stadt," *Antike Welt* 27, 1996, 305 ff.

[353] Aygül Süel and Mustafa Süel, "Šapinuwa. Découverte d'une ville hittite," *Archéologia* (Paris) 334, 1997, 68–74.

[354] Andreas Müller-Karpe, "Kuşaklı-Sarissa. A Hittite Town in the 'Upper Land,'" in: K. Aslihan Yener, Harry A. Hoffner Jr., and Simrit Dhesi (eds.), *Recent Developments in Hittite Archaeology and History. Papers in Memory of Hans G. Güterbock*, Winona Lake, IN 2002, 145–155.

[355] Aygül Süel, "Ortaköy-Šapinuwa," in: K. Aslihan Yener, Harry A. Hoffner Jr., and Simrit Dhesi (eds.), *Recent Developments in Hittite Archaeology and History. Papers in Memory of Hans G. Güterbock*, Winona Lake, IN 2002, 157–165.

Southern and Western Anatolia

[356] Albrecht Goetze, *Kizzuwatna and the Problem of Hittite Geography*, New Haven, CT 1940.

[357] Susanne Heinhold-Krahmer, *Arzawa. Untersuchungen zu seiner Geschichte nach den hethitischen Quellen*, Heidelberg 1977.

[358] Hans G. Güterbock et al., "The Hittites and the Aegean World," *American Journal of Archaeology* 87, 1983, 133–143.

[359] Hans G. Güterbock, "Hittites and Akhaeans: A New Look," *Proceedings of the American Philosophical Society* 128, 1984, 114–122.

[360] Fritz Schachermeyr, *Mykene und das Hethiterreich*, Vienna 1986.

[361] Heinrich Otten, "Das Land Lukka in der hethitischen Topographie," in: [415] Borchhardt and Dobesch, *Lykien-Symposion*, 1993, vol. 1, 117–121.

[362] Gerd Steiner, "Die historische Rolle der 'Lukka,'" in: [415] Borchhardt and Dobesch, *Lykien-Symposion*, 1993, vol. 1, 123–137.

[363] Frank Starke, "Troia im Kontext des historisch-politischen und sprachlichen Umfeldes Kleinasiens im 2. Jahrtausend," *Studia Troica* 7, 1997, 447 ff.

[364] Wolf-Dietrich Niemeier and Barbara Niemeier, "Milet 1994–1995. Projekt 'Minoisch-mykenisches bis protogeometrisches Milet.' Zielsetzung und Grabungen auf dem Stadionhügel und am Athenatempel," *Archäologischer Anzeiger* 1997, 189–248.

[365] John D. Hawkins, "Tarkasnawa King of Mira. 'Tarkondemos,' Boğazköy Sealings and Karabel," *Anatolian Studies* 48, 1998, 1 ff.

[366] Wolf-Dietrich Niemeier, "Milet in der Bronzezeit. Brücke zwischen der Ägäis und Anatolien," *Nürnberger Blätter zur Archäologie* 15, 1998–1999, 85–100.

[367] Éric Jean, Ali M. Dinçol, and Serra Durugönül (eds.), *La Cilicie: Espaces et pouvoirs locaux. Actes de la table ronde internationale d'Istanbul, 2–5 novembre 1999*, Paris 2001.

[368] Wolf-Dietrich Niemeier, "Ḫattusa and Aḫḫiyawa im Konflikt um Millawanda/Milet," in: [327] *Die Hethiter*, 2002, 294–299.

[369] Peter W. Haider, "Westkleinasien nach ägyptischen Quellen des Neuen Reiches," in: Christoph Ulf (ed.), *Der neue Streit um Troia. Eine Bilanz*, Munich 2003, 174 ff.

[370] Susanne Heinhold-Krahmer, "Aḫḫiyawa—Land der homerischen Achäer im Krieg mit Wiluša?" in: Christoph Ulf (ed.), *Der neue Streit um Troia. Eine Bilanz*, Munich 2003, 193–214.

[371] Wolf-Dietrich Niemeier, "The Minoans and Mycenaeans in Western Asia Minor. Settlement, Emporia or Acculturation?" *Aegaeum* 25, 2005, 199–204.

[372] Justus Cobet, Volkmar von Graeve, Wolf-Dietrich Niemeier, and Konrad Zimmermann (eds.), *Frühes Ionien—eine Bestandsaufnahme, Panionion Symposion Güzelcamlı, 26. 9.–1. 10. 1999*, Mainz 2007.

[373] Billie Jean Collins, Mary R. Bachvarova, and Ian C. Rutherford (eds.), *Anatolian Interfaces. Hittites, Greeks and Their Neighbours*, Oxford 2008.

[373a] Max Gander, *Die geographischen Beziehungen der Lukka-Länder*, Heidelberg 2010.

TROY AND THE NORTHWEST

[374] Moses I. Finley, "The Troian War," *Journal of Hellenic Studies* 84, 1964, 1 ff.

[375] Manfred Korfmann (ed.), *StTroica* 1, 1991 ff.; from 2006 Peter Jablonka, Ernst Pernicka, and Charles B. Rose (eds.).

[376] Frank Starke, "Troia im Kontext des historisch-politischen und sprachlichen Umfeldes Kleinasiens im 2. Jahrtausend," *StTroica* 7, 1997, 447 ff.

[377] Manfred Korfmann and Dietrich Mannsperger, *Troia. Ein historischer Überblick und Rundgang*, Darmstadt 1998.

[378] Manfred Korfmann, "Wilusa/(W)Ilios c. 1200 v. Chr.–Ilion c. 700 v. Chr.," in: *Troia— Traum und Wirklichkeit, Begleitband zur Ausstellung in Stuttgart*, Stuttgart 2001, 64–76.

[379] Joachim Latacz, *Troia und Homer. Der Weg zur Lösung eines alten Rätsels*, Munich and Berlin 2001.

[380] Dieter Hertel, *Troia. Archäologie, Geschichte, Mythos*, third ed., Munich 2008.

[381] Susanne Heinhold-Krahmer, "Zur Gleichsetzung der Namen Ilios-Wiluša und Troia-Taruiša," in: Christoph Ulf (ed.), *Der neue Streit um Troia. Eine Bilanz*, Munich 2003, 146–168.

[382] Frank Kolb, "War Troia eine Stadt?" in: Christoph Ulf (ed.), *Der neue Streit um Troia. Eine Bilanz*, Munich 2003, 120–145.

[383] Frank Kolb, "Ein neuer Troia-Mythos? Traum und Wirklichkeit auf dem Grabhügel von Hisarlık," in: Hans-Joachim Behr, Gerd Briegel, and Helmut Castritius (eds.), *Troia— Traum und Wirklichkeit. Ein Mythos in Geschichte und Rezeption, Tagungsband zum Symposion im Braunschweigischen Landesmuseum am 8. und 9. Juni 2001 im Rahmen der Ausstellung "Troia—Traum und Wirklichkeit,"* Braunschweig, Germany 2003, 8–39.

[384] Dieter Hertel, *Die Mauern von Troia. Mythos und Geschichte im antiken Ilion*, Munich 2004.

[385] Manfred Korfmann (ed.), *Troia. Archäologie eines Siedlungshügels und seiner Landschaft*, Mainz 2006.

Invasion of the Sea Peoples and the Dark Age (ca. 1200–800 BCE)

[386] Hermann Müller-Karpe (ed.), *Geschichte des 13. und 12. Jahrhunderts v. Chr.*, Munich 1977.

[387] Gustav Adolf Lehmann, "Zum Auftreten von Seevölker-Gruppen im östlichen Mittelmeerraum. Eine Zwischenbilanz," *SbWien* 418, 1983, 79–92.

[388] Nancy K. Sanders, *The Sea Peoples. Warriors of the Ancient Mediterranean*, second ed., London 1985.

[389] Kurt Bittel, "Die archäologische Situation in Kleinasien um 1200 v. Chr. und während der nachfolgenden vier Jahrhunderte," in: Sigrid Deger-Jalkotzy (ed.), *Griechenland, die Ägäis und die Levante während der Dark Ages vom 12.–9 Jh. v. Chr.*, Vienna 1983, 21–67.

[390] Gustav Adolf Lehmann, *Die mykenisch-frühgriechische Welt und der östliche Mittelmeerraum in der Zeit der Seevölker-Invasionen um 1200 v. Chr.*, Opladen, Germany 1985.

[391] Gustav Adolf Lehmann, "Die politisch-historischen Beziehungen der Ägäis-Welt des 15.–13 Jh. v. Chr. zu Ägypten und Vorderasien. Einige Hinweise," in: Joachim Latacz (ed.), *Zweihundert Jahre Homer-Forschung*, Stuttgart 1991, 105–126.

[392] Eliezer D. Oren, *The Sea Peoples and their World. A Reassessment*, Philadelphia 2000.

Small States, Peoples, and New Kingdoms (1000–ca. 550 BCE)

Late Hittites

[393] J. David Hawkins, "Karkamish and Karatepe: Neo-Hittite City-States in North Syria," in: Jack M. Sasson et al. (eds.), *Civilizations of the Ancient Near East* II, New York 1995, 1295 ff.

[394] Frank Starke, "Kleinasien C. Hethitische Nachfolgestaaten," in: *Der Neue Pauly* 6, 1999, 518 ff.

[395] John D. Hawkins, "Die Erben des Großreiches," in: [327] *Die Hethiter*, 2002, 56–59 and 264–273.

Urartians

[396] Friedrich W. König, *Handbuch der chaldischen Inschriften*, 2 vols., Graz 1955–1957.

[397] Thomas Beran, "Urartu," in: Hartmut Schmökel (ed.), *Kulturgeschichte des Alten Orients*, Stuttgart 1961, 606–657.

[398] Boris B. Piotrovski, *Il regno di Van. Urartu*, Rome 1966.

[399] Igor M. Diakonoff, *Hurrisch und Urartäisch*, Munich 1967.

[400] Ekrem Akurgal, *Urartäische und altiranische Kunstzentren*, Ankara 1968.

[401] Boris B. Piotrowski, *Urartu*, Munich, Geneva, and Paris 1969.

[402] Peter Frei, "Der Wagen von Gordion," *MusHelv* 29, 1972, 110–123.

[403] Stephan Kroll, "Urartus Untergang in anderer Sicht," *IstMitt* 34, 1984, 151–170.

[404] Volkert Haas, *Das Reich Urartu. Ein altorientalischer Staat im 1. Jahrtausend v. Chr.*, Konstanz 1986.

[405] Ralf-Bernhard Wartke, *Urartu. Das Reich am Ararat*, Mainz 1993.

[406] Mirjo Salvini, *Geschichte und Kultur der Urartäer*, Darmstadt 1995.

Armenia

[407] Charles Burney and David M. Lang, *The Peoples of the Hills. Ancient Ararat and Caucasus*, London 1971.

[408] Robert Drews, *The Coming of the Greeks*, Princeton, NJ 1988.

[409] Carl Friedrich Lehmann-Haupt, *Armenien einst und jetzt*, 3 vols., Berlin 1910–1931 (reprint Hildesheim, Zürich, and New York 1988).

Lycians, Carians, Sidetans, and Pisidians

LYCIANS

[410] Johann Jakob Bachofen, *Das lykische Volk und seine Bedeutung für die Entwicklung des Altertums*, Freiburg 1862.

[411] Oskar Treuber, *Geschichte der Lykier*, Stuttgart 1887.

[412] Philipp H. J. Houwink ten Cate, *The Luwian Population Groups of Lycia and Cilicia Aspera during the Hellenistic Period*, Leiden 1961.

[413] Trevor R. Bryce, *The Lycians in Literary and Epigraphic Sources*, Kopenhagen 1986.

[414] Peter Frei, "Solymer–Milyer–Termilen–Lykier. Ethnische und politische Einheiten auf der lykischen Halbinsel," in: [415] Borchhardt and Dobesch, *Lykien-Symposion*, 1993, vol. 1, 87–97.

[415] Jürgen Borchhardt and Gerhard Dobesch (eds.), *Akten des II. Internationalen Lykien-Symposions, 6.–12. Mai 1990*, 2 vols., Vienna 1993.

[416] Anthony G. Keen, *Dynastic Lycia. A Political History of the Lycians and Their Relations with Foreign Powers, c. 545–362 B. C.*, Leiden 1998.

[417] Anne-Valérie Schweyer, *Les Lyciens et la mort. Une étude d'histoire sociale*, Paris 2002.

[418] Mauro Giorgieri, Mirjo Salvini, Marie-Claude Trémouille, and Pietro Vannicelli (eds.), *Licia e Lidia prima dell'ellenizzazione*, Rome 2003.

[419] Isabella Benda-Weber, *Lykier und Karer. Zwei autochthone Ethnien Kleinasiens zwischen Orient und Okzident*, Bonn 2005.

[419a] Jürgen Borchhardt and Anastasia Pekridou-Gorecki (eds.), *Limyra. Studien zu Kunst und Epigraphik in den Nekropolen der Antike*, Vienna 2012.

CARIANS

[420] Olivier Masson, "Que savons-nous de l'écriture et de la langue des Cariens?," *Bulletin de la Societe de Linguistique de Paris* 69, 1973, 168 ff.

[421] Ignacio-Javier Adiego, *Studia Carica. Investigaciones sobre la escritura y lengua carias*, Barcelona 1993.

[422] Maria E. Giannotta et al. (eds.), *La Decifrazione del Cario. Atti del 1 Simposio Internazionale, Roma, 3–4 maggio 1993*, Rome 1994.

[423] Peter Frei and Christian Marek, *Die Karisch-Griechische Bilingue von Kaunos. Eine zweisprachige Staatsurkunde des 4. Jh. v. Chr.*, Berlin and New York 1997.

[424] Wolfgang Blümel, Peter Frei, and Christian Marek (eds.), *Colloquium Caricum*, Berlin and New York 1998.

[425] Peter Frei and Christian Marek, "Neues zu den karischen Inschriften von Kaunos," *Kadmos* 39, 2000, 85–132.

[419] Isabella Benda-Weber, *Lykier und Karer. Zwei autochthone Ethnien Kleinasiens zwischen Orient und Okzident,* Bonn 2005.

[426] Ignacio-Javier Adiego, *The Carian Language,* Leiden 2007.

[426a] Frank Rumscheid (ed.), *Die Karer und die Anderen. Internationales Kolloquium an der Freien Universität Berlin, 13.–15. Oktober 2005,* Bonn 2009.

[426b] Riet van Bremen and Jan-Matthieu Carbon (eds.), *Hellenistic Karia. Proceedings of the First International Conference on Hellenistic Karia, Oxford, 29 June–2 July 2006,* Bordeaux 2010.

Sidetans and Pisidians

[427] Clemens Emin Bosch, *Studien zur Geschichte Pamphyliens. Untersuchungen in der Gegend von Antalya,* Ankara 1957.

[428] Günter Neumann, "Die sidetische Schrift," *AnnPisa* 8/3, 1978, 869 ff.

[429] Hartwin Brandt, *Gesellschaft und Wirtschaft Pamphyliens und Pisidiens im Altertum,* Bonn 1992.

[430] Johannes Nollé, *Side im Altertum,* 2 vols., Bonn 1993–2001.

[431] Cristiana Doni, "The Pisidians: From Their Origin to Their Western Expansion," in: [286] Bru, Kirbihler, and Lebreton, *L'Asie Mineure,* 2009, 213–227.

Phrygians

[432] Richard D. Barnett, "Phrygia and the Peoples of Anatolia in the Iron Age," in: [4] *Cambridge Ancient History,* third edition, II 2, 1975, 417–442.

[433] Günter Neumann, *Phrygisch und Griechisch,* Vienna 1988.

[434] Roberto Gusmani, Mirjo Salvini, and Pietro Vannicelli (eds.), *Frigi e Frigio, Atti del 1° Simposio Internazionale, Roma, 16–17 ottobre 1995,* Rome 1997.

[435] Lynn E. Roller, *In Search of God the Mother. The Cult of Anatolian Cybele,* London 1999.

[436] Josef Wiesehöfer, "König Midas gibt Rätsel auf—Phrygien und das phrygische Reich," in: Rainer Albertz et al. (eds.), *Frühe Hochkulturen. Ägypter, Sumerer, Assyrer, Babylonier, Hethiter, Minoer, Phöniker, Perser,* Leipzig and Mannheim 2003, 257–263 and 356–357.

[437] Anne-Maria Wittke, *Mušker und Phryger. Ein Beitrag zur Geschichte Anatoliens vom 12. bis zum 7. Jh. v. Chr.,* Wiesbaden 2004.

Cimmerians

[438] Igor M. Diakonoff, "The Cimmerians," *ActaIranica* 21, 1981, 103 ff.

[439] Askold I. Ivantchik, *Les Cimmériens au proche-orient,* Göttingen 1993.

[440] Victor Parker, "Bemerkungen zu den Zügen der Kimmerier und der Skythen durch Vorderasien," *Klio* 77, 1995, 7–34, esp. 28–31.

[441] Sergej R. Tokhtasjev, "Die Kimmerier in der antiken Überlieferung," *Hyperboreus* 2, 1996, 1–46.

Lydians and the Kingdom of Lydia

[442] Georges Radet, *La Lydie et le monde grec aux temps des Mermnades (687–546),* Paris 1892.

[443] George M. A. Hanfmann, *Sardis und Lydien*, Wiesbaden 1960.

[444] John Griffiths Pedley, *Sardis and the Age of Croesus*, Norman, OK 1968.

[445] Clara Talamo, *La Lidia arcaica*, Bologna 1979.

[446] Peter Frei, "Die Rolle des Lyderreiches im internationalen System des 6. Jh. v. Chr., VIII," Türk Tarih Kongresi, Ankara 1979, 375–382.

[447] George M. A. Hanfmann and William E. Mierse, *Sardis from Prehistoric to Roman Times. Results of the Archaeological Exploration of Sardis, 1958–1975*, Cambridge, MA 1983.

[448] Walter Burkert, "Das Ende des Kroisos. Vorstufen einer Herodotischen Geschichtserzählung," in: Christoph Schäublin (ed.), *Catalepton*, Basel 1985, 4 ff.

[449] Crawford H. Greenewalt Jr., "When a Mighty Empire Was Destroyed. The Common Man at the Fall of Sardis, c. 546 B.C.," *Proceedings of the American Philosophical Society* 136, 1992, 247–271.

[450] Jack M. Balcer, "Herodotus, the Early State, and Lydia," *Historia* 43, 1994, 246 ff.

[451] Walter Burkert, "Lydia between East and West or How to Date the Trojan War. A Study in Herodotos," in: Christoph Riedweg (ed.), *Kleine Schriften* I: *Homerica*, Göttingen 2001, 218–232.

[452] Joachim Oelsner, "Review of R. Rollinger, *Herodots babylonischer Logos* (1993)," *AfO* 46–47, 1999–2000, 373–380.

[453] Giovanni B. Lanfranchi, Michael Roaf, and Robert Rollinger (ed.), *Continuity of Empire (?). Assyria, Media, Persia*, Padua 2003.

[418] Mauro Giorgieri, Mirjo Salvini, Marie-Claude Trémouille, and Pietro Vannicelli, *Licia e Lidia*, Rome 2003.

[454] Hasan Dedeoğlu, *The Lydians and Sardis*, İstanbul 2003.

[455] David M. Schaps, *The Invention of Coinage and the Monetization of Ancient Greece*, Ann Arbor, MI 2004.

[456] Nicholas D. Cahill (ed.), *Love for Lydia. A Sardis Anniversary Volume Presented to Crawford H. Greenwalt Jr.*, Cambridge and London 2009.

[264a] Chris Roosevelt, *The Archaeology of Lydia, from Gyges to Alexander*, Cambridge 2009.

Greeks

Robert M. Cook, "Ionia and Greece in the Eighth and Seventh Centuries B.C.," *JHS* 66, 1946, 67–98.

[458] Hermann Fränkel, *Dichtung und Philosophie des frühen Griechentums. Eine Geschichte der griechischen Epik, Lyrik und Prosa bis zur Mitte des fünften Jahrhunderts*, second ed., Munich 1962.

[459] John M. Cook, *The Greeks in Ionia and the East*, second ed., London 1965.

[460] Norbert Ehrhardt, *Milet und seine Kolonien. Vergleichende Untersuchungen zu den politischen Einrichtungen*, Frankfurt, Bern, and New York 1983.

[461] Jacques Vanschoonwinkel, *L'Égée et la Méditerranée Orientale à la fin du deuxième millénaire: témoignages archéologiques et sources écrites*, Louvain-la-Neuve, Belgium, and Providence, RI 1991.

[462] Martin West, *The East Face of Helicon. West Asiatic Elements in Greek Poetry and Myth*, London 1998.

[463] Sigrid Deger-Jalkotzy, "Kolonisation," *Der Neue Pauly* 6, 1999, 648–651.

[464] John Boardman, *The Greeks Overseas. Their Early Colonies and Trade*, fourth ed., London 1999.

[465] Peter Högemann, "Der Iliasdichter, Anatolien und der griechische Adel," *Klio* 82, 2000, 7 ff.

[466] Peter Högemann, "Zum Iliasdichter. Ein anatolischer Standpunkt," *StTroica* 10, 2000, 183 ff.

[467] Hartmut Blum, "Anatolien, die Ilias und die sogenannte 'Kontinuitätsthese,'" *Klio* 84/2, 2002, 275 ff.

[468] Walter Burkert, *Die Griechen und der Orient*, Munich 2003.

[469] Robert Rollinger, "Homer, Anatolien und die Levante. Die Frage der Beziehungen zu den östlichen Nachbarkulturen im Spiegel der schriftlichen Quellen," in: Christoph Ulf (ed.), *Der neue Streit um Troia. Eine Bilanz*, Munich 2003, 330–348.

[470] Elmar Schwertheim and Engelbert Winter (ed.), *Neue Forschungen zu Ionien*, FS Işık, Asia Minor Studien 54, Bonn 2005.

[372] Justus Cobet, Volkmar von Graeve, Wolf-Dietrich Niemeier, and Konrad Zimmermann (eds.), *Frühes Ionien—eine Bestandsaufnahme, Panionion Symposion Güzelcamlı, 26. 9.–1. 10. 1999*, Mainz 2007.

[471] Raoul Schrott, *Homers Heimat. Der Kampf um Troia und seine realen Hintergründe*, Munich 2008.

[472] Dieter Hertel, *Das frühe Ilion. Die Besiedlung Troias durch die Griechen (1020–650/25 v. Chr.)*, Munich 2008.

[473] Alan M. Greaves, *The Land of Ionia: Society and Economy in the Archaic Period*, London 2010.

[473a] Wolfram Hoepfner, *Ionien. Brücke zum Orient*, Stuttgart 2011.

[473b] Josef Fischer, "Zur Frühgeschichte von Ephesos bis auf die Zeit der Kimmereinfälle," in: Peter Mauritsch (ed.), *Akten des 13. Österreichischen Althistorikerinnen- und Althistorikertages, 18.–20. November 2010 in Graz*, Graz, Austria 2011, 29–44.

Persian Period (ca. 550–333 BCE)

[474] Walther Judeich, *Kleinasiatische Studien. Untersuchungen zur griechisch-persischen Geschichte des IV. Jahrhunderts v. Chr.*, Marburg 1892.

[475] Richard N. Frye, *The History of Ancient Iran*, Munich 1984.

[476] Bruno Jacobs, *Die Satrapienverwaltung im Perserreich zur Zeit Darius' III.*, Wiesbaden 1984.

[477] Gerold Walser, *Hellas und Iran. Studien zu den griechisch-persischen Beziehungen vor Alexander*, Darmstadt 1984.

[478] Peter Högemann, *Das alte Vorderasien und die Achämeniden. Ein Beitrag zur Herodot-Analyse*, Wiesbaden 1992.

[479] Pierre Briant, *Histoire de l'Empire Perse. De Cyrus à Alexandre*, Paris 1996. English edition: *From Cyrus to Alexander. A History of the Persian Empire*, Warsaw, 2002.

[416] Anthony G. Keen, *Dynastic Lycia. A Political History of the Lycians and Their Relations with Foreign Powers, c. 545–362 B.C.*, Leiden 1998.

[480] Pierre Debord, *L'Asie Mineure au IVe siècle (412–323 a.C.). Pouvoirs et jeux politiques*, Bordeaux 1999.

[481] Tomris Bakır et al. (eds.), *Achaemenid Anatolia. Proceedings of the First International Symposium on Anatolia in the Achaemenid Period (Bandırma 15.–18. August 1997)*, Leiden and Boston 2001.

[453] Giovanni B. Lanfranchi, Michael Roaf, and Robert Rollinger (eds.), *Continuity of Empire (?), Assyria, Media, Persia*, Padua 2003.

[482] Elspeth R. M. Dusinberre, *Aspects of Empire in Achaemenid Sardis*, Cambridge 2003.

[483] John Boardman, *Die Perser und der Westen. Eine archäologische Untersuchung zur Entwicklung der Achämenidischen Kunst*, trans. B. Jaros-Deckert, Mainz 2003. English edition: *Persia and the West: An Archaeological Investigation of the Genesis of Achaemenid Persian Art*, London 2000.

[484] Cristina Carusi, *Isole e peree in Asia Minore. Contributo allo studio dei rapporti tra poleis insulari e territori continentali dipendenti*, Pisa 2003.

[485] Olivier Casabonne, *La Cilicie à l'époque achéménide*, Paris 2004.

[486] Josef Wiesehöfer, *Das antike Persien*, Düsseldorf 2005.

[487] Pierre Briant, "L'Asie mineure en transition," in: Pierre Briant and Francis Joannès (eds.), *La Transition entre l'empire achéménide et les royaumes hellénistiques*, Paris 2006, 309–351.

[488] Josef Wiesehöfer, "Greeks and Persians," in: Kurt A. Raaflaub and Hans van Wees (eds.), *A Companion to Archaic Greece*, Oxford 2013.

[488a] Elspeth R. M. Dusinberre, *Empire, Authority, and Autonomy in Achaemenid Anatolia*, Cambridge 2013.

[488b] Engelbert Winter and Klaus Zimmermann, *Zwischen Satrapen und Dynasten. Kleinasien im 4. Jh. v. Chr.*, Bonn 2015.

Alexander and Hellenistic Period

General Works and Surveys

[489] Michael Rostovzeff, *The Social and Economic History of the Hellenistic World*, 3 vols., Oxford 1941.

[490] David Magie, *Roman Rule in Asia Minor to the End of the Third Century after Christ*, 2 vols., Princeton, NJ 1950.

[491] William Woodthorpe Tarn, *Hellenistic Civilisation*, third ed., London 1952.

[492] Christian Habicht, *Gottmenschentum und griechische Städte*, Munich 1970.

[493] Arnold H.M. Jones, *The Cities of the Eastern Roman Provinces*, second ed., Oxford 1971.

[494] Laura Boffo, *I re ellenistici e i centri religiosi dell'Asia Minore*, Florence 1985.

[495] Friedemann Quaß, *Die Honoratiorenschicht in den Städten des griechischen Ostens. Untersuchungen zur politischen und sozialen Entwicklung in hellenistischer und römischer Zeit*, Stuttgart 1993.

[496] Wolfgang Leschhorn, *Antike Ären*, Stuttgart 1993.

[497] Getzel M. Cohen, *The Hellenistic Settlements in Europe, the Islands, and Asia Minor*, Berkeley 1995.

[498] Maurice Sartre, *L'Asie Mineure et l'Anatolie d'Alexandre à Dioclétien*, Paris 1995.

[499] Christof Schuler, *Ländliche Siedlungen und Gemeinden im hellenistischen und römischen Kleinasien*, Munich 1998.

[500] Alain Bresson and Raymond Descat (eds.), *Les cités d'Asie Mineure occidentale au IIe siècle a.C.*, Bordeaux 2001.

[501] Maurice Sartre, *L'Anatolie hellénistique, de l'Égée au Caucase*, Paris 2003.

[484] Cristina Carusi, *Isole e peree in Asia Minore. Contributo allo studio dei rapporti tra poleis insulari e territori continentali dipendenti*, Pisa 2003.

[502] Sviatoslav Dmitriev, *City Government in Hellenistic and Roman Asia Minor*, Oxford 2005.

[502a] Anne-Valérie Pont, *Orner la cité. Enjeux culturels et politiques du paysage urbain dans l'Asie Mineure gréco-romaine*, Paris 2008.
[502b] Thibaut Boulay, *Arès dans la cité. Les poleis et la guerre dans l'Asie mineure hellénistique*, Pisa and Rome, 2014.

Alexander

[503] Johann Gustav Droysen, *Geschichte Alexanders des Großen*, Berlin 1833 (new editions and reprints).
[503a] Robin Lane-Fox, *Alexander the Great*, London 1973.
[504] Siegfried Lauffer, *Alexander der Große*, third ed., Munich 1993.
[504a] Paul Cartledge, *Alexander the Great. The Hunt for a New Past*, New York 2004.
[505] Hans-Ulrich Wiemer, *Alexander der Große*, Munich 2005.
[505a] Richard Stoneman, *Alexander the Great: A Life in Legend*, New Haven, CT 2008.
[505b] Alexander Demandt, *Alexander der Große*, Munich 2009.

Diadochi and Epigones

[506] Eduard Meyer, *Geschichte des Königreichs Pontos*, Leipzig 1879.
[507] Roger S. Bagnall, *The Administration of the Ptolemaic Possessions outside Egypt*, Leiden 1976.
[508] Getzel M. Cohen, *The Seleucid Colonies. Studies in Founding, Administration and Organization*, Wiesbaden 1978.
[509] Richard A. Billows, *Antigonos the One-Eyed and the Creation of the Hellenistic State*, Berkeley 1990.
[510] Amélie Kuhrt and Susan Sherwin-White, *From Samarkhand to Sardis. A New Approach to the Seleucid Empire*, Berkeley 1993.
[511] Jörn Kobes, *Kleine Könige. Untersuchungen zu den Lokaldynasten im hellenistischen Kleinasien (323–188 v. Chr.)*, St. Katharinen, Germany 1996.
[512] John Ma, *Antiochos III and the Cities of Western Asia Minor*, Oxford 1999.
[513] Christoph Michels, *Kulturtransfer und monarchischer "Philhellenismus." Bithynien, Pontos und Kappadokien in hellenistischer Zeit*, Göttingen 2009.

Galatians

[514] Felix Staehelin, *Geschichte der Kleinasiatischen Galater*, second ed., Leipzig 1907 (reprint Osnabrück 1973).
[515] Karl Strobel, *Die Galater. Geschichte und Eigenart der keltischen Staatenbildung auf dem Boden des hellenistischen Kleinasien, vol. 1. Untersuchungen zur Geschichte und historischen Geographie des hellenistischen und römischen Kleinasien*, Berlin 1996.

Rhodes and the Lycian League

[516] Hatto H. Schmitt, *Rom und Rhodos. Geschichte ihrer politischen Beziehungen seit der ersten Berührung bis zum Aufgehen des Inselstaates im römischen Weltreich*, Munich 1957.
[517] Ralf Behrwald, *Der lykische Bund. Untersuchungen zu Geschichte und Verfassung*, Bonn 2000.

[518] Hans-Ulrich Wiemer, *Krieg, Handel und Piraterie. Untersuchungen zur Geschichte des hellenistischen Rhodos*, Berlin 2002.

Pergamon and the Province of Asia

[519] Erwin Ohlemutz, *Die Kulte und Heiligtümer der Götter in Pergamon*, Würzburg 1940.

[520] Esther V. Hansen, *The Attalids of Pergamon*, second ed., Ithaca, NY 1971.

[521] Adrian N. Sherwin-White, "Rome, Pamphylia and Cilicia, 133–70 B.C.," *JRS* 66, 1976, 1 ff.

[522] Joachim Hopp, *Untersuchungen zur Geschichte der letzten Attaliden,* Munich 1977.

[523] Reginald E. Allen, *The Attalid Kingdom. A Constitutional History*, Oxford 1983.

[524] Hans-Joachim Schalles, *Untersuchungen zur Kulturpolitik der pergamenischen Herrscher im dritten Jahrhundert vor Christus*, Tübingen 1985.

[525] Wolfgang Radt, *Pergamon. Geschichte und Bauten einer antiken Metropole*, Darmstadt 1999.

[526] Michael Wörrle, "Pergamon um 133 v. Chr.," *Chiron* 30, 2000, 543 ff.

[527] Frank Daubner, *Bellum Asiaticum. Der Krieg der Römer gegen Aristonikos von Pergamon und die Einrichtung der Provinz Asia*, second ed., Munich 2006.

[527a] Martin Zimmermann, *Pergamon: Geschichte, Kultur und Archäologie*, Munich 2011.

Age of the Mithridatic Wars

[528] Théodore Reinach, *Mithradates Eupator, König von Pontos,* trans. A. Goetz, Leipzig 1895.

[529] Eckard Olshausen, "Mithradates VI. und Rom," *ANRW* I 1, 1972, 806 ff.

[530] Adrian N. Sherwin-White, *Roman Foreign Policy in the East*, London 1984.

[531] Eckart Olshausen and Joseph Biller, *Historisch-geographische Aspekte der Geschichte des Pontischen und Armenischen Reiches*, Wiesbaden 1984.

[532] Brian C. McGing, *The Foreign Policy of Mithridates VI Eupator, King of Pontus*, Leiden 1986.

[533] Robert M. Kallet-Marx, *Hegemony to Empire. The Development of the Roman Imperium in the East from 148 to 62 B.C.*, Berkeley 1995.

[534] Jakob Munk Højte (ed.), *Mithridates VI and the Pontic Kingdom*, Aarhus, Denmark 2009.

Pompey's Reorganization

[535] Gerhard Wirth, "Pompeius, Armenien, Parther. Mutmaßungen zur Bewältigung einer Krisensituation," *BJb* 183, 1983, 1–60.

[182] Christian Marek, *Stadt, Ära und Territorium in Pontus-Bithynia und Nord-Galatia*, Tübingen 1993.

[536] Ruprecht Ziegler, "Ären kilikischer Städte und Politik des Pompeius in Südostklein-asien," *Tyche* 8, 1993, 203–219.

[537] Martin Dreher, "Pompeius und die kaukasischen Völker. Kolcher, Iberer, Albaner," *Historia* 45, 1996, 188–207.

[538] Klaus M. Girardet, "'Imperia' und 'provinciae' des Pompeius 82 bis 48 v.Chr.," *Chiron* 31, 2001, 153–209.

Asia Minor under Caesar and Mark Antony

[539] Hans Buchheim, *Die Orientpolitik des Triumvirn M. Antonius. Ihre Voraussetzungen, Entwicklung und Zusammenhang mit den politischen Ereignissen in Italien*, Heidelberg 1960.
[540] Richard D. Sullivan, *Near Eastern Royalty and Rome, 100–30 B.C.*, Toronto 1990.
[541] Gerhard Dobesch, "Caesar und Kleinasien," *Tyche* 11, 1996, 51 ff.
[541a] Helmut Halfmann, *Marcus Antonius. Gestalten der Antike*, Darmstadt 2011.

Roman Imperial Period

General Works and Surveys

[490] David Magie, *Roman Rule in Asia Minor to the End of the Third Century after Christ,* 2 vols., Princeton, NJ 1950.
[542] Edward Dabrowa, *L'Asie Mineure sous les Flaviens. Recherches sur la politique provinciale,* Warsaw 1980.
[543] Maurice Sartre, *L'orient romain: provinces et sociétés provinciales en Méditerranée orientale d'Auguste aux Sévères*, Paris 1991.
[544] Stephen Mitchell, *Anatolia. Land, Men and Gods in Asia Minor*, 2 vols., Oxford 1993.
[496] Wolfgang Leschhorn, *Antike Ären*, Stuttgart 1993.
[498] Maurice Sartre, *L'Asie Mineure et l'Anatolie d'Alexandre à Dioclétien*, Paris 1995.
[545] Karl Christ, *Geschichte der römischen Kaiserzeit*, fifth ed., Munich 2005.
[546] Stephen Mitchell, *A History of the Later Roman Empire, AD 284–641*, Oxford 2007.

Individual Provinces

[547] Victor Chapot, *La province Romaine proconsulaire d'Asie depuis ses origins jusqu'à la fin du Haut-Empire*, Paris 1904 (reprint Rome 1967).
[548] Bernard Holtheide, *Römische Bürgerrechtspolitik und römische Neubürger in der Provinz Asia*, Freiburg 1983.
[182] Christian Marek, *Stadt, Ära und Territorium in Pontus-Bithynia und Nord-Galatia*, Tübingen 1993.
[549] Christian Marek, *Pontus et Bithynia. Die römischen Provinzen im Norden Kleinasiens*, Mainz 2003.
[549a] Margherita Cassia, *Cappadocia romana: strutture urbane e strutture agrarie alla periferia dell'impero. Testi e studi di storia antica* 15, Catania 2004.
[550] Hartwin Brandt and Frank Kolb, *Lycia et Pamphylia. Eine römische Provinz im Südwesten Kleinasiens*, Mainz 2005.
[550a] Gaetano Arena, *Città di Panfilia e Pisidia sotto il dominio romano*, second ed., Catania 2005.
[550b] John D. Grainger, *The Cities of Pamphylia*, Oxford 2009.

Imperial Administration: Territory, Personnel and Infrastructure, Military, Taxes, and Customs Duties

[551] Stephen Mitchell, "The Administration of Roman Asia from 133 B.C. to A.D. 250," in: Werner Eck (ed.), *Lokale Autonomie und römische Ordnungsmacht in den kaiserzeitlichen Provinzen vom 1.–3 Jh.*, Munich 1999, 18–46.

[552] Ruprecht Ziegler, "Das Koinon der drei Eparchien Kilikien, Isaurien und Lykaonien im späten 2. und frühen 3 Jh. n. Chr.," *Asia Minor Studien* 34, 1999, 137–152.

[553] Werner Eck, "Die politisch-administrative Struktur der kleinasiatischen Provinzen während der hohen Kaiserzeit," in: Gianpaolo Urso (ed.), *Tra Oriente e Occidente. Indigeni, Greci e Romani in Asia Minore, Colloquio della Fondazione Niccolò Canussio, Cividale del Friuli, 28–30 settembre 2006*, Pisa 2007, 189–207.

[554] Bernd Kreiler, *Die Statthalter Kleinasiens unter den Flaviern*, Augsburg 1975.

[555] Helmut Halfmann, *Die Senatoren aus dem östlichen Teil des Imperium Romanum bis zum Ende des 2 Jh. n. Chr.*, Göttingen 1979.

[556] Werner Eck, "Jahres- und Provinzialfasten der senatorischen Statthalter von 69/70 bis 138/9," *Chiron* 12, 1982, 281–362; *Chiron* 13, 1983, 147–237.

[557] Bernard Rémy, *L'évolution administrative de l'Anatolie aux trois premiers siècles de notre ère*, Lyon 1986.

[558] Bernard Rémy, *Les fastes sénatoriaux des provinces romaines d'Anatolie au Haut-Empire (31 avant J.-C.–284 après J.-C.)–Pont-Bithynie, Galatie, Cappadoce, Lycie-Pamphylie et Cilicie*, Paris 1988.

[559] Bernard Rémy, *Les carrières sénatoriales dans les provinces romaines d'Anatolie au Haut-Empire*, Paris 1989.

[560] Bengt E. Thomasson, *Laterculi praesidum* I–III, Göteborg 1984–1990.

[561] Rudolph Haensch, *Capita provinciarum. Statthaltersitze und Provinzialverwaltung in der römischen Kaiserzeit*, Mainz 1997.

[562] Eckard Meyer-Zwiffelhoffer, Πολιτικῶς ἄρχειν. *Zum Regierungsstil der senatorischen Statthalter in den kaiserzeitlichen griechischen Provinzen*, Wiesbaden 2002.

[563] Thomas Pekáry, *Untersuchungen zu den römischen Reichsstraßen*, Bonn 1968.

[564] David H. French, "The Roman Road-System of Asia Minor," *ANRW* II 7.2, 1980, 698–729.

[565] David H. French, *Roman Roads and Milestones of Asia Minor, Fasc. 2: An Interim Catalogue of Milestones*, 2 vols., Oxford 1988.

[194] Mustafa Adak and Sencer Şahin, *Stadiasmus Patarensis. Itinera Romana Provinciae Lyciae*, İstanbul 2007.

[566] Michael P. Speidel, "The Roman Army in Asia Minor. Recent Epigraphical Discoveries and Research," in: Steven Mitchell (ed.), *Armies and Frontiers in Roman and Byzantine Anatolia*, Oxford 1983, 7–34.

[567] Michael P. Speidel, "Legionaries from Asia Minor," *ANRW* II 7.2, 1980, 730–746.

[568] Michel Cottier, Michael Crawford et al. (eds.), *The Customs Law of Asia*, Oxford 2008.

[568a] Marco Vitale, *Eparchie und Koinon in Kleinasien von der ausgehenden Republik bis ins 3. Jh. n. Chr.*, Bonn 2012.

Population and Economic Foundations

[569] Thomas R. S. Broughton, "Roman Asia Minor," in: Tenney Frank (ed.), *An Economic Survey of Ancient Rome* IV, Baltimore, MD 1938, 499–950.

[570] Johannes Nollé, *Nundinas instituere et habere. Epigraphische Zeugnisse zur Einrichtung und Gestaltung von ländlichen Märkten in Afrika und der Provinz Asia*, Hildesheim 1982.

[571] Peter Herrmann, *Hilferufe aus römischen Provinzen. Ein Aspekt der Krise des römischen Reiches im 3 Jh. n. Chr.*, Hamburg 1990.

[429] Hartwin Brandt, *Gesellschaft und Wirtschaft Pamphyliens und Pisidiens im Altertum*, Bonn 1992.

[572] Silvia Bussi, *Economia e demografia della schiavitù in Asia Minore ellenistico-romana*, Milan 2001.

[573] Stephen Mitchell and Constantina Katsari (eds.), *Patterns in the Economy of Roman Asia Minor*, Swansea, UK 2005.

[574] Heinrich W. Drexhage, *Wirtschaftspolitik und Wirtschaft in der römischen Provinz Asia in der Zeit von Augustus bis zum Regierungsantritt Diokletians*, Bonn 2007.

[575] Onno M. van Nijf, *The Civic World of Professional Associations in the Roman East*, Amsterdam 1997.

[576] Imogen Dittmann-Schöne, *Die Berufsvereine in den Städten des kaiserzeitlichen Kleinasiens*, Regensburg 2001.

[577] Carola Zimmermann, *Handwerkervereine im griechischen Osten des Imperium Romanum*, Mainz 2002.

City and Country

[578] Wilhelm Liebenam, *Städteverwaltung im Römischen Kaiserreiche*, Leipzig 1900 (reprint Rome 1967).

[579] Jürgen Deininger, *Die Provinziallandtage der römischen Kaiserzeit. Von Augustus bis zum Ende des dritten Jahrhunderts n. Chr.*, Munich 1965.

[580] Wolfgang Leschhorn, *Gründer der Stadt. Studien zu einem politisch-religiösen Phänomen der griechischen Geschichte*, Stuttgart 1984.

[493] Arnold H. M. Jones, *The Cities of the Eastern Roman Provinces*, second ed., Oxford 1971.

[495] Friedemann Quaß, *Die Honoratiorenschicht in den Städten des griechischen Ostens. Untersuchungen zur politischen und sozialen Entwicklung in hellenistischer und römischer Zeit*, Stuttgart 1993.

[581] Michael Dräger, *Die Städte der Provinz Asia in der Flavierzeit. Studien zur kleinasiatischen Stadt- und Regionalgeschichte (69–96 n. Chr.)*, Bern and Frankfurt 1993.

[582] Tanja S. Scheer, *Mythische Vorväter. Zur Bedeutung griechischer Heroenmythen im Selbstverständnis kleinasiatischer Städte*, Munich 1993.

[583] Ruth Lindner, *Mythos und Identität. Studien zur Selbstdarstellung kleinasiatischer Städte in der römischen Kaiserzeit*, Stuttgart 1994.

[584] Maria D. Campanile, *I sacerdoti del koinon d'Asia (I sec. a.C.–III. sec. d. C.). Contributo allo studio del romanizzazione delle élites provinciali nell'Oriente greco*, Pisa 1994.

[585] Engelbert Winter, *Staatliche Baupolitik und Baufürsorge in den römischen Provinzen des kaiserzeitlichen Kleinasien*, Bonn 1996.

[499] Christof Schuler, *Ländliche Siedlungen und Gemeinden im hellenistischen und römischen Kleinasien*, Munich 1998.

[586] Helmut Halfmann, *Städtebau und Bauherren im römischen Kleinasien. Ein Vergleich zwischen Pergamon und Ephesos*, Tübingen 2001.

[587] Hertha Schwarz, *Soll oder Haben? Die Finanzwirtschaft kleinasiatischer Städte in der römischen Kaiserzeit am Beispiel von Bithynien, Lykien und Ephesos (29 v. Chr.–284 n. Chr.)*, Bonn 2001.

[588] Stefan Cramme, *Die Bedeutung des Euergetismus für die Finanzierung städtischer Aufgaben in der Provinz Asia*, Köln 2001.

[589] Daniela Pohl, *Kaiserzeitliche Tempel in Kleinasien unter besonderer Berücksichtigung der hellenistischen Vorläufer*, Bonn 2002.

[590] Christof Berns, Henner von Hesberg, Lutgarde Vandeput, and Marc Waelkens (eds.), *Patris und Imperium. Kulturelle und politische Identität in den Städten der römischen Provinzen Kleinasiens in der frühen Kaiserzeit, Kolloquium Köln, November 1998*, Löwen, Paris, and Dudley, MA 2002.

[591] Eckhard Stephan, *Honoratioren, Griechen, Polisbürger. Kollektive Identitäten innerhalb der Oberschicht des kaiserzeitlichen Kleinasien*, Göttingen 2002.

[592] Henri-Louis Fernoux, *Notables et élites des cités de Bithynie aux époques hellénistique et romaine (IIIe siècle av. J.-C.–IIIe siècle ap. J.-C.). Essai d'histoire sociale*, Lyon 2004.

[502] Sviatoslav Dmitriev, *City Government in Hellenistic and Roman Asia Minor*, Oxford 2005.

[593] Cédric Brélaz, *La sécurité publique en Asie Mineure sous le Principat (Ier–IIIème s. ap. J.-C.). Institutions municipales et institutions impériales dans l'Orient romain*, Basel 2005.

[594] Anna Heller, *Les bêtises des Grecs. Conflits et rivalités entre cités d'Asie et de Bithynie à l'époque romaine (129 a. C.–235 p. C.)*, Paris 2006.

[595] Marion Meyer, *Neue Zeiten—Neue Sitten. Zu Rezeption und Integration römischen und italischen Kulturguts in Kleinasien*, Vienna 2007.

[596] Tønnes Bekker-Nielsen, *Urban Life and Local Politics in Roman Bithynia*, Aarhus, Denmark 2008.

[597] Arjan Zuiderhoek, *The Politics of Munificence in the Roman Empire. Citizens, Elites and Benefactors in Asia Minor*, Cambridge 2009.

[598] Ursula Kunnert, *Bürger unter sich. Phylen in den Städten des kaiserzeitlichen Ostens*, Basel 2012.

Second Sophistic and Spectacles

[599] Louis Robert, *Les gladiateurs dans l'Orient grec*, Paris 1940 (reprint Amsterdam 1971).

[600] Glen W. Bowersock, *Greek Sophists in the Roman Empire*, Oxford 1969.

[601] Christopher P. Jones, *The Roman World of Dio Chrysostom*, Cambridge, MA, and London 1978.

[602] Louis Robert, "Discours d'ouverture," in: Chrysis Pelekides, Dina Peppa-Delmouzou, and Basileios Ch. Petrakos (eds.), ΠΡΑΚΤΙΚΑ ΤΟΥ Η ΔΙΕΘΝΟΥΣ ΣΥΝΕΔΡΙΟΥ ΕΛΛΗΝΙΚΗΣ ΚΑΙ ΛΑΤΙΝΙΚΗΣ ΕΠΙΓΡΑΦΙΚΗΣ, Athens 1984, 35 ff.

[603] Christopher P. Jones, *Culture and Society in Lucian*, Cambridge, MA and London 1986.

[187] Michael Wörrle, *Stadt und Fest im kaiserzeitlichen Kleinasien. Studien zu einer agonistischen Stiftung aus Oinoanda*, Munich 1988.

[604] Thomas Schmitz, *Bildung und Macht. Zur sozialen und politischen Funktion der Zweiten Sophistik in der griechischen Welt der Kaiserzeit*, Munich 1997.

Religion

[605] Josef Keil, "Die Kulte Lydiens," in: William H. Buckler and William M. Calder (eds.), *Anatolian Studies Presented to Sir William Mitchell Ramsay*, Manchester 1923, 239–266.

[606] Maarten J. Vermaseren, *Cybele and Attis: The Myth and the Cult*, London 1977.

[607] Pierre Debord, *Aspects sociaux et économiques de la vie religieuse dans l'Anatolie gréco-romaine*, Leiden 1982.

[608] Herbert William Parke, *The Oracles of Apollo in Asia Minor*, London 1985.

[609] *ANRW* II 18.3, 1990, with contributions on the cults and gods of various parts of Asia Minor: Richard E. Oster, "Ephesus as a Religious Center under the Principate," 1661–1728; Peter Frei, "Götterkulte Lykiens in der Kaiserzeit," 1729–1864; Eckart Olshausen, "Götter, Heroen und ihre Kulte in Pontos—ein erster Bericht, 1865–1906"; Thomas Drew-Bear and Christian Naour, "Divinités de Phrygie," 1907–2044; Theodora S. MacKay, "The Major Sanctuaries of Pamphylia and Cilicia," 2045–2129; Eugene N. Lane, "Men: A Neglected Cult of Roman Asia Minor," 2161–2174.

[610] Georg Petzl, *Die Beichtinschriften im römischen Kleinasien und der fromme und gerechte Gott*, Opladen 1998.

[611] Stephen Mitchell, "The Cult of Theos Hypsistos between Pagans, Jews, and Christians," in: Polymnia Athanassiadi and Michael Frede (eds.), *Pagan Monotheism in Late Antiquity*, Oxford 1999, 81–148.

[435] Lynn E. Roller, *In Search of God the Mother*, Berkeley 1999.

[612] Beate Dignas, *Economy of the Sacred in Hellenistic and Roman Asia Minor*, Oxford 2002.

[160] Johannes Nollé, *Kleinasiatische Losorakel*, Munich 2007.

[613] Maria Dzielska, *Apollonius of Tyana in Legend and History*, Rome 1986.

[614] Wolfgang Speyer, "Religiöse Betrüger. Falsche göttliche Menschen und Heilige in Antike und Christentum," in: *Frühes Christentum im antiken Strahlungsfeld. Ausgewählte Aufsätze*, Tübingen 1989, 440–462.

[615] Graham Anderson, *Sage, Saint and Sophist. Holy Men and Their Associates in the Early Roman Empire*, London and New York 1994.

[615a] Peter Herz and Jörn Kobes, *Ethnische und religiöse Minderheiten in Kleinasien: Von der hellenistischen Antike bis in das byzantinische Mittelalter*, Wiesbaden 1997.

[616] Peter Pilhofer, Manuel Baumbach, Jens Gerlach, and Dirk U. Hansen (eds.), *Lukian, Der Tod des Peregrinos. Ein Scharlatan auf dem Scheiterhaufen*, Darmstadt 2005.

[617] Kristoffel Demoen and Danny Praet (eds.), *Theios Sophistes. Essays on Flavius Philostratus' Vita Apollonii*, Boston 2009.

[618] Simon R. F. Price, *Rituals and Power. The Roman Imperial Cult in Asia Minor*, Cambridge 1984.

[619] Thomas Witulski, *Kaiserkult in Kleinasien. Die Entwicklung der kultisch-religiösen Kaiserverehrung*, Göttingen 2007.

[619a] Alexia Petsalis-Diomidis, *Truly beyond Wonders: Aelius Aristides and the Cult of Asklepios*, Oxford 2010.

Judaism and Early Christianity

[131] Joyce Reynolds and Robert Tannenbaum, *Jews and God-fearers at Aphrodisias. Greek Inscriptions with Commentary*, Cambridge 1987.

[620] Paul R. Trebilco, *The Jewish Communities in Asia Minor*, Cambridge 1991.

[621] William Mitchell Ramsay, *Saint Paul the Traveller and Roman Citizen*, London 1895.

[622] Friedrich Lauchert (ed.), *Die Kanones der wichtigsten altkirchlichen Concilien nebst den apostolischen Kanones*, Freiburg and Leipzig 1896.

[623] Heinrich Gelzer, Heinrich Hilgenfeld, and Otto Cuntz, *Patrum Nicaenorum nomina*, Leipzig 1898.

[624] Adolf von Harnack, *Die Mission und Ausbreitung des Christentums in den ersten drei Jahrhunderten*, 2 vols., third ed., Leipzig 1915.

[625] Adolf von Harnack, *Marcion. Das Evangelium vom fremden Gott*, second ed., Leipzig 1924.

[626] Willem Schepelern, *Der Montanismus und die phrygischen Kulte*, Tübingen 1929.

[627] François Blanchetière, *Le Christianisme asiate aux IIe et IIIe siècles*, Lille 1977.

[628] Elsa Gibson, *The "Christians for Christians" Inscriptions of Phrygia*, Missoula, MT 1978.

[629] August Strobel, *Das heilige Land der Montanisten: Eine religionsgeschichtliche Untersuchung*, Berlin 1980.

[630] Ronald E. Heine, *The Montanist Oracles and Testimonia*, Macon, GA 1989.

[544] Stephen Mitchell, *Anatolia. Land, Men and Gods in Asia Minor*, vol. II: *The Rise of the Church*, Oxford 1993.

[631] Louis Robert, *Le martyre de Pionios, prêtre de Smyrne, édité, traduit et commenté*, Washington, DC 1994.

[632] Peter Guyot and Richard Klein, *Das frühe Christentum bis zum Ende der Verfolgungen*, 2 vols., Darmstadt 1994.

[633] Peter Guyot, "Chaos in Pontos. Der 'kanonische Brief' des Gregorius Thaumaturgos als Dokument der politischen Geschichte," in: Ulrich Fellmeth and Holger Sonnabend (eds.), *Alte Geschichte: Wege, Einsichten, Horizonte*, FS Olshausen, Hildesheim 1998, 63–64.

[634] Thomas Witulski, *Die Adressaten des Galaterbriefes. Untersuchungen zur Gemeinde von Antiochia ad Pisidiam*, Göttingen 2000.

[635] Raymond van Dam, *Kingdom of Snow. Roman Rule and Greek Culture in Cappadocia*, Philadelphia 2002.

[636] Raymond van Dam, *Families and Friends in Late Roman Cappadocia*, Philadelphia 2003.

[637] Raymond van Dam, *Becoming Christian. The Conversion of Roman Cappadocia*, Philadelphia 2003.

[638] Paul Trebilco, *Early Christians in Ephesus from Paul to Ignatius*, Tübingen 2004.

[638a] Sophie Métivier, *La Cappadoce (IVe–VIe siècle). Une histoire provinciale de l'Empire romain d'Orient*, Paris 2005.

[639] Vera-Elisabeth Hirschmann, *Horrenda Secta. Untersuchungen zum frühchristlichen Montanismus und seinen Verbindungen zur paganen Religion Phrygiens*, Stuttgart 2005.

[640] Sabine Hübner, *Der Klerus in der spätantiken Gesellschaft Kleinasiens*, Stuttgart 2005.

[641] Thomas Witulski, *Die Johannesoffenbarung und Kaiser Hadrian: Studien zur Datierung der neutestamentlichen Apokalypse*, Göttingen 2007.

[642] William Tabbernee and Peter Lampe, *Pepouza and Tymion. The Discovery and Archaeological Exploration of a Lost Ancient City and an Imperial Estate*, Berlin 2008.

Index of Authors and Editors
Cited in the Bibliography

Index Locorum

1. Linear B, Cuneiform, Hieroglyphic, and Phoenician alphabetic Sources

PF (1404), 155

PY (Aa 792), 90
PY (Aa 798 + Ab 573), 90
PY (Ab 189), 90
PY (An 292), 90
PY (Fr 1206), 5–6

Anitta's proclamation (Rev. lines 47–51), 71
Annals of Assurbanipal (Cogan and Tadmor, *Orientalia* 46, 1977, 73), 112
Annals of Tudḫaliya (II 33 f.), 6
Apology of Ḫattusili III (§ I lines 5–6), 75
Apology of Ḫattusili III (§ 4 lines 42–50), 82
cuneiform tablet B. M. (62689), 205
Deeds of Suppiluliuma (Güterbock, *JCS* 10, 1956, 93 ff. [fr. 28]), 639n8
[61] Dercksen, *Copper Trade*, 1996 (No. 20, lines 24–26), 67
Hittite Laws (Tablet I § 7), 78
Instruction for temple officials (§ 19 line 78), 78
KUB (XXIII 92 Obv. lines 9–12), 76
KUB (XXXI 79, 4–20), 629n12
Merenptah Inscription (Kitchen, *Ramesside Inscriptions*, vol. 4, p. 4, 5:3), 94
Mursili II's second Plague Prayer (§ 9 lines 1–6), 82
Šaušagamuwa-Treaty (Rev. IV lines 12–18), 79
Telipinu's proclamation (Obv. II lines 34 f.), 72
Ten-Year Annals (§ 42, Rev. IV lines 44–48), 74
Treaty between Muwatalli II and Alaksandu of Wilusa (§ 14, III lines 10–12), 639n9
Treaty between Ḫattusili III and Ramses II (§ 18 [Obv. 60–64]), 75
Treaty between Suppiluliuma I and Ḫukkana of Hayasa (§ 6, lines 38–59), 79
Treaty between Mursili II and Manapa-Tarḫunta (A § 4 lines 60–62), 78

Phoenician Inscription from Cebel Ires Dağ (Mosca and Russell, *EpigrAnat* 9, 1987, 1–28), 126

2. Greek and Latin Inscriptions, Coins (Selection), and Papyri

AE (1905, 175), 348
AE (1915, 58), 388
AE (1968, 510), 345
AE (1975, 809), 382
AnSt (18, 1968, 115 no. 5) 679n213
BMC (4), 421
BMC (6), 418
BMC (89), 421
BMC (318) 478
CIG (2782), 664n102
CIG (3695), 679n210
CIG (Add. et Corr. 3846 l), 648n56
CIL (I² pp. 761–764), 258
CIL (II 1667), 660n16
CIL (III 6783), 418
CIL (V 5262), 344 + 664n82
CIL (VI 41075), 662n57
CIL (XIII 1807), 666n119
CIL (XVI 128), 385
FD (4, 132–135), 247
[199] Head, HN² (501), 656n140
[199] Head, HN² (577), 478
[199] Head, HN² (583), 478
[199] Head, HN² (716), 289
[199] Head, HN² (724 f.), 289
[199] Head, HN² (733), 417
[199] Head, HN² (749), 265, 648n69
[159] Herrmann and Malay (No. 32), 249
[171] I. Didyma (148), 362
[171] I. Didyma (479), 189
[171] I. Didyma (480), 189
[163] I. Pergamon (1), 240
[163] I. Pergamon (15), 210
[163] I. Pergamon (18 line 17), 240
[163] I. Pergamon (20), 214
[163] I. Pergamon (21–28), 215
[163] I. Pergamon (29), 215

3. Greek, Latin, and Syrian Literature

4. Old Testament

5. Apocryphal/Deuterocanonical Books

6. New Testament

Index

Sub-entries preceded by an arrow have been arranged alphabetically; otherwise, they have been arranged chronologically.